A BIBLIOGRAPHY OF NORTH CAROLINA
1589-1956

A BIBLIOGRAPHY
OF NORTH CAROLINA

1589-1956

COMPILED BY

MARY LINDSAY THORNTON

GREENWOOD PRESS, PUBLISHERS
WESTPORT, CONNECTICUT

The Library of Congress has catalogued this publication as follows:

Library of Congress Cataloging in Publication Data

Thornton, Mary Lindsay.
    A bibliography of North Carolina, 1589-1956.

    1. North Carolina--Bibliography. I. Title.
Z1319.T495 1973   015'.756   73-441
ISBN 0-8371-6765-5

Copyright 1958 by The University of North Carolina Press

Originally published in 1958
by The University of North Carolina Press, Chapel Hill

Reprinted with the permission
of The University of North Carolina Press

First Greenwood Reprinting 1973

Library of Congress Catalogue Card Number 73-441

ISBN 0-8371-6765-5

Printed in the United States of America

INTRODUCTION

The North Carolina Collection in the University Library which serves as a basis for this bibliography traces its beginning from material assembled at Chapel Hill by the Historical Society of North Carolina. In the Society's first report, published in 1845, collecting local publications is set forth as one of its main objects, and acquisition of thirty-two publications and eleven collections of manuscripts is recorded.[1] A few of these volumes, inscribed with the name of the Society, survive on the shelves of the North Carolina Collection today. In 1869, Fisk Brewer, in the first printed report of the University Librarian, called attention to the need for preservation of state publications, stating that 218 volumes of state laws, legislative records, and law reports, as well as a collection of University history, had been acquired.[2] A later society, chartered in Chapel Hill in 1875, issued a circular in which a plan was outlined "to collect and preserve historical material . . . especially such as pertain to North Carolina."[3]

Provision of an endowment for a North Carolina Collection and its organization in a special department of the Library followed the appointment of Louis R. Wilson as Librarian in 1901. In almost every report, Wilson recommended collection and special treatment of state material. In 1905, he called attention to the need for an endowment of North Carolina literature. A response came from John Sprunt Hill, Class of 1889, who set up a fund for this purpose as part of the library endowment raised to match the Carnegie gift of a new building. During the fifty-two years that have passed since his first gift, Hill's interest in the Library, and especially in the North Carolina Collection, has been demonstrated by a series of endowments culminating during the period following 1947 in the gift of several business properties in downtown Chapel Hill. His belief in libraries, first stated in an Alumni Association address delivered at the University in 1903, became a lifetime credo. At that time, he deplored the lack of library facilities in the state and, particularly, of the source material which nourishes the scholar "who digs down to the bottom of research and brings out the pure gold . . . from the treasure houses of the world." He called on "some great-hearted son or daughter of the Old North State [to] give our people a

1. Historical Society of the University of North Carolina, *First Report* [Chapel Hill, 1845], pp. 4-7.
2. Fisk Parsons Brewer, *The Library of the University of North Carolina* [Chapel Hill, 1870], pp. 5, 7-8.
3. North Carolina Historical Society, *An Appeal To Its Friends* [Chapel Hill, 1880]. This Society was active into the twentieth century.

great library . . . to illumine the homes of all the people."[4] That such a library now stands in Chapel Hill is due in large part to his interest and help. As Chairman of the Trustees Committee on Building and Grounds, he was active in the 1920's in the movement to secure appropriations by the state for the first unit of the building and again, in the same official capacity, was instrumental in approving plans for the enlargement which doubled its facilities in 1952. He provided an income for the support of the Library as a stipulation in his gift of the Carolina Inn to the University. He was charter member and first president of the Friends of the Library, an organization composed of alumni, faculty, and others interested in development of the Library. In recent years, he has extended the influence of the Library by financing publication of bibliographies.

An impoitant event in the history of the Collection was the purchase of the Stephen B. Weeks Collection of Caroliniana in 1918. The Weeks Collection, comprising ten thousand books, pamphlets, newspapers, maps, and a few manuscripts, was recognized as the most complete body of material relating to the state at that time. Dr. Weeks, Class of 1886, may have received the germ of a collector's zeal that directed his interest throughout life in meetings of the North Carolina Historical Society of which he was a member. In an enthusiastic account of his library, he traces his progress as a collector, beginning with the scrapbook method which he calls "the destructive stage," passing through stamps, single issues of newspapers, and coming finally in 1884 to ownership of his first North Carolina book, Moore's *Pioneers of Methodism in Virginia and North Carolina*, an important milestone for the state as his plan to build a great North Carolina collection became fixed at that point.[5] Acquisition of this library made the University a center of research on North Carolina and provided much material for regional research as well. Acquired at a time when collecting for the University was being accelerated by appointment of a special librarian for the North Carolina Collection, it became a model for future growth which followed its emphasis on ephemeral material of the present as well as the relics of the past. Pamphlets, bulletins, short-lived periodicals, newspapers, maps, state and federal documents, and books by local authors of little renown require the protection of an institutional library, or the care of some devoted bibliophile, from the time of their publication to escape destruction. A collection built on this plan approaches a complete depository of all local printing and provides a body of material on present conditions as well as a reservoir for historical research when the present

4. John Sprunt Hill, *Address Before the Alumni Association of the University of North Carolina* [Chapel Hill? 1903?], p. 21.
5. Stephen Beauregard Weeks, *The Weeks Collection of Caroliniana* [Raleigh, 1907], pp. 3-7.

becomes the past. Since the state has enjoyed its greatest progress in the past fifty years, preservation of source material of that period at the University has been especially fortunate. The Collection has furnished bibliography for many graduate students who carry out an important function of a state university in contributing to betterment of the state through study of its problems and achievements. "No isolated problem or process can be truly understood without a complete and accurate picture of the complex which makes up the environment."[6]

Another great private collection destined to come to the University by bequest in 1954 had its beginning before the turn of the century. Major Bruce Cotten, Class of 1895, has said that the urge to collect was aroused in him early in life when he volunteered to help his mother assemble an exhibit of state literature for the World's Fair at Chicago and found that only about twenty volumes could be located at the moment. This failure to present North Carolina to the world gave him an urge to do better. His pursuit of North Carolina material did not cease even during the migratory years of a long and distinguished service in the army, though Uncle Sam had to bear the expense of transporting volumes that soon numbered in the hundreds.[7] After his retirement to a permanent home in Baltimore, more concentrated collecting became possible. He became well-known as a book lover who had no rival for knowledge of books and zeal for finding them in his field. His special interest was in beautiful copies of the rarer volumes. Some of them which had always eluded him have come to his collection at Chapel Hill since his death by means of a substantial income which he established so that preservation of his state's bibliography in his name might be perpetuated.

Other private libraries, especially valuable as they reflect the interests, activities, and talents of their collectors, have come as gifts. Some of these which should be mentioned are: the Kemp Plummer Battle Collection given by his family following his death in 1919, a monument to a lifelong interest in history of the state as well as varied participation in its progress as President of the University and its first Professor of History; the Alexander Boyd Andrews Collection, invaluable source for the history of transportation with complete files of early North Carolina railroad reports gathered during his long service in their construction and administration; the James Sprunt Collection of Wilmington newspapers covering the period from 1846 to 1890, a remarkable source for the Civil War period when that port was the last refuge of blockade runners of the Confederacy; the Rowan County Historical Society file of Salisbury newspapers furnishing the longest files of

6. Donald Dean Parker, *Local History* [No place, 1944], p. vii.
7. Bruce Cotten, *Housed on the Third Floor* [Baltimore, 1941].

leading western North Carolina newspapers, 1820-1871; the Bennehan Cameron Collection, saved over a hundred years by a family prominent in the nineteenth century; the William Richardson Davie Collection of books illustrative of the earliest colonial period, the gift of Preston Davie, who continues to enrich its resources; the Nathan Wilson Walker Collection, reflecting the interest of a book lover in North Carolina literature as well as history. Two notable collections which memoralize individuals of international fame are the Sir Walter Raleigh Memorial Collection established in 1940 by the Roanoke Colony Memorial Association and the Thomas Wolfe Collection established by members of his family in 1951.

Collecting of rare and out of print material received a great impetus in 1930 when the Southern Historical Collection was established under the direction of J. G. de Roulhac Hamilton whose odyssey in tireless search for manuscripts for that department also garnered many an ancient book and pamphlet for the North Carolina Collection.

A lifetime of intimate association with highly specialized publications almost inevitably leads to bibliography as a natural progression from collecting, classifying, and cataloguing. Familiarity with the difficulties of those engaged in a type of research which demands the smallest components of history on the local level demonstrates the need for such an aid. No bibliography can be complete, but a collection representative of many years of effort offers the best possible basis for one. Publications listed are from the catalogue of the North Carolina Collection which includes material dealing with North Carolina and North Carollinians, writings of North Carolinians, and periodicals published in North Carolina.[8] In order to reduce the volume to manageable form, titles have been shortened, collation is limited to its simplest form, omitting preface paging in Roman numerals, illustrations, maps, and size, but imprint is given in full. Certain entries, already partially covered in published bibliographies and indexes, are omitted. They are state and federal documents, including publications of institutions supported by the state, newspapers, maps, manuscript theses, and articles appearing in periodicals. An index to general subject matter of titles which deal with North Carolina is included.

Mary L. Thornton, Librarian
North Carolina Collection
Louis Round Wilson Library

Chapel Hill, N. C.
May, 1958

8. North Carolinian is defined in its broader sense to mean an author whose work has been published during his established residence in the state as well as a native.

A BIBLIOGRAPHY OF NORTH CAROLINA
1589-1956

Abbot, Willis John. Blue jackets of '61. New York, Dodd, Mead & Co., 1886, 318 p. [1

Abbott, Allen O. Prison life in the South. New York, Harper & Brothers, 1865. 374 p. [2

Abbott, Frederick C. "North Carolina's finest town". [Charlotte, Observer Print, 1899] 16 p. [3

——Twenty-four years' growth in Charlotte real estate. [Charlotte, Queen City Printing Co., 1921] 10 p. [4

Abbott, John Stevens Cabot. Daniel Boone, the pioneer of Kentucky. [New York, Dodd, Mead and Co. c.1872] 331 p. [5

—— ——1898. [6

—— ——[c.1900] [7

Abbott's Creek Primitive Baptist Association. Minutes, 18 - 18 - NcU has 1844, 1845, 1848, 1900, 1903-1948, 1955 [8

Ein Abend-Gesprach zwischen drey Knaben in Nord-Carolina, betreffend dem vollsaufen und dessen üblen folgen. New Market, Va., Ambrose Henkel, 1811. 16 p. [9

Abernethy, Arthur Talmage. The apostles' creed; a romance in religion. Nashville, Tenn., Cokesbury Press, 1924. 104 p. [10

——Center-shots at sin; a series of evangelistic sermons. Cincinnati, Standard Publishing Co. [c.1918] 294 p. [11

——Christian's treasure island, a Restoration romance. St. Louis, Bethany Press [c.1927] 173 p. [12

——The Jew a Negro, being a study of the Jewish ancestry from an impartial standpoint. Moravian Falls, Dixie Publishing Co., 1910. 110 p. [13

——Mechanics and practice of the electric telegraph. Rutherford College, The Author, n.d. 35 p. [14

——Moonshine, being Appalachia's Arabian nights. Asheville, Dixie Publishing Co. [c.1924] 219 p. [15

——Roman Catholicism and the Protestant missionary. No place, no publisher, n.d. 14 p. [16

——A royal southern family; a biographical novel of facts. [Nashville] Parthenon Press [c.1934] 144 p. [17

——Twenty-five best sermons. Cincinnati, Standard Publishing Co. [c.1920] 367 p. [18

——Where are our dead? Rutherford College, The Author [1935?] 25 p. [19

Abernethy, W. E. Speeches. Danbury, Conn., Danbury Medical Printing Co., 1895. 124 p. [20

An account of Chang and Eng, the world renowned Siamese twins. New York, T. W. Strong, 1853. 91 p. [21

Acomb, Frances Dorothy. Anglophobia in France, 1763-1789. Durham, Duke University Press, 1950. 167 p. [22

Acorn, v. 1- 1907- Raleigh, Meredith College, 19 - NcU has v. [1-6, 9-24] [23

Ad valorem exposed by facts and figures. No place, no publisher [1859?] 4 p. [24

Ad valorem; or, Equal taxation. No place, no publisher, n.d. 4 p. [25

Ad valorem taxation, as proposed in North Carolina, the facts and figures, by an eastern Whig. Raleigh, Strother & Marcom's Book and Job Office, 1860. 8 p. [26

Adair, James. Adair's History of the American Indians, edited . . . by Samuel Cole Williams. Johnson City, Tenn., Watauga Press, 1930. 508 p. [27

——The history of the American Indians. London, E. and C. Dilly, 1775. 464 p. [28

Adams, Agatha (Boyd) joint ed. see **Knight, Edgar Wallace, ed.**

Adams, James McKee. Our Bible. Nashville, Tenn., The Sunday School Board of the Southern Baptist Convention [c.1937]   151 p.   [29

Adams, Juliette (Graves)   Studies in hymnology. Nashville, Tenn., Cokesbury Press [c.1938]   96 p.   [30

Adams, Mary Lizzie (Hall)   The Hall family history. [Athens, Ga., Speering Printing Co.] 1949.   443 p.   [31

Adams, Nicholson Barney. Brief French review grammar and composition. New York, H. Holt and Co. [c.1936]   179 p.   [32

——España, introducción a su civilización.   [New York] H. Holt [1947]   369 p.   [33

——The heritage of Spain. New York, H. Holt and Co. [1943]   331 p.   [34

——Lecturas modernas; a beginning reader in Spanish. New York, F. S. Crofts & Co., 1938.   176 p.   [35

——The romantic dramas of Garcia Gutierrez.   [New York] Instituto de las Españas en los Estados Unidos [c.1922]   149 p.   [36

Adams, Nicholson Barney, ed. Selections from Perez de Ayala; edited with introduction, notes and vocabulary by Nicholson B. Adams and Sterling A. Stoudemire. New York, W. W. Norton & Co., Inc. [c.1934]   239 p.   [37

Adams, Nicholson Barney, joint ed. see **Boggs, Ralph Steele, ed.**

Adams, Randolph Greenfield. Political ideas of the American Revolution. Durham, Trinity College Press, 1922.   207 p.   [38

——Three Americanists: Henry Harrisse, bibliographer, George Brinley, book collector, Thomas Jefferson, librarian. Philadelphia, University of Pennsylvania Press, 1939.   101 p.   [39

Adams, Raymond William. Intervals of contemplation; fifty-first annual Phi Beta Kappa address, Alpha Chapter of North Carolina, May 12, 1955. [Chapel Hill, 1955]   18 p.   [40

——Witnessing Walden; presidential address, the Thoreau Society, Concord, Massachusetts, July 10, 1954.   No place [1954]   6 p.   [41

Adams, Thomas. Proposed farm city in Pender County, North Carolina. [Ottawa] Farm Cities Corp., 1921.   24 p.   [42

Adams, William Jackson. The house in the horseshoe and other papers. No place, privately printed, n.d.   88 p.   [43

——Methodism in Moore County. Carthage, News-Blade Print, n.d.   27 p.   [44

——A sketch of Governor Benjamin Williams. Carthage, News-Blade Print, 1920. 15 p.   [45

——The World War. No place, no publisher, n.d.   16 p.   [46

Addington, Hugh M. Charles Kilgore of King's Mountain. Nickelsville, Va., Service Printery, 1935.   154 p.   [47

Addison, Alexander. Analysis of the report of the committee of the Virginia Assembly, on the proceedings of sundry of the other states in answer to their resolutions. Raleigh, Hodge & Boylan, pr., 1800.   54 p.   [48

An address to the freemen of North Carolina on the subject of amending the state constitution. Salisbury, Carolina Watchman, 1833.   7 p.   [49

——Raleigh, J. Gales & Son, 1833.   18 p.   [50

An address to the people in general who call themselves Christians. Raleigh, Printed for the Author, 1810.   32 p.   [51

An address to the voters of the electoral district composed by the counties of Anson, Richmond, Robeson, Cumberland, and Moore. Fayetteville, North-Carolina Journal, 1828.   p. defective copy p. 25—wanting.   [52

Adkins, Dorothy C. Factor analysis of reasoning tests, by Dorothy C. Adkins and Samuel B. Lyerly.   Chapel Hill, University of North Carolina Press, 1952. 221 p.   [53

Adney, Tappan. The Klondike stampede. New York, Harper & Brothers, 1900. 470 p.   [54

Advantages of Albemarle, N. C. No place, no publisher [1908?]   39 p.   [55

Advocate, pseud. see Reade, Edwin G.

Advocate [periodical] see North Carolina Christian advocate

African Methodist Episcopal Church. North Carolina Conference. Minutes, 1869- 1869-   NcU has 1869, 1870, 1884, 1924   [56

African Methodist Episcopal Zion Church. North Carolina Conference. Minutes, 18 - 18 - NcU has 1865, 1919 [57

Agora, the magazine of the South, v. 1, September, 1930-May, 1931. Chapel Hill, The Agora, 1930-1931. NcU has v. 1 [58

Agricola, pseud. see **Jeffreys, George W.**

Ahl, Frances Norene. Andrew Jackson and the Constitution. Boston, Christopher Publishing House [c.1939] 168 p. [59

Ake, Eli D. Ouaneetee, legend of Sunset Mountain. No place, no publisher [1902] 138 p. [60

Akers, Susan Grey. Simple library cataloguing. Chicago, American Library Association, 1927. 95 p. [61

—— ——1933. 173 p. [62

—— ——1944. 197 p. [63

—— ——1954. 250 p. [64

—— ——Tr. by Samuel Tsu Yung Seng. Winchang, Japan, Boone Library, 1929. 128 p. [65

—— ——Tr. into Japanese by Nakamura & Ouchi. [Tokio, Japan, Library Association, 1951] 258 p. [66

Alamance Co., N. C. Health Department. Report, 1949/50- [Graham? 1950- NcU has 1949/50 [67

Albemarle and Pantego Railroad, a brief description of the adjacent country and its advantages and natural resources. [Norfolk, Va., Christian Voice, 1887] 8 p. [68

Albemarle Normal and Industrial Institute, Albemarle. Announcement, 19 - 19 - NcU has 1912/13, 1913/14, 1915/16 [69

Albertson, Catherine Fauntleroy Seyton. In ancient Albemarle. Raleigh, Commercial Printing Co., 1914. 170 p. [70

——Legends of the dunes of Dare. Raleigh, Capital Printing Co., c.1936. 22 p. [71

——Roanoke Island in history and legend. [Elizabeth City, Independent Press, c.1934] 28 p. [72

——Wings over Kill Devil, and Legends of the dunes of Dare. No place, no publisher, n.d. 37 p. [73

Albion Academy, Franklinton, N. C. Catalogue, 18 - 18 - NcU has 1892/93, 1901/02 [74

Albright, Claribel. Some records of the Albright family. [St. Joseph, Mo., Prompt Printing Co.] 1951. [16] p. [75

——Additional findings on North Carolina Albright lineage. 1951. [16] p. [76

Albright, James W. Greensboro, 1808-1904, facts, figures, traditions, and reminiscences. [Greensboro, Jos. J. Stone and Co., 1904] 134 p. [77

——Guilford County and its resources. Greensboro, Thomas, Reece [1885?] 12 p. [78

——A sketch of Methodism in Greensboro, N. C. Greensboro, Joseph J. Stone and Co., n.d. 18 p. [79

Albright, William Thomas. History of the Widenhouse, Furr, Dry, Stallings, Teeter and Tucker families. [Greensboro? 1954?] 145 p. [80

Alcoholics, Anonymous. North Carolina. Groups in North Carolina 5th ed. Raleigh, 1956. [20] p. [81

Alden, John Richard. John Stuart and the southern colonial frontier. Ann Arbor, University of Michigan Press, 1944. 384 p. [82

Alderman, Edwin Anderson. Address delivered Oct. 15th, 1892, at the Guilford Battle Ground, on the occasion of the dedication of the monument to the Maryland soldiers. Greensboro, Guilford Battle Ground Co., 1893. 10 p. [83

——Address on the life of William Hooper . . . Guilford Battle Ground, July 4, 1894. Chapel Hill, University Press, n.d. 73 p. [84

——A brief history of North Carolina. Boston, Ginn and Co., 1896. 64 p. [85

—— ——1898. [85

——Classics old and new, a series of school readers. New York, University Publishing Co. [c.1906-07] 5 v. [86

——Freedom of the mind, address to the graduating classes finals of 1927, University of Virginia. No place, no publisher, n.d. 4 p. [87

——Function and needs of schools of education in universities and colleges. New York, General Education Board, 1917. 31 p. [88

——Inaugural address on installation as president of Tulane University, Louisiana, Tuesday, March 12, 1901. Boston, Geo. H. Ellis Co., pr., 1904. 22 p. [89

——Inauguration of President Edwin A. Alderman. Chapel Hill, University of North Carolina, 1897. (Its Record. Extra number) 41 p. [90

——J. L. M. Curry. [Brooklyn, Eagle Press] 1903. 23 p. [91

——J. L. M. Curry, a biography, by Edwin Anderson Alderman and Armistead Churchill Gordon. New York, Macmillan Co., 1911. 468 p. [92

——Magnanimitas, address to the graduating classes, finals of 1926, University of Virginia. [Charlottesville, Va., Michie Co., pr., 1926] 4 p. [93

——Sectionalism and nationality, speech before the New England Society in the city of New York, Dec. 22, 1906. No place, no publisher, n.d. 15 p. [94

——Value of southern idealism, brief address to the American Historical Association and the American Economic Association on the evening of Dec. 29th, 1903. No place, no publisher, n.d. 15 p. [95

——Virginia. New York, Chas. Scribner's Sons, 1916. 57 p. [96

——Virginia, address delivered in response to the toast "Virginia" at the banquet given by the citizens of Petersburg, Va., to the President of the United States and the Governor of Pennsylvania, on May 19, 1909. No place, no publisher, n.d. 11 p. [97

——Woodrow Wilson. Garden City, N. Y., Doubleday, Page & Co., 1925. 80 p. [98

Alderman, Jacob Oliver. Memories to keep. Garner, 1953. 20 p. [99

Alderman, John Thomas. Amariah Biggs Alderman (1819-1889) reminiscences and Civil War experiences. [Raleigh, W. A. Parker, 1954] 57 p. [100

Alderman, Sidney Sherrill. Three Americans in Paris, Spring, 1919. [Durham] Duke University Press, 1952. 126 p. [101

Alexander, Charles Beatty. Address delivered at the meeting of the North Carolina Society of the Cincinnati, April 23, 1921, Raleigh, N. C. No place, no publisher [1921?] 15 p. [102

——The hereditary friendship of the Cincinnati, address . . . May 10, 1917. [New York, 1917] 18 p. [103

Alexander, John Brevard. Biographical sketches of the early settlers of the Hopewell section and reminiscences of the pioneers and their descendants by families. Charlotte, Observer Printing and Publishing House, 1897. 104 p. [104

——The history of Mecklenburg County from 1740 to 1900. Charlotte, Observer Printing House, 1902. 431 p. [105

——Reminiscences of the past sixty years . . . Charlotte, N. C., 1908. Charlotte, Ray Printing Co. [1908] 513 p. [106

Alexander, Julia McGehee. Charlotte in picture and prose, an historical and descriptive sketch of Charlotte, North Carolina. [New York, Blanchard Press, c.1906] [60] p. [107

——Mothers of great men. Charlotte. Observer Printing House, 1916. 188 p. [108

[Alexander, Nancy] Here will I dwell (The story of Caldwell County) [Lenoir, Nancy Alexander, c.1956] 230 p. [109

Alexander, Samuel Caldwell. An historical address delivered at the centennial celebration of Thyatira Church, Rowan County, N. C., October 19, 1855. Salisbury, J. J. Bruner, pr. for the Session, 1855. 27 p. [110

——An historical address delivered at the dedication of Back Creek Church, March 21, 1857. Salisbury, Herald, 1857. 20 p. [111

——History of Back Creek Presbyterian Church, Rowan County, N. C., for 100 years, September, 1805 to March, 1857, by Rev. S. C. Alexander, and March, 1857 to September, 1905, by John K. Goodman. [Mooresville, Enterprise Job Print, 1905] 36 p. [112

Alexander Baptist Association. Minutes, 18 - 18 - NcU has 1876-1925, 1932, 1946-1953, 1955 [113

Alexander Cary McAlister. Asheboro, May 22, 1911. 3 p. [114

Alexander County Historical Association. 1847 to 1947: Alexander County homecoming and centennial celebration, June 5, 6, 7, 1947 . . . souvenir program. [Taylorsville, 1947] [62] p. [115

Alexander Rescue Home for Children, Charlotte, N. C.   Report, 18 - 18 - NcU
has 1894/95   [116
Allee, Marjorie (Hill)   The road to Carolina. Boston, Houghton Mifflin Co., 1932.
240 p.   [117
——Runaway Linda. Boston, Houghton Mifflin Co., 1930. 220 p.   [118
——Susanna and Tristram. Boston, Houghton Mifflin Co., 1929. 220 p.   [119
Alleghany Baptist Association.   Minutes, 18 - 18 - NcU has 1897, 1898, 1901,
1902, 1905-1918 [1923-1947]   [120
Allen, Don Cameron.   The star-crossed Renaissance; the quarrel about astrology
and its influence in England. Durham, Duke University Press, 1941. 280 p. [121
Allen, Gay Wilson, ed.   Literary criticism: Pope to Croce [edited by] Gay Wilson
Allen and Harry Hayden Clark. New York, American Book Company [c.1941]
659 p.   [122
Allen, Gay Wilson.   The solitary singer, a critical biography of Walt Whitman.
New York, Macmillan Co., 1955. 616 p.   [123
Allen, Gay Wilson, ed.   Walt Whitman abroad. [Syracuse, N. Y.] Syracuse Uni-
versity Press, 1955. 290 p.   [124
Allen, Gay Wilson.   Walt Whitman handbook. Chicago, Packard and Co., 1946.
560 p.   [125
Allen, Gay Wilson, ed.   Walt Whitman's poems; selections with critical aids,
edited by Gay Wilson Allen and Charles T. Davis. New York, New York University Press, 1955. 280 p.   [126
Allen, George.   Allen's Forty lessons in practical double entry bookkeeping. New-
bern, N. S. Richardson, pr., 1885. 40 p.   [127
—— ——Raleigh, Edwards, Broughton & Co., 1886. 96 p.   [128
—— ——1891. 136 p.   [129
—— ——1901.   [130
——The science of accounts made clear and simple. Graded school ed. Raleigh,
Edwards & Broughton Printing Co., 1909. 65 p.   [131
—— ——High school ed. 136 p.   [132
Allen, George H.   Forty-six months with the Fourth R. I. Volunteers, in the War
of 1861 to 1865. Providence, R. I., J. A. & R. A. Reid, pr., 1887. 389 p. [133
Allen, John Edward.   Review of progress in the public schools of Warren County.
Warrenton, Press Publishing Co. [1926] 50 p.   [134
——The Warren County schools, plans and objectives. [Warrenton, Warren
County Board of Education] 1945. 29 p.   [135
Allen, Mary Moore.   North Carolina sketch. [Goldsboro, The Author] 1946.
39 p.   [136
—— ——1949. 53 p.   [137
Allen, Nettie M., joint author, see **Foust, Julius Isaac**
Allen, Oliver Hicks.   My recollections of the bench and bar. Raleigh, Edwards
and Broughton Co., 1923. 32 p.   [138
—— ——supplement. No place, no publisher, n.d. 12 p.   [139
Allen, William Cicero.   The annals of Haywood County, North Carolina, historical,
sociological, biographical and genealogical. [Waynesville? The Author] 1935.
628 p.   [140
——Centennial of Haywood County, and its county seat, Waynesville, N. C.
Waynesville Courier [1908?] 184 p.   [141
——A child's history of North Carolina, a textbook for North Carolina schools.
New York, Authors' Cooperative Publishing Co. [c.1916] 480 p.   [142
——History of Halifax County. Boston, Cornhill Co. [c.1918] 231 p.   [143
——North Carolina history stories. Richmond, Va., B. F. Johnson Co., 1901.
5 parts.   [144
——The story of our state, North Carolina, by W. C. Allen in collaboration with
Clarence W. Griffin. Raleigh, Dixie Press, 1942. 358 p.   [145
Alley, Felix Eugene.   Random thoughts and the musings of a mountaineer. Salis-
bury, Rowan Printing Co. [1941] 539 p.   [146
——What think ye of Christ? A history. Salisbury, Rowan Printing Co. [1946]
491 p.   [147
Allison, Charles Walter.   Ney; Was Peter Stewart Ney, the Carolina schoolmaster

Marshal Michel Ney, the great French soldier? Charlotte, for sale at Efird's Book Shop, c.1946. 22 p.   [148

——Reverend John Tillett family history. [Charlotte, Observer Printing House, c.1955] 194, 64, 171 p.   [149

Allison, John. Address delivered on "King's Mountain Day, October 7" at the Tennessee Centennial Exhibition in Nashville, May 1 to October 31, 1897. Nashville, Tenn., Marshall and Bruce Co., n.d.   24 p.   [150

Allison, Mrs. John Phifer. A Confederate catechism for southern children. Newton, Enterprise Print, n.d.   8 p.   [151

Allison, Joseph. To the freemen of Orange County. Cedar Grove, February 12, 1832. [2] p.   [152

Allport, Floyd Henry. Social psychology. Boston, Houghton Mifflin Co. [c.1924] 453 p.   [153

Almy, John Jay. Incidents of the blockade. [Washington, 1892] (Military Order of the Loyal Legion of the U. S. District of Columbia. War papers, 9) 10 p. [154

Alston, Philip William Whitmell. Sermons . . . with a biographical notice and funeral sermon by the Rt. Rev. Jas. H. Otey. Philadelphia, Herman Hooker, 1854. 456 p.   [155

Altsheler, Joseph Alexander. My captive, a novel. New York, D. Appleton and Co., 1902. 281 p.   [156

Alvord, Clarence Walworth. First explorations of the trans-Alleghany region by the Virginians, 1650-1674, by Clarence Walworth Alvord and Lee Bidgood. Cleveland, Arthur H. Clark Co., 1912.   275 p.   [157

[Ambrose, Paul] Slavery, the mere pretext for the rebellion, not its cause; Andrew Jackson's prophecy in 1833. Philadelphia, C. Sherman, Son & Company, 1863. 16 p.   [158

Amendment catechism, 1900- Raleigh [N. C. State Democratic Executive Committee?] 1900- NcU has June, 1900.   [159

American, pseud. see **Strange, Robert, 1796-1854**

American Agricultural and Mineral Lane Company, New York. Letters and reports on Western North Carolina. New York, George Edward Sears, pr., 1868. 19 p. [160

American Association for Labor Legislation] Why North Carolina should adopt accident compensation. [New York, The Association, 1927?] 4 p.   [161

American Association for State and Local History. Historical societies in the United States and Canada, a handbook compiled and edited by Christopher Crittenden, editor, and Doris Godard, editorial associate. Washington, 1944. 261 p.   [162

American Association of University Women. North Carolina Division. Bulletin, v. 1- 193 - 193 - NcU has [1914-1956]   [163

[American Association of University Women. Western North Carolina Branch. Library Committee] Sondley Reference Library, a survey of research material. Asheville, 1940.   30 p.   [164

American Automobile Association. Guide to the Carolinas, Kentucky, Tennessee. Washington, c.1944. 120 p.   [165

——Southeastern accommodations directory, 19 - Washington, 19 - NcU has 1954/55   [166

——Southeastern tour book, 19 - Washington, 19 - NcU has 1954/55   [167

American Cancer Society. North Carolina Division. The 'forties and forward to cancer control. [Mt. Airy, 1950] 10 p.   [168

American Chemical Society. North Carolina Section. Annual announcement, 19 - 19 - NcU has 1904.   [169

American Church Institute for Negroes. Down where the need is greatest. New York [1936?] 46 p.   [170

American Civil Liberties Union. Justice—North Carolina style. New York, 1930. 14 p.   [171

American Cotton Manufacturers Association. Lest we forget. [Charlotte? 1946] 106 p.   [172

——The southern cotton spinners' association, United States of America. Charlotte, 1900. 28 p. [173

——Southern village costs and wage study. Charlotte, 1935. 21 p. [174

American Council on Education. Committee on Southern Regional Studies and Education. Channeling research into education, by John E. Ivey, Jr. Washington [1944] 187 p. [175

American Council on Public Affairs. The poll tax. [Washington, 1940] 23 p. [176

American Dialect Society. Word-lists from the South. Greensboro, 1944. (Its Publications, 2) 72 p. [177

American Emigrant Aid and Homestead Co. Resources of North Carolina. [New York, 1866] 7 p. [178

American Enka Corporation, Enka, N. C. Report, 1929- Enka, 1929- NcU has 1929-1953 [179

American Freedom Association. A. F. A. bulletin, v. 1- August, 1953- Salisbury, 1953- NcU has v. 1-5 [180

[American Freedom Association] Three kinds of peace and the religious basis of world law. [Salisbury, 1954] 8 p. [181

American fur animal and poultry digest, v. 1- July, 1928- Charlotte, Carolinas Rabbit and Cavy Breeders Association, 1928- NcU has v. 1-4 [5] [182

American Institute of Architects. N. C. Chapter. Centennial observance—February, 1957. [Durham, 1957] 23, 23 p. Half of booklet, including back cover and special title-page, is facsimile of North Carolina Chapter. Charter, constitution, by-laws. [183

American Jewish times-outlook, v. 1- April, 1936- Greensboro, 1936- NcU has v. 3, 4, 5-21 [184

American Legion. North Carolina. North Carolina public welfare child survey. No place [1934?] 34 p. [185

American Legion. North Carolina. Dysart-Kendall Post no. 29, Lenoir. History. Lenoir, 1955. 86 p. [186

American Legion. North Carolina. J. D. Monroe Post no. 42, Lumberton. History. Lumberton, 1956. 44 p. [187

American Legion Auxiliary. North Carolina. Constitution and by-laws. [Raleigh, 1932] 25 p. [188

——Proceedings, 1921- 1921- NcU has 1921-1932, 1935, 1938, 1941-1955 [189

American Legion Auxiliary. North Carolina. Pittsboro Post no. 280. The American guidebook. Pittsboro, 1945. unpaged. [190

American literature, a journal of literary history, criticism, and bibliography, v. 1- March, 1929- Durham, Duke University Press [1929- NcU has v. 1-28 [191
——Index, v. 1-20, March, 1929-January, 1949. 1 v.

American newspapers, 1821-1936, a union list of files available in the United States and Canada, edited by Winifred Gregory under the auspices of the Bibliographical Society of America. New York, The H. W. Wilson Co., 1937. 791 p. [192

American Philosophical Society. Calendar of the correspondence relating to the American Revolution of Brigadier-General George Weedon, Hon. Richard Henry Lee, and Major-General Nathanael Greene in the Library of the American Philosophical Society. Philadelphia, 1900. 255 p. [193

American Psychiatric Association. Central Inspection Board. Report on the state mental hospitals of North Carolina. No place, 1950. 136 p.

American Red Cross. Hurricane disasters of August and September, 1933. Washington, n.d. 41 p. [194

American Red Cross. Executive Board. History of the Raleigh Chapter of American Red Cross and of its branches and auxiliaries, 1916-1919. No place, 1920. 44 p. [195

American Red Cross. Southern Division. Social laws and agencies of North Carolina. Atlanta, 1920. 1705 paragraphs. [196

American Red Cross. Wilmington, N. C., Chapter. History Committee. History of Wilmington, N. C., chapter. No place [1919] 19 p. [197

American savings and loan news [North Carolina edition]   v. 1- 18 - Cincinnati, United States Savings and Loan League, 18 - NcU has [57-59] 61-64   [198

American society and the changing world, by C. H. Pegg [and others] 2d ed.   New York, F. S. Crofts, 1947.   673 p.   [199

American Society of Civil Engineers.   North Carolina Section.   Constitution and handbook.   Raleigh, 1919.   16 p.   [200

——Papers, no. 1- 1930- 1930- NcU has no. 1-2   [201

American Telephone and Telegraph Company.   North Carolina.   Constitutional provisions, general statutes and session laws relating to telepraph and telephone corporations.   In effect January 1, 1907.   New York, 1907.   57 p.   [202

American Tobacco Company.   The American Tobacco Company and its service to the public.   [New York? 1940]   75 p.   [203

——"Sold American!"   The first fifty years.   [New York, 1954]   144 p.   [204

American Tract Society.   Superintendent of Colportage in Virginia and North Carolina.   Annual report, 18 - 18 - NcU has 1852/53, 1854/55-1858/59   [205

American War Mothers of North Carolina.   Program, 192 - 192 - NcU has 1922, 1925-1927   [206

American Water Works Association.   North Carolina Section.   Journal . . . Proceedings of annual convention . . . and [of] Water Purification and Sewage Treatment Conference, 1923- 1923- NcU has 1923-1936, 1941-1955.   Not published 1921-1922.   [207

American Water Works Association.   North Carolina Section.   To the members of the General Assembly and the public; pertinent facts and suggested legislation.   No place [1926]   26 p.   [208

Ames, Adelbert.   Capture of Fort Fisher, January 15, 1865.   No place, privately printed, n.d.   24 p.   [209

Amis, Moses Neal.   Historical Raleigh from its foundation in 1792.   [Raleigh, Edwards and Broughton Co.]   1902.   230 p.   [210

——Historical Raleigh, with sketches of Wake County.   Raleigh, Commercial Printing Co., 1913.   289 p.   [211

Amis, Rufus.   To the free silver voters and delegates to the Democratic and Peoples' Party congressional conventions of the 5th district of North Carolina.   No place, no publisher [1895?]   [1] p.   [212

[**Amis, Rufus**]   Yellow tobacco: how to cultivate, how to cure, and prepare for market, the yellow wrapper, and bright smoker, by a Granville farmer.   No place, The Author, n.d.   20 p.   [213

Amity Associate Reformed Presbyterian Church, Iredell Co., N. C.   Directory.   No place, 1892.   8 p.   [214

Ammen, Daniel.   The Atlantic coast.   New York, C. Scribner's Sons, 1883.   273 p.   [215

——The navy in the Civil War, the Atlantic coast.   London, Sampson Low, Marston & Co., 1898.   [216

——A sketch of our second bombardment of Fort Fisher; a paper read before the District of Columbia Commandery of the Military Order of the Loyal Legion of the United States, November 2, 1887.   Washington, The Order, 1887.   8 p.   [217

Ammons, John.   Outlines of history of French Broad Association, and Mars Hill College.   Raleigh, Edwards & Broughton Printing Co., n.d.   96 p.   [218

Analyse des loix commerciales, avec les tarifs, des etats des deux Carolines, et de la Géorgie.   Fayetteville, Bowen & Howard, 1788.   17 p.   [219

An analysis: R. J. Reynolds Tobacco Company.   New York, E. F. Hutton & Co.   [1932]   14 p.   [220

Anchor, v. 1- April, 1885- Greensboro, Woman's Christian Temperance Union of N. C., 1885- NcU has v. [1-2]   [221

Anderson, Mrs. E. M.   Memorial poems.   [Durham, The Author? 1903] 119 p. [222

——Rays of light and words of love.   [Durham, The Author] n.d.   38 p.   [223

Anderson, Edward Hutchings.   The science of production organization, by E. H. Anderson and G. T. Schwenning.   New York, J. Wiley & Sons, 1938.   282 p. [224

Anderson, George A. Caswell County in the World War, 1917-1918 . . . edited by R. B. House. Raleigh, Edwards and Broughton Co., 1921. 201 p.   [225

Anderson, Lucy (London) The administration of Mrs. Livingston Rowe Schuyler, President-General, United Daughters of the Confederacy. No place, no publisher, n.d. 16 p.   [226

——North Carolina women of the Confederacy. [Fayetteville, Cumberland Printing Co. for Author] 1926. 141 p.   [227

——Pageant of the heroines of the Confederacy presented at Memphis general convention, U. D. C., November 17, 1932. No place, no publisher, 1932. [12] p. [228

Anderson, Micajah. The life of Micajah Anderson of Edgecombe County, by himself. Tarboro, Wm. A. Hearne's Printing and Publishing House, 1870. 47 p.   [229

Anderson, Richard Loree. Statistical theory in research [by] R. L. Anderson [and] T. A. Bancroft. New York, McGraw-Hill, 1952. 399 p.   [230

Anderson, Robert Campbell. The story of Montreat from its beginning, 1897-1947. Montreat, no publisher [c.1949] 237 p.   [231

Anderson, Rufus. Memoir of Catharine Brown, a Christian Indian of the Cherokee Nation. Boston, Crocker and Brewster, 1825. 144 p.   [232

Anderson, Sarah Travers Lewis (Scott) Lewises, Meriwethers and their kin. Richmond, Va., Dietz Press, 1938. 652 p.   [233

Anderson, T. C. Life of Rev. George Donnell, first pastor of the church in Lebanon; with a sketch of the Scotch-Irish race. Nashville, Tennessee, Author, 1858. 334 p.   [234

Anderson, Walter Wadsley. Kill 1, kill 2. New York, W. Morrow and Co., 1940. 284 p.   [235

Anderson, William E. Address delivered before the citizens of Wilmington, N. C., on the occasion of the third anniversary of Cape Fear Lodge no. 2, I. O. O. F. on the 13th day of May, 1845. Richmond, Va., Independent Odd Fellows, 1845. 16 p.   [236

Andrew, the king. Pittsburgh, John P. Hunt & Co., 1866. 12 p.   [237

Andrews, Alexander Boyd. Address of Alexander B. Andrews, Jr., Grand Master of the Grand Lodge of North Carolina. [Raleigh?] 1917. 57 p.   [238

——Address of Alexander B. Andrews, Jr., Right Eminent Grand Commander, 27th annual conclave, 1907. No place, no publisher, 1907. 22 p.   [239

——Address of the Grand High Priest. Durham, Seeman Printery, 1908. 22 p. [240

——A century of statistics of the Episcopal Church, 1832-1934. Raleigh, privately printed, 1937. 19 p.   [241

——A digest of the Masonic law of North Carolina, 1841 to 1906. Oxford, Grand Lodge of North Carolina, 1907. 57 p.   [242

——Fifteen years a Knight Templar. Raleigh, no publisher, 1914. 27 p.   [243

——Fifty years of statistics, 1876-1925 (also 1926-1930) of Protestant Episcopal Church in the United States of America. No place, no publisher, 1931. 26 p. [244

——Forecast of illiteracy in North Carolina, 1940 census. [Raleigh, Author] 1939. 4 p.   [245

——North Carolina's need of additional court facilities. [Raleigh] no publisher [1912] 19 p.   [246

——Per capita cost of courts. Raleigh, Mitchell Printing Co., 1921. 20 p.   [247

——Addendum of August 15, 1921. Richmond, Va., Whittet & Shepperson, pr., 1921. 8 p.   [248

——Revised addendum of January 6, 1922. 1922. 16 p.   [249

——Protestant Episcopal Church, U. S. A.: A. Forecast of statistics, 1931; B. Compiled statistics, 1931; C. Forecast of statistics for 1932. Raleigh, no publisher, 1932. 10 p.   [250

——Statistics on the population of lawyers in Arkansas. [Raleigh? no publisher, 1942] 6 p.   [251

——To the bishops, clergy and laity, Protestant Episcopal Church, United States of America. [Raleigh] no publisher, 1943. 9 p.   [252

Andrews, Charles McLean, ed. Narratives of the insurrections, 1675-1690. New York, C. Scribner's Sons, 1915. 414 p.   [253

Andrews, Columbus. Caldwell County, North Carolina, geography supplement. [Chapel Hill] University of North Carolina, 1927/28. 32 p.   [254

Andrews, Jane Virginia Hawkins. Revenge, a one-act play. Raleigh, Mitchell Printing Co., 1928. 16 p.   [255

Andrews, John. A brief essay on natural and moral inability embracing several important doctrines of the Gospel. Lexington, Ky., Printed, Salisbury, Reprinted by Francis Coupee, 1807. 62 p.   [256

Andrews, John. History of the war with America, France, Spain and Holland, commencing in 1775 and ending in 1783. London, J. Fielding, 1785-1786. 4 v. [257

Andrews, Marietta Minnigerode. The cross triumphant, a pageant of the Church in England and America . . . Cathedral Close, Washington, D. C. May 5 1922, for the benefit of St. Mary's School, Raleigh, N. C. No place, no publisher, n.d. 28 p.   [258

—— ——[Washington, Columbian Printing Co., 1922?] 29 p.   [259

—— ——Grounds of St. Mary's School, Raleigh, N. C., October 17, 1922. [Raleigh? 1922] 23 p. Program.   [260

Andrews, Melvin Brainerd. How to work your way through college. Greensboro [J. J. Stone and Co., pr.] 1921. 63 p.   [261

——A school boy's poems. No place, no publisher, n.d. 48 p.   [262

Andrews, Robert McCants. John Merrick, a biographical sketch. [Durham, Seeman Printery, c.1920] 229 p.   [263

Andrews, Sidney. The South since the war, as shown by fourteen weeks of travel and observation in Georgia and the Carolinas. Boston, Ticknor and Fields, 1866. 400 p.   [264

Andrews, Thomas Wingate. In memoriam, Frank Bell John, late principal of Boyden High School, Salisbury, N. C. No place [Printed for M. L. John, 1928] 20 p.   [265

Andrews, Wayne. The Vanderbilt legend, the story of the Vanderbilt family, 1794-1940. New York, Harcourt, Brace and Co. [c.1941] 454 p.   [266

Angell, Polly. Andy Jackson. New York, Aladdin Books, 1956. 192 p.   [267

Angier, N. C. Public High School. Announcement, 1912/13- Angier, 1912- NcU has 1912/13-1917/18   [268

Animadversions on Capt. Wilkinson's information. London, W. Davis, 1682· 18 (i.e. 20) p. NcU has photostat (positive)   [269

Animadversions on James Holland's Strictures on General Dickson's circular letter of the first of May, 1800. Lincolnton, John Martin Slump, pr., 1800. 15 p. [270

Annals of Southern Methodism, edited by C. F. Deems. New York, J. A. Gray, pr., 1856- NcU has 1855, 1856, 1857.   [271

Announcement and invitation, Greensboro's home-coming week, October 11-17, 1908. Greensboro, Harrison Printing Co., 1908. 8 p.   [272

Anson Co., N. C. Agricultural Extension Service. Anson County, 35 years of progress, 1911-1946. [Wadesboro, 1946?] [30] p.   [273

Anson Co., N. C. Bicentennial Corporation. Torchlight on the Pee Dee, 1749-1949; Anson County bicentennial celebration souvenir program, October 2-7, at 8:30 P.M. [Wadesboro, 1949] [36] p.   [274

Anson Co., N. C. Board of Education. Report of the public schools, 191 / - Wadesboro, 191 - NcU has 1912/13-1914/15   [275

Appalachian and Western North Carolina Railroad. Engineer. Some facts concerning Appalachian and Western North Carolina Railroad. Greensboro, Harrison Printing Co. [1924] 14 p.   [276

Appalachian Mountain Community Centre, Penland, N. C. Appalachian Mountain Community Centre under the auspices of the Protestant Episcopal Church. Penland, n.d. [3] p.   [277

Appalachian National Park Association. The Appalachian National Park . . . 4th ed., compiled by Dr. C. P. Ambler. Asheville, 1901. 31 p.   [278

Appalachian School, Penland, N. C. The Appalachian School Department of Fireside Industries. Penland [193?] [12] p.   [279

——Appalachian School summer camp. Penland, n.d. [5] p.   [280

Appalachian School, Penland, N. C., see also Appalachian Mountain Community Centre, Penland, N. C.; Penland School of Handicrafts, Penland, N. C.

Appalachian Trail Conference, Washington, D. C. The Appalachian trail. Washington, January, 1934. 35 p. [281

—— ——November, 1934. 36 p. [282

——Guide to the Appalachian trail in the Southern Appalachians. Washington, 1942. (Its Publication no. 8) Various paging. [283

—— ——3d ed. 1950. [284

——Guide to the Southern Appalachians. Washington, 1937. 187 p. [285

—— ——supplement. 1938. 81 p. [286

Apollonius of Ottaray, pseud. see Huger, Arthur Deveron

Archaeological Society of North Carolina. Bulletin, v. 1-4, March, 1934-February, 1938. Chapel Hill, 1934-1938. NcU has v. 1-4. [287

——News letter, no. 1- , May, 1938-. [Chapel Hill] 1938- NcU has no. 1-31 [288

Archdale, John. A new description of that fertile and pleasant province of Carolina. London, Printed for J. Wyat, 1707. 32 p. [289

Archibald Henderson. [Chapel Hill? Privately printed, 1939] 58 p. [290

Archibald Henderson and his books. [New York, D. Appleton and Co., 1927?] 8 p. [291

Archibald Henderson, the new Crichton . . . edited by Samuel Stevens Hood. New York, Beechhurst Press [1949] 252 p. [292

Archive, v. 37- January, 1925- Durham, Students of Duke University, 1925- NcU has v. 37, 40-54 [55-56] 57-59 [60-68] Preceded by Trinity archive [293

Archive, the Archive anthology . . . edited by R. P. Harriss. Durham, Duke University Press, 1926. 69 p. [294

Are North Carolinians freemen? No place, no publisher [1856] 8 p. [295

Arendell, F. B. Bingham School, 1793-1897. No place, no publisher, n.d. 12 p. [296

Argo, Fordyce Hubbard. Jesus' idea, a study of the real Jesus. Boston, R. G. Badger, c.1916. 282 p. [297

Aristides, pseud. see McKenney, Thomas Lorraine

Arkwright Club. Committee on Southern Competition. Report. No place, [1897?] 8 p. [298

Armfield, Eugene Morehead. Two short stories. New York, Cassowary Press, 1933. 36 p. [299

——Where the weak grow strong. New York, Covici-Friede [c.1936] 395 p. [300

Armfield, Lucile. Songs from the Carolina hills. New York [Doxey's, pr.] 1902. 68 p. [301

Armstrong, Zella. Notable southern families. Chattanooga, Tenn., Lookout Publishing Co., 1918-33. 6 v. [302

——Twenty-four hundred Tennessee pensioners, Revolution—War of 1812. Chattanooga, Tenn., Lookout Publishing Co. [c.1937] 121 p. [303

Arnett, Alex Mathews. Claude Kitchin and the Wilson war policies. Boston, Little, Brown and Co., 1937. 341 p. [304

——The story of North Carolina . . . with the collaboration of Walter Clinton Jackson. Chapel Hill, University of North Carolina Press, 1933. 496 p. [305

Arnett, Alex Mathews, joint author, see Kendrick, Benjamin Burks

Arnett, Ethel Stephens. Greensboro, North Carolina, the county seat of Guilford. Written under the direction of Walter Clinton Jackson. Chapel Hill, University of North Carolina Press [1955] 492 p. [306

Arnett, Thomas. Journal of the life, travels, and gospel labors of Thomas Arnett. Chicago, Association of Friends, 1884. 422 p. [307

——A solemn address to youth. Hillsborough, Printed and published by D. Heartt, 1823. 105 p. [308

Arnold, C. L. Centennial of the church and state, a sermon preached in St. James Church, Wilmington, N. C., April 30th, 1889. No place, no publisher, n.d. 14 p. [309

Arnold, Joseph D. Plain words for plain people. [Weldon, Harrell Printing House] n.d. 4 p. [310

Arnold, Robert. The Dismal Swamp and Lake Drummond. Norfolk, Va., Evening Telegram, pr., 1888. 53 p. [311

Arrington, B. F. Prophylactic care of the mouth with toothbrush and water. 3d ed. Goldsboro, Nash Bros., 1906. 23 p. [312

Arrington, Katherine (Pendleton) Jingles in a jiffy, by Katherine Pendleton Arrington and Adele Brenizer Dunn. [Wilmington? National Society of the Colonial Dames of America in the State of North Carolina, 1943?] [26] p. [313

Arrington, Pattie D. B. Is justice a farce? No place, no publisher [1893] 31 p. [314

Arthur, Glenn Dora (Fowler) Annals of the Fowler family. Austin, Tex., The Author, 1901. 327 p. [315

Arthur, John Preston. A history of Watauga County, North Carolina. Richmond, Va., Everett Waddey Co., 1915. 364 p. [316

——Western North Carolina; a history (from 1730 to 1913) Raleigh, Edwards and Broughton Printing Co., 1914. 710 p. [317

Asbury, Francis. The journal of the Rev. Francis Asbury, bishop of the Methodist Episcopal Church, from August 7, 1771, to December 7, 1815. New York, N. Bangs and T. Mason, 1821. 3 v. [318

[**Ash, Thomas**] Carolina; or, A description of the present state of that country. London, Printed for W. C., 1682. 40 p. [319

—— ——Tarrytown, N. Y., Reprinted, W. Abbatt, 1917. 23 p. [320

Ashburn, Jesse Anderson. History of the Fisher's River Primitive Baptist Association from its organization in 1832 to 1904. Laurel Fork, Va., F. P. Branscome, 1905. 205 p. [321

—— ——Reprinted with a second volume, from 1905 to 1953, by Francis Preston Stone. [Elon College, Primitive Baptist Publishing House, 1953] 350 p. [322

[**Ashe, S. W.**] The trial and death of Henry Wirz. Raleigh, E. M. Uzzell & Co., 1908. 62 p. [323

Ashe, Samuel, 1725-1813. A charge given to the Grand-Jury at Wilmington, November 30, 1782. No place, no publisher [1782?] [1] p. [324

Ashe, Samuel A'Court, ed., 1840-1938. Biographical history of North Carolina from colonial times to the present. Greensboro, C. L. Van Noppen, 1905-1917. 8 v. [325

——General index covering only the first eight volumes [1917?] 44 p.

[**Ashe, Samuel A'Court**] 1840-1938. A day with the professor and his friends. Raleigh, Edwards & Broughton Co., c.1895. 163 p. [326

Ashe, Samuel A'Court, 1840-1938. George Davis. Raleigh, Edwards & Broughton Printing Co., 1916. 25 p. [327

Ashe, Samuel A'Court, 1840-1938. History of North Carolina. Greensboro, C. L. Van Noppen, 1908-25. 2 v. [328

—— ——[Second ed.] v. 1. 1925. [329

[**Ashe, Samuel A'Court**] 1840-1938. An important document, the original first draught of the Mecklenburg Declaration recently brought to light. [No place, no publisher, 1916?] [4] p. [330

[**Ashe, Samuel A'Court**] 1840-1938. Mecklenburg Declaration; Governor Graham in line with Ashe's History. [Raleigh, Edwards & Broughton Printing Co., 1909] [7] p. [331

Ashe, Samuel A'Court, 1840-1938. Oration: General Robert E. Lee . . . Raleigh, N. C., January 20, 1904. Raleigh, W. S. Sherman & Co., pr., 1906. 23 p. [332

[**Ashe, Samuel A'Court**] 1840-1938. Reply of North Carolinians to the committee of bondholders. [Raleigh, no publisher, 1910] 16 p. [333

Ashe, Samuel A'Court, 1840-1938. Senator Simmons and his record. No place, no publisher [1912] 30 p. [334

Ashe, Samuel A'Court, 1840-1938. Should evolution be taught in the public schools? No place, no publisher, 1925. 2 p. [335

——Some facts about the Declaration. No place, no publisher, n.d. 3 p. [336

——A southern view of the invasion of the southern states. [Raleigh, The Author, 1935] 75 p. [337

Ashe, Samuel A'Court, 1874-1932. Raleigh from 1792 to 1888. Raleigh, Sun Publishing Co. [1888?] 24 p. [338

Ashe, William Willard. Cutting shortleaf pine so as to meet west coast competition.
No place, no publisher, n.d.   [339
——Forests and the cost of textile production.   [Raleigh? The Author? 1908]
11 p.   [340
Ashe Baptist Association. Minutes, 18 - 18 - NcU has 1891-1899, 1902-1910
[1929-1933] 1955   [341
Ashe Presbyterian, v. 1- June, 1923- Jefferson, Men of the Presbyterian Churches
of Ashe County, 1923- NcU has v. [1-6] 7-24 [25] 26-38   [342
Asheboro, N. C. Chamber of Commerce. Asheboro, North Carolina. Asheboro
[1939?] 24 p.   [343
——Directory, classified, business, professional service. Asheboro, 1946. 11 p. [344
——Facts about Asheboro, North Carolina. [Asheboro] n.d. 28 p.   [345
Asheville, N. C. Bar. Proceedings of the Bar of Asheville, July 28, 1902, upon the
death of Honorable Thomas Dillard Johnston. [Asheville? 1902] 24 p.   [346
Asheville, N. C. Board of Aldermen. Bourne's Asheville code. Asheville, Hackney
and Moale, 1909. 544 p.   [347
——Code of the city of Asheville. Asheville, Randolph & Hunt, pr., 1887. 405 p. [348
Asheville, N. C. Board of Commissioners. Pennell's Code of the city of Asheville.
[Asheville, Miller Press, pr., 1923?] 680 p.   [349
——Municipal bulletin, v. 1- January, 1916- Asheville, 1916- NcU has v. 1
[2]   [350
Asheville, N. C. Board of School Commissioners. Course of study for guidance of
teachers. 2d ed. Asheville, Hackney and Moale [1906] 135 p.   [351
——Courses of study for the public high school . . . prepared by R. V. Kennedy,
principal. Asheville, Hackney and Moale [1908] 26 p.   [352
——Report of city schools, 189 - Asheville, 189 - NcU has 1900/01-1908/09 [353
——Rules and regulations for the public schools. [Asheville, 1906] 43 p. [354
Asheville, N. C. Board of Trade. Asheville, N. C., America's beauty spot. [Ash-
ville, Inland Press, 1910?] 36 p.   [355
—— ——[Asheville, Hackney and Moale, 1911?] 31 p.   [356
—— ——[1915] 36 p.   [357
——Asheville, "the Land of the Sky". [Asheville, Hackney and Moale] n.d.
21 p.   [358
—— ——[1907?] 32 p.   [359
—— ——[1920] 20 p.   [360
——In the heart of the Blue Ridge. [Asheville, Hackney and Moale, 1917] 20 p. [361
——Opportunities, agricultural, Buncombe County. Asheville [1922] 24 p. [362
——To the health and pleasure-seeker. [Asheville, Citizen] 1898. 55 p.   [363
—— ——[Asheville, Citizen] 1899. 52 p.   [364
Asheville, N. C. Chamber of Commerce. Accomodations in Asheville and Western
North Carolina. Asheville, 1948. 48 p.   [365
—— ——1952-1953. Asheville, 1952. 47 p.   [366
——All the year: touring, sports, amusement, rest and joy. [Asheville, 192?]
39 p.   [367
——Asheville handbook, 192 - Asheville, 192 - NcU has 1929   [368
——Asheville "in the Land of the Sky". [Asheville, 192?] 16 p.   [369
—— ——[1922] 20 p.   [370
—— ——[1926?] 27 p.   [371
—— ——1927. 52 p.   [372
—— ——1929. 52 p.   [373
—— ——[1943?] 12 p.   [374
——Economic survey. [Asheville, 1947?] 44 p.   [375
——"In the Land of the Sky". [1937?] [11] p.   [376
Asheville, N. C. Chamber of Commerce. Industrial Bureau. Industry grows and
prospers in the Asheville district. [Asheville, 1927] [16] p.   [377
Asheville, N. C. Chestnut Street Methodist Episcopal Church, South. Annual
statement, 1920- [Asheville, 1920- NcU has 1920   [378
Asheville, N. C. Choral Society [Program] 1896/97- Asheville, 1896- NcU has
1898/99-1899/1900   [379

Asheville, N. C. Church of St. Lawrence. Altar Society. Guide to the history, art and architecture of the Church of St. Lawrence. [Asheville, 1923] 51 p. [380

Asheville, N. C. City Council. Budget, 19 - Asheville, 19 - NcU has 1952/53 [381
——The code of the city of Asheville. [Asheville, Miller Printing Co., 1945] 487 p. [382

Asheville, N. C. First Baptist Church. Pastor's tenth anniversary and sanctuary dedication. Asheville, 1954. [16] p. [383

Asheville, N. C. Health Department. Bulletin, no. 1-57, 1910-1915. Asheville, 1910-1915. NcU has no. 1-57 [384

Asheville, N. C. Mayor and Board of Aldermen. Year book, city of Asheville, North Carolina. Asheville, 1897- NcU has 1896/97 [385

Asheville, N. C. Mayor and Commissioner of Finance. Four years in review, and recommendations. [Asheville? 1927] [15] p. [386

Asheville, N. C. Mountain Sanitarium for Pulmonary Diseases. Biennial report, 1875/77- Baltimore, Sherwood & Co., pr., 1877- NcU has 1875/77 [387

Asheville, N. C. Music Festival. Official souvenir program, 1920- [Asheville] Asheville Music Festival Association, Inc., 1920- NcU has 1920-1922, 1927 [388

Asheville, N. C. Pen and Plate Club. Annual transactions, 1905- Asheville, 1906- NcU has 1905, 1906, 1907 [389
——The Pen and Plate Club of Asheville, N. C., 1904-1929. [Asheville, Inland Press, 1929] 49 p. [390
——The Pen and Plate Club of Asheville, N. C., 1904-1940. [Asheville, Stephens Press, 1940] 57 p. [391

Asheville, N. C. Sondley Reference Library. Leaves from the Sondley, v. 1-2, October, 1945-June, 1952. Asheville, 1945-1952. NcU has v. 1-2 [392

Asheville, N. C. Swannanoa Hotel. "Land of the Sky". [Asheville] 1891. 25 p. [393

Asheville, N. C. Trinity Church. Year Book. Asheville, 19 - NcU has 1904/05 [394

Asheville, N. C. Trinity Church. Woman's Guild. The kitchen counsellor. Asheville, Citizen, 1899. 84 p. [395

Asheville, N. C. Victoria Inn. Victoria Inn, Asheville, North Carolina. [Asheville, Inland Press] n.d. 15 p. [396

Asheville, N. C. Von Ruck Memorial Sanatorium. Advice to patients, rules and regulations. [Asheville?] n.d. 15 p. [397

Asheville-Biltmore College. Catalogue, 19 - Asheville, 19 - NcU has [1948/49-1955/56] [398

Asheville city directory, 188 - Asheville, Southern Directory Co., 18 - NcU has 1887 [399

Asheville city directory, compiled by J. S. McIlwaine, 1896- Atlanta, Ga., Franklin Printing and Publishing Co., 1896- NcU has 1896-1897 [400

Asheville Club, Asheville, N. C. Asheville Club. Asheville, 1908. 36 p. [401

Asheville Female College, Asheville, N. C. The constitution, charter, and by-laws. Asheville, R. M. Stokes, pr., 1869. [402
——Catalogue, 18 - Asheville, 18 - NcU has 1873/73, 1888/89 [403

Asheville Library Association. Catalogue. Asheville, Hackney and Moale, 1905. 100 p. [404

Asheville Normal and Teachers College. Catalogue, 18 - 18 - NcU has 1892/93 [1900/01-1940/41] [405

Asheville Normal and Teachers College. Department of Education. A survey of Liberty School district. [Asheville, 1918] 10 p. [406

Asheville Presbytery see Presbyterian Church in the U. S. Synod of North Carolina. Asheville Presbytery

Asheville School. Catalogue, 19 - Asheville, 19 - NcU has [1905/06-1941/42] [407

Asheville School review, v. 1- 19 - Asheville, 19 - NcU has v. [10, 16-22] [408

Asheville Senior High School dedication program, February 5, 1929. [Asheville, 1929] [16] p. [409

Ashley Horne for governor. No place, no publisher [1908] 20 p. [410

Ashmore, Harry S. The Negro and the schools. Chapel Hill, University of North Carolina Press [1954] 228 p. [411

—— ——Rev. ed. 239 p. [412

Asplund, John, comp. Annual register of the Baptist denomination in North America, [Pref. Southampton Co., Va., 1791] 70 p. [413

——Universal register of the Baptist denomination in North America. Boston, 1794. [414

Associated Committees on Southern Rural Development. Southern rural life. [Wilmington?] 1929. 28 p. [415

Associated General Contractors of America. Carolinas Branch. Roster of members, 194 - Charlotte, 194 - NcU has 1945, 1947, 1948, 1949, 1951, 1952, 1953, 1954, 1955 [416

——Special highway bulletin, no. 1- January 30, 1951- Charlotte, 1951- NcU has no. 1-15 [417

——Weekly bulletin, no. 1- 192 - NcU has [1934-1938, 1940-1942, 1946-1956] [418

Association of Clerks of the Superior Courts of North Carolina. Proceedings of the annual convention, 192 - Raleigh, 192 - NcU has 1923-1939, 1941, 1942 [419

Aston, Anna C. Princess Hilda. Chicago, Woman's Temperance Publishing Association, 1892. 59 p. [420

At home and abroad, v. 1-6, April, 1881-September, 1883. Wilmington, G. D. Bernheim, 1881-1883. NcU has v. 1-5 [6] [421

Aten, Henry J. History of the Eighty-fifth Regiment, Illinois Volunteer Infantry. Hiawatha, Kan., 1901. 506 p. [422

Athas, Daphne. The weather of the heart. New York, D. Appleton-Century Co. [1947] 276 p. [423

Atkin, Edmond. Indians of the Southern colonial frontier. Columbia, University of South Carolina Press [1954] 108 p. [424

Atkins, Emmet Day. Extracts from the diary of Benjamin Elberfield Atkins . . . 1848-1909. Gastonia, privately published, 1947. 97 p. [425

Atkins, James. The doctrines and polity of the Methodist Episcopal Church, South. Part first, by Rev. Wilbur F. Tillett . . . Part second, by Rev. James Atkins. Nashville, Tenn., Publishing House of the M. E. Church, South, 1905. 172 p. [426

——Help or hinder, a tract on missions. Asheville, Board of Missions of the Western North Carolina Conference, 1896. 24 p. [427

——The kingdom in the cradle. Nashville, Tenn., Publishing House of the M. E. Church, South, 1905. 325 p. [428

Atkins, S. G. President's address, North Carolina Negro Teachers' Association. No place, no publisher [1927] 15 p. [429

Atkins, Stewart. The halting gods. Emory University, Ga., Banner Press [1952] 64 p. [430

Atkins, Willard Earl. Labor attitudes and problems. New York, Prentice-Hall, 1924. 520 p. [431

——Worker in modern economic society. Chicago, University of Chicago Press [1923] 929 p. [432

Atkinson, James Oscar. These twain: Willis John Lee, Mary Jennet Lee. Greensboro, J. J. Stone & Co., n.d. 43 p. [433

Atkinson, Joseph Mayo. God, the giver of victory and peace. No place, no publisher [Pref. 1862] 15 p. [434

——The true path; or, The young man invited to the Savior. Philadelphia, Presbyterian Board of Publication. [c.1860] 300 p. [435

Atkinson, Thomas. Address delivered before the Historical Society of the University of North-Carolina, June 6, 1855. Raleigh, Holden & Wilson, 1855. 32 p. [436

——Authoritative ministerial teaching. Baltimore, D. Brunner, 1844. 19 p. [437

——Charge on the subject of sacramental confession. Raleigh, Daily News, 1874. 15 p. [438

——Christian duty in the present time of trouble. Wilmington, Fulton and Price, 1861. 14 p. [439

——Confirmation. No place, Published by order of the Convention, n.d.   13 p. [440
——Defence of the Charge on sacremental confession. No place, The Author, n.d.
39 p.   [441
——The episcopate, a stewardship.   Philadelphia, Episcopal Female Tract Society,
1860.   18 p.   [442
——Extract from the address . . . before the Council of the Protestant Episcopal
Church, held at Raleigh.   [Raleigh, J. C. Gorman, 1865]   13 p.   [443
——Extract from the annual address to the Convention of the Diocese of North
Carolina.   [Raleigh] Church Intelligencer, 1861.   8 p.   [444
——Free and open churches; a sermon preached in Holy Trinity Church, Brooklyn,
October 11, 1868.   No place, no publisher, n.d.   8 p.   [445
——The old paths; a sermon, preached in St. Luke's Church, Salisbury. Fayette-
ville, Edward J. Hale & Son, 1857.   16 p.   [446
——On the causes of our national troubles; a sermon delivered in St. James' Church,
Wilmington, N. C. . . . the 4th of January, 1861.   Wilmington, Herald Office,
1861.   15 p.   [447
——Primary charge to the clergy, delivered at the convention at Warrenton, May,
1855.   Fayetteville, Edward J. Hale & Son, 1855.   16 p.   [448
——A sermon commemorative of the Rt. Rev. William Rollinson Whittingham.
Baltimore, William K. Boyle, pr. [1879]   22 p.   [449
——A sermon in reference to the catastrophe which occurred on board the United
States Ship Princeton, on February 28, 1844.   Baltimore, D. Brunner, 1844.
16 p.   [450
——What is truth?   No place, no publisher [c.1859]   31 p.   [451
Atlanta and Richmond Air-Line Railway.   Atlanta and Richmond Air-Line Railway
Company from Atlanta, Ga., to Charlotte, N. C.   New York, E. W. Sackett, pr.,
1870.   19 p.   [452
Atlantic Baptist Association.   Minutes, 1884- 1884- NcU has 1884-1886 [1894-
1903] 1930-1933, 1936-1947, 1953-1955   [453
Atlantic Beach is calling you.   Morehead City, no publisher [1928]   5 p.   [454
Atlantic Christian College, Wilson.   Bulletin: Catalogue number, 19 - Wilson,
19 - NcU has 1907/08, 1911/12, 1912/13, 1915/16-1925/26 [1932/33-1937/38]
1939/40-1949/50, 1953/54-1955/56   [455
——Radiant, v. 1- 19 - Wilson, 19 - NcU has v. [1-4, 7-8, 11-12]   [456
Atlantic Coast Conference.   Constitution and by-laws. [Chapel Hill?] 1954.
28 p.   [457
——[Chapel Hill?] 1955.   29 p.   [458
——Yearbook, 1954/55-   [Chapel Hill, 1955- NcU has v. 1, v. 2, no. 2, v. 3,
no. 1   [459
Atlantic Coast Conference. Committee on Constitution and By-Laws.   Report.
[Chapel Hill? 1953]   24 p.   [460
Atlantic Coast Line news, v. 1- May, 1920- Wilmington, 1920- NcU has v. 5-37 [461
Atlantic Coast Line Railroad.   Annual report, 18 - Wilmington, 18 - NcU has
1901/02-1953/54   [462
——Class list. No place, n.d.   24 p.   [464
——A decade of progress, 1939-1948.   Wilmington, 1949.   39 p.   [465
——Distance and percentage tables between Weldon, N. C., and all points south and
southwest.   New York, Hosford & Sons, 1874.   28 p.   [466
Atlantic Collegiate Institute, Elizabeth City.   Catalogue, 190 - 190 - NcU has
1903/04-1905/06   [467
Atlantic Hotel, Morehead City, N. C.   Atlantic Hotel.   Raleigh, E. M. Uzzell, 1885.
31 p.   [468
——   ——[Washington, Southern Railway Co., 1895]   14 p.   [469
Atlantic sportsman, v. 1-2, September, 1931-December, 1933.   Winston-Salem,
Gordon Publishing Co., 1931-1933.   NcU has v. 1-2   [470
Atlantic, Tennessee, and Ohio Railroad.   Annual report, 18 - 18 - NcU has
1877/78, 1879/80, 1883/84   [471
——First mortgage bonds in North Carolina.   Charlotte, Journal Observer, pr.,
1883.   24 p.   [472

——Proceedings of stockholders, 18 - 18 - NcU has 1870 [473

Atson, William. Heart whispers. Philadelphia, H. Cowperthwait & Co., 1859. 368 p. [474

Atwood, Jesse Howell. Thus be their destiny; the personality development of Negro youth in three communities. Washington, American Council on Education, 1941. 96 p. [475

Audubon Society of North Carolina. Annual report, 1903-1911. No place, 1903-1911. Library has: 1903-1909, 1911. [476

——Constitution. No place, no publisher, n.d. 4 p. [477

——Constitution and by-laws. Greensboro, Charles G. Harrison Printing Co., 1905. 8 p. [478

——First one hundred sustaining members . . . November 15th, 1902. No place, n.d. 4 p. [479

——Leaflet, no. 1-6, 1902-1903. Raleigh, 1902-1903. NcU has no. 1-6 [480

Averill, Esther, ed. Daniel Boone. Paris, Domino Press [1931] [14] p. [481

—— ——New York, Harper & Brothers [1945] 56 p. [482

Avery, Alpohnso Calhoun. History of the Presbyterian churches at Quaker Meadows and Morganton from the year 1780 to 1913. Raleigh, Edwards & Broughton, 1913. 109 p. [483

——Memorial address on the life and character of Lieutenant General D. H. Hill, May 10th, 1893. Raleigh, Edwards & Broughton, 1893. 41 p. [484

Avery, Clifton K., ed. Official court record of the trial, conviction and execution of Francis Silvers, first woman hanged in North Carolina. [Morganton, The News-Herald, 1953] 12 p. [485

Avery, Isaac Erwin. Idle comments. Charlotte, Stone Publishing Co. [c.1905] 271 p. [486

Avery, William Bailey. The marine artillery with the Burnside expedition and the battle of Camden, N. C. Providence, N. B. Williams & Co., 1880. 28 p. [487

Avery, William Waightstill. Address delivered before the two literary societies of the University of North Carolina, June 4, 1851. Raleigh, William W. Holden, pr., 1851. 23 p. [488

——Address to the people of the 46th and 49th senatorial districts. No place, no publisher, 1861. 14 p. [489

Avery Baptist Association. Minutes, 191 - 191 - NcU has 1915, 1953 [490

Avery Co., N. C. Board of Education. Report of the public schools, 19 - [Newland, 19 - Library has : 1912/13 [491

Avirett, James Battle. Causes affecting church growth. No place, no publisher, n.d. 16 p. [492

——The memoirs of General Turner Ashby and his compeers. Baltimore, Selby & Dulany, 1867. 408 p. [493

——The old plantation; how we lived in great house and cabin before the war. New York, F. Tennyson Neely Co. [1901] 202 p. [494

——Who was the rebel—the traitor—the trans-Susquehanna man or the cis-Susquehanna man? [Winchester? 1897?] 30 p. [495

Aycock, Charles Brantley. Aycock on prohibition. No place, no publisher, n.d. 4 p. [496

——Speech accepting the nomination for govenor, April 11, 1900. Raleigh, Edwards & Broughton, 1902. 17 p. [497

Aycock, William Brantley. Military law under the Uniform code of military justice, by William B. Aycock and Seymour W. Wurfel. Chapel Hill, University of North Carolina Press, 1955. 430 p. [498

Aykroyd, James. A catalogue of vocal and instrumental music for sale by James Aykroyd, professor of music, Newbern, North Carolina. [New Bern?] n.d. 8 p. [499

Babcock, Mary Reynolds. First aid for flowers. [New York?] 1954. 53 p. [500

Babington, J. P. Biography of Mrs. Catherine Babington, the only woman Mason in the world and how she became a Blue Lodge Mason. Taylorsville, The Author, [1906?] 48 p. [501

[Back Bay Game Preservation Association, Norfolk, Va.] Documentary proof of imperative necessity for restoration of lock in Albemarle and Chesapeake Canal. [Norfolk, Va.? 1929?]   39 p.   [502

Bacon, George Washington. Life and speeches of President Andrew Johnson. London, Bacon and Co. [1865?]   106 p.   [503
—— ——London, Bacon and Co. [1866?]   137 p.   [504

Bacon, William J., ed. History of the Fifty-fifth Field Artillery Brigade. [Nashville, Tenn., Benson, pr., c.1920]   335 p.   [505

Badger, George Edmund. Address delivered before the Philanthropic and Dialectic societies at Chapel Hill, N. C., June 26, 1833. Richmond, Thomas W. White, pr., 1833.   21 p.   [506
——Examination of the doctrine declared and the powers claimed by the Rt. Rev. Bishop Ives in a pastoral letter to the clergy and laity of his diocese. Philadelphia, H. Hooker, 1849.   105 p.   [507

[Badger, George Edmund?] Letter from—— to Mr.—— containing an "extract" and other matters, besides a "P. S." [Raleigh? 1840] 7 p.   [508

Badger, George Edmund. Speech delivered at the great Whig meeting in the county of Granville, on Tuesday, the third day of March, 1840. Raleigh, Register, 1840.   24 p.   [509

Bagby, English. The psychology of personality; an analysis of common emotional disorders. New York, H. Holt and Co. [c.1928]   236 p.   [510

[Baggarly, Andrew] Eagle City, Iredell County, N. C. No place, The Author, 1856.   15 p.   [511

Bagpipe, 19 - [Maxton, Presbyterian Junior College] 19   -   NcU has v. 20   [512

Bahnsen, Jane Cutler, comp. Lawson's History of North Carolina, by John Lawson: index, 1951 edition, Garrett and Massie, publishers. Chapel Hill, University of North Carolina Library, 1956.   36 p.   [513

Bahnson, Charles F. North Carolina lodge manual. Farmington [Edwards and Broughton, 1905]   86 p.   [514

Bahnson, Henry Theodore. Days of the war, 1863-1865. [Winston-Salem?] n.d. 31 p.   [515

Bailey, Bernadine (Freeman) Picture book of North Carolina. Chicago, Albert Whitman and Co., c.1950. [28] p.   [516

Bailey, Christopher Thomas, comp. Baptism and the new version of the New Testament. Raleigh, Edwards and Broughton, 1881.   12 p.   [517

Bailey, Howard. The ABC's of play producing. New York, D. McKay Co. [1955] 276 p.   [518

Bailey, James Davis. Commanders at King's Mountain. Gaffney, S. C., E. H. De Camp, 1926.   431 p.   [519
——Sketch of the life and career of Col. James D. Williams.   No place, no publisher [1898] 91 p.   [520
——Some heroes of the American Revolution. Spartanburg, S. C., Band & White, pr., 1924.   287 p.   [521

Bailey, James Osler. Creative exercises in college English. New York, American Book Co. [c.1952]   248 p.   [522
——Proper words in proper places. New York, American Book Co. [1952] 473 p. [523
——The Southern Humanities Conference and its constituent societies. [Chapel Hill] University of North Carolina Press, 1951.   68 p.   [524
——Supplementary exercise: for use in English courses for engineers, prepared to accompany Howell's Handbook of English in engineering usage, 2d edition, by J. O. Bailey, Thomas B. Stroup, and A. C. Howell. New York, J. Wiley & Sons, Inc., 1940.   60 l.   [525
——Thomas Hardy and the cosmic mind; a new reading of The Dyna ts. Chapel Hill, University of North Carolina Press [1956]   223 p.   [526

Bailey, Josiah William. Condition of the farmers of North Carolina. Raleigh, Bynum Printing Co., [1921?]   19 p.   [527
——Elector's speech, 1909. No place, no publisher [1909] 13 p.   [528

——Four services of progress. Raleigh, Mitchell Printing Co. [1922] 8 p. [529

——Henry Groves Connor. No place, no publisher [1929] 19 p. [530

——The issues of the campaign. [Raleigh? 1924] 4 p. [531

——Needed changes in our tax system. [Raleigh] no publisher, 1924. 4 p. [532

——Proposed constitutional amendment on taxation. [Raleigh] no publisher, 1920. 12 p. [533

——The Republican and the Democratic program. Raleigh, Mitchell Printing Co. 1932. 16 p. [534

——The revaluation act. Raleigh [1920?] 16 p. [535

——Simmons for the Senate. [Raleigh, 1930] 31 p. [536

——Simmons—organizer of victory. No place, no publisher [1912] 16 p. [537

——To the Democratic voters of North Carolina, announcement of the candidacy of J. W. Bailey for the nomination for governor. Raleigh, Bynum Printing Co., [1924] [3] p. [538

——A valuable message to the farmers of North Carolina. No place, no publisher [1927?] 7 p. [539

——The wages and hours legislation. Washington, Washington Star, 1938. [8] p. [540

——The way of progress in North Carolina, opening speech at Raleigh, March 10, 1924. [Raleigh? 1924] 12 p. [541

Bailey, Josiah William, Jr. Gulf stream fishing guide for the Atlantic Beach—Morehead City area. [Morehead City, Herald Printing Co. 1947] [15] p. [542

Bailey, Loretto (Carroll) Job's kinfolks, a play of the mill people. Boston, Walter H. Baker Co. [c.1930] 126 p. [543

Bailey, Palmer Edwards. Conglomeration. Raleigh, P. E. Bailey [1947] 179 p. [544

——North Carolina compendium of trial law. Raleigh, Mitchell Printing Co., 1927. 365 p. [545

Bailey, William Henry. The detective faculty, as illustrated from judicial records and the actualities of experience. Cincinnati, Robert Clarke Co., 1896. 172 p. [546

——The effect of civil war upon the rights of persons and property. Salisbury, Lewis Hanes, pr., 1867. 22 p. [547

——The genealogy of the Latham, Hill, Montfort, Littlejohn, McCulloch, Campbell, and Brownrigg families. [Houston, Tex., no publisher, pref. 1899] 61 p. [548

——The onus probandi, preparation for trial, and the right to open and conclude. New York, Banks & Brothers, 1886. 712 p. [549

Baily, Waldron. Heart of the Blue Ridge. New York, W. J. Watt & Co. [c.1915] 275 p. [550

——The homeward trail. New York, Grosset and Dunlap [c.1916] 313 p. [551

——June gold. New York, W. J. Watt & Co. [c.1922] 281 p. [552

——When the cock crows. New York, Grosset and Dunlap [c.1918] 303 p. [553

Bain, Donald William. Edenton St. Sunday School of the Methodist Episcopal Church, South, Raleigh, N. C. Raleigh, Edwards & Broughton, 1881. 50 p. [554

Bain, Grady Lee. The circle's end. Boston, Meador Publishing Co., 1932. 224 p. [555

[Bain? John C.] The Bain family. Raleigh, Bynum Printing Co. [pref. 1928] 16 p. [556

Bain, William T. Letters and meditations on religious and other subjects. Raleigh, Register, pr., 1839. 148 p. [557

Bainton, Roland H. Friends in relation to the churches. Guilford College, 1954. (Ward lecture, November 12, 1954) 16 p. [557a

Baird, Nannie Clendinen (Catchings) The Clendinen, Myers, and Mills families, and various related families in the South by Mrs. J. R. Baird [and others] Atlanta, A. B. Caldwell, 1923. 188 p. [558

Baity, Elizabeth (Chesley) America before man. New York, Viking Press, 1953. 224 p. [559

——Americans before Columbus. New York, Viking Press, 1951. 256 p. [560

——Man is a weaver. New York, Viking Press, 1942. 334 p. [561

Bakeless, John Edwin. Daniel Boone. New York, W. Morrow & Co., 1939. 480 p. [562

——Fighting frontiersman, the life of Daniel Boone. New York, W. Morrow, 1948. 260 p. [563

Baker, Archibald. Address delivered before the two literary societies of Davidson College, N. C., July 31st, 1845. Raleigh, Weston R. Gales, n.d. 15 p.   [564

Baker, Blanche Egerton. Mrs. G. I. Joe [Goldsboro? 1951] 247 p.   [565

[Baker, Emma Eugenia (Hall)] The master of L'Etrange, by Eugene Hall. Philadelphia, T. B. Peterson & Brothers [c.1886] 346 p.   [566

——Vernal Dune, by Eugene Hall. New York, Neale Publishing Co., 1913. 251 p.   [567

Baker, James Millard. Contending the grade in India. [Asheville] The Biltmore Press, c.1947. 297 p.   [568

Baker, Richard Henry. The order of service for the consecration of the Reverend Richard Henry Baker, D. D., to be a bishop in the Church of God in the Diocese of North Carolina . . . January 25th, 1951. [Raleigh, Edwards and Broughton, 1951] 31 p.   [569

Baker, Webster B. History of Rust College. Greensboro, The Author, c.1924. 221 p.   [570

Bakersville, N. C. Historical Celebration Publications Committee. Bakersville, North Carolina, historical celebration. [Bakersville, 1956] 48 p.   [571

Balch, William S. The spirit life. Galesburg, Ill. Free Press Steam Printing House, 1868. 20 p.   [572

Baldwin, Alice Mary. The clergy of Connecticut in Revolutionary days. [New Haven] Yale University Press, 1936. 31 p.   [573

——The New England clergy and the American Revolution. Durham, Duke University Press, 1928. 222 p.   [574

Baldwin, Seth. Alas Lucinda! London, Denis Archer [1932] 300 p.   [575

Baldwin and Robersonian's Lumberton, North Carolina, city directory, 1938- Charleston, S. C., Baldwin Directory Co., c.1938- NcU has 1938   [576

Baldwin's Albemarle, North Carolina, city directory, 1937- Charleston, S. C., Baldwin Directory Co., 1937- NcU has 1937   [577

Baldwin's and Free Press' Kinston, North Carolina, city directory, 1936- Charleston, S. C., Baldwin Directory Co., 1936- NcU has 1936   [578

Baldwin's and Post's Salisbury, North Carolina, city directory, 1935- Charleston, S. C., Baldwin Directory Co., 1935- NcU has 1935   [579

Baldwin's and Review's Reidsville, North Carolina, city directory, 1935- Charleston, S. C., Baldwin Directory Co., 1935- NcU has 1935   [580

Baldwin's and Times' Thomasville, North Carolina, city directory, 1935- Charleston, S. C., Baldwin Directory Co., 1935- NcU has 1935   [581

Baldwin's Concord, North Carolina, city directory, 19 - Charleston, S. C., Baldwin Directory Co., 19 - NcU has 1938   [582

Baldwin's Goldsboro, North Carolina, city directory, 193 - Charleston, S. C., Baldwin Directory Co., c.19 - NcU has 1938   [583

Baldwin's Lexington, North Carolina, city directory, 1937- Charleston, S. C., Baldwin Directory Co., 1937- NcU has 1937   [584

Baldwin's New Bern, North Carolina, city directory, 1937- Charleston, S. C., Baldwin Directory Co., 1937- NcU has 1937   [585

Baldwin's Washington, North Carolina, city directory, 1937- Charleston, S. C., Baldwin Directory Co., 1937- NcU has 1937   [586

[Ball, W. W.] Kanuga Lake. No place, no publisher [pref. 1909] 11 p.   [587

[Ballard, B.] An examination of the opinion of the Supreme Court on the acts of 1784 regulating descents. Raleigh, Henderson, 1817. 32 p.   [588

Ballard, Robert E. Myrtle Lawn. Philadelphia, T. B. Peterson & Brother [c.1879] 288 p.   [589

Balliett, Carl J. World leadership in denims . . . dedicated to the founders of the Cone Mills at Greensboro, North Carolina. Proximity, Proximity Manufacturing Co. [c.1925] [67] p.   [590

Baltimore and North Carolina Copper and Gold Mine Company. Charter and by-laws. Baltimore, Hamilton & Co., pr., 1883. 8 p.   [591

Bandy, James Marcus. An analytical arithmetic, in six parts. Trinity College, Trinity Publication Society, 1890. 111 p. [592

Banks, Howard O. Report to the Charlotte observer of the celebration at Guilford Battle Ground, July 4th, 1893. [Charlotte?] n.d. 4 p. [593

Banks, James. The life and character of Flora McDonald. Fayetteville, Edward J. Hale & Son, pr., 1857. 24 p. [594

Bannister, Cowan & Company. Resources of North Carolina. Wilmington, 1869. 116 p. [595

[Bannister, Lemuel] Lake Waccamaw lands, Columbus and Brunswick counties, North Carolina. No place, no publisher, 1903. 7 p. [596

Bansemer, C. F. Inaugural address . . . North Carolina College. Charlotte, Daily Times and Weekly News, pr., 1868. 19 p. [597

Banvard, Joseph. Romance of American history. Boston, Guild and Lincoln, 1852. 306 p. [598

——Southern explorers and colonists. Boston, D. Lothrop & Co. [c.1880] 306 p. [599

Baptist, Leona. Daniel Boone. Charleston, W. Va., Children's Theatre Press, c.1940. 51 p. [600

Baptists. North Carolina. Advisory Council. Minutes of the Baptist Advisory Council held at Union Meeting House, Lenoir County, N. C., on the 11th, 12th, and 13th days of October, 1839. Raleigh, Thomas Loring, pr., 1840. 7 p. [601

Baptists. North Carolina. Associations see Name of the Association.

Baptists. North Carolina. Board of Missions. Curious and useful questions on the Bible. Goldsboro, 1864. 37 p. [602

——Kingdom building by North Carolina Baptists. Raleigh, 1923. 97 p. [603

——Report, 19 - 19 - NcU has [1901-1907] 1921 [604

Baptists. North Carolina. Convention at Zion Hill see United Baptist Association

Baptists. North Carolina. State Convention. Baptist Assembly grounds, adopted in Greensboro, 1906, Swannanoa Gap, Buncombe County. No place, n.d. 11 p. [605

——The growth of one hundred years. Raleigh [1930] 228 p. [606

——Minutes of annual meeting, 1830- 1830- NcU has 1830-1834, 1836-1839, [1845-1869] 1880-1955. [607

Baptists. North Carolina. Social Service Committee. Report. No place, n.d. 10 p. [608

Baptists. North Carolina. State Educational and Missionary Convention. Proceedings, 18 - 18 - NcU has [1891-1909] [609

Baptists. North Carolina. Sunday School Board. A catechism for little children. [Raleigh, W. W. Holden, pr., 1864] 32 p. [610

——Minutes, 18 - 18 - NcU has 1874, 1877-1878, 1880-1882, 1884, 1903, 1907 [611

Baptists. North Carolina. Woman's Missionary Union. Report, 189 - 189 - NcU has [1900-1909] 1911-1915, 1918-1931, 1933-1955 [612

Baptists (Colored) North Carolina. State Convention. Minutes, 18 - 18 - NcU has 1877, 1878, 1881, 1924, 1928 [613

Baptists, Primitive see Primitive Baptists

Baraca-Philathea herald, v. 1- 1904- 1904- NcU has v. [6, 11-15] [614

Barbee, David Rankin. An excursion in southern history, briefly set forth in the correspondence between Senator A. J. Beveridge and David R. Barbee. Asheville, Langbourne M. Williams, 1928. 64 p. [615

Barbee, Jennie M. Historical sketches of the Raleigh Public Schools, 1876-1941/42. [Raleigh, Barbee Pupils' Association, 1943] 109 p. [616

Barber-Scotia College, Concord, N. C. Catalogue, 18 - 18 - NcU has 1876/77 [1905/06-1953/54] [617

Barfield, J. M., joint author, see Harrison, T. F.

Barium messenger, v. 1- 192 - Barium Springs, Presbyterian Orphans' Home, 192 - NcU has v. [6-20] 21-33 [618

Barker, Addison. The magpie's nest. Mill Valley, Calif., Wings Press, 1950. 56 p. [619

Barker, Charles Ely. A little volume of songs and meditations. [Charlotte, Observer Printing House, c.1934] 48 p. [620

Barker, Tommie Dora. Libraries of the South. Chicago, American Library Association, 1936. 215 p. [621

Barksdale, Lane. Some notes on orchids of the Piedmont and Western North Carolina. Chapel Hill, M. A. Abernethy, 1936. 12 p. [622

Barlow, Arthur. The first voyage to Roanoke. 1584. [Boston, Directors of the Old South Work, 1898] (Old South leaflets [General ser., v. 4] no. 92) 20 p. [623

[Barlowe, Texie Horton] The Hortons of Western North Carolina. [Lenoir] n.d. 77 p. [624

Barnes, David A. An address delivered to the students of the Warrenton Male Academy . . . in June, 1850. Raleigh, Seaton Gales, 1850. 20 p. [625
——Speech on the subject of Negro slavery. No place, no publisher, 1851. 8 p. [626

Barnes, Willian Wright. The Southern Baptist Convention, 1845-1953. Nashville, Tenn., Broadman Press [1954] 330 p. [627

Barney, Caleb Henry. A country boy's first three months in the army. Providence, N. B. Williams & Co., 1880. (Personal narratives of events in the war of the rebellion, being papers read before the Rhode Island Soldiers and Sailors Historical Society, 2d ser., no. 2) 47 p. [628

Barnhardt, Jesse Homer. Looking them over. Boston, Stratford Co. [c.1931] 233 p. [629

[Barnwell, Lila Ripley] Hendersonville. [Hendersonville, Greater Hendersonville Club] n.d. [23] p. [630
——Hendersonville, North Carolina. [Asheville, Hackney and Moale, pr.] n.d. 18 p. [631

Barnwell, Mildred Gwin. Faces we see. Gastonia, Southern Combed Yarn Spinners Association, 1939. 112 p. [632

Barr, John. The history of John Barr. Philadelphia, George, Latimer and Co., 1833. 91 p. [633

Barrett, James F. Labor's appeal for minimum wage and maximum hour law for North Carolina. Raleigh, 1939. 17 p. [634
——Organized labor and child labor reform. New York, National Child Labor Committee, 1916. (Its Pamphlet 261, May, 1916) 4 p. [635

Barrett, John Gilchrist. Sherman's march through the Carolinas. Chapel Hill, University of North Carolina Press, 1956. 325 p. [636

Barrett, John Pressley, ed. Centennial of religious journalism. 2d ed. Dayton, O., Christian Publishing Association, 1908. 656 p. [637
——Iola; or, Facing the truth. Raleigh, Edwards and Broughton, 1886. 220 p. [638

Barrett, Solomon. A full grammatical analysis of British classical poetry adapted to Murray's English grammar, exercise and key, and intended as a supplement to the same . . . by Solomon Barrett and Simon S. Barrett. Milton, Gazette Office, 1830. 24 p. [639

[Barringer, Daniel Laurens] To the freemen of Orange, Person & Wake. No place, no publisher [1831] 3 p. [640
——To the freemen of the congressional district, composed of the counties of Orange, Person, and Wake. [Wake County, March 14, 1827] 3 p. [641

Barringer, Daniel Moreau. Address delivered before the alumni and graduating class of the University of North Carolina, Wednesday, June 3, 1840. Raleigh, Star, pr., 1840. 26 p. [642
——Address delivered before the Mecklenburg Agricultural Society at Charlotte, N. C., October 27, 1859. Charlotte, Western Democrat, 1860. 32 p. [643
——Letter, Raleigh, June 2, 1871. [Raleigh, 1871] 7 p. [644
——Oration delivered on the Fourth of July, 1837, at Concord, N. C. Charlotte, Thomas J. Holton, pr., 1837. 16 p. [645
——To the freemen of the second congressional district of North Carolina. No place, no publisher [1845] 4 p. [646

Barringer, Paul Brandon. The American Negro, his past and future. 3d ed. Raleigh, Edwards and Broughton, 1900. 23 p. [647
—— ——Charlotte, Observer Printing House, 1900. 15 p. [648
——The natural bent; the memoirs of Dr. Paul B. Barringer. Chapel Hill, University of North Carolina Press [1949] 280 p. [649
——"The sacrifice of a race"; an address delivered before the Race Conference at Montgomery, Alabama, May 10th, 1900. Raleigh, Edwards and Broughton, 1900. 30 p. [650

Barringer, Rufus. Address at the Luther commemoration in Concord, N. C., November 10th, 1883, on the early German settlers in eastern Cabarrus. No place, no publisher, n.d. 10 p. [651
——History of the North Carolina Railroad. Raleigh, News and Observer [1894] (Papers of the North Carolina Historical Society at the University of N. C.) 21 p. [652

Barrows, Harlan H. Geography . . . by Harlan H. Barrows . . . and Edith Putnam Parker. New York, Silver, Burdett and Co., c.1933. 4 v. "The geography of North Carolina, by Sallie B. Marks [and] Mary H. Hyman" 32 p. at the end of book four. [653

Bartlett, Frederick Orin. Big Laurel. Boston, Houghton Mifflin Company, 1922. 305 p. [654

Bartlett, William Irving. Jones Very, Emerson's "brave saint." Durham, Duke University Press, 1942. 237 p. [655

Bartram, John. Diary of a journey through the Carolinas, Georgia, and Florida, 1765-1766; Travels in Georgia and Florida, 1773-74, William Bartram, annotated by Francis Harper. [Philadelphia, The American Philosophical Society, 1942-43] (Its Transactions. New series, v. 33, parts 1-2) 242 p. [656

Bartram, William. The travels of William Bartram, edited by Mark Van Doren. New York, Barnes & Noble, 1940. 414 p. [657
—— ——New York, Dover [1947] [658
——Travels through North & South Carolina, Georgia, East & West Florida, the Cherokee country, the extensive territories of the Muscogulges, or Creek Confederacy, and the country of the Choctaws. Philadelphia, Printed by James & Johnson, 1791. 522 p. [659
—— ——Philadelphia, Printed by James and Johnson, 1791. London, Reprinted for J. Johnson, 1792. 520 p. [660
—— ——1794. [661
——Voyages dan les parties sud de l'Amérique Septentrionale, savoir: les Carolines Septentrionale et Méridionale, la Georgie, les Florides Orientale et Occidentale, le pays des Cherokées, le vaste territoire des Muscogulges ou de la confédération Creek, et le pays des Chactaws. Paris, Maradan, an IX [1801] 2 v. [662

Baskervill, Patrick Hamilton. The Hamiltons of Burnside, North Carolina, and their ancestors and descendants. Richmond, Va., W. E. Jones' Sons, 1916. 158 p. [663

Baskerville, Charles. Aids to teachers of School chemistry. Richmond, Va., B. F. Johnson Publishing Co., 1899. 42 p. [664
——Radium and radio-active substances, their application especially to medicine. Philadelphia, Williams, Brown & Earle [1905] 164 p. [665
——Rare-earth mordants, by Charles Baskerville and T. B. Faust. London, Eyre and Spottiswoode, 1904. 12 p. [665a
——School chemistry. Richmond, Va., B. F. Johnson Publishing Co., 1899. 159 p. [666

Bassett, John Spencer. Abraham Lincoln. [Durham? The Author, c.1909] 12 p. [667
——Anti-slavery leaders of North Carolina. Baltimore, The Johns Hopkins Press, 1898. (Johns Hopkins University Studies in historical and political science, 16th ser. VI) 74 p. [668
——The constitutional beginnings of North Carolina (1663-1729) Baltimore, The Johns Hopkins Press, 1894. (Johns Hopkins University Studies in historical and political science, 12th ser., III) 73 p. [669
——Expansion and reform, 1889-1926. New York, Longmans, Green, and Co., 1926. (Epochs of American history [v. 4] 355 p. [670
——The federalist system, 1789-1801. New York, Harper & Brothers, 1906. (The American nation, v. 11) 327 p. [671

——The League of Nations. New York, Longmans, Green, and Co., 1928. 415 p. [672
——The life of Andrew Jackson. New York, Doubleday, Page & Co., 1911. 2 v. [673
—— ——New ed. New York, Macmillan Co., 1925. 2 v. in 1. [674
——The lost fruits of Waterloo. New York, Macmillan Co., 1918. 289 p. [675
——Makers of a new nation. New Haven, Yale University Press, 1928. 344 p. [676
——The middle group of American historians. New York, Macmillian Co., 1917. [677
——Our war with Germany. New York, A. A. Knopf, 1919. 386 p. [678
——A short history of the United States, 1492-1920. New York, Macmillan Co., 1920. 942 p. [679
—— ——Revised ed. 1931. 976 p. [680
——Slavery and servitude in the colony of North Carolina. Baltimore, Johns Hopkins Press, 1896. (Johns Hopkins University in Studies historical and political science, 14th ser., 4-5) 86 p. [681
——Slavery in the state of North Carolina. Baltimore, Johns Hopkins Press, 1899. (Johns Hopkins University Studies in historical and political science, 17th ser., 7-8) 111 p. [682
——The southern plantation overseer as revealed in his letters. Northampton, Mass., Smith College, 1925 (Its fiftieth anniversary publications, v. [5]) 280 p. [683

Batchelor, Joseph Branch. Remarks at the presentation of the portrait of Judge William H. Battle to the Supreme Court of North Carolina, March 15, 1892. Raleigh, Edwards and Broughton Co., 1892. 20 p. [684

Batchelor, Oliver Douglas. My Alma Mater, a reverie. [Raleigh, Edwards and Broughton Co., pref. 1934] [9] p. [685

Bate, William Brimage. Andrew Jackson and the eighth of January. Nashville, Tenn., Foster and Webb, 1899. 31 p. [686

Bates, Morgan. Realistic description of life among the moonshiners of North Carolina. A mountain pink, by Morgan Bates and Elwyn A. Barron. Milwaukee, Riverside Printing Co., n.d. 24 p. [687

[Bath, N. C. SemiQuincentennial Committee] Program for celebrating the 250th anniversary of the incorporation of Bath, North Carolina, on March 8, 1705, October 1, 2, 3, 4, 1955. [Bath, 1955] 32 p. [688

Batten, John Mullin. Reminiscences of two years in the United States navy. Lancaster, Pa., Inquirer Printing and Publishing Co., 1881. 125 p. [689

Batterham, Rose. Pleasure piece. New York, Harper and Brothers, 1935. 290 p. [690

Batterson, Hermon Griswold. Sketch-book of the American episcopate. Philadelphia, J. B. Lippincott & Co., 1878. 322 p. [691

Battery Park Hotel, Asheville, N. C. . . . Asheville, N. C. Asheville, n.d. [15] p. [692
——1899. 12 p. [693
——[Philadelphia, E. A. Wright Co., pr.] n.d. 16 p. [694
——[Philadelplia, Elliott, pr.] n.d. [15] p. [695

Battle, George Gordon. Alfred E. Smith as I have known him; address at Raleigh N. C., April 12, 1928. [Raleigh? No publisher, 1928] 40 p. [696

[Battle, George Gordon] John Manning Battle, 1891-1918. No place, privately printed, n.d. 7 p. [697

Battle, Herbert Bemerton. The Battle book; a genealogy of the Battle family in America . . . completed by Lois Yelverton. Montgomery, Ala., Paragon Press, 1930. 768 p. [698
——The climate of Raleigh, N. C. [Raleigh, Edwards & Broughton Co., 1893?] 13 p. [699

Battle, Herbert Bemerton, joint author, see Dancy, Frank Battle

Battle, Jesse Mercer. Tributes to my father and mother and some stories of my life. St. Louis, Mangan Press, 1911. 230 p. [700

[Battle, Kemp Plummer] Ad valorem explained by questions and answers. No place, no publisher, n.d. 4 p. [701
——An address on the history of the buildings of the University of North Carolina . . . delivered on University day, 1883. Greensboro, Thomas, Reece & Co., pr., 1883. 15 p. [702
——An address on the history of the Supreme Court. Raleigh, Edwards & Broughton Co., 1889. 76 p. [703

——An address on the life and services of Brigadier General Jethro Sumner. Greensboro, Thomas, Reece and Company, pr., 1891. 51 p.   [704
——The Breckinridge Party a disunion party, read what Yancey, Holden, Clingman and others, supporters of Breckinridge say. No place, no publisher, n.d. 8 p. [705
——Early history of Raleigh; address delivered on the centennial celebration of the foundation of the city, October 18, 1892. Raleigh, Edwards and Broughton Co., 1893. 93 p.   [706
——The head and the hand, the practical side of college life, problems of the day; anniversary oration before the students of the South Carolina College, delivered June 23, 1886. [Goldsboro, The Messenger Publishing Co., 1886] 11 p.   [707
——The head and the hand. No place, no publisher [1908?] 10 p.   [708
——History of the University of North Carolina. Raleigh, Printed for the Author by Edwards and Broughton Printing Co., 1907-1912. 2 v.   [709

Battle, Kemp Plummer, ed. Letters and cocuments relating to the early history of the lower Cape Fear. Chapel Hill, The University, 1903. (James Sprunt historical monograph, no. 4) 135 p.   [710
——Letters of Nathaniel Macon, John Steele and William Barry Grove. Chapel Hill, The University [1902] (James Sprunt historical monograph, no. 3) 122 p. [711

Battle, Kemp Plummer. Memories of an old-time Tar Heel . . . edited by . . . William James Battle. Chapel Hill, University of North Carolina Press, 1945. 296 p.   [712
——The names of the counties of North Carolina and the history involved in them. Winston, W. A. Blair, 1888. 38 p.   [713
——Sketch of the life and character of Wilson Caldwell. Chapel Hill, University Press, 1895. 8 p.   [714
——Sketches of the early history of the city of Raleigh; centennial address, Fourth of July, 1876. Raleigh, Raleigh News, 1877. 71 p.   [715
——Sketches of the history of the University of North Carolina, together with a catalogue of officers and students, 1789-1889. [Chapel Hill] University, 1889. 242 p.   [716
——William Smith Battle . . . 1823-1915. No place [1915?] [4] p.   [717

Battle, Laura Elizabeth (Lee) Forget-me-nots of the Civil War; a romance containing reminiscences and original letters of two Confederate soldiers. St. Louis, Mo., A. R. Fleming Printing Co. [c.1909] 355 p.   [718

Battle, Richard Henry. Address at the laying of the cornerstone of Rex Hospital building. Raleigh, Edwards & Broughton Co., 1909. 16 p.   [719
——The ceremonies attending the unveiling of the bronze statue of Zeb B. Vance, L. L. D., in Capitol square, Raleigh, N. C., and the address of Richard H. Battle, L. L. D., August 22, 1900. Raleigh, Raleigh Advocate Co., pr. [1900] 74 p.   [720
——An historical sketch of St. Mary's School. [Charlotte, Observer, n.d.] 16 p. [721

Battle, Samuel Westray. Climate and the climatic treatment of disease with special reference to the merits of the Asheville plateau. Asheville, Randolph & Kerr, pr., 1888. 13 p.   [722
——Review of the mountain health resorts of North Carolina and their possibilities. Asheville, D. W. Furman, pr., 1892. 23 p.   [723

Battle, William Horn. An address delivered before the Philomathesian and Euzelian societies of Wake Forest College, June 18, 1840. Raleigh, Office of the Raleigh Register, 1840. 16 p.   [724
——Address delivered before the two literary societies of the University of North Carolina, June 1st, 1865. Raleigh, W. B. Smith & Co., 1866. 19 p.   [725

The Battle of Ancram Moor; or, Second lay of the lays of the muses; a poem founded on facts taken from Scottish history, by an unknown author. Portsmouth, Va., Bland & Hill, pr., 1837. 16 p. Dedication signed: The Author, Oak Grove, Gates County, N. C.   [726

Battles and leaders of the Civil War. New York, The Century Company [c.1884-1888] 4 v.   [727
——Grant-Lee edition [c.1884-1887] 4 v. in 8.   [728
—— ——New York, Thomas Yoseloff, Inc. [c.1956] 4 v.   [729
—— ——New York, Appleton-Century-Crofts [1956] 626 p.   [730

Baughan, Phoebe (Pegram) Things everyone should know. Franklin, The Franklin Press, 1933. 54 p.   [731

Baugher, Ruby Dell. Listening hills. New York, Hobson Book Press, 1947. 245 p.   [732

Baum, Helena Watts. The satiric & the didactic in Ben Jonson's comedy. Chapel Hill, University of North Carolina Press, 1947. 192 p.   [733

Baum, Paull Franklin, ed. Dante Gabriel Rosetti's letters to Fanny Cornforth. Baltimore, The Johns Hopkins Press, 1940. 142 p.   [734

Baum, Paull Franklin. The other harmony of prose. [Durham] Duke University Press, 1952. 230 p.   [735

——Tennyson sixty years after. Chapel Hill, University of North Carolina Press [1948] 331 p.   [736

Baver, Leonard David. Soil physics. New York, J. Wiley & Sons, 1940. 370 p.   [737

Baxter, Garrett. Ourselves. [Norfolk, Va.] Economic Press, 1930. 100 p.   [738

Baxter, John. Speech made in reply to Hon. T. L. Clingman, at Rutherfordton, 13th November, 1850. Asheville, Asheville Messenger Office, pr., 1850. 16 p.   [739

——To the voters of Henderson County. No place, no publisher, 1854. 8 p. [740

Baxter, Richard. The dying thoughts of the reverend, learned and holy Mr. Richard Baxter. Raleigh, Printed for and sold by William Glendinning, 1805. 96 p. [741

Bay leaves no. 1- 1950- Prize poems, Poetry Day contests, North Carolina. [Asheville] The Poetry Council of North Carolina, 1952- NcU has no. 1, 1950-51; no. 2, 1952-53; no. 3, 1954-55   [742

Bayard, [Thomas Francis] Mecklenburg's Declaration of Independence! 107th anniversary . . . with introductory remarks by Senators Ransom and Vance. Charlotte, Daily Charlotte Observer, pr., 1882. 15 p.   [743

Bays, W. W. The superannuate and other poems. [Concord, Times, c.1901] 6 p.   [744

Baysmore, Joseph. A historical sketch of the First Colored Baptist Church, Weldon, N. C., with the life and labor of Elder Baysmore. Weldon, Harrell's Printing House, 1887. 12 p.   [745

Beal, Fred E. Proletarian journay: New England, Gastonia, Moscow. New York, Hillman-Curl, 1937. 352 p.   [746

Beal, Marjorie. Libraries in North Carolina, a survey. Raleigh, North Carolina Library Associations, 1948. 90 p.   [747

Beale, Charles Willing. The ghost of Guir house. Cincinnati, The Editor Publishing Co., 1897. 184 p.   [748

Beale, Howard Kennedy. Are American teachers free? New York, C. Scribner's Sons [c.1936] 855 p.   [749

——The critical year; a study of Andrew Johnson and Reconstruction. New York, Harcourt, Brace and Co. [c.1930] 454 p.   [750

——A history of freedom of teaching in American schools. New York, C. Scribner's Sons [c.1941] 343 p.   [751

——Some fallacies of the interventionist view. [Washington, The Author, c.1941] 32 p.   [752

Beale, Maria (Taylor) Jack O'Doon; a novel. New York, H. Holt and Co., 1894. 277 p.   [753

Beall, Benjamin L. The Lord's supper. No place, no publisher [1910] 32 p. [754

Beaman, Charles Cotesworth. The national and private "Alabama claims" and their "final and amicable settlement". Washington, W. H. Moore, pr. [1871] 358 p.   [755

Bean, Eugene H. Rowan County, N. C., records; early settlers. Washington, Carnahan Press, 1914. 11 p.   [756

Bear Creek Primitive Baptist Association. Minutes, 18 - 18 - NcU has 1895, 1897, 1898, 1911-1955   [757

Beard, Ida May (Crumpler) Mississippi lawyer; or, Was it all a dream? [Winston-Salem, The Author, 1911] 63 p.   [758

——My own life; or, A deserted wife [2d ed.] Raleigh, Edwards & Broughton, 1900. 212 p.   [759

——[5th ed.] 212 p.   [760

——[7th ed.] [1911] 186 p.   [760a

——[18th ed.] c.1900. 186 p. [760b

Beard, James Melville. K. K. K. sketches, humorous and didactic, treating the more important events of the Ku-Klux Klan movement in the South. Philadelphia, Claxton, Remsen & Haffelfinger, 1877. 192 p. [761

Beard, John Grover. Latin for pharmacists. Chapel Hill, The Book Exchange, 1942. 72 (i. e. 74) numb. 1, 73-134 p. [762

——A list of therapeutic terms and common diseases, with definitions and glossary. Chapel Hill, A. A. Kluttz, 1913. 47 p. [763

——The pharmaceutical syllabus, outling the course of instruction for the degree of bachelor of science in pharmacy. 4th ed. [Chapel Hill] 1932. 168 p. [764

Beard, John Grover, joint author, see Howe, George, 1876-1936

[**Beasley, Charles Oscar**] Those American R's: Rule, ruin, restoration. Philadelphia, E. E. Wensley & Co., 1882. 335 p. [765

Beasley, Roland Fowler. Battle of Elizabethtown. [Greensboro?] Guilford Battle Ground Co., 1901. 17 p. [766

——Principles and machinery of social construction; an address at the North Carolina Social Service Conference, Raleigh, March 6, 1918. No place, no publisher, n.d. 30 p. [767

Beasley & Emerson's Charlotte directory for 1875-76. [Charlotte] Beasley & Emerson [1875] 146 p. [768

Beatie, Arthur Y. Walter W. Moore and Union Seminary; a short story of the life of a truly great man. Richmond, Va., Union Theological Seminary, 1927. 48 p. [769

[**Beaufort Co., N. C. Democratic Party Committee**] A brief analysis of the Republican hand-book, submitted to the voters of Beaufort County for their careful consideration. No place [1908?] [3] p. [770

Becker, Kate Harbes. Biography of Christian Reid. [Belmont? Author, 1941] 190 p. [771

——Paul Hamilton Hayne: life and letters. Belmont, Outline Co., 1951. 145 p. [772

——Was it worth while? Belmont, Outline Co., 1947. 186 p. [773

Beckerath, Herbert von. America desde la crisis mundial. Saragoza, Spain, F. Martinez, 1933. 15 p. [774

——El problema de la economía en la crisis de la cultura. Santiago de Chile, Ediciones Ercilla, 1938. 135 p. [775

Beckwith, Bosworth Clifton. John Bailey Beckwith, a biographical sketch, with a genealogy of the Beckwith family. Raleigh, E. M. Uzzell, pr., 1893. 55 p. [776

Bedell, Gregory Townsend. The desolations and the restoration of Zion. New York, T. and J. Swords, 1820. 23 p. [777

——The minister's most affectionate exhortation to his professing people. Fayetteville, Carney & Dismukes, 1820. 13 p. [778

[**Beecher, George**] Science and change in Alamance County; a background for the development of science studies in the schools of Alamance County, North Carolina. [Elon College, The Author] 1938. 140 p. [779

Beers, Alma Holland, joint author, see Coker, William Chambers

Beeson, Jasper Luther. Beeson genealogy. [Macon, Ga., Burke Co.] n.d. 144 p. [780

Beidler, Jacob Hoke. Marstella; or, The senator's wooing. No place, 1888. 43 p. NcU has microfilm (negative) [781

Belknap, Charles Eugene. Bentonville: what a bummer knows about it. [Washington, 1893] (Military Order of the Loyal Legion of the United States. Commandery of the District of Columbia. War papers, 12) 10 p. [782

Bell, Albert Q. Actors in the colony, 16th century. No place [pref. 1946] 50 p. [783

Bell, Corydon. John Rattling-Gourd of Big Cove. New York, Macmillan Co., 1955. 103 p. [784

Bell, James Munsie. Elements of physical chemistry, by James M. Bell and Paul M. Gross. New York, Longmans, Green and Co., 1929. 466 p.

Bell, Maria Locke. The Bell's and allied families. Columbia, S. C., The Compiler, 1953. 78 p. [785

Bell, Marjorie. A brief study of social work in rural North Carolina. New York, American Association for Organizing Family Social Work [pref. 1927] 29 p. [786

Bell, Thelma Harrington. Mountain boy, with drawings by Corydon Bell. New York, Viking Press, 1947. 39 p. [787

——Pawnee. New York, Viking Press, 1950. 60 p. [788

——Snow. New York, Viking Press, 1954. 55 p. [789

——Take it easy. New York, Viking Press, 1953. 172 p. [790

——Yaller-eye. New York, Viking Press, 1951. 87 p. [791

Bell, W. M., comp. The North Carolina flood, July 14, 15, 16, 1916. Charlotte [News Printing House] n.d. 68 p. [792

Bell, William H. Memorial to the Congress of the United States . . . in behalf of Capt. Bell's inventions for pointing cannon. [Washington] Metropolitan Office, 1836. 24 p. [793

Bell and Lawrence's North-Carolina almanack, 182 - Raleigh, Printed and sold by Bell and Lawrence, 182 - NcU has 1827 [794

Bellamy, Ellen Douglas. "Back with the tide". [Wilmington? Privately printed, 1941?] 35 p. [795

Bellamy, John Dillard. Address on the life and services of General Alexander Lillington. Washington, Press of Judd & Detweiler, 1905. 16 p. [796

——Bar of the lower Cape Fear. Raleigh, Mitchell Printing Co., 1925. 31 p. [797

——Memoirs of an octogenarian. [Charlotte, Observer Printing House, 1942] 201 p. [798

——Sketch of Maj. Gen. Robert Howe of the American Revolution. Wilmington, S. G. Hall, pr., 1882. 23 p. [799

Belmont, N. C. Presbyterian Church. History . . . 1890-1940. [Charlotte, Standard Printing Co., 1940?] 35 p. [800

Belmont Abbey College, Belmont, N. C. Bulletin, v. 1- 1937- Belmont, 1937- NcU has v. [1-19] [801

——Catalogue, 18 - 18 - NcU has [1885/86-1937/38] continues as its Bulletin, 1938/39- [802

Belo, Alfred Horatio. Memoirs . . . with a short introduction by Charles Peabody. Boston, Alfred Mudge & Son, pr., 1904. 75 p. [803

Bemis, Edward Webster. Local government in the South and Southwest. Baltimore, Johns Hopkins University, 1893. (Its Studies in historical and political science, 11th ser., no. 11) 94 p. [804

Bemis, Nettie Nichols. Life at Oxford. [Charlotte] Herald Press, 1937. 172 p. [805

Benedict, Cleo. A brief sketch of the work of Mrs. Crosby Adams and a list of her musical writings. [Chicago, Clayton F. Summy Co.] n.d. [6] p. [806

Benedict, David. A general history of the Baptist denomination in America and other parts of the world. Boston, Lincoln and Edmands, pr., 1813. 2 v. [807

——New York, Lewis Colby and Co., 1848. 970 p. [808

Benét, Laura. Caleb's luck. New York, Grosset & Dunlap, c.1942. [28] p. [809

Benge, Eugene Jackson. The right career for you. New York, Funk & Wagnalls [1950] 150 p. [810

Benjamin, Marcus. John Henry Boner. No place, no publisher, n.d. 9 p. [811

——Memorial of John Henry Boner. Washington, 1905. 38 p. [812

——Society of the Cincinnati. No place, no publisher, n.d. 7 p. [813

Benjamin, W. S. The great epidemic in New Berne and vicinity, September and October, 1864. New Bern, George Mills Joy, 1865. 38 p. [814

Bennett, Daniel K. Chronology of North Carolina. New York, J. M. Edney, 1858. 143 p. [815

Bennett, Hugh Hammond. Elements of soil conservation. New York, McGraw-Hill Book Co., 1947. 406 p. [816

——Soil conservation. New York, McGraw-Hill Book Co., 1939. 993 p. [817

——The soils and agriculture and the Southern States. New York, Macmillan Co., 1921. 399 p. [818

——The soils of Cuba, by Hugh H. Bennett and Robert V. Allison. Washington, Tropical Plant Research Foundation, 1928. 410 p. [819

——This land we defend, by Hugh Hammond Bennett and William Clayton Pryon. New York, Longmans, Green and Co., 1942. 107 p. [820

Bennett, Mark. Debate between Elder Mark Bennett . . . and Elder G. M. Thompson. Raleigh, Primitive Print, 1853. 86 p. [821

——Essay on the use of spirituous liquors. [Tarboro, Primitive Baptist] 1841. 15 p. [822

——Roger Williams and liberty of conscience. Raleigh, Biblical Recorder Office, 1854. 42 p. [823

Bennett, Simon Addison. The Christian denomination and Christian doctrine. Dayton, O., Christian Publication Association, n.d. 51 p. [824

Bennett, William W. Memorials of Methodism in Virginia, from its introduction into the state, in the year 1772, to the year 1829. Richmond, The Author, 1871. 741 p. The N. C. Conference was not organized until 1857 and until that time a large part of it was enbraced within the Virginia Conference. [825

Bennett College, Greensboro, N. C. Bulletin, 192 - Greensboro, 192 - NcU has v. [4-23] [826

——Catalogue, 19 - Greensboro, 19 - NcU has [1908/09-1920/21] Continues as its Bulletin [827

Benton, George H. and Company, New York. Prospectus of the North Carolina Land and Lumber Company. Newbern, N. S. Richardson and Son, pr. [1895?] 35 p. [828

Benton, Thomas Hart. Historical and legal examination of that part of the decision of the Supreme Court of the United States in the Dred Scott case, which declares the unconstitutionality of the Missouri Compromise Act. New York, D. Appleton and Co., 1857. 193 p. [829

——Thirty years' view; or, A history of the working of the American government for thirty years, from 1820 to 1850. New York, D. Appleton and Co., 1854. 2 v. [830

—— ——1903. 2 v. [831

[**Benton, William De Lancey**] In loving memory, Major John W. Graham, LL. D., Hillsboro, N. C. No place, no publisher [1928] 2 p. [832

[**Berea College, Berea, Ky.**] Berea College presents "Wilderness Road" [by Paul Green] [Berea, Ky., 1955] [32] p. Souvenir program. [833

Berean, pseud. A respectful appeal from the injurious charge of a wish to "Pluck with unhallowed hands, the crown from the head of the eternal". Raleigh, J. Gales & Son, 1830. 12 p. [834

Bernard, George S. War talks of Confederate veterans. Petersburg, Va., Fenn & Owen, 1892. 335 p. [835

Bernard, John. Retrospections of America, 1797-1811. New York, Harper & Brothers, 1887. 380 p. [836

Bernhard, Duke of, see Saxe-Weimer-Eisenach, Bernhard, Duke of

Bernheim, Gotthardt Dellmann. First twenty years of the history of St. Paul's Evangelical Church, Wilmington, N. C. Wilmington, S. G. Hall, pr., 1879. 71 p. [837

——The history of the Evangelical Lutheran and Ministerium of North Carolina. Philadelphia, Lutheran Publication Society, 1902. 191 p. [838

——History of the German settlements and the Lutheran Church in North and South Carolina. Philadelphia, Lutheran Book Store, 1872. 557 p. [839

——Localities of the Reformation, which were visited recently in a European tour. Wilmington, S. G. Hall, pr., 1877. 23 p. [840

Bernstein, Aline (Frankau) The journey down. New York, A. A. Knopf, 1938. 304 p. [841

—— ——1951. Third printing. [842

——Three blue suits: Mr. Froelich, Herbert Wilson, Eugene. New York, Equinox Cooperative Press, 1933. 74 p. [843

Bernstein, Edward Morris. Money and the economic system. Chapel Hill, University of North Carolina Press [c.1935] 516 p. [844

——Public utility rate making and the price level. Chapel Hill, University of North Carolina Press, 1937. 142 p. [845

Berry, Harry Jay. Living without fear. Asheville, Groves Printing Co., 1938. 72 p. [846

Berry, Lloyd E. Hudson Berry and his descendants. Pelzer, S. C., Berry-Gaines-Harrison Families, 1956. 106 p. [847

Berry, W. J. "God forbid": a brief exposition of the first eight chapters of Paul's Epistle to the saints at Rome. Elon College, Primitive Baptist Publishing House & Library, n.d. 32 p. [848

Bertie County Historical Association. Group of homes in colonial and ante-bellum Bertie County. Windsor, 1956. 8 p. [849

Bessemer City, N. C. School Board. Report of City Graded Schools, 1904/05- Bessemer City, 1905- NcU has [1904/05-1913/14] [850

Best, Harry. Blindness and the blind in the United States. New York, Macmillan Co., 1934. 714 p. Tables give state statistics. [851

——Deafness and the deaf in the United States. New York, Macmillan Co., 1943. 675 p. [852

Bethania, N. C. Bethania Congregation. [Program of service, 19 - Bethania, 19 - NcU has [December, 1929-March, 1934] [853

——Sesqui-centennial, 1759-1909. [Winston-Salem, Union Republican Publishing Co., 1909?] 79 p. [854

[Bethany Church, Iredell Co., N. C.] Centennial addresses on the life and character of Rev. James Hall, D. D., and short sketches of the ministers of the Gospel who have descended from James and Prudence Hall. Covington, Tenn., Tipton Record, 1885. [26] p. [855

Bethune, George Washington. Truth the strength of freedom; a discourse on the duty of a patriot, with some allusions to the life and death of Andrew Jackson. Philadelphia, Mentz & Rovoudt, 1845. 36 p. [856

Better health, v. 1-3, December, 1946-April, 1949. Raleigh, North Carolina Social Hygiene Society, 1946-1949. NcU has v. 1-3 [857

Betters, Paul Vernon, ed. State centralization in North Carolina. Washington, Brookings Institution, 1932. (Its Studies in administration, no. 26) 261 p. [858

Betts, Alexander Davis. Experience of a Confederate chaplain, 1861-64. No place no publisher, n.d. 103 p. [859

Betts, Doris. The gentle insurrection, and other stories. New York, Putnam [1954] 274 p. [860

Betts, Sylvester J. Criticism of Dr. Poteat's book . . . entitled "Can a man be a Christian today?" [Raleigh, no publisher, 1925] 12 p. [861

——The imminent second coming of Christ. Raleigh, Capital Printing Co., 1935. 96 p. [862

Betts, William Archibald. Brief studies in Methodist doctrines. No place, Smith and Lamar, 1903. 32 p. [863

——Brief study in Methodist biography and history. Raleigh, Edwards and Broughton Co., 1894. [864

Betts, William Archibald, ed. Charles Betts. Raleigh, Edwards and Broughton Co., 1893. 24 p. [865

—— ——[Bamberg, S. C. The Editor, 1942] [866

Betts, William Archibald. An instructive colloquy. No place, no publisher, n.d. 15 p. [867

[Betts, William Archibald] comp. Songs of the North Carolina University, compiled by W. A. B. '80. Charleston, D. L. Alexander, pr. 1880. 26 p. [868

Beulah Baptist Association. Minutes, 18 - 18 - NcU has [1845-1874] 1876-1883 [1886-1899] 1902-1906 [1923-1945] [869

Beust, Nora, comp. Graded list of books for children. Chicago, American Library Association, 1930. 149 p. [870

—— ——1936. 161 p. [871

Beveridge and Co.'s North Carolina state directory, 187 - [Raleigh, News Publishing Co.] 187 - NcU has 1877-78 [872

Bevington, Helen Smith. A change of sky and other poems. Boston, Houghton Mifflin, 1956. 144 p. [873

——Dr. Johnson's waterfall, and other poems. Boston, Houghton Mifflin Co., 1946. 164 p. [874

——Nineteen million elephants, and other poems. Boston, Houghton Mifflin, 1950. 115 p. [875

Biblical recorder, v. 1- January 7, 1835- New Bern, Raleigh, Biblical Recorder Co., 1835- NcU has v. [4-59] 60-63 [64-67] 68-74 [75-76] 77-87 [89] 90-121. Superseded The North Carolina Baptist interpreter, 1833-34.   [876

Bickett, Thomas Walter. The folks "down home"; speech delivered before the North Carolina Society in New York City, May 20, 1913. No place, no publisher [1913] 8 p.   [877

——Ho, for Carolina! Governor T. W. Bickett before the North Carolina Society of Pennsylvania, Philadelphia, December 4, 1920. [Raleigh, Edwards and Broughton Co., 1920] 6 p.   [878

——Speech of a southern governor; Hon. T. W. Bickett at the 56th anniversary of the North Carolina Conference of the A. M. E. Zion Church. Kinston, Committee of the Church, n.d. 16 p.   [879

——Triumph of the English people at Yorktown; address delivered at Moore's Creek Bridge, July 25, 1918. No place, no publisher, n.d. 6 p.   [880

——What will the Kaiser say? Extracts from speech of Governor Bickett. [Raleigh, 1918] [1] p.   [881

Biddle, Charles. Autobiography of Charles Biddle, Vice-President of the Supreme Executive Council of Pennsylvania. Philadelphia, E. Claxton and Co., 1883. 423 p.   [882

Biddle University see **Johnson C. Smith University, Charlotte, N. C.**

Bieseker, R. H. Hon. Zeb Vance Walser, candidate for the sixty-first Congress, seventh N. C. Congressional district. No place [1908?] [4] p.   [883

Biggs, Janes Crawford. Address before the North Carolina Bar Association: The power of the judiciary over legislation. Wilmington, Wilmington Stamp, pr. [1915?] 43 p.   [884

——Federal practice and procedure. [Raleigh, Mitchell Printing Co., 1926?] 16 p.   [885

Biggs, Joseph. A concise history of the Kehukee Baptist Association, from its original rise to the present time . . . Part I. Contains the history of the Kehukee Association, from its first organization until 1803, as compiled by Elders Burkitt and Read . . . Part II. Embraces a continuation of the history of the Association until the present time . . . by Joseph Biggs. [Tarboro?] G. Howard, 1834. 300 p.   [886

Biggs, Rosa (Fulghum) I take this squaw. Philadelphia, Dorrance and Co. [1942] 301 p.   [887

Bill, Alfred Hoyt. Rehearsal for conflict; the War with Mexico, 1846-1848. New York, A. A. Knopf, 1947. 342 p.   [888

Billings, Henry. All down the valley. New York, Viking Press, 1952. 208 p.   [889

Billingsley, Amos Stevens. The life of the great preacher, Rev. George Whitefield. Philadelphia, P. W. Ziegler [c.1878] 437 p.   [890

Biltmore, N. C. Biltmore Estate Company. General plan of Biltmore Forest. [Philadelphia, Ketterlinus, pr.] n.d. [7] p.   [891

Biltmore botanical studies, v. 1, no. 1-2, April 9, 1901-April 30, 1902. London, W. Wesley & Son; Biltmore, Biltmore Herbarium [1901-1902] 163 p. NcU has v. 1, no. 2.   [892

Biltmore Farms, Biltmore, N. C. Biltmore dairy farms on the famed Biltmore Estate. [Asheville, Miller Press, 1942?] [18] p.   [893

Biltmore Forest. Artisans' Shop, Biltmore, N. C. Antiques of the future. Biltmore, n.d. [34] p.   [894

Biltmore Forest Country Club, Biltmore, N. C. Year book, 1922/23- [Biltmore] 1922- NcU has: 1922/23, 1927/28, 1944/45   [895

Biltmore Forest School, Biltmore, N. C. Announcement, 18 - Biltmore, 18 - NcU has 1908, 1908/09, 1909/10   [896

——The working field of Biltmore Forest School. [Biltmore] n.d. 12 plates   [897

Biltmore House, Biltmore, N. C. [Asheville, Inland Press [n.d. [7] p.   [898

Biltmore House and gardens, Biltmore Estate, Biltmore—Asheville, North Carolina. [Asheville] n.d. [3] p.   [899

Biltmore Industries, Biltmore, N. C. Catalogue of hand-carved woodwork and hand woven homespun. Philadelphia, Ketterlinus, pr., n.d. [6] p.   [900

[Biltmore Industries, Asheville, N. C.]   The most remarkable discovery in health
clothing that ever has been made.   [Asheville, Homespun Shops, 1925]   8 p.   [901
Biltmore Nursery, Biltmore, N. C.   Flowering trees and shrubs.   Biltmore, c.1909.
63 p.   [902
Biltmore photogravures.   Brooklyn, N. Y., Albertype Co. [c.1900]   Unpaged.   [903
Bingham, Robert.   Address delivered at the annual communication of the Grand
Lodge, January 8, 1884.   Raleigh, Edwards and Broughton, 1884.   15 p.   [904
——The care of dependent children.   No place [Grand Lodge of North Carolina,
A. F. & A. M.] 1909.   16 p.   [905
——Co-education.   [Asheville? Pen and Plate Club?] n.d.   20 p.   [906
——The fifty years beyond 1857 and 1907, and beyond.   No place, no publisher
[1907?]   12 p.   [907
——The new South.   No place, no publisher [1884?]   22 p.   [908
——Response at the annual banquet of the New York Southern Society . . . to the
toast: "The status of the South in the past, the decadence of that status, its
restoration".   [Asheville, Pen and Plate Club, 1905]   16 p.   [909
——Secession in theory as the framers of the constitution viewed it, secession as
practised and sustained by the United States, secession as attempted by the Confederate States.   [Raleigh? North Carolina State Literary and Historical Association? 1908]   32 p.   [910
Bingham, William.   Bingham's elementary English grammar.   Philadephhia, T. H.
Butler & Co., 1881.   63 p.   [911
——A grammar of the English language.   Philadelphia, J. H. Butler and Co., [c.1867]
207 p.   [912
—— ——1871.   [913
——A grammar of the Latin language.   Greensboro, Sterling, Campbell & Albright,
1863. 304.   [914
—— ——Philadelphia, E. H. Butler & Co., 1875.   392 p.   [915
—— ——1877.   [916
—— ——1879.   [917
——A Latin reader.   Philadelplia, E. H. Butler & Co. [c.1869]   231 p.   [918
—— ——1882.   [919
—— ——[c.1886]   206 p.   [920
——Life and writings of Hugh Miller.   New York, George W. Wood, pr., 1859.
27 p.   [921
Bingham, William, ed.   Caesar's Commentaries on the Gallic War.   Greensboro,
Sterling, Campbell & Albright, 1864.   290 p.   [922
—— ——Philadelphia, E. H. Butler & Co. [c.1868]   348 p.   [923
—— ——Philadelphia, J. H. Butler & Co., 1874.   348 p.   [924
—— ——Philadelphia, J. H. Butler & Co., 1879.   290 p.   [925
—— ——Philadelphia, J. H. Butler & Co., 1880.   348 p.   [926
Bingham, William James.   Address delivered before the college temperance society,
at Chapel Hill, May 21st, 1836.   Raleigh, J. Gales and Son, pr., 1836.   16 p.   [927
Bingham School, Asheville, N. C.   Catalogue, 1891/92?-   Asheville, 1892?-   NcU
has [1899/1900-1904/05] 1924/25, 1926/27   [928
——Delivery of medals to the honor men.   [Asheville? 1895?]   5 p.   [929
——Where can I send my boy to a safe school?   [Asheville, 1907?]   [21] p. [930
—— ——[1909?]   52 p.   [931
Bingham School, Mebane, N. C.   The Bingham School, Orange County, North
Carolina.   [Mebane, n.d.]   3 p.   [932
——Catalogue, 18 - 18 - NcU has 1861/62-1871/72, 1877/78, 1879/80, 1883/84,
1886/87, 1889/90, 1896/97 [1903/04-1910/12]   [933
——Parent, a word with you about your boy.   [Mebane, n.d.]   14 p.   [934
Binkley, Olin Trivette.   Frontiers for Christian youth.   Nashville, Tenn., Broad-
man Press [c.1941]   116 p.   [935
Biographical sketch of Millie Christine, the Carolina twin, surnamed the two-
headed nightingale, and the eighth wonder of the world.   Cincinnati, Hennegan
and Co. [1900?]   32 p.   [936
Biographical sketch of Rev. Owen L. W. Smith.   No place, no publisher [1900?]
24 p.   [937

Biography of Joseph Lane . . . by Western. Washington, Congressional Globe Office, 1852. 40 p. [938

Bishop, Cortlandt Field. History of elections in the American colonies. New York, Columbia College, 1893. (Its Studies in history, economics and public law, v. 3, no. 1) 297 p. [939

Bishop, John Leander. A history of American manufactures, from 1608 to 1860. Philadelphia, E. Young & Co., 1861-64. 2 v. [940

Bishop, Nathaniel Holmes. Voyage of the paper canoe. Boston, Lee and Shepard, 1878. 351 p. [941

Bishop, W. L. Report on gold veins of Burke and Caldwell counties. No place, no publisher, n.d. 1 p. [942

——Report on the "Hercules group" gold mining properties. [Morganton, no publisher, 1901] 1 p. [943

——Report on the "Round Mountain" gold mining properties. [Morganton, no publisher, 1901] 1 p. [944

Bittinger, Lucy Forney. The Germans in colonial times. Philadelphia, J. B. Lippincott Co., 1901. 314 p. [945

[Bixley, O. H.] Incidents in Dixie, being ten months' experience of a Union soldier in the military prisons of Richmond, N. Orleans, and Salisbury. Baltimore, James Young, pr., 1864. 89 p. [946

Björkman, Edwin August. Old Barham's politics. Biltmore, Gollifox Press, 1936. 9 p. [947

——The soul of a child. New York, A. A. Knopf, 1922. 321 p. [948

——The wings of Azrael. [Biltmore, c.1934] 21 p. [949

Black, Archibald Ray. Report on public schools . . . New Hanover County, N. C. Wilmington, Engelhard & Price, pr., 1870. 12 p. [950

Black, C. J. A short history of Sandy Plains Baptist Church. No place, no publisher [1924?] 100 p. [951

Black, Ernest Watson. Living messages from the Canaan journey. [Kannapolis? 1948] 230 p. [952

Black, Jeremiah Sullivan. Eulogy on the life and character of General Andrew Jackson. Chambersburg, Pa., Weekly Messenger, pr., 1845. 23 p. [953

Black, Robert C. The railroads of the Confederacy. Chapel Hill, University of North Carolina Press [1952] 360 p. [954

Black and gold, v. 1- November, 1910- Winston-Salem, Students of Richard J. Reynolds High School, 1910- NcU has v. [1-15] [955

Black Beard; or, The desperate pirate and captive princess. London, J. L. Marks, n.d. 24 p. [956

Black Creek Primitive Baptist Association. Minutes, 18 - 18 - NcU has [1901-1938] [957

Black Mountain, N. C. Board of Trade. Here is recreation. [Asheville, Asheville Printing and Engraving Co.] n.d. [32] p. [958

Black Mountain College, Black Mountain, N. C. Black Mountain College. [Black Mountain] n.d. [32] p. [959

——Black Mountain College. [1940?] [15] p. [960

——Bulletin, 1934- 1934- NcU has [1934-1952] [961

Black Mountain review, no. 1- January, 1954- Black Mountain, 1954- NcU has no. 1-6 [962

Blackbeard, a page from the colonial history of Philadelphia. New York, Harper & Brothers, 1835. 2 v. [963

Blackbeard; or, The captive princess, a present for the New Year, 1818. No place, no publisher, n.d. 16 p. [964

Blackburn, William Maxwell. The architecture of Duke University. Durham, Duke University Press, 1936. 72 p. [965

—— ——1937. [966

—— ——1939. 74 p. [967

Blackburn, William Maxwell, ed. One and twenty, Duke narrative and verse, 1924 1945. Durham, Duke University Press, 1945. 297 p. [968

Blackmer [Luke?]   Address delivered in Lexington ,N. C., on the anniversary of St. John the Baptist.   Raleigh, Star, pr., A. L. 5849 [1849]   24 p.   [969
——Masonic address delivered in Franklinville, March 21 st, anno luci 5851.   Salisbury, J. J. Bruner, pr., 1851.   16 p.   [970

Blacknall, T. H. Kittrell Springs, North Carolina. [Kittrell Springs, 1872?] [1] p.   [971

Blackwell, Calvin S.   Elements of the art of expression.   [Elizabeth City?   The Author?] n.d.   [10] p.   [972

Blackwell, Gordon Williams, ed.   Church and community in the South . . . by Gordon W. Blackwell, Lee M. Brooks [and] S. H. Hobbs, Jr.   Richmond, Va., John Knox Press, 1949.   416 p.   [973

Blackwell, Gordon Williams.   Future citizens all [by] Gordon W. Blackwell and Raymond F. Gould.   Chicago, American Public Welfare Association, 1952.   181 p.   [974
——The role of the social sciences in general education.   [Chapel Hill, 1946?] 12 p.   [975

Blackwell, Gordon Williams, joint author, see Vance, Rupert Bayless

Blackwell's Durham Tobacco Company, Durham, N. C.   Charter and by-laws. [Durham? 1887?]   13 p.   [976

Bladen Baptist Association.   Minutes, 18 - 18 - NcU has [1895-1955]   [977

Blaine, James Cyril Dickson.   Enplaned airline traffic of the South, 1949-1950-Chapel Hill, Author, 1952- NcU has 1949-1951, and supplement 1951   [978
——North Carolina's urban markets as air passenger generating areas.   [Chapel Hill, Author, 1953]   16 p.   [979

Blair, David.   The first catechism containing common things necessary to be known at an early age.   Raleigh, J. Gales and Son, pr., 1826.   72 p.   [980

Blair, Joseph Addison.   Reminiscences of Randolph County.   Greensboro, Reece & Elam, pr., 1890.   57 p.   [981

Blair, William Allen.   Banking in North Carolina, 1834-1898.   No place, North Carolina Bankers Assocation, Group Five [1925?]   22 p.   [982
—— ——Supplement.   [1925]   5 p.   [983
——Easter in Salem.   No place, no publisher, n.d.   5 p.   [984
——A historical sketch of banking in North Carolina.   New York, B. Rhodes & Co., 1899.   21 p.   [985
——The Home Moravian Church, Winston-Salem, N. C.   [Winston-Salem, Union Republican, pr., 1934?]   12 p.   [986
——Memorial address on the occasion of the dedication of a portrait of George Pierce Pell, before the Supreme Court of North Carolina, Raleigh, North Carolina, December 11, 1940.   No place, no publisher, n.d.   13 p.   [987
——The Moravian graveyard, Salem, N. C.   [Winston-Salem, Home Moravian Church] n.d.   24 p.   [988

Blake, Bennett T.   Review of the sermon of the Rt. Rev. L. S. Ives at the consecration of the Rt. Rev. John Johns.   Raleigh, North Carolina Standard, 1843.   36 p.   [989

[Blake, Lillie (Devereux)]   Southwold, a novel . . . by Mrs. Lillie Devereus Umsted.   New York, Rudd & Carleton, 1859.   257 p.   [990

Blakey, Leonard Stott.   Sale of liquor in the South.   New York Columbia University, 1912.   (Its Studies in history, economics and public law, v. 51, whole no. 127)   56 p.   [991

Blanchard, Fessenden Seaver.   A cruising guide to the Inland Waterway and Florida.   New York, Dodd, Mead, 1954.   256 p.   [992

Bland, Edward.   The discovery of New Brittaine.   Began August 27, Anno Dom. 1650.   New York, Reprinted by J. Sabin and Sons, 1873.   16 p.   [993
—— ——London, 1651.   [Ann Arbor]   William L. Clements Library, University of Michigan, 1954.   16 p.   [944

Bland, John T.   These lowly lays of mine.   No place [The Author, 1920?]   63 p. [995

Bland, Margaret Clarkson.   First at Bethel.   New York, S. French, c.1935.   30 p.   [996
——Pink and patches.   New York, S. French, c.1928.   24 p.   [997
——The spinach spitters.   Boston, Walter H. Baker Co. [c.1935]   20 p.   [998

Blanding, A. Address to the citizens of Charleston . . . on the Louisville, Cincinnati, and Charleston Railroad. Columbia, S. C., A. S. Johnston, pr., 1836. 39 p.   [999

Blanding, Stephen F. Recollections of a sailor boy; the cruise of the gunboat Louisiana. Providence, E. A. Johnson & Co., 1886. 330 p.   [1000

Blanshard, Paul. Labor in southern cotton mills. New York, The New Republic [c.1927] 88 p.   [1001

Bledsoe, Mary Lina. Shadows slant north. Boston, Lothrop, Lee & Shepard Co., 1937. 398 p.   [1002

Bleeker, Sonia. The Cherokee, Indians of the mountains. New York, Morrow, 1952. 159 p.   [1003

Blessner, Gustave. Grand march of the University of North Carolina, composed expressly for the Commencement of 1844. Philadelphia, A. Fiot, pr., c.1844. 5 p.   [1004

Blockaded British subject, pseud. see Hopley, Catherine Cooper

[Blome, Richard] The present state of His Majesties isles and territories in America. London, H. Clark for D. Newman, 1687. 262 p.   [1005

Blomquist, Hugo Leander. Ferns of North Carolina. Durham, Duke University Press, 1934. 131 p.   [1006

——The grasses of North Carolina. Durham, Duke University, 1948. 276 p. [1007

——A guide to the spring and early summer flora of the Piedmont, North Carolina, by H. L. Bomquist and H. J. Oosting. 2d ed. [Durham, Seeman Printery] 1936. 138 p.   [1008

—— ——1940. 144 p.   [1009

——Laboratory manual of general botany, by H. L. Blomquist and N. F. Wilkerson. Durham, Duke University Press, 1926. 122 p.   [1010

Blomquist, Hugo Leander, joint author, see Greene, Wilhelmina F.

Bloodworth, Mattie. History of Pender County, North Carolina. Richmond, Dietz Printing Co., 1947. 240 p.   [1011

Blount, William Augustus. The North Carolina tidewater country. [Chapel Hill? The Author, 1920?] 20 p.   [1012

[Blount, Wilson] Exact and candid statement of transactions with Messrs. Jonathan and William Simpson, administrators to the estate of Anthony Letchmere] [Newbern, John S. Pasteur, pref. January 29, 1801] 30 p. Title page wanting in NcU copy   [1013

Blue Mont, "the beauty spot in the Land of the Sky", the home of the Southern Baptist Assembly, eighteen miles east of Asheville. [Raleigh, Edwards and Broughton Co.] n.d. 15 p.   [1014

Blue Ridge Association, Blue Ridge, N. C. Glorious days and restful nights in the heart of the Blue Ridge Mountains. [Nashville, Tenn., 1930] Folder   [1015

——In the Land of the Sky, a royal retreat. Blue Ridge [1929] Folder   [1016

——In the land of the Sky, by motor to the heart of playland. [1931] Folder [1017

——Out of doors in the Blue Ridge. [Blue Ridge, 19 - NcU has 1920, 1922 [1018

——Southern student conference, 19 - Blue Ridge, 19 - NcU has 1919, 1923, 1940   [1019

Blue Ridge Parkway Associated Chambers of Commerce. Accommodations and services along Blue Ridge Parkway, Virginia, North Carolina, 195 - [Asheville, Miller Printing Co.] 19 - NcU has 1951, 1952-53   [1020

Blue Ridge Parkway guide, 19 - Asheville, 19 - NcU has 1946   [1021

Blue Ridge Railroad. Conditions and prospects. Charleston, S. C., Walker, Evans, & Co., 1868. 24 p.   [1022

——The narrow gauge, a report of the chief engineer. Columbia, S. C., Carolina Printing Co., 1871. 36 p.   [1023

——Report, 18 - Charleston, Walker, Evans & Co., 18 - NcU has 1855/56, 1856/57   [1024

Blue Ridge voice, v. 1-8, November, 1919-June, 1927. Nashville, Tenn., Blue Ridge Association, 1919-1927. NcU has v. 1-8   [1025

Blumenthal, Walter Hart. American Indians dispossessed; fraud in land cessions forced upon the tribes. Philadelphia, G. S. MacManus Co., 1955. 200 p.   [1026

Blum's farmers' and planters' almanac, 18　-　Salem, Blum, 18　-　NcU has 1829-
1838, 1840-1842, 1844-1956.　　　　　　　　　　　　　　　　　　　[1027

Blum's farmers' and planters' almanac.　A selection of tales and anecdotes compiled
from Blum's farmers' and planters' almanac for the past 75 years. 3d ed. Winston-
Salem, Crist and Keehln, 1913.　64 p.　　　　　　　　　　　　　[1028

Blythe, LeGette. Alexandriana. Harrisburg, Pa., Stackpole Sons [c.1940] 445 p. [1029

——Bold Galilean.　Chapel Hill, University of North Carolina Press, 1948.
317 p.　　　　　　　　　　　　　　　　　　　　　　　　　　　[1030

——James W. Davis, North Carolina surgeon.　Charlotte, William Loftin, 1956.
227 p.　　　　　　　　　　　　　　　　　　　　　　　　　　　[1031

——Marshal Ney, a dual life.　New York, Stackpole Sons, 1937.　356 p.　[1032

——The old rock house.　[Charlotte, Daughters of the American Revolution] n.d.
[4] p.　　　　　　　　　　　　　　　　　　　　　　　　　　　[1033

——A tear for Judas.　Indianapolis, Bobbs-Merrill [1951]　338 p.　　　[1034

——Voice in the wilderness, a play.　Charlotte, William Loftin, 1955.　87 p.　[1035

——William Henry Belk, merchant of the South.　Chapel Hill, University of North
Carolina Press [1950]　225 p.　　　　　　　　　　　　　　　　　[1036

Blythe, LeGette, joint author,　see Sloop, Mary T. (Martin)

Boardman, Henry Augustus.　A word of friendly counsel to young men; a sermon on
the death of George M. Ramseur, of North Carolina.　Philadelphia, Hayes &
Zell, 1856.　30 p.　　　　　　　　　　　　　　　　　　　　　　[1037

Bobbitt, William E.　A brief history of Rocky Mount, North Carolina.　Rocky
Mount, Chamber of Commerce, 1950.　18 p.　　　　　　　　　　　[1038

Boddie, John Bennett.　Southside Virginia families.　Redwood, Calif., Pacific Coast
Publishers, 1955.　422 p.　　　　　　　　　　　　　　　　　　　[1039

Boddie, John Thomas.　Boddie and allied families, by John Thomas Boddie and
John Bennett Boddie.　[Chicago?] Privately printed, 1918.　250 p.　　[1040

[Boddie, William Willis]　In memory of Lucy Williams Perry.　No place [1925?]
[7] p.　　　　　　　　　　　　　　　　　　　　　　　　　　　[1041

Boddie, William Willis, comp.　Marion's men, a list of twenty-five hundred. [Charles-
ton, S. C., Heisser Printing Co., c.1938]　24 p.　　　　　　　　　　[1042

Boehm, Henry.　Reminiscences, historical and biographical, of sixty-four years in
the ministry.　New York, Carlton and Porter, 1865.　493 p.　　　　[1043

Boehme, Anton.Wilhelm.　Das verlangte nicht erlangte Canaan bey den lustgräbern.
Franckfurt und Leipzig [Andrea] 1711.　[12] 127 p.　NcU has photostat (negative) from original in New York Public Library　　　　　　　　　[1044

Boerner, Trilby.　Oh college dear, to you, by Trilby Boerner and Norma Cofer.
[Greensboro, privately printed, 1953]　[42] p.　　　　　　　　　　[1045

Bogart, William Henry.　The border boy and how he became the great pioneer of
the West; a life of Daniel Boone.　Boston, Lee and Shepard [c.1884]　464 p. [1046

——Daniel Boone, and the hunters of Kentucky.　New York, Miller, Orton &
Mulligan, 1856.　464 p.　　　　　　　　　　　　　　　　　　　[1047

——　——New York, G. M. Saxton, 1859.　464 p.　　　　　　　　[1048

Boggs, Martha Frye.　Jack Crews.　New York, G. W. Dillingham Co., 1899.
273 p.　　　　　　　　　　　　　　　　　　　　　　　　　　　[1049

Boggs, Ralph Steele.　Bibliography of Latin American folklore.　New York, H. W.
Wilson Co., 1940.　109 p.　　　　　　　　　　　　　　　　　　　[1050

——Leyendas épicas de España; prosificación moderna . . . de Ralph S. Boggs . . .
y Carlos Castillo.　Boston, D. C. Heath and Co. [c.1935]　221 p.　　[1051

——Outline history of Spanish literature.　Boston, D. C. Heath and Co. [c.1937]
154 p.　　　　　　　　　　　　　　　　　　　　　　　　　　　[1052

Boggs, Ralph Steele, ed.　Spanish folktales, edited with exercises, notes, and vocabulary by R. S. Boggs and N. B. Adams.　New York, F. S. Crofts & Co., 1932.
161 p.　　　　　　　　　　　　　　　　　　　　　　　　　　　[1053

Boggs, Ralph Steele, comp.　Tentative dictionary of medieval Spanish, compiled
by R. S. Boggs [and others] Chapel Hill, 1946.　2 v.　　　　　　　[1054

Boggs, Ralph Steele.　Three golden oranges and other Spanish folk tales, by Ralph
Steele Boggs and Mary Gould Davis.　New York, Longmans, Green & Co., 1936.
137 p.　　　　　　　　　　　　　　　　　　　　　　　　　　　[1055

Boggs, William Robertson. Military reminiscences of Gen. Wm. R. Boggs. Durham, Seeman Printery, 1913. (The John Lawson monographs of the Trinity College Historical Society, v. 3)   115 p.   [1056

Boies, Andrew J.   Record of the Thirty-third Massachusetts Volunteer Infantry, from Aug. 1862 to Aug. 1865. Fitchburg, Sentinel Printing Co., 1880. 168 p.   [1057

Boiling Springs College, Boiling Springs, N. C.   Catalogue, 19 - 19 - NcU has [1912/13-1918/19] 1941/42   [1058

Bond, Octavia Louise (Zollicoffer)   The family chronicle and kinship book of Maclin, Clack, Cocke, Carter, Taylor, Cross, Gordon and other related American lineages. [Nashville, Tenn., McDaniel Printing Co., c.1928]   663 p.   [1059

Bond, Richmond Pugh, ed.   Chesterfield: Letters and other pieces, selected and edited by Richmond P. Bond. Garden City, N. Y., Doubleday, Doran & Co. [c.1935]   321 p.   [1060

Bond, Richmond Pugh.   English burlesque poetry, 1700-1750.   Cambridge, Harvard University Press, 1932.   (Harvard studies in English, v. 6)   483 p.   [1061

——Queen Anne's American kings.   Oxford, Clarendon Press, 1952.   148 p.   [1062

Bond, Richmond Pugh, joint author, see Weed, Katharine Kirkley

Bond, William Marion.   Our government, its courts and their critics. Raleigh, Commercial Printing Co., 1916.   15 p.   [1063

Bond, William R.   Pickett or Pettigrew? An historical essay. Weldon, Hall & Sledge [c.1888]   49 p.   [1064

—— ——2d ed.   Scotland Neck, W. L. L. Hall [c.1888]   91 p.   [1065

—— ——3d ed.   Scotland Neck, W. L. L. Hall, 1901.   94 p.   [1066

Bond Conference of Banks of the Fifth Federal Reserve District, Richmond, 1940.   Fundamentals of bank investment. [Richmond] Conference Committee, 1940. 226 p.   [1067

Boner, John Henry.   Poems. New York, Neale Publishing Co., 1903.   122 p. [1068

—— ——Charlotte, Stone Publishing Co. [c.1903]   122 p.   [1069

——Some new poems. Washington, George E. Howard, 1901.   10 p.   [1070

——Whispering pines, poems. New York, Brentano Brothers, 1883.   167 p. [1071

—— ——Winston-Salem, J. F. Blair, 1954.   116 p.   [1072

Bonham, Milledge L.   The British consuls in the Confederacy. New York, Columbia University, 1911.   (Its Studies in history, economics, and public law, v. 43, no. 3)   267 p.   [1073

Bonnamy, Francis, pseud. see Walz, Audrey

Bonnell, Allen Thomas.   German control over international economic relations, 1930-1940. Urbana, The University of Illinois Press, 1940.   (Its Studies in the social sciences, v. 26, no. 1)   167 p.   [1074

Bonner, Eugene.   Sicilian roundabout. New York, Coward-McCann [1952] 193 p.   [1075

Bonner, Lottie Hale.   Colonial Bath and Pamlico section, North Carolina. Aurora, The Author, 1939.   46 p.   [1076

Booker, John Manning.   A Middle English bibliography. Heidelberg, C. Winter, 1912.   76 p.   [1077

Boone, Daniel.   Life and adventures of Col. Daniel Boon . . . written by himself. Brooklyn, C. Wilder, 1823. [Reprinted for Daniel Boone Club] n.d.   42 p.   [1078

Boone bulletin, no. 1- April, 1925- [Buffalo, N. Y.? Boone Family Association] 1925- NcU has no. 1-3   [1079

Borden, Mattie Fuller.   Song poems. No place, no publisher, c.1906.   5 p.   [1080

Borden, Walter E.   Banking and business ethics by W. E. Borden and Cyrus Lauron Hooper. Chicago, Rand, McNally & Co. [c.1921]   223 p.   [1081

Borden, William.   An address to the inhabitants of North-Carolina. Williamsburg, Va., Printed by William Parks, 1746.   26 p. NcU has photostat from the original in Massachusetts Historical Society Library   [1082

Bosley, Harold Augustus.   A firm faith for today. New York, Harper & Brothers [1950]   283 p.   [1083

——Main issues confronting Christendom. New York, Harper & Brothers [1948] 204 p.   [1084

Bost, Annie (Kiser)   Notice of intention to marry.   No place, Legislative Council of N. C. Women [1928]   [3] p.   [1085

Bost Caleb Ervin.   John H. Bost of North Carolina.   Miami, Fla., no publisher, 1923.   28 p.   [1086

Bost, Emma Ingold.   Songs in many keys.   [Hickory, no publisher, c.1920]   80 p.   [1087

Bost, Ralph Walton, comp.   Bibliography of organic sulfur compounds.   [New York] American Petroleum Institute [c.1930]   187 p.   [1088

Bost, Tom.   Dealing with the Deacs.   Wake Forest, Wake Forest News Bureau, 1949.   56 p.   [1089

Boston, Charles Anderson.   Address before the North Carolina State Bar Association at Chapel Hill, North Carolina, on July 24, 1931.   [Chapel Hill? 1931]   42 p.   [1090

Boston and North Carolina Turpentine Company, Boston.   Prospectus.   Boston [1865?]   [1] p.   [1091

Boston Athenaeum.   Confederate literature.   [Boston] 1917.   213 p.   [1092

Bothwell, Jean.   Lost colony.   Philadelphia, John C. Winston Co. [1953]   182 p.   [1093

Botkin, Benjamin Albert.   A treasury of Southern folklore.   New York, Crown Publishers [1949]   776 p.   [1094

Boutell, Henry Sherman.   The obligations of culture to democracy, address . . . at the one hundred and tenth annual commencement of the University of North Carolina, Chapel Hill, May 31st, 1905.   Wash., Globe Printing Co., 1905.   45 p.   [1095

Bouvé, Pauline Carrington (Rust)   Their shadows before, a story of the Southampton insurrection.   Boston, Small, Maynard & Co., 1899.   202 p.   [1096

Bowers, Claude Gernade.   Making democracy a reality: Jefferson, Jackson, and Polk.   Memphis, Memphis State College Press, 1954.   170 p.   [1097

——The party battles of the Jackson period.   Boston, Houghton Mifflin Co., 1922.   506 p.   [1098

—— ——[pref. 1928]   506 p.   [1099

——Rediscovering the Old South.   No place, North Carolina Division, United Daughters of the Confederacy [1930]   [12] p.   [1100

——The tragic era; the revolution after Lincoln.   Cambridge, Houghton Mifflin Co., 1920.   567 p.   [1101

Bowker, Richard Rogers, comp.   State publications.   New York, Publishers' Weekly, 1908.   1 v. in 4 parts.   North Carolina, part 4, p. 735-780   [1102

Bowman, Charles Wesley.   Bowman genealogy.   Wash., Law Reporter Printing Co., 1912.   104 p.   [1103

Bowman, Clarice Margurette.   Spiritual values in camping.   New York, Association Press, 1954.   240 p.   [1104

Bowman, Elizabeth Skaggs.   Land of high horizons.   Kingsport, Tenn., Southern Publishers, 1938.   212 p.   [1105

Bowman, Samuel Millard.   Sherman and his campaigns . . . by Col. S. M. Bowman and Lt.-Col. R. B. Irwin.   New York, C. F. Vent & Co., 1865.   512 p.   [1106

Bowman, William Dodgson, ed.   Bristol and America, a record of the first settlers in the colonies of North America, 1654-1685.   London, R. Sydney Glover [1929]   182 p.   [1107

——Index to Bristol and America.   [1931]   xvi p.   [1108

Bownas, Samuel.   An account of the life, travels, and Christian experiences in the work of the ministry of Samuel Bownas.   London, J. Phillips, 1795.   196 p.   [1109

Bowyer, James T.   The witch of Jamestown.   Richmond, Va., J. W. Randolph & English, 1890.   151 p.   [1110

Boyce, Benjamin.   The polemic character, 1640-1661; a chapter in English literary history.   [Lincoln] University of Nebraska Press [1955]   160 p.   [1111

Boyce, Warren Scott.   Economic and social history of Chowan County, North Carolina, 1880-1915.   New York, Columbia University, 1917.   (Its Studies in history, economics and public law, v. 76, no. 1)   293 p.   [1112

Boyd, Boston Napoleon Bonapart.   Revised search light on the seventh day Bible

and x-ray, by organic, supernatural and artificial science. Greenville, no publisher, 1924.   250 p.   [1113
——Search light on the seventh wonder. Greenville, no publisher, 1905. 260 p. [1114

Boyd, Charles Rufus. Resources of South-West Virginia. New York, John Wiley & Sons, 1881. 321 p. Includes chapters on Ashe & Alleghany counties, N. C.   [1115

Boyd, James. Bitter Creek. New York, Charles Scribner's Sons, 1939. 422 p.   [1116
——Drums. New York, Charles Scribner's Sons, 1925.   490 p.   [1117
——Drums, with pictures by N. C. Wyeth. New York, Charles Scribner's Sons [c.1928]   409 p.   [1118
——Eighteen poems. New York, Charles Scribner's Sons, 1944.   29 p.   [1119

Boyd, James, ed. The Free Company presents . . . a collection of plays about the meaning of America. New York, Dodd, Mead & Co. [c.1941]   312 p.   [1120

Boyd, James. Long hunt. New York, C. Scribner's Sons, 1930.   376 p.   [1121
——Marching on. New York, Charles Scribner's Sons, 1927.   426 p.   [1122
——Mr. Hugh Dave MacWhirr looks after his $1.00 investment in The Pilot newspaper. Southern Pines, The Pilot, 1943.   64 p.   [1123
——Old pines and other stories. [Chapel Hill] University of North Carolina Press [1952]   165 p.   [1124
——Roll river. New York, Charles Scribner's Sons, 1935.   603 p.   [1125

Boyd, James Penny. The life of General William T. Sherman. [Philadelphia] Publishers' Union, 1891. 608 p.   [1126

Boyden, Nathaniel. To the people of the sixth congressional district of North Carolina. [Washington? 1868?]   16 p.   [1127

Boyd, Thomas Alexander. Light-horse Harry Lee. New York, C. Scribner's Sons, 1931.   359 p.   [1128

Boyd, William Kenneth. The ecclesiastical edicts of the Theodosian code. New York, Columbia University, 1905. (Its Studies in history, economics and public law, v. 24, no. 2)   122 p.   [1129
——The federal period, 1783-1860. Chicago, Lewis Publishing Co., 1919. (History of North Carolina, by Robert Digges Wimberly Connor, William Kenneth Boyd, and J. G. de Roulhac Hamilton, v. 2)   407 p.   [1130

Boyd, William Kenneth, ed. Military reminiscences of Gen. William R. Boggs. Durham, Seeman Printery, 1913. (The John Lawson monographs of the Trinity College Historical Society, v. 3)   115 p.   [1131

Boyd, William Kenneth. Selected bibliography and syllabus of the history of the South, 1584-1876, by William K. Boyd and Robert P. Brooks. Athens, University of Georgia, 1918. (Its Bulletin, v. 18, no. 6)   133 p.   [1132
——The story of Durham, city of the new South. Durham, Duke University Press, 1925.   345 p.   [1133
——A syllabus of North Carolina history, 1584-1876, by William K. Boyd and J. G. de R. Hamilton,   Durham, Seeman Printery, 1913.   101 p.   [1134

Boyer, Frederick Q. Industrial opportunities in the Asheville district, 1899-1925. [Asheville, Chamber of Commerce, 1926?]   7 p.   [1135

Boyer, Marie Louise. Early days, All Souls' Church and Biltmore Village. Biltmore, 1933.   22 p.   [1136

Boylan's North-Carolina almanack for the year of Our Lord, 180 - Raleigh, Printed by William Boylan, 180 - NcU has 1806-1812.   [1137

Boyle, John Richards. Soldiers true, the story of the One Hundred and Eleventh Regiment, Pennsylvania Veteran Volunteers, and of its campaigns in the war for the union. New York, Eaton & Mains, 1903.   368 p.   [1138

Boynton, Charles Brandon. The history of the navy during the rebellion. New York, D. Appleton & Co., 1867-68.   2 v.   [1139

Boynton, Henry Van Ness. Oration delivered at Guilford Battle Ground, July 4, 1900. Greensboro, Guilford Battle Ground Co., 1900.   14 p.   [1140
——Sherman's historical raid, the memoirs in the light of the record. Cincinnati, Wilstach, Baldwin & Co., 1875.   276 p.   [1141

Boynton, Percy Holmes. America in contemporary fiction. Chicago, University of Chicago Press [c.1940]   273 p.   Chapter 12: Thomas Wolfe.   [1142

Brabham, William Mouzon. History of Sunday school work in the North Carolina

Conference, Methodist Episcopal Church, South. Greensboro, North Carolina Christian Advocate, 1925. 47 p.   [1143

Bradlee, Francis Boardman Crowinshield. Blockade running during the Civil War and the effect of land and water transportation on the Confederacy. Salem, Mass., Essex Institute, 1925. 340 p.   [1144

Bradley, George S. The star corps; or, Notes of an army chaplain, during Sherman's famous "march to the sea". Milwaukee, Jermain & Brightman, pr., 1865. 304 p.   [1145

Bradshaw, George Samuel, comp. and ed. The history of the first North Carolina reunion at Greensboro, N. C., October eleventh, twelfth, and thirteenth, nineteen hundred and three. Greensboro, J. J. Stone & Co., 1905. 176 p.   [1146

——Mrs. Kerenhappuch Turner, a heroine of 1776; an address on occasion of the unveiling of a monument to her memory at the Guilford Battle Ground, July 4, 1902 Greensboro [1902?] 6 p.   [1147

——Presentation of the portrait of Gov. Morehead to Guilford County . . . September 5, 1921. No place, no publisher, n.d. 14 p.   [1148

Bradway, John Saeger. Legal aid clinic instruction at Duke University. Durham, Duke University Press, 1944. 126 p.   [1149

Brady, Cyrus Townsend. American fights and fighters. New York, McClure, Phillips & Co., 1900. 326 p.   [1150

——Commodore Paul Jones. New York, D. Appleton and Co., 1900. 480 p. [1151

——The true Andrew Jackson. Philadelphia, J. B. Lippincott Co., 1906. 504 p. [1152

——When blades are out and love's afield. Philadelphia, J. B. Lippincott Co., 1901. 305 p.   [1153

Bragaw, John Goldsmith. Random shots. [Raleigh, Edwards and Broughton Co.] 1905. 356 p.   [1154

Bragg, Ada Satterthwaite. Forget-me-nots of Bath, N. C. Bath, M. E. Price [c.1926] 35 p.   [1155

Braithwaite, Joseph Bevan. Memoirs of Joseph John Gurney, with selections from his journal and correspondence. 2d ed. Norwich, Fletcher and Alexander, 1855. 2 v.   [1156

Branch, Houston. Diamond Head. [New York] Farrar, Straus, 1948. 371 p. [1157

Branch, Lawrence O'Bryan. Letter to his constituents. [Washington] Lemuel Towers, pr. [1858] 16 p.   [1158

Branch, Mary Jones (Polk) Memoirs of a southern woman "within the lines" and a genealogical record. Chicago, Joseph G. Branch Publishing Co. [c.1912] 107 p. [1159

Brandon, Edgar Ewing, ed. A pilgrimage of liberty; a contemporary account of the triumphal tour of General Lafayette through the southern and western states in 1825. Athens, O., Lawhead Press, 1944. 487 p.   [1160

Brandon, Evan. Green Pond. New York, Vanguard Press [1955] 506 p.   [1161

Brannon, Clarence Ham. Allen H. Godbey, a biography. Boston, Christopher Publishing House [1949] 470 p.   [1162

——An introduction to the Bible. [Raleigh? 1951, c.1950] 292 p.   [1163

Branscomb, Bennett Harvie. The Gospel of Mark. New York, Harper and Bros., n.d. 314 p.   [1164

——Jesus and the law of Moses. New York, R. R. Smith, 1930. 296 p.   [1165

——Teaching with books; a study of college libraries. Chicago, Association of American Colleges, American Library Association, 1940. 239 p.   [1166

——The teachings of Jesus. Nashville, Tenn., Cokesbury Press [1931] 384 p. [1167

Branson, Eugene Cuningham. Common school speller. Atlanta, B. F. Johnson Publishing Co. [c.1900] 104 p.   [1168

——Farm life abroad; field letters from Germany, Denmark, and France. Chapel Hill, University of North Carolina Press, 1924. 303 p.   [1169

——Farm prosperity and the local market problem in Mecklenburg. Charlotte, Union National Bank [1917?] [19] p.   [1170

——Farm prosperity in Forsyth. Winston-Salem, Board of Trade, 1917. 29 p. [1171

——Methods in teaching arithmetic. Boston, D. C. Heath & Co., 1896. 39 p. [1172

——Pasquotank today and tomorrow. Elizabeth City, First National Bank, n.d. 19 p.   [1173

——Public port terminals in North Carolina. [Chapel Hill, Author, 1924] 16 p. [1174
——Reading methods with chapter on spelling. Boston, D. C. Heath & Co., 1896.
39 p.   [1175
——Supplementary notes, Waymarks for teachers, by Sarah Louise Arnold. New
York, Silver, Burdett & Co. [c.1900]   32 p.   [1176
——The University serves. [Greensboro?] Guilford County Alumni, n.d. 15 p. [1177

Branson, Levi. Branson's hand book of North Carolina authors. Raleigh, Levi
Branson, 1900. 13 p.   [1178
——Directory of the business and citizens of Durham City, 1887- Raleigh, Levi
Branson, 1887- NcU has 1887   [1179

Branson, Levi, ed. The elementary spelling-book, rev. from Webster. Raleigh,
Branson, Farrar and Co., n.d.   152 p.   [1180

Branson, Levi. First book in composition, applying the principles of grammar to
the art of composing. Raleigh, Branson, Farrar & Co., 1863.   139 p.   [1181
——Moore County business directory. Raleigh, Levi Branson, 1898.   125 p. [1182
——Randolph County business directory. Raleigh, L. Branson, 1894.   146 p. [1183

Branson, Levi, ed. North Carolina sermons. Raleigh, L. Branson, 1881-1893.
3 v.   [1184

[Branson, Thomas A.?] The Jack Morgan songster, compiled by a capt. in Gen.
Lee's army. Raleigh, Branson & Farrar, 1864.   [1185

Branson magazine of genealogies, v. 1, no. 1-2, June, 1898-June, 1899. Raleigh, L.
Branson, 1898-1899. NcU has v. 1, no. 1-2.   [1186

Branson's North Carolina agricultural almanac see **North Carolina** agricultural
almanac

Branson's North Carolina business directory, 1866/67- Raleigh, Levi Branson,
1866- NcU has 1866/67, 1867/68, 1869, 1872, 1877-78, 1884, 1890, 1896 [1187

Brantley, Allen Patterson. The enchanted cross. New York, Fleming H. Revell
Co. [c.1937]   214 p.   [1188

Brawley, Benjamin Griffith, ed. Early Negro American writers, selections with
biographical and critical introductions. Chapel Hill, University of North Carolina Press, 1935.   305 p.   [1189

Brawley, Benjamin Griffith. Negro builders and heroes. Chapel Hill, University
of North Carolina Press, 1937.   315 p.   [1190
——A new survey of English literature. New York, A. A. Knopf, 1925. 388 p. [1191
——A short history of the American Negro. Revised ed. New York, MacMillan
Co., 1922.   280 p.   [1192
——A social history of the American Negro. New York, Macmillan Co., 1921.
420 p.   [1193

Brawley, James Shober. The Rowan story, 1753-1953, a narrative history of Rowan
County, North Carolina. Salisbury, Rowan Printing Co., 1953.   402 p.   [1194

Brayton, Patience. Life and religious labours of Patience Brayton, late of Swansey
in the State of Massachusetts. New York, Isaac Collins and Sons, 1801. NcU
has typewritten copy of the North Carolina sections.   [1195

Brearley, Harrington Cooper. Homicide in the United States. Chapel Hill, University of North Carolina Press, 1932. 249 p.   [1196

Brearley, Harrington Cooper, ed. The rural South, a reading guide . . . edited by
H. C. Brearley and Marian Tippit. Nashville, Southern Rural Life Council,
George Peabody College for Teachers [1946]   86 p.   [1197

Breazeale, J. W. M. Life as it is. Knoxville, Printed by J. Williams, 1842.
256 p.   [1198

[Breckinridge, Robert Jefferson] An address to the American people. No place,
no publisher [1836?]   12 p.   [1199

Breckinridge, Robert Jefferson. Papism in the XIX century in the United States,
being select contributions to the papal controversy during 1835-1840. Baltimore,
David Owen & Sons, 1841.   343 p.   [1200

The Breckinridge Party a disunion party! No place, no publisher [1860?] 8 p. [1201

Breed, William Pratt. Presbyterians and the Revolution. Philadelphia, Presbyterian Board of Publication [c.1876]   205 p.   [1202

Breedlove, Joseph Penn. Duke University Library, 1840-1940. Durham, The Friends of Duke University Library, 1955. (Library notes, no. 30) 81 p. [1203

Brett, Thomas. True moderation, a sermon on Philip, IV, 5. Raleigh, Bell & Lawrence, 1825. 15 p. [1204

Brevard, N. C. Board of Trade. Brevard, N. C., the land of waterfalls. Buffalo, N. Y., Matthews-Northrup for Brevard Board of Trade, n.d. 11 p. [1205

—— ——n.d. [20] p. [1206

Brevard, N. C. The Franklin. The Franklin for rest and recreation. Brevard, Bryan Lawrence [1908?] 16 p. [1207

Brevard College, Brevard, N. C. Bulletin, v. 1- March, 1935- Brevard, 1935- NcU has v. [1-4, 8-23] v. 17-28 omitted in numbering. [1208

Brevoort, James Carson. Verrazano, the navigator. New York [Albany, N. Y., Argus Co., pr.] 1874. 159 p. [1209

Brewer, Fisk Parsons. The Library of the University of North Carolina. No place, no publisher [1870?] 8 p. [1210

——Memoir of Hon. David Lowry Swain. Boston, David Clapp & Son, 1870. 8 p. [1211

[Brewer, Warren Harold] History of Brewer family. [Terre Haute? Ind., 1936?] 70 numb. leaves. [1212

Brewster, J. C. & Co., Raleigh, N. C. Tobacco culture. Raleigh, Edwards and Broughton Co., 1885. 46+ p. p. 47—wanting in NcU copy. [1213

Brick Junior College see Joseph Keasbey Brick Agricultural, Industrial and Normal School

Brickell, John. The natural history of North-Carolina. Dublin, Printed by J. Carson for the Author, 1737. 408 p. [1214

—— ——[Raleigh, Reprinted by authority of the Trustees of the Public Libraries, 1911] 417 p. [1215

Bridenbaugh, Carl. Myths and realities, societies of the colonial South. Baton Rouge, Louisiana State University Press [1952] 208 p. [1216

Bridgers, Ann Preston. Coquette, a play in three acts, by George Abbott and Ann Preston Bridgers. New York, Longmans, Green and Co., 1928. 137 p. [1217

—— ——New York, Samuel French [c.1926] 92 p. [1218

Bridgers, John L., joint author, see Turner, Joseph Kelly

Bridges, Earley Winfred. Chorazin Chapter no. 13, Royal Arch Masons, a historical survey of one of North Carolina's outstanding chapters. Staunton, Va., McClure Printing Co., 1953. 163 p. [1220

——Greensboro Lodge no. 76, A. F. & A. M. Staunton, Va., McClure Printing Co., 1951. 469 p. [1221

——The Guilford Battle Ground gavel. Greensboro, E. A. Woodell & Co., 1954. 12 p. [1222

——The Masonic governors of North Carolina. Greensboro, no publisher, 1937. 279 p. [1223

——Tokens . . . by Earley Winfred Bridges and William Moseley Brown. Staunton, Va., McClure Printing Co., 1954. 81 p. [1224

A brief description of the province of Carolina on the coasts of Floreda, and more particularly of a new-plantation begun by the English at Cape-Feare . . . together with a most accurate map of the whole province. London, Printed for R. Horne, 1666. 10 p. [1225

——Reproduced in facsimile with an introduction by John Tate Lanning. Charlottesville, The Tracy W. McGregor Library, University of Virginia, 1944. 23 p. [1226

Brief history of Col. David Fanning; also, Naomi Wise . . . and Randolph's manufacturing. Weldon, Harrell's Printing House, 1888. 121 p. [1227

Brief history of our synodical orphans' home. Barium Springs [Presbyterian Orphan Home] n.d. 18 p. [1228

Brief history of the Moravian Church, prepared by teachers and friends of the Salem Home Sunday School, Winston-Salem, N. C., January, 1909. Raleigh, Edwards & Broughton Printing Co. [1909] 146, 23 p. [1229

Brief inquiry into some of the objections urged against the election of Andrew Jack son to the office of President of the United States. No place, no publisher, n.d. 35 p. [1230

Brief memoir concerning Abel Thomas, a minister of the Gospel of Christ in the Society of Friends. Philadelphia, Benjamin & Kite, 1824. 51 p. [1231

Brief memoir of Nathan Hunt. London, W. and F. G. Cash, 1854. 27 p. [1232

Brief replies to several charges against James Buchanan . . . compiled by a North Carolinian. Washington, Printed at the Capital City Office, 1856. 16 p. [1233

Brief sketch of Helen Pugh. [Greensboro, Hackney and Moale? n.d.] 6 p. [1234

Brier Creek Baptist Association. Minutes, 18 - 18 - NcU has [1852-1876] 1880-1886, 1897, 1904-1906 [1929-1939] [1235

Briggs, Thomas Henry. Curriculum problems. New York, Macmillan Co., 1927. 138 p. [1236

——The great investment, secondary education in a democracy. Cambridge, Harvard University Press, 1930. 143 p. [1237

——Improving instruction. New York, Macmillan Co. [1939] 587 p. [1238

——The junior high school. New York, Houghton Mifflin Co. [c.1920] 350 p. [1239

——Outline questions for the study of Silas Marner. No place, no publisher [c.1909] 15 p. [1240

——Reading in public schools by Thomas H. Briggs and L. D. Coffman. Rev. ed. Chicago, Row, Peterson & Co. [c.1911] 332 p. [1241

——Secondary education. New York, Macmillan Co., 1933. 577 p. [1242

——Ways to better English . . . by Thomas H. Briggs and Isabel McKinney. Boston, Ginn and Co. [c.1924] 331 p. [1243

Briggs, Willis G. First Baptist Church, Raleigh, N. C. [Raleigh, 1952] [7] p. [1244

——Henry Potter, 1766-1857. Raleigh, Edwards & Broughton Co., 1953. 20 p. [1245

——Statement of fact, fourth congressional district, North Carolina, Delegates James C. Stancil and Willis G. Briggs to the National Republican Convention, Chicago . . . June 16, 1908. No place, no publisher [1908] 10 p. [1246

Brigham, Clarence Saunders, comp. Bibliography of American newspapers, 1690-1820. Part X: North Carolina. Worcester, Mass., American Antiquarian Society, 1919 (Its Proceedings, n.s., v. 28) North Carolina, p. 291-322. [1247

——History and bibliography of American newspapers, 1690-1820. Worcester, Mass., American Antiquarian Society, 1947. 2 v. North Carolina, v. 2, p. 785-782. [1248

Bright, John Morgan. Oration delivered at the centennial celebration of the Mecklenburg Declaration of Independence at Charlotte, N. C., May 20, 1875. Nashville, Tenn., Roberts & Purvis, pr., 1875. 18 p. [1249

Brimley, Clement Samuel. Outlines of lectures on zoology. Biltmore, Biltmore Forest School, n.d. 20 p. [1250

Brimley, Herbert Hutchinson. A North Carolina naturalist, H. H. Brimley, selections from his writings, edited by Eugene P. Odum. Chapel Hill, University of North Carolina Press [1949] 205 p. [1251

Brink, Wellington. Big Hugh, the father of soil conservation. New York, Macmillan Co., 1951. 167 p. [1252

Brinkley, Roberta Florence, ed. Coleridge on the seventeenth century. Durham, Duke University Press, 1955. 704 p. [1253

Brinton, Howard Haines. The function of a Quaker college. Guilford College, 1951. (Ward lectures, November 9, 1951) 22 p. [1254

Britt, James Jefferson. Life and character of Andrew Johnson. [Greenville, Tenn.?] n.d. 15 p. [1255

——Memorial address on the life and character of Judge Jeter Conley Pritchard. [Asheville? First Baptist Church? 1921] 19 p. [1256

Brittain, I. J. Brittain's poems. Winston-Salem, [The Author] c.1918. 80 p. [1257

——Tragedy of Naomi Wise. Life of Andrew Jackson. First English baby in America. The lost little girl. Mrs. David Caldwell. A Tory beauty. Winston-Salem, The Author, n.d. 47 p. [1258

Britton, Nathaniel Lord. North American trees. New York, H. Holt and Co., 1908. 894 p. [1259

Broad, Carter. The North Carolina shrimp survey. Morehead City, Institute of Fisheries Research [1950] 62 p. [1260
——Pink doubloons in Key West waters. Morehead City, Institute of Fisheries Research, 1950. 8 p. [1261
——The shrimp fishery of the Florida keys. Morehead City, University of North Carolina, Institute of Fisheries Research, 1950. 13 p. [1262

Broaddus, Andrew. Doctrine of justification by the imputed righteousness of Jesus Christ, opened and defended in a sermon on Romans, X, 4. Raleigh, Printed by William Boylan for Robert T. Daniel, 1806. 32 p. [1263

Broadfoot, Charles Wetmore. Address at the centennial celebration of St. John's Church, Fayetteville, N. C. . . . April 15, 1917. [Fayetteville?] n.d. 34 p. [1264
——Excerpts from the letters, addresses, and papers of Colonel Charles W. Broadfoot. Washington, Philip W. Wiley, pr., 1928. 88 p. [1265

Broadhurst, Edgar David. Old North State copies [by] Edgar D. Broadhurst, Mary I. Tinnin, J. A. Matheson, the letter forms and two stories of Carolina and Raleigh. No place, North State Publishing Co. [c.1906] 6 v. [1266

Broadwell, Julius H. Life of John E. Starling, the supposed double-murderer. Smithfield, The Herald, 1890. 13 p. [1267

Brock, Henry Irving. Archibald Henderson, a sketch. New York, D. Appleton and Co., 1932. 10 p. [1268

Brockman, Zoe Kincaid. Heart on my sleeve. Emory University, Ga., Banner Press [1951] 73 p. [1269

Brockmann, Charles Raven. Adams, Caruthers, Clancy, Neely, and Townsend descendants. Charlotte, 1950. 118 leaves. [1270

Brodie, David Arthur. Mecklenburg County, North Carolina, seventy-five years of progressive farming at a glance. Washington, The Author [c.1925] 8 p. [1271

Brodin, Piérre. Thomas Wolfe. Asheville, Stephens Press [c.1949] 41 p. [1272

Brogden, Curtis Hooks. Address to the voters of the second congressional district. No place, n.d. [2] p. [1273
——Opinion on the impeachment trial of William W. Holden. Raleigh, Sentinel, 1871. 15 p. [1274
——Speech delivered before the Wayne County Republican Convention, at the Town Hall, in Goldsboro, N. C., Saturday, May 29, 1880. Goldsboro, Messenger, 1880. 16 p. [1275

Brogden, Willis James. Address: The message of the college to modern life, at Wake Forest Commencement, June 4th, 1931. No place, no publisher, 1931. 22 p. [1276

Brooke, Henry K. Book of pirates. Philadelphia, J. B. Perry, 1841. 216 p. [1277

Brookings Institution, Washington. Report on a survey of the organization and administration of county government in North Carolina. [Washington? 1931] 152 p. [1278
——Report on a survey of the organization and administration of the state government of North Carolina. [Washington? 1930] 323 p. [1279

Brooks, Aubrey Lee. An address before the North Carolina Bar Association at Asheville, N. C., July 3rd, 1917. No place, no publisher, 1917. 29 p. [1280
——An address before the North Carolina Bar Association at Wrightsville Beach, July 1st, 1914. [Greensboro, Harrison Printing Co., 1914?] 15 p. [1281
——A. L. Brooks replies to anonymous attack on Angus Wilton McLean. No place, no publisher [1923] 8 p. [1282
——Chief Justice Walter Clark, memorial address . . . before the North Carolina Bar Association, Asheville, N. C., July 2, 1925. No place, no publisher [1925?] 10 p. [1283

Brooks, Aubrey Lee, ed. The papers of Walter Clark, ed. by Aubrey Lee Brooks and Hugh Talmage Lefler. Chapel Hill, University of North Carolina Press [1948-1950] 2 v. [1284

Brooks, Aubrey Lee. Selected addresses of a southern lawyer. Chapel Hill, University of North Carolina Press [1954] 165 p. [1285
——A southern lawyer, fifty years at the bar. Chapel Hill, University of North Carolina Press [1950] 214 p. [1286

——Walter Clark, fighting judge. Chapel Hill, University of North Carolina Press [1944] 278 p.   [1287

Brooks, E. M.   History of Rocky River Baptist Church. [Albemarle, The Author] 1928. 104 p.   [1288

Brooks, Eugene Clyde. Agricultural supplement to Milne's Progressive arithmetic, second book, North Carolina edition, prepared by E. C. Brooks . . . and I. O. Schaub. New York, American Book Co. [1914] p. 305-320   [1289
——Building of a system of high schools in North Carolina. [Durham? Trinity College, 1908] (Its Department of Education Bulletin, no. 1) 28 p.   [1290
——A comparison of school systems. [Durham, Trinity College, 1910?] (Its Department of Education Bulletin, no. 2) 23 p.   [1291
——Dodge's geography of North Carolina, by Eugene C. Brooks . . . and William D. Carmichael. [Chicago] Rand, McNally and Co. [c.1911] 32 p.   [1292
——Education for democracy. Chicago, Rand, McNally and Co. [c.1919] 263 p. [1293
——Inaugural address . . . The need of a new educational content . . . North Carolina Teachers' Assembly, Greensboro, November 27, 1912. Raleigh, E. M. Uzzell & Co., pr., 1913. 16 p.   [1294

Brooks, Eugene Clyde, ed. North Carolina poems, selected and edited with an introduction, notes, and biographical sketches. Raleigh, North Carolina Education, 1912. 160 p.   [1295

Brooks, Eugene Clyde. Our dual government. Chicago, Raleigh, McNally and Co. [c.1924] 246 p.   [1296
——Stories of South America. Richmond, Va., Johnson Publishing Co. [c.1922] 272 p.   [1297
——The story of corn and the westward migration. Chicago, Rand, McNally and Co. [c.1916] 308 p.   [1298
——The story of cotton and the development of the cotton states. Chicago, Rand, McNally & Co. [c.1911] 370 p.   [1299
——Woodrow Wilson as president. Chicago, Row, Peterson and Co. [c.1916] 572 p.   [1300

Brooks, Evelyn (Cheney) joint author, see Brooks, Lee Marshall

Brooks, J. H.   Oration delivered before the Euzelian and Philomathesian societies of the Wake Forest Institute, July 4, 1838. Raleigh, Recorder Office, pr., 1838. 12 p.   [1301

Brooks, John Rives. An earnest appeal to preachers, college professors, and other Christians. Nashville, Tenn., Publishing House of the M. E. Church, South, n.d. p. 388-413   [1302
——Scriptural sanctification; an attempted solution of the holiness problem. Nashville, Tenn., Publishing House of the M. E. Church, South, 1904. 413 p.   [1303

Brooks, Lee Marshall. Adventuring in adoption, by Lee M. Brooks and Evelyn C. Brooks. Chapel Hill, University of North Carolina Press, 1939. 225 p.   [1304
——Evaluation of teaching in the social sciences. [Chapel Hill, 1946?] 20 p. [1305
——Manual for southern regions to accompany Southern regions of the United States by Howard W. Odum, by Lee M. Brooks . . . in collaboration with Wayland J. Hayes [and others] Chapel Hill, University of North Carolina Press, 1937. 194 p.   [1306
——Urban communities of the South, by Lee M. Brooks . . . with the assistance of Sara E. Smith . . . and Evelyn C. Brooks. Chapel Hill, Institute for Research in Social Science, 1946. 112 numbered leaves.   [1307

Brooks, Lee Marshall, joint author, see Groves, Ernest Rutherford

Brougham, John. Dred; or, The Dismal Swamp, a play in five acts . . . from Mrs. Harriet Beecher Stowe's novel. New York, S. French, c.1856. 43 p.   [1308

Broughton, Joseph Melville. An address and presentation of a portrait of Judge Robert Watson Winston to the Wake County Bar Association. [Raleigh? 1946] 7 p.   [1309
——The language of the law; an address delivered at the annual convention of the North Carolina Bar Assocation, Asheville, North Carolina, July 9, 1936. [Raleigh? The Author? 1936?] 15 p.   [1310

Broughton, Leonard Gaston. In His way. Nashville, Tenn., Sunday School Board of the Southern Baptist Convention [c.1936] 183 p.   [1311

——Revival of a dead church. Chicago, Bible Institute Colportage Association [c.1900] 131 p.   [1312

——Soul consciousness after death. Nashville, Tenn., Sunday School Board of the Southern Baptist Convention [c.1924] 159 p.   [1313

Brow, Francis W. Useful hints, ideas, notes, tips, suggestions for the home gardener. [Biltmore, The Author, c.1951] 15 p.   [1314

Brower, Lee Carlton. The organ grinder, a book of verse. Otsego, Mich., The Verseland Press, 1937. 94 p.   [1315

Brown, A. J. Vindication of the Evangelical Lutheran Tennessee Synod . . . by the Rev. A. J. Brown and Rev. A. Miller. Salem, Blum & Son, 1838. 46 p.   [1316

Brown, Aaron Vail. Address delivered before the two literary societies of the University of North Carolina. Raleigh, William C. Doub, 1854. 27 p.   [1317

Brown, Aaron Venable. Speeches, congressional and political, and other writings, of ex-Governor Aaron V. Brown. Nashville, Tenn., J. L. Marling and Co., 1854. 606 p.   [1318

Brown, Alexander. The genesis of the United States. Boston, Houghton, Mifflin and Co., 1890. 2 v.   [1319

Brown, Arch Burfoot. Historic sands of Eastern Carolina. [Washington? c.1937] 39 p.   [1320

Brown, Aycock. The birth of aviation, Kitty Hawk, N. C. Winston-Salem, Collins Co., c.1953. Unpaged.   [1321

Brown, Bedford. Address delivered before the two literary societies of the University of North Carolina . . . June, 1839. Raleigh [T. Loring, pr.] 1839. 39 p.   [1322

Brown, Bertram E. A list of historical relics displayed in the hall of Calvary Parish House, Tarboro, N. C. [Raleigh, Edwards and Broughton Co.] n.d. 139 p. [1323

Brown, Cecil Kenneth. Introduction to economics. New York, American Book Co. [1941] 534 p.   [1323a

——The state highway system of North Carolina, its evolution and present status. Chapel Hill, University of North Carolina Press, 1931. 260 p.   [1324

——A state movement in railroad development. Chapel Hill, University of North Carolina Press, 1928. 300 p.   [1325

Brown, Charlotte (Hawkins) The correct thing to do-to say-to wear. Sedalia, The Author, 1940. 109 p.   [1326

Brown, Frank Clyde. Elkanah Settle, his life and works. Chicago, University of Chicago Press [c.1910] 170 p.   [1327

Brown, Frederick J. Northward movement of the colored population. Baltimore, Cushing & Co. [c.1897] 50 p.   [1328

Brown, Henry Clay. Address before the North Carolina Retail Merchants' Association at its annual convention held in Greensboro, June 9, 1907. Raleigh, E. M. Uzzell, 1908. 12 p.   [1329

Brown, Henry N. A speech delivered to Orange Republicans at the court house, September 14th. No place, no publisher, Sept. 14, 1878. [1] p.   [1330

[**Brown, J. Parsons**] Tuckahoe Christian Church, 1849-1936. [Jacksonville, The Jacksonville Record, 1941] [21] p.   [1331

Brown, John Mason. Daniel Boone. New York, Random House [1952] 181 p. [1332

Brown, John P. Old frontiers; the story of the Cherokee Indians. Kingsport, Tenn., Southern Publishers, 1938. 570 p.   [1333

Brown, Joseph Gill. Address delivered at the convention of the American Bankers' Association at New Orleans, November 22nd, 1911. Raleigh, Edwards and Broughton Co., 1911. 17 p.   [1334

——The new South; address delivered at the convention of the American Bankers' Association at New Orleans, Nov. 11, 1902. Raleigh, Edwards and Broughton Co., 1902. 18 p.   [1335

Brown, Laura Morrison. Historical sketch of the Morrison family. [Charlotte, Presbyterian Standard] 1919. 51 p.   [1336

Brown, Leslie Hubert. Genealogy of the Farrior family. Wilmington, 1948. 345 p.   [1337

Brown, Marion Lea. Pickles and preserves. New York, Wilfred Funk [1955] 282 p. [1338

——The Southern cook book. Chapel Hill, University of North Carolina Press [1951] 371 p. [1339

—— ——New York, Pocket Books, Inc. [1953] 414 p. [1340

Brown, Minnie McIver. History of Wilmington Presbyterial Auxiliary, 1888-1922. Raleigh, Edwards and Broughton Co., 1923. 84 p. [1341

Brown, Richard L. A history of the Michael Brown family of Rowan County, North Carolina. [Granite Quarry] Michael Brown Family Association [c.1921] 190 p. [1342

Brown, Rome G. Muckraking the constitution; address before the State Bar Association of North Carolina . . . Wrightsville Beach, N. C., June 30, 1914. Washington, Byron S. Adams, pr., n.d. 28 p. [1343

Brown, Roy Melton. Public poor relief in North Carolina. Chapel Hill, University of North Carolina Press, 1928. 184 p. [1344

Brown, Roy Melton, joint author, see **Steiner, Jesse Frederick**

Brown, Samuel Windsor. The secularization of American education as shown by state legislation, state constitutional provisions and state supreme court decisions. New York, Teachers College, Columbia University, 1912. (Its Contributions to education, no. 49) 160 p. [1345

Brown, Tarleton. Memoirs of Tarleton Brown, a captain of the Revolutionary army. New York, privately printed, 1862. 65 p. [1346

Brown, Thelma Sharman. By way of Cherokee. Atlanta, Home Mission Board, Southern Baptist Convention [1944] 127 p. [1347

Brown, William Garrott. The foe of compromise, and other essays. New York, Macmillan Co., 1903. 224 p. [1348

Brown Creek Baptist Association. 18 - 18 - NcU has [1857-1876] 1880-1883 [1349

Browne, Edward Tankard, joint author, see **Lasley, John Wayne**

Brownell, William Arthur. Arithmetic in grades I and II. Durham, Duke University Press, 1941. (Duke University Research studies in education, no. 6) 175 p. [1350

——The effect of unfamiliar settings on problem-solving. Durham, Duke University Press, 1931. (Duke University Research studies in education [no. 1]) 86 p. [1351

——Learning the multiplication combinations, by William A. Brownell and Doris V. Carper. Durham, Duke University Press, 1943. (Duke University Research studies in education, no. 7) 177 p. [1352

——Learning as reorganization. Durham, Duke University Press, 1939. (Duke University Research studies in education [no. 3]) 87 p. [1353

——Meaningful vs. mechanical learning. Durham, Duke University Press, 1949. (Duke University Research studies in education, no. 8) 207 p. [1353a

[Browning, Raymond] After-study meditations. No place, no publisher [pref. 1906] 31 p. [1354

——Phantom anvil, and other melodies. No place, no publisher, n.d. 38 p. [1355

——The phoenix. Littleton, Phoenix Publishing Co., n.d. 29 p. [1356

Brownlee, Frederick L. The John C. Campbell Folk School, 1925-1952. [Brasstown, 1952?] 23 p. [1357

Brownlow, William Gannaway. Americanism contrasted with foreignism, Romanism, and bogus democracy, in the light of reason, history, and Scripture. Nashville, Tenn., The Author, 1856. 208 p. [1358

Brownlow, William Gannaway. The great iron wheel examined. Nashville, Tenn., The Author, 1856. 331 p. [1359

——Helps to the study of Presbyterianism . . . to which is added a brief account of the life and travels of the author, interspersed with anecdotes. Knoxville, Tenn., F. S. Heiskell, pr., 1834. 299 p. [1360

Bruce, Henry Addington Bayley. Daniel Boone and the Wilderness road. New York, Macmillan Co., 1910. 349 p. [1361

Bruce, James C. An address delivered before the alumni and graduating class of

the University of North Carolina . . . June third, 1841.   Raleigh, North Carolina Standard, pr., 1841. 26 p.   [1362
—— ——Baltimore, John Cox's Sons, 1898.   28 p.   [1363

Bruce, Jerome. Studies in black and white. New York, Neale Publishing Co., 1906. 472 p.   [1364

Brucker, Margaretta. A doctor for Barbara. New York, Avalon Books [1956] 224 p.   [1365

Brumfield, Lewis Floyd. How to grow and market capons. [Elkin, Elkin Printing Co.] c.1933. 42 p.   [1366

Bruner, James Dowden, ed. Le roman d'un jeune homme pauvre, par Octave Feuillet. Boston, D. C. Heath & Co., 1904. 283 p.   [1367
——Hernani, par Victor Hugo. New York, American Book Co. [c.1906] 264 p. [1368

Bruner, James Dowden. Studies in Victor Hugo's dramatic characters. Boston, Ginn and Co., 1908. 171 p.   [1369

Brunner, Edmund de Schweinitz. Church life in the rural South. New York, George H. Doran Co. [c.1923] 117 p.   [1370

Brushfield, Thomas Nadauld. A bibliography of Sir Walter Raleigh. 2d ed. Exeter, J. G. Commin, 1908. 181 p.   [1371

Brushy Mountain Baptist Association. Minutes, 1872- 1872- NcU has 1872-1906 [1928-1954]   [1372

Brushy Mountain Land Company. The famous Brushy Mountain Iron and Lithia Springs and valuable fruit farms. North Wilkesboro [1910] 23 p.   [1373

Bruton, John Fletcher. Address . . . Wilmington, N. C., May 11, 1892. Raleigh, Edwards and Broughton Co., 1892. 23 p.   [1374

Bry, Theodor de, ed. [America, pt. 1-13] Frankfort, T. de Bry, 1590-1634. 13 parts in 14 volumes with individual title pages. Known as "Grand Voyages". NcU has 1st ed. (Latin)   [1375
——Historia antipodum oder newe Welt. Frankfort, Bey denen Merianischen erben, 1655. 661 p.   [1376
——Voyages en Virginie et en Floride. Paris, Dvchartre et Van Bvggenhovt, 1927. 661 p.   [1377

Bryan, Daniel. The mountain muse, comprising the adventures of Daniel Boone. Harrisonburg, Printed for the Author by Davidson & Bourne, 1813. 252 p. [1378

Bryan, Ferrebee Catharine. At the gates, life story of Matthew Tyson and Eliza Moring Yates of China. Nashville, Tenn., Broadman Press [c.1949] 374 p. [1379
——His golden cycle, the life story of Robert Thomas Bryan. Richmond, Va., Rice Press, 1938. 297 p.   [1380

Bryan, James West. An oration on the death of William H. Harrison. Newbern, John I. Pasteur, pr., 1841. 12 p.   [1381

Bryan, John Heritage. Memoir of Hon. Frederick Nash. Chapel Hill, Neathery and Jones, pr., 1859. 7 p.   [1382
——An oration delivered at Chapel Hill, on Wednesday, the 23rd June, 1830. Newbern, J. I. Pasteur, pr., 1830. 19 p.   [1383
——Orations on the death of Thomas Jefferson and John Adams, delivered at the request of the citizens of Newbern, on the 17th and 24th July, 1826, by the Hon. John H. Bryan and the Hon. John Stanly. Newbern, Watson & Machen, pr., 1826. 31 p.   [1384

Bryan, Mary Norcott. Echoes from the past. [New Berne, privately printed, 1921] 48 p.   [1385
——A grandmother's recollection of Dixie. [New Bern, Owen G. Dunn, pr.] n.d. 43 p.   [1386

Bryan, Thomas Conn. Confederate Georgia. Athens, University of Georgia Press [1953] 299 p.   [1387

Bryant, Buck, see Bryant, Henry Edward Cowan

Bryant, Edwin Eustace. History of the Third regiment of Wisconsin Veteran Vol-unteer Infantry, 1861-1865. Madison, Wis., Veteran Association of the Regiment, 1891. 445 p.   [1388

Bryant, Gilmore Ward. First lessons in piano playing. 10th ed. Durham, The Author, c.1905. 19 p. [1389

Bryant, Henry Edward Cowan. A fool about a hound. [Washington, D. C., The Author] n.d. 24 p. [1390

——Joseph Pearson Caldwell, 1853-1911. Statesville, Brady Printing Co., 1933. 70 p. [1391

——A little despot. [Washington, D. C., W. F. Roberts, pr., 1937?] 23 p. [1392

——Miss Eva. Matthews, The Author, 1944. 39 p. [1393

——Simmons, a real Senate leader. No place, no publisher [1919?] 4 p. [1394

——Tar Heel tales. Charlotte, Stone & Barringer Co., 1910. 218 p. [1395

Bryant, Samuel S. An address delivered at the laying of the cornerstone of the Asylum for the Deaf, Dumb, and Blind, in the city of Raleigh, N. C. on the fourteenth April, 1848. Raleigh, Office of the Star, pr., 1848. 16 p. [1396

——Sermon on the obligation and benefits of infant baptism. Greensborough, Swaim and Sherwood, 1843. 23 p. [1397

Bryant, Victor Silas, 1867-1920. Address on fire insurance rates and conditions in North Carolina, delivered . . . New Bern, North Carolina, August 10, 1915. No place, no publisher, n.d. 14 p. [1398

Bryant, Victor Silas, 1898- Academic freedom. [Chapel Hill, Oliver Max Gardner Award, 1954] 25 p. [1399

——Address and presentation of a portrait of Judge Robert Watson Winston to the Durham Bar Association . . . on the 21st day of January, 1946. [Durham? 1946] 17 p. [1400

——The responsibilites of trustees of a state university; an address before the Faculty Club of the University of North Carolina at Chapel Hill, October 2, 1956. [Chapel Hill, 1956] 19 p. [1401

[Bryant, William Cullen] Picturesque America; or, The land we live in. New York, D. Appleton and Co. [c.1872-74] 2 v. The French Broad, v. 1, p. 132-149. [1402

Bryne, James. Address before the North Carolina Bar Association at Wrightsville Beach, N. C., Wednesday, June 29, 1910. Wilmington, Jackson and Bell Co., 1910. 23 p. [1403

Buchan, John. Salute to adventurers. New York, George H. Doran Co. [c.1917] 348 p. [1404

Buck, Charles Neville. Flight to the hills. Garden City, Doubleday, Page & Co., 1926. 348 p. [1405

Buck, John E. Vance County, 1881-1931. Henderson, The Author [1931?] 15 p. [1406

Buckalew, Charles Rollin. Opinion on the impeachment of Andrew Johnson. [Washington, 1867?] 15 p. [1407

Buckingham, James Silk. The slave states of America. London, Fisher, Son, and Co. [1842] 2 v. [1408

Buckner, Irene Sutphin. Rhymes of living. Pittsboro [The Author] 1951. 23 p. [1409

Bud, a collection of experiments in creative writing as done in English 53, at the University of North Carolina, 1933- Chapel Hill, 1933- NcU has 1933-1953 [1410

Budington, William Giles. Memorial of Giles F. Ward, Jr., late First Lieut., Twelfth New York Cavalry. New York, Anson D. F. Randolph, 1866. 99 p. [1411

Buell, Augustus C. History of Andrew Jackson. New York, C. Scribner's Sons, 1904. 2 v. [1412

——Paul Jones. New York, C. Scribner's Sons, 1900. 2 v. [1413

Buford, Marcus Bainbridge. History and genealogy of the Buford family in America. LeBelle, Mo., Mildred Buford Minter [c.1924] 512 p. [1414

[Buie, Robert Bernard] The Scotch family Buie. No place, privately printed [1950] [80] p. [1415

Buies Creek Academy see Campbell College, Buies Creek, N. C.

Builders, v. 1- June, 1923- Wilmington, North Carolina Educational League, 1923- NcU has v. [1-3] [1416

Bullard, Henry A. A discourse on the life and character of the Hon. François Xavier Martin. New Orleans, J. B. Steel, pr., 1847. 35 p. [1417

Bullions, Peter. An analytical and practical grammer of the English language revised by Rev. B. Craven. Raleigh, North Carolina Christian Advocate Publishing Co., 1864. 190 p.   [1418

Bullock, Charles Jesse. Essays on the monetary history of the United States. New York, Macmillan Co., 1900. 292 p. No. 2. Paper currency of North Carolina.   [1419

Bullock, Ralph W. In spite of handicaps; brief biographical sketches . . . of outstanding Negroes. New York, Association Press, 1927. 140 p. Includes Charles C. Spaulding and Matthew W. Bullock.   [1420

Bumgardner, Edward. The life of Edmund G. Ross. Kansas, Mo., Fielding-Turner Press, 1949. 117 p.   [1421

Bumpass, Frances Moore (Webb) Autobiography and journal, compiled by Miss Eugenia H. Bumpass. Nashville, Tenn., Publishing House of Methodist Episcopal Church, South, 1899. 82 p.   [1422

Bumpass, Sidney D. Sermon on offenses. Greensborough, Swaim and Sherwood, pr., 1847. 24 p.   [1423

Bunch, Elizabeth. The bunch of poems. [Statesville, Statesville Printing Co.] n.d. 40 p.   [1424

Buncombe Baptist Association. Minutes, 18 - 18 - NcU has 1893, 1911, 1912 [1926-1953]   [1425

Buncombe Co., N. C. Board of Education. Directory of the public schools of Buncombe County, N. C., 1927-1928. No place, [1927?] 28 p.   [1426
——Handbook for teachers of the elementary department of the Buncombe County Schools. [Asheville? 1927?] 75 p.   [1427
——High school course of study, English, grades eight and nine [ten and eleven] Asheville, Buncombe County Schools, 1931. (Its Curriculum bulletin, no. 2, 3) 2 v.   [1428

Buncombe Co., N. C. Board of Financial Control. Assessor's manual, 1933. Asheville, 1933. 69 p.   [1429

Buncombe Co., N. C. Board of Health. Rules and regulations . . . for the control of infectious diseases. [Asheville] 1914. 14 p.   [1430

Buncombe Co., N. C. Community School Guild. Asheville and Buncombe County community schools. Asheville, 1935. [11] p.   [1431

Buncombe County, N. C. Good Roads Association see Good Roads Association of Asheville and Buncombe County, N. C.

[Bunker, Benjamin] Ways and byways of Chapel Hill. Chapel Hill, Wootten-Moulton, 1939. [28] p.   [1432

[Bunting, John N?] Mose's letters. Life as it is: or, The writings of "our Mose". Raleigh, Whitaker & Bunting, 1858. 156 p.   [1433

Burch, Viola S. Designs in my quilt. Boston, B. Humphries [1943] 62 p.   [1434

Burder, George. A plain argumentative sermon on the doctrine of the Holy Trinity. Milton, Benjamin Cory, 1823. 12 p.   [1435

Burgess, Caleb Kight. A Christian's relationship to strong drink. Raleigh, Temperance Education Bureau [1935] [15] p.   [1436
——The greatest of these is love. Raleigh, Brotherhood Press [c.1953] 245 p. [1437

Burgess, Frederick Ross. Randolph County, economic and social. [Chapel Hill, The advertisers therein] 1924. 104 p.   [1438

Burgiss, L. Grady. A historical background of the Roanoke Association. [Greenville, 1954] 12 p.   [1439
——A history of the Roanoke Baptist Association, 1908-1955. [Greenville, 1955] 25 p.   [1440

[Burgwin, John] North-Carolina; a table of the number of taxables in this province from the year 1748 . . . to the year 1770. [Newbern, James Davis, 1771] NcU has reproduction of original in Massachusetts Historical Society Library, Boston. [1] p.   [1441

Burgwyn, Henry King] Considerations relative to a southern confederacy, by a citizen of North-Carolina. Raleigh, Standard Office, pr., 1860. 40 p.   [1442
——Our currency: Some of its evils, and remedies for them, by a Citizen of North Carolina. Raleigh, John W. Syme, 1861. 47 p.   [1443

Burgwyn, Mebane (Holoman) Lucky Mischief. New York, Oxford University Press, 1949. 246 p. [1444
——Moonflower. Philadelphia, J. B. Lippincott Co. [1954] 186 p. [1445
——Penny Rose. New York, Oxford University Press, 1952. 223 p. [1446
——River treasure. New York, Oxford University Press, 1947. 159 p. [1447
——True love for Jenny. Philadelphia, Lippincott [1956] 189 p. [1448

Burgwyn, William Hyslop Sumner. Address on the military and civil services of Gen. Matt. W. Ransom . . . May 10, 1906. [Greensboro, C. L. Van Noppen, n.d.] 52 p. [1449
——The necessity of preserving the memorials of the past and of transmitting to posterity a just and impartial history of North Carolina. Raleigh, Edwards & Broughton, pr., 1890. 30 p. [1450

Burke, Fielding, pseud. see Dargan, Olive (Tilford)

[Burke, Joseph K.] To the voters of Rowan County. No place, no publisher, [1870] 4 p. [1451

Burkett, Charles William. Agriculture for beginners, by Charles William Burkett . . . Frank Lincoln Stevens . . . and Daniel Harvey Hill. Boston, Ginn and Co., 1903. 267 p. [1452
—— ——[c.1903] 347 p. [1453
——Cotton, its cultivation, marketing, manufacture, and the problems of the cotton world, by Charles William Burkett . . . and Clarence Hamilton Poe. New York, Doubleday, Page & Co., 1906. 331 p. [1454
——The feeding of farm animals. Raleigh, Edwards & Broughton, pr., 1902. 125 p. [1455
——How to teach agriculture, by the authors of Agriculture for beginners. Boston, Ginn & Company, [c.1906] 23 p. [1456

Burkett, John M. Descendants of Jehu Burket. No place, Burket-Fouts group, 1940. 10 p. [1457

Burkhead, Liryum Skidmore, ed. Centennial of Methodism in North Carolina. Raleigh, John Nichols, 1876. 427 p. [1458
——The mode of baptism, a catechism for children, large and small. Raleigh, P. W. Wiley & Co., 1884. 138 p. [1459

Burkhimer, Eloise Bernheim. Rise and fall of the Confederacy, historical pageant presented at Charlotte, North Carolina, June 5th, 1929. Charlotte, no publisher, 1929. [7] p. Program. [1460

Burkitt, Henry Lemuel. Burkitt's maxims and guide to youth. [Philadelphia, Collins, pr.] 1882. 172 p. [1461

[Burkitt, Lemuel] An argument between a Baptist and a Methodist relative to the ordinance of baptism in a series of dialogues. Edenton, Wills and Beasley, 1806. 48 p. [1462
——A concise history of the Kehukee Baptist Association from its original rise to the present time, by Elders Lemuel Burkitt and Jesse Read. Halifax, A. Hodge, pr., 1803. 319 p. [1463
—— ——Revised by Henry L. Burkitt. Philadelphia, Lippincott, Grambo and Co., 1850. 351 p. [1464

Burkitt, Lemuel, joint author, see Biggs, Joseph

Burlage, Henry Matthew, ed. Fundamental principles and processes of pharmacy, by Henry M. Burlage . . . editor [and others] New York, McGraw-Hill Book Co., 1944. 615 p. [1465

Burlage, Henry Matthew. Laboratory manual for principles and processes of pharmacy [by] Henry M. Burlage [and others] New York, McGraw-Hill Book Co., 1946. 271 p. [1466

Burlington, N. C. Board of Aldermen. The code of the city of Burlington, Charlottesville, Va., Michie Co., 1939. 376 p. [1467
—— ——1946. 283 p. [1468
——Revenue ordinances, as amended . . . 1941-42. Charlottesville, Va., Michie Co., 1941. 71 p. [1469

Burlington, N. C. Board of Education. Burlington, N. C. catechism . . . on school bond issue. [Burlington, n.d.] 8 p. [1470

Burlington, N. C. Chamber of Commerce. Builders of Alamance. Burlington,
1951. 69 p.   [1471
——Burlington, North Carolina, the ideal industrial center. [1943?] Folder. [1472
——Burlington, N. C., the opportunity city. [Burlington, 1946] [11] p.   [1473
——Industrial directory for Burlington and Alamance County, North Carolina.
[Burlington, 1947] 20 p.   [1474
——Things to know about Burlington. [1943?] Folder   [1475
——Why Burlington? [1934?] 36 p.   [1476
—— ——[1940?] 40 p.   [1477

Burlington, N. C. First Reformed Church. First Reformed Church, forty-fourth
anniversary, 1889-1933. [Burlington? 1933?] [16] p.   [1478

Burlington, Graham, and Haw River, N. C., city directory, 19 - Asheville, Commercial Service Co., 19 - NcU has 1920-21, 1924-25.   [1479

Burlington Foundation. James Lee Love educational loan fund. [Greensboro,
1948?] [6] p.   [1480

Burlington Mills Corporation. Report, 192 - 192 - NcU has 1940/41-1952/53 [1481
——Thirty years of the Burlington story. [New York? 1954] 39 p.   [1482

Bur-Mil review, v. 1-5, February, 1950-April, 1954. [Greensboro] Burlington Mills,
1950-1954. NcU has: v. 1-5   [1483

Burnaby, Andrew. Travels through the middle settlements in North America, in
the years 1759 and 1760. London, T. Payne, 1798. 209 p.   [1484

Burnett, Edmund Cody. The Continental Congress. New York, Macmillan Co.,
1941. 757 p.   [1485

Burnett, Edmund Cody, ed. Letters of members of the Continental Congress.
Washington, Carnegie Institution of Washington, 1921-1936. (Its Publication
no. 299, v. 1-8)   [1486

Burnett, Frances Hodgson. Esmeralda, a comedy drama in four acts, by Frances
Hodgson Burnett and William H. Gillette. New York, Samuel French [c.1881]
59 p.   [1487
——In connection with the De Willoughby claim. New York, Charles Scribner's
Sons, 1899. 445 p.   [1488
——Louisiana. New York, Charles Scribner's Sons, 1907. 163 p.   [1489
—— ——1880.   [1490
—— ——1909.   [1491

Burnett, John Franklin. Rev. Barton Warren Stone. No place, no publisher,
n.d. 32 p.   [1492
——Rev. James O'Kelly, a champion of religious liberty. No place, no publisher,
n.d. 36 p.   [1493

Burnham, George. Billy Graham: a mission accomplished. [Westwood, N. J.]
Revell [1955] 158 p.   [1494

Burns, Walter Francis. Captain Otway Burns, patriot, privateer, and legislator.
New York, no publisher, 1905. 166 p.   [1495

Burnside, Ambrose Everett. The Burnside expedition. Providence, N. B. Williams
and Co., 1882. (Personal narratives of events in the war of the rebellion read
before the Rhode Island Soldiers and Sailors Historical Society, 2d ser., no. 6)
33 p.   [1496

Burnt Swamp Baptist Association. Minutes, 18 - 18 - NcU has 1884   [1497

Burr, James Green. Old mansions of Cape Fear: the Hermitage. Wilmington,
no publisher, 1885. 16 p.   [1498

[Burr, James Green] The Thalian Association of Wilmington, N. C. Wilmington,
J. A. Engelhard, pr., 1871. 52 p.   [1499

Burrage, Henry Sweetser, ed. Early English and French voyages, chiefly from
Hakluyt, 1534-1608. New York, C. Scribner's Sons, 1906. 451 p.   [1500

Burrington, George. An answer to Dr. William Brakenridge's letter concerning the
number of inhabitants within the London bills of mortality. London, J. Scott,
1757. 40 p.   [1501
——Seasonable considerations on the expediency of a war with France. London,
F. Cogan, 1743. 60 p.   [1502

Burroughs, Paul H. Southern antiques. Richmond, Garrett & Massie [c.1931] 191 p. [1503

Burroughs, Prince Emanuel. Teacher-training in southern Baptist educational institutions, 1925-1927. Nashville, Tenn., Sunday School Board, Sunday Baptist Convention [1927?] 32 p. [1504

Burrus, John T. Address . . . January 31, 1922. No place, no publisher [1922?] 12 p. [1505

Burt, Clare Louise. Bowl of petunias. Ellerbe, Ellerbe School Press, 1936. 19 numbered leaves. [1506

——Call me not dead. Raleigh, Capital Printing Co., 1940. 55 p. [1507

——Darkest hour. Raleigh, The Author, 1939. 19 p. [1508

——Ordered chaos. Boston, Christopher Publishing House [c.1937] 88 p. [1509

——Wicks in earthenware. Raleigh, The Author, 1937. 17 p. [1510

Burt, Katharine (Newlin) The branding iron. Boston, Houghton Mifflin Co., 1919. 310 p. [1511

——Captain Millett's island. Philadelphia, Macrae-Smith-Co., 1944. 256 p. [1512

——Close pursuit. New York, C. Scribner's Sons, 1947. 320 p. [1513

——Lady in the tower. Philadelphia, Macrae-Smith-Co., 1946. 284 p. [1514

——No surrender. Philadelphia, Macrae-Smith-Co., 1940. 258 p. [1515

——Quest. Boston, Houghton Mifflin Co., 1925. 376 p. [1516

——The red lady. Boston, Houghton Mifflin Co., 1920. 241 p. [1517

——Still Water. Philadelphia, Macrae-Smith-Co., 1948. 287 p. [1518

——Strong citadel. New York, C. Scribner's Sons, 1949. 281 p. [1519

Burt, Maxwell Struthers. Along these streets. New York, C. Scribner's Sons, 1942. 608 p. [1520

——Chance encounters. New York, C. Scribner's Sons, 1921. 287 p. [1521

——The delectable mountains. New York, C. Scribner's Sons, 1927. 463 p. [1522

——Entertaining the islanders. New York, C. Scribner's Sons, 1933. 458 p. [1523

——Escape from America. New York, C. Scribner's Sons, 1936. 255 p. [1524

——Festival. New York, C. Scribner's Sons, 1931. 388 p. [1525

——The interpreter's house. New York, C. Scribner's Sons, 1924. 445 p. [1526

——Malice in Blunderland. New York, C. Scribner's Sons, 1935. 31 p. [1527

——Philadelphia, holy experiment. Garden City, New York, Doubleday, Doran & Co., 1945. 396 p. [1528

——Powder River: let'er buck. New York, Farrar & Rinehart [c.1938] 389 p. [1529

——Songs and portraits. New York, C. Scribner's Sons, 1920. 78 p. [1530

——They could not sleep. New York, C. Scribner's Sons, 1928. 323 p. [1531

——War songs. New York, C. Scribner's Sons, 1942. 46 p. [1532

——When I grew up to middle age. New York, C. Scribner's Sons, 1925. 94 p. [1533

Burt, Nathaniel. Question on a kite. New York, C. Scribner's Sons, 1950. 43 p. [1534

Burt, William Henry. A field guide to the mammals, giving field marks of all species found north of the Mexican boundary. Boston, Houghton Mifflin Co., 1952. 200 p. [1535

Burton, Robert. The English empire in America. 7th ed. London, A. Bettesworth and C. Hitch, 1739. 192 p. [1536

Burwell, Armistead. Address, May 10th, 1898, Confederate memorial services, Elmwood cemetery. No place, no publisher [1898?] [3] p. [1537

——The ideal Confederate soldier, address, unveiling Confederate monument, Cornelius, N. C., August 4th, 1910. No place, no publisher [1910?] [3] p. [1538

Burwell, Convere Jones. How do you know? A study of Hegelian epistemology. Chapel Hill, Department of Philosophy, University of North Carolina, 1936. (Studies in philosophy, no. 10) 22 p. [1539

——The relation of Hegelian epistemology to the development of individuality. Chapel Hill, Department of Philosophy, University of North Carolina, 1937. (Studies in philosophy, no. 12) 108 p. [1540

——A study of the process of the Hegelian Dialectic. Chapel Hill, Department of Philosophy, University of North Carolina, 1935. (Studies in philosophy, no. 9) 31 p. [1541

Busbee, Jacques. American history and travel including the North Carolina collection of Jacques Busbee . . . July 1, 1921. New York, The Walpole Galleries, 1921. 30 p. [1542

Busby, Levi E. Life-sketch of Rev. Charles A. Rose. Salisbury, Smith & Irvin, pr., n.d. 102 p. [1543

Business Foundation of North Carolina, Inc. Business and education seeking a common goal. [Chapel Hill] 1951. 26 p. [1544
——The Business Foundation of North Carolina. [Chapel Hill, 1946] [25] p. [1545
——Report, 19 - [Chapel Hill] 19 - NcU has 1948/49, 1953/54. [1546

[Butel-Dumont, Georges Marie] Histoire et commerce des colonies angloises dans l'Amerique Septentrionale. Haye, La Compagnie, 1755. 246 p. [1547

Butler, Benjamin Franklin. Autobiography and personal reminiscences. Boston, A. M. Thayer & Co., 1892. Various paging. [1548
——Speech, against further delays in the trial of impeachment . . . of Andrew Johnson. [Washington. Congressional Globe Office, 1868] 7 p. [1549
——Speech upon the campaign before Richmond, 1864 . . . with an appendix: The two attacks on Fort Fisher. Boston, Wright & Potter, pr., 1865. 88 p. [1550

Butler, Bion H. The church on Quintuple Mountain. Southern Pines, Foss, Stradley & Butler, 1912. 271 p. [1551
——Old Bethesda, at the head of Rockfish. New York, Grosset & Dunlap [c.1933] 288 p. [1552
——The story of Ravenwood. New Bern, Owen G. Dunn, pr., n.d. 36 p. [1553

Butler, George E. The Croatan Indians of Sampson County, N. C. [Durham, Seeman Printery, 1916] 65 p. [1554

Butler, Marion. Addresses of Marion Butler, president, and Cyrus Thompson, lecturer, to the North Carolina Farmers' State Alliance. Raleigh, Barnes Bros., pr., 1893. 10 p. [1555
——Another Democratic lie nailed, the facts about the collection of the 2d mortgage North Carolina bonds. No place, no publisher [1908] [2] p. [1556
——Magna Charta, the birthplace of civil and religious liberty not at Runnymede, but on North Carolina soil. No place, no publisher, n.d. [3] p. [1557
——Marion Butler's Raleigh speech, delivered Nov. 4, 1910. 2d ed. No place, no publisher [1911] 66 p. [1558
——Progress and prosperity will return. No place, no publisher [1918] [4] p. [1559
——Senator Butler's position on the proposed constitutional amendment and the Simmons-Goebel election law. No place, no publisher [1900] 7 p. [1560
——Some correspondence between the state chairmen of two political organizations. No place, no publisher [1900] 8 p. [1561
——State v. Butler, from Guilford. No place, no publisher, n.d. 93 p. [1562

Butterworth, Hezekiah. A zigzag journey in the sunny South. Boston, Estes and Lauriat, 1887. 320 p. [1563

Buxton, Claude E. Latent learning and the goal gradient hypothesis. Durham, Duke University Press, 1940. (Contributions to psychological theory, v. [II, no. 2, serial no. 6]) 75 p. [1564

Buxton, Jarvis Barry. Parish sermons. New York, D. Appleton & Co., 1852. 694 p. [1565
——The rector's farewell. [Asheville, Randolph-Kerr Printing Co., 1890?] 12 p. [1566
——Regeneration and conversion. Asheville, Furman & Stone, pr., 1883. 14 p. [1567
——Sermon in exposition of the situation wants and prospects of the church in the Diocese of North Carolina. New York, Pott & Amery, 1867. 21 p. [1568

Buyers' guide to southern hosiery and knitwear manufacturers, 193 - Charlotte, Clark Publishing Co., 193 - NcU has 1941/42, 1943/44-1944/45, 1946-1952 [1569

Byfield, Thomas and Company. The case of Thomas Byfield, and Company, owners of the ship Dove . . . relating to the bill for importing naval stores from the plantations. No place, no publisher, n.d. NcU has photostat. [1570

Bynum, Curtis. Destiny. [Asheville, Stephens Press, c.1943] 29 p. [1571

Bynum, Curtis, comp. Marriage bonds of Tryon and Lincoln counties, North Carolina, abstracted and indexed. [Asheville, The Compiler] 1929. 184 p. [1572
——The reality and appearance of morals. Chapel Hill, University Press, 1903. (Worth prize thesis, 1903) 18 p. [1573

Bynum, Jefferson Carney. The climate of Chapel Hill. [Chapel Hill] University of North Carolina [1929?] 2 p. [1574

Bynum, Jesse Atherton. An address to the reflecting men of Northampton County, North Carolina. No place, Blair and Rives, pr., n.d.   15 p.   [1575
——An exposition of the misrepresentations contained in a publication issued by Robert Potter against Jesse A. Bynum and others.   [Halifax, Free Press, 1825] 42 p.   [1576
Bynum, John Gray. An address to the people of North Carolina on the subject of constitutional reform.   [Asheville, J. M. Edney, 1851]   8 p.   [1577
Bynum, Minna Curtis see **Henderson, Barbara**
Bynum, William Preston. Address on law in its relation to economic freedom and morality before the North Carolina Bar Association at Asheville, N. C., 1915. Wilmington, Wilmington Stamp & Printing Co. [1915?]   31 p.   [1578
——Address presenting a portrait of the late Chief Justice David M. Furches to the Supreme Court of North Carolina, May 11, 1909.   Raleigh, E. M. Uzzell & Co., 1909.   12 p.   [1579
——Address presenting the portrait of Thomas Settle to the Supreme Court, November seventh, nineteen hundred and five.   No place, no publisher, n.d.   61 p.   [1580
——A guide to magistrates, mayors, and coroners in criminal proceedings.   Greensboro, C. F. Thomas, 1895.   18 p.   [1581
——State rights and federal power, address delivered at Asheville, June 29th, 1920. Greensboro, Jos. J. Stone and Co., n.d.   54 p.   [1582
Byrd, Charles Wesley. Prayers.   [Asheville, Central Methodist Church, 1918?] 37 p.   [1583
Byrd, John W. Reasons why the Negro should remain in the South.   Wilson, P. D. Gold Publishing Co., 1904.   12 p.   [1584
Byrd, Sam. The Duplin County Historical Association, Inc., presents The Duplin story.   Wilmington, Wilmington Printing Co., 1949.   [46] p.   [1585
—— ——1950.   [56] p.   [1586
——Hurry home to my heart.   Boston, Houghton Mifflin Co., 1945.   150 p.   [1587
——Small town, South.   Boston, Houghton Mifflin Co., 1942.   237 p.   [1588
Byrd, William. Description of the Dismal Swamp and a proposal to drain the swamp. Metuchen, N. J., C. F. Heartman, pr., 1922.   32 p.   [1589
——History of the dividing line, and other tracts.   Richmond, Va., 1866.   2 v. [1590
——A journey to the land of Eden, and other papers.   [New York] Macy-Masius, 1928.   367 p.   [1591
——The Westover manuscripts.   Petersburg [Va.] E. and J. C. Ruffin, pr., 1841. 141 p.   [1592
——William Byrd's Natural history of Virginia; or, The newly discovered Eden (edited and translated from a German version) by Richmond Croom Beatty . . . and William J. Mulloy.   Richmond, Dietz Press, 1940.   95, 109 p.   [1593
——The writings of "Colonel William Byrd of Westover in Virginia, esq." New York, Doubleday, Page & Co., 1901.   461 p.   [1594
Byrnes, Charles Metcalfe. The relative individual.   Chapel Hill [Philosophy Department, University of North Carolina]   1902.   (Worth prize thesis, 1902) 15 p.   [1595
Byrum, J. T. History of Ballard's Bridge Church.   Raleigh, Edwards and Broughton Co., 1908.   38 p.   [1596
Cabarrus Baptist Association. Minutes, 19 - 19 -   NcU has 1953-1955   [1597
Cabarrus Black Boys, a short historical sketch of a daring deed.   Concord, Times Presses, 1909.   7 p.   [1598
Cabarrus Co., N. C. Board of County Commissioners. Rules and regulations for working the public roads.   Concord, Times Job Print, n.d.   8 p.   [1599
Cabarrus Co., N. C. Board of Education. Handbook for Cabarrus County teachers, 1919/20.   [Concord, Times Tribune, pr., 1919?]   23 p.   [1600
——Report of County Superintendent of Schools, 190 -   [Concord, 19 -   NcU has 1905/06, 1910/11, 1912/13.   [1601
Cabarrus Co., N. C. War Records Committee. A history of Cabarrus County in the wars.   [Concord] War Records Collection Committee [1947]   430 p.   [1602
Cabell, James Alston. An address . . . preceding the launching of the U. S. Cruiser North Carolina.   Richmond, William Ellis Jones, pr., 1907.   7 p.   [1603

Cabinet. Philadelphia, J. Laval and S. F. Bradford [1829] [150] p. [1604

Cadbury, Henry Joel. The church in the wilderness, North Carolina Quakerism as seen by visitors. [Guilford College] North Carolina Friends Historical Society [1948] 14 p. [1605

——A Quaker approach to the Bible. [Guilford College, 1953?] (Ward lecture, November 9, 1953) 15 p. [1606

Cade, Baylus. The preacher's opportunity in the twentieth century. No place, no publisher, 1909. 22 p. [1607

Cahen, Alfred. Statistical analysis of American divorce. New York, Columbia University Press, 1932. 149 p. [1608

Cain, William. Brief course in the calculus. New York, D. Van Nostrand, 1905. 280 p. [1609

—— ——3d ed., rev. 1911. 281 p. [1610

——Commencement exercises of the Citadel, 1917. Address. Charleston, S. C., 1918. 19 p. [1611

——Earth pressure, retaining walls and bins. New York, John Wiley & Sons, 1916. 287 p. [1612

——Maximum stresses in framed bridges. New York, D. Van Nostrand, 1878. 192 p. [1613

—— ——1914. 182 p. [1614

——Practical designing of retaining walls. New York, D. Van Nostrand, 1888. 169 p. [1615

——A practical theory of vouissoir arches. New York, D. Van Nostrand, 1874. 118 p. [1616

——Sanitary engineering. Raleigh, Edwards and Broughton Co., 1879. 29 p. [1617

—— ——2d ed. 1880. 86 p. [1618

—— ——3d ed. 1885. 90 p. [1619

——Symbolic algebra. New York, D. Van Nostrand, 1884. 131 p. [1620

——Theory of solid and braced elastic arches. New York, D. Van Nostrand, 1879. 172 p. [1621

——Theory of steel-concrete arches and of vaulted structures. 3d ed., rev. New York, D. Van Nostrand, 1903. 181 p. [1622

—— ——6th ed., rev. New York, D. Van Nostrand, 1918. 215 p. [1623

——Theory of vouissoir arches. 2d ed., rev. New York, D. Van Nostrand, 1893. 201 p. [1624

——Vouissoir arches applied to stone bridges, tunnels, domes and groined arches. New York, D. Van Nostrand, 1879. 196 p. [1625

Cairns, John S. List of the birds of Buncombe County, North Carolina. No place, no publisher [1902?] 18 p. [1626

Caius Victor, pseud. see **Hooper, Archibald MacLaine**

Caldwell, Arthur Bunyan. History of the American Negro and his institutions. Atlanta, A. B. Caldwell Publishing Co., 1921. v. 4: North Carolina edition. 864 p. [1627

Caldwell, Bettie D., comp. Founders and builders of Greensboro, 1808-1908. Greensboro, J. J. Stone & Co., 1925. 356 p. [1628

Caldwell, Charles. Autobiography of Charles Caldwell, with a preface, notes, and appendix by Harriot W. Warner. Philadelphia, Lippincott, Grambo and Co., 1855. 454 p. [1629

——Memoirs of the life and campaigns of the Hon. Nathaniel Greene. Philadelphia, R. Desilver, T. DeSilver, 1819. 452 p. [1630

Caldwell, Howard Haine. Oliatta and other poems. New York, Redfield, 1855. 200 p. [1631

Caldwell, Joseph. Address to the senior class. Raleigh, J. Gales and Son, 1827. 12 p. [1632

——Autobiography and biography. Chapel Hill, J. B. Neathery, pr., 1860. 68 p. [1633

——Compendious system of elementary geometry. Philadelphia, William Fry for the Author, 1822. 391 p. [1634

——A discourse delivered at the University of North-Carolina, at the Commencement in July, 1802. Raleigh, J. Gales, pr., 1802. 50 p. [1635

——Eulogy on General Washington, pronounced in Person-Hall at the University of North-Carolina, on the twenty-second day of February, 1800. Raleigh, J. Gales, pr., 1800. 34 p. [1636

[Caldwell, Joseph] Letters on popular education addressed to the people of North-Carolina. Hillsborough, Dennis Heartt, pr., 1832. 54, 48 p. [1637

[Caldwell, Joseph] The numbers of Carlton, addressed to the people of North Carolina, on a central rail-road through the state. New York, G. Long, 1828. 232 p. [1638

Caldwell, Joseph. Sermon delivered at the ordination of the Rev. Samuel Paisley . . . April 4, 1813. Raleigh, J. Gales, pr., n.d. 23 p. [1639

Caldwell, Joseph Pearson, comp. The judgment of the fourth estate; editorials by J. P. Caldwell, Josephus Daniels, Dr. A. J. McKelway, and J. W. Bailey. Raleigh, Johnson-Wynne Co., 1904. 7 p. [1640

[Caldwell, Thomas] A brief explanation of the revelation of Jesus Christ to St. John. Fayetteville, Edward J. Hale, pr., 1842. 100 p. [1641

Caldwell, Wallace Everett. An address by M. W. Wallace E. Caldwell, Grand Master, before the Conference of Grand Masters of North America at Washington, D. C. [Chapel Hill? Author? 1951] 14 p. [1642

——The ancient world. New York, Farrar & Rinehart, Inc. [c.1937] 590 p. [1643

——Masonry and democracy. No place, n.d. 8 p. [1644

——The new popular history of the world . . . [by] Wallace E. Caldwell [and] Edward H. Merrill. New York, Greystone Press [1950] 870 p. [1645

Caldwell, Wallace Everett, tr. Thebes . . . by Jean Capart. New York, Dial Press, 1926. 362 p. [1646

Caldwell, Wallace Everett. Two addresses. [Chapel Hill? The Author? 1950?] 19 p. [1647

——World history . . . [by] Wallace E. Caldwell [and] Edward H. Merrill. Chicago, B. H. Sanborn [c.1949] 870 p. [1648

Caldwell Baptist Association. Minutes, 1885- 1885- NcU has 1885, 1886, 1888-1943 [1945-1953] [1649

Caldwell Co., N. C. Board of Education. Report of County Superintendent of Schools, 190 - [Lenoir?] 190 - NcU has 1904/05 [1650

Caldwell Institute. Trustees. Plan of the Caldwell Institute. Richmond, Va., 1836. 11 p. [1651

Calfee, John Edward. Doing the impossible. New York, Fleming H. Revell Co. [c.1925] 116 p. [1652

——Rural arithmetic. Berea, Ky., Printing Dept., 1912. 64 p. [1653

——What next? Talks to young people. New York, Fleming H. Revell Co. [c.1932] 148 p. [1654

Calhoon, Richard Percival. Influencing employee behavior [by] Richard P. Calhoon [and] C. A. Kirkpatrick. New York, McGraw-Hill [1956] 312 p. [1655

——Problems in personnel administration. New York, Harper [1949] 540 p. [1656

——Relationships between wages, wage payment methods, and personnel efficiency in the furniture industry. Chapel Hill, Bureau of Business Services and Research, School of Business Administration, 1951. 30 p. [1657

Calhoun, Frederick Harvey Hall. Geological resources, Seaboard Air Line Railway territory. [Savannah, Ga., Seaboard Air Line Railroad] 1925. 51 p. [1658

A call for a North Carolina sanitary convention in Raleigh on Wednesday, February 6th, 1889. No place, no publisher, 1889. [2] p. [1659

Callahan, North. Smoky Mountain country. New York, Duell, Sloan & Pearce [1952] 257 p. [1660

[Calvert, Caroline (Beall)] Beallmont, Linwood, North Carolina. No place, The Author [1926] [6] p. [1661

Camak, David English. June of the hills, the Junaluska prize novel. Waynesville, Junaluska Woman's Club [c.1927] 252 p. [1662

Cameron, Duncan. [Letter to his constituents] Raleigh, December 21, 1805. [1] p. [1663

——[Letter to his constituents, December 21, 1806] [1] p. [1664

——To the freemen of Orange County. Raleigh, December 19, 1807. [1] p. [1665

——To the freemen of the district composed of the counties of Wake, Orange and Chatham. Orange, June, 1808. [1] p.   [1666

[Cameron, Duncan] To the freemen of Orange County. [Raleigh, T. Henderson, pr., December 25, 1813] 16 p.   [1667

Cameron, Duncan. To the people of Orange County. [Orange County, 22d July, 1820] 2 p.   [1668

Cameron, Frank Kenneth. Les constituants minéraux des solutions des sols par Frank K. Cameron et James M. Bell. Montpelier, Coulet et Fils, 1907. 87 p. [1669

——A study of the reaction of certain diazo compounds with the alcohols. Baltimore, Deutsch Lithographing & Printing Co., 1894. 30 p.   [1670

Cameron, John Donald. Glimpses of a land of beauty, by John D. Cameron and Walter S. Cushman. Asheville, Asheville Printing Co. [1896?] 66 p.   [1671

——Prospectus of the Hillsboro' recorder. Hillsboro, Oct. 1872. [1] p.   [1672

——Sketch of the tobacco interests in North Carolina. Oxford, W. A. Davis & Co., 1881. 109 p.   [1673

Cameron, Kenneth Walter. Authorship and sources of "Gentleness and nobility". Raleigh, The Thistle Press, 1941. 132 p.   [1674

——The background of John Heywood's "Witty and witless". Raleigh, The Thistle Press, 1941. 46 p.   [1675

——The Christian view of sex. [Raleigh] Y. M. C. A. Press of North Carolina State College, 1942. 9 p.   [1676

Cameron, Kenneth Walter, ed. Gentleness and nobility (1522-1523) by John Heywood. Raleigh, Thistle Press, 1941. 36 p.   [1677

Cameron, Kenneth Walter. John Heywood's "Play of the wether". Raleigh, Thistle Press, 1941. 65 p.   [1678

Cameron, Kenneth Walter, ed. Nature (1836) by Ralph Waldo Emerson. New York, Scholars' Facsimiles & Reprints, 1940. Various paging.   [1679

——Ralph Waldo Emerson's reading. Raleigh, Thistle Press, 1941. 144 p.   [1680

Cameron, Paul Carrington. Address before the Orange County Society for the Promotion of Agriculture, the Mechanic Arts, and Manufactures, at the first annual fair of the Society. Hillsborough, D. Heartt & Son, 1855. 41 p.   [1681

——Extracts of will. No place, no publisher [1891] 8 p.   [1682

——Will. No place, no publisher [1891] 17 p.   [1683

[Cameron, Rebecca] Salted with fire, by H. M. LeGrange [pseud.] 2d ed. New York, E. J. Hale, 1872. 177 p.   [1684

Cameron, Thomas N. An address before the Medical Society of the State of North Carolina at its first annual communication, in Raleigh. Raleigh, Seaton Gales, 1850. 16 p.   [1685

Camp, Carol E. Snapshots, a season in Korea. New York, Pageant Press, Inc. [c.1956] 106 p.   [1686

Camp, Cordelia. North Carolina by problems; a handbook for teachers. [Asheville, c.1929] 94 p.   [1687

——The settlement of North Carolina, by Cordelia Camp and Eddie W. Wilson. [Cullowhee] The Author, 1942. 44 p.   [1688

——Sketches of Burke County. 1935. 11 p. NcU has microfilm.   [1689

Camp Bragg and Fayetteville; sketches of camp and city. Richmond, Central Publishing Co., c.1919. 72 p.   [1690

Camp life in Western North Carolina. No place, Greater Western N. C. Association, 1914. 39 p.   [1691

Campbell, Doak Sheridan. Problems in the education of college women. Nashville, Tenn., Division of Surveys and Field Studies, George Peabody College for Teachers, 1933. 80 p.   [1692

Campbell, Evelyn. Survival. New York, Lincoln MacVeagh, Dial Press, 1928. 306 p.   [1693

Campbell, Sir George. White and black. London, Chatto & Windus, 1879. 441 p.   [1694

Campbell, Helen (Stuart) The easiest way in housekeeping and cooking. New York, Fords, Howard, & Hulbert, 1881. 283 p.   [1695

Campbell, J. D., joint author, see Sterling, Richard

Campbell, John Charles. The southern highlander and his homeland. New York, Russell Sage Foundation, 1921. 405 p. [1696

Campbell, John Charles. Folk School, Brasstown, N. C. see **John C. Campbell Folk School, Brasstown, N. C.** [1697

Campbell, John M. Asheville, nature's sanitarium. Asheville, J. M. Campbell [ca. 1895] [23] p. [1698

Campbell, Olive Arnold (Dame) The Danish folk school; its influence in the life of Denmark and the North. New York, Macmillan Co., 1928. 359 p. [1699

——English folk songs from the southern Appalachians . . . collected by Olive Dame Campbell and Cecil J. Sharp. New York, G. P. Putnam's Sons, 1917. 341 p. [1700

Campbell, Olive Arnold (Dame) comp. Southern highland schools maintained by denominational and independent agencies. New York, Russell Sage Foundation, 1921. 16 p. [1701

Campbell, Olive Arnold (Dame) The Southern highlands. New York, Russell Sage Foundation Library [1920] 4 p. [1702

——Southern mountain schools maintained by denominational and independent agencies. New York, Russell Sage Foundation, 1929. 15 p. [1703

Campbell, Orville. Way up in North Carolina . . . by Orville Campbell and Hank Beebe. Chapel Hill, Charles Music Co. [c.1951] [3] p. [1704

Campbell, Robert Clifford. Around the cross. Nashville, Tenn., Broadman Press [c.1942] 195 p. [1705

Campbell, Robert Fishburne. The dog in literature and life. No place, no publisher, n.d. 20 p. [1706

——Inter-relations of the individual and the institutions of society. [Asheville] n.d. 12 p. [1707

——Mission work among the mountain whites in Asheville Presbytery, North Carolina. Asheville, Citizen, 1899. 10 p. [1708

—— ——2d ed. 10 p. [1709

——Some aspects of the race problem in the South. Asheville, Asheville Printing Co., 1899. 31 p. [1710

—— ——2d ed. Asheville, Citizen, 1899. 24 p. [1711

——Three years of home mission work in Asheville Presbytery. No place, no publisher [1900] 7 p. [1712

Campbell, Tom W. Two fighters and two fines; sketches of the lives of Matthew Lyon and Andrew Jackson. Little Rock, Ark., Pioneer Publishing Co., 1941. 557 p. [1713

Campbell College, Buies Creek, N. C. Bulletin, v. 1- 19 - Buies Creek, 19 - NcU has v. [10-44] [1714

——Campbell College, a purpose to fulfill. [Buies Creek, 1949?] [20] p. [1715

——Catalogue, 188 - Buies Creek, Campbell College, 188 - NcU has [1900/01-1919/20] Continues as its Bulletin. [1716

Camping in Carolina. v. 1- August, 1926- Charlotte, Observer Publishing Co., 1926- NcU has v. 1, no. 1-2 [1717

Canada, John William. Life at eighty. [La Porte, Tex., 1952] 198 p. [1718

Canaday, Julia. Big end of the horn. New York, Vantage Press [1956] 171 p. [1719

[Candler, Isaac] A summary view of America. London, T. Cadell, 1824. 503 p. [1720

Candour, pseud. Irenicum. No place, no publisher [182?] 8 p. [1721

Canfield, Mary Grace. Lafayette in Vermont. No place, privately printed, 1934. 38 p. [1722

Cannon, Brenda, pseud. see **Moore, Bertha B.**

Cannon, Mrs. Charles A. see **Cannon, Ruth C.**

Cannon, James. History of Southern Methodist missions. Nashville, Tenn., Cokesbury Press, 1926. 356 p. [1723

Cansler, Edwin Thomas. Presentation of the portrait of the late Associate Justice of the Supreme Court, Platt Dickinson Walker. [Raleigh? 1926?] 20 p. [1724

Cantrell, Clyde Hull. Southern literary culture; a bibliography of masters' and doctors' theses, by Clyde H. Cantrell and Walton R. Patrick. [University] University of Alabama Press, 1955. 124 p. [1725

Cantwell, Edward. Benjamin Franklin; a lecture delivered before the Franklin Society . . . Oxford, N. C., Friday, 14th Dec. 1866. Oxford, Franklin Society, 1867. 32 p. [1726

——How to learn; an address, delivered before the students of Holly Springs Academy, Wake county, N. C., Third·of June, 1859. Raleigh, R. H. Whitaker, Democratic Press, 1859. 22 p. [1727

——Oration delivered before the Wilmington Light Infantry, on their twenty-fourth anniversary, May 20th, 1877. Wilmington, S. G. Hall, pr., 1877. 26 p. [1728

——The practice at law in North Carolina. v. 1. Raleigh, Strother and Marcom, 1860. 1 v. [1729

——Swaim's justice—revised. The North Carolina magistrate, a practical guide to the laws of the state, and the decisions of the Supreme Court. Raleigh, H. D. Turner, 1856. 575 p. [1730

Cape Fear Agricultural Association. Regulations, premium list and awarding committees for the . . . annual fair. 1st- 1869- Wilmington, 1869- NcU has 1869, 1870, 1871, 1914, 1918 [1731

——To the patrons and friends of the Cape Fear Agricultural Association. Wilmington, 1870. 3 p. [1732

Cape Fear Baptist Association. Minutes, 18 - 18 - NcU has 1856 [1866-1914] [1733

Cape Fear Baptist Sunday School Convention. Minutes, 18 - 18 - NcU has 1877, 1881, 1884, 1886. [1734

Cape Fear Club, Wilmington, see **Wilmington, N. C. Cape Fear Club**

Cape Fear-Columbus Association. Minutes, 1899- 1899- NcU has [1899-1936] [1735

Cape Fear Free-Will Baptist Conference. Minutes, 185 - 185 - NcU has 1894-1912, 1898, 1902, 1921, 1930, 1951-1954 [1736

Cape Fear Rice Company, Wilmington. Cape Fear Rice Company, incorporated under the laws of North Carolina. Wilmington, n.d. [9] p. [1737

Cape Fear Valley Festival, Inc. Cape Fear Valley Festival souvenir program commemorating the 200th anniversary of Cumberland County. [Fayetteville] 1954. 36 p. [1738

Cape Fear Valley Scottish Festival. The Cape Fear Valley Scottish Festival, City Auditorium, Fayetteville, N. C., souvenir program. Second autumn season, October 14-November 2, 1940. [Fayetteville, 1940] 40 p. [1739

Capehart, L. C. Reminiscences of Isaac and Sukey, slaves of B. F. Moore, of Raleigh, N. C. Raleigh, Edwards and Broughton Printing Co., 1907. 11 p. [1740

Capers, Ellison. Sermon commemorative of the late Theodore Benedict Lyman. Raleigh, E. M. Uzzell, pr., 1894. 21 p. [1741

Capital Highway Association. [Capital highway between Pinehurst, N. C. and Sanford, N. C., and between Sanford, N. C. and Raleigh, N. C.] [Pinehurst, The Association, c.1911] 4 p. [1742

[Capps, W. R.] Condensed history of the Battle of King's Mountain. Charlotte, Harper J. Elam, 1880. 32 p. [1743

Car owner see **Go**

Caraleigh Mills Co., Raleigh. Statement relatve to $100,000 of first mortgage bonds issued by the Caraleigh Mills Co. Raleigh, E. M. Uzzell, pr. [1893] 24 p. [1744

Carawan, George Washington. Trial of the Rev. George W. Carawan, Baptist preacher, for the murder of Clement H. Lassiter, schoolmaster. New York, Printed for the Proprietor, 1854. 123 p. [1745

—— ——2d ed. New York, no publisher, 1854. 123 p. [1746

Carlton, Helen T. The practical and fancy cook book for every household. Louisville, Ky., Courier-Journal Job Printing Co., n.d. 95 p. [1747

Carmichael, Peter Archibald. The nature of freedom. Chapel Hill, Dept. of Philosophy, University of North Carolina [1930?] 48 p. [1748

Carmichael, Roderick Leland, comp. The Scottish highlander Carmichaels of the Carolinas. [Washington] The Compiler, 1935. 143 p. [1749

Carmichael, William Donald, joint author, see **Brooks, Eugene Clyde**

[Carolina] pseud. An address to the citizens of North-Carolina on the subject of the presidential election. No place, no publisher [1823] 15 p. [1750

Carolina. The two charters granted by King Charles II to the Proprietors of Carolina, with the first and last fundamfntal [!] constitutions of that colony. London, Printed and are to be sold by R. Parker [1705?] 60 p. [1751

Carolina. Proprietors. Commissions and instructions from the Lords Proprietors of Carolina to public officials of South Carolina, 1685-1715, ed. by A. S. Salley, Jr. [Columbia, S. C.] Printed for the Historical Commission of South Carolina by the State Co., 1916. 292 p. [1752

Carolina a.id North-western Railway Co. Information for 1903, Summer homes. No place [1903?] [16] p. [1753

——People's own line. Richmond, J. W. Fergusson & Son, pr., n.d. [32] p. [1754

—— ——No place, 1897. 7 p. [1755

Carolina and the southern cross, v. 1-2, March, 1913-August, 1914. Kinston [1913-14] NcU has v. 1-2 [1756

Carolina Arcanian, v. 1- 1914- Wilmington, 1914- NcU has v. [2-5] [1757

Carolina babies, v. 1- June, 1945- Greensboro, Children's Home Society, 1945- NcU has v. 1-8 [1758

Carolina Baptist Association. Minutes, 18 - 18 - NcU has [1911-1949] [1759

[Carolina Beach, N. C. Chamber of Commerce] Sunny Carolina Beach, North Carolina. No place [1948?] [32] p. [1760

Carolina Beach, N. C. Chamber of Commerce. Visitor's guide. [Carolina Beach?] n.d. 58 p. [1761

Carolina Beach, N. C. City Manager. Report, 1949/50- Carolina Beach, 1950- NcU has 1949/50 [1762

Carolina churchman see North Carolina churchman

Carolina, Clinchfield, and Ohio Railway. Carolina, Clinchfield and Ohio Railway, the quick service short line between the Central West and the South East. [Chicago, Poole] n.d. 38 p. [1763

——Clinchfield route. Johnson City, Tenn. [1909] 30 p. [1764

——A national asset. [Chicago, Poole] n.d. 16 p. [1765

——The playground above the clouds. [Chicago, Poole] n.d. 15 p. [1766

—— ——[Chicago, Poole] n.d. 30 p. [1767

——Report, 1911-1924. [1912-1925] NcU has 1911-1924. Continues as Clinchfield Railroad, 1925- [1768

——[Table of mountain peaks of the Appalachian range] Johnson City, Tenn., 1915. 4 p. [1769

——[Through the Appalachian wonderland] [Chicago, Poole, 1915] 38 p. [1770

——$22,150,000 first mortgage 4 per cent bonds, series A . . . dated September 1, 1940, due September 1, 1965. [New York, 1940] 47 p. [1771

Carolina College, Maxton, N. C. Catalogue, 19 - Maxton, 19 - NcU has [1913/14-1917/18] [1772

Carolina community, v. 1- June, 1952- Charlotte, Carolinas United, 1952- NcU has v. 1-4 [1773

Carolina Construction Company, Philadelphia. Norfolk, Wilmington and Charleston Railroad Company. [Philadelphia, Continental Trust and Finance Co., 1890?] 30 p. [1774

Carolina Cooperative Council. Tenth anniversary souvenir booklet. [Greensboro, Jos. J. Stone for Carolina Cotton and Woolen Mills Co., 1930] 52 p. [1775

Carolina co-operator, v. 1- 1922- Raleigh, North Carolina Cotton Growers Cooperative Association, 1922- NcU has v. [1-4] 5-12 [13] 14-26 [27] 28 [1776

Carolina cultivator, v. 1- 1855- Raleigh, Wm. D. Cooke, 1855- NcU has v. 1-2 [3] [1777

Carolina described more fully than heretofore. Dublin, 1684. 56 p. NcU has microfilm (positive) from original in New York Public Library [1778

The Carolina farmer, v. 1- 1910- Cary, 1910- NcU has v. 5-6 [1779

The Carolina farmer, v. 1- 194 - Greensboro, 194 - NcU has v. [4-5] 8-10 [1780

The Carolina farmer, v. 1- 19 - Raleigh, Tarheel Electric Membership Association, 19 - NcU has v. 8-10 [1781

The Carolina farmer, a monthly magazine, v. 1- 1868- Wilmington, W. H. Bernard, 1868- NcU has v. 1-4; ser. II, v. [1-3] [1782

Carolina Folk Festival, Chapel Hill, N. C. Annual Carolina Folk Festival, 194 - Chapel Hill 194 - NcU has 1952 (a poster) [1783

Carolina fur animal see American fur animal and poultry digest

Carolina homes, designed by Carolina architects. [Statesville] Brick and Tile Service [c.1948] 39 p. [1784

[Carolina Hotel, Pinehurst, N. C.] Make your winter home in Pinehurst. [Pinehurst, 1955] 15 p. [1785

Carolina Institute of International Relations. Findings, 19 - Greensboro, 19 - NcU has 1945 [1786

Carolina Inter-state Building and Loan Association, Wilmington, N. C. The Carolina Inter-state Building and Loan Association, Wilmington, N. C. [Wilmington] Jackson & Bell, 1892. 20 p. [1787

Carolina Israelite, v. 1- 194 - Charlotte, 194 - NcU has [1952-1956] [1788

Carolina live stock journal, v. 1, 1885-1886. Asheville, J. A. Williams, 1885-1886. NcU has v. 1 [1789

Carolina medical journal see North Carolina medical journal

Carolina Military Institute, Charlotte, N. C. Catalogue, 18 - Charlotte, 18 - NcU has 1874/75, 1877/78 [1790

Carolina Motor Club. Map itinerary, Carolinas historic and scenic tour, October 14-25, 1935. No place, 1935. [15] p. [1791

——Official garage and service station directory for North and South Carolina. [Greensboro, 1929] [15] p. [1792

——Proposed legislative program, 1929. [Greensboro, 1928] [10] p. [1793

——Vacationing in North Carolina, 1929- Greensboro, 1929- NcU has 1929, 1930 [1794

——What we do for you. Greensboro [1928?] 48 p. [1795

Carolina Motor Club. Committee on Highway Safety. This slaughter must stop. [Greensboro? 1934] 9 p. [1796

Carolina Motor Club. Committee on Motor Vehicle Taxation and Diversion of Highway Funds. Report on motor vehicle taxation and diversion of highway funds in North Carolina. No place, 1934. 52 p. [1797

Carolina Motor Club. Committee on Statewide Drivers' License. Summary of proposed drivers' license bill. Charlotte [1935?] [5] p. [1798

Carolina motor news see Go

Carolina motorist see Go

Carolina Mountain Club, Asheville, N. C. Guide to trails in Western North Carolina. Asheville [1933] 15 p. [1799

Carolina Oil and Creosote Co., Wilmington, N. C. Carolina Oil and Creosote Company, manufacturers of carbonized and wood-creosoted timber and cross-ties. Washington, D. C., Anderson & Moore, pr. [1886?] 24 p. [1800

Carolina Petroleum Co., Washington, D. C. Carolina Petroleum Company: details of its plan to develop oil fields along the Atlantic. Washington [192?] 15 p. [1801

Carolina Power and Light Company, Raleigh, N. C. Dedication of Eastern North Carolina's billion kilowatt-hour generating plant, Goldsboro, N. C. [Raleigh?] 1951. [13] p. [1802

——Notice of special meeting of stockholders to be held February 4, 1952. Raleigh, 1952. 31 p. [1803

——Prospectus: 156,158 shares $5 preferred stock without nominal or par value. [Raleigh?] 1945. 46 p. [1804

——Report, 19 - Raleigh, 19 - NcU has [1914-1933] 1937-1955 [1805

——Statement to the North Carolina Board of Conservation and Development. [Raleigh, 1951] 11 p. [1806

——Story of an opportunity at home. No place [1920] 7 p. [1807

[Carolina Power and Light Company, Raleigh, N. C.] 25 years of power progress. [Raleigh, 1951] [21] p. [1808

Carolina road builders, v. 1- September, 1946- Raleigh, Carolina Road Builders Association, 1946- NcU has v. 1-4 [1809

A Carolina sampler; an anthology of prose and poetry. New York, Harbinger House [c.1941] 137 p. [1810

Carolina School Supply Company, Charlotte, N. C. Views of a few representative school buildings of North and South Carolina, equipped with furniture manufactured by the American Seating Company. [Charlotte, Queen City Printing Co.] n.d. [1811

Carolina shopping list, v. 1- 1921- Charlotte, Observer Printing House, 1921- NcU has v. 1-2 [1812

Carolina Steel and Iron Company, Greensboro, N. C. Carolina steel. Greensboro [1952?] 69 p. [1813

Carolina union farmer, v. 1- 1907- Charlotte, Union Farmer Publishing Co., 1907- NcU has v. 5-7 [1814

The Carolinas, v. 1-9, June, 1932-June, 1940. Charlotte, 1932-40. NcU has v. 1-6 [7] 8-9 [1815

Carolinas Advertising Executives Association. The $3,266,800,000 "double feature" Carolinas market. No place [1948] [28] p. [1816

Carolinas hardware quarterly, v. 1- 192 - Charlotte, Hardware Association of the Carolinas, 192 - NcU has v. [4-9] [1817

Carolina's Hollywood in the Land of the Sky, the city inevitable. [Asheville? Hamilton Barrett Syndicate, 1925?] [17] p. [1818

Carolinas United community services. [Charlotte, Carolinas United, 1955] [8] p. [1819

Carolinian, pseud. The South and the North; being a reply to a lecture . . . by Ellwood Fisher, delivered before the Young Men's Mercantile Library Association of Cincinnati, January 16, 1849. Washington, Buell & Blanchard, 1849. 32 p. [1820

Carolinian (J. J. P.) pseud. see Pettigrew, James Johnston

Carpenter, Ernest Willoughby. A consideration of Plato's scheme of education in "The Republic". Chapel Hill, University of North Carolina, 1927. 29 p. [1821

Carpenter, H. K. Behind the microphone. [Raleigh, The Author] c.1929. 52 p. [1822

Carpenter, Hugh. King's Mountain, an epic of the Revolution. Knoxville, Tenn., The Author, 1936. 137 p. [1823

Carpenter, Kinchen Jahu. War diary of Kinchen Jahu Carpenter, Company I, Fiftieth North Carolina Regiment, War between the States. Rutherfordton, 1955. 17 p. [1824

Carpet-Bagger, pseud. see Green, John Paterson

Carr, Edward Parrish. The significance of the French Revolution. Chapel Hill, University Press, 1896. 18 p. [1825

Carr, Evander McNair. Advanced arithmetic, oral and written, on the eclectic method. Richmond, Va., B. F. Johnson Publishing Co., 1899. 373 p. [1826
——Beginners' objective arithmetic on the objective method. Richmond, B. F. Johnson Publishing Co., 1898. 89 p. [1827
——A primary arithmetic, oral and written, on the eclectic method. Richmond, Va., B. F. Johnson Publishing Co., 1899. 245 p. [1828

Carr, James Ozborn. Argument on behalf of the Cape Fear bar pilots, by James Ozborn Carr and George Rountree. Raleigh, Edwards & Broughton, n.d. 35 p. [1829
——The Carr family of Duplin County. Wilmington, Wilmington Stamp and Printing Co., 1939. 65 p. [1830

Carr, James Ozborn, joint author, see Rountree, George

Carr, John. Early times in middle Tennessee. Nashville, Tenn., Published for E. Carr, by E. Stevenson & F. A. Owen, 1857. 248 p. [1831

Carr, John Winder. Factors affecting distribution of trained teachers among rural white elementary schools of North Carolina. New York, Teachers College, Columbia University, 1927. (Teachers college, Columbia University. Contributions to education, no. 269) 91 p. [1832

Carr, Julian Shakespeare. Address delivered . . . at the Charlotte Poultry Show, January 7, 1902. [Charlotte, B. S. Davis, 1902?]   16 p.   [1833
——Address . . . "The Confederate soldier", reunion, Richmond, Va., June 2, 1915. [Durham? 1915?]   28 p.   [1834
——[Address to the veterans of the Southern Confederacy] delivered at Wilmington, N. C., May the 10th, 1894. No place, no publisher, n.d.   23 p.   [1835
——Letter to ex-Confederates; the old soldiers will not be disfranchised. [Durham? 1900]   16 p.   [1836
——The Hampton Roads conference. [Durham, 1917?]   36 p.   [1837
——A heart to heart talk with my old comrades. No place, no publisher, n.d. 14 p.   [1838
——In loving remembrance of our brother in gray; an address delivered at Windsor, Bertie County, N. C. . . . Thursday, Aug. 1st, 1895. No place, no publisher [1895?]   20 p.   [1839
——The issues of the campaign stated; an open letter to Van B. Sparrow. No place, no publisher [pref. 1898]   22 p.   [1840
[**Carr, Julian Shakespeare?**] Ladies, fellow countrymen and veterans of North Carolina. No place, no publisher, n.d.   10 p.   [1841
Carr, Julian Shakespeare. Local taxation . . . letter to Hon. C. H. Mebane. Chapel Hill, Summer School of the University of N. C., 1897.   1 p.   [1842
——Memorial address on the life and character of Col. Eugene Morehead, delivered before the Commonwealth Club, Durham, N. C., March 18th, 1889. No place, no publisher, n.d.   9 p.   [1843
[**Carr, Julian Shakespeare**] Our altars and our fires. [Durham? The Author?] n.d.   12 p.   [1844
——A plea for the Confederate veteran (extract from memorial address on the death of Captain Thomas D. Johnston) No place, no publisher [190?]   4 p.   [1845
Carr, Julian Shakespeare. The problem of the hour: will the colored race save itself from ruin?   An address delivered before the . . . North Carolina College of Agriculture and the Mechanic Arts, at Greensboro, May, 1899. Durham, Seeman Printery, 1899.   36 p.   [1846
—— . . . Solomon's wealth and wisdom, I Kings iv: 25-34 . . . Trinity Sunday School. [Durham? The Author? 1896]   23 p.   [1847
——Speeches. [Durham? The Author?] n.d.   20 p.   [1848
——These remarks are affectionately dedicated to the Confederate soldiers of the "rank and file", and to Henry L. Wyatt . . . delivered at Wilmington, N. C., May the 10th, 1894. No place, no publisher, n.d.   23 p.   [1849
[**Carr, Julian Shakespeare**] To the people of North Carolina. [Charlotte, Charlotte Daily Observer, 1900]   2 p.   [1850
Carr, Julian Shakespeare. Unveiling Bennett house memorial, November 8th, 1923; address . . . Peace with honor, Durham, N. C. Durham, Seeman Printery [1923] 20 p.   [1851
Carraway, Daphne. A teachers' book of stories adapted for the story hour. [Raleigh, The Graphic Press, Inc., c.1946]   43 p.   [1852
Carraway, Gertrude Sprague. Camp Lejeune leathernecks, Camp Lejeune, N. C. New Bern, Owen G. Dunn Co., 1946.   100 p.   [1853
——Carolina crusaders; history of North Carolina Federation of Women's Clubs. New Bern, Owen G. Dunn, 1941.   142 p.   [1854
——Crown of life; history of Christ Church, New Bern, N. C., 1715-1940. New Bern, O. G. Dunn, 1940.   245 p.   [1855
——Historic New Bern; guide book. New Bern, New Bern Merchants Association and Chamber of Commerce, 1934.   [23] p.   [1856
—— ——3d ed. c.1938.   51 p.   [1857
—— ——4th ed.   c.1939.   56 p.   [1858
—— ——5th ed.   1942.   64 p.   [1859
—— ——7th ed.   1947.   64 p.   [1860
—— ——8th ed.   1950.   64 p.   [1861
——New Bern, second oldest city in North Carolina. [New Bern] City of New Bern, c.1943.   36 p.   [1862
——The United States Marine Corps Air Station, Cunningham Field, Cherry Point, North Carolina. New Bern, Owen G. Dunn Co., 1946.   80 p.   [1863

——Years of light; history of St. John's Lodge, no. 3, A. F. & A. M., New Bern, North Carolina, 1772-1944, 5772-5944, A. L. (anno lucis, year of light) New Bern, Owen G. Dunn Co., 1944. 256 p. [1864

Carrigan, Daisy Patterson. Lyrics and songs of other days. Burlington, The Author, 1926. 60 p. [1865

Carrington, Elizabeth Scott. Historical sketch of Hawfields Presbyterian Church, by Elizabeth Scott (Mrs. George Carrington) . . . brought down to date by Mrs. R. W. Scott and Mrs. W. Kerr Scott, with excerpts from history by Mildred White. No place, n.d. 74 p. [1866

Carring*on, Henry Beebee. Battle maps and charts of the American Revolution. New York, A. S. Barnes & Co. [1881] 88 p. [1867

——Battles of the American Revolution, 1775-1781. New York, A. S. Barnes & Co. [c.1888] 712 p. [1868

Carroll, Bartholomew Rivers, ed. Historical collections of South Carolina. New York, Harper & Brothers, 1836. 2 v. [1869

Carroll, Eber Malcolm. Germany and the great powers, 1866-1914. New York, Prentice-Hall, Inc., 1938. 852 p. [1870

——Origins of the Whig party. Durham, Duke University Press, 1925. 260 p. [1871

Carroll, James Elwood. History of the North Carolina annual conference of the Methodist Protestant Church. [Greensboro, McCulloch & Swain, pr., c.1939] 112 p. [1872

Carroll, Robert Sproul. The grille gate. Boston, R. G. Badger [c.1922] 401 p. [1873

——The mastery of nervousness based upon reeducation. New York, Macmillan Co., 1917. 346 p. [1874

——Old at forty or young at sixty, simplifying the science of growing old. New York, Macmillan Co., 1920. 147 p. [1875

——Our nervous friends; illustrating the mastery of nervousness. New York, Macmillan Co., 1919. 258 p. [1876

——The soul in suffering. New York, Macmillan Co., 1919. 241 p. [1877

Carroll, Ruth (Robinson) Beanie, by Ruth and Latrobe Carroll. New York, Oxford University Press, 1953. Unpaged. [1878

——Digby, the only dog, by Ruth and Latrobe Carroll, New York, Oxford University Press, 1955. 47 p. [1879

——Peanut, by Ruth and Latrobe Carroll. New York, Oxford University Press, 1951. 45 p. [1880

——Salt and Pepper, by Ruth and Latrobe Carroll. New York, Oxford University Press, 1952. 30 p. [1881

——Tough Enough, by Ruth and Latrobe Carroll. New York, Oxford University Press, 1954. unpaged. [1882

——Tough Enough's trip, by Ruth and Latrobe Carroll. New York, Oxford University Press, 1956. 64 p. [1883

Carroll, Thomas Henry, ed. Business education for competence and responsibility. Chapel Hill, University of North Carolina Press [1954] 67 p. [1884

Carson, Hampton Lawrence, ed. History of the celebration of the one hundredth anniversary of the promulgation of the Constitution of the United States. Philadelphia, under the direction and by the authority of the Commission, by J. B. Lippincott Co., 1889. 2 v. [1885

Carson, Hampton Lawrence. History of the Supreme Court of the United States; with biographies of all the chief and associate justices . . . A. D. 1790-1902. Philadelphia, P. W. Ziegler and Co., 1902. 2 v. [1886

Carson, Rachel Louise. The edge of the sea. Boston, Houghton Mifflin, 1955. 276 p. [1887

——Under the sea-wind. New York, Oxford University Press, 1952. 314 p. [1888

Carson, Samuel Price. Circular to the freemen of the twelfth congressional district of North Carolina. [Washington, no publisher, May 20, 1828] 7 p. [1889

—— ——Washington, Printed by Duff Green, 1829. 8 p. [1890

——To the freemen of the twelfth congressional district of the state of N. C. No place, no publisher [183?] 8 p. [1891

Carter, A. G. To the free-holders of Rowan and Davie counties. Salisbury, no publisher, 1844. [1] p. [1892

Carter, Bruce. The Wright brothers. London, Newnes Educational Publishing Co. Ltd. [1955] 47 p. [1893

Carter, David Wendel. Carter of Tennessee, including the Taylors; descendants of Colonel John Carter. Chattanooga, Tenn., Lookout Publishing Co. [c.1927] 31 p. [1894

Carter, Eva M. Gleanings from nature. New York, Abbey Press [c.1901] 147 p. [1895

——Princess Florina in Natureland. New York, Abbey Press [c.1903] 64 p. [1896

Carter, J. W. Truth and righteousness; baccalaureate sermon to the Class of '92. Raleigh, Edwards & Broughton, pr., 1892. 23 p. [1897

Carter, Jane, ed. A picture book of Old Salem. Winston-Salem, Collins Co. [c.1956] unpaged. [1898

Carter, Joseph E. Distinctive Baptist principles: A sermon delivered before the Western Baptist Convention of North Carolina, at Enon Church, Transylvania County, October 20th, 1883. Raleigh, Edwards, Broughton & Co., 1883. 46 p. [1899

Carter, Laura Lindsay. An historical sketch of the Protestant Episcopal Church in the state of North Carolina. Asheville [Inland Press] 1906. 19 p. [1900

Carter, Mary Nelson. North Carolina sketches. Chicago, A. C. McClurg & Co., 1900. 313 p. [1901

Carteret Co., N. C. Board of Education. Consolidation of Carteret County schools. No place, no publisher [1923?] 23 p. [1902

——Handbook for Carteret County teachers, 1927-1928. No place, no publisher [1927?] 30 p. [1903

Carteret County school news, v. 1- November, 1925- NcU has v. 1-3 [4-6] [1904

Carthage, N. C. Board of Trade. Carthage, North Carolina, its industrial, agricultural, and residential advantages. [Carthage, Board of Trade, 1914] 28 p. [1905

—— ——Supplement. [Carthage, Board of Trade, 192?] [3] p. [1906

Carthage, N. C. Tyson and Jones Buggy Company see **Tyson and Jones Buggy Company, Carthage, N. C.**

Carthage Academic Institute, Carthage, N. C. Catalogue, 18 - Carthage, 18 - NcU has 1887/88 [1907

Carthagenian, v. 1- 1935/36- Carthage, Moore County News Press, 1937- NcU has v. 1 [1908

Cartland, Fernando Gale. Southern heroes. Cambridge, Riverside Press, 1895. 480 p. [1909

—— ——Poughkeepsie, N. Y., The Author, 1897. 480 p. [1910

Cartledge Creek Baptist Church, Richmond County, N. C. Building program rally, held on Tuesday, Nov. 16, 1948, at W. H. (Billy) Covington "spring". [Rockingham, Post-Dispatch, pr., 1948] [16] p. [1911

Caruthers, Eli Washington. A discourse delivered at Alamance Academy, July 4th, 1848. Greensborough, Printed by Swaim and Sherwood, 1848. 40 p. [1912

——Interesting Revolutionary incidents. 2d series. Philadelphia, Hayes & Zell, 1856. 448 p. [1913

——Revolutionary incidents. Philadelphia, Hayes & Zell, 1854. 431 p. [1914

——A sketch of the life and character of the Rev. David Caldwell. Greensborough, Printed by Swaim and Sherwood, 1842. 302 p. [1915

Cary, N. C. Cary High School. Catalogue, 1900/01- Cary, 1901- NcU has 1900/01-1902/03, 1904/05-1927/28 [1916

Cary, N. C. Chamber of Commerce. A brief history of the town of Cary, Wake County, North Carolina. [Cary] n.d. 8 p. [1917

The case of the Church of England in Carolina, humbly offer'd to the consideration of both Houses of Parliament. No place, no publisher, n.d. 4 p. NcU has photostat (positive) [1918

Cash, Walter. Articles of faith and rules of decorum of the Primitive Baptist Church. St. Joseph, Mo., Messenger of Peace, n.d. [23] p. [1919

Cash, Wilbur Joseph. The mind of the South. New York, A. A. Knopf, 1941. 429 p. [1920

—— ——Garden City, N. Y., Doubleday and Co., 1954. 444 p. [1921

The casket; periodical of the Chowan Female Collegiate Institute, Murfreesborough, N. C., v. 1- Murfreesborough, 185 - NcU has v. 2, no. 1 [1922

Casper Company, Winston-Salem, N. C. Honest whiskies. Winston-Salem [1905?] 32 p. [1923

Castalia Preparatory School. Castalia, N. C. Catalogue, 19 - Castalia, 19 - NcU has 1908/09-1910/11 [1924

Castlemon, Harry, pseud. see Fosdick, Charles Austin

Catalogue of paintings, Davenport Female College, April 22, 1861. No place, no publisher [1861?] 2 p. [1925

Catawba College, Salisbury, N. C. Catawba College bulletin, v. 1- April, 1925- Salisbury, 1925- NcU has v. 1-2 [3-31] [1926

——Catalogue, 189 - Newton, 189 - NcU has [1898/99-1921/22] Continues as its Bulletin, 1925- [1927

Catawba County Historical Association. A history of Catawba County. Salisbury, Rowan Printing Co., 1954. 526 p. [1928

Catawba County, North Carolina. [Newton, Shuford National Bank, 1915] [11] p. [1929

Catawba County school news, v. 1- December, 1925- Newton, 1925- NcU has v. 1-3 [4-6] [1930

Catawba Industrial Association. Second annual fair at Hickory, N. C., October 19th, 20th, 21st and 22d. Hickory, Piedmont Press, n.d. [1] p. [1931

Catawba River Baptist Association. Minutes, 18 - 18 - NcU has 1843, 1849, 1854, 1878, 1882-1886, 1897, 1921, 1927, 1932-1941, 1953 [1932

Catchings, Fermine Baird. Baird and Beard families. Nashville, Tenn., Baird-Ward [c.1918] 230 p. [1933

Catesby, Mark. Die Beschreibung von Carolina, Florida, und den Bahamischen inseln. Noȗrnberg, J. M. Seligmann [1755] [62] p. [1934

——Hortus Europae americanus; or, A collection of 85 curious trees and shrubs, the produce of North America. London, Printed for J. Millan, 1767. 41 p. [1935

——The natural history of Carolina, Florida, and the Bahama Islands. London, Printed for C. Marsh, 1754. 2 v. [1936

—— ——London, Printed for B. White, 1771. 2 v. [1937

Cathey, Cornelius Oliver. Agricultural developments in North Carolina, 1783-1860. Chapel Hill, University of North Carolina Press, 1956. (James Sprunt Studies in history and political science, v. 38) 229 p. [1938

Cathey, James Harrison. The genesis of Lincoln. [Atlanta, Franklin Printing and Publishing Co. [c.1899] 307 p. [1939

——Truth is stranger than fiction. [1899] 185 p. [1940

Catholic Church. Catechisms. English. A catechism of Christian doctrine. Nazareth, Truth [c.1885] 67 p. [1941

Catholic Layman. Religious liberty in danger. No place, no publisher [1844?] 16 p. [1942

Catholicus [pseud.] Argumentum ad hominem. No place, no publisher, n.d. 7 p. [1943

Cedar Creek Baptist Association. Minutes, 18 - 18 - NcU has 1861, 1876-1879, 1885-1886, 1906-1908 [1944

Cedar Grove Missionary Baptist Association. Minutes, 19 - 19 - NcU has 1917, 1918 [1945

Central Baptist Association. Minutes, 18 - 18 - NcU has [1864-1874] 1876-1914 [1917-1933] [1946

Central Carolina Fair, Greensboro, N. C. List of premiums and rules and regulations, 1st- 189 - Greensboro, 189 - NcU has [1900-1921] [1947

Central Conference. Original Free Will Baptist Church. Minutes, 18 - 18 - NcU has [1924-1955] [1948

Central Hickory Club, Washington, D. C. Address of the Central Hickory Club, to the Republican citizens of the United States. Washington, 1832. 23 p. [1949

Central Jackson Committee. Address to the freemen of North Carolina; electoral ticket of North Carolina. Raleigh, Lawrence & Lemay, 1828. 16 p. [1950

——Case of the six militia men fairly stated. Raleigh, Lawrence & Lemay, 1828. 47 p.   [1951

The Central Protestant, v. 1- 1874- Greensboro, Methodist Protestant Church, 1874- NcU has v. [1-10]   [1952

A century of social thought; a series of lectures delivered at Duke University . . . 1938-1939. Durham, Duke University Press [c.1939] 172 p.   [1953

Chace, Elizabeth (Buffum) Two Quaker sisters. New York, Liveright Publishing Corporation [1937] 183 p.   [1954

Chadbourn, James Harmon, 1853- History of North Carolina Waterways Association; an address . . . on the occasion of President Taft's reception at Wilmington . . . November 9th, 1909. [Wilmington, 1909] 8 p.   [1955

Chadbourn, James Harmon, 1905- Lynching and the law. Chapel Hill, The University of North Carolina Press, 1933. 221 p.   [1956

Chadsey, Charles Ernest. . . . The struggle between President Johnson and Congress over reconstruction. New York, 1896. (Columbia University Studies in history, economics and public law, v. VIII, no. 1) 142 p.   [1957

Chaffee, Allen. The Wilderness trail. New York, T. Nelson and Sons, 1936. 72 p.   [1958

Chaffin, Nora Campbell. Trinity College, 1839-1892: the beginnings of Duke University. Durham, Duke University Press, 1950. 584 p.   [1959

Chalkley, Thomas. Journal of the life, travels, and Christian experiences of Thomas Chalkley, written by himself. London, Edward Marsh, 1850. 374 p.   [1960

Chalmers, George. Political annals of the present united colonies, from their settlement to the peace of 1763. Book I. London, Printed for the Author: and sold by J. Bowen, 1780. 695 p.   [1961

Chalmers, James, tr. A literal translation of Demosthenes On the crown, translated . . . by James Chalmers . . . rev. and cor. . . . by F. S. Goode and R. L. Patterson. Chapel Hill, New York, Printed for the Authors, 1849. 81 p.   [1962

Chalmers, Mary Letitia (Strong) Our kith and kin; or, A history of the Harris family. [Philadelphia, American Printing House, 1895?] 167 p.   [1963

Chaloner, John Armstrong. Four years behind the bars of "Bloomingdale". Roanoke Rapids, Palmetto Press, 1906. Various paging.   [1964

Chamberlain, Henry. Cotton gins. Tarborough, Printed at the Office of the Free Press, 1833. [1] p.   [1965

Chamberlain, Hope Summerell. History of Wake County, North Carolina. Raleigh, Edwards & Broughton Printing Co., 1922. 302 p.   [1966

——Old days in Chapel Hill, being the life and letters of Cornelia Phillips Spencer. Chapel Hill, University of North Carolina Press, 1926. 325 p.   [1967

——This was home. Chapel Hill, University of North Carolina Press [c.1938] 328 p.   [1968

Chamberlain, Olivia Hart. Science as a particular. Chapel Hill, Department of Philosophy, University of North Carolina [1932] (Studies in philosophy, no. 5) 8 p.   [1969

Chambers, J. C. Address delivered before the Alumni Association of Davidson College, N. C., July 14th, 1859. Yorkville, S. C., Printed by Lewis M. Grist, 1859. 15 p.   [1970

Chambers, Joseph Lenoir. The breed and the pasture. Charlotte, Stone & Barringer Co., 1910. 125 p.   [1971

Chambers, Maxwell. Last will. Salisbury, J. J. Bruner, pr., 1856. 15 p.   [1972

Chambers, Robert William. The mystery lady. New York, Grosset & Dunlap [c.1925] 335 p.   [1973

——The rogue's moon. New York, D. Appleton & Co., 1929. 261 p.   [1974

Chambers, William Nisbet. Old Bullion Benton, senator from the new West: Thomas Hart Benton, 1782-1858. Boston, Little, Brown [1956] 517 p.   [1975

Champion, Richard. Considerations on the present situation of Great Britain and the United States of America. 2d ed. London, J. Stockdale, 1784. 274 p. [1976

Champion of democracy, Senator Frank P. Graham fights communism and dictatorships. [Raleigh? 1950] 7 p.   [1977

[Champion Paper and Fibre Company, Hamilton, Ohio] An industrial forest policy in Western North Carolina. Canton, n.d. [8] p.   [1978
——The story of the Canton Division. [Hamilton, Ohio? 1948?] 39 p.   [1979
Chandler, Helen Deane. A brief description of the Battle of Kings Mountain. Gastonia, Publicity Committee of the Sesqui-centennial Celebration Committee, 1930. 47 p.   [1980
The Chanticleer, v. 1- 1912- Durham, Organizations of Trinity College, 1912- NcU has 1912, 1920   [1981
Chapel Hill, N. C. Baptist Church. Year book and directory, 19 - 19 - NcU has 1912, 1920   [1982
[Chapel Hill, N. C. Baptist Church] Your church in the college community. Chapel Hill [1948] [8] p.   [1983
Chapel Hill, N. C. Board of Aldermen. Building zone ordinance for the town of Chapel Hill, N. C. [Chapel Hill, 1928] 14 p.   [1984
—— ——[1938] 16 p.   [1985
——Report concerning the extension of the town limits. Chapel Hill, June 26, 1950. 13 p.   [1986
——Sanitary ordinance of the town of Chapel Hill, adopted . . . 1922. [Durham, Seeman Printery] 1922. 15 p.   [1987
Chapel Hill, N. C. Board of Commissioners. Ordinances and charter for the government of the town of Chapel Hill, N. C., ratified Feb. 15th, 1896. Chapel Hill, University Press, 1896. 31 p.   [1988
——Ordinances passed for the town of Chapel Hill, on the 19th day of February, 1829. Hillsborough, D. Heartt & Son, 1829. 8 p.   [1989
Chapel Hill, N. C. Board of Trustees of Chapel Hill Graded School. Record, 1912/13- Chapel Hill, 1913- NcU has 1912/13   [1990
——Statement showing that the town of Chapel Hill cannot do less than it is now doing for the education of its children. No place, no publisher [1922?] 3 p. [1991
——Statement to the citizens of Chapel Hill, discussing the issues in the school election called for May 30, 1922. No place, no publisher [1922?] 7 p.   [1992
Chapel Hill, N. C. Chapel Hill Country Club. The Chapel Hill Country Club, membership and dues, social regulations and golf rules. Chapel Hill, March, 1940. [6] p.   [1993
——Membership, January 11, 1927. [Chapel Hill, 1927] [1] p.   [1994a
Chapel Hill, N. C. Chapel of the Cross. The Cross roads, v. 1- 1929- Chapel Hill, 1929- NcU has v. [1-30]   [1994
——Handbook, 1940. [Chapel Hill, 1940] [11] p.   [1995
——"Our appointed task, for others, for ourselves." Chapel Hill [1955] [10] p. [1996
——Special service in the new Chapel of the Cross . . . on the third Sunday after Easter, May 8, 1949. [Chapel Hill, 1949] 22 p.   [1997
——Year book. Chapel Hill [1921] 24 p.   [1998
—— ——1923. 32 p.   [1999
Chapel Hill, N. C. Choral Society. Concert, first season- 1898- Chapel Hill, 1898- NcU has 1st-2d seasons   [2000
Chapel Hill, N. C. Citizens. A message to our fellow citizens. [Chapel Hill, Chapel Hill Weekly, 1928] [1] p.   [2001
Chapel Hill, N. C. Community Club. The Community Club, Chapel Hill, North Carolina, 1921/22- Chapel Hill, 1921- NcU has 1914/15-1916/17, 1921/22- 1929/30, 1941/42, 1944/45, 1947/48-1953/54   [2002
——Constitution and by-laws of the Community Club of Chapel Hill, N. C. [Chapel Hill] n.d. [3] p. .   [2003
Chapel Hill, N. C. Community Council. Calendar of meetings scheduled by Chapel Hill organizations, 1949- [Chapel Hill, 1949-] NcU has 1949   [2004
——List of Chapel Hill organizations. [Chapel Hill, 1949] [1] p.   [2005
—— ——[1952] 6 p.   [2006
Chapel Hill, N. C. Junior Service League. Carolina cooking, Chapel Hill, 1953. 123 p.   [2008
——Population survey and school census of the Chapel Hill school attendance district. Chapel Hill, 1948. 3 p.   [2009

Chapel Hill, N. C. Kiwanis Club. Roster of members, committees, 19 - Chapel Hill, 19 - NcU has 1957 [2010

[Chapel Hill, N. C. League of Women Voters] Local government; a handbook for citizens of Chapel Hill and Orange County, North Carolina. [Chapel Hill, 1952] 26 p. [2011

——Your local government, 1948. [Chapel Hill] 1948. 16 p. [2012

Chapel Hill, N. C. Long and McCauley. To the public. Chapel Hill, 1871. [1] p. [2013

Chapel Hill, N. C. Methodist Church. The Chapel Hill Methodist Church presents a challenge to the Methodists of North Carolina. [Durham, Seeman Printery] 1917. 9 p. [2014

——Dedication of the Methodist Church . . . Sunday, April 7, 1935. [Chapel Hill, 1935] [3] p. [2015

——Presenting a plan for a new church education building. Chapel Hill [1955] [12] p. [2016

——Steeple views, v. 1- October, 1944- Chapel Hill, 1944- NcU has v. 1-2 [2017

——University Methodist Church, Church School directory, 19 - Chapel Hill, 19 - NcU has 1953/54 [2018

Chapel Hill, N. C. Presbyterian Church. The first hundred years . . . 1849-1949. Chapel Hill [1950] 39 p. [2019

——Our Church in Chapel Hill. [Chapel Hill, 1956] [8] p. [2020

——Statements of the treasurers, 19 - [Chapel Hill, 19 - NcU has 1926/27 [2021

Chapel Hill, N. C. Presbyterian Church. Woman's Auxiliary. The Chapel Hill cook book. [Chapel Hill, Orange Print Shop, 1935] 88 p. [2022

Chapel Hill, N. C. Rock Hill Baptist Church. The seventy-sixth anniversary celebration of the Rock Hill Baptist Church . . . April 7-28, 1946. [Chapel Hill 1946. [3] p. [2023

Chapel Hill, N. C. School of religion. By-laws. Chapel Hill, no publisher, 1926. 18 p. [2024

Chapel Hill, N. C. Town Business Manager. Report to the Board of Aldermen, 1st- 1922/23- Chapel Hill, 1923- NcU has 1922/23 [2025

[Chapel Hill-Carrboro Merchants Association] Chapel Hill, North Carolina, a village of the old South and the new South. [Chapel Hill, Orange Print Shop, 1947] Folder. [2026

[Chapel Hill Insurance and Realty Co.] Chapel Hill: a brief sketch. [Chapel Hill? 1925?] [6] p. [2027

Chapel Hill, N. C., University and community. [Chapel Hill, Orange Print Shop, 1952] 16 p. [2028

Chapel Hill School, Chapel Hill, N. C. Register, 1897/98- Chapel Hill, 1898- NcU has 1897/98, 1898/99 [2029

Chapel Hill transfer company and general livery office. Weldon, Harrell's Print, n.d. [2] p. [2030

Chapel Hillian, v. 1- November 4, 1890- Chapel Hill, Walter A. Bonitz and S. A Ashe, Jr., 1890- NcU has v. [1] [2031

Chapin, George H. Health resorts of the South. Boston, The Author, 1893. 222 p. [2032

Chapman, Alvan Wentworth. Flora of the southern United States. New York, Ivison, Blakeman, Taylor & Co., 1860. 621 p. [2033

—— ——2d ed. New York, Ivison, Blakeman & Co., 1889. 698 p. [2034

Chapman, John Stanton Higham see Chapman, Maristan, pseud.

Chapman, Maristan, pseud. Rogue's March. Philadelphia, J. B. Lippincott Co. [1949] 384 p. [2035

Chapman, Mary (Ilsley) see Chapman, Maristan, pseud.

Chapman, Paul Wilber. Southern crops, by Paul W. Chapman and Roy H. Thomas. Atlanta, Turner E. Smith & Co. [1953] 503 p. [2036

—— ——1939. 558 p. [2037

Chapman, Robert Hett. A funeral sermon delivered in the Presbyterian Church of Asheville, North Carolina, on the tenth of July, 1857, at the interment of the Rev. Elisha Mitchell. Asheville, Printed at the Spectator Office, 1857. 12 p. [2038

Chapone, Hester (Mulso) Letters on the improvement of the mind. Newbern, Printed by John S. Pasteur, 1802. 2 v. in 1   [2039

Chappell, Louis Watson. Folk-songs of Roanoke and the Albemarle. Morgantown, W. Va., Ballad Press, 1939. 203 p.   [2040

Charitable Brotherhood of North Carolina. Constitution and by-laws. Raleigh, Edwards & Broughton Printing Co. [1916?] 30 p.   [2041

Charles Ross, Lillington, N. C., candidate in Democratic primary for Attorney General. No place, no publisher [1924] Folder   [2042

Charles W. Chesnutt in platform readings. No place, no publisher, n.d. [6] p. [2043

Charleston, S. C. Committee on Railroad from Ohio to S. C. Proceedings of the citizens of Charleston. Charleston, S. C., A. E. Miller, pr., 1835. 27 p. [2044

Charlotte, N. C. American Trust Co. Fifty years of banking service . . . 1901-1951. [Charlotte, 1951] [28] p.   [2045

Charlotte, N. C. Anti-saloon League. It helps business and is a blessing. Charlotte [1908] 32 p.   [2046

Charlotte, N. C. Board of Aldermen. The code of the city of Charlotte. Charlotte, Hirst Printing Co., 1887. 137 p.   [2047
—— ——Charlotte, Observer, 1895. 180 p.   [2048
—— ——Charlotte, Washburn Press, 1915. 429 p.   [2049

Charlotte, N. C. Board of Commissioners. Ordinances of the town of Charlotte. [Charlotte] 1859. [1] p.   [2050

Charlotte, N. C. Board of School Commissioners. By-laws and rules. Charlotte, Queen City Printing Co., 1926. 40 p.   [2051
——Courses of study of the Charlotte City Schools, Grades 1-6, 192 - Charlotte, 192 - NcU has 1925/26, 1926/27   [2052
——Courses of study of the Charlotte City Schools, Junior and Senior High Schools . . . 1925-26. [Charlotte] n.d. 110 p.   [2053
——Reports, courses of study, by-laws and rules, 1890/91- [Charlotte, 1890?- NcU has 1892/93, 1898/99 [1901/02-1904/05, 1915/16-1925/26]   [2054

[Charlotte, N. C. Business and Professional Women's Club] Won't you tarry a while with me? [Charlotte, News] n.d. [12] p.   [2055

Charlotte, N. C. Chamber of commerce. Charlotte, North Carollna, "distribution center in war and peace." Charlotte [1942?] [30] p.   [2056
——Charlotte, North Carolina . . . diversified industrial and commercial center. [Charlotte, Observer Printing House, 1930] [63] p.   [2057
——Charlotte, now a city of more than 100,000 population. [Charlotte, 194?] 14 p.   [2058
——Charlotte the center; list of Charlotte manufacturers. Charlotte, 1930. [4] p.   [2059
——Charlotte "the friendly city". Charlotte, 1937. 14 p.   [2060
——Charlotte, the industrial center of the Carolinas. Charlotte, 1947. 24 p. [2061
——Charlotte, North Carolina, focal point of the Carolinas. 6th ed. Charlotte, 1946. [34] p.   [2062

[Charlotte, N. C. Chamber of Commerce] City of Charlotte. [Charlotte, 1938?] 16 p.   [2063

Charlotte, N. C. Chamber of Commerce. Directory of Charlotte manufacturers. Charlotte, 1950. 17 p.   [2064
——"In the heart of the Piedmont". Charlotte. [Charlotte, Observer] n.d. 24 p. [2065
——Know Charlotte, Queen City of the South. Charlotte, 1930. [18] p.   [2066
——Sketches of Charlotte, the Queen City. Charlotte, Hirst Printing Co., 1888. 46 p.   [2067
——Temperature averages, precipitation, growing season for Charlotte. Charlotte, n.d. [2] p.   [2068

Charlotte, N. C. City Attorneys. The code of the city of Charlotte. Charlotte, News, 1902. 286 p.   [2069
——Charter [Charlotte, 1955] 58 p.   [2070

Charlotte, N. C. City Council. City of Charlotte budget, 19 - Charlotte, 19 - NcU has 1945/46-1951/52, 1952/53, 1954/55, 1955/56   [2071
——The code of the city of Charlotte. Charlotte, Observer Printing House, 1931. 581 p.   [2072

——[Financial report]   19   -   Charlotte, 19   -   NcU has 1952/53, 1954/55 [2073

——Report, 1st- 1929/30- [Charlotte, 1930?- NcU has 1929/30, 1933/34, 1935/36, 1937/38   [2074

——Zoning code amended and rewritten . . . and adopted by the City Council . . . on April 23, 1951. Charlotte, 1951. 14 p.   [2075

Charlotte, N. C. City Engineer. Report of City Engineer and Superintendent of Streets, 19   -   [Charlotte, 19   -   NcU has 1933/34   [2076

Charlotte, N. C. Covenant Presbyterian Church. [To the greater glory of God] [Charlotte, 1953]   12 p.   [2077

Charlotte, N. C. Fire Department. Report of the Chief of Fire Department, 19   - [Charlotte, 19   -   NcU has 1934, 1937-1940, 1942, 1945-1954   [2078

Charlotte, N. C. First Presbyterian Church. Directory. [Charlotte?] February, 1913. 112 p.   [2079

——Year book, report of Christian activities and list of members, 19   -   Charlotte, 19   -   NcU has 1909   [2080

Charlotte, N. C. Good Samaritan Hospital. Report, 1892- Charlotte, 1892- NcU has 1892, 1893, 1909-1911   [2081

Charlotte, N. C. Greater Charlotte Club. Charlotte, city of electrical energy. [Charlotte] n.d.   [4] p.   [2082

——Charlotte, North Carolina. Charlotte, 1913. [62] p.   [2083

Charlotte, N. C. Housing authority. Report, 1938/39- [Charlotte, 1940- NcU has 1938/39-1942, 1943/44, 1945/47   [2084

Charlotte, N. C. Independence Trust Co. Ten years of progress, 1912-1922. No place, no publisher [1922?]   [2085

Charlotte, N. C. Made-in-Carolinas Association. see **Made-in-Carolinas Association, Charlotte, N. C.**   [2086

Charlotte, N. C. Memorial Hospital. All the facts about Charlotte Memorial Hospital [Charlotte, n.d.]   [8] p.   [2087

——Bulletin, no. 1-3, January-June, 1944. Charlotte, 1944. NcU has no. 1-3 [2088

Charlotte, N. C. Mining Board. Statistics of mines and minerals in North Carolina. Charlotte, Observer Print, 1878. 15 p.   [2089

Charlotte, N. C. Mint Museum of Art. Catalogue, inaugural exhibition . . . [October 1, 1936-January 1, 1937] Charlotte [1936]   [28] p.   [2090

——The Mint museum of art. [Charlotte, 1938?] Folder.   [2091

—— ——[1944] [19] p.   [2092

Charlotte, N. C. Myers Park Presbyterian Church. Myers Park pulpit, v. 1- [Charlotte, 195 - NcU has v. 2-4   [2093

Charlotte, N. C. North Carolina Building and Loan Association   see **North Carolina Building and Loan Association, Charlotte**

Charlotte, N. C. North State Agency Co. Certificate, articles of incorporation, by-laws. [Charlotte, Ray Printing Co., 1908]   11 p.   [2094

Charlotte, N.·C. Oasis Temple see **Freemasons. Charlotte, N. C. Oasis Temple of A. A. O. N. M. S.**

Charlotte, N. C. Old Ladies' Home. Old Ladies' Home, Charlotte, N. C.   [Charlotte] 1914. 15 p.   [2095

Charlotte, N. C. Police Department. Report, 19   -   Charlotte, 19   -   NcU has 1932, 1933   [2096

Charlotte, N. C. Public Library.   . . . Directory of clubs and organizations in Charlotte and Mecklenburg county, 19   -   Charlotte, 19   -   NcU has 1943, 1946, 1952, 1953   [2097

——Magazines, newspapers and services received regularly. [Charlotte] 1949. [11] p.   [2098

——Report, 1903- Charlotte 1904- NcU has 1903, 1937/38, 1943/44-1945/46, 1950/51, 1952/53   [2099

——Why Charlotte and Mecklenburg County need better library service. Charlotte, Board of Trustees, Public Library, 1946. 16 p.   [2100

Charlotte, N. C. Railroad Convention, April 27-28, 1847. Proceedings. No place, no publisher, 1847. 4 p.   [2101

Charlotte, N. C. St. Martin's Episcopal Church. St. Martin's Chapel . . . 1887-
1937. [Charlotte, 1937] 18 p.   [2102

[Charlotte, N. C. St. Peter's Catholic Church] Souvenir, St. Peter's Catholic
Church, 1851-1901. Charlotte, Elam and Dooley, pr. [190?] 44 p.   [2103

Charlotte, N. C. St. Peter's Episcopal Church. A century of Christian progress
. . . 1844, 1944. Charlotte, 1944. 32 p.   [2104

——The consecration of St. Peter's Protestant Episcopal Church . . . May 15, 1921.
[Charlotte] 1921. 15 p.   [2105

——Dainty recipes. [Charlotte, Dooley Printing Co.] n.d. 32 p.   [2106

——Directory of communicants and contributors, 1893. Charlotte, Hirst Printing
Co., 1893. 13 p.   [2107

Charlotte, N. C. St. Peter's Hospital. Report, 187 - Charlotte, 187 - NcU has
1881-1890, 1893, 1907, 1909, 1911   [2108

——Rules for the management of St. Peter's Home and Hospital. Charlotte, Observer Power Press, 1887. 15 p.   [2109

——St. Peter's Hospital (Episcopal) a hospital with a heart. Charlotte, 1924.
[20] p.   [2110

Charlotte, N. C. Southern Manufacturers' Club. By-laws and house rules, incorporated Dec. 15, 1894. Charlotte, Queen City Printing Co., 1911. 48 p. [2111

—— ———1905. 36 p.   [2112

——Charlotte, North Carolina. [Charlotte, Queen City Printing Co., 190?]
[8] p.   [2113

Charlotte, N. C. Treasurer. Mecklenburg County & City of Charlotte invite your
bid on library bonds. [Charlotte, 1955] No paging.   [2114

Charlotte, N. C. Tryon St. Methodist Episcopal Church, South. List of officers
and societies. Charlotte, Blakey Printing House, 1892. 48 p.   [2115

Charlotte and South Carolina Railroad. Proceedings of the annual meeting, 1848-
Columbia, S. C., 1848- NcU has 1848-1861, 1863-1869   [2116

——Proceedings of a convention of the stockholders, held for the purpose of organization, at Charlotte, N. C., Sept. 9th, 1847. Columbia, S. C., South Carolinian,
1847. 16 p.   [2117

——Proceedings of the convention of stockholders, held at Chesterville, S. C., on
Thurs. and Fri., Jan. 13 and 14, 1848. Columbia, A. G. Summer, 1848. 21 p. [2118

——Report of the president. Columbia, S. C., Printed by A. S. Johnston, 1847.
11 p.   [2119

Charlotte and South Carolina Railroad. Superintendent. Rates of freight. Columbia, S. C., June 1st, 1854. [1] p.   [2120

Charlotte, Columbia and Augusta Railroad. The Charlotte, Columbia & Augusta
R. R. Co. cotton case. Columbia, S. C., Presbyterian Publishing House, 1879.
20 p.   [2121

——General rules applying to officers and employees of the Transportation Department. Richmond, Baughman Brothers, pr., 1881. 130 p.   [2122

——Proceedings of stockholders at their annual meeting, 1870- Columbia, S. C.,
1870- NcU has 1870-1884   [2123

——The railroad bill. Columbia, S. C., Presbyterian Publishing House, 1881.
16 p.   [2124

——Resolutions adopted at meeting of Board of Directors, held at Columbia, S. C.,
1st June, 1883. No place, 1883. 3 p.   [2125

Charlotte College, Charlotte, N. C. Catalogue, 194 - Charlotte, 194 - NcU has
1949/50-1954/55   [2126

Charlotte Literary & Library Association. Constitution, by-laws, and regulations,
with the act of incorporation. Charlotte, Hirst Printing Co., 1891. 17 p. [2127

[Charlotte Master Printers Association] The fifth industry, the mother of progress.
[Charlotte] n.d. 13 p.   [2128

Charlotte Medical Journal see Southern Medicine and Surgery

Charlotte Merchants Association, Inc. Report, 192 - [Charlotte, 192 - NcU has
1923/24   [2129

Charlotte News, Charlotte, N. C. Better health for North Carolinians; a factual
survey of state health. Charlotte, February 11, 1947. 51 p.   [2130

——100, 899: the story of "the Queen City of the Carolinas". [Charlotte, 1941]
[32] p.   [2131

Charlotte, North Carolina, city directory, 19 - Asheville, Piedmont Directory Co.,
Inc., 19 - NcU has 1911, 1918, 1923-24   [2132

Charlotte the center, v. 1- 1920- Charlotte, Charlotte Chamber of Commerce,
1920- NcU has v. 1   [2133

Charlotte "the friendly city" and Mecklenburg County, North Carolina, welcome
the General Assembly of North Carolina, in special session, Charlotte, N. C.,
February 22, 1939. [Charlotte? 1939?] 24 p.   [2134

The Charlottean, v. 1, 1932. Charlotte, The Civic Clubs of Charlotte, 1932. NcU
has v. 1   [2135

Charnley, Mitchell Vaughn. The boys' life of the Wright brothers. New York,
Harper & Brothers [c.1928] 291 p.   [2136

Chase, Harry Woodburn. Inauguration of Harry Woodburn Chase, president of
the University of North Carolina. No place, no publisher, n.d. 23 p.   [2137
——State university and the new South; being the proceedings of the inauguration
of Harry Woodburn Chase as president of the University of N. C. Chapel Hill,
April 28, 1920. 104 p.   [2138
——The University and the state. Chapel Hill, Central Alumni Office [1925?]
15 p.   [2139

Chase, Lucien Bonaparte. History of the Polk administration. New York, G. P.
Putnam, 1850. 512 p.   [2140

Chase, Philip Stephen. Battery F, First Regiment Rhode Island Light Artillery in
the Civil War, 1861-1865. Providence, Snow and Farnham, pr., 1892. 332 p. [2141
——Organization and service of Battery F, First Rhode Island Light Artillery, to
January 1st, 1863. Providence, N. Bangs Williams & Co., 1880. (Personal nar-
ratives of events in the war of the rebellion, being papers read before the Rhode
Island Soldiers and Sailors Historical Society, 2d ser., no. 3) 48 p.   [2142

Chase, Richard, ed. Grandfather tales; American-English folk tales. Boston,
Houghton Mifflin Co., 1948. 239 p.   [2143

Chase, Richard, comp. Hullabaloo, and other singing folk games. Boston,
Houghton Mifflin Co., 1949. 57 p.   [2144

Chase, Richard. Jack and the three sillies. Boston, Houghton Mifflin Co., c.1950.
39 p.   [2145

Chase, Richard, ed. The Jack tales, told by R. M. Ward and his kindred in the
Beech Mountain section of Western North Carolina. [Boston] Houghton Mifflin
Co., 1943. 201 p.   [2146
——Old songs and singing games. Chapel Hill, University of North Carolina Press
[c.1938] 52 p.   [2147
——Traditional ballads, songs, and singing games. Chapel Hill, Institute of Folk
Music, 1935. [37] p.   [2148

The Chat, bulletin of the North Carolina Bird Club, v. 1- March, 1937- Raleigh,
1937- NcU has v. 1-19   [2149

Chataigne's North Carolina state directory and gazetteer, 18 - Raleigh, J. H.
Chataigne, 18 - NcU has 1883-84   [2150

Chataigne's Raleigh city directory, 187 - No place, J. H. Chataigne, 187 - NcU
has 1875-76   [2151

Chatham County school news, v. 1- January, 1917- Pittsboro, 1917- NcU has
v. [1-3]   [2152

Chatham Manufacturing Co., Elkin, N. C. Catalogue, 1879- Elkin, Elkin Times
Power Press, 1879- NcU has 1900   [2153

The Chatham Railroad and its connections. No place, no publisher, n.d. 16 p. [2154
——64 p.   [2155

Cheatham, Edwin Goode. Oration delivered before Henderson Lodge, no. 229,
Dec. 27, 1872. Raleigh, John Nichols & Co., pr., 1873. 10 p.   [2156

Cheatham, Thaddeus Ainsley. I believe in life. Pinehurst, privately printed, 1941.
79 p.   [2157

Cheek, John Morgan. An examination of the theory of the organic unity of society.

Raleigh, Edwards and Broughton, 1893. (North Carolina, University Philosophy
Dept. Worth prize thesis. 1893) 27 p. [2158
——The perception of time. [Morganton, Herald] 1891. 13 p. [2159

Cheek, Philip Macon. . . . Seraphic dust. Philadelphia, Dorrance & Co. [1944]
283 p. [2160

Cheek, Roma Sawyer. The pardoning power of the governor of North Carolina.
Thesis (Ph. D.) Duke University. [Durham? Author?] 1932. 188 p. [2161
——Sleeping "Tar-Heels". [Durham, 1956] 95 p. [2162

Chenery, William H. Reminiscences of the Burnside expedition. Providence, R. I.,
The Society, 1905. (Personal narratives of events in the war of the rebellion,
being papers read before the Rhode Island Soldiers and Sailors Historical Society.
7th ser. no. 1) 48 p. [2163

Cherokee Baptist Association. Minutes, 18 - 18 - NcU has 1935, 1936 [2164

Cherokee Historical Association. The Cherokee Historical Association . . . presents Unto these hills, a drama of the Cherokee by Kermit Hunter. [Cherokee]
1950- NcU has 1950-1954 [2165

Cherry, Lina Vandegrift (Denison) Ancestry of my three children. [Little Rock?
Ark.] 1945. 743 p. [2166

Cherry, Noah. The murder of the Worley family in Wayne County, N. C., and the
arrest, trial and execution of Noah Cherry, Robert Thompson and Harris Atkinson.
Goldsboro, Messenger, 1878. 68 p. [2167

Cheshire, Joseph Blount. Address before the one hundred and first annual convention of the Diocese of North Carolina, 1917. Raleigh, Edwards & Broughton,
1917. 26 p. [2168
——Address . . . before the one hundred and second annual convention of the
Diocese of North Carolina, 1918. Raleigh, Edwards & Broughton Printing Co.,
1918. 23 p. [2169
——Address: colonial church history; St. Thomas's Church, Bath, and its colonial
rectors. Raleigh, Bynum Printing Co. [1926] 15 p. [2170

[Cheshire, Joseph Blount] Address of the bishop. No place, no publisher, 1901.
25 p. [2171
—— ——No place, no publisher [1907] 21 p. [2172
—— ——1908. n.d. 24 p. [2173
—— ——1909. n.d. 22 p. [2174
—— ——1910. 21 p. [2175
—— ——1912. 24 p. [2176
—— ——[1913] 24 p. [2177
—— ——[1924] 24 p. [2178

Cheshire, Joseph Blount. Address on the occasion of the dedication of the memorial
vestibule in Christ Church, Raleigh. [Charlottesville, Va., Michie Co., pr.]
1927. 14 p. [2179

[Cheshire, Joseph Blount] Annual address of the bishop. [Raleigh? 1895?] 22 p. [2180
——Appendix A: Address of the bishop. No place, no publisher [1915?] [2181

Cheshire, Joseph Blount. Bishop Cheshire's convention address. No place, no
publisher [1903] 24 p. [2182
——Charge of the bishop. No place, n.d. 9 p. [2183
——The Church in the Confederate States. New York, Longmans, Green, and Co.,
1912. 291 p. [2184

[Cheshire, Joseph Blount] Convention of the Diocese of North Carolina: Address of
the bishop. No place, no publisher, 1911. 64 p. [2185
——Diocese of North Carolina: address of the bishop . . . 1919. Raleigh, Edwards
and Broughton Printing Co., 1919. 23 p. [2186
——Diocese of North Carolina, convention 1900: Address of the bishop. No place,
no publisher [1900?] 24 p. [2187

Cheshire, Joseph Blount, comp. The early conventions, held at Tawborough Anno
Domini 1790, 1793, and 1794. Raleigh, Spirit of the Age, 1882. 29 p. [2188

Cheshire, Joseph Blount. Fifty years of church life in North Carolina; an address
on the fiftieth anniversary of the Rev. Robert B. Drane, D. D. as rector of St.
Paul's Church, Edenton, N. C., All Saints' Day, 1926. Edenton, no publisher,
n.d. 14 p. [2189

[Cheshire, Joseph Blount] Fishers of men; a charge to the clergy of the jurisdiction of Asheville. No place, no publisher, 1896. 9 p. [2190

Cheshire, Joseph Blount. Fragments of colonial church history: 1. Public libraries. No place, no publisher [1886] 14 p. [2191
——Fragments of colonial church history: II. The first settlers of North Carolina not religious refugees. No place, no publisher [1886] 16 p. [2192
——An historical address delivered in Saint Matthew's Church, Hillsboro, N. C. on Sunday, August 24, 1924. [Durham, Christian & King Printing Co., 1925] 35 p. [2193

[Cheshire, Joseph Blount] In memoriam: Mrs. Martha A. Battle. [Raleigh, 1913] [4] p. [2194

Cheshire, Joseph Blount. Milnor Jones, deacon and missionary. Raleigh, Mutual Publishing Co., pr., 1920. 84 p. [2195
——The name of this church . . . address, 1903. No place, no publisher, n.d. 8 p. [2196
——Nonnulla. Chapel Hill, University of North Carolina Press, 1930. 255 p. [2197
——Public worship in the church . . . delivered at the . . . convocations of Raleigh and Charlotte, in October, nineteen hundred and twelve. No place, no publisher, n.d. 26 p. [2198
——Saint Mark's Church, Mecklenburg County, North Carolina. [Charlotte, Southern Printing Co.] 1927. 26 p. [2199
——St. Peter's Church, Charlotte, N. C. [Charlotte, Observer, 1921] 44 p. [2200

[Cheshire, Joseph Blount] ed. Sketches of church history in N. C. Wilmington, Wm. L. DeRosset, Jr., 1892. 456 p. [2201

Cheshire, Joseph Blount. White Haven Parish. No place, no publisher [1885] 39 p. [2202

Chesney, Alexander. Journal. Columbus, Ohio State University, 1921. (Its Bulletin. Oct., 1921. v. 26, no. 4) 166 p. [2203

Chesney, Charles Cornwallis. Essays in military biography. New York, Henry Holt and Co., 1874. 398 p. [2204

Chesney, Louisa (Fletcher) Life of the late General F. R. Chesney by his wife and daughter [Louisa Fletcher Chesney and Jane Chesney O'Donnell] London, Eden, Remington & Co., 1893. 477 p. [2205

Chesnutt, Charles Waddell. The colonel's dream. New York, Doubleday, Page & Co., 1905. 294 p. [2206
——Conjure woman. Boston, Houghton, Mifflin and Co., 1900. 229 p. [2207
—— ——[c.1897-1927] [2208
——The house behind the cedars. Boston, Houghton, Mifflin and Co., 1901. 294 p. [2209
——The marrow of tradition. Boston, Houghton, Mifflin and Co., 1901. 329 p. [2210
——The wife of his youth, and other stories of the color line. Boston, Houghton, Mifflin and Co., 1899. 323 p. [2211

Chesnutt, Helen M. Charles Waddell Chesnutt, pioneer of the color line. Chapel Hill, University of North Carolina Press [1952] 324 p. [2212

[Chester] pseud. The campaigns of a "conqueror". No place, no publisher, n.d. [2] p. [2213

Chester and Lenoir Narrow Gauge Railroad. Proceedings of annual convention of stockholders, 187 - 187 - NcU has 1875 [2214

Cheyney, Edward Gheen. Scott Burton in the Blue Ridge. New York, D. Appleton and Co., 1924. 268 p. [2215
—— ——1926. [2216

Chidsey, Donald Barr. Sir Walter Raleigh. New York, John Day Co. [c.1931] 315 p. [2217

Child, Frank Samuel. An unknown patriot. Boston, Houghton, Mifflin and Co., 1899. 396 p. [2218

Children's Home Society of North Carolina, Greensboro. Report, 19 - 19 - NcU has 1934, 1944-49 (as one) [2219

Chimney Rock Mountains, Inc. Lake Lure. [Charlotte, Queen City Printing Co., 1927?] Folder. [2220

——A new empire in Western North Carolina. [Clinton, S. C., Jacobs & Co., 1924?]
[20] p.   [2221

Chimney Rock Mountains, Inc., owners and developers of Lake Lure. No place,
no publisher [1926?]   19 p.   [2222

Chipman, Luzene. Earnest entreaties and appeals to the unconverted. Raleigh,
Weekly Post, 1852.   192 p.   [2223

——A wonderful revelation of heaven by an angel sent from God. Raleigh, John
Nichols, 1877.   23 p.   [2224

Chowan Baptist Association. Minutes, 180 - 180 - NcU has 1822-1825 [1846-
1912] 1917-1923, 1925-1955   [2225

Chowan Baptist Female Institute   see Chowan College

Chowan College, Murfreesboro, N. C. Catalogue, 18 - Murfreesboro, 18 -
NcU has 1853/54, 1887/88, 1898/99 [1902/03-1907/08] 1909/10-1919/20, 1921/22-
1931/32 [1933/34-1953/54]   [2226

——Views of Chowan College. [Murfreesboro, May, 1922] [1] p.   [2227

Chowan Co., N. C. Chamber of Commerce. Points of interest in Edenton. [Eden-
ton?] n.d. [3] p.   [2228

Chowan Co., N. C. People's Party Executive Committee. People's Party convention. [Edenton] 1900. [1] p.   [2229

Chowan Female Collegiate Institute   see Chowan College

Chowanoka, 19 - [Murfreesboro] Senior Class of Chowan College, 19 - NcU
has 1913   [2230

Chreitzberg, Abel McKee. Early Methodism in the Carolinas. Nashville, M. E.
Church, South, Publishing House, 1897. 364 p.   [2231

Christian Advocate   see North Carolina Christian Advocate

The Christian almanac for North Carolina, 18 - Raleigh, American Tract Society,
18 - NcU has 1828-1830   [2232

Christian Church (Disciples of Christ)   see Disciples of Christ

Christian Church (General Convention) Christian annual, 18 - 18 - NcU has
[1882-1921]   [2233

——Principles and government. Suffolk, Va., Christian Board of Publication, 1867.
120 p.   [2234

—— ——Raleigh [1894]   147 p.   [2235

——Revised ritual of the Christian Church. Raleigh, Raleigh Advocate, 1901.
64 p.   [2236

Christian educator, v. 1- 1896- Durham, Trinity College, 1896- NcU has v. [2] [2237

Christian frontiers, a journal of Baptist life and thought, v. 1-2, January, 1946-
January, 1949. Chapel Hill, Baptist Book Club, 1946-1949. NcU has v. 1-2 [2238

Christie, Susan Cantrill. The Cantrill-Cantrell genealogy. New York, Grafton
Press [c.1908] 271 p.   [2239

Christmas, L. T. An evil router from all the walks of life. Raleigh, Edwards &
Broughton, 1900. 24 p.   [2240

Christy, Samuel Preston, defendant. The Muddy Creek murder mystery. No
place, no publisher, n.d. 128 p.   [2241

Chsite, 19 - Cary, Senior Class of the Cary High School, 1914- NcU has 1916,
1918, 1927   [2242

Chunn, Ida F. Descriptive illustrated guide-book to North Carolina mountains.
New York, E. J. Hale & Son, 1881. 87 p.   [2243

Church, John R. A bird's eye view of God's plan. Winston-Salem [c.1936] 85 p. [2244

Church, William E., comp. A guide book for administrators, executors, collectors,
guardians and trustees. Winston-Salem, Penry-Aitchison Printing Co., 1934.
64 p.   [2245

Church council bulletin, v. 1- September, 1940- [Greensboro] North Carolina
Council of Churches, 1940- NcU has v. 1-16   [2246

Church intelligencer, v. 1-7, March 1, 1860-March 7, 1867. Raleigh, T. S. W. Mott,
1860-1867. NcU has v. [1-7]   [2247

Church Leaders Conference, Blue Ridge, N. C. An appeal to the Christian people of the South; . . . Blue Ridge, N. C., August 18-21, 1920.   No place, no publisher, n.d.   16 p.   [2248

Church messenger, v. 1-   May 18, 1879- Winston, Diocese of North Carolina, 1879- NcU has v. [1-7]   [2249

Church of Scotland.   The larger catechism.   Raleigh, Printed by T. Henderson, June, 1815.   60 p.   [2250

The churches, v. 1- 19 - Salisbury, 19 - NcU has v. [23-26]   [2251

Churchill, Winston.   The crossing.   New York, Macmillan Co., 1904.   598 p. [2252

Churchland, N. C.   High School.   Catalogue, 19 - Churchland, 19 - NcU has [1909/10-1916/17]   [2253

[**Cincinnati, Cumberland Gap, and Charleston Railroad.   Committee to Secure Aid**] Report.   [Morristown, Tenn., June 5, 1869]   10 p.   [2254

Cincinnati, Cumberland Gap, and Charleston Railroad.   Engineer.   A report by the chief engineer.   Washington, Chronicle Publishing Co., n.d.   13 p.   [2255

Cincinnati, Cumberland Gap and Charleston Railroad.   President.   Report, 185 - 185 -   NcU has 1856/57, 1866/67, 1870/71   [2256

[**Citizen and Soldier**] pseud.   To the people of the district of Edenton.   No place, no publisher [1788]   13 p.   [2257

Citizen of North Carolina, pseud.   see **Burgwyn, Henry King, 1764-1877**

Citizen of Pittsylvania, pseud.   A letter to a member of the General Assembly of North Carolina, on the navigation of the Roanoke.   Richmond, Printed by John O'Lynch, 1811.   66 p.   [2258

Citizen of the South, pseud.   see **Wiley, Calvin Henderson**

Citizens' Conference on Education, Greensboro, N. C.   Committee of Twenty-five. Report of the committee . . . appointed at the educational conference, May 4-5, 1920.   No place, no publisher, n.d.   [1] p.   [2259

Citizens of Winston-Salem . . . now we are asked to invest $800,000 in the education of our children.   No place, no publisher [1919?]   6 p.   [2260

City directory and classified business guide, Washington, N. C., 19 - [New Bern, Dunn] 19 - NcU has 1923   [2261

The city of Raleigh.   Raleigh, Edwards & Broughton, 1887.   152 p.   [2262

Civil and military history of Andrew Jackson.   New York, P. M. Davis, 1825. 359 p.   [2263

Claremont College, Hickory, N. C.   Catalogue, 18 - 18 - NcU has [1901/02-1913/14]   [2264

Clarendon, Edward Hyde, 1st earl of.   The life of Edward, earl of Clarendon. Oxford, Clarendon Printing-House, 1759.   523 p.   [2265

Clark, Barrett Harper.   An introduction to the plays of Paul Green.   Reprinted from Lonesome road by Paul Green, New York, Robert M. McBride & Co. [c.1926] 18 p.   [2266

——Paul Green.   New York, Robert M. McBride & Co., 1928.   36 p.   [2267

Clark, Charles C.   Address before the Grand Lodge of North Carolina, A. F. & A. M., annual communication, December 4th, 1871.   Raleigh, Nichols & Gorman, 1872. 14 p.   [2268

Clark, Charles Dunning.   Big Foot, the guide.   New York, Beadle and Co. [1866] 91 p.   [2269

Clark, Charles E.   Prince and boatswain.   Greenfield, Mass., E. A. Hall & Co. [c.1915]   105 p.   [2270

Clark, D. L.   The roving artist.   High Point, c.1895.   127 p.   [2271

Clark, David.   Blue Ridge facts and legends.   Charlotte, Clark Publishing Co. [1955]   132 p.   [2272

Clark, Eva Lee (Turner)   Gill.   New York, Richard R. Smith, 1939.   196 p. [2273

Clark, James W.   An address to the citizens of Edgecombe County in vindication of his vote, as member of the Assembly of 1811.   [Raleigh, Gales and Seaton, 1812] 19 p.   [2274

[**Clark, James W.?**]   Address to the freemen of North Carolina by a member of their late General Assembly.   Raleigh, Gales and Seaton, 1812.   24 p.   [2275

Clark, James W. An appeal from the wishes of an interested to the deliberate judgment of an impartial and constitutional tribunal. Raleigh, Minerva Press by Alexander Lucas, 1814. 30 p. [2276

Clark, Kenneth. An architectural monograph: an Eastern North Carolina town house, the Smallwood-Jones residence. New York, R. F. Whitehead, c.1927. (The white pine series of architectural monographs, v. XIII, no. 3) Paged continuously with the two preceding numbers of this volume of the series, p. 51-72. [2277

Clark, Kenneth Willis. Eight American praxapostoloi. Chicago, University of Chicago Press [1941] 204 p. [2278

Clark, Thomas Dionysius, ed. Travels in the Old South, a bibliography. Norman, University of Oklahoma Press [1956- v. NcU has v. 1-2] [2279

Clark, Victor Selden. History of manufactures in the United States. Washington, D. C., Carnegie Institution of Washington, 1916-28. 2 v. [2280

Clark, Walter, 1846-1924. Address at Cooper Union, New York City, 27 January, 1914: Government by judges. 2d ed. No place, no publisher, n.d. 24 p. [2281

——Address at Richmond, Va., 30 Jan. 1914: Equal suffrage. No place, no publisher, n.d. 18 p. [2282

——Address before the Federation of Women's Clubs, New Bern, N. C., 8 May, 1913: The legal status of women in North Carolina. No place, no publisher, n.d. 23 p. [2283

——Address before the University Law school, Chapel Hill, 25 Jan. 1924. No place, no publisher [1924?] 16 p. [2284

——Address on reform in law and legal procedure . . . before the North Carolina Bar Association at Wrightsville Beach, N. C., Tuesday, June 30, 1914. Wilmington, Wilmington Stamp & Printing Co. [1914?] 16 p. [2285

——Address on the life and services of Gen. William R. Davie, at the Guilford Battle Ground, July 4, 1892. Greensboro, Reece & Elam, pr., 1892. 36 p. [2286

——Address to the law class at the University of North Carolina, 31 January, 1919. [Raleigh, Mitchell Printing Co., 1919] 23 p. [2287

——Ballots for both; an address at Greenville, N. C., 8 Dec. 1916. [Raleigh, Commercial Printing Co.] n.d. 16 p. [2288

——The Bible in the public schools. [Raleigh] no publisher [1913] 2 p. [2289

——Caldwell County, N. C. in the great war of 1861-5; address on the occasion of the unveiling of the monument to the Confederate soldiers from Caldwell County at Lenoir, June 3rd, 1910. Hickory, Clay Printing Co., 1910. 53 p. [2290

——Can a prior registered mortgage acknowledged before a duly appointed and acting deputy clerk, be set aside merely because the deputy happens to be a woman? Dissenting opinion. Raleigh, Edwards & Broughton Printing Co., 1916. 10 p. [2291

——Centennial of the Supreme Court of North Carolina; response to addresses, 4 Jan., 1919. No place, no publisher, n.d. 16 p. [2292

——Chief Justice Clark to Messers. J. C. B. Ehringhaus and L. T. Hartsell. [Raleigh] no publisher [1923] 6 p. [2293

——Chief Justice Merrimon; remarks . . . at the memorial meeting of the bar. Raleigh, Edwards & Broughton, 1893. 8 p. [2294

——Child labor, dangerous place to work in. No place, no publisher, n.d. 5 p. [2295

——Equal suffrage; address before the Equal Suffrage League, Greensboro, N. C., 22 Feb., 1915. No place, no publisher, n.d. 8 p. [2296

——Everybody's book; some points in law. Raleigh, P. M. Hale, 1882. 29 p. [2297

——Gospel of progress; an address at Elon College, N. C., 6 June, 1911. No place, no publisher, n.d. 11 p. [2298

Clark, Walter, 1846-1924, ed. Histories of the several regiments and battalions from North Carolina, in the great war 1861-'65, written by members of the respective commands. Raleigh, E. M. Uzzell, pr., 1901. 5 v. Vols. 2-5 have imprint: Goldsboro, N. C. Nash Brothers pr., 1901. (v. 2 not dated) [2299

Clark, Walter, 1846-1924, comp. History of the Raleigh and Augusta Air-Line Railroad Co. Raleigh, News, 1877. 77 p. [2300

Clark, Walter, 1846-1924. History of the Supreme Court Reports of North Carolina. [Raleigh] no publisher [1918] 2 p. [2301

Clark, Walter, 1846-1924, comp. An index of the cases decided in the Supreme

Court of North Carolina, which have been overruled, modified, limited, explained, denied, doubted, and distinguished.   Raleigh, News, 1876.   32 p.   [2302

Clark, Walter, 1846-1924.   Labor day address . . . at Wilmington, N. C., Sept. 7, 1914.   Roanoke, Va., Industrial Era, 1914.   12 p.   [2303

——Lecture, American Correspondence School of Law; pleading and practice.   Chicago, American Correspondence School of Law [c.1908]   23 p.   [2304

——The legal profession; remarks accepting for the court the portrait of Hon. W. T. Dortch, 23 May, 1916.   Raleigh, Edwards & Broughton, 1916.   5 p.   [2305

——Legal status of women in North Carolina . . . address before the Federation of Women's Clubs, New Bern, N. C., 8 May, 1913.   No place, no publisher, n.d. 24 p.   [2306

——Life and services of Gen. William R. Davie.   Greensboro, Reece and Elam, 1892.   36 p.   [2307

——Memorial address upon the life of General James Green Martin; delivered at Raleigh, N. C., May 10, 1916.   No place, no publisher [1916?]   21 p.   [2308

——Millions of dollars of "tax-free" stocks advertised for sale, but no "tax-free" lands or mules on the market.   [Raleigh, 1920]   4 p.   [2309

——More reason for labor's protest of today than for revolt of our forefathers against Great Britain.   No place, no publisher [1922?]   [4] p.   [2310

——The next constitutional convention of the United States; . . . address before the University of Pennsylvania, at Philadelphia, 27 April, 1906.   Raleigh, E. M. Uzzell & Co., pr., 1906.   22 p.   [2311

——North Carolina at Gettysburg, and Pickett's charge a misnomer; also, Sixty years afterwards and the Rearguard of the Confederacy.   No place, no publisher [1921]   31 p.   [2312

——Old foes with new faces; address before Bar Association of Va. at Hot Springs, Va., 25 August, 1903.   No place, no publisher, n.d.   16 p.   [2313

——On Roanoke Island.   Goldsboro, Nash Brothers, pr. [1902?]   9 p.   [2314

——The papers of Walter Clark.   Chapel Hill, University of North Carolina Press [1948-1950]   2 v.   [2315

——People vs. privilege.   No place, no publisher, n.d.   24 p.   [2316

——Platform of Walter Clark, candidate for U. S. Senate, in the Democratic primary, 5 November, 1912.   Raleigh [1912?]   [1] p.   [2317

——"The right of women to make a living"; dissenting opinion . . . in Bickett vs. Knight.   No place, no publisher, n.d.   9 p.   [2318

——Some of the discriminations against women in North Carolina.   No place, no publisher, n.d.   6 p.   [2319

——Some points in law of every-day use to farmers, merchants and business men generally.   New ed., rev.   Raleigh, P. M. Hale, 1886.   45 p.   [2320

——Suggestions as to taxation.   No place, no publisher, n.d.   [2] p.   [2321

——Taxation; injustice in exempting $500,000,000 or more of stocks . . . in reply to Gov. Bickett.   No place, no publisher [1920]   12 p.   [2322

Clark, Walter, 1885-1933.   Paper presented to the State Federation of Women's Clubs by Walter Clark, Jr. and J. Melville Broughton, Jr.   Raleigh [N. C. Federation of Women's Clubs] 1914.   26 p.   [2323

Clark, William Alexander Graham.   Clark's weave room calculations.   2d ed. [Charlotte, Clark Publishing Co., c.1926]   262 p.   [2324

Clark, William Bell.   Ben Franklin's privateers; a naval epic of the American Revolution.   Baton Rouge, Louisiana State University Press [c.1956]   198 p.   [2325

——The first Saratoga.   Baton Rouge, Louisiana State University Press [c.1953] 199 p.   [2326

Clarke, Dumont.   Scripture thinking.   New York, General Council, Presbyterian Church in the U. S. A., n.d.   26 p.   [2327

Clarke, Ednah Proctor.   An opal; verses.   Boston, Lamson, Wolffe and Co., 1896. 89 p.   [2328

Clarke, Jennie Thornley, comp. and ed.   Songs of the South.   Philadelphia, J. B. Lippincott Co., 1896.   333 p.   [2329

Clarke, Mary Bayard (Devereux)   Clytie and Zenobia.   New York, E. P. Dutton and Co., 1871.   65 p.   [2330

——Mosses from a rolling stone . . . by Tenella [pseud.]   Raleigh, W. B. Smith & Co., 1866.   168 p.   [2331

——Poems. New York, Broadway Publishing Co. [c.1905]   193 p.   [2332

[Clarke, Mary Bayard (Devereux)] comp. Wood-notes; or, Carolina carols . . .
compiled by Tenella. Raleigh, Warren L. Pomeroy, 1854. 2 v.   [2333

Clarke, Mary Patterson. Parliamentary privilege in the American colonies. New
Haven, Yale University Press, 1943. (Yale historical publications. Miscellany,
XLIV)   303 p.   [2334

Clarke, William John. Circular to the freemen of the sixth congressional district of
North Carolina. No place, The Author, June 30, 1849. [1] p.   [2335

——Harp of the south, a poem by a sophomore of the University of N. C. Raleigh,
W. W. Holden, pr., 1846. 8 p.   [2336

Clark's directory of cotton oil mills, 19 - Charlotte, Clark Publishing Co., 19 -
NcU has 1921   [2337

Clark's directory of southern cotton mills, 1912- Charlotte, Clark Publishing Co.,
1912- NcU has [1912-1924] 1926-1945, 1948-1956   [2338

Clarkson, Francis Osborne. St. Andrew's Church, Charlotte, North Carolina.
[Charlotte] 1945. 23 p.   [2339

Clarkson, Heriot. Address at Charlotte, North Carolina, June 10, 1926, graduating
class, Belmont vocational school. [Charlotte? 1926?]   15 p.   [2340

——Address at the Memorial Day exercises of the Johnston Pettigrew Chapter,
United Daughters of the Confederacy, May 10th, 1933, Raleigh, N. C. [Raleigh?
1933?] 12 p.   [2341

——Address at the 71st Founders' Day anniversary exercises of Johnson C. Smith
University, April 7, 1938. [Raleigh ? 1938] 12 p.   [2342

——Address . . . August 8th, 1930, at Georgetown, S. C. No place, no publisher
[1930?] 14 p.   [2343

——Address . . . August 21, 1937, at the eighteenth district bar association meeting
at the Marion Lake Club. [Raleigh? 1937?] 6 p.   [2344

——Address before the Daughters of the American Revolution, Guilford Battle
Chapter, February 21, 1931, at the King Cotton Hotel, Greensboro, N. C. No
place, no publisher, n.d. 18 p.   [2345

——Address . . . before the Woman's Christian Temperance Union on January 16th,
1930, at Charlotte . . . subject: Law enforcement. No place, no publisher, 1930.
20 p.   [2346

——Address . . . presenting the portrait of Justice Alfred Moore of the Supreme
Court of the United States to the Law School of the University of North Carolina,
. . . February 10th, 1934. No place [1934?] 8 p.   [2347

——Address, unveiling at St. Marks Church, memorial tablet to Rt. Rev. Joseph
Blount Cheshire, Jr., and Rev. Edwin Augustus Osborne, . . . November 26th,
1933. [Charlotte? 1933] 5 p.   [2348

——Heroic incidents in the life of Gen. Francis Marion: address delivered at the
banquet of the Society of the Cincinnati . . . at Charlotte, April 19, 1907. Raleigh, Commercial Printing Co. for the Society, 1907. 8 p.   [2349

——Heroic incidents in the life of Gen. Francis Marion; address delivered at the
banquet of the Society of the Cincinnati . . . at Charlotte, Apr. 19, 1907; Part II,
The hornet's nest. [Charlotte, Honeycutt, n.d.] 29 p.   [2350

——History of the Law Library Association of Charlotte, N. C. . . . also, A sketch of
the lawyers of the Mecklenburg County bar. [Charlotte] 1941. 24 p.   [2351

——Memorial to Capt. Samuel A'Court Ashe, in Capitol Square, Raleigh, N. C.
[Raleigh? 1941?] 8 p.   [2352

[Clarkson, Heriot?] Statement as to the foundation of the Church of the Resurrection and Geneva Hall at Little Switzerland, N. C. [Raleigh? 1934?] 4 p. [2353

Clarkson, Heriot. A story of the progress of the kingdom through the Young Men's
Christian Association of the Carolinas . . . at the sixtieth annual meeting and
seventy-seventh anniversary of the organization of the Raleigh Y. M. C. A.,
Saturday, March 28th, 1936. No place, no publisher [1936] [12] p.   [2354

[Clarkson, Mary Osborne] The Church of the Resurrection, Du Bose memorial.
[Little Switzerland, The Church, 1949] 30 p.   [2355

Clarkson, Paul Stephen. A bibliography of William Sydney Porter (O. Henry)
Caldwell, Id., The Caxton Printers, Ltd., 1938. 161 p.   [2356

Clary, John. The trial and conviction of John Clary of Perquimans, for adultery.
No place, printed for the publisher, 1810. 30 p.   [2357

Clason, Augustus Wood. Seven conventions. New York, D. Appleton and Co., 1888. 174 p. [2358

Classroom teachers bulletin, v. 1- March, 1940- [Charlotte?] Department of Classroom Teachers, North Carolina Education Association, 1940- NcU has v. [1-6] [2359

Claude Wayland Wilson, 1867-1922. Raleigh, Edwards & Broughton, 1922. 43 p. [2360

Claxton, Philander Priestley. Effective English, by Philander P. Claxton . . . and James McGinniss. Boston, Allyn and Bacon [c.1922] 553 p. [2361

——The work of the Conference for Education in the South. [Washington, Executive Board of the Southern Conference for Education and Industry, 1914?] [7] p. [2362

Clay, Clifton, pseud. see **Coburn, A. L.**

Clay, Henry. Annexation of Texas; opinions of Messers. Clay, Polk, Benton and Van Buren. No place, no publisher [1844] 16 p. [2363

——Mr. Clay's speech; delivered in the city of Raleigh, April 13th, 1844. No place, no publisher, n.d. 17 p. [2364

——Speeches of the Hon. Henry Clay, at Raleigh, N. C., April 13th, 1844, and of Hon. John M. Clayton, at Wilmington, Del., June 15th, 1844. Hartford, Journal Office Press, 1844. 24 p. [2365

Clayton, Daniel B. Forty-seven years in the Universalist Ministry. Columbia, S. C., 1889. 370 p. [2366

Clayton, Edith May. Fight on for U. S. A.; a Mecklenburg declaration of war. Charlotte, The Author [1941?] [1] p. [2367

Cleland, James Tough. Nisi dominus frustra; baccalaureate sermon- for UNC, Class of 1948. Chapel Hill, Phi Delta Fraternity, 1949. 7 p. [2368

——The true and lively Word. New York, Charles Scribner's Sons, 1954. 120 p. [2369

Clemenceau, Georges Eugène Benjamin. American reconstruction, 1865-1870, and the impeachment of President Johnson. New York, L. MacVeagh, Dial Press, 1928. 300 p. [2370

Clemens, William Montgomery, ed. North and South Carolina marriage records from the earliest colonial days to the Civil War. New York, E. P. Dutton [c.1927] 295 p. [2371

Clements, Marie. Lillian De Vere. Chicago, Scroll Publishing Co. [c.1902] 334 p. [2372

Clemmons, Peter. Poor Peter's call to his children. Salisbury, Printed by Coupee and Crider, 1812. 153 p. [2373

Clemmons School, Clemmons, N. C. Catalogue, 1900/01- Clemmons, 1901- NcU has [1900/01-1911/12] [2374

Clerc, Jean-Louis. Cinq possédés de l'impossible. Lausanne, L'Abbaye du Livre, 1945. 262 p. [2375

Clergy-House Association, Saluda, N. C. The Clergy-House Association, Saluda, North Carolina. [Saluda, Sept. 1907] [3] p. [2376

Cleveland, James M. Biographical sketch of Charles Manly, late governor of North Carolina. Raleigh, Printed at the Office of the Southern Weekly Post, 1853. 11 p. [2377

Cleveland, Sallie (Sadler) Things I remember. [Chapel Hill, 1948] 47 p. [2378

Cleveland College. Executive Committee. Resolution on the death of Dr. A. Caswell Ellis. [Cleveland, 1948] [2] p. [2379

Cleveland Co., N. C. Board of County Commissioners. Delightful homes for thousands in Cleveland County, N. C. Raleigh, Edwards and Broughton, 1884. 12 p. [2380

[**Cleveland Co., N. C. Board of Education**] The public schools of Cleveland County for the year, 190 - Charlotte, 190 - NcU has 1907/08 [2381

Clewell, John Henry. History of Wachovia in North Carolina. New York, Doubleday, Page & Co., 1902. 365 p. [2382

Clewell, John Henry, comp. Jubilee celebration: Fiftieth anniversary of the Rt. Rev. Edward Rondthaler. Salem, Republican Steam Print, 1893. 21 p. [2383

Clewell, John Henry. Moravian Easter, Salem, North Carolina. No place, no publisher, n.d. 16 p. [2384

Clinard, Walter B. Stray poems. [Winston-Salem, Barber Printery, c.1912] 14 p. [2385

Clinchfield Railroad Company. Report of general manager to Atlantic Coast Line Railroad Company and Louisville and Nashville Railroad Company, lessees, first- 1925- [Erwin, Tenn.? 1926- NcU has 1925-1954 [2386

Clinchfield Railroad Company see also Carolina, Clinchfield, and Ohio Railway

Cline, Alvin W. Practical points on probation. Winston-Salem [The Author?] 1935. 64 p. [2387

Clingman, Nixon Poindexter. A poet and his songs: being a memoir of N. P. Clingman, and a selection of his best essays and poems, prefaced by a few poems of his mother, Emily Magee Clingman. Baltimore, Arundel Press, 1900. 153 p. [2388

Clingman, Thomas Lanier. Address. No place, no publisher [1853] 16 p. [2389
——Address at Davidson College, 1873. [Salisbury, J. J. Bruner, 1873] 15 p. [2390
——Address at the commencement of the University of the South . . . August 5th, 1875, at Sewanee, Tennessee. Asheville, F. P. Davis, 1875. 12 p. [2391
——Address . . . on the recent senatorial election. To the freemen of the first congressional district of North Carolina. [Washington] J. & G. S. Gideon, pr. [1849] 16 p. [2392
——Address on the political condition and prospects of the country to the freemen of the eighth congressional district of North Carolina. [Washington, 1856] 8 p. [2393

[**Clingman, Thomas Lanier**] Address to the citizens of North Carolina. Raleigh, March 10, 1870. 16 p. [2394

Clingman, Thomas Lanier. Follies of the positive philosophers; address to the University Normal School of North Carolina . . . Chapel Hill, June 26, 1878. Raleigh, John Nichols, pr., 1878. 25 p. [2395
——Gold Hill Mine in Rowan County, North Carolina. Washington, M'Gill & Witherow, pr., 1875. 13 p. [2396
——Letter [to Dr. Ladson A. Mills] Raleigh, October 8, 1852. [1] p. [2397
——Letter of Hon. T. L. Clingman to his constituents. [Washington, The Author, 1856] 4 p. [2398
——Measurements of the Black Mountain, letter of T. L. Clingman. Washington, G. S. Gideon, pr. [1856] 16 p. [2399
——Memoranda of the late affair of honor between Hon. T. L. Clingman, of North Carolina, and Hon. William L. Yancey, of Alabama. [Washington? 1845] 8 p. [2400
——Selections from the speeches and writings. Raleigh, John Nichols, pr., 1877. 623 p. [2401
—— ——2d ed. 1878. [2402
——State Agricultural Society of N. C., annual address, delivered at the fair grounds, on Thursday, Oct. 21, 1858. Washington, Gideon, pr., n.d. 22 p. [2403
——The tobacco remedy. New York, Orange Judd Co. for the Author, 1885. 42 p. [2404
——Valedictory address to the freemen of the eighth congressional district of North Carolina. Washington, Gideon [1858] 8 p. [2405

Clingman Tobacco Cure Company, Durham, N. C. Clingman's tobacco remedies. Durham, n.d. [3] p. [2406

Clinton, Sir Henry. The American rebellion. New Haven, Yale University Press, 1954. 658 p. [2407
——A letter . . . to the commissioners of public accounts, relative to some observations in their seventh report. London, Printed for J. Debrett, 1784. 31 p. [2408

[**Clinton, Sir Henry**] Memorandums, &c. &c. respecting the unprecedented treatment which the army have met with respecting plunder taken after a siege. London, 1794. 106 p. [2409

Clinton, Sir Henry. Narrative . . . relative to his conduct during part of his command of the King's troops in North America, particularly to that which respects the unfortunate issue of the campaign in 1781. London, Printed for J. Debrett, 1783. 115 p. [2410
——Narrative of the campaign in 1781 in North America. Philadelphia, J. Campbell, 1865. 115 p. [2411
——Observations on Mr. Stedman's History of the American war. London, Printed for J. DeBrett, 1794. 34 p. [2412

——Observations on some parts of the Answer of Earl Cornwallis to Sir Henry Clinton's Narrative. London, Printed for J. Debrett, 1783. 113 p.   [2413

Clinton. N. C.   St. Paul's Episcopal Church.   Dedication of St. Paul's parish house and memorials and celebration of the 124th anniversary St. Paul's organization . . . September 5, 1954.   Clinton, 1954.   18 p.   [2414

Clodhopper, pseud.   see Lawrence, Joshua

Cloudland Hotel, on top of Roan Mountain, in East Tennessee and Western North Carolina.   Buffalo, Matthews, Northrup & Co. [1885?]   Folder.   [2415
——[Memphis, Tenn., B. C. Toof & Co., 1900?]   [20] p.   [2416

Clyde, Paul Hibbert.   The Far East.   New York, Prentice-Hall, 1948.   862 p. [2417

Coat of arms of North Carolina.   Raleigh, E. M. Uzzell, 1889.   8 p.   [2419

Coate, Samuel.   Guide to true happiness.   Newbern, Printed for Jeremiah Mastin and David B. Mintz, 1806.   177 p.   [2420

[Coates, Albert]   Law school association.   No place, no publisher [1928]   18 p. [2421
——Out of a classroom in Chapel Hill.   [Chapel Hill, 1951]   41 p.   [2422

Coates, Albert.   Outline of tentative plan for country, district and statewide schools of governmental officers for the study of governmental institutions and processes in . . . North Carolina.   [Chapel Hill, The Author, 1932?]   62 p.   Country is probably misprint for county.   [2423
——Preliminary draft of a plan for county, district and statewide schools of law enforcing officers.   [Chapel Hill, The Author] n.d.   [7] p.   [2424
——Robert Burton House of Chapel Hill and North Carolina; address.   [Chapel Hill, 1951]   [10] p.   [2425
——Statement, speaking for William B. Umstead, Governor of North Carolina, in presenting the new addition to Venable Hall to the University of North Carolina, 24 October 1953.   [Chapel Hill, 1953]   6 p.   [2426
——The story of the Institute of Government, the University of North Carolina, Chapel Hill.   Bloomington, Ind., National University Extension Association [1944]   (National University Extension Association.   Studies in university extension education, no. 2)   76 p.   [2427
——A task of legal education in North Carolina.   [Chapel Hill, The Author] n.d.   57 p.   [2428

Coatsworth, Elizabeth Jane.   Aunt Flora.   New York, Macmillan and Co., 1953.   64 p.   [2429

Cobb, Collier.   An American man of letters, George Horton, the Negro poet.   [Chapel Hill, The Author, n.d.]   8 p.   [2430
——Evolution and Christianity; address before the Young Men's Christian Association of Waseda University, Tokio, Japan, Nov. 15, 1920.   No place, no publisher, n.d.   4 p.   [2431
——Excerpts from the lectures on human geography.   No place, no publisher, n.d.   [4] p.   [2432
——North Carolina supplement, Tarr and McMurry's New geographies.   New York, Macmillan Co., 1916.   31 p.   [2433
——Pocket dictionary of common rocks and rock minerals.   Chapel Hill, Dept. of Geology, University of North Carolina [c.1914]   37 p.   [2434
—— ——2d ed.   1915.   53 p.   [2435
——Presentation of portrait of Governor Benjamin Smith to the state of North Carolina . . . November 15, 1911, by the North Carolina Society of the Sons of the Revolution; address.   [Raleigh, 1911]   14 p.   [2436
——Topographic features and physiographic processes in relation to North Carolina ports and terminals.   No place, no publisher [1924]   7 p.   [2437

Cobb, Darius.   The novelette number 94, containing the story complete of Adeline Desmond; or, The spy of Newbern.   Boston, Office American Union, Flag of Our Union, and Dollar Monthly [c.1863]   49 p.   [2438

Cobb, Enoch.   The Free Will Baptist hymn book.   Newbern, William G. Hall, 1846.   327 p.   [2439

Cobb, Irvin Shrewsbury.   North Carolina.   New York, George H. Doran Co. [c.1924]   61 p.   [2440

Cobb, Lucy Maria.   Animal tales from the Old North State, by Lucy M. Cobb and Mary A. Hicks.   New York, E. P. Dutton & Co., Inc., 1938.   200 p.   [2441

——To O. Henry. No place, no publisher [c.1922] [1] p. [2442

Cobb, Needham Bryan. Poetical geography of North Carolina, . . . and other poems. Cambridge [Mass.] Riverside Press, 1887. 63 p. [2443

Cobb, Robert A. True life of Maj. Lewis Richard Redmond, the notorious outlaw. Raleigh, Edwards & Broughton, 1882. 32 p. [2444

Cobb, Sanford Hoadley. The rise of religious liberty in America. New York, Macmillan Co., 1902. 541 p. [2445

Cobb, Whitfield, Jr. Study of God and values. Chapel Hill, Dept. of Philosophy, University of North Carolina, 1934. (Studies in philosophy, no. 8) 24 p. [2446

Cobbett, William. Life of Andrew Jackson. New York, Harper & Brothers, 1834. 196 p. [2447

Coble Dairy Products, Inc., Lexington, N. C. New issue, 20,000 shares. Raleigh, Kirchofer & Arnold, 1946. 27 p. [2448

——Report, 19 - Lexington, 19 - NcU has 1946-1953 [2449

Coblentz, Catherine (Cate) Sequoya. New York, Longmans, Green and Co., 1946. 199 p. [2450

Coble's home almanac and rural directory of Guilford county, 19 - Greensboro, Coble, 19 - NcU has 1923, 1925-1930 [2451

Coburn, A. L. The life of Clifton Clay. Charlotte, Ray Printing Co. [1904?] 179 p. [2452

—— ——Raleigh, Christian Sun, 1895. 145 p. [2453

Cochran, Hamilton. Rogue's holiday. Indianapolis, Bobbs-Merrill Co. [1947] 297 p. [2454

Cocke, Norman A. A ten-year review of the work of the Duke Endowment. Charlotte, Duke Endowment [1934?] 11 p. [2455

[Cocke, William M.] Prospectus of the mineral lands of Wm. M. Cocke, Jr., & W. H. Lester, located in the counties of Sevier and Cocke, in Tennessee, and in Swain and Haywood counties, in North Carolina. Asheville, News Print, n.d. 4 p. [2456

Coe, Jeffrey. The picture story of Daniel Boone. New York, Wonder Books, Inc. [c.1956] 64 p. [2457

Coenen, Frederic Edward, ed. Auf höherer Warte; deutsche Dichtungen der Neuzeit. New York, Reynal & Hitchcock [c.1941] 176 p. [2458

Coenen, Frederic Edward. Franz Grillparzer's portraiture of men. Chapel Hill, 1951. (North Carolina. University. Studies in the Germanic languages and literatures, no. 4) 135 p. [2459

Coffey, Laurence H. Thomas Coffey and his descendants. Chattanooga, N. Sanders, 1931. 102 p. [2460

Coffin, Addison. Life and travels. Cleveland, O., W. G. Hubbard, 1897. 570 p. [2461

Coffin, Elijah. The life of Elijah Coffin. No place, E. Morgan & Sons, 1863. 307 p. [2462

Coffin, Helen Watts. Carolina memories. [Kingsville, Texas, Students of the Texas-Mexican Industrial Institute, 1946?] 66 p. [2463

Coffin, Levi. Reminiscences of Levi Coffin, the reputed president of the underground railroad. Cincinnati, R. Clarke & Co. [c.1876] 712 p. [2464

—— ——2d ed. 1880. 732 p. [2465

Coffin, Oscar Jackson. State house anthology. Raleigh, Edwards & Broughton, 1917. 79 p. [2466

Coffin, Percival Brooks. Charles F. Coffin, a Quaker pioneer; preceded by Earliest historical period of the Coffin family, by Mary Coffin Johnson. Richmond, Ind., Nicholson, 1923. 214 p. [2467

Coffman, George Raleigh, ed. Five significant English plays. New York, T. Nelson and Sons, 1930. 433 p. [2468

——Studies in language and literature. Chapel Hill, University of North Carolina Press, 1945. 344 p. First issued as no. 3, vol. XLII (1945) of Studies in philology as its contribution to the sesquicentennial celebration of the University of North Carolina. [2469

Coggins, James Caswell. Abraham Lincoln, a North Carolinian. Asheville, Advocate [1925] 100 p [2470

—— ——2d ed., rev.   Gastonia, Carolina Printing Co., c.1927.   194 p.   [2471
——The eugenics of President Abraham Lincoln.   Milligan College, Tenn., Good-
will Press [c.1940]   284 p.   [2472
——A new philosophy of life. New York, Broadway Publishing Co., 1911. 108 p. [2473
——. . . The star crowned woman.   Robersonville, The Watch Tower, 1915.
64 p.   [2474
Cogswell, Joseph Green.   Life of Joseph Green Cogswell as sketched in his letters.
Cambridge, Mass., privately printed at the Riverside Press, 1874.   377 p.   [2475
Cohen, Sanford.   State labor legislation, 1937-1947.   Columbus, Bureau of Busi-
ness Research, College of Commerce and Administration, Ohio State University
[1948]   150 p.   [2476
Coile, Theodore Stanley.   Relation of soil characteristics to site index of loblolly and
shortleaf pines in the lower Piedmont region of North Carolina.   Durham, 1948.
(Duke University, Durham, N. C.   School of Forestry.   Bulletin 13)   78 p. [2477
——. . . Soil changes associated with loblolly pine succession on abandoned agri-
cultural land of the Piedmont plateau.   Durham [Printed by the Seeman Print-
ery] 1940.   (Duke University.   School of Forestry.   Bulletin 5)   85 p.   [2478
Coit, Charles Guernsey.   The Federal Reserve Bank of Richmond.   New York,
Columbia University Press, 1941.   140 p.   [2479
Coker, Robert Ervin.   Establishment of the Institute of Fisheries Research; a talk
given at . . . Morehead City, October 19, 1949.   [Chapel Hill] 1949.   8 p. [2480
[Coker, Robert Ervin]   The need for research.   [Chapel Hill] 1945.   7 p.   [2481
Coker, Robert Ervin.   Streams, lakes, ponds.   Chapel Hill, University of North
Carolina Press [1954]   327 p.   [2482
——This great and wide sea.   Chapel Hill, University of North Carolina Press [1947]
325 p.   [2483
—— ——Rev. ed. [c.1949]   [2484
Coker, William Chambers.   The Boletaceae of North Carolina, by William Cham-
bers Coker and Alma Holland Beers.   Chapel Hill, The University of North Caro-
lina Press, 1943.   96 p.   [2485
——The Clavarias of the United States and Canada.   Chapel Hill, University of
North Carolina Press, 1923.   209 p.   [2486
——The Gasteromycetes of the eastern United States and Canada, by William
Chambers Coker and John Nathaniel Couch.   Chapel Hill, University of North
Carolina Press, 1928.   201 p.   [2487
——Laboratory guide in general botany, by William Chambers Coker and Henry
Roland Totten.   Chapel Hill, The Authors, 1920.   70 p.   [2488
—— ——Rev. ed. 1926.   75 p.   [2489
—— ——3d ed.   1931.   97 p.   [2490
——The plant life of Hartsville, S. C.   Columbia, State Co., 1912.   129 p.   [2491
——The Saprolegniaceae, with notes on other water molds.   Chapel Hill, Uni-
versity of North Carolina Press, 1923.   201 p.   [2492
——The stipitate hydnums of the eastern United States, by William Chambers
Coker and Alma Holland Beers.   Chapel Hill, University of North Carolina Press,
1951.   211 p.   [2493
Coker, William Chambers, ed.   Studies in science.   Chapel Hill, University of
North Carolina Press, 1946.   375 p.   [2494
Coker, William Chambers.   The trees of North Carolina, by W. C. Coker and H. R.
Totten.   Chapel Hill, W. C. Coker, 1916.   106 p.   [2495
—— ——Key to the Trees of N. C.   [Chapel Hill] n.d.   18 p.   [2496
——Trees of the Southeastern States . . . by William Chambers Coker and Henry
Roland Totten. Chapel Hill, University of North Carolina Press, 1934. 399 p. [2497
—— ——2d ed.   1937.   417 p.   [2498
Cole, Arthur Charles.   The Whig party in the South.   Washington, American
Historical Association, 1913.   392 p.   [2499
Cole, Henderson.   New Hanover County and the city of Wilmington, North Caro-
lina.   Wilmington, Merchants' Association [190?]   19 p.   [250(
Cole, James Reid.   Miscellany.   Dallas, Texas, Press of Ewing B. Bedford, 1897
303 p.   [250
Cole, Taylor.   The Canadian bureaucracy, a study of Canadian civil servants an(

other public employees, 1939-1947. Durham, Duke University Press, 1949. 292 p.   [2502
——European political systems. New York, A. A. Knopf, 1953. 699 p.   [2503
Coleman, Charles Thaddeus   see Stanley, Win, pseud.
Coleman, Elliott.   . . . An American in Augustland. Chapel Hill, University of North Carolina Press [c.1940] 82 p.   [2504
Coleman, Roy V.   Liberty and property. New York, Charles Scribner's Sons, 1951. 606 p.   [2505
[Coleman, Thaddeus Charles]   The Land of the Sky. [Asheville, Furman's Print] n.d. 22 p.   [2506
Coleman, William Macon.   An epitome of Fearne on contingent remainders and executory devises. Philadelplia, T. & J. W. Johnson & Co., 1878. 105 p.   [2507
——The history of the primitive Yankees. Washington, Columbia Publishing Co., 1881. 62 p.   [2508
——Jesus a revolutionary socialist. 2d ed. Washington, no publisher, n.d. 17 p. [2509
——The snare of the men and religion forward movement. Washington, no publisher [1912?] 23 p.   [2510
Coleraine, George Hanger, 4th baron.   An address to the army; in reply to strictures, by Roderick M'Kenzie . . . on Tarleton's History of the campaigns of 1780 and 1781. London, Printed for J. Ridgway, 1789. 138 p.   [2511
[College English Association. North Carolina, Virginia, West Virginia Division] Training in English for leadership in business. [Raleigh, Dept. of English at State College, 1954] 30 p.   [2512
College message, v. 1- 188 - Greensboro, Students of Greensboro College for Women, 1886- NcU has v. [2-12, 18, 24, 28-30]   [2513
Collins, George.   Short account of the rise and progress of the African M. E. Church in America, by Christopher Rush with . . . George Collins. New York, The Author, 1866. 106 p.   [2514
Collins, Hugh W.   To the voters of the 1st congressional district. Edenton, July 26, 1839. [1] p.   [2515
[Collins, James Potter]   Autobiography of a Revolutionary soldier. Clinton, La., Feliciana Democrat, pr., 1859. 176 p.   [2516
Collins, Willis E.   Sententia. [Flat Rock? 1931?] 27 p.   [2517
Collins, Winfield Hazlitt.   The domestic slave trade of the Southern States. New York, Broadway Publishing Co. [1904] 154 p.   [2518
Collins' travelbook of North Carolina, 194 - [Winston-Salem, Collins Co.] 1947- NcU has 1950, 1951, 1953-54—1956-57   [2519
Col. W. T. Jones of Carthage . . . our candidate. No place, no publisher, n.d. 3 p.   [2520
Colonial churches. Richmond, Southern Churchman, 1907. 319 p.   [2521
Colonial Dames of America. North Carolina Society. Addresses delivered under the auspices of the North Carolina Society of the Colonial Dames of America, 1900-1926. [Wilmington, 1926?] 192 p.   [2522
——By-laws and directory, 1904-5. [Wilmington, Wilmington Stamp Works, pr., 1905?] 34 p.   [2523
——Constitution and by-laws; officers and members. Wilmington [The Society] 1903. 28 p.   [2524
—— ——1913. 30 p.   [2525
—— ——1921. 32 p.   [2526
—— ——1927. 33 p.   [2527
—— ——1936. 36 p.   [2528
——Constitution of the National Society with by-laws of the Society of Colonial Dames of North Carolina. Wilmington, Jackson and Bell Co., 1898. 23 p. [2528a
——Eligibility list and qualification to membership. No place, The Society, n.d. 4 p.   [2529
[Colonial Dames of America. North Carolina Society] The fourth house. [Winston-Salem, 1948?] [2] p.   [2530
Colonial Dames of America. North Carolina Society. Historical addresses, delivered at the ruins of Saint Philip's church. [Wilmington] 1901. [46] p.   [2531

——Historical papers on Cabarrus County, North Carolina. No place, 1935-36. Various paging. [2532

——Jamestown day for the public schools of North Carolina. [Wilmington, 1907] 15 p. [2533

——Minutes of the annual meeting, 1894- 1894- NcU has 1896-1900, 1906-1955 [2534

——The North Carolina Society of the Colonial Dames of America, 1900. Wilmington, Jackson & Bell, 1900. 58 p. [2535

—— ————Supplement no. 1, 1900-1904. Wilmington, DeRosset Press, 1904. 43 p. [2536

[Colonial Dames of America. North Carolina Society] Orton plantation. [Wilmington? n.d.] [4] p. [2537

Colonial Dames of America. North Carolina Society. Presentation and unveiling of the tablet commemorating the Mecklenburg Declaration of Independence, May 20th, 1775 . . . Raleigh . . . May 20th, 1912. No place, no publisher, 1912. [2] p. Program. [2538

——Register. Raleigh, Printed for the Society, 1912. 233 p. [2540

—— ————Wilmington, 1924. 289 p. [2541

—— ————1939. 378 p. [2542

——Rules for candidates. Wilmington, 1937. [3] p. [2543

——Supplement to Register, North Carolina Society, Colonial Dames, 1927. [Wilmington?] n.d. 49 p. [2544

Colter, John R. The town that found itself. New York, Community Service National Headquarters [1919?] 16 p. [2545

Colton, Arthur Willis. Bennie Ben Cree. New York, Doubleday & McClure, 1900. 138 p. [2546

Colton, Henry E. Andrew Jackson's place in history; an address . . . over WSM Nashville, Tennessee, March 15, 1938, under auspices of Ladies' Hermitage Association. [Nashville, Tenn.?] Ladies' Hermitage Association [1938?] [6] p. [2547

——Guide book to the scenery of Western North Carolina. Asheville, Printed at the Western Advocate Office, 1860. 16 p. [2548

——Mountain scenery; the scenery of the mountains of Western North Carolina and Northwestern South Carolina. Raleigh, W. L. Pomeroy, 1859. 111 p. [2549

Colton, Simeon. An address delivered at his inauguration to the presidency of Mississippi College, July 30, A. D. 1846. Jackson, Southron Office, 1846. 29 p. [2550

——Address delivered before the Philomathesian and Euzelian societies, in Wake Forest College June 16, 1842. Fayetteville, Edward J. Hale, pr., 1842. 22 p. [2551

——Documents connected with the trial of the Rev. Simeon Colton; printed by order of Fayetteville Presbytery. Fayetteville, Edward J. Hale, pr., 1839. 107 p. [2552

Columbian University, Washington, D. C. In memory of Emil Alexander de Schweinitz . . . March 5, 1904. [Washington, Judd and Detweiler] n.d. 38 p. [2553

Columbus, pseud. see Orne, Henry

Columbus Baptist Association. Minutes, 189 - 189 - NcU has 1892, 1897, 1937-1939, 1943, 1948, 1953 [2554

Columbus Co., N. C. Board of Education. A pamphlet of information issued for the benefit of teachers, school-committeemen, and others. [Whiteville, 1909] 18 p. [2555

——Report of the Public Schools of Columbus County, 191 / - [Whiteville?] 191 - NcU has 1915/16 [2556

Columbus Co., N. C. Development Committee. Columbus County, North Carolina. [Whiteville, 1950] 48 p. [2557

[Colwell, Joseph] Address to the people of the United States on the subject of the presidential election. No place, Printed for the Proprietor, 1828. 47 p. [2558

Colyar, Arthur St. Clair. Life and times of Andrew Jackson. Nashville, Tenn., Marshall & Bruce Co., 1904. 2 v. [2559

Colyer, Vincent. Report of the Christian mission to the United States army . . . from April 1861 to Aug. 1862. New York, George A. Whitehorne, pr. [1862?] 24 p. [2560

——Report of the services rendered by the freed people to the United States army in North Carolina in the spring of 1862.   New York, The Author, 1864.   63 p.   [2561

Comitatus, Zedekiah, pseud.   Reconstruction on "my policy".   Skaggaddahunk, Scantlewood, Timberlake & Co., 1866.   29 p.   [2562

Commemoration of the close of twenty-one years of pastorate of Charles F. Deems. New York, Wilbur B. Ketcham, 1887.   48 p.   [2563

Commercial directory; containing a topographical description, extent and productions of different sections of the Union.   Philadelphia, J. C. Kayser & Co., 1823.   242 p.   [2564

Commission on Inter-racial Cooperation.   Cooperation in southern communities. Atlanta, Ga. [c.1921]   67 p.   [2565
——Progress report for Virginia and North Carolina.   No place, 1935.   [6] p.   [2566

Committee of Editors and Writers of the South.   Voting restrictions in the 13 southern states.   [Atlanta, 1945]   [26] p.   [2567

Communist Party of the United States of America.   Carolina District.   Bulletin, v. 1-   December, 1940-   Greensboro, 1940-   NcU has v. [1-3]   [2568
——Don't let this happen to you.   Winston-Salem [1949]   [1] p.   [2569

Community Chests and Councils, Inc.   Survey, social welfare problems and agencies, Durham, North Carolina, conducted April 14 to May 15, 1941.   [New York? 1941]   101 p.   [2570
——Welfare portrait of Asheville, North Carolina.   [New York?] 1940.   87 p.   [2571

Community Council of Charlotte and Mecklenburg County.   Directory of social resources of Charlotte and Mecklenburg County, 1946.   Charlotte [1946] 37 p.   [2572

Community health, v. 1-   194 -   Chapel Hill, Hospital Saving Association, 194 - NcU has v. [6-10]   [2573

Compagnie de Wilmington.   Prospectus.   [Paris? 1797]   4 p.   NcU has photostat (negative) of original in Library of Congress.   [2574

A compendium of logic for the use of the sophomore class in Davidson College. Charlotte, Smith for Class of 1870, Davidson College, 1870.   47 p.   [2575

Compher, C. Morgan.   The challenge of Jesus.   Lynchburg, Va., Dulaney-Boatwright Co., pr., n.d.   9 p.   [2576
——Notes of the Christmas music.   No place, no publisher, n.d.   11 p.   [2577

Compton, Lucius Bunyan.   Life of Lucius B. Compton, the mountain evangelist. Cincinnati, Office of God's Revivalist [c.1903]   102 p.   [2578

Concerning the Clark-Kilgo matter.   No place, no publisher [1898?]   [2] p.   [2579

A concise system of farriery.   Newbern, J. C. Osborn & Co., 1798.   186 p.   NcU has photostat of original in American Antiquarian Society Library.   [2580

Concord, N. C.   Cabarrus Memorial Hospital.   Volunteers.   The volunteers' cook book.   Concord, 1953.   118 p.   [2581

Concord, N. C.   Corbin St. School.   Sixth Grade.   A short history of Cabarrus County and Concord.   [Concord, Snyder Printing Co.] 1933.   60 p.   [2582

Concord, N. C.   Forest Hill Methodist Episcopal Church.   Official directory and register of membership for the year 1892.   Greensboro, Thomas Bros., pr., 1892. 24 p.   [2583

Concord, N. C.   Ordinances, etc.   The code of the city of Concord, North Carolina, 1947.   Charlottesville, Va., Michie City Publications Co., 1947.   203 p.   [2584

Concord, North Carolina, city directory, 19 -   Asheville, Piedmont Directory Co., inc., 19 -   NcU has 1916-17, 1922-23   [2585

Concord Presbytery   see **Presbyterian Church in the U. S. Synod of North Carolina. Concord Presbytery**

Concordia College, Conover, N. C.   Catalogue, 18 -   Conover, 18 -   NcU has [1887/88-1918/19]   [2586

Conduct of the administration.   Boston, Stimpson & Clapp, 1832.   86 p.   [2587

Cone, Bernard M.   Some present day problems of the textile industry, February 3, 1930.   No place, no publisher [1930]   [19] p.   [2588

Cone Export & Commission Co.   Half century book, 1891-1941.   [Greensboro, c.1941]   [45] p.   [2589

Cone Mills Corporation, Greensboro, N. C.   The story of Cone denim.   Greensboro, 1950.   [22] p.   [2590

A Confederate, pseud.   The grayjackets: and how they lived, fought and died for Dixie.   Richmond, Va., Jones Brothers & Co. [c.1867]   574 p.   [2591

The Confederate boarding house, no. 15, Fayetteville Street, Raleigh, N. C.   No place, no publisher [186?]   [1] p.   [2592

The Confederate cruiser Shenandoah.   New York, Powers, MacGowan & Slipper, pr., 1873.   13 p.   [2593

Confederate Memorial Literary Society, Richmond, Va.   Confederate Museum. Catalogue, North Carolina Room of the Confederate Museum.   Richmond, Va., Dietz Printing Co., 1933.   53 p.   [2594

Confederate Memorial Literary Society, Richmond, Va.   Southern Historical Manuscripts Commission.   A calendar of Confederate papers, with a bibliography. Richmond, Va., The Confederate Museum, 1908.   620 p.   [2595

Confederate Veterans   see United Confederate Veterans

Confederated Southern Memorial Association.   History of the Confederated Memorial Associations of the South.   Rev. and authorized ed.   [New Orleans, Graham Press, 1904]   318 p.   [2596

Confederates insulted.   No place, no publisher [1900?]   2 p.   [2597

Conference for Education in the South.   Proceedings of the 1st-16th Conference, 1899-1913.   Raleigh, 1899-1913.   NcU has 1899-1901, 1903-1913   [2598

Conference for Progressive Labor Action.   The Marion murder . . . funeral addresses by Francis J. Gorman . . . Tom Tippett . . . A. J. Muste.   New York, 1929.   (Progressive labor library.)   Pamphlet no. 2)   17 p.   [2599

Conference of Superior Court Judges of North Carolina.   Proceedings, 1956-   Raleigh, 1956-   NcU has 1956   [2600

Conference of Teachers and Friends of Education, Raleigh, N. C., 186?   Address to the people of North Carolina.   No place, no publisher [186?]   15 p.   [2601

Conference of York Rite Masons, Asheville.   To the several subordinate chapters, councils, and commanderies throughout North Carolina. No place, n.d. 8 p. [2602

Conference on the Measurement of County Income.   County income estimates for seven Southeastern States.   Charlottesville, Bureau of Population and Economic Research, University of Virginia, 1952.   246 p.   [2603

Conference on the Measurement of County Income.   Technical Committee. Methods for estimating income payments in counties; a technical supplement to County income estimates for seven Southeastern States.   Charlottesville, Bureau of Population and Economic Research, University of Virginia, 1952.   108 p. [2604

Conference on Negro Education in N. C., Raleigh, N. C., Nov. 3, 1923.   Conference on Negro education in North Carolina, Shaw University. [Raleigh] 1923. 8 p. [2605

Conference on Regional Planning and Development, Chapel Hill, Nov. 18-19, 1950. Regional planning and development.   Chapel Hill, Department of City and Regional Planning and the Institute for Research in Social Science, University of North Carolina, 1951.   82 p.   [2606

Conference on Research and Regional Welfare, University of North Carolina, 1945. Research and regional welfare.   Chapel Hill, University of North Carolina Press, 1946.   229 p.   [2607

Congregational and Christian Churches, Inc.   Southern Convention.   Minutes of the thirty-fourth regular session . . . Greensboro, North Carolina, April 30 to May 2, 1940.   [Greensboro? 1940]   47 p.   [2608

Congregational Churches.   North Carolina.   Minutes, 187 - 187 - NcU has [1883-1920]   [2609

Connecticut.   General Assembly.   Addresses delivered in the Senate and House of Representatives of Connecticut, in honor or Colonel Charles L. Russell.   New Haven, Babcock & Sizer, State Printers, 1862.   35 p.   [2610

Connelly Springs Co.   Prospectus of the Connelly Springs Co., Connelly Springs P. O., Western N. C. Division, Richmond and Danville Railroad.   Salisbury, Herald, 1892.   18 p.   [2611

Connery, Robert Hough. The Navy and the industrial mobilization in World War II. Princeton, N. J., Princeton University Press, 1951. 527 p. [2612

Connolly, Paul, pseud. see Wicker, Tom

Connor, Henry Groves. Address presenting the portrait of Hon. William T. Dortch to the Supreme Court of North Carolina, and its acceptance . . . by Chief Justice Walter Clark. Raleigh, Edwards & Broughton, 1916. 18 p. [2613

——The constitution of the state of North Carolina, annotated by H. G. Connor and J. B. Cheshire, Jr. Raleigh, Edwards & Broughton Printing Co., 1911. 510 p. [2613a

——George Davis . . . delivered at the unveiling of a statue of George Davis at Wilmington, N. C., April 20, 1911. [Wilmington? 1911?] 53 p. [2614

——George Howard, 1829-1905; an address . . . Feb. 13, 1917. Raleigh, Edwards & Broughton, 1917. 19 p. [2615

——John Archibald Campbell; annual address delivered before the Alabama State Bar Association. Birmingham, no publisher, 1917. 54 p. [2616

——John Archibald Campbell, associate justice of the United States Supreme Court, 1853-1861. Boston, Houghton Mifflin Co., 1920. 310 p. [2617

——Paper read before the Society of the Colonial Dames of N. C., at their annual pilgrimage to St. Philips Church, Old Brunswick . . . July 6th, 1902. Goldsboro, Nash Brothers pr. [1902?] 23 p. [2618

——Remarks upon the opening of the Federal court room, Raleigh, N. C., Jan. 18, 1915, and in accepting the portraits of Hon. Asa Biggs and Hon. George W. Brooks. Raleigh, Edwards & Broughton Printing Co., 1915. 25 p. [2619

——Sketch of the constitutions of the state of North Carolina. Raleigh, Edwards & Broughton Printing Co., 1911. 35 p. [2620

Connor, Robert Digges Wimberly. Address on Alfred Moore Scales . . . May 10, 1907. Raleigh, E. M. Uzzell & Co., pr., 1907. 33 p. [2622

——. . . Ante-bellum builders of North Carolina. [Greensboro] The College, 1914. (North Carolina State Normal & Industrial College. Historical publications, no. 3) 149 p. [2623

——Cornelius Harnett; an essay in North Carolina history. Raleigh, Edwards & Broughton Printing Co., 1909. 209 p. [2624

Connor, Robert Digges Wimberly, comp. A documentary history of the University of North Carolina, 1776-1799. Chapel Hill, University of North Carolina Press, 1953. 2 v. [2625

Connor, Robert Digges Wimberly. History of North Carolina. v. 1. The colonial and Revolutionary periods, 1584-1783. Chicago, Lewis Publishing Co., 1919. v. 1 of 6 volumes published with title History of North Carolina. [2626

——The life and speeches of Charles Brantley Aycock, by R. D. W. Connor and Clarence Poe. Garden City, N. Y., Doubleday, Page & Co., 1912. 369 p. [2627

——Makers of North Carolina history. Raleigh, Thompson Publishing Co., 1911. 317 p. [2628

—— ——Supplementary pages. 1921. 20 p. [2629

—— ——2d ed. Raleigh, Alfred Williams and Co., 1930. 350 p. [2630

——Memorial day, an interpretation; an address before the John W. Dunham Chapter of the United Daughters of the Confederacy at Wilson, N. C., May 11. 1909. Raleigh, Edwards & Broughton Printing Co., n.d. 22 p. [2631

——North Carolina; address at the commencement of Goldsboro High School . . . May 26, 1911. Goldsboro, Goldsboro Argus, pr., 1911. 8 p. [2632

——North Carolina, rebuilding an ancient commonwealth, 1584-1925. Chicago, American Historical Society, Inc., 1929. 4 v. [2633

—— ——Special limited [biographical] supplement. 1927. 322 p. [2634

——North Carolina's priority in the demand for a Declaration of Independence. [Raleigh, 1909] 23 p. [2635

——"Our federal archives"; speech . . . broadcast over a nation-wide network of the National Broadcasting Company . . . November 25, 1935. [Washington] The Evening Star, 1935. [6] p. [2636

——. . . Race elements in the white population of North Carolina. [Raleigh] The College, 1920. (North Carolina State Normal & Industrial College. Historical publications, no. 1) 115 p. [2637

——. . . Revolutionary leaders of North Carolina. [Greensboro] The College, 1916.] (North Carolina State Normal and Industrial College. Historical publications, no. 2) 125 p. [2638

——Samuel Johnston, governor of North Carolina. Raleigh, Edwards & Broughton Printing Co., 1912. 29 p. [2639

——A state experiment in higher education; an address delivered at . . . the University of North Carolina . . . December 4, 1946. Chapel Hill, Committee on Convocations and Lectures of the University of North Carolina [1947] 15 p. [2640

——A state library building and department of archives and records; an address . . . before the North Carolina Literary and Historical Association at Raleigh, November 15, 1906. Raleigh, Edwards & Broughton Printing Co. [1906] 20 p. [2641

——The story of the Old North State. Philadelphia, J. B. Lippincott Co. [c.1906] 180 p. [2642

——The story of the United States, for young Americans. Raleigh, Thompson Publishing Co., 1916. 403 p. [2643

—— ——Supplementary pages. 1921. 15 p. [2644

Conrad, Donald Williams. The golden censer. New York, Fleming H. Revell Co. [c.1932] 106 p. [2645

Conrad, Earl. Gulf Stream north. Garden City, N. Y., Doubleday, 1954. 253 p. [2646

Conrad Hill Gold and Copper Company, Baltimore. Prospectus. Baltimore, The Sun, 1881. 16 p. [2647

Constantine, Gus A., ed. Bibliography of materials on state and local history in North Carolina. Durham, Duke University, Department of Education [1954] 8 p. [2648

Contempo; a review of books and personalities, v. 1-3, May, 1931-February 15, 1934. Chapel Hill [Contempo, Ltd.] 1931-1934. NcU has v. 1-3. [2649

Contempo, v. 4, no. 1-2, April-May, 1933. Durham, Contempo, 1933. NcU has v. 4, no. 1-2. Published under same name and simultaneously with above periodical published at Chapel Hill. [2650

Contentnea Baptist Association. Minutes, 18 - 18 - NcU has 1831-1847, 1871, 1886, 1889, 1893, 1895 [1899-1937] [2651

Continental Plant Company, Kittrell, North Carolina. Modern methods in growing strawberries, blackberries, dewberries . . . etc., and also how to can and preserve. Richmond, Va., W. C. Hill, pr., n.d. 96 p. [2652

Conval, Ronleigh de, pseud. see Pollock, John Alfred

Convention for the Purpose of Memorializing Congress on the Subject of Reopening Roanoke Inlet, Edenton, N. C., Feb. 1830. Proceedings. No place, no publisher [1830?] 4 p. [2653

Convention of Northern Residents of the South, Charlotte, N. C., January 15, 1879. What northern men say of the South. Charlotte, Observer, pr., 1879. 63 p. [2654

Convention of Teachers of the Confederate States, Columbia, S. C., 1863. Proceedings . . . April 28th, 1863. Macon, Ga., Burke, Boykin & Co., 1863. 19 p. [2655

Convention of the Representatives of the Railroad Lines between Washington and Kingsville, S. C. Proceedings of a railroad convention held at Richmond, Va., Apr. 3rd and 4th, 1867. Richmond, Gary & Clemmitt, pr., 1867. 8 p. [2656

Convocation of Raleigh see **Raleigh Convocation**

Conway, C. B. History 119th Infantry, 60th Brigade, 30th Division, U. S. A.; operations in Belgium and France, 1917-1919. [Compiled by C. B. Conway and George A. Shuford] Wilmington, Chamber of Commerce [1920] 140 p. [2657

Conway, James H. The North Carolina calculator. Salisbury, Printed by J. Krider, 1819. 238 p. [2658

Conway, Katherine Pendleton. Random thoughts. No place, 1953. 13 p. [2659

Conway, N. C. Parent-Teacher Association. History of Conway School District, 1870-1951. Conway, 1951. 62 p. [2660

Conyngham, David Power. Sherman's march through the South. New York, Sheldon and Co., 1865. 431 p. [2661

Coogler and Dugger. No place, no publisher, n.d. 3 p. [2662

Cook, Charles Thomas. The Billy Graham story. Wheaton, Ill., Van Kampen Press [1954] 128 p. [2663

Cook, Claiborn. Reply to Doctor Hare. No place, no publisher [1819] 6 p. [2664

Cook, Dyrus. Donkeying through seven states. No place, privately printed, 1933. 55 p. [2665

Cook, Earl A. . . . Cook history and genealogy of families in, or originating in, North Carolina from 1760 to 1941. [2d ed.] Albemarle, The Church Press [1941] 92 p. [2666

Cook, Mrs. James P. see **Cook, Margaret Norfleet**

Cook, John Harrison. A study of the mill schools of North Carolina. New York, Teachers College, Columbia University, 1925. (Its Contributions to education, no. 178) 56 p. [2667

Cook, Margaret Norfleet. Captain John Cowper, Revolutionary patriot. No place, no publisher, 1926. 8 p. [2668

Cook, Olan Victor, comp. Incunabula in the Hanes Collection of the Library of the University of North Carolina. Chapel Hill, 1940. (Hanes Foundation publications, no. 1) 125 p. [2669

[Cook, Staley A.] "Men of affairs" in the public-industrial life of Burlington and North Carolina. [Burlington?] D. C. Johnson [1940?] 80 p. [2670

Cooke, Arthur Wayland. Independent Church of God of the Juda Tribe of Israel, the black Jews. No place, no publisher [c.1925] 32 p. [2671

Cooke, C. L. To the voters of the 7th congressional district of North Carolina. No place [1882] [1] p. [2672

Cooke, Charles S. The Governor, Council, and Assembly in royal North Carolina. Chapel Hill, 1912. (James Sprunt historical publications; pub. under the direction of the North Carolina Historical Society, v. 12, no. 1) p. [5]-40 [2673

Cooke, Dennis Hargrove. Humanizing educational administration. 2d preliminary ed. [Nashville] c.1944. 131 p. [2674

——The white superintendent and the Negro schools in North Carolina. Nashville, Tenn., George Peabody College for Teachers, 1930. (Contribution to education, pub. under the direction of George Peabody College for Teachers. no. 73) 176 p. [2675

Cooke, William D., comp. Revolutionary history of North Carolina, in three lectures, by Rev. Francis L. Hawks . . . Hon. David L. Swain . . . and Hon. Wm. A. Graham. Raleigh, W. D. Cooke, 1853. 236 p. [2676

Cool, R. C. The scuppernong grape, its growth and care. Raleigh, Edwards & Broughton Printing Co., 1913. 15 p. [2677

Coon, Charles Lee. Course of study for primary schools (four years). Charlotte, Observer, 1901. 39 p. [2678

——Facts about southern educational progress. No place, no publisher [pref. 1905] 124 p. [2679

——First year: Spelling and preparation for reading. Charlotte, Observer, 1901. 2 v. [2680

Coon, Charles Lee, ed. The handy register; ed. by Charles L. Coon and J. A. Matheson. Greensboro, Wills Book and Stationery Co., n.d. Unpaged. [2681

Coon, Charles Lee. Hints and suggestions for the teaching of drawing in graded and ungraded schools. New York, Silver, Burdett & Co. [c.1902] 15 p. [2682

——Need of a constructive educational policy for North Carolina; being the president's address before the N. C. Teachers' Assembly, Raleigh, Nov. 30th, 1911. No place, no publisher [pref. 1911] 14 p. [2683

——The North Carolina public school register. [Raleigh, E. M. Uzzell & Co., 1912. Unpaged. [2684

—— ——[1915] [2685

[Coon, Charles Lee] The 1000 words Ayers' list, World and Everyday speller compared. [Wilson? Charles L. Coon, 1919] 7 p. [2686

Coon, Charles Lee. Our responsibility to the Negro. New York, American Missionary Association [1913?] 12 p. [2687

——Public schools of Wilson County, North Carolina, ten years, 1913-14 to 1923-24. [Wilson, Barrett for Board of Education of Wilson County] 1924. 100 p. [2688

——Public taxation and Negro schools; paper read before the twelfth Annual Conference for Education in the South . . . Atlanta, Ga. April 14, 15, and 16, 1909. Cheyney, Pa., Committee of Twelve for the Advancement of the Interests of the Negro Race, n.d. 11 p. [2689

——Suggestions and omissions, Milne arithmetics I-III. No place, no publisher [1919] 9 p. [2690

[Coon, Charles Lee] Test questions on Rapeer's How to teach the elementary subjects, and Colvin's High school teaching. [Wilson? The Author, 1919] 10 p. [2691
——Test questions on the North Carolina school law. [Wilson? 1919] 8 p. [2692

Coon, Charles Lee. Useful phonic facts. [Wilson, The Author, Oct., 1923] [4] p. [2693

Cooper, Alonzo. In and out of rebel prisons. Oswego, N. Y., R. J. Oliphant, pr., 1888. 335 p. [2694

Cooper, Charles Logan. Major factors involved in the vocational choices of Negro college students. Ithaca, N. Y., 1935. [6] p. Abstract of thesis (Ph. D.)—Cornell University, 1935. [2695

[Cooper, Francis Hodges] . . . Some colonial history of Beaufort County, North Carolina. Chapel Hill, The University, 1916. (University of North Carolina. James Sprunt historical publications, pub. under the direction of the North Carolina Historical Society, v. 14, no. 2) 45 p. [2696

Cooper, Francis Hodges. Some colonial history of Craven County. Chapel Hill, 1920. (James Sprunt historical publications; pub. under the direction of the North Carolina Historical Society, v. 17, no. 1) p. [27]-74 [2697

Cooper, Guy Carlton. Tips on press work on cylinder and platen presses. [Salisbury, Rowan Printing Co., Inc., c.1939] 111 p. [2698

Cooper, Mrs. James Crawford see Cooper, Lucy (Parham)

Cooper, Lucy (Parham) A nightingale singing. Philadelphia, Dorrance & Co. [c.1949] 71 p. [2699

Cooper, Morley. Cruising to Florida via the intracoastal waterway. New York, Whittlesey House, McGraw-Hill Book Co., Inc. [1946] 201 p. [2700

Cooper, Murphy Rowe. The Cooper family history and genealogy, 1681-1931. Richmond, Printed by Garrett and Massie [c.1931] 116 p. [2701

Cooper, N. M. The three baptisms of Our Lord and Savior, Jesus Christ. No place, no publisher, n.d. 8 p. [2702

Cooper, Susan Fenimore, ed. William West Skiles; a sketch of missionary life at Valle Crucis . . . 1842-1862. New York, James Pott & Co., 1890. 141 p. [2703

Cooper, Walter Gerald, ed. The Piedmont region, embracing Georgia, Alabama, Florida and the Carolinas. Atlanta, Ga., C. P. Byrd, 1895. 104 p. [2704

Cooper, William Arthur. Catalogue of paintings and biographical sketch. [Charlotte, A. M. E. Zion, pr., 1935] 4 p. [2705
——A portrayal of Negro life. [Durham, Seeman Printery, Inc.] 1936. 110 p. [2706

Cooper, William James, ed. Four plays; written and produced during . . . 1923 by members of the Dramatic Club of Davidson College. W. J. Cooper and E. T. Woolfolk, editors. Davidson, Blue Pencil Club of Sigma Upsilon, 1923. 99 p. [2707

Cooperative Committee on Library Building Plans. The North Carolina conference . . . held at Chapel Hill and Durham, North Carolina, March 18-19, 1947. Philadelphia, Stephenson Brothers, 1947. 32 p. [2708

Co-operative digest, v. 1-3, July, 1940-January, 1943. Raleigh, 1940-43. NcU has v. 1-3 [2709

Coppock, W. R. Carolina dance. New York, Firth and Hall, c.1844. 7 p. [2710

Coppridge, William Maurice. The presentation to the University of North Carolina of the portrait of Dr. William deBerniere MacNider; address . . . December 15, 1946. [Chapel Hill] privately printed [1947] 27 p. [2711

[Copy of correspondence relating to Angus Wilton McLean's record] No place, no publisher [1924] 13 p. [2712

Corbett, Maurice N. The harp of Ethiopia. Nashville, Tenn., National Baptist Publishing Board, 1914. 276 p. [2713

Corbitt, David Leroy. Chart showing origin of North Carolina counties, by D. L. Corbitt and L. Polk Denmark. [Raleigh? Authors, c.1940] [1] p. [2714

Corby, Ruth Rosemary. Heart's haven. New York, Arcadia House, Inc., 1939. 256 p. [2715

Cornwallis, Charles Cornwallis, 1st marquis. An answer to that part of the Narrative of Lieutenant-General Sir Henry Clinton, K. B. which relates to the conduct of Lieutenant-General Earl Cornwallis, during the campaign in North-America, in the year 1781. London, Printed for J. Debrett, 1783. 260 p. [2716

——Correspondence of Charles, first marquis Cornwallis. London, J. Murray, 1859. 3 v. [2717

Corporal, pseud. see **Haines, Zenas T.**

Corresponding Primitive Baptist Association (Negro) Minutes, 18 - 18 - NcU has [1900-1924] [2718

[**Cosby, Dabney**] A memorial to the General Assembly of North Carolina [by Dabney Cosby and John W. Cosby] Raleigh, Charles C. Raboteau, 1851. 8 p. [2719

Cotten, Bruce. An adventure in Alaska during the gold excitement of 1897-1898. Baltimore, The Sun Printing Office, 1922. 107 p. [2720

——As we were; a personal sketch of family life. Baltimore, privately printed for the family only, 1935. 76 p. [2721

——Housed on the third floor; being a collection of North Caroliniana formed by Bruce Cotten. Baltimore [Horn-Shafer Co.] 1941. 65 p. [2722

——The mirrors of Bensboro. [Baltimore] The Author, 1925. 36 p. [2723

Cotten, Edward R. Life of the Hon. Nathaniel Macon, of North Carolina. Baltimore, Printed by Lucas & Deaver, 1840. 272 p. [2724

Cotten, Lyman Atkinson. Keep on the target; a service song. New York, Charles H. Hoyt & Co., c.1906. 7 p. [2725

Cotten, Sallie Southall. The clubwoman's hymn. No place, N. C. Federation of Women's Clubs [c.1923] 2 p. [2726

——History of the North Carolina Federation of Women's Clubs, 1901-1925. Raleigh, Edwards & Broughton Printing Co., 1925. 214 p. [2727

——Negro folk lore stories. Charlotte, Queen City for N. C. Federation of Women's Clubs, 1923. 22 p. [2728

——The white doe; the fate of Virginia Dare. Philadelphia, J. B. Lippincott Co., 1901. 89 p. [2729

—— ——Manteo, Roanoke Island Historical Association, 1937. 89 p. [2730

Cotterill, Robert Spencer. The old South. 2d ed. rev. Glendale, Calif., The Arthur H. Clark Co., 1939. 354 p. [2731

——The southern Indians. Norman, University of Oklahoma Press [1954] 255p. [2732

Cottom's edition Richardson's Virginia and North Carolina almanac see **The Warrock-Richardson** Maryland, Virginia, and North Carolina almanack

Cottom's Virginia & North Carolina almanack for the year of our Lord, 181 - Richmond, Printed and published annually by Peter Cottom, [181 - NcU has 1819, 1820, 1828, 1829, 1833] [2733

Cotton, Ella Earls. A spark for my people. New York, Exposition Press [1954] 288 p. [2734

Cotton boll, 1917- Winterville, Societies of Winterville High School, 1917- NcU has 1917, 1918 [2735

Cotton Manufacturers' Association of South Carolina. Rules for the purchase of cotton . . . July 1, 1910, known as Carolina mill rules. Rev. June, 1915. No place, 1915. 11 p. [2736

Couch, John Nathaniel. The genus Septobasidium. Chapel Hill, University of North Carolina Press, 1938. 480 p. [2737

Couch, John Nathaniel, joint author, see **Coker, William Chambers**

Couch, William Terry. Book-making in the South. Chapel Hill [University of North Carolina Press] 1938. [16] p. [2738

Couch, William Terry, ed. Culture in the South. Chapel Hill, University of North Carolina Press, 1934. 711 p. [2739

—— ——1935. [2740

Coulter, Ellis Merton. The Cincinnati Southern Railroad and the struggle for southern commerce, 1865-1872. Chicago, The American Historical Society, Inc., 1922. 68 p. [2741

——The Civil War and readjustment in Kentucky. Chapel Hill, University of North Carolina Press, 1926. 468 p. [2742

——College life in the old South. New York, Macmillan Co., 1928. 381 p.   [2743
——The Confederate States of America, 1861-1865. [Baton Rouge] Louisiana State University Press, 1950. (A History of the South, v. 7) 644 p.   [2744
——Georgia. rev. and enl. ed. of· A short history of Georgia. Chapel Hill, University of North Carolina Press, 1947. 510 p.   [2745

Coulter, Ellis Merton, ed. Georgia's disputed ruins: Certain tabby ruins on the Georgia coast, by Marmaduke Floyd. Chapel Hill, University of North Carolina Press, 1937. 275 p.   [2746

Coulter, Ellis Merton. The Granville District. Durham, 1913. (James Sprunt historical publications, pub. under the direction of the North Carolina Historical Society, v. 13, no. 1) p. [33]-56   [2747
——History of Georgia [by] Ellis Merton Coulter [and others] New York, American Book Co. [1954] 448 p.   [2748
——John Jacobus Flournoy, champion of the common man in the antebellum South. Savannah, Georgia Historical Society, 1942. 112 p.   [2749

Coulter, Ellis Merton, ed. A list of the early settlers of Georgia, ed. by E. Merton Coulter and Albert b. Śaye. Athens, University of Georgia Press [1949] 103 p. [2750

Coulter, Ellis Merton. A short history of Georgia. Chapel Hill, University of North Carolina Press, 1933. 457 p.   [2751
——The South during Reconstruction, 1865-1877. [Baton Rouge] Louisiana State University Press, 1947. (A History of the South, v. 8) 426 p.   [2752
——. . . Thomas Spalding of Sapelo. University, La., Louisiana State University Press, 1940. 334 p.   [2753
——Travels in the Confederate States, a bibliography. Norman, University of Oklahoma Press, 1948. 289 p.   [2754
——William G. Brownlow, fighting parson of the southern highlands. Chapel Hill, University of North Carolina Press, 1937. 432 p.   [2755
——Wormsloe; two centuries of a Georgia family. Athens, University of Georgia Press [1955] 322 p.   [2756

Coulter, William Robert, ed. History of the Golden Fleece, 1903-1950, University of North Carolina, Chapel Hill. [Chapel Hill, 1950] [2] p.   [2757

[Council, Anne (Cromartie)] comp. The William Cromartie family. No place [The Cromartie Clan] 1946. 27 p.   [2758

Council Against Intolerance in America. The Council Against Intolerance in America invites you to a regional conference . . . Durham, North Carolina, Saturday, March 1, 1941. [Durham? 1941?] [4] p. Program.   [2759

Councill, Judson. Hodges Councill of Virginia and descendants. Baltimore [J. H. Furst Co.] 1941. 108 p.   [2760

Country life, v. 1- September, 1890- Trinity College, Randolph County Farmers' Alliance, 1890- NcU has v. [1-2]   [2761

Country Line Primitive Baptist Association. Minutes, 18 - 18 - NcU has [1839-1847] 1849-1860 [1863-1906]   [2762

County year book of timely information for home and business . . . special for Durham and Wake counties, 19 - Greensboro, National Directory Co., 19 - NcU has 1923/24   [2763

Coupee's North-Carolina almanac for the year, 18 - Salisbury, Francis Coupee, 18 - NcU has 1809   [2764

Cousin Charles. No place, no publisher, n.d. [1] p.   [2765

Covell, Elizabeth Greene. The two Williams, William King Covell, 1802-1890, William King Covell, 1833-1919; a story of nineteenth century Newport, Rhode Island and Wilmington, North Carolina. Cambridge, Mass., University Press, 1954. 137 p.   [2766

Covington, James Robert, ed. Nods and becks, a review of 25 years. Charlotte, Mercury Printing Service, 1954. [75] p.   [2767

Covington, Nina Holland. Guide book of Raleigh, N. C. [Raleigh, Capital Printing Co., 192?] 64 p.   [2768

Cowan, Robert H. [Oration commemorative of . . . Edward B. Dudley; delivered before the stockholders of the W. & W. Railroad Co., Nov. 8th, 1855] 16 p. Title page wanting in NcU copy.   [2769

Cowden, Dudley Johnstone, joint author, see Croxton, Frederick Emory

Coweta Indians. King (Hoboyetly) The humble submission of the kings, princes, generals, &c. to the Crown of England. London, Printed and sold by A. Baldwin, 1707. [1] p. NcU has photostat. [2770

Cowles, Andrew D. A card to the Republican Party of Iredell County. Statesville, Oct. 29, 1894. [1] p. [2771

Cowles, William Henry Harrison, 1840-1901. Memorial day: subject, The life and services of General James B. Gordon; address delivered in Metropolitan Hall, Raleigh, N. C., May 10th, 1887. Raleigh, Edwards & Broughton, 1887. 20 p. [2772

Cowles, William Henry Harrison, 1891- A text book of trigonometry for colleges and engineering schools, by William H. H. Cowles and James E. Thompson. New York, D. Van Nostrand Co., Inc., 1936. 373 p. [2773

Cowley, Charles. Leaves from a lawyer's life, afloat and ashore. Lowell, Mass., Penhallow Printing Co., 1879. 245 p. [2774

[Cowper, Mary O.] The Australian ballot system. No place, Legislative Council of N. C. Women [1928] 3 p. [2775

——Working hours for children in North Carolina. No place, Legislative Council of N. C. Women [1928] [3] p. [2776

Cowper, Pulaski. Sketch of the life of Gov. Thomas Bragg. Raleigh, Edwards & Broughton, 1891. 33 p. [2777

Cowper, Roswell. The Ella waltz. Baltimore, F. D. Benteen, c.1847. [2] p. [2778

Cox, Aras B. Foot prints on the sands of time. Sparta, Star Publishing Co., 1900. 162 p. [2779

Cox, Charles Lea. Pharmaceutical review no. 1, by C. L. Cox and E. V. Howell. Chapel Hill, University of North Carolina, 1913. 36 p. [2780

Cox, Cordelia. A day's work. No place, Southern Woman's Educational Alliance, n.d. [6] p. [2781

Cox, Daisy Kelly. A history of the Methodist Church, Jonesboro Heights, Sanford, North Carolina. [Durham] The Author, 1955. 109 p. [2782

——A history of the Morris Chapel Methodist Church, Jonesboro Heights Station, Sanford, North Carolina. [Sanford, Morris Chapel Methodist Church] 1956. 12 p. [2783

——Our heritage. Sanford, privately printed by the Author, 1952. 68 p. [2784

Cox, David Samuel. Blackie Bear. Wilmington, Wilmington Stamp and Printing Co., c.1931. [55] p. [2785

—— ——Bear Creek, Blackie Bear's Organization, c.1937. [28] p. [2786

Cox, E. Victor. A representative Republican for the amendment. No place, no publisher [1900] [2] p. [2787

Cox, George H. Beginnings of the Lutheran Church in N. C.; delivered at the 120th annual convention of the United Evangelical Lutheran Synod of N. C. No place, Lutheran Synod of N. C. [1923?] 12 p. [2788

——History of Organ Church, Rowan County, N. C. Newberry, S. C., Aull & Houseal, 1894. 46 p. [2789

Cox, Jacob Dolson. . . . The march to the sea; Franklin and Nashville. New York, C. Scribner's Sons, 1886. (The army in the Civil War, v. X) 265 p. [2790

Cox, John Harrington, ed. Folk-songs of the South. Cambridge, Harvard University Press, 1925. 545 p. [2791

Cox, Lula Price (O'Conner) . . . The O'Conner-Conner-Simmons families. Southern Pines, W. E. Cox, Jr., 1941. 81 p. [2792

Cox, Macy. Berean class songs. No place, The Author [c.1921] [2] p. [2793

Cox, Reavis. Competition in the American tobacco industry, 1911-1932. New York, Columbia University Press, 1933. (Studies in history, economics and public law, ed. by the Faculty of Political Science of Columbia University, no. 381) 372 p. [2794

Cox, Samuel Sullivan. . . . Three decades of federal legislation, 1855 to 1885. Providence, R. I., J. A. & R. A. Reid, 1894. 726 p. [2795

Cox, William Edward. The heart of the prayer book. Richmond, Va., Dietz Press, Inc., 1944. 162 p. [2796

——. . . Our family genealogy. [Southern Pines] The Mary Nelson Smith family, 1938. 109 p.   [2797

——Practical observance of Lent; an address delivered at . . . the Convocation of Norfolk . . . St. John's Church, Hampton, Va., Nov. 21, 1923. No place, Printed by request of the Richmond clericus, n.d. 11 p.   [2798

——Southern sidelights. Raleigh, Edwards & Broughton Co., 1942. 170 p. [2799

Cox, William Ruffin. Address delivered at Raleigh, N. C., Oct. 16, 1907, at the laying of the corner stone of Masonic Temple. Raleigh, Edwards & Broughton, 1907. 11 p.   [2800

——Address delivered before the Oakwood Memorial Association, Richmond, Va., May 10, 1911. [Richmond, F. J. Mitchell Printing Corp.] n.d. 16 p.   [2801

——Address on the life and character of Maj. Gen. Stephen D. Ramseur . . . May 10, 1891. Raleigh, E. M. Uzzell & Co., 1891. 54 p.   [2802

——Address on the life and services of Gen. James H. Lane . . . Dec. 4, 1908. No place, no publisher, n.d. 23 p.   [2803

——Address on the life and services of General Marcus J. Wright . . . February 26th, 1915. No place, no publisher [1915?] 15 p.   [2804

[Cox, William Ruffin] comp. In fond and loving memory of Fanny Lyman Cox. No place, privately printed [1885?] 77 p.   [2805

Coxe, Daniel. A description of the English province of Carolana. London, Printed for B. Cowse, 1722. 122 p.   [2806

—— ——London, Printed for E. Symon, 1727.   [2807

—— ——[London] Printed for and sold by O. Payne, 1741.   [2808

—— ——St. Louis, Churchill, 1840.   [2809

Coy, Harold. The Prices and the Moores. [New York, International Press, 1944] 330 p.   [2810

——The real book about Andrew Jackson. Garden City, N. Y., Garden City Books [1952] 192 p.   [2811

[Coyler, Leigh] Water power on the Catawba River known as Catawba Falls. [Charlotte, D. A. Tompkins, c.1902] 26 p.   [2812

Crabb, Alfred Leland. Home to the Hermitage. Indianapolis, Bobbs-Merrill Co. [1948] 318 p   [2813

Crabtree, Carrie Martin. Kindred spirits. Bear Creek, Beacon Printers, n.d. 87 p.   [2814

Craddock, Charles Egbert, [pseud.] In the clouds. Boston, Houghton, Mifflin and Co., 1887. 452 p.   [2815

——The prophet of the Great Smoky Mountains. Boston, Houghton, Mifflin and Co., 1899. 308 p.   [2816

—— ——[c.1885]   [2817

——Story of old Fort Loudon. New York, Macmillan Co., 1899. 409 p.   [2818

[Crafford, John] A new and most exact account of the fertiles [!] and famous colony of Carolina. Dublin, Printed for Nathan Tarrant, 1683. 7 p. NcU has microfilm (negative) of original in New York Public Library   [2819

[Craig, Burton] To the public. [Salisbury, no publisher, 1833] 7 p.   [2820

Craig, David Irvin. Historical sketch of New Hope Church in Orange County, N. C. Reidsville, S. W. Paisley, pr., 1886. 47 p.   [2821

—— ——[Rev. ed.] Reidsville, 1891. 54 p.   [2822

——History of the development of the Presbyterian Church in North Carolina. Richmond, Whittet & Shepperson, pr. [c.1907] 192 p.   [2823

Craig, Hardin. Forty-fifth annual Phi Beta Kappa address . . . The problem of progress. [Chapel Hill, 1949] [11] p.   [2824

——Freedom and renaissance. Chapel Hill, University of North Carolina Press, 1949. 117 p.   [2825

——An interpretation of Shakespeare. New York, Dryden Press [1948] 400 p. [2826

——Literary study and the scholarly profession. Seattle, University of Washington Press, 1944. 150 p.   [2827

——Literature and the community. [Chapel Hill, Friends of the Library, 1946] 13 p.   [2828

——A North Carolina renaissance; an address . . . in Memorial Hall, April, 3, 1946. [Chapel Hill, University of North Carolina, 1946] 9 p.   [2829

——"Responsibility and crisis"; an address . . . in Chapel Hill, October 10, 1947. Chapel Hill, Sigma Phi Epsilon Fraternity [1948?] 9 p. [2831
——Task of the future; an address . . . at Davidson College, November 20, 1946. Davidson College, Public Relations Department, 1946. 7 p. [2832

Craig, James A. To the editors of the National intelligencer. Hawfields, 1829. [1] p. [2833

Craig, Locke. Legacy of the Confederacy; speech . . . at Raleigh, N. C., June 10, 1914. Raleigh, Edwards & Broughton, 1914. 8 p. [2834
——Memoirs and speeches. Asheville, Hackney and Moale, 1923. 284 p. [2835
——Mitchell's Peak and Dr. Mitchell. Raleigh, Edwards & Broughton, 1915. 23 p. [2836

Craig, Marjorie. Family records of Henrietta Alberta Ratcliffe and Jasper Newton Craig. Reidsville, The Author, 1955. Unpaged. [2837
——The known way. Francestown, N. H., Golden Quill Press [c.1955] 80 p. [2838

Craighead, James Geddes. The Craighead family, Philadelphia, Printed for the descendants [Sherman & Co., pr.] 1876. 173 p. [2839
——Scotch and Irish seeds in American soil. Philadelphia, Presbyterian Board of Publication [c.1878] 348 p. [2840

Craighill, Francis H. How the church came to us. Rocky Mount, 1936. [4] p. [2841

Cram, Thomas Jefferson. Discussion of the problem of probable profit to be expected from the gold and mercury amalgamating mill . . . at Gold Hill Mine. Philadelphia, Collins, pr., 1874. 31 p. [2842
——Report upon the mine and mills, with estimates for the use of the "North Carolina Gold Amalgamating Co." Philadelphia, Collins, pr., 1874. 36 p. [2843

Cramer, Stuart Warren. Useful information for cotton manufacturers. 2d ed. [Charlotte, Queen City Printing and Paper Co.] 1904-09. 4 v. NcU has v. 1. [2844

Cramerton Mills, Inc. Cramerton Mills, Inc., fine cotton spinners and doublers. Cramerton, 1925. [24] p. [2845

Crandall, Marjorie Lyle. Confederate imprints; a check list based principally on the collection of the Boston Athenaeum. [Boston] Boston Athenaeum, 1955. 2 v. [2846

Crane, Verner Winslow. The southern frontier, 1670-1732. Durham, Duke University Press, 1928. 391 p. [2847

Cranford, Henry C. The North Carolina good health program. [Raleigh? 1948] 14 p. [2848

Craven, Avery Odelle. The coming of the Civil War. New York, C. Scribner's Sons, 1942. 491 p. [2849
——Democracy in American life. Chicago, University of Chicago Press [1941] 149 p. [2850
——Edmund Ruffin, southerner. New York, D. Appleton and Co., 1932. 283 p. [2851
——The growth of Southern nationalism, 1848-1861. [Baton Rouge] Louisiana State University Press [and] the Littlefield Fund for Southern History of the University of Texas, 1953. (A History of the South, v. 6) 433 p. [2852
——The repressible conflict, 1830-1861. University, La., Louisiana State University Press, 1939. 97 p. [2853
——Soil exhaustion as a factor in the agricultural history of Virginia and Maryland, 1606-1860. Urbana, University of Illinois [c.1926] (University of Illinois Studies in the social sciences, v. XIII, no. 1) 179 p. [2854

[Craven, Braxton] Mary Barker, by Charlie Vernon [pseud.] 2d ed. Raleigh, Branson & Farrar, 1865. 69 p. [2855

Craven, Braxton. Methodism, a sermon by . . . President of Trinity College, North Carolina. Baltimore, Innes and Co., pr., 1868. 25 p. [2856

[Craven, Braxton] Naomi Wise; or, The wrongs of a beautiful girl. Pinnacle, W. C. Phillips, pr., n.d. 27 p. [2857
—— ——[pref. 1884] 17 p. [2858
—— ——[Randleman, Randleman News] n.d. 21 p. [2859

Craven, Bruce, comp. Title guaranty law of North Carolina, ratified Mar. 8, 1913, effective Jan. 1, 1914. Charlotte, Observer Printing House, 1913. 108 p. [2860

Craven, Charles. Charles Craven's kind of people. Chapel Hill, Colonial Press, Inc. [c.1956] 106 p. [2861

Craven, George B. Fayetteville, North Carolina. No place, no publisher [1924] 3 p.   [2862

Craven, Wesley Frank. The southern colonies in the seventeenth century, 1607-1689. [Baton Rouge] Louisiana State University Press, 1949. (A History of the South, v. 1) 451 p.   [2863

Craven, William W. In the shadows. Charlotte, n.d. [2] p.   [2864

Craven Co., N. C. Board of Commissioners. County debt statement, August 31, 1869. [New Bern?] 1869. [1] p.   [2865

——Report, 18 - New Bern, Dunn, 18 - NcU has 1887/90, 1891/94, 1908/10, 1910/11, 1912/14, 1915/16   [2866

——Statement of compensation allowed county commissioners. [New Bern?] August 31, 1869. [1] p.   [2867

Craven Co., N. C. Board of Education. Handbook of Craven County Schools, 1927-1928. New Bern, Owen G. Dunn, pr. [1927?] 22 p.   [2868

——Vote for the constitutional amendment giving the schools a six months term instead of four months. [New Bern? 1918] [1] p.   [2869

Craven Co., N. C. Board of Superintendents of Common Schools. Common schools. [New Bern?] 1851. [2] p.   [2870

Craven Co., N. C. Public Meeting. Public meeting. No place, no publisher, n.d. [1] p.   [2871

Craven County Farm-Life School, Vanceboro, N. C. Announcement, 1913/14-Vanceboro, 1913- NcU has 1913/14-1918/19, 1922/23-1924/25   [2872

Cravner, Marie. Zither of many strings. [Asheville, Stephens Press] privately printed, 1949. 59 p.   [2873

Crawford, Alexander W. North Carolina, the great opportunity. Greensboro, Home Mission Committee of the Synod of N. C., 1923. 41 p.   [2874

Crawford, Dugald. Searmoin chuaidh a liobhairt ag an Raft-Swamp, Le D. Crauford, minster. Fayetteville, Howard & Rowlston, 1791. 50 p. NcU has photograph of original in First Presbyterian Church, Fayetteville   [2875

——A sermon preached before the Cape-Fear Union Lodge of the Ancient and Honourable Order of . . . Masons . . . at Fayetteville on December 27, 1786. Fayetteville, Printed by Hodge and Blanchard, 1787. 18 p.   [2876

Crawford, Leonidas Wakefield. Life and work of Charles Duncan McIver, funeral sermon. [Greensboro, J. Stone & Co., pr., 1906?] 7 p.   [2877

Crawford, Nelson Antrim. The press and the public, an ethical problem; an address delivered at the Newspaper Institute at Chapel Hill, January 13-15, 1926. No place, no publisher [1926] 5 p.   [2878

[**Crawford, William Thomas**] Locke Craig for Governor. [Asheville? 1907] 4 p. [2879

Creasman, Clarence Dixon. Moore of Mars Hill; introduction by Gerald W. Johnson. Nashville, Tenn., The Author, c.1950. 136 p.   [2880

Credle, Ellis. Across the cotton patch. New York, T. Nelson and Sons, 1935. [59] p.   [2881

——The adventures of Tittletom. New York, Oxford University Press, 1949. 79 p.   [2882

——Big doin's on Razorback Ridge. New York, T. Nelson and Sons [1956] 125 p.   [2883

——Down, down the mountain. New York, T. Nelson and Sons, 1934. [47] p. [2884

——The flop-eared hound. London, Oxford University Press [c.1938] [61] p. [2885

——The goat that went to school. New York, Grosset & Dunlap [c.1940] [28] p. [2886

——Here comes the Showboat New York, T. Nelson and Sons [1949] 95 p. [2887

——Johnny and his mule. New York, Oxford University Press, 1946. [44] p. [2888

——Little Jeemes Henry. New York, T. Nelson and Sons, 1936. 44 p.   [2889

——My pet Peepelo. New York, Oxford Univ. Press, 1948. 62 p.   [2890

——Pepe and the parrot. New York, T. Nelson and Sons, 1937. [47] p.   [2891

——Pig-o-wee. New York, Rand, McNally & Co. [c.1936] [44] p.   [2892

Creecy, James R. Scenes in the South. Washington, T. McGill, pr., 1860. 294 p. [2893

Creecy, Richard Benbury. Grandfather's tales of North Carolina history. Raleigh, Edwards & Broughton, pr., 1901. 301 p.   [2894

——Memoirs of the Creecy and Benbury families. No place, no publisher, n.d. [3] p. Proof sheets.   [2895

——The tribute of Col. Creecy, editor of the Elizabeth City (N. C.) Economist, to the late James Robert Bent Hathaway. [Edenton, 1903] 6 p. Published as supplement, North Carolina historical and genealogical register, July, 1903. v. 3, no. 3. [2896

Creel, Mrs. Henry. White pussy cat and little gray mouse. New York, The Poetry Digest, 1950. 23 p. [2897

Creeley, Robert. All that is lovely in men. Asheville, Jonathan Williams, 1955. [46] p. [2898

Crenshaw, Ollinger. The slave states in the presidential election of 1860. Baltimore, The Johns Hopkins Press, 1945. (Johns Hopkins University Studies in historical and political science . . . Ser. LXIII, no. 3) 332 p. [2899

Crescent, 1916- Dover, Senior Class of Dover High School, 1916- NcU has 1920. [2900

The Crescent monthly; a magazine of literature, art, science and society, v. 1- April, 1866- New Orleans, William Evelyn and Co., Raleigh, William B. Smith and Co., 1866- NcU has v. [2] [2901

Crews, Hall. Old Salem, now a part of Winston-Salem, North Carolina. New York, R. F. Whitehead, c.1929. (The monograph series recording the architecture of the American colonies and the early republic, v. XV, no. 2) 44 p. [2902

Crisp, Lucy Cherry. Brief testament; verse. North Montpelier, Vt., Driftwind Press, 1947. 114 p. [2903

——Spring fever and other dialect verse. Greensboro, Jos. J. Stone and Co. for the Author [c.1935] 41 p. [2904

Crittenden, Charles Christopher. The commerce of North Carolina, 1763-1789. New Haven, Yale University Press, 1936. (Yale historical publications. Miscellany, xxix) 196 p. [2905

——History for the people. [Raleigh? 1941?] 8 p. [2906

——. . . North Carolina newspapers before 1790. Chapel Hill, University of North Carolina Press, 1928. (James Sprunt historical studies, v. 20, no. 1) 83 p. [2907

——Preserving New England history. [Raleigh] 1954. 18 p. [2908

Crittenden, Edward B. [pseud.?] The entwined lives of Miss Gabrielle Austin . . . and of Redmond, the outlaw. Philadelphia, Barclay and Co. [c.1880] 80 p. [2909

—— ——[c.1885] [2910

——Das Leben des Fraüleins Gabrielle Austin. [c.1879] 63 p. [2911

Crockett, David. The adventures of Davy Crockett. New York, C. Scribner's Sons, 1934. 258 p. [2912

——A narrative of the life of David Crockett. Philadelphia, E. L. Carey and A. Hart, 1834. 211 p. [2913

Crockett, G. F. H. Discourse on the necessity of revelation to the knowledge of the existence of God; being the substance of two lectures, delivered in Wake Forest College, and the University of North Carolina, in Sept. and Oct., 1855. Richmond, H. K. Ellyson, pr., 1856. 50 p. [2914

Crofts, Margaret Lee. Armed with light. Garden City, N. Y., Doubleday, Doran and Co., Inc., 1937. 292 p. [2915

Croke, Sir Alexander. The genealogical history of the Croke family, originally named Le Blount. Oxford, Printed by W. Baxter for J. Murray, 1823. 2 v. [2916

Cronin, John William. A bibliography of William Henry Harrison, John Tyler, James Knox Polk, compiled by John W. Cronin and W. Harvey Wise, Jr. Washington, Riverford Publishing Co., 1935. 60 p. [2917

Croom, Hardy Bryan. A catalogue of plants . . . in the vicinity of New Bern, North Carolina. New York, G. P. Scott and Co., pr., 1837. 52 p. [2918

——Oration delivered before Capt. J. H. Byrd's company of volunteers on the fourth of July, 1825, at Kinston. Newbern, Pasteur and Watson at the office of the Carolina Sentinel, 1826. 12 p. [2919

Cross, Arthur Lyon. The Anglican episcopate and the American colonies. New York, Longmans, Green, and Co., 1902. (Harvard historical studies . . . v. ix) 368 p. [2920

Crossley, William J. Extracts from my diary, and from my experiences while boarding with Jefferson Davis in three of his notorious hotels . . . from July, 1861, to June, 1862. Providence, Rhode Island Soldiers and Sailors Historical Society,

1903. (Personal narratives of events in the war of the rebellion. Sixth series, no. 4)   49 p.   [2921

Crossnore School. Bulletin, v. 1- 193 - Crossnore, 193 - NcU has v. [6-7] 8-30   [2922

——Weaving department, Crossnore school, Crossnore, N. C. No place, no publisher, n.d.   4 p.   [2923

Crouch, John. Address on the life and character of Col. Benjamin Cleveland, delivered at Guilford Battle Ground, on July 4, 1908. Greensboro, Guilford Battle Ground Co., n.d.   13 p.   [2924

——Historical sketches of Wilkes County. Wilkesboro, J. Crouch, 1902. 141 p. [2925

Crouch, W. Perry. Guidance for Christian home life. Nashville, Tenn., Convention Press [1955]   129 p.   [2926

Crouse, A. L. Biblical exceptions to the modern evangelistic system. 2d ed. Conover, The Author, 1891.   24 p.   [2927

——A Christian catechism for little children. 8th ed. Hickory ,Crouse, n.d. 20 p.   [2928

——Divisions; a sermon preached in St. Stephen's E. L. Church, Catawba County, N. C., Nov. 15, 1903. Taylorsville, Crouse, 1903.   12 p.   [2929

——Memorial address on Luther's parents, birth, and education, and a sermon on justification. New Market, Va., Henkel & Co., pr., [1883?]   22 p.   [2930

——Pulpit and altar fellowship. Hickory, no publisher ,1893.   28 p.   [2931

Crow, John Armstrong. The epic of Latin America. Garden City, N. Y., Doubleday & Co., Inc., 1946.   756 p.   [2932

——Spanish American life. [New York] H. Holt and Co. [c.1941]   288 p.   [2933

Crowder, Wilbur S. Up to infinity. New York, Comet Press [c.1954]   88 p. [2934

Crowe, Charles M., ed. Great southern preaching. New York, Macmillan Co., 1926.   280 p.   [2935

Crowell, John Franklin. Government war contracts. New York, Oxford University Press, 1920. (Preliminary economic studies of the war, ed. by D. Kinley, no. 25)   357 p.   [2936

——Personal recollections of Trinity College, North Carolina, 1887-1894. Durham, Duke University Press, 1939.   280 p.   [2937

——Program of progress; an open letter to the General Assembly of North Carolina of 1891. [Durham] Printed for the School of Political and Social Science, Trinity College [1891]   (Trinity College publication, no. 3)   35 p.   [2938

Crowell, L. A. Old age deferred. Lincolnton, n.d. [12] p.   [2939

Croxton, Frederick Emory. Practical business statistics, by Frederick E. Croxton and Dudley J. Cowden. 2d ed. New York, Prentice-Hall, 1948.   550 p.   [2940

Crozet, C. Report of C. Crozet, engineer, to the president and directors of the Portsmouth and Roanoke Railroad Co. Norfolk, Va., Shields & Ashburn, pr., 1832. 16 p.   [2941

Crozier, William Armstrong, ed. Crozier's general armory. New York, Published for the Genealogical Association by Fox, Duffield & Co., 1904. 155 p. [2942

Crozier, William Armstrong. A key to southern pedigrees. 2d ed. Baltimore, Southern Book Co., 1953.   80 p.   [2943

Crudup, Josiah. The temple and other essays in verse. [New Orleans, Press of Dameron-Pierson Co., Ltd., c.1934]   96 p.   [2944

Cruising the Caribbean in the wake of pirates. [New York] United Fruit Co., c.1915.   31 p.   [2945

Crum, Mason. Gullah; Negro life in the Carolina Sea islands. Durham, Duke University Press, 1940.   351 p.   [2946

——The Southern Christian advocate. [Columbia, S. C., Southern Christian Advocate] 1945.   48 p.   [2947

——The story of Lake Junaluska. Greensboro, The Piedmont Press, 1950. 117 p.   [2948

Crump, S. A. Speech, delivered at the reunion of the N. C. Confederate veterans, Greensboro, Aug. 20th, 1902. [Macon, Ga., Macon Evening News, 1902?] 14 p.   [2949

Crumpler, Thomas N., joint author, see **Ramsay, James Graham**

The cub, 19 - [New Bern, New Bern High School Students, 19 - NcU has 1927   [2950

Culbertson, Anne Virginia. At the big house, where Aunt Nancy and Aunt 'Phrony held forth on the animal folks. Indianapolis, Bobbs-Merrill [c.1904] 348 p. [2951

Culbreth, James Marvin. Pathways to the abundant life. Nashville, Cokesbury Press [c.1933] 221 p. [2952

Cullen, Andrews Battle, patriot, orator, soldier. No place, no publisher [1905?] [15] p. [2953

Cullom, W. R. Christmas and good will to men. [Wake Forest, 1949?] 8 p. [2954

Cullum, George W. Biographical sketch of Brigadier-General Joseph G. Swift. New York, Charles A. Coffin, pr., 1877. 26 p. [2955

Cumberland Baptist Association. Minutes, 19 - 19 - NcU has [1910-1928] [2956

Cumberland Co., N. C. Board of Education. [Report of the Superintendent of Public Schools, 19 - [Fayetteville, 19 -] NcU has 1903/05 [2957

Cumberland Co., N. C. Board of Superintendents of Common Schools. Report, 18 - Fayetteville, 1849- NcU has 1848/49 [2958

Cumberland Co., N. C. Citizens. Jno. G. Shaw for lieutenant governor. No place, no publisher, n.d. [1] p. [2959

Cumberland Co., N. C. Commissioners. General and special road law of Cumberland County, N. C. No place, County Commissioners [1905?] 21 p. [2960

Cundiff, Ruby Ethel, ed. School libraries in the South. Nashville, Tenn., Peabody Library School, 1936. (Peabody contributions to librarianship, no. 6) [43] p. [2961

Cuninggim, Jesse Lee. The family of God. Nashville, Parthenon Press [1948] 124 p. [2962

Cunningham, Bert. Laboratory manual for general zoology: achordates. Rev. ed. Durham, Seeman Printery, 1933. 68 p. [2963

Cunningham, H. B. Christian temperance; a sermon preached in Hopewell Church, N. C., July 18th, 1852. Charlotte, North Carolina Whig, pr., 1853. 14 p. [2964
——Two sermons delivered by the . . . pastor of the congregations of Hopewell and Paw-Creek, Mecklenburg County, N. C. Charlotte, Hornets' Nest Office, pr., 1849. 28 p. [2965

Cunningham, John Rood. William Henry Belk; an address at the banquet . . . of the Charlotte Chamber of Commerce, September 26, 1945, in honor of Mr. Belk. [Charlotte, 1945] [6] p. [2966

Cunningham, William. The real book about Daniel Boone. Garden City, N. Y., Garden City Books [1952] 192 p. [2967

Current, Richard Nelson. Daniel Webster and the rise of national conservatism. Boston, Little, Brown [1955] 215 p. [2968

Currituck Co., N. C. Board of Education. Report of the Public Schools of Currituck County, 19 - [Jarvisburg?] 19 - NcU has 1914/15 [2969

Curry, Jabez Lamar Monroe. Address delivered before the Association of Confederate Veterans, Richmond, Va., July 1, 1896. Richmond, B. F. Johnson Publishing Co. [1996?] 31 p. [2970
——Civil history of the government of the Confederate States. Richmond, B. F. Johnson Publishing Co., 1901. 318 p. [2971
——Proceedings of the Winthrop Training School on Memorial Day, May 12, 1889, with the memorial address of Hon. Jabez L. M. Curry. Columbia, S. C., Bryan Printing Co., 1889. 29 p. [2972
——The southern states of the American union. [Students ed.] Richmond, Va., B. F. Johnson Publishing Co., 1895. 272 p. [2973
——Speech . . . delivered before the North Carolina legislature, Jan. 21, 1891. Raleigh, Josephus Daniels, 1891. 15 p. [2974

Curry, Kathryn (Worth) see Worth, Kathryn

Curtis, Lillian Johnson. The Laos of North Siam. Philadelphia, Westminster Press, 1903. 338 p. [2975

Curtis, Moses Ashley. Sacerdotal absolution; a sermon preached before the . . . Diocese of North Carolina, 1843. New York, James A. Sparks, 1844. 33 p. [2976
—— ——1843. [2977

Curtis, Nathaniel Cortlandt. Elements of graphics, descriptive geometry, shades and shadows, and perspectives. Cleveland, O., J. H. Jansen, 1924. 100 p. [2978

——Elements of graphics, orthographic projections, shades, shadows, and perspective. [Auburn, Ala.] The Author, 1909. 34 p. [2979

——New Orleans; its old houses, shops and public buildings. Philadelphia, J. B. Lippincott Co., 1933. 267 p. [2980

Curtis, W. A. Annual address delivered before the Charles L. Robinson Camp no. 947, U. C. V., of Franklin, N. C., March 31, 1899. Franklin, Franklin Press, 1899. 16 p. [2981

Curtis, W. A., joint author, see Smith, C. D.

Curtis, Walter Gilman. . . . Reminiscences, 1848-1900. For thirty years state quarantine surgeon for the port of Wilmington. Southport, Herald [c.1905] 64 p. [2982

Curtiss, John Shelton. The Russian church and the Soviet state, 1917-1950. Boston, Little, Brown [1953] 387 p. [2983

Cushman, Ralph Spaulding. The prayers of Jesus, with meditations and verse for devotional use. New York, Abingdon Press [1955] 125 p. [2984

——More hilltop verses and prayers . . . poems of Ralph Spaulding Cushman, with prayers by Robert Earl Cushman. New York, Abingdon-Cokesbury Press [1949] 96 p. [2985

Cushman, Rebecca. Swing your mountain gal. Boston, Houghton Mifflin Co., 1934. 150 p. [2986

Cushman, Walter S. Selections from newspaper articles. No place, no publisher [1878?] 4 p. [2987

Cushman, Walter S., joint author, see Cameron, John Donald

Cutchin, Walter Thaddeus. The book of Revelation. [Chapel Hill] Orange Printshop for the Author, 1923. 71 p. [2898

Cutten, George Barton. College education—what is it? A talk to Freshmen. [Chapel Hill, 1953] 11 p. [2989

——Forty-ninth annual Phi Beta Kappa address, Alpha Chapter of North Carolina: The nonconformist makes God an optimist. [Chapel Hill, 1953] 12 p. [2990

——The silversmiths of Virginia, together with watchmakers and jewelers, from 1694 to 1850. Richmond, Va., Dietz Press, 1952. 259 p. [2990a

Cuyler, Cornelius C. The question answered, whose children are entitled to baptism? A sermon . . . New-York . . . 6th June, 1816. Raleigh, Printed by Joseph Gales, 1817. 37 p. [2991

Cyclopedia of eminent and representative men of the Carolinas of the nineteenth century. Madison, Wis., Brant & Fuller, 1892. 2 v. [2992

Cyrus B. Watson for Judge Clark. [Raleigh] no publisher, n.d. 16 p. [2993

D., W. see Williamson, Hugh, 1735-1819

Dabney, Charles William. Note on cassiterite from King's Mountain, N. C. [Raleigh, no publisher, 1884] 3 p. [2994

——Universal education in the South. Chapel Hill, University of North Carolina Press [c.1936] 2 v. [2995

Dabney, Robert Lewis. Christ our penal substitute. Richmond, Presbyterian Committee of Publication [c.1898] 115 p. [2996

Daggett, Parker Hayward. National Council State Boards of Engineering; presidential address at the seventh annual convention. Philadelphia, 1926. 12 p. [2997

Dairy Council, Durham, N. C. The Dairy Council, what it is, what it does. [Durham, 1949?] 10 p. [2998

Dairy goat bulletin, v. 1- January, 1943- Charlotte, 1943- NcU has v. [1] 2, 3 [2999

Dale, J. Acrostics, serious, religious, sentimental, mirthful, etc. Raleigh, The Author, n.d. 60 p. [3000

Dallas, George Mifflin. Obsequies in honor of Andrew Jackson: Eulogium by George M. Dallas, vice president of the United States. Philadelphia, Mifflin & Parry, pr., 1845. 16 p. [3001

Dalton, Archibald Carter. Individualism. Chapel Hill, Published by the University, 1906. (N. C. University. Philosophy Department. Worth prize thesis, 1906) 21 p. [3002

——Warning to women voters of High Point. No place, no publisher [1930] [1] p. [3003

Dalton, John H. Land and Negroes at public sale . . . at the late residence of Placebo Houston. [Statesville] Iredell Express, Feb. 9, 1859. [1] p.   [3004

Dalton, William Reid. The deadly parallel; let the Democratic votes choose between the two, Simmons or Bailey. Reidsville, The Author, May 19, 1930. [1] p. [3005

——A tree is known by its fruit, being an answer to attacks of Bailey . . . on Senator Simmons. [Reidsville, The Author, March 31, 1930] [2] p.   [3006

Daly, Augustin. . . . "Frou frou"; a play. New York, S. French, c.1897. 59 p. [3007

Daly, Joseph Francis. The life of Augustin Daly. New York, Macmillan Co., 1917. 672 p.   [3008

Dan River Steam-Electric Plant, Rockingham County, N. C. Dan River Steam-Electric Plant, Duke Power Company. [Charlotte, Duke Power Company, 1950] [12] p.   [3009

Dan River Steam Navigation Co., Inc. Dan River Steam Navigation Company, incorporated by state of North Carolina, Feb. 14th, 1855. Baltimore, John W. Woods, pr., 1855. 7 p.   [3010

Dan Valley Missionary Baptist Association. Minutes, 19 - 19 - NcU has 1948-1955   [3011

Dancy, Frank Battle. Chemical conversion tables . . . By F. B. Dancy and H. B. Battle. Raleigh, The Authors, 1885. 42 p.   [3012

Dancy, William Francis. Oration pronounced at Tarborough, N. C., the 22d of May, 1850 . . . to the memory of Louis D. Wilson. Raleigh, William W. Holden, pr., 1850. 12 p.   [3013

Daniel, Ella Mae. Hunger, a tragedy of North Carolina farm folk. Minneapolis, Minn., Northwestern Press, c.1938. 24 p.   [3014

——A new Carolina folk-play: Hunger. [Chapel Hill? Carolina Playmakers? 1935] 32 p.   [3015

——A new Carolina folk-play: Yours and mine. [Chapel Hill? Carolina Playmakers? 1935?] 32 p.   [3016

——"A pageant of education" celebrating one hundred years of public education in North Carolina. Chapel Hill, Bureau of Community Drama [1937?] 32 p. [3017

Daniel, James Walter. The girl in checks. Columbia, S. C., L. L. Pickett, 1892. 208 p.   [3018

Daniel Boone. Boston, Educational Publishing Co., 1898. (Young folk's library of choice literature, v. 5, no. 98) 32 p.   [3019

Daniels, Adelaide Worth (Bagley) Recollections of a cabinet minister's wife, 1913-1921. [Raleigh, Mitchell Printing Co., 1945] 199 p.   [3020

Daniels, Frank Arthur. Address on presentation of a portrait of the late George Vaughan Strong to the Supreme Court of North Carolina . . . 28 May 1934. No place, no publisher, n.d. 8 p.   [3021

——Henry Groves Connor; address delivered before the Superior Court of Wilson County . . . Feb. 12, 1926. Raleigh, Edwards & Broughton, 1926. 34 p. [3022

——History of Wayne County. Address . . . at opening of Wayne County's new court house, November 30, 1914. [Goldsboro? 1914?] 43 p.   [3023

——Presentation of the portrait of the late Justice of the Supreme Court, William Reynolds Allen, Sept. 6, 1922. No place, no publisher [1922?] 16 p.   [3024

Daniels, Jonathan Worth. Clash of angels. New York, Brewer and Warren, Inc., 1930. 288 p.   [3025

——The end of innocence. Philadelphia, J. B. Lippincott Co. [1954] 351 p.   [3026

——Frontier on the Potomac. New York, Macmillan Co., 1946. 262 p.   [3027

——The man of Independence. Philadelphia, J. B. Lippincott Co. [1950] 384 p. [3028

——. . . A southerner discovers New England. [New York] Macmillan Co., 1940. 398 p.   [3029

——. . . A southerner discovers the South. New York, Macmillan Co., 1938. 346 p.   [3030

——Tar heels; a portrait of North Carolina. New York, Dodd, Mead & Co., 1941. 347 p.   [3031

Daniels, Josephus. Address on the occasion of the Edison centennial celebration. Minneapolis, Minn., no publisher, 1947. 26 p.   [3032

——Editor in politics. Chapel Hill, University of North Carolina Press, 1941. 644 p.   [3033

——First fallen hero; a biographical sketch of Worth Bagley, Ensign, U. S. N. Norfolk, Sam W. Bowman, c.1898. 88 p. [3034

——Fourth of July address by Ambassador Daniels . . . at the American Embassy, July 4th, 1940. [Mexico City? 1940?] 6 p. [3035

——Freedom in the University . . . remarks at the Alumni luncheon, Chapel Hill, June 10, 1935. [Raleigh, 1935] 16 p. [3036

——Henry Groves Connor . . . address presenting the portrait of Judge Connor. No place, no publisher, 1929. 48 p. [3037

——The life of Woodrow Wilson. Philadelphia, John C. Winston Co. [c.1924] 381 p. [3038

——The navy and the nation; war-time addresses. New York, George H. Doran Co. [c.1919] 348 p. [3039

——Our navy at war. Washington, D. C., Pictorial Bureau, 1922. 374 p. [3040

——Shirt-sleeve diplomat. Chapel Hill, University of North Carolina Press, 1947. 547 p. [3041

——Tar heel editor. Chapel Hill, University of North Carolina Press, 1939. 544 p. [3042

——Thanksgiving address by Ambassador Daniels at the Union Church, Mexico City, Thanksgiving Day, 1936. [Mexico City, 1936] 6 p. [3043

——Universal education; address delivered to . . . seminar in Mexico City, Thursday, July 26th, 1934. No place, no publisher [1934?] 6 p. [3044

——The Wilson era; years of peace, 1910-1917. Chapel Hill, University of North Carolina Press, 1944. 615 p. [3045

——The Wilson era; years of war and after, 1917-1923. Chapel Hill, University of North Carolina Press, 1946. 654 p. [3046

Daniels, Mrs. Josephus see **Daniels, Adelaide Worth (Bagley)**

Daniels, Lucy. Caleb, my son; a novel. Philadelphia, J. B. Lippincott Co. [1956] 125 p. [3047

Danson, Mary, appellant. [Case of Mary Danson, widow, heard at the bar of the House of Lords on March 27th, 1729; . . . involving title to one eighth part of the Province of Carolina]. [London, 1729] Various paging. [3048

Darby, Ada Claire. Island girl. Philadelphia, J. B. Lippincott Co. [1951] 215 p. [3049

Darby, John. Botany of the Southern States. New York, A. S. Barnes & Co., 1855. 612 p. [3050

Darby, William. View of the United States, historical, geographical, and statistical. Philadelplia, H. S. Tanner, 1828. 654 p. [3051

Darden, John W. Morrattock Church is suggested as shrine. No place, n.d. [1] p. [3052

Dare, birthplace of America (Motion picture) Made and released by Communication Center, University of North Carolina, 1952. 22 min., 16mm. [3053

Dare County, N. C. Chamber of Commerce. Carolina's greatest ocean county. Manteo, Dare County Chamber of Commerce [1933?] Folder. [3054

Dare County, N. C. Historians. Dare County and its matchless history, 1584-1927. Manteo [1927] 15 p. [3055

[Dargan, Olive (Tilford)] Call home the heart, a novel by Fielding Burke [pseud.] London, Longmans, Green and Co., 1932. 432 p. [3056

Dargan, Olive (Tilford) The cycle's rim. New York, C. Scribner's Sons, 1916. 73 p. [3057

——The flutter of the goldleaf, and other plays, by Olive Tilford Dargan and Frederick Peterson. New York, C. Scribner's Sons, 1922. 114 p. [3058

——From my highest hill: Carolina mountain folks. Philadelphia, J. B. Lippincott Co. [c.1941] 221 p. [3059

——Highland annals. New York, C. Scribner's Sons, 1925. 286 p. [3060

——Lords and lovers, and other dramas. New York, C. Scribner's Sons, 1906. 315 p. [3061

——Lute and furrow. New York, C. Scribner's Sons, 1922. 140 p. [3062

——The mortal gods, and other plays. New York, C. Scribner's Sons, 1912. 303 p. [3063

——Path flower, and other verses. London, J. M. Dent & Sons, Ltd., 1914. 119 p. [3064

——Semiramis, and other plays. New York, Brentano's, 1904. 255 p. [3065

[Dargan, Olive (Tilford)] Sons of the stranger, by Fielding Burke [pseud.] New York, Longmans, Green and Co., 1947. 405 p. [3066

——A stone came rolling; a novel by Fielding Burke [pseud.] New York, Longmans, Green and Co., 1935. 412 p. [3067

Dark, N. J. One cotton farmer writes to another. [Raleigh] N. C. Cotton Growers Cooperative Association, 1924. 6 p. [3068

Darst, Thomas C. Diocesan convention address . . . read at Greenville, North Carolina, January 28, 1931. No place, no publisher [1931?] 11 p. [3069

Dashiell, John Frederick. An experimental manual in psychology. Boston, Houghton Mifflin Co. [c.1931] 160 p. [3070

——Fundamentals of objective psychology. Boston, Houghton Mifflin Co. [c.1928] 588 p. [3071

——Fundamentals of general psychology. Boston, Houghton Mifflin Co. [c.1937] 655 p. [3072

——Manual to accompany Fundamentals of general psychology. Boston, Houghton, Mifflin Co. [c.1937] 117 p. [3073

Dau, William Herman Theodore. Review of Prof. R. A. Yoder's "Situation in North Carolina" by a committee [W. H. T. Dau and others] No place, no publisher, ca.1895. 47 p. [3074

Daugherty, Adam Mast. Paradise on Rich Mountain, N. C., Sept. 26th, 1904. No place, no publisher, n.d. 4 p. [3075

Daugherty, James Henry. Daniel Boone. New York, Viking Press, 1939. 94 p. [3076

Daughters of the American Colonists. North Carolina. The North Carolina Society, Daughters of the American Colonists . . . Roster, 1943-1946. [Oxford? 1947?] [5] p. [3077

Daughters of the American Revolution. Lineage book, National Society of the Daughters of the American Revolution, [v. 1]-166, 1890/91-1921. Harrisburg, Pa., 1895; Washington, D. C. 1895-1939. NcU has v. 1-166 [3078

——Lineage books. (Indexes) Index of the Rolls of honor (ancestor's index) in the Lineage books of the National Society of the Daughters of the American Revolution, volumes 1 to 160. Pittsburgh, Pa., Press of Pierpont, Siviter & Co., 1916-1940. 4 v. NcU has v. 1-4 [3079

Daughters of the American Revolution. North Carolina. By-laws. [Charlotte, Observer] 1904. 11 p. [3080

——By-laws of the National Society of the Daughters of the American Revolution in North Carolina. [Charlotte] 1913. 15 p. [3081

——Daughters of the Revolution, North Carolina State Society. [Raleigh, 1895] [3] p. [3082

——N. C. D. A. R. genealogical register, members and Revolutionary ancestors . . . 1890 through 1947. New Bern, 1948. 185 p. [3083

——Programme of the unveiling and dedication of the tablet in memory of the fifty-one signers of the Edenton tea party resolves in the Capitol . . . October the twenty-fourth, nineteen hundred and eight. No place, no publisher [1908] [2] p. [3084

——Roster of the soldiers from North Carolina in the American Revolution. [Durham] 1932. 709 p. [3085

——Souvenir programme, Kings Mountain historical pageant, October 6 and 7, 1930. No place, 1930. [16] p. [3086

——Year book and report of the annual state conference, 1st- 1901- 1901- NcU has 1901-1956. Not published 1918. [3087

Daughters of the American Revolution. North Carolina. Benjamin May Chapter, Farmville. George Washington bi-centennial, 1931-1932. Farmville [1931] [7] p. [3088

Daughters of the American Revolution. North Carolina. Caswell Nash Chapter, Raleigh. The Kirmiss under the auspices of the Daughters of the Revolution, May 30th and 31st. Raleigh, 1905. [20] p. Program. [3089

Daughters of the American Revolution. North Carolina. Craighead-Dunlap Chapter, Wadesboro. Anson County in the World War 1917-1919. Raleigh, Edwards and Broughton, 1929. 464 p. [3090

Daughters of the American Revolution. North Carolina. Dorcas Bell Love Chapter, Waynesville, N. C. In memoriam, Mary Love Stringfield Wulbern, 1873-1907. No place, n.d. 43 p.   [3091

Daughters of the American Revolution. North Carolina. Mecklenburg Declaration of Independence Chapter, Charlotte. By-laws of the Mecklenburg Chapter. Charlotte, Dooley Printing Co., 1928. 18 p.   [3092

——Memoir of Mrs. Stonewall Jackson. [Charlotte? 1915?] 24 p.   [3093

Daughters of the American Revolution. North Carolina. Stamp Defiance Chapter, Wilmington. Wilmington, historic colonial city. Wilmington, Floyd W. Cox, Jr., 1952. 74 p.   [3094

Daughters of the Confederacy see United Daughters of the Confederacy

Daughters of Temperance of the State of North Carolina, see North Carolina Daughters of Temperance

Davega, A. H. Correspondence between Dr. A. H. Davega and Col. Wm. Johnston No place, no publisher [187?] 23 p.   [309

Davenport, William Henry. The anthology of Zion Methodism. Charlotte, A. M. E. Zion Publishing House, 1925. 32 p.   [3096

——Membership in Zion Methodism. Charlotte, A. M. E. Zion Publishing House [c.1936] 107 p.   [3097

Davenport College, Lenoir, N. C. Catalogue, 18 - Lenoir, 18 - NcU has [1860/61-1930/31]   [3098

——Davenport Female College, Lenoir, N. C. Atlanta, Franklin Printing and Publishing Co., 1900. 7 p.   [3099

Daves, Edward Graham. Address to the Massachusetts Cincinnati. No place, no publisher, n.d. [4] p.   [3100

——. . . Maryland and North Carolina in the campaign of 1780-1781. Baltimore [Printed by J. Murphy & Co.] 1893. ([Maryland Historical Society] Fund-publication, no. 33) 100 p.   [3101

Daves, Graham. In memoriam, John A. Guion, M. D., New Bern, N. C., 1816-1894. [New Bern, no publisher, 1894?] 8 p.   [3102

——A sketch of the military career of Captain John Daves. Baltimore, Press of the Friedenwald Co., 1892. 16 p.   [3103

David, Paul Theodore. Presidential nominating politics in 1952, prepared by Paul T. David, Malcolm Moos [and] Ralph M. Goldman. Baltimore, Johns Hopkins Press [1954] 5 v.   [3104

David, Anderson Covington, 1884-1909. No place, no publisher [1909?] 12 p. [3105

Davidson, Chalmers Gaston. Cloud over Catawba. [Charlotte] Published under the sponsorship of the Mecklenburg Historical Society, 1949. 210 p.   [3106

——Friend of the people; the life of Dr. Peter Fayssoux of Charleston, South Carolina. Columbia, Medical Association of South Carolina, 1950. 151 p.   [3107

——Gaston of Chester. [Davidson? 1956] 146 p.   [3108

——Mid-point for '28; a summary of the achievements . . . of the Davidson College Class of 1928. Davidson, Davidson College, 1953. 65 p.   [3109

——Major John Davidson of "Rural Hill," Mecklenburg County, N. C. Charlotte, Lassiter Press, Inc., 1943. 93 p.   [3110

——Piedmont partisan; the life and times of Brigadier-General William Lee Davidson. Davidson, Davidson College, 1951. 190 p.   [3111

Davidson, Donald. The Tennessee. New York, Rinehart & Co., Inc. [1946-1948] (Rivers of America) 2 v.   [3112

Davidson, Elizabeth Huey. Child labor legislation in the southern textile states. Chapel Hill, University of North Carolina Press, 1939. 302 p.   [3113

Davidson, George Samuel Franklin. Partial catalogue of the library of George Samuel Franklin Davidson, planter, of Iredell County, N. C. No place, 1942. [11] p.   [3114

Davidson, James Wood. The living writers of the South. New York, Carleton, 1869. 635 p.   [3115

Davidson, Theodore F. Reminiscences and traditions of Western North Carolina; paper read before the Pen and Plate Club of Asheville, N. C. at its November, 1928, meeting. Asheville, Service Printing Co., n.d. 25 p.   [3116

Davidson, Theodore F., joint author, see Sondley, Foster Alexander

Davidson College, Davidson, N. C. Abroad in the land, the Davidson story. Davidson, 1949. 24 p. [3117

——Alumni catalogue of Davidson College . . . 1837-1924. Charlotte, Presbyterian Standard Publishing Co., 1924. 315 p. [3118

——Catalogue of the officers and students, 183 - 183 - NcU has [1840/41-1860/61] 1868/69-1900/01. Continues as its Davidson College Bulletin, v. 1- 1902- [3119

——Catalogue of the officers, professors, and alumni of Davidson College from 1837-1881. Raleigh, E. M. Uzzell & Co., pr., 1881. 31 p. [3120

——Celebration of the seventy-fifth anniversary of the founding of Davidson College. Davidson, 1912. 4 p. [3121

——Davidson College. [Davidson, n.d.] 4 p. [3122

—— ——1901. 6 p. [3123

—— ——[1943?] [42] p. [3124

——Davidson College bulletin, v. 1- February, 1902- Davidson, 1902- NcU has v. [1-55] [3125

——General catalogue of students of Davidson College, 1837-1887. Raleigh, E. M. Uzzell, pr., 1887. 61 p. [3126

——Laws of Davidson College, 1872. [Salisbury, J. J. Bruner, pr., 1872?] 15 p. [3127

——The next step forward. Davidson, 1942. [22] p. [3128

——Publications of the faculty, 19 - Davidson, 19 - NcU has 1938/39, 1945, 1953-1955 [3129

——Rules and regulations for students of the College, 19 - Davidson, 19 - NcU has 1934/35-1937/38, 1939/40-1948/49 [3130

——Semi-centennial catalogue of Davidson College . . . 1837-1887. Raleigh, E. M. Uzzell, pr., 1891. 194 p. [3131

——Souvenir calendar of Davidson College. [Charlotte, Ray Printing Co.] 1906. 6 mounted plates [3132

——Talking points for Davidson College. [Davidson] n.d. 34 p. [3133

Davidson College, Davidson, N. C. Board of Trustees. Charter and by-laws of the Trustees of Davidson College, revised February 16, 1938. [Davidson, 1938?] 39 p. [3134

——Charter and by-laws of the Trustees of Davidson College, with revisions to February 20, 1946. [Davidson, 1946] 44 p. [3135

——Circular. Davidson College, 1872. [4] p. [3136

[Davidson College, Davidson, N. C. Board of Trustees] Constitution and charter of Davidson College, adopted . . . June 14-16, 1887. [Davidson] n.d. 24 p. [3137

Davidson College, Davidson, N. C. Centennial Program Committee. Davidson, an interpretation. Davidson [1937] 8 p. [3138

Davidson College, Davidson, N. C. Davidson College Historical Association. Studies in history, v. 1, no. 1, March, 1898. Davidson, 1898. 71 p. No more published. [3139

[Davidson College, Davidson, N. C. General Alumni Association] An analysis of the opinions of Davidson College alumni regarding the needs of the College. [Davidson, 194?] 30 p. [3140

——For such a time as this. [Davidson, 1943] 15 p. [3141

Davidson College, Davidson, N. C. Library. Davidson College Library handbook. Davidson, 1948. 13 p. [3142

——Dedication, Hugh A. and Jane Parks Grey Memorial Library . . . May 1, 1942. [Davidson, 1942] [5] p. [3143

——Handbook. [Davidson] n.d. 37 p. [3144

Davidson College, Davidson, N. C. Philanthropic Society. Constitution and by-laws. [Davidson] n.d. 72 p. [3145

Davidson College, Davidson, N. C. Sophomore Class. The Freshmen and Juniors' mirror. Davidson College [Sophomore Class] n.d. 62 p. [3146

Davidson College, Davidson, N. C. Young Men's Christian Association The Wildcat handbook, 19 - Davidson, 19 - NcU has 1924/25-1926/27, 1928/29, 1930/31, 1931/32, 1933/34, 1934/35, 1939/40-1947/48, 1949/50 [3147

Davidson College magazine, v. 1- 1870- Davidson, Students of Davidson College, 1870- NcU has v. [1-20] 21-22 [23-24] 25-28 [29-40] [3148

Davidson College Presbyterian Church. Brief history of Davidson College Presbyterian Church with roll of members . . . Dec. 15, 1925. Statesville [1925] 15 p. [3149

Davie, William Richardson. Instructions to be observed for the formations and movements of the cavalry. Halifax, Printed by Abraham Hodge, 1799. 180 p. [3150

——. . . William Richardson Davie: a memoir by J. G. de Roulhac Hamilton . . . followed by his letters. Chapel Hill, The University, 1907. (University of North Carolina. James Sprunt historical monograph, no. 7)   75 p.   [3151

Davie Co., N. C.   Board of Education.   Directory of schools, 19   -   [Mocksville?] 19   -   NcU has 1914/15   [3152

Davie County Agricultural and Mechanical Society. The Davie County Agricultural and Mechanical Society will hold its sixth annual fair at Farmington.   Salisbury, Watchman, n.d.   [1] p.   [3153

Davies, William Watkins.   Transfusion.   Louisville, Ky., John P. Morton Co., 1923.   56 p.   [3154

Davis, Burke. Gray Fox; Robert E. Lee and the Civil War. New York, Rinehart & Co. [1956]   466 p.   [3155

——The ragged ones.   New York, Rinehart & Co., Inc. [1951]   336 p.   [3156

—— ——New York, Pocket Books [1953]   353 p.   [3157

——Roberta E. Lee.   Winston-Salem, J. F. Blair [1956]   unpaged   [3158

——They called him Stonewall. New York, Rinehart & Co., Inc. [1954] 470 p. [3159

——Whisper my name. New York, Rinehart & Co., Inc. [1949]   282 p.   [3160

——Yorktown.   New York, Rinehart & Co., Inc. [1952]   306 p.   [3161

Davis, Champion McDowell.   Atlantic Coast Line, fragments of its history.   New York, The Newcomen Society in North America, 1950.   28 p.   [3162

——A discussion of the revitalized Atlanta, Birmingham and Coast Railroad Company. [Birmingham? Atlantic Coast Line Railroad Co.] 1954.   19 p.   [3163

——An informal look at Atlantic Coast Line; address before the New York Society of Security Analysts . . . December 18, 1951. [Wilmington? Atlantic Coast Line Railroad Co.?] 1951.   28 p.   [3164

[Davis, Charles Augustus] Letters of J. Downing, major [pseud.] . . . to his old friend, Mr. Dwight, of the New-York advertiser. New York, Harper & Brothers, 1834.   270 p.   [3165

——The life of Andrew Jackson . . . By Major Jack Downing [pseud.] Philadelphia, T. K. Greenbank, 1834.   263 p.   [3166

Davis, Charles Henry. Good roads everywhere. Washington [National Highway Association, 1913]   27 p.   [3167

Davis, Charles Lukens. A brief history of the North Carolina troops on the Continental establishments in the war of the Revolution. Philadelphia, no publisher, 1896.   106 p.   [3168

——North Carolina Society of the Cincinnati. Boston [Riverside Press] 1907. 106 p.   [3169

Davis, E. G. & Sons Company. Diamond jubilee. Henderson, 1950.   45 p.   [3170

Davis, Edward Hill. Historical sketches of Franklin County. Raleigh, Edwards & Broughton Co., 1948.   298 p.   [3171

Davis, George. Address delivered before the two literary societies of the University of North-Carolina, June 6, 1855. Raleigh, Holden & Wilson, 1855.   36 p.   [3172

——Address delivered before the young ladies of Greensboro Female College, 14th May, 1856. Greensborough, Times, 1856.   20 p.   [3173

——Eulogy on the life and services of Henry Clay, delivered in the Presbyterian Church, Wilmington, N. C., on the 15th July, 1852. Wilmington, Herald, 1852. 18 p.   [3174

——A study in colonial history: a lecture delivered before the Historical Society of Wilmington, the 26th day of November, A. D. 1879. Wilmington, Jackson & Bell, pr., 1880.   34 p.   [3175

Davis, Hannah Martin (Barham) Heartleaves. Warrenton, Jones Printing Co. [for Author, 1951?]   116 p.   [3176

Davis, Harold Lenoir. Beulah Land. New York, William Morrow & Co., 1949. 314 p.   [3177

[Davis, James?] James Davis, Sen. was born the 21st of October in the Year of our

Lord MDCCXXI. [New Bern? James Davis?] n.d. [1] p. NcU has photostat (positive) of original belonging to T. L. Davis, Wilson, N. C. [3178

Davis, James. The office and authority of a justice of peace. Newbern, Printed by James Davis, 1744. 2 p. 1, 404 [3] p. Official publications of James Davis are listed in Thornton, Mary Lindsay. Official publications of the colony and state of North Carolina. Chapel Hill, University of North Carolina Press, 1954. [3179

Davis, James Wagner. Notes on bacteriology. Charlotte, Queen City Printing Co. [c.1927] 85 p. [3180

Davis, Jefferson. Ex-President Davis' last paper of a public nature . . . The occasion—the centennial celebration of the ratification, by North Carolina, of the Constitution of the United States, at Fayetteville, November 21st, 1889. Fayetteville, Wharton J. Green, c.1896. [1] p. [3181

Davis, Josephine Rhoades. Our legacy; a tribute to George Fox and William Edmundson, a history play. No place, no publisher [1929] [18] p. [3182

Davis, Junius. Alfred Moore and James Iredell, Revolutionary patriots, and associate justices of the Supreme Court of the United States. [Raleigh, North Carolina Society of the Sons of the Revolution] 1899. 37 p. [3183

Davis, R. L. Thirteen years of prohibition in N. C. and what it has wrought. Raleigh, Anti-saloon League [1922?] 8 p. [3184

Davis, Randolph David. Public big roads of God. 2d ed. [Newberry, S. C., Herald and News, c.1901] 48 p. [3185

Davis, Rebecca Harding. Silhouettes of American life. New York, C. Scribner's Sons, 1892. 280 p. [3186

Davis, Richard Bryant. A manual of tobacco culture. Hickory, Hall Brothers, n.d. 30 p. [3187

Davis, Robert Hobart. The caliph of Bagdad, being Arabian night flashes of the life, letters, and work of O. Henry . . . [by] Robert H. Davis and Arthur B. Maurice. New York, D. Appleton and Co., 1931. 411 p. [3188

——People, people everywhere. New York, Frederick A. Stokes Co., 1936. 355 p. [3189

[Davis, Ruth] Tourist's and shopper's guide, Boone, Blowing Rock, and Linville, N. C. [Boone? The Author] n.d. 30 p. [3190

Davis, S. M. Children in front. Shelby, Babington, Roberts & Co., 1888. 47 p. [3191

Davis, Thomas Frederick, 1804-1870. Address delivered before the two literary societies of the University of North Carolina . . . in June, 1845. Raleigh, Printed by W. R. Gales [1845] 16 p. [3192

[Davis, Thomas Frederick] 1804-1870. Church Home; the sermon and reports at the third anniversary celebration of the Church Home . . . June 11th, 1853. Charleston, Printed by A. E. Miller, 1853. 13 p. [3193

Davis, Thomas Frederick, 1877- A genealogical record of the Davis, Swann and Cabell families of North Carolina and Virginia. [Jacksonville, Fla., c.1934] 40 p. [3194

Davis, Thomas Walker. The bar, it's [!] duties and burdens; the president's address . . . at the twenty-third annual session of the North Carolina Bar Association . . . July 5, 1921. [Charlotte? 1921?] 14 p. [3195

Davison, Wilburt Cornell. The compleat pediatrician . . . 3d ed. Durham, Duke University Press, 1940. [316] p. [3196

Dawley, Thomas Robinson. The child that toileth not; the story of a government investigation. New York, Gracia Publishing Co. [c.1912] 490 p. [3197

The dawn, 1921- Durham, Student Body of the Durham Business School, 1921- NcU has 1921 [3198

Dawn of day, no. 1- 188 - Asheville and Waynesville, Convocation of Asheville, 188 - NcU has new series, no. 169-192. [3199

Dawson and Co., Charlotte, N. C. 2,000,000 acres of land for sale! No place, no publisher, n.d. 1 p. [3200

Day, David L. My diary of rambles with the 25th Mass. Volunteer Infantry, with Burnside's coast division. [Milford, Mass., King & Billings, pr., 1884] 153 p. [3201

Day, W. A.　True history of Company 1, 49th Regiment, North Carolina troops, in the great Civil War.　Newton, Enterprise, 1893.　127 p.　　　　　　　[3202

A day at a North Carolina association.　Baltimore, Maryland Baptist Mission Rooms, n.d.　[15] p.　　　　　　　　　　　　　　　　　　　　　[3203

The deadly parallel, Ashe vs. Lacy. ¨ No place, no publisher]1908?]　1 p.　　[3204

The Deaf Carolinian　see **The North Carolinian**

Deal, Romulus Columbus.　. . . Deal-Stafford genealogical history, compiled by Rom C. Deal and Miss Kelsie Deal.　[Taylorsville] Printed by the Taylorsville Times, c.1939.　150 p.　　　　　　　　　　　　　　　　　　　　[3205

Deal, Walter E.　The county of Macon and the town of Franklin, North Carolina. Franklin, Franklin Press, 1904.　30 p.　　　　　　　　　　　　　　　[3206

Dean, John Ward.　Sketch of the life of Frederic Kidder.　Boston, Printed for private circulation, 1887.　16 p.　　　　　　　　　　　　　　　　　[3207

Debnam, Waldeman Eras.　The story of "Oxford 26".　No place [Smith-Douglass Co., Inc.] n.d.　[13] p.　　　　　　　　　　　　　　　　　　　　[3208
——Then my old Kentucky home, good night!　[Raleigh, 1955]　135 p.　　[3209
——This is Debnam.　[Raleigh, WPTF [1946?]　16 p.　　　　　　　　　[3210
——Weep no more, my lady.　[Raleigh, Graphic Press, Inc., c.1950]　60 p.　　[3211
—— ——64 p.　　　　　　　　　　　　　　　　　　　　　　　[3212

De Bow, James Dunwoody Brownson.　The southern states.　Washington, 1856. 560 p.　　　　　　　　　　　　　　　　　　　　　　　　　[3213

De Bry, Theodore　see **Bry, Theodor de**

De Conval, Ronleigh, pseud.　see **Pollock, John Alfred**

De Costa, Benjamin Franklin.　Verrazano the explorer: being a vindication of his letters and voyage.　New York, A. S. Barnes & Co., 1880.　82 p.　　　[3214

Dedication and unveiling of marker of Appalachian Indian road and buffalo trail, October 5, 1930.　No place, no publisher [1930]　[3] p.　　　　　　　[3215

Dedication of a memorial in memory of Nannie Graham Parrish Carr, Trinity Church, Durham, N. C.　No place, no publisher, 1920.　2 p.　　　　　[3216

Dedication of the Alston Grimes Memorial Auditorium, Grimesland High School, May 20, 1915.　No place, no publisher [1915?]　11 p.　　　　　　[3217

Dedication of the City Building, Asheville, N. C.　[Asheville, Jarrett's Press, 1928] 12 p.　　　　　　　　　　　　　　　　　　　　　　　　[3218

Deems, Charles Force.　Address delivered before the Grand Division of the Order of the Sons of Temperance of North Carolina, in the Presbyterian Church, Raleigh . . . 19th of Oct. 1847.　Philadelphia, The Society, 1847.　28 p.　　[3219
——An address delivered before the literary societies of Randolph-Macon College June, 1847.　Philadelphia, Sorin and Ball, 1847.　27 p.　　　　　　[3220
——Autobiography and memoir by his sons, E. M. Deems and F. M. Deems.　New York, Fleming H. Revell Co. [c.1897]　365 p.　　　　　　　　　[3221
——Deems birthday-book; selections from the writings of Rev. Charles F. Deems. New York, Funk & Wagnalls, 1882.　397 p.　　　　　　　　　　[3222
——Devotional melodies.　Raleigh, Published by Th. Jefferson Lemay, 1841. 48 p.　　　　　　　　　　　　　　　　　　　　　　　　　　[3223
——Discourse delivered in the Methodist Episcopal Church, at Raleigh, N. C. on Sunday, 20th of November, 1842.　Raleigh, Printed by Thomas Loring, 1842. 15 p.　　　　　　　　　　　　　　　　　　　　　　　　　[3224
——Dr. Deems' sermons; forty-eight discourses.　New York, Funk & Wagnalls, 1886.　304 p.　　　　　　　　　　　　　　　　　　　　　　[3225
——Gospel of commonsense as contained in the canonical epistle of James.　New York, Wilbur B. Ketcham [c.1888]　322 p.　　　　　　　　　　[3226
——Gospel of spiritual insight, being studies in the Gospel of St. John.　New York, Wilbur B. Ketcham [c.1891]　365 p.　　　　　　　　　　　　[3227
——Home altar.　New York, M. W. Dodd, 1851.　281 p.　　　　　　[3228
—— ——1855.　　　　　　　　　　　　　　　　　　　　　[3229
—— ——New York, Published by Hurd and Houghton, 1878.　　　　[3230
——Jesus.　New York, U. S. Publishing Co., 1872.　756 p.　　　　　　[3231
——The light of the nations.　New York, Gay Brothers & Co. [c.1884]　755 p.　[3232
——My septuagint.　New York, Cassell Publishing Co. [c.1892]　207 p.　　[3233

——A Scotch verdict in re-evolution. New York, John W. Lovell Co. [c.1885] 108 p.   [3234
——Sketch of a sermon, delivered before the North Carolina Bible Society . . . Raleigh . . . 12th of Dec., 1841. Raleigh, Weston R. Gales, 1841. 16 p.   [3235
——Speech on the trial of Rev. Wm. A. Smith, D. D. for immorality, before the Va. conference, Dec. 1855. Wilmington, Fulton & Price, pr., 1858. 168 p.   [3236
[Deems, Charles Force] The triumph of peace, and other poems. New York, D. Fanshaw, 1840. 96 p.   [3237
——Twelve college sermons. Philadelphia, Sorin and Ball, 1846. 256 p.   [3238
Deems, Cnarles Force. Twelve sermons. New York, The Author, 1855. 244 p. [3239
—— ——1856.   [3240
——What it has done, and what we must do; an address delivered before the Grand Division of the Order of the Sons of Temperance of North Carolina . . . Raleigh . . . 19th of October, 1847. 2d ed. Philadelphia, T. K. and P. G. Collins, pr., 1847. 28 p.   [3241
——What now? For young ladies leaving school. New York, M. W. Dodd, 1852. 130 p.   [3242
——What now? A present for young ladies. 1854.   [3243
——Who was Jesus? New York, J. Howard Brown [c.1880] 756 p.   [3244
Deep River Mining and Transportation Co. Charter and by-laws. Albany, Weed, Parsons & Co., 1851. 14 p.   [3245
[Defoe, Daniel] The case of Protestant dissenters in Carolina. London, Printed in the year 1706. 67 p. NcU has photostat.   [3246
——Party-tyranny: or, An occasional bill in miniature. London, Printed in the year 1705. 30 p.   [3247
[De Fontaine, Felix Gregory] Marginalia; or, Gleanings from an army note-book. By "Personne" [pseud.] Columbia, S. C., F. G. DeFontaine & Co., pr., 1864. 248 p.   [3248
deGraffenried, Christopher   see Graffenried, Christopher, baron von

De Grummond, Jane Lucas. Envoy to Caracas; the story of John G. A. Williamson. Baton Rouge, Louisiana State University Press [1951] 228 p.   [3249
De Jean, Louis Leon. Junior citizen. New York, Philosophical Library [1948] 204 p.   [3250
De Koven, Anna (Farwell) A fictitious Paul Jones masquerading as the real. [New York, The New York Times, c.1906] 30 p.   [3251
——The life and letters of John Paul Jones. New York, C. Scribner's Sons, 1913. 2 v.   [3252
Delakas, Daniel L. Thomas Wolfe, la France, et les romanciers francais. Paris, Jouve & Cie., 1950. 154 p.   [3253
De La Torre, Lillian. The white rose of Stuart; the story of Flora Macdonald. New York, T. Nelson [1954] 214 p.   [3254
De Laubenfels, Max Walker. Ecology of the sponges of a brackish water environment, at Beaufort, N. C. Durham, Duke University Press, 1947. (Duke University. Marine Station, Beaufort, N. C. Bulletin, no. 4) 46 p.   [3255
Delaval; a novel. Newbern, Franklin & Garrow, 1804. 345 p.   [3256
Delille, Jacques Montanier, called. The rural philosopher; or, French Georgics, a didactic poem trans. from the original . . . L'homme des champs, by John Maunde. Newbern, Franklin and Garrow, 1804. 172 p.   [3257
Delke, James Almerius. History of the North Carolina Chowan Baptist Association, 1806-1881. Raleigh, Edwards, Broughton & Co., 1882. 111 p.   [3258
Dell School, Delway, N. C. Catalogue, 190 - Delway, 190 - NcU has [1904/05-1919/20]   [3259
Delta Kappa Epsilon. Beta. North Carolina University. Delta Kappa Epsilon, one hundred years of Beta, University of North Carolina, Chapel Hill, N. C. [Chapel Hill, 1951] [20] p.   [3260
Delta Kappa Gamma Society. North Carolina State Organization. Some pioneer women teachers of North Carolina. No place, The Society, 1955. 213 p. [3261
Demerath, Nicholas J., joint ed.   see Vance, Rupert Bayless, ed.
De Mille, Henry Churchill. The plays of Henry C. De Mille, written in collabora-

tion with David Belasco. Princeton, N. J., Princeton University Press, 1941.
[America's lost plays, v. xvii]   342 p.   [3262

De Mille, William Churchill.   "Food"; a tragedy of the future.   New York, Samuel
French, Ltd., c.1914.   16 p.   [3263
——The forest ring: a play in three acts, by William C. De Mille and Charles Bar-
nard.   New York, Samuel French, c.1921.   56 p.   [3264
——Hollywood saga.   New York, E. P. Dutton & Co., Inc. [c.1939]   319 p.   [3265
——"In 1999"; a problem play of the future.   New York, Samuel French, c.1914.
15 p.   [3266
——"Poor old Jim"; a sketch in one act.   New York, Samuel French, c.1914.
16 p.   [3267
——Strongheart; an American comedy drama in four acts.   New York, Samuel
French, c.1909.   98 p.   [3268

Deming, Frederick L.   Disposal of southern war plants, by Frederick L. Deming and
Weldon A. Stein.   [Washington, National Planning Association, 1949?] (NPA
Committee of the South.   Reports, no. 2)   74 l.   [3269

Democratic Party. National Committee, 1852-1856. Sketches of the lives of
Franklin Pierce and Wm. R. King, candidates of the Democratic Republican
Party for the presidency and vice presidency of the United States. [No place,
1852]   36 p.   [3271

Democratic rule in Beaufort County from 1898 to 1908.   No place, no publisher, n.d.
22 p.   [3272

Democratic State Rights Convention, Britton's Cross Roads, N. C., May 4, 1839.
Address to the people of the second congressional district of N. C.   [Britton's
Cross Roads, no publisher, 1839]   6 p.   [3273

Democratic text-book, containing the lives of Pierce and King.   Philadelphia,
Printed by James Fullerton [1852?]   48 p.   [3274

Democrats on the run; a change of base; Simmons reverses his whole policy and bids
for the Negro vote.   No place, no publisher [1898]   4 p.   [3275

DeMond, Robert O.   The loyalists in North Carolina during the Revolution.   Durham, Duke University Press, 1940.   286 p.   [3276

De Morgan, John.   Marion and his men.   Philadelphia, David McKay [c.1892]
214 p.   [3277

Denham, Adeline.   Monotheism; a prize thesis in competition for the Graham Kenan
fellowship.   [Chapel Hill, Department of Philosophy of the University of N. C.]
1922.   7 p.   [3278

Denny, George Vernon.   Democracy and leadership; an address delivered at the
commencement exercises of Temple University . . . June 13, 1940.   [Philadel-
phia? 1940?]   9 p.   [3279
——Free speech in wartime.   New York, The Town Hall [1942?]   [2] p.   [3280

Denny, Joseph Waldo.   Wearing the blue in the Twenty-fifth Mass. Volunteer Infantry, with Burnside's coast division.   Worcester, Putnam & Davis, 1879.
523 p.   [3281

Denny, Sidney B.   Wilson Primitive Baptist Church, Wilson, North Carolina.
[Wilson, 1946]   52 p.   [3282

Denson, Claude Baker.   Address delivered in Raleigh, N. C. on Memorial Day,
May 10, 1895; containing a memoir of the late Maj.-Gen. William Henry Chase
Whiting of the Confederate army.   Raleigh, Edwards & Broughton, 1895.
56 p.   [3283
——An address in memory of Thomas M. Holt, governor of North Carolina . . .
delivered in . . . Raleigh, October 27, 1898.   Raleigh, Alford, Bynum & Christophers, pr., 1899.   30 p.   [3284
——Address, upon the invitation of the Daughters of the Confederacy of N. C.,
delivered . . . in Raleigh, Oct. 10, 1900.   No place, no publisher, n.d.   20 p. [3285
——Price list . . . Kelvyn gardens, Pittsboro, Chatham County, N. C., 18 - Raleigh, 18 - NcU has 1870, 1874, and a later issue not dated.   [3286

Dental Foundation of North Carolina, Inc.   The background, the School of Den-
tistry, the Dental Foundation, your opportunity.   [Chapel Hill] The Dental
Foundation [1951]   [15] p.   [3287

Denver Academy, Denver, N. C. Catalogue, 1889/90- Lincolnton, 1890- NcU has 1889/90 [3288

DePew, E. Douglas. Land of waterfalls; text and photographs by E. Douglas DePew and Bob Tinsley. Asheville, Stephens Press, 1954. Unpaged. [3289

De Peyster, John Watts. Battle, or Affair of King's Mountain, Saturday, 7th Oct., 1780; being the address delivered at the annual meeting of the New York Historical Society . . . 4th Jan., 1881. No place, no publisher, n.d. 8 p. [3290

Derby, William P. Bearing arms in the Twenty-seventh Massachusetts Regiment of Volunteer Infantry during the Civil War. Boston, Wright & Potter Printing Co., 1883. 607 p. [3291

Derendinger, Ernst. Art survey . . . lecture course, 1934/35- Salisbury, Catawba College [c.1934- NcU has 1934/35 [3292

De Rosset, Armand John. Dissertatio medica inauguralis de febribus intermittentibus quam annuente summo numine sub moderamine viri admodum reverendi, Gulielmi Smith, S. T. P. Academiae Philadelphiensis praefecti. Philadelphiae, Typis Thomae Dobson, 1790. 34 p. [3293

DeRosset, William Lord, ed. Pictorial and historical New Hanover County and Wilmington, North Carolina, 1723-1938. Wilmington, W. L. deRosset, 1938. [110] p. [3294

DeRosset, William Lord. Wilmington, the port city of North Carolina. Wilmington, The Author, 1937. [46] p. [3295

Derrick, Samuel Melanchthon. Centennial history of South Carolina Railroad. Columbia, S. C., The State Co., 1930. 335 p. [3296

Dershem, Elsie. Outline of American state literature. Lawrence, Kansas, World Co., 1921. 187 p. [3297

Description du pays nommé Caroline. No place, no publisher, n.d. 3 p. NcU has photostat. [3299

DeVane, William Clyde. A Browning handbook. New York, F. S. Crofts & Co., 1935. 533 p. [3300

——Browning's Parleyings; the autobiography of a mind. New Haven, Yale University Press, 1927. 306 p. [3301

Devereux, Margaret. Plantation sketches. Cambridge, privately printed at the Riverside Press, 1906. 168 p. [3302

Deveron, Hugh, pseud. see Huger, Arthur Deveron

Devin, Robert I. History of Grassy Creek Baptist Church, from its foundation to 1880. Raleigh, Edwards & Broughton, 1880. · 150 p. [3303

De Weese, Fred C. Transmission lines. New York, McGraw-Hill Book Co., 1945. 297 p. [3304

Dewey, Thomas Webber. Christ the Lord is risen today! Richmond, Whittet & Shepperson, pr., n.d. 13 p. [3305

Dewitt, David Miller. The impeachment and trial of Andrew Johnson. New York, Macmillan Co., 1903. 646 p. [3306

Dey, William Morton, ed. Adolphe, par Benjamin Constant. New York, Oxford University Press, 1918. 164 p. [3307

A dialogue between two ministers of the Gospel on the subject of Masonry. [Tarboro, Free Press] n.d. 8 p. [3308

Diamond Cotton Chopper and Cultivator Company, Fayetteville, N. C. Read and circulate! The greatest labor-saver of the 19th century. Fayetteville [1874] 59 p. [3309

Dibble, Roy Floyd. Albion W. Tourgée. New York, Lemcke & Buechner, 1921. 160 p. [3310

Dick, Robert Paine. Address delivered at Chapel Hill, N. C., Wed. June 7th, 1893, commencement day. Greensboro, Thomas Brothers, pr., 1893. 29 p. [3311

——Bible pictures. Greensboro, New North State , 1873. 27 p. [3312

——Children in history . . . delivered before the Guilford County Sunday School Convention in 1880. Greensboro. Thomas Brothers, pr., 1891. 35 p. [3313

——Discourse upon the life and character of Hon. Thomas Ruffin . . . on the 27th of August, 1889. Greensboro, Bar of Guilford Co., 1889. 22 p. [3314

——Hebrew poetry; Sunday afternoon lectures before the Greensboro Law School. Greensboro, Thomas Brothers, pr., 1883. 205 p.   [3315
——Introductory lecture before the Law School, Greensboro, N. C., 1880- Greensboro, Jos. M. Reece, pr., 1880- NcU has first and second sessions, 1880, 1881; first sessions, 1885, 1887, 1888   [3316
——Legend of light; a lecture read before the Sunday School Bible class of the First Presbyterian Church of Greensboro, Jan. 27th, 1895. Greensboro, Thomas Bros., pr., 1895. 21 p.   [3317

[Dick, Robert Paine?] Letters of an old citizen. No place, no publisher [1895?] 17 p.   [3318

Dick, Robert Paine. Memorial address on the life and character of Richard Mumford Pearson, chief justice of North Carolina . . . on the occasion of the unveiling of the statue erected to his memory in Oakwood Cemetery, June 8th, 1881. Raleigh, News and Observer Book and Job Print [1881?] 21 p.   [3319

[Dick, Mrs. Robert Paine] The making of toothsome tit-bits. No place, no publisher [pref. 1897] 8 p.   [3320

Dickerson, Oliver Morton. American colonial government, 1696-1765. Cleveland, Ohio, Arthur H. Clark Co., 1912. 390 p.   [3321

Dickeson, Montroville Wilson. Report of the geological survey and condition of the Rhea Mine, in the county of Mecklenburg, North Carolina. Philadelphia, J. B. Chandler, pr., 1860. 10 p.   [3322
——Report of the geological survey and condition of the Twin Mine in the county of Guilford, N. C. Philadelphia, J. B. Chandler, pr., 1860. 11 p.   [3323

Dickey, Luther Samuel. History of the 103d Regiment, Pennsylvania Veteran Volunteer Infantry, 1861-1865. Chicago, L. S. Dickey, 1910. 400 p.   [3324

Dickins, Samuel. To the electors of the district composed of the counties of Wake, Orange, and Person. [Raleigh, July 6, 1816] [2] p.   [3325

Dicks, Russell Leslie. And peace at the last; a study of death . . . by Russell L. Dicks and Thomas S. Kepler. Philadelphia, Westminster Press [1953] 94 p. [3326
——My faith looks up. Philadelphia, Westminster Press [1949] 96 p.   [3327
——Pastoral work and personal counseling. Rev. ed. New York, Macmillan Co., 1949. 195 p.   [3328

Dickson, Charlie Monroe. Fireside philosophy. Boston, Christopher Publishing House [c.1940- NcU has v. 1   [3329

Dickson, J. A. An address delivered before the members of "Piedmont Lodge" I. O. O. F. in Morganton, on the 23d of October, 1850. Lincolnton, Printed by Thomas J. Eccles, 1851. 11 p.   [3330

Dickson, James Henderson. Address delivered before the Alumni Association of the University of North Carolina, June, 1853. Raleigh, Southern Weekly Post, 1853. 43 p.   [3331

[Dickson, John] Questions for self-examination for the young. [Asheville? 184?] [2] p.   [3332

Dickson, Sallie O'Hear. Poems, by "O. H." Richmond, Whittet & Shepperson, pr., 1900. , 62 p.   [3333
——Ralph Fabian's mistakes. New York, Broadway Publishing Co. [c.1908] 175 p.   [3334
——Reuben Delton, preacher: a sequel to "The story of Marthy." Richmond, Va. Presbyterian Committee of Publication [c.1900] 296 p.   [3335
——Stories for Grandma Bright's missionary evenings. [Winston-Salem?] n.d. 32 p.   [3336
——Story of Marthy. Richmond, Presbyterian Committee of Publication [c.1898] 269 p.   [3337
——"Within our doors"; our work among the Negroes. Richmond, Presbyterian Board of Publication [1913] 32 p.   [3338

Dickson, Thomas J. The world war; major tactics of the greatest battle in history, July 18 to November 11, 1918. Washington, Park Press for Charles M. Stedman, c.1929. Folder   [3339

Dickson, William. The Dickson letters; comp. and ed. by James O. Carr. Raleigh, Edwards & Broughton, pr., 1901. 42 p.   [3340

Diet of the Evangelical Lutheran Church in the South. Minutes of the Diet . . .

held at Court House, Salisbury, N. C., November 12th and 13th, 1884. New Market, Va., Henkel & Co., pr. [1884] 14 p. [3341

Digger, v. 1- 191 - Asheville, Literary Societies of Fruitland Institute, 191 - NcU has v. 3 [3342

Digges, George A., comp. Buncombe County, North Carolina, grantee deed index. Asheville, Miller Press, Inc. [c.1927] 2 v. [3343
——Buncombe County, North Carolina, grantor deed index. Asheville, Miller Press, Inc. [c.1926] 3 v. [3344

Digges, George A. Historical facts concerning Buncombe County government. [Asheville] 1935. 316 p. [3345

Dill, Alonzo Thomas. Governor Tryon and his palace. Chapel Hill, University of North Carolina Press [1955] 304 p. [3346

Dillard, Richard. At autumn time. Norfolk, Burke & Gregory, 1907. [15] p. [3347
——A brief history of Edenton and its environs, . . . compiled by Dr. Richard Dillard and Capt. Richard D. Dixon. [Elizabeth City, Independent] n.d. 8 p. [3348
——Captain Jake's place, a reminiscence of "Old Edenton". NcU has microfilm [3349
——The Civil War in Chowan County. No place, no publisher, 1916. 30 p. [3350
——Curious experience with the tombstone of a pirate. [Edenton, no publisher, 1906] 7 p. [3351
——The golden treasure of the Albemarle. Edenton, Transcript Printery, 1907. 12 p. [3352
——The historic tea-party of Edenton, October 25th, 1774; an incident connected with British taxation. [Edenton, 1898] 16 p. [3353
—— ——[Norfolk, Burke and Gregory, 1907] 16 p. [3354
—— ——[6th ed.] [Edenton? 1925] 17 p. [3355
——Historical reminiscences, Centre Hill. No place, no publisher [1918] 7 p. [3356
——Little Marie's papa. [Edenton, 1925] [7] p. [3357
——Old Brownrigg Mill and its memories. No place, no publisher [1924] 16 p. [3358
——Old Gaskin's funeral, from a physician's diary. NcU has microfilm [3359
——The poetic beauty and literary value of the Song of Solomon. No place, no publisher, n.d. 15 p. [3360
——Points of interest in and near Edenton. No place, no publisher, n.d. Folder. [3361
——Some legends of Eastern North Carolina. Edenton, no publisher [1926] 22 p. [3362
——The song of the south wind. [Edenton?] 1913. [1] p. [3363
——That affair of Gordon's. [Edenton? The Author?] n.d. [4] p. [3364

Dinkins, Charles [Roundtree] Lyrics of love. Columbia, S. C., The State Co. [1904] 230 p. [3365

Diocese of N. C. Protestant Episcopal Church **see Protestant Episcopal Church. Diocese of N. C.**

. . . Directory of American society, Georgia, Louisiana, . . . North and South Carolina . . . v. 1- 1929- New York, Town Topics [c.1929- NcU has v. 1 [3366

Directory of Charlotte, N. C., 189 - Charlotte, Blakey Printing House for J. S. Drakeford, 189 - NcU has 1893-94 [3367

Directory of Granville County, N. C., 19 - No place, no publisher, 19 - NcU has 1908 [3368

Directory of greater Durham, North Carolina, v. 1- 189 - Durham, Samuel L. Adams, 189 - NcU has 1902 [3369

Directory of life insurance agents . . . North Carolina, 193 - Raleigh, Dixie Underwriter Publishing Co., 1931- NcU has 1931/32 [3370

Directory of Moore County, Carthage, Pinehurst, Hemp, Southern Pines, Vass, Cameron and Aberdeen; May, 1925. [Albemarle, Selders' Directory Co., 1925] 124 p. [3371

Directory of Negro businesses and professions, Durham, N. C. [Durham, Senior Commercial Class of 1938, Hillside Park High School, 1938] [14] p. [3372

Directory of rural residents; comprising the names of rural residents in the vicinity of Durham and Raleigh, North Carolina. Norfolk, Va., Directories Publishing Corporation, 1906. 42 p. [3373

Directory of rural residents, series D, no. 7, comprising the names of rural residents in the vicinity of Greensboro, High Point, and Winston-Salem, N. C., Norfolk, Va., Directories Publishing Corporation, 1906. 32 p.   [3374

Directory of students of Methodist preference and affiliation at the University of N. C., 1926-7. No place, no publisher, n.d. 8 p.   [3375

Directory of the business and citizens of Durham city, 1887- Raleigh, Levi Branson, 1887- NcU has 1887   [3376

Directory of the city of Raleigh, North Carolina, 1887- Raleigh, Edwards, Broughton & Co., 1887- NcU has 1887   [3377

Directory of the city of Raleigh, 1888- Raleigh, Observer Printing Co., 1888- NcU has 1888   [3378

Directory of the city of Raleigh, N. C., 189 - [Raleigh] Raleigh Stationery Co. [1896- NcU has 1896-7   [3379

Directory of the city of Wilmington, N. C., 18 - Wilmington, J. A. Bonitz, 18 - NcU has 1889   [3380

Directory of the drug stores in North Carolina, January, 1922, compiled by J. G. Beard for the North Carolina Pharmaceutical Association. [Durham, Seeman Printery] 1922. 31 p.   [3381

Directory of Wake county taxpayers, 192 - Raleigh, Mattison Advertising Co., 192 - NcU has 1929, 1930, 1933   [3382

Disciples of Christ. North Carolina. Carolina enlargement campaign. Raleigh, Commercial Printing Co., 1920. 13 p.   [3383

——Disciples of Christ in North Carolina; articles of incorporation, constitution and by-laws. Wilson, North Carolina Christian Missionary Convention [1945?] 12 p.   [3384

——Minutes of N. C. Christian Missionary Convention, 18 - 18 - NcU has 1887-1907, 1909-1947. Title varies, 1912- : Yearbook.   [3385

——Program, eighty-third annual meeting . . . Golden jubilee convention . . . Kinston, N. C., Nov. 8-10, 1927. No place, 1927. [4] p.   [3387

——Tar Heel Disciples, 1841-1852. New Bern, Owen G. Dunn Co., 1942. 104 p. [3388

Discussion between the gubernatorial candidates, at Goldsboro. No place, no publisher, n.d. 14 p.   [3389

Dismal Swamp Canal Company. Memorial and other papers to the Senate and House of Representatives of the United States of America, December, 1877. [Norfolk, Va.? 1877] 17 p.   [3390

——Memorial to the Senate and House of Representatives . . . December, 1877. [Norfolk, Va.? 1877] 6 p.   [3391

[Distributive, Processing and Office Workers of America] A brief history of the organizing struggles of the workers in the R. J. Reynolds plants in Winston-Salem, N. C. since 1942. No place, 1951?] 10 p.   [3392

Ditterlane, T. Sketch of the battles of Gettysburg, July 1st, 2d, and 3d, 1863. New York, C. A. Alvord, pr., 1863. 24 p.   [3393

Division of Cooperation in Education and Race Relations. Proceedings of conference, May 20-21, 1935- [Chapel Hill] 1935- NcU has 1925, 1936   [3394

The Dixie dog news, v. 1- March, 1926- Raleigh, W. T. Scarborough, 1926- NcU has v. [1-4]   [3395

The Dixie druggist, v. 1- April-July, 1913- Hickory, 1913- NcU has v.. 1, no. 1-4   [3396

Dixie underwriter, a magazine of facts . . . for those engaged in the business of insurance, v. 1- January, 1930- Raleigh, 1930- NcU has v. 1-4 [5] Title varies, v. 1, no. 1-2: Tar Heel underwriter   [3397

Dixon, Amzi Clarence. Evangelism old and new. New York, American Tract Society [c.1905] 209 p.   [3398

——Milk and meat; twenty-four sermons. New York, Baker and Taylor Co. [c.1893] 275 p.   [3399

[Dixon, Arthur Wilson] Greenland, 1943-1945. [Gastonia, 1945] 14 p.   [3400

Dixon, Benjamin Franklin. Peter Francisco; an address delivered at the unveiling of a tablet to his memory at Guilford Battle Ground, July 4th, 1910. Greensboro, Guilford Battle Ground Co. [1910?] 12 p.   [3401

Dixon, Helen (Cadbury) Alexander.   A. C. Dixon, a romance of preaching.   New York, G. P. Putnam's Sons, 1931.   324 p.   [3402

Dixon, Margaret Collins (Denny)   Denny genealogy, by Margaret Collins Denny Dixon and Elizabeth Chapman Denny Vann.   New York, National Historical Society, 1944-1951.   v. 2, Rutland, Vt., Tuttle Publishing Co., 1947; v. 3, Richmond, Va., 1951.   3 v.   [3403

Dixon, Thomas.   The black hood. New York, D. Appleton and Co., 1924. 336 p. [3404

——. . . The clansman. New York, American News Co., c.1905. [58] p. [3405

——The clansman. New York, Doubleday, Page & Co., 1905. 374 p.   [3406

—— ——1907.   [3407

——Campanions. New York, Otis Publishing Corporation, 1931. 303 p.   [3408

——Comrades. New York, Doubleday, Page & Co., 1909. 319 p.   [3409

—— ——New York, Grosset and Dunlap [c.1909]   [3410

——Dixon on Ingersoll; ten discourses delivered in Association Hall, New York. New York, Ogilvie, 1892. 198 p.   [3411

——Dixon's sermons; delivered in the Grand Opera House, New York, 1898-1899. New York, F. L. Bussey & Co., 1899. 156 p.   [3412

——Failure of Protestantism in New York and its causes. New York, Victor O. A. Strauss, 1896. 186 p.   [3413

——The fall of a nation, a sequel to The birth of a nation. New York, D. Appleton and Co., 1916. 361 p.   [3414

——The flaming sword. Atlanta, Monarch Publishing Co., 1939. 562 p.   [3415

——The foolish virgin. New York, D. Appleton and Co., 1915. 352 p.   [3416

——The inside story of the Harding tragedy, by Harry M. Daugherty . . . in collaboration with Thomas Dixon. New York, Churchill Co., 1932. 323 p.   [3417

——The leopard's spots. New York, Doubleday, Page & Co., 1902. 465 p.   [3418

—— ——New York, Grosset & Dunlap [c.1902]   469 p.   [3419

—— ——New York, Doubleday, Page & Co., 1903.   [3420

—— ——1906.   [3421

——The life worth living, a personal experience. New York, Doubleday, Page & Co., 1905. 140 p.   [3422

—— ——1914.   [3423

——Living problems in religion and social science. New York, Charles T. Dillingham, 1889. 253 p.   [3424

——The love complex. New York, Boni & Liveright, 1925. 287 p.   [3425

——The man in gray. New York, D. Appleton and Co., 1921. 427 p.   [3426

——A man of the people; a drama of Abraham Lincoln. New York, D. Appleton and Co., 1920. 155 p.   [3427

——The one woman. New York, Doubleday, Page & Co., 1903. 350 p.   [3428

—— ——New York, Grosset and Dunlap [c.1903]   [3429

——Root of evil. New York, Doubleday, Page & Co., 1911. 407 p.   [3430

—— ——New York, Grosset and Dunlap [c.1911]   [3431

——The sins of the father. New York, D. Appleton and Co., 1912. 462 p. [3432

——The southerner; a romance of the real Lincoln. New York, D. Appleton and Co., 1913. 543 p.   [3433

—— ——1915.   [3434

——The traitor. New York, Doubleday, Page & Co., 1907. 331 p.   [3435

—— ——New York, Grosset and Dunlap [c.1907]   [3436

——The victim; a romance of the real Jefferson Davis. New York, D. Appleton and Co., 1914. 510 p.   [3437

——The way of a man. New York, D. Appleton and Co., 1919. 295 p.   [3438

——Wildacres in the Land of the Sky. Little Switzerland, Wildacres Development Co., c.1926. [28] p.   [3439

Doak, Frances Renfrow.   Why North Carolina voted dry; read before a convention of the United Dry Forces in Greensboro, January 16, 1934. Raleigh, Capital Printing Co., 1934. 26 p.   [3440

Doak, Henry Melvil.   The Wagonauts abroad. Two tours in the wild mountains of Tennessee and North Carolina . . . By A. T. Ramp [pseud.] Nashville, Tenn., Southwestern Publishing House, 1892. 300 p.   [3441

Dobbin, James Cochran.   Address delivered before the two literary societies of the

University of North Carolina, June 5, 1850.   Fayetteville, Edward J. Hale, pr.,
1850. 23 p.   [3442
—— ——2d ed.   Chapel Hill, Published by James M. Henderson, Printer to the
University, 1859. 24 p.   [3443
Dobbins, D. P. Descriptive sketch of Winston-Salem, its advantages and sur-
roundings . . . compiled under auspices of the Chamber of Commerce. Winston,
Sentinel Job Print, 1888. 96 p.   [3444
Dobbs, Arthur. An account of the countries adjoining to Hudson's Bay in the north-
west part of America. London, Printed for J. Robinson, 1744. 211 p.   [3445
——An essay on the trade and improvement of Ireland. Dublin, Printed by A.
Rhames for J. Smith and W. Bruce on the Blind-Key, 1729. 99 p.   [3446
[Dobbs, Arthur] Some thoughts concerning government in general, and our present
circumstances in Great Britain and Ireland . . . by A. D. esq. Dublin, Printed by
and for S. Hyde, 1731. 60 p.   [3447
Dockery, A. V. Black bass and other fishing in North Carolina. Raleigh, Com-
mercial Printing Co., 1909. 176 p.   [3448
Dockery, James C. Oration delivered before the Philomathesian and Euselian
societies, at Wake Forest Institute, July 4, 1835. Raleigh, J. Gales & Son, pr.,
1835. 18 p.   [3449
Dockery at the lowest depth. No place, no publisher [1888] [1] p.   [3450
Dockery; the life and times of Oliver Hart Dockery—a colored narrative. No place,
no publisher [1888?] 23 p.   [3451
Dockery voting for Negro nominees. No place, no publisher [1888?] [1] p. [3452
Dr. Tyre York, the coalition candidate for Congress in the seventh congressional
district. No place, no publisher [1882] 4 p.   [3453
Documents shewing that Mecklenburg County, North-Carolina, declared her independence of Great-Britain, May 20, 1775. Raleigh, Printed by J. Gales & Son,
1822. 15 p.   [3454
Dodd, Rebekah (Young) Reminiscences, 1811-1911. [Henderson? The Author?]
1941. [37] p.   [3455
Dodd, William Edward. Ambassador Dodd's diary, 1933-1938; edited by William
E. Dodd, Jr., and Martha Dodd. New York, Harcourt, Brace and Co. [c.1941]
464 p.   [3456
——The cotton kingdom. New York, Yale University Press, 1921. (The chronicles
of America series [v. 27]) 161 p.   [3457
——Expansion and conflict. Boston, Houghton Mifflin Co. [c.1915] (The River-
side history of the United States [III]) 329 p.   [3458
——Jefferson Davis. Philadelphia, George W. Jacobs & Co. [1907] 396 p.   [3459
——The life of Nathaniel Macon. Raleigh, Edwards & Broughton, pr., 1903.
443 p.   [3460
——Lincoln or Lee. New York, Century Co. [c.1928] 177 p.   [3461
——The old South; struggles for democracy. New York, Macmillan Co., 1937.
312 p.   [3462
——Statesmen of the old South; or, From radicalism to conservative revolt. New
York, Macmillan Co., 1911. 242 p.   [3463
——Thomas Jeffersons rückkehr zur Politik 1796. Leipzig, Grübel & Sommerlatte,
pr. [1900?] 88 p. Thesis (Ph. D.)—University of Leipzig.   [3464
——Woodrow Wilson and his work. New York, Doubleday, Page & Co., 1920.
369 p.   [3465
—— ——New and rev. ed. New York, P. Smith, 1932. 454 p.   [3466
Dodge, Constance (Woodbury) . . . The dark stranger. Philadelphia, Penn Pub
lishing Co. [c.1940] 439 p.   [3467
——Weathercock. New York, Dodd, Mead & Co., 1942. 370 p.   [3468
Dodge, David, pseud. Lincoln as the South should know him. 2d ed. Raleigh
[Edwards and Broughton for] Manly's Battery Chapter, Children of the Con-
federacy [1915] 21 p.   [3469
—— ——3d ed. [Raleigh, Commercial Printing Co. for Manly's Battery Chap-
ter, Children of the Confederacy, 1915]. 20 p.   [3470
[Dodge, David] pseud. A protest against Lincoln worship at the South. Richmond,
Va., W. C. Hill Printing Co., 1915. 20 p.   [3471

Dodge, Richard Irving. Our wild Indians; thirty-three years' personal experience among the red men of the great West. Hartford, A. D. Worthington and Co., 1882. 650 p.   [3472

Dods, John Bovee. Thirty short sermons on various important subjects. 12th ed. Boston, James M. Usher, 1855. 348 p.   [3473

Does baptism mean immersion? Newbern, Thomas Watson, pr., 1832. 18 p. [3474

Does it pay? No place, no publisher, n.d. 1 p.   [3475

Does this system suit you? No place, no publisher [1930] [3] p.   [3476

Donaldson Academy and Manual Labor School, Fayetteville, N. C. Catalogue, 1833/34- Fayetteville, 1834- NcU has 1834/35   [3477

——Donaldson Academy located near Fayetteville, N. C. [Fayetteville, 1848?] [1] p.   [3478

Donnelly, Grant Lester. Alcohol and the habit-forming drugs. Raleigh, A. Williams & Co. [c.1936] 218 p.   [3479

Dooley, Albert Joseph. State taxation of motor vehicles. Philadelphia [University of Pennsylvania] 1934. 171 p. Thesis (Ph. D.)—University of Pennsylvania [3480

Dooley, Dennis A., ed. Index to state bar association reports and proceedings. New York, Baker, Voorhis & Co., Inc., 1942. 640 p.   [3481

Doran, Joseph I. Pennsylvania Society of Colonial Governors: Sir Walter Raleigh, address before the Council of the Society, February sixth, nineteen eleven. No place, n.d. 22 p.   [3482

Dorr, Louise S. Fountain spray and miscellaneous poems. Raleigh, E. M. Uzzell & Co., 1885. 100 p.   [3483

Dorrance, Ethel. Flames of the Blue Ridge, by Ethel and James Dorrance. New York, Macaulay Co. [c.1919] 342 p.   [3484

Dorris, Jonathan Truman. Pardon and amnesty under Lincoln and Johnson. Chapel Hill, University of North Carolina Press [1953] 459 p.   [3485

Dortch, William Theophilus. "Dortch answers Abernathy." No place, no publisher [1918] 14 p.   [3486

[**Dosier, J. F.**] Immersion or pouring and sprinkling, which? High Point, W. C. Phillips, pr., 1906. 13 p.   [3487

Doub, Belle [and others] Our heritage; a pageant of local history comprising the counties of Nash and Edgecombe. [Rocky Mount, Evening Telegram, 1919] 34 p.   [3488

Doub, Peter. Address delivered before the Grand Division of North Carolina, Sons of Temperance, at the Oct. session, 1852. Raleigh, Spirit of the Age, 1853. 37 p.   [3489

Doughton, J. K. Suggestions to bank directors. [Raleigh, no publisher, 1909] 19 p.   [3490

Douglas, John. History of Steele Creek Church, Mecklenburg, N. C. Columbia, S. C., Presbyterian Publishing House, 1872. 81 p.   [3491

—— ——Charlotte, Observer Printing Office, 1901. 83 p.   [3492

Douglas, Mary Teresa (Peacock) The teacher-librarian's handbook. 2d ed. Chicago, American Library Association, 1949. 166 p.   [3493

Douglas, Robert Dick, 1875- Administration of estates in North Carolina. Charlottesville, Va., Michie Co., 1948. 278 p.   [3494

Douglas, Robert Dick, 1875- ed. Douglas' Forms; a . . . compilation of legal and business forms for use in . . . North Carolina. Charlottesville, Va., The Michie Co., 1941- 5 v.   [3495

——Forms. 2d ed., rev. and enl. by Robert D. Ussery. Charlottesville, Va., Michie Co., 1953. 4 v.   [3496

——Greensboro as the location for a branch of the Federal Reserve Bank of Richmond to serve the Carolinas. Greensboro, Greensboro Clearing House Association [1924] 32 p.   [3497

Douglas, Robert Dick, 1912- A boy scout in the grizzly country. New York, G. P. Putnam's Sons, 1929. 181 p.   [3498

——In the land of the Thunder Mountains; adventures with Father Hubbard among the volcanoes of Alaska. New York, Brewer, Warren and Putnam, 1932. 160 p.   [3499

Douglas, Robert Dick, 1912- [and others] Three boy scouts in Africa, on safari with Martin Johnson. New York, G. P. Putnam's Sons, 1928. 149 p. [3500

Douglas, Robert Martin. Addresses. [Greensboro, J. Stone & Co., pr., 1897?] 25 p. [3501

——Claim of Rob't M. and Stephen A. Douglas, of Rockingham County, North Carolina, for their private cotton and other property taken . . . in March, 1863 . . . by a portion of the army of the United States. Wash., Printed by Powell & Ginck, 1872. 57 p. [3502

——Demands a square deal; a second open letter by candidate for corporation commissioner. [Greensboro, J. M. Reece & Co., 1906] 2 p. [3503

——Life and character of Gov. Alexander Martin. No place, no publisher, n.d. 15 p. [3504

——Railroad rates and taxation; an open letter to the people of N. C. [Greensboro, J. M. Reece & Co., 1906] 8 p. [3505

——Speech delivered at Statesville, North Carolina, Tuesday, Oct. 19, 1880. No place, no publisher, n.d. 7 p. [3506

——Stephen A. Douglas' attitude toward slavery. [Greensboro, no publisher, 1908] 4 p. [3507

——Trade combinations and strikes. No place, no publisher [1893] 15 p. [3508

Douglas, William W. Relief of Washington, North Carolina, by the Fifth Rhode Island Volunteers. Providence, The Society, 1886. (Personal narratives of events in the war of the rebellion, being papers read before the Rhode Island Soldiers and Sailors Historical Society. 3d ser. no. 17) 28 p. [3509

Douglass, Elisha P. Rebels and Democrats. Chapel Hill, University of North Carolina Press [c.1955] 368 p. [3510

Douglass, John Jordan. The bells. [Charlotte, Presbyterian Standard Publishing Co.] 1919. 104 p. [3511

——The gates of dreams. Newton, Martha Taylor Douglass, 1940. 315 p. [3512

——Girdle of the great. New York, Broadway Publishing Co. [c.1908] 197 p. [3513

——The quest of the star. Columbia, S. C., The State Co., n.d. [32] p. [3514

Douty, Harry Mortimer. . . . Wage and hour legislation for the South. Chapel Hill, University of North Carolina Press, 1937. (Southern policy papers, no. 9) 26 p. [3515

Dow, Lorenzo. Extracts from original letters to the Methodist bishops mostly from their preachers and members in North America giving an account of the work of God since the year 1800. Liverpool, Printed by H. Forshaw, 1806. 76 p. [3516

——A hint to the public. 3d ed. Salisbury, Printed by Coupee and Crider, 1811. 24 p. [3517

——History of Cosmopolite; or, The writings of Rev. Lorenzo Dow. 6th ed. Rev. and cor. with notes. Cincinnati, Queen City Publishing House, 1856. 720 p. [3518

——Life, travels, labors, and writings of Lorenzo Dow. New York, C. M. Saxton, 1859. 508 p. [3519

[Dow] Lorenzo. Quintessence of Lorenzo's works. 3d ed., cor. and enl. Philadelphia, Printed by Joseph Rakestraw, 1816. 700 p. [3520

Dow, Lorenzo. The Yankee spy; or, Cosmopolite's interesting analects of common sense. 5th ed., improved. Raleigh, Printed at the Minerva Press by Alex. Lucas, 1814. 110 p. [3521

Dow, Neal. The concept and term "nature" in Montaigne's Essays. Philadelphia, 1940. 68 p. Thesis (Ph. D.)—Univ. of Pennsylvania, 1938. [3522

Dowd, Clement. Life of Zebulon B. Vance. Charlotte, Observer Printing and Publishing House, 1897. 493 p. [3523

Dowd, Jerome. Burr and Hamilton; a New York tragedy in five acts. New York, Geo. W. Wheat, pr., 1884. 34 p. [3524

——Democracy in America. Oklahoma City, Harlow Publishing Co., 1921. 506 p. [3525

——Life of Braxton Craven. Raleigh, Edwards & Broughton, 1896. 246 p. [3526

——The life of Braxton Craven; a biographical approach to social science. Durham, Duke University Press, 1939. 246 p. [3527

——The Negro in American life. New York, Century Co. [c.1926] 611 p. [3528

——The Negro races, a sociological study. New York, Macmillan Co., 1907-1914. 2 v. [3529

——Shall clergymen be politicians? Criticism upon Dr. Van Dyke's article in the North American review. [New York, 1885] 8 p. [3530
——Sketches of prominent living North Carolinians. Raleigh, Edwards & Broughton, pr., 1888. 320 p. [3531

[Dowd, William Carey] The new conception of the countryside. [Charlotte, Charlotte News] n.d. 23 p. [3532

Dowdey, Clifford. The proud retreat; a novel of the lost Confederate treasure. Garden City, N. Y., Doubleday, 1953. 318 p. [3533

Dowell, Willard L. What is a sales tax? And why North Carolina should not adopt it. Raleigh, N. C. Merchants Association [1931?] 16 p. [3534

Dowling, Morgan E. Southern prisons. Detroit, William Graham, 1870. 506 p. [3535

Down homer, v. 1- 1910?- Elizabeth City, W. O. Saunders, 1910?- NcU has v. [1-7] [3536

Down in Dixie, Southern Pines, N. C. No place, no publisher, n.d. 54 p. [3537

Downing, Frances (Murdaugh) Nameless. Raleigh, W. B. Smith & Co., 1865. 232 p. [3538

[Downing, Frances (Murdaugh)] Pluto. Raleigh, John Nichols, pr., 1867. 35 p. [3539

Downing, J., major, pseud., see Davis, Charles Augustus, 1795-1867

Downs, Posey Edgar. The Captain Benjamin Newton-William Downs and other lineage history. [Shelby, Downs-Newton Ancestral Ass'n., 1954?] 373 p. [3540

Downs, Robert Bingham. American humorous folklore. Minneapolis, University of Minnesota Press for the University Library [c.1950] 42 p. [3541
——American library resources. Chicago, American Library Association, 1951. 428 p. [3542
——Books that changed the world. Chicago, American Library Association, 1956. 200 p. [3543
—— ——[New York] New American Library [c.1956] 200 p. [3544
——National Diet Library. Tokyo, National Diet Library, 1948. 31 p. [3545
——Resources of New York city libraries. Chicago, American Library Association, 1942. 442 p. [3546

Downs, Robert Bingham, ed. Resources of southern libraries. Chicago, American Library Association, 1938. 370 p. [3547
——Union catalogs in the United States. Chicago, American Library Association, 1942. 409 p. [3548
——A survey of research materials in North Carolina libraries. [Chapel Hill, The University of North Carolina Library, 1936] [3549

Downum, James Monroe. Lays of life from the Southern Appalachians. [Boone, The Author] n.d. 94 p. [3550

Doyle, John Alexander. The English in America; Virginia, Maryland, and the Carolinas. London, Longmans, Green, and Co., 1882. 556 p. [3551

[Doyle, John E. P.] Tar-heel tales in vernacular verse, by Major Jep Joslynn [pseud.] New York, M. Doolady, 1873. 69 p. [3552
—— ——New York, J. E. P. Doyle, 1881. [64] p. [3553

Dozier, Howard Douglas. A history of the Atlantic Coast Line Railroad. Boston, Houghton Mifflin Co., 1920. 197 p. [3554

Drake, James Madison. The history of the Ninth New Jersey Veteran Vols. A record of its service from September 13th, 1861, to July 12th, 1865. Elizabeth, N. J., Journal Printing House, 1889. 501 p. [3555

Drake, Samuel Gardiner. Brief memoir of Sir Walter Raleigh. Boston, The Author, 1862. 35 p. [3556

Drake, William E. The American school in transition. New York, Prentice-Hall, 1955. 624 p. [3557

Drane, Robert Brent. Address delivered in St. James' Church, Wilmington, N. C., at the interment of Dr. Thomas H. Wright, Monday, Sept. 23d, 1861. Wilmington, Fulton & Price, pr., 1861. 11 p. [3558

[Drane, Robert Brent] St. Paul's Edenton, N. C., parish organized 1701, this building begun 1736. No place, no publisher [1930] [3] p. [3559

Drane, Robert Brent. Sketch of St. James parish, Wilmington, N. C., from the

Historical notices of Rev. R. B. Drane. New York, E. J. Hale & Son, 1874. 84 p.   [3560

——A sketch of the life of Tristrim·Lowther Skinner, major of First Regiment, North Carolina Volunteers, Confederate States Army. [Edenton, The Author, 1931] 10 p.   [3561

Draper, Lyman Copeland. King's Mountain and its heroes. Cincinnati, P. G. Thomson, 1881. 612 p.   [3562

—— ——Facsimile reprint. New York, Dauber & Pine Bookshops, Inc., 1929.   [3563

—— ——Marietta, Ga., Continental Book Co., 1954.   [3564

Draper, William Franklin. Recollections of a varied career. Boston, Little, Brown and Co., 1908. 411 p.   [3565

Draughon, Wallace R. North Carolina genealogical reference; a research guide. Durham [The Author] 1956. 231 p.   [3566

Drayton, John. Memoirs of the American Revolution . . . as relating to the state of South-Carolina, and occasionally refering [!] to the states of North-Carolina and Georgia. Charleston, S. C., Printed by A. E. Miller, 1821. 2 v.   [3567

Drehar, Daniel I. A sermon delivered by . . . pastor of St. James' Church, Concord, N. C. June 13, 1861, day of humiliation and prayer. Salisbury, Watchman Office, 1861. 16 p.   [3568

Dreier, Theodore. [Report on the first fifteen years of Black Mountain College] Brooksville, Fla., 1949. 10 p.   [3569

Dress parade, 18 - Oak Ridge, The Cadet Corps of Oak Ridge Military Institute, 18 - NcU has 1952   [3570

Drewry, William Sidney. The Southampton insurrection. Washington, Neale Co., 1900. 201 p.   [3571

Driver, Carl Samuel. John Sevier, pioneer of the old Southwest. Chapel Hill, University of North Carolina Press, 1932. 240 p.   [3572

Drummond's pictorial atlas of North Carolina. Charlotte, Albert Y. Drummond [c.1924] 148 p.   [3573

Drury, Frank S. Baptism, a treatise, with scriptural references. [Morganton? 1937?] 16 p.   [3574

——The laymen's lancet; tentative issue, revised Jan. 1919. Morganton, The Author, c.1918. 18 p.   [3575

—— ——Supplement . . . Sept. 15, 1920. [Morganton? The Author, 1920?] [11] p.   [3576

Drysdale, William. Pine Ridge plantation. New York, T. Y. Crowell & Co. [1901] 320 p.   [3577

Duffey, Frank Marion. The early cuadro de costumbres in Colombia. Chapel Hill, University of North Carolina Press, 1956. (North Carolina. University. Studies in the Romance languages and literatures, no. 26) 116 p.   [3578

Duffy, Annie V. Glenalban, and other poems. New York, E. J. Hale & Son [c.1878] 155 p.   [3579

Duggan, Janie Prichard. A Mexican ranch. Philadelphia, American Baptist Publication Society [1903] 377 p.   [3580

Dugger, Shepherd Monroe. The balsam groves of the Grandfather Mountain. Banner Elk, Printed by J. B. Lippincott Co., 1892. 187 p.   [3581

—— ——Banner Elk, The Author, 1895.   [3582

—— ——1907. 300 p.   [3583

—— ——1934. 310 p.   [3584

——The war trails of the Blue Ridge. Banner Elk, The Author, 1932. 324 p. [3585

Duke, Angier Buchanan, Memorial, Inc. Angier B. Duke Memorial, Inc. report. New York [1951] 17 p.   [3586

Duke, Basil W. Morgan's cavalry. New York, Neale Publishing Co., 1906. 441 p.   [3587

Duke, James Buchanan. Indenture of James B. Duke establishing the Duke Endowment, with provisions of the will. [Charlotte, Duke Endowment, pref. July 13, 1932] 89 p.   [3588

Duke, Jane Taylor. Kenmore and the Lewises. Garden City, N. Y., Doubleday, 1949. 268 p. [3589

Duke, Walter Garland. Henry Duke, councilor, his descendants and connections. Richmond, Va., Dietz Press, 1949. 452 p. [3590

Duke, Washington, Sons & Company, Durham, N. C. Costumes of all nations. Durham, n.d. 21 plates. [3591

——The heroes of the Civil War. No place, n.d. 51 plates [3592

[Duke, Washington, Sons & Company, Durham, N. C.] [Histories of generals] New York, Knapp and Co., c.1888. 50 booklets [3593

Duke almuni register, v. 11- January, 1925- Durham, Duke University, 1925- NcU has v. 11-41. Preceded by Trinity alumni register, v. 1-10, 1915-1924 [3594

The Duke Bar Association journal, v. 1-10, March, 1933-1941/42. Durham, School of Law, Duke University, 1933-1942. NcU has v. 1-10 [3595

Duke Endowment. Addresses delivered at the eighth anniversary of the Duke Endowment . . . held at the First Methodist Episcopal Church, South, Charlotte, North Carolina, December 11, 1932. [Charlotte] 1932. 60 p. [3596

——Addresses delivered at the ninth anniversary of the Duke Endowment, sponsored by the city of Greenville, South Carolina. [Greenville, S. C., Keys Printing Co.] 1933. 63 p. [3597

——Financial statements, December 31, 1949?- Charlotte, 1950- NcU has 1949- 1954 [3598

——Year book, no. 1- 1924/28- [Charlotte, 1929- NcU has no. 1-23 [3599

Duke Endowment. Hospital Section. Annual report, 1925-1939. [Charlotte, 1926-1940] NcU has 1925-1939 [3600

——A system of hospital accounting. [Charlotte] 1926. (Its Bulletin no. 1. November, 1926) 44 p. [3601

Duke Endowment. Orphan Section . . . Annual report, 1926-1939. [Charlotte, 1927-1940] NcU has 1926-1939 [3602

——A system of accounting for children's homes. [Charlotte] December, 1927. (Its Bulletin no. 2, December, 1927) 6 p. [3603

Duke engineer, v. 1- 193 - Durham, Duke University, 193 - NcU has v. [11- 13] [3604

Duke Hospital, Durham, N. C. Information for patients, 19 - [Durham, 19 - NcU has 1950, 1951 [3605

Duke Hospital. Library. Print collection in reading room of the Duke Hospital Library. Durham, 1938. 16 p. [3606

Duke mathematical journal, v. 1- March, 1935- Durham, Duke University Press [1935- NcU has v. 1-23 [3607

Duke Power Co. Industrial Department. Piedmont Carolinas where wealth awaits you. Charlotte, Duke Power Co. [1927] 47 p. [3608

Duke power magazine, v. 1- 191 - Charlotte, Duke Power Co., 191 - NcU has v. [7] 8-20 [21] 22-41. Title varies, 191 - March, 1935: Southern public utilities magazine [3609

Duke University, Durham, N. C. Bulletin, v. 1- 1929- Durham, 1929- NcU has v. [1-2] 3-18 [19-28] [3610

——Campus views, Duke University (centennial ed.) Durham [1938?] [14] p. [3611

——Catalogue, 1924/25-1928/29. Durham, 1925-1929. NcU has 1924/25-1926/27 and 1927/28-1928/29 undergraduate catalogue. Continues as Duke University, Durham, N. C. Bulletin, 1929- [3612

——The Chapel of Duke University. Durham, 1932. 19 p. [3613

——The dedication of the University Chapel . . . Sunday, June the second, nineteen hundred and thirty-five. [Durham, 1935] [22] p. [3614

——Duke. [Durham, The Duke University Development Program, 1949] 20 p. [3615

——Duke University and the war. Durham, Alumni Office, Duke University, 1943. [30] p. [3616

——Duke University at work. Centennial ed. [Durham, 1936?] 23 p. [3617

——The Duke University centennial conference on teacher training. Durham, Duke University Press, 1953. (Historical papers of the Trinity College Historical Society, ser. 30) 119 p. [3618

——Duke University . . . Union Institute, 1835; Normal College, 1851; Trinity College, 1859; Duke University, 1924. [Durham, 1931] 27 p.   [3619
——History and government of Duke University. Durham, 1936. 27 p.   [3620
——In memoriam, William Kenneth Boyd, January 10, 1879-January 19, 1938. Durham, Duke University Press, 1938. (Historical papers of the Trinity Historical Society, ser. 22) 97 p.   [3621
——The inauguration of William Preston Few . . . November 9, 1910. [Chicago, University of Chicago Press, 1910?] 173 p.   [3622
——Order of exercises for the dedication of the Duke University School of Medicine and the Duke Hospital, April the twentieth, 1931. [Durham] 1931. [3] p.   [3623
——A program of coöperation, Duke University, the University of North Carolina. Durham, Chapel Hill [Duke University, the University of N. C.] 1935. 15 p. [3624
——Programs of organ recitals presented during the academic year, 19   -   Durham, 19   -   NcU has 1941/42, 1943/44   [3625
——Report on recent cooperative activities between Duke University and the University of North Carolina. [Durham? 1937] [2] p.   [3626
Duke University, Durham, N. C. Alumni Association. Alumni directory, Duke University School of Law, 1935. Durham, 1935. 54 p.   [3627
——In the service of Alma Mater; constitutions of alumni and alumnae organizations of Duke University. [Durham, Duke University, 1925?] 24 p.   [3628
Duke University, Durham, N. C. Americana Club. American studies in honor of William Kenneth Boyd. Durham, Duke University Press, 1940. 377 p.   [3629
Duke University, Durham, N. C. Art Association. Initial exhibition of the Art Association. [Durham, 1931] 27 p.   [3630
Duke University, Durham, N. C. Department of Psychology. The first ten years of the Parapsychology Laboratory. Durham, 1940. [18] p.   [3631
Duke University, Durham, N. C. Divinity School. Bulletin, v. 1- February, 1936- Durham, 1936- NcU has v. 1-13 [14-17] 18-20   [3632
Duke University, Durham, N. C. Divinity School. Library. The Isaiah scroll. [Durham, 1950] [6] p.   [3633
Duke University, Durham, N. C. History Dept. Historical background of the world today; a synopsis. New York, Rinehart & Co., Inc., 1947. 128 p. [3634
Duke University, Durham, N. C. Institute of International Relations. Lecture notes from the Institute of International Relations, Duke University . . . June 11th-23rd, 1934. Washington, D. C., Paul Harris, Jr., 1934. Various paging. [3635
Duke University, Durham, N. C. Institute of Teachers of Mathematics. High lights of the annual mathematics institute, 1st- 19   -   Durham, 194   -   NcU has 1948   [3636
Duke University, Durham, N. C. Interfraternity Council. Fraternities at Duke, 1948-1949, a handbook for Freshmen. [Durham, 1948] [29] p.   [3637
Duke University, Durham, N. C. Library. . . . Bulletin, no. 1-7, Oct. 1929-Dec. 1933. Durham, 1929-1933. NcU has no. 1-7   [3638
——Catalogue of the Whitman collection. Durham, 1945. 148 p.   [3639
——The centennial exhibit of the Duke University Library, consisting of material from the George Washington Flowers Memorial Collection . . . April 5-June 5, 1939. Durham, 1939. 60 p.   [3640
——Checklist of Alabama pamphlets in the Duke University Library, 1823-1941. [Durham? 1942] 53 p.   [3641
——. . . Check list of the Paul Hamilton Hayne Library. Durham, 1930. (Its Bulletin, no. 2, July, 1930) 109 p.   [3642
——. . . A checklist of United States newspapers (and weeklies before 1900) in the General Library. Durham, 1932-37. 6 v.   [3643
——A guide to the manuscript collections in the Duke University Library. Raleigh, Historical Records Survey, 1939. 165 p.   [3644
—— ————Durham, Duke Univ. Press, 1947. (Historical papers of the Trinity College Historical Society, ser. 27-28) 362 p.   [3645
——Handbook of the Duke University libraries. Durham, 1931. 32 p.   [3646
——Scientific journals in the libraries of Duke University. Durham, 1935. 81 p. [3647
—— ————1st supplement. 1937. 30 p.   [3648
——The Trent Collection in the rare book room of the Duke University Library. Durham [1943] [7] p.   [3649

Duke University, Durham, N. C. Library, Frank C. Brown Collection of North Carolina Folklore. The Frank C. Brown Collection of North Carolina Folklore. Durham, Duke University Press [1952-   v. 1-3 (5 v. when completed)   [3650

Duke University, Durham, N. C. Marine Station. Bulletin, no. 1-   1943-   Durham, Duke University Press, 1943-   NcU has no. 1-5   [3651

Duke University, Durham, N. C. President. The Duke Endowment and Duke University, by W. P. Few, president. [Durham] n.d.   8 p.   [3652

Duke University, Durham, N. C. Press. Catalogue, 1926-   Durham, 1926-   NcU has 1926, 1928/29-1931/32, 1936/37, 1943, 1948/49, Summer and Fall, 1949, 1950/51, Spring and Summer, 1956   [3653

Duke University, Durham, N. C. School of Forestry. Bulletin, no. 1-   February, 1935-   Durham, 1935-   NcU has no. 1-9   [3654

——Duke University School of Forestry lectures, no. 1-   Durham, 1941-   NcU has no. 1-8   [3655

Duke University, Durham, N. C. School of law. Bulletin, v. 1-11, September, 1931-March, 1942. Durham, 1931-1942. NcU has v. [1-3] 4-10 [11]   [3656

Duke University, Durham, N. C. School of Law. Department of Legislative Research and Drafting. Legislation in North Carolina. Durham, Duke University Press, 1932. 98 p.   [3657

Duke University, Durham, N. C. School of Law. Library. Annual report, 19 - Durham, 19 -   NcU has 1938/39-1942/46   [3658

——Bulletin, v. 1-5, October, 1930-March? 1936. Durham, 1930-1936. NcU has v. [1-5]   [3659

——Current legal publications, no. 1-105, September, 1941-April, 1943. Durham, 1941-1953. NcU has no. 1-105   [3660

——Law school bulletin, v. 1-   September, 1931-   [Durham, 1931-   NcU has v. [1-3] 4-10 [11]   [3661

Duke University, Durham, N. C. School of Law. Legal Aid Clinic. Report, 1931/32- [Durham] 1932-   NcU has 1933/34-1942/43   [3662

Duke University, Durham, N. C. School of Law. Samuel Fox Mordecai Law Society. Constitution; with a tribute to Mr. Mordecai by Sidney S. Alderman. No place, no publisher, n.d.   9 p.   [3663

Duke University, Durham, N. C. School of Medicine. Fourteen distinguished physicians and surgeons; brief sketches of eminent men for whom Duke Hospital wards are named. [Durham, 1931?]   19 p.   [3664

Duke University, Durham, N. C. Stadium Committee. The stadium for Duke University. [Durham, The Committee, 1928]   4 p.   [3665

Duke University, Durham, N. C. Trinity College Historical Society. Historical papers, Series I-   Durham, 1897-   NcU has ser. 1-32   [3666
—— ——Contents. 1941.

Duke University, Durham, N. C. Y. M. C. A. Directory [of] faculty, administration and students, Duke University, 19 -   [Durham, 19 -   NcU has 1933/34-1936/37   [3667

Duke writers and rhymers, poems, tales, essays by students of creative writing (English 65-66) 1940/41-   [Durham, 1941-   NcU has 1940/41   [3668

Dula, William C., ed. Durham and her people. Durham, 1951.   295 p.   [3669

Dumont, N., ed. North Carolina as a place for investment, manufactures, mining, stock raising, fruit and farming. Raleigh, Observer, 1879.   86 p.   [3670

Duncan, Eula Griffin. Big Road Walker. New York, Frederick A. Stokes Co., 1940.   121 p.   [3671

Duncan, Hannibal Gerald.   . . . Race and population problems. New York, Longmans, Green and Co., 1929.   424 p.   [3672

Duncan, Norvin C. People, places, things. [Asheville? Privately printed, c.1944] 77 p.   [3673
—— ——[Asheville? c.1955]   96 p.   [3674

Dunlap, George T. Lest we forget! Recollections of wartime restrictions and other trivia. [Pinehurst] privately printed, 1948.   48 p.   [3675

Dunlap, Isaac H. Some experiences during my 80 years. Bonlee, The Author [1945?]   11 p.   [3676

Dunlap, John, pseud., see Sawyer, Lemuel, 1777-1852

[Dunlap, Roberta K.]   Mabel Gordon. A novel. By R. K. D.   New York, J. S.
Ogilvie Publishing Co., 1901.   250 p.   [3677

Dunn, Adele Brenizer.   Jingles in a jiffy, North Carolina A-B-C-' -S. [Wilmington?]
National Society of the Colonial Dames of America in the State of North Carolina
[1943?] [26] p.   [3678

Dunn, Adele Brenizer, joint author,   see Arrington, Katherine Pendleton

Dunn, Ernest Windley.   How to get well, how to keep well. [New Bern, Owen G.
Dunn, pr.] n.d.   15 p.   [3679

Dunn, Robert A.   History of the First Presbyterian Church of Charlotte, N. C.
. . . November, 1932. [Charlotte? 1945?]   54 p.   [3680

Dunn, N. C., city directory, v. 1- 19 - Asheville, Miller Press, 192 - NcU has
1926-27   [3681

[Dunnagan, Macon Rush] comp.   Opinions of governors and others about Macon
Rush 'Mike' Dunnagan. [Winston-Salem? The Author, 1936?] [4] p.   [3682

Dunne, William F.   Gastonia, citadel of the class struggle in the new South. New
York, National Textile Workers Union [c.1929]   58 p.   [3683

Dunston, C. H.   To the public. Raleigh, 1875.   [1] p.   [3684
—— ——[Raleigh, 1875?]   3 p.   [3685

Du Pont, Henry Algernon.   Address upon the unveiling of Major General Ramseur's
monument. [Winterthur, Del., H. A. Du Pont, c.1920]   14 p.   [3686

Du Pont, Henry B.   Blueprint for disaster; a speech before Chamber of Commerce,
Kinston, North Carolina, October 1, 1953. [Kinston, 1953]   13 p.   [3687

Durden, Chauncey Wright.   The epic of Jesus. New York, Fleming H. Revell Co.
[c.1934]   187 p.   [3688

Durham, Carl Thomas.   Speech of Congressman Carl T. Durham before the Junior
Chamber of Commerce, Greensboro, North Carolina, Thursday, July 15, 1954.
[Greensboro? 1954]   4 p.   [3689

Durham, Ernest Creecy.   An appreciation of the Christian ministry. No place, no
publisher, c.1915.   27 p.   [3690
——If evolution is true.   2d ed. rev. and enl. [Newbern, Owen G. Dunn for the
Author] 1922.   72 p.   [3691
——Poems of a lifetime. [Nashville, Tenn., Parthenon Press, c.1948]   128 p.   [3692
——Roses. [Durham, Seeman Printery, Inc.] 1920.   91 p.   [3693
——Strugglin' along. Durham, Christian and King, 1925.   109 p.   [3694

Durham, Plato Tracy.   Ave atque vale, frater! To Angier Buchanan Duke. [At-
lanta, The Author, pref. 1923]   [18] p.   [3695

Durham, Robert Lee.   The call of the South. Boston, L. C. Page & Co., 1908.
439 p.   [3696

Durham, Robert Lee]   O Duke, alma mater, and other songs and verse of Trinity
College and Duke University. [Buena Vista, Va., c.1933]   15 p.   [3697

Durham, Robert Lee.   Since I was born. Richmond, Whittet & Shepperson, 1953.
217 p.   [3698

Durham, N. C.   Board of Aldermen.   Charter and ordinances of the city of Durham
. . . revised and adopted . . . April, 1899. [Durham? 1899?]   67 p.   [3699

[Durham, N. C.   Board of Charities and Public Welfare]   Board of Charities and
Public Welfare, Durham, North Carolina. [Durham, 1922?]   24 p.   [3700

Durham, N. C.   Board of Commissioners.   Charter and ordinances of the town of
Durham, revised and adopted . . . March 1st, 1892. Durham, Whitaker Printing
House, March, 1892.   100 p.   [3701
——Charter of the town of Durham, North Carolina, incorporating all the recent
amendments . . . adopted . . . April 2d, 1889, revised and corrected by W. J.
Exum. Durham, D. W. Whitaker, 1889.   84 p.   [3702
——Ordinances and resolutions for the government of the town of Durham. Ra-
leigh, Edwards and Broughton, 1873.   16 p.   [3703

[Durham, N. C.   Board of Education?]   Book suggestions for the pupils of the city
schools, Durham, N. C. [Durham?] December, 1904.   14 p.   [3704

Durham, N. C. Board of Education. Durham City Schools, Directory of school personnel, 19 - Durham, - NcU has 1918/19, 1945/46, 1946/47 [3705
——Report of the superintendent, Durham city schools, 19 - Durham, 19 - NcU has 1914/15, 1922/23, with summary, 1914/1923, 1933/34 [3706
——Teachers' qualifications and salary schedule, Durham City Schools, 19 - Durham, 19 - NcU has 1920 [3707

Durham, N. C. Board of Health. Dairy regulations of the city and county of Durham, North Carolina. Durham, Seeman Printery, n.d. 33 p. [3708

Durham, N. C. Central Labor Union. Durham's labor review annual, union directory and buyers' guide, 192 - Durham, Central Labor Union, 192 - NcU has 1927, 1928, 1935, 1936, 1939, 1943 [3709

Durham, N. C. Chamber of Commerce. Dinner program, given by the citizens of Durham under the auspices of the Durham Chamber of Commerce in honor of our manufacturers and educators . . . Washington Duke Hotel . . . Nov. 18, 1927. [Durham, Seeman Printery] n.d. 42 p. [3710
——Durham, North Carolina. [Durham, Seeman Printery, 1906] 30 p. [3711
——Durham, North Carolina, a center of industry and education. [Durham, Seeman Printery, 1926] 39 p. [3712
——Durham, North Carolina, city of education, industry, medicine; an economic summary. Durham [1948] 8 p. [3713
——Facts about Durham, North Carolina. [Durham, 1924?] 5 p. [3714
—— ——[1955] 8 p. [3715

[Durham, N. C. Chamber of Commerce] What we have done, what we propose doing, and the cost. [Durham, 1921] 12 p. [3716

Durham, N. C. Citizens. Proposal submitted by the citizens of Durham for the North Carolina school of medicine. [Durham, 1923] 15 p. [3717

Durham, N. C. City Council. Code of ordinances of the city of Durham, 1928. [Durham? 1928?] 190 p. [3718
——The code of the city of Durham, North Carolina, the charter . . . and the general ordinances . . . effective November 1, 1940. Charlottesville, Va., Michie Co., 1940. 515 p. [3719
—— ——1943 supplement. 1943. 93 p. [3720
——The code of the city of Durham, North Carolina, 1947. Charlottesville, Va., Michie City Publications Co., 1947. 552 p. [3721
——Instructions to bidders; proposal, specifications, and contract for Third Fork disposal plant for Durham, N. C. Durham, Gilbert C. White Co. [1927] 44 p. [3722
——License and privilege tax ordinance, city of Durham, 1927-28, adopted June 18, 1927. [Durham, Seeman Printery, 1927] 47 p. [3723
——Report by City Manager, 19 - Durham, 1922- NcU has 1922/23 [3724

[Durham, N. C. City Council] War emergency ordinance of the city of Durham, North Carolina, effective January 19, 1942. [Durham, 1942] 24 p. [3725

Durham, N. C. City Manager. Before the Corporation Commission of North Carolina in the matter of the proceeding . . . in connection with electric rates and charges of the Durham Public Service Company. [Durham? 1932] 59 p. [3726

Durham, N. C. Commercial Club. Durham, North Carolina. [Durham, Seeman Printery, 1913?] 30 p. [3727

Durham, N. C. Committee of 100. Durham, North Carolina; a word-picture story. [Durham, 1956] [12] p. [3728

Durham, N. C. Democratic Executive Committee. Rules and regulations for holding a primary for the nomination of Democratic candidates for mayor, aldermen, and police and fire commissioner of the city of Durham. [Durham, 1911] 7 p. [3729

Durham, N. C. Depositors National Bank. Report, 1933- Durham, 1933- NcU has [1936-1950] [3730

Durham, N. C. Durham Council of Social Agencies. Social service directory, Durham, North Carolina, 1936-1937. Durham, 1936. 48 p. [3731

Durham, N. C. Durham Realty and Insurance Co. Durham Realty and Insurance Co. No place, no publisher, n.d. 6 p. [3732

Durham, N. C. Educational Planning Council. Educational Planning Council, Durham City Schools, organized, January, 1945. Durham, 1946. 41 p. [3733

Durham, N. C.   Farmers Mutual Exchange   see Farmers Mutual Exchange, Durham, N. C.

Durham, N. C.   Fidelity Bank. Wills and ways. [Durham, Fidelity Bank, 1935?] 15 p.   [3734

Durham, N. C.   First Baptist Church. Centennial Committee. First Baptist Church . . . 1845-1945. Durham [1945] [32] p.   [3735

Durham, N. C.   First National Bank. Forty years, 1887-1927. Durham [pref. 1927] 65 p.   [3736

Durham, N. C.   First National Trust Co. A safe administrator. No place, no publisher [c.1917] 8 p.   [3737

Durham, N. C.   First Presbyterian Church. Roster of members, April 1, 1927. [Durham, Seeman Printery, 1927?] 64 p.   [3738

Durham, N. C.   Health Department. Annual report, 19 - Durham, 1914- NcU has 1916   [3739

[Durham, N. C. John Avery Boys' Club, Inc.] Guidance in health, physical, mental and character development for our citizens of tomorrow. [Durham, 1949] [12] p.   [3740

Durham, N. C.   League of Women Voters. Here is Durham: a handbook on Durham city and county government. Durham, City Manager, 1953. 40 p. [3741

Durham, N. C.   Mutual Land and Manufacturing Co. The Mutual Land and Manufacturing Company, Durham, N. C. Durham, D. W. Whitaker, pr., 1890. 10 .p.   [3742

Durham, N. C.   North Carolina News Company. Souvenir folder of Duke University and Durham, North Carolina. Chicago, Curt Teich and Co., Inc., c.1941. Folder.   [3743

Durham, N. C.   Public Library. Report, 1924- Durham, 1924- NcU has 1928-1940, 1941/45 (as one)   [3744

Durham, N. C. Rotary Club. Constitution and by-laws. Durham, n.d. 15 p.   [3745
——Three prize-winning essays in a high school senior contest conducted by . . . the Rotary Club of Durham. [Durham, 1952] 15 p.   [3746

Durham, N. C.   Saint Philip's Church. Committee of Women Assisting in Raising a Fund for a New Church Building. Tucks and puckers . . . Thanksgiving, 1903, November 26, Durham, N. C. [Durham?] 1903. [32] p.   [3747

Durham, N. C.   Social Planning Council. Youth Committee. Report of the Youth Committee . . . December 1, 1943. Durham, 1944. 99 p.   [3748
——Summary of report of the Youth Committee of the Durham Social Planning Council. [Durham, 1944?] 20 p.   [3749

Durham, N. C.   Trinity Methodist Church. Diamond jubilee, 1861-1936. [Durham, 1936?] 41 p.   [3750

Durham, N. C.   Watts Hospital see Watts Hospital, Durham, N. C.

Durham, N. C.   Watts Street Baptist Church. Directory, 19 - Durham, 19 - NcU has 1929   [3751

Durham almanac, 189 - Durham, N. A. Ramsey, 189 - NcU has 1896, 1897, 1898   [3752

Durham Business School, Durham, N. C. Durham Business School. [Durham, 1927?] 24 p.   [3753

Durham Civic Association. Durham Civic Association. Durham, n.d. 10 p. [3754

Durham Co., N. C. Board of Education. Course of study for Durham County Public Schools, elementary and grammar grades, 1912/13. [Durham? 1912?] 16 p.   [3755
——Durham County Public Schools, apportionments, 19 - [Durham? 19 - NcU has Spring term, 1915, Spring term, 1919   [3756
——Durham County school bulletin, v. 1- September, 1915- Durham, 1915-NcU has v. [1-3]   [3757
——Primary plan book for Durham County Schools, 1913/14. [Durham? 1913?] 13 p.   [3758
——Report, 1902/03- Durham [1903- NcU has 1902/03-1913/14, 1915/16, 1918/19, 1914/23   [3759

——We always train our fine horses and dogs; should our children be equally as well trained and educated? [Durham? 1915] [4] p.   [3760

Durham Co., N. C. Citizens. To the voters of Durham County. Durham, 1911. [3] p.   [3761

Durham Co., N. C. County Manager. Budget, Durham County, North Carolina, 19 - Durham, 19 - NcU has 1953/54-1956/57   [3762
——Financial statement, 19 - [Durham, 19 - NcU has [1940/41-1949/50] each with budget for next fiscal year   [3763

Durham Co., N. C. Juvenile Court. Juvenile Court of the city and county, Durham, N. C., annual report, 19 - Durham, 19 - NcU has 1945/46-1947/48, 1948/49 with history 1934/1949   [3764

[**Durham County Bar Association**] The presentation of a portrait of Howard Alexander Foushee, Durham, North Carolina, July 24th, 1946. [Durham, 1946] 28 p.   [3765

Durham Fact-Finding Conference, Durham, N. C. Report, 1929- [Durham, 1929- NcU has 1929   [3766

Durham high school bulletin, Durham, North Carolina: Courses of study, 19 - [Durham, Seeman Printery, 192 - NcU has 1922/23   [3767

Durham Hosiery Mills, Durham, N. C. Constitution and by-laws for the house of representatives, the senate, and the cabinet, employee representation plan of the Durham Hosiery Mills. [Durham, Seeman Printery] 1919. 17 p.   [3768

Durham railroad guide, fire alarm boxes and business directory. Raleigh, Edwards and Broughton, n.d. [8] p.   [3769

Durham Water Company. . . . Rules, regulations and tariff of water rates, April, 1900. [Durham? 1900?] 11 p.   [3770

Durling, Dwight Leonard, ed. Biography; varieties and parallels, edited by Dwight Durling . . . and William Watt. New York, Dryden Press [c.1941] 501 p. [3771

Dusenbery, Benjamin M., comp. Monument to the memory of General Andrew Jackson: containing twenty-five eulogies and sermons delivered on occasion of his death. Philadelphia, Walker & Gillis, 1846. 416 p.   [3772

Duttera, William Babylon. Descendants of George Philip Duddra or Dodderer. Salisbury, 1934. 148 p.   [3773

Duyckinck, Evert Augustus. A memorial of Francis L. Hawks; read before the New York Historical Society, May 7, 1867. New York, New York Historical Society, 1871. 166 p.   [3774

Dwelle, Mary (Myers) Introducing Queen Charlotte to her namesake. Charlotte, Lassiter Press, 1935. 24 p.   [3775

Dyer, Gustavus Walker. Democracy in the South before the Civil War. Nashville, Tenn., Publishing House of the Methodist Episcopal Church, South, Smith & Lamar [c.1905] 90 p.   [3776

Dyer, Oliver. General Andrew Jackson. New York, R. Bonner's Sons, 1891. 378 p.   [3777
——Life of General Jackson. New York, R. Bonner's Sons [1892] 378 p. Reissue of his General Andrew Jackson.   [3778

Dykemann, Wilma. The French Broad. New York, Rinehart & Co. [1955] (Rivers of America) 371 p.   [3779

Earnest, Ernest. John and William Bartram, botanists and explorers. Philadelphia, University of Pennsylvania Press, 1940. 187 p.   [3780

[**Easley, Philip Samuel**] The "low-down" on Floridy, by Joshuway Whipple [pseud.] Statesville, Brady Printing Co. [1926] 48 p.   [3781
——Romancin' through Floridy with Mandy and me. By Joshuway Whipple [pseud.] Statesville, Link-Pickens Publishing Co. [c.1926] 78 p.   [3782

East, Louise P. President's message, forty-seventh annual convention, N. C. State Nurses' Association, High Point, N. C., October 24-27, 1949. No place [1949?] 6 p.   [3783

East Carolina Folk Festival. The first- 1952- Kenansville, The Duplin Times, 1952- NcU has 1952.   [3784

[**East Tennessee and Western N. C. Railroad and Linville River Railroad**] [The scenic route through the heart of the Blue Ridge] [Atlanta, Ga., Dillard Jacobs Agency] n.d. 14 p.   [3785

Eastern Baptist Association. Minutes, 18 - 18 - NcU has [1865-1955] [3786

Eastern Carolina Chamber of Commerce, Inc. Builders of Eastern North Carolina. Kinston, [c.1931- v. NcU has v. 1, 1931   [3787

Eastern Carolina Chamber of Commerce, Kinston, N. C. Eastern Carolina "tell the world". Kinston [1925] 64 p.   [3788

——Eastern North Carolina, where prosperity is perennial, invites you! [Wilmington, National Press, 1924?] 49 p.   [3789

—— ——"where life is really worth while", invites you! 2d ed. [Kinston, 1925?] 44 p.   [3790

——Sixty-nine progressive and prosperous towns of Eastern North Carolina, "where life is really worth while", invite you. Kinston [1925?] 48 p.   [3791

Eastern Carolina Exposition and Automobile Shows, Kinston, N. C. Pageant, "Eastern Carolina in action, 12 counties." Kinston, N. C., April 11th, 1924. New Bern, Owen G. Dunn [1924?] 7 p.   [3792

Eastern Carolina Exposition and Automobile Shows, Smithfield, N. C. Programme and handbook . . . April 13th to 18th, 1925. Wilmington, National Press [1925?] 64 p.   [3793

Eastern national park to park guide, Shenandoah National Park to Great Smoky Mountains National Park, 193 - Asheville, Park-to-Park Publishing Co., 193 - NcU has 1935, 1939-1941   [3794

Eastern star news, v. 1- 193 - Charlotte, Order of the Eastern Star, 193 - NcU has v. 7-25   [3795

Eastern States Archeological Federation. Bulletin, no. 1- October, 1941- 1941- NcU has no. 1-14   [3796

Eaton, Allen Hendershott. Handicrafts of the Southern highlands. New York, Russell Sage Foundation, 1937. 370 p.   [3797

Eaton, Charles Edward. The bright plain. Chapel Hill, University of North Carolina Press, 1942. 92 p.   [3798

——The greenhouse in the garden. New York, Twayne Publishers [1955] 64 p. [3799

——The shadow of the swimmer. New York, Fine Editions Press, 1951. 88 p. [3800

Eaton, Clement. Freedom of thought in the Old South. Durham, Duke University Press, 1940. 343 p.   [3801

——A history of the Old South. New York, Macmillan Co., 1949. 636 p. [3802

——A history of the Southern Confederacy. New York, Macmillan Co., 1954. 351 p.   [3803

Eaton, John, defendant. Circuit Court of the United States, North-Carolina District, Hamilton versus Eaton; declaration . . . June term, 1792. [Newbern? F. X. Martin? 1792?] 77 p.   [3804

Eaton, John Henry. Candid appeal to the American public, in reply to Messrs. Ingham, Branch, and Berrien. Washington, Printed at the Globe Office, 1831. 55 p.   [3805

[**Eaton, John Henry**] The complete memoirs of Andrew Jackson. New York, Hurst & Co. [1885?] 362 p.   [3806

Eaton, John Henry. Leben des generals-majors Andreas Jackson. Reading [Pa.] Gedruckt bey J. Ritter und comp., 1831. 419 p.   [3807

——The life of Andrew Jackson. Philadelphia, M. Carey and Son, 1817. 425 p. [3808

—— ——Philadelplia, Samuel F. Bradford, 1824. 468 p.   [3809

——The life of Andrew Jackson, major-general in the service of the United States. Cincinnati, Hatch & Nichols, 1827. 454 p. Chapters 1-4 by John Reid. [3810

——The life of Major General Andrew Jackson . . . 3d ed. rev. and cor. Philadelphia, McCarty & Davis, 1828. 335 p.   [3811

[**Eaton, John Henry**] Memoirs of Andrew Jackson . . . comp. by a citizen of Massachusetts. Boston, C. Ewer, 1828. 334 p.   [3812

——The life of Major General Andrew Jackson . . . 3d ed. rev. and cor. Philadelphia, McCarty & Davis, 1828. 335 p.   [3811

—— ——Philadelphia, no publisher, 1834. 334 p.   [3813

—— ——1845.   [3814

—— ——1848.   [3815

Eaton, William. Address delivered before the Eumenean and Philanthropic societies of Davidson College, N. C., July 13th, 1859. Raleigh, Institution for the Deaf
and Dumb and the Blind, 1859. 24 p.   [3816
——Address delivered before the two literary societies of the University of N. C.,
May 31, 1848. Fayetteville, Edward J. Hale, 1848. 23 p.   [3817
——Book of practical forms . . . intended as a manual to the practising lawyer . . .
of North Carolina. Philadelphia, Lindsay and Blakiston, 1854. 380 p.   [3818
—— ——2d ed. rev. Baltimore, Printed by John Murphy & Co., 1867. 654 p. [3819

Eaton, William Richard. History of the Raleigh Baptist Association of North
Carolina. [Zebulon] Raleigh Baptist Association, 1955. 83 p.   [3820

[Eaves, John Amelia Logan?] Sketch of lineal descendants of Samuel Wilson, Sr.,
by Mrs. J. B. Eaves. [Rock Hill, S. C., London Printery] n.d. 117 p.   [3821

Ebbs, Eloise Buckner. Carolina mountain breezes. Asheville, Miller Press, Inc.
[c.1929] 213 p.   [3822

Echo, 19 - Greensboro, Students' Association of Greensboro College for Women,
19 - NcU has 1921   [3823

The Echo, v. 1-16, 1940-1954. Pisgah Forest, Employees of the Ecusta Paper
Corporation, 1940-1954. NcU has v. 10-16   [3824

Ecological monographs, v. 1- Jan. 1931- Durham, Duke University Press [1931-
NcU has v. 2-26   [3825

Ecusta Paper Corporation, Pisgah Forest, N. C. The fifth anniversary record of a
new American industry. Pisgah Forest [c.1944] 69 p.   [3826

Edelweiss, v. 1- 19 - Charlotte, The Presbyterian College, 19 - NcU has
1907   [3827

Edenton, N. C. St. Paul's Church. The religious and historic commemoration of
the two hundred years of St. Paul's parish, Edenton, N. C., observed in the parish
church, May 22nd and 24th, A. D. 1901. Goldsboro, Nash Brothers, pr. [1901]
49 p.   [3828

[Edenton, N. C. St. Paul's Church] St. Paul's Church, 1701-1925, Edenton, N. C.
[Edenton] 1925. [4] p.   [3829
——200th anniversary of the building of St. Paul's Episcopal Church. [Edenton,
Chowan Herald, 1936] 23 p.   [3830

[Edenton, N. C. Theater] The last night of performance at Edenton, this season.
On Thursday evening, the 20th of July, 1797, will be exhibited, the beauties of the
comic opera of Inkle and Yarico. No place [1797] [1] p. NcU has photostat
(negative) of original in Playbill Collection, Colonial Williamsburg, Inc.   [3831

[Edenton, N. C. Woman's Club] Historic Edenton and countryside, incorporated
1722. [Edenton, 1953] [26] p.   [3832

Edenton-Chowan Chamber of Commerce. Edenton, North Carolina. Edenton,
1937. 27 p.   [3833

Edgar, Patrick Nisbett. American race-turf register, sportsman's herald, and general
stud book. New York, Press of Henry Mason, 1933. 2 v. NcU has v. 1.   [3834

Edge, Frederick Milnes. Slavery doomed; or, The contest between free and slave
labour in the United States. London, Smith, Elder and Co., 1860. 224 p.   [3835

Edgecombe Agricultural & Mechanical Fair Association. Premium list and rules and
regulations . . . annual fair, 1st- 1881- Tarboro, 1881- NcU has 1st-3d   [3836

Edgecombe Agricultural Works, Tarboro, N. C. The Edgecombe cotton plow, a
specialty. Tarboro, Enquirer Press, n.d. Folder.   [3837

Edgecombe Co., N. C. Board of Commissioners. Annual statement, 19 - NcU
has 1903/04, 1905/06, 1906/07, 1910/11   [3838

Edgecombe Co., N. C. Board of Education. Report, 19 - [Tarboro, 19 - NcU
has 1925/26, 1926/27   [3839

[Edgecombe Co., N. C. Board of Education] Teacher's handbook, Edgecombe
County Schools. New Bern, Owen G. Dunn, n.d. 32 p.   [3840

Edgecombe Co., N. C. Board of Health. Report, 19 - [Tarboro, 19 - NcU
has 1936-1938   [3841

Edgecombe County, North Carolina, foremost in agriculture, good schools, and
churches. [Tarboro, C. F. Clayton's Print] n.d. [2] p.   [3842

Edgecombe County, North Carolina, her people and resources. Raleigh, Edwards & Broughton, pr., 1891. 40 p. [3843

Edgecombe County school bulletin, v. 1- February, 1915- Tarboro, 1915- NcU has v. [1-2] [3844

Edgecombe farm-journal, v. 1- September, 1860- Tarboro, W. B. Smith, 1860- NcU has v. [1] [3845

Edgecombe Homestead and Loan Association, Tarboro, N. C. The Edgecombe Homestead and Loan Association, 1889-1939. [Tarboro? 1939?] [11] p. [3846

Edgecombe school news, v. 1- January, 1929- Tarboro, 1929- NcU has v. [1] [3847

Edgemont, N. C. Mountain Home Club. History, prospectus, contract, articles of agreement, charter, constitution, and by-laws and rules. Charlotte, Queen City Printing Co., 1908. 40 p. [3848

Edgerton, Polly Lynette. The Guilford Scholarship Society, history and directory, by Polly Lynette Edgerton and Dorothy Lloyd Gilbert. Guilford College, 1952. 31 p. [3849

Edgerton Touring Co., Greensboro, N. C. From the Atlantic to the Pacific. Greensboro, 1922. 56 p. [3850

Edgeville, Edward. Castine. Raleigh, Wm. B. Smith & Co., 1865. 32 p. [3851

Edgeworth Female Seminary, Greensboro, N. C. Catalogue, 184 - Greensboro, 184 - NcU has [1853/54-1860/61] [3852

Edinburgh. National Library of Scotland. National library of Scotland, valuable documents of Flora MacDonald. [Edinburgh, 1938] 4 p. [3853

Edmonds, Helen G. The Negro and fusion politics in North Carolina, 1894-1901. Chapel Hill, University of North Carolina Press [1951] 260 p. [3854

Edmonds, Richard Hathaway. Facts about the South. Baltimore, no publisher, 1902. 37 p. [3855

—— ——c.1898. 30 p. [3856

—— ——Baltimore, Manufacturers' Record Publishing Co., 1907. 72 p. [3857

——The South's amazing progress. [Charlotte, Southern Power Co.] n.d. 28 p. [3858

——The South's redemption. From poverty to prosperity. Baltimore, Manufacturer's Record Co., 1890. 63 p. [3859

Edmonds, Richard Woods. Cotton mill labor conditions in the South and New England. Baltimore, Manufacturers' Record, 1925. 61 p. [3860

Edmondston, Catherine (Devereux) The journal of Catherine Devereux Edmondston, 1860-1866. Mebane, privately printed [1954] 111 p. [3861

Edmunds, Pocahontas Wight. Land of sand; legends of the North Carolina coast. Richmond, Va., Garrett and Massie, Inc. [c.1941] 35 p. [3862

Edmundson, Mildred. Dramatizing democracy, by Mildred Edmundson . . . in collaboration with Edward Lee Edmundson, Jr. Raleigh, Edwards & Broughton Co. [c.1947-50] 2 v. [3863

Education bulletin, v. 1, Jan. 15, 1934–Jan. 1, 1935. Raleigh, Public Relations Committee of the North Carolina Education Association, 1934-1935. NcU has v. 1 [3864

Educational Publishing Co., Atlanta, Ga. Complete list [of] North Carolina library books and new free premium offer order sheet. [Atlanta] n.d. 15 p. [3865

Edward William Faucette, born in Alamance County, N. C., Aug. 5th, 1826. [Lenoir, no publisher, 1901] 1 p. [3866

Edwards, Charles William. The problem of teaching physics in North Carolina; a paper read before North Carolina Academy of Science . . . Wake Forest, April 29, 1910. No place, no publisher [1910?] [8] p. [3867

Edwards, Edward. The life of Sir Walter Ralegh. [London] Macmillan & Co., 1868. 2 v. [3868

Edwards, Emma R. A history of North Carolina's Association of Jewish Women. [Greensboro? 1941?] 43 p. [3869

——Jewish war record, Goldsboro, North Carolina. [Goldsboro, 1945] 12 p. [3870

——North Carolina Congress of Parents and Teachers: History, vol. 1, 1919-1944. [Greensboro? 1945] 128 p. [3871

Edwards, John Ellis. The Confederate soldier; being a memorial sketch of George

N. and Bushrod W. Harris, privates in the Confederate army. New York, Blelock & Co., 1868. 139 p. [3872

——Life of Rev. John Wesley Childs. Richmond, Va., J. Early for Methodist Episcopal Church, South, 1852. 295 p. [3873

——The log meeting-house, and the McIlhanys. Nashville, Tenn., Southern Methodist Publishing House, 1885. 343 p. [3874

Edwards, Leila Taylor. The evidence, by Leila Taylor Edwards and Bernice Kelly Harris. New York, Samuel French [c.1931] 26 p. [3875

Edwards, Richard, ed. Statistical gazetteer of the states of Virginia and North Carolina. Richmond, Published for the Proprietor, 1856. 601 p. [3876

Edwards, Sallye Lee Oakes. Thoughts for a lonely hour. Richmond, Va., Published for the Author by Presbyterian Committee of Publication [c.1929] 87 p. [3877

Edwards, Weldon Nathaniel. Address to his constituents, the freemen of Warren County. No place [1853] 19 p. [3878

——Memoir of Nathaniel Macon, of North Carolina. Raleigh, Raleigh Register Steam Power Press, 1862. 22 p. [3879

E. Earle Rives for Congress, sixth district. [Greensboro, 1946] Folder [3880

Ege, Thompson P. Dodson Genealogy, 1600-1907. Philadelphia, Deemer & Jaisohn, 1908. 434 p. [3881

Eggers, Graydon, tr. The owl and the nightingale; translated into verse by Graydon Eggers. [Durham] Duke University Press, 1955. 62 p. [3882

Eggleston, George Cary. Carolina cavalier. Boston, Lothrop Publishing Co. [c.1901] 448 p. [3883

Eggleston, Joseph Dupuy. Distinguished descendants of Colonel Clement Read. No place, no publisher, n.d. 44 p. [3884

Ehle, John Marsden. American adventure (Series I) Programs no. 1-13. [Chapel Hill, Communications Center, University of North Carolina] 1953. Various paging. [3885

—— ——(Series II) Production scripts. Programs no. 14-26. 1955. Various paging. [3886

——The road to Orange, a bi-centennial pageant for Orange County, North Carolina. [Chapel Hill, 1953] 53 (i. e. 54) p. [3887

Ehringhaus, John Christoph Blucher. State government at the crossroads . . . delivered at the twenty-eighth annual convention of the Association of Life Insurance Presidents, at New York, December 14, 1934. No place, no publisher [1934?] 7 p. [3888

Eichelberger, L. The worth of life illustrated . . . an address delivered before the Crescent and Philalaethian societies of Western Carolina Academy, Mt. Pleasant, N. C. . . . September 16th, 1857. Salisbury, J. J. Bruner, 1857. 16 p. [3889

Eichhorn, Hermene Warlick. North Carolina composers as represented in the Holograph Collection, by Hermene Warlick Eichhorn and Treva Wilkerson Mathis. Greensboro, Woman's College Library, Woman's College of the University of North Carolina, 1945. 39 p. [3890

Eiker, Mathilde. The lady of stainless raiment. Garden City, N. Y., Doubleday, Doran and Co., 1928. 340 p. [3891

Elam, Harper J. Sketch of the Battle of Guilford Courthouse. Greensboro, Thomas Brothers, 1887. 36 p. [3892

Elder, Alphonso. Freshmen and seniors in the Negro colleges in North Carolina. Durham, North Carolina College for Negroes, 1927. 62 p. [3893

Eldredge, Daniel. . . . The Third New Hampshire and all about it. Boston, Press of E. B. Stillings and Co., 1893. 1054 p. [3894

Eldridge, T. B. Manual of style; rules observed in . . . Commercial Printing Co., Raleigh, N. C. [Raleigh, Commercial Printing Co.] 1918. 39 p. [3895

Eldridge, T. B., comp. Rules of composition for the guidance of printers and proof-readers . . . of Edwards and Broughton. [Raleigh, Edwards & Broughton] 1915. 33 p. [3896

Eley, Peter Harden. An epoch in history. [Roanoke, Va., Hammond's Printing Works, 1904] 92 p. [3897

Elfreth, Emily Allen. War echoes. Southern Pines [privately printed, c.1944] 38 p. [3898

Eliada Home for Children, Inc. The Eliada Home for Children (Incorporated) R. F. D. 4, Asheville, North Carolina. No place [1941?] [13] p. [3899

Eliason, Minnie Hampton. Fort Dobbs. Statesville, Fort Dobbs Chapter, Daughters, American Revolution [1915] 19 p. [3900

Eliason, Norman Ellsworth. Tarheel talk; an historical study of the English language in North Carolina to 1860. Chapel Hill, University of North Carolina Press [1956] 324 p. [3901

Elisha Mitchell Scientific Society, Chapel Hill, N. C. . . . Journal, v. 1- 1883/84- Raleigh [etc.] 1884- NcU has v. 1-72 [3902
—— ——Index to vols. 1-31. 1915. (In v. 31 of Journal)
—— ——Index to vols. 32-37. 1922. (In v. 37 of Journal)
—— ——Index to vols. 38-44. 1929. (In v. 44 of Journal)
—— ——Index to vols. 45-58. 1942. (In v. 58 of Journal)
—— ——Index to vols. 59-69. 1953. (In v. 69 of Journal)

Elizabeth City, N. C. Auditor. Report, 18 - 18 - NcU has 1896/97, 1899/1903 1908/09, 1937/38 [3903

Elizabeth City, N. C. Board of Aldermen. Ordinances of Elizabeth City, N. C., adopted July 3d, 1899. No place, no publisher, n.d. 24 p. [3904
—— ——adopted June 3d, 1901. Elizabeth City, Ed. F. Snakenberg, pr., 1901. 28 p. [3905
—— ——adopted July 6th, 1903. Elizabeth City, Tar Heel, pr., 1903. 32 p. [3906
—— ——Elizabeth City, Carolinian, 1905. 32 p. [3907

Elizabeth City, N. C. Board of Commissioners. Ordinances of Elizabeth City, N. C. for the year 1890-91. Elizabeth City, Economist Job Print, 1890. 13 p. [3908
—— ——1891-92. Weldon, Harrell's Printing House, 1891. 19 p. [3909
—— ——passed and adopted June 27th, 1897. Elizabeth City, Carolinian, 1897. 21 p. [3910
—— ——passed and adopted June 20th, 1898. 1898. 21 p. [3911

Elizabeth City, N. C. Board of Trustees of the Graded Schools. Graded Schools, session, 190 - Elizabeth City, 190 - NcU has 1908/09-1912/13 [3912
——Rules and regulations governing the Graded Schools of Elizabeth City . . . rev. and adopted . . . September 20th, 1915. [Elizabeth City, 1915] 18 p. [3913

Elizabeth City, N. C. Chamber of Commerce. Greeting and invitation from the city on the Pasquotank. No place, no publisher, n.d. 12 p. [3914

[Elizabeth City, N. C. Chamber of Commerce] Inviting you to Elizabeth City. [Elizabeth City? 1940?] [10] p. [3915

Elizabeth City, N. C. Christ Church. Yearbook, 1918. [Elizabeth City, 1918?] [14] p. [3916

Elizabeth City, N. C. City Council. The code . . . containing the ordinances of the city of Elizabeth City . . . to January 3, 1933. [Elizabeth City, Advance Printery, 1933?] 164 p. [3917

Elizabeth City, N. C. Ehringhaus for Governor Club. Ehringhaus the man, as seen by his neighbors of the Albemarle region of North Carolina. [Elizabeth City, Daily Advance] 1932. [3] p. [3918

Elizabeth College and Conservatory of Music, Charlotte, N. C. Catalogue, 18 - 1914/15? Charlotte, 18 - 1915? NcU has [1904/05-1914/15] Merged with Elizabeth College, Salem, Va., 1916. [3919
——Elizabeth College and Conservatory of Music for Women. Charlotte, N. C. [Charlotte, Washburn Press] n.d. 15 plates, with illustrations on both sides. [3920
—— ——[Charlotte, Queen City Printing Co.] n.d. 15 plates with illustrations on both sides. [3921

Elizabethtown, N. C. Presbyterian Church. Historical sketch of the Elizabethtown Presbyterian Church. Elizabethtown [1936] [7] p. [3922

Elkin Baptist Association. Minutes, 18 - 18 - NcU has 1880-1886, 1897, 1928, 1953, 1954 [3923

Ellenwood, Henry S. Lecture on elocution . . . delivered . . . before the North Carolina Institute of Education . . . June 20th, 1832. Newbern, John I. Pasteur, 1832. 16 p. [3924

Eller, Adolphus Hill. Guide-posts in preparing wills, by A. H. Eller and Gilbert T. Stephenson. Winston-Salem, Barber Printing Co., 1919. 79 p. [3925

—— ——[Winston-Salem, c.1925] [3926

——My will. (An excerpt from Eller and Stephenson's Guide-posts in preparing wills) [Winston-Salem] Wachovia Bank and Trust Co. [c.1919] 32 p. [3927

——The new university; an oration delivered at the one hundredth annual commencement of the University of North Carolina, June 5th, 1895. No place, no publisher, n.d. 14 p. [3928

Eller, Ernest McNeill. "The houses of peace" . . . account of the Moravians and their settlement of Salem in North Carolina. New York, Fleming H. Revell Co. [c.1937] 287 p. [3929

Eller, Franklin Plato. Institutions the result of growth; a speech by a student of the University of North Carolina, 1892. No place, no publisher, 1892. 9 p. [3930

Eller, Walter F. Poems for smiles and thought. Raleigh, The Author, c.1947. 39 p. [3931

Ellerbe, N. C. Public School. Activities and units of work, the Ellerbe school. Ellerbe [1935] Various paging. [3932

Ellerbe, North Carolina, the ideal spot. No place, no publisher [1907] 8 p. [3933

Ellerbe Springs; the finest water and finest grove in North Carolina. [Raleigh, Edwards & Broughton Printing Co.] 1907. 6 p. [3934

Ellet, Elizabeth Fries (Lummis) Pioneer women of the West. Philadelphia, Porter & Coates, n.d. 434 p. [3935

——Rambles about the country. New York, Harper and Bros., 1847. 257 p. [3936

——The women of the American Revolution. 2d ed. New York, Baker and Scribner, 1848-50. 3 v. [3937

—— ——Philadelphia, G. W. Jacobs & Co. [1900] 2 v. [3938

Ellicott, John Morris. The life of John Ancrum Winslow, rear-admiral, United States Navy. New York, G. P. Putnam's Sons, 1902. 281 p. [3939

Elliot, Henry. Address at the second annual meeting of the Agricultural Society of Cumberland County, N. C. Fayetteville, Edward J. Hale and Son, 1853. 22 p. [3940

Elliot, Jonathan, ed. The debates in the several state conventions on the adoption of the federal Constitution, as recommended by the general convention at Philadelphia in 1787. Washington, Printed by and for the Editor, 1836-45. 5 v. [3941

——The debates, resolutions, and other proceedings, in convention [of the states] on the adoption of the federal Constitution. Washington, The Editor, 1827-30. 4 v. [3942

Elliott, Charles. History of the great secession from the Methodist Episcopal Church in the year 1845, eventuating in . . . the Methodist Episcopal Church, South. Cincinnati, Swormstedt and Poe, 1855. 1143 p. [3943

Elliott, James Carson. The southern soldier boy; a thousand shots for the Confederacy. Raleigh, Edwards & Broughton Printing Co. [c.1907] 77 p. [3944

Elliott, Robert Neal. The Raleigh register, 1799-1863. Chapel Hill, University of North Carolina Press, 1955. (James Sprunt studies in history and political science, v. 36) 133 p. [3945

Elliott, Sarah A. Days long ago; a novelette. Raleigh, Uzzell & Wiley, 1881. 57 p. [3946

——Mrs. Elliott's housewife, containing practical receipts in cookery. New York, Hurd & Houghton, 1872. 346 p. [3947

—— ——Philadelphia, Claxton, Remsen & Haffelfinger, 1877. 347 p. [3948

Ellis, Edward Sylvester. . . . In the days of the pioneers. Philadelphia, H. T. Coates & Co. [c.1897] (Boone and Kenton series, no. 3) 368 p. [3949

——The life and times of Col. Daniel Boone, hunter, soldier, and pioneer. Philadelphia, Porter & Coates [c.1884] 269 p. [3950

——The life and times of Col. Daniel Boone, the hunter of Kentucky. New York, Beadle and Co. [c.1860] (Beadle's dime biographical library, no. 2) 96 p. [3951

——. . . The phantom of the river. Philadelphia, H. T. Coates & Co. [c.1896] (Boone and Kenton series, no. 2) 352 p. [3952

——. . . Shod with silence. Philadelphia, H. T. Coates & Co. [c.1896] (Boone and Kenton series, no. 1) 363 p. [3953

Ellis, John Willis. Eulogy on the life and character of Thomas James Memory, delivered at Whiteville, Oct. 6th, 1872. No place, no publisher, n.d. 9 p.   [3954

——Speech . . . delivered before the Democratic state convention, in Raleigh, March 9, 1860. Raleigh, Standard Office Print, 1860. 15 p.   [3955

Ellis, William B. Sanity for sale; the story of the rise and fall of William B. Ellis, by himself. Advance, The Advance Publishing Co., 1928. 179 p.   [3956

[**Ellms, Charles, comp.**] Pirates own book. Salem, Mass., Marine Research Society, 1924. (Marine research society. Publication no. 4) 469 p.   [3957

Ellms, Charles. Tragedy of the seas. Philadelphia, W. A. Leary, 1848. 432 p.   [3958

Ellwood, Charles Abram. A history of social philosophy. New York, Prentice-Hall, Inc., 1938. 581 p.   [3959

——Man's social destiny in the light of science. Nashville, Tenn., Cokesbury Press, 1929. 219 p.   [3960

——Methods in sociology. Durham, Duke University Press, 1933. 214 p.   [3961

——The story of social philosophy. New York, Prentice-Hall, Inc., 1938. 581 p. Published also in the Prentice-Hall sociology series under title: A history of social philosophy.   [3962

——The world's need of Christ. New York, Abingdon-Cokesbury Press [c.1940] 237 p.   [3963

—— ——rev. [1946] 213 p.   [3964

Elon College, Elon College, N. C. Bulletin, v. 1- 1905- Elon College, 1905- NcU has v. [1-49]   [3965

——Catalogue, 18 - Elon College, 18 - NcU has [1895/96-1899/1900] Continues as its Bulletin, 1905-   [3966

——Elon College alumni directory, 1948. Elon College, General Alumni Association, 1948. 104 p.   [3967

Elsom, P. G. The feast of Belshazzar. No place, no publisher, n.d. 15 p.   [3968

——Your chickens will come home to roost. [Asheville, Inland Press] n.d. 29 p.   [3969

Elson, William Harris. Good English, oral and written . . . by William H. Eslon . . . Lura E. Runkel . . . James F. Royster. Teacher's edition. Chicago, Scott, Foresman and Co. [c.1922] 3 v.   [3970

—— ——Special state edition, by James F. Royster. Chicago, Scott, Foresman and Co. [c.1921] NcU has Book 1.   [3971

Ely, Ezra Stiles. Duty of Christian freemen to elect Christian rulers; a discourse delivered on the Fourth of July, 1827, in the Seventh Presbyterian Church, in Philadelphia. Philadelphia, Printed by William F. Geddes, 1828. 32 p.   [3972

Embury, Aymar. An architectural monograph: New England influence on North Carolina architecture, New Bern—Part II. New York, R. F. Whitehead, 1927. (White Pine Series, Folio 13, pt. 2) 24 p.   [3973

Emerson, Bettie Alder (Calhoun) comp. Historic southern monuments. New York, Neale Publishing Co., 1911. 466 p.   [3974

Emerson, Charles, comp. North Carolina tobacco belt directory; embracing the counties of Alamance, Durham, Forsyth, Granville, Guilford, Orange, Rockingham, Vance, and Wake. Raleigh, Edwards, Broughton & Co., 1886. 763 p.   [3975

Emerson, Charles and Co. Charles Emerson and Co.'s Newbern directory, 1880-'81. Raleigh, Edwards, Broughton & Co., 1880. 157 p.   [3976

——Chas. Emerson & Co.'s Raleigh directory, 1880-'81. Raleigh, Edwards, Broughton & Co., 1879. 212 p.   [3977

Emery, E. B. Letters from the South, on the social, intellectual, and moral condition of the colored people. Boston, T. Todd, pr., 1880. 19 p.   [3978

Emilio, Luis F. Roanoke Island, its occupation, defense, and fall: a paper read before the Roanoke Associates, New York City, Feb. 9th, 1891. No place, Printed for the Associates, 1891. 18 p.   [3979

Emison, James Wade. The Emison families. Vincennes, Ind., 1947. 243 p.   [3980

—— ——1954. 360 p.   [3981

Emma Lydia Rankin, third daughter of Rev. Jesse and Ann Delight Rankin, July 29, 1838-Feb. 28, 1908. No place, no publisher, n.d. 40 p.   [3982

Emmerson, John Cloyd, comp. The steam-boat comes to Norfolk Harbor, and the log of the first ten years: 1815-1825. [Portsmouth? Va.] 1949. 455 p.   [3983

——Steam navigation in Virginia and Northeastern North Carolina waters, 1826-1836. [Portsmouth? Va., 1950] 453 p. [3984

Emmerton, James Arthur. A record of the Twenty-third Regiment Mass. Vol. Infantry in the war of the rebellion, 1861-1865. Boston, W. Ware & Co., 1886. 352 p. [3985

Emmons, Ebenezer. Manual of geology. Philadelphia, Sower, Barnes & Co., 1860. 290 p. [3986

—— ——2d ed. New York, A. S. Barnes & Co., 1867. 297 p. [3987

Emory, Samuel Thomas. . . . Bright tobacco in the agriculture, industry and foreign trade of North Carolina. [Chicago] 1939. 154 p. Thesis (Ph. D.)—University of Chicago. [3988

Empie, Adam. The official character and duty of the gospel messenger; a sermon preached in St. Paul's Church, Edenton, N. C. April 30, 1820. Fayetteville, Carney and Dismukes, 1820. 49 p. [3989

——Remarks on the distinguishing doctrine of modern Universalism. New York, Printed by T. and J. Swords, 1825. 139 p. [3990

——Sermons on various subjects, written and preached at different places and times. New York, Dana and Co., 1856. 511 p. [3991

Engelhard, Joseph Adolphus. Address before the Philanthropic and Dialectic societies of the University of North Carolina, June, 1878. Raleigh, Edwards, Broughton & Co., 1879. 26 p. [3992

[Engelhardt, Nickolaus Louis] The Richard J. Reynolds High School. Winston-Salem [City Public Schools] 1921. 14 p. [3993

Engelhardt, Nickolaus Louis. School building programs in American cities. New York, Teachers College, Columbia University, 1928. 560 p. [3994

England, John. Pastoral letter of the Right Reverend Dr. England, Roman Catholic bishop of Charleston, to his flock in the states of North and South-Carolina and Georgia. Charleston, A. E. Miller, 1821. 12 p. [3995

English, Oliver Spurgeon. Fathers are parents, too . . . by O. Spurgeon English and Constance J. Foster. New York, G. P. Putnam's Sons [1951] 304 p. [3996

——Your behavior problems, by O. Spurgeon English and Constance J. Foster. Chicago, Science Research Associates, c.1952. 49 p. [3997

English forum, v. 1-2, October, 1923-May, 1925. High Point, North Carolina Council of Teachers of English, 1923-1925. NcU has v. 1-2 [3998

Enka voice, v. 1—Jan. 1930- Enka, American Enka Corporation Employees, 1930- NcU has v. [2-5] 6-9 [10] 11-26 [3999

Enniss, James H. Catalogue of photographs for sale at N. C. book store, next door to Capitol Square, Raleigh, N. C. Raleigh, n.d. [1] p. [4000

——A catalogue of publications and importations embracing valuable standard books in historical, law, medical, school, and general literature. Raleigh, For sale by J. H. Enniss, 1869. 71 p. [4001

——Importance of economy on the farm; agricultural address delivered at the N. C. Grange encampment . . . at Mt. Holly encampment, Gaston County, Aug. 8th to 13th. No place, no publisher [1887] 12 p. [4002

——J. H. Enniss' advertiser, for the use of parents, teachers, and the public generally. Salisbury, n.d. [4] p. [4003

Enniss, Peyton Hervey. The ancient stones cry out. New York, Biblical Treasures [c.1939] 124 p. [4004

Ensign, John. My camp book, stewards in God's world, by John and Ruth Ensign. Richmond, Va., John Knox Press for the Cooperative Publication Association [c.1953] 65 p. [4005

——Stewards in God's world, a guide for junior high camp leaders, by John and Ruth Ensign. Richmond, Va., John Knox Press [c.1954] 144 p. [4006

Eos; a magazine of standard fiction at a popular price, v. 1- June, 1906- Greensboro, Eos Publishing Co., June, 1906- NcU has v. 1, no. 1-4. [4007

Episcopal School of North Carolina, Raleigh, N. C. Prospectus of the Episcopal School of North Carolina, near the city of Raleigh. Raleigh, Joseph Gales & Son, 1834. 24 p. [4008

——Report on the state of the Episcopal School of North Carolina, November, 1834- Raleigh, 1834- NcU has November, 1834; November, 1835 [4009

Episcopal School of North Carolina, Raleigh, N. C. Trustees. Address of the Trustees . . . to the public. Raleigh, Printed by T. J. Lemay, 1836. 10 p. [4010

Epitaphs in the grave-yard at Bonarva Lake, Phelps, North-Carolina. New York, Protestant Episcopal Press, 1834. 8 p. [4011

Epoch Producing Corporation, New York. Souvenir, The birth of a nation. New York [c.1915] [16] p. [4012

Eppes, Allen. Eveless Eden. New York, Gateway Books, 1940. 255 p. [4013
——Meet the prince. New York, William Godwin, Inc. [c.1934] 279 p. [4014

Eppes, Susan (Bradford) Through some eventful years. Macon, Ga., Press of the J. W. Burke Co., 1926. 378 p. [4015

Epstein, Beryl (Williams) Francis Marion, Swamp Fox of the Revolution, by Beryl Williams and Samuel Epstein. New York, J. Messner [1956] 192 p. [4016

Epstein, Florence. That girl Ava; the life and loves of a fabulous female. No place, Literary Enterprises, Inc., c.1955. Unpaged. [4017

Epstein, Samuel. The real book about pirates, by Samuel Epstein and Beryl Williams. Garden City, N. Y., Garden City Books [1952] 192 p. [4018

Equal taxation; injustice done to the West by Gov. Ellis. No place, no publisher, n.d. 8 p. [4019

Equal taxation; young slaves, the best investment. Raleigh, Book and Job Office, n.d. 4 p. [4020

Erickson, E. T. Whither are we drifting? Radio talk by E. T. Erickson . . . Soil Conservation Service, over Station WDNC . . . January 1, 1936. No place, 1936. 6 p. [4021

Ericson, Eston Everett. The use of swa in Old English. Göttingen, Vandenhoeck & Ruprecht, 1932. (Hesperia. Ergänzungsreihe: Schriften zur englischen Philologie . . . 12. hft.) 89 p. [4022

Ernul, J. B. Life of a Confederate soldier in a federal prison. [New Bern, Owen G. Dunn] n.d. 15 p. [4023

Erskine, Edith Deaderick. Clouds, chords and calico [by] Marie Smith Inzer, Louise Godfrey Ogle [and] Edith Deaderick Erskine. Emory University, Ga., Banner Press [1943] 79 p. [4024
——From sea to sky. Emory University, Ga., Banner Press [1954] 59 p. [4025
——Here they live and die. Dallas, Texas, Story Book Press [c.1953] 64 p. [4026
——The power flows. Dallas, Texas, Story Book Press [c.1950] 48 p. [4027

Erskine, Payne. A girl of the Blue Ridge. Boston, Little, Brown, and Co., 1915. 401 p. [4028
——Joyful Heatherby. New York, A. L. Burt Co. [1913] 449 p. [4029
——The mountain girl. Boston, Little, Brown, and Co., 1912. 312 p. [4030
——When the gates lift up their heads. Boston, Little, Brown, and Co., 1901. 445 p. [4031

Ervin, Catharine E. History of woman's work . . . First Presbyterian Church, Morganton, N. C. [Morganton? First Presbyterian Church, 1944] 86 p. [4032

Ervin, Samuel James. The provincial agents of North Carolina. Chapel Hill, The University, 1919. (James Sprunt historical publications, v. 16, no. 2) p. [61]-77[4033

Ervin, William Carson. Catawba Valley and highlands, Burke County, Western North Carolina. Morganton, Morganton Land and Improvement Co., c.1896. 40 p. [4034

Ervin for Congress Committee. Joe W. Ervin for Congress. No place [1944] 15 p. [4035

Erwin, Ira. The church of Christ . . . first sermon delivered in the Sunday-school room of the new Centenary M. E. Church of Greensboro, N. C. . . . March 19, 1905. No place, no publisher, n.d. 20 p. [4036

Erwin, Marcus. Address to the people of the 46th and 49th senatorial districts, [by Marcus Erwin and W. W. Avery] No place, no publisher, 1861. 14 p. [4037

Eseeola Inn, Linville, N. C. Eseeola Inn and annex, Linville, N. C. [Philadelphia, Loughead, 191?] 14 p. [4038

Eskridge, Thomas Joseph. Growth in understanding of geographic terms in grades IV to VII. Durham, Duke University Press, 1939. (Duke University. Research studies in education [no. 4]) 67 p. [4039

[Esso Standard Oil Co.] To be rather than to seem. No place, n.d. [28] p. [4040

Etheredge, Hamlin. The enthusiastic Spring. New York, Pegasus Co. [c.1937] 255 p. [4041

Ethridge, Mark. The South and its prospects; an address delivered in Chapel Hill . . . October 12, 1938. [Chapel Hill] Junior-Senior Cabinet of the University YMCA [1938] 15 p. [4042

Eubank, W. Hampton, joint author, see Harris, William Shakespeare

Eure, Thaddeus Armie. Accomplishments of the 1935 session of the General Assembly of North Carolina; radio address . . . delivered over station WPTF, Raleigh . . . May 11, 1935. [Raleigh, 1935] 8 p. [4043

Eustis, Helen. The fool killer. New York, Pocket Books, Inc. [1955] 181 p. [4044

Eutsler, Roland Byerly. Transportation in North Carolina. Philadelphia, 1929. 65 p. Thesis (Ph. D.)—University of Pennsylvania. [4045

Evangelical Lutheran Church in the Confederate States of America. Minutes, 186 - Savannah, 186 - NcU has 1866 (3d) [4046

Evangelical Lutheran Church in the Southern States. Diet see Diet of the Evangelical Lutheran Church in the South

Evangelical Lutheran Synod of North Carolina. Constitution . . . and ministerium of North Carolina. Wilmington, Lutheran Publication Co., 1888. 35 p. [4047

——Constitution . . . and ministerium of North Carolina, adopted August 27-28, 1889. Newberry, S. C., Aull & Houseal, 1890. 45 p. [4048

——Minutes of the annual convention, 18 - 18 - NcU has 1803-1810 (published as one in 1811, German) 1812 (English and German) 1813-17 (German) 1819 (German) 1825 (German) [1821-1881] 1883-1893, 1923-1955 [4049

◄——Minutes of the Evangelical Lutheran Synod of North Carolina from 1803-1826, twenty-three conventions, translated from the German protocol by Rev. F. W. E. Peschau. Newberry, S. C., Aull & Houseal, 1894. 67 p. [4050

Evangelical Lutheran Synod of North Carolina. Luther League of America. Minutes of the annual convention, 1st- 1920- 1920- NcU has 1st-7th, 9th-18th, 20th [4051

Evangelical Lutheran Synod of North Carolina. Woman's Missionary Society. Minutes, 1885- 1885- NcU has [1889-1917] [4052

Evans, James Gilbert, Jr. Basic economics in a democratic society using a machine technology. Chapel Hill, University of North Carolina Press, 1934. 139 p. [4053

Evans, Virginia Fraser. The story of the First Presbyterian Church of Statesville, North Carolina, 1753-1953. [Statesville, 1953] 30 p. [4054

Evans, W. P. Address delivered before the Catawba Synodical Sunday School Convention. Norfolk, Va., Guide Publishing Co., Inc., 1926. 14 p. [4055

Evans, Sir William David. Essays on the action for money had and received, on the law of insurances, and on the law of bills of exchange and promissory notes. Liverpool, Merritt & Wright; Newbern, Martin & Ogden, 1802. Various paging. [4056

Everest, Charles William. Songs of the fireside. Hartford, Brockett & Co., 1852. 127 p. [4057

Everett, Lillie (Moore) Seven times seven; a history of the seven Sabbaths of years in the North Carolina Conference Woman's Missionary Society, December 1, 1878-Dec. 31, 1928. Greensboro, Piedmont Press, 1929. 459 p. [4058

Everett, Reuben Oscar. Does the constitution of the United States meet the demands of today? An address delivered over WDNC . . . on September 17, 1936, in celebration of Constitution Week. [Durham? 1936?] 8 p. [4059

——William Jennings Bryan. Durham, no publisher, 1926. 24 p. [4060

——The world court; an address at the dedication of Geneva Hall, Little Switzerland, North Carolina, August 1, 1928. No place, no publisher [1928] 23 p. [4061

Everett, Robinson O. Military justice in the armed forces of the United States. Harrisburg, Pa., Military Service Pub. Co. [1956] 338 p. [4062

Everett, William Nash. In which some questions regarding the central alumni office are answered by Pres. Everett. [Chapel Hill, General Alumni Office, University of N. C., 1925?] 4 p. [4063

——The record of North Carolina democracy's administration of public affairs; address before the State Democratic Convention . . . at Raleigh, April 17, 1924. No place, no publisher [1924?] 29 p. [4064

Evergreen monthly, v. 1- October, 1850- Ashborough, B. Craven and R. H. Brown, 1850- NcU has v. [1] [4065

Everywoman's magazine, v. 1- 1916- Raleigh, 1916- NcU has v. [1-4] [4066

Ewing, Cortez Arthur Milton. Primary elections in the South. Norman, University of Oklahoma Press [c.1953] 112 p. [4067

Ewing, Linda (Cunningham) My forebears; history and genealogy of the Cunningham, Knox, Gibson, Borders, [and] Ewing families. [Atlanta, J. T. Hancock, 1946] 112 p. [4068

Ewing, Tempe Berry, ed. History of the Albemarle Chapter, United Daughters of the Confederacy, from 1906 to 1932. [Albemarle, Press Printing Co., 1932] 18 p. [4069

Ewing, Thomas. Historical papers and reports read before the Empire State Society, Sons of the American Revolution; Historical address—Gen. Thomas Ewing: Battle of Guilford Court House. [New York? The Society, Feb. 28, 1899] (Historical papers and reports. 1899. v. 1, no. 1) 48 p. [4070

[Exquemelin, Alexandre Olivier] The buccaneers and marooners of America. Popular ed. London, T. Fisher Unwin, 1897. 403 p. [4071

Exquemelin, Alexandre Olivier. The buccaneers of America. London, Swan Sonnenschein & Co., Ltd., n.d. 508 p. Reprinted from the first English edition of 1684. [4072

[Exquemelin, Alexandre Olivier] The history of the bucaniers of America. London, Printed for J. Walker, 1810. 660 p. [4073

Extracts of letters, containing some account of the work of God since the year 1800, written by the preachers and members of the Methodist Episcopal Church to their bishops. Barnard, Vt., Published by Joseph Dix, March, 1812. 120 p. [4074

Ezell, Robert A. Speech delivered before the Democratic Association of Warren, N. C. Richmond, Shepherd and Colin, 1840. 29 p. [4075

Facts about Charlotte and its government [Charlotte] 1955. 4 p. [4076

Facts about Flora Macdonald College. [Charlotte, Presbyterian Standard] 1920. Folder. [4077

Facts about Fort Bragg, North Carolina. [Fayetteville, Cumberland Printing Co. 192?] 57 p. [4078

Facts about the school tax election in Chapel Hill. Chapel Hill [Group of Citizens] 1933. [4] p. [4079

Facts about Winston-Salem, Forsyth County, North Carolina, U. S. A. Salem, Press Electric Print [1891?] 15 p. [4080

[Facts in brief about Greensboro, N. C.] [Greensboro, Chamber of Commerce, 1921] 2 p. [4081

Facts! Relating to hard times in Brunswick County. No place, no publisher, n.d. [1] p. [4082

Fagin, Nathan Bryllion. William Bartram, interpreter of the American landscape. Baltimore, Johns Hopkins Press, 1933. 299 p. [4083

Fain, John Tyree. Fain's critical and analytical index and genealogical guide to Ramsey's Annals of Tennessee. Nashville, Tenn., Printed for subscribers by P. Hunter, 1920. 86 p. [4084

Fairbrother, Al, joint author, see Hopkins, Lindsay

Fairchild, C. B. Price list and descriptive catalogue of greenhouse and bedding plants, flower and garden seeds, bulbs and small fruits, Raleigh, N. C., 1880. Raleigh, Edwards, Broughton & Co., 1880. 27 p. [4085

Fairview Farm, Raleigh, N. C. . . . Catalogue of highly bred trotting stock owned by B. P. Williamson. [New York, M. J. Hendrick] 1890. 27 p. [4086

Fairview Institute and Commerical College, Gibsonville, N. C. Catalogue, 1884- Gibsonville 1884- NcU has [1889/90-1895/96] [4087

Faison, W. E. The dignity and responsibility of organized labor; Labor Day address, Greensboro, N. C., Sept. 4, 1905. [Raleigh, Allied Printing Trades Council, 1905?] 15 p. [4088

Faison Male Academy, Faison, N. C. Catalogue, 1901/02- Faison, 1902- NcU has [1903/04-1909/10] [4089

Faithful, Mamie. Poems. Wilson, Barrett's Print, n.d. 47 p. [4090

Fales, James M. Prison life of Lieut. James M. Fales, by George N. Bliss. Providence, N. B. Williams & Co., 1882. (Personal narratives of events in the war of the rebellion, being papers read before the Rhode Island Soldiers and Sailors Historical Society, 2d ser., no. 15) 70 p. [4091

Falk, Isidore Sydney. . . . A community medical service organized under industrial auspices in Roanoke Rapids, North Carolina, by I. S. Falk [and others] Chicago, Ill., University of Chicago Press [1932] (Publications of the Committee on the costs of medical care, no. 20) 109 p. [4092

Fallow, Amy C., joint author, see **Hassell, Allene B.**

Fanning, David. Col. David Fanning's Narrative of his exploits and adventures as a loyalist of North Carolina in the American Revolution. Toronto, Reprinted from the Canadian Magazine, 1908. 55 p. [4093
——The narrative of Colonel David Fanning (a Tory in the Revolutionary war with Great Britain;) giving an account of his adventures in North Carolina, from 1775 to 1783. Richmond, Va., Printed for private distribution, 1861. (Historical documents relating to the Old North State, no. 1) 92 p. [4094
—— ——New York, Reprinted for J. Sabin, 1865. 86 p. [4095

Faria, Francisco de. The information of Francisco de Faria, delivered at the bar of the House of Commons, Munday, the first day of November, in the year of our Lord, 1680. Lond., Printed by the assigns of John Bill, Thomas Newcomb, and Henry Hills, 1680. 12 p. [4096

Faris, John Thomson. Roaming the eastern mountains. New York, Farrar & Rinehart, Inc. [c.1932] 327 p. [4097
——Romance of forgotten towns. New York, Harper and Bros., 1924. 355 p. [4098

Farish, Hunter Dickinson. The circuit rider dismounts; a social history of Southern Methodism, 1865-1900. Richmond, Va., Dietz Press, 1938. 400 p. [4099

Farmer, Foy (Johnson) Hitherto; history of North Carolina Woman's Missionary Union. Raleigh, Woman's Missionary Union of North Carolina, 1952. 171 p. [4100
——King's way: Catharine of Argyll. Birmingham, Ala., Woman's Missionary Union [1953] 23 p. [4101
——Sacrifice and song. Nashville, Tenn., Broadman Press [c.1953] 136 p. [4102

Farmer, James S. Tape of time. New York, Vantage Press [c.1953] 46 p. [4103

Farmer, John W. Dear Sir. No place, no publisher, n.d. [1] p. [4104

Farmer Institute, Farmer, N. C. Catalogue, 18 - Farmer, 18 - NcU has 1899/1900 [4105

Farmer's advocate, v. 1- August, 1838- Jamestown, John Sherwood, 1838- NcU has v. [1-3] [4106

[Farmer's and Mechanic's Life Assurance Association] To the members of our General Assembly. [Raleigh, 1870] 5 p. [4107

Farmers Consolidated Tobacco Company, Greenville, N. C. Some extracts from report, O. L. Joyner, president, at the fifth annual meeting of the Company, April 20th, 1908. [Greenville, 1908] [8] p. [4108
——To the tobacco farmers of Eastern North Carolina. [Greenville] n.d. [1] p. [4108a

Farmers' Cooperative Council of North Carolina. Articles of incorporation. [Raleigh, 1935] 5 p. [4109

Farmer's dollar magazine, v. 1- March, 1870- Ridgeway, T. M. Hughes, 1870- NcU has v. [1] [4110

Farmers' Educational & Co-operative Union of America. North Carolina. Constitution and by-laws to govern North Carolina. [Marshville? Carolina Union Farmer? 1902?] 20 p. [4111
——Minutes, 19 - 19 - NcU has 1916 [4112

Farmers' Federation, Inc., Asheville, N. C. The country church at work with the Lord's acre plan. [Asheville, 1935?] 11 p. [4113
——The Farmers' Federation handbook, 19 - Asheville, 193 - NcU has 1935, 1946 [4114

Farmers' Federation news, v. 1- September, 1920- Asheville, Farmers' Federation, Inc., 1920- NcU has v. [5] 8-9, 13-16, 19-22. 24-25 [26-27] 29-37 [4115

Farmer's journal, v. 1-3, April, 1852-1854. Bath, J. F. Tompkins, 1852-1854. NcU has v. 1-3. [4116

Farmers, merchants, and manufacturers trade journal, and housekeeper's receipt book. Raleigh, Edwards & Broughton, 1872. 48 p. [4117

Farmers Mutual Exchange, Durham, N. C. Durham Farmers Mutual Exchange, explanation and by-laws, March, 1930. Durham [1930] 14 p. [4118

——10 years of progress . . . Annual meeting, 1940. [Durham, 1940] [12] p. [4119

Farmer's mutual patron, v. 1- April, 1946- Raleigh, Farmer's Cooperative Exchange, 1946- NcU has v. [1, 9-11] [4120

Farmers' National Congress, Raleigh, N. C. Proceedings of the twenty-ninth annual convention, held at Raleigh, North Carolina, November 4th to 9th, nineteen hundred and nine. No place [1909] 131 p. [4121

——Raleigh, Durham, Greensboro, Friday, Nov. 5, itinerary and historical. No place, no publisher, 1909. 8 p. [4122

Farrar, Frederic William. Sir Walter Raleigh and America; a sermon preached at St. Margaret's Church, Westminster, on May 14, 1882, at the unveiling of the Raleigh window. London, Anglo-American Times Press [1882?] 21 p. [4123

Farrell, Louis. McCallums: Daniel McCallum, Isabel Sellars, their antecedents, descendants and collateral relatives . . . by Louis Farrell [and] Flora Janie Hamer Hooker. [Nashville] Published by the Compilers for private distribution, 1946. 234 p. [4124

Farris, Edward N. Reasons for the Charlotte-Wilmington military highway, by E. N. Farris, Heriot Clarkson, W. C. Wilkinson, committee. [Charlotte, Huneycutt Printing Co., 1918?] [3] p. [4125

Farriss, Charles Sherwood. The American soul; an appreciation of the four greatest Americans and their lesson for present Americans. Boston, Stratford Co., 1920. 89 p. [4126

——Robert E. Lee, a play. Boston, Richard G. Badger [c.1924] 131 p. [4127

Farriss, James Joseph. High Point in word and picture. [High Point, Enterprise, 1908?] [116] p. [4128

——High Point, N. C.; a brief summary of its manufacturing enterprises. No place, 1896. 78 p. [4129

—— ——3d ed. [High Point, Enterprise Printing Co.] 1903. [168] p. [4130

—— ——5th ed. [1909] [204] p. [4131

—— ——6th ed. [High Point? Daily Enterprise? 1911?] [196] p. [4132

—— ——7th ed. 1912. [194] p. [4133

Fassifern School, Hendersonville, N. C. Catalogue, 19 - Hendersonville, 190 - NcU has [1908/09-1948/49] [4134

Fassifern School. English Department. The blue book . . . containing specimens of the work of that department, together with names and addresses of Fassifern faculty and student body. No place, no publisher, 1925. [17] p. [4135

Fast, Howard Melvin. . . . Patick Henry and the frigate's keel, and other stories of a young nation. New York, Duell, Sloan and Pearce [1945] 253 p. [4136

"The father of rural free delivery" . . . tribute to Senator Butler. No place, no publisher [1915] [6] p. [4137

Father Price of Maryknoll; a short sketch of the life of Reverend Thomas Frederick Price. Maryknoll, N. Y., Catholic Foreign Mission Society of America [c.1923] 93 p. [4138

Faulkner, Nancy. Pirate quest. Garden City, N. Y., Doubleday & Co., Inc., 1955. 256 p. [4139

Faun, v. 1, no. 1-6, Oct. 9, 1926-Nov. 20, 1926. Chapel Hill, 1926. NcU has v. 1 [4140

Faust, Albert Bernhardt. The German element in the United States. Boston, Houghton Mifflin Co., 1909. 2 v. [4141

—— ——New York, The Steuben Society of America, 1927. 2 v. in one. [4142

——Guide to the materials for American history in Swiss and Austrian archives. Washington, D. C., Carnegie Institution of Washington, 1916. (Carnegie Institution of Washington. Publication no. 220) 299 p. [4143

——Lists of Swiss emigrants in the eighteenth century to the American colonies. Washington, D. C., National Genealogical Society, 1920-25. 2 v. [4144

Faust, Bernard Christoph. Catechism of health; translated from the German. 3d American ed. Raleigh, Printed at the Star Office by Thomas Henderson, 1812. 90 p.   [4145

Favorite quotations of representative people who are, or have been, associated with Wilson. No place, no publisher, n.d. 46 p.   [4146

Fayetteville, N. C. Banking House of P. A. Wiley and Co. Banking house of P. A. Wiley & Co., in Bank of Fayetteville, N. C. Fayetteville, Presbyterian Office, 1866. 15 p.   [4147

Fayetteville, N. C. Board of Aldermen. Ordinances, the charter, continuing contracts and franchises of the city of Fayetteville, North Carolina, adopted on May 11, 1925. [Fayetteville, Cumberland Printing Co., 1925?] 185 p.   [4148

Fayetteville, N. C. Chamber of Commerce. Buyer's guide, Fayetteville, N. C. . . . a classified directory, 1948- [Fayetteville] 1948- NcU has 1948   [4149
——Facts and figures relating to Fayetteville, North Carolina. Fayetteville, 1899. 8 p.   [4150
—— ——[Fayetteville, Baptist Print, 1904] 17 p.   [4151
——Fayetteville, North Carolina. [Fayetteville, 1950?] [4] p.   [4152
——Stop over point, Fayetteville, North Carolina, furtherest inland port. [Fayetteville, 193?] 28 p.   [4153
——Stop over point, Fayetteville, North Carolina, on the shortest all-paved route south. [Fayetteville] n.d. [27] p.   [4154

Fayetteville, N. C. Cross Creek Lodge No. 4 of the I. O. O. F. of North Carolina see Independent Order of Odd Fellows. North Carolina. Cross Creek Lodge No. 4, Fayetteville

Fayetteville, N. C. Lafayette Division of the Sons of Temperance see North Carolina Sons of Temperance. Lafayette Division No. 2, Fayetteville

Fayetteville, N. C. Phoenix Lodge No. 8, Masons see Freemasons. Phoenix Lodge No. 8, Fayetteville, N. C.

[Fayetteville, N. C. Theater] An evening's lounge; or, Antidote for the spleen. No place [1795] [1] p. NcU has photostat (negative) of original in Playbill Collection, Colonial Williamsburg, Inc.   [4155
——Fayetteville in North Carolina. On Monday evening next, will be performed at the theatre . . . comic entertainments. No place, n.d. [1] p. NcU has photostat (negative) of original in Playbill Collection, Colonial Williamsburg, Inc. [4156
——Possitively (!) the last night. An evening's lounge; or, Antidote for the spleen. No place [1795] [1] p. NcU has photostat (negative) of original in Playbill Collection, Colonial Williamsburg, Inc.   [4157

Fayetteville, N. C. Treasurer. Annual statement for the year ending May 5th, 1878. Fayetteville, no publisher, 1878. [1] p.   [4158

Fayetteville Area Industrial Development Corporation. Fayetteville, North Carolina, industrial location data, December, 1955. Fayetteville [1955] 43 p.   [4159

Fayetteville-Davidson Academy, Fayetteville, N. C. Announcement, 1901/02- Fayetteville, 1901- NcU has 1901/02   [4160

Fayetteville Female High School, Fayetteville, N. C. Catalogue, 1855/56- Fayetteville, 1856- NcU has 1855/56   [4161

[Fayetteville Historical Celebration, Inc.] The highlanders, 1739-1939. [Fayetteville, 1939] [16] p.   [4162

Fayetteville illustrated. Fayetteville, McKee Barclay, n.d. 20 p.   [4163

Fayetteville, North Carolina, the city of history and hospitality. No place, no publisher, n.d. 12 p.   [4164

Fayetteville, North Carolina, the trading point for the upper Cape Fear section. Richmond, Va., Central Publishing Co. [1916] 31 p.   [4165

Fayetteville Presbytery see Presbyterian Church in the U. S. Synod of N. C. Fayetteville Presbytery

The feast of Belshazzar and its end. [Goldsboro, Board of Missions, n.d.] 4 p. [4166

Featherstonhaugh, George William. A canoe voyage up the Minnay Sotor. London, R. Bentley, 1847. 2 v.   [4167
——Excursion through the slave states, from Washington on the Potomac to the frontier of Mexico. London, J. Murray, 1844. 2 v.   [4168

Federal Reserve Bank of Richmond, Va. Business indicators, North Carolina, 194 - Richmond, 194 - NcU has [December, 1948-December, 1956] [4169
——Index . . . North Carolina, 19 - Richmond, 195 - NcU has 1950 [4170
——Member banks of Federal Reserve District no. 5, 19 - [Richmond, 19 - NcU has 1914, 1919 [4171
——Monthly review, credit, business, and agricultural conditions, 19 - Richmond, Va., 19 - NcU has June-December, 1921; Feb. 1922-Jan. 1923; April-June, 1925; Sept. 1925-May 1926; July-Aug. 1926; [Nov. 1929-Dec. 1937] 1938-1956 [4172
——Report, 1915-1936. Richmond, Va., 1916-1937. NcU has 1920-1936. [4173
——Report on subscriptions to the Fourth Liberty Loan of 1918 for the Fifth Federal Reserve District. [Richmond, Va.] n.d. 62 p. [4174
——Supplemental brief in support of application in the matter of the application . . . for the establishment at Wilmington, N. C. of a branch of the Federal Reserve Bank of Richmond, Va. Wilmington, National Press, 1924. 45 p. [4175

Federal Writers' Project. . . . The intracoastal waterway, Norfolk to Key West. Washington, U. S. Govt. Print. Off., 1937. 143 p. [4176
——. . . The ocean highway; New Brunswick, New Jersey to Jacksonville, Florida. New York, Modern Age Books, Inc. [c.1938] 244 p. [4177
——These are our lives, as told by the people and written by members of the Federal Writers' Project. Chapel Hill, University of North Carolina Press, 1939. 421 p. [4178
——. . . U. S. one, Maine to Florida. New York, Modern Age Books, Inc. [c.1938] 344 p. [4179

Federal Writers' Project. North Carolina. . . . North Carolina, a guide to the Old North State. Chapel Hill, University of North Carolina Press, 1939. 601 p. [4180
——The North Carolina guide, ed. by Blackwell P. Robinson. Chapel Hill, University of North Carolina Press [1955] 649 p. [4181

Fellowship of Reconciliation. Can guns settle strikes? A study of violent aspects of the 1934 textile strike in three southern states. New York, 1935. (Fellowship pamphlet. 1935 series, no. 2) 27 p. [4182

Felton, Augustus Cicero. Descendants of Robert & Michael Barnett. Macon, Ga., 1956. 159 p. [4183
——The Felton family of North Carolina and Georgia. Macon, Ga., 1954. 154 p. [4184
—— ——Supplement, 1955. Macon, Ga., 1955. [23] p. [4185

The female foundling; a novel. Newbern [Francois-Xavier Martin?] 1802. Unpaged. [4186

Fender, Robert Bryan. Sentimental poems. Winston-Salem, Clay Printing Co., 1938. [31] p. [4187

Fenollosa, Mary (McNeil) Christopher Laird, by Sidney McCall [pseud.] New York, Dodd, Mead and Co., 1919. 338 p. [4188

Ferber, Edna. A peculiar treasure. New York, Literary Guild of America, 1939. 398 p. [4189

Ferebee, London R. Brief history of the slave life of Rev. L. R. Ferebee, and the battles of life . . . written from memory to 1882. Raleigh, Edwards & Broughton, 1882. 24 p. [4190

Ferguson, James. Two Scottish soldiers, a soldier of 1688 and Blenheim, a soldier of the American Revolution, and A Jacobite laird. Aberdeen, D. Wyllie & Son, 1888. 162 p. [4191

Ferguson, Maxwell . . . State regulation of railroads in the South. New York, Columbia University, 1916. (Studies in history, economics and public law, ed. by the Faculty of Political Science of Columbia University, v. LXVII, no. 2; whole no. 162) 228 p. [4192

[Ferguson, Sue Ramsey Johnston] A syllabus of historical sketches showing the curious commixture of the ancestors of James Rufus Ferguson at Liledoun. No place, privately printed [1944] [26] p. [4193

Ferguson, Thomas Wiley. Home on the Yadkin. Winston-Salem, Clay Printing Co. [1956] 242 p. [4194

Ferguson, William Burder. Shipbuilding cost & production methods. New York, Cornell Maritime Press, 1944. 232 p. [4195

Ferrell, John Atkinson. The role of the architect in the program of the Medical Care Commission. Raleigh, North Carolina Medical Care Commission [1948] 6 p. [4196

Fesler, James William. Area and administration. University, University of Alabama Press, 1949. 158 p. [4197

——The merit system in the states, an address delivered to the Public Welfare Institute meeting in Chapel Hill, N. C., October 24, 1939. [Chapel Hill, 1939] 8 p. [4198

Fesperman, Edward L., comp. Hand-book of Raleigh, 1908-9; a guide to the city. Raleigh, Novelty Publisher, n.d. 72 p. [4199

Fesperman, Joseph Hamilton. The life of a sufferer; an autobiography. Utica, Young Lutheran Co., 1892. 127 p. [4200

Few William Preston. Constructive educational leadership; an address delivered before the N. C. Teachers' Assembly at Morehead City, N. C. June 17, 1909. [Raleigh, Edwards & Broughton, 1909?] 13 p. [4201

——Papers and addresses. [Durham] Duke University Press, 1951. 369 p. [4202

A few facts about the Charlotte medical journal . . . established 1877. No place, no publisher, n.d. 8 p. [4203

A few of the many reviews and testimonials received by the publisher, Biographical history of N. C. Greensboro, Charles L. Van Noppen, [1906] 24 p. [4204

A few reasons why the Bingham School, Orange County, near Mebane, N. C. is the best place to educate your boy. Raleigh, Edwards & Broughton [1899?] 9 p. [4205

A few reasons why the citizens of Raleigh should subscribe more liberally towards the building of the Raleigh and Eastern North Carolina Railroad. No place, no publisher [1901] 5 p. [4206

Field, Louise Randall. Sea anemones and corals of Beaufort, North Carolina. Durham, Duke University Press, 1949. (Duke University. Marine station. Bulletin, no. 5) 39 p. [4207

The fifth quinquennial meeting of the association known as the eleven branches of the house of William Barnard. No place, no publisher, 1905? 19 p. [4208

Fiftieth anniversary of the ordination to the priesthood of the Right Rev. Theodore Benedict Lyman. New York, James Pott & Co., 1892. 24 p. [4209

Fiftieth anniversary, Salem Fire Department, celebrated on . . . Sept. 16, 1893. Salem, Crist & Keehln, pr., 1893. 20 p. [4210

Filson, John. Histoire de Kentucke, nouvelle colonie á l'ouest de la Virginie. Paris, Buisson, 1785. 234 p. [4211

——Life and adventures of Colonel Daniel Boone. Brooklyn, Printed for C. Wilder, 1823. Tarrytown, N. Y., Reprinted, W. Abbatt, 1932. (The magazine of history with notes and queries. Tarrytown, N. Y., 1932. Extra number. no. 180) p. [5]-29 [4212

Finch, Josiah John. A sermon on the conditions of discipleship delivered in the Baptist Church in Newbern on . . . April 24, 1842. Newbern, Published for Mrs. E. Washington, 1842. 24 p. [4213

——Sermons, with a memoir of his life. Charleston, Southern Baptist Publication Society, 1853. 314 p. [4214

Finch, Robert. The desert shall rejoice. New York, Samuel French [1940] 31 p. [4215

——Heroes just happen; a comedy . . . by Robert Finch and Betty Smith. New York, Samuel French, c.1940. 97 p. [4216

Finch, Robert, joint author, see Smith, Betty

The find out book, v. 1-2. Chapel Hill, University of North Carolina Press, [c.1934-37] 2 v. [4217

Finger, Sidney Michael. Address to the Department of Superintendence of the National Educational Association, at Washington, D. C., on the educational and religious interests of the colored people of the South, Feb. 24, 1886. No place, no publisher, n.d. [1] p. [4218

——Civil government in North Carolina and the United States. New York, University Publishing Co., 1894. 184 p. [4219

—— ——1898. [4220

Fink, Paul. That's why they call it . . . The names and lore of the Great Smokies. [Jonesboro, Tenn., c.1956] 20 p. [4221

Fink, Robert Mathias. Technically trained personnel in North Carolina. Raleigh, North Carolina State Planning Board, 1947. 9 p. Condensed from his Thesis (Ph. D.)—University of North Carolina. [4222

Finlay, Hugh. Journal kept by Hugh Finlay, surveyor of the post roads on the continent of North America . . . begun the 13th of Septr., 1773, and ended 26th June 1774. Brooklyn, F. H. Norton, 1867. 94 p. NcU has microfilm (negative) from original in Virginia State Library. [4223

Finley, A. E. and Associates. 20 years of service, 1931-1951. [Raleigh? 1951] Unpaged. [4224

Finley, William Wilson. Address at a meeting of farmers in Salisbury, N. C., Nov. 17, 1909. 8 p. [4225

——Address of W. W. Finley, president, Southern Railway Company, to the citizens of Asheville, N. C., September 23, 1910. No place, no publisher, n.d. 8 p. [4226

——Address . . . to the employees . . . at Spencer, N. C. on the occasion of the formal opening of the Y. M. C. A. Building, March twenty-third, 1907. [Wash. 1907?] [3] p. [4227

——Reply of W. W. Finley . . . to toast at the annual banquet of the Merchants and Manufacturers Club of Greensboro, N. C., April 3, 1907. No place, no publisher, 1907. 10 p. [4228

——Reply to toast at annual banquet of the Greater Charlotte Club, Charlotte, N. C., Nov. 15, 1907. No place, no publisher [1907?] 4 p. [4229

——Reply . . . to toast at a banquet of the North Carolina State Bankers' Association, Winston-Salem, N. C., May 23, 1907. [Wash. 1907?] 4 p. [4230

Finley High School, Lenoir, N. C. [Announcement, 186 - [Lenoir, 186 - NcU has 1872/73 [4231

Firestone, Clark Barnaby. Bubbling waters. New York, R. M. McBride and Co., 1938. 296 p. [4232

First drill for recruits, and the manual exercise for infantry . . . arranged . . . by an officer of the militia of the state of North Carolina. Fayetteville, Printed at the Observer Press by Carney and Dismukes, n.d. 12 p. [4233

First reader for southern schools. Raleigh, Christian Advocate Co., 1864. 24 p. [4234

Fish, Carl Russell. Restoration of the southern railroads. Madison, Wis., University of Wisconsin, 1919. (University of Wisconsin Studies in the social sciences and history, no. 2) 28 p. [4235

Fishburne, Stuart P. Here's the story of how a North Carolina farmer made himself a $10,000-a-year-man. Richmond, Federal Reserve Bank of Richmond, 1950. 14 p. [4236

Fisher, Charles. The address . . . to the anti-tariff meeting held in Salisbury, on Thursday of August court. Salisbury, Western Carolinian, 1832. 16 p. [4237

[Fisher, Charles] Address to the citizens of Rowan County. No place, no publisher [1832?] 15 p. [4238

Fisher, Charles. Once again to men of candid minds. No place, no publisher [1816] [1] p. [4239

——To men of candid minds. No place, no publisher, n.d. [1] p. [4240

——To the freemen of the tenth congressional district. [Salisbury, no publisher, June 15, 1839] 16 p. [4241

——To the freemen of Rowan County. No place, no publisher [1833] [1] p. [4242

—— ——No place, no publisher [1833] [1] p. [4243

—— ——No place, no publisher [1833] [1] p. [4244

—— ——[Salisbury, no publisher, 1833] [1] p. [4245

——To the freemen of the counties of Rowan, Davie, Davidson, Randolph, and Chatham. No place, no publisher [1839?] 14 p. [4246

——To the freemen of the second congressional district. No place, no publisher, n.d. 8 p. [4247

——To the freemen of the tenth congressional district. [Salisbury, no publisher, 1839] 3 p. [4248

——To the freemen of the tenth congressional district. [No place, no publisher, 1841] 12 p. [4249

——To the people of Rowan County. No place, no publisher, n.d. [1] p. [4250

——To the public. No place, no publisher, n.d. [1] p. [4251

—— ——[Salisbury, no publisher, 1833?] 12 p. [4252

Fisher, Miles Mark. Keep Negro "churches" central; recognition address . . . president of the Ministerial Alliance of Durham and vicinity, . . . October 2, 1946, White Rock Baptist Church, Durham, North Carolina. [Durham? The Author, c.1946] 10 p. [4253

——Negro slave songs in the United States. Ithaca, Cornell University Press for the American Historical Association [1953] 223 p. [4254

——A short history of the Baptist denomination. Nashville, Tenn., Sunday School Publishing Board [1933] 188 p. [4255

Fisher, S. J. The American Negro, a study. Rev. ed. Pittsburgh, Pa., Board of Missions for Freedmen of the Presbyterian Church in the U. S. A. [1912?] 136 p. [4256

Fishers River Primitive Baptist Association. Minutes of the annual session, 18 - 18 - NcU has 1859 [1904-1916] 1918-1936, 1943-1951 [4257

Fishwick, Marshall William. Virginians on Olympus; a cultural analysis of four great men. Richmond, 1951. 74 p. [4258

Fisk, Charles B. Reports of chief engineer to the stockholders of the Yadkin Navigation Co. on reconnoissance and a survey . . . made in . . . 1856. Salisbury, J. J. Bruner, pr., 1856. 20 p. [4259

Fiske, John. Old Virginia and her neighbors. Boston, Houghton, Mifflin and Co., 1900. 2 v. [4260

Fiske, Maude. Brenau College presents This heritage; a play concerning Eleanor Dare . . . May 24, 1940, 8:30 P. M. [Gainesville, Ga., Brenau College, c.1940] 58 p. [4261

Fitch, Charles L. Through rates and proportions between New Orleans, Mobile, Montgomery and Columbus, and the northern and eastern cities. New York, Sanford, Harroun & Co., pr., 1866. 46 p. [4262

Fitch, William Edwards. The Battle of Alamance. Burlington, Alamance Battle Ground Commission, 1939. 80 p. [4263

——First founders in America, with facts to prove that Sir Walter Raleigh's Lost Colony was not lost; an address . . . before the New York Society of the Order of the Founders and Patriots of America . . . New York, Oct. 29, 1913. [New York, The Society, 1913?] 40 p. [4264

——Origin, rise, and downfall of the state of Franklin . . . an address . . . before the N. Y. Society of the Order of the Founders and Patriots of America . . . New York, March 11, 1910. No place, Published by the Society, 1910. 24 p. [4265

——Some neglected history of North Carolina; being an account of the revolution of the Regulators. New York, Neale Publishing Co., 1895. 307 p. [4266

—— ——1905. [4267

—— ——2d ed. New York, The Author, 1914. 307 p. [4268

——Some things the colony of North Carolina did, and did first . . . an address . . . before the New York Society of the Order of the Founders and Patriots of America . . . New York, December 11, 1908. [New York] The Society [1908] (Society Publication no. 23) 23 p. [4269

Fitts, James Harris. Genealogy of the Fitts or Fitz family in America. Albany, N. Y., Fort Orange Press, 1897. 170 (i. e. 171) p. [4270

[Fitzgerald, Mrs. Mary Newman] The Cherokees, 1540-1937. [Knoxville, Tenn., Clarence F. Coleman Co., c.1937] 33 p. [4271

Fitzgerald, Oscar Penn. California sketches. New series. Nashville, Tenn., Southern Methodist Publishing House, 1881. 288 p. [4272

——Centenary cameos, 1784-1884. Nashville, Southern Methodist Publishing House, 1886. 352 p. [4273

——Christian growth. Nashville, Southern Methodist Publishing House, 1882. 130 p. [4274

——Eminent Methodists: Lovick Pierce. Nashville, Barbee and Smith, Jan. 1896. 32 p. [4275

——Eminent Methodists; twelve booklets in one book, by Bishop O. P. Fitzgerald and Bishop C. B. Galloway. Nashville, Tenn., M. E. Church, South, 1897. 375 p. [4276

——Epworth book, in five parts. Nashville, Southwestern Publishing House, 1893. 318 p. [4277

——Fifty years: observations—opinions—experiences. Nashville, Tenn., Publishing House of the M. E. Church, South, 1903. 253 p. [4278

——John B. McFerrin; a biography. Nashville, Tenn., Publishing House of the M. E. Church, South, 1888. 448 p. [4279

——Judge Longstreet; a life sketch. Nashville, Tenn., Publishing House of the Methodist Episcopal Church, South, 1891. 318 p. [4280

——Sunset views in three parts. Nashville, Tenn., Barbee & Smith, 1901. 343 p. [4281

Fitzgibbon, Maurice. Popular lectures embracing all the new discoveries in electricity and magnetism. Norfolk, Norfolk Beacon, n.d. [1] p. [4282

Fitz-Simons, Foster. Bright Leaf. New York, Rinehart & Co., Inc. [1948] 631 p. [4283

——Four on a heath, a fantasy in one act. Evanston, Ill., Row, Peterson and Co. [c.1933, 1935] 21 p. [4284

A five minutes talk . . . Vote on Nov. 5th for the best man in N. C. No place, no publisher [1912?] 4 p. [4285

Flack, Horace Edgar. Spanish-American diplomatic relations preceding the war of 1898. Baltimore, Johns Hopkins Press, 1906. (Johns Hopkins Studies in historical and political science, ser. 24, no. 1-2) 95 p. [4286

Flake, Elijah W. Battle between the Merrimac and the Monitor. Polkton, The Author [c.1914] 12 p. [4287

Le flambeau, 19 - [Asheville, St. Genevieve's, 19 - NcU has 1917 [4288

Flannagan, Roy Catesby.• The story of Lucky Strike. [New York, c.1938] 94 p.

—— ——[c.1953] [50] p. [4289

Flat River Baptist Association. Minutes, 18 - Raleigh, 18 - NcU has 1811, [1833-1935] [4290

Fleet School, Highland Lake, Flat Rock, N. C. Fleet School, 191 - Flat Rock, 191 - NcU has 1914/15, 1915/16. [4291

Fleharty, Stephen F. Our regiment; a history of the 102d Illinois Infantry Volunteers, with sketches of the Atlanta campaign, the Georgia raid, and the campaign of the Carolinas. Chicago, Brewster & Hanscom, pr., 1865. 192 p. [4292

Fleming, John K., joint author, see **Ramsay, James Graham**

Fleming, Patrick Henry. Bible reading course. No place, no publisher, n.d. 4 p. [4293

——The Christian church; annual address before the N. C. and Va. Christian Conference. Raleigh, Christian Sun, 1893. 26 p. [4294

——The lost legacy. Raleigh, Christian Sun, 1889. 16 p. [4295

——Mother's answered prayer. Elon College, Printed for the Author by the Christian Sun, 1905. 97 p. [4296

Fleming, Robert. Sketch of the life of Elder Humphrey Posey, first Baptist missionary to the Cherokee Indians. [Philadelphia] Western Baptist Association of Ga., 1852. 103 p. [4297

Fleming, Walter Lynwood. The freedmen's savings bank. Chapel Hill, University of N. C. Press, 1927. 170 p. [4298

——Prescript of Ku-Klux Klan. No place, no publisher, n.d. 22 p. [4299

[Fletcher, Arthur Lloyd] History of the American Legion and American Legion Auxiliary, Department of North Carolina, 1919-1929. [by Arthur Lloyd Fletcher and Mae Pitzer Fletcher] Raleigh, Commercial Printing Co., 1930. 376 p. [4300

——History of the 113th Field Artillery, 30th Division. Raleigh, N. C. History Committee of 113th Field Artillery [c.1920] 262 p. [4301

Fletcher, Beale. How to improve your social dancing with the Fletcher count system. New York, A. S. Barnes [1956] 136 p. [4302

Fletcher, Inglis. Bennett's welcome. Indianapolis, Bobbs-Merrill Co. [1950] 451 p. [4303

—— ——Garden City, N. Y. Garden City Books [1951] 451 p. [4304

—— ——Garden City, N. Y. Permabooks [1952] 446 p. [4305

—— ——Abridged. New York, Omnibook, Inc., 1951. Extract from Omnibook. April, 1951. v. 31, no. 5. p. [80]-127 [4306

——El esfuerzo de los bravos. [Barcelona, Spain] Jose Janes, 1950. 521 p. [4307

——Så föddes en nation. Stockholm, Ljus [1941] 741 p. [4308

——Förlig vind till Carolina. Stockholm, Ljus [1945] 567 p. [4309

——Förtrollad jord. Stockholm, Ljus [1942] 378 p. [4310

——Frihetens kavaljerer. Stockholm, Ljus [1943] 416 p. [4311
——Gabrielle. Kjobenhavn, Arnold Busck, 1946. 614 p. [4312
——Guvernørens datter. [Oslo] Nasjonalflorlaget [1948] 2 v. [4313
——Hundrede Mand til Virginia. Copenhagen, NYT Nordisk Forlag, Arnold Busck, 1950. 357 p. [4314
——Lusty wind for Carolina. London, Hutchinson & Co., Ltd., n.d. 348 p. [4315
—— ——Indianapolis, Bobbs-Merrill Co. [1944] 509 p. [4316
—— ——Garden City, N. Y., Permabooks [1951] 477 p. [4317
—— ——Garden City, N. Y., Garden City Books [1951] 470 p. [4318
——Men of Albemarle. Indianapolis, Bobbs-Merrill Co. [1942] 566 p. [4319
—— ——Garden City, N. Y., The Sun Dial Press [1943] 566 p. [4320
—— ——Garden City, N. Y., Permabooks [1952] 512 p. [4321
——En nasjon blir til. [Oslo] Nasjonalforlaget [1946] 599 p. [4322
——Queen's gift. Indianapolis, Bobbs-Merrill Co. [1952] 448 p. [4323
—— ——Garden City, N. Y., Permabooks [1954] 440 p. [4324
——Raleigh's Eden. Indianapolis, Bobbs-Merrill Co. [c.1940] [4325
—— ——New York, The Sun Dial Press [1942] 662 p. [4326
—— ——(abridged) Garden City, N. Y., Permabooks [c.1953] 480 p. [4327
——Roanoke Hundred. Indianapolis, Bobbs-Merrill Co. [1948] 492 p. [4328
——The Scotswoman. Indianapolis, Bobbs-Merrill Co. [1955, c.1954] 480 p. [4329
——Toil of the brave. Indianapolis, Bobbs-Merrill Co. [1946] 547 p. [4330
—— ——Garden City, N. Y., Permabooks [1953] 504 p. [4331
——Vinden blåser mot Carolina. [Oslo] Nasjonalforlaget [1948] 547 p. [4332
——The White Leopard, a tale of the African bush. Indianapolis, Bobbs-Merrill Co. [c.1931] Reprinted 1948. 304 p. [4333
——The young commissioner, a tale of the African bush. London, Hutchinson & Co., Ltd., n.d. 264 p. [4334

Fletcher, James Floyd. A history of the Ashe County, North Carolina and New River, Virginia, Baptist associations. Raleigh, Commercial Printing Co., 1935. 133 p. [4335

Fletcher, William James. The Gee family. Rutland, Vt., Tuttle Publishing Co., Inc. [c.1937] 154 p. [4336

Flint, Thomas. The Carolinian spelling book. Hillsborough, Printed and published by D. Heartt, 1827. 120+ p. Pages 1-6?, 121-? wanting in NcU copy. [4337

Flint, Timothy. The life and adventures of Daniel Boone . . . New ed. New York, Hurst [c.1868] 256 p. [4338
—— ——Cincinnati, Published by U. P. James, 1868. 256 p. [4339

Flora, Jerome B. An historical sketch of ancient Pasquotank County, North Carolina, 1586?-1793. Elizabeth City, Chamber of Commerce [1950] 14 p. [4340

Flora Macdonald College, Red Springs, N. C. Bulletin, no. 1- November, 1915- Red Springs, 1915- NcU has no. [1-24] 26-61 [63-95] and v. [13-37] [4341
——Catalogue, 18 - Red Springs, 1897- NcU has [1899/1900-1907/08] 1911/12-1914/15-1915 Continues as its Bulletin, 1915- [4242
——Financial facts about Flora Macdonald College. [Charlotte, Presbyterian Standard Publishing Co.] 1920. 4 p. [4343

[Flora Macdonald College, Red Springs, N. C.] More than a college. [Red Springs, 1953?] [8] p. [4344

Flora Macdonald College, Red Springs, N. C. Library. Treasure tales; a guide to Scottish relics in the Library, Flora Macdonald college, 1896-1946. [Red Springs, 1946] [4] p. [4345

Floral College, Robeson Co., N. C. Catalogue, 18 - 18 - NcU has 1856/57 [4346

Flournoy, Martha Watkins. A short history of the Public library of Charlotte and Mecklenburg County, Charlotte, N. C. Charlotte, 1952. 23 p. [4347

Flournoy, Thomas Stanhope. Address delivered at the second annual exhibition of the Union Agricultural Society of Virginia and North Carolina. 24 p. Title page defective in NcU copy. [4348

Floyd, Joe Summers. Effects of taxation on industrial location. Chapel Hill, University of North Carolina Press [1952] 155 p. [4349
——This changing South [by] John M. Maclachlan and Joe S. Floyd, Jr. Gainesville, University of Florida Press, 1956. 154 p. [4350

Flue cured (bright leaf) tobacco, producers and total sales, 19   -   [Greenville] R. C. Rankin, c.1940-   NcU has 1933-1943 (as one) 1954, 1955   [4351

Flutist, v. 1-v. 10, no. 2, 1920-1929. Asheville, Emil Medicus, 1920-1929. NcU has v. 3-10   [4352

Flynn, Edward Joseph.   Address of the Honorable Edward J. Flynn . . . at the . . . University of North Carolina, Chapel Hill, N. C. . . . March 26, 1941. No place, 1941. 5 p.   [4353

Foard, John F.   North America and Africa, their past, present, and future. No place, no publisher [c.1904] 67 p.   [4354

Foerster, Norman.   American criticism. Boston, Houghton Mifflin Co., 1928. 273 p.   [4355

Foerster, Norman, ed.   American ideals, ed. by Norman Foerster . . . and W. W. Pierson, Jr. Boston, Houghton Mifflin Co. [c.1917] 326 p.   [4356

Foerster, Norman.   American ideals: a syllabus. Chapel Hill, University of North Carolina, 1918. 14 p.   [4356a

——The American scholar. Chapel Hill, University of North Carolina Press, 1929. 66 p.   [4357

Foerster, Norman, ed.   Essays for college men . . . chosen by Norman Foerster, F. A. Manchester, Karl Young. New York, Henry Holt [c.1913] 390 p.   [4358

Foerster, Norman.   Nature in American literature. New York, Macmillan Co., 1923. 324 p.   [4359

——New viewpoints in American literature. Boston, Houghton Mifflin Co. [1925] [12] p.   [4360

——Outlines and summaries. New York, Henry Holt and Co. [c.1915] 105 p. [4361

——Ralph Waldo Emerson, his appreciation of nature. New York, Macmillan Co., 1924. 54 p.   [4362

Foerster, Norman, ed.   The reinterpretation of American literature. New York, Harcourt, Brace and Co., 1928. 271 p.   [4363

Foerster, Norman.   Sentences and thinking . . . by Norman Foerster . . . and J. M. Steadman, Jr. Boston, Houghton Mifflin Co. [c.1919] 121 p.   [4364

—— ——[Rev. and enl. ed.] [c.1923] 329 p.   [4365

Foley, Martha, ed.   U. S. stories; regional stories from the forty-eight States, selected . . . by Martha Foley and Abraham Rothberg. New York, Hendricks House-Farrar Straus [1949] 683 p.   [4366

Folger, Alfred M.   The family physician, being a domestic work . . . by . . . one of the attending physicians in the Cherokee Hospital. Spartanburg, S. C., Z. D. Cottrell, 1845. 320 p.   [4367

Folk, Edgar Estes.   . . . W. W. Holden, . . . editor of North Carolina standard, 1843-1865. Nashville, Tenn., George Peabody College for Teachers, 1934. ([George Peabody College for Teachers] Abstract of Contribution to education no. 156) 12 p.   [4368

Folk, Reau Estes.   Battle of New Orleans, its real meaning. [Nashville, Ladies' Hermitage Association, c.1935] 45 p.   [4369

Follett, Mrs. C. M. V.   Jehovah-rapha (The Lord that healeth) 2d ed. Durham [Seeman Printery] n.d. 16 p.   [4370

Foltz, Henry Wesley, comp.   Descendants of Adam Spach; autobiography and memoirs of Adam Spach and his wife, translated . . . by Adelaide L. Fries. Raleigh, Edwards for Wachovia Historical Society, 1924. 170 p.   [4371

—— ——Index to family names contained in Descendants of Adam Spach. No place, Spach Family, n.d. 11 p.   [4372

Foltz, Henry Wesley.   Winston fifty years ago. [Winston-Salem, The Author] 1926. [16] p.   [4373

Fonvielle, W. F.   Reminiscences of college days. [Raleigh] Printed for the Author by Edwards and Broughton, 1904. 143 p.   [4374

The fool-killer, v. 1- 1910?- Moravian Falls, James Larkin Pearson, 1910- NcU has v. [3-4]   [4375

Foote, Henry Stuart.   Eulogy upon the life and character of James K. Polk . . . delivered at Washington City, July 9, 1849. Washington, Thomas Ritchie, pr., 1849. 16 p.   [4376

Foote, James H. "Methodist armor" reviewed; The rise and progress of the Baptists, and . . . History of the Brier Creek Association. Statesville, Landmark, 1888. 223 p.   [3477

Foote, William Henry. Sketches of North Carolina, historical and biographical. New York, Robert Carter, 1846. 557 p.   [4378

—— ——New York, Robert Carter, 1846. Reprinted, 1912, by the Reprint Co., Dunn, N. C.   [4379

For sale: elegant country home of the late Governor Thomas M. Holt, near Haw River in Alamance County, N. C. Raleigh, Edwards & Broughton, n.d. [6] p. [4380

Forbes, Edward M. Oral catechism for the use of small children. 2d ed. Newbern, Pool & Whitaker, 1869. 88 p.   [4381

Forbes-Lindsay, Charles Harcourt Ainslie. Daniel Boone, backwoodsman. Philadelphia, J. B. Lippincott Co., 1908. 319 p.   [4382

—— ——1912.   [4383

Forbus, Ina B. The magic pin. New York, Viking Press, 1956. 138 p.   [4384

Forbus, Wiley Davis. Reaction to injury. Baltimore, Williams & Wilkins Co., 1943. 797 p.   [4385

Force, Manning Ferguson. . . . General Sherman. New York, D. Appleton and Co., 1899. 353 p.   [4386

Ford, Arthur Peronneau. Life in the Confederate army . . . and Some experiences and sketches of southern life, by Marion Johnstone Ford. New York, Neale Publishing Co., 1905. 136 p.   [4387

Ford, Henry Jones. The Scotch-Irish in America. New York, P. Smith, 1941. 607 p.   [4388

—— ——Princeton, N. J., Princeton University Press, 1915. 607 p.   [4389

Fore, Mrs. James Albert. A catechism for the Children of the Confederacy of the North Carolina Division, United Daughters of the Confederacy. [Charlotte, Observer Printing House] n.d. [8] p.   [4390

——First Presbyterian Church, Charlotte, North Carolina, 1832-1932. [Charlotte, First Presbyterian Church Auxiliary, 1932] 32 p.   [4391

[Fore, Mrs. James Albert] North Carolina; some facts about the Old North State. [Charlotte, Observer Printing House] n.d. 6 p.   [4392

Foreman, Grant. Indian removal; the emigration of the Five Civilized Tribes of Indians. [New ed.] Norman, University of Oklahoma Press [1953] 415 p. [4393

——Sequoyah. Norman, University of Oklahoma Press, 1938. 90 p.   [4394

Foreman, Paul Breck. The Negro in the United States: a bibliography . . . by Paul B. Foreman . . . and Mozell C. Hill. Stillwater [1947] (Bulletin of the Oklahoma A. and M. college, v. 44, no. 5. February, 1947) 24 p.   [4395

Forest, Herman Silva. Handbook of algae, with special reference to Tennessee and the Southeastern United States. Knoxville, University of Tennessee Press, 1954. (Contribution from the Botanical Laboratory, University of Tennessee, New ser., no. 155) 467 p.   [4396

Forney, Edward J. The essentials of bookkeeping. [Greensboro] no publisher, n.d. [23] p.   [4397

——High speed on the typewriter. Greensboro, no publisher [c.1901] 6 p. [4398

——Leaves from the stenographers' note books; side lights on Dr. McIver at work. Greensboro, Harrison Printing Co., n.d. 23 p.   [4399

——The student's book of style. [Greensboro, The Author] n.d. [11] p.   [4400

——A trip en route to Florida; landscape, atmosphere, locale. [Greensboro, The Author, 1934] 6 p.   [4401

Forrest, William S. Norfolk and the interior. Norfolk, T. G. Broughton & Son, pr., 1852. 83 p.   [4402

Forster, Anthony. Sermons, chiefly of a practical nature. Raleigh, Joseph Gales, 1821. 335 p.   [4403

Forster, Garnet Wolsey. Agricultural economics laboratory manual. Raleigh, 1932. [42] p.   [4404

——Farm organization and management. Ann Arbor, Mich., Edwards Brothers, Inc., 1935. 210 p.   [4405

—— ——New York, Prentice-Hall, Inc., 1938. 432 p.   [4406

—— ——1953. 430 p. [4406a

Forsyth Co., N. C. Board of Education. Report of the public schools, 19 - Winston-Salem, 19 - NcU has 1912/13-1914/16 [4407

Forsyth Co., N. C. County Commissioners. Soil erosion control and land-use program, Deep River and Reedy Fork projects . . . Special handbook issued . . . November 1, 1934. No place, 1934. 32 p. [4408

[Forsyth Co., N. C. Long-Range Agricultural Program] Forsyth faces the future. [Winston-Salem?] n.d. [20] p. [4409

Forsyth County Bar Association. Proceedings on presentation of portrait of Clement Manly, Esquire, October 20, 1927. No place, no publisher, n.d. 14 p. [4410

Forsyth County school news, v. 1- December, 1920- Winston-Salem, 1920- NcU has v. [1-4] [4411

Fort Bragg at war, the station complement. [Atlanta, Foote & Davies, 1945] 121 p. [4412

Fort Fisher. No place, Printed for the Author [Knowles Anthony & Co., pr., 1865. 11 p. [4413

Fort Macon, North Carolina's number one state park, Beaufort, N. C. Morehead City, Deegee's Shop, 1936. Folder. [4414

[Fosdick, Charles Austin] . . . Marcy, the blockade-runner, by Harry Castlemon [pseud.] Philadelphia, John C. Winston Co. [c.1891] 428 p. [4415

——. . . Marcy, the refugee, by Harry Castlemon [pseud.] Philadelphia, Porter & Coates [c.1892] 432 p. [4416

Fosdick, Lucian D. The two commonwealths, Massachusetts, North Carolina: address . . . at the reception . . . Stoughton St. Baptist church, Bost., Mass., to the N. C. delegates and visiting Friends, Sat. July 13, 1895. No place, no publisher [1895?] 3 p. [4417

Foster, Alfred G. Address before the Randolph County Society for the Promotion of Agriculture . . . at the annual fair of the Society, Oct. 26th, 1855. Lexington, Printed by James B. Shelton, 1855. 23 p. [4418

Foster, Constance J., joint author, see English, Oliver Spurgeon

Foster, Genevieve (Stump) Andrew Jackson. New York, Charles Scribner's Sons [1951] 112 p. [4419

Foster, James L. Sermon to the Jr. O. U. A. M. . . . Nov. 18, 1894, in the Christian Church, Raleigh, N. C. Raleigh, Barnes for Raleigh Council, No. 1, Jr. O. U. A. M., 1894. 17 p. [4420

Foster, John. Dark heritage. New York, Fawcett Publications [1955] 160 p. [4421

Foster, Lillian, comp. Andrew Johnson, president of the United States; his life and speeches. New York, Richardson & Co., 1866. 316 p. [4422

Fountain, Alvin Marcus. Descendants of John R. Fountain. Raleigh, The Author, 1952. 37 p. [4423

——Place-names on State College campus. Raleigh, 1956. 52 p. [4424

Fountain, Richard Tillman. An address delivered by R. T. Fountain, candidate for Governor over Radio Station WPTF. [Raleigh? 1932?] 11 p. [4425

Foushee, Alexander Roundtree. Reminiscences . . . life in Person County in former days. Roxboro [Durham, Seeman Printery] 1921. 81 p. [4426

Foust, Julius Isaac. . . . North Carolina, by J. I. Foust . . . and Nettie M. Allen. New York, Macmillan Co., 1906. 76 p. [4427

——A spelling book, by Julius I. Foust . . . Isaac C. Griffin . . . Thomas R. Foust. Raleigh, A. Williams & Co., 1906. 124 p. [4428

—— ——rev. and enl. 1911. 188 p. [4429

Foust, Thomas Bledsoe, joint author, see Baskerville, Charles

Fowler, Grover Parsons. The house of Fowler; a history of the Fowler families of the South. Hickory, The Author, 1940. 754 p. [4431

Fowler, Keith. All the skeletons in all the closets. New York, Macaulay [c.1934] 312 p. [4432

Fowler, Malcolm. They passed this way: a personal narrative of Harnett County history. No place, Harnett County Centennial, Inc., c.1955. 167 p. [4433

Fowler, Marion Butler. Durham County: economic and social, [by] W. M. Up-church and M. B. Fowler. [Durham] John Sprunt Hill [1918] 62 p. [4434

Fowler, Stanley G. Farms and farm lands along the Seaboard Air Line. [Chicago] Rand, McNally, 1896. 48 p. [4435

Fox, George. The journal of George Fox, edited . . . by Norman Penney. Cambridge, The University Press, 1911. 2 v. [4436

——A journal or historical account of the life, travels, sufferings . . . of . . . George Fox. 4th ed. New York, Printed by Isaac Collins, 1800. 2 v. [4437

Fox, John A. Address . . . before the North Carolina Waterways Association, November 5, 1907. [Wilmington, N. C., Waterways Association, 1907] 12 p. [4438

Fox, Junius B. Biography of Rev. Alfred J. Fox, M. D., Evangelical Lutheran minister of the Tennessee Synod. Philadelphia, Published for the Author by Lutheran Publication Society, 1885. 150 p. [4439

Foy, Joseph H. Going back to Jerusalem. St. Louis, Christian Publishing Co., 1878. 48 p. [4440

[Foy, Joseph H.] To the public. No place, no publisher [1863] 15 p. [4441

Frances Bridges Atkinson; a record of her life prepared by her friends. New York, National Board of the Y. W. C. A. of the U. S. A., 1908. 148 p. [4442

Francis, Mary Cornelia. A son of destiny; the story of Andrew Jackson. New York, Federal Book Co., 1902. 459 p. [4443

Francis Hilliard School, Oxford, N. C. The Francis Hilliard School, 18 - Oxford, 18 - NcU has 1898/99 [4444

Frank W. Hancock, Jr., worthy of your support. [Oxford, no publisher, 1930] [4] p. [4445

Franklin, John Hope. The free Negro in North Carolina, 1790-1860. Chapel Hill, University of North Carolina Press, 1943. 271 p. [4446

——From slavery to freedom. New York, A. A. Knopf, 1947. 622 p. [4447

——The militant South, 1800-1861. Cambridge, Mass., Belknap Press, 1956. 317 p. [4448

[Franklin, Meshach] [Circular to his constituents] Washington, no publisher, April 13th, 1808. 3 p. [4449

Franklin, Meshach. To the freemen of the 13th congressional district of the state of North Carolina. Salisbury, Philo White [182?] [1] p. [4450

Franklin, N. C. Chamber of Commerce. Franklin, N. C., scenic center of the Nantahalas. Franklin, 1949. [56] p. [4451

[Franklin, N. C. Rotary Club?] Franklin, North Carolina. [Franklin, 192?] [11] p. [4452

Franklin, N. C. St. Agnes Church. St. Agnes Church, Franklin, N. C., the first fifty years, . . . 1888 to . . . 1938. [Franklin, 1938] 16 p. [4453

Franklin Co., N. C. Bickett Club. Bickett for governor, the record is the reason. No place, 1915. 21 p. [4454

Franklin Co., N. C. Health Department. Report, 193 - Louisburg, 193 - NcU has 1937/38-1940/41 [4455

Franklin Co., N. C. Home Demonstration Clubs. Federation of Home Demonstration Clubs favorite recipes. [Louisburg, 1950] 181 p. [4456

Franklin Gold Mining Co., Mecklenburg Co., North Carolina. Charter, with amendment and description of their mines. New York, W. M. Mercein and Son, pr., 1835. 18 p. [4457

[Franklinton, N. C. Public School. Fifth Grades] The Old North State. [Franklinton, 1938?] [24] p. [4458

Franklinton Christian College, Franklinton, N. C. Catalogue, 18 - Franklinton, 18 - NcU has 1908/09 [4459

Fraps, George Stronach. Principles of dyeing. New York, Macmillan Co., 1916. 270 p. [4460

[Frayser, Lou H.] Then and now; or, Hope's first school, by Zillah Raymond [pseud.] Wilmington, Jackson & Bell, 1883. 231 p. [4461

Frazer, Charles R. Nicholas Franklin Roberts, pioneer in religion, education, and

civic relations in the state of North Carolina.   [Raleigh] Shaw University [1954?]
26 p.   [4462

Frazer, William H. Bible notes. Charlotte, Presbyterian Standard, 1924. 158 p. [4463
——Challenging mantles; a series of chapel talks.   [Charlotte, Queen City, pr., pref.
1926]   180 p.   [4464
——Fireside musings of "Uncle" Rastus and "Aunt" Randy.   Charlotte, Murrill
Press, 1925.   101 p.   [4465
——The possumist, and other stories.   Charlotte, Murrill Press, 1924.   68 p. [4466

Free Man, pseud.,   see Snelling, William Joseph

Free Voter, pseud. To the voters of the 10th congressional district.   No place, no
publisher [184?]   [1] p.   [4467

Free Will Baptist, v. 1- 18 - Ayden, Free Will Baptist Press, 18 - NcU has
v. 55-61 [62-63] 64-71   [4468

Free Will Baptist Church (Original) Central Conference.   Minutes, 18 - 18 -
NcU has 1879, 1927, 1928, 1930   [4469

Freeman, Douglas Southall. Lee's lieutenants. New York, C. Scribner's Sons,
1942-1944. 3 v.   [4470

[Freeman, George Washington] An appendix to the documents printed by the
vestry, connected with the resignation of the rector of Christ Church. [Raleigh,
1840]   12 p.   [4471

Freeman, George Washington. Rights and duties of slaveholders; two discourses
delivered . . . Nov. 27, 1836, in Christ Church, Raleigh, N. C. Raleigh, Joseph
Gales, 1836. 43 p.   [4472
—— ——Charleston, A. E. Miller, Printer for Protestant Episcopal Society in
S. C., 1837. 40 p.   [4473
——Valedictory sermon, delivered in Christ Church, Raleigh, N. C. Raleigh,
Joseph Gales, 1841. 19 p.   [4474

Freemasons. Asheville, N. C. Mount Hermon Lodge No. 118. By-laws. Asheville, Groves Printing Co. [1942?]   16 p.   [4475

Freemasons. Charlotte, N. C. Oasis Temple of A. A. O. N. M. S. Official directory. Charlotte, 1908. 31 p.   [4476

Freemasons. Durham, N. C. Durham Lodge No. 352.   . . . The presentation of
a portrait of James Southgate, first master of Durham Lodge no. 352. [Durham?
1944]   [16] p.   [4477

Freemasons. Edenton, N. C. Unanimity Lodge, No. 54. Bye laws of Unanimity
Lodge, no. 54, Edenton. Edenton, James Wills, pr., 1816. 27 p.   [4478

Freemasons. Fayetteville, N. C. Phoenix Lodge No. 8. Bye-laws, adopted June
1829. Fayetteville, E. J. Hale, pr., 1829. 11 p.   [4479

Freemasons. Greensboro, N. C. Corinthian Lodge No. 542. 50th anniversary
. . . January 7, 1956. [Greensboro, 1956] [17] p.   [4480

Freemasons. Kinston, N. C. St. John's Lodge No. 4. By-laws of St. John's Lodge
no. 4, A. F. & A. M., North Carolina. Raleigh, Edwards & Broughton, pr., 1917.
11 p.   [4481

Freemasons. Mocksville, N. C. Mocksville Lodge. By-laws for the government
of Mocksville Lodge. Salisbury, Printed at the Carolina Watchman Office, 1851.
8 p.   [4482

Freemasons. New Bern, N. C. Eureka Chapter No. 7 of Royal Arch Masons.
By-laws. Newbern, Printed at the Commercial Office, 1867. 8 p.   [4483

Freemasons. New Bern, N. C. New Bern Lodge No. 245, of Ancient York Masons.
By-laws. New Berne, Commercial Office, 1867. 16 p.   [4484
—— ——Printed at the Daily Times Office, 1869.   [4485

Freemasons. New Bern, N. C. St. John's Lodge No. 3 of Ancient York Masons.
By-laws. Newbern, Printed at the Daily Progress, 1860. 12 p.   [4486

Freemasons. N. C. Grand Chapter of Royal Arch Masons.   . . . Capitular reviews,
19 - 192 - NcU has 1926-1928; 1930; 1932   [4487
——Constitution and by-laws. Durham, Seeman Printery, 1906. 75 p.   [4488
——The Grand Royal Arch constitution for the state of North-Carolina. Fayetteville, Printed at the Observer Press, 1824. 12 p.   [4489

——Proceedings, 18 - 18 - NcU has [1823-1830] 1847-1852 [1855-1865] 1866-1945 [4490

——[Report of] a special committee to investigate conditions of the craft in North Carolina. Concord, 1930. [8] p. [4491

——The York rite of Freemasonry, the chapter, the council, the commandery. No place, The Grand York Rite Bodies of North Carolina, n.d. 11 p. [4492

Freemasons. N. C. Grand Commandery of Knights Templar. Constitution; to which is appended the constitution and by-laws of subordinate lodges working under its jurisdiction adopted . . . May 29th, 1867. Raleigh, Spirit of the Age Office, 1873. 31 p. [4493

——Proceedings, 18 - 18 - NcU has 1872, 1873, 1881-1945 [4494

——Report of Grand Worthy Chief Templar, 18 - New Bern, 18 - NcU has 1878 [4495

——Report of Grand Worthy Treasurer, 18 - 18 - NcU has 1877/78 [4496

——Report of representative to Right Worthy Grand Lodge. New Bern, 1878. 4 p. [4497

——Templar reviews, 19 - [Oxford, Oxford Orphanage] 192 - NcU has 1925, 1928, 1929 [4498

[Freemasons. N. C. Grand Commandery of Knights Templar] What is my duty? A tract for good Templars. No place, n.d. 4 p. [4499

Freemasons. N. C. Grand Council of Royal and Select Masters. Constitution. No place, 1904. 14 p. [4500

——. . . Cryptic reviews, 19 - 19 - NcU has 1928 [4501

——Masonic shrine at Black Camp Gap entrance to Great Smoky Mountains National Park. [Waynesville? 1938?] 36 p. [4502

——Names of Master Masons in North Carolina, 19 - 19 - NcU has October 31, 1905 [4503

——Proceedings, 18 - 18 - NcU has 1822 (reprint) 1860, 1866, 1867, 1869-1883, 1894-1898, 1900-1945. Not issued 1823-1859, 1862-1865 [4504

——Proceedings of a convocation for the purpose of organizing a Grand Council for the State of North Carolina . . . Wilmington . . . 6th day of June, 1860. Salisbury, J. J. Bruner, 1860. 7 p. [4505

——Reports [of officers] 19 - 19 - NcU has 1921 [4506

——Statutes and regulations . . . adopted May 12, 1920. [Raleigh?] 1920. 16 p. [4507

Freemasons. N. C. Grand Lodge. Circular on the subject of education to all the Masonic lodges of N. C. No place, no publisher [1847] 10 p. [4508

——Constitution and by-laws of the Grand Lodge of North Carolina. Raleigh, Printed by W. C. Doub, Star Office, 1856. 31 p. [4509

—— ——Raleigh, Nichols and Gorman, 1870. 38 p. [4510

——The constitution of the Grand Lodge of North-Carolina. Halifax, Printed by Brother A. Hodge, 1798. 12 p. NcU has photostat (positive) and microfilm (negative) [4511

——Constitution of the Grand Lodge of North Carolina, Ancient, Free, and Accepted Masons, with regulations. Oxford, Press of Oxford Orphanage, 1924. 252 p. [4512

——List of lodges under jurisdiction of the Grand Lodge of North Carolina, 19 - Oxford, 19 - NcU has 1916 [4513

——Masonic code of North Carolina. Raleigh, John Nichols, 1875. 154 p. [4514

—— ——Raleigh, Edwards & Broughton, 1892. 152 p. [4515

—— ——Oxford, Oxford Orphan Asylum, 1897. 186 p. [4516

—— ——Raleigh, Edwards & Broughton, 1905. 175 p. [4517

—— ——5th ed. [Raleigh, 1912] 148 p. [4518

—— ——5th ed. [sic.] [Raleigh, 1915] 254 p. [4519

——Masonic reviews, 1926- [Oxford, Press of Oxford Orphanage, 1926- NcU has 1926-1940 [4520

——Proceedings . . . Annual communication, 17 - Raleigh, 17 - NcU has 1804-1840 (reprint as one) 1834-1836, 1839-1947 [4521

——Proceedings of the special communication of the Grand Lodge of North Carolina, A. F. & A. M., held at Raleigh, January 14, A. L. 5871, A. D. 1871; Centennial anniversary of the Grand Lodge. Raleigh, John Nichols, 1871. 18 p. [4522

——Program: corner stone Masonic Temple. Raleigh, 1907. 6 p. [4523

——Standards of recognition of the Grand Lodge of North Carolina. Oxford, Press of Masonic Orphanage, 1925. 14 p. [4524

——Uniform code of by-laws for the government of subordinate lodges . . . adopted at the annual communication of 1871. Raleigh, John Nichols, 1872. 8 p. [4525

——You are invited to be present at the presentation to the North Carolina Historical Commission of a bust of Governor Samuel Johnston. No place, 1912. [4] p.   [4526

Freemasons. North Carolina. Grand Lodge. Loan Fund Committee. Report, 1921- Raleigh, 1923- NcU has 1921/23, 1925, 1926, 1930, 1931   [4527

Freemasons. North Carolina. Grand Lodge. Committee on Negro Lodges. Report to the Grand Lodge of North Carolina. Raleigh, Key-stone Office, 1866. 15 p.   [4528

Freemasons. North Carolina. Grand Lodge. School Committee. Proceedings . . . on the establishment of a seminary of learning for the education of orphans and indigent children of Masons and others. Raleigh, Printed by Thomas Loring, Office of the Independent, 1844. 8 p.   [4529

Freemasons. North Carolina. Grand Lodge. Committee on the York Rite Library Fund. Report, No place [1926] 8 p.   [4530

Freemasons. North Carolina. Grand Lodge of Ancient York Masons. Constitution . . . A. L. 5821. Raleigh, Tho. Henderson, Jr., pr., 1821. 8 p.   [4531

—— ——. . . A. L. 5837. Raleigh, Thos. J. Lemay, pr., 1838. 9 p.   [4532

——Constitution, as amended . . . December, 1846. No place [1846?] 20 p. [4533

—— ——No place [1851?] 21 p.   [4534

Freemasons. North Carolina and Tennessee. Grand Lodge. The Ahiman rezon and Masonic ritual. Newbern, John C. Sims and Edward G. Moss, 5805. Various paging.   [4535

Freemasons. Raleigh, N. C. Hiram Lodge No. 40. Bye-laws of Hiram Lodge no. 40 . . . to which is annexed the constitution of the Grand Lodge of North Carolina. Raleigh, Thos. J. Lemay, 1846. 16 p.   [4536

Freemasons. Raleigh, N. C. William G. Hill Lodge No. 218. Complete roster. Oxford, Press of Oxford Orphanage, 1942. 32 p.   [4537

Freemasons. Rocky Mount, N. C. Sudan Temple of A. A. O. N. M. S. Spring ceremonial. New Bern, Presses of Hill Printing Co., 1917. 12 p.   [4538

Freemasons. Salisbury, N. C. Davie Chapter of Royal Arch Masons. Constitution and by-laws of Davie Chapter No. 32. Salisbury, Printed at the Watchman Office, 1867. 8 p.   [4539

Freemasons. Tarborough, N. C. Concord Lodge No. 58. Bye-laws of Concord Lodge, no. 58, Tarborough. Raleigh, Printed at the Minerva Office, 1813. 14 p.   [4540

Freemasons. Wadesboro, N. C. Kilwinning Lodge No. 64. By-laws. Raleigh, Nichols & Gorman, 1870. 14 p.   [4541

——By-laws, revised and adopted May 2d, 1856. Salisbury, Printed at the Watchman Office, 1856. 8 p.   [4542

Freemasons. Warrenton, N. C. Johnson Caswell Lodge No. 10. By-laws . . . adopted May 22, A. D. 1865, Warrenton, N. C. Raleigh, John Nichols, 1866. 8 p.   [4543

Freemasons. Washington, N. C. Washington Lodge No. 15. Laws for the regulation of Washington Lodge No. 15, Washington, constituted by charter . . . dated April 4th, 1802, and incorporated by Act of Assembly at Raleigh, 1803. Newbern, John S. Pasteur, pr., 1804. 16 p.   [4544

Freemasons. Wilmington, N. C. Concord Chapter No. 6 of Royal Arch Masons. Constitution & bye-laws of the Concord Royal Arch Chapter no. 6. Wilmington, Printed by William Hollinshead for Thomas Loring, 1818. 8 p.   [4545

Freemasons. Wilmington, N. C. Orient Lodge No. 395. Banquet in honor of her twenty-fifth anniversary, Masonic Temple, Wilmington . . . January fourteenth, nineteen hundred and ten. [Wilmington, 1910] [7] p.   [4546

——Orient lodge no. 395 . . . Twenty-fifth anniversary. No place, no publisher, n.d. 62 p.   [4547

Freemasons. Wilmington, N. C. St. John's Lodge No. 1. A record of the bicentennial celebration, St. John's Lodge No. 1, A. F. & A. M. Wilmington, 1955. [29] p.   [4548

——St. John's day, June 24th, 1909, Lumina, Wrightsville Beach, N. C. [Wilmington? 1909?] 12 p. [4549

——Souvenir program, one hundred and sixty-eighth annual communication of the Grand Lodge of A. F. & A. M. of North Carolina and the bicentennial celebration of St. John's Lodge No. 1, A. F. & A. M. Wilmington, 1955. [12] p. [4550

Freemasons. Wilson, N. C. Mount Lebanon Chapter No. 27 of Royal Arch Masons. By-laws approved by the Grand Royal Arch Chapter of North Carolina . . . June 24th, 1866. Raleigh, Nichols, Gorman & Neathery, 1866. 11 p. [4551

Freemasons. Windsor, N. C. Charity Lodge No. 78. By-laws. No place, n.d. 8 p. [4552

——By-laws of Charity Lodge No. 78, Windsor. New York, Printed for Brother John F. Sibell, 1827. 14 p. [4553

Fremont, S. L., defendant. General orders no. 17, War Department, Adjutant General's Office, Washington, March 3, 1843. Wash., Adjutant General's Office, 1843. 2 p. [4554

Fremont Institute, Fremont, N. C. Catalogue, 1888/89- [Fremont, 1889- NcU has 1888/89 [4555

French, Alfred Llewellyn. A farmer's musings. Raleigh, Edwards & Broughton Printing Co., 1920. 102 p. [4556

French, Janie Preston (Collup) The Crockett family and connecting lines, [by] Janie Preston Collup French and Zella Armstrong. Bristol, Tenn., King Printing Co. [c.1928] (Notable southern families, v. 5) 611 p. [4557

——Davy Crockett and the Crockett family, by Janie Preston Collup French and Zella Armstrong. Chattanooga, The Lookout Publishing Co. [1952?] [19] p. [4558

——. . . The Doak family. Chattanooga, Tenn., The Lookout Publishing Co. [c.1933] ([Armstrong, Zella] Notable southern families, v. 6) 98 p. [4559

French Broad Missionary Baptist Association. Session, 18 - 18 - NcU has 1879 [1908-1930] 1938-1946 [4560

Freudenthal, Elsbeth Estelle. Flight into history; the Wright brothers and the air age. Norman, Univ. of Oklahoma Press, 1949. 268 p. [4561

Friedenberg, Walter, joint author, see McIlwain, William

Frieden's Evangelical Lutheran Church, Guilford County, N. C. Annual memorial and historical day, 19 - [Gibsonville, 19 - NcU has 1925, 1932 [4562

Friederich, Werner Paul. Bibliography of comparative literature, by Fernand Baldensperger and Werner P. Friedrich. Chapel Hill, 1950. (North Carolina. University. Studies in comparative literature, 1) 701 p. [4563

——Dante's fame abroad, 1350-1850. Roma, Edizioni di Storia e letteratura, 1950. (Storia e letteratura, n. 31) 582 p. [4564

——Kurze Geschichte des deutschen Volkes. New York, F. S. Crofts & Co., 1939. 184 p. [4565

——An outline-history of German literature. New York, Barnes & Noble [1948] 326 p. [4566

——Outline of comparative literature from Dante Alighieri to Eugene O'Neill. Chapel Hill, University of North Carolina Press, 1954. (University of North Carolina Studies in comparative literature, 11) 451 p. [4567

——Die Schweiz. Chicago, J. B. Lippincott Co. [c.1938] 90 p. [4568

——Spiritualismus und Sensualismus in der englischen Barocklyrik. Wien, Braumüller, 1932. (Wiener beiträge zur englischen philologie . . . LVII. bd.) 303 p. [4569

——Werden und Wachsen der U. S. A. in 300 Jahren, politische und literarische charakterköpfe von Virginia Dare bis Roosevelt. Bern, Verlag A. Francke ag. [c.1939] 271 p. [4570

Friederich, Werner Paul, ed. Yearbook of comparative and general literature, no. 1- Chapel Hill, University of North Carolina Press, 195 - (North Carolina. University. Studies in comparative literature, no. 6, 7, 9, 16) NcU has Yearbook, no. 1-4 [4571

Friedrich, Gerhard. When Quakers meet, and other poems. [Guilford College] Guilford College, 1943. 50 p. [4572

Friend o' wildlife, v. 1- 1945?- Raleigh, North Carolina Wildlife Federation, 1945?- NcU has v. [2-3] [4573

The Friendly news letter, v. 1- 1933- Guilford College, North Carolina Yearly Meeting, 1933- NcU has v. [1-15] 17-19   [4574

Friends, Society of. Book of meetings; containing an account of the times and places of holding the meetings . . . in America, together with a list of recorded ministers. Columbus, O., Joseph H. Miller, 1884. 207 p.   [4575

[Friends, Society of] The Society of Friends, commonly called Quakers. No place [T. A. F. of N. C.] n.d. 8 p.   [4576

Friends, Society of. Board on Religious Education. . . . Lessons in Friends history and belief. [Richmond, Ind., G. O. Ballinger Co.] 1923. 28 p.   [4577

Friends, Society of. Deep River, N. C. Deep River Friends Meeting, Route 1, High Point, North Carolina; bicentennial 1754-1954. [High Point, 1954] [8] p.   [4578

Friends, Society of. London. Yearly Meeting. The epistle from the Yearly Meeting held in London, 184 - Jamestown, J. Sherwood, pr., 18 - NcU has 1843-46, 1848-1851, 1853-1860, 1867, 1871-72, 1874, 1876, 1878-79, 1881, 1883, 1888 [4579
——A salutation in the love of Christ . . . to all who bear the name of Friends. Greensborough, Reprinted at the Patriot and Flag Office, 1857. 8 p.   [4580

Friends, Society of. New York. Yearly Meeting. Third report of a committee of the representatives of New York Yearly Meeting of Friends upon the condition and wants of the colored refugees, 1864. No place, 1864. 23 p.   [4581

Friends, Society of. North Carolina. Yearly Meeting. An account of the sufferings of Friends of North Carolina Yearly Meeting, in support of their testimony against war, from 1861 to 1865. Baltimore, W. K. Boyle, 1868. 28 p.   [4582
—— ——2d ed. No place, Peace Association of Friends, 1868.   [4583
——Constitution and discipline for the American Yearly Meetings . . . with some additions made in 1906. Greensboro, Jos. J. Stone, n.d. 113 p.   [4584
—— ——with some additions and changes made from 1906 to 1923. 111 p. [4585
—— ——with some additions and changes made from 1906 to 1937. 98 p. [4586
——[Copy of An appeal on the iniquity of slavery and the slave trade received and read, in the 11th month, 1844] No place [1844?] [4] p.   [4587
——The discipline of Friends, revised and approved of by the Yearly Meeting, held at New-Garden, in Guilford County, North Carolina . . . 1809. Raleigh, Thomas Henderson, Jr., pr., 1809. 29 p.   [4588
—— ——1822. Hillsborough, Dennis Heartt, pr., 1823. 28 p.   [4589
—— ——1836. Jamestown, J. Stanton, pr., 1837. 55 p.   [4590
—— ——1854. Greensboro, Printed at the Patriot Office, 1855. 39 p.   [4591
—— ——Greensboro, Society of Friends, 1869. 74 p.   [4592
—— ——Rev., 1869. Greensboro, Patriot Office, 1870. 74 p.   [4593
—— ——Rev. 1876. Greensboro, Jos. M. Reece, pr., 1877. 82 p.   [4594
—— ——Rev. 1876. Columbus, O., Friends Publishing House, 1880. 85 p. [4595
—— ——Rev., 1893. Richmond, Ind., Nicholson Mfg. Co., 1893. 97 p.   [4596
——Epistle of the Yearly Meeting of Friends of N. C. for the year 1827. Baltimore, Providence, reprinted, H. H. Brown, 1828. 12 p.   [4597
——From the meeting for sufferings instituted . . . for the purpose of acting in behalf of the . . . interests of the Society. [Greensborough, William Swaim, pr., 1831] [2] p.   [4598
——The memorial of the religious Society of Friends . . . of New-Garden Yearly Meeting, Guilford County, to the General Assembly of North Carolina. No place, no publisher, n.d. [1] p.   [4599
——Memorial to the General Assembly of the state of North Carolina. No place, no publisher, n.d. [1] p.   [4600
——Minutes of the North Carolina Yearly Meeting, 1845- 1845- NcU has 1845, 1848-1861, 1863-1955   [4601
——Names, times and places of holding North Carolina Yearly Meeting. Jamestown, J. Sherwood, pr., 1845. 14 p.   [4602
——Narrative of some of the proceedings of North Carolina Yearly Meeting on the subject of slavery within its limits. Greensborough, Swaim and Sherwood, 1848. 40 p.   [4603
——A narrative of the cruelties inflicted upon Friends of North Carolina . . . during the years 1861 to 1865, in consequence of their . . . view of the unlawfulness of war. London, E. Newman, pr., 1868. 28 p.   [4604

——Rules of discipline of the Yearly Meeting of Friends of North Carolina, together with some of the Christian doctrines of the Society. Woodland, 1908. 91 p. [4605
——The Society of Friends in North Carolina, 1672-1953, some important dates and events. Guilford College [1953] [15] p. [4606
——Views of ancient Friends, on the origin of, and impropriety in adopting the popular appellations of the months and days of the week; and also, using the plural number to a single person. From our Yearly Meeting . . . 1803. No place, no publisher, n.d. [1] p. NcU has photostat (negative) [4607
—— ——No place, Reprinted 1858. 4 p. [4608

Friends messenger, v. 1- February, 1904- High Point, Society of Friends of North Carolina Yearly Meeting, 1904- NcU has v. [1-9] 10-17 [19-31] 32-40 [41] [4609

Friends of Temperance. North Carolina. Proceedings of the North Carolina State Council, 1st- 18 - Raleigh, 186 - NcU has 4th, 1870; 6th, 1872 [4610

Friends of Temperance. North Carolina. Guilford County. People of Guilford, read this! Resolutions . . . passed, July Fourth, 1854. No place [1854] [1] p. [4611

Fries, Adelaide Lisetta. Distinctive customs and practices of the Moravian Church. Bethlehem, Pa., Commenius Press, 1949. 64 p. [4612
——Forsyth, a county on the march. Chapel Hill, University of North Carolina Press, 1949. 248 p. [4613
——Forsyth County. Winston, Stewarts' Printing House, 1898. 132 p. [4614
——Historical sketch of Salem Female Academy. Salem, Crist & Keehln, pr., 1902. 32 p. [4615
——The Mecklenburg Declaration of Independence as mentioned in records of Wachovia. Raleigh, Edwards & Broughton Printing Co., 1907. 11 p. [4616
——The Moravian Church yesterday and today, by Adelaide L. Fries and J. Kenneth Pfohl. Raleigh, Edwards & Broughton, 1926. 153 p. [4617
——Moravian customs; our inheritance. [Winston-Salem, privately printed] 1936. 62 p. [4618
——The Moravians in Georgia, 1735-1740. Raleigh, Printed for the Author by Edwards & Broughton [c.1905] 252 p. [4619
——Parallel lines in Piedmont North Carolina Quaker and Moravian history; the historical lecture delivered at the two hundred and fifty-second session of North Carolina Yearly Meeting . . . 1949. [Guilford College] North Carolina Friends Historical Society [1950?] (North Carolina Friends Historical Society. Publication no. 3) 16 p. [4620

Fries, Adelaide Lisetta, ed. . . . Records of the Moravians in North Carolina. Raleigh, Edwards & Broughton Printing Co., 1922-1954. 8 v. [4621

Fries, Adelaide Lisetta. The road to Salem. Chapel Hill, University of North Carolina Press [c.1944] 316 p. [4622
——Sigma Phi Alpha; an operetta for ladies' voices; the book of words. Words by Adelaide L. Fries. Music by Charles S. Skilton. Salem, no publisher, c.1896. 26 p. [4623
——Some Moravian heroes. Bethlehem, Pa., Comenius Press, 1936. 118 p. [4624
——The town builders. Winston-Salem [Edwards & Broughton Printing Co., Raleigh] 1915. 19 p. [4625

Fries, Francis Henry. Conservatism; an address delivered before the Trust Company section of the American Bankers' Association in New York City, Sept. 13, 1904. Winston-Salem, Lanier Press, n.d. 29 p. [4626

Fries, Henry Elias. Along life's pathway; poems. Winston-Salem [The Author, c.1947] 47 p. [4627

[Fries, Henry Elias] ed. In memory of Robert Curtis Ogden. [Garden City, N. Y.] Privately published [Country Life Press] 1916. 55 p. [4628

Fries, John William. The banking plan proposed by the monetary commission, discussed from a southern standpoint. No place, no publisher, n.d. 16 p. [4629

Frost, James Raleigh. Fighting tobacco the successful way. St. Louis, Mo., Frost & Dectiar [c.1930] 24 p. [4630
——The universal empire. Mocksville, The Author, c.1925. 147 p. [4631

[Frost, John] Pictorial life of Andrew Jackson. Philadelphia, Lindsay and Blakiston, 1845. 183 p. [4632

Frost, John. Pictorial life of Andrew Jackson. Hartford, Belknap and Hamersley, 1847. 560 p. [4633

——The presidents of the United States. Boston, Phillips, Sampson and Co., 1855. 455 p.   [4634

Frost, S. Milton. A Thanksgiving sermon, delivered in Wilmington, North Carolina, Oct. 25, 1855. Wilmington, Fulton & Price, pr., 1855. 11 p.   [4635

Frothingham, Earl Hazeltine. Forest research . . . an address given at the 13th annual meeting of the North Carolina Forestry Association . . . Washington . . . 1924. Wilmington [N. C. Forestry Association] 1924. 13 p.   [4636

Fruitland Institute, Hendersonville, N. C. Catalogue, 1899/1900- [Hendersonville, 1900- NcU has 1913/14, 1919/20   [4637

Fugitt, James Preston. . . . Our country and slavery; a friendly word to the Rev. Francis L. Hawks . . . and other northern clergymen. Baltimore, Joseph Robinson, pr., 1861. 36 p.   [4638

[Fulghum, Susan] A manual for teachers based on a spelling book (revised and enlarged) by Julius I. Foust [and others] Raleigh, Alfred Williams and Co., 1912. 28 p.   [4639

Full report of the great meeting at Southport, N. C., Sept. 28, 1909, to push forward the construction of the . . . South-Atlantic and Trans-continental Railroad. Asheville, Hackney and Moale [1909?] 19 p.   [4640

Fuller, Edwin Wiley. The angel in the cloud. New York, E. J. Hale & Son, 1871. 107 p.   [4641
——   ——1872. 119 p.   [4642
——   ——1881. 153 p.   [4643
——Sea-gift. New York, E. J. Hale & Son, 1873. 408 p.   [4644
——   ——New York, E. J. Hale & Son, 1873. Reprinted by Gavin H. Dortch, 1940. 348 p.   [4645

Fuller, Richard. Addresses of Rev. Dr. H. M. Scudder of the Reformed Dutch Church, Arcot, India; and of Rev. Dr. Richard Fuller of the Baptist Church, Baltimore, Md., at the anniversary of the American Tract Society, New York, May, 1860. No place, no publisher, n.d. 16 p.   [4646

Fuller, Thomas C. First annual address before the law class of the University of North Carolina, Commencement, 1898. Wilson, Advance, 1898. 29 p.   [4647
——   ——Raleigh, Edwards & Broughton, 1898. 24 p.   [4648

Fuller, Thomas Oscar. Pictorial history of the American Negro. Memphis, Tenn., Pictorial History, Inc., 1933. 375 p.   [4649

[Fuller, Walter Pliny] Bascom Lee Field, 1890-1918. No place, no publisher, n.d. 61 p.   [4650

Fuller, Williamson Whitehead. Address at Durham, North Carolina, Monday, October 15th, 1928. [Durham? 1928?] 7 p.   [4651
——By-paths; a collection of occasional writings. [New York] privately printed, 1926. 110 p.   [4652
——A tribute to William H. Osborn. [Oxford, no publisher, 1921] [6] p.   [4653

Fullwood, Anne Hunt. Itinerary of thoughts. New York, Caruthers Co., 1935. 28 p.   [4654

Fulmer, John Leonard. Agricultural progress in the cotton belt since 1920. Chapel Hill, University of North Carolina Press [1950] 236 p.   [4655

[Fulton, David Bryant] "Eagle clippings," by Jack Thorne [pseud.] [Brooklyn, N. Y., D. B. Fulton, c.1907] 116 p.   [4656
——Hanover; or, The persecution of the lowly, a story of the Wilmington massacre, by Jack Thorne [pseud.] No place, M. C. L. Hill, n.d. 128+ p. p. 129- missing in NcU copy.   [4657
——A plea for social justice for the Negro woman. Yonkers, N. Y., Negro Society of Historical Research, 1912. 11 p.   [4658
——Poem, Abraham Lincoln, by "Jack Thorne" [pseud.] No place, no publisher, n.d. 5 p.   [4659
——Recollections of a sleeping car porter, by Jack Thorne [pseud.] Jersey City, Doan & Pilson, pr., 1892. 45 p.   [4660

Fulton, Harry Rascoe. Essentials of botany. West Raleigh, The Author, 1915. 42 p.   [4661

Fulton, Maurice Garland, ed.   College life, its conditions and problems.   New York, Macmillan Co., 1915.   524 p.   [4662
——National ideals and problems; essays for college English.   New York, Macmillan Co., 1918.   415 p.   [4663
——Southern life in southern literature.   Boston, Ginn and Co. [c.1917]   530 p. [4664

Fulton, Robert.   Report of the practicability of navigating with steam boats, on the southern waters of the United States.   2d ed.   Philadelphia, Thomas Town, pr., 1828.   12 p.   [4665

Functions of an angle.   Durham, W. T. Blackwell, n.d.   4 p.   [4666

The fundamentalist, v. 1-   1926-   Charlotte, 1926-   NcU has v. 1, no. 1   [4667

Funeral of the Honorable William Gaston.   [New Bern, 1844]   [1] p.   [4668

The funeral services of D. A. Davis.   [Salisbury?] n.d.   [1] p.   [4669

Funeral services of the late Col. R. L. Patterson, Salem, N. C., July 16, 1879.   Salem, L. V. & E. T. Blum, pr., 1879.   11 p.   [4670

Fuquay Springs, N. C.   Board of Commissioners.   Plumbing ordinance of the town of Fuquay Springs, North Carolina. [Fuquay Springs] 1937.   23 p.   [4671

Fuquay Springs Academy, Fuquay Springs, N. C.   Prospectus.   [Fuquay Springs] 1906.   [2] p.   [4672

Furches, David Moffatt.   Address delivered at the Masonic picnic given for the benefit of the Oxford Orphan Asylum, Mocksville, N. C. Aug. 8th, 1901.   No place [The Author?] n.d.   13 p.   [4673

Furgurson, W. H.   The burial of radicalism in N. C., Nov. 7, 1876.   No place, no publisher, n.d.   Cartoon.   [4674

Furman, Richard.   The mode and subjects of baptism; two discourses delivered before the Cedar Creek Baptist Church, North Carolina . . . September 10, 1843.   Cheraw, S. C., John Stubs, pr., 1843.   55 p.   [4675
——Review of the Rev. A. B. Smith's pamphlet on the mode of baptism.   Cheraw, Farmers' Gazette Office, 1845.   57 p.   [4676

Furniss, William.   Tetra-Chordon: a pot pourri of rhythms and prose.   New York, American News Co., 1874.   144 p.   [4677

Furniture merchandising for manufacturer and retailer, v. 1-   189?-   High Point, Southern Furniture Journal, 189?-   NcU has v. 18-21, 33-34, 43-63   [4678

Furniture South, v. 1-   192 -   High Point, 192 -   NcU has v. 6-9 [10-11] 16-34 [4679

Furr, William.   "Tomorrow achieved"; a novel.   Kansas City, Chapman Publishers, Inc. [c.1946]   331 p.   [4680

Fussler, Irene Graham (Howe)   In the shadow of the cross, yesterday and today.   Boston [Walter H. Baker Co., c.1938]   51 p.   [4681

G., J. C.,   see Gorman, John C.

Gabrielson, Ira Noel.   Wildlife refuges.   New York, Macmillan Co., 1943. 257 p. [4682

[Gaddy, Hazel Ross]   Lockhart Gaddy with his friends, the wild geese.   Asheville, Miller Printing Co., n.d.   64 p.   [4683

Gage, Moses D.   From Vicksburg to Raleigh.   Chicago, Clarke & Co., 1865.   356 p.   [4684

Gaines, Francis Pendleton.   The inauguration of Francis Pendleton Gaines as the eighth president of Wake Forest College, April 25, 1928.   Wake Forest [Wake Forest College, 1928]   73 p.   [4685
——The southern plantation.   New York, Columbia University, 1924.   243 p. [4686

Gaines, George Towns.   Fighting Tennesseans.   [Kingsport, Tenn.] Privately printed [Kingsport Press] 1931.   127 p.   [4687

Gaines, Wesley John.   African Methodism in the South; or, Twenty-five years of freedom.   Atlanta, Franklin Publishing House, 1890.   305 p.   [4688

Gaither, Frances Ormond (Jones)   Little Miss Cappo.   New York, Macmillan Co., 1937.   254 p.   [4689

The Galax, v. 1-   1906?-   Lenoir, Senior Class of Davenport College, 1906?-   NcU has 1911   [4690

Gales, Mrs. Joseph   see Gales, Winifred (Marshall)

[Gales, Winifred (Marshall)] Matilda Berkely, or, Family anecodotes. Raleigh, Printed by J. Gales, 1804. 224 p. [4691

Gales' North Carolina almanack, 18 - Raleigh, Joseph Gales, 18 - NcU has 1805, 1807, 1808, 1812 (defective) 1814-1818, 1821-1827, 1829-1830, 1831 (defective) 1832-1838 [4692

Galloway Primitive Baptist Association. Minutes, 1842- Tarboro, Tarboro Press, 1842- NcU has 1842 [4693

Galvin, Hoyt Rees, ed. Planning a library building, the major steps; proceedings of the institute sponsored by the American Library Association Buildings Committee at S. Paul, Minnesota, June 19-20, 1954, Hoyt R. Galvin, editor, Kathryn A. Devereaux, assistant editor. Chicago, American Library Association, 1955. 80 p. [4694

Ganderson, Harry. World federal government or international anarchy. [Greensboro, The Democrat, 1947] 11 p. [4695

Gano, John. Biographical memoirs. New York, Printed by Southwick and Hardcastle for John Tiebout, 1806. 151 p. [4696

Ganse, H. D. Bible slaveholding not sinful; a reply to "Slaveholding not sinful", by Samuel B. Howe. New York, R. & R. Brinkerhoff, 1856. 85 p. [4697

Gantt, Mrs. Robert M. Why women should vote for Governor Smith. [Durham? Durham County Women's Democratic Club, 1928?] 8 p. [4698

Garber, Paul Neff. John Carlisle Kilgo, president of Trinity College, 1894-1910. Durham, Duke University Press, 1937. 412 p. [4699
——The Methodist meeting-house. New York, Board of Missions and Church Extension, the Methodist Church [1941] 121 p. [4700
——The Methodists are one people. Nashville, Cokesbury Press [c.1939] 144 p. [4701
——The romance of American Methodism. Greensboro, Piedmont Press, 1931. 343 p. [4702
——That fighting spirit of Methodism. Greensboro, Piedmont Press, 1928 [i. e. 1929] 199 p. [4703

Garden, Alexander. Anecdotes of the American Revolution. 2d series. Charleston [S. C.] A. E. Miller, pr., 1828. 240 p. [4704
—— ——Brooklyn, N. Y., Reprinted, 1865. 3 v. NcU has v. 1-2, 1st ser.; v. 3, 2d ser. [4705
——Anecodotes of the Revolutionary war in America [1st ser.] Charleston [S. C.] Printed for the Author by A. E. Miller, 1822. 459 p. [4706

Garden Club of North Carolina. Year book, 1931- 1931- NcU has 1931-1940/41 [4707

Gardiner, Asa Bird. The discovery of the remains of Major-General Nathanael Greene, first president of the Rhode Island Cincinnati; address . . . delivered in . . . State House, Newport, R. I., July 4th, 1901. [New York, Blumenberg Press, c.1901] 30 p. [4708

Gardner, Anna. Harvest gleanings, in prose and verse. New York, Fowler & Wells, 1881. 200 p. [4709

[Gardner, Augustus Peabody] Gardner or Daniels? New York, American Defense Society [1915] 22 p. [4710

Gardner, E. Norfleet. Magnifying the church. [Nashville, Tenn., Broadman Press, c.1947] 143 p. [4711

[Gardner, James Browne] Massachusetts memorial to her soldiers and sailors who died in the Department of No. Carolina, 1861-1865, dedicated at New Bern, No. Carolina, November 11, 1908. [Boston, Gardner & Taplin, 1909] 102 p. [4712

Gardner, Oliver Max. . . . Banking and government. Washington, Treasury Department, 1946. 8 p. [4713
——Franklin D. Roosevelt, a man of courage; address . . . before a rally of Young Democrats in Guilford County . . . September 17, 1932. Raleigh, Capital Printing Co. [1932] 8 p. [4714
——New conditions demand new remedies; an address . . . before . . . the General Assembly of the State of Iowa, at Des Moines, Iowa, January 9, 1933, and . . . at Oklahoma City, Oklahoma, February 17, 1933. No place [1933] 15 p. [4715
——The significance of the citizens' library movement. [Raleigh] North Carolina Library Association, 1929. [5] p. [4716

——War, not Democratic Party, causing low-priced cotton. [Raleigh? 1915?] 4 p. [4717

Gardner, Paris Cleveland. List of captains and information on Confederate leaders from Cleveland. No place, no publisher [1930] [1] p. [4718

Gardner-Webb College, Boiling Springs, N. C. Catalogue, 19 - Boiling Springs, 19 - NcU has [1946/47-1955/56] [4719

——Gardner-Webb College, Boiling Springs, North Carolina. [Boiling Springs] n.d. [16] p. [4720

——Gardner-Webb College, founded 1907, golden anniversary plans. [Boiling Springs] n.d. [11] p. [4721

[**Garibaldi, Linn Dunklin**] Joseph Garibaldi. New York, James T. White & Co., 1940. [6] p. [4722

Garner, Wightman Wells. The production of tobacco. Rev. 1st ed. Philadelphia, Blakiston Co., 1951. 520 p. [4723

Garnett, Theodore Stanford. The Virginia Bar Association: Paper entitled, The impeachment and trial of Andrew Johnson, read . . . at the fourteenth annual meeting held at Hot Springs . . . August 5, 6, and 7, 1902. Richmond, Everett Waddey Co., 1902. 27 p. [4724

Garrett, J. W. B. Prospectus of The Ratoon. Hillsborough, May 3, 1848. [1] p. [4725

Garrett, Mitchell Bennett. . . . The Estates general of 1789. New York, D. Appleton-Century Co., Inc. [c.1935] 268 p. [4726

——Europe since 1815, by Mitchell B. Garrett and James L. Godfrey. New York, F. S. Crofts, 1947. 763 p. [4727

——European history, 1500-1815. New York, American Book Co. [c.1940] 715 p. [4728

——. . . Sixty years of Howard college, 1842-1902. Birmingham, Ala., Howard College [1927] (Howard college bulletin, v. LXXXV, no. 4, October, 1927) 167 p. [4729

Garrett, William Robertson. History of the South Carolina cession and the northern boundary of Tennessee. Nashville, Tenn., Southern Methodist Publishing House, 1884. (Tennessee Historical Society. Papers) 32 p. [4730

Garrison, Karl Claudius. An analytic study of rational learning. Nashville, Tenn., George Peabody College for Teachers, 1928. (Its Contributions to education, no. 44) 52 p. [4731

——Educational psychology [by] Karl C. Garrison & J. Stanley Gray. New York, Appleton-Century-Crofts [c.1955] 505 p. [4732

——Growth and development. New York, Longmans, Green, 1952. 559 p. [4733

——The psychology of adolescence. Rev. ed. New York, Prentice-Hall, Inc., 1940. 477 p. [4734

—— ——3d ed. 1946. 375 p. [4735

—— ——1951. 377 p. [4736

——The psychology of exceptional children. New York, Ronald Press Co. [c.1940] 351 p. [4737

—— ——[1943] 351 p. [4738

Garrison, Sidney Clarence. Fundamentals of psychology in secondary education, by S. C. Garrison . . . and K. C. Garrison. New York, Prentice-Hall, Inc., 1936. 599 p. [4739

Garth, John Goodall. The idyll of the Shepherd. 2d ed. Charlotte, Standard Printing Co., c.1932] 64 p. [4740

——Sixty years of home missions in the Presbyterian Synod of North Carolina. [Charlotte, The Synod, 1949?] 86 p. [4741

[**Gascoyne, Joel**] A true description of Carolina. [London, Printed for J. Gascoin and R. Greene, 1682] 4 numbered leaves. NcU has photostat from original in the John Carter Brown Library. [4742

Gasparin, Agénor Étienne de. Reconstruction; a letter to President Johnson. New York, Loyal Publication Society, 1865. 70 p. [4743

Gasque, Jim. Bass fishing; technique, tactics, and tales. New York, A. A. Knopf 1945. 203 p. [4744

——Hunting and fishing in the Great Smokies. New York, A. A. Knopf, 1948. 210 p. [4745

[Gaston, A. P.]   Partisan campaigns of Col. Lawrence M. Allen, commanding the 64th Regiment, North Carolina State Troops, during the late Civil War.   Raleigh, Edwards & Broughton, 1894.   28 p.   [4746

Gaston, William.   An address delivered before the American Whig and Cliosophic societies of the College of New Jersey, Sept. 29, 1835.   Princeton, John Bogart, pr., 1835.   42 p.   [4747

——Address delivered before the Dialectic and Philanthropic societies, at Chapel Hill, N. C., June 20, 1832.   Raleigh, Joseph Gales, 1832.   16 p.   [4748

—— ——1849.   23 p.   [4749

—— ——5th ed.   Chapel Hill, J. M. Henderson, 1858.   27 p.   [4750

——Circular.   Washington, April 19, 1814.   [3] p.   [4751

——Circular.   [Washington, A. Lucas, March 1, 1815]   15 p.   [4752

——The old North State.   No place, no publisher, n.d.   [1] p.   [4753

—— ——a patriotic song.   Philadelphia, Lee and Walker [c.1844]   (National and patriotic songs.   No. 15)   [3] p.   [4754

—— ——Band arrangement.   [Raleigh] N. C. State College of Agriculture and Engineering, n.d.   2 p.   [4755

—— ——Washington, Rotary Club of Washington, n.d.   [1] p.   [4756

—— ——(traditional air as sung in 1926) collected and arranged by Mrs. E. E. Randolph.   [Charlotte, Standard Printing Co. of North Carolina Daughters of the American Revolution, c.1950]   [2] p.   [4757

——To the freemen of the counties of Johnston, Wayne, Greene . . . composing the fourth congressional district.   Newbern, March 15th, 1813.   [1] p.   [4758

—— ——June 12th, 1815.   [1] p.   [4759

—— ——[Newbern, September 19, 1808]   17 p.   [4760

Gaston College, Dallas, N. C.   Catalogue, 18 - [Dallas, 18 - NcU has [1882/83-1898/99]   [4761

Gaston Co., N. C.   Board of County Commissioners.   Some facts about Gaston County, N. C.   [Gastonia, Gazette Printing House] 1905.   11 p.   [4762

Gaston Co., N. C.   Board of Education.   Public education in Gaston County, 19   - Gastonia, 19   -   NcU has 1905/06, 1915/16   [4763

Gaston County Baptist Association.   Annual session, 1919-   1919-   NcU has [1920-1954]   [4764

[Gastonia, N. C.   Board of Commissioners]   City of Gastonia, report of audit, 19   - Gastonia, 19   -   NcU has 1923/24   [4765

Gastonia, N. C.   Chamber of Commerce.   Gastonia, North Carolina, the combed yarn manufacturing center of America.   [Gastonia, 193?]   Folder.   [4766

——Manufacturers of Gaston County, N. C.   [Gastonia, 1950]   9 p.   [4767

—— ——[1952?]   23 p.   [4768

[Gastonia, N. C.   Chamber of Commerce]   Not fancies, but facts, about Gastonia.   [Gastonia, 1943?]   [3] p.   [4769

——Promoting progress in 1955.   Gastonia [1955]   [7] p.   [4770

Gastonia, N. C.   City Council.   The Code of the city of Gastonia, North Carolina, 1952.   Charlottesville, Va., Michie City Publications Co., 1952.   293 p.   [4771

Gastonia, N. C.   Loray Baptist Church.   Directory . . . 1923-1924.   [Gastonia, 1924]   30 p.   [4772

Gastonia Commercial Club.   Illustrated handbook of Gastonia, N. C.   [Charlotte, Ray Printing Co., 1906.   73 p.   [4773

Gastonia, North Carolina, city directory, 19   -   Asheville, Commercial Service Co., Inc., 19   -   NcU has 1921/22   [4774

[Gatchell, Edwin A.]   The standard guide to Asheville and Western North Carolina.   Asheville, F. L. Jacobs, 1887.   65 p.   [4775

Gatchell, Horatio P.   Western North Carolina; its resources, climate, scenery and salubrity.   New York, A. L. Chatterton Publishing Co., 1885.   32 p.   [4776

—— ——Milwaukee, Starr and Son, pr., 1870.   24 p.   [4777

Gates, Theophilus R.   Life and writings.   2d ed.   Philadelphia, Dickinson, 1818.   514 p.   [4778

——The trials, experiences, exercises of mind and first travels of Theophilus R. Gates, written by himself.   Poughkeepsie, C. C. Adams for the Author, 1810.   214 p.   [4779

Gates Co., N. C. Board of Education. Report of County Superintendent of Schools, 19 - [Gatesville?] 19 - NcU has 1911/12, with a summary for 1901/02-1910/11 [4780

Gatling, John. A card. No place, no publisher, n.d. [1] p. [4781
——Sale of land. Warrenton, 1875. [1] p. [4782

Gauss, Christian. The city of man; an address delivered at . . . the University of North Carolina . . . April 9, 1947. [Chapel Hill] Committee on Convocations and Lectures of the University of North Carolina, 1947. 10 p. [4783

Gay, J. E. Onward. No place, Board of Missions of the Western North Carolina Conference, 1906. [24] p. [4784

Gay, James. A collection of various pieces of poetry, chiefly patriotic. Raleigh, William Boylan, pr., 1810. 42 p. [4785

Gay, John Lenoir. True story of Marshall Ney and other notable Frenchmen. St. Louis, Woodward & Tiernan Printing Co., n.d. 45 p. [4786

Gee, Joshua. Trade and navigation of Great Britain considered. A new ed. Glasgow, Printed for Robert Urie, 1767. 267 p. [4787

Gee, Pattie Williams. Ode to North Carolina. [Hasbrouck Heights, N. J., The Author, 1906] 8 p. [4788
——The palace of the heart, and other poems of love. Boston, R. G. Badger, 1904. 63 p. [4789

Gee, Wilson. The cotton cooperatives in the Southeast, by Wilson Gee and Edward Allison Terry. New York, D. Appleton-Century Co., Inc., 1933. (University of Virginia Institute for Research in the Social Sciences. Institute monographs, no. 17) 271 p. [4790
——Research barriers in the South. New York, Century Co. [c.1932] 192 p. [4791

Gegenheimer, Albert Frank. . . . Thomas Godfrey: protégé of William Smith. Philadelphia, 1943. 37 p. Essential portion of thesis (Ph. D.)—University of Pennsylvania, 1940. [4792

Geismar, Maxwell David. Writers in crisis; the American novel between two wars. Boston, Houghton Mifflin Co., 1942. 299 p. [479

Genealogy of Philander Priestley Claxton. No place, n.d. [3] p. [4794

Gen. Andrew Jackson and the Rev. Ezra Stiles Ely. [N. Y. George H. Evans, pr.] n.d. 8 p. [4795

A general directory of Mount Airy, North Carolina, rural routes and suburbs, 19 - [Mount Airy? J. Edwin Carter and A. Kyle Sydnor, Compilers] 19 - NcU has 1913-14 [4796

General Federation of Women's Clubs. Public Welfare Department. A review of health conditions and needs in Granville County, North Carolina. New York, Metropolitan Life Insurance Co. [1930] 15 p. [4797

General Graphite Co. Graphite. No place, no publisher, n.d. [12] p. [4798

General Jackson vetoed; being a review of the veto message on the Bank of the U. S. [New York, 1832?] 24 p. Title page wanting in NcU copy. [4799

General Motors Corporation, New York. A tribute to North Carolina. New York, 1932. Various paging. [Program and tribute by Bruce Barton] [4800

General Southern Land Agency, New York. Descriptive catalogue of southern lands for sale or lease. New York, 1865. 62 p. [4801
——The North Carolina Land Agency. New York, November 20, 1865. [1] p. [4802

General Tract Agency, Raleigh, N. C. General Tract Agency, Raleigh, N. C. [Raleigh? Dec. 1, 1862] 4 p. [4803

Genth, Friedrich August Ludwig Karl Wilhelm. Mineral resources of North Carolina . . . Read before the Franklin Institute at the monthly meetings of Nov. and Dec., 1871. Philadelphia, 1871. 31 p. [4804

George, Arthur Allen. The history of Johnson C. Smith University, 1867 to the present. Ann Arbor, University Microfilms [1955] ([University Microfilms, Ann Arbor, Mich.] Publication no. 10,661) Collation of the original: 5, vii, 241, 95 leaves. [4805

George, Wesley Critz. Race, heredity, and civilization. [Chapel Hill, 1954] 7 p. [4806

—— ——[1955?] 11 p.   [4807
——The race problem from the standpoint of one who is concerned about the evils of miscegenation. [Chapel Hill] 1946? 9 p.   [4808
—— ——Birmingham, Ala. American States Rights Association, 1955. 14 p. [4809

George Peabody College for Teachers. Survey of the school system of New Hanover County, N. C., 1920. [Wilmington, Wilmington Printing Co. for Board of Education] 1920. 114 p.   [4810

George Peabody College for Teachers, Nashville. Division of Surveys and Field Studies. Libraries in the accredited high schools of the Association of Colleges and Secondary Schools of the Southern States. [Nashville] 1930. 72 p.   [4811
——A study of Baptist higher education in North Carolina (a tentative report) Nashville, Tenn., 1939. 54 p.   [4812

George Peabody College for Teachers, Nashville, Tenn. English Class in Southern Life and Literary Culture. The South, a suggested reading list. Nashville, Tenn., 1944. (Contribution to southern life and literature, no. 2) 29 p.   [4813
——Southern regional literature for children. Nashville, Tenn., 1946. (Southern life and literary culture series, no. 3) 34 p.   [4814

George Peabody College for Teachers, Nashville. Regional Materials Service• Your region's resources. Nashville [1947] 149 p.   [4815

Georgetown and Charlotte Railroad. Statement and estimate of the cost and equipment of the Georgetown and Charlotte R. R. No place, no publisher [1870] 7 p.   [4816

German Kali Works, New York. Tobacco culture. New York [189?] 98 p. [4817

Gerson, Noel B. The Cumberland Rifles. Garden City, N. Y., Doubleday & Co., Inc., 1952. 314 p.   [4818

Gewehr, Wesley Marsh. The great awakening in Virginia, 1740-1790. Durham, Duke University Press, 1930. 292 p.   [4819

Gholson, Edward. From Jerusalem to Jericho. Boston, Chapman & Grimes [1943] 122 p.   [4820
——Musings of a minister. Boston, Christopher Publishing House [1943] 101 p. [4821
——The Negro looks into the South. Boston, Chapman & Grimes [1947] 115 p. [4822

Gholson, Thomas Saunders. Valedictory address . . . delivered before the Union Agricultural Society of Virginia and North Carolina, October 27, 1854. [Petersburg, Va.] Printed at the Office of the Southern Farmer, 1854. 14 p.   [4823

Gibbes, Robert Wilson. Documentary history of the American Revolution. New York, D. Appleton & Co., 1853-57. 3 v.   [4824

Gibbon, John H. Report on the utility of an uniform system in measures, weights, fineness and decimal accounts, for the standard coinage of commercial nations. Charleston, Steam Power Press, 1854. 19 p.   [4825

Gibbon, James, cardinal. [Reminiscences of Catholicity in North Carolina] No place, no publisher [1891] 16 p.   [4826
——The sacrament of penance and the moral influence of sacramental confession. Richmond, Simons & Keiningham, 1874. 24 p.   [4827

Gibson, John Mendinghall. Physician to the world; the life of General William C. Gorgas. Durham, Duke University Press, 1950. 315 p.   [4828

[Gibson, Julia Amanda (Springs)] Lineage and tradition of the family of John Springs III. Atlanta, Foote & Davies Co., 1921. 418 p.   [4829

Gibson, Roland. Cotton textile wages in the United States and Great Britain . . . 1860-1945. New York, King's Crown Press, 1948. 137 p.   [4830

Gibson, William Marion. Constitutions of Colombia. Durham, Duke University Press, 1948. 478 p.   [4830a

Giduz, Hugo, ed. Les contes des sept sages, adapted by Hugo Giduz and Urban T. Holmes. New York, Farrar & Rinehart, Inc. [c.1938] 61 p.   [4831

Giduz, Hugo. French verb drill test pad. [Chapel Hill] The Author, c.1939. [23] p.   [4832
——Sept contes de la vieille France, by Hugo Giduz and Urban T. Holmes. Boston, D. C. Heath and Co. [c.1930] 96 p.   [4833

Giduz, Hugo, joint author, see Staab, Hermann Henry

Gielow, Martha S.   Old Andy, the moonshiner.   New York, Fleming H. Revell Co.
[c.1909]   46 p.   [4834
——Uncle Sam.   New York, Fleming H. Revell Co. [c.1913]   61 p.   [4835
Gilbert, Allan H.   Dante's conception of justice.   Durham, Duke University Press,
1925.   244 p.   [4836
——Literary criticism, Plato to Dryden.   New York, American Book Co. [c.1940]
704 p.   [4837
——Machiavelli's Prince and its forerunners; The Prince as a typical book de
regimine principum.   Durham, Duke University Press, 1938.   266 p.   [4838
——On the composition of Paradise lost.   Chapel Hill, University of North Carolina
Press, 1947.   185 p.   [4839
Gilbert, Allan H., ed. and tr.   Orlando furioso; an English translation with introduc-
tion, notes, and index by Allan Gilbert.   New York, S. F. Vanni [1954]   2 v. [4840
——The Prince, and other works.   Chicago, Packard and Co. [1946]   322 p. [4841
Gilbert, Allan H.   The symbolic persons in the masques of Ben Johson.   Durham,
Duke University Press [1948]   297 p.   [4842
Gilbert, Dorothy Lloyd.   Distinction in Quaker education.   Guilford College, Guil-
ford College Bulletin [1946]   14 p.   [4843
——Guilford, a Quaker college.   [Greensboro, Printed for Guilford College by J. J.
Stone & Co.] 1937.   359 p.   [4844
——In faith and in unity; three scenes in the life of Guilford College and North
Carolina.   [Guilford College, 1942]   26 p.   [4845
[**Gilbert, Dorothy Lloyd**]   Two hundred years at Rocky River Friends Meeting,
Siler City, N. C., Route 1, 1753-1953.   [Siler City? 1954?]   16 p.   [4846
Gilbert, Katharine (Everett)   Aesthetic studies: architecture and poetry.   [Durham,
Duke University Press, 1952.   145 p.   [4847
——A history of esthetics, by Katharine Everett Gilbert and Helmut Kuhn.   New
York, Macmillan Co., 1939.   582 p.   [4848
——Maurice Blondel's philosophy of action.   Chapel Hill, Dept. of Philosophy,
University of N. C., 1924.   (University of N. C. studies in philosophy no. 1)
94 p.   [4849
——Studies in recent aesthetic.   Chapel Hill, University of N. C. Press, 1927.
178 p.   [4850
Gilchrist, Adam.   Annual sermon, delivered before the students of the Fayetteville
Female High School, on Tuesday evening, July 15, 1856.   Fayetteville, Edward J.
Hale & Son, pr., 1856.   15 p.   [4851
Giles, Janice (Holt)   The Kentuckians.   Boston, Houghton Mifflin Co., 1953.
272 p.   [4852
Gill, Edwin.   De Witt Clinton, the man on the cigarette stamp.   Raleigh, Edwards
and Broughton [pref. 1953]   30 p.   [4853
——Oliver Max Gardner—the man; an address on the occasion of the dedication of
Gardner Hall, North Carolina State College, Raleigh, May 6, 1953.   [Raleigh,
1953]   14 p.   [4854
Gill, Everett.   A. T. Robertson.   New York, Macmillan Co., 1943.   250 p.   [4855
Gill, Henry M., comp.   The South in prose and poetry.   New Orleans, F. F. Hansell
& Bro., Ltd. [c.1916]   438 p.   [4856
Gill, John.   An abridgment of an exposition of The book of the Prophet Isaiah.
Halifax, Printed at the Office of the North-Carolina Journal for Richard Poindexter
and Jesse Read, 1806.   276 p.   [4857
Gillen, Martin James.   A new economic yardstick of taxation and public credit for
states and their political subdivisions.   No place, no publisher, 1932.   20 p. [4858
Gillenson, Lewis W.   Billy Graham, the man and his message.   Greenwich, Conn.,
Fawcett Publications, c.1954.   32 p.   [4859
Gillespie, Joseph Halstead.   Elsinore, and other poems.   Raleigh, Edwards &
Broughton, 1888.   33 p.   [4860
Gillett, Ezra Hall.   History of the Presbyterian Church in the U. S.   Philadelphia,
Presbyterian Publication Committee [c.1864]   605 p.   [4861
Gillett, Mary (Bledsoe)   see Bledsoe, Mary Lina

Gilliam's Academy, Altamahaw, N. C. Catalogue, 19 - 19 - NcU has 1911/12-
1913/14   [4862

Gillin, John Philip.   Cultural sociology, a revision of An introduction to sociology,
by John Lewis Gillin [and] John Philip Gillin.   New York, Macmillan Co., 1948.
844 p.   [4863

——The culture of security in San Carlos.   New Orleans, 1951.   (Tulane University of Louisiana.   Middle American Research Institute.   Publication no. 16)
128 p.   [4864

Gillin, John Philip, ed.   For a science of social man . . . by Howard Becker [and
others]   New York, Macmillan Co. [1954]   289 p.   [4865

——The ways of men, an introduction to anthropology.   New York, D. Appleton-
Century Co. [1948]   649 p.   [4866

Gillis, Adolph.   Old Hickory, a semi-historical play.   New York, Liveright Publishing Corporation [c.1938]   142 p.   [4867

Gilman, Caroline (Howard)   The poetry of travelling in the United States, with
additional sketches, by a few friends; and A week among autographs, by Rev. S.
Gilman.   New York, S. Colman, 1838.   430 p.   [4868

Gilman, Glenn.   Human relations in the industrial Southeast.   Chapel Hill, University of North Carolina Press [1956]   327 p.   [4869

[Gilmer, George Rockingham]   Sketches of some of the first settlers of upper
Georgia, of the Cherokees, and the Author.   Americus, Ga., Americus Book Co.,
1926.   458 p.   [4870

[Gilmer, Robert D.]   The trial of the sparrow for killing Cock Robin.   [New York,
Russell Brothers] c.1889.   15 p.   [4871

Gilmore, James Roberts.   The advance-guard of western civilization.   New York,
D. Appleton and Co., 1888.   343 p.   [4872

[Gilmore, James Roberts]   Among the pines; or, South in secession-time.   By Edmund Kirke [pseud.]   New York, The Author, 1862.   310 p.   [4873

Gilmore, James Roberts.   John Sevier as a commonwealth builder.   New York, D.
Appleton and Co., 1887.   321 p.   [4874

——A mountain-white heroine.   New York, Belford, Clarke and Co., 1889.
240 p.   [4875

[Gilmore, James Roberts]   My Southern friends.   . . . By Edmund Kirke [pseud.]
New York, Carleton, Publishers, 1863.   308 p.   [4876

Gilmore, James Roberts.   The rear-guard of the Revolution.   New York, D. Appleton and Co., 1889.   323 p.   [4877

Gilmour, A. D. Pollock.   Woodrow Wilson, the Christian; an address . . . at a memorial service . . . First Presbyterian Church, Wilmington, N. C. . . . February 10,
1924.   [Wilmington, National Press, Inc., 1941]   18 p.   [4878

Gilpatrick, Delbert Harold.   Jeffersonian democracy in North Carolina, 1789-1816.
New York, Columbia University Press, 1931.   (Studies in history, economics and
public law, ed. by the Faculty of Political Science of Columbia University, no. 344)
257 p.   [4879

Gist, Christopher.   Christopher Gist's journals with historical, geographical and
ethnological notes.   Pittsburgh, J. R. Weldin & Co., 1893.   296 p.   [4880

Givler, John Paul.   Laboratory directions for general biology, by John Paul Givler
and E. Inez Coldwell.   [7th ed.]   Greensboro, Woman's College of the University
of North Carolina [1938]   78 p.   [4881

—— ——[9th ed.]   [1943]   106 p.   [4882

Glade Valley High School, Cherry Lane, N. C.   Catalogue, 1911/12-   Cherry Lane,
1912-   NcU has 1911/12   [4883

Glasson, William Henry.   . . . Federal military pensions in the United States.   New
York, Oxford University Press, 1918.   305 p.   [4884

Glazier, Willard.   The capture, the prison pen, and the escape, giving a complete
history of prison life in the South.   Hartford, Conn., H. E. Goodwin, 1868.
400 p.   [4885

Gleason, Eliza Atkins.   The southern Negro and the public library.   Chicago, Ill.,
University of Chicago Press [1941]   218 p.   [4886

Gleitsmann, William.   . . . Western North Carolina as a health resort, read before

the American Public Health Association, November, 1875, at Baltimore. Baltimore, Sherwood & Co., 1876. 8 p. [4887

Glen Alpine Springs Hotel, Burke Co., N. C. Glen Alpine Springs. Morganton,
1879] 6 p. [4888
——Glen Alpine Springs, near Morganton, Burke county. Weldon, Harrell's Book
and Job Printing House, 1880. 8 p. [4889

Glen Anna Seminary, Thomasville, N. C. Catalogue, 18 - Thomasville, 18 -
NcU has 1858/59 [4890

Glendinning, William. . . . The life of William Glendinning, preacher of the gospel.
Philadelphia, Printed for the Author at the Office of W. W. Woodward, 1795.
154 p. [4891

Glenn, Robert Broadnax. What prohibition will do for North Carolina . . . the
Selma speech . . . on Mar. 29, 1908. No place, no publisher, n.d. 12 p. [4892

Glenn, Theodosia Wales. The bells of old St. Paul's; the celebration of the fiftieth
year of the rectorship of Rev. Robert Brent Drane . . . being the 225th of the
founding of the parish. [Edenton? 1926?] 24 p. [4893
——Joseph Hewes in historic review; an historical pageant. [Elizabeth City, Printed
by Pell, 1932] 22 p. [4894

The globe girdler, 194 - Fallston, Fallston High School, 194 - NcU has 1943 [4895

Glover, Mortimer. Unfinished symphony, a sermon . . . preached in St. James
Church, Wilmington, N. C., April 15, 1945. No place, no publisher, n.d. [2] p. [4896
——"Wisdom of the spirit"; a sermon in memory of the Rev. William Hammond
Milton . . . preached in St. James Church, June 30, 1946. [Wilmington?] 1946.
[3] p. [4897

Go, v. 1- October, 1922- Greensboro, Carolina Motor Club, 1922- NcU has
v. 1-18 [19-23] 24-32 Title varies: Carolina motorist; Car owner [4898

Gobbel, Luther Lafayette. Church-state relationships in education in North Carolina since 1776. Durham, Duke University Press, 1938. 251 p. [4899

Godbey, Allen Howard. Ancient oriental history, Pre-Mosaic Hebrew religion; in-
ductive outlines for students. St. Louis, Mo., John S. Swift Co., Inc., 1935.
102 p. [4900
——For the Methodist Judicial Council . . . open letter to Dr. Charles W. Tadlock.
[Durham, 1940] 11 p. [4901
——Information for the Methodist Judicial Council and for each annual conference.
No place, 1941. 19 p. [4902
——An open letter to Dr. Elbert Russell. [Durham, 1931] 28 p. [4903
——An open letter to President W. P. Few, April 26, 1932. [Durham, 1932]
42 p. [4904
——What Rabbi Yeshua thought of soldiers, and Ante-Nicene Christian soldiers.
Durham, 1941. 30 p. [4905

Godbey, Allen Howard, comp. Reactions of scholars and of Duke university students and alumni on the open letters to Dr. Russell and President Few. [Durham,
1933] 80 p. [4906

Godbold, Albea. The church college of the old South. Durham, Duke University
Press [1944] 221 p. [4907

Goddard, Frederick Bartlett. Where to emigrate and why. Philadelphia, Peoples
Publishing Co., 1869. 591 p. [4908

Godfrey, James Logan, ed. The Graduate School dissertations and theses; ed. . . .
by James L. Godfrey, Fletcher M. Green [and] W. W. Pierson. Chapel Hill, University of North Carolina Press, 1947. 184 p. [4909

Godfrey, James Logan. Revolutionary justice; a study of the . . . Paris Tribunal,
1793-1795. Chapel Hill, University of North Carolina Press, 1951. (James
Sprunt studies in history and political science, v. 33) 166 p. [4910

Godfrey, Thomas. Juvenile poems on various subjects; with, The prince of Parthia,
a tragedy. Philadelphia, Printed by Henry Miller, 1765. 223 p. [4911
——The prince of Parthia. Boston, Little, Brown, and Co., 1917. 189 p. [4912

Goerch, Carl. Carolina chats. Raleigh, Edwards & Broughton Co., 1944. 403 p. [4913
——Characters . . . always characters. Raleigh, Edwards & Broughton Co., 1945.
296 p. [4914

——Down home. Raleigh, Edwards & Broughton Co., 1943. 375 p. [4915

——Just for the fun of it. Raleigh [Printed by Edwards & Broughton] 1954. 256 p. [4916

——Ocracoke. Raleigh, The Author, 1956. 223 p. [4917

Goff, George P. Nick Baba's last drink, and other sketches. Lancaster, Pa., Inquirer, 1879. 84 p. [4918

Gohdes, Clarence Louis Frank. American literature in nineteenth-century England. New York, Columbia University Press, 1944. 191 p. [4919

Gohdes, Clarence Louis Frank, ed. Faint clews & indirections; manuscripts of Walt Whitman and his family, ed. by Clarence Gohdes and Rollo G. Silver. Durham, Duke University Press, 1949. 250 p. [4920

——The periodicals of American transcendentalism. Durham, Duke University Press, 1931. 264 p. [4921

Gold, Daisy Hendley. It was forever. Philadelphia, Dorrance and Co. [c.1940] 281 p. [4922

——Tides of life. Wilson, P. D. Gold [1927?] 58 p. [4923

Gold, Pleasant Daniel. Gold generations in England and America. [Silver Spring, Md., 1946] 126 p. [4924

——History of Duval County, Florida. St. Augustine, Fla., The Record Co., 1928. 693 p. [4925

——In Florida's dawn. Jacksonville, Fla., H. & W. B. Drew Co., 1926. 411 p. [4926

——A treatise on the Book of Joshua. Wilson, Zion's Landmark Print, 1889. 173 p. [4927

Gold, Thomas J. Glimpses of Shelby, N. C. Shelby, Star, 1905. 25 p. [4928

Gold Star mother's day, November 11, 1949, Shelby, N. C. [Shelby, 1949] [3] p. [4929

Golden, Harry Lewis. Jewish roots in the Carolinas. [Charlotte, The Carolina Israelite] c.1955. 72 p. [4930

——Jews in American history . . . by Harry L. Golden and Martin Rywell. [Charlotte, H. L. Martin Co., 1950] 498 p. [4931

Goldsboro, N. C. Bank of Wayne. Facts of North Carolina history. Goldsboro, n.d. [18] p. [4932

Goldsboro, N. C. Board of Trustees of the Graded Schools. Report, 1888/89- Goldsboro, 1889- NcU has 1888/89, 1909/10 [4933

[**Goldsboro, N. C.** Chamber of Commerce] Goldsboro, the gate city of Eastern North Carolina. [Goldsboro, 1924?] 34 p. [4934

——Goldsboro, Wayne County, North Carolina. [Goldsboro, 1956] 22 p. [4935

——Visit Goldsboro, North Carolina, industrial & recreational center of Eastern North Carolina. [Goldsboro] n.d. Folder. [4936

Goldsboro, N. C. St. Stephen's Church. Eightieth anniversary history and church directory . . . 1933. [Goldsboro] 1933. [23] p. [4937

Goldsboro bulletin, v. 1, no. 1-4, Feb.-May, 1921. Goldsboro, City of Goldsboro, 1921. NcU has v. [1] and supplement. [4938

[**Goldsboro Centennial Commission, Inc.**] Goldsboro centennial celebration, 1847- 1947. [Goldsboro, 1947] 76 p. [4939

Goler, William H. The funeral sermon over the body of Rev. J. C. Price, D. D., President of Livingstone College . . . October 28, 1893. [Salisbury] Livingstone Press [1893] 15 p. [4940

Golterman, Guy. The book of the Presidents; a gallery of famous portraits. St. Louis, c.1953. 1 v. [4941

Gonecke, J. F. General Calvin Jones grand march. Philadelphia, G. Willig's Musical Magazine, n.d. [2] p. [4942

[**Gooch, Joseph Henry**] Brief history of the organization of Memorial Primitive Baptist Church, Stem, N. C., December 31, 1923. [Oxford, Oxford Orphanage] 1923. 26 p. [4943

Good Roads Association of Asheville and Buncombe County, N. C. Good roads bulletin, v. 1- 1900- Asheville, 1900- NcU has v. [1] [4944

——Constitution and report of work accomplished . . . October 1st, 1909. 2d ed. [Asheville?] 1912. 14 p. [4945

Good Roads Institute, Chapel Hill, N. C. Program of Road Institute, University of

North Carolina, Chapel Hill, N. C., February 23-27, 1915. [Chapel Hill, 1915]
[5] p. [4946
——. . . Road Institute, 191 - Chapel Hill, [1916- NcU has 1916, 1918 [4947
Goode, Walter Everett. The superlative Christianity of the crucified man. New
York, American Press [1956] 127 p. [4948
Goodloe, Daniel Reaves. The birth of the republic. Chicago, Belford, Clarke &
Co. [1889] 400 p. [4949
——Emancipation and the war; compensation essential to peace and civilization.
[Washington, 1861] 12 p. NcU has microfilm. [4950
Goodloe, Daniel Reaves, comp. Federalism unmasked. No place, no publisher
[1860?] 15 p. [4951
Goodloe, Daniel Reaves. A history of the demonetization of silver. Washington,
C. R. Gray, pr., 1890. 48 p. NcU has microfilm. [4952
——Information for the people; two tracts . . . "Negro slavery, no evil", by B. F.
Stringfellow . . . "Is it expedient to introduce slavery into Kansas", by D. R.
Goodloe. Boston, Alfred Mudge and Son, pr., for N. E. Emigrant Aid Co., 1855.
56 p. [4953
[Goodloe, Daniel Reaves?] Inquiry into the causes which have retarded the accumu-
lation of wealth and increase of population in the Southern States. Washington,
W. Blanchard, pr., 1846. 27 p. [4954
Goodloe, Daniel Reaves. Is it expedient to introduce slavery into Kansas? [Cincin-
nati, American Reform Tract and Book Society, 1854?] 24 p. [4955
——Letter to Hon. Charles Sumner, on the situation of affairs in North Carolina.
Raleigh, 1868. 16 p. [4956
[Goodloe, Daniel Reaves] The marshalship in North Carolina; being a reply to
charges made by . . . Senators and Representatives of the state. No place, no
publisher [pref. 1869] 12 p. [4957
——The South and the North; being a reply to a lecture . . . by Ellwood Fisher . . .
Cincinnati, January 16, 1849. Washington, Buell and Blanchard, pr., 1849.
32 p. [4958
Goodloe, Daniel Reaves. The southern platform. Boston, John P. Jewett & Co.,
1858. 79 p. [4959
——Synopsis of congressional legislation for a century. No place, no publisher,
n.d. 12 p. [4960
Goodman, Hattie S. The Knox family. Richmond, Whittet & Shepperson, 1905.
266 p. [4961
Goodman, John K., joint author, see Alexander, Samuel Caldwell
Goodrich, Charles Augustus. Lives of the signers to the Declaration of Inde-
pendence. New York, William Reed & Co., 1829. 460 p. [4962
—— ——Hartford, Huntington, 1841. 479 p. [4963
[Goodrich, Frances Louisa] Allanstand cottage industries. No place, no publisher
[1902] 7 p. [4964
Goodrich, Frances Louisa. Mountain homespun. New Haven, Yale University
Press, 1931. 91 p. [4965
——The story of the Allanstand cottage industries. [Asheville] n.d. [4] p. [4966
Goodwin, Adolph Oettinger. Who's who in Raleigh. Raleigh, Commercial Print-
ing Co., 1916. [140] p. [4967
Goodwin, Edwin McKee. The North Carolina Institution for the Deaf and Dumb
and the Blind, Raleigh, North Carolina, 1845-1893. [Raleigh, 1893] 9 p. [4968
Goodwin, Maud Wilder. White aprons; a romance of Bacon's rebellion, Virginia,
1676. Boston, Little, Brown and Co., 1896. 339 p. [4969
Goodwin, Philo A. Biography of Andrew Jackson. Hartford, Clapp and Benton,
1832. 422 p. [4970
Goodwyn, Albert Taylor. Address of General A. T. Goodwyn, commander-in-chief
of the United Confederate Veterans at their 39th reunion . . . Charlotte, N. C.,
June 5th, 1929. [Montgomery, Ala., Beers, 1929?] 22 p. [4971
Gordon, Caroline. Green centuries. New York, C. Scribner's Sons, 1941. 469 p. [4972
Gordon, Elizabeth Southall (Clarke) Gordon Biddle. Days of now and then.
Philadelphia, Dorrance & Co. [1945] 259 p. [4973

Gordon, George Henry. Speech delivered at Newburyport, Mass., Oct. 28, 1868. 16 p.   [4974

Gordon, Ian. After innocence [New York, Dell Publishing Co., 1955] 191 p. [4975

——The whip hand. New York, Crown Publishers [1954] 200 p.   [4976

Gordon, James & Co., Norfolk, Va. A letter from James Gordon & Co. . . . on direct trade between Europe and Norfolk. Norfolk, Va., C. W. Wilson and Co., 1873. 27 p.   [4977

Gordon, Jan. On wandering wheels, through roadside camps from Maine to Georgia, by Jan Gordon and Cora J. Gordon. New York, Dodd, Mead and Co., 1928. 336 p.   [4978

Gore, Daniel L. A review of political history in the state. [Wilmington? 1923?] [2] p.   [4979

[**Gorman, John C.**] Lee's last campaign, by Captain J. C. G. Raleigh, W. B. Smith & Co., 1866. 59 p.   [4980

[**Gorman, Maxwell J.**] Our Raleigh letter . . . the gubernatorial candidates. [Raleigh, 1900] 3 p.   [4981

Gorrell, Joseph Hendren. Indirect discourse in Anglo-Saxon. Baltimore, Modern Language Association of America, 1895. 144 p.   [4982

Gorrell, Ralph. Address to the farmers of Guilford, Feb. 19, 1852. Greensboro, Samuel W. James, pr., 1852. 26 p.   [4983

——Influence of educated men upon society; an address . . . before the two literary societies of Davidson College, on the 13th day of Aug. 1851. Greensborough, Printed by Swaim and Sherwood, 1851. 22 p.   [4984

Goshen Baptist Association. Minutes, 18 - 18 - NcU has [1828-1843]   [4985

Gospel messenger, devoted to the Primitive Baptist cause, v. 1-45, 1878-1923. Williamston, 1878-1923. NcU has v. [1-4] 7-9 [10] 11 [12] 13-15 [16-17] 18 [19] 20-23 [24] 27 [28] 29-45   [4986

Gosse, Edmund William. . . . Raleigh. New York, D. Appleton and Co., 1886. 248 p.   [4987

Gosse, Philip. The pirates' who's who. London, Dulau and Co., Ltd., 1924. 328 p.   [4988

[**Gould, Daniel?**] Reasons for not being a Baptist. Charlotte, Thomas J. Holton for Daniel Gould, 1834. 62 p.   [4989

Gould, Maggy. The dowry, a novel. New York, W. Morrow, 1949. 244 p. [4990

Govan, Gilbert Eaton. The Chattanooga country, 1540-1951 . . . by Gilbert E. Govan and James W. Livingood. New York, Dutton, 1952. 509 p.   [4991

Government. No place [T. A. F. in N. C.] n.d. 4 p.   [4992

Governmental guide, North Carolina edition, 19 - [Nashville, Tenn.] Carl Hardaway Boone, 19 - NcU has 1955, 1956   [4993

Gov. Jarvis says about Capt. S. A. Ashe's work in the white supremacy campaign of 1898. No place, no publisher [1908?] 2 p.   [4994

Gov. Kitchin's service to labor. No place, no publisher [1912?] [1] p. [4995

Gov. Vance's record. [Raleigh, Sentinel, 187?] 24 p.   [4996

Governor William Hawkins of the state of North Carolina. No place, Brant and Fuller, n.d. [1] p.   [4997

Gowen, Harry W. Story of the Right Worshipful Joseph Montfort, provincial grand master of Masons . . . from A. L. 5771 to A. L. 5776. [Halifax, The Author, c.1907] 24 p.   [4998

Grabs, William F. Memoir of William Samuel Schaub. Culler, Phillips the Printer, 1893. 31 p.   [4999

——Sunday school speeches for the young folks. Randleman, W. C. Phillips, pr., 1888. 119 p.   [5000

Grady, Benjamin. John Grady (1710-1787) of Dobbs and Duplin, with some of his descendants, by Benjamin Grady, assisted by Louis Carr Hendry. Wilson, P. D. Gold Publishing Co., 1930. 93 p.   [5001

[**Grady, Benjamin Franklin**] An agricultural catechism. Wilmington, Engelhard & Price, 1867. 40 p.   [5002

Grady, Benjamin Franklin. The burdens of the southern people. Revised and amended. [Clinton, The Author, 1913] 20 p. [5003
——The case of the South against the North; or, Historical evidence justifying the southern states of the American union in their long controversy with the northern states. Raleigh, Edwards & Broughton, 1899. 345 p. [5004
——Sectionalism and some of its fruits. Goldsboro, Nash Brothers, 1909. 40 p. [5005
——The South's burden; or, The curse of sectionalism in the United States. Goldsboro, Nash Brothers, pr., 1906. 147 p. [5006
Grady, Henry Alexander. Address at the first annual meeting of the Grady-Outlaw Historical Association at the B. F. Grady High School in Duplin County, N. C., August 29, 1930. No place, no publisher [1930?] 16 p. [5007
——Address at Moore's Creek Battle Ground, August 13, 1925, with original poem, entitled "Mary Slocumb's ride". No place, no publisher [1925?] [15] p. [5008
——The Mecklenburg Declaration of Independence of May 20, 1775, delivered before the New Hanover Bar Association, May 14, 1929. [Wilmington, Wilmington Stamp, pr., 1929?] [12] p. [5009
Grady, Robert Gibson. Sales tax. [Wilmington, The Author, 1928] 33 p. [5010
Graffenried, Thomas Pritchett de. History of the deGraffenried family from 1191 A. D. to 1925. [New York] The Author, 1925. 282 p. [5011
Graham, Alexander. Prologue, events forming background of Mecklenburg Declaration of Independence, May 20, 1775. Charlotte, Charlotte Chamber of Commerce, 1924. 14 p. [5012
[Graham, Annie Leo] ed. Souvenir, the General Assembly, 1927. [Raleigh? The Editor, 1927] 26 p. [5013
Graham, Augustus Washington. Mistakes of Captain Ashe in regard to change of views of Governor W. A. Graham as to date of Mecklenburg Declaration of Independence, and Governor Graham's real views set forth. [Raleigh, Mutual, pr., 1911] 8 p. [5014
——Retail Merchants' Association ask candidates for a show-down. [Oxford?] n.d. [1] p. [5015
Graham, Billy see Graham, William Franklin
Graham, Edward Kidder. Education and citizenship, and other papers. New York, G. P. Putnam's Sons, 1919. 253 p. [5016
——The function of the state university, being the proceedings of the inauguration of Edward Kidder Graham as president of the University of North Carolina. Chapel Hill, 1915. 100 p. [5017
Graham, Frank Porter. American aspects of the crisis in democracy; address at Williamstown Institute of Human Relations, August 28, 1935. [Chapel Hill, 1935] 9 p. [5018
——Cameron Morrison. [Charlotte, privately printed, 1956] 25 p. [5019
——Charles Brantley Aycock of North Carolina, the South's greatest educational governor. [Raleigh, 1951] 18 p. [5020
——Christian leadership and today's world, Frank P. Graham, John C. Schroeder; addresses to the National Council, Young Men's Christian Associations of the United States, Pittsburgh, Pennsylvania, October 25 and 26, 1940. [New York, Association Press, 1940?] 30 p. [5021
——Commencement Day address. [Chapel Hill] 1947. [5] p. [5022
——The faith and hope of an American. [New York, Spiral Press, 1952] [7] p. [5023
——The first university of the people in the peoples' war for the peoples' freedom and the peoples' peace [Chapel Hill, 1944. [11] p. [5024
——Letter dated 18 December 1951 to the Secretary-General transmitting his second report to the Security Council. [New York, United Nations, 1951] (United Nations. Security Council. General S/2448) 49 p. [5025
——The need for spiritual reenforcement of the United Nations in its quest for freedom and security in the atomic age; a lecture delivered under the auspices of The Walter J. Shepard Foundation, May 9, 1954. Columbus, The Foundation [1954] 15 p. [5026
——Should the War Labor Board prescribe maintenance of union membership for the duration? Speakers: Dr. Frank Graham . . . John A. Sellers. Columbus, O., American Education Press, Inc., 1944. (Town meeting, v. 10, no. 5) 23 p. [5027
——A statement of democratic principles in a time of crisis; excerpts from an address

on the occasion of the opening of the University, September 14, 1939. [Greensboro, North Carolina League for Progressive Democracy, 1939?] [3] p.   [5028
——A tribute to Chapel Hill. [Chapel Hill] n.d. [1] p.   [5029
——The University and national defense; convocation address delivered in Chapel Hill on September 27, 1940, opening the 147th session of the University. [Chapel Hill, General Alumni Association, 1940] (Alumni review, supplement, October, 1940) 8 p.   [5030
——The University and the press. [Chapel Hill, 1926] 7 p.   [5031
——The University today; inaugural address at the University of North Carolina, November 11, 1931. [Chapel Hill, 1931] 12 p.   [5032

Graham, George Washington. The Mecklenburg Declaration of Independence, May 20, 1775, and lives of its signers. New York, Neale Publishing Co., 1905. 205 p.   [5033
——Why North Carolinians believe in the Mecklenburg Declaration of Independence of May 20th, 1775. 2d ed., rev. and enl. Charlotte, Queen City Printing and Paper Co., 1895. 43 p.   [5034

Graham, Henry Tucker. Some things for which the South did not fight in the war between the states. No place, no publisher, n.d. 12 p.   [5035

Graham, Ian Charles Cargill. Colonists from Scotland; emigration to North America, 1707-1783. Ithaca, N. Y., Published for the American Historical Association [by] Cornell University Press [1956] 213 p.   [5036

Graham, James, 1793-1851. Circular to the citizens of the twelfth congressional district of North Carolina. Rutherfordton, Carolina Gazette Office, 1837. 7 p.   [5037
—— ——March 15, 1839. [Washington, 1839] 16 p.   [5038
——Circular to the people of the twelfth congressional district in North Carolina. [Washington, March 4, 1843] 28 p.   [5039

[**Graham, James**] 1793-1851. To the freemen of the twelfth congressional district in North Carolina [Washington, 1835] 3 p.   [5040

Graham, James, 1793-1851. To the freemen of the twelfth congressional district of North Carolina. [Washington, 1840] 8 p.   [5041

[**Graham, James**] 1793-1851. To the freemen of the twelfth congressional district of North Carolina. [Washington, July 4, 1842] 8 p.   [5042

Graham, James, fl. 1858. The life of General Daniel Morgan, of the Virginia line of the army of the United States, with portions of his correspondence. New York, Derby & Jackson, 1858. 475 p.   [5043

Graham, James Augustus. The James A. Graham papers, 1861-1884, edited by H. M. Wagstaff. Chapel Hill, University of North Carolina Press, 1928. (James Sprunt historical studies, v. 20, no. 2) 324 p.   [5044

Graham, John Washington. Presentation of the Murphey portrait to the Supreme Court of North Carolina. [Raleigh? 1908] 14 p.   [5045
——Some events in my life; address before the North Carolina Bar Association, session 1918. [No place, no publisher, 1918?] 21 p.   [5046
——To the voters of the 4th congressional district. No place, n.d. [1] p.   [5047

Graham, Joseph. North Carolina centennial celebration of the Mecklenburg Declaration of Independence: Programme. [Charlotte] 1875. [1] p.   [5048

Graham, Matthew John. The Ninth Regiment, New York Volunteers (Hawkins' Zouaves) being a history of the regiment and veteran association from 1860 to 1900. New York [E. P. Coby & Co.] 1900. 634 p.   [5049

Graham, Samuel L. Revivals of religion; a sermon preached before the Synod of North Carolina, at Hillsborough, N. C., October 15, 1831. Hillsborough, Dennis Heartt, 1832. 20 p.   [5050

Graham, William Alexander, 1804-1875. Address delivered before the two literary societies of the University of North Carolina, June 6, 1849. Raleigh, Seaton Gales, 1849. 16 p.   [5051
——The address on the Mecklenburg Declaration of Independence of the 20th of May, 1775; delivered at Charlotte, on the 4th day of Feb'y, 1875, by request of the citizens of Mecklenburg County; with accompanying documents. New York, E. J. Hale & Son, 1875. 167 p.   [5052
——Discourse in memory of the life and character of the Hon. Geo. E. Badger, de-

livered . . . at Raleigh, July 19th, 1866.   Raleigh, Nichols, Gorman & Neathery, pr., 1866.   34 p.   [5053
——Life and character of Gen. Nathaniel Greene, with an epitome of North Carolina's services in the Revolutionary War; an address delivered at Greensboro, N. C., December, 1860.   Lincolnton, Journal Printing Co., 1901.   26 p.   [5054
——Life and character of the Hon. Thomas Ruffin, late chief justice of North Carolina; a memorial oration, delivered before the Agricultural Society of the state, by its request, at the annual fair in Raleigh, Oct. 21st, 1870.   Raleigh, Nichols & Gorman, pr., 1871.   34 p.   [5055
——Speech . . . delivered in Tucker Hall, Raleigh, N. C., on being called to preside over the Conservative State Convention of N. C., February 5, 1868.   Raleigh, Sentinel, 1868.   19 p.   [5056
Graham, William Alexander, 1839-1923.   General Joseph Graham and his papers on North Carolina Revolutionary history; with appendix: An epitome of North Carolina's military services in the Revolutionary war and of the laws enacted for raising troops.   Raleigh, Published for the Author, by Edwards & Broughton, 1904. 385 p.   [5057
——General William Lee Davidson; an address delivered at the unveiling of a monument to General Davidson, voted by Congress, at the Guilford Battle Ground, July 4th, 1906.   Greensboro, Guilford Battle Ground Co., 1906.   31 p.   [5058
——History of the South Fork Baptist Association.   Lincolnton, Journal Printing Co., 1899.   27 p.   [5059
——The history of the South Fork Baptist Association; or, The Baptists for one hundred years in Lincoln, Catawba, and Gaston counties, North Carolina.   Lincolnton, Journal Printing Co., 1901.   196 p.   [5060
——Memorial of Wm. A. Graham, trustee of the State Business Agency Fund, W. H. Worth, the state business agent, and W. S. Barnes, secretary and treasurer of the Farmer's State Alliance of North Carolina, to the Senate of North Carolina and its Committee on Agriculture.   [Raleigh? 1893?]   4 p.   [5061
Graham, William Archibald.   Abilities of pupils in the public elementary schools, Kinston, North Carolina, October, 1931.   Kinston, 1931.   21 p.   [5062
Graham, William Franklin.   Peace with God.   Garden City, N. Y., Doubleday, 1953.   222 p.   [5063
—— ——New York, Permabooks [1955]   248 p.   [5064
——The secret of happiness; Jesus' teaching on happiness as expressed in the Beatitudes.   Garden City, N. Y., Doubleday, 1955.   117 p.   [5065
——The 7 deadly sins.   Grand Rapids, Mich., Zondervan Publishing House [c.1955] 113 p.   [5066
Graham, N. C. Presbyterian Church.   Manual.   [Graham? n.d.]   14 p.   [5067
Graham Collegiate Institute, Marshallberg, N. C.   Catalogue, 19 - Marshallberg, 19 - NcU has 1901/02, 1902/03, 1904/05   [5068
Graham Institute, Graham, N. C.   Circular.   [Graham?] n.d.   [1] p.   [5069
Gramley, Dale Hartzler.   Where are we now?   An address.   Winston-Salem, Winston-Salem Traffic Club, 1950.   [9] p.   [5070
Grand Army of the Republic. Department of Virginia and North Carolina.   Roster, 18 - No place, 18 - NcU has 1894   [5071
Grand Camp Confederate Veterans. Department of Virginia. History Committee.   Official report . . . by Hon. Geo. L. Christian, chairman . . . North Carolina and Virginia in the Civil War.   [Richmond, 1904]   26 p.   [5072
Grand Lodge of North Carolina see Freemasons. North Carolina. Grand Lodge
Grandfather Orphans' Home, proposed addition to Lees-McRae Institute.   Charlotte, Presbyterian Standard Publishing Co., n.d.   [1] p.   [5073
Grandma, pseud., see Parker, Annie (Moore)
Grandy, Moses.   Narrative of the life of Moses Grandy, late a slave in the United States of America.   London, C. Gilpin, 1843.   72 p.   [5074
—— ——2d American from the last London ed.   Boston, Oliver Johnson, 1844. 45 p.   [5075
Granite Falls, N. C. Superintendent of Schools.   The policies of administration, Granite Falls Public Schools.   New and revised ed.   Granite Falls, 1930.   57 p. [5076
Grant, Daniel Lindsey, comp.   Alumni history of the University of North Carolina.   Chapel Hill [General Alumni Association] 1924.   950 p.   [5077

Grant, Daniel Lindsey. Handbook of alumni work, the University of North Carolina. [Chapel Hill] Central Alumni Office of the General Alumni Association [c.1925]   205 p.   [5078

Grant, Dorothy (Fremont)   Devil's food, a novel.   New York, Longmans, Green, 1949.   282 p.   [5079

——John England, American Christopher.   Milwaukee, Bruce Publishing Co. [1949] 167 p.   [5080

Grant, H. L.   The present development and future possibilities of Washington, North Carolina, setting forth the commercial, industrial and other advantages of Washington, North Carolina, and her environments. [Greensboro, Jos. J. Stone and Co.] n.d.   52 p.   [5081

[Grant, Hiram L.]   G. A. R.   General Meade Post no. 39, Department of Virginia and North Carolina, Raleigh, N. C., Commander C. H. Beine. [Raleigh? 1908] 16 p.   "Memorial address . . . by Hiram L. Grant".   [5082

Grant, James.   Address of the Hon. James Grant, of Davenport, Iowa, to the alumni of the University of N. C. at Chapel Hill, on the 6th of June, 1878.   Raleigh, Edwards, Broughton & Co., 1878.   29 p.   [5083

Grantham, George Kenneth.   When did Mr. Bailey become the friend of the farmer? His record discussed.   Dunn, The Author, 1924.   [3] p.   [5084

Grantham, Katherine E.   Principles of the drama uncovered by the Greeks.   Chapel Hill, Department of Philosophy, 1929.   (University of North Carolina Studies in philosophy, no. 3)   53 p.   [5085

Granville, John Carteret, earl.   Devisees.   Charge of Judge Potter in the suit of the devisees of the Earl Granville against Josiah Collins in the Circuit Court of the United States, December term, 1805.   Raleigh, J. Gales [1806?]   16 p.   [5086

Granville, Roger.   The history of the Granville family, traced back to Rollo, first duke of Normandy, with pedigrees, etc.   Exeter, W. Pollard & Co., 1895. 489 p.   [5087

[Granville Co., N. C. Board of Education]   A la française. [Oxford] n.d. [1] p.   [5088

——Condition of Granville County Public Schools . . . July 1, 1926.   Oxford, Board of Education of Granville County, 1926.   14 p.   [5089

——Special taxation for schools.   Oxford [1908?]   [8] p.   [5090

Granville Co., N. C. Democratic Executive Committee.   Democratic county convention!   Monday, October 1!   Oxford, Ledger Print, n.d.   [1] p.   [5091

Granville Co., N. C. Schools. Country Life Club.   Constitution and by-laws . . . prepared by Mary G. Shotwell.   Oxford, Oxford Orphanage, pr., n.d.   15 p. [5092

Granville Grays, Oxford, N. C.   Constitution and by-laws, approved February, 1885.   Oxford, Orphan Asylum Printing Office, 1885.   16 p.   [5093

Granville Institute, Oxford, N. C.   Catalogue, 18 - Oxford, 18 - NcU has 1893/94   [5094

Graphic sketches from old and authentic works, illustrating the costume, habits, and character of the aborigines of America; together with rare and curious fragments relating to the discovery and settlement of the country. [pt. 1]   New York, J. and H. G. Langley, 1841.   15 [22] 24 plates.   The John White drawings.   [5095

Grass Roots Opera Company, Raleigh, N. C.   Leaves from Grass Roots Opera, an American heritage born in Raleigh. [Raleigh, 1952?]   [22] p.   [5096

Grasty, John S.   A discourse on the death of General Zachary Taylor, delivered at Yanceyville, N. C., July 24th, 1850.   Danville, Va., Register Office, 1850. 16 p.   [5097

——Memoir of Rev. Samuel B. McPheeters . . . with an introduction by Rev. Stuart Robinson.   St. Louis, Southwestern Book and Publishing Co., 1871. 384 p.   [5098

Graves, Charles M.   Master plan for recreation, city of Greensboro, North Carolina, July, 1951, prepared for the Greensboro Council of Social Agencies, the City Council of Greensboro, the Park and Recreation Commission. Atlanta [1915] 178 p. [5099

Graves, Ernest.   The line man's Bible; a foot-ball text book of detailed instruction. [New York, Book Publishers Press] c.1921.   158 p.   [5100

Graves, James Robinson.   The great iron wheel; or, Republicanism backwards and

Christianity reversed. 11th ed. Nashville, Graves, Marks, and Rutland, 1856. 570 p. [5101

Graves, Louis. North Carolina progressive. [Pinehurst? Pinehurst, Inc., 1924] 23 p. [5102

[Graves, Ralph Henry] Ten days, a crisis in American history, by George Grey [pseud.] New York, Duffield and Green [c.1933] 58 p. [5103

Graves, Ralph Henry. The triumph of an idea, the story of Henry Ford. Garden City, N. Y., Doubleday, Doran & Co., Inc., 1934. 184 p. [5104

Graves, William Brooke. Uniform state action; a possible substitute for centralization. Chapel Hill, University of North Carolina Press, 1934. 368 p. [5105

Gravier, Gabriel. Les voyages de Giovanni Verrazano sur les côtes d'Amerique avec des marins normands, pour le compte du roi de France en 1524-1528. Rouen, E. Cagniard, 1898. 32 p. [5106

Gray, Alexander. To the free citizens of Rowan, Chatham, & Randolph. Salisbury, Coupee and Crider, 1813. [1] p. [5107

Gray, Mrs. E. A., comp. Handbook for the Woman's Foreign Missionary Society of the M. E. Church, South. [Nashville, Tenn.? M. E. Church, South?] n.d. 40 p. [5108

Gray, Edna. One woman's life, the steppings of faith; Edna Gray's story. Atlanta, Ga., Franklin Printing and Publishing Co., 1898. 335 p. [5109
—— ——Rev. ed. 1900. 352 p. [5110
—— ——1903. [5111
——Thoughts when a sightless invalid; a story in verse of an eventful life. Atlanta Ga., Mutual Printing Co., 1898. 24 p. [5112

Gray, Elizabeth Janet. Jane Hope. New York, Viking Press, 1933. 276 p. [5113
——Meggy MacIntosh. Garden City, N. Y., Doubleday, Doran & Co., Inc., 1930. 274 p. [5114
——Women in the Society of Friends. Guilford College, 1955. (Guilford College. Ward lecture, Nov. 11, 1955) 23 p. [5115

Gray, Gordon. Founder's Day address, delivered at the 118th anniversary celebration of Guilford College on November 10, 1954. No place [1954] 10 p. [5116
——The inauguration of Gordon Gray as President of the Consolidated University of North Carolina. [Chapel Hill, University of North Carolina, 1954] 95 p. [5117
——President Gordon Gray's Inaugural address. [Chapel Hill] University News Bureau [1950] 14 p. [5118

Gray, Idyl Dial, ed. Azure-lure, a romance of the mountains. Asheville, Advocate Publishing Co. [c.1924] 400 p. [5119

Gray, Robert Terelius. A statement concerning the municipal indebtedness of the city of Raleigh, N. C., and other matters relating thereto. Raleigh, E. M. Uzzell, pr., 1889. 27 p. [5120

Gray Memorial Botanical Association. Bulletin, v. 1-6, March, 1933-May, 1939. Fayetteville, H. A. Rankin, 1933-1939. NcU has v. 1-6. Moved to Marietta, Ohio, October, 1940. [5121

Gray's Creek Baptist Association. Minutes, 18 - 18 - NcU has 1879 [5122

[Great Bridge Lumber and Canal Co.] The Great Bridge Lumber and Canal Company. [Norfolk? 1855] 16 p. [5123

Great Britain. Court of King's Bench. Cases determined in the Court of King's Bench, during the I, II, & III years of Charles I. [1624-1627] Collected by John Latch . . . Tr. into the English language by François-Xavier Martin. Newbern, From the Translator's Press, 1793. 275 (i. e. 215) [20] p. [5124

Great Britain. Sovereigns, etc., 1603-1625 (James I) A proclamation declaring His Maiesties pleasure concerning Sir Walter Rawleigh, and those who adventured with him. London, Bonham Norton and Iohn Bill, pr., 1618. [1] p. NcU has photostát. [5125

Great Britain. Sovereigns, etc., 1625-1649 (Charles I) By the King: A proclamation for setling the Plantation of Virginia; with an introduction by Thomas Cary Johnson, Jr. · Charlottesville, Va., Tracy W. McGregor Library, University of Virginia, 1946. 39 p. [5126

Great Britain. Sovereigns, etc., 1727-1760 (George II) Instructions given with letters of marque against France. [Kensington, High Court of Admiralty, 1756] 8 p. NcU has photostat.   [5127

Great Britain. Sovereigns, etc., 1760-1820 (George III) By authority: Charlestown, March 26, 1781 [London] R. Wells & Son, pr., 1781. [1] p. NcU has photostat. [5128

The great destroyer. Put the liquor traffic out. No place, no publisher, n.d. [1] p.   [5129

Great improvement in the administration of county affairs. No place [People's Party of North Carolina, 1900?] 2 p.   [5130

Great services to the state and party, Simmons. No place, no publisher, n.d. [4] p.   [5131

Great Smoky Mountains Conservation Association, Knoxville, Tenn. Great Smoky Mountains. Knoxville, Tenn. [1925?] [28] p.   [5132

Great Smoky Mountains, Inc., Asheville, N. C. Save our mountains. [Asheville, 1925?] 7 p.   [5133

The Great Smoky Mountains National Park. Knoxville, Tenn., J. L. Caton, c.1937. [29] p.   [5134

The Great Smoky Mountains National Park, Tennessee and North Carolina. Knoxville, Tenn., Great Smoky Mountains Publishing Co., Inc., c.1928. [80] p. [5135

Greater Charlotte Club, Charlotte, N. C. Charlotte, North Carolina. Charlotte, The Greater Charlotte Club, 1913. [64] p.   [5136

——Introducing Charlotte, Queen City of the Carolinas. [Charlotte, Queen City Printing Co., 1921?] 3 p.   [5137

Greater Western North Carolina Association. Greater Western North Carolina. [Asheville, Inland Press, 1913?] 119 p.   [5138

——Information to visitors concerning Western North Carolina. [Asheville, Inland Press] 1913. 83 p.   [5139

Greeley and Brown Club of North Carolina. Constitution. Raleigh, Sentinel Book and Job Print, 1872. 4 p.   [5140

Green, Ashbel, joint author, see Willison, John

Green, Charles Sylvester. B. W. Spilman, the Sunday school man. Nashville, Broadman Press [1953] 154 p.   [5141

Green, Charles Sylvester, ed. General Julian S. Carr, greathearted citizen. Durham, Seeman Printery, 1946. 114 p.   [5142

Green, Charlotte (Hilton) Birds of the South; permanent and winter birds commonly found in gardens, fields, and woods. Chapel Hill, University of North Carolina Press [c.1933] 277 p.   [5143

——Trees of the South. Chapel Hill, University of North Carolina Press, 1939. 551 p.   [5144

Green, Elizabeth (Lay) Balanced diet; a one-act comedy. New York, Samuel French [c.1928] 31 p.   [5145

Green, Erma. Fixin's; the tragedy of a tenant farm woman, by Erma and Paul Green. New York, S. French [c.1934] 40 p.   [5146

Green, Fletcher Melvin, ed. The Chapel Hill Methodist Church; a centennial history, 1853-1953. Chapel Hill, 1954. 66 p.   [5147

Green, Fletcher Melvin. Constitutional development in the South Atlantic states, 1776-1860. Chapel Hill, University of North Carolina Press, 1930. 328 p. [5148

Green, Fletcher Melvin, ed. The Lides go south; the record of a planter migration in 1835. Columbia, University of South Carolina Press, 1952. 51 p.   [5149

Green, Fletcher Melvin. A style book for theses and dissertations. Chapel Hill, Department of History, University of North Carolina, 1954. 14 p.   [5150

——Writing and research in southern history; address delivered before the annual meeting of the South Carolina Historical Association, held in Charleston, South Carolina, April 18, 1942. Spartanburg, S. C., Band and White, pr. [1942] 16 p. [5151

Green, Fletcher Melvin, joint editor, see Godfrey, James Logan, ed.

Green, Grace E. The pilgrim from the hills- a biography of Lucius Bunyan Compton. [Asheville? Eliada Home of Children? 1952?] 210 p.   [5152

Green, John Paterson. Fact stranger than fiction; seventy five years of a busy life. Cleveland, O., Riehl Printing Co., 1920. 368 p.   [5153

[Green, John Paterson] Recollections of the inhabitants, localities, superstitions and Kuklux outrages of the Carolinas, by a "carpet-bagger" who was born and lived there. [Cleveland? O.] 1880. 205 p. [5154

[Green, John Pugh] Essays on miscellaneous subjects, by a self-educated colored youth. Cleveland, O., Nevins' Steam Printing House, 1866. 48 p. [5155

Green, Paul. Challenge to citizenship. [Chapel Hill] Alpha Chapter of Phi Beta Kappa, 1956. 24 p. [5156
——Christmas prayer. Chapel Hill [Author, 1943?] [1] p. [5157
——The common glory, a symphonic drama of American history, with music, commentary, English folksong and dance. Chapel Hill, University of North Carolina Press [1948] 273 p. [5158
——The common glory song book, songs, hymns, dances and other music from Paul Green's symphonic drama "The common glory" composed, compiled, and collected with additional lyrics by Paul Green, edited by Adeline McCall. New York, Carl Fischer, c.1951. 47 p. [5159
——The critical year; a one-act sketch of American history and the beginning of the Constitution. New York, S. French, c.1939. 40 p. [5160
——Dog on the sun, a volume of stories. Chapel Hill, University of North Carolina Press [1949] 178 p. [5161
——Dramatic heritage. New York, S. French [1953] 177 p. [5162
——The enchanted maze; the story of a modern student in dramatic form. New York, S. French, 1939. 126 p. [5163
——The field god and In Abraham's bosom. New York, Robert M. McBride Co., 1927. 317 p. [5164
——Forever growing; some notes on a credo for teachers. Chapel Hill, University of North Carolina Press [1945] 42 p. [5165
——Franklin and the King, historical play in one act. New York, Dramatists Play Service, Inc. [c.1939] 29 p. [5166
——The Free Company presents . . . A start in life [New York, The Free Company, c.1941] 23 p. [5167
——The hawthorn tree; some papers and letters on life and the theatre. Chapel Hill, University of North Carolina Press [1943] 157 p. [5168
——The Highland call; a symphonic play of American history in two acts, with hymn tunes, folksongs, ballads, and dance. Chapel Hill, University of North Carolina Press, 1941. 280 p. [5169
——The house of Connelly, and other plays: The house of Connelly; Potter's field; Tread the green grass. New York, S. French, 1931. 308 p. [5170
——The house of Connelly, at the Martin Beck Theatre. [New York, New York Theatre Program Corporation, 1931] 24 p. Program. [5171
——Hymn to the rising sun; a play in one act. New York, Samuel French [c.1936] 36 p. [5172
——Ibsen's Peer Gynt. American version. New York, Samuel French [c.1951] 167 p. [5173
——In Abrahams Schoss, die Lebensgeschichte eines Negers in sieben Scenen, autorisierte deutsche übertragung aus dem englishchen von Elisabeth Loos. Berlin, Oesterheld & Co., c.1929. 98 p. [5174
——In the valley, and other Carolina plays. New York, S. French, 1928. 308 p. [5175
——Johnny Johnson; the biography of a common man, in three acts; music by Kurt Weill. New York, S. French, 1937. 175 p. [5176
——The last of the Lowries; a play of the Croatan outlaws of Robeson County, North Carolina. New York, Samuel French [c.1925] p. 233-264 [5177
——The laughing pioneer. New York, Robert M. McBride, 1932. 282 p. [5178
——Lonesome road; six plays for the Negro theatre, with an introduction by Barrett H. Clark. New York, Robert M. McBride and Co., 1926. 217 p. [5179
——The Lord's will, a tragedy of a country preacher; play in one act. New York, Samuel French [c.1925] 45 p. [5180
——The Lord's will and other Carolina plays . . . with a foreword by Frederick H. Koch. New York, Henry Holt, 1925. 264 p. [5181
——The lost colony; an outdoor play in two acts (with music, pantomime, and dance) Chapel Hill, University of North Carolina Press, 1937. 138 p. [5182
——The lost colony; a symphonic drama in two acts (with music, pantomime, and dance) Chapel Hill, University of North Carolina Press [1939] 138 p. [5183
—— ——1946. 202 p. [5184

——The lost colony; a symphonic drama of American history.   Roanoke Island ed.
Chapel Hill, University of North Carolina Press, 1954.   70 p.   [5185
——The lost colony song-book; songs, hymns, dances, and other music from the play
. . . special music by Lamar Stringfield, additional settings by Lamar Stringfield
and Adeline McCall.   New York, Carl Fischer, Inc., c.1939.   39 p.   [5186
——. . . The lost colony, Wednesday, August 23, 1939, 9:00-10:00 P.M. EDST,
broadcast from Roanoke Island, N. C. [New York?] Columbia Broadcasting
System, 1939.   59 p.   [5187
——The man who died at twelve o'clock; a Negro comedy in one act. New York,
Samuel French, c.1927.   18 p.   [5188
——Native son (the biography of a young American) a play in ten scenes by Paul
Green and Richard Wright, from the novel by Richard Wright.   New York,
Harper & Brothers [c.1941]   148 p.   [5188a
——The no 'count boy; play in one act.   New York Samuel French [c.1928]   p. 177-
202   [5189
——The no 'count boy; a one-act comedy of American country life.   New York,
Samuel French [c.1953]   29 p.   [5190
——On looking into Horace Williams, gadfly of Chapel Hill, by Robert Watson
Winston. [Chapel Hill, privately printed, 1943]   6 p.   [5191
——Out of the South, the life of a people in dramatic form.   New York, Harper &
Brothers, 1939.   577 p.   [5192
——Preface for professors (from a talk at graduating time) [Chapel Hill, 1942]
15 p.   [5193
——Provincetown playbill . . . In Abraham's bosom. [New York, Provincetown
Playhouse, 1927]   4 p.   Program.   [5194
——Roll sweet chariot; a symphonic play of the Negro people, in four scenes. New
York, S. French, 1935.   107 p.   [5195
——Salvation on a string, and other tales of the South.   New York, Harper &
Brothers [1946]   278 p.   [5196
——Shroud my body down, a play in four scenes; with four rubber-cuts by Richard
Gates.   Iowa City, Clio Press, 1935.   203 p.   [5197
——Song in the wilderness, cantata for chorus and orchestra, with baritone solo;
poem by Paul Green, music by Charles Vardell.   Chapel Hill, University of North
Carolina Press, 1947.   79 p.   [5198
——The southern cross; a play in one act.   New York, S. French, Inc., c.1938.
42 p.   Includes music.   [5199
——This body the earth.   New York, Harper & Brothers, 1935.   422 p.   [5200
——This declaration; a play in one act.   New York, Samuel French, Inc. [c.1954]
18 p.   [5201
——The vocal score of Johnny Johnson; play by Paul Green, music by Kurt Weill.
New York, S. French, Inc., c.1940.   94 p.   [5202
——White dresses, drama in one act.   New York, S. French, Inc., c.1935.   25 p. [5203
——Wide fields.   New York, Robert M. McBride & Co., 1928.   380 p.   [5204
——Wilderness Road; a symphonic outdoor drama.   New York, Samuel French
[1956]   166 p.   [5205

Green, Paul, joint author, see Green, Erma

Green, Thomas Jefferson.   Journal of the Texian expedition against Mier.   New-
York, Harper & Brothers, 1845.   487 p.   [5206
—— ——Austin, Tex., Steck Co., 1935.   487 p.   A facsimile reproduction. [5207

Green, Wharton Jackson.   Recollections and reflections; an auto of half a century
and more. [Raleigh] Edwards and Broughton Printing Co., 1906.   349 p. [5208
[**Green, Wharton Jackson**]   Tokay vineyard, near Fayetteville, N. C.; with essay on
grape-culture. [Boston, Rand, Avery and Co., 188?]   37 p.   [5209

Green, William F.   Address delivered before the students of Morning Star Institute,
Nashville, N. C., May 29, 1857.   Raleigh, Holden & Wilson, pr., 1857.   22 p. [5210
——Sketch of the history and resources of Franklin County, prepared for North
Carolina State Exposition.   Franklinton, Franklinton Weekly, 1884.   10 p. [5211

Green, William Mercer.   Address delivered before the Board of Trustees, August 2,
1880. [Sewanee, Tenn., University of the South, 1880?]   16 p.   [5212
[**Green, William Mercer**]   Bishop Ravenscroft.   No place, no publisher [1870?]
28 p.   [5213
Green, William Mercer.   The divine origin and unbroken transmission of ministerial

authority; a sermon preached in St. Andrew's Church, Jackson, Miss., February 8th, 1852. 2d ed. Philadelphia, H. Hooker, 1853. 32 p. [5214

——The influence of Christianity upon the welfare of nations; an oration delivered at Chapel Hill, on Wednesday, June 22, 1831. Hillsborough, Dennis Heartt, 1831. 32 p. [5215

——Memoir of the Rt. Rev. James Hervey Otey, the first bishop of Tennessee. New York, James Pott and Co., 1885. 359 p. [5216

Green Park Hotel, Blowing Rock, N. C. Green Park, Blowing Rock, N. C. New York, South Publishing Co., n.d. 15 p. [5217

——Green Park Hotel, Green Park, North Carolina. [Louisville, Ky., F. C. Nunemacher Press] n.d. [6] p. [5218

——The Green Park, Green Park, Watauga County, N. C., is the place to go. Charlotte, Blakey Printing House [1891?] 12 p. [5219

Green River Baptist Association. A century of growth in the Green River and Sandy Run Baptist associations of North Carolina, celebrating the centennial anniversary . . . Spindale, N. C., Thursday, April 11, 1940. No place [1940] 8 p. [5220

——Minutes, 1840?- 1840?- NcU has [1854-1872] 1876-1898 [1899-1952] [5221

Greene, Caro Mae. The universal-individual relation (Crowned with the Mildred Williams Buchan prize) Chapel Hill, University of North Carolina, 1925. 10 p. [5222

Greene, Evarts Boutell. American population before the federal census of 1790. New York, Columbia University Press, 1932. 228 p. [5223

Greene, Francis Vinton. General Greene. New York, D. Appleton and Co., 1893. 332 p. [5224

Greene, George Washington. The life of Nathanael Greene, major-general in the army of the Revolution. New York, G. P. Putnam and Son, 1867-71. 3 v. [5225

——Nathanael Greene, an examination of some statements concerning Major-General Greene, in the ninth volume of Bancroft's History of the United States. Boston, Tichnor and Fields, 1866. 86 p. [5226

Greene, Henry F. Pastoral address to the parishioners of Christ Church, Newbern, N. C. [Chicago? Author, 1855] 6 p. [5227

Greene, Ivery C. A disastrous flood, a true and fascinating story. [Richmond, William Byrd Press, Inc., c.1941] 103 p. [5228

Greene, Nathanael. Letters by and to Gen. Nathanael Greene, with some to his wife. New York, George H. Richmond, 1906. 39 p. A calendar of papers offered for sale by George H. Richmond. [5229

Greene, Talbot. American nights' entertainments, compiled from pencilings of a United States senator: entitled, A winter in the Federal city. Jonesborough, Tenn., W. A. Sparks & Co., pr., 1860. 266 p. [5230

Greene, Ward. Cora Potts; a pilgrim's progress. New York, J. Cape and H. Smith [c.1929] 270 p. [5231

——Death in the deep South; a novel about murder. New York, Stackpole Sons [c.1936] 283 p. [5232

Greene, Ward, ed. Star reporters and 34 of their stories. New York, Random House [1948] 402 p. [5233

Greene, Ward. Weep no more. New York, Harrison Smith, 1932. 311 p. [5234

Greene, Wilhelmina F. Flowers of the South, native and exotic, by Wilhelmina F. Greene and Hugo L. Blomquist. Chapel Hill, University of North Carolina Press [1953] 208 p. [5235

Greene County school news, v. 1- February, 1924- Snow Hill, 1924- NcU has v. [1-2] [5236

Greeneville, Tenn. Andrew Johnson Woman's Club. From tailor shop to the White House. [Greenville, Tenn., 1928?] [24] p. [5237

Greenlaw, Edwin Almiron, ed. Builders of democracy. Chicago, Scott, Foresman and Co. [c.1918] 347 p. [5238

——The great tradition . . . by Edwin Greenlaw and James Holly Hanford. Chicago, Scott, Foresman and Co. [c.1919] 679 p. [5239

——Knickerbocker's History of New York (Books III-VII) by Washington Irving. New York, Macmillan, 1923. 288 p. [5240

——Literature and life . . . by Edwin Greenlaw, William H. Elson, and Christine M. Keck. Chicago, Scott, Foresman and Co. [c.1922-24]   4 v.   [5241

Greenlaw, Edwin Almiron. An outline of the literature of the English Renaissance. Chicago, B. H. Sanborn & Co., 1916. 136 p.   [5242

Greenlaw, Edwin Almiron, ed. Selections from Chaucer. Chicago, Scott, Foresman and Co. [1907?]   316 p.   [5243

Greenlaw, Edwin Almiron. A syllabus of English literature. Chicago, Benj. H. Sanborn & Co., 1923. 319 p.   [5244

Greensboro, N. C. Asheboro Street Friends Meeting. A survey of Asheboro Street Friends Meeting. Greensboro, 1927. 16 p.   [5245

Greensboro, N. C. Bank of Guilford. Charter and by-laws, January 1st, 1889. [Greensboro? 1889?]   17 p.   [5246

Greensboro, N. C. Biggs Hygienic Sanitarium. The Biggs treatment. Greensboro, n.d. 34 p.   [5247

Greensboro, N. C. Board of Aldermen. Charter and ordinances of the city of Greensboro, North Carolina. [Greensboro?] 1906. 192 p.   [5248

——Charter and ordinances of the city of Greensboro, compiled . . . by John S. Michaux, esq. Greensboro, Reece & Elam, pr., 1894. 223 p.   [5249

Greensboro, N. C. Board of Commissioners. City tax ordinance. [Greensboro? 1912]   15 p.   [5250

——Code of the city of Greensboro . . . compiled by A. W. Cooke. [Greensboro] 1912. 290 p.   [5251

——Ordinances of the city of Greensboro, adopted . . . June 1st, 1873. Greensboro, Patriot, pr., 1873. 15 p.   [5252

[**Greensboro, N. C. Board of Education**] Bulletin and outlines of primary work [by] Janet McKenzie, Supervisor. [Greensboro] n.d. 29 p.   [5253

Greensboro, N. C. Central Carolina Fair see **Central Carolina Fair, Greensboro, N. C.**

Greensboro, N. C. Chamber of Commerce. Album of Greensboro, N. C. No place, n.d. 43 p.   [5254

——The battle-ground oak, Revolutionary battlefield, March 15th, 1781. [Greensboro] n.d. [10] p.   [5255

——City government by commission. [Greensboro?] n.d. 65 p.   [5256

[**Greensboro, N. C. Chamber of Commerce**] Exhibit submitted jointly by city of Greensboro, N. C., city of High Point, N. C., Guilford County, N. C., to Civil Aeronautics Board. [Greensboro] 1944. 55 p.   [5257

Greensboro, N. C. Chamber of Commerce. Facts and figures about Greensboro, North Carolina. Greensboro, 1956. 15 p.   [5258

——General Nathanael Greene speaks. Greensboro, 1928. 4 p.   [5259

——Greensboro and 50 mile area . . . the South's most important market. [Greensboro, 1945] [7] p.   [5260

——Greensboro, master key to the South's best markets. [Greensboro, 1924?] 16 p.   [5261

——Greensboro, North Carolina. [Greensboro, 1907?]   14 p.   [5262

—— ——1911. [24] p.   [5263

—— ——[1921?] [3] p.   [5264

—— ——[1938] Folder.   [5265

—— ——[1941?] Folder.   [5266

—— ——[1943] Folder.   [5267

——Greensboro steps to the forefront in effective schools and colleges. Greensboro, 1928. 14 p.   [5268

——Guilford County, N. C. [Greensboro, 1921?] [2] p.   [5269

——Industries in Greensboro, North Carolina. Greensboro, 1956. [24] p.   [5270

——Report, 1887/88- Greensboro, 1889- NcU has 1887/88   [5271

Greensboro, N. C. Chamber of Commerce. Commercial Development Bureau. A survey of the Greensboro retail trading area . . . conducted by David S. Lindeman. Greensboro, 1933. 61 p.   [5272

Greensboro, N. C. Chamber of Commerce. Transportation Committee. Report . . . January 15, 1908, on freight rates. [Greensboro, 1908] 9 p.   [5273

Greensboro, N. C. City Council. Budget, 19 - Greensboro, 19 - NcU has 1955/56 [5274

——City of Greensboro plumbing code, adopted . . . September 7, 1948. [Greensboro, 1948] 65 p. [5275

——City of Greensboro, North Carolina, revised proposal for refunding bonds and bond anticipation notes, June 29, 1933. Greensboro, 1933. 26 p. [5276

——The code of the city of Greensboro . . . compiled and revised by Robert Moseley. [Greensboro] 1930. 693 p. [5277

——The code of the city of Greensboro. Charlottesville, Va., Michie Co., 1941. 785 p. [5278

——Municipal activities . . . report of the city manager, 1911/12- [Greensboro, 1912- NcU has 1911/12, 1939/40, 1940/41, 1941-1952 (in one) [5279

Greensboro, N. C. Eclectic Literary Club. Constitution and by-laws, as amended and adopted, January 21st, A.D. 1870. Greensboro, Patriot Office, 1870. 8 p. [5280

Greensboro, N. C. First Presbyterian Church. Action taken upon the resignation of their pastor, Rev. Egbert W. Smith, D. D., 1893-1905. [Greensboro, 1905?] 18 p. [5281

——Directory . . . with a brief sketch of its history. [Greensboro?] 1906. 45 p. [5282

—— ——1909. 39 p. [5283

Greensboro, N. C. Geodetic, Topographic and Block Survey. Report. Toledo, O., R. H. Randall and Co., 1926. 125 p. [5284

Greensboro, N. C. Juvenile Commission. Report, 192 - Greensboro, 192 - NcU has 1930/31, 4th [5285

[Greensboro, N. C. Library Club] Union list of periodicals in the libraries of Greensboro Public Library, Greensboro College, Guilford College, and Woman's College of the University of North Carolina [Greensboro] 1945. 38 p. [5286

Greensboro, N. C. Parent-Teacher Association. Directory, 1919/20- Greensboro [1919- NcU has 1919/20, 1920/21 [5287

Greensboro, N. C. Planning and Zoning Commission. Thoroughfares for Greensboro. [Greensboro, 1948] 12 p. [5288

Greensboro, N. C. Presbyterian Church of the Covenant. Brief history . . . twenty-fifth anniversary, May 17, 1931. [Greensboro] 1931. 16 p. [5289

——Presbyterian Church of the Covenant, 35th anniversary. [Greensboro? 1941] [8] p. [5290

Greensboro, N. C. Public Library. Directory of clubs and organizations in Greensboro, 19 - Greensboro, 19 - NcU has Fall, 1952, Fall, 1953, Fall, 1954, September, 1955, September, 1956 [5291

Greensboro, N. C. Security National Bank. Statement, 19 - 19 - NcU has 1945-1956 [5292

Greensboro, N. C. Socialist Party. City Socialist platform, Greensboro, N. C., 1909. [Greensboro, 1909] 4 p. [5293

Greensboro, N. C. Southern Loan and Trust Co. Southern Loan and Trust Co., Greensboro, N. C. [Greensboro? 1904?] 6 p. [5294

Greensboro, N. C. Washington Street Baptist Church. Membership, manual, and directory, 1900. [Greensboro? 1900?] 12 p. [5295

Greensboro, N. C. West End Hose Company no. 5. Constitution and by-laws. [Greensboro, 1909?] 21 p. [5296

Greensboro, N. C. West Market Street Methodist Episcopal Church, South. West Market Street Methodist Episcopal Church, South, a history. Greensboro, 1934. 29 p. [5297

Greensboro, N. C. Young Men's Christian Association see Young Men's Christian Association. Greensboro, N. C.

Greensboro, North Carolina. [Greensboro? 1932?] 16 p. [5298

Greensboro, N. C. directory, 1903-1904- Richmond, Va., Hill Directory Co., 1903- NcU has 1933, 1935, 1943, 1947-48, 1951-52 [5299

Greensboro Bar Association. The Greensboro bar. [Greensboro] 1939. 63 p. [5300

Greensboro Bar Association. Committee on Legislation. A bill providing for the conferring of civil jurisdiction on the Municipal Court of the City of Greensboro. [Greensboro, 1930?] 11 p. [5301

Greensboro Bible Training School, Greensboro, N. C.   Catalogue, 190 - Greensboro, 190 - NcU has 1907/08   [5302
Greensboro College, Greensboro, N. C.   Bulletin, v. 1- July, 1913- Greensboro, 1913- NcU has v. 1-5 [6-14] 15-22 [23-36] 37-39 [40].   Called Greensboro Female College, 1838-1912, Greensboro College for Women, 1913-1919   [5303
——Catalogue, 18 - Greensboro, 18 - 1913.   NcU has 1846/47, 1857/58-1858/59 [1860/61-1899-1900] 1901/02-1902/03, 1905/06-1912/13.   Continues as its Bulletin, 1913-   [5304
Greensboro Community Chest, Inc.   Annual meeting, 193 - Greensboro, 193 - NcU has 1951   [5305
Greensboro Conference on Children and Youth, November 2-4, 1949.   [Papers] Greensboro, 1949.   Various paging.   [5306
Greensboro Female College   see Greensboro College
Greensborough: its population, schools, health, &c.   [Greensborough, 1846?] 8 p.   [5307
Greensborough Mutual Insurance Co.   Circular, by-laws, and act of incorporation. Greensboro', Patriot, 1851.   30 p.   [5308
Greensville and Roanoke Railroad.   Report, 18 - No place, 18 - NcU has 1854/55   [5309
——Report to auditor, 18 - Petersburg, Va., 18 - NcU has 1847/48   [5310
Greenville, N. C.   Board of Aldermen.   Charter and code of the City of Greenville, North Carolina, 1949.   Charlottesville, Va., Michie City Publications Co., 1949. 283 p.   [5311
——An ordinance to regulate the use of the sewage system.   Raleigh, Edwards and Broughton, pr., 1907.   13 p.   [5312
——Ordinances of the town of Greenville, North Carolina, adopted August 9, 1904. Raleigh, Edwards and Broughton, pr. [1904?]   73 p.   [5313
Greenville, N. C.   Board of Trustees of Public Schools.   Report, 190 - Greenville, 190 - NcU has 1914/15-1915/16   [5314
Greenville, N. C.   Chamber of Commerce.   Greenville, North Carolina.   [Greenville, 1940?]   4 p.   [5315
——Greenville, Pitt County, North Carolina.   [Raleigh, 1944]   [7] p.   [5316
Greenville, N. C.   city directory, 192 - Asheville, Commercial Service Co., 192 - NcU has 1926-27   [5317
Greenville and French Broad Railroad Co.   Memorial to the South Carolina Legislature.   No place [185?]   8 p.   [5318
——Report on the survey.   No place, 1859.   16 p.   [5319
Greenville and French Broad Railroad.   Engineer.   Chief Engineer's Report of the late survey from Butt Mountain Gap to Spartanburg.   Asheville, July 29, 1874. No place [1874?]   4 p.   [5320
——Report of the survey from Greenville, S. C. to Butt Mountain Gap, N. C. Greenville, S. C., July 24, 1874.   No place [1874?]   [1] p.   [5321
Greenwood, Bernard.   The dealings of God with a laborer.   Raleigh, Edwards, Broughton and Co., 1884.   222 p.   [5322
Greer, Guy.   Your city tomorrow.   New York, Macmillan Co., 1947.   210 p. [5323
Greer, Louise.   Browning and America.   Chapel Hill, University of North Carolina Press [1952]   355 p.   [5324
[Gregg, Alexander]   An appeal of southern bishops in behalf of St. Augustine's Normal School, Raleigh, N. C.   [Philadelphia, Church of the Holy Trinity, 1883] 3 p.   [5325
Gregory, Margaret (Overman)   Fifty years of service: history of the National Society, Daughters of the American Revolution of North Carolina.   New Bern, Owen G. Dunn Co., pr., 1950.   164 p.   [5326
——Forty years of service.   No place [1940?]   44 p.   [5327
[Gregory, Nelle Haynes]   History of St. Mark's Episcopal Church, Halifax, N. C., 1855-1955.   [Halifax, 1955]   [4] p.   [5328
[Gregory, W. O.]   Stonewall Jackson.   No place, no publisher, n.d.   8 p.   [5329
Grellet, Stephen.   Memoirs of the life and gospel labors of Stephen Grellet.   Philadelphia, Friends' Book Store [1890]   916 p.   [5330

Gretter, John A. The power to forgive. Fayetteville, Presbyterian Office, 1859. 32 p.   [5331

Grey, George, pseud., see **Graves, Ralph Henry**

Grier, M. B. Sermon to young men, delivered in the Presbyterian Church, Wilmington, N. C., November 17th, 1854. Wilmington, Herald, 1855. 13 p. [5332

Griffin, Clarence. The Bechtlers and Bechtler coinage, and Gold mining in North Carolina, 1814-1830. Forest City, Forest City Courier, 1929. 15 p.   [5333
——The beginning of the press in North Carolina. Forest City, Author [1951?] [10] p.   [5334
——Centennial history of Pleasant Grove Methodist Church, 1838-1938. [Forest City] Pleasant Grove Centennial Committee [1938]   20 p.   [5335
——Descendants of Chisolm Griffin. Spindale, C. Griffin, 1931.   163 leaves   [5336
——Essays on North Carolina history. Forest City, Forest City Courier, 1951. 284 p.   [5337
——History of old Tryon and Rutherford counties, North Carolina, 1730-1936. Asheville, Miller Printing Co., 1937.   640 p.   [5338
——History of Rutherford County, 1937-1951. Asheville, Inland Press, 1952. 136 p.   [5339
——Public officials of Rutherford County, N. C., 1779-1934. Forest City, Forest City Courier, 1934.   41 p.   [5340
——Revolutionary service of Col. John Walker and family, and Memoirs of Hon. Felix Walker. Forest City, Forest City Courier, 1930.   23 p.   [5341
——Semi-centennial history of First Methodist Church, Forest City, North Carolina, 1889 . . . 1939. Forest City, Semi-Centennial Committee [1939]   16 p.   [5342
——Western North Carolina sketches. Forest City, Forest City Courier, 1941. 96 p.   [5343

Griffin, Clarence, joint author see **Allen, William Cicero**

Griffin, J. C. "Hell"; or, Endless punishment of the wicked. New Bern [Author] n.d.   26 p.   [5344

Griffin, Margarette Glenn, see **Williams, Ruth Smith**

Griffin, T. N. Biographical sketch of the Kerns family of Mecklenburg County, North Carolina. Huntersville, 1927-1928.   15 p.   [5345

Griffith, Andrew. What it was was football. [Chapel Hill, Bentley Music Company, c.1953]   [2] p.   [5346

Griffith, John. Journal of the life, travels, and labours in the work of the ministry of John Griffith. Philadelphia, Joseph Crukshank, 1780.   426 p.   [5347

Grime, William. A sermon preached at All Saints Church, Great Neck, New York, on Sunday morning, December 15th, 1929, at the memorial service to the late Rev. Kirkland Huske. No place, no publisher [1929?]   15 p.   [5348

[Grimes, Alston] Grimesland, Pitt County, N. C. [by Alston and J. Bryan Grimes] [Grimesland, 1907]   [5] p.   [5349

Grimes, Bryan. Extracts of letter to his wife, written while in active service in the Army of Northern Virgina . . . compiled from original manuscripts by Pulaski Cowper. Raleigh, Edwards, Broughton & Co., 1883.   137 p.   [5350
——————Raleigh, A. Williams & Co., 1884.   134 p.   [5351

Grimes, Green. A secret worth knowing, a treatise on insanity. New York, William H. Graham, 1847.   92 p.   [5352

Grimes, John Bryan. Agricultural resources and opportunities of the South. No place, no publisher [1905?]   19 p.   [5353
——Judge Shepherd and his vindication. [Grimesland, August 13, 1888]   4 p. [5354
——A peace protectorate for Mexico, letter to William Jennings Bryan, secretary of state. [Raleigh] no publisher [1914]   7 p.   [5355
——Resolution introduced in the Farmers' National Congress for the establishment of a parcels post. [No place, n.d.]   [1] p.   [5356
——Unveiling of the Virginia-North Carolina Monument and Wyatt Memorial, at Bethel, Virginia, June 10, 1905, speech by J. Bryan Grimes. No place, no publisher, n.d.   10 p.   [5357

Grimes, John Bryan, joint author, see **Grimes, Alston**

Grimes Real Estate Co., Washington, N. C. Coastal plain region of North Carolina. [Washington, 1899?]   24 p.   [5358

——Eastern North Carolina as a home for farmers and investors. Washington, N. C., Grimes Real Estate Co. [1899] 8 p.   [5359
——Washington, North Carolina, some of its advantages as a home for investors. [Washington] n.d. 3 p.   [5360
Grimm Brown Stone and Improvement Co., Raleigh, N. C. Prospectus . . . office, Raleigh, N. C., quarries, near Carthage, Moore County, N. C. Raleigh, Edwards, Broughton & Co., 1891. 33 p.   [5361
Grissom, Eugene. Address delivered before the Masonic fraternity and the public at Wilmington, N. C., on St. John's day, December 27th, 1881. Oxford, Orphans' Friend, pr., 1882. 22 p.   [5362
——Mania transitoria, read before the Medical Society of North Carolina at its meeting in Fayetteville, N. C., May 4th, 1876. Raleigh, Edwards, Broughton & Co., 1876. 48 p.   [5363
——Mechanical protection for the violent insane. No place, no publisher, n.d. 32 p.   [5364
——Medical science in conflict with materialism, address delivered before the Medical Society of North Carolina, May 13th, 1880. Wilmington, Jackson & Bell, pr., 1880. 31 p.   [5365
——Medical hygiene for pupil and teacher, a lecture delivered before the Normal School at Chapel Hill, North Carolina, August 4, 1877. Raleigh, John Nichols, 1877. 36 p.   [5366
——Proceedings of the Alumni Society of the Medical Department of the University of Pennsylvania for 1885, with the annual address of Eugene Grissom, delivered March 24, 1885. Philadelphia, Matlack & Harvey, pr., 1885. 29 p.   [5367
Grissom, William Lee. History of Methodism in Davie County. [Farmington, no publisher, 1890] 53 p.   [5368
——History of Methodism in North Carolina from 1772 to the present time . . . Volume 1, from the introduction of Methodism in North Carolina to the year 1805. Nashville, Tenn., M. E. Church, South, 1905. 373 p. No more published. [5369
Groome, Pinckney Lafayette. Rambles of a southerner in three continents. Greensboro, Thomas Brothers, pr., 1889. 345 p.   [5370
—— ——1891. 335 p.   [5371
Grove, William Barry. Letters, edited by Henry McGilbert Wagstaff. Chapel Hill, University of North Carolina, 1910. (The James Sprunt Historical Publications, v. 9, no. 2) [45]-88 p.   [5372
Grove Academy, Kenansville, N. C. Bulletin, 19 - Raleigh, 19 - NcU has [1907/08] and one issue without date.   [5373
Grove Institute, Kenansville, N. C. Catalogue, 191 - 191 - NcU has 1919/20 [5374
Grove Park Inn, Sunset Mountain, Asheville, North Carolina. [Asheville, Inland Press] n.d. [22] p.   [5375
Grove Park Inn, the finest resort hotel in the world. [Asheville, 1913] 14 p. [5376
——[Asheville?] n.d. 15 p.   [5377
Grove Park School, Asheville, N. C. Catalogue, 19 - Asheville, 19 - NcU has [1922/23-1926/27]   [5378
Groves, Catherine. Get more out of life. New York, Association Press, 1941. 136 p.   [5379
Groves, Ernest Rutherford. The American family. Chicago, J. B. Lippincott Co. [c.1934] 500 p.   [5380
——American marriage and family relationships, by Ernest Rutherford Groves . . . and William Fielding Ogburn. New York, H. Holt and Co. [c.1928] 497 p. [5381
——The American woman. New York, Greenberg [c.1937] 438 p.   [5382
——Case book of marriage problems. New York, H. Holt and Co., c.1941. 40 p. [5383
——Christianity and the family. New York, Macmillan Co., 1942. 229 p.   [5384
——Conserving marriage and the family. New York, Macmillan Co., 1944. 138 p.   [5385
——The family and its relationships, by Ernest R. Groves . . . Edna L. Skinner . . . [and] Sadie J. Swenson. Chicago, J. B. Lippincott Co. [c.1932] 321 p. [5386
—— ——[c.1941] 583 p.   [5387
——The family and its social functions. Chicago, J. B. Lippincott Co. [c.1940] 631 p.   [5388

——Introduction to mental hygiene, by Ernest R. Groves . . . and Phyllis Blanchard. New York, H. Holt and Co. [c.1930] 467 p. [5389

——An introduction to sociology. New York, Longmans, Green and Co., 1928. 568 p. [5390

—— ——New rev. ed. New York, Longmans, Green and Co., 1932. 741 p. [5391

——An introduction to sociology, by Ernest R. Groves and Harry Estill Moore. New York, Longmans, Green and Co. 1941. 737 p. [5392

——Marriage. New York, H. Holt and Co. [c.1933] 552 p. [5393

—— ——Revised ed. New York, H. Holt and Co. [c.1941] 671 p. [5394

——The marriage crisis. New York, Longmans, Green and Co., 1928. 242 p. [5395

——Parents and children, by Ernest R. Groves . . . and Gladys Hoagland Groves. Philadelphia, J. B. Lippincott Co. [c.1928] 196 p. [5396

——Personality and social adjustment. New ed., rev. New York, Longmans, Green and Co., 1931. 353 p. [5397

——Preparation for marriage. New York, Greenberg [c.1936] 124 p. [5398

Groves, Ernest Rutherford, ed. Readings in mental hygiene, edited by Ernest R. Groves . . . and Phyllis Blanchard. New York, H. Holt and Co. [c.1936] 596 p. [5399

——Readings in the family, by Ernest R. Groves and Lee M. Brooks. Chicago, J. B. Lippincott Co. [c.1934] 526 p. [5400

Groves, Ernest Rutherford. Sex fulfillment in marriage, by Ernest R. Groves . . . Gladys Hoagland Groves . . . [and] Catherine Groves. New York, Emerson Books, Inc. [c.1943] 1947. 319 p. [5401

——Sex in childhood, by Ernest R. Groves and Gladys Hoagland Groves. New York, Macaulay Co. [c.1933] 247 p. [5402

——Sex in marriage, by Ernest R. Groves and Gladys Hoagland Groves. New York, Macaulay Co., 1931. 250 p. [5403

——The sociologic aspects of marriage conservation . . . presented before the American Congress on Obstetrics and Gynecology, Cleveland, Ohio, September 11-15, 1939. No place, no publisher, n.d. 7 p. [5404

——Sociology, by Ernest R. Groves. Philadelphia, J. B. Lippincott Co., 1931. 160 p. [5405

——Understanding yourself. New York, Emerson Books, Inc. [c.1941] 279 p. [5406

——Wholesome childhood, by Ernest R. Groves . . . and Gladys Hoagland Groves. Boston, Houghton Mifflin Co., 1924. 183 p. [5407

—— ——1927. 239 p. [5408

—— ——1931. 201 p. [5409

——Wholesome parenthood, by Ernest R. Groves and Gladys Hoagland Groves. Boston, Houghton Mifflin Co., 1929. 320 p. [5410

Groves, Gladys (Hoagland) Marriage and family life. New York, Henry Holt and Co. [1946, c.1942] 564 p. [5411

Groves, Gladys (Hoagland) joint author, see Groves, Ernest Rutherford

Groves, Joseph Asbury. The Alstons and Allstons of North and South Carolina. Atlanta, Ga., Franklin Printing and Publishing Co., 1901. 554 p. [5412

Gudger, Owen. A small bit of history. No place [1956] 13 p. [5413

Guerrant, Edward O. Galax gathers, the gospel among the highlanders. Richmond, Va., Onward Press [c.1910] 216 p. [5414

Guerrant, Edward O., 1911- Roosevelt's good neighbor policy. Albuquerque, University of New Mexico Press, 1950. (Its Inter-Americana studies, 5) 235 p. [5415

[Guess, William Conrad] County government in colonial North Carolina . Chapel Hill, The University, 1911. (James Sprunt historical publications, v. 11, no. 1) 39 p. [5416

Guide book of N. W. North Carolina, containing historical sketches of the Moravians in North Carolina, a description of the country and its industrial pursuits. Salem, L. V. & E. T. Blum, 1878. 109 p. [5417

Guide to North Carolina's periodical literature, v. 1- 1946- Winston-Salem, Winston-Salem Teachers College, c.1946- NcU has 1946-1949 [5418

Guilford Battle Ground Co., Greensboro, N. C. Addresses of Hon. Chas. B. Aycock and R. F. Beasley, esq., on the occasion of the unveiling of the colonial column and the monument to Captain James Morehead, at Guilford Battle Ground, July 4, 1901. Greensboro, 1901. 17 p. [5419

——Charters and amendments, by-laws and ordinances, collated May 5th, 1891. [Greensboro? 1891] 9 p. [5420

—— ——collated August 1, 1906, by Jos. M. Morehead, president. [Greensboro, 1906] 12 p. [5421

——Extracts from the Memorial volumes of the Guilford Battle Ground Company. Greensboro, 1894. 17 p. [5422

——Meeting of the stockholders, 18 - [Greensboro, 18 - NcU has 1891 [5423

——Memorial volume. Greensboro, Reece & Elam, pr., 1893. 142 p. [5424

——Report of the President, 1887- Greensboro, 1887- NcU has 1887, 1888, 1904, 1907, 1908 [5425

[Guilford Battle Sesqui-Centennial Commission] Battle of Guilford Court House Sesqui-Centennial celebration, July 4th, 1931. [Greensboro, 1931] [10] p. [5426

Guilford College, Guilford College, N. C. Bulletin, v. 1- 1908- Guilford College, 1908- NcU has v. 1-5 [6-13] 14-47 [5427

——Catalogue, 18 - Guilford College, 18 - NcU has 1867/68, 1871-72-1881/82, 1884/85-1898/99 [1900/01-1907/08] Continues, 1908- as Guilford College. Bulletin [5428

[Guilford College, Guilford College, N. C.] Personality in education. [Guilford College] n.d. 14 p. [5429

Guilford College, Guilford College, N. C. Girls Aid Committee. Girls aid report, 1889-1915. Guilford College [1915] 8 p. [5430

Guilford College, Guilford College, N. C. Y. M. C. A. Students' hand-book, 189 - Guilford College, 189 - NcU has 1893/94 [5431

Guilford collegian, v. 1-26, 1888-1914. Guilford College, Literary Societies, 1888-1914. NcU has v. [1-3] 4-12 [13] 14-15 [16] 17-19 [20] 21-22 [23-26] [5432

Guilford Co., N. C. Board of Education. Handbook for Guilford County teachers, 1927-1928. [Greensboro? 1927] 36 p. [5433

——Progress of public education in Guilford County, North Carolina, 1902-1905. [Greensboro, 1905] 11 p. [5434

Guilford Co., N. C. Board of Health. Special babies bulletin. [Greensboro] n.d. 7 p. [5435

Guilford Co., N. C. Domestic Relations Court. Court receiving home needs of Guilford County. [Greensboro?] 1956. 2, 15 p. [5436

Guilford County Literary and Historical Association. Constitution. [Greensboro] n.d. 8 p. [5437

——Publications, v. 1, 1908. Greensboro, 1908. NcU has v. 1. No more published. [5438

Guilford Land Agency. Facts for capitalists and parties desirous to settle in North Carolina. Lynchburg, Va., Johnson & Schaffter, pr., 1867. 12 p. [5439

Guilford Nurseries and Fruit Farm. Descriptive catalogue of select fruits and fruit and ornamental trees, flowering plants, etc. Greensboro, Thomas, Reece & Co., 1884. 50 p. [5440

Guilford Pomological Gardens and Nurseries. Catalogue of fruit trees, grape vines, strawberries, etc. Greensboro, Patriot Office, 1855. 15 p. [5441

[Guion, Haywood Williams] The comet; or, The earth in her varied phases . . . by Non Quis? New York, E. J. Hale & Son, 1869. 547 p. [5442

Guirey, William. The pattern in the mount, the substance of a sermon delivered in the state house of North Carolina, Aug. 10, 1806, on the ordination of James Lockhart. 2d ed. Raleigh, Members of the Christian Church, 1808. 35 p. [5443

Gulledge, Virginia (Wooten) The North Carolina Conference for Social Service. [Chapel Hill] North Carolina Conference for Social Service, 1942. 75 p. [5444

Gulliver, Lucile. Daniel Boone. New York, Macmillan Co., 1924. 244 p. [5445

Gunn, William H. Cotton factories, an address delivered in the Court House at Hertford, N. C., February 28, 1880. No place, no publisher, [1880?] [4] p. [5446

Gustin, Margaret. Activities in the public school, by Margaret Gustin . . . and Margaret L. Hayes. Chapel Hill, University of North Carolina Press, 1934. 290 p. [5447

Guthrie, Laurence Rawlin. American Guthrie and allied families. Chambersburg, Pa., Kerr Printing Co. [c.1933] 743 p. [5448

[Guthrie, William Anderson] McDuffie's discovery of the natural causes for the variations of the magnetic needle of the compass. Durham, Seeman Printery, 1910. 36 p. [5449

[Guthrie, William Anderson] Opinion of a lawyer on the constitutionality of the proposed amendment to the constitution of North Carolina. [Durham? Author? 1899] 15 p. [5450

Guthrie, William Anderson. Supplemental address to the People's Party voters of North Carolina. Raleigh, Author, 1896. [1] p. [5451

Gwathmey, John Hastings. Fly-fishing in the South. Richmond, Va., Dietz Press, 1942. 74 p. [5452

Gwynn, John Minor. Curriculum principles & social trends. New York, Macmillan Co., 1943. 630 p. [5453

Gwynn, Price Henderson. The freedom of the individual. Chapel Hill, University of North Carolina, 1913. (Its Worth prize theses. 1913) 15 p. [5454
——Leadership in the local church. Philadelphia, Cooperative Association by the Westminster Press [1952] 157 p. [5455

Gwynn, Walter. Report of Walter Gwynn, chief engineer of the Blue Ridge Railroad Company in South Carolina to a meeting of stockholders, held in Charleston, the 22d Nov. 1856. Charleston, S. C., Walker, Evans and Co., pr., 1856. 32 p. [5456
——Report to the President and Directors of the Portsmouth and Roanoke Railroad Company. Norfolk, T. G. Broughton, pr., 1833. 10 p. [5457

Habel, Samuel Tilden. All the way, Choo Choo, a sermon. Chapel Hill, The Wayside Pulpit, 1949. 11 p. [5458
——Baptists stand for freedom! [Chapel Hill, Author, 1952] 20 p. [5459
——Centennial monograph celebrating the first hundred years of the Baptist Church at Chapel Hill. Chapel Hill, 1954. 58 p. [5460
——The difference that matters, a sermon. [Chapel Hill, 1949] 12 p. [5461
——Enter Jesus, a sermon. [Chapel Hill, 1949?] 11 p. [5462
——On honesty, a sermon. [Chapel Hill, 1949?] 12 p. [5463
——Stand up and be counted! [Chapel Hill, 1951?] 17 p. [5464
——The twelve Apostles. Ft. Lauderdale, Fla., Creighton's Restaurant Corp. [c.1956] 156 p. [5465

Hackett, Frank Warren. Flusser and the Albemarle. [Washington, 1899] (Military Order of the Loyal Legion of the United States. Commandery of the District of Columbia. War papers, 31) 23 p. [5466

Hackney, J. D. The New Testament on baptism. No place, no publisher, n.d. 8 p. [5467

Haddock's Wilmington, N. C. directory and general advertiser . . . compiled by T. M. Haddock. Wilmington, P. Heinsberger, 1871. 263 p. [5468

Hader, Robert John. Introduction to statistics for engineers. [Raleigh] North Carolina State College, 1956. Various paging [5469

Hadley, Chalmers. Notes on the Quaker family of Hadley. [Denver, Carson-Harper Co.] 1916. 59 p. [5470

Hadley, John Vestal. Seven months a prisoner, or, Thirty-six days in the woods . . . by an Indiana soldier. Indianapolis, J. M. & F. J. Meikel, 1868. 180 p. [5471

Hagood, Margaret Jarman. Mothers of the South; portraiture of the white tenant farm woman. Chapel Hill, University of North Carolina Press, 1939. 252 p. [5472
——Statistics for sociologists. New York, Reynal and Hitchcock, Inc., 1941. 934 p. [5473

Hahn, George W. The Catawba soldier of the Civil War. Hickory, Clay Printing Co., 1911. 385 p. [5474

[Haines, Zenas T.] Letters from the Forty-Fourth Regiment M. V. M., a record of the experience of a nine months' regiment in the Department of North Carolina in 1862-3. By "Corporal" [pseud.] Boston, Herald Job Office, pr., 1863. 121 p. [5475

Hairston, Elizabeth Seawell (Hairston) The Hairstons and Penns and their relations. Roanoke, Va. [Walters Printing and Manufacturing Co.] 1940. 193 p. [5476

Hakluyt, Richard. A discourse concerning western planting written in the year 1584. Cambridge [Mass.] J. Wilson and Son, 1877. (Collections of the Maine Historical Society, 2d ser. [v. 2]) 253 p. [5477

——Heroes from Hakluyt, edited by Charles J. Finger. New York, Henry Holt Co. [c.1928]   331 p.   [5478

——The principall navigations, voiages and discoveries of the English nation. London, George Bishop and Ralph Newberie, 1589.   825 (i.e. 822) p.   [5479

——The principal navigations, voyages, traffiques & discoveries of the English nation.   Glasgow, J. MacLehose and Sons, 1903-1905.   12 v.   [5480

—— ——London, J. M. Dent & Sons, New York, E. P. Dutton & Co., 1927-28.   10 v.   [5481

——Voyages of the Elizabethan seamen to America.   Oxford, Clarenden Press, 1893.   272 p.   [5482

——Voyages of the Elizabethan seamen to America; select narratives from the 'Principal navigations' of Hakluyt, ed. by Edward John Payne.   2d series . . . 2d ed.   Oxford, Clarendon Press, 1900.   298 p.   [5483

——The voyages of the English nation to America.   Collected by Richard Hakluyt, preacher, and edited by Edmund Goldsmid.   Edinburg, E. & G. Goldsmid, 1889-90.   4 v.   [5484

Hale, Edward Everett, ed.   Original documents, from the State-Paper Office, London, and the British Museum, illustrating the history of Sir Walter Raleigh's first American colony, and the colony at Jamestown; with an appendix containing a memoir of Sir Ralph Lane, the governor of the colony of Roanoke.   [Worcester, Mass.]   American Antiquarian Society, 1860.   (Its Archaeologia americana. Transactions and collection, v. 4)   65 p.   [5485

Hale, Edward Jones.   Republican and Democratic national platforms compared. [Raleigh, E. M. Uzzell & Co., pr., 1908]   8 p.   [5486

[Hale, Edward Jones]   Short sketch of the life of Major E. J. Hale, issued by the Fayetteville Committee, Oct. 1, 1910. [Fayetteville] no publisher [1910]   8 p. [5487

Hale, Edward Joseph.   History of the canalization of the Cape Fear River, being a compilation of pertinent publications in the Fayetteville observer from 1900 to 1915.   [Fayetteville] Judge Printing Co., 1917.   86 p.   [5488

——How to prevent freight discriminations against North Carolina, paper read before the convention of the North Carolina Press Association, at Charlotte, N. C. Apr. 23, 1908.   No place, no publisher [1908?]   10 p.   [5489

——Improvement of the Cape Fear River.   Fayetteville, Chamber of Commerce, 1907.   15 p.   [5490

——Improvement of the upper Cape Fear River, brief, January, 1910.   Fayetteville?] no publisher [1910]   3 p.   [5491

——To the North Carolina delegation in Congress.   Fayetteville, E. J. Hale, 1920. 49 p.   [5492

——Unveiling of the Wyatt statue, Raleigh, June 10, 1912, address.   Fayetteville, Judge Printing Co., 1912.   16 p.   [5493

[Hale, James W.]   An historical account of the Siamese twin brothers, from actual observations.   New York, Elliot and Palmer, pr., 1831.   16 p.   [5494

—— ——3d ed.   [5495

Hale, John Peter.   Daniel Boone.   Wheeling, L. Baker & Co., pr., n.d.   18 p. [5496

Hale, Peter Mallett, ed.   In the coal and iron counties of North Carolina.   Raleigh P. M. Hale, 1883.   425 p.   [5497

——The woods and timbers of North Carolina.   Raleigh, P. M. Hale, 1883. 272 p.   [5498

Haliburton, Margaret Winifred.   The Haliburton primer.   Boston, D. C. Heath, 1911.   131 p.   [5499

——Teaching poetry in the grades, by Margaret W. Haliburton . . . and Agnes G. Smith.   Boston, Houghton Mifflin Co. [c.1911]   167 p.   [5500

Halifax Co., N. C. Bar.   Minimum fees.   No place, n.d.   [1] p.   [5501

Halifax Co., N. C. Board of Education.   Halifax County teachers' handbook, 1926-1927.   [Oxford, Oxford Orphanage, pr., 1926?]   83 p.   [5502

——Handbook of the Halifax County Public Schools, 1927-1928.   No place [1927?] 39 p.   [5503

[Hall, Allen A.]   The counterfeit detector; or, The leaders of "The Party" exposed. [Nashville, Tenn., Republican Banner Office, 1839]   48 p.   [5504

Hall, Alonzo C.   Outlines of English literature, by Alonzo C. Hall and Leonard B. Hurley.   Boston, D. C. Heath and Co. [c.1930]   292 p.   [5505

——A topical outline of American literature. Greensboro, Harrison Printing Co. [c.1925]   244 p.   [5506

Hall, Basil. Forty etchings, from sketches made with the camera lucida, in North America, in 1827 and 1828. Edinburgh, Simpkin & Marshall, 1829. [21] plates. [5507

——Travels in North America, in the years 1827 and 1828. Philadelphia, Carey, Lea & Carey, 1829.   2 v.   [5508

Hall, Charles Henry. The call to work; a baccalaureate sermon to the senior class of the University of North Carolina . . . June 2, 1886. Raleigh, Edwards, Broughton & Co. 1886.   21 p.   [5509

Hall, Charles Mercer. Catholic principles . . . a sermon preached at St. Mary's, Asheville, N. C. on the eixth Sunday after Trinity, A.D. 1915. Asheville, Inland Press, 1915]   11 p.   [5510

Hall, Clifton Rumery. Andrew Johnson, military governor of Tennessee. Princeton, Princeton University Press, 1916.   234 p.   [5511

Hall, Eli W. An address delivered before the members of Cape Fear Lodge, no. 2, Independent Order of Odd Fellows . . . Wilmington, N. C., on the 13th of May, 1850. Wilmington, T. Loring, pr. [1850]   14 p.   [5512

Hall, Eugene, pseud., see Baker, Emma Eugenia (Hall)

Hall, Everett Wesley. Modern science and human values; a study in the history of ideas. Princeton, N. J., D. Van Nostrand Co. [1956]   483 p.   [5513

——What is value? An essay in philosophical analysis. New York, Humanities Press, 1952.   255 p.   [5514

Hall Francis. Travels in Canada and the United States in 1816 and 1817. London, 1818.   543 p.   [5515

Hall, Frank Gregory. Laboratory manual for general zoology (Zoology 1) [Durham, Duke University Press, 1929]   75 p.   [5516

Hall, James. A brief history of the Mississippi Territory. Salisbury, Francis Coupée, pr., 1801.   70 p.   [5517

——A narrative of a most extraordinary work of religion in North Carolina; also a collection of interesting letters from the Rev. James M'Corkle. Philadelphia, William W. Woodward, 1802.   52 p.   [5518

——A sermon, preached at Suga-Creek, on Thursday, February 21, 1792, at the ordination of Mr. Samuel Caldwell. Halifax, Abraham Hodge, pr., 1795.   43 p. NcU has photograph.   [5519

Hall, James King. Bettie Waddell Murphy (Mrs. P. L. Murphy) February 10, 1854-February 7, 1933, an appreciation. [Morganton, Samuel McDowell Tate Chapter, U. D. C., 1933?]   12 p.   [5520

Hall, Jane. 1896-1946: Saint Agnes Hospital; the past, the present, the future. [Raleigh] 1946.   [25] p.   [5521

Hall, Joseph Kirkland. History of Goshen Church, presented at the celebration of the 175th anniversary . . . October 15th, 1939. No place [1939?]   13 p.   [5522

——The Rev. James Davidson Hall and his descendants. [Belmont? Author? 1935?]   15 p.   [5523

—— ——rev. ed. Belmont, 1946.   21 p.   [5524

——Sardis Church; a historical sketch read at the centennial of the Church. [Lillington, 1916]   14 p.   [5525

Hall, Joseph Sargent. The phonetics of Great Smoky Mountain speech. New York, King's Crown Press, 1942.   110 p.   [5526

Hall, Thomas H. Circular to the freemen of the 3d congressional district of N. C. [Tarboro] Free Press, 1831.   8 p.   [5527

——To the citizens of the 3d congressional district of North-Carolina. No place, no publisher [1825]   [4] p.   [5528

——To the qualified voters of the 3d congressional district of N. C. No place, no publisher [June, 1835]   [2] p.   [5529

Halliburton, Cecil D. A history of St. Augustine's College, 1867-1937. Raleigh, St. Augustine's College, 1937.   97 p.   [5530

Hallock, R. E., comp. Souvenir of Asheville, N. C. for the soldiers of U. S. A. General hospital no. 12. [Asheville?] no publisher, n.d.   [47] p.   [5531

Hallowell, John Hamilton. The decline of liberalism as an ideology with particular reference to German politico-legal thought. Berkeley, University of California Press, 1943. 145 p.   [5532

——Main currents in modern political thought. New York, Henry Holt [1950] 759 p.   [5533

——The moral foundation of democracy. [Chicago] University of Chicago Press [1954] 134 p.   [5534

Hall-Quest, Alfred Lawrence. The University afield. New York, Macmillan Co., 1926. 292 p.   [5535

Halyburton, Edgar. Shoot and be damned. New York, Covici, Friede [c.1932] 452 p.   [5536

Hamblen, Edwin Crowell. Endocrine gynecology. Springfield, Ill., C. C. Thomas [c.1939] 453 p.   [5537

——Endocrinology of woman. Springfield, Ill., C. C. Thomas, 1945. 571 p.   [5538

——Facts about the change of life. Springfield, Ill., C. Thomas [1949] 86 p.   [5539

——Facts for childless couples. Springfield, Ill., C. C. Thomas [1942] 103 p.   [5540

Hamill, Howard Melancthon. The Bible and its books. Nashville, Tenn., M. E. Church, South, 1905. 142 p.   [5541

Hamilton, Earl Jefferson. Money, prices, and wages in Valencia, Aragon, and Navarre, 1351-1500. Cambridge, Mass., Harvard University Press, 1936. 310 p.   [5542

Hamilton, John. To the honorable the speakers and members of the General Assembly of the state of North-Carolina: The petition of John Hamilton, esquire, his Britannic Majesty's Consul for the State of Virginia, in behalf of himself and of Archibald Hamilton & Co. late merchants of Halifax County, in the state of North Carolina. [Newbern, 1791] [2] p. NcU has photograph from original in Duke University Library.   [5543

[Hamilton, Joseph Gregoire de Roulhac] Benjamin Sherwood Hedrick. Chapel Hill, The University, 1910. (James Sprunt historical publications, v. 10, no. 1) 42 p.   [5544

——Commencement exercises of The Citadel . . . Address. Charleston, S. C., Daggett Printing Co., 1917. 29 p.   [5545

——Henry Ford, the man, the worker, the citizen. New York, H. Holt and Co. [c.1927] 322 p.   [5546

—— ——London, George Allen & Unwin, Ltd. [1928] 322 p.   [5547

——Henry Ford, zijn leven en werken verteld voor vaders en jongens. 's-Gravenhage, H. P. Leopold, 1928. 191 p.   [5548

——North Carolina since 1860. Chicago, The Lewis Publishing Co., 1919. v. 3 of 6 v. work entitled: History of North Carolina.   [5549

Hamilton, Joseph Gregoire de Roulhac, ed. Letters of John Rust Eaton. Chapel Hill, The University, 1910. (James Sprunt historical publications, v. 9, no. 1) p. [25]-59.   [5550

Hamilton, Joseph Gregoire de Roulhac. Life of Andrew Johnson. Greeneville, Tenn., Custodian of the Andrew Johnson Tailor Shop Memorial, 1928. 29 p. [5551

—— ——2d ed. 1930. 34 p.   [5552

——The life of Robert E. Lee for boys and girls, by J. G. de Roulhac Hamilton and Mary Thompson Hamilton. Boston, Houghton Mifflin Co., 1917. 209 p.   [5553

——The making of citizens, by J. G. de Roulhac Hamilton and Edgar W. Knight. Chicago, A. C. McClurg & Co., 1922. 146 p.   [5554

——Our republic, by Franklin L. Riley, J. A. C. Chandler, and J. G. de R. Hamilton. Raleigh, Thompson Press, 1911. 570 p.   [5555

—— ——1918.   [5556

——Party politics in North Carolina. [Chapel Hill, The University, 1916] (James Sprunt historical publications, v. 15) 212 p.   [5557

——Presentation of portrait of Governor Abner Nash to the State of North Carolina . . . November 15, 1909. [Raleigh, 1909] 15 p.   [5558

——Reconstruction in North Carolina. Raleigh, Edwards & Broughton [c.1906] 264 p.   [5559

—— ——New York, Columbia University, 1914. (Its Studies in history, economics and public law, v. 58, whole no. 141) 683 p.   [5560

——Suggestions for the modern teaching of history based on Our republic. Richmond, Va., Riley and Chandler, n.d. 15 p.   [5561

——Suggestions for the modern teaching of United States history in the sixth and seventh grades, by F. L. Riley, J. A. C. Chandler, J. G. de R. Hamilton. No place, Author, n.d. 18 p. Based upon Our republic. [5562

Hamilton, Joseph Gregoire de Roulhac, joint author, see Boyd, William Kenneth

Hamilton, Mary Thompson, joint author, see Hamilton, Joseph Gregoire de Roulhac

Hamilton, Robert A. Mission of the Patrons of Husbandry; Birds and insects; two addresses before Young's Cross Roads Grange, Granville County, N. C., delivered April 3d and July 3d, 1875. Petersburg, Va., Nash & Rogers, 1875. 13 p. [5563

Hamilton, W. J., pseud., see Clark, Charles Dunning

Hamilton, William Baskerville. A preliminary list of the printed writings of William Thomas Laprade. Durham, Seeman Printery, 1952. 32 p. [5564

Hamlin, Charles Hunter. Conflicting forces in North Carolina education. Nashville, Tenn., George Peabody College for Teachers, 1941. (Its Abstract of Contribution to education, no. 288) 8 p. [5565

——Educators present arms; the use of the schools and colleges as agents of war propaganda, 1914-1918. [Zebulon, Record Publishing Co.] c.1939. 47 p. [5566

——Lobbyists and lobbying in the North Carolina legislature. [Wilson, Author, 1933] 43 p. [5567

——Ninety bits of North Carolina biography. [New Bern, Owen G. Dunn Co., 1946] 148 p. [5568

Hamlin, Griffith Askew. The life and influence of Dr. John Tomline Walsh. [Wilson, Author, c.1942] 43 p. [5569

Hamlin, Talbot Faulkner. We took to cruising; from Maine to Florida afloat [by] Talbot and Jessica Hamlin. New York, Sheridan House [1951] 320 p. [5570

Hammel, William Charles Adam. Industrial education in the public school. Greensboro, State Normal and Industrial College [1910?] 13 p. [5571

Hammer, Carl. Rhinelanders on the Yadkin; the story of the Pennsylvania Germans in Rowan and Cabarrus. [Salisbury, Rowan Printing Co., 1943] 130 p. [5572

Hammer, Minnie Lee (Hancock) Courier representative's travelogue. [Asheboro? 1910?] 37 p. [5573

Hammond, John Martin. Winter journeys in the South. Philadelphia, J. B. Lippincott Co., 1916. 261 p. [5574

Hammond, William Alexander. Insanity in its medico-legal relations; opinions relative to the testamentary capacity of the late James C. Johnston, of Chowan County, North Carolina. 2d ed. New York, Baker, Voorhis & Co., 1867. 81 p. [5575

——An open letter to Eugene Grissom, superintendent of the Asylum for the Insane, at Raleigh, N. C. New York, Trow's Printing and Bookbinding Co., 1878. 13 p. [5576

—— ——2d ed. 1878. 16 p. [5577

——A second open letter to Dr. Eugene Grissom. 1878. 18 p. [5578

——To the medical profession. No place, no publisher [1879] 4 p. [5579

Hammonds, Oliver Wendell. The attorney general in the American colonies. New York, New York University School of Law, 1939. (Its Anglo-American legal history series, ser. 1, no. 2) 24 p. [5580

Hampden, August Charles Hobart see Hobart-Hampton, Augustus Charles

Hampton, Frank A. For the Senate, Furnifold M. Simmons [Washington? 1930?] 32 p. [5581

Hampton, John S. North Carolina guide and business office companion. Raleigh, News, 1877. 42 p. [5582

Hampton, Lura Jimison. Nightfall. Winston-Salem, Clay Printing Co., 1949. 87 p. [5583

Hancock, Frank Willis. Truth, Democracy's bulwark; a speech before a Democratic rally in the Forsyth County Court House . . . Oct. 11, 1940. No place [1940] 25 p. [5584

Hand-book for county officers. Raleigh, Nichols & Gorman, 1868. 203 p. [5585

——2d ed. 1869. 306 p. [5586

Handbook of American institutions for delinquent juveniles, 193 - New York, Osborne Association, Inc. [c.1938- NcU has 1938, v. 4, Virginia-North Carolina.   [5587

Hand-book of Durham, N. C. Durham, Educator Co., 1895. 96 p.   [5588

Hanes, Frank Borden. Abel Anders, a narrative. New York, Farrar, Straus and Young [1951] 209 p.   [5589
——The Bat brothers. New York, Farrar, Straus and Young [1953] 304 p. [5590

Hanes, Frederick Moir. An African diary. No place, no publisher, n.d. 52 p. [5591

Hanes, Leigh. Song of the new Hercules, and other poems. Boston, The Four Seas Co. [c.1930] 65 p.   [5592

Hanft, Frank William. You can believe; a lawyer's brief for Christianity. Indianapolis, Bobbs-Merrill [1952] 187 p.   [5593

Hanna, Alfred Jackson. Flight into oblivion. [Richmond] Johnson Publishing Co. [c.1938] 306 p.   [5594

Hanna, Charles Augustus. The Scotch-Irish; or, The Scot in North Britain, North Ireland, and North America. New York, G. P. Putnam's Sons, 1902. 2 v. [5595

Hanna, George B. Minerals of the Piedmont section of North Carolina and the best method of developing them; address before the Charlotte Chamber of Commerce, Tuesday evening, April 7, 1891. [Charlotte, 1891] 16 p.   [5596

Hannum, Alberta (Pierson) The gods and one. New York, Duel, Sloan and Pearce [c.1941] 272 p.   [5597
——The hills step lightly. New York, W. Morrow & Co., 1934. 280 p.   [5598
——Thursday April. New York, Harper & Brothers, 1931. 285 p.   [5599

Hanson, J. H. Doctrine of repentence; being a review of A pastoral letter to the clergy and laity of his diocese by the Rt. Rev. L. Silliman Ives. New York, Stanford and Swords, 1849. 32 p.   [5600

Harbaugh, Thomas Chalmers. Under Greene's banner; or, The boy heroes of 1781. Philadelphia, David McKay [c.1904] 213 p.   [5601

Harden, Earl Louis. Rythmical treasure. Macon, Ga., J. W. Burke Co. [1950] 99 p.   [5602

Harden, John William. The Devil's tramping ground, and other North Carolina mystery stories. Chapel Hill, University of North Carolina Press [1949] 178 p. [5603
——Tales of Tarheelia, nos. 1-22 [May 1, 1946]-September 25, 1946. Raleigh, Station WPTF, 1946. 22 parts.   [5604
——Tar Heel ghosts. Chapel Hill, University of North Carolina Press [1954] 178 p.   [5605

Hardesty, Irving. Neurological technique. Chicago, University of Chicago Press, 1902. 183 p.   [5606

Hardin, Dan S. History of Missionary Methodism, 1913-1948. Forest City, Forest City Courier, 1948. 40 p.   [5607

[Harding, Edmund Hoyt] Saint Peters Parish, Washington, North Carolina. Charlotte, Queen City Printing Co., 1922. 47 p.   [5608

Harding, N. D. Sermon on the life, character, and death of Gen. Andrew Jackson, delivered at Yanceyville, N. C., July 18th, 1845. Richmond, John B. Martin and Co., 1845. 18 p.   [5609

Harding, William Proctor Gould. The federal reserve system, what it is, and what it is not; address at the "Made in Carolinas" Exposition at Charlotte, N. C., Sept. 22, 1921. [Richmond, Va.] Federal Reserve Bank of Richmond, 1921. 24 p.   [5610

Hardison, Osborne Bennett. This University is doing great work for the Navy; Commencement address at the University of North Carolina, February 25, 1945. [Chapel Hill, 1945] [20] p.   [5611

Hardre, Jacques. Existentialism and humanism. Chapel Hill, 1951. 11 p. [5612

Hardware Association of the Carolinas. Constitution and by-laws, adopted at Spartanburg, S. C., June 9, 1925. [Charlotte, News Printing House] 1925. 8 p.   [5613

Hardwicke, Henry. The art of rising in the world. New York, Useful Knowledge Publishing Co. [c.1896] 182 p.   [5614

——History of oratory and orators. New York, G. P. Putnam's Sons, 1896. 454 p. [5615

Hardy, J. F. E. Second annual address delivered before the Asheville Temperance Society, on the 4th of July, 1832 . . . with the Executive Committee's First annual report. Rutherfordton, Roswell Elmer, Jr., pr., 1832. 12 p. [5616

Hardy Evergreen Gardens, Marion, N. C. American plants for American gardens. [Marion? 1929?] 16 p. [5617

Hargan, Thomas J. Asheville, Western North Carolina, in the heart of the Alleghanies. Asheville, J. M. Wood, pr. [1890?] 40 p. [5618

Hargrave, Carrie Guerphan. Jean and Tom in Casablanca. New York, Exposition Press [1953] 103 p. [5619

Hargrave, Will Loftin. Wallannah, a colonial romance. Richmond, Va., B. F. Johnson, 1902. 429 p. [5620

Hargrove, Marion. The girl he left behind; or, All quiet on the Third Platoon. New York, Viking Press, 1956. 191 p. [5621
——See here, Private Hargrove. New York, H. Holt and Co. [1942] 211 p. [5622
—— ——New York, Pocket Books, Inc. [c.1942] 166 p. [5623
—— ——Garden City, N. Y., The Sun Dial Press [1943] 211 p. [5624
—— ——London, Hodder and Stoughton [1943] 192 p. [5625
——Something's got to give. New York, W. Sloane Associates [1948] 312 p. [5626

Hariot, Thomas. Admiranda narratio, fida tamen, de commodis et incolarvm ritibvs Virginiae . . . Anglico scripta sermone á Thoma Hariot . . . nunc avtem primvm Latio donata à C. C. A. Francoforti ad Moenvm, Typis I Wecheli, svmtibvs T. de Bry, 1590. (Bry, Theodor de [America. pt. 1. Latin]) 34 [91] p. [5627
——A brief and true report of the new found land of Virginia . . . a facsimile edition of the 1588 quarto, with an introduction by the late Randolph G. Adams. New York, History Book Club, 1951. [48] p. [5628
—— ——Ann Arbor, Edwards Brothers, 1931. (Ann Arbor facsimile series, no. 1) [48] p. [5629
——A briefe and true report of the new found land of Virginia, of the commodities, and of the nature and manners of the naturall inhabitants. A reproduction of the edition printed at Frankfort, in 1590 . . . ed. by W. Harry Rylands. Manchester, Holbein Society, 1888. 33 p. 48 leaves [5630
—— ——[New York, Reprinted by J. Sabin & Sons, 1871] 33 p. 47 leaves [5631
——A briefe and true report of the new found land of Virginia, of the commodities there found and to be raysed, as well merchantable, as others for victuall. London, 1588, New York [1902] (The Bibliographer, v. 1) [48] p. [5632
——A briefe and true report of the new found land of Virginia, Sir Walter Raleigh's colony of MDLXXXV . . . with an introduction. London, privately printed [by C. Wittingham for Henry Stevens] 1900. 84 p. [5633
——A briefe and true report of the new found land of Virgina, reproduced in facsimile from the first edition of 1588, with an introductory note by Luther S. Livingston. New York, Dodd, Mead & Co., 1903. (Dodd, Mead & Company's facsimile reprints, historical series, no. 1) 24 leaves [5634
——A briefe and true report of the newfoundland of Virginia. London, 1588. [Monroe, Nocalore Press, n.d.] [46] p. [5635
——Narrative of the first English plantation of Virginia. First printed at London in 1588, now reproduced after De Bry's illustrated edition printed at Frankfort in 1590, the illustrations having been designed in Virginia in 1585 by John White. London, B. Quaritch, 1893. 111 p. [5636

Harkness, David James. Literary profiles of the Southern States; a manual for schools and clubs. Knoxville, Division of University Extension, University of Tennessee, 1953. 79 p. [5637

Harllee, William Curry. Kinfolks. New Orleans, La., Searcy & Pfaff, pr., 1934-1937. 3 v. with index in separate v. [5638

Harman, Henry Elliot. At the gate of dreams. Atlanta, Authors Publishing Co., 1905. [44] p. [5639
——A bar of song. Columbia, S. C., State Co. [c.1914] 124 p. [5640
——Collected poems and The window of souls. Columbia, S. C., State Co. [c.1922] 299 p. [5641
——Dreams of yesterday. Columbia, S. C., State Co. [c.1911] 110 p. [5642

——Gates of twilight. Charlotte, Stone & Barringer Co. [c.1910] 134 p.   [5643
——The history of famous songs and poems. Atlanta, Industrial Press [c.1925]
197 p.   [5644
——Idle dreams of an idle day. Columbia, S. C., State Co. [c.1917] 88 p.   [5645
——In love's domain, and The call of the woods. Charlotte, Stone & Barringer Co.
[c.1909] 82 p.   [5646
——In peaceful valley. Dalton, Ga., A. J. Showalter Co., 1901. 45 p.   [5647
——Songs of Florida shores. Charlotte, Stone Publishing Co. [c.1921] 48 p. [5648

Harman, Henry Elliot, comp. The tobacco planter's guide. Wilmington, Atlantic
Coast Line Railroad, n.d. 50 p.   [5649

Harman, Henry Elliot. Yuletide and you, with other love songs. Charlotte, Stone
Publishing Co., n.d. 48 p.   [5650

Harman, John Newton. Harman genealogy (southern branch) with biographical
sketches, 1700-1924. Richmond, Va., W. C. Hill, pr., 1925. 376 p.   [5651

Harmon, George Dewey. Sixty years of Indian affairs, political, economic, and
diplomatic, 1789-1850. Chapel Hill, University of North Carolina Press, 1941.
428 p.   [5652

Harmon, Nolan Bailey. The organization of the Methodist Church; historic development and present working structure. Nashville, Tenn., Abingdon-Cokesbury
Press [1948] 281 p.   [5653

Harned, Jessie M. Medical terminology made easy. Chicago, Physicians' Record
Co., 1951. 275 p.   [5654

[Harnett Co., N. C. Board of County Commissioners] Financial survey, 19 - Lillington, 19 - NcU has 1925/26   [5655

Harnett Co., N. C. Board of Education. Report of the public schools, 19 - Raleigh, 19 - NcU has 1911/14, 1915/17   [5656

[Harnett Co., N. C. Republican Executive Committee] [Election ballot] No
place [1870] [1] p.   [5657

Harper, Alice. Via lucis, and other poems. Nashville, Tenn., Publishing House of
the Methodist Episcopal Church, South [c.1911] 63 p.   [5658

Harper, Frank M. Legal status of the city school superintendent. [Raleigh, no
publisher, 1917] 4 p.   [5659

[Harper, George Washington Finley] Emma Lydia Rankin. [Lenoir? Author,
1908?] 40 p.   [5660

Harper, George Washington Finley. Reminiscences of Caldwell County, N. C., in
the great war of 1861-65. Lenoir, Author, 1913. 59 p.   [5661
——Sketch of the Fifty-eighth Regiment (Infantry) North Carolina Troops. [Lenoir?
1910] 23 p.   [5662

Harper, Ralph Moore. A Bible study of life's problems. Boston, Brotherhood of
Saint Andrew, 1911. 62 p.   [5663
——G-suiting the body, a secret of poise. [Boston, E. C. Schirmer Music Co.]
c.1946. 30 p.   [5664
——The process of religion, a valid variety. [Chapel Hill, Horace Williams Philo-
sophical Society, 1946?] [8] p.   [5665
——The voice governor, give it a chance; correct body mechanics does it. Boston,
Mass., E. C. Schirmer Music Co. [c.1940] 142 p.   [5666

Harper, Wilhelmina, comp. Where the redbird flies, stories from the Southeastern
States. New York, E. P. Dutton & Co., 1946. 277 p.   [5667

Harper, William Allen. Character building in colleges. New York, Abingdon Press
[c.1928] 237 p.   [5668
——The church in the present crisis. New York, Fleming H. Revell Co. [c.1921]
272 p.   [5669
——An integrated program of religious education. New York, Macmillan Co.,
1926. 152 p.   [5670
——The making of men. Dayton, O., Christian Publishing Association [c.1915]
173 p.   [5671
——The minister of education. Ashland, O., University Post Publishing Co.
[c.1939] 159 p.   [5672
——The new church for the new time, a discussion of principles. New York, Fleming H. Revell [c.1918]   [5673

——The new layman for the new time, a discussion of principles. New York, Fleming H. Revell [c.1917] 160 p. [5674

Harper, William Allen, ed. Preparing the teacher; teacher training course of the Southern Christian Convention, Book one-Book two, edited by W. A. Harper, W. P. Lawrence, W. C. Wicker. Elon College, Southern Christian Publishing Board [1910] 2 v. [5675

Harper, William Allen. Reconstructing the church. New York, Fleming H. Revell Co. [c.1920] 188 p. [5676

——Youth and truth. New York, Century Co. [c.1927] 225 p. [5677

Harrell, Eugene G., comp. The North Carolina speaker . . . comp. by Eugene G. Harrell and John B. Neathery. Raleigh, A. Williams & Co., 1887. 200 p. [5678

——Songs and hymns for North Carolina schools. Raleigh, A. Williams & Co., 1893. 53 p. [5679

Harrell, Isaac Samuel. Loyalism in Virginia. Philadelphia, 1926. 203 p. [5680

Harrell, William Bernard. Up with the flag, composed and respectfully dedicated to the Fourth N. C. troops. Richmond, Geo. Dunn and Co., c.1863. [3] p. [5681

Harrer, Gustave Adolphus. Studies in the history of the Roman province of Syria. Princeton, Princeton University Press, 1915. 94 p. [5682

Harrer, Gustave Adolphus, joint ed., see Howe, George, 1876-1936

Harrington, Karl Pomeroy. 'Neath the oaks. [Chapel Hill?] n.d. [4] p. [5683

——The song of the A. B. [Chapel Hill? Author, c.1897] [3] p. [5684

Harris, Agnes (Roueche) Grandmother dear; or, One who held a lighted torch; a history of the Catholic Church in Salisbury, N. Carolina. [Salisbury, privately printed, 1939] 149 p. [5685

Harris, Bernice (Kelly) Folk plays of eastern Carolina. Chapel Hill, University of North Carolina Press [c.1940] 294 p. [5686

——Hearthstones, a novel of the Roanoke River country in North Carolina. Garden City, N. Y., Doubleday and Co., 1948. 273 p. [5687

——Janey Jeems. Garden City, N. Y., Doubleday and Co., 1946. 306 p. [5688

——Portulaca. Garden City, N. Y., Doubleday, Doran and Co., 1941. 335 p. [5689

——Purslane. Chapel Hill, University of North Carolina Press [c.1939] 316 p. [5690

——Sage quarter. Garden City, N. Y., Doubleday, Doran and Co., 1945. 259 p. [5691

——Sweet Beulah land. Garden City, N. Y., Doubleday, Doran & Co., 1943. 389 p. [5692

——Wild Cherry Tree Road. Garden City, N. Y., Doubleday and Co., 1951. 282 p. [5693

Harris, Bernice (Kelly), joint author, see Edwards, Leila Taylor

Harris, Charles Nelson. Truth vs. untruth; a study for the benefit of mankind. Raleigh, Edwards & Broughton Co., 1939. 123 p. [5694

Harris, Charles Wilson. The Harris letters [ed.] by H. M. Wagstaff. [Durham, Seeman Printery, 1916] (James Sprunt historical publications, University of North Carolina, v. 14, no. 1) 91 p. [5695

Harris, Cicero Willis. A glance at government; short essays on the rise and basis of government, the study of politics, the unity of sovereignty, and the saving principle. Philadelphia, J. B. Lippincott Co., 1896. 46 p. [5696

——The sectional struggle; an account of the troubles between the North and the South. Philadelphia, J. B. Lippincott Co., 1902. 343 p. [5697

Harris, Closs Peace. Where's my baby? Boston, B. Humphries, Inc. [c.1940] 32 p. [5698

Harris, Cora A. Auto tours in Western North Carolina; a complete guide to tourist travel. [Charlotte, Author, c.1934] 31 p. [5699

Harris, Fletcher. Sermons on important subjects, to which is prefixed a memoir of the author's life, Granville County, N. C. New York, Willis Harris, 1821. 339 p. [5700

Harris, Governor Ellis. North Carolina constitutional reader. Raleigh, St. Augustine's School Printing Office, 1903. 117 p. [5701

Harris, Hunter Lee. Twilight songs and other youthful poems. Raleigh, [Author?] 1890. 16 p. [5702

Harris, James Coffee. The personal and family history of Charles Hooks and Margaret Monk Harris. [Rome? Ga.] c.1911. 116 p.   [5703

Harris, James Morrison. Discourse on the life and character of Sir Walter Raleigh. Baltimore, Maryland Historical Society, 1846. 71 p.   [5704

Harris, James Sidney. Historical sketches of the Seventh Regiment, North Carolina Troops. Mooresville, Mooresville Printing Co. [1893?] 70 p.   [5705

Harris, Jane Yancey. Thoroughly tested, a drama in six acts. Raleigh, Edwards and Broughton Co., n.d. 56 p.   [5706

Harris, Mattie Virginia. Weddin' trimmin's. New York, Exposition Press [1949] 233 p.   [5707

Harris, Mrs. Richard Sadler. History of the First Presbyterian Church, Concord, N. C., from its organization, 1804, to the completion of the present new church building. Concord, Tribune, 1905. 18 p.   [5708

Harris, Seale. James Coffee Harris and his family. Birmingham, 1935. 49 p. [5709

Harris, Wade Hampton, ed. The city of Charlotte and the County of Mecklenburg. Charlotte, Chamber of Commerce, 1924. 63 p.   [5710

[**Harris, Wade Hampton**] Letters to The Charlotte observer. Charlotte, Observer Printing House [1927] 95 p.   [5711

Harris, Wade Hampton. My school days; reconstruction experiences in the South. New York, Neale Publishing Co., 1914. 57 p.   [5712

——Sketches of Charlotte. Charlotte, Board of Aldermen, 1896. 39 p.   [5713

—— ——Charlotte, Observer, 1899. 51 p.   [5714

—— ——1902. 58 p.   [5715

—— ——7th ed. Charlotte, Author, 1907. 60 p.   [5716

—— ——8th ed. [Charlotte, Author, c.1909] 48 p.   [5717

Harris, William Shakespeare. Historical sketch of Poplar Tent Church . . . read before Concord Presbytery, April 22nd, 1872. Charlotte, Jones & McLauglin, pr., 1873. 17 p.   [5718

——Historical sketch of Poplar Tent Church. Concord, Tribune, 1901. 18 p. [5719

——Historical sketch of Poplar Tent Church, with introduction and brief resume of the history of Poplar Tent Church from 1873 to 1923, to which is appended an article on Rev. Hezekiah James Balch and the Mecklenburg Declaration of Independence, by W. Hampton Eubank. Concord, Times, pr., 1924. 39 p.   [5720

Harris Granite Quarries Co. Balfour pink, "the granite eternal". New York, Harris Granite Quarries Co. [c.1916] 13 p.   [5721

Harrison, Fairfax. The future of the Southern Railway in N. C. Raleigh, Chamber of Commerce, 1914. 4 p.   [5722

——A history of the legal development of the railroad system of Southern Railway Company. Washington, D. C., 1901. 1519 (i.e. 1523) p.   [5723

——What the Southern Railway Company means to Charlotte and North Carolina, an address before the Chamber of Commerce, Charlotte, North Carolina, February 16, 1916. [Charlotte? 1916?] 7 p.   [5724

Harrison, Joshua. This booklet contains the evidence of the Beasley-Harrison kidnapping case. Elizabeth City, Tar Heel Office, n.d. 28 p.   [5725

Harrison, Michael. Airborne at Kitty Hawk; the story of the first heavier-than-air flight made by the Wright brothers, December 17, 1903. London, Cassell and Co. [1953] 118 p.   [5626

Harrison, T. F. History of the Free Will Baptists of North Carolina, by Elds. T. F. Harrison and J. M. Barfield. No place, no publisher, n.d. 430 p.   [5727

Harrison, Thomas Perrin. Address to graduating class of The Citadel, on Tuesday, June 9th, 1925. Charleston, S. C., The Citadel [1925] 12 p.   [5728

——Recollections of Andersonville, 1864-1878. [Asheville, Stephens Press, 1947] 9 p.   [5729

Harriss, Robert Preston. The foxes. Boston, Houghton Mifflin Co., 1936. 239 p.   [5730

[**Hart, Alban J.**] Attempts at rhyming, by an old field teacher. Raleigh, Thomas J. Lemay, pr., 1839. 124 p.   [5731

Hart, Hornell Norris. Autoconditioning, the new way to a successful life. Englewood Cliffs, N. J., Prentice-Hall, 1956. 263 p.   [5732

——Can world government be predicted by mathematics? A preliminary report. Durham, 1944. 16 p. [5733

Hart, Hornell Norris, comp. The "great debate" on American foreign policy. Durham, Duke Consensus Project, 1951. 101 p. [5734

Hart, Hornell Norris. Personality and the family. Rev. and enl. ed. by Hornell Hart and Ella B. Hart. Boston, D. C. Heath and Co. [c.1941] 526 p. [5735

[**Hart, Hornell Norris, ed.**] Toward consensus for world law and order. Durham, Duke University, 1949. 57 p. [5736

Hart, John. An inaugural thesis on sensation & motion, submitted to the examination of the Rev. John Andrews . . . the trustees and medical professors of the University of Pennsylvania, on the 21st day of April, 1806, for the degree of Doctor of Medicine. Philadelphia, 1806. 12 p. [5737

Hart, Sophie L. Fireside musings; or, Grandfather's true story. Goldsboro [Author] n.d. 47 p. [5738

Hart, Thomas Roy. The School of Textiles, N. C. State College; its past and present. [Raleigh, North Carolina State College Print Shop, 1951] 230 p. [5739

Hartley, Cecil B. Life and times of Colonel Daniel Boone. Philadelphia, G. G. Evans, 1859. 351 p. [5740

——Life of Daniel Boone, the founder of the state of Kentucky. New York, A. L. Burt Co. [c.1902] 385 p. [5741

—— ——355 p. [5742

—— ——New York, A. L. Burt Co. [1936?] 385 p. [5743

——Life of Major General Henry Lee, commander of Lee's Legion in the Revolutionary War. New York, Derby & Jackson, 1859. 352 p. [5744

Hartley, Joseph L. Walking for health and traveling to eternity; combined with Singing on the mountain. Linville, n.d. 23 p. [5745

Hartley, Lodwick Charles, ed. Harvest, 1948, an anthology of student short stories. Raleigh, North Carolina State College, 1948. 51 p. [5746

——Patterns in modern drama [ed. by] Lodwick Hartley [and] Arthur Ladu. New York, Prentice-Hall, 1948. 496 p. [5747

Hartley, Lodwick Charles. This is Lorence, a narrative of the Reverence Laurence Sterne. Chapel Hill, University of North Carolina Press [1943] 302 p. [5748

——William Cowper, humanitarian. Chapel Hill, University of North Carolina Press, 1938. 277 p. [5749

Hartman, Olga. The marine annelids of North Carolina. Durham, Duke University Press, 1945. (Duke University. Marine Station. Bulletin, 2) 51 p. [5750

Hartness, James Alexander. Stone Mountain, the old South, General Robert E. Lee, the South's comeback, World War veterans. Raleigh, Edwards & Broughton Co., 1932. 10 p. [5751

Hartridge, Clifford Wayne. Manteo. New York, F. C. Osberg [c.1935] 340 p. [5752

The Harvey family. No place, no publisher, n.d. 8 p. [5753

Hassell, Allene B. Personal analysis and future planning, by Allene B. Hassell . . . and Amy C. Fallaw. [Raleigh, Edwards and Broughton Co., c.1951] 99 p. [5754

——Personal analysis and future planning, by Allene B. Hassell, Amy C. Fallaw, and Peggie L. Webb. Winston-Salem, Hunter Publishing Co. [c.1956] 414 p. [5755

Hassell, Cushing Biggs. Friendly greetings across the water; or, The love letters of Elders Garrard & Hassell. New York, Chatterton and Crist, pr., 1847. 26 p. [5756

——History of the Church of God, from the creation to A. D. 1885; including especially the history of the Kehukee Primitive Baptist Association, by Elder Cushing Biggs Hassell, revised and completed by Elder Sylvester Hassell. Middletown, N. Y., G. Beebe's Sons [1886] 1008 p. [5757

—— ——[Reprinted Atlanta, Turner Lassetter, 1948] [5758

Hassell, Sylvester. The apostolic church. No place, Author [1912?] p. 269-326. A revision of the ninth chapter of History of the Church of God, by Cushing Biggs Hassell and Sylvester Hassell. [5759

——The articles of faith of Smithwick's Creek Primitive Baptist Church. [Williamston, Author? 1928] [3] p. [5760

[**Hassell, Sylvester**] Evolution. [Williamston, Author] n.d. [4] p. [5761

——Evolution: supplement to article in December (1925) Advocate amd messenger. Raleigh, Edwards and Broughton, 1926. [2] p.   [5762

Hassell, Sylvester. Life of Elder C. B. Hassell. No place, no publisher, n.d. 9 p.   [5763

——The old paths. Columbus Ga., Thomas Gilbert, pr., n.d. 15 p.   [5764

[Hassell, Sylvester] Principles of The Gospel messenger. [Williamston, The Gospel Messenger] n.d. 8 p.   [5765

—— ——[1901] 4 p.   [5766

——Supplement; undesigned testimony of the latest and greatest evolutionists against evolution. No place, no publisher, n.d. [1] p.   [5767

Haughawaut, A. H. Address to the colored voters of Orange County. No place, n.d. [1] p.   [5768

[Hauser, Margaret Louise] Boy dates girl . . . by Gay Head [pseud.] New York, Scholastic Corporation [1953] 123 p.   [5769

——Etiquette for young moderns. New York, Scholastic Corporation for Teen Age Book Club [1954] 160 p.   [5770

——Hi there, high school! New York, Teen Age Book Club, c.1953. 94 p.   [5771

Havens, Jonathan. The Pamlico section of North Carolina. New Bern, N. S. Richardson & Son, pr., 1886. 88 p.   [5772

Hawes, Herbert Bouldin. The daughter of the blood. Boston, Four Seas [c.1930] 427 p.   [5773

Hawfield, Samuel Glenn. History of the Stonewall Jackson Manual Training and Industrial School, Concord, North Carolina. Concord, Stonewall Jackson Training and Industrial School, 1946. 125 p.   [5774

Hawk, Emory Quinter. Economic history of the South. New York, Prentice-Hall, Inc., 1934. 557 p.   [5775

Hawkins, Benjamin. Creek Indian history as comprised in Creek Confederacy, by W. B. Hodgson and The Creek country, by Col. Benjamin Hawkins. Americus, Ga., Americus Book Co., 1938. 80 p.   [5776

——Letters of Benjamin Hawkins, 1796-1806. Savannah, Ga., Georgia Historical Society, 1916. (Collections of the Georgia Historical Society, v. 9) 500 p. [5777

Hawkins, Dean. Skull Mountain. Garden City, N. Y., Doubleday, Doran & Co., Inc., 1941. 275 p.   [5778

Hawkins, Ernest. Historical notices of the missions of the Church of England in the North American colonies. London, B. Fellowes, 1845. 447 p.   [5779

Hawkins, J. R. The educator; a condensed statement of the Department of Education of the African Methodist Church. No place, no publisher [1900?] 104 p. [5780

[Hawkins, John Davis] Address. No place, Author [1841] 12 p.   [5781

Hawkins, John Davis. Oration commemorative of Col. Philemon Hawkins, senior . . . delivered on the 28th day of Sept. 1829. Raleigh, Lawrence and Lemay, 1829. 10 p.   [5782

—— ——Raleigh, Weaver and Houseman, 1906. 17 p.   [5783

Hawkins, Rush Christopher. An account of the assassination of loyal citizens of North Carolina, for having served in the Union army, which took place at Kingston in the months of February and March, 1864. New York [J. H. Folan, pr.] 1897. 46 p.   [5784

Hawkins, Walter Everette. Chords and discords. Boston, R. G. Badger [c.1920] 100 p.   [5785

Hawkins, William George. Lunsford Lane; or, Another helper from North Carolina. Boston, Crosby & Nichols, 1863. 305 p.   [5786

—— ——1864.   [5787

Hawks, Elizabeth H. (Rose) A distant field, memoirs of a nonagenarian. [Warrenton] n.d. 96 p.   [5788

[Hawks, Francis Lister] The adventures of Daniel Boone . . . by the author of "Uncle Philip's conversations." New York, D. Appleton & Co., 1844. 174 p. [5789

—— ——1854.   [5790

—— ——1856.   [5791

——The adventures of Henry Hudson . . . by the author of "Uncle Philip's conversations". New York, D. Appleton & Co., 1873. 161 p.   [5792

——The adventures of Hernan Cortes, the conqueror of Mexico. New York, D. Appleton & Co., 1856. 186 p. [5793

——The American forest; or, Uncle Philip's conversations with the children about the trees of America. New York, Harper & Brothers, 1845. 250 p. [5794

——Auricular confession in the Protestant Episcopal Church. New York, Geo. P. Putnam, 1850. 132 p. [5795

Hawks, Francis Lister. Documentary history of the Protestant Episcopal Church in the United States of America: South Carolina. New York, James Pott, 1862. 33 p. [5796

[**Hawks, Francis Lister**] The early history of the Southern States: Virginia, North and South Carolina, and Georgia. . . . by Lambert Lilly, schoolmaster. Philadelphia, Key, Mielke and Biddle, 1832. 192 p. [5797

—— ——Boston, Ticknor, Reed and Fields, 1852. 192 p. [5798

—— ——Boston, Wm. D. Ticknor, 1854. [5799

——Evidences of Christianity; or, Uncle Philip's conversations with children about the truth of the Christian religion. New York, Harper & Brothers, 1844. 209 p. [5800

——Hints on the internal improvement of North Carolina . . . by a North Carolinian. New York, John F. Trow, 1854. 50 p. [5801

—— ——2d ed. Fayetteville, Edward J. Hale, pr., 1854. 32 p. [5802

——The history of the middle states. . . . by Lambert Lilly, schoolmaster. Boston, William D. Ticknor and Co., 1844. 167 p. [5803

—— ——Boston, Ticknor, Reed and Fields, 1850. 167 p. [5804

——The history of New England . . . by Lambert Lilly, schoolmaster. Boston, W. Hyde, 1831. 184 p. [5805

Hawks, Francis Lister. History of North Carolina. Fayetteville, E. J. Hale & Son, 1857-58. 2 v. [5806

—— ——2d ed. 1857. v. 1 only. [5807

—— ——3d ed. 1859. v. 1 only. [5808

[**Hawks, Francis Lister**] The history of the Western States . . . by Lambert Lilly, schoolmaster. Boston, W. D. Ticknor, 1835. 156 p. [5809

—— ——1838. [5810

—— ——1852. 167 p. [5811

[**Hawks, Francis Lister?**] A letter to the Right Rev. L. Silliman Ives, bishop of the Protestant Episcopal Church in ths state of North Carolina occasioned by his late address to the convention of his diocese. Washington, Buel and Blanchard [1846] 15 p. [5812

Hawks, Francis Lister. The monuments of Egypt; or, Egypt a witness for the Bible. New York, G. P. Putnam, 1850. 256, 162 p. [5813

——Narrative of the expedition of an American squadron to the China seas and Japan . . . compiled from the original notes and journals of Commodore Perry and his officers . . . by Francis L. Hawks. New York, D. Appleton and Co., 1856. 624 p. [5814

—— ——Abridged and edited by Sidney Wallach. London, MacDonald and Co. [c.1952] 304 p. [5815

[**Hawks, Francis Lister**] Natural history; or, Uncle Philip's conversations with the children about tools and trades among inferior animals. New York, Harper and Brothers, 1844. 213 p. [5816

Hawks, Francis Lister. Poems, hitherto uncollected. New York, privately printed by Charles L. Moreau, 1873. 27 p. [5817

——Revolutionary history of North Carolina, in three lectures, by Francis L. Hawks . . . Hon. David L. Swain, and Hon. Wm. A. Graham . . . comp. by William D. Cooke. Raleigh, W. D. Cooke, 1853. 236 p. [5818

[**Hawks, Francis Lister**] The story of the American Revolution . . . by Lambert Lilly, schoolmaster. Boston, William D. Ticknor, 1839. 204 p. [5819

Hawks, Lena James. Between the lines; a history of three pioneer families of Warren County, North Carolina, as read from county court records. [Warrenton, Author, 1949] 109 p. [5820

Haworth, Sara Richardson. Springfield, 1773-1940; a history . . . of Springfield Monthly Meeting of Friends. [High Point, Barber-Hall Printing Co., 1940] 34 p. [5821

Hay, Gertrude May (Sloan) comp. Chapter histories of the North Carolina Daughters of the American Revolution. [Durham] Seeman Press, 1930. v. 1. [5822

Hay, James. The hidden woman. New York, Dodd, Mead and Co., 1929. 258 p. [5823

——The winning clue. New York, Dodd, Mead & Co., 1919. 298 p. [5824

Hayden, Harry. The story of the Wilmington rebellion. [Wilmington] c.1936. 32 p. [5825

Haydn, Hiram Collins. The time is noon. New York, Crown Publishers [1948] 561 p. [5826

Haydon, Glen. Introduction to musicology. New York, Prentice-Hall, Inc., 1941. 329 p. [5827

Hayes, Charles Willard. The Southern Appalachians. New York, American Book Co., 1895. (National geographic monographs, v. 1, no. 10) 336 p. [5828

Hayes, Hubert. The red spider; a mystery play in three acts. Boston [Walter H. Baker Co., c.1937] 128 p. [5829

——Smoky Joe; a comedy in three acts. Boston [Walter H. Baker Co., c.1936] 133 p. [5830

Hayes, Johnson J. The Wake Forest speech of Hon. Johnson J. Hayes . . . February 9, 1950. [Greensboro, Greensboro Chapter of Wake Forest Alumni, 1950] 16 p. [5831

Hayes, Kenneth Crawford. The logical development of the concept of light. Chapel Hill, Department of Philosophy, University of North Carolina, 1936. (Mildred Williams Buchan prize thesis, 1936) 22 p. [5832

Hayne, Joseph E. The black man; or, The natural history of the Hametic race. Raleigh, Edwards and Broughton Co., 1894. 144 p. [5833

Hayne, Robert Young. Address in behalf of the Knoxville Convention to the citizens of the several states interested in the proposed Louisville, Cincinnati and Charleston Railroad. Charleston, A. E. Miller, 1836. 38 p. [5834

Haynes, Hubert Calvin. Relation of teacher intelligence, teacher experience, and type of school to types of questions. Nashville, Tenn., George Peabody College for Teachers, 1935. (Its contributions to education, no. 150) 41 p. [5835

Haynes, Ina (Fortune) Raleigh Rutherford Haynes, a history of his life and achievements, by Mrs. Grover C. Haynes, Sr. Cliffside, privately printed [c.1954] 99 p. [5836

Haynes, Lowell Q. Dreaming and doing. No place, no publisher [1917] 28 p. [5837

——Millennial thought. No place, no publisher, 1918. 30 p. [5838

Haynes, Williams. Sandhills sketches. New York, D. O. Haynes & Co. [c.1916] 95 p. [5839

Hays, Benjamin K. Is stone in the kidney primarily a surgical disease? Richmond, Va., Williams Printing Co., n.d. 8 p. [5840

Hayward, Arthur Lawrence. The book of pirates. New York, Roy Publishers [1956?] 239 p. [5841

Haywood, Edmund Burke. Ligation of right-external iliac artery for traumatic aneurism of femoral artery. Raleigh, Nichols & Gorman, 1870. 7 p. [5842

——Valedictory address delivered before the Medical Society of the State of North Carolina. Raleigh, Nichols and Gorman, 1869. 20 p. [5843

Haywood, Edward Graham. Tribute to the memory of Bartholomew Figures Moore. Raleigh, Edwards and Broughton Co., 1879. 56 p. [5844

Haywood, Ernest, ed. Dedication of Hill-King Memorial Methodist Church, near to the Green Hill residence, southeast of Louisburg in Franklin County, N. C., Sunday, July 31, 1938. Raleigh, 1938. 31 p. [5845

Haywood, Ernest. Memorial of Armistead Jones . . . North Carolina Bar Association, Wrightsville Beach, N. C., July 1, 1926. No place, no publisher [1926?] [4] p. [5846

——Presentation of the portrait of Hon. George Edmund Badger as a gift from his granddaughter, Mrs. Kate Badger Moore. No place, no publisher [1933] 7 p. [5847

——Presentation of the portrait of Hon. George Haywood Snow, as a gift from his children. No place, no publisher [1936?] 7 p. [5848

Haywood, Ernest, ed. Proceedings of Lambda Chapter of the Phi Kappa Sigma Fraternity, at its first reunion and banquet, held at Raleigh, N. C., June 7, 1884. Raleigh, Uzzell & Gatling, 1884. 23 p. [5849

Haywood, Ernest. Sketch of Mr. Alfred Williams of Raleigh, N. C., and incidentally of "Mr. John King—preacher of the Gospel". Raleigh, privately printed, 1933. 15 p. [5850

——Some notes in regard to the eminent lawyers whose portraits adorn the walls of the Superior Court Room at Raleigh, North Carolina. [Raleigh? 1936] 20 p. [5851

Haywood, Gertrude W. The whir of wings, the chronicle of the short but shining earth-path of Ernest Eagles Haywood, September, 1902-May, 1928. Raleigh, Edwards and Broughton Co., 1929. 236 p. [5852

Haywood, Hubert Benbury. A sketch of the Haywood family in North Carolina. [Raleigh? Author, 1956] 78 p. [5853

[Haywood, John] The Christian advocate, by a Tennesseean. Nashville, Thomas G. Bradford, 1819. 357 p. [5854

Haywood, John. The civil and political history of the state of Tennessee, from its earliest settlement up to the year 1796. Knoxville, Tenn., Heiskell & Brown, 1823. 504 p. [5855

—— ——with a biographical sketch of Judge John Haywood, by Col. A. S. Colyar. Nashville, Tenn., Publishing House of the Methodist Episcopal Church, South, 1891. 518 p. [5856

—— ——Index compiled by Zella Armstrong. Chattanooga, Tenn., Lookout Publishing Co., 1939. 26 p. [5857

——The natural and aboriginal history of Tennessee, up to the first settlements therein by the white people, in the year 1768. Nashville, G. Wilson, pr., 1823. 390 p. [5858

Haywood, John D. John D. Haywood, breeder of thoroughbred Wyandottes. [Raleigh, Author] n.d. [4] p. [5859

Haywood, Marshall De Lancey. Ballads of courageous Carolinians. Raleigh, Edwards & Broughton Printing Co., 1914. 51 p. [5860

——The beginnings of Freemasonry in North Carolina and Tennessee. Raleigh, Weaver & Lynch, pr., 1906. 86 p. [5861

——Calvin Jones, physician, soldier, and Freemason, 1775-1846. [Oxford] Oxford Orphanage [1919] 31 p. [5862

——Colonel Edward Buncombe, Fifth North Carolina Continental Regiment. Raleigh, Alford, Bynum and Christophers, pr., 1901. 20 p. [5863

——Governor George Burrington, with an account of his official administration in the colony of North Carolina, 1724-1725, 1731-1734. Raleigh, Edwards & Broughton, pr., 1896. 34 p. [5864

——Governor William Tryon, and his administration in the province of North Carolina, 1765-1771. Raleigh, E. M. Uzzell, pr., 1903. 223 p. [5865

——Joel Lane, pioneer and patriot. Raleigh, Alford, Bynum and Christophers, pr., 1900. 23 p. [5866

—— ——2d ed., rev. Raleigh, Alfred Williams & Co., 1925. 30 p. [5867

—— ——3d ed. Raleigh, Wake County Committee of the Colonial Dames of America, 1952. 31 p. [5868

——[Leaflet . . . designed to aid those who have occasion to search for records of the services of Revolutionary ancestors in North Carolina] [Raleigh? Author? 1904?] 4 p. [5869

——Lives of the bishops of North Carolina. Raleigh, Alfred Williams & Co., 1910. 270 p. [5870

——Sir Walter Raleigh, an address. Raleigh, Edwards & Broughton Co., pr., [1913?] 52 p. [5871

—— ——[Raleigh, Roanoke Colony Memorial Association] 1937. 47 p. [5872

——William G. Hill . . . an address delivered before William G. Hill Lodge no. 218, Raleigh, N. C., April 26, 1926. [Raleigh] Published by the Lodge [1926] 15 p. [5873

Haywood, Richard Bennehan. Memoir of Dr. Wm. G. Hill, late president of the Raleigh Academy of Medicine, read before that body. Raleigh, Observer, pr., 1877. 7 p. [5874

——Valedictory speech, delivered at Asheville, June 1st, 1881, before the North Carolina Medical Society at the 28th annual meeting. Wilmington, Jackson and Bell, pr. [1881?] 14 p. [5875

Haywood, William Henry. Address to the people of North Carolina. Washington, Blair and Rives, 1846. 29 p. [5876

——To the freemen of Wake County. [Raleigh, Philo White, January 14, 1835] 24 p. [5877

Haywood County Baptist Association. Minutes, 18 - 18 - NcU has [1894- 1955] [5878

Hazen, Whipple & Fuller, New York. Report on Durham Water Company, Durham, North Carolina, with appraisal of its plant as of January 1, 1916. [New York? 1916?] 27, 39 p. [5879

Head, Gay, pseud., see **Hauser, Margaret Louise**

Headley, Joel Tyler. Grant and Sherman; their campaigns and generals. New York, E. B. Treat & Co., 1865. 608 p. [5880

——The lives of Winfield Scott and Andrew Jackson. New York, C. Scribner, 1852. 341 p. [5881

Heafner, Bruce Franklin. Encyclopedic digest of North Carolina Supreme Court decisions on automobile civil cases: cases reported, index, decisions and principles of law. Lincolnton [c.1956] various paging [5882

Heagney, Anne. The magic pen. Milwaukee, Bruce Publishing Co. [1949] 168 p. [5883

Health educators at work, v. 1- May, 1847- Chapel Hill, University of North Carolina, 1947- NcU has v. 1-7 [5884

Healthiest place in America, the ideal summer resort, Hot Springs, North Carolina. New York, South Publishing Co. [1891] [4] p. [5885

Heard, Alexander. Money and politics. [New York, Public Affairs Committee, 1956] (Public affairs pamphlet, no. 242) 28 p. [5886

——Southern primaries and elections, 1920-1949 [by] Alexander Heard and Donald S. Strong. University, Ala., University of Alabama Press, 1950. 206 p. [5887

——A two-party South? Chapel Hill, University of North Carolina Press [1952] 334 p. [5888

Hearn, Rufus K., comp. Zion's hymns, for the use of the original Free-Will Baptist Church of North Carolina . . . compiled from various authors by Rufus K. Hearn, Joseph S. Bell, and Jesse Randolph. Falkland, Pitt County, Compilers, 1854. 303 p. [5889

Hearn, S. W. The Stone-Hearn libel suit. Wadesboro, Intelligence, pr., 1888. 72 p. [5890

Heath, Jesse. The Free Will Baptist hymn book for the use of the United Churches of Christ commonly called Free Will Baptists in North Carolina, and for all denominations, by Jesse Heath and Elias Hutchins. Newbern, Thomas Watson, 1832. 268 p. Title page mutilated in NcU copy. [5891

Heath, John R. The strange case of Thomas Wolfe. [Chicago] Chicago Literary Club, 1949. 32 p. [5892

Heath, Milton Sydney. Constructive liberalism; the roll of the state in economic development in Georgia to 1860. Cambridge, Harvard University Press, 1954 448 p. [5893

Heatherley, Erskine X. Salmagundi; rhyme-or-nots. [Danville, Va., J. T. Townes Printing Co.] c.1934. 46 p. [5894

Heck, Charles McGee, comp. Contemporaneous accounts of the coming of the first train to Raleigh, N. C. Raleigh [Author, 1940] 19 p. [5895

Heck, Fannie Exile Scudder. Everyday gladness. New York, Fleming H. Revell Co. [c.1915] 93 p. [5896

——In royal service, the mission work of southern Baptist women. Richmond, Va., Educational Department, Foreign Mission Boards, Southern Baptist Convention, 1913. 380 p. [5897

——Sunrise, and other poems. New York, Fleming H. Revell Co. [c.1916] 47 p. [5898

Heck, William Harry. Mental discipline & educational values. New York, J. Lane Co., 1909. 147 p. [5899

Hedden, Worth Tuttle. Love is a wound. New York, Crown Publishers [1952] 467 p. [5900

——The other room, a novel. New York, Crown Publishers [1947] 274 p. [5901

——Two and three make one, by Winifred Woodley [pseud.] New York, Crown Publishers [c.1956] 167 p. [5902

Hedley, Fenwick Y. Marching through Georgia; pen-pictures of every-day life in General Sherman's army. Chicago, Donohue, Henneberry & Co., 1890. 490 p. [5903

Hedley, George Percy. The minister behind the scenes. New York, Macmillan Co., 1956. 147 p. [5904

Hedrick, Henry Grady. Notes on torts . . . taught in the Law School of Trinity College. Durham [Seeman Printery] 1918. 51 p. [5905

Heer, Clarence. Income and wages in the South. Chapel Hill, University of North Carolina Press, 1930. 68 p. [5906

Heiberg-Jurgensen, Kai see **Jurgensen, Kai**

Heide, R. E. Report of Vice-Consul R. E. Heide, on the resources, trade, and commerce of North Carolina. Wilmington, North Carolina Presbyterian Publishing House, 1875. 25 p. [5907

Heidelberg Academy, Flat Rock, N. C. Heidelberg Academy, 19 - Flat Rock, 19 - NcU has one issue not dated [5908

Heinzerling, Sarah Anderson (Chance) The call. Statesville, Brady Printing Co., 1936. 45 p. [5909

——The pines of Rockingham and other poems. Boomer, Pearson Printing Co., 1934. 44 p. [5910

——Songs of Iredell. Statesville, Brady Printing Co., 1934. 46 p. [5911

Heiskell, Samuel Gordon. Andrew Jackson and early Tennessee history. 2d ed. Nashville, Tenn., Ambrose Printing Co., 1920. 2 v. [5912

Heitman, Francis Bernard. Historical register of officers of the Continental Army during the War of the Revolution, April, 1775, to December, 1783. Washington [Baltimore, Press of Nichols, Killam & Maffitt] 1893. 525 p. [5913

—— ——New, rev. and enl. ed. Washington, Rare Book Co., 1914. 685 p. [5914

The Hellenian, 1890-1900. Chapel Hill, Fraternities of the University of North Carolina, 1890-1900. NcU has 1890-1900. [5915

Helme, R. H. An address delivered before the Agricultural Society of North Carolina, at Raleigh, December 16, 1822. Raleigh, J. Gales and Son, pr. [1822] 12 p. [5916

[**Helmstaedt Mission Society**] Lehrbucher fur die Jugend in Nordcarolina. Leipzig, Siegfried Lebrecht Crusius, 1788-1789. [16] 32, 24 p. [5917

Helper, Hardie Hogan. Address to the people of the 6th congressional district. [Salisbury, June 22, 1870] 8 p. [5918

Helper, Hinton A. Asheville, Western North Carolina, nature's trundle-bed of recuperation for tourist & health-seeker. New York, Southern Railway Co. [1886?] 64 p. [5919

Helper, Hinton Rowan. Compendium of the Impending crisis of the South. New York, Burdick Brothers, 1860. 214 p. [5920

——Dreadful California . . . ed. by Lucius Beebe and Charles M. Clegg. Indianapolis, Bobbs-Merrill [1948] 162 p. First published under title: The land of gold. [5921

——The impending crisis of the South: how to meet it. New-York, Burdick Brothers, 1857. 420 p. [5922

—— ——Enlarged ed. New York, George W. Carleton and Co., 1857. 438 p. [5923

—— ——Enlarged ed. New York, A. B. Burdick, 1860. 438 p. [5924

—— ——1860. 420 p. [5925

——The land of gold; reality versus fiction. Baltimore, Author, 1855. 300 p. [5926

Helper, Hinton Rowan, comp. The Negroes in Negroland; the Negroes in America; and Negroes generally. New York, G. W. Carleton, 1868. 254 p. [5927

Helper, Hinton Rowan. Nojoque; a question for a continent. New York, G. W. Carleton & Co., 1867. 479 p. [5928

——Noonday exigencies in America. New York, Bible Brothers, 1871. 211 p. [5929

——Oddments of Andean diplomacy. St. Louis, W. S. Bryan, 1879. 480 p. [5930

——The three Americas railway. St. Louis, W. S. Bryan, 1881. 473 p. [5931

——To the public. New York, August 25, 1857. [1] p. [5932

Helton, Roy Addison. Nichey Tilley, a novel. New York, Harper & Brothers, 1934. 352 p. [5933

——Their own day. London, Cassell and Co. [1934] 315 p. Original title: Nichey Tilley. [5934

Helvetische Societät (Virginia, 18th cent.) Neu-gefundenes Eden. Oder: Ausführlicher Bericht von Süd-und Nord-Carolina, Pensilphania, Mary-Land & Virginia. No place, In Truck verfertiget durch Befelch der Helvetischen Societät, 1737. 288 (i.e. 228) p. NcU has microfilm (negative) from original in Library of Congress. [5935

Hembree, James Willis. Smoky Mountain songs. Knoxville, Tenn., Clarence F. Coleman Co. [c.1931] 70 p. [5936

Henderlite, Rachel. A call to faith. Richmond, Va., John Knox Press [1955] 217 p. [5937

Henderson, Archibald. Bernard Shaw, playboy and prophet. New York, D. Appleton and Co., 1932. 871 p. [5938

——The campus of the first state university. Chapel Hill, University of North Carolina Press, 1949. 412 p. [5939

——The changing drama. New York, H. Holt and Co., 1914. 321 p. [5940

—— ——London, Grant Richards [c.1914] [5941

——The Church of the Atonement and the Chapel of the Cross at Chapel Hill, North Carolina. Hartford, Conn., Church Missions Publishing Co., 1938. (Story and Pageant, Publication no. 59) 57 p. [5942

——The conquest of the old Southwest. New York, The Century Co., 1920. 395 p. [5943

——Contemporary immortals. New York, D. Appleton and Co., 1930. 208 p. [5944

——Cradle of liberty; historical essays concerning the Mecklenburg Declaration of Independence. [Charlotte] Mecklenburg Historical Association, 1955. 53 p. [5945

——Derivation of the Brianchon configuration from two spatial point-triads. [Chapel Hill?] n.d. 6 p. [5946

——European dramatists. London, Grant Richards, 1914. 395 p. [5947

—— ——Cincinnati, Stewart & Kidd Co., 1918. 429 p. [5948

——First editions and autograph letters by George Bernard Shaw, the property of Dr. Archibald Henderson, Chapel Hill, N. C.; unrestricted public sale, Monday, January 16, at 2:15 P.M. New York, Anderson Galleries, 1933. (Sale no. 4015) 52 p. [5949

——Forty-sixth annual Phi Beta Kappa address . . . The undying flame, the story of its lighting. [Chapel Hill, University of North Carolina, 1950] [12] p. [5950

——The founding of Nashville, second of the Transylvania towns. Henderson, Ky., The Transylvanians, 1932. [15] p. [5951

——George Bernard Shaw, his life and works, a critical biography. Cincinnati, Stewart & Kidd Co., 1911. 528 p. [5952

—— ——London, Hurst and Blackett, 1911. 523 p. [5953

—— ——New York, Boni and Liveright, 1918. 528 p. [5954

——George Bernard Shaw: man of the century. New York, Appleton-Century-Crofts [1956] 969 p. [5955

——The history of St. Luke's Parish, and the beginnings of the Episcopal Church in Rowan County. [Salisbury? 1924?] 34 p. [5956

——In memoriam, Joseph Hyde Pratt, delivered at the annual session of the North Carolina Society for the Preservation of Antiquities . . . December 2, 1942. [Raleigh? 1942?] [8] p. [5957

——Interpreters of life and the modern spirit. New York, M. Kennerley, 1911. 330 p. [5958

—— ——London, Duckworth and Co., 1911. 330 p. [5959

——Is Bernard Shaw a dramatist? A scientific, but imaginary symposium in the neo-Socratic manner, conducted by Bernard Shaw's biographer. New York, M. Kennerley, 1929. 33 p. [5960

——Mark Twain. London, Duckworth & Co., 1911. 230 p. [5961

——North Carolina, the Old North State and the new. Chicago, Lewis Publishing Co., 1941. 5 v. v. 3-5: "North Carolina biography by a special staff of writers". [5962

——O. Henry, a memorial essay. [Raleigh, Mutual Publishing Co., pr., 1914] 32 p. [5963

Henderson, Archibald, ed. Pioneering a people's theatre. Chapel Hill, University of North Carolina Press, 1945. 104 p. Also issued as v. 17, no. 1 of The Carolina play-book. [5964

Henderson, Archibald. Revolution in North Carolina in 1775, Transylvania, Craven, Anson, and Mecklenburg. No place, no publisher [1916] 18 p. [5965
——The significance of the Transylvania Company in American history. No place, no publisher [1935?] 16 p. [5966
——The South's awakening; address before the Alpha Chapter, Phi Beta Kappa, of Tulane University. New Orleans [Tulane Press] 1915. 15 p. [5967
——The star of empire; phases of the westward movement in the old Southwest. Durham, Seeman Printery, 1919. 86 p. [5968
——Table-talk of G. B. S. Conversations on things in general between George Bernard Shaw and his biographer. New York, Harper & Brothers, 1925. 162 p. [5969
——The theory of relativity, studies and contributions, by Archibald Henderson, Allan Wilson Hobbs, and John Wayne Lasley, Jr. Chapel Hill, University Press, 1924. 98 p. [5970
——The Transylvania Company and the founding of Henderson, Kentucky. No place, no publisher [1929] 15 p. [5971
——The twenty-seven lines upon the cubic surface. Cambridge, University Press, 1911. (Cambridge tracts in mathematics and mathematical physics, no. 13) 100 p. [5972
——Washington the traveler. Washington, United States George Washington Bicentennial Commission, 1931. (Its Pamphlet, no. 11) 44 p. [5973
——Washington's southern tour, 1791. Boston, Houghton Mifflin Co., 1923. 339 p. [5974

Henderson, Barbara. Of wars and rumors of war. [Charlotte, privately printed, c.1950] [21] p. [5975

[Henderson, Le Grand] Augustus drives a jeep, by Le Grand [pseud.] Indianapolis, Bobbs-Merrill Co. [1944] 125 p. [5976
——Tom Benn and Blackbeard, the pirate. Nashville, Abingdon Press [1954] 63 p [5977

Henderson, Pleasant. To the freemen of Surry County. [Surry County, N. C. July 3, 1835] [1] p. [5978

Henderson, Thomas Johnston. Ann of the Ku Klux Klan- a partly fictional story of the Old South, centered around the Kirke-Holden War and the murder of John Walter ('Chicken') Stephens. [Yanceyville, Author, 1942] 13 p. [5979
——Homespun yarns. [Yanceyville? 1943] 37 p. [5980
——Honeysuckles and bramblebriars. [Yanceyville?] n.d. 38 p. [5981
——"Judge Cooke". [Yanceyville? 1942?] 21 p. [5982
——Plain tales from the country. [Yanceyville? 1942] 36 p. [5983
—— ——Book two. [Yanceyville? 1943] 40 p. [5984

Henderson, W. A. King's Mountain and its campaign. Greensboro, Guilford Battleground Co., n.d. 24 p. [5985

Henderson, N. C. Board of Commissioners. Code of the town of Henderson . . . compiled by J. H. Bridgers. Henderson, D. E. Aycock, pr., 1893. 92 p. [5986

Henderson, N. C. Board of School Trustees. Report of the Henderson Public Schools, 1902/03- Henderson, 1903- NcU has 1902/03-1922/23 [5987

Henderson, N. C. H. Leslie Perry Memorial Library. North Carolina books. [Henderson? 1941] [3] p. [5988

Henderson, N. C. Home Telephone and Telegraph Co. Charter and by-laws 1903. Raleigh, Edwards and Broughton Co., 1903. 24 p. [5989

Henderson County Baptist Association. Minutes, 188 - 188 - NcU has 1886 [5990

Henderson magazine, v. 1- July, 1926- Henderson, Chamber of Commerce, 1926- NcU has v. 1, no. 1-3 and October, 1929 (not numbered) [5991

Henderson's almanack for the year of our Lord, 18 - Raleigh, Thomas Henderson, 18 - NcU has 1811-1814, 1816, 1818-1823 [5992

Hendersonville, N. C. Board of Trade. Hendersonville illustrated. Hendersonville [190?] [30] p. [5993
——Hendersonville, Western North Carolina. [Hendersonville] n.d. 19 p. [5994

Hendersonville, N. C. Board of Trustees of the Graded Schools. Report, 1901/02- Hendersonville, 1902- NcU has 1911/12 [5995

Hendersonville, N. C. First Baptist Church. History of the First Baptist Church of Hendersonville, N. C. [Hendersonville] 1944. 35 p. [5996

Hendersonville, N. C. First Methodist Church. Anniversary yearbook, 1852-1952. [Hendersonville, 1952] [15] p. [5997

Hendersonville, N. C. Greater Hendersonville Club. Hendersonville, N. C., Land of the Sky. [Hendersonville] n.d. 28 p. [5998

Hendersonville, N. C. Presbyterian Church. One hundredth anniversary, Sunday, November 23, 1952. [Hendersonville, 1952] [9] p. [5999

Hendersonville, North Carolina [Hendersonville?] n.d. [16] p. [6000

Hendersonville, N. C. city directory, 19 - Asheville, Commercial Service Co., Inc., 19 - NcU has 1926-27, 1937-38, 1943-44, 1948-49, 1950-51, 1952-53 [6001

Hendersonville, N. C. in the Land of the Sky. [Hendersonville? 1918?] 10 p.[6002

Hendersonville Academy, Hendersonville, N. C. Announcement, 18 - Hendersonville, 18 - NcU has 1897 [6003

Hendrick, Burton Jesse. The life and letters of Walter H. Page. Garden City, N. Y., Doubleday, Page & Co., 1922-25. 3 v. [6004
—— ——Garden City, N. Y., Doubleday, Page & Co., 1922. 2 v. [6005
—— ——1923. [6006
—— ——1924. 4 v. [6007
—— ——adapted for school use by Rollo L. Lyman. 1925. 349 p. [6008
—— ——1927. 2 v. [6009
——The training of an American; the earlier life and letters of Walter H. Page, 1855-1913. Boston, Houghton Mifflin Co., 1928. 444 p. [6010

Hendricks, Garland A. Biography of a country church. Nashville, Broadman Press [1950] 137 p. [6011

Hendrickson, C. R. A knowledge of the Bible essential to complete scholarship; an address delivered before the literary societies of Wake Forest College, North Carolina, June 13, 1850. Richmond, H. K. Ellyson, 1850. 21 p. [6012

Henkel, David. Answer to Joseph Moore, the Methodist; with a few fragments on the doctrine of justification. New Market, Va., Printed in S. Henkel's Office, 1825. 188 p. [6013
——Carolinian herald of liberty, religious and political. Salisbury, Printed by Krider and Bingham, 1821. 65 p. [6014
——Heavenly flood of regeneration; or, A treatise on holy baptism. Salisbury, Bingham & White, 1822. 48 p. [6015
——A treatise on the person and incarnation of Jesus Christ, in which some of the principal arguments of the Unitarians are examined. New Market, Va., Printed in S. Henkel's Office, 1830. 119 p. [6016

[Henkel, P. C.] P. C. Henkel vindicates himself against the foul calumnies and misrepresentations of the so called "Evangelical Lutheran Tennessee Synod Reorganized". Salem, Printed by Blum & Son, 1851. 30 p. [6017

Henkel, Socrates. History of the Evangelical Lutheran Tennessee Synod. New Market, Va., Henkel & Co., 1890. 275 p. [6018

Henkels, Stanislaus V. Andrew Jackson and the Bank of the United States. [Philadelphia] privately printed for Stan. V. Henkels, Jr., 1928. [8] p. [6019

Henle, Mary. An experimental investigation of dynamic and structural determinants of substitution. Durham, Duke University Press, 1942. (Its Contributions to psychological theory [v. 2, no. 3, serial no. 7]) 112 p. [6020

Henley, Nettie (McCormick) The home place. New York, Vantage Press [1955] 182 p. [6021

Henly, Rachel Cornie, comp. Echoes from the pines. [Greensboro, J. J. Stone, pr., 1914] 20 p. [6022

Hennessee, William E. Your family coat of arms. Salisbury, Author, c.1952. [23] p. [6023

Henri, Florette. Kings Mountain. Garden City, N. Y., Doubleday, 1950. 340 p. [6024

Henry, Beulah Louise. Silent chords, by Sereca Trelsoe (Beulah Louise Henry) [Charlotte, Author, c.1914] 54 p. [6025

Henry, Louis D. Correspondence between Louis D. Henry . . . and the committee appointed to inform him of his nomination as the Democratic candidate for the office of governor of the state of North Carolina. Fayetteville, W. H. Bayne, pr., 1842. 12 p. [6026

Henry, Mellinger Edward. A bibliography for the study of American folk-songs with many titles of folk-songs (and titles that have to do with folk-songs) from other lands. London, Mitre Press [1937] 142 p. [6027

Henry, Mellinger Edward, ed. Folk-songs from the southern highlands. New York, J. J. Augustin [1938] 460 p. [6028

Henry, Mellinger Edward, comp. Songs sung in the Southern Appalachians, many of them illustrating ballads in the making. London, Mitre Press [1934] 253 p. [6029

Henry, O., pseud., see Porter, William Sydney

Henry, Reginald Buchanan. Genealogies of the families of the presidents. Rutland, Vt., Tuttle Co., 1935. 340 p. [6030

Henry, Robert. Narrative of the Battle of Cowan's Ford, February 1st, 1781, by Robert Henry, and Narrative of the Battle of Kings Mountain, by Captain David Vance. Greensboro, Reece & Elam for D. Schenck, 1891. 50 p. [6031

Henry, Walter Richard. Cotton and the commission merchants. 2d ed. Raleigh, P. W. Wiley, pr., 1883. 29 p. [6032

——Story of progress of the Queen City Charlotte and Mecklenburg County, North Carolina. Charlotte, Ray Printing Co., 1910. 34 p. [6033

——To the bankers of North Carolina, South Carolina, and Alabama, and other southern states. No place, no publisher [1907] 4 p. [6034

Henry Armand London. No place, no publisher, n.d. 5 p. [6035

Henty, George Alfred. True to the old flag, a tale of the American war of independence. London, Blackie and Son, n.d. 390 p. [6036

Hentz, Caroline Lee (Whiting) Lovell's folly. Cincinnati, Hubbard and Edmonds, 1833. 333 p. NcU has microfilm. [6037

Hentz, Nicholas Marcellus. A classical French reader, selected from the best writers of that language, in prose and poetry. Boston, Richardson & Lord, 1831. 270 p. [6038

——A manual of French phrases, and French conversations, adapted to Wanostrocht's grammar. Boston, Richardson and Lord, 1822. 154 p. [6039

Herald of health, v. 1- October, 1891- Kinston, H. O. Hyatt, 1891- NcU has v. 1-2. Discontinued following v. 2, no. 8? [6040

Herbst, Josephine. New green world. New York, Hastings House [1954] 272 p. [6041

Here is more proof that a property qualification is to follow the "amended" amendment. No place, no publisher [1900] [1] p. [6042

Hergesheimer, Joseph. Swords and roses. New York, A. A. Knopf, 1929. 327 p. [6043

Herman, Margery L. First aid in illness and injury. Raleigh, Edwards and Broughton Co., pr., 1917. 22 p. [6044

Herren, Sam C. The rise and decline of the Roman empire; an address delivered before the Irving Literary Club, at the residence of Judge R. P. Dick, April 25, 1880. [Greensboro? 1880?] [1] p. [6045

Herring, Harriet Laura. Passing of the mill village. Chapel Hill, University of North Carolina Press [1949] 137 p. [6046

——Southern industry and regional development. Chapel Hill, University of North Carolina Press, 1940. 103 p. [6047

——Southern resources for industrial development. Richmond, Dietz Press, 1948. (Southern Association of Science and Industry. Mongraph no. 2) 31 p. [6048

——Welfare work in mill villages; the story of extra-mill activities in North Carolina. Chapel Hill, University of North Carolina Press, 1929. 406 p. [6049

——Worker and public in the southern textile problem. Greensboro, Industrial Seminar for Ministers, 1930. 21 p. [6050

Herring, Needham Bryan. The lantern of Diogenes. Raleigh, E. M. Uzzell & Co., pr., 1910. 289 p. [6051

Herrington, W. D. The captain's bride; a tale of the war. Raleigh, William B. Smith, 1864. (Illustrated mercury novelette no. 1) 22 p. [6052

——The deserter's daughter. Raleigh, William B. Smith, 1865. (Southern field and fireside novelette, new series, no. 3) 27 p. [6053

Hersey, John. Inquiry into the character and condition of our children, and their claim to a participation in the privileges and blessings of the Redeemer's kingdom on earth. Raleigh, Thomas J. Lemay, pr., 1839. 36 p. [6054

Hertford Co., N. C. Bar. At a meeting of the Bar of Hertford County, on June 9th, 1937, the following resolution was introduced and duly considered. No place 1937. [8] p. [6055

Hertford County year book, 194 - Ahoskie, Parker Brothers, Inc., 194 - NcU has 1947-48. [6056

Herty, Charles Holmes. Per cent tables for oil in cotton-seed products, with method of analysis. Chapel Hill, University Press, 1908. 50 p. [6057

——An urgent message to the South. No place, Barrett Co., n.d. [16] p. [6058

—— ——delivered before the Association of Southern Agricultural Workers, Atlanta, Ga., January 31, 1935. No place, 1935. 6 p. [6059

Hess, Paul. Wilmington, N. C., annual meteorological summary, with comparative data from 1871 to 1923. Wilmington, Chamber of Commerce [192?] 3 p. [6060

Hesseltine, William Best. Civil War prisons; a study in war psychology. Columbus, O., Ohio State University Press, 1930. (Its Contributions in history and political science, no. 12) 290 p. [6061

Hewitt, Andrew. Pickapot, and other poems. Charlotte, Peak & Pine Press [1956] unpaged. [6062

——Traveler to April. Charlotte, Blue Ridge Press [1949] [51] p. [6063

Hewitt, Robert L. Work horse of the western front; the story of the 30th Infantry Division. Washington, Infantry Journal Press [1946] 356 p. [6064

Hexner, Ervin. International cartels. Chapel Hill, University of North Carolina Press [1945] 555 p. [6065

——The international steel cartel. Chapel Hill, University of North Carolina Press, 1943. 339 p. [6066

——Studies in legal terminology. Chapel Hill, University of North Carolina Press, 1941. 150 p. [6067

Heyward, DuBose. Angel. New York, George H. Doran Co. [c.1926] 287 p. [6068

——Lost morning. New York, Farrar & Rinehart, Inc. [c.1936] 270 p. [6069

——Skylines and horizons. New York, Macmillan Co., 1924. 74 p. [6070

Heyward, Frank A. The Norfolk & Southern Railroad and its commercial tributaries. [Norfolk] Norfolk Landmark Publishing Co., 1891. 64 p. [6071

Heywood, Susan (Merrick) Maum Nancy. Atlanta, Mabel Loeb & Virginia Pairo, 1937. 82 p. [6072

Hibbard, Clarence Addison, ed. The lyric South; an anthology of recent poetry from the South. New York, Macmillan Co., 1928. 279 p. [6073

Hibbard, Clarence Addison. Review of literature in the South—1925. [Chapel Hill, University News Bureau, 1926] [1] p. [6074

Hibbard, Clarence Addison, ed. Stories of the South, old and new. Chapel Hill, University of North Carolina Press [c.1931] 520 p. [6075

Hickerson, Thomas Felix. Beam deflection when I is constant or variable. [Chapel Hill] Author [1955] 100 p. [6076

——Happy valley, history and genealogy. Chapel Hill, Author [c.1940] 244 p. [6077

——Highway curves and earthwork. New York, McGraw-Hill Book Co., Inc., 1926. 382 p. [6078

——Highway surveying and planning; formerly published under the title of Highway curves and earthwork. 2d ed. New York, McGraw-Hill Book Co., Inc., 1936. 422 p. [6079

——Latitude, longitude and azimuth by the sun or stars; formerly published under the title of Navigational handbook with tables. 2d ed. Chapel Hill, Author, c.1947. 101 p. [6080

——Magnetic compass. [Durham, Seeman Printery, c.1918] 15 p. [6081

——Navigational handbook with tables. Chapel Hill, Author, c.1944. 75 p. [6082

——New field method for laying out circular curves. [Chapel Hill] Author, c.1920. 4 p. [6083

——Route location and surveying; formerly published under the title of Highway surveying and planning. 3d ed. New York, McGraw-Hill Book Co., Inc., 1953. 543 p. [6084
——Statically indeterminate frameworks. Chapel Hill, University of North Carolina Press, 1937. 205 p. Earlier edition called Structural frameworks. [6085
——Structural frameworks; a new method of analysis, with tables. Chapel Hill, University of North Carolina Press, 1934. 147 p. [6086

Hickerson Waterwheel Company, Chapel Hill, N. C. Farm waterworks; Hickerson improved waterwheel and pump-attachment for supplying country homes with running water. Chapel Hill [1915?] [3] p. [6087

Hickman, Franklin Simpson. A child in the midst of democracy; delivered at the tenth anniversary of the Duke Endowment, Orphan Section (Group meeting) Raleigh, North Carolina, December 11, 1934. Charlotte, Duke Endowment [1934] 14 p. [6088
——The possible self; a study in religious education. New York, Abingdon Press [c.1933] 128 p. [6089
——Signs of promise. New York, Abingdon-Cokesbury Press [1943] 186 p. [6090

Hickory, N. C. Chamber of Commerce. Hickory. [Hickory? 191?] 28 p. [6091
——Hickory, North Carolina. [Hickory, 1939] [14] p. [6092
——A survey and classified directory of Hickory. Hickory, 1946. 60 p. [6093

Hickory, N. C. City Council. The charter and the code of general ordinances. Charlottesville, Va., Michie City Publications Co., 1949. 452 p. [6094
——Handbook, Hickory City Schools, 19 - [Hickory, 19 - NcU has 1915/16, 1921/22 [6095
——Municipal survey, city of Hickory, North Carolina, six year period, ended June 30, 1938. [Hickory, 1938] 32 p. [6096

[Hickory, N. C. Community Council] Hickory, North Carolina. [Hickory, 1937] [15] p. [6097

Hicks, Archibald Arrington. Hon. A. A. Hicks addresses the Colonial Dames of America, delivered at St. John's Church, at Williamsboro, on Saturday, April 26. [Williamsboro? n.d.] [1] p. [6098

Hicks, Georgia. Interesting facts concerning North Carolina . . . compiled from the histories of North Carolina. No place, Author, 1924. 8 p. [6099
—— ——1925. 12 p. [6100
——Where North Carolina leads. No place, Author [1916?] [1] p. [6101

Hicks, John Donald. The Populist revolt; a history of the Farmers' Alliance and the People's Party. Minneapolis, University of Minnesota Press [c.1931] 473 p. [6102

Hicks, Mary A., joint author, see Cobb, Lucy Maria

Hicks, Thurston Titus. An address delivered before the North Carolina Bar Association, at Asheville, N. C., July 2nd, 1909. No place [Author, 1909?] 17 p. [6103
——Address presenting a portrait of Judge Walter A. Montgomery to the Supreme Court of North Carolina at Raleigh, October 30, 1923. No place, no publisher [1923?] 19 p. [6104
——The Democrats and Butler. No place [Author, 1916] [4] p. [6105
——The Supreme Court of the future; an address delivered at the celebration of the centennial . . . January 4, 1919. Raleigh, Edwards & Broughton Printing Co., 1919. 13 p. [6106
——Views of Mr. Hicks; honors the Governor for bouncing the directors . . . Growth of the Southern's "pull" during twenty years. Henderson, Author, [1896?] [1] p. [6107

Higby, Chester Penn. Present status of modern European history in the United States. Chapel Hill, University of North Carolina Press, 1926. (James Sprunt historical studies, v. 19, no. 1) 48 p. [6108

High, Stanley. Billy Graham; the personal story of the man, his message, and his mission. New York, McGraw-Hill [1956] 274 p. [6109

High Hampton Inn and Country Club, Cashiers, N. C. No place, High Hampton Inn [1931] Folder. [6110

High life, v. 1- 1920- Greensboro, Greensboro High School, 1920- NcU has v. 9 [6111

High Point, N. C. Board of Aldermen. Ordinances of the city [of] High Point . . . September 5th, 1907. [High Point, 1907] 35 p.   [6112

High Point, N. C. Board of Education. Report of the Superintendent of the High Point Graded Schools, 1897/98- High Point, 1898- NcU has 1897/98-1907/08, 1912/13.   [6113

High Point, N. C. Centennial Executive Committee. 1851-1951, High Point, N. C. centennial and festival celebration, July 9-14 . . . featuring Then & now. High Point, Chamber of Commerce, 1951. 104 p.   [6114

High Point, N. C. Chamber of Commerce. The building and the builders of a city. High Point [1947] 329 p.   [6115
——A few facts about High Point, the industrial city of the South. [High Point] 1922. 5 p.   [6116
——High Point, N. C., the industrial city of the South. [High Point, 192?] 22 p. [6117

[High Point, N. C. Chamber of Commerce] Pertinent facts about High Point, North Carolina. [High Point, 1944] Folder.   [6118
——Pioneer days and progress of High Point, N. C., 1859-1948. High Point [1949?] 48 p.   [6119
——What's made in High Point and who makes it, 19 - [High Point, 19 - NcU has [1937?] 1944 [1952] and one issue not dated.   [6120

High Point, N. C. First Presbyterian Church. Service of dedication and historical chronology. [High Point, 1946] 12 p.   [6121

High Point, N. C. High Point Furniture Co. The new premier line. [High Point, 1936?] [8] p.   [6122

High Point, N. C. Library. Report, 19 - [High Point, 19 - NcU has 1949/50, 1950/51   [6123

High Point, N. C., city directory, 19 - Asheville, Piedmont Directory Co., 19 - NcU has 1923-24   [6124

High Point College, High Point, N. C. High Point College bulletin: Catalogue number, 19 - High Point, 19 - NcU has 1926/27, 1931/32, 1933/34-1955/ 56   [6125

High school journal, v. 1- January, 1918- Chapel Hill, University of North Carolina Press [1918- NcU has v. 1-39   [6126

High Shoals, Gaston County, N. C., a southern cotton mill town. Charlotte, Observer Printing House [c.1908] 44 p.   [6127

High Shoals, North Carolina, 1750, 1800, 1850, 1900. [Charlotte? D. A. Tompkins, c.1902] Folder.   [6128

High tops in the Land of the Sky, a guide to Western North Carolina, 1947- [Asheville, High Tops] 1947- NcU has 1947, 1948, 1949, 1951, 1952   [6129

The highland churchman, 19 - Asheville, Diocese of Western North Carolina, 19 - NcU has v. [13-21] 22-25   [6130

Highland House and cottages, Pine Bluff, N. C. [Pine Bluff] n.d. 16 p.   [6131

Highland Pines Inn, Weymouth Heights, Southern Pines, N. C. No place, n.d. 22 p.   [6132

Highlands Biological Station, Inc., Highlands, N. C. The Highlands Biological Station, 1930- Highlands, 1930- NcU has 1930, 1931, 1939, 1943-1945, 1952. Title varies, 1930-39: Publication.   [6133
——25th anniversary, the Highlands Biological Station (established 1927, incorporated 1930) Highlands, 1952. 11 p.   [6134

Highsmith, James Albert. Relation of the rate of response to intelligence. Princeton, N. J., Psychological Review Co. [1924] (Psychological review publications. Psychological monographs, v. 34, no. 3) 33 p.   [6135

Highsmith Hospital, Green and Old Streets, Fayetteville, N. C. [Fayetteville?] n.d. 14 p.   [6136

Hight, William B. A collection of hearts. No place [1956] 156 p.   [6137
——Odd moments. [Henderson, Author, 1946] [17] p.   [6138

Hilker, Elmer Albert. It does add up. Boston, Christopher Publishing House [1948] 142 p.   [6139

Hill, Charles Applewhite. An improved American grammar of the English language for the use of schools, by C. A. Hill, A. M. principal of the Warrenton Academy, North-Carolina. Raleigh, J. Gales, pr., 1818.   82 p.   [6140

Hill, Daniel Harvey, 1821-1889.   College discipline; an inaugural address delivered at Davidson College, N. C., on the 28th February, 1855.   Salisbury, Watchman Office, 1855.   19 p.   [6141

——The Confederate soldier in the ranks; an address before the Virginia Division of the Association of the Army of Northern Virginia, at Richmond, Virginia, on Thursday evening, October 22d, 1885.   Richmond, The Association, 1885. 28 p.   [6142

——Consideration of the Sermon on the mount.   Philadelphia, William S. & Alfred Martien, 1858.   282 p.   [6143

——The crucifixion of Christ.   Philadelphia, William S. & Alfred Martien, 1859. 345 p.   [6144

——Essay on military education, delivered at Wilmington, N. C., November 14th, 1860, before the State Educational Convention.   Charlotte, Daily Bulletin, 1860. 18 p.   [6145

——The old South; an address delivered at Ford's Grand Opera House, on Memorial Day, June 6, 1887, before the Society of the Army and Navy of the Confederate States in the State of Maryland.   Baltimore, Andrew J. Conlon, pr., 1887. 23 p.   [6146

Hill, Daniel Harvey, 1859-1924.   Bethel to Sharpsburg.   Raleigh, Edwards & Broughton Co., 1926.   2 v.   [6147

——The Hill readers, by Daniel Harvey Hill, Frank Lincoln Stevens, and Charles William Burkett.   Boston, Ginn & Co. [c.1906]   5 v.   [6148

——North Carolina.   [Atlanta, Confederate Publishing Co., 1899]   (Evans, C. A., ed.   Confederate military history.   Atlanta, v. 4)   813 p.   [6149

——Southern histories; a paper read before the Southern Educational Association at Chattanooga, Tenn., July, 1891.   Raleigh, Edwards & Broughton Co., 1892. 10 p.   [6150

——Young people's history of North Carolina.   Charlotte, Stone and Barringer Co. [c.1907]   410 p.   [6151

—— ——revised and enlarged, 1923.   Raleigh, Alfred Williams & Co. [c.1916] 451 p.   [6152

Hill, George Canning.   Daniel Boone, the pioneer of Kentucky.   New York, Worthington Co. [c.1859]   262 p.   [6153

——Chicago, Donohue, Henneberry & Co. [c.1859]   262 p.   [6154

[Hill, George F.]   Brief history of Christ Episcopal Church Parish, Elizabeth City?] 1948.   18 p.   [6155

Hill, Jim Dan.   Sea dogs of the sixties; Farragut and seven contemporaries.   Minneapolis, Minn., University of Minnesota Press, 1935.   265 p.   [6156

Hill, John.   An address delivered before the two literary societies, of the University of North Carolina . . . under the appointment of the Dialectic Society.   Raleigh, W. R. Gales, pr., 1843.   18 p.   [6157

Hill, John Sprunt.   Address before the Alumni Association of the University of North Carolina, June 2, 1903.   No place, no publisher, n.d.   24 p.   [6158

Hill, John Sprunt, ed.   Against fluoridation of water; authorities collected by John Sprunt Hill.   Durham, Editor [1952?]   10 p.   [6159

Hill, John Sprunt.   Anniversary speech, March seventeenth, nineteen hundred and and fifty-two, Durham, North Carolina.   Durham, privately printed [1952] 10 p.   [6160

——La Carolina del Norte; una historia de democracia triunfante.   No place, no publisher [1924]   21 p.   [6161

——Co-operation and the work of the American Commission in Europe; speech . . . at the State Convention of Farmers.   [Durham, Seeman Printery] 1913.   16 p. [6162

——Co-operation in Hungary; speech . . . delivered at Budapest, Hungary, May 26, 1913.   [Durham, 1948?]   12 p.   [6163

——A co-operative plan to provide 5 per cent money for farmers . . . delivered at Conference for Education in the South, Southern Educational Association, Louisville, Ky., April 9th, 1914.   No place [1914]   20 p.   [6164

——Democracy regulated by law vs. bureaucrats and budgeteers.   [Durham, Author, 1931]   [3] p.   [6165

——Facts about state road law; square deal vs. pork barrel. [Durham, Author, 1931] [3] p. [6166

——Five per cent money for farmers and a system of taxation. Washington, Conference for Education in the South, n.d. 23 p. [6167

——North Carolina, a story of triumphant democracy; address delivered at annual meeting of Retail Merchants.' Association, Atlanta, Ga., January 28, 1924. [Durham? Author? 1924?] 22 p. [6168

——Organized credit, the hope of the Mecklenburg farmer; speech delivered at a meeting of merchants and farmers, Charlotte, N. C., December 18, 1915. [Durham? Author? 1915?] 16 p. [6169

——Organized credit, the paramount need of the Tar Heel farmer; speech . . . delivered at State Convention of Organized Farmers, Durham, North Carolina, November 16, 1915. [Durham, Author? 1915] 19 p. [6170

——A progressive program for building and maintaining a great primary system of state highways in North Carolina; address delivered at meeting of Good Roads Association, Asheville, N. C., June 17, 1920. [Durham? 1920?] 16 p. [6171

——Rural credits; speech delivered at State Convention of Farmers, Raleigh, N. C., August 26, 1915. [Durham? 1915?] 16 p. [6172

——State highway, Oxford to Durham, decision on location. Durham, 1923. 13 p. [6173

——A study of the new plan of operation of the Consolidated University of North Carolina. [Durham? Author] 1936. 24 p. [6174

[Hill, John Sprunt]   Uncle Peter fights a ghost; or, Heroes of Cedarhurst. [Durham] 1948. 9 p. [6175

——Waterloo. [Durham, 1949] 13 p. [6176

Hill, Joseph Alston.   Address delivered at Chapel Hill before the North Carolina Institute of Education, on Wednesday, June 26, 1833. Chapel Hill, Isaac C. Patridge, 1833. 16 p. [6177

Hill, Joseph M.   Biography of Daniel Harvey Hill, lieutenant general, Confederate States of America, educator, author, editor. [Little Rock] Arkansas History Commission [1946?] 37 p. [6178

Hill, Lewis Webb.   Lectures in pediatrics to the North Carolina post-graduate course, 1916. [Raleigh, Edwards & Broughton Co., c.1916] 66 p. [6179

Hill, Mildred Martin.   A traipsin' heart. New York, W. Malliet and Co., 1942. 61 p. [6180

Hill, Reuben.   Families under stress. New York, Harper & Bros. [1949] 443 p. [6181

Hill, Reuben, ed.   Family, marriage, and parenthood. 2d ed., edited by Howard Becker and Reuben Hill, Boston, Heath [c.1955] 849 p. [6182

Hill, Reuben.   When you marry [by] Evelyn Millis Duvall [and] Reuben Hill. Rev. ed. New York, Association Press [1953] 466 p. [6183

Hill, Theophilus Hunter.   Hesper and other poems. Raleigh, Strother and Marcom, 1861. 96 p. [6184

——Passion flower, and other poems. Raleigh, P. W. Wiley, 1883. 119 p. [6185

——Poems. New York, Hurd and Houghton, 1869. 155 p. [6186

Hill, William J., joint author, see Satchwell, S. S.

Hill, William Lauriston.   Bluebird songs of hope and joy, by Wm. Laurie Hill . . . and Rev. Halbert G. Hill. Boston, R. G. Badger [c.1916] 192 p. [6187

——The master of the Red Buck and the Bay Doe. Charlotte, Stone Publishing Co., 1913. 297 p. [6188

Hill, William W.   A discourse delivered in the Baptist Church at Raleigh . . . in explanation of the views, and in defence of the principles of the Associated Methodists. Raleigh, Lawrence and Lemay, 1830. 12 p. [6189

[Hill, William W.]   Stroke at the root; or, A contest between the love of liberty and the pride of office. Halifax, Office of the Free Press, 1825. 13 p. [6190

The Hillbilly, 19 - Asheville, Senior Class of Asheville High School, 19 - NcU has 1922, 1923, 1926 [6191

Hilldrup, Robert Leroy.   The life and times of Edmund Pendleton. Chapel Hill, University of North Carolina Press, 1939. 363 p. [6192

Hilliard, Henry Washington.   De Vane; a story of plebians and patricians. New-York, Blelock & Co., 1865. 2 v. in one, paged continuously 552 p. [6193

——Speeches and addresses. New York, Harper & Brothers, 1855. 497 p.   [6194

Hillife, 1925-   Chapel Hill, Seniors of Chapel Hill High School, 1925-   NcU has 1925, 1926   [6195

Hill's Albemarle (Stanly [County] N. C.) city directory, 19 - Richmond, Va., Hill Directory Co., Inc., 19 - NcU has 1951   [6196

Hill's Burlington (Alamance County, N. C.) city directory, 1935- Richmond, Va., Hill Directory Co., Inc., c.1935- NcU has 1935, 1943, 1950-51, 1952-53   [6197

Hill's Charlotte (North Carolina) city directory, 1932- Richmond, Va., Hill Directory Co., Inc., c.1932- NcU has 1935, 1943, 1947, 1951, 1952, 1953   [6198

Hill's Concord (Cabarrus County, N. C.) city directory, 19 - Richmond, Va., Hill Directory Co., Inc., 19 - NcU has 1949, 1952   [6199

Hill's Durham (Durham County, N. C.) city directory, 190 - Richmond, Va., Hill Directory Co., Inc., 190 - NcU has 1905-06, 1923, 1932, 1934, 1943, 1947, 1950, 1951, 1952.   [6200.

Hill's Fayetteville (Cumberland County, N. C.) city directory, 19 - Richmond, Va., Hill Directory Co., Inc., 19 - NcU has 1943, 1946, 1951, 1953   [6201

Hill's Gastonia (Gaston County, N. C.) city directory, 1934- Richmond, Va., Hill Directory Co., Inc., c.1934- NcU has 1934, 1942, 1947, 1951, 1953   [6202

Hill's Goldsboro (Wayne County, N. C.) city directory, 1906-1907- Richmond, Va., Hill Directory Co., Inc., 1906- NcU has 1934, 1945, 1950-51, 1952-53   [6203

Hill's Greensboro (Guilford County, N. C.) city directory, 1903-4- Richmond, Va., Hill Directory Co., Inc., 1903- NcU has 1933, 1935, 1943, 1947-48, 1951-52 [6204

Hill's High Point (Guilford County, N. C.) city directory, 1933- Richmond, Va., Hill Directory Co., Inc., c.1933- NcU has 1933, 1942-43, 1948, 1951-52, 1953, 1954   [6205

Hill's Kannapolis (Cabarrus County, N. C.) city directory, 19 - Richmond, Va., Hill Directory Co., Inc., 19 - NcU has 1951   [6206

Hill's Kinston (Lenoir County, N. C.) city directory, 19 - Richmond, Va., Hill Directory Co., Inc., 19 - NcU has 1928, 1951, 1953   [6207

Hill's Raleigh (Wake County, N. C.) city directory, 1903- Richmond, Va., Hill Directory Co., Inc., 1903- NcU has 1903, 1905-06, 1907-08, 1909-10, 1911-12, 1913-14, 1915-16, 1917, 1918-19, 1919-20, 1921-22, 1922-23, 1923-24, 1924, 1925, 1926, 1927, 1928, 1929, 1930, 1931, 1932, 1933, 1934, 1935, 1936, 1937, 1938, 1939, 1940, 1941, 1942, 1948   [6208

Hill's Reidsville (North Carolina) city directory, 1932- Richmond, Va., Hill Directory Co., Inc., c.1932- NcU has 1932   [6209

Hill's Rocky Mount (Edgecombe County, N. C.) city directory , 19 - Richmond, Va., Hill Directory Co., Inc., 19 - NcU has 1934, 1942, 1948, 1952   [6210

Hill's Sanford (Lee County, N. C.) city directory, 19 - Richmond, Va., Hill Directory Co., Inc., 19 - NcU has 1952   [6211

Hill's Wilmington (New Hanover Co., N. C.) city directory, 1897- Richmond, Va., Hill Directory Co., Inc., c.1897- NcU has 1897, 1905, 1907, 1909-10, 1911-12, 1912-13, 1917, 1918, 1919-20, 1922, 1926, 1928, 1930, 1932, 1934, 1943, 1947, 1952, 1953   [6212

Hill's Winston-Salem (Forsyth County, N. C.) city directory, 1932- Richmond, Va., Hill Directory Co., Inc., c.1932- NcU has 1933, 1935, 1943, 1947-48, 1952, 1953   [6213

Hillsboro, N. C.   Board of Commissioners. Acts of the General Assembly for the regulation of the town of Hillsborough, revised by John Scott. Hillsborough, Dennis Heartt, 1842. 19 p.   [6214

——Ordinances for the government of the town of Hillsborough. Hillsborough, Dennis Heartt, 1823. 11 p.   [6215

———— ————1838. 12 p.   [6216

———— ————Hillsborough, Democrat, 1849. 15 p.   [6217

———— ————Hillsborough, Dennis Heartt, 1858. 31 p.   [6218

———— ————Hillsborough, Hillsborough Recorder, 1871. 20 p.   [6219

———— ————Durham, Whitaker Printing House, 1892. 15 p.   [6220

Hillsboro, N. C.   Presbyterian Church.   Women of the Church. Selected Hillsboro recipes. Hillsboro, 1952. 124 p.   [6221

Hillsboro, N. C. Public Schools. Grade Six. History of the historic town of Hillsboro . . . written by the pupils of Grade Six, Hillsboro Public School, 1927-1928. [Hillsboro, 1928?] 30 p.   [6222

Hillsboro Academy. Polemic Society. Constitution and temporary laws. Hillsborough, Dennis Heartt, 1841. 11 p.   [6223

Hillsboro Commercial Club, Hillsboro, N. C. Charter and by-laws. Durham, Seeman Printery, 1909. 15 p.   [6224

Hillsboro Military Academy, Hillsboro, N. C. Hillsborough Military Academy, 1859- [Hillsborough, 1860- NcU has 1866/67 [1867/68, 1877/78]   [6225
——Semi-annual register of the officers and cadets, 1860- Hillsboro, 1860- NcU has Aug. 1, 1860, Nov. 23d, 1860, December 23d, 1860   [6226

Hillsboro Savings Institution, Hillsboro, N. C. Charter and by-laws . . . incorporated February 16th, 1859. Hillsborough, Dennis Heartt, 1859. 18 p.   [6227

Hillsborough Academy, Hillsborough, N. C. Catalogue, 18 - Hillsborough, 18 - NcU has 1838/39   [6228

Hillyard, M. B. The new South; a description of the Southern States, noting each state separately. Baltimore, Manufacturers' Record Co., 1887. 413 p.   [6229

Hilton, William. A relation of a discovery lately made on the coast of Florida (from lat. 31. to 33. deg. 45 min. north-lat.) . . . giving an account of the nature and temperature of the soyl, the manners and disposition of the natives, and whatsoever else is remarkable therein. Together with proposals made by the Commissioners of the Lords Proprietors to all such persons as shall become the first setlers. London, Printed by J. C. for S. Miller, 1664. (Force, Peter. Tracts. Washington, 1836-46. v. 4, no. 2, 1846) 27 p.   [6230

Himes, Joseph S. Social planning in America; a dynamic interpretation. Garden City, N. Y., Doubleday, 1954. (Doubleday short studies in sociology, SSS3) 59 p.   [6231

[Hines, Charles Anderson] Let us reason together. No place, no publisher [1930] [4] p.   [6232

Hines, Peter Evans. Memoir of Dr. C. E. Johnson . . . delivered at Fayetteville, N. C., May 4th, 1876. Raleigh, Edwards, Broughton & Co., 1876. 11 p. [6233

Hinsdale, John Wetmore. Address before the North Carolina Bar Association at Wrightsville Beach, N. C., Wednesday, June 29, 1910. Wilmington, Jackson & Bell Co., n.d. 44 p.   [6234
——Removal of causes from state courts to federal courts: Briefs. Raleigh, Edwards, Broughton & Co., 1896. 290 p.   [6235
——Should the term of office for state officials be limited to two terms? [Raleigh? Author?] n.d. [1] p.   [6236

Hinshaw, Ida Clifton. Bits of verse. Winston-Salem, Clay Printing Co., 1952. 23 p.   [6237
——The green satin lady; a Christmas story. [Winston-Salem, Winston Printing Co.] n.d. 22 p.   [6238

Hinshaw, William Wade. Encyclopedia of American Quaker genealogy, [compiled by T. W. Marshall] Ann Arbor, Mich., Edwards Bros.; [distributors: Friends Book and Supply House, Richmond, Ind.] 1936- NcU has v. 1-5. 6 v. have been published. v. 1: North Carolina.   [6239

Hinson, Estelle Elizabeth. A few rhymes and rhythms. Boston, Stratford Co., 1925. 25 p.   [6240

Hirsch, Arthur Henry. The Huguenots of colonial South Carolina. Durham, Duke University Press, 1928. 338 p.   [6241

Hirsch, Nathaniel David Mttron. An experimental study upon three hundred school children over a six-year period; from the Department of Psychology of Duke University. Worcester, Mass., Clark University, c.1930. (Genetic psychology monographs, v. 7, no. 6) p. 487-549   [6242

Hispanic American historical review, v. 6- February, 1926- Durham, Duke University, 1926- NcU has v. 6-36. Published Baltimore, Williams and Wilkins, 1918-1922; discontinued, 1922-1925.   [6243

Historical and descriptive review of the state of North Carolina, including the manufacturing and mercantile industries. Charleston, S. C., Empire Publishing Co., 1885. 2 v.   [6244

Historical Foundation of the Presbyterian and Reformed Churches, Montreat, N. C.
A great collection of Presbyterian and Reformed literature. Montreat, 1944.
8 p.   [6245
——The Historical Foundation and its treasures, by Thomas Hugh Spence, Jr.
Montreat, 1956. 174 p.   [6246
——Historical foundation news, v. 1- November 1, 1944- Montreat, 1944- NcU
has v. 1-12   [6247
——The Historical Foundation of the Presbyterian and Reformed Churches, Mon-
treat, N. C. [Montreat? 1935] [4] p.   [6248
——In appreciation: Mrs. Samuel Mills Tenney. Montreat, 1943. 16 p.   [6249
——Pictorial guide. Montreat, 1949. Folder.   [6250
——Survey of records and minutes in the Historical Foundation of the Presbyterian
and Reformed Churches, compiled by Thomas H. Spence, curator. Montreat,
1943. 46 p.   [6251

History news, v. 1- July, 1941- Chapel Hill, American Association for State and
Local History, 1941- NcU has v. 5-11   [6252

History of the Carolina, Cumberland Gap, and Chicago Railway. New York, Trow's
Printing and Bookbinding Co., 1882. 175 p.   [6253

History of the life and public services of Major-General Andrew Jackson, impartially
compiled from the most authentic sources. No place, no publisher, 1828.
37 p.   [6254

History of North Carolina. Chicago and New York, Lewis Publishing Co., 1919.
6 v. Contents. v. 1. The colonial and Revolutionary periods, 1584-1783, by
R. D. W. Connor.—v. 2. The federal period, 1783-1860, by W. K. Boyd.—v. 3.
North Carolina since 1860, by J. G. deR. Hamilton. v. 4-6. North Carolina
biography, by special staff of writers.   [6255

History of the organization of the Methodist Episcopal Church, South. Nashville,
Tenn., South-Western Christian Advocate, 1845. 267 p.   [6256

History of the Seaboard and Roanoke Railroad Company, including the Acts of the
assemblies of the states of Virginia and North Carolina relating thereto. No
place, no publisher, n.d. 128 p.   [6257

History of the Siamese youths. London, Cowie and Strange, n.d. 8 p.   [6258

History of the Sixtieth U. S. Infantry, 1917-1919. No place, no publisher, n.d.
85 p.   [6259

History of the stars and bars, designed by O. R. Smith, February, 1861, at Louisburg,
N. C., adopted by Congress of the Confederate States of America at Montgomery,
Ala., March 4, 1861. Raleigh, Edwards & Broughton Co., 1913. 30 p.   [6260

Hitchcock, Henry. Marching with Sherman . . . edited with an introduction, by M.
A. De Wolfe Howe. New Haven, Yale University Press, 1927. 332 p.   [6261

Hiwassee Dam Library. Library service at the camp library, Hiwassee Dam, North
Carolina, July, 1927 to June, 1940. [Hiwassee, 1940] 4 p.   [6262

Hobart, Alice Burridge. No elfin wings. [Dexter, Mo., Candor Press] c.1954.
52 p.   [6263

[Hobart-Hampden, Augustus Charles] Never caught; personal adventures with
twelve successful trips in blockade-running during the American Civil War. By
Captain Roberts [pseud.] London, John Camden Hotten, 1867. 123 p.   [6264
—— ——Reprinted, New York, W. Abbatt, 1908. (The magazine of history
with notes and queries, Extra no. 3) 65 p.   [6265
——Sketches from my life, by the late Admiral Hobart Pasha. 2d ed. London,
Longmans, Green and Co., 1886. 282 p.   [6266

Hobbs, Allan Wilson, joint author, see Henderson, Archibald

[Hobbs, Mary (Mendenhall)] Girls' aid work at Guilford College, North Carolina.
[Guilford College, 1905?] 7 p.   [6267
——Letters to Gertrude, 1910-1913, edited by Mary I. Shamburger. Philadelphia,
John C. Winston Co., 1936. 175 p.   [6268

Hobbs, Richard Junius Mendenhall. The cultural resources of the triangle cities:
Chapel Hill, Durham, Raleigh. [Chapel Hill, 1955] Various paging.   [6269

Hobbs, Samuel Huntington. North Carolina economic and social. Chapel Hill,
University of North Carolina Press, 1930. 403 p.   [6270

——North Carolina today, by S. H. Hobbs, Jr. and Majorie N. Bond. Chapel Hill, University of North Carolina Press [1947] 420 p. [6271

——Rural communities of the South . . . with the assistance of Solomon Sutker. Richmond, Va., Presbyterian Committee of Publication, c.1946. 111 p. [6272

Hocutt, Hilliard Manly. Struggling upward; a brief story of the upward struggle of Rev. and Mrs. J. D. Hocutt and their fourteen children of Burgaw, North Carolina. [Asheville, Author, 1951] 76 p. [6273

Hodge, Abraham. In the press, and shortly will be published, Instructions to be observed for the formation and movements of the cavalry . . . by William R. Davie. Halifax, 1799. [1] p. NcU has photostat (negative) of original in North Carolina State Department of Archives and History, Raleigh. [6274

Hodge and Bolyan's North-Carolina almanack see **Hodge's North-Carolina almanack**

Hodges, J. E. A history of Balls Creek Camp Ground, 1853-1929, including sketches of Rock Springs, St. Matthews and Wesley Chapel Camp Grounds. No place, no publisher [1929] [23] p. [6275

Hodges, J. E. Jesse Boone, his ancestors and descendants. Maiden, Author, 1953. 6 p. [6276

Hodges, Le Roy. Petersburg, Virginia, economic and municipal. Petersburg, Va., Petersburg Chamber of Commerce, Inc., 1917. 166 p. [6277

Hodges, Luther Cranston. Run and find the arrows. Winston-Salem, Bradford Printing Service, 1955. 127 p. [6278

Hodge's North-Carolina almanack for the year of our Lord, 179 - Halifax, Printed and sold by Abraham Hodge, [179 - NcU has 1794-1805. Called Hodge & Boylan's North-Carolina almanack, 1800-1805. [6279

Hodgin, David Reid. Tall Tom Wolfe. [Asheville, Stephens Press, c.1949] [6] p. [6280

Hoey, Clyde Roark, comp. In memory of Bess Gardner Hoey, who died in Shelby, N. C., February 13th, 1942. [Shelby? 1942] 37 p. [6281

——The position of Clyde R. Hoey on issues of the day. No place, no publisher [1950] 16 p. [6282

——The real Al Smith; speech delivered . . . before a county mass meeting, Shelby, N. C., Tuesday night, July 24th, 1928, opening the campaign. [Shelby, Star Publishing Co., 1928] [4] p. [6283

Hoffman, Frederick Ludwig. Malaria in Virginia, North Carolina, and South Carolina. Newark, N. J., Prudential Press, 1933. 30 p. [6284

Hoffman, Laban Miles. Our kin. Charlotte, D. E. Rhyne, L. L. Jenkins, and L. M. Hoffman, 1915. 584 p. [6285

Hoffman, Max Ellis. The Hoffmans of North Carolina. Asheville, M. E. Hoffman [c.1938] 192 p. [6286

Hoffmann, Margaret Jones. Miss B's first cookbook; 20 family-sized recipes for the youngest cook. Indianapolis, Bobbs-Merrill Co. [1950] [48] p. [6287

——Sew easy, for the young beginner. New York, Dutton, 1956. 93 p. [6288

The Hog Back Mountain Club, Tryon, North Carolina. [Clinton, S. C., Jacobs and Co., pr.] n.d. 24 plates [6289

Hoge, Peyton Harrison. The progressiveness of Christianity; a sermon delivered August 5, 1888, in the First Presbyterian Church, Wilmington, N. C. Richmond, Whittet & Shepperson, 1888. 22 p. [6290

Hogg, Thomas D. Northwestern mining interests. Raleigh, E. M. Uzzell, pr., 1894. 34 p. [6291

——Proposed bill for remedying the condition of the streets of Raleigh. Raleigh, E. M. Uzzell, pr., 1881. 11 p. [6292

——The streets of Raleigh, their condition and the remedy. Raleigh, E. M. Uzzell, pr., 1881. 20 p. [6293

Hogue, Richard Wallace. Commencement sermon of 1906, preached in St. Mary's Chapel, Sunday, May 27th. [Raleigh, St. Mary's School, 1906?] 15 p. [6294

——Spindrift; a volume of verse. [Remington? Va.] 1949. 72 p. [6295

Holcombe, James Philemon. An address delivered before the Society of Alumni of the University of Virginia at its annual meeting, held in the public hall, June 29, 1853. Richmond, MacFarlane & Fergusson, pr., 1853. 43 p. [6296

Holden, Jean (Stansbury) Oddments, bitments, and remainders. [Tryon, Pacelot Publishing Co., 1931?] 45 p. [6297

Holden, Joseph William. Hatteras and other poems. Raleigh, Edwards and Broughton Co., 1925. 51 p. [6298

Holden, William Woods. Address delivered before the Cumberland County Agricultural Society at Fayetteville, November 3d, 1859. Fayetteville, E. J. Hale, 1859. 22 p. [6299

——Address delivered before the Duplin County Agricultural Society, November 6, 1857. Raleigh, The Standard, 1857. 29 p. [6300

——Address delivered before the State Educational Association of North Carolina, at Warrenton, July 1st, 1857. Raleigh, Holden and Wilson, pr., 1857. 32 p. [6301

——Address delivered before the young ladies of the Raleigh Female Seminary, June 7, 1859. Raleigh, W. W. Holden, 1859. 16 p. [6302

——Address on the history of journalism in North Carolina delivered at the ninth annual meeting of the Press Association of North Carolina, held at Winston, June 21, 1881. Raleigh, News and Observer Book and Job Print [1881?] 23 p. [6303

——Lecture read before the Raleigh Merchanics' Association on the 4th anniversary, July 12, 1842. Raleigh, Star, 1842. 20 p. [6304

——Memoirs of W. W. Holden. Durham, Seeman Printery, 1911. (The John Lawson monographs of the Trinity College Historical Society, v. 2) 199 p. [6305

——Oration delivered in the city of Raleigh, North Carolina, July 4th, 1856. Raleigh, W. W. Holden, 1856. 20 p. [6306

——The President's plan considered; the proposed constitutional amendment explained, and its adoption urged. Raleigh, September 20, 1866. [1] p. [6307

——Union meeting in Raleigh; Alfred Dockery nominated for governor. [Raleigh? 1866] 16 p. [6308

The Holden record, no. 1, 3-6, March 19-April 16, 1868. Raleigh [H. H. Helper] 1868. NcU has no. 1, 3-6 [6309

[**Holding, Joseph**] The liberal soul shall be made fat and the honest statesmen and politician shall be rewarded and their labor and works will follow them through life. [Tarboro, Press, 1845] 4 p. [6310

Holding, W. W. Facts about Holding's certified early planting cotton seed. Raleigh, Commercial Printing Co. [1918?] 18 p. [6311

Holeman, Mary Russell. To the women of the Confederacy. [Durham, c.1915] 2 p. [6312

Holiday handbook of North Carolina, 1947- Charlotte, Tarheel Publications, 1947- NcU has 1947 [6313

Holiness Church   see **Pilgrim Holiness Church**

Holland, F. R. A sermon delivered in the Moravian Church at Salem, N. C., on the late national fast day, January 4, 1861. Salem, L. V. and E. T. Blum, 1861. 15 p. [6314

Hollander, Jacob Harry, ed. Studies in state taxation with particular reference to the Southern States. Baltimore, The Johns Hopkins Press, 1900. (Johns Hopkins University. Studies in historical and political science, ser. 18, no. 1-4) 253 p. [6315

Holley, Irving Brinton. Ideas and weapons; exploitation of the aerial weapon by the United States during World War I. New Haven, Yale University Press, 1953. (Yale historical publications. Miscellany, 57) 222 p. [6316

Hollingsworth, Jesse Gentry. History of Surry County, or, Annals of Northwest North Carolina. [Greensboro, W. H. Fisher Co., pr., c.1935] 280 p. [6317

Holloway, Roland Funk. Five months in "The Old North State". Chicago, privately printed, 1914. 94 p. [6318

Holman Association, Inc. An informal report of the work of Miss Lydia Holman in the mountains of North Carolina, October 1914, to October, 1915. [Boston? Boston Committee, 1915?] [14] p. [6319

——Report, 1st- 1911- Baltimore [1912- NcU has v. 1 [6320

Holme, Benjamin. A collection of the epistles and works of Benjamin Holme; to which is prefixed an account of his life and travels in the work of the ministry. London, Luke Hinde, 1754. 194 p. [6321

Holmes, Edison Parker. The disadvantages of being a preacher's son. Winston-Salem, Clay Printing Co., 1950. 167 p.   [6322

——Nothin' ain't no good. Winston-Salem, Clay Printing Co. [1955] 123 p. [6323

Holmes, Joseph Austin. Notes on the Indian burial mounds of Eastern North Carolina. No place, no publisher, n.d. 6 p.   [6324

Holmes, Mary Bynum see Pierson, Mary Bynum (Holmes)

Holmes, Oscar E. A true story of how I lost my hearing. [Winston-Salem, Stewart's Printing House, 1908] 6 p.   [6325

Holmes, Mrs. T. C. History of St. David's Church and Parish, Creswell, North Carolina. [Creswell, 1954?] 16 p.   [6326

Holmes, Urban Tigner. At the cross roads on the hill; a pageant celebrating the hundredth anniversary of the founding of the parish of the Chapel of the Cross in Chapel Hill, North Carolina. Chapel Hill, Chapel of the Cross, 1942. 48 p. [6327

——Daily living in the twelfth century, based on the observations of Alexander Neckam in London and Paris. Madison, University of Wisconsin Press, 1952. 337 p.   [6328

——A French composition, consisting of original French text with English paraphrase. Columbia, Mo., Lucas Brothers [c.1926] 134 p.   [6329

——A history of Old French literature, from the origins to the year 1300. Chapel Hill, Book Exchange, 1930. 224 p.   [6330

—— ——Chapel Hill, R. Linker, 1937. 351 p.   [6331

——A history of the French language, by Urban T. Holmes, Jr. . . . and Alexander H. Schutz. Columbus, O., H. L. Hedrick, 1933. 196 p.   [6332

—— ——1935.   [6333

—— ——New York, Farrar & Rinehart, Inc. [c.1938] 184 p.   [6334

——A source book for the History of the French language. Columbus, O., H. L. Hedrick, 1940. 122 p.   [6335

Holmes, Urban Tigner, ed. Romance studies presented to William Morton Dey on the occasion of his seventieth birthday by his colleagues and former students; edited by Urban T. Holmes, Jr., Alfred G. Engstrom and Sturgis E. Leavitt. Chapel Hill [University of North Carolina] 1950. 196 p.   [6336

Holmes, Urban Tigner. Samuel Pepys in Paris, and other essays. Chapel Hill, University of North Carolina Press [1954] (Its Studies in the Romance languages and literatures, no. 24) 57 p.   [6337

Holmes, Urban Tigner, ed. The works of Guillaume de Salluste, sieur Du Bartas, a critical edition with introduction, commentary, and variants . . . by Urban Tigner Holmes, Jr., John Coriden Lyons, Robert White Linker. Chapel Hill, University of North Carolina Press, 1935-1940. 3 v.   [6338

Holmes, Urban Tigner, joint author, see Giduz, Hugh

Holt, C. E. Autobiographical sketch of a teacher's life including a residence in the northern and southern states, California, Cuba, and Peru. Quebec [Canada] James Carrel, 1875. 104 p.   [6339

Holt, Eugene. Edwin Michael Holt and his descendants, 1807-1948. [Richmond, Va., privately printed, 1949] 221 p.   [6340

Holt, J. Robert, ed. Heavenly chimes; new soul-stirring songs for the Sabbath School, singing schools and revivals. Greensboro, J. Robert Holt, c.1907. 62 p.   [6341

[Holt, John Saunders] What I know about Ben Eccles, by Abraham Page. Philadelphia, J. B. Lippincott & Co., 1869. 407 p.   [6342

The holy shield. No place, no publisher, n.d. 8 p.   [6343

Home mission college review, v. 1-4, May, 1927-May, 1930. Raleigh, Shaw University under the auspices of the American Baptist Home Mission Society of New York, 1927-1930. NcU has v. 1-4. Discontinued following v. 4, no. 1, May, 1930.   [6344

Homespun, v. 1- November, 1925- Greensboro, Students of the Central High School of Greensboro, 1925- NcU has v. 1-5 [6-8]   [6345

Honigmann, John Joseph. Culture and personality. New York, Harper and Brothers [1954] 499 p.   [6346

Hood, Frazer, ed. If ye know these things; the Presbyterian task in North Carolina. Charlotte, Presbyterian Standard Publishing Co., 1927. 240 p.   [6347
——Seeing men as trees walking; a psychological study of Mark 8:14-26. No place, no publisher, n.d. 13 p.   [6348
Hood, George Ezekiel. The origin of man. Goldsboro, Author, 1926. 111 p. [6349
Hood, Gurney Pope. Chartering of banks; address . . . before first session, Regional Banking Conference . . . Atlanta, Georgia, March 25, 1937. [Raleigh? 1937] 6 p.   [6350
——Taxation and its relationship to the future of our banking structure; an address delivered before the 40th annual convention of the National Association of Supervisors of State Banks, St. Paul, Minn., September 25, 1941. [Raleigh? 1941?] 7 p.   [6351
Hood, Robin. Industrial social security in the South. Chapel Hill, University of North Carolina Press, 1936. (Southern policy papers, no. 5) 22 p.   [6352
Hood, Samuel Stevens. Archibald Henderson. [Chapel Hill?] 1946. 20 p. [6353
Hook, James William. James Hook and Virginia Eller; a family history and genealogy. New Haven, Conn., Tuttle, Morehouse & Taylor Co., 1925. 171 p. [6354
Hook and Sawyer, Architects, Charlotte, N. C. Some designs. [Charlotte, Queen City Printing and Paper Co.] 1902. 19 plates with illus. on both sides.   [6355
Hooker, Flora Janie (Hamer) John Hicks Hamer, 1765-1842; his antecedents, descendants and collateral families, 1744-1949, a compilation. [Hamer, S. C.] Compiler [1949] 350 p.   [6356
Hooks, Arah. Mr. Nosey. New York, D. Appleton-Century Co. [1945] [31] p. [6357
Hoole, William Stanley. Alias Simon Suggs; the life and times of Johnson Jones Hooper. University, Ala., University of Alabama Press, 1952. 283 p.   [6358
[Hooper, Archibald MacLaine] Defence of the administration of Andrew Jackson against the calumnies of the Whig press in relation to the removal of the Wilmington collector [by Caius Victor] No place, no publisher, n.d. 83 p.   [6359
Hooper, Archibald MacLaine. A memoir of Gen. John Ashe of the Revolution by the late A. M. Hooper and G. J. McRee. Wilmington, Daily Herald, pr., 1854. 16 p.   [6360
[Hooper, Johnson Jones] Simon Suggs' adventures and travels . . . with Widow Rugby's husband, and twenty-six other humorous tales of Alabama. Philadelphia, T. B. Peterson [1848] 201, 169 p.   [6361
Hooper, Johnson Jones. Simon Suggs' adventures . . . together with 'Taking the census' and other Alabama sketches. Philadelphia, T. B. Peterson & Brothers [c.1881] 217 p.   [6362
Hooper, William. Address delivered before the North Carolina Bible Society, December, 1819. No place, no publisher, n.d. 8 p.   [6363
——Address on female education, delivered at Raleigh before the Sedgwick Female Seminary, February 27, 1847. Raleigh, Weston R. Gales, 1848. 24 p.   [6364
——Discipline of the heart, to be connected with the culture of the mind; a discourse on education, delivered to the students of the college, at Chapel Hill, N. C., August 22, 1830. New York, Sleight and Robinson, 1830. 24 p.   [6365
——A discourse delivered before the Masonic Society, at Chapel-Hill, June 23d, 1827, on the occasion of celebrating the anniversary of St. John the Baptist. Hillsborough, D. Heartt, 1827. 16 p.   [6366
——Fifty years since; an address before the Alumni Association of the University of North Carolina . . . June 1st, 1859. Raleigh, Holden and Wilson, 1859. 34 p. [6367
—— ——2d ed. Chapel Hill, John B. Neathery, 1861. 34 p.   [6368
——The force of habit; a discourse delivered to the students of the University of North Carolina, at Chapel Hill, March 31st, 1833. Philadelphia, J. W. Martin and W. K. Boden, 1833. 21 p.   [6369
—— ——2d ed. Raleigh, A. M. Gorman, 1851. 21 p.   [6370
—— ——Wilmington, Messenger, 1890. 16 p.   [6371
——The happy choice; a sermon occasioned by the death of Mrs. Mallett, wife of Peter Mallett, Esq., of Fayetteville, N. C. Philadelphia, W. W. Woodward, 1824. 28 p.   [6372
——Human inventions make vain the worship of God; a discourse delivered before

the Chowan Association, North Carolina, May, 1851. Raleigh, North Carolina Institution for the Deaf and Dumb and the Blind, pr., 1851. 29 p. [6373
——Latin prosody for the use of schools. 3d ed. Boston, Hilliard, Gray and Co., 1836. 55 p. [6374
——A lecture on the imperfections of our primary schools and the best method of correcting them, delivered before the North Carolina Institute of Education at Chapel Hill, June 20th, 1832. Newbern, John I. Pasteur, pr., 1832. 28 p. [6375
——An oration delivered at Chapel Hill, on Wednesday, June 24th, 1829, being the day before the commencement of the college according to the annual appointment of the two literary societies. Hillsborough, Dennis Heartt, pr., 1829. 27 p. [6376
——Professor Hooper's address delivered before the Literary Society of Pittsborough. Hillsborough, Dennis Heartt, pr., 1835. 24 p. [6377
——The sacredness of human life and American indifference to its destruction; an address before the literary societies of Wake Forest College, June 10th, 1857. Raleigh, Holden and Wilson, pr., 1857. 32 p. [6378
——A sermon on the deceitfulness and wickedness of the heart. No place, no publisher, n.d. 12 p. [6379
——A short system of Latin prosody, containing all the necessary rules. Philadelphia, Lydia R. Bailey, pr. for the Author, 1819. 36 p. [6380
——A valedictory address delivered to the students of the University of North Carolina, January 21, 1838. Raleigh, Raleigh Register, pr., 1838. 25 p. [6381
Hoover, Calvin Bryce. Dictators and democracies. New York, Macmillan Co., 1937. 110 p. [6382
——The economic life of Soviet Russia. New York, Macmillan Co., 1931. 361 p. [6383
——Economic resources and policies of the South [by] Calvin B. Hoover [and] B. U. Ratchford. New York, Macmillan Co. [1951] 464 p. [6384
——Germany enters the Third Reich. New York, Macmillan Co., 1933. 243 p. [6385
Hoover, David. Memoir of David Hoover, a pioneer of Indiana. Richmond, Ind., James Elder, 1857. 44 p. [6386
Hope, James Barron, joint author, see Vance, Zebulon Baird
Hopkins, Lindsey. Discovered! The winning and giving of a million [by] Lindsey Hopkins [and] Al Fairbrother. [Greensboro, 1910?] [60] p. [6387
[Hopley, Catherine Cooper] Life in the South, from the commencement of the war, by a blockaded British subject. London, Chapman and Hall, 1863. 2 v. [6388
Horace Kephart Memorial Association, Asheville, N. C. Horace Kephart Memorial Association. [Asheville] 1932. [4] p. [6389
[Horn, Josiah R.] To the public. [Tarboro, Free Press, 1829] 8 p. [6390
Horn, Stanley Fitzgerald. Gallant rebel, the fabulous cruise of the C. S. S. Shenandoah. New Brunswick, Rutgers University Press, 1947. 292 p. [6391
——The Hermitage, home of Old Hickory. Richmond, Va., Garrett & Massie, 1938. 225 p. [6392
Horne, Herman Harrell. Christ in man-making. New York, Abingdon Press [c.1926] 101 p. [6393
——The democratic philosophy of education; companion to Dewey's Democracy and education. New York, Macmillan Co., 1932. 547 p. [6394
——Free will and human responsibility; a philosophical argument. New York, Macmillan Co., 1912. 197 p. [6395
——The function of a school of pedagogy. No place, no publisher [1909] [6] p. [6396
——Idealism in education; or, First principles in the making of men and women. New York, Macmillan Co., 1910. 183 p. [6397
——Jesus as a philosopher, and other radio talks. New York, Abingdon Press [c.1927] 208 p. [6398
——Jesus—our standard. New York, Abingdon Press [c.1918] 307 p. [6399
——Leadership of Bible study groups. New York, Association Press, 1912. 62 p. [6400
——Modern problems as Jesus saw them. New York, Association Press, 1918. 137 p. [6401
——The philosophy of Christian education. New York, Fleming H. Revell Co. [c.1937] 171 p. [6402
——The philosophy of education. New York, Macmillan Co., 1904. 295 p. [6403
——The principle underlying modern physical education. No place, no publisher [1910] 7 p. [6404

——The psychological principles of education. New York, Macmillan Co., 1906.
435 p.   [6405
——Shakespeare's philosophy of love. [Raleigh, Edwards & Broughton Co., pr.]
1945. 205 p.   [6406
——Story-telling, questioning and studying. New York, Macmillan Co., 1917.
181 p.   [6407
——The teacher as artist; an essay in education as an aesthetic process. Boston,
Houghton Mifflin Co. [c.1917] 62 p.   [6408
——This new education. New York, Abingdon Press [c.1931] 280 p.   [6409
——What is religion? Chapel Hill, University Press, 1895. (University of North
Carolina, Department of Philosophy, Worth prize, 1895) 18 p.   [6410

Horne, Ida Carolina Harrell. Romantic rambles, letters home from abroad, edited
by her son, Herman Harrell Horne. Raleigh, Edwards & Broughton Co., 1926.
165 p.   [6411
——Simple southern songs, edited by Herman Harrell Horne. No place, privately
printed, 1916. 198 p.   [6412
——Songs of sentiment . . . edited by her son, Herman Harrell Horne. New York,
Neale Publishing Co., 1917. 155 p.   [6413

Horner, Junius Moore. The educational problem of the South.[Asheville? Prot-
estant Episcopal Church, Missionary District of Asheville?] n.d. [8] p. [6414
——An Epiphany pastoral to the clergy and laity of the Missionary District of
Asheville, N. C. No place, no publisher [1916] 13 p.   [6415
——School work, Southern Appalachian Mountains. [Asheville? Protestant Episco-
pal Church, Diocese of Western North Carolina?] n.d. [3] p.   [6416
——The Southern Appalachian highlanders. [Asheville? Protestant Episcopal
Church, Diocese of Western North Carolina? 1927] [21] p.   [6417

Horner, William Edwin. Good afternoon. [Sanford, 1955] 144 p.   [6418
—— ——Sanford, 1956. unpaged.   [6419

Horner & Graves's School, Hillsboro, N. C. [Catalogue, 1872/73- Hillsboro, 1873-
NcU has 1872/73, 1874/75   [6420
——Rules and regulations, 1874. Raleigh, Edwards, Broughton & Co., 1874.
12 p.   [6421

Horner Military School, Oxford and Charlotte, N. C. Catalogue, 18 - Oxford,
Charlotte, 18 - NcU has 1880/81, 1882/83,1893/94, 1895/96, 1898/99, 1899/
1900, 1900/01, 1903/04, 1904/05, 1905/06, 1906/07, 1908/09, 1912/13, 1913/14,
1914/15, 1916/17.   [6422

[Hornot, Antoine] Anecodotes américaines; ou, Histoire abrégée des principaux
événements arrivés dans le nouveau monde. Paris, Chez Vincent, 1776. 782 p. [6423

Horry, Peter. The life of Gen. Francis Marion, a celebrated partisan officer in the
Revolutionary War, against the British and Tories in South Carolina and Georgia,
by Brig. Gen. P. Horry . . . and M. L. Weems. 11th ed. Frankford, Pa.,
Joseph Allen, 1825. 252 p.   [6424
—— ——Philadelphia, J. B. Lippincott and Co., 1857.   [6425
—— ——1860.   [6426

[Horton, George Moses] [The hope of liberty; or, Poems by a slave. 2d ed.
Philadelphia, 1837] 23 p. Title page wanting in NcU copy   [6427

Horton, George Moses. The poetical works of George M. Horton, the colored bard
of North-Carolina, to which is prefixed the life of the author, written by himself.
Hillsborough, D. Heartt, pr., 1845. 96 p.   [6428

Hosack, David. A biographical memoir of Hugh Williamson . . . delivered on the
first of November, 1819, at the request of the New-York Historical Society. New-
York, C. S. Van Winkle, pr., 1820. 91 p.   [6429
—— ——New-York, E. Bliss and E. White, 1821. 78 p.   [6430

Hospital Saving Association of North Carolina, Inc., see North Carolina Hospital
Saving Association, Inc.

Hoss, May Dikeman. The pike. New York, Appleton-Century-Crofts [1954]
303 p.   [6431

Hot and Warm Springs Hotel, Madison County, N. C. Hot and Warm Springs
Hotel, Madison County, N. C. [New York, Leve and Alden, 1884] NcU has
defective copy, p. 29—wanting.   [6432

—— ——Raleigh, Edwards, Broughton & Co., 1883. 16 p.   [6433

Hot Springs, N. C. Mountain Park Hotel. The Hot Springs of North Carolina. Hot Springs, [1886?] [2] p.   [6434
——Mountain Park Hotel. Columbia, S. C., State Co., pr., n.d. 7 p.   [6435

Hot Springs Hotel and Sanitarium, Hot Springs, N. C., "the recreation center of the South". [Asheville Inland Press] n.d. 15 p.   [6436

Hotel Albert, New Berne, N. C. A long felt want supplied, the new Hotel Albert, New Berne, North Carolina. New Berne, Journal Job Print, 1887. 32 p.   [6437

Hotel Chattawka, Newbern, North Carolina, the favorite winter resort. [Newbern, W. T. Hill and Co., n.d.] [6] p.   [6438

Hotel Raleigh, Raleigh, N. C. No place, no publisher, n.d. [1] p. 10 plates. [6439

Hotten, John Camden, ed. The original lists of persons of quality; emigrants; religious exiles; political rebels; serving men sold for a term of years; apprentices; children stolen; maidens pressed; and others who went from Great Britain to the American plantations, 1600-1700. New York, J. W. Bouton, 1874. 580 p.   [6440
—— ——New York, G. A. Baker and Co., Inc., 1931. Facsimile re-issue. [6441

Hough, Emerson. The way to the West, and the lives of three early Americans, Boone—Crockett—Carson. New York, Grosset & Dunlap [1903] 446 p.   [6442

House, Homer Doliver. Woody plants of Western North Carolina. Darmstadt, Germany, C. F. Winters, 1913. 34 p.   [6443

House, Robert Burton. Miss Sue and the Sheriff. Chapel Hill, University of North Carolina Press, 1941. 118 p.   [6444
——Miss Sue and the Sheriff, a chapter in the biography of a home. [Chapel Hill] n.d. 11 p.   [6445

Houser, George. We challenged Jim Crow! [New York, The Fellowship of Reconciliation, 1948?] 15 p.   [6446

Houston, Martha Lou, comp. Census of 1840 (list of persons aged 80-100) Iredell County, North Carolina. Washington, D. C., 1936. 3 numb. leaves. [6447

Houston, Noel. The great promise, a novel. New York, Reynal & Hitchcock [1946] 502 p.   [6448

Houston, W. M. My drummer. Greensboro, Thomas, Reece and Co., pr., 1883. [1] p.   [6449

Hovey, Alvah. Memoir of the life and times of the Reverend Isaac Backus. Boston, Gould and Lincoln, 1859. 369 p.   [6450

How should our judges be appointed? No place, no publisher [1891?] [4] p. [6451

Howard, George. Free textbooks in public schools. New York, 1924. 75 p. [6452

Howard, John Hamilton. In the shadow of the pines. New York, Eaton & Mains [c.1906] 249 p.   [6453

Howard, Oliver Otis. Autobiography of Oliver Otis Howard, major-general, United States Army. New York, Baker & Taylor Co., 1907. 2 v.   [6454

Howard, T. Levron. The TVA and economic security in the South. Chapel Hill, University of North Carolina Press, 1936. (Southern policy papers, no. 7) 11 p.   [6455

Howard Alexander Foushee, 1870-1916. No place, no publisher [1916?] 43 p. [6456

[Howard W. Odum Memorial Fund] The Howard W. Odum Memorial Fund. [Chapel Hill] 1956. 12 p.   [6457

Howe, Charles Kent. Solving the riddle of the Lost Colony. [Beaufort, M. P. Skarren, pr., 1947] 45 p.   [6458

Howe, George, 1802-1883. The value and influence of literary pursuits; an oration delivered before the Eumenean and Philanthropic societies of Davidson College, N. C., on commencement day, August 13th, 1846. Columbia, S. C., I. C. Morgan, pr., 1846. 27 p.   [6459

Howe, George, 1876-1936. Fasti sacerdotum p.r. publicorum aetatis imperatoriae. Lipsiae, In Aedibus B. G. Teubneri, 1904. 96 p.   [6460

Howe, George, 1876-1936, ed. Greek literature in translation, selected and edited by George Howe . . . and Gustave Adolphus Harrer. New York, Harper & Brothers, 1924. 642 p.   [6461

Howe, George, 1876-1936. A handbook of classical mythology, by George Howe and G. A. Harrer. New York, F. S. Crofts & Co., 1929. 301 p.   [6462
——Latin for pharmacists, by George Howe . . . and John Grover Beard. Philadelphia, P. Blakiston's Son & Co. [c.1916]   134 p.   [6463
——Latin sight reader. Raleigh, Thompson Publishing Co., 1912.   87 p.   [6464
—— ——1917.   [6465
Howe, George, 1876-1936, ed. Roman literature in translation, selected and edited by George Howe . . . and Gustave Adolphus Harrer. New York, Harper & Brothers, 1924.   630 p.   [6466
Howe, Joseph William. Winter homes for invalids. New York, G. P. Putham's Sons, 1875.   205 p.   [6467
Howe, Margaret, pseud.,   see Brucker, Margaretta
Howell, Almonte Charles. Ensayos sobre literatura northeamericana. Guatemala, C. A., 1948.   80 p.   [6468
——Forty-seventh annual Phi Beta Kappa address, Alpha Chapter of North Carolina: Meditations on a pawned Phi Beta Kappa key.   [Chapel Hill, 1951] [10] p.   [6469
——A handbook of English in engineering usage. New York, J. Wiley & Sons, Inc., 1930.   308 p.   [6470
—— ——2d. ed.   New York, J. Wiley & Sons, Inc., 1940.   433 p.   [6471
——A history of the Chapel Hill Baptist Church, 1854-1924. Chapel Hill, [Chapel Hill Baptist Church] 1945.   32 p.   [6472
——The Kenan professorships. Chapel Hill, University of North Carolina Press, 1956.   343 p.   [6473
——Military correspondence and reports. New York, McGraw-Hill Book Co., Inc., 1943.   190 p.   [6474
Howell, Andrew Jackson. Anniversaries, prepared for the congregation of the First Presbyterian Church, Wilmington, North Carolina. Wilmington, Wilmington Stamp and Printing Co., 1913.   31 p.   [6475
——The book of Wilmington. [Wilmington?] no publisher [1930]   206 p.   [6476
——Cornelius Harnett, a Revolutionary patriot. Wilmington, Wm. L. deRosset, Jr., 1896.   48 p.   [6477
——A history of First Presbyterian Church, Wilmington, North Carolina. [Wilmington, First Presbyterian Church, 1951]   16 p.   [6478
——Money Island. [Wilmington, Commercial Printing Co., c.1908]   68 p.   [6479
——Songs of summer nights. Wilmington, Wilmington Stamp and Printing Co., 1937.   72 p.   [6480
Howell, Edward Vernon. Latin for pharmacist and physician. [Chapel Hill?] no publisher, n.d.   20 p.   [6481
——Latin for physician and pharmacist. Chapel Hill [University Press] 1900. 49 p.   [6482
Howell, Gertrude Jenkins. The Woman's Auxiliary of the Synod of North Carolina. Wilmington, Wilmington Stamp and Printing Co. [1938?]   69 p.   [6483
Howell, Logan Douglass. The first Christmas. New York, Howell and Co., c.1911. 8 p.   [6484
——How to teach reading; a revised manual for teachers of the New Howell primer, by Logan Douglass Howell . . . and Frances S. Williams. New York, Howell & Co., 1919.   119 p.   [6485
——The Howell reader. New York, Howell and Co. [c.1910] v. NcU has v. 1-2 [6486
——The new Howell reader. New York, Howell and Co. [c.1917]   v. NcU has v. 1-2   [6487
Howell, Louise H. Tomorrow's vintage, a book of poems. Boston, B. Humphries, Inc. [1942]   38 p.   [6488
Howell, Mabel Katharine. Women and the kingdom; fifty years of kingdom building by the women of the Methodist Episcopal Church, South, 1878-1928. Nashville, Tenn., Cokesbury Press, 1928.   283 p.   [6489
Howell, Peter. The life and travels of Peter Howell, written by himself. Newbern, W. H. Mayhew [1849]   320 p.   [6490
Howell, Robert Boyte Crawford. An oration delivered before the Knights Templars, and the Masonic lodges of the city of Richmond and Manchester, at the festival of

John the Baptist, June 24, 1850. Richmond, Va., H. K. Ellyson's Power Press, pr., 1850. 21 p. [6491

[Howell, Robert Boyte Crawford] The relations of woman to human happiness; an address before the Chowan Female Collegiate Institute, at the anniversary at Murfreesborough, North Carolina, August 10, 1853. Richmond, Va., H. K. Ellyson, pr., 1853. 22 p. [6492

Howerton, William H. Card to the public. [Raleigh, Author, 1876] 8 p. [6493

Howie Mining Co., Chicago. The Howie Mining Co., Inc., capitalization $2,000,000.00, Mines in Union County, N. C. Chicago, Howie Mining Co., 1906] 32 p. [6494

The Howler, 190 - Wake Forest, Philomathesian and Euzelian Literary Societies of Wake Forest College, 190 - NcU has 1915, 1917, 1918, 1929, 1933 [6495

Hoxie, Richard Leveridge. Improvement of the upper Cape Fear; report of hearing at Fayetteville by Lieut. Col. Hoxie and Committee of the Board of Engineers, January 24th, 1907. No place, no publisher [1909?] 20 p. [6496

Hoyle, Bernadette. Tar Heel writers I know. Winston-Salem, J. F. Blair, 1956. 215 p. [6497

Hoyle, Kenneth Roger. The "whole" record sustains Kitchin; Mr. J. W. Bailey denies what is not charged and artfully dodges what is charged. [Sanford, no publisher, 1912] 2 p. [6498

Hoyle, Vinton Asbury, joint author, see Mackie, Ernest Lloyd

Hoyt, William Henry. The Mecklenburg Declaration of Independence. New York, G. P. Putham's Sons, 1907. 284 p. [6499

Hubbard, Fordyce Mitchell. Lives of William Richardson Davie and Samuel Kirkland [by Fordyce M. Hubbard and Samuel K. Lothrop] Boston, Charles C. Little and James Brown, 1848. (The Library of American biography, conducted by Jared Sparks, 2d. ser., v. 15) 461 p. [6500

——The North-Carolina reader, no. 1. New York, A. S. Barnes & Co. [c.1855] 110 p. [6501

—— ———1856. [6502

——The North-Carolina reader, number II. New York, A. S. Barnes & Co., 1856. 195 p. [6503

—— ———Wilmington, S. W. Whitaker, 1856. [6504

—— ———New York, A. S. Barnes & Burr, 1858. [6505

—— ———1859. [6506

—— ———New York, A. S. Barnes & Co., 1873. [6507

Hubbard, Margaret Ann. The Hickory Limb. New York, Macmillan Co., 1942. 291 p. [6508

[Hubbard, Simeon] Address to the citizens of Connecticut by the friends of Andrew Jackson in Norwich and vicinity. Norwich, L. H. Young, 1828. 26 p. [6509

Hubbell, Jay Broadus, ed. American life in literature. New York, Harper & Brothers, 1936. 2 v. in 1. [6510

Hubbell, Jay·Broadus. The enjoyment of literature. New York, Macmillan Co., 1929. 289 p. [6511

Hubbell, Jay Broadus, comp. An introduction to drama, by Jay B. Hubbell . . . and John O. Beaty. New York, Macmillan Co., 1937. 849 p. [6512

Hubbell, Jay Broadus, ed. The last years of Henry Timrod, 1864-1867. Durham, Duke University Press, 1941. 184 p. [6513

Hubbell, Jay Broadus. Lives of Franklin Plato Eller and John Carlton Eller. [Durham] privately printed, 1910. 245 p. [6514

——The South in American literature, 1607-1900. [Durham] Duke University Press, 1954. 987 p. [6515

Hubbs, Carl Leavitt. Endemic fish fauna of Lake Waccamaw, North Carolina, by Carl L. Hubbs and Edward C. Raney. Ann Arbor, University of Michigan Press, 1946. (Its Miscellaneous publications, Museum of Zoology, no. 65) 30 p. [6516

Huckleberries, v. 1- 1942- Hendersonville, Huckleberry Mountain Camp, 1942- NcU has v. [2-6] [6517

Huddle, John Warfield, ed. A laboratory manual for beginning students in general

geology, edited by John W. Huddle . . . and John C. McCampbell.   Chapel Hill
[Ann Arbor, Mich., Edwards Brothers, Inc., 1944]   99 p.   [6518
Hudson, Arthur Palmer.   But mine was different: cystolithectomy, embolism,
pleurisy, Memorial Hospital, Chapel Hill, April 28-May 20, 1955.   Chapel Hill,
University of North Carolina Press, 1955.   16 p.   [6519
—— ——2d ed., rev. and enl.   23 p.   [6520
——Folksongs of Mississippi and their background.   Chapel Hill, University of
North Carolina Press, 1936.   321 p.   [6521
——Folk tunes from Mississippi collected by Arthur Palmer Hudson and edited by
George Herzog.   New York, National Play Bureau, 1937.   (Works Progress Ad-
ministration, National Play Bureau.   Publication no. 25)   45 p.   [6522
——Functional college composition, by Authur Palmer Hudson . . . Earl H. Hart-
sell . . . W. Lester Wilson.   New York, Thomas Y. Crowell Co. [c.1936-1937]
2 v.   [6523
Hudson, Arthur Palmer, ed.   Humor of the old deep South.   New York, Macmillan
Co., 1936.   548 p.   [6524
Hudson, Arthur Palmer, comp.   Nelson's college carvan . . . [by] Arthur Palmer
Hudson . . . Leonard Burwell Hurley . . . [and] Joseph Deadrick Clark.   New
York, T. Nelson and Sons, 1936.   4 v. in 1.   [6525
—— ——1939.   4 v.   [6526
Hudson, C. R.   My experience as a "co-op".   Raleigh, North Carolina Cotton
Growers Cooperative Association, 1924.   [3] p.   [6527
Hudson, Hilary Thomas.   Children's lamp; or, A standard catechism on the leading
truths of Christianity, as believed and taught by the Methodist Episcopal Church,
South.   Shelby, J. P. Babington, pr., 1884.   162 p.   [6528
——The Gospel an antidote to death's fears, a sermon preached in the Methodist
Church, Chapel Hill, April 13, 1856.   Raleigh, A. M. Gorman, pr., 1856.   16 p. [6529
——The Methodist armor.   Shelby, Aurora Book and Job Print, 1882.   247 p. [6530
—— ——rev. and enl.   Nashville, Tenn., Southern Methodist Publishing House
for the Author, 1884.   342 p.   [6531
—— ——1889.   [6532
—— ——1891.   [6533
—— ——1893.   355 p.   [6534
—— ——1896.   [6535
——The shield of the young Methodist; or, The Methodist armor, abridged and
arranged in the form of a catechism.   Shelby, Babington & Roberts, pr., 1883.
211 p.   [6536
—— ——Nashville, Tenn., Publishing House, M. E. Church, South, 1904.
226 p.   [6537
Huey, Lillian Olive (Gribble)   Rosemary and rue, and other poems.   Winston-
Salem, Children's Home Printship, 1921.   50 p.   [6538
Huffman, Minna R.   Come into my garden, and other poems.   Durham, Religion
& Health Press [c.1955]   58 p.   [6539
Hufham, James Dunn.   Memoir of Rev. John L. Prichard, late pastor of the First
Baptist Church, Wilmington, N. C. Raleigh, Hufman & Hughes, 1867. 182 p. [6540
[Huger, Arthur Deveron]   The heresies of our age; Christianity versus civilization,
or, Faith versus facts, by Apollonius of Ottaray.   [Burnsville? Author] 1916.
54 p.   [6541
——A rosary of the ridges, by Hugh Deveron and Ruellia Kernestaffe of the Over
Hills of Ottaray.   Burnsville, Edwards Printery, 1919.   48 p.   [6542
——Waifs from the wayside, by Vernon Revier.   Burnsville [Edwards Printery]
1923.   36 p.   [6543
Huggins, Edith Warren.   In all its glory.   Philadelphia, Dorrance & Co. [1945]
209 p.   [6544
Hughes, Harvey Hatcher.   Hell-bent fer heaven; a play in three acts.   New York,
Harper and Brothers, 1924.   187 p.   [6545
—— ——New York, Samuel French [c.1924]   187 p.   [6546
——Ruint; a folk comedy in four acts.   New York, Harper and Brothers, 1925.
214 p.   [6547
——Wake up, Jonathan; a comedy in a prologue and three acts, by Hatcher Hughes
and Elmer L. Rice.   New York, Samuel French, c.1928.   98 p.   [6548

Hughes, John. The Christian law of charity; a discourse delivered before the graduating class of the University of North Carolina, June 5th, 1860. Chapel Hill, John B. Neatherly, pr., 1860. 8 p.   [6549
——Lawrence O'Brien Branch; oration delivered at Raleigh, May 10th, 1884. No place, no publisher, n.d.   14 p.   [6550
Hughes, Nicholas Collin. Genesis and geology, the harmony of the scriptural and geological records. Chocowinity, Author, 1887. 142 p.   [6551
——Hendersonville in Civil War times, 1860-1865, as written in the memory of a very small child. Hendersonville, Blue Ridge Specialty Printers, 1936. 30 p. [6552
——Is Christ divided? A sermon delivered before the Edenton Convocation, in St. Peter's Church, Washington, N. C., on Sunday the 29th September, 1878. No place, no publisher [1878?]   8 p.   [6553
Hughson, Shirley Carter. The Carolina pirates and colonial commerce, 1670-1740. Baltimore, The Johns Hopkins Press, 1894. (Johns Hopkins University Studies in historical and political science, 12th ser., 5-7)   134 p.   [6554
Hughson, Walter, comp. The church's mission to the mountaineers of the South. Hartford, Conn., Church Missions Publishing Co. [c.1908]   131 p.   [6555
Hulbert, Archer Butler. Boone's wilderness road. Cleveland, O., A. H. Clark Co., 1903. (Historic highways of America, v. 6) 207 p.   [6556
Hulme, Francis Pledger. Come up the valley; ballads and poems. New Brunswick, Rutgers University Press, 1949. 92 p.   [6557
Hulme, William. Gentlemen. Raleigh, December 2, 1815. [1] p.   [6558
——To the citizens of Wilkes County [Raleigh, December 28, 1816] [1] p.   [6559
[Hulse, E. G.] History of the great world war ... illustrated with photographic reproductions of the men from Granville County who took part in this unparalleled conflict. [Oxford] Oxford Orphanage Press, 1920. 214 p.   [6560
Human relations bulletin, no. 1- May, 1955- Charlotte, North Carolina Council on Human Relations, 1955- NcU has no. 1-9   [6561
Humanities in the South, no. 1- April, 1951- Chapel Hill, Southern Humanities Conference, 1951- NcU has no. 1-4   [6562
[Humber, Robert Lee] The declaration of the federation of the world. [Raleigh, Edwards and Broughton Co., 1940] 8 p.   [6563
Hume, Martin Andrew Sharp. Sir Walter Raleigh; the British dominion of the West. London, T. Fisher Unwin, 1926. 292 p.   [6564
Hume, Thomas. Helps to the study of Hamlet in questions and suggestions. Waynesboro, Va., Semi-Weekly Print, 1884. 11 p.   [6565
Humphrey, Willis C. The great contest: a history of military and naval operations during the Civil War in the United States of America, 1861-1865. Detroit, C. H. Smith & Co., 1886. 691 p.   [6566
Humphreys, David. An historical account of the incorporated Society for the Propagation of the Gospel in Foreign Parts. London, J. Downing, pr., 1730. 356 p.   [6567
Humphries, John David. Georgia descendants of Nathaniel Pope of Virginia, John Humphries of South Carolina, and Allen Gay of North Carolina. [Atlanta? Ga., 1934] 40 p.   [6568
[Hunnicutt, F. H.] Hot-shot truths about Raleigh city affairs. [Raleigh, Allied Printing Trades, 1917] 6 p.   [6569
Hunnicutt, Samuel J. Twenty years of hunting and fishing in the Great Smoky Mountains. Knoxville, Tenn., S. B. Newman & Co. [c.1926] 216 p.   [6570
Hunt, Cornelius E. The Shenandoah; or, The last Confederate cruiser. New York, G. W. Carleton & Co., 1867. 273 p.   [6571
Hunt, Gaillard, comp. Fragments of Revolutionary history. Brooklyn, Historical Printing Club, 1892. 167 p.   [6572
Hunt, Mabel Leigh. Benjie's hat. New York, Frederick A. Stokes Co., 1938. 119 p.   [6573
——Ladycake Farm. Philadelphia, J. B. Lippincott Co. [1952] 126 p.   [6574
——Little grey gown. New York, Frederick A. Stokes Co., 1939. 168 p.   [6575
Hunt, R. F. Longing, poetry by Mrs. Mathilda Raven, von Beckman, music composed and respectfully dedicated to Miss Minna Raven, teacher at Edgeworth

Female Seminary, Greensboro, N. C., by R. F. Hunt. New York, S. T. Gordon, c.1858. 5 p.   [6576
——Souvenir d'Edgeworth, polka mazurka. Philadelphia, Beck & Lawton, c.1858. 7 p.   [6577

Hunt, Thomas Poage. The Bible Baptist; or, What does the Bible say on the mode of baptism. No place, Thomas Loring, 1834. 24 p.   [6578
—— ——Albany, N. Y., J. Munsell, 1843.   [6579
——Life and thoughts of Rev. Thomas P. Hunt; an autobiography. Wilkes-Barre, Pa., R. Baur & Son, 1901. 400 p.   [6580

Hunt, William. Memoirs of William and Nathan Hunt, taken chiefly from their journals and letters. Philadelphia, Uriah Hunt & Son, 1858. 159, 160 p. [6581

Hunter, Alexander. The huntsman in the South, v. 1- New York, Neale Publishing Co., 1908- NcU has v. 1. No more issued?   [6582

Hunter, Charles N. The story of a check. [Raleigh] n.d. [1] p.   [6583

Hunter, Cyrus Lee. Sketches of Western North Carolina, historical and biographical. Raleigh, Raleigh News Steam Job Print, 1877. 357 p.   [6584
—— ——Raleigh, Edwards & Broughton Co., 1930. 356 p.   [6585

Hunter, David. Correspondence, orders, etc., between Major-General David Hunter, Major-General J. G. Foster, and Brigadier-General Henry M. Naglee, and others, February and March, 1863. Philadelphia, J. B. Lippincott & Co., 1863. 60 p. [6586

Hunter, Floyd. Community power structure; a study of decision makers. Chapel Hill, University of North Carolina Press [1953] 297 p.   [6587

Hunter, Joshua Allen. Dear Doctor Dick; the story of a small-town physician. New York, Exposition Press [1955] 53 p.   [6588

Hunter, Kermit Houston. Chucky Jack; the story of Tennessee. Gatlinburg, Tenn., Great Smoky Mountains Historical Association, c.1956. 48 p.   [6589
——The eleventh hour; a drama of Woodrow Wilson. No place, c.1956. 47, 23 p.   [6590
——Forever this land; a drama of Lincoln's New Salem. Petersburg, Ill., New Salem Lincoln League, Inc., c.1951. 68 p.   [6591
—— ——[2d year revision]   [6592
——Horn in the West; a drama of the Southern Appalachian highlands. Boone, Southern Appalachian Historical Association, c.1952. 62 p.   [6593
——Unto these hills; a drama of the Cherokee. [Chapel Hill] University of North Carolina Press [1951, c.1950] 100 p.   [6594
——Voice in the wind; the story of Florida. No place, Florida Outdoor Drama Association, c.1955. 64 p.   [6595

Hunter, Mary Moseley, comp. Southern Baptist foreign missionaries. Nashville, Tenn., Broadman Press, 1940. 143 p.   [6596

Hunter, Osborne. Essay delivered at the second annual meeting of the North Carolina Educational Association in the House of Representatives, at Raleigh, N. C., July 9th, 1874. Raleigh, John Nichols & Co., 1874. 8 p.   [6597

Hunter, Robert. Quebec to Carolina in 1785-1786, being the travel dairy and observations of Robert Hunter, Jr., a young merchant of London, ed. by Louis B. Wright and Marion Tinling. San Marino, Calif., Huntington Library, 1943. 393 p.   [6598

Hunter, William May. The Hunter family, the generation of Henry Hunter. Charlotte, Observer Printing House, 1920. 144 p.   [6599

Hurd, Anna C. First lessons in speech. Morganton, School for the Deaf and Dumb, n.d. [79] p.   [6600

Hurdle, Carolyn. Guide me, sacred song; lyric by Pattie Viola Battle, music by Carolyn Hurdle. Bristol, Tenn., Hollembeak Music Co. [c.1914] 5 p.   [6601

Hurewicz, Witold. Dimension theory, by Witold Hurewicz and Henry Wallman. Princeton, Princeton University Press, 1941. (Princeton mathematical series, 4) 165 p.   [6602

Hurley, James Franklin. The prophet of Zion-Parnassus, Samuel Eusebius McCorkle, by James F. Hurley and Julia Goode Eagan. Richmond, Va., Presbyterian Committee of Publication for the Authors [c.1934] 121 p.   [6603

Hurley, Leonard B., joint author, see Hall, Alonzo C.

Hurley, M. L., ed. Five cardinal principles of the Christian Church defined. Raleigh, Christian Board of Publication, 1886. 130 p. [6604

Hurst, Martha. Some aspects of the problem of time. Chapel Hill, Department of Philosophy, University of North Carolina, 1934. (Its Studies in philosophy, no. 7) 102 p. [6605

[**Husband, Herman**] A fan for Fanning and a touch-stone to Tryon, containing an impartial account of the rise and progress of the so much talked of Regulation in North-Carolina, by Regulus [pseud.] Boston, Printed and sold at the Printing-Office, opposite the seat of William Vassel, 1771. 80 p. NcU has microfilm (negative) from original in Library of Congress [6606
——An impartial relation of the first rise and cause of the recent differences in publick affairs in the province of North-Carolina. No place, Printed for the Compiler, 1770. 104 p. NcU has imperfect copy completed by photostat. [6607

Huse, Howard Russell, tr. The divine comedy; a new prose translation. New York, Rinehart [1954] 492 p. [6608

Huse, Howard Russell. The illiteracy of the literate; a guide to the art of intelligent reading. New York, D. Appleton-Century Co., Inc., 1933. 272 p. [6609
——The psychology of foreign language study. Chapel Hill, University of North Carolina Press, 1931. 231 p. [6610
——Reading and speaking foreign languages. Chapel Hill, University of North Carolina Press [1945] 128 p. [6611

Huske, Joseph Caldwell. Christ our peace; a sermon preached in St. John's Church, Fayetteville, N. C., on the seventh Sunday after Trinity, August 7, 1859. Fayetteville, E. J. Hale, 1859. 16 p. [6612
——In memoriam; a sermon preached in St. John's Church, Fayetteville, N. C. . . . July 14th, 1872, on the occasion of the death of Charles Beatty Mallett. [Fayetteville? 1872] 14 p. [6613
——Sermon, delivered Sunday, July 1, 1894, upon occasion of the death of Mr. Samuel Johnston Hinsdale. Raleigh, Edwards, Broughton and Co., 1894. 12 p. [6614

Hutchins, Elias, joint author, see **Heath, Jesse**

Hutchins, James. A sketch of the Yancey Collegiate Institute, Burnsville, N. C. Burnsville, Edwards Printing Co. [1951?] 40 p. [6615

Hutchins, James Hill. My native town. New Bern, New Bern Historical Society Foundation [1955] unpaged. [6616

Hutchins, Thomas. Description topographique de la Virginie, de la Pensylvanie, du Maryland et de la Caroline Septentrionale. Paris, Le Rouge, 1781. 68 p. [6617
——A topographical description of Virginia, Pennsylvania, Maryland and North Carolina. London, Printed for the Author, and sold by J. Almon, 1778. 67 p. [6618
—— ——Reprinted from the original edition of 1778; ed. by Frederick Charles Hicks. Cleveland, O., Burrows Brothers Co., 1904. 143 p. [6619

Hutchins, W. L. Withered weeds. Winston-Salem, Clay Printing Co., 1950. 81 p. [6620

Hutchinson, Crete. In Cloudland, Mayview Park, Blowing Rock, North Carolina. [Washington, Judd & Detweiler, Inc., c.1920] [64] p. [6621

Hutchinson, Ruth Gillette. State-administered locally-shared taxes; development in the state and local tax systems of the United States. New York, Columbia University Press, 1931. 157 p. [6622

Hutchison, James Lafayette. China hand. Boston, Lothrop, Lee and Shepard Co., 1936. 418 p. [6623
——One-two-three-four; a nocturne. Boston, Lothrop, Lee and Shepard Co., 1935. 196 p. [6624

Hutchison, James M. Free-men of Mecklenburg County. No place, no publisher [January 22, 1835] 2 p. [6625

Hutchison Manufacturing Co., Chapel Hill, N. C. Farm water-works, the Hutchison-Hickerson combination water wheel and pump. Chapel Hill [1915] 10 p. [6626

Hutt, Mrs. William Nichol. How to organize a club of "United Farm Women" with 1915 programs. [Raleigh] The Progressive Farmer [1915?] 15 p. [6627

Hutto, Jasper C. Tomorrow can be better; an address delivered before the North

Carolina Association of Chamber of Commerce Executives, at Wilson, North Carolina, September 19, 1949. [Lumberton? Author? 1949] [6] p.   [6628

Hutton, Joseph. The wounded hussar; or, Rightful heir, a musical afterpiece. Philadelphia, Thomas T. Stiles, pr., 1809. 24 p.   [6629

Hyams, Charles W. Sergeant Hallyburton, the first American soldier captured in the World War. Moravian Falls, Dixie Publishing Co., 1923. 79 p.   [6630

Hyatt, Sybil. Calling all children. No place, no publisher, 1939. 32 p.   [6631

Hyde Co., N. C. Chamber of Commerce. Annual convention, Ocracoke Island, 193 - No place, 193 - NcU has 1939.   [6632

Hyman, Mary H., joint author, see Barrows, Harlan H.

Hymns for the camp. Raleigh, Biblical Recorder Print, 1864. 127 p.   [6633
——3d ed., rev. and enl. No place, no publisher, n.d. 127 p.   [6634

Icenhour, Walter E. My native land. No place, no publisher [1910] [3] p. [6635
——Sweet rhymes on nature. Brookside, W. H. McGuire's Job Print, 1908. [7] p.   [6636

Iden, Susan Franks. Edenton Street Methodist Sunday School, Raleigh, N. C.; historical sketch commemorating the opening of the new Sunday School Building, April 28, 1912. Raleigh, Edwards & Broughton Co. [1912?] 102 p.   [6637

Idol, Vera. Paths of shining light. New York, Abingdon Press [1956] 111 p. [6638

If you are an American, if you are a North Carolinian, if you love your country, read this. No place, no publisher [1949] [4] p.   [6639

Illinois Infantry. 55th Regt., 1861-1865. The story of the Fifty-Fifth Regiment, Illinois Volunteer Infantry in the Civil War, 1861-1865. [Clinton, Mass., W. J. Coulter, pr.] 1887. 519 p.   [6640

Illinois Infantry. 92d Regt., 1862-1865. Ninety-Second Illinois Volunteers. Freeport, Ill., Journal Steam Publishing House and Bookbindery, 1875. 390 p. [6641

Illinois Infantry. 103rd Regt., 1862-1865. Reminiscences of the Civil War, from diaries of members of the 103d Illinois Volunteer Infantry, 1904. Chicago, J. F. Leaming & Co. [c.1905] 293 p.   [6642

Illinois. University. Installation of Harry Woodburn Chase as president of the University of Illinois, May 1, 1931. Urbana, University of Illinois [1931] 97 p. [6643

Illustrating modern consolidated schools in Wake County, North Carolina. [Raleigh, Southern School Supply Co., 1926?] 7 p.   [6644

Ilsen, Isa Maud. Chimney Rock anthology, from Indian to white man. [Asheville, Hackney and Moale] c.1921. 8 p.   [6645

An imaginary conversation between President Jackson and the ghost of Jefferson. Columbia, S. C., Telescope Office, 1831. 22 p.   [6646

Immanuel Lutheran College, Greensboro, N. C. Catalogue, 190 - Greensboro, 190 - NcU has 1914/15-1916/17[1927/28?]   [6647

An impartial and true history of the life and services of Major General Andrew Jackson. No place, no publisher, n.d. 31 p.   [6648

In cloudland, Mayview Manor, Blowing Rock, N. C. [Baltimore, Thomas-Ellis, pr.] n.d. 9 p.   [6649
——Blowing Rock, Mayview Manor [1929] Folder.   [6650

In cloudland, Mayview Park, Blowing Rock, North Carolina. Blowing Rock, W. L. Alexander [1924?] 22 p.   [6651

In memoriam: Alexander Doak McClure, D. D. [Raleigh, Edwards & Broughton Co., 1920] 71 p.   [6652

In memoriam: Allen J. Tomlinson, 1843-1900. No place, no publisher [1900?] 31 p.   [6653

In memoriam: Anna Marguerite Fries, 1892-1916. No place, no publisher [1916?] 35 p.   [6654

In memoriam: Charles Campbell Coddington, 1878, 1928. [Charlotte? 1928?] [25] p.   [6655

In memoriam: David Gaston Worth, born December 17th, 1831, died November 21st, 1897. No place, no publisher, n.d. 91 p.   [6656

In memoriam: Elder Shubal Stearns, pastor of the Sandy Creek Baptist Church, from its organization, November, 1755, to the year 1771. [Greensboro, W. H. Eller, 1902]   4 p.   [6657

In memoriam: Eugene Morehead, died February 27, 1889. [Durham, Seeman Printery, 1889?]   56 p.   [6658

In memoriam: Emil A. de Schweinitz, 1864-1904.   No place, no publisher [1904?] 21 p.   [6659

In memoriam: Florie Lane Graham, 1866-1900.   No place, privately printed [1900?]   [24] p.   [6660

In memoriam: George Hubbard Brown, late associate justice of the Supreme Court of North Carolina.   Raleigh, Bynum Printing Co. [1927?]   29 p.   [6661

In memoriam: Henry Theodore Bahnson, 1845-1917. [Winston-Salem] 1917?] [17] p.   [6662

In memoriam: Hon. John M. Morehead.   Raleigh, Nichols & Gorman, pr., 1868. 84 p.   [6663

In memoriam: James Harmon Chadbourn, Wilmington, N. C.   No place, no publisher [1902?]   43 p.   [6664

In memoriam: John Franklin Reinhardt, 1844-1913.   No place, no publisher, n.d. 7 p.   [6665

In memoriam: Joseph Henry Gooch, 1866-1935. [Stem? Privately printed, 1935] 32 p.   [6666

In memoriam: Julius A. Gray, born September 6, 1833, died April 14, 1891.   [Philadelphia, Allen, Lane & Scott, pr., 1892?]   42 p.   [6667

In memoriam: Lysander D. Childs, born July 6th, 1855, died September 12th, 1899. No place, no publisher, n.d.   85 p.   [6668

In memoriam: Mrs. Jennie Britt Armfield, October 22, 1850, March 10, 1915.   [High Point?] Privately printed [1915?]   24 p.   [6669

In memoriam: Mrs. Mary A. Dixon, Mrs. Mary A. Payne.   No place, no publisher, n.d.   11 p.   [6670

In memoriam: Mrs. Nancy R. White.   No place, no publisher, n.d.   15 p.   [6671

In memoriam of John Cameron Buxton.   No place, no publisher [1917?]   21 p. [6672

In memoriam: Rev. J. Henry Smith, D. D., born in Lexington, Va., August 13, 1820, died in Greensboro, N. C., November 22, 1897.   [Baltimore, Printed by the family for private distribution, 1900]   110 p.   [6673

In memoriam: Rev. Mr. George McNeil, 1720-1805, delivered June 7, 1905.   No place, no publisher [1905?]   17 p.   [6674

In memoriam: Rev. Robert Ernest Caldwell, D. D., born October 18, 1858, died January 3, 1904.   [Baltimore, privately printed, 1905]   100 p.   [6675

In memoriam: Rt. Rev. Thomas Atkinson, D. D., LL. D., bishop of North Carolina. No place, no publisher, n.d.   NcU has defective copy, p. 25—wanting   [6676

In memoriam: The memorial window placed in Christ Church, Raleigh, to Mrs. Lucy M. Battle.   [Raleigh, 1874?]   [1] p.   [6677

In memoriam: Thomas Jefferson Moore, M. D., born, 30th April, 1840, died, 24th February, 1898.   [Richmond? 1898?]   [16] p.   [6678

In memoriam: William Houston Patterson, 1832-1904.   No place, no publisher, n.d.   17 p.   [6679

In memory of Alston Grimes, 1866-1914.   No place, no publisher [1914]   9 p. [6680

In memory of the late Edward William Pou; proceedings of the Bar of the county of Johnston.   Raleigh, Edwards and Broughton, pr., 1892.   19 p.   [6681

In the beautiful Sapphire country, Glenville Park Estates.   Glenville, Glenville Park Estates [1926?]   [21] p.   [6682

Incog, pseud.   A collection of poems.   Newbern, Newbernian Office, pr., 1845. 122 p.   [6683

The independent citizen; or, The majesty of the people asserted against the usurpations of the legislature of North-Carolina, in several acts of assembly, passed in the years 1783, 1785, 1786, and 1787.   [Newbern, F. X. Martin, 1787]   21 p. NcU has photostat of original in Library of Congress.   [6684

Independent Order of Odd Fellows.   North Carolina.   Code for conducting trials

in subordinate lodges of R. W. Grand Lodge, 1877.   Raleigh, Edwards, Broughton
& Co., 1877.   14 p.   [6685
——Constitution and by-laws of the Grand Lodge of North Carolina, together with
the resolutions now in force, and rules for the conduction of trials.   Raleigh, W. C.
Doub, pr., 1856.   12 p.   [6686
——Constitution, by-laws, and rules of the Right Worthy Grand Encampment of
Patriarchs of the Independent Order of Odd Fellows of the state of North Carolina.
Wilmington, Stringer's Job Press, 1848.   19 p.   [6687
——Constitution; or, General laws for the government of subordinate lodges, as
amended 1908.   No place, no publisher [1908?]   8 p.   [6688
——Digest of the laws, decisions, and enactments of the Grand Lodge of North
Carolina, Independent Order [of] Odd Fellows.   Raleigh, Edwards, Broughton &
Co., 1886.   100 p.   [6689
——Journal of proceedings of the Right Worthy Grand Lodge, from its organization,
1843, to 1851; together with the constitution of the Grand Lodge of the United
States, v. 1.   Raleigh, P. G. H. P. William D. Cooke, 1851.   314 p.   [6690
——Journal of annual session, 1843-   1843-   NcU has 1843-1857 [1860-1900] 1903-
1916, 1918-1940   [6691

Independent Order of Odd Fellows.   North Carolina.   Cold-water Lodge no. 62,
Concord.   Constitution, by-laws and rules of order.   Chapel Hill, James M.
Henderson, pr., 1858.   16 p.   [6692

Independent Order of Odd Fellows.   North Carolina.   Cross Creek Lodge no. 4,
Fayetteville.   Bye-laws . . . to which are appended the general rules of the order.
Fayetteville, Edward J. Hale, pr., 1843.   19 p.   [6693

Independent Order of Odd Fellows.   North Carolina.   Edgecombe Lodge no. 50,
Tarboro.   Constitution, by-laws, and rules of order.   Tarboro', Southerner Job
Office, pr., 1882.   16 p.   [6694

Independent Order of Odd Fellows.   North Carolina.   Hardenburgh Lodge no. 39,
Germantown. Constitution and by-laws. Salem, Blum & Son, pr., 1853. 24 p. [6695

Independent Order of Odd Fellows.   North Carolina.   Hope for All Lodge no. 2645,
Raleigh.   Constitution and by-laws.   [Raleigh? 1928?]   27 p.   [6696

Independent Order of Odd Fellows.   North Carolina.   McRee Encampment of
Patriarchs no. 15, Raleigh.   Constitution, by-laws and rules of order.   Raleigh,
Nichols and Gorman, 1871.   40 p.   [6697

Independent Order of Odd Fellows.   North Carolina.   Manteo Lodge no. 8, Raleigh.   By-laws, instituted January 13, 1846.   Raleigh, North Carolina Institution for the Deaf and Dumb, pr., 1848.   28 p.   [6698
——By laws.   Raleigh, Seaton Gales, 1849.   16 p.   [6699
——Constitution and general laws.   No place, n.d.   7 p.   [6700

Independent Order of Odd Fellows.   North Carolina.   Neuse Lodge no. 6, Goldsboro.   By-laws.   Wilmington, W. Stringer's Job Office, 1848.   15 p.   [6701

Independent Order of Odd Fellows.   North Carolina.   Ocracoke Lodge no. 194,
Ocracoke.   By-laws.   No place [1902]   17 p.   [6702

Independent Order of Odd Fellows.   North Carolina.   Olive Branch Lodge no. 37,
Smithfield.   Constiution (!) and by-laws.   Raleigh, W. W. Holden, 1853.
27 p.   [6703

Independent Order of Odd Fellows.   North Carolina.   Raleigh Encampment no. 5,
Raleigh.   By-laws and rules of order.   Raleigh, North Carolina Institution for
the Deaf and Dumb and the Blind, 1851.   23 p.   [6704

Independent Order of Odd Fellows.   North Carolina.   Rebekah State Assembly.
Proceedings, 1909-   Raleigh, 1909-   NcU has 1913-1923, 1925-1935, 1937-
1943   [6705

Independent Order of Odd Fellows.   North Carolina.   Reidsville Lodge.   Odd
Fellows anniversary!   Reidsville, Mayo's Print, 1890.   [1] p.   [6706

Indorsement of Judge Thomas H. Calvert for Judge of Superior Court.   Raleigh,
Commercial Printing Co., n.d.   [1] p.   [6707

Industrial School and Music Academy, Kinston, N. C.   Bulletin, 19 - Kinston,
19 - NcU has 1918/19, 1919/20   [6708

Information Service, New York.   The strikes at Marion, North Carolina.   New

York, Department of Research and Education, Federal Council of the Churches of Christ in America, 1929. (Its [Publication] v. 8, no. 47)   15 p.   [6709

Ingle, Edward. Southern sidelights; a picture of social and economic life in the South a generation before the war. New York, T. Y. Crowell & Co. [1896]   373 p. [6710

Inglis Fletcher of Bandon, chronicler of North Carolina. Indianapolis, Bobbs-Merrill [1946]   18 p.   [6711

Ingold, Mrs. Arthur M. The power of music. No place, no publisher [c.1921] 32 p.   [6712

Ingram, S. M. The thorough-bred jack, Bedford, sired by an imported Malta jack of Tennessee, will stand the ensuing season at terms. Wadesborough, Argus Office, February, 1851. [1] p.   [6713

Inklings, 19 -   Waynesville, Waynesville Township High School Students, 19   - NcU has June, 1929.   [6714

Institute for Young Ladies, Charlotte, N. C. Circular, 1878/79- Raleigh, 1878- NcU has 1878/79   [6715

Insurance record, v. 1- March, 1898- Raleigh, Carolina Benevolent Association, 1898- NcU has v. 1, no. 1, March, 1898.   [6716

Internal Improvement Convention, Salisbury, N. C., October 10-12, 1836. Proceedings . . . with an appendix. Salisbury, Watchman, pr., 1836.   17 p.   [6717

International Order of King's Daughters and Sons. North Carolina. Conference, 188 - 188 - NcU has 1902-1905, 1908, 1909, 1911-1914   [6718

International Order of King's Daughters and Sons. North Carolina. Whatsoever Circle, Winston-Salem. The twin-city housewife. Winston-Salem, Winston Printing Co., 1915.   108 p.   [6719

International Typographical Union of North America. Raleigh Union no. 54. Proceedings of special meeting . . . January 31, 1943 . . . presentation forty-year button to Hon. Josephus Daniels. [Raleigh, 1943]   39 p.   [6720

Interstate notes, v. 1-15, June, 1905-September, 1918. Charlotte, Young Men's Christian Associations of the Carolinas, 1905-1918. NcU has v. [1-15]   [6721

Iola Mining Co., Baltimore. Prospectus of the Iola Mining Company. Baltimore [1903?]   8 p.   Incorporated by the North Carolina General Assembly, 1901 and 1903.   [6722

[Iredell, James] 1751-1799. Answers to Mr. Mason's objections to the new constitution recommended by the late convention at Philadelphia by Marcus. To which is added An address to the freemen of North-Carolina by Publicola. [Newbern, Printed by Hodge and Wills, 1788]   12 p.   NcU has photostat of the original in Harvard Library.   [6723

Iredell, James, 1751-1799. Life and correspondence see **McRee, Griffith John.**

Iredell, James, 1788-1853. Address delivered before the Dialectic and Philanthropic societies at Chapel Hill, N. C., June 25, 1834. Chapel Hill, Isaac C. Patridge, pr., 1834.   16 p.   [6727
——A card. Raleigh, August 4, 1840. [1] p.   [6728

[Iredell Co., N. C. Board of Education] Manual for Iredell County teachers, 1915/16. Statesville [1915?]   34 p.   [6729

Iredell Co., N. C. Board of Education. Report of Iredell County Public Schools, 190 - [Statesville, 190 - NcU has 1909/10, 1915/17   [6730

[Iredell Co., N. C. Board of Education] A report to the people, Iredell County Schools [Statesville, 1953]   48 p.   [6731

Irelan, John Robert. History of the life, administration, and times of Andrew Johnson. Chicago, Fairbanks and Palmer Publishing Co., 1888. (Irelan, John Robert. The Republic, v. 18)   630 p.   [6732

Irvin, Oscar William. State budget control of state institutions of higher education. New York, Teachers College, Columbia University, 1928. (Its Contributions to education, no. 271)   122 p.   [6733

Irving, William Henry. John Gay, favorite of the wits. Durham, Duke University Press, 1940.   334 p.   [6734
——The providence of wit in the English letter writers. Durham, Duke University Press, 1955.   382 p.   [6735

Irwin, Harriet (Morrison) The hermit of Petraea; a tale, written with the hope of throwing a charm around the out-of-door life so necessary to invalids . . . by Mrs. James P. Irwin. Charlotte, Hill & Irwin, 1871. 60 p. [6736

Irwin, Laetitia (McDonald) The golden hammock. Boston, Little, Brown, 1951. 373 p. [6737

Is it right? No place, no publisher [1908?] [1] p. [6738

Is this "white supremacy"? No place, no publisher [1900?] 4 p. [6739

Isaacs, I. J., ed. Progressive Greensboro, the gate city of North Carolina. Greensboro, J. J. Stone & Co., pr., 1903. 111 p. [6740

Isbell, Robert Lee. The world of my childhood, compiled by Nancy (Mrs. W. E.) Alexander; edited by Kearney C. Pearce. Lenoir, News-Topic [1955] 208 p. [6741

Ives, Elizabeth (Stevenson) My brother Adlai, by Elizabeth Stevenson Ives and Hildegrade Dolson. New York, Morrow, 1956. 308 p. [6742

Ives, Levi Silliman. The apostles' doctrine and fellowship. New York, D. Appleton & Co., 1844. 189 p. [6743

——The Christian bishop approving himself to God; the sermon at the consecration of the Rt. Rev. John Johns, D. D., assistant bishop of Virginia. Richmond, Va., P. D. Bernard, pr., 1842. 30 p. [6744

——The duties now especially called for to preserve the faith of the church; a charge to the clergy of the Diocese of North Carolina . . . May 8th, 1836. Raleigh, J. Gales & Son, pr., 1836. 30 p. [6745

——Humility, a ministerial qualification; an address to the students of the General Theological Seminary of the Protestant Episcopal Church in the United States . . . June 28, 1840. New York, Swords, Stanford & Co., 1840. 22 p. [6746

——The importance of Christian education; a charge delivered to the convention of the Protestant Episcopal Church in the Diocese of North Carolina . . . June 1st, 1833. Fayetteville, Edward J. Hale, pr., 1833. 14 p. [6747

——The introductory address of the Historical Society of the University of North Carolina, delivered in the University Chapel, June 5th, 1844. Raleigh, T. Loring, 1844. 18 p. [6748

——A letter from the Rt. Rev. Bishop Ives in answer to certain questions concerning confession and absolution. New-York, Stanford and Swords, 1850. 36 p. [6749

——New manual of devotions, in three parts . . . A new edition to which is added, A friendly visit to the house of mourning by the Rev. Richard Cecil. New York, Swords, Stanford & Co., 1842. 372 p. [6750

——New manual of private devotions, in three parts . . . 3d New York ed. New York, T. and J. Swords, 1831. 367 p. [6751

——"The obedience of faith"; seven sermons delivered on his visitations to the churches in his diocese, during 1848-49. New York, Stanford and Swords, 1849. 161 p. [6752

——A pastoral letter addressed to the Diocese of North-Carolina, February 4th, 1835. Raleigh, J. Gales and Son, 1835. 26 p. [6753

——A pastoral letter to the clergy and laity of his diocese. New York, Stanford and Swords, 1849. 77 p. [6754

——The 'perfect peace' of the Christian; a sermon occasioned by the death of Mrs. May Catharine Cairns . . . 23d Sunday after Trinity, November 6th, 1836. Raleigh, J. Gales & Son, pr., 1836. 20 p. [6755

——The protection of destitute Catholic children; a lecture delivered at Cooper Institute, November 23d, 1864. New York, D. & J. Sadlier & Co., 1864. 24 p. [6756

——The relative positions and duties of the clergy and laity; a charge to the clergy of the Diocese of North Carolina . . . May 9th, 1841. Fayetteville, Edward J. Hale, pr., 1841. 30 p. [6757

——A sermon at the opening of the first convention after his entering on the duties of his episcopate . . . May, 1832. New-York, Protestant Episcopal Press, 1832. 26 p. [6758

——The struggle of sense against faith; the sermon at the opening of the triennial convention of the Protestant Episcopal Church in the United States of America . . . October 2, 1844. Philadelphia, George & Wayne, 1844. 24 p. [6759

——The trials of a mind in its progress to Catholicism; a letter to his old friends. Boston, Patrick Donahoe, 1854. 233 p. [6760

Ivey, Fritz Henry. "Good and faithful servant"; memorial address on the life and character of Rev. W. M. Wingate, D. D., late president of Wake Forest College,

N. C., delivered at the annual commencement, June 12, 1879.   Raleigh, Edwards, Broughton & Co., 1879.   20 p.   [6761

Ivey, George Franks. Carding and spinning; a book for practical mill men. Hickory, G. F. Ivey & Co. [1904]   220 p.   [6762
——Humor and humanity. Hickory, Southern Publishing Co. [1945]   243 p. [6763
——The Ivey family in the United States. Hickory, Southern Publishing Co. [1941?]   113 p.   [6764
——Loom-fixing and weaving. Shelby, C. P. Roberts, pr., 1896.   109 p.   [6765
——The physical properties of lumber. Hickory, Southern Publishing Co. [c.1934] 263 p.   [6766

Ivey, George M. Voice of Charlotte . . . fifth talk in a series broadcast over radio station WBT by the Charlotte Chamber of Commerce, Friday, March 6th, 1931. Charlotte [1931]   10 p.   [6767

Ivey, John Eli. Building Atlanta's future, by John E. Ivey, Jr., Nicholas J. Demerath [and] Woodrow W. Breland. Chapel Hill, University of North Carolina Press [1948]   305 p.   [6768
——The summary report of a laboratory study of southeastern regional problems, potentialities, and planning . . . [by] John E. Ivey, Jr., and Abbott L. Ferriss. Chapel Hill, Institute for Research in Social Science, University of North Carolina, 1942.   70 num. leaves   [6769
——Teacher education in the social sciences. [Chapel Hill, 1946?]   20 p.   [6770

Ivey, Joseph Benjamin. My memoirs. [Greensboro, Piedmont Press, c.1940] 368 p.   [6771

Ivey, Thomas Neal. Bildad Akers, his book; the notions and experiences of a quaint rural philosopher who thinks for himself. Raleigh, Mutual Publishing Co. [c.1909] 205 p.   [6772
——Green Hill; edited with genealogical notes by J. Edward Allen. [Oxford, Oxford Orphanage, pr.] n.d.   25 p.   [6773

Ivy, Thomas Parker. Forestry problems in the United States. Hendersonville, 1906.   47 p.   [6774
——I. Here and hereafter, or, The reality of things. II. Evolution, man, and God. No place, no publisher [1925?]   15 p.   [6775
——Long leaf pine. Southern Pines, Sandhill Citizen Print [1923]   16 p.   [6776

J. Bryan Grimes, candidate for nomination for secretary of state before the Democratic State Convention to be held at Charlotte, N. C., June 24, 1908. No place, no publisher [1908]   3 p.   [6777
——June 6, 1912. [1912]   10 p.   [6778
——June, 1916. [1916]   14 p.   [6779

Jack, Edward. Prospectus of 57,484 acres of land, the property of James A. Bryan, of New Bern, N. C. New Bern, N. S. Richardson, 1899.   31 p.   [6780
——Reports on the agricultural advantages, timber wealth, and hunting advantages of 57,484 acres of land, situated in Craven, Carteret, and Jones counties, N. C., owned by James A. Bryan, esq., of New-Berne, N. C., by Edward Jack . . . and H. A. Brown. [New Bern? J. A. Bryan? n.d.]   29 p.   [6781

Jackman, Lyman. History of the Sixth New Hampshire Regiment in the war for the Union. Concord, Republican Press Association, 1891.   630 p.   [6782

Jackson, Andrew, Pres. U. S. Annual messages, veto messages, protest, &c. 2d ed. Baltimore, Edward J. Coale & Co., 1835.   272 p.   [6783
——Correspondence between Gen. Andrew Jackson and John C. Calhoun . . . on the subject of the course of the latter in the deliberations of the cabinet of Mr. Monroe in the Seminole War. Washington, Duff Green, 1831.   52 p.   [6784
——Correspondence of Andrew Jackson, edited by John Spencer Bassett. Washington, Carnegie Institution of Washington, 1926-1935.   7 v.   [6785
——Gen. Jackson's farewell address to the people of the United States, together with his Proclamation to South Carolina. Harrisburg, J. M. G. Lescure, pr., 1850. 25 p.   [6786
——Messages of Gen. Andrew Jackson, with a short sketch of his life. Concord, N. H., John F. Brown and William White, 1837.   429 p.   [6787
—— ——Concord, N. H., John F. Brown and William White, 1837.   432 p. [6788
——A short account of the trial of Gen. Andrew Jackson, before the Hon. Dominick A. Hall, judge of the District Court of the United States for the Louisiana Dis-

trict . . . accompanied by Gen. Jackson's defence, and sundry other documents relative to the case. No place, no publisher [1827?] 16 p. [6789

——The statesmanship of Andrew Jackson as told in his writings and speeches, edited by Francis Newton Thorpe. New York, Tandy-Thomas Co. [c.1909] 538 p. [6790

——Two eighteenth century indentures. Memphis, Southwestern University, 1956. (Burrow Library monograph no. 1) 12 p. [6791

Jackson, Charles T. Brief sketch of the North Carolina Gas-Coal Company with report of Charles T. Jackson . . . and of Oswald Heinrich. Philadelphia, M. P. Williams, pr., 1856. 26 p. [6792

——Report of the coal lands of Egypt, Belmont, Evans, Palmer & Wilcox plantations on Deep River, North Carolina. New-York, George F. Nesbitt and Co., pr., 1853. 24 p. [6793

——Report of the copper mine of the North Carolina Copper Company in Guilford County, North Carolina. [New York, G. F. Nesbitt and Co., 1853?] 8 p. [6794

Jackson, Crawford. Near nature's heart; a volume of verse. Atlanta, Foote & Davies Co., pr. [c.1923] 96 p. [6795

Jackson, David Kelly, comp. The contributors and contributions to the Southern literary messenger (1834-1864) Charlottesville, Va., Historical Publishing Co., Inc., 1936. 192 p. [6796

——Poe and the Southern literary messenger, with a foreword by J. H. Whitty. Richmond, Va., Press of the Dietz Printing Co., 1934. 120 p. [6797

Jackson, Dudley. I'm in love with love, words by W. A. Watson, music by Dudley Jackson. Deep Gap, W. A. Watson, n.d. [2] p. [6798

Jackson, Edgar Allan. Letters of Edgar Allan Jackson, September 7, 1860-April 15, 1863. [Franklin? Va., 193?] 22 p. [6799

Jackson, Elmo L. The pricing of cigarette tobaccos; a study of the process of price development in the flue-cured and burley auction markets. Gainesville, University of Florida Press, 1955. 239 p. [6800

Jackson, Frederick. Il recrutio, a comic opera as originally produced by members of the Forty-fourth Regiment, in barracks, at Newbern, N. C. . . . 1863 . . . Words by Frederick Jackson, Zenas T. Haines, and Wm. G. Reed; music arranged by Charles C. Chickering. No date, n. p. 15 p. [6801

Jackson, George Pullen, ed. Another sheaf of white spirituals. Gainesville, University of Florida Press, 1952. 233 p. [6802

——Down-east spirituals, and others. [2d ed.] Locust Valley, N. Y., J. J. Augustin [1953] 296 p. [6803

——Spiritual folk-songs of early America. [2d ed.] Locust Valley, N. Y., J. J. Augustin [1953] 254 p. [6804

——White and Negro spirituals, their life span and kinship. New York, J. J. Augustin [1944] 349 p. [6805

——White spirituals in the southern uplands. Chapel Hill, University of North Carolina Press, 1933. 444 p. [6806

Jackson, James. The most useful and pleasing hymns and spiritual songs. Raleigh, Wm. Boylan, pr., 1809. 93 p. [6807

Jackson, John. A faithful account of the massacre of the family of Gerald Watson, of Fayetteville County, N. C. Boston, N. Coverly, pr., 1819. 24 p. [6808

Jackson, Mary Anna (Morrison) Mrs. "Stonewall" Jackson. Julia Jackson Christian, by her mother. Charlotte, Stone & Barringer Co. [c.1910] 57 p. [6809

——Life and letters of General Thomas J. Jackson . . . with an introduction by Henry M. Field. New York, Harper and Brothers, 1892. 479 p. [6810

——Memoirs of Stonewall Jackson by his widow. [2d ed.] Louisville, Ky., Prentice Press [1895] 647 p. [6811

Jackson, Walter Clinton. A boys' life of Booker T. Washington. New York, Macmillan Co., 1922. 147 p. [6812

[Jackson, Walter Clinton] John Thomas Battle, M. D. [Raleigh? Meredith College, 1945] 46 p. [6813

Jackson, Walter Clinton, joint ed., see White, Newman Ivy, ed.

Jackson, Walter M. Alabama's first United States Vice-President, William Rufus King. Decatur, Ala., Decatur Printing Co., 1952. 48 p. [6814

Jackson Co., N. C. Superintendent of Schools. Public school record. Raleigh, Edwards & Broughton Co. [190?] Unpaged. Form.   [6815

The Jackson wreath; or, National souvenir . . . containing a biographical sketch of General Jackson until 1829, by Robert Walsh, Jr., esq. with a continuation until the present day . . . by Dr. James M'Henry. Philadelphia, J. Maas, 1829. 88 p.   [6816

Jacksonville, N. C. Town Planning Board. Jacksonville today and tomorrow. [Jacksonville] 1955. 39 p.   [6817

Jacksonville (Onslow County, N. C.) city directory, v. 1- 1948- Wilmington, Carolina Publishing Co., c.1948- NcU has 1948   [6818

Jacobs, William Plumer. The pioneer. Clinton, S. C., Jacobs & Co., 1935. 126 p.   [6819

Jacobson, Nathan. Continuous groups. [1939] 93 p.   [6820

——The theory of rings. New York, American Mathematical Society, 1943. (Mathematical surveys, no. II) 150 p.   [6821

James, Bessie (Rowland) The courageous heart; a life of Andrew Jackson for young readers, by Bessie Rowland James and Marquis James. Indianapolis, Bobbs-Merrill Co. [c.1934] 273 p.   [6822

——The happy animals of Atagahi. Indianapolis, Bobbs-Merrill Co. [c.1935] 260 p.   [6823

James, Horace. Annual report of the Superintendent of Negro Affairs in North Carolina, 1864; with an appendix containing the history and management of the freedmen in this department up to June 1st, 1865. Boston, W. F. Brown & Co. [1865?] 64 p.   [6824

James, Horace, defendant. Trial of Rev. Horace James, before a special military commission, convened by direction of Andrew Johnson, president of the United States, in September, 1866. [Raleigh, 1866?] 29 p.   [6825

James, Horace. The two great wars of America; an oration delivered in Newbern, North Carolina, before the Twenty-fifth Regiment Massachusetts Volunteers, July 4, 1862. Boston, W. T. Brown & Co., 1862. 30 p.   [6826

James, James Alton. Our government, local, state, and national, by J. A. James . . . and A. H. Sanford . . . [North Carolina ed.] New York, C. Scribner's Sons, 1904. 235 p.   [6827

James, John G., ed. Southern student's hand-book of selections for reading and oratory. New York, A. S. Barnes & Co., 1879. 407 p.   [6828

James, Marquis. Andrew Jackson, portrait of a president. Indianapolis, Bobbs-Merrill Co. [c.1937] 627 p.   [6829

——Andrew Jackson, portrait of a president. New York, Garden City Publishing Co. [c.1937, 1940] 627 p.   [6830

——Andrew Jackson, the border captain. Indianapolis, Bobbs-Merrill Co. [c.1933] 461 p.   [6831

——The life of Andrew Jackson, complete in one volume. Indianapolis, Bobbs-Merrill Co. [c.1938] 972 p.   [6832

James, Martha Elizabeth McArthur. A mixed-up family. Clinton, Mrs. Taft Bass [1955] 35 p.   [6833

James, Powhatan Wright. George W. Truett, a biography, with an introduction by Douglas Southall Freeman. New York, Macmillan Co., 1939. 281 p.   [6834

—— ——1941. 277 p.   [6835

—— ——Memorial ed. [c.1953] 311 p.   [6836

James, William Dobein. A sketch of the life of Brig. Gen. Francis Marion, and a history of his brigade, from its rise in June, 1780, until disbanded in December, 1782 . . . containing also, an appendix, with copies of letters which passed between several of the leading characters of that day, principally from Gen. Greene to Gen. Marion. Charleston, S. C., Gould and Riley, pr., 1821. 182, 39 p.   [6837

—— ——Marietta, Ga., Continental Book Co., 1948. 182, 39 p.   [6838

James Daniel Moore. No place, no publisher, n.d. 60 p.   [6839

James K. Polk's position on the tariff defined. [Washington, Gideon's Office, 1844?] 4 p.   [6840

James Sprunt, a tribute from the city of Wilmington. Raleigh, Edwards & Broughton Co., 1925. 114 p. [6841

James Sprunt Institute, Kenansville, N. C. Catalogue, 19 - Kenansville, 19 - NcU has 1907/08, 1908/09, 1910/11, 1916/17, 1917/18 supplement, 1918/19, supplement. Continues, 1919/20 as Grove Institute [6842

The James Sprunt studies in history and political science, [v.] 1- Chapel Hill, University of North Carolina Press, 1900- NcU has v. 1-38. Title varies, v. 1-8: James Sprunt historical monograph; 9-18: The James Sprunt historical publications; 19-22: The James Sprunt historical studies. [6843

[Jameson, S. Keith] ed. WDNC, Durham. Peoria, Illinois, National Radio Personalities, Inc., c.1941. [23] p. [6844

Jamestown Corporation, Williamsburg, Va. The common glory by Paul Green, the souvenir program, first showing, 1947- Williamsburg, Va., 1947- NcU has 1947-1955 [6845

Janson, Charles William. The stranger in America. London, J. Cundee, 1807. 499 p. [6846

—— ——Reprinted . . . with an introducation and notes by Dr. Carl S. Driver. New York, Press of the Pioneers, Inc., 1935. 502 p. [6847

Jarratt, Devereux. The life of the Reverend Devereux Jarratt, rector of Bath Parish, Dinwiddie County, Virginia. Baltimore, Warner & Hanna, pr., 1806. 84 p. [6848

——Sermons on various and important subjects in practical divinity, adapted to the plainest capacities, and suited to the family and closet. Raleigh, Printed for and sold by William Glendinning, 1805. 452 p. [6849

Jarrell, Randall. Losses. New York, Harcourt, Brace [1948] 68 p. [6850
——Pictures from an institution. New York, A. A. Knopf, 1954. 277 p. [6851
——Poetry and the age. New York, A. A. Knopf, 1953. 271 p. [6852
—— ——London, Faber and Faber [1955] 240 p. [6853
——Selected poems. New York, A. A. Knopf, 1955. 205 p. [6854
——The seven-league crutches. New York, Harcourt, Brace [1951] 94 p. [6855

Jarrett, J. P. A voyage to the three continents and theology from the pew. No place, no publisher, n.d. 186 p. [6856

Jarrett, Robert Frank. Back Home, and other poems. Asheville, Inland Press, 1911. 48 p. [6857
——Occoneechee, the maid of the mystic lake. New York, Shakespeare Press, 1916. 284 p. [6858

Jarvis, Samuel. [Broadside signed by Samuel Jarvis, Solomon Perkins and Nathan Poyner, of Currituck County, and Isaac Gregory and Jonathan Hearring, of Pasquotank County, explaining their reason for withdrawing from the Provincial Convention, held at Newbern, April 3, 1775] [Newbern? 1775?] [1] p. [6859

Jarvis, Samuel Farmar. A voice from Connecticut, occasioned by the late pastoral letter of the Bishop of North Carolina to the clergy and laity of his diocese. Hartford, Conn., A. C. Goodman & Co., 1849. 43 p. [6860

Jarvis, Thomas Jordan. Address delivered by Hon. Thos. J. Jarvis, governor of North Carolina, before the Society of Alumni of Randolph Macon College, June 15th, 1881. Richmond, Va., Johns & Goolsby, pr., 1881. 20 p. [6861
——Schools vs. saloons; Governor Jarvis on the eternal conflict. No place, no publisher, n.d. [1] p. [6862
—— ——[Raleigh, Edwards & Broughton Printing Co., n.d.] [2] p. [6863
——[Some questions involved in the election] Greenville, May 20th, 1908. [1] p. [6864

Jay, Allen. Autobiography of Allen Jay, born 1831, died 1910. Philadelphia, John C. Winston Co. [c.1910] 421 p. [6865

Jay, William. A letter to the Right Rev. L. Silliman Ives . . . occasioned by his late address to the convention of his diocese. 3d ed. New York, William Harned, 1848. 32 p. [6866

Jaynes, R. T. The old Waxhaws. No place, no publisher, n.d. 22 p. [6867

Jefferson Academy and Business School, McLeansville, N. C. Catalogue, 189 - McLeansville, 189 - NcU has 1903/04, 1905/06, 1907/08 [6868

Jefferson School, Jefferson, N. C. Catalogue, 191 - Jefferson, 191 - NcU has 1920/21 [6869

Jefferson Standard Life Insurance Co., Greensboro, N. C. Report, 19 - Greensboro, 19 - NcU has 1924-1955 [6870

The Jeffersonian, 19 - Greensboro, Jefferson Standard Life Insurance Co., 19 - NcU has January, 1947-December, 1956 [6871

[Jeffreys, George Washington] A series of essays on agriculture & rural affairs, in forty-seven numbers, by "Agricola", a North Carolina farmer. Raleigh, Joseph Gales, 1819. 223 p. [6872

Jeffreys, Raymond John. Life will begin at 100. Columbus, O., Capitol College Press [1955] 239 p. [6873

——Must they sell apples again? Columbus, O., Capitol College Press [1956] 101 p. [6874

Jellicoe, George Patrick John Rushwork, 2nd earl. The Elizabethan spirit, text of address . . . delivered in Waterside Theatre at Fort Raleigh, Roanoke Island at the 363d anniversary celebration, birth of Virginia Dare, August 18, 1950. Manteo, 1950. 7 p. [6875

Jellife, Belinda (Dobson) For dear life. New York, C. Scribner's Sons, 1936. 355 p. [6876

Jemison, George Meredith. The effect of basal wounding by forest fires on the diameter growth of some southern Appalachian hardwoods. Durham, Duke University, School of Forestry, 1944. (Its Bulletin, 9) 63 p. [6877

Jenkens, Charles Augustus, ed. Baptist doctrines. St. Louis, Mo., Chancy R. Barns, 1880. 566 p. [6878

——The bride's return; or, How Grand Avenue Church came to Christ, a story with a supreme purpose. Charlotte, C. H. Robinson & Co. [c.1911] 342 p. · [6879

——Good gumption; or, The story of a wise fool. Nashville, Tenn., Southwestern Co. [c.1907] 400 p. [6880

——What made me a Baptist. Goldsboro, Book and Job Printers [1901] 147 p. [6881

Jenkins, James. Experience, labours, and sufferings of Rev. James Jenkins, of the South Carolina Conference. No place, printed for the Author, 1842. 232 p. [6882

Jenkins, John. A candid inquiry into the nature and design of Christian baptism Milton, J. Campbell, Jr., pr., 1827. 72 p. [6883

Jenkins, John Stilwell. James Knox Polk, and a history of his administration, embracing the annexation of Texas, the difficulties with Mexico, the settlement of the Oregon question, and other important events. Auburn and Buffalo, N. Y., John E. Beardsley [c.1850] 395 p. [6884

Jenkins, John Stilwell, ed. Life and public services of Gen. Andrew Jackson . . . ed. by John S. Jenkins . . . with the eulogy delivered at Washington city, June 21, 1845, by Hon. George Bancroft. Buffalo, George H. Derby and Co., 1851. 397 p. [6885

Jenkins, John Wilber. James B. Duke, master builder. New York, George H. Doran Co. [c.1897] 302 p. [6886

Jenkins, Joseph. A defence of the Baptists against the aspersions and misrepresentations of Mr. Peter Edwards . . . in his book entitled, Candid reasons for renouncing the principles of antipaedobaptism. Halifax, W. Boylan, pr., 1805. 128 p. NcU has defective copy p. 113—mutilated or wanting. [6887

Jenkins, W. J. Mountain rhythms; or, Poems of a mountaineer. No place, no publisher, 1922. 58 p. [6888

Jenkins, William Adrian. What is religion? Chapel Hill, [Department of Philosophy] University of North Carolina, 1907. (Worth prize thesis, 1907) 15 p. [6889

Jenkins, William Sumner. Bill Jenkins' Christmas booklet. [Chapel Hill, 1950] [28] p. [6890

——Collected public documents of the states; a check list. Boston, 1947. 87 p. [6891

——Jayhawking over the state records microfilm project. Chapel Hill, Author, 1952. 9, 9 p. [6892

——An overture for a public records research laboratory. [Chapel Hill, 1953?] 7 p. [6893

——Photoduplication and checklisting of state documents . . . A paper delivered to the annual meeting of the American Association of Law Libraries in Miami, Florida, June 30, 1954. [Chapel Hill? 1954] 7 p. [6894

——Pro-slavery thought in the old South. Chapel Hill, University of North Carolina Press, 1935. 381 p. [6895

——Public documents resources of the University Library. [Chapel Hill? 1946?] 25 p. [6896

——Some selected materials relating to the microfilm collection of early state records (introductory format) [Chapel Hill, 1953] 6, 9 p. [6897

——State documents microfilm project progress report, 1947/48- [Chapel Hill, 1948- NcU has 1947/48 [6898

——A stock inventory of state records resources available for the proposed public records collection and research center at the University of North Carolina. Chapel Hill, 1954. 17 p. [6899

Jenks, Almet. The huntsman at the gate. Philadelphia, J. B. Lippincott Co. [1952] 115 p. [6900

Jennett, Jesse, comp. A collection of the most approved hymns and spiritual songs now in use. Wilmington, 1807. 42 p. [6901

Jennings, Al J. Through the shadows with O. Henry. New York, H. K. Fly Co. [c.1921] 320 p. [6902

Jennings, Augustus Campbell. A linguistic study of the Cartulario de San Vincente [!] de Oviedo. New York, 1940. 326 p. "Vincente" misprint for "Vicente" [6903

Jensen, Zora S. List of native plants and shrubs that can be planted for bird food. Chapel Hill, n.d. [1] p. [6904

Jernigan, Muriel Molland. Forbidden City. New York, Crown Publishers [1954] 346 p. [6905

Jernigan, Thomas R. China in law and commerce. New York, Macmillan Co., 1905. 408 p. [6906

Jerome, Edward Columbus. North Carolina civil procedure. Charlottesville, Va., Michie Co., 1928. 719 p. [6907

Jerome, Thomas J. Ku Klux Klan no. 40. Raleigh, Edwards & Broughton, pr., 1895. 259 p. [6908

Jeter, Jeremiah Bell. Don't swear! [Raleigh, Board of Missions of the North Carolina Baptist State Convention, n.d.] (No. 10) 8 p. [6909

——Memoir of Abner W. Clopton. Richmond, Va., Yale & Wyatt, 1837. 283 p. [6910

——Popular charges against the Baptists refuted. [Charleston, S. C., Southern Baptist Publication Society, 1853] 25 p. [6911

Jewish New Year book, 192 - Greensboro, The Jewish New Year Book, 192 - NcU has v. 4, 1932 [6912

Jillson, Willard Rouse. The Boone narrative . . . to which is appended a sketch of Boone and a bibliography of 238 titles. Louisville, Ky., Standard Printing Co., Inc., 1932. 16 p. [6913

——Tales of the dark and bloody ground; a group of fifteen original papers on the early history of Kentucky. Louisville, Ky., C. T. Dearing Printing Co., 1930. 149 p. [6914

Jocher, Katharine, joint author, see Odum, Howard Washington

John C. Campbell Folk School, Brasstown, N. C. [Bulletin] no. 1- 192 - Brasstown, 192 - NcU has no. [8-31] [6915

——Calendar notebook, 1955. Brasstown [1954] Unpaged. [6916

John Pendleton King. No place, privately printed, n.d. 80 p. [6917

Johns, Annie Eliza. Cooleemee; a tale of southern life. Rockingham County, Leaksville Gazette, 1882. 225 p. [6918

——Our Chautauqua. No place, no publisher, 1884. [1] p. [6919

Johns Hopkins University, Baltimore. Walter Hines Page School of International Relations. The Walter Hines Page School of International Relations. New York [1925?] 15 p. [6920

Johnson, Albert Sidney. Obituary of Alva C. Springs originally written for the Christian observer. Charlotte [1932?] [3] p. [6921

Johnson, Andrew, Pres. U. S. A full and impartial report: The great impeachment trial of Andrew Johnson. Philadelphia, Barclay & Co. [c.1868] 122 p. [6922

——The great impeachment and trial of Andrew Johnson. Philadelphia, T. B. Peterson & Brothers [c.1868] 289 p. [6923
——Issues of the day, speech at the new Memphis Theater, Saturday evening, May 16th, 1874. [Memphis] Daily Memphis Avalanche Print, 1874. 11 p. [6924
——Message of Andrew Johnson, governor of Tennessee, to both houses of the General Assembly, October 6, 1857. Nashville, Tenn., G. C. Torbett & Co., 1857. 26 p. [6925
——Speeches . . . with a biographical introduction by Frank Moore. Boston, Little, Brown and Co., 1866. 494 p. [6926

Johnson, Bradley Tyler, ed. A memoir of the life and public service of Joseph E. Johnston. Baltimore, R. H. Woodward & Co., 1891. 362 p. [6927

Johnson, Cecil. British West Florida, 1763-1783. New Haven, Yale University Press, 1943. (Yale historical publication. Miscellany, 42) 258 p. [6928

Johnson, Charles. A general history of the pyrates. 2d ed. London, T. Warner, 1724. 427 p. NcU has film (negative) from original in Library of Congress. [6929
—— ——4th ed. London, T. Woodward, 1726. 2 v. [6930
——A general history of the robberies and murders of the most notorious pirates, edited by Arthur L. Hayward. London, Routledge & Kegan Paul [1955] 603 p. [6931

Johnson, Charles B. A brief history of the descendants of Samuel Johnson, founder of the Cape Fear Johnsons. Champaign Ill., Times Job Print, 1907. 29 p. [6932

Johnson, Charles Earl. An address before the Medical Society of North Carolina at its second annual meeting, in Raleigh, May, 1851. Raleigh, Seaton Gales, 1851. 32 p. [6933
——An address delivered before the Medical Society of North Carolina, at its second annual meeting, in Raleigh, May, 1851. Raleigh, Southern Weekly Post, 1854. 139 p. [6934
——An essay on the position and duties of the medical profession in the middle of the nineteenth century. Raleigh, Raleigh Register, 1858. 25 p. [6935

[Johnson, Charles Earl] The medico-legal relations of insanity considered upon general principles. No place, no publisher, 1867. 36 p. [6936

Johnson, Charles Earl. The question of insanity and its medico-legal relations considered upon general principles. Raleigh, T. M. Hughes, pr., 1869. 250 p. [6937

Johnson, Charles F. The long roll; being a journal of the Civil War. East Aurora, N. Y., The Roycrofters, 1911. 241 p. [6938

Johnson, Charles Hampton. Heart-felt songs. East Bend, Author [c.1913] 26 p. [6938a
——North Carolina in rhyme. Winston-Salem, Union Republican Publishing Co., c.1911. 79 p. [6939
——Songs. East Bend, Author, c.1917. 24 p. [6940
——Your Uncle Charlie's poetical love letters. East Bend, Author, 1913. 44 p. [6941

Johnson, Charles Spurgeon. The collapse of cotton tenancy; summary of Field studies and statistical surveys, 1933-35, by Charles S. Johnson, Edwin R. Embree [and] W. W. Alexander. Chapel Hill, University of North Carolina Press, 1935. 81 p. [6942
——Into the main stream, a survey of best practices in race relations in the South, by Charles S. Johnson and associates. Chapel Hill, University of North Carolina Press, 1947. 355 p. [6943
——The Negro college graduate. Chapel Hill, University of North Carolina Press, 1938. 399 p. [6944
——Statistical atlas of southern counties . . . by Charles S. Johnson and associates. Chapel Hill, University of North Carolina Press, 1941. 355 p. [6945

Johnson, Clarence Walter. The history of the 321st Infantry, with a brief historical sketch of the 81st Division. Columbia, S. C., R. L. Bryan Co., 1919. 201 p. [6946

Johnson, Douglas Wilson. The origin of the Carolina bays. New York, Columbia University Press, 1942. (Columbia geomorphic studies, ed. by Douglas Johnson, no. 4) 341 p. [6947
——Stream sculpture on the Atlantic slope; a study in the evolution of Appalachian rivers. New York, Columbia University Press, 1931. (Columbia geomorphic studies) 142 p. [6948

Johnson, Edward Augustus. History of Negro soldiers in the Spanish-American War. Cincinnati, W. H. Ferguson Co., 1899. 228 p. [6949
——Light ahead for the Negro. New York, Grafton Press [c.1904] 132 p. [6950

——A school history of the Negro race in America, from 1619 to 1890. Raleigh, Edwards & Broughton, pr., 1890. 194 p. [6951
——A school history of the Negro race in America, from 1619 to 1890. No place, no publisher [c.1891] 447 p. [6952
—— ———Rev. ed. Chicago, W. B. Conkey Co., 1893. 200 p. [6953
——A school history (Fourth reader grade) of the Negro race in the U. S. Rev. ed. under the supervision of S. M. Finger and W. B. Kendrick. Raleigh, Edwards & Broughton, 1894. 188 p. [6954
—— ———Rev. ed. 1911. 400 p. [6955
Johnson, Edwin R. Save Currituck; statement and argument for the installation of a tidal guard lock in the Albemarle and Chesapeake Canal. [Wash., National Publishing Co., 1930?] 21 p. [6956
Johnson, Elbert Neil. The master is here; Jesus' presence in fact and experience. New York, American Press [1955] 141 p. [6957
Johnson, Elmer Douglass. A brief history of Cherokee County, South Carolina. Gaffney, S. C., Chamber of Commerce, 1952. [30] p. [6958
Johnson, Gerald White. American heroes and hero-worship. New York, Harper & Brothers [1943] 284 p. [6959
——America's silver age; the statecraft of Clay-Webster-Calhoun. New York, Harper & Brothers, 1939. 280 p. [6960
——Andrew Jackson; an epic in homespun. New York, Minton, Balch & Co., 1927. 303 p. [6961
—— ———New York, Bantam Books, Inc. [1956] 244 p. [6962
——By reason of strength. New York, Minton, Balch & Co. [c.1930] 221 p. [6963
——The first captain, the story of John Paul Jones. New York, Coward-McCann [1947] 312 p. [6964
——An honorable Titan, a biographical study of Adolph S. Ochs. New York, Harper & Brothers [1946] 313 p. [6965
——Incredible tale; the odyssey of the average American in the last half century. New York, Harper and Brothers [1950] 301 p. [6966
——Liberal's progress. New York, Coward-McCann [1948] 268 p. [6967
——A little night-music; discoveries in the exploitation of an art. New York, Harper & Brothers, 1937. 125 p. [6968
——The making of a southern industrialist; a biographical study of Simpson Bobo Tanner. Chapel Hill, University of North Carolina Press [1952] 84 p. [6969
——Mount Vernon; the story of a shrine . . . together with pertinent extracts from the diaries and letters of George Washington concerning the development of Mount Vernon, selected and annotated by Charles Cecil Wall. New York, Random House [1953] 122 p. [6970
——Number thirty-six, a novel. New York, Minton, Balch & Co., 1933. 315 p. [6971
——Our English heritage. Philadelphia, J. B. Lippincott [1949] 253 p. [6972
——Pattern for liberty; the story of old Philadelphia. New York, McGraw-Hill [1952] 146 p. [6973
——"A proud tower in the town"; an address delivered before the Edgar Allan Poe Society of Baltimore at the commemorative exercises in Westminster Church, January 19, 1937. Baltimore, Edgar Allan Poe Society, 1937. 8 p. [6974
——Randolph of Roanoke; a political fantastic. New York, Minton, Balch & Co., 1929. 278 p. [6975
——Roosevelt: dictator or democrat? New York, Harper & Brothers [c.1941] 303 p. [6976
——The secession of the southern states. New York, G. P. Putnam's Sons, 1933. 176 p. [6977
——Speech before the Democratic Congressional Wives Workshop, March 19, 1954. Washington, Publicity Division, Democratic National Committee, 1954. 4 p. [6978
——The Sunpapers of Baltimore, by Gerald W. Johnson, Frank R. Kent, H. L. Mencken, [and] Hamilton Owens. New York, A. A. Knopf, 1937. 430 p. [6979
——This American people. New York, Harper & Brothers [1951] 205 p. [6980
——The undefeated. New York, Minton, Balch & Co., 1927. 120 p. [6981
——Viewpoint, July 4, 1952- Baltimore, WAAM, Inc., 1952- NcU has July 4, 1952-December 26, 1954 [6982
——The wasted land. Chapel Hill, University of North Carolina Press, 1937. 110 p. [6983

——What is news? A tentative outline. New York, A. A. Knopf, 1926. (Borzoi handbooks of journalism, ed. by N. A. Crawford) 98 p.   [6984

——Woodrow Wilson . . . with the collaboration of the editors of Look magazine. New York, Harper & Brothers [1944] 293 p.   [6985

Johnson, Guion Griffis. Ante-bellum North Carolina; a social history. Chapel Hill, University of North Carolina Press, 1937. 935 p.   [6986

——A social history of the Sea Islands, with special reference to St. Helena Island South Carolina. Chapel Hill, University of North Carolina Press, 1930. 245 p. [6987

Johnson, Guy Benton. Folk culture on St. Helena Island, South Carolina. Chapel Hill, University of North Carolina Press, 1930. 183 p.   [6988

——John Henry; tracking down a Negro legend. Chapel Hill, University of North Carolina Press, 1929. 155 p.   [6989

Johnson, Guy Benton, joint author, see **Odum, Howard Washington**

Johnson, Herschel Vespasian. Nationalism and internationalism; an address delivered at a convocation of the University of North Carolina, Friday, January 24, 1947. Chapel Hill, University of North Carolina [1947] 14 p.   [6990

Johnson, J. Henry. How influence transforms life. Everetts, Author [c.1908] 25 p.   [6991

Johnson, J. W. Robert Lucas, a booklet . . . Andrew Jackson, a sketch. Circleville, O. [Privately printed? 1930] 40 p.   [6992

Johnson, James Asa. Sanctuary, a book of verse. Genesee, Pa., Johnson Print Shop [c.1931] 33 p.   [6993

Johnson, James Gibson. Southern fiction prior to 1860. Charlottesville, Va., Michie Co., pr., 1909. 126 p.   [6994

Johnson, James MacNeill. Free verse and paraphrase. [Raleigh, Author? c.1929] 125 p.   [6995

——A thousand years with royalty; a story of the English kings. [Lynchburg, Va., J. P. Bell Co., Inc., c.1913] 94 p.   [6996

Johnson, John. A sermon commemorative of the Rt. Rev. Thomas Frederick Davis, D. D., late bishop of the Diocese of South Carolina, preached 10th of December, 1871, in Grace Church, Camden. Charleston, S. C., Walker, Evans, & Cogswell, 1872. 21 p.   [6997

Johnson, John A. My wife, her lover and I. An autobiography. Norfolk, Va., c.1883. 53 p.   [6998

Johnson, Joseph. Traditions and reminiscences, chiefly of the American Revolution in the South. Charleston, S. C., Walker & James, 1851. 592 p.   [6998a

Johnson, Lemuel. An elementary arithmetic, designed for beginners. Raleigh, Branson & Farrar, 1864. 154 p.   [6999

Johnson, Leonard E. Men of achievement in the Carolinas . . . by Leonard E. Johnson and Lloyd M. Smith. [Charlotte, Men of Achievement, Inc. c.1952] 341 p.   [7000

Johnson, Livingston. Christian statesmanship. 2d ed. Raleigh, Edwards and Broughton Co., 1915. 130 p.   [7001

——History of the North Carolina Baptist State Convention. Raleigh, Edwards & Broughton Printing Co., 1908. 153 p.   [7002

Johnson, Margaret Sweet. Stowaway cat. New York, W. Morrow, 1955. 62 p. [7003

[**Johnson, Mary Lynch**] Elizabeth Avery Colton; an educational pioneer in the South. No place, North Carolina Division of the South Atlantic Section of the American Association of University Women, n.d. 10 p.   [7004

Johnson, Mary Lynch. The grotesque in Browning. Raleigh, Meredith College, 1926. (Its Bulletin, Series 20, no. 1) 19 p.   [7005

——A history of Meredith College. Raleigh, Meredith College, 1956.. 301 p. [7006

Johnson, Pamela Hansford. Hungry Gulliver. New York, S. Scribner's Sons, 1948. 170 p.   [7007

——Thomas Wolfe; a critical study. London, W. Heinemann [1947] 138 p. [7008

Johnson, Richard Carroll. A story of six loves. New York, Pageant Press [1955] 52 p.   [7009

Johnson, Rozelle Parker. Compositiones variae, from Codex 490, Biblioteca capitolare, Lucca, Italy. Urbana, University of Illinois Press, 1939. 116 p.   [7010

Johnson, Talmage Casey. The Christian differential. Nashville, Tenn., Cokesbury Press [c.1936] 192 p.   [7011
——The crucifiers, then and now. Nashville, Tenn., Broadman Press [1942] 116 p.   [7012
——Life's intimate relationships. New York, Abingdon-Cokesbury Press [c.1941] 205 p.   [7013
——Look for the dawn! Sermons of courage, hope, and faith for crucial war and postwar days. Nashville, Tenn., Broadman Press [1943] 173 p.   [7014
——The story of Kinston and Lenoir County. Raleigh, Edwards & Broughton, 1954. 413 p.   [7015

Johnson, Thomas. Every man his own doctor; or, The poor man's family physician. Salisbury, Author, 1798. 50 p.   [7016

Johnson, Thomas Cary. A history of the southern Presbyterian Church, with appendix. New York, Christian Literature Co., 1894. 487 p.   [7017

Johnson, Walter Nathan. The release of power in churches vitalized to save our modern world. Raleigh, Laboratory of Church Vitalization [c.1946] 33 p. [7018
——The southern Baptist crisis, a readjustment for efficiency. Thomasville, Charity and Children [1914] 37 p.   [7019

Johnson, Walter Rogers. Report on the coal lands of the Deep River Mining and Transportation Company, in Chatham and Moore counties, North Carolina. Albany, N. Y., Weed, Parsons, and Co., 1851. 39 p.   [7020

Johnson, William. Sketches of the life and correspondence of Nathanael Greene, major general of the armies of the United States, in the war of the Revolution. Charleston [S. C.] Printed for the Author, by A. E. Miller, 1822. 2 v.   [7021

Johnson, William Eugene. The federal government and the liquor traffic. Westerville, O., American Issue Publishing Co. [c.1911] 275 p.   [7022

Johnson, Willis Fletcher. Life of Wm. Tecumseh Sherman. [Philadelphia] Edgewood Publishing Co., 1891. 607 p.   [7023

Johnson, Wingate Memory. The true physician. New York, Macmillan Co., 1936. 157 p.   [7024
——The years after fifty. New York, Whittlesey House [1947] 153 p.   [7025

Johnson C. Smith University, Charlotte, N. C. Bulletin, v. 1- 1934- Charlotte, 1934- NcU has v. [1-20]   [7026
——Catalogue, 1867/68- Charlotte, 1868- NcU has [1867/68-1919/20] 1921/22-1933/34. Continues as its Bulletin, v. 1- 1934- Called Biddle University, 1867-1922   [7027

Johnston, Charles Hughes. High school education. New York, C. Scribner's Sons, 1912. 555 p.   [7028

Johnston, Frances Benjamin. The early architecture of North Carolina; a pictorial survey by Frances Benjamin Johnston, with an architectural history by Thomas Tileston Waterman. Chapel Hill, University of North Carolina Press, 1941. xxiii, 290 p.   [7029
—— ——xxvii, 290, xxxiii-xxxv p. Limited edition. Varies in preface only. [7030

Johnston, Ira Thomas. Judge Tam C. Bowie worthy of your support, candidate for Democratic nomination for United States Senator. No place, no publisher [1931] 3 p.   [7031

Johnston, James C. Edward Wood and others, ex'rs of Jas. C. Johnston vs. his heirs at law and next of kin. [Raleigh?] n.d. 12 p.   [7032

Johnston, Joseph Eggleston. Narrative of military operations, directed, during the late war between the states. New York, D. Appleton and Co., 1874. 602 p. [7033

Johnston, Joseph Henry, joint author, see **Williams, Lester Alonzo**

Johnston, Josiah Stoddard. First explorations of Kentucky; Dr. Thomas Walker's Journal of an exploration of Kentucky in 1750 . . . also Colonel Christopher Gist's Journal of a tour through Ohio and Kentucky in 1751, with notes and sketch, by J. Stoddard Johnston. Louisville, Ky., J. P. Morton and Co., 1898. 222 p.   [7034

Johnston, Mary. Croatan. Boston, Little, Brown and Co., 1923. 298 p.   [7035
—— ——New York, A. L. Burt Co. [c.1923] 298 p.   [7036

Johnston, Robert Zenas. Historical sketch of Goshen Presbyterian Church, Gaston County, N. C., 1889. Shelby, C. P. Roberts, pr., 1889. 9 p.   [7037

——Historical sketch of Little Brittain Presbyterian Church, Rutherford County, N. C. . . . 1888. [Lincolnton] Lincoln Courier, 1889. 10 p. [7038]

Johnston, Ruby F. The development of Negro religion. New York, Philosophical Library [1954] 202 p. [7039]

Johnston, Thomas P. Fellow citizens of the seventh congressional district. No place, n.d. [1] p. [7040]

Johnston, William. Atlantic, Tennessee and Ohio Railroad; a card to the stock-holders . . . and to the citizens of the counties of Iredell and Mecklenburg. No place, n.d. [1] p. [7041]

Johnston, William, joint author see Davega, A. H.

Johnston Co., N. C. Board of Commissioners. Itemized statement of expendi-tures, 188 - No place, 188 - NcU has 1880/81 [7042]

Johnston County, N. C. Board of Education. Report of Johnston County Public Schools, 19 - [Smithfield? 19 - NcU has 1908/09 (with history, 1901-1909)] [7043]

Johnston County Baptist Association. Minutes, 1903- 1903- NcU has 1903-1906 [1928-1949] [7044]

Johnstone, Herrick. The secret shot; or, The rivals of Misty Mount. New York, Frank Starr [c.1874] (Frank Starr's ten cent American novels, no. 154) 44 p. [7045]

Joint Committee of the North Carolina English Teachers Association and the North Carolina Library Association. North Carolina authors: a selective Handbook. Chapel Hill, University of North Carolina Library, 1952. (Its Library extension publication, v. 18, no. 1) 136 p. [7046]

Jolly, William. Flora Macdonald in Uist, a study of the heroine in her native surroundings. Perth [Scotland] S. Cowan & Co. [1886?] 93 p. [7047]

Jolts and scrambles; or "We uns and our doin's". Philadelphia (privately printed) 1884. 93 p. [7048]

Jones, A. On the relations of Christians to the appointments of the churches of which they are members; a sermon preached at Hillsboro, N. C. . . . September, 1854. Richmond, Va., H. K. Ellyson's Steam-Power Press, 1855. 14 p. [7049]

Jones, Alexander Hamilton. Knocking at the door; Alex. H. Jones, member-elect to Congress. Washington, McGill & Witherow, pr., 1866. 38 p. [7050]

Jones, Cadwallader. A genealogical history. Columbia, S. C., Ye Bryan Printing Co., 1900. 73 p. [7051]

Jones, Charles P. Roman Catholicism scripturally considered; or, The Church of Rome, the great apostasy. New York, M. W. Dodd, 1856. 396 p. [7052]

Jones, Claude C. Reminiscences of North Carolina. [Wilson, Carolina Discipliana Library, 1954] 7 p. [7053]

Jones, Decatur. The impure hand. Prairie City, Ill., Decker Press [c.1948] 72 p. [7054]

Jones, Edmund. Fellow citizens . . . Raleigh, January 20, 1837. [1] p. [7055]

Jones, Gilmer Andrew. Songs from the hills. [Franklin? 1950] 57 p. [7056]

Jones, Hamilton Chamberlain, 1798-1868. Circular to the freemen of Rowan County. No place, no publisher [1833] 4 p. [7057]

Jones, Hamilton Chamberlain, 1884- Address . . . upon the occasion of the pre-sentation of the portrait of Chief Justice William Alexander Hoke, Supreme Court, Raleigh, N. C., 2d September, 1930. No place, no publisher, 1930. 23 p. [7058]

Jones, Howard Mumford. The convocation ode. No place, no publisher [c.1916] 11 p. [7059]

Jones, Mrs. Howard Mumford see Mumford, Elizabeth

Jones, Hugh. The present state of Virginia. New York, Reprinted for J. Sabin, 1865. (Sabin's reprints, no. 5) 151 p. [7060]

——The present state of Virginia; from whence is inferred a short view of Maryland and North Carolina, edited . . . by Richard L. Morton. Chapel Hill, University of North Carolina Press for Virginia Historical Society [1956] 295 p. [7061]

[Jones, I. W.] An appeal to the Old Whigs and Union Democrats of Rowan County. [Vallambroso, July 12th, 1870] 7 p. [7062]

[Jones, James Athearn]　Tales of an Indian camp.　London, Henry Colburn, 1829. (The new British novelist, v. 43-45)　3 v.　[7063

Jones, James Sawyer.　Life of Andrew Johnson.　Greeneville, Tenn., East Tennessee Publishing Co. [1901]　400 p.　[7064

Jones, Joe.　1-B soldier.　New York, Harper & Brothers [1944]　162 p.　[7065

Jones, John Beauchamp.　Wild western scenes . . . wherein the conduct of Daniel Boone, the great American pioneer, is particularly described.　Philadelphia, J. B. Lippincott Co., 1860.　263 p.　[7066

Jones, Joseph Addison, Construction Company, Inc., Charlotte, N. C.　J. A. Jones Construction Company, Inc., fiftieth anniversary. [Charlotte, 1946?] 102 p. [7067

Jones, Joseph Seawell.　A defence of the Revolutionary history of the state of North Carolina from the aspersions of Mr. Jefferson.　Boston, C. Bowen; Raleigh, Turner and Hughes, 1834.　343 p.　[7068

[Jones, Joseph Seawell]　The mammoth humbug; or, The adventures of Shocco Jones, in Mississippi, in the summer of 1839, including the history of his visit to Alabama, and "the way he come it over" certain members of its legislature, &c., &c.　Memphis, 1842.　22 p.　[7069

Jones, Joseph Seawell.　Memorials of North Carolina.　New-York [Printed by Scatcherd & Adams] 1838.　87 p.　[7070

Jones, Katharine M., ed.　New Confederate short stories.　Columbia, University of South Carolina Press, 1954.　202 p.　[7071

Jones, Kimbrough.　To the freemen of Wake County.　No place, Author, August 6, 1836.　[1] p.　[7072

Jones, Lewis Hampton.　Captain Roger Jones, of London and Virginia.　Albany, N. Y., J. Munsell's Sons, 1891.　295 p.　[7073
—— ——1891.　442 p.　[7074

Jones, Mary Best.　Songs of seasons.　New York, American Book Co. [c.1909] 108 p.　[7075

Jones, May F., ed.　Memoirs and speeches of Locke Craig.　Asheville, Hackney and Moale, 1923.　284 p.　[7076

Jones, Nellie (Rowe)　see Rowe, Nellie M.

Jones, Oleona May.　My colorful days.　Boston, Christopher Publishing House [c.1940]　119 p.　[7077

Jones, S. Armistead.　Compliments of Waynesville, N. C., in the land and country God lifted close to the sky.　Asheville, Hackney & Moale [1905?]　75 p.　[7078
——Compliments of Waynesville, N. C., in the Land of the Sky. [1906?] 32 p. [7079

Jones, Samuel Porter.　Hogs worth more than men!　No place, no publisher, n.d. 1 p.　[7080

[Jones, Sarah (Bailey)]　Fifty years of organized work of the Woman's Missionary Union of North Carolina, auxiliary to the Baptist State Convention, 1886-1936. [Raleigh? Baptist State Convention of North Carolina, 1936]　20 p.　[7081

Jones, Shocco　see Jones, Joseph Seawell

Jones, Stephen Collins.　The Hamrick generations, being a genealogy of the Hamrick family.　Raleigh, Edwards & Broughton Printing Co., 1920.　207 p.　[7082

Jones, Thomas H.　Experience and personal narrative of Uncle Tom Jones, who was for forty years a slave.　Boston, J. E. Farwell & Co., 1855.　54 p.　[7083
——The experience of Thomas H. Jones, who was a slave for forty-three years. Worcester, Mass., Printed by Henry J. Howland, 1857.　48 p.　[7084
—— ——[3d ed.] New Bedford, Mass., E. Anthony & Sons, pr., 1885. 84 p. [7085

Jones, Tiberius Gracchus.　Mind and woman, an address delivered before the Chowan Female Collegiate Institute, Murfreesboro', N. C., July 25th, 1855. Richmond, Va., H. K. Ellyson, 1855.　24 p.　[7086
——The true man, an oration before the Philomathesian and Euzelian societies of Wake Forest College, N. C., delivered June 7, 1854.　Philadelphia, C. Sherman, pr., 1854.　35 p.　[7087

Jones, Walter Burgwyn.　John Burgwin, Carolinian; John Jones, Virginian; their ancestors and descendants.　[Montgomery, Ala.] Privately printed, 1913. 119 p.　[7088

Jones, William Francis. The constitution and the Supreme Court of the United States. Wilmington, Jackson & Bell, pr. [1937]   80 p.   [7089

Jones, William Robert. John Paul Jones and his ancestry . . . together with His last days, by Joseph G. Branch. Chicago, Joseph G. Branch Publishing Co. [c.1927]   284 p.   [7090

Jonesboro High School, Jonesboro, N. C. Catalogue, 18 - Jonesboro, 18 - NcU has 1887/88   [7091

Jonesville Male and Female Academies, Jonesville, N. C. Catalogue, 18 - Jonesville, 18 - NcU has 1855/56, 1857/58   [7092

Jong, Herman Holland de. Experimental catatonia, a general reaction-form of the central nervous system, and its implications for human pathology. Baltimore, Williams & Wilkins Co., 1945.   225 p.   [7093

Jordan, Alphonso. Prayers offered by the Reverend Alphonso Jordan, chaplain, at the opening of the daily sessions of House of Representatives, General Assembly of North Carolina, session 1955. [Raleigh, 1955]   Unpaged.   [7094

Jordan, Arthur Melville. Children's interests in reading. Rev. ed. Chapel Hill, University of North Carolina Press, 1926.   103 p.   [7095

——Educational psychology. New York, H. Holt and Co. [c.1928]   460 p.   [7096

——Educational psychology. Rev. ed. New York, H. Holt and Co. [c.1933] 522 p.   [7097

—— ——3d ed. New York, H. Holt and Co. [1942]   597 p.   [7098

——Educational psychology; growth and learning. 4th ed. New York, H. Holt and Co. [1956]   600 p.   [7099

——Experiments in educational psychology. New York, H. Holt and Co. [c.1933] 94 p.   [7100

——How to study. Boston, Christopher Publishing House [c.1936]   97 p.   [7101

——Measurement in education. New York, McGraw-Hill, 1953.   533 p.   [7102

Jordan, Chester A. Importance in war of minor seaports and adjoining coastal areas. [Portland, Me., Author, c.1950]   10 p.   [7103

Jordan, Francis Marion. Life and labors of Elder F. M. Jordan. Raleigh, Edwards & Broughton, pr., 1899.   325 p.   [7104

Jordan, Gerald Ray. Adventures in radiant living. New York, Round Table Press, Inc., 1938.   197 p.   [7105

——Beyond despair; when religion becomes real. New York, Macmillan Co., 1955. 166 p.   [7106

——Courage that propels. Nashville, Cokesbury Press [c.1933]   182 p.   [7107

——Faith that propels. Nashville, Cokesbury Press [c.1935]   208 p.   [7108

——The hour has come. New York, Abingdon-Cokesbury Press [1948] 152 p. [7109

——Intimate interests of youth. Nashville, Tenn., Cokesbury Press [c.1931] 164 p.   [7110

——The intolerance of Christianity. New York, Fleming H. Revell Co. [c.1931] 160 p.   [7111

——Look at the stars! New York, Abingdon-Cokesbury Press [1942]   204 p. [7112

——We believe! A creed that sings. New York, Abingdon-Cokesbury Press [1944] 135 p.   [7113

——We face Calvary—and life! Nashville, Tenn., Cokesbury Press [c.1936] 160 p.   [7114

——What is yours? And other sermons. New York, Fleming H. Revell Co. [c.1930]   156 p.   [7115

——Why the cross? New York, Abingdon-Cokesbury Press [c.1941]   138 p. [7116

Jordan, Grace Welch, comp. Bibliography of the books and articles written by Ernest R. Groves at the University of North Carolina, 1927-1945. [Chapel Hill, 1945]   [5] p.   [7117

Jordan, Marea, comp. Statesville Public Schools song book, compiled and arranged by Misses Marea Jordan, Nell Armfield, and others. [Statesville, Statesville Printing Co.] n.d.   55 p.   [7118

Jordan, Richard. Journal of the life and religious labours of Richard Jordan, a minister of the Gospel in the Society of Friends. Philadelphia, Thomas Kite, 1829.   172 p.   [7119

Jordan, Stroud. Chocolate evaluation. New York, Applied Sugar Laboratories, Inc., 1934.   225 p.   [7120

——Confectionery problems. Chicago, National Confectioners' Association, 1930. 347 p.   [7121
——Confectionery standards. New York, Applied Sugar Laboratories, Inc., 1933. 370 p.   [7122

Jordan, Weymouth T. George Washington Campbell of Tennessee, western states-man. Tallahassee, Florida State University, 1955. (Florida State University studies, no. 17) 214 p.   [7123

Jordan, William Hill. An address delivered before the two literary societies of Wake Forest College, on the 10th of June, 1847, at the solicitation of the Euzelian Society. Raleigh, W. W. Holden, 1847. 36 p.   [7124
——An address delivered to the students of the Warrenton Male Academy . . . in June, 1849. Baltimore, John D. Toy, pr., 1850. 23 p.   [7125
——The fragility of human life and human glory, a sermon on occasion of the death of Gen. Zachary Taylor. Raleigh, Raleigh Times, 1850. 15 p.   [7126

Joseph Keasbey Brick Agricultural, Industrial and Normal School, Enfield, N. C. Catalogue, 189 - Enfield, 189 - NcU has 1904/05-1911/12 [1914/15-1932/33] Called Brick Junior College, 192 -   [7127
——Joseph Keasby Brick Agricultural, Industrial, and Normal School, Bricks, N. C. No place, [1920?] Folder.   [7128

Joseph K. Brick news, v. 1- 189 - Enfield, 189 - NcU has v. [9-20]   [7129

Josephine Gilmer, celebrated American prima donna soprano. No place, no pub-lisher, 1915. [8] p.   [7130

Josey, Charles Conant. Psychology and successful living. New York, Charles Scribner's Sons [1952] 405 p.   [7131
——The psychology of religion. New York, Macmillan Co., 1927. 362 p.   [7132
——Race and national solidarity. New York, C. Scribner's Sons, 1923. 227 p. [7133
——The social philosophy of instinct. New York, C. Scribner's Sons [c.1922] 274 p.   [7134

Joslynn, Jep, pseud. see **Doyle, John E. P.**

Joubert, William H. Southern freight rates in transition. Gainesville, University of Florida Press, 1949. 424 p.   [7135

Journal of American poetry, v. 1, no. 1-3, Spring, 1927-Autumn-Winter, 1928/29- Charlotte, Journal of American Poetry, 1927-1928. NcU has v. 1, no. 1-3. Dis-continued following v. 1, no. 3.   [7136

Journal of legal education, v. 1- Autumn, 1948- Durham, Association of American Law Schools, 1948- NcU has v. 1-8   [7137

Journal of parapsychology, v. 1- March, 1937- Durham, Duke University Press [1937- NcU has v. [1-5] 6-20   [7138

Journal of social forces see Social forces

Joyner, E. N. Rosborough number two. Lenoir, Author, 1917. 15 p.   [7139

[Joyner, James Yadkin] Address at the annual meeting of the State Association of County Superintendents: Our task and our opportunity. [Raleigh? 1913] 7 p. [7140

Joyner, James Yadkin. Address before the North Carolina Press Association at Montreat, July 1, 1915. No place, no publisher [1915?] 6 p.   [7141
——Dr. J. Y. Joyner pleads cause of Sandy Graham for governor . . . radio address over Station WPTF . . . May 22 [1926] [Raleigh? 1936] 7 p.   [7142

Joyner, O. L. Eastern North Carolina as a tobacco producing section. [Greenville, no publisher, 1898] 34 p.   [7143

Judson, Clara (Ingram) Andrew Jackson, frontier statesman. Chicago, Follett Publishing Co. [1954] 224 p.   [7144

Judson College, Hendersonville, N. C. Catalogue, 18 - Hendersonville, 18 - NcU has 1884/85, 1887/88   [7145

Julian, George Washington. The rank of Charles Osburn as an anti-slavery pioneer. Indianapolis, Bowen-Merrill Co., 1891. (Indiana Historical Society Publications, v. II, no. 6) 37 p.   [7146

Julius Shakespeare Harris, born February 17, 1845, died March 19, 1936. No place, no publisher, n.d. 7 p.   [7147

Junaluskan. Souvenir ed. [Lake Junaluska, Southern Assembly, Methodist Epis-copal Church, South, 1923] 46 p.   [7148

——Program number. 1936. [24] p. [7149

Junior College Work Conference, Chapel Hill, June 27-30, 1954. Summary report. Chapel Hill [1954] 45 p. [7150

Junior Order of United American Mechanics. North Carolina. Proceedings, 1891?-1891?- NcU has 1915 [7151

Junior Order of United American Mechanics. North Carolina. Edgemont Council no. 473, Durham, N. C. Constitution and by-laws. Durham [Seeman Printery] 1916. 32 p. [7152

Junior Settlement, Montgomery Co., N. C. Announcement of an institution for boys, city born and from families of the landless class in the South. [New York, Oscar Haywood, c.1910] [18] p. [7153

Jurgensen, Kai, joint editor, see Schenkkan, Robert Frederic, ed.

Jusserand, Jean Adrien Antoine Jules. Rochambeau and the French in America . . . an address delivered before the State Literary and Historical Association of North Carolina at Raleigh on November 21, 1913. [Raleigh, 1913] 37 p. [7154

Justus, May. Children of the Great Smoky Mountains. New York, E. P. Dutton and Co., 1952. 158 p. [7155

——Dixie decides. New York, Random House [1942] 295 p. [7156

Kahler, Hugh MacNair. MacIvor's folly. New York, D. Appleton and Co., 1925. 287 p. [7157

Kaighn, Raymond P. How to retire and like it. [2d ed., rev.] New York, Association Press, 1951. 149 p. [7158

[Kaler, James Otis] Boy spies at the defense of Fort Henry . . . by James Otis. New York, A. L. Burt Co. [c.1900] 365 p. [7159

——Boy spies with the Regulators. New York, A. L. Burt Co. [c.1901] 303 p. [7160

——With the Regulators. New York, A. L. Burt Co. [c.1901] 303 p. [7161

Kane, Harnett Thomas. Gentlemen, swords and pistols. New York, Wm. Morrow and Co., 1951. 306 p. [7162

Kane, Hope Frances. Colonial promotion and promotion literature of Carolina, Pennsylvania and New Jersey, 1660-1700. [Ann Arbor, Mich., Edwards Brothers, 1948] 23 p. [7163

Kanuga Lake, a co-operative resort colony in the North Carolina mountains. No place [Kanuga Club?] n.d. 27 p. [7164

Karig, Walter. Don't tread on me; a novel of the historic exploits, military and gallant, of Commodore John Paul Jones. New York, Rinehart & Co. [1954] 442 p. [7165

Karraker, Cyrus Harreld. Piracy was a business. Rindge, N. H., R. R. Smith, 1953. 244 p. [7166

Karsner, David. Andrew Jackson, the gentle savage. New York, Brentano's, 1929. 399 p. [7167

Kattsoff, Louis Osgood. The design of human behavior. St. Louis, Educational Publisher [1953] 402 p. [7168

——Elements of philosophy. New York, Ronald Press Co. [1953] 448 p. [7169

——A philosophy of mathematics. Ames, Iowa State College Press, 1948. 266 p. [7170

Kazin, Alfred. On native grounds, an interpretation of modern American prose literature. New York, Reynal & Hitchock [1942] 541 p. [7171

Keckley, Elizabeth (Hobbs) Behind the scenes . . . or, Thirty years a slave, and four years in the White House. New York, G. W. Carleton & Co., 1868. 371 p. [7172

Keech, James Maynard. Workmen's compensation in North Carolina, 1929-1940. Durham, Duke University Press, 1942. 198 p. [7173

Keen, T. G. The times we live in, an address delivered before the Philomathesian and Euzelian societies of Wake Forest College, N. C., June 13, 1860. Raleigh, Strother & Marcom, Book and Job Printers, 1860. 24 p. [7174

Kehukee Baptist Association. Minutes, 17 - 17 - NcU has 1769-1778 (film of manuscript) 1791-1792 (photograph of original printing) 1794, 1796 (photograph) 1798 (photograph) 1827-1849 [1858-1902] 1903-1933 [1934-1956] [7175

——Minutes of the Kehukey Association (Baptist) with letter of Joel Battle Fort, and with introduction and notes by Kemp Plummer Battle, LL. D. [Chapel Hill]

The University, 1904. (James Sprunt historical monograph, no. 5) 32 p. Includes Minutes, 1769-1777. [7176

Keidel, George Charles. The early life of Professor Elliott, paper read before the Romance Club of Johns Hopkins University, Oct. 12, 1916. Washington, privately printed, 1917. 10 p. [7177

Keiser, Albert. The Indian in American literature. New York, Oxford University Press, 1933. 312 p. [7178

Keith, Alice Barnwell, joint author, see Wallace, Lillian Parker

Keith, Benjamin F. Memories; "truth and Honesty will conquer". Raleigh, Bynum Printing Co., 1922. 159 p. [7179

Kell, John McIntosh. Recollections of a naval life, including the cruises of the Confederate States steamers "Sumter" and "Alabama". Washington, Neale Co., 1900. 307 p. [7180

Kellam, Ida (Brooks) Brooks and kindred families. [Wilmington?] 1950. 384 p. [7181

Keller, Franklin J. Proposed program for the new Negro industrial high school at Winston-Salem, North Carolina, prepared in conference by Drs. Franklin J. Keller and J. L. Meader. [Winston-Salem, 1930] 12 p. [7182

Keller, Hans Gustav. Christoph von Graffenried und die Gründung von Neu-Bern in Nord-Carolina. Bern, Buchdruckerei Feuz, 1953. 42 p. [7183

Keller, John Esten, tr. The book of the wiles of women. Chapel Hill, University of North Carolina Press [1956] (North Carolina. University. Studies in the Romance languages and literatures, no. 27) 60 p. [7184

Kelley, Mary Sullivan. Alma Mater's children, a class day play. [Reidsville?] c.1939. 24 p. [7185

——Attic memories, a class day play. [Reidsville, Reidsville Printing Co.] c.1938. 18 p. [7186

——In honored glory, a patriotic class day pageant. [Reidsville] c.1942. 23 p. [7187

——Isle of our dreams. [Reidsville] c.1941. 32 p. [7188

——Sails at dawn, a class day play. [Reidsville] c.1942. 20 p. [7189

——A senior in wonderland, a class day play. [Reidsville] c.1939. 24 p. [7190

Kelley, Welbourn. So fair a house. New York, W. Morrow & Co., 1936. 310 p. [7191

Kelley's Wilmington directory, 18 - Wilmington, G. H. Kelly, 18 - NcU has 1860-61 [7192

Kelling, Lucile. Index verborum Iuvenalis, by Lucile Kelling and Albert Suskin. Chapel Hill, University of North Carolina Press, 1951. 139 p. [7193

Kells, Lucas Carlisle, Typical methods of thinking in science and philosophy. New York, Columbia University, 1910. 39 p. [7194

Kelly, Fred Charters. The Wright brothers, a biography authorized by Orville Wright. New York, Harcourt, Brace and Co. [1943] 340 p. [7195

—— ——New York, Ballantine Books [c.1950] 214 p. [7196

Kemp, Leila Rush. Ventures in verse. San Antonio, Southern Literary Institute, 1934. 36 p. [7197

[Kenan, Thomas Stephen, ed.] Sketch of the Forty-Third Regiment, North Carolina Troops (Infantry) [Raleigh, 1895] 26 p. [7198

Kenan, William Rand. A concise description of the electrical apparatus employed at the Sault Ste. Marie Works of the Union Carbide Company. No place, no publisher, n.d. [2] p. [7199

——Discovery and identification of calcium carbide in the U. S. A. [Lockport, N. Y., Author, 1939] 27 p. [7200

——History of Randleigh Farm. Lockport, N. Y., W. R. Kenan, Jr., 1935. 116 p. [7201

—— ——2d ed. Lockport, N. Y., 1937. 298 p. [7202

—— ——3d ed. c.1940. 256 p. [7203

—— ——4th ed. 1942. 348 p. [7204

—— ——5th ed. c.1947. 227 p. [7205

—— ——6th ed. 1950. 377 p. [7206

—— ——7th ed. 1953. 246 p. [7207

——Incidents by the way; lifetime recollections and reflections. [Lockport? N. Y. privately printed, 1946] 186 p. [7208

——Incidents by the way; more recollections. 2d ed. [1949] 105 p. [7209
—— ——3d ed. [Lockport? N. Y., 1952] 85 p. [7210
—— ——4th ed. [Lockport? N. Y.] 1955. 128 p. [7211

Kendall, Henry Plimpton. Early maps of Carolina and adjoining regions, together with early prints of Charleston from the collection of Henry P. Kendall; catalogue comp. by Priscilla Smith, ed. by Louis C. Karpinski. No place, no publisher [1930] 47 p. [7212
—— ——2d ed. [1937] 67 p. [7213

Kendrick, Benjamin Burks. The South looks at its past, by Benjamin Burks Kendrick and Alex Mathews Arnett. Chapel Hill, University of North Carolina Press, 1935. 196 p. [7214

Kenilworth Inn, Biltmore, N. C. see Biltmore, N. C. Kenilworth Inn

Kennaway, John Henry. On Sherman's track; or, The South after the war. London, Seeley, Jackson, and Halliday, 1867. 320 p. [7215

Kennedy, Edwin Wexler. Quit-rents and currency in North Carolina, 1663-1776. Baltimore, J. W. Bond Co., pr., 1902. 35 p. [7216

[Kennedy, John Pendleton] Horse Shoe Robinson; a tale of the Tory ascendency, by the author of "Swallow barn". Philadelphia, Carey, Lea & Blanchard, 1835. 2 v. First edition. [7217

Kennedy, John Pendleton. Horse Shoe Robinson. New York, J. W. Lovell Co. [1883?] 554 p. [7218
—— ——Rev. ed. New York, G. P. Putnam's Sons, 1899. 598 p. [7219
—— ——New York, A. L. Burt Co., n.d. 483 p. [7220
—— ——New York, G. P. Putnam's Sons, 1907. 598 p. [7221
—— ——condensed for use in schools, with introductory and explanatory notes. New York, University Publishing Co., 1897. 192 p. [7222

Kennedy, Sara Beaumont (Cannon) Joscelyn Cheshire, a story of Revolutionary days in the Carolinas. New York, Doubleday, Page & Co., 1906. 338 p. [7223
——The wooing of Judith, colonial Virginia. New York, Doubleday, Page & Co., 1906. 399 p. [7224

Kennel and field, v. 1- December, 1931- Raleigh, W. T. Scarborough, 1931- NcU has v. [1] [7225

Kent, Charles William, comp. Southern poems, selected, arranged, and ed. with biographical notes. Boston, Houghton Mifflin Co. [c.1913] 112 p. [7226

Kent, Rosemary (May) An evaluation of the health education program of the American Cancer Society, North Carolina Division, Inc. Chapel Hill, 1949 [i.e. 1950] 159 leaves. [7227

Kephart, Horace. Camp cookery. New York, Macmillan Co., 1926. 154 p. [7228
——Camping and woodcraft; a handbook for vacation campers and for travelers in the wilderness. New York, Macmillan Co. [1947] 2 v. in 1. [7229
——The Cherokees of the Smoky Mountains. Ithaca, N. Y. [Atkinson Press] 1936. 36 p. [7230
——Our southern highlanders. New York, Outing Publishing Co., 1913. 395 p. [7231
—— ——New and enl. ed. New York, Macmillan Co., 1922. 469 p. [7232

Kepler, Hazel Cloughley. Food for little people, by Hazel Kepler and Elizabeth Hesser. New York, Funk & Wagnalls [1950] 276 p. [7233

Kern, John Dwight. Constance Fenimore Woolson, literary pioneer. Philadelphia, University of Pennsylvania Press, 1934. 198 p. [7235

Kern, Paul Bentley. The basic beliefs of Jesus; a study of the assumptions behind a life. Nashville, Tenn., Cokesbury Press [c.1935] 247 p. [7236
——Methodism has a message! The Jarrell lectures for 1941 at Emory University. New York, Abingdon-Cokesbury Press [c.1941] 188 p. [7237

[Kerner, Jane (Donnell) ed.] Memorial of Robah Bascom Kerner, esq., containing some of his speeches, edited by his wife, assisted by a friend. Richmond, Va., B. F. Johnson Publishing Co., 1894. 158 p. [7238

Kernersville High School, Kernersville, N. C. Kernersville High School, male and female. [Kernersville] 1858. [1] p. [7239

Kerr, pseud. see Pinnix, Hannah Courtney (Baxter)

Kerr, John. A sermon on the general resurrection and final judgment, delivered at the funeral of Col. Joseph Williams, late of Surry County, N. Carolina, on the first Lord's Day in November, 1828. Richmond, Va., Printed by Thomas W. White [1828?] 22 p.   [7240

Kester, John Marcus. The life beyond death. Nashville, Tenn., Sunday School Board of the Southern Baptist Convention [c.1930] 102 p.   [7241

Kester, Vaughan. The prodigal judge. Indianapolis, Bobbs-Merrill Co. [c.1911] 448 p.   [7242

Ketchum, Everett Phoenix. George Washington's vision, and other poems . . . by Everett Phoenix Ketchum and Lillian Floyd Ketchum. Asheville, Inland Press, pr. [1950] 64 p.   [7243

Ketring, Ruth Anna. Charles Osborn in the anti-slavery movement. Columbus, O., Ohio State Archaeological and Historical Society, 1937. 95 p.   [7244

Kettell, Thomas Prentice. Southern wealth and northern profits, as exhibited in statistical facts and official figures. New York, G. W. & J. A. Wood, 1860. 173 p.   [7245

Key, Alexander. With Daniel Boone on the Caroliny trail.   Philadelphia, John C. Winston Co. [c.1941] 223 p.   [7246

Key, Valdimer Orlando. Southern politics in state and nation [by] V. O. Key, Jr. with the assistance of Alexander Heard. New York, A. A. Knopf, 1949. 675 p. [7247

**Key-Stone, v. 1- 1865?- Raleigh, William B. Smith, 1865?- NcU has v. [1-3] [7248

Keyes, Charles A. The parson of the hills. New York, Vantage Press [1956] 103 p.   [7249

Kidder, Grier. The world, the flesh, and the devil. Wilmington, 1888. 17 p.   [7249a

Kidder, Maurice Arthur. Prayer: the sacrament of abiding power. Chapel Hill, Author [1954] 31 p.   [7250

Kidney, John Steinfort. Catawba River, and other poems. New-York, Baker and Scribner, 1847. 119 p.   [7251

Kilgo, John Carlisle. Chapel talks . . . ed. by D. W. Newsom. Nashville, Tenn., Publishing House, M. E. Church, South, 1922. 173 p.   [7252

——Christian education, its aims and superiority. No place, no publisher, n.d. 8 p.   [7253

——Hon. Robert Oswald Burton: a study. No place, no publisher, n.d. 28 p. [7254

——In memory of Mr. Washington Duke, exercises held in Craven Memorial Hall, Trinity College, Durham, N. C., June 4, 1905; memorial address [by] President John C. Kilgo, expressions from the faculty. [Durham, Trinity College, 1905] 26 p.   [7255

Kilgo, John Carlisle, defendant. Report of the proceedings of the investigation of the charges brought by Justice Walter Clark against Dr. John C. Kilgo, president of Trinity College, August 30 and 31, 1898, together with certain correspondence and proceedings preliminary thereto. Durham, Educator Co., pr., 1898. 166 p. [7256

——Suppressions and omissions in the so-called "minutes" of the so-called "investigation" of Dr. J. C. Kilgo, by the Board of Trustees of Trinity College, August 30-31, 1898. No place, no publisher, n.d. 63 p.   [7257

Kilgo, John Carlisle. William Wallace Duncan, an appreciation. [Durham, Seeman Printery] 1908. 68 p.   [7258

Kill Devil Hills Memorial Association. Kill Devil Hills Memorial Association, its genesis and its aims. [Elizabeth City, 1927] 8 p.   [7259

Killebrew, Joseph Buckner. The battle of Guilford Court House; an address before the Tennessee Division of the Sons of the American Revolution, at Nashville, March 15, 1901. Knoxville, Tenn., S. B. Newman & Co., pr., 1902. 15 p.   [7260

——The South, its opportunities for the investment of capital; an address delivered at a convention held in Southern Pines, N. C., April 19, 1899. No place, By request of bankers of Nashville, Tenn. [1899?] 22 p.   [7261

Kimrey, Grace Saunders. Glimpses of beauty. [Atlanta] Emory University [c.1955] 60 p.   [7262

——Songs of Sunny Valley. Emory University, Ga., Banner Press [1954] 60 p. [7263

Kincaid, Robert Lee. The Wilderness road. Indianapolis, Bobbs-Merrill Co. [1947] 392 p.   [7264

—— ———Harrogate, Tenn., Lincoln Memorial University Press, 1955.   [7265

King, Alice M.   The festival of the harvest moon.   Emory University, Ga., Banner Press [c.1931]   30 p.   [7266

King, Cardenio Flournoy.   The light of four candles.   Boston, Author, 1908. 510 p.   [7267

King, E. Sterling.   The wild rose of Cherokee; or, Nancy Ward, "the Pocahontas of the West".   Nashville, Tenn., University Press, 1895.   119 p.   [7268

King, Edward.   The great South; a record of journeys in Louisiana, Texas, the Indian Territory, Missouri, Arkansas, Mississippi, Alabama, Georgia, Florida, South Carolina, North Carolina, Kentucky, Tennessee, Virginia, West Virginia, and Maryland.   Hartford, Conn., American Publishing Co., 1875.   802 p.   [7269
——The southern states of North America; a record of journeys.   London, Blackie & Son, 1875.   806 p.   [7270

King, Henry Thomas.   Sketches of Pitt County; a brief history of the county, 1704-1910.   Raleigh, Edwards and Broughton, 1911.   263 p.   [7271

King, John L.   Reply to the so-called special report of the Superintendent of the North Carolina Insane Asylum of April 15th, 1885. [Greensboro? 1887] 18 p. [7272

King, Marie Halbert.   Call to remembrance.   [San Antonio, Texas, Carleton Printing Co. for the Author] c.1951.   74 p.   [7273

King, Pendleton.   Life and public services of Grover Cleveland.   New York, G. P. Putnam's Sons, 1884.   224 p.   [7274

[King, Pendleton]   The nomination of Mr. Cleveland.   No place [Author, 1892] 14 p.   [7275

King, Pendleton.   Remarks on the tariff.   No place, no publisher, n.d.   34 p. [7276

King, Samuel.   To the freemen composing the counties of Surry, Iredell, Wilkes, and Ashe.   Salisbury, Philo White, 1825.   [1] p.   [7277
——To the freemen of Surry, Iredell, Wilkes and Ashe.   No place, no publisher [1833]   [1] p.   [7278

King, Spencer Bidwell.   Selective Service in North Carolina in World War II.   Chapel Hill, University of North Carolina Press, 1949.   451 p.   [7279

King, Victor C.   Charlotte, N. C., story of the origin of the city of Charlotte.   [Charlotte, 1954]   31 p.   [7280

King, Victor C., comp.   Lives and times of the 27 signers of the Mecklenburg Declaration of Independence of May 20, 1775.   Charlotte [Anderson Press] 1956. 225 p.   [7281

King, William.   A manual of electricity.   Newbern, 1825.   83 p.   [7282

King, William J.   Address delivered before the young ladies of Louisburg Female College on thirty-first May, 1877.   Raleigh, Raleigh News Steam Job Print, 1877. 18 p.   [7283

King, William Rufus.   Address to the citizens of the fifteenth electoral district.   No place, no publisher [1840]   [1] p.   [7284
——Address to the people of the slave holding states.   No place, no publisher, 1840. 16 p.   [7285
——Last will and testament of William R. King, probated, May 11, 1853.   No place, no publisher [1929]   [3] p.   [7286

King Cotton Hotel, Greensboro, N. C.   The King Cotton guide.   [Greensboro] n.d. [16] p.   [7287

King's Business College, Raleigh, N. C.   Catalogue, 190 - Raleigh, 190 -   NcU has 4 issues without date issued around 1905, 1912, 1916, 1918   [7288

Kings Mountain, N. C.   First Baptist Church.   Directory, December, 1925.   [Kings Mountain?] Herald Print [1925?]   [16] p.   [7289

Kings Mountain Baptist Association.   Minutes, 185 - 185 -   NcU has 1877-1879, 1882-1883, 1885, 1897 [1899-1906] 1923-1954   [7290

Kings Mountain Baptist Association.   Historical Committee.   The history of the Kings Mountain Baptist Association from November 7, 1851 to November 7, 1951.   No place [1952?]   191 p.   [7291

King's Mountain Centennial Association.   Battle at King's Mountain, October 7, 1780.   Proposed centennial celebration, October 7, 1880.   [Yorkville, S. C. Printed at the Office of the Enquirer, 1880?]   48 p.   [7292

King's Mountain Mining Company, Charlotte, N. C.   Information in regard to the property of the King's Mountain Mining Company near Charlotte, North Carolina.   Philadelphia, Allen, Lane & Scott, pr., 1877.   12 p.   [7293

Kings Mountain Railroad Company.   Report, 1852/54-   Yorkville, S. C., 1854-NcU has 1852/54   [7294

[Kings Mountain Sesqui-Centennial Celebration Committee]   Official programme of the sesqui-centennial celebration of the Battle of Kings Mountain on the battle-ground in York County, South Carolina, Tuesday, October 7, 1930.   No place, [1930]   28 p.   [7295

Kingsbury, Theodore Bryant.   The Bible, its influence upon the world; an address delivered before the Clio Society of Oxford Female College, Thursday, June 28th, 1866.   Raleigh, Biblical Recorder Book and Job Printing Establishment, 1866. 22 p.   [7296

Kingsbury, Theodore Bryant, ed.   The International Exhibition guide for the southern states.   Philadelphia, Pa., and Raleigh, R. T. Fulghum, 1876.   100 p. At head of title: 1776.   The first hundred years.   1876.   [7297

Kingsbury, Theodore Bryant.   Oration on the life and character of the late Reverend Thomas G. Lowe, delivered at Haywood's Church, Halifax County, June 24th, 1882.   Weldon, Methodists of Halifax County, 1882.   25 p.   [7298
——What is baptism?   Or, Some of the reasons and facts which made me a Baptist. Petersburg, Va., Index Office for the Author, 1867.   275 p.   [7299

Kingsley, Charles.   Sir Walter Raleigh and his time, with other papers.   Boston, Ticknor and Fields, 1859.   461 p.   [7300

Kinnear, John R.   History of the Eighty-sixth Regiment, Illinois Volunteer Infantry, during its term of service.   Chicago, Tribune Company's Book and Job Printing Office, 1866.   139 p.   [7301

Kinston, N. C.   Chamber of Commerce.   Kinston and Lenoir County, N. C.   [Richmond, Va., Whittet and Shepperson, pr.] 1917.   [12] p.   [7302
——Kinston, North Carolina, key city of Eastern North Carolina.   [Kinston, 1942?] [7] p.   [7303

Kinston, N. C.   City Council.   The code of the city of Kinston, North Carolina, 1946.   Charlottesville, Va., Michie City Publications Co., 1946.   264 p.   [7304

Kinston, N. C.   Queen Street Methodist Church.   Annual, 191 -   [Kinston, 191 -NcU has 1917/18   [7305

Kinston, N. C.   Queen Street Methodist Church.   Young Woman's Aid Society. The housewife's aid.   New Bern, Owen G. Dunn, pr., n.d.   88 p.   [7306

Kinston, N. C.   Rotary Club.   Kinston Rotarians brag.   [Kinston? 1921?] 3 p.   [7307

Kinston College, Kinston, N. C.   Catalogue, 188 -   Kinston, 188 -   NcU has 1888/89   [7308

Kinston Collegiate Institute, Kinston, N. C.   Catalogue, 187 -   Kinston, 187 -NcU has 1878/79   [7309

Kinston, Whitehall and Goldsboro (North Carolina) expedition, December, 1862. New York, W. W. Howe, 1890.   92 p.   [7310

[Kirby, George F.]   In memoriam, Eugene M. Armfield, September 25, 1869-August 11, 1908.   No place, no publisher, n.d.   46 p.   [7311

Kirk, J. Allen.   Statement of facts concerning the bloody riot in Wilmington, N. C., of interest to every citizen of the United States.   No place, no publisher, n.d. 16 p.   [7312

Kirke, Edmund, pseud.   see Gilmore, James Roberts

Kirkham, J. H.   J. H. Kirkham, land and pension agent, Raleigh, North Carolina, has valuable information for the following named widows of Revolutionary soldiers.   Raleigh, Author, n.d.   [1] p.   [7313

Kirkland, Winifred Margaretta.   The Easter people; a pen-picture of the Moravian celebration of the resurrection.   New York, Fleming H. Revell Co. [c.1923] 61 p.   [7314
——The joys of being a woman, and other papers.   Boston, Houghton Mifflin Co., 1918.   281 p.   [7315
——My little town.   New York, E. P. Dutton & Co. [c.1917]   32 p.   [7316
——The new death.   Boston, Houghton Mifflin Co., 1918.   173 p.   [7317

——The view vertical, and other essays. Boston, Houghton Mifflin Co., 1920. 270 p.   [7318
——Where the star still shines. New York, Fleming H. Revell Co. [c.1924] 64 p. [7319

Kirkpatrick, Charles Atkinson. Salesmanship; helping prospects buy. Cincinnati, Southwestern Publishing Co. [1951]   483 p.   [7320
—— ——[2d ed.] [1956]   631 p.   [7321

Kirkpatrick, Charles Atkinson, joint author, see **Calhoon, Richard Percival**

Kirkpatrick, G. F. Historical sketches of Laurel Hill and Smyrna Presbyterian churches. No place, no publisher [1931?]   42 p.   [7322

Kirkpatrick, Thomas Leroy. Key note speech before the Mecklenburg County Democratic convention, May 11, 1940. [Charlotte, 1940]   9 p.   [7323

Kirton, W. H. The dispensary reviewed, its character and methods exposed and overwhelmingly condemned as a hybrid monstrosity. [Raleigh, Edwards and Broughton Co.] n.d.   71 p.   [7324

[Kirwan, Thomas] Soldiering in North Carolina . . . By "one of the Seventeenth". Boston, T. Kirwan, 1864.   126 p.   [7325

Kiser, Clyde Vernon. Group differences in urban fertility; a study derived from the national health survey. Baltimore, Williams & Wilkins Co., 1942.   284 p. [7326
——Sea island to city; a study of St. Helena islanders in Harlem and other urban centers. New York, Columbia University Press, 1932.   272 p.   [7327

Kitchin, Claude. Do you advocate peace or war? What the preparedness program means, by William Jennings Bryan and Claude Kitchin. No place, no publisher [1915]   47 p.   [7328
——Response of Hon. Claude Kitchin at the sixteenth annual Appomattox day banquet, Monday evening, April 9, 1906, Auditorium, Chicago, to the toast "The South". [Chicago] Hamilton Club [1906?]   16 p.   [7329

Kitchin, Thurman Delna. Address to the National Association of Private Psychiatric Hospitals at the 8th annual meeting, May 7th, 1941, Richmond, Virginia.   No place [1941?]   [8] p.   [7330
——The doctor and citizenship. Boston, Christopher Publishing House [c.1934] 89 p.   [7331

Kitchin, William Walton. Bryan's second warning. No place, 1912.   [1] p. [7332
——The North Carolina suffrage amendment; speech in the House of Representatives, Thursday, May 3, 1900. [Raleigh, Edwards and Broughton Co., 1900] 20 p.   [7333
——The record confirms Kitchin's speech. No place, no publisher [1912?]   [1] p. [7334
——Speech on Democratic fidelity, delivered in Raleigh, February 16, 1912.   No place, no publisher [1912?]   16 p.   [7335
——Speech on the record of Senator Simmons, delivered at Greensboro, March 18, 1912; to which are added extracts from a speech of Vance and the national Democratic platform. [Raleigh, Commercial Printing Co., 1912]   8 p.   [7336

Kittrell, Flemmie Pansy. A study of Negro infant feeding practices in a selected community of North Carolina. Ithaca, N. Y., 1935.   [6] p.   [7337

Kittrell, N. C. Board of Education. The Kittrell Public School; course of study and manual of government to be used in primary, elementary, and high school, Kittrell, North Carolina, 1916-1917. [Kittrell] 1916.   [10] p.   [7338

Kittrell College, Kittrell, N. C. Catalogue, 189 - Kittrell, 189 - NcU has 1906/ 07, 1915/16   [7339
——Report, 189 - Kittrell, 189 - NcU has 1900/01-1903/04   [7340

Kjelgaard, James Arthur. Buckskin brigade. New York, Holiday House [1947] 310 p.   [7341
——Rebel siege. New York, Holiday House [1943]   221 p.   [7342

Klain, Zora. Quaker contributions to education in North Carolina.   Philadelphia, Westbrook Publishing Co., 1925.   351 p.   [7343

Klapp, Russell. Guilford wedding bells—and homes, prepared in the interest of new homes and homemakers in Guilford County. Greensboro, R. Klapp [c.1927] 127 p.   [7344

Kleppel, Placid, father. The ballad of Marshal Ney and other poems, by Dom Placid. Belmont Abbey, Abbey Press, 1935.   45 p.   [7345
——Benedict; a life in verse. [Belmont] Abbey Press, 1933.   48 p.   [7346

——A bibliography of North Carolina poetry. Belmont, Abbey Press, 1934. 15 p. [7347
——From the hid battlements. Caldwell, Id., Caxton Printers, Ltd., 1934. 238 p. [7348
——Paintings and other poems. Belmont, Abbey Press, 1933. 42 p. [7349
——Silver maid and other poems. Belmont, Abbey Press, 1933. 45 p. [7350
——Twelve o'clock cat, a simple Chinese tale. No place, no publisher, n.d. [5] p. [7351
Kline, Henry B. Freight rates; the interregional tariff issue. Nashville, Tenn., Vanderbilt University Press, 1942. (Papers of the Institute of Research and Training in the Social Sciences, Vanderbilt University, no. 3) 47 p. [7352
[Kline, W. S. and Co., Kinderhook, New York] Greensboro illustrated "the gate city", 1904-1905. [Kinderhook, N. Y., 1904?] 26 p. [7353
Kline, W. S. and Co., Kinderhook, New York. Illustrated Durham, North Carolina. [Kinderhook, N. Y.] 1905. 16 p. [7354
Klingberg, Frank Wysor. The Southern Claims Commission. Berkeley, University of California Press, 1955. 261 p. [7355
Knapp, Seaman Ashahel. Better conditions for southern farmers; address . . . before the Conference of Education in the South, held at Pinehurst, N. C., April, 1907. No place, no publisher [1907?] [11] p. [7356
Knight, Edgar Wallace. Among the Danes. Chapel Hill, University of North Carolina Press, 1927. 236 p. [7357
——The butter curriculum. [Chapel Hill, privately printed, 1944] [3] p. [7358
Knight, Edgar Wallace, ed. A documentary history of education in the South before 1860. Chapel Hill, University of North Carolina Press [1949-1953] 5 v. [7359
Knight, Edgar Wallace. Education in the South. Chapel Hill, University of North Carolina Press, 1924. 31 p. [7360
——Education in the United States. Boston, Ginn and Co. [c.1934] 613 p. [7361
—— ——3d rev. ed. Boston, Ginn and Co. [1951] 753 p. [7362
——Education has suffered severer blows in this depression than in any one before. [Chapel Hill, 1934] [3] p. [7363
——Education in the United States. Boston, Ginn and Co. [c.1929] 588 p. [7364
—— ——New ed. [c.1934] 613 p. [7365
—— ——2d rev. ed. [c.1941] 669 p. [7366
——Fifty years of American education, a historical review and critical appraisal. New York, Ronald Press Co. [1952] 484 p. [7367
Knight, Edgar Wallace, ed. The Graduate School research and publications, ed. with a foreword by Edgar W. Knight and Agatha Boyd Adams. Chapel Hill, University of North Carolina Press, 1946. (University of North Carolina Sesquicentennial publications) 461 p. [7368
Knight, Edgar Wallace. Improvement of instruction and the work of the Commission on Curricular Problems and Research. [Chapel Hill, 1946] 4 p. [7369
——Influence of Reconstruction on education in the South. New York, Teachers' College, Columbia University, 1913. 100 p. [7370
——Notes on education. Chapel Hill [Seeman Printery for Author] 1927. 64 p. [7371
——Our state government; an elementary text in government and citizenship for use in North Carolina. Chicago, Scott, Foresman and Co. [c.1926] 152 p. [7372
——Progress and educational perspective. New York, Macmillan Co., 1942. (The Kappa Delti Pi lecture series [no. 14]) 148 p. [7373
——Public school education in North Carolina. Boston, Houghton Mifflin Co. [c.1916] 384 p. [7374
——Public education in the South. Boston, Ginn and Co. [c.1922] 482 p. [7375
Knight, Edgar Wallace, ed. Readings in American educational history, by Edgar W. Knight and Clifton L. Hall. New York, Appleton-Century-Crofts [1951] 799 p. [7376
——Readings in educational administration. New York, Henry Holt and Co. [1953] 534 p. [7377
——Reports on European education, by John Griscom, Victor Cousin [and] Calvin E. Stowe, edited by Edgar W. Knight. New York, McGraw-Hill Book Co., Inc., 1930. 319 p. [7378
Knight, Edgar Wallace. Some principles of teaching as applied to the Sunday-School. Boston, Pilgrim Press [c.1915] 157 p. [7379

——A study of Hampton Institute, by Edgar W. Knight and consultants. Chapel Hill, 1937. 3 v. [7380

——A study of higher education for Negroes in Alabama by the Survey Staff, Edgar W. Knight, director, Gould Beech, R. E. Cammack, E. G. McGehee, Jr., R. E. Tidwell. Montgomery, 1940. Various paging. [7381

——Twenty centuries of education. Boston, Ginn and Co. [c.1940] 622 p. [7382

Knight, Edgar Wallace, ed. What college presidents say. Chapel Hill, University of North Carolina Press, 1940. 377 p. [7383

Knight, Edgar Wallace, joint author, see Hamilton, Joseph Gregoire de Roulhac

Knight, Ken, ed. The wonders of North Carolina. Winston-Salem, Collins Co., c.1954. Unpaged. [7384

Knights of Pythias. North Carolina. Grand Lodge. Proceedings, 187 - 187 - NcU has 1895, 1922-23, 1923-24, 1924-25, 1931 [7385

Knowles, Morris, Inc., engineers. Report upon certain phases of a city plan for the city of High Point, N. C., July, 1928. [High Point, Barber-Hall Printing Co., 1929] 83 p. [7386

Knox, Joe. Little Benders. Philadelphia, J. B. Lippincott Co. [1952] 255 p. [7387

Knox, Rose Bell. Gray caps. Garden City, N. Y., Doubleday, Doran & Co., Inc., 1932. 304 p. [7388

——Marty and Company on a Carolina farm. Garden City, N. Y., Doubleday, Doran & Co., Inc., 1933. 280 p. [7389

—— ——1946. [7390

Koch, Dorothy (Clarke) Gone is my goose. [New York] Holiday House, c.1956. unpaged. [7391

——I play at the beach. [New York] Holiday House, c.1955. Unpaged. [7392

Koch, Frederick Henry, ed. American folk plays. New York, D. Appleton-Century Co., Inc., 1939. 592 p. [7393

——Carolina folk comedies. New York, S. French, 1931. 311 p. [7394

——Carolina folk-plays. New York, H. Holt and Co. [c.1928] 267 p. [7395

——Carolina folk-plays, with an introduction on folk-play making. New York, H. Holt and Co., 1922. 160 p. [7396

——Carolina folk-plays, with an introduction on making a folk theatre. New York, H. Holt and Co., 1924. 173 p. [7397

——Carolina folk-plays, first, second, and third series. New York, H. Holt and Co. [c.1941] 493 p. [7398

Koch, Frederick Henry. The Carolina Playmakers. Chapel Hill, University of North Carolina, n.d. 4 p. [7399

——Drama in the South; the Carolina Playmakers coming of age. [Chapel Hill? University of North Carolina, 1940] 14 p. [7400

——Raleigh, the shepherd of the ocean; a pageant-drama . . . designed to commemorate the tercentenary of the execution of Sir Walter Raleigh, with a foreword by Edwin Greenlaw. Raleigh, Edwards & Broughton Printing Co., 1920. 95 p. [7401

Koger, M. V. Index to the names of 30,000 immigrants, German, Swiss, Dutch, and French, into Pennsylvania, 1727-1776, supplementing the I. Daniel Rupp ship load volume. [Pennington Gap, Va., M. V. Koger, 1936] 232 p. [7402

Kollock, Shepard Koscusko. The doctrine of the perseverance of the saints, illustrated, proved, and applied. Philadelphia, Presbyterian Tract and Sunday School Society, 1837. 20 p. [7403

——A Sermon occasioned by the death of Edmunds Mason, student of the University of North-Carolina, preached in the college chapel, August 8, 1824. Raleigh, J. Gales & Son, pr., 1824. 23 p. [7404

Kolodny, Joseph. 4000 years of service; the story of the wholesale tobacco industry and its pioneers. New York, Farrar, Straus and Young [1953] 309 p. [7405

Konkle, Burton Alva. James Wilson and the constitution, the opening address in the official series of events known as the James Wilson Memorial, delivered before the Law Academy of Philadelphia, on November 14, 1906. [Philadelphia] The Law Academy, 1907. 40 p. [7406

——John Motley Morehead and the development of North Carolina, 1796-1866 . . . with an introduction by Hon. Henry G. Connor. Philadelphia, William J. Campbell, 1922. 437 p. [7407

Koonce, D. S. The Devil and mother Eve. Ocean, Author [1920] [16] p. [7408

Koos, Frank H. Winston-Salem City Public Schools; our schools today, a radio talk, American Education Week. [Winston-Salem] 1930. 13 p. [7409

Korstian, Clarence Ferdinand. The Duke forest, a demonstration and research laboratory, by Clarence F. Korstian . . . and William Maughan. Durham, Duke University, 1935. (Duke University. School of Forestry. Bulletin, no. 1) 74 p. [7410

——Forestry in the South. Richmond, Dietz Press, Inc., 1948. (N. C. University. Institute for Research in Social Science. Southern resource monograph, no. 1) 57 p. [7411

——Forestry on private lands in the United States. Durham, Duke University, 1944. (Duke University. School of Forestry. Bulletin, no. 8) 234 p. [7412

——Plant competition in forest stands, by Clarence F. Korstian . . . and Theodore S. Coile. Durham, Duke University, 1938. (Duke University. School of Forestry. Bulletin, no. 3) 125 p. [7413

Kramer, Dale. The heart of O. Henry. New York, Rinehart & Co., Inc. [c.1954] 323 p. [7414

Kreutzer, William. Notes and observations made during four years of service with the Ninety-eighth N. Y. Volunteers, in the war of 1861. Philadelphia, Grant, Faires & Rodgers, pr., 1878. 368 p. [7415

Kroll, Harry Harrison. Darker grows the valley. Indianapolis, Bobbs-Merrill Co. [1947] 400 p. [7416

——My heart's in the hills. Philadelphia, Westminster Press [1956] 188 p. [7417

——Summer gold. Philadelphia, Westminster Press [1955] 176 p. [7418

Kropff, Frederick C. Report on the Lewis Mine in Union County, N. C. Philadelphia, John C. Clark, 1849. 11 p. [7419

Kuder, George Frederic. Exploring children's interests, by G. Frederic Kuder [and] Blanche B. Paulson. Chicago, Science Research Associates [1951] 49 p. [7420

Kuhn, Helmut. Freedom forgotten and remembered. Chapel Hill, University of North Carolina Press, 1943. 267 p. [7421

Ku Klux Klan (1915-) Papers read at the meeting of Grand Dragons, Knights of the Ku Klux Klan, at their first annual meeting held at Asheville, N. C., July, 1923. No place, n.d. 136 p. [7422

Kurfees, John W. Everybody read! The fight is on! The issue is clear cut. [Winston-Salem, 1926?] [4] p. [7423

Kyle, J. K. and Co., Fayetteville, N. C. New goods! Fayetteville, News Office, n.d. [1] p. [7424

Kyles, Alpheus Alexander. A short history of Hickory Grove Methodist Episcopal Church, South, 1844-1935. No place, 1935. 23 p. [7425

L. C. W. see Wood, Mrs. L. C.

Labaree, Leonard Woods, ed. Royal instructions to British colonial governors, 1670-1776. New York, D. Appleton-Century Co., Inc. [c.1935] 2 v. [7426

LaBarre, Maurine (Boie) New York City's baby book; a handbook for parents. New York, Department of Health [1947] 136 p. [7427

La Barre, Weston. The human animal. [Chicago] University of Chicago Press [1954] 371 p. [7428

Labatt, D. C., comp. The importation law, showing the importable and prohibited articles, together with the tariff of the Confederate States, and the recent regulations in relation to foreign commerce. [Wilmington? Compiler? 1864?] 48 p. [7429

Labor Institute, Charlotte, N. C., August 9-10, 1941. "Labor and national defense" . . . sponsored by North Carolina State Federation of Labor, with the cooperation of North Carolina and Workers Education Bureau of America. [Charlotte? 1941] [3] p. Program. [7430

Labor Research Association, New York. Southern labor in wartime. [New York, International Publishers Co., Inc., c.1942] 31 p. [7431

Laboulaye, Édouard René Lefebvre de. Locke, législateur de la Caroline. Paris, Chez Durand, 1850. 31 p. [7432

Lachicotte, Virginia Wilson. The runaway path, and other poems. New York, Galleon Press, 1936. 63 p. [7433

Lacy, Benjamin Rice. George W. Watts, the Seminary's great benefactor; a memorial address delivered at the First Presbyterian Church, Durham, North Carolina. [Durham, privately printed] 1937. 28 p.   [7434
——Revivals in the midst of the years. Richmond, Va., John Knox Press, 1943. 167 p.   [7435

Lacy, Dan Mabry. Books and the future: a speculation. New York, New York Public Library, 1956. (R. R. Bowker Memorial Lectures, no. 17) 27 p. [7436

Lacy, Drury. Address delivered at the General Military Hospital, Wilson, N. C., on the day appointed by the President as a day of fasting, humiliation, and prayer. Fayetteville, Edward J. Hale & Sons, 1863. 15 p.   [7437
——A sermon preached on occasion of the death of the Rev. Henry Pattillo to his former congregations in Granville County, North Carolina, October 11th, 1801. Philadelphia, William W. Woodward, 1803. 32 p.   [7438
——A Thanksgiving discourse, delivered in the Presbyterian Church, Raleigh, N. C., on Thursday, the 27th November, 1851. Raleigh, Seaton Gales, pr., 1851. 18 p.   [7439

Lacy, William Sterling. Historical address delivered on the occasion of the centennial of Buffalo Church, August 12, 1897. Sanford, Cole Steam Printing Co. [1897?] 28 p.   [7440
——Sermon preached at Buffalo Church, Moore County, January 24th, 1882, on the occasion of the death of Walter Temple Jones. Fayetteville, Garrett [1882?] 8 p.   [7441
——William Sterling Lacy: memorial, addresses, sermons. Richmond, Va., Presbyterian Committee of Publication [1900] 198 p.   [7442

Ladies' Hermitage Assocation, Nashville, Tenn. The Hermitage, home of General Andrew Jackson, near Nashville, Tennessee . . . compiled by Mrs. Mary C. Dorris, revised, May 4, 1913, by Louise G. Lindsley. [Nashville, Tenn., 1913] 28 p. [7443
—— ——revised, June 11, 1937 [by] Mrs. Jesse M. Overton, Mrs. Paul De Witt. [Nashville, Tenn., 1937] 63 p.   [7444
—— ——revised, June, 1949 [by] Mrs. Robert F. Jackson, Miss Martha Lindsey. [Nashville, Tenn., 1949] 63 p.   [7445

Ladies' Memorial Association of New Bern, N. C. Confederate memorial addresses, Monday, May 11, 1885, New Bern, N. C. Richmond, Va., Whittet & Shepperson, 1886. 32 p.   [7446

Ladu, Arthur Irish. Manual of notary public practice in North Carolina. Raleigh, Edwards & Broughton Co., 1939. 73 p.   [7447

Lafayette Military Academy, Fayetteville, N. C. Announcement, 189 - Fayetteville, 189 - NcU has 1894/95   [7448

Lafferty, R. H. A fast-day sermon, preached in the Church of Sugar Creek, Mecklenburg County, N. C., February 28th, 1862. Fayetteville, Presbyterian Office, pr., 1862. 16 p.   [7449

Lafferty, Robert H., ed. History of the Second Presbyterian Church, Charlotte, North Carolina, 1873-1947. [Charlotte, Covenant Presbyterian Church, 1953] 118 p.   [7450
——The North Carolina Medical College, Davidson and Charlotte, North Carolina. [Charlotte, 1946] 61 p.   [7451

Lager Fackel; Wochenzeitung der deutschen Kriegsgefangenen, v. 1-2, September 23, 1945-April 4, 1946. Camp Butner, 1945-1946. NcU has v. [1-2]   [7452

LaGrange, H. M., pseud. see Cameron, Rebecca

LaGrange Collegiate Institute, LaGrange, N. C. Catalogue, 187 - LaGrange, 187 - NcU has 1883/84   [7453

Lake, Isaac Beverly. Discrimination by railroads and other public utilities. Raleigh, Edwards & Broughton Co., 1947. 346 p.   [7454

Lake James, near Morganton. [Morganton, News-Herald] n.d. Folder. [7455

Lake Waccamaw Missionary Baptist Association. Minutes, 188 - 188 - NcU has 1903   [7456

LaMar, A. Fitch, pseud. see Tilden, Mrs. Charles W. F.

Lamb, Elizabeth. Historical sketch of Hay St. Methodist Episcopal Church, South, Fayetteville, North Carolina. [Fayetteville?] 1934. 96 p.   [7457

Lamb, Roger. An original and authentic journal of occurrences during the late American war, from its commencement to the year 1783. Dublin, Wilkinson and Courtney, 1809. 438 p. [7458

Lambert, John R. Arthur Pue Gorman. Baton Rouge, Louisiana State University Press [1953] 397 p. [7459

Lambeth, J. J. The signs of the times. Raleigh, Edwards, Broughton & Co., 1885. 181 p. [7460

Lancaster, Bruce. Phantom fortress. Boston, Little, Brown, 1950. 310 p. [7461
—— ——Garden City, N. Y., Permabooks [1952] 384 p. [7462

Land, Marie (Long) The story of the Sallie Southall Cotten loan fund . . . its aims, its growth, its accomplishments. [Statesville] North Carolina Federation of Women's Clubs, 1929?] 14 p. [7463

Land of the sky, v. 1- Asheville, Natt Atkinson, 1886- NcU has v. 1, no. 2, September, 1886 [7464

"The Land of the Sky" and Great Smoky Mountains National Park. Asheville, Great Smoky Mountains Publishing Co., Inc., c.1929. [81] p. [7465

[Land of the Sky, views on the Western North Carolina Railroad] New York, A. Wittemann, c.1887] plates. [7466

Land we love, v. 1-6, May, 1866-March, 1869. Charlotte, James P. Irwin and D. H. Hill, 1866-1869. NcU has v. 1-6. In April, 1869, this magazine was incorporated with The new eclectic, Baltimore. [7467

Lander, Samuel. Our own primary arithmetic. 2d ed. Greensboro, Sterling, Campbell & Albright [c.1863] 130 p. [7468
——Our own school arithmetic. Greensboro, Sterling, Campbell & Albright, 1863. 223 p. [7469

Landon, Charles Edward. Transportation; principles, practices, problems. New York, Sloane [1951] 618 p. [7470

Landrum, John Belton O'Neall. Colonial and Revolutionary history of upper South Carolina . . . with a general review of the entire military operations in the upper portion of South Carolina and portions of North Carolina. Greenville, S. C., Shannon & Co., pr., 1897. 364 p. [7471

Lane, Elinor (Macartney) Katrine; a novel. New York, Harper & Brothers [c.1909] 314 p. [7472

Lane, Sir Ralph. Raleigh's first Roanoke colony, the account by Ralph Lane. [Boston, Directors of the Old South Work, 1902] (Old South leaflets [general ser. v. 5] no. 119) 24 p. [7473

Laney, T. B. Meditations. No place, no publisher, c.1924. 87 p. [7474

The Langren, Asheville, N. C., J. Baylis Rector, manager. [Asheville, Inland Press] n.d. [21] p. [7475
——[22] p. [7476

Langston, Allen, comp. In the beginning. Raleigh, Author, 1951. 15 p. [7477

Langston, John Dallas. Can North Carolina afford to pay the price? [Goldsboro? 1930] 8 p. [7478
——[Reply to a letter from J. J. Laughinghouse referring to the comparative qualities of Ex.-Gov. Aycock, Senator Simmons, and W. W. Kitchin] [Goldsboro, 1912?] [1] p. [7479

Lanier, James Franklin Doughty. Sketch of the life of J. F. D. Lanier. New York, privately printed, 1871. 62 p. [7480

Lanier, John Jabez. Washington, the great American Mason. New York, Macoy Publishing & Masonic Supply Co. [c.1922] 288 p. [7481

Lanman, Charles. Adventures in the wilds of the United States and British American provinces. Philadelphia, J. W. Moore, 1856. 2 v. [7482
——Letters from the Alleghany Mountains. New-York, G. P. Putnam, 1849. 198 p. [7483

Lanning, John Tate. Academic culture in the Spanish colonies. London, Oxford University Press, 1940. 149 p. [7484
——The diplomatic history of Georgia; a study of the epoch of Jenkins' ear. Chapel Hill, University of North Carolina Press, 1936. 275 p. [7485

——The Spanish missions of Georgia. Chapel Hill, University of North Carolina Press [c.1935] 321 p. [7486

——The university in the Kingdom of Guatemala. Ithaca, N. Y., Cornell University Press [1955] 331 p. [7486a

Lansdell, J. J. The Biblical catechism designed for Sabbath schools: No. I. Raleigh, Biblical Recorder Print, 1863. 108 p. [7487

Lansdell, Thomas. The Christian race; a sermon delivered in the Baptist Church in Hillsboro', April 13, 1856. Raleigh, Biblical Recorder, pr., 1856. 8 p. [7488

Laprade, William Thomas. British history for American students. New York, Macmillan Co., 1926. 913 p. [7489

——England and the French Revolution, 1789-1797. Baltimore, The Johns Hopkins Press, 1909. 232 p. [7490

——Public opinion and politics in the eighteenth century England to the fall of Walpole. New York, Macmillan Co., 1936. 463 p. [7491

Larew, Ada Campbell. Wauhonhasee, an Indian legend of Blowing Rock. [Knoxville, Author, c.1927] 11 p. [7492

La Rochefoucauld Liancourt, François Alexandre Frédéric, duc de. Travels through the United States of North America, the country of the Iroquois, and Upper Canada, in the years 1795, 1796, and 1797. London, R. Phillips, 1799. 2 v. [7493

La Roque, Oscar K. What is past is prologue . . . address delivered . . . before Maryland Council of Insured Savings and Loan Associations, in Baltimore, Md., January 27, 1944. [Winston-Salem? Federal Home Loan Bank? 1944] [7] p. [7494

[LaSelle, Evelyn] The black sheep, by Qui. Raleigh, Edwards & Broughton Co., 1895. 347 p. [7495

Lashley, Loraine. None but the melody. New York, Charles Leon Tumasel, 1938. 47 p. [7496

Lasley, John Wayne. Introductory mathematics, by J. W. Lasley, Jr., and E. T. Browne. Chapel Hill, The Authors, 1931. 225 p. [7497

—— ——1st ed. New York, McGraw-Hill Book Co., 1933. 439 p. [7498

Lasley, John Wayne, joint author, see Henderson, Archibald

Lassiter, Mable S. The twilight hour. Burlington [Author] 1952. 24 p. [7499

Lassiter, Margaret C. Lift up thine eyes unto the hills from whence cometh thy strength. No place, no publisher, 1956. 9 p. [7500

Lassiter, William Carroll. Law and press; the legal aspects of news reporting, editing and publishing in North Carolina. Rev. ed. Raleigh, Edwards & Broughton, 1956. 262 p. [7501

Latham, Edythe. The sounding brass. Boston, Little, Brown [1953] 465 p. [7502

Latham, Frank Brown. The fighting Quaker; the southern campaigns of General Nathanael Greene. New York, Aladdin Books, 1953. 192 p. [7503

Latham, Lois. Hit's man's business, a comedy-drama. New York, Row, Peterson & Co. [c.1940] 32 p. [7504

Lathan, Robert, fl. 1880. Historical sketch of the Battle of King's Mountain . . . October 7, 1780. Yorkville, S. C., Enquirer, 1880. 18 p. [7505

——History of the Associate Reformed Synod of the South, to which is prefixed A history of the Associate Presbyterian and Reformed Presbyterian churches. Harrisburg, Pa., Author, 1882. 418 p. [7506

Lathan, Robert, 1881-1937. A look into the future; an address delivered at the Newspaper Institute at Chapel Hill, 1926. No place, no publisher [1926] 7 p. [7507

Lathrop, Virginia Terrell. Educate a woman; fifty years of life at the Woman's College of the University of North Carolina. Chapel Hill, University of North Carolina Press, 1942. 111 p. [7508

[Latrobe, John Hazelhurst Boneval] In memory of Major Mordecai. No place, n.d. 13 p. [7509

Latshaw, Harry Franklin. The Lohr-Latshaw Latin form test for high schools. Chapel Hill, Bureau of Educational Research, School of Education, University of North Carolina, 1923. (Its Studies in education, no. 1) 47 p. [7510

Latta, Estelle (Cothran) Controversial Mark Hopkins, in collaboration with Mary L. Allison. New York, Greenberg [1953] 195 p. [7511

Latta, Morgan London. The history of my life and work. Raleigh, M. L. Latta [1903] 371 p. [7512

Latta, W. A. Catalogue of watches, clocks, gold pens, jewelry, silverware, canes, spectacles, &c., for sale. Monroe, Enquirer and Express Office, 1885. 50 p. [7513

Latta University, West Raleigh, N. C. Catalogue, 189 - Raleigh, 189 - NcU has 1908/09, 1919/20 [7514

Laughinghouse, Joseph J. I am writing to ask your support for Governor Kitchin in this Senatorial race. Raleigh, October 7, 1911. [1] p. [7515

Laughlin, Clara Elizabeth. So you're going south! (To the South Atlantic States) Boston, Little, Brown and Co., 1940. 639 p. [7516

Laura Lazenby, 1864-1941. [Statesville?] Privately printed, 1945. 41 p. [7517

Laura Valinda Watts. No place, no publisher [1915?] 16 p. [7518

Laurinburg, N. C. Presbyterian Church. Semi-Centennial Committee. Historical sketches and addresses delivered at the semi-centennial of the Laurinburg, N. C., Presbyterian Church and dedication of new church, March 3-7, 1909. [Richmond, Va., Whittet & Shepperson, 1909] 102 p. [7519

Laurinburg Normal and Industrial Institute, Laurinburg, N. C. [Catalogue] 191 - Laurinburg, 191 - NcU has 1914/15, 1926/27 [7520

——Report, 190 - Laurinburg, 190 - NcU has 1913/14 [7521

Laurinburgh High School for Boys, Laurinburgh, N. C. Catalogue, 187 - Laurinburgh, 187 - NcU has 1883/84 [7522

Law and contemporary problems, v. 1- December, 1933- [Durham] School of Law, Duke University, 1933- NcU has v. 1-21 [7523

Law and Order Conference, Blue Ridge, N. C., August 4-6, 1917. Lawlessness or civilization, which? Report of addresses and discussions . . . ed. by W. D. Weatherford. Nashville, Tenn., Williams Printing Co. [1917?] 126 p. [7524

Lawrence, Elizabeth L. A southern garden, a handbook for the middle South. Chapel Hill, University of North Carolina Press, 1942. 241 p. [7525

Lawrence, Eva J., comp. A bibliography of North Carolina county histories, compiled by Eva J. Lawrence and William S. Powell. [Raleigh, 1952] 13 p. [7526

[**Lawrence, Joshua**] The American telescope, by a clodhopper of North Carolina. Philadelphia, Printed for the Author, 1825. 24 p. [7527

Lawrence, Joshua. Basket of fragments, for the children. Tarborough, Office of The Free Press, 1833. 126 p. [7528

[**Lawrence, Joshua**] The mouse, trying to gnaw out of the Catholic trap. [Tarboro, Tarboro Press] n.d. 20 p. [7529

——The North-Carolina Whig's apology, for the Kehukee Association. Tarborough, Office of the "North-Carolina Free Press", 1830. 56 p. [7530

Lawrence, Joshua. A patriotic discourse, delivered at the Old Church in Tarborough, N. C., on Sunday, the 4th of July, 1830. 2d ed. [Tarboro, Free Press] n.d. 24 p. [7531

Lawrence, Robert Carbelle. Address . . . at the third annual convention of Clerks of Superior Court at Wrightsville Beach, July 2, 1919. No place, no publisher [1919?] 25 p. [7532

——Here in Carolina. Lumberton, 1939. 302 p. [7533

Lawrence, Ruth, ed. Burwell, Spotswood, Dandridge, West, and allied family histories, genealogical and biographical. New York, National Americana Publications, Inc., 1943. 29 p. [7534

Lawrence, Thomas. The inspiration of the Scriptures, or, The divine and human in the written word. Wilmington, Jackson & Bell, pr., 1882. 14 p. [7535

Lawrence and Lemay's North Carolina almanack, 18 - Raleigh, Lawrence and Lemay, 18 - NcU has 1828, 1830-1833, 1835-1838. Called Lemay's North Carolina almanack, 1837-1838 [7536

Lawrence's reliable friend and almanac, 18 - Wilson, J. J. Lawrence, 18 - NcU has 1867, 1872 [7537

Laws, Romulus Don. "Hot stuph; or, The Yellow jacket boiled down". Moravian Falls, The Yellow Jacket Press, 1909. 397 p. [7538

Lawson, J. S. Progressive air brake examination. Raleigh, Edwards & Broughton & Co., c.1906. 63 p. [7539

[Lawson, John] Allerneuste Beschreibung der provintz Carolina in West-Indien. Hamburg, T. von Wierings erben, 1712. 365 p. [7540

Lawson, John. The history of Carolina; containing the exact description and natural history of that country, together with the present state thereof. And a journal of a thousand miles, travel'd thro' several nations of Indians. Giving a particular account of their customs, manners, &c. London, Printed for W. Taylor and J. Baker, 1714. 258 p. [7541

—— ——London, Printed for T. Warner, 1718. 258 p. [7542

—— ——Raleigh [O. H. Perry & Co.] Printed by Strother & Marcom, 1860. 390 p. [7543

——History of North Carolina. Being a reprint of the copy now in the North Carolina State Library, presented by President James Madison, in the year 1831. Charlotte, Observer Printing House, 1903. 171 p. [7544

——Lawson's History of North Carolina, containing the exact description and natural history of that country, together with the present state thereof and a journal of a thousand miles traveled through several nations of Indians, giving a particular account of their customs, manners, etc., etc. London, Printed for W. Taylor and F. Baker, 1714. Richmond, Va., Garrett and Massie, 1937. 259 p. [7545

——Lawson's History of North Carolina, containing the exact description and natural history of that country, together with the present state thereof, and a journal of a thousand miles traveled through several nations of Indians, giving a particular account of their customs, manners, etc., etc. London, Printed for W. Taylor . . . and F. Baker . . . 1714. [Edited by Frances Latham Harriss. 2d ed.] Richmond, Garrett and Massie, 1951 [i.e. 1952] 259 p. [7546

—— ——Index; compiled by Jane C. Bahnsen. Chapel Hill, University of North Carolina Library, 1956. 36 p. [7547

——Mr. Lawson's Allerneueste Beschreibung der Gross-Britannischen provintz Carolina in West-Indien. Hamburg, T. von Wierings erben, 1722. 396 p. [7548

——A new account of Carolina. London, J. Knapton, 1709. (Stevens, John, ed. A new collection of voyages and travels, v. 1) 60 p. [7549

——A new voyage to Carolina; containing the exact description and natural history of that country: together with the present state thereof. And a journal of a thousand miles, travel'd thro' several nations of Indians. Giving a particular account of their customs, manners, &c. London, Printed in the year 1709. 258 p. [7550

Lawson, Laura Burnett. Leonora, a tale of the Great Smokies. New York, Neale Publishing Co., 1904. 247 p. [7551

Lawson McGhee Library, Knoxville, Tenn. Calvin Morgan McClung historical collection of books, pamphlets, manuscripts, pictures, and maps, relating to early western travel and the history and genealogy of Tennessee and other southern states, presented to Lawson McGhee Library by Mrs. Calvin M. McClung. Knoxville, Tenn., Knoxville Lithographing Co., 1921. 192 p. [7552

Lay, Ellen Balch, joint author, see **Stout, Wilbur White**

Lay, George William. "Ye are the light of the world"; the sermon delivered at the opening of Trinity Cathedral, Easton, Maryland, Thursday, July 9th, 1891. No place [Author? 1891?] 8 p. [7553

Lay, Henry Champlin. The "ardent longing" of the Anglican communion for peace and unity; a sermon preached on the occasion of the consecration of the Rt. Rev. Theodore Benedict Lyman, assistant bishop of North Carolina, December 11, 1873. Baltimore, Innes and Co., pr., 1873. 30 p. [7554

—— ——New York, American Church Press Co., 1874. 27 p. [7555

——Letters to a man bewildered among many counsellors. Rev. and enl. 3d ed. New York, General Protestant Episcopal Sunday School Union, 1853. 65 p. [7556

——Sermon commemorative of the late Thomas Atkinson, bishop of North Carolina, delivered in Christ Church, Raleigh, before the Convention of North Carolina, May 18, 1881. Winston, Church Messenger Publishing House, n.d. 27 p. [7557

—— ——New York, James Pott, n.d. 52 p. [7558

Layman of Mississippi, pseud. see **Yerger, George S.**

Lazard Freres and Company, New York. State of North Carolina: revised financial study. New York, Lazard Frères & Co. [1939] 15 leaves. [7559

Lazenby, Mary Elinor, comp. Catawba frontier, 1775-1781; memories of pensioners. Washington, 1950. 109 p. [7560

——Herman Husband, a story of his life . . . Book I. In Maryland. Book II. In North Carolina. Book III. In Pennsylvania. Washington, Old Neighborhoods Press, 1940. 180 p. [7561

[**Lazenby, Mary Eleanor**] Lewis grave yard with mention of some early settlers along Fifth Creek, Iredell County, N. C. [Statesville, Author, 1944] 11 p. [7562

Lea, Reba (Fitzpatrick) The Lea family in Nelson County, Virginia, their history and genealogy. [Lynchburg, Va., Brown-Morrison Co., 1946] 245 p. [7563

Leach, J. T. Circular letter on equal taxation to the voters of Johnston County. No place, no publisher [1859?] 8 p. [7564

Leach, John P. Prospectus of the Montauk water-power, Curls Hill Falls, Roanoke River, Halifax County, N. C. . . . with report of survey made by Professor W. C. Riddick. Raleigh, E. M. Uzzell, pr., n.d. 5 p. [7565

Leach, Lucie Maynard. Scattered leaves. New York, E. J. Hale & Son, 1877. 143 p. [7566

Leak, Walter F. Address delivered before the Agricultural Society of Cumberland County, N. C., at its seventh annual fair, November 15, 1860. Fayetteville, Edward J. Hale & Sons, pr., 1860. 16 p. [7567

Leaksville Woolen Mills, Leaksville, N. C. Catalog. [Leaksville?] n.d. 14 p. [7568

Leaksville-Spray Institute, Leaksville, N. C. Catalogue, 1905/06- Leaksville, 1906- NcU has 1905/06 [7569

Leary, Lewis Gaston, ed. Articles on American literature, appearing in current periodicals, 1920-1945. Durham, 1947. 337 p. [7570

—— ——1900-1950. Durham, Duke University Press, 1954. 437 p. [7571

——The literary career of Nathaniel Tucker, 1750-1807. Durham, Duke University Press, 1951. (Historical papers of the Trinity College Historical Society, ser. 29) 108 p. [7572

[**Leary, William James**] An address to the people of Chowan County. [Edenton, 1900] 4 p. [7573

Leary, William James. A speech, in a joint discussion between himself and H. S. Ward, also a candidate for solicitor, at Hertford, N. C., Sept. 24, 1906. [Edenton? 1906] 15 p. [7574

Leavitt, Alga E., ed. Stories and poems from the Old North State. Durham, Seeman Printery, Inc. [c.1923] 324 p. [7575

Leavitt, Dorothy. Adventure on the Tennessee. Boston, Little, Brown, 1952. 195 p. [7576

Leavitt, Sturgis Elleno. Argentine literature; a bibliography of literary criticism, biography, and literary controversy. Chapel Hill, University of North Carolina Press, 1924. (University of North Carolina studies in language and literature, no. 1) 92 p. [7577

Leavitt, Sturges Elleno, ed. Amalia . . . por José Mármol. Boston, D. C. Heath & Co. [c.1928] 222 p. [7578

——Concise Spanish grammar, by Sturgis E. Leavitt and Sterling A. Stoudemire. New York, H. Holt and Co. [1942] 167 p. [7579

Leavitt, Sturgis Elleno, ed. Eduardo Marquina: Las flores de Aragón. New York, Century Co. [c.1928] 222 p. [7580

——Elements of Spanish, by Sturgis E. Leavitt and Sterling A. Stoudemire. New York, H. Holt and Co. [c.1935] 133 p. [7581

——The Estrella de Sevilla and Claramonte. Cambridge, Mass., Harvard University Press, 1931. 111 p. [7582

——Hispano-American literature in the United States; a bibliography of translations and criticism. Cambridge, Mass., Harvard University Press, 1932. 54 p. [7583

—— ——1932-1934 (with additional items from earlier years) Chapel Hill, University of North Carolina Press, 1935. 21 p. [7584

——Inter-American student exchange: a key to better understanding. New York, Office of the Bicentennial of Columbia University, 1954. 24 p. [7585

——Latin American studies at the University of North Carolina; report to the Rockefeller Foundation. Chapel Hill, 1947. 12 p. [7586

Leavitt, Sturgis Elleno, ed.   Por los siglos, an anthology of Hispanic readings [edited by] Sturgis E. Leavitt [and] Sterling A. Stoudemire.   [New York] H. Holt and Co. [1942]   335 p.   [7587

[Leavitt, Sturgis Elleno]   Proposal to the Carnegie Corporation for support of cooperation in the Latin American field.   [Chapel Hill] 1947.   17 p.   [7588

Leavitt, Sturgis Elleno.   Report on the acquisition of Latin American materials by the University of North Carolina, July 1, 1940-July 1, 1948.   Chapel Hill, 1941-1948.   NcU has 1940/41-1944/45, 1940/48 (final report)   [7589

——Sound Spanish [by] Sturgis E. Leavitt [and] Sterling A. Stoudemire.   New York, H. Holt and Co. [1950]   119 p.   [7590

[Leavitt, Sturgis Elleno]   Supplementary report on cooperation in Latin American studies between Duke University, Tulane University, and the University of North Carolina, Latin American Institutes, made to Frank P. Graham for transmission to the Rockefeller Foundation.   Chapel Hill, 1940.   Various paging.   [7591

Leavitt, Sturgis Elleno.   A tentative bibliography of Bolivian literature.   Cambridge, Mass., Harvard University Press, 1933.   23 p.   [7592

——A tentative bibliography of Colombian literature, by Sturgis E. Leavitt . . . and Carlos García-Prada.   Cambridge, Mass., Harvard University Press, 1934. 80 p.   [7593

——A tentative bibliography of Peruvian literature.   Cambridge, Mass., Harvard University Press, 1932.   37 p.   [7594

Leavitt, Sturgis Elleno, ed.   Tres cuentos sud-americanos [by] Ugarte and Latorre. New York, F. S. Crofts & Co., 1935.   163 p.   [7595

Leavitt, Sturgis Elleno.   ¡Vamos a leer!   [By] Sturgis E. Leavitt and Sterling A. Stoudemire.   [New York] H. Holt and Co. [c.1938]   237 p.   [7596

—— ——[New York] H. Holt and Co. [c.1944]   260 p.   [7597

——¡Vamos a ver!   A Spanish workbook by Sturgis E. Leavitt and Sterling A. Stoudemire.   New York, Henry Holt and Co., [c.1936]   90 p.   [7598

—— ——[1937.]   90 p.   [7599

Lebanon Syrian-American Association of North Carolina   see **Syrian-American Association of North Carolina**

LeClerc, Jean.   The life and character of Mr. John Locke, author of the essay concerning humane understanding . . . done into English by T. F. P.   London, Printed for John Clark, 1706.   31 p.   [7600

Lederer, John.   The discoveries of John Lederer, in three several marches from Virginia to the west of Carolina, and other parts of the continent, begun in March, 1669, and ended in September, 1670; together with a general map of the whole territory which he traversed; collected and translated out of Latine from his discourse and writings, by Sir William Talbot.   London, Printed by J. C. for S. Heyrick, 1672.   27 p.   NcU has microfilm.   [7601

—— ——[Charleston, S. C., Walker, Evans & Cogswell Co., 1891]   47 p.   [7602

—— ——London, Printed by J. C. for S. Heyrick, 1672 [Reprinted for G. P. Humphrey, Rochester, N. Y., 1902]   30 p.   [7603

Ledford, Preston Lafayette.   Ready calculator.   No place, Author, c.1910.   32 p. [7604

——Reminiscences of the Civil War, 1861-1865.   Thomasville, News Printing House, 1909.   104 p.   [7605

Lee, Charles.   Memoirs of the life of the late Charles Lee, esq . . . second in command in the service of the United States of America during the Revolution.   2d American ed.   New-York, T. Allen, pr., 1793.   284 p.   [7606

Lee, Henry, 1756-1818.   Memoirs of the war in the southern department of the United States.   Philadelphia, Bradford and Inskeep, 1812.   2 v.   [7607

—— ——A new ed. with revisions, and a biography of the author, by Robert E. Lee.   New York, University Publishing Co., 1869.   620 p.   [7608

Lee, Henry, 1787-1837.   The campaign of 1781 in the Carolinas; with remarks, historical and critical, on Johnson's Life of Greene.   To which is added an appendix of original documents, relating to the history of the Revolution.   Philadelphia, E. Littell, 1824.   511 p.   [7609

——Observations on the writings of Thomas Jefferson, with particular reference to the attack they contain on the memory of the late Gen. Henry Lee.   New-York, C. De Behr, 1832.   237 p.   [7610

Lee, James Kendall. The volunteer's hand book, containing an abridgement of Hardee's Infantry tactics. Raleigh, Institution for the Deaf & Dumb & the Blind, pr., 1861. 96 p. [7611

Lee, James R. To the voters of the sixteenth senatorial district, Harnett, Cumberland and Sampson counties. No place, Author, February 15, 1869. [1] p. [7612

Lee, Jesse. Memoir of the Rev. Jesse Lee, with extracts from his journals, by Minton Thrift. New York, N. Bangs and T. Mason, for the Methodist Episcopal Church, 1823. 360 p. [7613

Lee, Laura Elizabeth see Battle, Laura Elizabeth Lee

Lee, Leroy M. The life and times of the Rev. Jesse Lee. Charleston, S. C., John Early for the Methodist Episcopal Church, South, 1848. 517 p. [7614

Lee, Robert Earl. North Carolina family law. Winston-Salem, College Book Store, Wake Forest College, 1955. 150 leaves. [7615

Lee, Thomas Mossette. The boys that broke the line. No place, no publisher, n.d. 2 p. [7616

Lee, Wallace. Math miracles. [Durham, Seeman Printery, Inc., c.1950] 83 p. [7617

Lee, William States. Fertilization our greatest problem. [Charlotte, Queen City Printing Co.] n.d. 7 p. [7618

Lee School, Blue Ridge, N. C. Boy life at Lee School. Blue Ridge [1929] 2 p. [7619

Lees-McRae College, Banner Elk, N. C. Catalogue, 191 - Banner Elk, 191 - NcU has [1935/36-1945/46] 1947/48-1951/52, 1955/56 [7620

——Chaffee Center, Lees-McRae College. [Banner Elk, 1955] 15 p. [7621

——Pinnacles, v. 1- 1916- Banner Elk, 1916- NcU has v. [11-40] [7622

Leesville High School, Flint, N. C. Catalogue, 1900/01?- Raleigh, 1901?- NcU has 1903/04-1905/06 [7623

Lefferts, Aleeze. Carteret County, economic and social, by Aleeze Lefferts, H. C. Lay, and C. W. Lewis. Chapel Hill, University of North Carolina Press, [1926] (University of North Carolina. Extension Division Bulletin, v. 5, no. 13) 99 p. [7624

Leffingwell, William Bruce. The happy hunting grounds, also fishing, of the South . . . the game laws of . . . the states penetrated by the Southern Railway. Chicago, Donohue & Henneberry, pr., 1895. 64 p. [7625

Lefler, Hugh Talmage. A guide to the study and reading of North Carolina history. Chapel Hill, University of North Carolina Press [1955] 89 p. [7626

——Hinton Rowan Helper, advocate of a "white America". Charlottesville, Va., Historical Publishing Co., Inc., 1935. (Southern sketches, no. 1) 45 p. [7627

——History of North Carolina. New York, Lewis Historical Publishing Co. [1956] 4 v. v. 3-4, comp. by Publisher have subtitle: Family and personal history [7628

Lefler, Hugh Talmage, ed. North Carolina history told by contemporaries. Chapel Hill, University of North Carolina Press [c.1934] 454 p. [7629

—— ——[2d ed. rev.] [c.1948] 502 p. [7630

—— ——[3d ed. rev. and enl.] [c.1956] 528 p. [7631

Lefler, Hugh Talmage. North Carolina, the history of a southern state, by Hugh Talmage Lefler and Albert Ray Newsome. Chapel Hill, University of North Carolina Press [1954] 676 p. [7632

Lefler, Hugh Talmage, ed. Orange County, 1752-1952, ed. by Hugh Lefler and Paul Wager. Chapel Hill [Orange Printshop] 1953. 389 p. [7633

Lefler, Hugh Talmage, joint author, see Newsome, Albert Ray; also, Walser, Richard Gaither

Lefler, Hugh Talmage, joint ed. see Brooks, Aubrey Lee, ed.

Legislative Council of North Carolina Women. The Australian ballot system. No place, n.d. [2] p. [7634

——The Australian ballot system; what will it give to North Carolina? No place [1928] [2] p. [7635

——Notice of intention to marry. No place, n.d. [3] p. [7636

——Program, 1929. No place, 1929. 2 p. [7637

——Working hours for children in North Carolina. No place, n.d. [2] p. [7638

Legislative record, giving the acts passed session ending March, 1877. Together with sketches of the lives and public acts of the members of both houses, v. 1, no. 1. Raleigh, Edwards, Broughton & Co., pr., 1877. 52 p. [7639

Le Grand, pseud. see **Henderson, Le Grand**

Le Grange, H. M., pseud. see **Cameron, Rebecca**

Lehman, Benjamin Harrison. Carlyle's theory of the hero; its sources, development, history, and influence on Carlyle's work; a study of a nineteenth century idea. Durham, Duke University Press, 1928. 212 p. [7640

Lehman, Emma A. Poems. New York, Grafton Press [1904] 47 p. [7641
——Sketches of European travel, May, 1890. Winston, Republican Steam Print, 1890. 115 p. [7642

Leigh, Hezekiah Gilbert. Address delivered before the two literary societies of Randolph Macon College on the day preceding commencement, June, 1841. Raleigh, Raleigh Star, 1841. 17 p. [7643

Leighton, Clare Veronica Hope. Southern harvest, written and engraved by Clare Leighton. New York, Macmillan Co., 1942. 157 p. [7644
——Tempestuous petticoat, the story of an invincible Edwardian. New York, Rinehart & Co., Inc., 1947. 272 p. [7645

Leiper, Bart, ed. Home companies of Carolinas are rugged guardians at the portals of progress. Charlotte, News Publishing Co. [1933?] 32 p. [7646

Leland, John Adams. Othneil Jones. Philadelphia, J. B. Lippincott Co. [1956] 253 p. [7647

Leland, Waldo Gifford. Robert Digges Wimberly Connor, 1878-1950, first archivist of the United States, 1934-1941; an address on the occasion of the unveiling of a portrait at the National Archives, October 10, 1952. [Wash., 1952] 10 p. [7648

Lemay, Thomas J. An address delivered before Hiram Lodge no. 40, in the Masonic Hall, Raleigh, on the twenty-fourth June, 1846. Raleigh, Raleigh Star, 1847. 15 p. [7649

Lemay's North Carolina almanack see **Lawrence and Lemay's North Carolina almanack**

Lemert, Benjamin Franklin. The cotton textile industry of the Southern Appalachian Piedmont. Chapel Hill, University of North Carolina Press, 1933. 188 p. [7650
——North Carolina geography; a study of how we live in North Carolina [by] Benjamin Franklin Lemert and Martha Langston Harrelson. Prelim. ed. Oklahoma City, Harlow Publication Corporation, 1953. 188 p. [7651
—— ——1954. 190 p. [7652
——The tobacco manufacturing industry in North Carolina. Raleigh, National Youth Administration of North Carolina, 1939. 107 p. [7653

Lemmon, Kathleen. House in the woods; a biographical sketch of Juliette and Crosby Adams. [Asheville, Inland Press, Inc., c.1956] 89 p. [7654

Lemond, Marcus Monroe. Genealogy of the families of Milas and Mary Means Lemmond and of their brothers and sisters. Brooklyn, privately printed, 1937. 162 p. [7655

Lennox Development Corporation, Durham, N. C. Glen Lennox, Chapel Hill, N. C., 1953- Chapel Hill, 1953- NcU has December 12, 1953 [7656

[Lenoir, Walter Waightstill] Atlantic, Tennessee and Ohio Railroad. No place, [1854] 10 p. [7657

Lenoir, William. To the citizens of the twelfth election district, in the state of North Carolina. Fort Defiance, July 30, 1806. [1] p. [7658

Lenoir, William A. N. Carolina system of railroads! [Fort Defiance, January 3, 1850 and July 12, 1854] [1] p. [7659

Lenoir, N. C. Bank of Lenoir. 60th anniversary souvenir, open house, May 4, 1954. Lenoir, 1954. 16 p. [7660

Lenoir, N. C. Bill May Memorial Committee. Bill May Memorial Fund for Education. [Lenoir, 1941?] 15 p. [7661

Lenoir, N. C. Board of Trade. Lenoir, North Carolina, "furniture manufacturing center of the South" . . . compiled by Lenoir Board of Trade and Lenoir News-Topic. [Lenoir, Lenoir News-Topic, 1938?] 16 p. [7662

Lenoir, N. C. Chamber of Commerce. A protest addressed to the Office of Defense Transportation, the Interstate Commerce Commission, the North Carolina Utilities Commission, in respect to the application of ODT Order no. 47 and the past, present and future passenger train service of the Carolina and North Western Railway. Lenoir [1945] 16 p. [7663

Lenoir, N. C. Citizens Building and Loan Association. Souvenir, fortieth anniversary, 1888-1928. [Lenoir, News-Topic, 1928] 4 p. [7664

Lenoir, N. C. First Presbyterian Church. Centennial program for the observance of the one hundredth anniversary of the First Presbyterian Church, Lenoir, North Carolina. [Lenoir, 1952] 24 p. [7665

Lenoir Academy, Lenoir, N. C. Catalogue, 188 - Lenoir, 188 - NcU has 1889/90 [7666

Lenoir Academy and Commercial Institute, Lenoir, N. C. [Catalogue] 1905/06?- Lenoir, 1906?- NcU has 1906/07 [7667

Lenoir Circuit see Methodist Episcopal Church, South. North Carolina Conference. Lenoir Circuit

Lenoir College see Lenoir Rhyne College, Hickory, N. C.

Lenoir Collegiate Institute, Lenoir Institute, N. C. Catalogue, 1855/56?- Kinston, 1857?- NcU has 1857/58 [7668

Lenoir Co., N. C. Auditor. Lenoir, County, North Carolina, financial statement, 19 - [Kinston, 19 -] NcU has 1943/42, 1943/44-1955/56 [7669

Lenoir Co., N. C. Board of Education. Report, Public Schools of Lenoir County, 19 - Kinston, 19 - NcU has 1909/10, 1914/15 [7670

[Lenoir Realty and Insurance Company] Where is Lenoir, N. C.? [Lenoir] n.d. 10 p. [7671

Lenoir Rhyne College, Hickory, N. C. Bulletin, v. 1- 1910?- Hickory, 1910?- NcU has v. [3-45] [7672

——Catalogue, 18 - Hickory, 18 - NcU has 1891/92, 1895/96. Continues as its Bulletin, v. 1- 1910- [7673

——Lenoir College: Address list of graduates and ex-students. [Lenoir, 1922?] [4] p. [7674

Lenski, Louis. Blue Ridge Billy, written and illustrated by Louis Lenski. New York, J. B. Lippincott Co. [1946] 203 p. [7675

——Peanuts for Billy Ben. Philadelphia, J. B. Lippincott Co., 1952. 128 p. [7676

Lent, George Eidt. The impact of the undistributed profits tax, 1936-1937. New York, 1948. 203 p. [7677

Leon, Louis. Diary of a Tar Heel Confederate soldier. Charlotte, Stone Publishing Co. [c.1913] 87 p. [7678

Leon, Mita, pseud. see Rivenback, Mrs. R. W.

Leonard, Burgess. One-man backfield. Philadelphia, J. B. Lippincott Co. [1953] 180 p. [7679

——Phantom of the foul-lines. Philadelphia, J. B. Lippincott Co. [1952] 184 p. [7680

——The rookie fights back. Philadelphia, J. B. Lippincott Co. [1954] 192 p. [7681

——Rookie southpaw. Philadelphia, J. B. Lippincott Co. [1951] 218 p. [7682

——Second-season jinx. Philadelphia, J. B. Lippincott Co. [1953] 216 p. [7683

——Victory pass. Philadelphia, J. B. Lippincott Co. [1950] 221 p. [7684

Leonard, Colvin T. History of the Presbyterian Church of the Covenant, Greensboro, N. C. [Greensboro, 1945] 11 p. [7685

Leonard, J. S. Carolina harmony; a book of new tunes especially adapted to the hymns for which they were composed with concise rudiments. Statesville, Author, c.1895. 89 p. [7686

Leonard, Jacob Calvin. Centennial history of Davidson County, North Carolina. Raleigh, Edwards & Broughton Co., 1927. 523 p. [7687

——The great commission. No place, no publisher, n.d. 9 p. [7688

——History of Catawba College, formerly located at Newton, now at Salisbury, N. C. No place [Trustees of Catawba College, c.1927] 352 p. [7689

——The Sabbath, a day of worship. No place, no publisher, n.d. 10 p. [7690

——Salient facts in the history and doctrine of the Reformed Church. Thomasville, News Printing House, 1903. 13 p. [7691

——The Southern Synod of the Evangelical and Reformed Church. Lexington [Raleigh, Edwards and Broughton Co.] 1940. 373 p. [7692

Le Page du Pratz. The history of Louisiana, or of the western parts of Virginia and Carolina, containing a description of the countries that lie on both sides of the river Mississippi, with an account of the settlements, inhabitants, soil, climate, and products. Tr. from the French. London, T. Becket, 1774. 2 v. [7693

—— ——A new ed. [New Orleans, Pelican Press, Inc., 1947] 387 p. [7694

Lepawsky, Albert. State planning and economic development in the South. [Washington] Committee of the South, National Planning Association [1949] (Its Report no. 4) 193 p. [7695

LePrince, Joseph Albert Augustin. The relation of storage water supply lakes to malaria; a paper delivered before fifth annual meeting of the North Carolina section, American Water Works Association, September 13, 14, 15, 1925. No place, 1925. 11 p. [7696

Lequeux, H. D. Palmetto leaves. Hickory, Hickory Printing Co., 1892. 29 p. [7697

Lesley, J. Peter. Corundum. No place, no publisher [1873?] 4 p. [7698

——The titaniferous iron ore range of N. C. Philadelphia, M'Calla and Stavely, 1871. 34 p. [7699

Lester, William Stewart. The Transylvania colony. Spencer, Ind., S. R. Guard & Co., 1935. 288 p. [7700

A letter from a member of the General Assembly to one of his constituents, respecting the change in the judiciary system, together with the substance of Mr. Mebane's speech on the same subject. Raleigh, Thomas Henderson, 1818. NcU has microfilm. [7701

Letter on the subject of the vice-presidency, in favor of the claims of James K. Polk, of Tennessee, to the nomination of the Democratic National Convention, by a Tennessean. Washington, Globe, 1844. 7 p. [7702

Levin, Peter R. Seven by chance: the accidental presidents. New York, Farrar, Straus, 1948. 374 p. [7703

Levin, Ron. I, the city, and other poems. Chapel Hill, New Sounds Publishers [c.1956] 13 p. [7704

——Rebellion. Chapel Hill, Old Well Publishers, 1955. (Old Well contemporary poets series, 1955 [no.] 2) 13 p. [7705

Lewis, Alfred Henry. When men grew tall; or, The story of Andrew Jackson. New York, D. Appleton & Co., 1907. 331 p. [7706

Lewis, Charles Bertrand. Mad Dan, the spy of 1776. New York, Beadle and Adams [1873] 154 p. [7707

Lewis, Charles Lee. Philander Priestley Claxton, crusader for public education. Knoxville, University of Tennessee Press, 1948. 369 p. [7708

Lewis, Cornelia Battle see **Lewis, Nell Battle**

Lewis, Edwin A. Newbern; or, True to the old flag, a drama of the southern rebellion in prologue and three acts. No place, no publisher [c.1883] 49 p. [7709

Lewis, Emily Roberts. For you; words by D. B. Fulton, music by Emily Roberts Lewis. New York, John T. Hall [c.1914] 5 p. [7710

Lewis, George C. The soldier's companion; containing an abridgement of Hardee's Infantry tactics. Raleigh, John Spelman, pr., 1863. 325 p. [7711

Lewis, Henry Wilkins. Northampton parishes. Jackson, 1951. 120 p. [7712

Lewis, Joseph Volney. Determinative mineralogy, with tables for the determination of minerals by means of their chemical and physical characters. New York, J. Wiley & Sons, 1913. 151 p. [7713

——A manual of determinative mineralogy, with tables for the determination of minerals. 3d rev. and enl. ed. New York, John Wiley & Sons, Inc., 1921. 298 p. [7714

—— ——4th ed. rev. [c.1931] 254 p. [7715

Lewis, Kate (Porter) Alabama folk plays, edited, with an introduction by Frederick H. Koch. Chapel Hill, University of North Carolina Press [1943] 152 p. [7716

Lewis, Lloyd. Sherman, fighting prophet. New York, Harcourt, Brace and Co. [c.1932] 690 p. [7717

Lewis, McDaniel. Honorable E. B. Jeffress, his contribution to Greensboro; an address at a testimonial dinner at Greensboro Country Club. [Greensboro, Chamber of Commerce, 1955] 3 p. [7718

——The story of North Carolina municipal bonds. Greensboro, McDaniel Lewis & Co. [1954] 14 p. [7719

Lewis, Nell Battle, ed. The power of prayer as set forth in the words of Jesus of Nazareth. [Raleigh, Author, 1941] 31 p. [7720

——The way; studies in the teachings of Jesus of Nazareth. [Raleigh, Author, 1942] 130 p. [7721

Lewis, P. Loyd. James Lewis and Ann Elizabeth Stewart Lewis of North Carolina and Missouri. [Ferguson, Mo., Author, 1934] 23 p. [7722

Lewis, Richard Henry. Higher medical education and how to secure it; the annual address before the Alumni Association of the University of Maryland. No place, no publisher [1889] 20 p. [7723

——How to make cheap silos. [Raleigh] n.d. 2 p. [7724

——How we see . . . a lecture delivered before the University Normal School at Chapel Hill, July 31st, 1877. Raleigh, Edwards, Broughton & Co., 1878. 23 p. [7725

Lewis, Sinclair. Cheap and contented labor; the picture of a southern mill town in 1929. [New York?] United Feature Syndicate, Inc. c.1929. 32 p. [7726

Lewis, William Terrell. Genealogy of the Lewis family in America, from the middle of the seventeenth century down to the present time. Louisville, Ky., Courier-Journal Job Printing Co., 1893. 454 p. [7728

Lewis and Hall, Greensboro, N. C. North Carolina, description, including maturities of state bonds outstanding, February 1, 1934. Greensboro, 1934. [3] p. [7729

——North Carolina, state and county financial information, May 1, 1939. Greensboro, 1939. [4] p. [7730

Lewis Fork Baptist Association. Minutes, 1836- 1836- NcU has 1838-1859, 1867 [7731

Lexington, N. C. Board of Commissioners. The code of the city of Lexington, North Carolina, 1947. Charlottesville, Va., Michie City Publications Co., 1947. 317 p. [7732

Lexington Primitive Baptist Association. Minutes, 18 - 18 - NcU has 1842-1847 [7733

Lexington Seminary, Lexington, N. C. Catalogue, 188 - Lexington, 188 - NcU has 1889/90 [7734

Liancourt, François Alexandre Frédéric, duc de la Rochefoucauld. see La Rochefoucauld Liancourt, François Alexandre Frédéric, duc de

Libby, Orin Grant. The geographical distribution of the vote of the thirteen states on the federal constitution, 1787-8. Madison, Wis., University of Wisconsin, 1894. (Its Bulletin, economics, political science, and history ser., v. 1, no. 1) 116 p. [7735

Liberation, v. 7-13, 1937-1940. Asheville, Pelley Publishers, 1937-1940. NcU has v. 7-8 [9-10] 11-13. Moved from North Carolina following November 28, 1940, issue. Title varies, 1937: The new liberation. [7736

Liberty Baptist Association. Minutes, 1832- 1832- NcU has 1832 [1845-1866] 1868-1905 [1906-1922] 1924-1942 [1946-1956] [7737

Liberty Normal College, Liberty, N. C. Catalogue, 188 - Liberty, 188 - NcU has 1902/03 [7738

Liberty-Piedmont Institute, Wallburg, N. C. Catalogue, 1903/04?- Wallburg, 1904?- NcU has 1909/10-1912/13 [7739

Library notes, no. 1- April 4, 1955- Chapel Hill, Louis R. Wilson Library, 1955- NcU has no. 1-91 [7740

Library notes, v. 1- March, 1936- Durham, Friends of Duke University Library, 1936- NcU has v. 1-4 and no. 7-30 [7741

Lichtenstein, Gaston. Early history of Tarboro, North Carolina; also, Collated colonial public claims of Edgecombe County, and Easter Sunday in Savannah, Ga. Richmond, Va., W. E. Jones, pr., 1908. 16 p. [7742

——Early social life in Edgecombe; also, Early history of Edgecombe, and a Tarborean's experience abroad. Richmond, Va., W. E. Jones, pr., 1904. 16 p. [7743

——From Richmond to North Cape. Richmond, Va., William Byrd Press, 1922. 160 p. [7744

——George Washington's lost birthday. History of Meridian Lodge. Also, other articles written at various times. Richmond, Va., William Byrd Press, 1924. 115 p. [7745

——History of the Jews of Richmond, from 1769 to 1917, by Gaston Lichtenstein and H. T. Ezekiel. Richmond, Va., H. T. Ezekiel, pr., 1917. 374 p. [7746

——Louis D. Wilson, Mexican war martyr, also, Thos. H. Hall, Andrew Johnson as he really was, and Our town common. Richmond, Va., H. T. Ezekiel, pr., 1911. 20 p. [7747

Lichtenstein, Gaston, comp. Repatriation of prisoners of war from Siberia, a documentary narrative. Richmond, Va., William Byrd Press, 1924. 177 p. [7748

Lichtenstein, Gaston. Thomas Jefferson as war governor; also, Three travel articles, and Some North Carolina history. Richmond, Va., William Byrd Press, 1925. 112 p. [7749

——The Virginia Lichtensteins. Richmond, Va., Herbert T. Ezekiel, pr., 1912. 16 p. [7750

——A visit to Young's Pier at Atlantic City, N. J., also, When Edgecombe was a-borning, The word sheriff, and Products of colonial North Carolina. Richmond, Va., W. E. Jones, pr., 1908. 15 p. [7751

——When Tarboro was incorporated; also, Reverend James Moir, Edgecombe changes her county seat, and Germantown, Pennsylvania. Richmond, Va., Capitol Printing Co., 1910. 27 p. [7752

Liddell, Anna Forbes. Alexander's space, time and deity, a critical consideration. Chapel Hill, Department of Philosophy, University of North Carolina [1925] (Its Studies in philosophy, no. 2) 70 p. [7753

Lief, Arthur. The wee cooper of Fife, folk songs from North Carolina, SATBB. New York, Music Press [1947] 10 p. [7754

Life, adventures, and anecdotes of "Beau" Hickman, prince of American bummers. Washington, Potomac Publishing Co., 1879. 60 p. [7755

The life and public services of the Hon. James Knox Polk. Baltimore, N. Hickman, 1844. 47 p. [7756

The life, confession, and execution of the Jew and Jewess, Gustavus Linderhoff, and Fanny Victoria Talzingler, who were hung in Asheville, North Carolina, Oct. 27, 1855, for the triple murder of Abner, Benjamin and Charles Ecclangfeldt. Baltimore, A. R. Orton, 1856. 50 p. [7757

Life Insurance Association of the Carolinas. Meeting, 1891- 1891- NcU has 1893 [7758

Life of Andrew Jackson, embracing anecdotes illustrative of his character. Philadelphia, Lindsay and Blakiston [c.1846] 183 p. [7759

Life of General Marion, embracing anecdotes illustrative of his character. Philadelphia, Lindsay and Blakiston [c.1847] 208 p. [7760

[Liggett and Myers Tobacco Co., Durham, N. C.] Tobaccoland, U. S. A. [Durham? c.1940] [40] p. [7761

—— ——The new Tobacco land, U. S. A. [1949?] [38] p. [7762

—— ——[1950] [38] p. [7763

—— ——14th ed. [Durham, 1951?] [40] p. [7764

[Light, George W.] The North and the South; an important enterprise for promoting the triumph of freedom in 1860. [Boston, The National Era, 1859?] 4 p. [7765

Lightfoot, Florence Jean Richards. Bits of Arden. [Fayetteville, Cumberland Printing Co., c.1923] [14] p. [7766

——Bubbles, by Florie Jean Lightfoot and Lucia Starnes Monroe. [Pinebluff, George E. Wells, pr., c.1924] [21] p. [7767

——For you, just you. [New York, Gebhardi Press] n.d. [1] p. [7768

——Immortelles. [Raleigh, Author, c.1935] [16] p. [7769

——Mother mine. [New York, Gebhardi Press] n.d. [2] p. [7770

Lilienthal, David Eli. TVA; democracy on the march. New York, Harper & Brothers [1944] 248 p. [7771

—— ——[1953]   294 p.   [7772

Lilley, Kader. My life and experience. [Williamston, 1903]   27 p.   [7773

Lillington, John Alexander. To our constituents. No place, no publisher [1851?]
[1] p.   [7774

Lillington, N. C. Public High School and Farm Life School. Announcement,
catalogue, 1914/15- Lillington, 1914- NcU has 1914/15-1917/18. Called Lillington Farm Life School, 1914/15.   [7775

Lilly, David Clay. Faith of our fathers. Richmond, Va., Presbyterian Committee
of Publication, 1935.   143 p.   [7776

——Safeguarding civilization, Deuteronomy VI, 6-7: the opening sermon of the Conference on Christian Education at Montreat, North Carolina, July 19th, 1925.
[Louisville, Ky., Presbyterian Church in the United States, Department of Christian Education, 1925?]   16 p.   [7777

Lilly, Lambert, schoolmaster, pseud. see Hawks, Francis Lister

Lillybridge, C. A review of the Rev. Geo. W. Langhorne's inquiry into the antiquity
of the Baptist Church. Elizabeth City, Printed by J. Howell at the Office of the
Old North State, 1841.   60 p.   [7778

Lillycrop, William Arthur. The awakening of St. Timothy's League. Milwaukee,
Wis., Morehouse Publishing Co., 1933.   59 p.   [7779

Lincoln Hospital, Durham, N. C. Report, 19 - Durham, 19 - NcU has 1927,
1930, 1933, 1938   [7780

Lincoln Lithia Club, Lincolnton, N. C. Prospectus and articles of agreement.
Lincolnton, News Print, n.d.   20 p.   [7781

Lincoln Lithia Water Co. Lincoln lithia water. Lincolnton, n.d.   16 p.   [7782

Lincolnton, N. C. High School. Library. May I show you around? Study
manual for library assistants. Lincolnton, 1939.   47 p.   [7783

Lincolnton, N. C. Presbyterian Church. Memorial tributes, Rev. Robert Zenas
Johnston, 1834-1908. Durham, Seeman Printery, 1908.   32 p.   [7784

——Reports and directory, 190 - Lincolnton, 190 - NcU has 1907/08   [7785

Lincolnton Female Seminary, Lincolnton, N. C. Catalogue, 18 - Lincolnton,
18 - NcU has 1870   [7786

Lindesay, M. Batterham. The first shearing. Richmond, Va., Whittet & Shepperson, 1904.   299 p.   [7787

Lindley, Maybon. Carillons and cow bells. San Antonio, Naylor Co. [1949]
55 p.   [7788

Lindley, Percy Elliott. How build the new world? Address given before the Rotary
Club of High Point, November 16, 1944. [High Point, Author, 1944?]   20 p. [7789

——Rise up and walk. Boston, Chapman & Grimes [1949]   167 p.   [7790

Lindquist, Ruth. The family in the present social order; a study of needs of American
families. Chapel Hill, University of North Carolina Press, 1931.   241 p.   [7791

Lindsay, Margaret Isabella. The Lindsays of America, a genealogical narrative.
Albany, N. Y., J. Munsell's Sons, 1889.   275 p.   [7792

Lindsay, Maud McKnight. Posey and the peddler. New York, Lothrop, Lee and
Shepard Co., 1938.   186 p.   [7793

Lindsay, Nicholas Vachel. A handy guide for beggars . . . made while afoot and
penniless in Florida, Georgia, North Carolina, Tennessee, Kentucky, New Jersey,
and Pennsylvania. New York, Macmillan and Co., 1920.   205 p.   [7794

Lindsey, Thomas H. Lindsey's guide book to Western North Carolina. Asheville,
Randolph-Kerr Printing Co., 1890.   92 p.   [7795

Lindsey and Brown's descriptive catalogue of photographic views of the Land of the
Sky; or, Beauties of Western North Carolina. Asheville, Lindsey and Brown,
n.d.   23 p.   [7796

The line up; Which side are you on? No place, no publisher, n.d.   15 p.   [7797

Linebarger, Paul Myron Anthony. The China of Chiang K'ai-shek, a political
study. Boston, World Peace Foundation, 1941.   449 p.   [7798

——A family of five republics; a sketch of the origin of the Leyenberger-Linebarger-
Lionberger families, by Paul Myron Linebarger and Walter Franklin Lineberger.
Hammond, Ind., W. B. Conkey Co., 1925.   43 p.   [7799

——Government in republican China. New York, McGraw-Hill Co., Inc., 1938. 203 p. [7800

Lingle, Thomas Wilson. History of Thyatira Church, 1753 to 1925, including address delivered by Rev. S. G. Alexander at the centennial celebration held on October 17, 1885. Statesville, Brady Printing Co., 1925. 61 p. [7801

Lingle, Walter Lee. The burning of Servetus. No place, no publisher, n.d. 14 p. [7802
——The first general assembly and the events leading up to it. Philadelphia, Publicity Department of the General Assembly [1938] 22 p. [7803
——Memories of Davidson College. Richmond, Va., John Knox Press [1947] 157 p. [7804
——Presbyterians, their history and beliefs. Richmond, Va., Presbyterian Committee of Publication [c.1928] 199 p. [7805
——Thyatira Presbyterian Church, Rowan County, North Carolina, 1753-1948. Statesville, Brady Printing Co. [1949?] 71 p. [7806

Linguistic Society of America. The Linguistic Institute under the auspices of the Linguistic Society of America and the University of North Carolina, Summer Session, 1941, June 12-July 19. [Chapel Hill, 1941] 12 p. [7807

Link, Arthur Stanley. American epoch; a history of the United States since the 1890's. New York, A. A. Knopf, 1955. 724 p. [7808
——Wilson, the new freedom. Princeton, N. J., Princeton University Press, 1956. 504 p. [7809
——Wilson, the road to the White House. Princeton, N. J., Princeton University Press, 1947. 570 p. [7810
——Woodrow Wilson and the progressive era, 1910-1917. New York, Harper and Brothers [c.1954] 331 p. [7811

Linker, Joseph Burton. Mathematics of finance [by] J. B. Linker and M. A. Hill, Jr. New York, H. Holt [1948] 175 p. [7812

Linker, Robert White, ed. Aucassin et Nicolete. Chapel Hill, Author, c.1937. 43 p. [7813
—— ——Chapel Hill, University of North Carolina Press [1948] 49 p. [7814
——Li chevaliers au Lyon, ou, Yvain. Chapel Hill, Author, 1940. 146 p. [7815

Linker, Robert White, ed. A provençal anthology. [Chapel Hill, Author] c.1934. [88] p. [7816
——A Provençal anthology. Columbus, O., H. L. Hedrick [c.1940] 104 p. [7817
——Roman de Renart, branches I-III. Chapel Hill, Author, c.1947. 84 p. [7818
——Li Romanz de la Rose. Chapel Hill, c.1937. 83 p. [7819
——Tannhäuser. Chapel Hill, Author, 1936. 59 p. [7820
——The works of François Villon, M. A. Chapel Hill, Author, c.1935. 106 p. [7821

Linscott, Henry Farrar. Pure scholarship, its place in civilization. No place, no publisher, n.d. 10 p. [7822

Linville, N. C. Linville Improvement Co. Grandfather Mountain toll road. Linville [1935?] Folder. [7823

Lions Club, Asheville, N. C. The Lions Club of Asheville . . . roster, officers, code of ethics and by-laws. [Asheville, 1939?] Unpaged. [7824

Lipscomb, Victor H. Statement of Dr. V. H. Lipscomb. No place, no publisher, n.d. [1] p. [7825

Liquor is labor's worst enemy. No place, no publisher, n.d. 1 p. [7826

List of heads of families on R. F. D. routes leaving Oxford. [Oxford, Oxford Orphanage, pr.] n.d. 14 p. [7827

List of North Carolina fairs, 19 - 19 - NcU has 1954 [7828

List of persons convicted of felony or other infamous crimes in Granville County since March 12, 1877. No place, no publisher [1894] [1] p. [7829
——Since November term of Granville Superior Court, 1894. [1896] [1] p. [7830

List of private schools and colleges in the several counties in North Carolina, 1890. No place, no publisher, 1890. 19 p. [7831

List of regular lodges, Masonic, 19 - Blomington, Ill., Pantagraph Printing & Stationery Co. [c.19 - NcU has 1920, 1928 North Carolina edition with cover note: Issued by Grand Lodge of North Carolina. [7832

Litchford, Henry E. The Torrens system of land registration; an address before the

North Carolina State Bankers Association, at Wrightsville, N. C., June 24, 1910.
No place, no publisher [1910?]   6 p.   [7833

Literary South, v. 1, no. 1-3, January, February, August, 1937. Lincolnton, James
Larkin Pearson, 1937.   NcU has v. 1.   No more published.   [7834

Literary world, v. 1-   March? 1880-   Monroe, J. D. Davis, 1880-   NcU has v.
[1-3, 5]   [7835

Little, Henry F. W.   The Seventh Regiment New Hampshire Volunteers in the war
of the rebellion.   Concord, N. H., I. C. Evans, pr., 1896.   567 p.   [7836

Little, Lacy LeGrand.   Rivershade, a historical sketch of Kiangyin Station, China.
No place, no publisher [1933]   63 p.   [7837

Little, Luther.   Manse dwellers.   Charlotte, Presbyterian Standard Publishing Co.,
1927.   314 p.   [7838

Little, William Myers.   The Little scrapbook, being selections from the varied newspaper writings of William M. Little. Atlanta, privately printed, 1952. 103 p. [7839

Little Alma, a true story of early piety.   Raleigh, Raleigh Baptist Sabbath School,
1868.   48 p.   [7840

Little River Baptist Association.   Minutes, 18 - 18 - NcU has 1876-1881, 1883-
1886, [1895-1953]   [7841

Little River Primitive Baptist Association.   Minutes, 18 - 18 - NcU has [1871-
1934]   [7842

——Synopsis of churches of the Little River Primitive Baptist Association of North
Carolina and collective statement of Juniper Conference held August, 1893. Raleigh, Edwards and Broughton Co., 1910.   90 p.   [7843

Little River record, v. 1-   April, 1898-   Buie's Creek, Little River Baptist Association, 1898-   NcU has v. [1-2]   [7844

The little Smith barn; a story of the triangular plot now called Pritchard Park, Asheville, North Carolina [Asheville, The Bank of Asheville?] n.d.   [12] p.   [7845

Little Switzerland.   No place, no publisher, 1916.   22 p.   [7846

Little Switzerland, North Carolina, nature's playground, the beauty spot of the Blue
Ridge.   No place, no publisher, 1931.   11 p.   [7847

Littleton Female College, Littleton, N. C.   Catalogue, 18 - Littleton, 18 - NcU
has 1901/02, 1904/05-1908/09, 1913/14-1915/16, 1917/18   [7848

Live at home, buy at home.   Charlotte, Clark Publishing Co., 1930.   38 p.   [7849

Lively, Robert A.   Fiction fights the Civil War; an unfinished chapter in the literary
history of the American people.   Chapel Hill, University of North Carolina Press
[1957]   230 p.   [7850

——The South in action; a sectional crusade against freight rate discrimination.
Chapel Hill, University of North Carolina Press, 1949.   (James Sprunt studies in
history and political science, v. 30)   98 p.   [7851

Livermore, Mary Hoyland.   Songs of the quiet hour.   Raleigh, Edwards and
Broughton Co., 1909.   50 p.   [7852

Lives of Andrew Jackson and General Marion, embracing anecdotes of their characters.   Boston, Lee and Shepard, 1881.   208 p.   [7853

Living preacher, v. 1-   January? 1885-   Durham, J. J. Lansdell, 1885-   NcU has
v. [1]   [7854

Living water for the thirsty.   Goldsboro, Board of Missions, n.d.   4 p.   [7855

[Livingstone, John A.]   Risden Tyler Bennett, born June 18, 1840, died July 21,
1913.   No place, no publisher [1933?]   21 p.   [7856

Livingstone College, Salisbury, N. C.   Catalogue, 18 - Salisbury, 18 - NcU
has [1895/96-1952/53]   [7857

Lloyd, Arthur Young.   The slavery controversy, 1831-1860.   Chapel Hill, University of North Carolina Press, 1939.   337 p.   [7858

Lloyd, Charles Allen.   We who speak English and our ignorance of our mother
tongue.   New York, Thomas Y. Crowell Co. [c.1938]   308 p.   [7859

Local designations of Confederate troops.   No place, no publisher, n.d.   152 p. [7860

[Locke, David Ross]   Ekkoes from Kentucky, by Petroleum V. Nasby [pseud.]
Boston, Lee, 1868.   324 p.   [7861

——"Swingin round the cirkle" by Petroleum V. Nasby [pseud.]   Boston, Lee and Shepard, 1867.   299 p.   [7862

Locke, John. A collection of several pieces of Mr. John Locke, never before printed, or not extant in his works. London, Printed by J. Betterham for R. Francklin, 1720.   362 p.   [7863

——The fundamental constitutions of Carolina, 1669.   [Boston, Directors of the Old South Work, 1906]   (Old South leaflets [General series, v. 7] no. 172)   24 p. [7864

Lockhart, Luther Bynum, Jr.   American lubricants, from the standpoint of the consumer.   Easton, Pa., Chemical Publishing Co., 1918.   236 p.   [7865

Lockhart, Walter Samuel.   A handbook of the law of evidence for North Carolina. Cincinnati, W. H. Anderson Co. [c.1915]   384 p.   [7866

—— ——2d ed., rev., extended and enl. with the assistance of Richmond Rucker. Cincinnati, W. H. Anderson Co. [c.1931]   540 p.   [7867

Lockmiller, David Alexander.   The consolidation of the University of North Carolina.   Raleigh, Chapel Hill, University of North Carolina, 1942.   160 p.   [7868

——History of the North Carolina State College of Agriculture and Engineering of the University of North Carolina, 1889-1939.   Raleigh [Edwards & Broughton, pr.] 1939.   310 p.   [7869

——Magoon in Cuba, a history of the second intervention, 1906-1909.   Chapel Hill, University of North Carolina Press, 1938.   252 p.   [7870

——Sir William Blackstone.   Chapel Hill, University of North Carolina Press, 1938. 308 p.   [7871

Lodge, Henry Cabot.   A short history of the English colonies in America.   New York, Harper & Brothers, 1881.   560 p.   [7872

Loftin, George Augustus.   Harp of life, its harmonies and discords.   Nashville, Tenn., J. R. Florida & Co. [1896]   463 p.   [7874

Logan, George Bryan.   Liberty in the modern world.   Chapel Hill, University of North Carolina Press, 1928.   142 p.   [7873

Logan, John Henry.   A history of the upper country of South Carolina, from the earliest periods to the close of the war of independence.   Vol. I.   Charleston, S. G. Courtenay & Co.; Columbia, P. B. Glass, 1859.   521 p.   A part of the manuscript for v. 2 was published in Historical collections of Joseph Habersham Chapter, D. A. R., v. 3, 1910.   [7875

Logan, John Randolph.   Sketches, historical and biographical of the Broad River and King's Mountain Baptist Associations, from 1800 to 1882, with an introductory sketch of the author, by R. L. Ryburn.   Shelby, Babington, Roberts & Co., 1887.   605 p.   [7876

Logan, Rayford Whittingham, ed.   The attitude of the southern white press toward Negro suffrage, 1932-1940.   Washington, Foundation Publisher, 1940.   115 p. [7877

——What the Negro wants.   Chapel Hill, University of North Carolina Press [1944] 352 p.   [7878

Lomax, Thomas H.   Silver anniversary of Rt. Rev. Thomas H. Lomax, D. D., episcopacy in African Methodist Episcopal Zion Church, Charlotte, North Carolina, March 8, 9, 10, 1904, Grace A. M. E. Zion Church.   Raleigh, Edwards and Broughton Co. [1904]   12 p.   [7879

London, Henry Armand.   An address on the Revolutionary history of Chatham County, N. C., at the centennial celebration at Pittsborough, N. C., on the fourth of July, 1876.   Sanford, Cole Printing Co. [1894]   27 p.   [7880

——Memorial address of the life and services of Bryan Grimes, a major-general in the provisional army of the Confederate States, delivered on Memorial Day, May 10th, 1886, at Raleigh, N. C.   Raleigh, E. M. Uzzell, pr., 1886.   22 p.   [7881

London, Isaac Spencer.   Pictures and sketches of my son, Isaac Spencer London, Jr. . . . and a bit of genealogical data.   [Rockingham, Author] 1947.   44 p.   [7882

[London, John B.]   The Chapel, its history and purpose, and an explanation of its design.   Charlotte, Charlotte Memorial Hospital [1940]   19 p.   [7883

London, Lawrence Foushee.   Bishop Joseph Blount Cheshire, his life and work. Chapel Hill, University of North Carolina Press, 1941.   140 p.   [7884

[London, M.]   A dialogue.   No place, no publisher [1874]   8 p.   [7885

Long, Augustus White, ed.   American patriotic prose, with notes and biographies. Boston, D. C. Heath & Co. [c.1917]   389 p.   [7886

——American poems, 1776-1900, with notes and biographies. New York, American Book Co. [c.1905] 368 p. [7887

Long, Augustus White. Son of Carolina. Durham, Duke University Press, 1939. 280 p. [7888

Long, Benjamin Franklin. The criminal guide for justices of the peace, mayors of towns and coroners. Statesville, Landmark, 1889. 20 p. [7889

Long, Daniel Albright. The divine law of giving. No place, no publisher, n.d. 8 p. [7890

——Jefferson Davis, an address delivered at Concord, N. C., June 3, 1921. Raleigh, Edwards and Broughton Co., 1923. 20 p. [7891

Long, Eugene Hudson. O. Henry, the man and his work. Philadelphia, University of Pennsylvania Press, 1949. 158 p. [7892

Long, Hollis Moody. Public secondary education for Negroes in North Carolina. New York, Teachers College, Columbia University, 1932. (Its Contributions to education, no. 529) 115 p. [7893

[**Long, Jacob Alston**] To the people of North Carolina. [Graham, 1906] [4] p. [7894

Long, John. Circular to the freemen of the tenth congressional district in North Carolina. Washington, no publisher, 1827. 8 p. [7895

——To the citizens of the tenth congressional district of North-Carolina, composed of the counties of Rowan, Davidson, Randolph, and Chatham. No place, April 29, 1823. [1] p. [7896

——To the freemen of the tenth congressional district in North Carolina. Washington, no publisher, 1828. 6 p. [7897

—— ——[1829] 8 p. [7898

Long, John Wesley. Early history of the North Carolina Medical Society. No place, no publisher [1917?] 18 p. [7899

——Remarks made at the meeting of the American College of Surgeons, Washington, D. C., November 16th, 1914. No place, no publisher [1914?] 3 p. [7900

Long, John Wesley, comp. Transactions of the Southern Surgical and Gynecological Association general index, v. I-XXV, 1887-1912. No place, no publisher, n.d. 615 p. [7901

Long, Joseph Kindred. Trends in the equalization of educational opportunity in North Carolina. Nashville, Tenn., George Peabody College for Teachers, 1936. (Its Abstract of Contribution to education no. 178) 19 p. [7902

Long, Mary Alves. High time to tell it. Durham, Duke University Press, 1950. 314 p. [7903

Long, Mary Rutherford (Harsh) General Griffith Rutherford and allied families. Milwaukee, Wis., Cuneo Press, 1942. 194 p. [7904

Long, Mildred. Triumph of faith. Durham, Religion & Health Press [c.1954] 29 p. [7905

Long, Stephen Harriman. Col. Long's report to the Estillville Convention. [Abingdon, Va., James Alexander, pr., 1831] 40 p. [7906

Long Creek Gold Mining Co. Long Creek Gold Mining Co., Gaston County, North Carolina, Henry W. Clark, president, George A. Parker, secretary, capital $500,000, 50,000 shares. [Boston, Cordner Bros. & Co., 1880?] 7 p. [7907

Lonn, Ella. The colonial agents of the southern colonies. Chapel Hill, University of North Carolina Press, 1945. 438 p. [7908

Lorant, Stefan, ed. The new world; the first pictures of America, made by John White and Jacques Le Moyne and engraved by Theodore De Bry, with contemporary narratives of the Huguenot settlement in Florida, 1562-1565, and the Virginia colony, 1585-1590. New York, Duell, Sloan & Pearce [1946] 292 p. [7909

Lord, William. Nature notes on the Blue Ridge Parkway. Waynesboro, Va., Blue Ridge Parkway Association [c.1953] [30] p. [7910

Lord Rivers, a novel. New Bern [Francois-Xavier Martin] 1802. Unpaged. [7911

Lore, Adelaide McKinnon. The Morrison family of the Rocky River settlement of North Carolina; history and genealogy by Adelaide and Eugenia Lore and Robert Hall Morrison. [Charlotte? 1950] 543 p. [7912

Lorenz, Lincoln. The admiral and the Empress: John Paul Jones and Catherine the Great. New York, Bookman Associates [1954] 194 p. [7913

——John Paul Jones, fighter for freedom and glory.   Annapolis, Md., United States Naval Institute, 1943.   846 p.   [7914
Loring, Emilie (Baker)   Rainbow at dusk.   Boston, Little, Brown and Co., 1942. 311 p.   [7915
Lossing, Benson John.   Biographical sketches of the signers of the Declaration of American Independence. New York, G. F. Cooledge & Brother [c.1848] 384 p. [7916
——The pictorial field-book of the Revolution.   New York, Harper & Brothers, 1851-52.   2 v.   [7917
Lott Carey Baptist Foreign Mission Convention.   Minutes, 189 - 189 - NcU has [1920-1931]   [7918
The Lotus, 19   -   Raleigh, Students of Peace Institute, 19   -   NcU has 1915, 1916, 1919, 1921, 1924   [7919
Lou, Herbert H.   Juvenile courts in the United States.   Chapel Hill, University of North Carolina Press, 1927.   277 p.   [7920
Louis Round Wilson; papers in recognition of a distinguished career in librarianship. Chicago, Ill., University of Chicago Press [1942]   339-773 p.   Published also as v. XII, no. 3, of The Library quarterly.   [7921
Louisa Avery Lenoir . . . Bessie Lenoir.   [Lenoir] Topic Press [1877?]   13 p.   [7922
Louisburg, N. C.   St. Paul's Church   [Letter to the friends of the Church]   [Louisburg? 1894]   2 p.   [7923
Louisburg College, Louisburg, N. C.   Book of views, the campus, equipment, buildings, recreation.   [Louisburg?] 1927.   [2] p.   25 illustrations.   [7924
—— ——1929.   26 p.   [7925
—— ——1930.   26 p.   [7926
——Bulletin, v. 1-   1924- Louisburg, 1924- NcU has v. [2-14]   [7927
——Catalogue, 18   -   Louisburg, 18   -   NcU has [1895/96-1903/04] 1905/06-1917/18, 1919/20-1921/22, 1923/24-1924/25, 1926/27-1936/37, 1938/39.   Published as Catalogue issue of its Bulletin, 1939/40-   [7928
——Louisburg College, North Carolina, 1802-1918.   Raleigh, Commercial Printing Co. for Louisburg College [1918?]   15 p.   [7929
——Student organization, constitution and by-laws.   [Raleigh, Commercial Printing Co. for Louisburg College] n.d.   12 p.   [7930
Louisiana.   Supreme Court.   The celebration of the centenary of the Supreme Court of Louisiana.   [New Orleans, 1913]   66 p.   [7931
The Louisiana amendment the same as ours. No place, no publisher [1900] [2] p. [7932
Louisville, Cincinnati, and Charleston Railroad.   Charter.   Columbia, S. C., A. S. Johnston, 1836.   23 p.   [7933
——Proceedings, 183 - Charleston, S. C., 183 - NcU has 1838.   [7934
Loula Fries Moore Foundation, Montreat, N. C.   An ode to Montreat.   Montreat, c.1943.   [15] p.   [7935
Lounsberry, Alice.   Southern wild flowers and trees, together with shrubs, vines, and various forms of growth found through the mountains, the middle district and the low country of the South.   New York, F. A. Stokes Co. [1901]   570 p. [7936
Louthan, Doniphan.   The poetry of John Donne, a study in explication.   New York, Bookman Associates [1951]   193 p.   [7937
Love, James Franklin, ed.   The southern Baptist pulpit.   Philadelphia, American Baptist Publication Society, 1895.   365 p.   [7938
Love, James Lee.   The good neighbor at Harvard University.   [Burlington, privately printed, 1944]   [2] p.   [7939
——The Lawrence Scientific School in Harvard University, 1847-1906.   Burlington, privately printed, 1944.   26 p.   [7940
——Reprint of a Harvard Report, by James Lee Love.   Burlington, privately printed, 1944.   18 p.   [7941
——'Tis sixty years since.   Chapel Hill, 1945.   48 p.   [7942
—— ——2d ed. 1945.   55 p.   [7943
Love, Jane Groome.   Earth-child.   Dallas, Tex., Kaleidoscope Publishers, 1931. 41 p.   [7944
Love, John D.   The copy-book primer; or, An easy way of learning to read and write. 2d ed.   Wilmington, Author, 1873.   48 p.   [7945

Love, Robert A. General Thomas Love of Western North Carolina and Western Tennessee and his brothers Robert and James. St. Petersburg, Fla., Author, n.d. 43 p. [7946

Lovejoy, Gordon Williams. Paths to maturity; findings of the North Carolina Youth Survey, 1938-1940. Sponsored by Cooperative Personnel Study, University of North Carolina [Raleigh] 1940. 310 p. [7947

Loveland, Charles Welling. The mountain men, and other poems. Shelby, 1950. 68 p. [7948

Lovell, Walter Raleigh. Lyrics of love and other poems. No place, no publisher, 1921. 46 p. [7949

Lowdermilk, Walter Clay. The untried approach to the Palestine problem. [New York, American Christian Palestine Committee, 1948?] 11 p. [7950

Lowe, James Roy. Roosevelt and other poems. Boston, Meador Publishing Co., 1935. 61 p. [7951

Lowe, John Adams. Report of a survey of the Charlotte Public Library to the Board of Trustees of the Charlotte Public Library, the City Council of the city of Charlotte, and the Board of County Commissioners of Mecklenburg County, North Carolina, April, 1944, by John Adams Lowe . . . and Tommie Dora Barker. Chicago, American Library Association, 1944. 107 numbered leaves. [7952

——Survey of the Charlotte Public Library: summary. [1944?] 21 leaves [7953

Lower Country Line Primitive Baptist Association. Minutes, 1907- Wilson, 1907- NcU has 1907-1955 [7954

Lower Creek Baptist Association, 1854?- 1854?- NcU has 1855 [7955

Lucas, Eric. Swamp fox brigade; adventures with General Francis Marion's guerrillas. New York, International Publishers [1945] 128 p. [7956

Lucas, John Paul, 1885-1940. Charlotte is urged as center to distribute farm products. [Charlotte, Chamber of Commerce, 1938?] [2] p. [7957

——The Charlotte market for Carolinas produced livestock, poultry, and ordinary milk. [Charlotte, Chamber of Commerce, 1938?] 11 p. [7958

Lucas, John Paul, Jr. The king of Scuffletoun, a Croatan romance, by John Paul Lucas, Jr., and Bailey T. Groome. Richmond, Va., Garrett and Massie, Inc. [c.1940] 238 p. [7959

Lucas and Abraham H. Boylan's North-Carolina almanack see Boylan's North-Carolina almanack

Lumber River Baptist Association. Minutes, 18 - 18 - NcU has 1880 [7960

Lumberton, N. C. Chamber of Commerce and Agriculture. A look at Lumberton, North Carolina. Lumberton [1941?] [8] p. [7961

Lumberton, N. C. Chamber of Commerce and Industry. Lumberton looks to aviation. Lumberton [1945] 15 p. [7962

——Lumberton, North Carolina "Queen City of the rich and beautiful Lumber River valley". [Lumberton, 1945] Folder. [7963

——The story of Robeson County, North Carolina. Lumberton [1946?] [8] p. [7964

Lumberton, N. C. First Baptist Church. The First Baptist Church, Lumberton, North Carolina; one hundred years of Christian witnessing, 1855-1955. [Lumberton, 1955] 92 p. [7965

Lundholm, Helge. The aesthetic sentiment; a criticism and an original excursion. Cambridge, Mass., Sci-Art Publishers [c.1941] 223 p. [7966

——The manic-depressive psychosis. Durham, Duke University Press, 1931. (Duke University psychological monographs [no. 1]) 86 p. [7967

——Schizophrenia. Durham, Duke University Press, 1932. (Duke University psychological monographs [no. 2]) 117 p. [7968

Lunsford, Bascom Lamar. It's fun to square dance, Southern Applachian calls and figures, by Bascom Lamar Lunsford and George Myers Stephens. 2d printing. [Asheville, Stephens Press, c.1942] [16] p. [7969

——Thirty and one folksongs (from the southern mountains) compiled and arranged by Bascom Lamar Lunsford and Lamar Stringfield. New York, Carl Fischer [c.1929] 56 p. [7970

Lutheran Synod. North Carolina see United Evangelical Lutheran Synod of North Carolina

Lutterloh, C. Catalogue of select green-house and hardy plants, fruit and ornamental trees, evergreens, shrubs, roses, grape-vines, raspberries, strawberries, bulbs, &c., cultivated and for sale. 4th ed. Fayetteville, Edward J. Hale, pr., 1857. 16 p. [7971

Lutz, Grace Livingston Hill see **Hill, Grace Livingston**

Lyceum, v. 1- June, 1890- Asheville, Tilman R. Gaines, 1890- NcU has v. [1-2] [7972

Lyde, Augustus Foster. Buds of spring; poetical remains, with addenda. Boston, Perkins and Marvin, 1838. 150 p. [7973

Lyell, Sir Charles, 1st bart. Lyell's travels in North America in the years 1841-2; abridged and ed. by John P. Cushing. New York, C. E. Merrill Co. [c.1909] 172 p. [7974

——A second visit to the United States of North America. New York, Harper & Brothers, 1849. 2 v. [7975

——Travels in North America, in the years 1841-2; with geological observations on the United States, Canada, and Nova Scotia. New York, Wiley and Putnam, 1845. 2 v. [7976

Lyle, Guy Redvers. The administration of the college library. New York, H. W. Wilson Co., 1944. 601 p. [7977

——Classified list of periodicals for the college library, by Guy R. Lyle . . . and Virginia M. Trumper. 2d ed., rev. and enl. Boston, F. W. Faxon Co., 1938. 96 p. [7978

Lyle, Samuel Harley. Brain shapes. Macon, Ga., Randall Printing Co., 1913. 31 p.

——By-ways. Franklin, S. H. Lyle, Jr., 1912. 28 p. [7979

——Leaves of life. Athens, Ga., McGregor Co., 1910. 90 p. [7980

——Ways of men. Franklin, S. H. Lyle, Jr., 1911. 74 p. [7981

Lyman, Charles E. A few verses. [Asheville, Inland Press, c.1915] 18 p. [7982

Lyman, Theodore Benedict. Address to the annual convention of the Diocese of North Carolina, 1892. Raleigh, Edwards and Broughton Co., 1892. 36 p. [7983

——Address to the sixth-fourth annual convention of the Diocese of North Carolina, May, 1880. Raleigh, Uzzell & Wiley, pr., n.d. 29 p. [7984

——Address to the sixty-fifth annual convention of the Diocese of North Carolina, May 19, 1881. No place, no publisher, n.d. 34 p. [7985

——Address to the sixty-sixth annual convention of the Diocese of North Carolina, May, 1882. No place, no publisher, n.d. 33 p. [7986

——Address to the sixty-eighth annual convention of the Diocese of North Carolina, May 15, 1884. No place, no publisher [1884?] 27 p. [7987

——Address to the sixty-ninth annual convention of the Diocese of North Carolina, May 28th, 1885. No place, no publisher, n.d. 36 p. [7988

——Address to the seventieth annual convention of the Diocese of North Carolina, May 20th, 1886. Raleigh, Edwards and Broughton Co., 1886. 36 p. [7989

——Address to the seventy-first annual convention of the Diocese of North Carolina, May 12th, 1887. Raleigh, Edwards and Broughton Co., 1887. 34 p. [7990

——The apostolic witness; the sermon preached in the Church of the Epiphany, Washington, D. C., on Thursday, January 8th, 1885, at the consecration of the Rev. William Paret, D. D., as Bishop of Maryland. New York, James Pott & Co., 1885. 30 p. [7991

——Christ through the Church the light of the world; the sermon preached at the consecration of the Church of the Holy Spirit, Nice, France, Thursday, Dec. 13th, 1888. London, Spottiswoode & Co., 1888. 15 p. [7992

——Continuity and perpetuity of the Episcopal office; the sermon delivered in St. James Church, Wilmington, April 17, 1884, at the consecration of Rev. Alfred Augustin Watson, D. D., as bishop of East Carolina. No place, Published by request of the bishops and other clergy [1884?] 21 p. [7993

[Lyman, Theodore Benedict] Letter from the bishop of North Carolina. [New York? 1884] [2] p. [7994

Lyman, Theodore Benedict. The manifestation of the truth; a sermon delivered before the Associate Alumni of the General Theological Seminary of the Protestant Episcopal Church, in St. Peter's Church, New York, June 28th, 1859. New York, Daniel Dana, 1859. 16 p. [7995

——The old paths; two sermons delivered on the 22d and 23d Sundays after Trinity,

1843, in St. John's Church, Hagerstown, Md. Hagerstown, William Stewart, 1843. 47 p. [7996

——Sermon preached on the occasion of the opening services in St. John's Church, Hagerstown, Md., November the 11th, 1875. Hagerstown, Md., Mail Steam Job Printing Office [1875?] 8 p. [7997

Lynch, James D. Columbia saluting the nations. No place, no publisher, n.d. 6 p. [7998

Lynchburg and Durham Railroad. Annual meeting of the stockholders, 1890- Lynchburg, J. P. Bell, pr., 1890- NcU has 1890. [7999

——[The Lynchburg and Durham Railroad Company] [Lynchburg? 1887?] 24 p. Title page wanting in NcU copy. [8000

Lynde, Francis. The master of Appleby; a novel tale concerning itself in part with the great struggle in the two Carolinas. New York, Grosset & Dunlap [c.1902] 580 p. [8001

Lyon, Ralph Muse. The basis for constructing curricular materials in adult educa- tion for Carolina cotton mill workers. New York, Teachers College, Columbia University, 1937. 129 p. (Teachers College, Columbia University. Contribu- tions to education, no. 678) 129 p. [8002

Lyon, Winfield Hancock, ed. Commentaries on equity jurisprudence as administer- ed in England and America, by Joseph Story. 14th ed., by W. H. Lyon, Jr. Boston, Little, Brown and Co., 1918. 3 v. [8003

Lyons, John Coriden, ed. Eight French classic plays, by Corneille, Racine, and Molière, edited by J. C. Lyons . . . and Colbert Searles. New York, H. Holt and Co. [c.1932] 609 p. [8004

——Reading French [by] J. C. Lyons and W. L. Wiley. New York, H. Holt and Co. [1942] 205 p. [8005

Mabry, George S. Sketch of Alamance County, N. C., for the colored exhibit to the Cotton States and International Exposition, Atlanta, Ga. No place, no publisher [1895?] 4 p. [8006

Mabry, William Alexander. The Negro in North Carolina politics since Reconstruc- tion. Durham, Duke University Press, 1940. (Historical papers of the Trinity College Historical Society, ser. XXIII) 87 p. [8007

McAfee, Lee Mangum. Address delivered before the Theta Delta Chi Society at the annual convention held in Washington City, May 25th, 1858. Greensboro, Cole and Albright at the Times Office, 1858. 31 p. [8008

McAlister, Alexander Worth. The eternal verities of golf; a study in philosophy and the ancient game. [Greensboro, J. J. Stone & Co., pr., c.1911] [36] p. [8009

——The 1915 legislature of North Carolina will pass on the matter of fire insurance rates and practices; a solution of the problem. [Greensboro, Joseph J. Stone, pr., 1914] 15 p. [8010

McAllister, David Smith. Genealogical record of the descendants of Col. Alexander McAllister, of Cumberland County, N. C.; also of Mary and Isabella McAllister. Richmond, Va., Whittet & Shepperson, 1900. 244 p. [8011

McAllister, Quentin Oliver. Business executives and the humanities. Chapel Hill, University of North Carolina Press, 1951. (Southern Humanities Conference. Bulletin no. 3) 114 p. [8012

McAtee, Waldo Lee. Chips from an old block. [Chapel Hill, privately printed, 1952] [8] p. [8013

——Elliott Coues as represented in The Nation, 1873-1900. [Chapel Hill, privately printed, 1955] 12 p. [8014

——For 1953. [Chapel Hill, Author, 1953] [7] p. [8015

Macauley, Robie. The disguises of love. New York, Random House [1952] 282 p. [8016

McBain, Howard Lee. How we are governed in North Carolina and the nation, by Howard Lee McBain and Nathan Wilson Walker. New York, Howard Lee McBain, 1916. 272 p. [8017

McBee, May Wilson, comp. Anson County, North Carolina, abstracts of early records. [Greenwood, The Compiler, c.1950] 180 p. [8018

McBee, Silas. An eirenic itinerary; impressions of our tour, with addresses and papers on the unity of Christian churches. New York, Longmans, Green, and Co., 1911. 225 p.   [8019

McBride, Robert Martin. Portrait of an American loyalist, James Cotton of Anson County, North Carolina. Nashville, 1954. 64 p.   [8020

McCain, Paul M. The county court in North Carolina before 1750. Durham, Duke University, 1954. (Historical papers of the Trinity College Historical Society, ser. 31) 163 p.   [8021

McCall, Adeline (Denham) Getting ready for the children's concert. [Chapel Hill] Children's Concert Division, North Carolina Symphony Orchestra [1956] 18 p.   [8022

——Symphony stories, 194 - [Chapel Hill] North Carolina Symphony Orchestra, 194 - NcU has [194 - Spring, 1951] Spring, 1952, two issues; Spring, 1955, two issues; Spring, 1956, 2 issues.   [8023

McCall, Ettie (Tidwell) McCall-Tidwell and allied families. Atlanta, Ga., Author, 1931. 663 p.   [8024

McCall, S. M. Address upon the evils of prohibition to the patriotic voters of Caldwell County, N. C., during the campaign between patriotism and fanaticism prior to May 26, 1908. No place, no publisher, n.d. 8 p.   [8025

McCall, Sidney, pseud. see **Fenollosa, Mary (McNeil)**

McCall, William Anderson. Cherokees and pioneers. Asheville, Stephens Press, pr. [1952] 106 p.   [8026

——The McCall speller, by William A. McCall and J. David Houser. Chicago, Laidlaw Brothers [c.1925] 2 v.   [8027

McCallum, C. J. Historical sketch of Ashpole Presbyterian Church. No place, no publisher [1936] 20 p.   [8028

McCants, Elliott Crayton. In the red hills; a story of the Carolina country. New York, Doubleday, Page & Co., 1904. 340 p.   [8029

——Ninety Six, a novel. New York, Thomas Y. Crowell Co. [c.1930] 325 p. [8030

MacCarthy, Edward Thomas. Incidents in the life of a mining engineer. London, G. Routledge and Sons, Ltd. [1918] 384 p.   [8031

McCarthy, Gerald, joint author, see **Wood, Thomas F.**

McClamroch, James Gwaltney Westwarren. A discussion of justice of the peace courts in North Carolina; address before the North Carolina Bar Association, Pinehurst, May 3, 1930. Raleigh, Edwards & Broughton Co., 1930. 19 p. [8032

——Greensboro's water and stream pollution problem, delivered over television station WFMY . . . 10 November 1953. [Greensboro, 1953] 5 p.   [8033

[**McClamroch, James Gwaltney Westwarren**] Line of descent from James G. W. MacClamroch back to the Emperor Charlemagne. [Greensboro, 1956] 6 p. [8033a

McClane, William. Letter on the supply of bituminous coal from North Carolina. New York, George F. Nesbitt & Co., 1854. 12 p.   [8034

MacClenny, Wilbur E. Life of Rev. James O'Kelly, and the early history of the Christian Church in the South. Raleigh, Edwards & Broughton Printing Co., 1910. 253 p.   [8035

McClure, Alexander Kelly. The South, its industrial, financial, and political condition. Philadelphia, J. B. Lippincott Co., 1886. 257 p.   [8036

McClure, Clarence Henry. Opposition in Missouri to Thomas Hart Benton. Nashville, Tenn., George Peabody College for Teachers, 1927. 238 p.   [8037

McClure, Marjorie (Barkley) John Dean's journey. New York, Minton, Balch & Co., 1932. 323 p.   [8038

McClure, Robert Edwin. Presbyterianism, Leaksville and vicinity, 1832-1872; a brief sketch. [Leaksville? 1924?] 8 p.   [8039

[**McConkey, Rebecca**] The hero of Cowpens; a centennial sketch. New York, A. S. Barnes & Co. [c.1881] 295 p.   [8040

McConnaughey, James. Village chronicle. New York, Farrar & Rinehart, Inc. [c.1936] 357 p.   [8041

McConnell, James Rogers. Flying for France with the American escadrille at Verdun. Garden City, N. Y., Doubleday, Page & Co., 1917. 157 p.   [8042

McConnell, Joseph Moore, ed. Southern orators; speeches and orations. New York, Macmillan Co., 1910. 351 p. [8042a

McConnell, Roland Calhoun. The Negro in North Carolina since Reconstruction. New York, New York University, 1949. 25 p. Abridgement of thesis, New York University. [8043

McCorkle, George W. Rhymes from the Delta. 2d ed., rev. High Point, Author [1948] 159 p. [8044

McCorkle, Lutie Andrews. Old time stories of the Old North State. Boston, D. C. Heath & Co. [c.1903] 159 p. [8045

—— ——Boston, D. C. Heath & Co. [c.1921] 163 p. [8046

McCorkle, Samuel Eusebius. A charity sermon. Halifax, Abraham Hodge, 1795. 64 p. [8047

——A discourse on the doctrine and duty of keeping the Sabbath. Salisbury, John M. Slump at Michael Brown's English and German Printing-Office, 1798. 36 p. [8048

——Four discourses on the general first principles of Deism and Revelation contrasted. Salisbury, Francis Coupee, 1797. 56 p. [8049

—— ——1798. 42 p. [8050

——A sermon on the comparative happiness and duty of the United States of America contrasted with other nations, particularly the Israelites. Halifax, Abraham Hodge, 1795. 43 p. [8051

——Three discourses on the terms of Christian communion . . . Discourse I. Salisbury, Francis Coupee and John M. Slump, 1798. 49 p. [8052

——The work of God for the French Republic, and then, her reformation or ruin; or, The novel and useful experiment of national Deism to us and all future ages. Salisbury, Francis Coupee, 1798. 45 p. [8053

McCorkle, William P. Anti-Christian sociology as taught in the Journal of social forces, presenting a question for North Carolina Christians. Burlington, Author, [1925?] 32 p. [8054

—— ——Rev. ed. [1925?] 32 p. [8055

——Christian Science; or, The false Christ of 1866. Richmond, Va., Presbyterian Committee of Publication [1899] 321 p. [8056

McCormac, Eugene Irving. James Knox Polk, a political biography. Berkeley, Calif., University of California Press, 1922. 746 p. [8057

McCormick, John Gilchrist. Personnel of the convention of 1861, by John Gilchrist McCormick. Legislation of the convention of 1861, by Kemp Plummer Battle. Chapel Hill [University Press] 1900. (James Sprunt historical monographs, no. 1) 144 p. [8058

McCoy, George William. Archibald Henderson, artist and scientist. No place, no publisher, 1930. 24 p. [8059

——Archibald Henderson, pioneer of the new South. No place, no publisher [1928?] 15 p. [8060

——A bibliography for the Great Smoky Mountains. [Asheville, Author, 1932] 31 p. [8060a

——A brief history of the Great Smoky Mountains National Park movement in North Carolina. Asheville, Inland Press, 1940. 42 p. [8061

——The First Presbyterian Church, Asheville, N. C., 1794-1951. Asheville, 1951. 67 p. [8062

——Guide to the Great Smoky Mountains National Park, by George W. McCoy and George Masa. Asheville, Inland Press, c.1933. 142 p. [8063

——Official data on Western North Carolina's 223 highest mountain peaks. Asheville, Asheville Citizen-Times Co., 1946. 20 p. [8064

——Western North Carolina's 223 highest mountain peaks. 2d printing. 1949. 20 p. [8065

McCracken, Duane. Strike injunctions in the new South. Chapel Hill, University of North Carolina Press, 1931. 290 p. [8066

McCrady, Edward. The history of South Carolina under the proprietary government, 1670-1719. New York, Macmillan Co., 1897. 762 p. [8067

——The history of South Carolina in the Revolution, 1775-1780. New York, Macmillan Co., 1901. 899 p. [8068

—— ——1780-1783. 1902. 787 p. [8069

McCrary, John Raymond. Boone memorial booklet. High Point, Enterprise, n.d. 15 p.   [8070

——Thoughts about things I love. Cleveland, O., Central Publishing House [c.1941] 70 p.   [8071

[**McCrary, Madeline P.**] Services provided for the blind of North Carolina by the N. C. State Commission for the Blind, the N. C. State Association for the Blind, the more than 300 Lions Clubs in North Carolina [Raleigh, North Carolina State Association for the Blind, 1953?] 10 p.   [8072

McCrimmon, Donald. Ecclesiastical proceedings in the case of Mr. Donald Mc-Crimmon, a ruling elder of the Presbyterian Church who was suspended from sealing ordinances, and from the exercise of his office, by the Session of Ottery's Church, for marrying the sister of his deceased wife . . . to which is added A speech . . . by Colin McIver. Fayetteville, Author, 1827. 42 p.   [8073

McCubbins, Benjamin David. The Court of Justice of the Peace. Atlanta, Harrison Co. [c.1940] 183 p.   [8074

McCullen, A. Captured by demons! Who will go to the rescue? [Sanford, Cole Printing Co.] n.d. 12 p.   [8075

McCullers, Carson (Smith) The heart is a lonely hunter. Boston, Houghton Mifflin Co., 1940. 356 p.   [8076

——Reflections in a golden eye. [Boston] Houghton Mifflin Co., 1941. 182 p. [8077

[**McCulloch, Maude**] Junaluska. Atlanta, Ga., Byrd Printing Co., n.d. 32 p. [8078

McCullock Copper and Gold Mining Co. Report, July, 1853. New York, McSpedon & Baker, pr., 1853. 23 p.   [8079

[**McCulloh, Henry**] A miscellaneous essay concerning the courses pursued by Great Britain in the affairs of her colonies, with some observations on the great importance of our settlements in America, and the trade thereof. London, Printed for R. Baldwin, 1755. 134 p.   [8080

——Miscellaneous representations relative to our concerns in America, submitted to the Earl of Bute; now first printed from the original ms. with biographical and historical introduction by W. A. Shaw. London, George Harding, n.d. 16, 22 p.   [8081

——The wisdom and policy of the French in the construction of their great offices so as best to answer the purposes of extending their trade and commerce and enlarging their foreign settlements, with some observations in relation to the disputes now subsisting between the English and French colonies in America. London, Printed for R. Baldwin, 1755. 133 p.   [8082

McCurdy, Harold Grier. The personality of Shakespeare; a venture in psychological method. New Haven, Yale University Press, 1953. 243 p.   [8083

——A straw flute. Raleigh, Meredith College, 1946. [35] p.   [8084

McCurry, Betsy, pseud. see Moore, Bertha B.

McCurry, Mrs. Mack D. see Moore, Bertha B.

McCutchan, John Wilson, comp. '31 plus twenty-five; a short review of those who matriculated at Davidson College in 1927 and who subsequently became members of the Class of 1931. Davidson, Davidson College, 1956. 71 p.   [8085

McDaniel, J. Gaskill. This town of mine; a collection of original radio poems [New Bern, Owen G. Dunn Co., pr., 1943?] [24] p.   [8086

——————2d ed. [New Bern, Richardson Printing Co., c.1944] [40] p.   [8087

McDaniel, James. The chief excellence of female character; a sermon preached before the graduating class of Oxford Female College, N. C., May 30th, 1860. Fayetteville, A. T. Banks, 1860. 16 p.   [8088

——A sermon preached to the students of the United Baptist Institute, at Taylorsville, N. C., June 4th, 1857, at the request of the Ciceronian Society of the Institute. Fayetteville, Observer Office, 1857. 22 p.   [8089

McDaniel, R. Examination of Rev. L. Rosser on open communion. Raleigh, Biblical Recorder Office, 1859. 110 p.   [8090

MacDavis, E. An additional word about the dwellers in the remote mountain coves of the South. No place, no publisher, n.d. 5 p.   [8091

McDermott, Malcolm Mallette. The lawyer's place in an upset world . . . condensation of a memorable address before North Carolina Bar Association, October

22, 1943. [New York, Committee for Constitutional Government, Inc.] n.d.
4 p.   [8092
——National socialism or the American way; which for US?   Greensboro, Greens-
boro Chamber of Commerce [1943?]   15 p.   [8093
McDiarmid, Katherine.   Special libraries, North Carolina.   Raleigh, Textiles Li-
brary, North Carolina State College [1951]   [15] p.   [8094
MacDonald, Allan Reginald, ed.   The truth about Flora MacDonald.   Inverness,
Scotland, The Northern Chronicle Office, 1938.   126 p.   [8095
Macdonald, James Alexander.   Flora Macdonald; a history and a message.   [Wash-
ington, D. C., James William Bryan Press, c.1916]   32 p.   [8096
MacDonald, Lois.   Southern mill hills; a study of social and economic forces in
certain mill villages.   New York, Alex. L. Hillman, 1928.   151 p.   [8097
MacDonald, William.   Jacksonian democracy, 1829-1837.   New York, Harper and
Brothers, 1906.   (The American nation . . . ed. by A. B. Hart, v. 15) 345 p. [8098
[McDonald for Governor Club]   For Governor, Ralph McDonald.   [Raleigh? 1944]
11 p.   [8099
McDougald, Daniel A., defendant.   The trial of D. A. McDougald for the murder of
Simeon Conoley, at Fayetteville, N. C., by Z. W. Whitehead and Hamilton Mc-
Millan.   [Fayetteville? 1891?]   188 p.   [8100
McDougall, Kenneth Dougal.   Sessile marine invertebrates of Beaufort, North Caro-
lina.   [Durham, Duke University, 1943]   (Duke University.   Marine Station.
Bulletin no. 1)   p. [321]-374   [8101
McDougall, William.   Character and the conduct of life; practical psychology for
everyman.   New York, G. P. Putnam's Sons, 1927.   394 p.   [8102
——The energies of men; a study of the fundamentals of dynamic psychology.   New
York, C. Scribner's Sons, 1933.   395 p.   [8103
——The frontiers of psychology.   London, Nisbet [1934]   235 p.   [8104
——Modern materialism and emergent evolution.   London, Methuen & Co., Ltd.
[1929]   295 p.   [8105
——Religion and the sciences of life, with other essays on allied topics.   London,
Methuen & Co., Ltd. [1934]   263 p.   [8106
——What to read on psychology.   Leeds, Public Libraries, 1928.   20 p. [8107
——World chaos; the responsibility of science.   New York, Covici, Friede [c.1932]
117 p.   [8108
McDowell, A.   Systematic benevolence.   Raleigh, Baptist S. S. & Publication
Board, n.d.   14 p.   [8109
McDowell, Franklin Brevard.   The Battle of King's Mountain, October 7, 1780;
address delivered before the Society of the Cincinnati in the state of North Caro-
lina, at Charlotte, April 19, 1907.   Raleigh, Commercial Printing Co., 1907.
11 p.   [8110
——The broad axe and the forge; or, A narrative of Unity Church neighborhood,
from colonial times until the close of the Civil War.   Charlotte, Observer Pub-
lishing House, 1897.   21 p.   [8111
——A Scotch-Irish neighborhood, before the Mecklenburg Historical Society, at
Charlotte, N. C., May 23d, 1895.   Charlotte, Observer Publishing House, 1895.
15 p.   [8112
McDowell, John Hugh.   History of the McDowells and connections.   Memphis,
C. B. Johnston & Co., 1918.   680 p.   [8113
McDowell, Mrs. Robert E., comp.   A list of those buried in historic Steele Creek
burying grounds, Mecklenburg County, Charlotte, North Carolina, 1760-1953.
[Charlotte, Steele Creek Church] 1953.   79 p.   [8114
MacDuffie, Laurette.   The stone in the rain.   Garden City, N. Y., Doubleday &
Co., Inc., 1946.   246 p.   [8115
McEachern, Daniel Purcell, ed.   All about Robeson County.   Lumberton, Board
of County Commissioners, 1884.   20 p.   [8116
McElroy, Isaac Stuart.   Some pioneer Presbyterian preachers of the Piedmont North
Carolina.   [Gastonia, Loftin and Co.] n.d.   50 p.   [8117
MacElyea, Annabella Bunting (MacCallum)   The MacQueens of Queensdale . . .
with an introduction containing a history of the origin of the Clan MacQueen by
Hon. A. W. McLean.   [Charlotte, Observer Printing House, 1916]   261 p. [8118

MacFadyen, Virginia. At the sign of the sun, a novel. New York, Albert & Charles Boni, 1925. 248 p.   [8119
——Bittern Point. New York, Albert & Charles Boni, 1926. 214 p.   [8120
——Windows facing west. New York, Albert & Charles Boni, 1924. 288 p. [8121

McFarland, Alice, comp. Songs of remembrance: an anthology. [Nashville? Parthenon Press ? 1935] 67 p.   [8122

McFarland, Wilbur Galloway. Turner Allen's forebears, a sketch. [Durham] 1946. 102 p.   [8123

McGeachy, Archibald A. Fishers of men. [Atlanta, Executive Committee of Home Missions, Presbyterian Church in the United States] n.d. [8] p.   [8124

McGeachy, Neill Roderick. A history of the Sugaw Creek Presbyterian Church, Mecklenburg Presbytery, Charlotte, North Carolina. Rock Hill, S. C., Record Printing Co., 1954. 195 p.   [8125

McGee, Julian Murrill. Modern health guide. Greensboro, Murrill Press, c.1939. 243 p.   [8126

McGehee, Lucius Polk. Due process of law under the federal Constitution. Northport, Long Island, N. Y., Edward Thompson Co., 1906. 451 p.   [8127

McGehee, Montford. Life and character of William A. Graham; a memorial oration delivered before the bench and bar of the Supreme Court, in the hall of the House of Representatives, in Raleigh, June 8, 1876. Raleigh, News Job Office, 1877. 57 p.   [8128

McGinnis, Howard Justus. The state teachers college president. Nashville, Tenn., George Peabody College for Teachers, 1932. (Its Contribution to education, no. 104) 187 p.   [8129

McGirt, James Ephraim. Avenging the Maine, A drunken A. B., and other poems. Raleigh, Edwards & Broughton, pr., 1899. 86 p.   [8130
—— ——1900. 109 p.   [8131
—— ——1901. 119 p.   [8132
——For your sweet sake, poems. Philadelphia, John C. Winston Co. [c.1906] 79 p.   [8133

M'Gready, James. Posthumous of the Reverend and pious James M'Gready, late minister of the Gospel, in Henderson, Kentucky, edited by the Rev. James Smith. Louisville, Ky., W. W. Worsley, 1831-1833. 2 v.   [8134

MacGregor, Alexander. The life of Flora Macdonald. Stirling, MacKay, 1901. 152 p.   [8135

McHugh, Gelolo. Developing your child's personality. New York, D. Appleton-Century Co. [1947] 234 p.   [8136
——Training for parenthood. Durham, Family Life Publications [1950, c.1947] 234 p.   [8137

McIlvaine, Charles Pettit. The apostolical commission; the sermon at the consecration of the Rt. Rev. Leonidas Polk, D. D., missionary bishop for Arkansas, in Christ Church, Cincinnati, December 9, 1838. Gambier, O., G. W. Myers, 1838. 43 p.   [8138

McIlwain, William. Legends of Baptist Hollow, tales of Wake Forest College, by Bill McIlwain and Walt Friedenberg. Wake Forest, Delta Publishing Co., 1949. 67 p.   [8139

McIlwain, William E. Historical sketch of the Presbytery of Mecklenburg, from its orgainization, October 16th, 1869, to October 1st, 1884. Charlotte, Hirst Printing Co., 1884. 91 p.   [8140
——Twenty-three years of home mission work in the Presbytery of Mecklenburg, Synod of North Carolina. Birmingham, Dispatch, 1893. 35 p.   [8141

McIlwaine, Shields. The southern poor-white from Lubberland to Tobacco Road. Norman, University of Oklahoma Press, 1939. 274 p.   [8142

McIntosh, Atwell Campbell. North Carolina practice and procedure in civil cases. St. Paul, West Publishing Co., 1929. 1228 p.   [8143
——Selected cases on the law of contracts, with annotations. Raleigh, Edwards & Broughton Printing Co., 1908. 615 p.   [8144
—— ——2d ed. Cincinnati, W. H. Anderson Co., 1915. 693 p.   [8145

McIntosh, Atwell Campbell, joint ed. see Mordecai, Samuel Fox, ed.

McIntosh, Charles Eugene. A brief digest of the general report of the North Carolina Youth Survey, "Paths to maturity". [Raleigh, National Youth Survey, 1940?] 30, 10 p. [8146]

McIntosh, William Alexander. Public health administration in North Carolina, by William A. McIntosh and John F. Kendrick. [Raleigh] 1940. 190 p. [8147]

[**McIntyre, Peter**] James Menzies Sprunt, born at Perth, Scotland, January 14th, 1818, died at Kenansville, N. C., Dec. 6th, 1884. Wilmington, DeRosset & Meares, 1885. 13 p. [8148]

McIver, Charles Duncan. Discussions of our school problems by educational statesmen, Dr. Walter B. Hill, Dr. Charles D. McIver. Atlanta, Ga., State Educational Campaign Committee, n.d. 18 p. [8149]

McIver, Colin. An humble attempt to illustrate the character and obligations of a minister of the gospel of Christ, in a sermon preached . . . the 30th day of July, 1819, in the Presbyterian Church of Fayetteville, North-Carolina, at the ordination of the Rev'd William D. Snodgrass. Fayetteville, Carney & Dismukes, 1820. 32 p. [8150]

McIver, Colin, ed. The Rev. Matthew Henry's aphorisms on the ministry, the church, and other kindred subjects. Princeton, N. J., George Thompson, 1847. 197 p. [8151]

——The southern preacher: a collection of sermons from the manuscripts of several eminent ministers of the gospel residing in the southern states. Philadelphia, Published by the Editor and Proprietor, William Fry, pr., 1824. 419 p. [8152]

McIver, Colin. A speech prepared for delivery before the Synod of North Carolina, October, 1839, on the reference to that Synod by the Presbytery of Fayetteville of the case of the Rev. Simeon Colton. Cheraw, Printed by Wm. Potter, 1840. 41 p. [8153]

McIver, Helen H. Genealogy of the McIver family of North Carolina. [Fort Slocum, N. Y., Compiler] 1922. 168 p. [8154]

—— ——Richmond, Va., Whittet & Shepperson, 1943. 53 p. Called Part I. [8155]

Mack, Edward. A laboratory manual of elementary physical chemistry, by Edward Mack, Jr. . . . and Wesley G. France. New York, D. Van Nostrand Co., Inc., 1928. 195 p. [8156]

Mack, Joseph Bingham. A historical sketch of Rocky River Church from 1775 to 1875, to which is appended a fore-word and an afterword by Morrison Caldwell. [Concord, Concord Job Printery] 1913. 39 p. [8157]

Mackay, Alexander. The western world; or, Travels in the United States in 1846-47. 3d ed. London, R. Bentley, 1850. 3 v. [8158]

McKay, Elizabeth Whitfield. Fruits in season. New York, New Voices Publishing Co. [1952] 57 p. [8159]

McKay, James Iver. Democratic Congressional address. [Tarboro?] Free Press [1838] 10 p. [8160]

McKay, John Archibald. "A plain talk by a plain man" to producers and taxpayers of North Carolina and everywhere. Dunn, Author [1930] 11 p. [8161]

——The "stop sign" at the parting of the ways; the tragedy of the untrained child. Dunn, Author [c.1930] 64 p. [8162]

——The wheels of Juggernaut and the crushing effects of his worship, showing the well-beaten trail from the temples of this god to the gates of our prisons. [Raleigh, Mitchell Printing Co. c.1932] 150 p. [8163]

McKay, Neill. A centenary sermon delivered before the Presbytery of Fayetteville at the Bluff Church, the 18th day of October, 1858. Fayetteville, Presbyterian Office, 1858. 19 p. [8164]

McKee, William John. New schools for young India; a survey of educational, economic and social conditions in India with special reference to more effective education. Chapel Hill, University of North Carolina Press, 1930. 435 p. [8165]

McKeithan, W. A. Leland. The authority of the grand jury. [Raleigh, Conference of Superior Court Judges of North Carolina, 1956] 14 p. [8166]

McKellar, Kenneth Douglas. Tennessee senators as seen by one of their successors. Kingsport, Tenn., Southern Publishers, Inc., 1942. 625 p. [8167]

McKelway, Alexander Jeffrey.   Child labor in the Carolinas; account of investigations made in the cotton mills of North and South Carolina, by Rev. A. E. Sedden, A. H. Ulm, and Lewis W. Hine, under the direction of the southern office of the National Child Labor Committee.   [New York? 1909]   [20] p.   [8168

——Christianity and war. Pinehurst, Pinehurst Community Church, 1934. 9 p. [8169

——Do not grind the seed corn, the child's appeal to the state for protection against the evils of child labor. No place, no publisher, n.d.   15 p.   [8170

McKenna, Helen.   Young Hickory, a dramatization of Andrew Jackson's boyhood. Charleston, W. Va., Children's Theatre Press, c.1940.   48 p.   [8171

[McKenney, Thomas Lorraine]   Essays on the spirit of Jacksonism as exemplified in its deadly hostility to the Bank of the United States and in the odious calumnies employed for its destruction, by Aristides. Philadelphia, Jesper Harding, 1835. 151 p.   [8172

McKenney, Thomas Lorraine.   Memoirs, official and personal; with sketches of travels among northern a d r uthern Indians. New York, Paine and Burgess, 1846.   2 v. in 1.   [8173

Mackenzie, Lieut. Roderick   Strictures on Lt.-Col. Tarleton's History "of the campaigns of 1780 and 1781, in the southern provinces of North America". London, Printed for the Author, 1787.   186 p.   [8174

MacKethan, Lula B.   Fayetteville, city of historic charm and modern progress. Fayetteville, Fayetteville Chamber of Commerce, n.d.   [2] p.   [8175

Mackey, Albert Gallatin.   A defence of Freemasonry; an address delivered on the 24th of June, 1851, before Catawba Valley Lodge, at Morganton, N. C.   Charleston, Walker and James, pr., 1851.   16 p.   [8176

Mackie, Ernest Lloyd.   Elementary college mathematics, by Ernest Lloyd Mackie and Vinton Asbury Hoyle. Boston, Ginn and Co. [c.1940]   331, 77 p.   [8177

McKie, George McFarland.   The speaker and the speech. Ann Arbor, Mich., Edwards, n.d.   49 p.   [8178

McKimmon, Jane (Simpson)   When we're green we grow. Chapel Hill, University of North Carolina Press [1945]   353 p.   [8179

McKinley, Albert Edward.   The suffrage franchise in the thirteen English colonies in America. Philadelphia, For the University, 1905. (Publications of the University of Pennsylvania. Series in history, no. 2)   518 p.   [8180

MacKinney, Loren Carey.   Early medieval medicine, with special reference to France and Chartres. Baltimore, Johns Hopkins Press, 1937. (Publications of the Institute of the History of Medicine, Johns Hopkins University, 3d ser., v. 3) 247 p.   [8181

——The medieval world. New York, Farrar & Rinehart, Inc. [c.1938] (The civilization of the western world, v. 2)   81, 801 p.   [8182

MacKinney, Loren Carey, ed.   A state university surveys the humanities, edited with a foreword by Loren C. MacKinney, Nicholson B. Adams [and] Harry K. Russell. Chapel Hill, University of North Carolina Press, 1945.   262 p.   [8183

McKinney, Richard Ishmael.   Religion in higher education among Negroes. New Haven, Yale University Press, 1945.   (Yale studies in religious education, XVIII) 165 p.   [8184

McKinney, Theophilus Elisha, ed.   Higher education among Negroes; addresses delivered in celebration of the twenty-fifth anniversary of the presidency of Dr. Henry Lawrence McCrorey of Johnson C. Smith University. Charlotte, Johnson C. Smith University [c.1932]   124 p.   [8185

McKinnon, Mary Narcissa.   Parsifal: a day at the Wagner-Bayreuth festival. Raleigh, Edwards & Broughton Co., 1898.   43 p.   [8186

McKnight, John P.   The papacy, a new appraisal. New York, Rinehart [1952] 437 p.   [8187

—— ——London, McGraw-Hill Publishing Co. [c.1953]   400 p.   [8188

McKnight, William Albert, comp.   Bibliography of contemporary Spanish literature, no. 1- 1953- Chapel Hill, 1954- NcU has no. 1-2.   [8189

McKoy, Elizabeth Francinia, comp.   Inscriptions copied from stones in St. James graveyard during the months of March and April, 1939. [Wilmington, Compiler, 1948]   40 p.   [8190

McKoy, Henry Bacon. The McKoy family of North Carolina and other ancestors including Ancrum, Berry, Halling, Hasell, Usher. Greenville, S. C., 1955. 198 p.   [8191

Maclaine, Archibald. An address to the people of North-Carolina, with the charges against the judges in the last assembly, the protests in both houses, and other papers relative to that business. [Newbern, Hodge and Blanchard, 1787?] 16 p. NcU has photograph.   [8192

McLauchlin, James A. Pensa prima latina, containing a primary Latin grammar, selections from Cornelius Nepos, and three books of Caesar's Gallic War. Raleigh, Edwards & Broughton, 1896. 316 p.   [8193

—— ——Richmond, Va., B. F. Johnson Publishing Co., 1897. 316 p.   [8194

McLaughlin, Glenn Everett. Why industry moves south; a study of factors influencing the recent location of manufacturing plants in the South, by Glenn E. McLaughlin [and] Stefan Robock. [Washington] Committee of the South, National Planning Association [1949]   148 p.   (NPA Committee of the South. Report no. 3)   [8195

McLaughlin, James A. Ra-cruits (a three-act play) [Asheville, Inland Press, 1938] 83 p.   [8196

McLean, Angus Wilton. Attitude of A. W. McLean, candidate for governor, in regard to labor. No place, no publisher [1924?] [3] p.   [8197

——International organization and its relation to the treaty of peace; address delivered before the North Carolina Bar Association at its annual meeting at Wrightsville Beach, N. C., June 27th, 1918. No place, no publisher, n.d. 34 p.   [8198

——Lumber River Scots and their descendants; the McLeans, the Torreys, the Purcells, the McIntyres, the Gilchrists, by Angus Wilton McLean, John Edwin Purcell I, Archibald Gilchrist Singletary [and] John Edwin Purcell II.   [Richmond, Va., William Byrd Press, Inc.] 1942.   839 p.   [8199

——Presentation address . . . upon the occasion of the ceremonies attending the presentation and unveiling of the North Carolina Memorial on the Battlefield of Gettysburg, Wednesday, July 3d, 1929. [Raleigh? 1929?]   15 p.   [8200

——Remarks to the graduates of the University of North Carolina following his presentation of the diplomas at the 133d annual commencement, Memorial Hall, Chapel Hill, N. C., June 11, 1928. New Bern, Owen G. Dunn, pr., 1928. 5 p. [8201

——Some business problems of today; an address before the Chamber o {Commerce of Charlotte, N. C., March 15th, 1922.   No place, no publisher [1922?]   16 p. [8202

——Statement of Angus Wilton McLean, candidate for governor of North Carolina. [Lumberton, 1924]   4 p.   [8203

——Training of the engineer for overseas engineering projects; an address delivered before the Conference on Business Training for Engineers and Engineering Training for Students of Business at Washington, D. C.   No place, no publisher, n.d. 12 p.   [8203a

——Woodrow Wilson, an appreciation; address delivered before the literary societies of Antioch State High School. [Charlotte, Observer Printing House] 1914. 24 p.   [8204

McLean, Carrie L. First Baptist Church, Charlotte, N. C., 1832-1916.   Charlotte, Washburn Press, 1917.   107 p.   [8205

McLean, Eddie, pseud. see MacNair, Colin

McLean, Harry Herndon. The Wilson family, Somerset and Barter Hill branch. Washington [c.1950]   102 p.   [8206

MacLean, John Allan. The most unforgettable character I've ever met. Richmond, Va., John Knox Press [c.1945]   223 p.   [8207

MacLean, John Patterson. Flora Macdonald in America, with a brief sketch of her life and adventures. Lumberton, A. W. McLean, 1909.   84 p.   [8208

——An historical account of the settlements of Scotch Highlanders in America prior to the peace of 1783.   Cleveland, Helman-Taylor Co., 1900.   459 p.   [8209

McLean, McDougald. Tuberculosis; a primer and philosophy for patient and public.   New York, Journal of Outdoor Life Publishing Co., 1922.   168 p. [8210

McLeod, John. To the people of Johnston County.   [Raleigh] no publisher [1834] 6 p.   [8211

McLeod, John Angus. From these stones: Mars Hill College, the first hundred years. [Mars Hill] Mars Hill College, 1955.   291 p.   [8212

McLeod, Randall Alexander. Historical sketch of Long Street Presbyterian Church, 1756 to 1923. [Sanford, Cole, pr.] n.d. 19 p.   [8213

McMahon, John Robert. The Wright brothers, fathers of flight. Boston, Little, Brown and Co., 1930. 308 p.   [8214

McMahon, Mrs. Philip, ed. Studies in citizenship for North Carolina women. Charlotte, North Carolina League of Women Voters, 1926. 109 p.   [8215

McMaster, W. H. Modern Sabbath questions for the people. Raleigh, Edwards & Broughton, 1910. 106 p.   [8216

McMillan, Hamilton. Sir Walter Raleigh's lost colony. Wilson, Advance Presses, 1888. 27 p.   [8217

——————Rev. ed. Raleigh, Edwards & Broughton Printing Co. [c.1907] 46 p.   [8218

Macmillan, Margaret (Burnham) The war governors in the American Revolution. New York, Columbia University Press, 1943. (Studies in history, economics and public law, ed. by the Faculty of Political Science of Columbia University, no. 503) 309 p.   [8219

McMillan, Mary Lee (Swann) My favorite recipes. No place, no publisher [c.1930] 316 p.   [8220

MacMillan, William Dougald, comp. Catalogue of the Larpent plays in the Huntington Library. San Marino, Calif., Huntington Library, 1939. (Its Library lists, no. 4) 442 p.   [8221

——Drury Lane calendar, 1747-1776. Oxford, Clarendon Press, 1938. 364 p. [8222

MacMillan, William Dougald, ed. Plays of the restoration and eighteenth century as they were acted at the theatres-royal by Their Majesties' servants, ed. by Dougald MacMillan and Howard Mumford Jones. New York, H. Holt and Co. [c.1931] 896 p.   [8223

McMullan, Thomas Shelton. The southron's burden. No place, no publisher, n.d. 88 p.   [8224

McMurtrie, Douglas Crawford. Eighteenth century North Carolina imprints, 1749-1800. Chapel Hill, University of North Carolina Press, 1938. 198 p.   [8225

——A note on North Carolina printing history. Chicago, privately printed, 1928. 6 p.   [8226

[**MacNair, Colin**] The race crisis. Uncle Sam, the innocent old Negro. [Henderson?] 1904. 22 p.   [8227

——The sweet old days in Dixie, by Eddie McLean. Raleigh, Edwards & Broughton Co., 1907. 180 p.   [8228

McNair, James Birtley, comp. McNair, McNear, and McNeir genealogies. Chicago, Author, 1923. 315 p.   [8229

—— ——————Supplement, 1928, compiled by James Birtley McNair. 1929. 240 p. [8230

—— ——————Supplement, 1955. Los Angeles, Author [c.1955] 457 p.   [8231

McNair, Lura Thomas, comp. Cantos amorosos, the sort of love songs you have longed to own. Puxico, Mo., Candor Magazine [1939] [42] p.   [8232

——Caravansary. Jonesboro, Grotto Studio Press [1939] [46] p.   [8233

——Friends'and gardens. Lowell, Mass., Alentour House, 1938. [21] p.   [8234

McNair, Lura Thomas. Humming birds in the mimosas. 1937. [11] p.   [8235

McNair, Lura Thomas, comp. A mother's day bouquet. Shelbyville Ind., Blue River Press, 1937. [40] p.   [8236

——Peace poems. Charleston, S. C., Scimitar and Song [1948?] [50] p.   [8237

——Scimitar and song year book, v. 1- 1936- Wendell, Gold Leaf Press [1936- NcU has v. 1, 1936; v. 2, n.d., v. 3 [1939]   [8238

McNair, Lura Thomas. Scenes along life's highway, by Lura Thomas McNair and Loren Phillips. Shelbyville, Ind., Blue River Press, n.d. [54] p.   [8239

McNair, Lura Thomas, comp. Thanksgiving and other autumn poems. Shelbyville, Ind., Blue River Press [1937] [10] p.   [8240

——Villanelles and triolets. Jonesboro, Grotto Studio Press [1939] [14] p.   [8241

——With clash of sword and cymbal. Cleveland, Pagasus Studios, 1938. 34 p. [8242

McNairy, C. Banks. Eugenics, read at the Onslow County Medical Society, Jacksonville, N. C., January 21, 1916. The growth of a North Carolina idea, read at the Seaboard Medical Society, Norfolk, Va., December 8-9, 1915. No place, no publisher, n.d. 22 p.   [8243

McNamara, J. V. What did Dr. Pritchard say? Review of a "Treatise on infant baptism" by Thomas H. Pritchard. Part one. Boston, Patrick Donahoe, 1871. 46 p.   [8244

McNeer, May Yonge. The story of the southern highlands. New York, Harper & Brothers [1945] [32] p.   [8245

McNeil, Kin. Strange stories of Carolina. Canton, South Literary Service, c.1947. 42 p.   [8246

MacNeil memorial, Red Springs, N. C. No place [Clan MacNeil Association of America] 1928. 24 p.   [8247

McNeill, Duncan. Life of Rev. Daniel White, with incidents in Scotland and America. Raleigh, Edwards, Broughton & Co. [1879?] 64 p.   [8248
——condensed in the following digest form by Arch M. McMillan. [Wake Forest?] 1955. 7 p.   [8249

[McNeill, Franklin] Angus Wilton McLean, successful lawyer, business man, farmer, publicist, candidate for governor. [Raleigh, 1924] 6 p.   [8250

McNeill, G. B., comp. Discipline of the faith and practice of the United American Free Will Baptists, written under the direction of their general conference. Raleigh, Edwards & Broughton Co., 1903. 16 p.   [8251

McNeill, John Charles. Lyrics from cotton land. Charlotte, Stone & Barringer Co. [c.1907] 189 p.   [8252
—— ——[c.1922]   [8253
—— ——[Chapel Hill, University of North Carolina Press, c.1949]   [8254
——Select prose of John Charles McNeill, by Jasper L. Memory, Jr. Wake Forest, Jasper L. Memory, Jr., c.1936. 106 p.   [8255
——Songs, merry and sad. Charlotte, Stone & Barringer Co., 1906. 106 p. [8256
—— ——Chapel Hill, University of North Carolina Press [c.1932]   [8257
——The sunburnt boys. [Cllnton, S. C., Jacobs and Co.] n.d. 4 p.   [8258

McNeill, Robert Hayes. Annual literary address, delivered at commencement of Flora MacDonald College, May 26th, 1926. [Red Springs, 1926] 16 p. [8259

McNeill, Thomas Alexander. Address on presentation of a portrait of the late William Foster French to the county of Robeson by his family. No place, privately printed, 1942. 16 p.   [8260

MacNider, William de Berniere. The good doctor, and other selections from the essays and addresses of William de Berniere MacNider, with tributes by Robert B. House, William M. Coppridge [and] Victor S. Bryant, ed. by William W. McLendon and Shirley Graves Cochrane. Chapel Hill, University of North Carolina Press [1953] 179 p.   [8261

McNinch, Frank Ramsay. The case against Governor Smith, speech . . . delivered at Newbern, N. C., October 12, 1928, with introduction by Senator F. M. Simmons. No place, no publisher, 1928. 16 p.   [8262
——Governor Al Smith's real position on immigration. No place, no publisher [1928] [6] p.   [8263

McNutt, Franklin Holbrook. The mother of professions; acceptance of the sixth annual O. Max Gardner award. [Chapel Hill, 1954] [2] p.   [8264

Macon County Baptist Association. Minutes, 1904?- 1904?- NcU has 1906, 1910, 1916   [8265

McPherson, Hannah Elizabeth (Weir) [History of five families, Gaston, Harvey, Reid, Simonton, Tomlinson] [Washington, Author, 1939] 50 p.   [8266
——The Holcombes, nation builders. [Washington, Lewin Dwinnell McPherson and Elizabeth Weir McPherson, c.1947] 1345 p.   [8267

McPherson, Holt. Churchmen, let's go to press; a short manual in the writing of church news. Shelby, Star Publishing Co., n.d. 11 p.   [8268
——Rotary in a rapidly changing age. [Charlotte, Charlotte Conference, Rotary International, 1947] 12 p.   [8269

McPherson, J. P. Our obligations to the Bible; a sermon, preached before the Robeson County Bible Society, at Philadelphus Church, June 4, 1853. Raleigh, Seaton Gales, 1853. 31 p.   [8270

McPherson, Lewin Dwinell. Kincheloe, McPherson, and related families. [Washington] c.1951. 505 p.   [8271

McPherson, Neill. The petition and information of Tho. S. Ashe . . . in the behalf and upon the relation of Neill McPherson. [Fayetteville?] March 27, 1847. [1] p. [8272

McQueen, Hugh. An address delivered before the alumni and graduating class of the University of North Carolina, on the afternoon preceding commencement day in Gerard Hall, June 26, 1839. Raleigh, Raleigh Register, 1839. 46 p. [8273
——The orator's touchstone; or, Eloquence simplified. New York, Harper & Brothers, 1854. 327 p. [8274

McRae, Alexander H. The soldier's instructor, compiled by Alexander H. McRae, inspector of the 4th Brigade of North Carolina Militia. [Fayetteville, E. J. Hale, pr.] 1825. 51 p. [8275

McRae, Cameron. The book of common prayer . . . a sermon preached during the session of the convention of the Diocese of North Carolina, 1849. Richmond, Va., H. K. Ellyson, 1849. 16 p. [8276

Macrae, David. The Americans at home. New York, E. P. Dutton & Co., 1952. 606 p. [8277

McRae, Duncan G. et al. Trial of the murderers of Archibald Beebee; argument of Ed. Graham Haywood . . . February 11, 1867. Raleigh, R. Avery, 1867. 94 p. [8278

McRae, Duncan Kirkland. Oration in the city of New Berne on the occasion of the planting of a memorial tree in honor of the late William Gaston by the Graded School of that city. Wilmington, Morning Star Presses, 1883. 14 p. [8279

MacRae, Hugh. Bringing immigrants to the South; address delivered before the North Carolina Society of New York, December 7, 1908. No place, no publisher, n.d. 12 p. [8280

MacRae, James Cameron. Address delivered under the auspices of the Johnston Pettigrew Chapter, United Daughters of the Confederacy, in the hall of the House of Representatives, Raleigh, N. C., January 19th, 1907. Durham, Seeman Printery, 1907. 21 p. [8281

McRae, John C. and Co. A defence of John C. McRae & Company from the imputations cast upon them as contractors on the North Carolina Railroad by the report of a joint select committee of the last legislature of North Carolina. No place, n.d. 25 p. [8282

[MacRae, Lawrence] Descendants of Duncan and Ann (Cameron) MacRae of Scotland and North Carolina. No place, no publisher [1928] 62 p. [8283

McRary, R. B. Address delivered at the New Auditorium, Raleigh, N. C., October 26, 1911; and, A tribute to the memory of the late Reverence Augustus Shepard, D. D., by Rev. J. A. Whitted. [Raleigh, Commerical Printing Co., 1911] 9 p. [8284

McRee, Griffith John. Memoir of Major Griffith J. McRee. No place, no publisher, n.d. 21 p. [8284a
——Life and correspondence of James Iredell, one of the associate justices of the Supreme Court of the United States. New York, D. Appleton and Co., 1857-1858. 2 v. [8284b
—— ——Index compiled by Helen Dortch Harrison. Chapel Hill, University of North Carolina Library, 1955. 151 p. [8284c
—— ——New York, Peter Smith, 1949. 2 v. in one. Micro-Offset. [8284d

McRee, Griffith John, joint author see Hooper, Archibald MacLaine

McRee, James. An eulogium; or, Funeral discourse, delivered at Salisbury, on the 22d February, 1800, in commemoration of the death of General George Washington, Salisbury, Printed by Francis Coupee, 1800. 20 p. NcU has photograph [8285

McSpadden, Joseph Walker. Pioneer heroes. New York, Thomas Y. Crowell Co. [c.1929] 300 p. [8286
——Storm center, a novel about Andy Johnson. New York, Dodd, Mead & Co., 1947. 393 p. [8287

McSweeney, Edward F. Gastons. [Boston] privately printed [c.1926] 235 p. [8288

McTyeire, Holland Nimmons. A manual of the discipline of the Methodist Episcopal Church, South. [13th ed.] Nashville, Tenn., M. E. Church, South, 1899. 306 p. [8289

MacWhirr, Hugh Dave, pseud. see Boyd, James

Maddry, Charles Edward. Charles E. Maddry; an autobiography. Nashville, Tenn., Broadman Press [1955] 141 p. [8290

——Christ's expendables. Nashville, Tenn., Broadman Press [1949] 182 p. [8291

——Day dawn in Yoruba land. Nashville, Tenn., Broadman Press [c.1939] 217 p. [8292

——History of the First Baptist Church of Hillsboro, North Carolina. [Raleigh, Edwards and Broughton Co.] 1953. 31 p. [8293

Made-In-Carolinas Association, Charlotte, N. C. Some Carolinas products. Charlotte, News [1922?] 16 p. [8294

Madison, N. C. Presbyterian Church. Centennial Committee. Memorial program for the one hundredth anniversary . . . 1851-1951. [Madison, 1951] [11] p. [8295

Maffitt, Emma (Martin) The life and services of John Newland Maffitt. New York, Neale Publishing Co., 1906. 436 p. [8296

Maffitt, John Newland. Nautilus, or, Cruising under canvas. New York, United States Publishing Co., 1871. 352 p. [8297

Magie, David. Debts; the substance of three sermons, delivered in the Second Presbyterian Church, Elizabeth-Town. Elizabeth-Town, Sanderson and Brookfield, pr., 1830. 32 p. [8298

Magnus, Sir Philip Montefiore, bart. Sir Walter Raleigh. London, Falcon Educational Books [1952] 126 p. [8299

Magoon, Elias Lyman. A useful life and a peaceful death; a discourse delivered before the legislature of North Carolina, December 18, 1842. Richmond, Va., H. K. Ellyson, 1843. 20 p. [8300

Mahaffey, James Ervin. What ails the world. [Charlotte, Observer Printing House, Inc., c.1918] 192 p. [8301

Mahan, Alfred Thayer. Letters to Samuel A'Court Ashe (1858-59) ed. by Rosa Pendleton Chiles. Durham, 1931. (Duke University. Library. Bulletin, no. 4) 121 p. [8302

Mahoney, James W. The Cherokee physician; or, Indian guide to health, as given by Richard Foreman, a Cherokee doctor. Asheville, Edney and Dedman, 1849. 308 p. [8303

Mahoney, John. Parousia, and other poems. [Detroit, Mich., Harlo Printing and Publishing Co., c.1955] 21 p. [8304

Maine. Salisbury Monument Commission. Report of the Maine Commissioners on the monument erected at Salisbury, N. C., 1908. Waterville, Sentinel Publishing Co., 1908. 27 p. [8305

Maine Infantry. 11th Regt., 1861-1866. The story of one regiment; the Eleventh Maine Infantry Volunteers in the war of the rebellion, comp. by a committee of the regimental association. New York [J. J. Little & Co.] 1896. 435 p. [8306

Mais, Stuart Petre Brodie. From Shakespeare to O. Henry; studies in literature. New York, Dodd Mead and Co. [1918] 313 p. [8307

Major General Stephen D. Ramseur. No place, no publisher, n.d. 25 p. [8308

Major Jno. W. Graham; give the West a showing. No place [1885?] [1] p. [8309

Makers of America. Washington, B. F. Johnson, 1915- v. NcU has v. 1-3 [8310

Mallary, Charles Dutton. Memoirs of Elder Jesse Mercer. New-York, J. Gray, pr., 1844. 455 p. [8311

Mallet, E. Pierre. A doctor looks at psychic research; from telepathy to telekenisis. Hendersonville, n.d. 17 p. [8312

Mallett, Edward Jones. Address to the graduating class at the University of North Carolina at commencement, June 2d, 1881. Raleigh, Edwards, Broughton & Co., 1881. 8 p. [8313

——Memoirs of Edward J. Mallett, a birthday gift for each of his children. No place, privately printed, 1880. 53 p. [8314

Malone, Bartlett Yancey. The diary of Bartlett Yancey Malone, edited by William Whatley Pierson, Jr. Chapel Hill, University of North Carolina, 1919. (James Sprunt historical publications, v. 16, no. 2) 59 p. [8315

Malone, Dumas. Edwin A. Alderman, a biography. New York, Doubleday, Doran & Co., Inc., 1940. 392 p. [8316

Malone, Henry Thompson. Cherokees of the Old South; a people in transition. Athens, University of Georgia Press [1956]   238 p.   [8317

Maloney's Asheville, N. C., city directory, v. 1- 189 - Richmond, Va., J. L. Hill Printing Co., 189 - NcU has 1899-1900   [8318

Maloney's . . . Raleigh, N. C. city directory . . . v. 1- 189 - Atlanta, Ga., Maloney Directory Co., c.189 - NcU has 1899-1900, 1901   [8319

Maltby, Frances (Goggin) The dimity sweetheart; O. Henry's own love story. Richmond, Va., Dietz Printing Co., 1930.   84 p.   [8320

Manchester, Alan Krebs. British preeminence in Brazil, its rise and decline; a study in European expansion. Chapel Hill, University of North Carolina Press, 1933.   371 p.   [8321

The Manettism, v. 1- June 25, 1927- Monroe, Manetta Mills, Monroe Plant, 1927- NcU has v. [1-8]   [8322

Mangum, Adolphus Williamson. A funeral sermon on the death of James W. Harriss, of Halifax County, N. C. Salisbury, Watchman, 1861.   8 p.   [8323

[**Mangum, Adolphus Williamsson**] Morven and Linda; or, The token star, the tale of a soldier's faithful love. Raleigh, Branson & Farrar, 1863.   16 p.   [8324

Mangum, Adolphus Williamson. Myrtle leaves; or, Tokens at the tomb. Philadelphia, H. B. Ashmead, pr., 1858.   123 p.   [8325

————————Raleigh, Branson & Farrar, 1864.   132 p.   [8326

————The safety lamp; or, Light for the narrow way. Salisbury, J. J. Bruner, pr., 1866.   80 p.   [8327

————Your life work, what shall it be? An address to boys and young men. Nashville, Tenn., Southern Methodist Publishing House, 1885.   80 p.   [8328

Mangum, Charles Staples. The legal status of the Negro. Chapel Hill, University of North Carolina Press, 1940.   436 p.   [8329

————The legal status of the tenant farmer in the Southeast. Chapel Hill, University of North Carolina Press [1952]   478 p.   [8330

Mangum, Dewitt C. Biographical sketches of the members of the legislature of North Carolina, session 1897. Raleigh, Edwards & Broughton Co., 1897. 39 p. [8331

Mangum's directory of Durham and suburbs, 189 - Durham, Educator Co., pr. 189 - NcU has 1897, 1902   [8332

Manley, Joe F. Fishing in the Great Smoky Mountains National Park and adjacent waters. Gatlinburg, Tenn., J. F. Manley [c.1938]   79 p.   [8333

Manly, Basil, comp. The Baptist psalmody, a selection of hymns for the worship of God, by Basil Manly, D. D., and B. Manly, Jr. Charleston, S. C., Southern Baptist Publication Society [c.1850]   809 p.   [8334

————The choice, a new selection of approved hymns for Baptist churches. Louisville, Ky., Baptist Book Concern, 1891.   161 p.   [8335

————A sermon, preached by appointment of the senior class of the University of North Carolina, June 2, 1856. [Raleigh?] The Class, 1856.   16 p.   [8336

————Sunday school questions of the four gospels, together with a condensed harmony. Raleigh,. Baptist Sunday School Board of North Carolina, 1864.   v.   NcU has v. 1   [8337

Manly, Charles. An address delivered before the alumni and the senior class of the University of North Carolina, in Gerard Hall, on the day preceding the annual commencement, in June, 1838. Raleigh, T. Loring, pr., 1838.   22 p.   [8338

Manly, Louise. Early life and marriage of Charlotte Elizabeth Whitfield Manly. Columbia, S. C., George Whitfield Manly, 1922.   46 p.   [8339

————The Manly family; an account of the descendants of Captain Basil Manly of the Revolution, and related families. Greenville, S. C. [Keys Printing Co.] 1930. 351 p.   [8340

————Southern literature from 1579-1895; a comprehensive review, with copious extracts and criticisms. Richmond, Va., B. F. Johnson Publishing Co., 1895. 514 p.   [8341

Mann, Albert William, comp. History of the Forty-fifth Regiment, Massachusetts Volunteer Militia. [Boston, W. Spooner, pr., c.1908]   562 p.   [8342

Mann, J. E. Should the North Carolina Conference be divided? A reply to the criticisms of Reverends S. D. Adams and W. S. Chaffin. Goldsboro, Messenger, pr., 1885.   54 p.   [8343

Manndale Institute, Manndale, N. C. Catalogue, 1903/04?- Manndale, 1904?-
NcU has [1907/08-1915/16]   [8344

Manning, Isaac Hall. Dr. I. H. Manning memorial luncheon, Carolina Inn, Chapel
Hill, January 22nd, 1947, 1:30 P. M. [Chapel Hill] 1947. [9] p.   [8345

Manning, James Smith. North Carolina laws made plain; laws and legal forms prepared for the use of farmers, mechanics and business men, compiled by Hon. James
S. Manning . . . and John H. Manning. Kansas City, Mo., Bankers Law Publishing Co., c.1924. 100 p.   [8346

Manning, John. Address before the Alumni Association of the University of North
Carolina. Greensboro, Thomas, Reece & Co., pr., 1884. 16 p.   [8347
——Commentaries on the first book of Blackstone. Chapel Hill, University Press,
1899. 268 p.   [8348

Manning, John N. An address delivered before the annual meeting of the North
Carolina and Virginia Christian Conference, convened at Pleasant Hill, Chatham
County, N. C., October 11th, 1860. Suffolk, Va., W. B. Wellons, 1860. 20 p. [8349

Manning, Thomas Courtland. The performance of political duties the great need of
the present day; address delivered before the literary societies of the University of
North Carolina, at Chapel Hill, June 6th, 1883. No place, no publisher [1883]
13 p.   [8350

The Manor, Asheville. In America, an English Inn. [Asheville? 1926?] [14] p. [8351
——The Manor, Albemarle Park, Asheville, N. C. [New York, J. C. & W. E. Powers,
pr.] n.d. 14 p.   [8352

Manteo, N. C. Graded School. Manteo Graded School, 190 - Manteo, 190 -
NcU has 1903/04, 1908/09   [8353

Manufacturers' record, Baltimore, Md. Blue book of southern progress, 1909-
Baltimore, Manufacturers Record [c.1909- NcU has 1922-1924, 1926-1956 [8354

Maple, James. Discourses on heaven. Raleigh, Christian Sun Office, 1853.
204 p.   [8355

[March, W. B.] A card to the voters of Rowan and Davie counties. No place
1870?] 4 p.   [8356

Marion, N. C. First Presbyterian Church. First Presbyterian Church, 1845-1945.
[Marion? 1945?] 40 p.   [8357

Marion, N. C. Hardy Evergreen Gardens. American plants for American gardens.
No place, no publisher [1929?] 16 p.   [8358
——Sterling evergreens. [Marion, 1928?] 8 p.   [8359

Marion Improvement Co. [To the stockholders.] No place, no publisher [1896?]
8 p.   [8360

Marion Sprunt Memorial Hospital, Wilmington, N. C. Dedicatory exercises, May
26, 1917. [Wilmington, Wilmington Printing Co.] 1917. 14 p.   [8361

Market Research, Inc., Indianapolis. This is an unbiased report describing the
retail shopping area of Winston-Salem, North Carolina. [Indianapolis] c.1932.
38 p.   [8362

Marks, Sallie B., joint author, see Barrows, Harlan H.

The Maroon and gray, v. 1- 19 - Durham, North Carolina College, 19 - NcU
has v. 5, 1948   [8363

Marriott, Alice Lee. Sequoyah, leader of the Cherokees. New York, Random
House [1956] 180 p.   [8364

Mars Hill, N. C. Baptist Church. Centennial observance of the Mars Hill Baptist
Church, 1856-1956. Mars Hill, 1956. [8] p.   [8365

Mars Hill College, Mars Hill, N. C. Catalogue, 185 - Mars Hill, 195 - NcU has
1901/02, 1902/03, 1903/04. Continues as its Mars Hill College quarterly,
1904-   [8366
——Fifty years at Mars Hill for Christ and youth. [Mars Hill, 1947] [6] p. [8367

[Mars Hill College, Mars Hill, N. C.] Holding fast to that which is good, reaching
forth unto those things which are before. [Mars Hill, 1956?] [8] p.   [8368
——Mars Hill College quarterly, v. 1- 1904- NcU has v. [1-19] 20-23 [24] 25-29
[30] 31-52   [8369

Mars Hill College, Mars Hill, N. C. Baptist Union. Handbook [1927-28] No place, n.d. 22 p. [8370

Marshall, Beatrice. Sir Walter Raleigh. New York, Frederick A. Stokes Co. [c.1914] 191 p. [8371

Marshall, Helen E. Dorothea Dix, forgotten Samaritan. Chapel Hill, University of North Carolina Press, 1937. 298 p. [8372

[**Marshall, Matthias M.**] In memoriam: Mrs. Margaret Bennehan Mordecai. Raleigh, Edwards and Broughton, n.d. [1] p. [8373

Marshall, Matthias M. Ministers and members of Christ . . . a sermon preached before the fifty-sixth convention of the Diocese of N. C., in . . . Salisbury . . . May 29th, 1872. New York, Deller & Walrath Printing Co., 1872. 19 p. [8374

Marshall, Rachelle. College wife. [Yellow Springs, Ohio] Antioch Press [1950] 62 p. [8375

Marshall, Robert K. Julia Gwynn: an American Gothic tale. New York, Duell, Sloan and Pearce [1952] 228 p. [8376
——Little Squire Jim. New York, Duell, Sloan and Pearce [1949] 255 p. [8377

Marshall, Roy Kenneth. The Easter story. Chapel Hill, Morehead Planetarium, University of North Carolina, c.1950. 12 p. [8278
——The Morehead Planetarium. Chapel Hill, Morehead Planetarium, University of North Carolina, c.1949. 16 p. [8379
——The nature of things. New York, Holt [1951] 188 p. [8380
——The star of Bethlehem. Chapel Hill, The Morehead Planetarium, c.1949. 23 p. [8381

Marshville Academy, Marshville, N. C. Catalogue, 189 - Marshville, 189 - NcU has 1898/99 [8382

Marteena, Constance Hill. Achievements of Afro-American women of the twentieth century, a checklist, compiled under the sponsorship of the North Carolina Negro Library Association. Greensboro, 1949. 67 p. [8383

Martenet, May Davies. Taw Jameson. New York, Knopf, 1953. 352 p. [8384

Martin, A. C. Key to the trees of Wake County, North Carolina, by A. C. Martin and I. V. Shunk. [Raleigh] North Carolina State College, 1935. 18 p. [8385

[**Martin, Alexander**] A new scene interesting to the citizens of the United States, additional to the historical play of Columbus, by a Senator. [Philadelphia] Benjamin Franklin Bache, pr., 1798. NcU has microcard [8386

Martin, Charles Haddon. Dora; the maid of Meherrin, rev. and enl.; and A sermon to lawyers. Raleigh, Edwards & Broughton, 1910. 13 p. [8387

Martin, Charles Henry. Negro problem a factor in the prohibition of the South. No place, no publisher, n.d. 4 p. [8388

Martin, Elizabeth L. Only a factory girl. Charlotte, Mill News Printing Co. [c.1909] 97 p. [8389

Martin, Eugene S. . . . An essay: The nebular hypothesis; read April 5th, 1882. Wilmington, S. G. Hall, 1882. 11 p. [8390

Martin, Frances Gardiner (McEntee) Pirate island. New York, Harper & Brothers [1955] 215 p. [8391

[**Martin, François-Xavier?**] tr. An account of Louisiana. Newbern, Franklin and Garrow, 1804. 272 p. [8392

Martin, François-Xavier. A funeral oration on . . . Major-General Richard Caswell . . . delivered in Christ-Church . . . Newbern . . . the 29th of November, 5789. Newbern, Printed at the expence of the Lodge, 5789. 6 p. NcU has photograph [8393

[**Martin, François-Xavier**] tr. Historical memoirs of Stephanie Louise de Bourbon Conti. Newbern [F. X. Martin] 1801. 172 p. [8394

Martin, François-Xavier. The history of Louisiana. New Orleans, J. A. Gresham, 1882. 469 p. [8395
——The history of North Carolina, from the earliest period. New Orleans, Printed by A. T. Penniman & Co., 1829. 2 v. [8396
——Martin's treatise on the powers and duties of executors and administrators according to the law of North-Carolina. Raleigh, Printed by J. Gales, 1820. 203 p. [8397

——The office and authority of a justice of the peace, and of sheriffs, coroners, &c. Newbern, F. X. Martin, 1791. 307 p.   [8398

—— ——new ed. Newbern, Martin & Odgen, 1804. 415 p.   [8399

——Proposals for printing by subscription a digested index to the American Reports. Newbern, November 15, 1803. [1] p.   [8400

——Treatise on the powers and duties of a constable, according to the law of North Carolina. Newbern, John C. Sims, 1806. 40 p.   [8401

——Treatise on the powers and duties of a coroner, according to the law of North Carolina. Newbern, John C. Sims, 1806. 31 p.   [8402

——Treatise on the powers and duties of a sheriff, according to the law of North Carolina. Newbern, John C. Sims, 1806. 287 p.   [8403

——A treatise on the powers and duties of executors and administrators, according to the law of North-Carolina. Newbern, Martin & Ogden, 1803. 320 p. [8404

Martin, François-Xavier, tr. see **Great Britain. Court of King's Bench;** also, **Pothier, Robert Joseph;** also **Riccoboni, Marie Jeanne (de Heurles Laboras de Mézières)**

Martin, James Walter. . . . Southern state and local finance trends and the war. Nashville, Tenn., Vanderbilt University Press, 1945. (Papers of the Institute of Research and Training in the Social Sciences, Vanderbilt University, no. 8) 106 p.   [8405

——Taxation of manufacturing in the South, by James W. Martin and Glenn D. Morrow. University, Bureau of Public Administration, Univ. of Alabama, 1948. (Alabama. University. Bureau of Public Administration. Publications, 29) 110 p.   [8406

Martin, R. H. How W. P. Canaday lost his position at custom house . . . the fraud exposed by a colored mechanic. Wilmington, 1882. [1] p.   [8407

Martin, Sidney Walter. Florida's Flagler. Athens, Univ. of Georgia Press [1949] 280 p.   [8408

Martin, Silas N. Educational: Cape Fear Teachers' Association meeting . . . Lillington . . . 12th April, 1873; an address delivered by Silas N. Martin. [Wilmington, S. G. Hall, pr., 1873] 12 p.   [8409

Martin, Thomas Wesley. Power and the public; address at convention of Southeastern Division, National Electric Light Association, Memphis, Tenn., April 14, 1927. No place, no publisher, n.d. 11 p.   [8410

Martin, William. The self vindication of Colonel William Martin against certain charges and aspersions made against him by Gen. Andrew Jackson and others. Nashville, Printed by John S. Simpson, 1829. 48 p.   [8411

Mary Jordan White, 1859-1909. No place, no publisher, n.d. 24 p.   [8412

Mary Magdelene, sister, see **Becker, Kate Harbes**

Masa, George, joint author, see **McCoy, George William**

Mason, John Young. Address before the alumni association of the University of North Carolina . . . June 2, 1847. Washington, Printed by J. and G. S. Gideon, 1847. 24 p.   [8412a

—— ——2d ed.   [8413

Mason, Julian. Search party; a collection of poems. New York, Pageant Press [1953] 49 p.   [8414

Mason, Lucy Randolph. Standards for workers in southern industry. No place, Printed by National Consumers' League, 1931. 46 p.   [8415

——To win these rights; a personal story of the CIO in the South. New York, Harper & Brothers [1952] 206 p.   [8416

[**Mason, Mary**] A wreath from the woods of Carolina. New York, General Protestant Episcopal Sunday School Union and Church Book Society, 1859. 154 p.   [8417

Mason, Mary. The young housewife's counsellor and friend. Philadelphia, J. B. Lippincott & Co., 1875. 380 p.   [8418

[**Mason, Richard Sharp**] A letter to the Bishop of North Carolina on the subject of his late pastoral on the Salisbury Convention. New-York, Stanford and Swords, 1850. 71 p.   [8419

Mason, Richard Sharp. The baptizing of infants defended from the objections of the anti-paedo-Baptists. New York, E. J. Hale & Son, 1874. 126 p.   [8420

Mason, Robert Lindsay. The lure of the Great Smokies. Boston, Houghton Mifflin Co., 1927. 320 p.   [8421

Mason, Thomas William. Address before the Ladies' Memorial Association, at the
laying of the cornerstone of the Confederate monument, Raleigh, N. C., May 20,
1895. Raleigh, E. M. Uzzell, pr., 1898. 13 p.   [8422

Mason, Van Wyck. Golden Admiral. Garden City, N. Y., Doubleday & Co., Inc.,
1953. 435 p.   [8423

Masonic and Eastern Star Home, Greensboro, N. C. Report, 191 - Greensboro,
191 - NcU has 1925   [8424

Masonic Institute, Germanton, N. C. Catalogue of the officers and students of the
Masonic Institute for the scholastic year MDCCCLII-III. Germanton, 1853.
12 p.   [8425

Masonic monitor, v. 1- March, 1872- Goldsboro, J. A. Bonitz, 1872- NcU has
v. [1]   [8426

Masonic Seminary. Trustees. Report of the Trustees and speech of J. M. Lovejoy
on the subject of the Masonic Seminary. No place, Grand Lodge of North Carolina, 1848. 16 p.   [8427

Masonry vindicated: "A review" reviewed, by a craftsman. Raleigh, Square and
Compass, 1868. 48 p.   [8428

Masons see **Freemasons**

Massachusetts. Labor and Industries Dept. Report of a special investigation into
conditions in the textile industry in Massachusetts and the Southern States.
Boston, Printed for the Arkwright Club, n.d. 24 p. Report submitted in 1923. [8429

Massachusetts. State Library, Boston. ... Hand-list of legislative sessions and
session laws ... Prepared by Charles J. Babbitt. [Boston, Wright & Potter
Printing Co., State Printers, 1912] 634 p.   [8430

Massachusetts Infantry. 44th Regiment, 1862-1863. Record of the service of the
Forty-fourth Massachusetts Volunteer Militia in North Carolina, August 1862 to
May 1863. Boston, privately printed, 1887. 364 p.   [8431

Massee, James C. Evangelism in the pew. Chicago, Winona Publishing Co.
[c.1907] 177 p.   [8432

Massey, Mary Elizabeth. Ersatz in the Confederacy. Columbia, University of
South Carolina Press, 1952. 233 p.   [8433

Massey, Wilbur Fisk. The know what to do; or, Brains vs. muscle; a lecture delivered before the ... North Carolina College of Agriculture and Mechanic Arts,
April 30, 1892. Raleigh, Edwards and Broughton, 1892. 16 p.   [8434

——Massey's garden book for the southern states. Raleigh, Progressive Farmer
Co. [c.1918] 127 p.   [8435

Masters, Victor Irvine. Baptist missions in the South. [Atlanta, Townley & Co.,
pr., c.1915] 239 p.   [8436

Masterson, William Henry. William Blount. Baton Rouge, Louisiana State University Press [1954] 378 p.   [8437

Matherly, Walter Jeffries. Business education in the changing South. Chapel Hill,
University of North Carolina Press, 1939. 342 p.   [8438

——The manager's task in industry. Durham, Christian and King Printing Co.,
1925. 132 p.   [8439

——A number of things. Boston, Richard G. Badger [c.1921] 80 p.   [8440

——Survey of Hickory, North Carolina ... prepared by Walter J. Matherly and
others. Hickory, Hickory Chamber of Commerce, 1925. 37 p.   [8441

Mathews, Cornelius. Big Abel and the Little Manhattan. New York, Wiley and
Putnam, 1845. 93 p.   [8442

Mathewson, Alice Clarke. Ali-Mat takes off. Raleigh, Forest Hills Distributors,
n.d. 152 p.   [8443

Mathis, Alexander. The lost citadel. New York, Pageant Press [1954] 273 p. [8444

Mattamuskeet Railway Co. Prospectus. Raleigh, Edwards and Broughton, 1909.
27 p.   [8445

Matteson, Maurice. Beech Mountain folk-songs and ballads, collected ... with
piano accompaniments by Maurice Matteson, texts edited ... by Mellinger Ed-

ward Henry.   New York, G. Schirmer, Inc. [c.1936]   (Schirmer's American folk-song series. Set 15)   58 p.   [8446

Matthews, Brinsley, pseud.   see Pearson, William Simpson

Matthews, C. Turner.   The Carolina motor club.   Greensboro, W. H. Fisher Co. [c.1929]   186 p.   [8447

Matthews, Ches.   This is your America . . . the newest of the nation's playgrounds. Asheville, Stephens Press, c.1950.   [35] p.   [8448

Matthews, Essie (Collins)   Aunt Phebe, Uncle Tom and others; character studies among the old slaves of the South.   Columbus, O., Champlin Press, 1915. 140 p.   [8449

Matthews, Etta Lane.   Over the blue wall.   Chapel Hill, University of North Carolina Press, 1937.   328 p.   [8450

Matthews, Luther Preston.   Is the principle of Isaiah the true principle of religion? Chapel Hill, University, 1908.   (N. C. University. Philosophy Department. Worth prize thesis. 1908)   9 p.   [8451

Matthews, Martin Taylor.   Experience-worlds of mountain people. New York City, Teachers College, Columbia University, 1937. (Teachers College. Columbia University. Contributions to education, no. 700)   210 p.   [8452

Matthews, Mary Green.   Wheels of faith and courage; a history of Thomasville, North Carolina, by Mary Green Matthews and M. Jewell Sink. [Thomasville? 1952]   216 p.   [8453

Matthews, Thomas Edwin.   General James Robertson, father of Tennessee. Nashville, Parthenon Press [c.1934]   588 p.   [8454

Matthews, Velma Dare.   Studies on the genus Pythium.   Chapel Hill, University of North Carolina Press, 1931.   136 p.   Ph. D. thesis, with additions—University of North Carolina, 1930.   [8455

Maughan, William, ed.   A guide to forestry activities in North Carolina, South Carolina, and Tennessee.   [Asheville, Miller Printing Co. for] Appalachian Section, Society of American Foresters, 1939.   287 p.   [8456

[Mauldin, Guy E.]   Supplement to Legal history of the lines of railroad of the Southern Railway Company.   Washington, 1921.   108 p.   [8457

[Maull, Allen]   Eastern North Carolina, the farmer's road to wealth.   Wilmington, Agricultural and Immigration Dept. of the Atlantic Coast Line [1916?]   32 p. [8458

Maull, Allen.   Eastern North Carolina, "the land of the best", calls you, Mr. Farmer and Investor.   Wilmington, Atlantic Coast Line, n.d.   12 p.   [8459

——Eastern North Carolina for the farmer.   Wilmington, Passenger Traffic Dept. of the Atlantic Coast Line [1916?]   32 p.   [8460

Maurice, Arthur Bartlett.   O. Henry.   New York, Doubleday Page for O. Henry Memorial Association, 1925.   56 p.   [8461

Maurice, George H.   On the trail of Daniel Boone in North Carolina.   Eagle Springs, Author, 1955.   19 p.   [8462

Maury, Matthew Fontaine.   Manual of geography.   Rev. ed.   New York, University Publishing Co., 1898.   136 p.   North Carolina edition.   [8463
—— ——1899.   [8464

Maxwell, Allen Jay.   Address, Friday, May 15, 1936, over radio stations WPTF, Raleigh, WBT, Charlotte, and WWNC.   Asheville; subject. . . . Refutation of . . . misrepresentations . . . by one of the candidates for governor. [Raleigh, Author? 1936]   16 p.   [8465

——A balanced program of progress for North Carolina; A. J. Maxwell for governor. [Raleigh? 1940]   16 p.   [8466

——Classified taxation of reproducing timber lands; address to the Southern Forestry Congress, Memphis . . . Apr. 11, 1930.   14 p.   [8467

——Collateral issues before the people of North Carolina. [Raleigh, Capital Printing Co., 1932]   12 p.   [8468

——An issue and a program. [Raleigh, Bynum Printing Co., 1931]   24 p.   [8468a

——Neglected North Carolina; radio address on program of North Carolina woman's clubs . . . November 17, 1937. [Raleigh?] 1937.   7 p.   [8469

——The record . . . by A. J. Maxwell . . . [and] by J. Y. Joyner. [Raleigh, 1916?] 23 p.   [8470

[Maxwell, Phillip Herbert] Valhalla in the Smokies. Cleveland, O., G. A. Exline, 1938. Unpaged. [8471

Maxwell, Raymond C. Life and works of Allen Jay Maxwell, 1873-1946. [Raleigh, Author] 1949. 213 p. [8472

Maxwell, William Cary. Reimwortuntersuchungen im deutschen. Heidelberg, Carl Winter [1932] 55 p. [8473

May Hosiery Mills, Inc., Burlington, N. C. The story of hosiery. Burlington [c.1931] 101 p. [8474

Mayerberg, Samuel Spier. Chronicle of an American crusader; alumni lectures delivered at the Hebrew Union College, Cincinnati, Ohio, December 7-10, 1942. New York, Bloch Publishing Co., 1944. 148 p. [8475

Mayo, Robert. The affidavit of Andrew Jackson, taken by the defendants in the suit of Robert Mayo vs. Blair & Rives for a libel. Washington City, D. C., Printed for the Plaintiff, 1840. 23 p. [8476

——Political sketches of eight years in Washington; in four parts . . . [Part 1] Baltimore, F. Lucas, Jr., 1839. 216 p. No more published. [8477

Mayo Baptist Association. Minutes, 18 - NcU has 1840, 1872, 1925, 1931, 1932, 1942 [8478

[Mazzei, Filippo] Recherches historiques et politiques sur les États-Unis de l'Amérique Septentrionale. Colle, Froullé, 1788. 4 v. [8479

Mead, Martha Elizabeth (Norburn) Asheville, in Land of the Sky. Richmond, Va., Dietz Press, 1942. 188 p. [8480

Meade, Julian Rutherford. Teeny and the tall man. Garden City, N. Y., Doubleday, Doran & Co., Inc., 1936. 155 p. [8481

Meader, Stephen Warren. The sea snake. New York, Harcourt, Brace and Co. [1943] 255 p. [8482

Meadowcroft, Enid (La Monte) On Indian trails with Daniel Boone. New York, Thomas Y. Crowell Co. [1947] 136 p. [8483

——The story of Andrew Jackson. New York, Grosset & Dunlap [1953] 182 p. [8484

Meadows, Leon Renfroe. Reveries. New York, Exposition Press [1949] 125 p. [8485

Means, Alexander. A cluster of poems. New York, E. J. Hale & Son, 1878. 216 p. [8486

Means, George W. 1903 Red Cuban games as bred by Geo. W. Means. Concord, 1903. 14 p. [8487

Meares, Catherine Douglass (De Rosset) Annals of the De Rosset family. [Columbia, S. C., R. L. Bryan Co., 1906] 91 p. [8488

——A group of my ancestral dames of the colonial period. Goldsboro, Nash Bros., pr. [1901?] 17 p. [8489

Meares, George D. Ode to our Confederate dead . . . sung at the . . . unveiling of the Confederate monument at Raleigh, May 20th, 1895. Raleigh, Author, c.1895. 3 p. [8490

Meares, Iredell. An address on the administration of the law . . . delivered . . . at Wilmington, N. C., April 21st, 1892. Wilmington, Jackson & Bell, 1892. 10 p. [8491

——The confiscation fact; or, National honor demands the return of enemy-owned property. Wilmington, Del., Star Publishing Co., c.1924. 71 p. [8492

——God not in the covenant; the League of Nations doomed. [Wilmington? Author, 1920?] 14 p. [8493

——Is the South to be humiliated? No place, no publisher [1908?] 15 p. [8494

——Mix brains and ballots. [Wilmington, no publisher, 1908] 4 p. [8495

[Meares, Iredell] [Presidents who have visited Wilmington, N. C.] [Raleigh, Edwards and Broughton, 1909] 47 p. [8496

Mebane, A. W. Address to the people of Northampton, Martin, Hertford, and Bertie. No place, no publisher [1840] 15 p. [8497

Mebane, Albert Leonidas. Lessons with nature for school, garden, farm, and home. Greensboro, W. H. Fisher Co., pr. [1917] 62 p. [8498

Mebane, Banks Holt. Law: an outline of its definition, origin and object. Chapel Hill, University, 1915. (N. C. University. Philosophy department. Worth prize thesis. 1915) 15 p. [8499

Mebane, George Allen. "The Negro problem" as seen and discussed by southern white men in conference at Montgomery, Ala. . . . prepared and comp. for the National Afro-American Council. New York, Alliance Publishing Co., 1900. 40 p. [8500

Mebane, James. To the freemen of the counties of Orange, Wake & Person. No place, 1813. 2 p. [8501

Mechanic, pseud. Paper currency and constitutional currency. No place, no publisher, n.d. [1] p. [8502

[Mechanics' liens.] No place, no publisher, n.d. 24 p. Title page wanting in NcU copy [8503

Mecklenburg Baptist Association. Minutes, 1886?- 1886?- NcU has 1897, 1904-1906 [1932-1951] Called Mecklenburg-Cabarrus Association, -1935. [8504

Mecklenburg Co., N. C. Board of Commissioners. Budget appropriations resolution, 19 - [Charlotte? 19 - NcU has 1935/36, 1936/37, 1955/56 [8505
——Recapitulation of outstanding bonds of Mecklenburg County. [Charlotte?] 1936. 13 p. [8506

Mecklenburg Co., N. C. Board of Education. Catalogue of Public Schools in Mecklenburg County, North Carolina, 19 - Charlotte [19 - NcU has 1901-1907, issued as one [8507

Mecklenburg Co., N. C. Democratic Executive Committee. What everybody ought to know about this campaign. Charlotte [1928] 32 p. [8508

Mecklenburg Co., N. C. Department of Public Welfare. Report, 19 - [Charlotte] 19 - NcU has 1919/1921 [8509

Mecklenburg Co., N. C. Planning Board. A planning program for Mecklenburg, Charlotte. [Charlotte? 1953?] 40 p. [8510

Mecklenburg Co., N. C. Superior Court. Trial jurors' handbook. [Charlotte, Published at the request of Charlotte League of Women Voters, 1949] 23 p. [8511

Mecklenburg County Home Guard. Rules and regulations of Mecklenburg County Home Guard, North Carolina Council of Defense. Charlotte, 1917. 8 p. [8512

The Mecklenburg Declaration of Independence, May 20, 1775. Charlotte, 1954. [2] p. [8513

Mecklenburg Declaration of Independence, May 20th, 1775; souvenir edition, May 20, 1898. Charlotte, Queen City Printing and Paper Co. [c.1898] 26 p. [8514
——May 18, 19, 20, 1909. [1909] [8515

Mecklenburg Drainage Commission. Mecklenburg Drainage Commission, 1913. No place, no publisher, n.d. 24 p. [8516

Mecklenburg Historical Society. Constitution and by-laws. [Charlotte?] n.d. 4 p. [8517

Mecklenburg Historical Society, Inc., Charlotte, N. C. Souvenir program, Shout freedom, May 20th-June 3rd. [Charlotte] 1948. 32 p. [8518

Mecklenburg Monument Association, Charlotte, N. C. Unveiling of the monument to the signers of the Mecklenburg Declaration of Independence at Charlotte, N. C. May 20, 1898. Charlotte, Observer Print. and Pub. House, 1898. 37 p. [8519

The Mecklenburg Presbyterian, v. 1- June, 1941- Charlotte, Mecklenburg Presbytery, 1941- NcU has v. 1-16 [8520

Mecklenburg Presbytery see **Presbyterian Church in the U. S. Synod of N. C. Mecklenburg Presbytery**

The medical brief, v. 1- July, 1873- Wilson, J. J. Lawrence, 1873- NcU has v. [1] [8521

The Medical journal of North Carolina, v. 1-3, August, 1858-September, 1861. Edenton and Raleigh, State Medical Society, 1858-1861. NcU has v. 1-3 [8522

Medical Society of the State of North Carolina. Constitution, adopted, April 7th, 1849, with by-laws, resolutions, amendments and laws of state in regard to practice of medicine. Tarboro, C. G. Bradley, pr., 1888. 38 p. [8523
——Constitution and by-laws . . . revised May 10th, 1893. [1893] 7 p. [8524
—— ——revised April 28, 1925. Lynchburg, 1925. 24 p. [8525
—— ——revised April 28, 1930. [1930?] [8526
—— ——revised May 1, 2, 3, 1944. [1944] [8527

——Memoranda. [Raleigh, Edwards and Broughton, pr., 1902] 18 p.   [8528
——Officers, committees, and roster of fellows, 1948- Winston-Salem, North Carolina Medical Journal, 1948- (North Carolina medical journal, 1948- Supplement) NcU has 1948-1955   [8529
——Officers and committees, constitution and by-laws. Raleigh, Edwards and Broughton, 1903. 43 p.   [8530
——Program, 18 - 18 - NcU has [1916-1934] 1938-1944 [1947-1950]   [8531
——Transactions of the Medical society of the state of North Carolina, 1849-1939. 1849-1939. NcU has 1849-1939. Continues, 1940- in North Carolina medical journal.   [8532

Medical Society of the State of North Carolina. Confederate Veterans Committee. Provisional record of Confederate medical officers. No place, n.d. 57 p. [8533

Medical Society of the State of North Carolina. Rural Health Committee. People can work for health and freedom at the same time. [Raleigh, 1951] [16] p. [8534

Medical Society of the State of North Carolina. State Medicine and Medical Jurisprudence Section. An appeal for state care for all the insane . . . by Isaac M. Taylor . . . May 28th, 1891. Wilmington, Jackson & Bell, pr., 1891. 9 p. [8535

Medley, John. The sermon at the consecration of Thomas Frederick Davis . . . and Thomas Atkinson . . . New York . . . October 17, 1853. New York, Church Depository, 1853. 25 p.   [8536

Medley, Mary Louise. Dogwood winter, poems. Raleigh, Wolf's Head Press, 1952. 64 p.   [8537

[Medley, Mary Louise] State Society of County and Local Historians tours in 1952. No place, 1952. 5 p.   [8538

Meek, Sterner St. Paul. Surfman, the adventures of a Coast Guard dog. New York, Alfred A. Knopf, 1950. 267 p.   [8539

Meekins, Victor. The old sea captain and the drummer. Manteo [The Times Printing Co., Inc., c.1950] 120 p.   [8540

Meeting of the Governors of the States of Virginia, North Carolina, South Carolina, Georgia, Alabama and Mississippi, Augusta, Ga., 1864. Letter from the Governor of Virginia communicating a series of resolutions passed. [Richmond, 1864] 3 p. NcU has microfilm (negative) from original in Library of Congress   [8541

Meier, Frank. Hurricane warning. New York, E. P. Dutton, 1947. 254 p. [8542

Meigs, William Montgomery. The life of Thomas Hart Benton. Philadelphia, J. B. Lippincott Co., 1904. 535 p.   [8543

Meiklejohn, Kenneth. Southern labor in revolt. New York, Intercollegiate Student Council of the League for Industrial Democracy, 1930. 24 p.   [8544

Melbourn, Julius. Life and opinions of Julius Melbourn, with sketches of the lives and characters of Thomas Jefferson . . . and several other . . . American statesmen. Syracuse, Hall and Dickson, 1847. 239 p.   [8545

Melish, John. Travels through the United States of America, in the years 1806 & 1807, and 1809, 1810, & 1811. Philadelphia, Author, 1815. 2 v.   [8546

Mellen, George W. F. An argument on the unconstitutionality of slavery. Boston, Saxton & Peirce, 1841. 440 p.   [8547

Melton, Anson Gustavus. Where is love? And other poems. Boiling Springs, Author, 1938. 100 p.   [8548
——The wicked house, and other poems. Ellenboro, Author [c.1917] 98 p. [8549

Melton, Frances Jones. A daughter of the highlanders. Boston, Roxburgh Publishing Co. [c.1910] 376 p.   [8550

Melville Farm, Haw River, N. C. Dispersal sale, August 1st, Melville farm jerseys and Shetland ponies, R. W. Scott, proprietor. Raleigh, Commercial Printing Co. [1917?] 21 p.   [8551

Memminger, Edward Read. An historical sketch of Flat Rock. Flat Rock, Mrs. Walter M. Norment [c.1954] 26 p.   [8552

Memoir of Colonel William McRee. [Wilmington, 184?] 17 p.   [8553

Memoir of Mrs. Margaret M. Vance, and Mrs. Harriette Espy Vance. Raleigh, Edwards and Broughton, 1878. 35 p.   [8554

Memoir of our late sister, Ann Lavinia Zevely, who departed this life at Salem, N. C., June 11th, 1862. Salem, L. V. & E. T. Blum, 1862. 6 p. [8555

Memoir of Susan Dimock, resident physician of the New England Hospital for Women and Children. Boston [Press of John Wilson & Son] 1875. 103 p. [8556

Memorial addresses on the life and character of Rev. Evander McNair, D. D. delivered at Sardis church, Cumberland County, N. C. May 28, 1886. Richmond, Whittet & Shepperson, 1886. 58 p. [8557

Memorial Associations of the South. To the women of North Carolina. [Raleigh? 1875?] [1] p. [8558

Memorial meeting, Walter Hines Page; held at the Brick Presbyterian Church . . . New York, on April the twenty-fifth, 1919. New York, Doubleday, Page & Co., 1920. 56 p. [8559

Memorial of Alexander Lacy Phillips. [Richmond, Richmond Press, Inc., 1915?] 32 p. [8560

Memorial of Micajah Cox. Goldsboro, Nash Bros., 1915. 8 p. [8561

Memorial of Nash Cheek. No place, no publisher [1904?] 10 p. [8562

Memorial of Rev. Joseph C. Huske . . . rector emeritus of St. John's Episcopal Church, Fayetteville, N. C. No place, no publisher, n.d. 69 p. [8563

Memorial of Rev. R. H. Wills. Greensboro, Thomas Brothers, 1891. 24 p. [8564

Memorial of Rev. William H. Wills. No place, no publisher, n.d. 7 p. [8565

Memorial of the First Presbyterian Church, Wilmington, N. C., seventy-fifth anniversary, 1817-1892. Richmond, Whittet & Shepperson, 1893. 101 p. [8566

A memorial of the Hon. George Davis . . . senator from . . . North Carolina in the Congress of the Confederate States of America. Wilmington, Chamber of Commerce, 1896. 33 p. [8567

[Memorial of Thomas Greely Stevenson] Cambridge, Mass., Welch, Bigelow & Co., pr., n.d.] 129 p. [8568

Memorial of William Royall Hobgood. No place, no publisher, n.d. 31 p. [8569

Memorial proceedings, and tributes of respect to the memory of the late Asa Biggs. Norfolk, Va., Thomas O. Wise, pr., 1878. 36 p. [8570

Memorials, Mrs. William A. Smith, the good Samaritan and heroine. Wadesboro, John Lowe and Son, 1914. 14 p. [8571

Men of mark in Georgia; containing biographies of William Few, Jr., by Marion Letcher and Benjamin Few, by L. D. Carman. Atlanta, Ga., A. B. Caldwell, n.d. 20 p. [8572

Mendall, Charles. Two poems, written on the occasion of the birthdays of R. H. DeLuce and Frank W. Wellington of the Twenty-Fifth Regiment . . . at Newbern, N. C. Worcester, Edward R. Fiske, 1864. 10 p. [8573

Mendelsohn, Samuel. The criminal jurisprudence of the ancient Hebrews. Baltimore, M. Curlander, 1891. 270 p. [8574

——A square deal, or Equitable rates for veteran Arcanians. Wilmington, No publisher, 1906. 32 p. [8575

Mendenhall, Nereus. An address delivered before the Springfield Agricultural Club, of Guilford County, N. C. . . . Sept. 30, 1868. [Greensboro, Patriot and Times Office for the Club, 1868?] 7 p. [8575a

Mental hygiene news, v. 1- July, 1939- Charlotte, North Carolina Mental Hygiene Society, 1939- NcU has v. [1-8] [8576

Mercantile Association of the Carolinas. Reference book. Wilmington, Jackson & Bell, pr., 18 - NcU has 1889-1891 [8577

Mercer, Alexander G. American citizenship, its faults and their remedies; a sermon for the day of national fast, Jan. 4, 1861. Boston, Little, Brown and Co., 1861. 41 p. [8578

Mercer, S. E. Why has Dr. J. A. Van Valzah been denied license? No place, no publisher, n.d. 2 p. [8579

[Merchant] pseud. Silver; points for Senator Butler to answer. Charlotte, 1895. 40 p. [8580

The mercury, devoted to polite Southern literature, 186 - Raleigh, Wm. B. Smith, 186 - NcU has v. 4, no. 15, Aug. 6, 1864 [8581

Meredith, Clement Orestes. The partes orationis as discussed by Virgilius Maro Grammaticus. [Guilford, Printed by J. M. Purdie, 1916] 75 p. Thesis (Ph. D.)— Johns Hopkins University, 1912. [8582

Meredith, Hugh. An account of the Cape Fear country, 1731. Perth Amboy, N. J., C. F. Heartman, 1922. 29 p. [8583

Meredith, Thomas. Address delivered before the literary societies at the Wake Forest Institute, N. C., Nov. 24, 1836. Newbern, Recorder, 1837. 14 p. [8584

Meredith College, Raleigh, N. C. Bulletin, v. 1- 1907- Raleigh, 1907- NcU has v. [1-6] 7-35 [36-49] [8586

——Catalogue, 1899/1900- Raleigh, 1900- NcU has 1899/1900, 1902/03-1907/08. Continues as its Bulletin, 1907- [8587

——Report of the president, report of the treasurer, report of the bursar, 19 - Raleigh, 19 - NcU has 1915/16-1916/17, 1919/1920-1930/31, 1934/35-1938/39 [8588

Meredith College, Raleigh, N. C. Student Government Association. Hand-book, 1918/19 - Raleigh, 1918- NcU has 1918/19, 1929/30 [8589

Mereness, Newton Dennison, ed. Travels in the American colonies. New York, Macmillan Co., 1916. 693 p. [8590

Meroney & Brother, Salisbury, N. C. Catalogue of foreign and domestic fancy goods, wood and willow ware, fancy groceries. Philadelphia, Henry B. Ashmead, pr., n.d. 51 p. [8591

Merrick, Elliott. Frost and fire. New York, C. Scribner's Sons, 1939. 334 p. [8592

——Green Mountain farm. New York, Macmillan Co., 1948. 209 p. [8593

——Passing by. New York, Macmillan Co., 1947. 234 p. [8595

Merrick, Pliny. Eulogy on General Andrew Jackson . . . delivered in Faneuil Hall, July 9, 1845, at the request of the municipal authorities. Boston, J. H. Eastburn, 1845. 32 p. [8596

Merrill, Allen. Freedom and responsibility, by Allen Merrill, Charles M. Robinson, Jr. Chapel Hill, Department of Philosophy, University of North Carolina, 1939. (Buchan prize theses) 30 p. [8597

Merrill, Daniel. The mode and subjects of baptism examined in seven sermons . . . 6th edition. Raleigh, Printed by Joseph Gales, 1807. 108 p. [8598

Merrill, Samuel. The Seventieth Indiana Volunteer Infantry in the war of the rebellion. Indianapolis, Bowen-Merrill Co. [1900] 372 p. [8599

Merrill, William Ernest. Captain Benjamin Merrill and the Merrill family of North Carolina. No place, no publisher [pref. 1935] 90 p. [8600

—— ——Supplement. 1951. p. 91-121. [8601

[Merrimon, Maud L.] Memoir, Augustus Summerfield Merrimon. No place, no publisher, n.d. 100 p. [8602

Message [Greensborough periodical] see Weekly message

A message to our fellow citizens. [Chapel Hill, Chapel Hill Weekly, 1928] [1] p. [8602a

Messenger, 1921- Durham, Senior Class of Durham High School, 1921- NcU has 1922, 1934, 1937, 1938 [8603

Messick, John Decatur. The discretionary powers of school boards. Durham, Duke Univ. Press, 1949. 147 p. [8604

——Personality and character development. New York, Fleming H. Revell Co. [c.1939] 192 p. [8605

Metcalf, Bryce. Original members and other officers eligible to the Society of the Cincinnati, 1783-1938. Strasburg, Va., Shenandoah Publishing House, Inc., 1938. 390 p. [8606

Metcalf, Paul C. Will West. Asheville, Jonathan Williams, 1956. 68 p. [8607

Metcalf, Zeno Payne. An introduction to zoology, through the study of the vertebrates. Springfield, Ill., C. C. Thomas, 1932. 425 p. [8608

——Research, the handmaiden of teaching. [Raleigh, 1955] [5] p. [8609

Metcalfe, Samuel Lytler, comp. A collection of some of the most interesting narratives of Indian warfare in the West. Lexington, Ky., Printed by W. G. Hunt, 1821. 270 p. [8610

Methodist advance, v. 1 Goldsboro, W. M. Robey, 1880?- NcU has v. [2, 4-7] [8611

Methodist Church (United States) North Carolina Conference. Journal, first session- 1939- 1939- NcU has 1939-1955 [8612

Methodist Church (United States) North Carolina Conference. Durham Regional Personnel Committee. [Report] May 6, 1946. Durham, 1946. 26 p. [8613

Methodist Church (United States) North Carolina Conference. Woman's Society of Christian Service. Report, 1941- 1941- NcU has 1941-1955 [8614

Methodist Church (United States) N. C. Conference. Youth Fellowship. Louisburg Assembly song book. [Delaware, O., Cooperative Song Service] n.d. 72 p. [8615

Methodist Church (United States) Western North Carolina Conference. Minutes of the first- session, 1939- [1940- NcU has 1939-1955 [8616

Methodist Church (Wesleyan) see Wesleyan Methodist Connection (or Church) of America

Methodist College Foundation of North Carolina, Inc. For youth and the kingdom! [Greensboro, 1952] [6] p. [8617

Methodist Episcopal Church. Catechisms of the Wesleyan Methodists . . . revised and adapted to the use of . . . the Methodist Episcopal Church: No. I.—For children of tender years. Greensboro, Sterling, Campbell & Albright, 1863. 16 p. [8618

Methodist Episcopal Church. Conferences. Minutes of the annual conferences of the Methodist Episcopal Church, for the years, 1773-1845. New-York, T. Mason and G. Lane for the Methodist Episcopal Church, 1840. 3 v. [8619

——Minutes of the Methodist conferences, annually held in America; from 1773 to 1813, inclusive. Volume the first. New-York, Published by Daniel Hitt and Thomas Ware, for the Methodist Connexion in the United States, John C. Totten, pr., 1813. 611 p. [8620

Methodist Episcopal Church. Blue Ridge—Atlantic Conference. Journal, 1877-1938. 1877-1938. NcU has 1916-1938 [8621

Methodist Episcopal Church, African see African Methodist Episcopal Church

Methodist Episcopal Church, South. Catechisms of the Wesleyan Methodists . . . adapted to the use of . . . the Methodist Episcopal Church, South: No. II.—For children of seven years of age and upwards. Rev. ed. Raleigh, N. C. Publishing Co., n.d. 64 p. [8622

——Child's Scripture question book, Southern edition. Macon, Ga., John W. Burke, 1862. 194 p. [8623

——The doctrines and discipline of the Methodist Episcopal Church, South. Nashville, Tenn., Southern Methodist Publishing House, 1882. 375 p. [8624

—— ——1886. 403 p. [8625

—— ——edited by W. P. Harrison. 1890. 442 p. [8626

—— ——1894. 380 p. [8627

—— ——1902. 415 p. [8628

—— ——1906. 441 p. [8629

——Hymn and tune book of the Methodist Episcopal Church, South. Character note edition. Nashville, Tenn. Publishing House of the Methodist Episcopal Church, South, 1889. 558 p. [8630

——The Methodist hymnal. Nashville, Tenn., 1905. 798 p. [8631

——Minutes of the annual conferences, 18 - Richmond, Va., 184 - NcU has 1858-1863 [8632

——Missionary yearbook, 19 - Nashville, Tenn., Board of Missions of the Methodist Episcopal Church, South, 19 - NcU has 1928 [8633

Methodist Episcopal Church, South. Department of Education and Promotion. Education and child labor in the Southern States. Nashville, Tenn. [193?] 15 p. [8634

Methodist Episcopal Church, South. Holston Conference. The Holston annual, 18 - 18 - NcU has 1860, 1875, semi-centennial number; 1880 [8635

Methodist Episcopal Church, South. N. C. Conference. Journal, 18 - 1938. NcU has [1860-1869] 1872-1898, 1900-1938 Continues as Methodist Church (United States) 1939 - [8636

——Proceedings of annual Methodist Educational Convention of the N. C. conferences, 189 - 189- NcU has 1891, 1892 (program) [8637

Methodist Episcopal Church, South. N. C. Conference. Charlotte District. Proceedings, 187 - Monroe, Monroe Enquirer, 187- NcU has 1877, 1879   [8638

Methodist Episcopal Church, South. N. C. Conference. Fayetteville District. Centenary directory of the Fayetteville District Conference. Jonesboro, 1884. 20 p.   [8639

Methodist Episcopal Church, South. N. C. Conference. Historical Society. Historical papers, 1897- 1897- NcU has 1897, 1901, 1912, 1925. 1912 published as Trinity College Historical Society Papers, series 9.   [8640

Methodist Episcopal Church, South. N. C. Conference. Lenoir Circuit. Directory of Lenoir Circuit. [Lenoir] Racket Job Print, 1889. 21 p.   [8641

Methodist Episcopal Church, South. N. C. Conference. Local Ministers Association. Minutes, 18 - 18 - NcU has 1870 [1882-1892]   8642

Methodist Episcopal Church, South. N. C. Conference. Salisbury District. Proceedings, 18 - 18 - NcU has 1880   [8643

Methodist Episcopal Church, South. N. C. Conference. Sunday School Board. Some achievements and objectives of Sunday School Board. No place [1926] 14 p.   [8644

——Year book, 1905- 1905- NcU has 1905, 1907, 1909   [8645

Methodist Episcopal Church, South. N. C. Conference. Woman's Foreign Missionary Conference. Minutes, 187 - 1912. 187 - 1912. NcU has [1886-1912]   [8646

Methodist Episcopal Church, South. N. C. Conference. Woman's Missionary Society. Session, 1st-28th, 1913-1940. 1913-1940. NcU has 1913-1940 [8647

Methodist Episcopal Church, South. Virginia Conference. Proceedings in the trial of W. A. Smith, on charges preferred by C. F. Deems, D. D., at the session of 1855. Richmond, Va., Charles H. Wynne, pr., 1856. 52 p.   [8648

Methodist Episcopal Church, South. Western North Carolina Conference. Minutes of the annual conference, 1st-49th, 1890-1938. 1891-1939. NcU has 1890-1938   [8649

Methodist Episcopal Church, South. Western N. C. Conference. Woman's Missionary Society. Minutes, 1891-1938. 1891-1938. NcU has 1891 [1900-1931] [8650

Methodist Episcopal Church, South. Western N. C. Conference and N. C. Conference. Report of joint commission on church building at Chapel Hill. No place [pref. 1926] 4 p.   [8651

Methodist Episcopal Church, South see also Methodist Church (United States)

Methodist Protestant Church. N. C. Conference. Journal, 18 - 1938. 18 - 1938. NcU has 1843, 1868, 1885, 1887-1938   [8652

Methodist Protestant Church see also Methodist Church (United States)

Methodist Protestant Female College, Jamestown, N. C. Catalogue, 18 - 18 - NcU has 1859/60   [8653

Methodist Protestant herald, v. 1-45, 1894-1939. Greensboro, North Carolina Conference of the Methodist Protestant Church, 1894-1939. NcU has v. [41-42] 43-45.   [8654

Metropolitan Railroad. Report of a survey of a railroad route between Raleigh and Cheraw by John Childe and Thomas S. O'Sullivan. Fayetteville, Edward J. Hale, 1848. 16 p.   [8655

Meyer, Alfred Masten. . . . A history of the Southern Association of Colleges and Secondary Schools. Nashville, Tenn., George Peabody College for Teachers, 1936. ([George Peabody college for teachers, Nashville] Abstract of Contribution to education, no. 173) 9 p.   [8656

Meyer, Gladys Eleanor. The magic circle. New York, A. A. Knopf, 1944. 313 p. [8657

Meyer, Harold Diedrich. Community recreation, a guide to its organization and administration, by Harold D. Meyer and Charles K. Brightbill. Boston, D. C. Heath [1948] 704 p.   [8658

——. . . Financing extra curricular activities [by] Harold D. Meyer . . . and Samuel McKee Eddleman. New York, A. S. Barnes and Co., 1929. 132 p.   [8659

——A handbook of extra-curricular activities in the high school. New York, A. S. Barnes and Co., 1926. 402 p.   [8660

——Recreation administration, a guide to its practices [by] Harold D. Meyer [and] Charles K. Brightbill. Englewood Cliffs, N. J., Prentice-Hall, 1956. 496 p. [8661

——. . . The school club program. New York, A. S. Barnes and Co., Inc., 1931. 178 p. [8662

Meynardie, Elias J. Address delivered on the anniversary of St. John the Baptist, June 26th, 1855 . . . before Catawba Valley Lodge, no. 100, A. F. M., at Morganton, N. C. Charleston, Printed by A. J. Burke, 1855. 19 p. [8663

Michael, Olin Bain. Yadkin College, 1856-1924. Salisbury, Rowan Printing Co., 1939. 182 p. [8664

Michaux, André. Flora boreali-americana. Parisiis et Argentorati, apud fratres Levrault, 1803. 2 v. [8665

——Travels west of the Alleghanies made in 1793-96 by André Michaux; in 1802 by F. A. Michaux; and in 1803 by Thaddeus Mason Harris. Cleveland, Arthur H. Clark Co., 1904. 382 p. [8666

Michaux, Anna Meade. Phonic drills; . . . by Anna Meade Michaux, Mary Owen Graham, J. A. Matheson. Chicago, Rand McNally & Co. [c.1910-11] 43 p. [8667

Michaux, François André. North American sylva; or, A description of the forest trees of the U. S., Canada, and Nova Soctia . . . by François André Michaux and T. Nuttall. Philadelphia, D. Rice & A. N. Hart, 1857. 5 v. [8668

——Travels to the westward of the Alleghany mountains, in the states of the Ohio, Kentucky, and Tennessee, and return to Charlestown, through the upper Carolinas. London, J. Mawman, 1805. 350 p. [8669

—— ——London, Printed for R. Phillips, 1805. (Phillips, R., pub. Collection of modern and contemporary voyages & travels, v. 1) 96 p. [8670

——Voyage a l'ouest des monts Alléghanys, dans les états de l'Ohio, du Kentucky, et du Tennessée. Paris, Levrault, Schoell et cie., 1804. 312 p. [8671

Michaux, John Lafayette. The blessing and the departure; a discourse on the life and death of Dr. C. J. H. W. Hester, delivered at Union Chapel, Granville County, N. C. . . . October 31st, 1875. Greensboro, Printed at Central Protestant Office, 1875. 17 p. [8672

Michaux, Richard Randolph. Sketches of life in North Carolina. Culler, W. C. Phillips, pr., 1894. 247 p. [8673

Michie, Allan A. Dixie demagogues, by Allan A. Michie and Frank Ryhlick. New York, Vanguard Press [c.1939] 298 p. [8674

Michigan. University. William L. Clements Library of American History. A brief account of Ralegh's Roanoke colony of 1585. Ann Arbor, Michigan, 1935. (Bulletin xxii of the William L. Clements Library) 18 p. [8675

——British headquarters maps and sketches used by Sir Henry Clinton . . . 1775-1782; a descriptive list of the original manuscripts and printed documents . . . in the William L. Clements library. Ann Arbor, William L. Clements Library, 1928. 144 p. [8676

Micklejohn, George. On the important duty of subjection to the civil powers. A sermon preached before . . . William Tryon . . . Governor . . . of the Province of North-Carolina, and the troops raised to quell the late insurrection at Hillsborough . . . September 25, 1768. Newbern, Printed by James Davis, 1768. NcU has photograph [8677

Middle South wool book. Leaksville, Leaksville Woolen Mills, 1900. 95 p. [8678

Middleton, Christopher. A vindication of the conduct of Captain Christopher Middleton, in a late voyage on board His Majesty's ship the Furnace, for discovering a north-west passage. London, Printed by the Author's appointment; and sold by J. Robinson, 1743. 206 p. [8679

Middleton, Lamar. Revolt, U. S. A. New York, Stackpole Sons [c.1938] 313 p. [8680

Middleton, Robert Lee. Thinking about God; devotional meditations. Nashville, Broadman Press [1955] 119 p. [8681

Midland Improvement and Construction Company. . . . Statement of W. J. Best, president. No place [1883] 16 p. [8682

Midland North Carolina Railway. Circular. Newbern, 1881. [1] p. [8683

——Report of president and directors, July 15, 1882. No place [1882?] 24 p. [8684

Midland North Carolina Railway. Engineer. Report of J. W. Andrews, chf. eng. &

supt. . . . on the condition of the A. & N. C. railroad.   Newbern, N. S. Richardson, pr., 1882.   20 p.   [8685

Miers, Earl Schenck. The general who marched to hell: William Tecumseh Sherman and his march to fame and infamy.   New York, A. A. Knopf, 1951.   349 p.   [8686

Milan.   Esposizione Universale, 1906. Comitato "I valdesi all' estero".   I valdesi in America.   Torino, Unione Tipografico-Editrice, 1906.   127 p.   [8687

Milburn, Frank Pierce. [Designs from the work of Frank P. Milburn, architect, Columbia, S. C.]   No place, no publisher [1901?]   [5] p.   [8688
——Designs from the work of Frank P. Milburn.   [Columbia, S. C., State, 1903?] [7] p.   [8689

Milburn, Frank Pierce and Co. Specifications for a library building for the University of the state of North Carolina . . . at Chapel Hill, N. C.   Washington, n.d.   42 p.   [8690

Milburn, Heister, and Co. Book of designs.   [Columbia, State] 1905.   3 p. 84 plates.   [8691

[**Milburn, Heister, and Co.**]   [Selections from the latest work of Milburn, Heister, and co., architects.]   No place, no publisher, n.d.   48 plates.   [8692

Miles, Herbert De la Haye. Look up, O world.   Boston, B. Humphries [1948] 151 p.   [8693

Milham, Willis Isbister. Early American observatories.   Northfield, Minn., Goodsell Observatory of Carleton College, 1937.   28 p.   [8694
——Early American observatories.   Which was the first astronomical observatory in America?   Williamstown, Mass., Williams College, 1938.   58 p.   [8695

Milhollen, Hirst Dillon. Presidents on parade, by Hirst D. Milhollen and Milton Kaplan.   New York, Macmillan Co., 1948.   425 p.   [8696

Military Conventions, Goldsboro, N. C., July 11, 1860, Salisbury, N. C., Nov. 14-15, 1860. Proceedings.   Salisbury, Printed by J. J. Bruner, 1860.   34 p.   [8697

Military Historical Society of Massachusetts, Boston. Operations on the Atlantic coast, 1861-1865, Virginia, 1862, 1864, Vicksburg.   Boston, 1912.   (Papers of the Military Historical Society of Massachusetts [v. IX])   585 p.   [8698

The military movement of Gov. Holden.   [Raleigh? 1871]   [2] p.   NcU has microfilm (negative) from original in Library of Congress   [8699

Military Order of the Loyal Legion of the United States.   Ohio Commandery. Sketches of war history, 1861-1865; papers read before the Ohio Commandery . . . 1883-19   v. 1-   Cincinnati, R. Clarke & Co., 1888-19   v. NcU has v. 5   [8700

Miller, A. A vindication of the Evangelical Lutheran Tennessee Synod; reply to a sermon delivered by the Rev. John Bachman . . . by the Rev. A. J. Brown and Rev. A. Miller.   Salem, Printed by Blum & Son, 1838.   46 p.   [8701

Miller, Alexander F. Safety, security and the South, by Alexander F. Miller and Mozell Hill.   Atlanta, Southern Regional Council [1951?]   28 p.   [8702

Miller, Allen Guivere. Along life's way; selections from his best short pieces . . . and from those of his sister, M. M. W.   Boston, Meador Publishing Co., 1938. 87 p.   [8703
——As once I passed this way.   Boston, Meador Publishing Co., c.1935.   143 p. [8704

[**Miller, Allen Guivere**]   Guy Ego's average philosophy.   Asheville, Light [1906?] 16 p.   [8705

Miller, Allen Guivere. Light on life's meanings.   Kalmia, Author, 1940.   32 p.   [8706
——Lyrics of life.   Boston, Meador Press, 1937.   48 p.   [8707
——The meaning of life.   Kalmia, Author [1946]   27 p.   [8708
——Thoughts.   Kalmia, Author [1939]   32 p.   [8709
——What we and the world should be and do, songs and sense we'd send to you. Kalmia, Author, 1943.   32 p.   [8710

Miller, Arnold deWilles. Descriptive catalogue of the library of the late Dr. A. W. Miller, of Charlotte, N. C.   No place, no publisher [1892?]   69 p.   [8711
——The General Assembly of 1879 on the force of past deliverances touching worldly amusements.   St. Louis, Presbyterian Publishing Co., n.d.   99 p.   [8712
——Memorial sketches of Rev. Robert Hall Morrison, by Rev. A. W. Miller and Gen. D. H. Hill.   Charlotte, Hirst Printing Co., 1889.   16 p.   [8713

——The restoration of the Jews. Atlanta, Constitution Publishing Co., 1887. 59 p. [8714

Miller, Barnette. Beyond the Sublime Porte; the Grand seraglio of Stambul. New Haven, Yale University Press, 1931. 281 p. [8715

Miller, Carolyn. William R. Davie. No place, no publisher, n.d. [2] p. [8716

Miller, David Reed. The Red Swan's Neck; a tale of the North Carolina mountains. Boston, Sherman, French & Co., 1911. 328 p. [8717

Miller, Elva E. Fertilizing for profit. Raleigh, Presses Mutual Publishing Co., 1910. 106 p. [8718

Miller, Francis Pickens, ed. . . . The southern press considers the Constitution. Chapel Hill, University of North Carolina Press, 1936. (Southern policy papers, no. 6) 28 p. [8719

Miller, Frank T. Plan and report on grade crossing elimination for the city of Charlotte, North Carolina. Greensboro, Author, 1950. 30 p. [8720

——A plan and report with estimates and recommendations covering railway and street grade crossing elimination for the city of Thomasville, North Carolina. Greensboro, Author, 1948. 19 p. [8721

Miller, Helen (Topping) Hawk in the wind. New York, D. Appleton-Century Co., Inc., 1938. 256 p. [8723

——Her Christmas at the Hermitage; a tale about Rachel and Andrew Jackson. New York, Longmans, Green, 1955. 89 p. [8724

——The horns of Capricorn. New York, Appleton-Century-Crofts[1950] 282 p [8725

——Sharon. Philadelphia, Penn Publishing Co. [c.1931] 311 p. [8727

——Slow dies the thunder. Indianapolis, Bobbs-Merrill Co. [1955] 310 p. [8728

——The sound of chariots; a novel of John Sevier and the State of Franklin. Indianapolis, Bobbs-Merrill Co. [1947] 288 p. [8729

——Splendor of eagles. Philadelphia, Penn Publishing Co. [c.1935\ 312 p. [8730

——Whispering river. New York, D. Appleton-Century Co., Inc., 1936. 280 p. [8731

Miller, Henry W. Address before the Sons of Temperance at the celebration in Raleigh, August 11, 1849. No place, no publisher, n.d. 12 p. [8732

——An address delivered before the Euzelian and Philomathesian societies of Wake Forest College. Raleigh, Raleigh Register, 1839. 22 p. [8733

——Address delivered before the N. C. Military and Scientific Academy in . . . Raleigh . . . 30th October, 1845. Raleigh, W. W. Holden, 1846. 18 p. [8734

——Address delivered before the Philanthropic and Dialectic societies of the University of North-Carolina, June 3, 1857. Raleigh, Holden & Wilson, 1857. 34 p. [8735

——Address to the young ladies, patrons and friends of the Louisburg Female Seminary. Raleigh, Printed at the Office of the Carolina Cultivator, 1855. 16 p. [8736

——The eighteenth century; address written and delivered in North Carolina in 1856 for the benefit of the Mt. Vernon Ladies' Association. Leaksville, Gazette, 1896. 30 p. [8737

——Eulogy on the life and character of General Zachary Taylor; delivered at the request of the citizens of Raleigh . . . July 20th, 1850. Raleigh, Spirit of the Age, 1850. 16 p. [8738

——Speech delivered at Oxford, North Carolina, November 5, 1850, in reply to Hon. A. W. Venable. No place, no publisher [1850] 8 p. [8739

Miller, J. B. Watauga boys in the great Civil War. No place, no publisher, n.d. 15 p. [8740

Miller, Justin Handbook of criminal law. St. Paul, Minn., West Publishing Co., 1934. 649 p. [8741

——Preventive justice and the law. New York, National Probation Association, 1930. 19 p. [8742

Miller, Kelly. As to the leopard's spots; an open letter to Thomas Dixon, Jr. Washington, Hayworth Publishing Co. [1905] 21 p. [8743

Miller, Norman Mickey. I took the sky road, by Comdr. Norman M. Miller, USN, as told to Hugh B. Cave. New York, Dodd, Mead & Co., 1945. 212 p. [8744

Miller, Robert Johnston. An introduction to the knowledge of the Christian religion. Salisbury, Printed by John M. Slump at Michael Brown's Printing Office, 1799. 50 p. [8745

Miller, Robert V. The eternal purpose. New York, Charles C. Cook, 1911. 31 p. [8746

Miller, Stephen Franks. The bench and bar of Georgia: memoirs and sketches. Philadelphia, J. B. Lippincott & Co., 1858. 2 v.   [8747

Miller's Asheboro, N. C., city directory, v. 1- 1937- Asheville, Southern Directory Co., 1937- NcU has 1937-38, 1941-42, 1947-48, 1951-52   [8748

Miller's Asheville (Buncombe County, N. C.) city directory, 190 - Richmond, Piedmont Directory Co., 190 - NcU has 1913, 1927, 1935, 1943, 1947, 1951, 1953, 1954   [8749

Miller's Canton, N. C., city directory, 1937-38- Asheville, Southern Directory Co., 1937- NcU has 1937-38, 1942-43   [8750

Miller's Elizabeth City, N. C., city directory, 192 - Asheville, Southern Directory Co., 192 - NcU has 1936-37, 1938-39, 1942-43   [8751

Miller's Greenville, N. C., city directory, 193 - Asheville, Southern Directory Co., 193 - NcU has 1936-37, 1942-43, 1947-48, 1951-52   [8752

Miller's Henderson, N. C., city directory, 1938-39- Asheville, Southern Directory Co., c.1938- NcU has 1938-39, 1940-41, 1947-48   [8753

Miller's Hendersonville, N. C., city directory, 192 - Asheville, Commercial Service Co., Inc., 192 - NcU has 1926-27, 1937-38, 1943-44, 1948-49, 1950-51, 1952-53   [8754

Miller's Hickory, N. C., city directory, 19 - Asheville, Southern Directory Co., c.19 - NcU has 1925-26, 1937-38, 1943-44, 1947-48, 1951-52   [8755

Miller's Lenoir, N. C., city directory, 193 - Asheville, Southern Directory Co., 193 - NcU has 1937-38, 1939-1940, 1943-44, 1948-49, 1950-51, 1953-54   [8756

Miller's Lexington, N. C., city directory, 192 - Asheville, Miller Press, 192 - NcU has 1925-26, 1941-42, 1947-48, 1951-52   [8757

Miller's Marion, N. C., city directory, 1940-41- Asheville, Southern Directory Co., 1940- NcU has 1940-41   [8758

Miller's Mooresville, N. C., city directory, 1939-1940- Asheville, Southern Directory Co., 1939- NcU has 1939-1940, 1950-51   [8759

Miller's Morganton, N. C., city directory, 1939-1940- Asheville, Southern Directory Co., c.1939- NcU has 1939-1940, 1943-44, 1948-49   [8760

Miller's Mount Airy, N. C., city directory, 194 - Asheville, Southern Directory Co., 194 - NcU has 1949-1950   [8761

Miller's New Bern, N. C., city directory, 19 - Asheville, Southern Directory Co., 19 - NcU has 1947-48   [8762

Miller's North Wilkesboro, N. C., city directory, including Wilkesboro, 1939/40- Asheville, Southern Directory Co., c.1939- NcU has 1939/40, 1948/49   [8763

Miller's Oxford, N. C., city directory, 19 - Asheville, Southern Directory Co., 19 - NcU has 1942-1943   [8764

Miller's Reidsville, N. C., city directory, 193 - Asheville, Southern Directory Co., 193 - NcU has 1941-1942, 1948-49, 1952-53   [8765

Miller's Roanoke Rapids, N. C., city directory, 1938-39- Asheville, Southern Directory Co., 1938- NcU has 1938-39, 1942-43, 1948-49, 1950-51   [8766

Miller's Shelby, N. C., city directory, 193 - Asheville, Southern Directory Co., c.193 - NcU has 1937-38, 1939-1940, 1941-42, 1943-44, 1947-48, 1951-52   [8767

Miller's Statesville, N. C., city directory, 191 - Asheville, Piedmont Directory Co. (Inc.) 191 - NcU has 1916-17, 1922-23, 1930-31, 1932-33, 1940-41, 1942-43, 1948-49, 1952-53   [8768

Miller's Washington, N. C., city directory, 1916-17- Asheville, Southern Directory Co., 1916- NcU has 1916-17, 1948-49   [8769

Millett, Fred Benjamin. Contemporary American authors; a critical survey and 219 bio-bibliographies. New York, Harcourt, Brace and Co., 1940. 716 p.   [8770

Milling, Chapman James. Red Carolinians. Chapel Hill, University of North Carolina Press, 1940. 438 p.   [8771

Millis, Mary (Raoul) The family of Raoul. [Asheville] Privately printed. [The Miller Printing Co.] 1943. 224 p.   [8772

Mills, Charles. The choice. New York, Macmillan Co., 1943. 424 p.   [8773

Mills, George H. History of the Sixteenth North Carolina Regiment (originally 6th N. C. Regiment) in the Civil War. [Rutherfordton, Sun Printing Co., 1902] 76 p. [8774

Mills, John Haymes. About children; blood and diet, walking and talking, books and schools. Raleigh, Ferrell, Booker & Co., 1879. 27 p. [8775
——French spelling book, grammar, and reader. Raleigh, W. L. Pomeroy, 1860. 64 p. [8776

Mills, Mary Hampton. Be ye beggar or king. Asheville, Advocate Publishing Co., n.d. 176 p. [8777

Mills, Quincy Sharpe. Editorials, sketches and stories. New York, G. P. Putnam's Sons, 1930. 863 p. [8778
——One who gave his life; war letters of Qunicy Sharpe Mills, with a sketch of his life and ideals . . . by James Luby. New York, G. P. Putnam, 1923. 490 p. [8779

Mills Home, Inc., Thomasville, N. C. see **Baptist Orphanage, Thomasville, N. C.**

Milner, Clyde Alonzo. The dean of the small college. Boston, Christopher Publishing House [c.1936] 151 p. [8780

Milton, George Fort. . . . The age of hate; Andrew Johnson and the radicals. New York, Coward-McCann, Inc., 1930. 787 p. [8781

Milton, William Hammond. The call of the hour; two sermons preached in Saint James' Church, Wilmington, North Carolina . . . in Lent, 1917. [Wilmington? 1917?] 27 p. [8782
——The great adventure . . . at a memorial service in St. James Church, Wilmington, North Carolina, January 5th, 1919. [Wilmington? 1919?] 16 p. For Frank Lenox Williams. [8783
——Ventures of the soul; sermons preached in St. James' Church, Wilmington, N. C., during the Lenten and Easter seasons of 1911. Wilmington, Jackson & Bell Co., n.d. 126 p. [8784

Mims, Edwin. The advancing South. Garden City, N. Y., Doubleday, Page & Co., 1926. 319 p. [8785
——John Maurice Webb, 1847-1916; an address delivered at Webb School commencement, June 5, 1946. Nashville, Tenn., 1946. 25 p. [8786
——Sidney Lanier. Boston, Houghton Mifflin Co., 1905. 386 p. [8787

Mims, Edwin, ed. Southern prose and poetry for schools, by Edwin Mims . . . and Bruce R. Payne. New York, Charles Scribner's Sons, 1910. 440 p. [8788

"Mine angel before thee." New York, E. P. Dutton and Co., 1872. 48 p. [8789

Miner, William Harvey. Daniel Boone; contribution toward a bibliography. New York, The Dibdin Club, 1901. 32 p. [8790

Minor, Charles Launcelot. What you should know about tuberculosis. New York, National Tuberculosis Association [1925] 32 p. [8791

Minton, William Thomas. Life of Hosanna Baker. No place, n.d. [6] p. [8792
——Signs of the times; a . . . recital of the oppression of the "toiling masses of humanity". Richmond, Va., L. H. Jenkins [1912?] 50 p. [8793
——The Turko-Balkan war. Richmond, Hermitage Press, 1913. 142 p. [8794

Mintz, David B. The spiritual song book, designed as an assistant for the pious of all denominations. Halifax, Printed by Abraham Hodge, 1805. 65 p. [8795

A minute and circumstantial narrative of the loss of the stream-packet Pulaski . . . on the coast of North-Carolina, June 14, 1828. Providence, H. H. Brown, 1838. 24 p. [8796

Miranda, Francisco de. The diary of Francisco de Miranda, tour of the United States, 1783-1784. New York [The Hispanic Society of America] 1928. 206 p. [8797

Misrepresentations about Aycock. No place, no publisher [1900] [2] p. [8798

Mission herald, v. 1- 18 - Plymouth, N. C. Diocese of East Carolina, 18 - NcU has v. [23, 25-31] 36-70 [8799

Missionary District of Asheville see **Protestant Episcopal Church. Missionary District of Asheville**

Misstatements as to Hoke county corrected. No place, no publisher [1909?] 3 p. [8800
. . . **Mr. Clay** and General Jackson . . . a complete history of the case. [Baltimore, 1827] 16 p. [8801

Mitchell, Allen & Company, Newbern, N. C. . . . North Carolina agricultural house and hardware store . . . catalogue. Newbern, W. I. Vestal, pr., 1866. 36 p. [8802

Mitchell, Broadus. The industrial revolution in the South, by Broadus Mitchell . . . and George Sinclair Mitchell. Baltimore, Johns Hopkins Press, 1930. 298 p. [8803

——Rise of cotton mills in the South. Baltimore, Johns Hopkins, 1921. (Johns Hopkins studies in historical and political science. Ser. 19, no. 2) 281 p. [8804

Mitchell, Elisha. Arguments for temperance; a sermon addressed to the students of the University of N. C., March 13th, 1831. Raleigh, Printed by J. Gales & Son, 1831. 29 p. [8805

——Catalogue of books and instruments belonging to Dr. E. Mitchell, for sale at his late residence. Chapel Hill, Gazette, 1857. 15 p. [8806

——. . . Diary of a geological tour . . . in 1827 and 1828, with introduction . . . by Dr. Kemp P. Battle. Chapel Hill, The University, 1905. (University of North Carolina. James Sprunt historical monograph no. 6) 73 p. [8807

——Elements of geology, with an outline of the geology of North Carolina. No place, no publisher, 1842. 141 p. [8808

——A lecture on the subject of common schools, delivered before the North Carolina Institute of Education, at Chapel Hill, June 26, 1834. Chapel Hill, Printed by Isaac C. Patridge, 1834. 12 p. [8809

[**Mitchell, Elisha?**] Natural history. No place, no publisher, n.d. 27 p. [8810

—— ——28 p. [8811

——The other leaf of the book of nature and the word of God. No place, no publisher, 1948 (misprint for 1848) 74 p. [8812

——Remarks on Bishop Ravenscroft's answer to the statements contained in Professor Mitchell's printed letter of the 12th of February last. Raleigh, Printed by J. Gales & Son, 1825. 48 p. [8813

——Statistics, facts, and dates, for the Sunday recitations of the Junior Class in the University. Raleigh, Register, 1843. 16 p. [8814

Mitchell, Elisha, joint author, see **Ravenscroft, John Stark**

Mitchell, George Sinclair. Textile unionism and the South. Chapel Hill, University of North Carolina Press, 1931. 92 p. [8815

Mitchell, Joseph. McSorley's wonderful saloon. New York, Duell, Sloan and Pearce [1943] 253 p. [8816

——My ears are bent. New York, Sheridan House [c.1938] 284 p. [8817

——Old Mr. Flood. New York, Duell, Sloan and Pearce [1948] 111 p. [8818

Mitchell, Samuel Augustus. Mitchell's traveller's guide through the United States. Philadelphia, Thomas, Cowperthwait & Co. [c.1836] 78 p. [8819

—— ——Philadelphia, Mitchell & Hinman, 1837. [8820

Mitchell College, Statesville, N. C. Bulletin, ser. 1- 192 - Statesville, 192 - NcU has ser. [5-27] catalogue issue only [8821

Mitchell Co., N. C. Board of Education. Discovering Mitchell County, 1939-40: a cooperative study. Bakersville [1940?] 58 p. [8822

[**Mitchell Co., N. C. Board of Education**] The heritage of Toe River Valley; a drama of county history . . . produced . . . 1941-42. [Bakersville, 1942?] 73 p. [8823

Mitchell Co., N. C. Board of Education. Improving science teaching in Mitchell County, 1940-41. Bakersville [1941?] 55 p. [8824

——Then and now, Mitchell County Schools. Bakersville [1953] 19 p. At head of title: 1922, 1952. [8825

Mitchell County Baptist Association. Minutes, 188 - 188 - NcU has 1897, 1906 [8826

Mode, Peter G. Source book and bibliographical guide for American church history. Menasha, Wisconsin, George Banta Publishing Co. [c.1921] 735 p. [8827

Model school, spelling class up. No place, no publisher [1878?] 1 p. [8828

The Mohisco, 19 - Monroe, Monroe High School, 19 - NcU has 1916, 1917 [8829

Molton, Thomas Hunter. Molton family and kinsmen; Hooks, Hunter, Whitfield, . . . and others. [Birmingham, Ala., Birmingham Publishing Co., 1922] 145 p. [8830

Moment, Alfred H. Temperance in the light of the letter and spirit of the Bible; a sermon preached before the N. C. state convention of the Woman's Christian Temperance Union . . . Raleigh, N. C., Oct. 1st, 1905. [Raleigh, Edwards & Broughton, n.d.] 8 p. [8831

——The will of God to man and man's duty to God. Richmond, Va., Presbyterian Committee of Publication, n.d. 16 p.   [8832

Money, Hernando De Soto. Extracts from Senator Money's great speech in reply to Senator Pritchard. Raleigh, E. M. Uzzell, pr., 1900. 16 p.   [8833

Moneymaker, Berlen Clifford. . . . Stratigraphy and structural geology of the Hiwassee River basin in vicinity of Coleman dam site. Knoxville, Tenn., 1934. (Tennessee Valley Authority. General engineering and geology division. Geologic bulletin, no. 2) 29 p.   [8834

Monroe, John. Faith and baptism; two discourses, delivered at Spring Hill, N. C., November 22, 1857. Fayetteville, Edward J. Hale & Son, pr., 1858. 96 p. [8835

Monroe, N. C. Public Schools. Course of study, 1912/13. Monroe, 1912. 15 p. [8836

Monroe, North Carolina, city directory, 1922/23- Asheville, Commercial Service Co., 1922- NcU has 1922-23, 1942-43   [8837

Montgomery, Elizabeth Wilson. The Saint Mary's of olden days. Raleigh, Bynum Printing Co., 1932. 28 p.   [8838

——Sketches of old Warrenton, North Carolina. Raleigh, Edwards & Broughton, 1924. 451 p.   [8839

Montgomery, Walter Alexander, 1845-1921. Address and poem; delivered at the unveiling of the monument . . . to the . . . Confederate dead of Warren County, N. C., Aug. 27, 1903. Raleigh, Edwards & Broughton, 1906. 20 p.   [8840

——The days of old and the years that are past. [Charlottesville, Va.? Privately printed, 1939?] 67 p.   [8841

——Life and character of Major-General W. D. Pender; memorial address, May 10, 1894. Raleigh, Edwards & Broughton, 1894. 27 p.   [8842

Montgomery, Walter Alexander, 1872-1949. Memorial address, May 26, 1940, under the auspices of the Albemarle Chapter of the United Daughters of the Confederacy. [Charlottesville, Va.? 1940?] 10 p.   [8843

Montgomery, William. To the people of the state of N. C. [by William Montgomery and M. T. Hawkins] No place, no publisher [1840] 8 p.   [8844

Montgomery Baptist Association. Minutes, 188 - 188 - NcU has 1902, 1907 [1926-1954]   [8845

Monthly magazine, v. 1, no. 1-4, December, 1872-April, 1873. Statesville, Chas. R. Jones, pr., 1872-73. NcU has v. 1. (v. 1, no. 1, defective)   [8846

Monthly visitor, v. 1- May, 1869- New Bern, N. C. Masonic Mutual Life Insurance Co., 1869- NcU has v. [1]   [8847

Montreat College, Montreat, N. C. Catalogue, 19 - 19 - NcU has 1946/47, 1952/53   [8848

Montreat Normal School for Young Women, Montreat, N. C. Catalogue, 1916/17?- Montreat, 1917?- NcU has 1918/19   [8849

Montreat, where is it? [Raleigh, Edwards & Broughton] 1902. 14 p.   [8850

Monvert, Adolphe de, pseud. see **Vermont, Adolph**

Moon, Anna Mary. Sketches of the Shelby, McDowell, Deaderick, Anderson families. [Chattanooga, c.1933] 150 p.   [8851

Moore, Albert Burton. Conscription and conflict in the Confederacy. New York, Macmillan Co., 1924. 367 p.   [8852

Moore, Alfred. Address delivered before the North Carolina Institute of Education at their annual meeting, June 19th, 1832. Newbern, Printed by John L. Pasteur, 1832. 16 p.   [8853

Moore, Anne. Children of God and winged things. Boston, Four Seas Co., 1921. 126 p.   [8854

——A misty sea. Portland, Me., Southworth-Anteoensen Press, 1937. 154 p. [8855

Moore, Augustus. To the public. [Norfolk, Va., T. G. Broughton, pr., 1833] 29 p.   [8856

Moore, Bartholomew Figures. Address before the Euzelian and Philomathesian societies of Wake Forest College . . . June 11, 1856. Raleigh, Biblical Recorder, 1856. 20 p.   [8857

——Address delivered before the two literary societies of the University of North Carolina, June 5th, 1846. Raleigh, Recorder, 1846. 26 p.   [8858

——Address on life, character, and public services of Henry Clay, delivered on the
. . . day of Aug. 1852, at Weldon, North Carolina. Raleigh, Southern Weekly
Post, 1853. 27 p.   [8859
——B. F. Moore's will. No place [1878] 10 p.   [8860
——Speech before the Young Men's Scott and Graham Club, Raleigh, July 13th,
1852. No place, no publisher [1852?] [1] p.   [8861
——To the voters of Wake County. Raleigh, Sept. 12, 1865. [1] p.   [8862
Moore, Bertha B. As by fire. Grand Rapids, Mich., William B. Eerdmans Pub-
lishing Co., 1939. 192 p.   [8863
——Autumn on Breezy Hill, a story for pre-school children, by Betsy McCurry.
Grand Rapids, Zondervan Pub. House [1956] 56 p.   [8864
——The Baers' Christmas. Grand Rapids, Mich., Wm. B. Eerdmans Publishing
Co., 1953. 86 p.   [8865
——Black top. Grand Rapids, W. B. Eerdmans Pub. Co., 1956. 151 p.   [8866
——Bread for the hungry, by Brenda Cannon [pseud.] Chicago, Bica Press [c.1940]
159 p.   [8867
——Dan and Jack find a pal, by Brenda Cannon [pseud.] Chicago, Moody Press
[c.1955] 127 p.   [8868
——Doctor Happy. Grand Rapids, Mich., Wm. B. Eerdmans Publishing Co., 1938.
184 p.   [8869
——Eyes unto the hills. Grand Rapids, Mich., Wm. B. Eerdmans Publishing Co.,
1953. 192 p.   [8870
——From palms to pines. Grand Rapids, Mich., Wm. B. Eerdmans Publishing Co.,
1947. 181 p.   [8871
——The girl of the listening heart. Grand Rapids, Mich., Wm. B. Eerdmans Pub-
lishing Co., 1937. 188 p.   [8872
——Go with him twain. Grand Rapids, Mich., Wm. B. Eerdmans Publishing Co.,
1941. 171 p.   [8873
——The healing hills, by Betsy McCurry. Findlay, O., Fundamental Truth Pub-
lishers [c.1941] 175 p.   [8874
——The Jolly J's have a reunion, by Brenda Cannon [pseud.] Chicago, Moody
Press [c.1952] 128 p.   [8875
——The Jolly J's make decisions, by Brenda Cannon [pseud.] Chicago, Moody
Press [1951] 125 p.   [8876
——The Jolly J's of Silver Creek, by Brenda Cannon [pseud.] Chicago, Moody
Press [1949] 126 p.   [8877
——Joy shop stories. Springfield, Mo., Gospel Publishing House [c.1929] 71 p. [8878
——Joyous Judy. Grand Rapids, Mich., Wm. B. Eerdmans Publishing Co. [1936]
226 p.   [8879
——Laborers together. Grand Rapids, W. B. Eerdmans Publishing Co., 1952.
206 p.   [8880
——Listen, the bells. Grand Rapids, Mich., Wm. B. Eerdmans Publishing Co.,
1949. 168 p.   [8881
——Mary Sunshine. Grand Rapids, Mich., Wm. B. Eerdmans Publishing Co.,
1939. 191 p.   [8882
——Mercy forever, a novel, by Bertha B. McCurry. Grand Rapids, Mich., W. B.
Eerdmans Publishing Co., 1954. 201 p.   [8883
——Never forgotten. Grand Rapids, Mich., Eerdmans Publishing Co., 1940.
192 p.   [8884
——A new song. Grand Rapids, Mich., Wm. B. Eerdmans Publishing Co. [1946]
166 p.   [8885
——On Silver Creek knob, by Brenda Cannon [pseud.] Chicago, Moody Press
[c.1939] 123 p.   [8886
——One master. Grand Rapids, Wm. B. Eerdmans Publishing Co., 1947. 183 p. [8887
——Ordered steps. Grand Rapids, Mich., Wm. B. Eerdmans Publishing Co., 1940.
3d ed. 192 p.   [8888
——Rock of decision. Grand Rapids, Mich., Wm. B. Eerdmans Publishing Co.
[c.1931] 259 p.   [8889
——Silver Creek's Camp Jolly, by Brenda Cannon [pseud.] Chicago, Moody Press
[c.1954] 128 p.   [8890
——Spring on Breezy Hill. Grand Rapids, Mich., Zondervan Publishing House
[1952] 56 p.   [8891
——Strength of the hills, by Brenda Cannon [pseud.] Chicago, Moody Press [1952]
252 p.   [8892

——These, my people. Grand Rapids, Mich., Wm. B. Eerdmans Publishing Co., 1942. 168 p. [8893

——The three Baers. Grand Rapids, Mich., Wm. B. Eerdmans Publishing Co., 1938. 88 p [8894

——To these also. Grand Rapids, Mich., Wm. B. Eerdmans Publishing Co., 1940. 216 p. [8895

——The time of their coming. Grand Rapids, Wm. B. Eerdmans Publishing Co., 1946. 168 p. [8895a

——Tomorrow begins today. Grand Rapids, Mich., Wm. B. Eerdmans Publishing Co., 1938. 136 p. [8896

——The touch of Polly Tucker. Grand Rapids, Mich., Wm. B. Eerdmans, 1950. 189 p. [8897

——The triplets become good neighbors. Grand Rapids, Mich., Wm. B. Eerdmans Publishing Co., 1945. 87 p. [8898

——The triplets fly high. Grand Rapids, Mich., Wm. B. Eerdmans Publishing Co., 1950. 87 p. [8899

——The triplets go places. Grand Rapids, Mich., Wm. B. Eerdmans Publishing Co., 1942. 72 p. [8900

——The triplets go south. Grand Rapids, Mich., Wm. B. Eerdmans Publishing Co., 1940. 86 p. [8901

——The triplets go to camp. Grand Rapids, Mich., Wm. B. Eerdmans Publishing Co., 1952. 83 p. [8902

——The triplets have an adventure. Grand Rapids, W. B. Eerdmans Publishing Co., 1947. 89 p. [8903

——The triplets in business. Grand Rapids, Mich., Wm. B. Eerdmans Publishing Co., 1939. 88 p. [8904

——The triplets make a discovery (eleventh in this series) Grand Rapids, Mich., W. B. Eerdmans Publishing Co., 1948. 89 p. [8905

——The triplets over J. O. Y. Grand Rapids, Mich., Wm. B. Eerdmans Publishing Co., 1941. 79 p. [8906

——The triplets receive a reward. Grand Rapids, Mich., Wm. B. Eerdmans Publishing Co. [1946] 88 p. [8907

——The triplets sign up. Grand Rapids, Wm. B. Eerdmans Publishing Co., [c.1943] 66 p. [8908

——The triplets take over. Grand Rapids, W. B. Eerdmans Publishing Co., 1953. 89 p. [8909

——The triplets try television. Grand Rapids, W. B. Eerdmans Publishing Co., 1954. 86 p. [8910

Moore, Charles C. C. C. Moore, candidate for the nomination for commissioner of agriculture. [Charlotte, Author, 1908] [4] p. [8911

Moore, Charles H. Report of Prof. Chas. H. Moore, state inspector of Negro schools . . . before the North Carolina State Teachers' Association . . . Greensboro, June 23, 1916. [Durham, Durham Reformer, pr.] 1916. 18 p. [8912

Moore, Frank, comp. Rebel rhymes and rhapsodies. New York, George P. Putnam, 1864. 299 p. [8913

Moore, Gabriel T. To the freemen of Stokes County. No place, 1830. [2] p. [8914

Moore, Harry. The Liberty Boys after Cornwallis. New York, Frank Tousey, 1905. (The Liberty Boys of "76". No. 236. July 7, 1905) 28 p. [8915

——The Liberty Boys and Flora MacDonald. New York, Frank Tousey, 1904. (The Liberty Boys of "76". No. 177. May 20, 1904) 28 p. [8916

——The Liberty Boys and General Greene. New York, Frank Tousey, 1903. (The Liberty Boys of "76". No. 140. Sept. 4, 1903) 28 p. [8917

——The Liberty Boys at Guilford Court House. New York, Frank Tousey, 1905. (The Liberty Boys of "76". No. 211. Jan. 13, 1905) 28 p. [8918

——The Liberty Boys at Hanging Rock. New York, Frank Tousey, 1904. (The Liberty Boys of "76". No. 209. Dec. 30, 1904) 28 p. [8919

——The Liberty Boys "going it blind". New York, Tousey, 1902. (The Liberty Boys of "76". No. 87. Aug. 29, 1902) 28 p. [8920

Moore, Harry Estill. . . . What is regionalism? Chapel Hill, University of North Carolina Press, 1937. (Southern policy papers, no. 10) 16 p. [8921

Moore, Harry Estill, joint author, see **Odum, Howard Washington**

Moore, Harry F. S. Murder goes rolling along. Garden City, New York, Pub. for the Crime Club by Doubleday, Doran and Co., Inc., 1942. 273 p. [8922

Moore, Helen Trafford. My thoughts and I. Boston, Richard G. Badger, [c.1929] 44 p. [8923

Moore, Hight C. The country Sunday school. Philadelphia, American Baptist Publication Society [c.1906] 27 p. [8924

——The man of mark in the church tomorrow. Raleigh, Mutual Publishing Co. [1912] 150 p. [8925

——Memorial sketch of William Bradshaw Moore, by his nephew. Morehead City, Author, 1891. 49 p. [8926

——Normal studies for Sunday school workers: 2. The books of the Bible. Nashville, Tenn., Southern Baptist Convention, 1902. 134 p. [8927

——North Carolina poets and their work. Goldsboro, Nash Brothers, pr. [1903?] 14 p. [8928

——Seaside sermons. Morehead City, Author, 1892. 54 p. [8929

Moore, Hight C., comp. Select poetry of North Carolina. Raleigh, Edwards & Broughton, 1894. 210 p. [8930

Moore, Horatio Newton. The life and times of Gen. Francis Marion. Philadelphia, John B. Perry [c.1845] 210 p. [8931

Moore, Ida L. . . . Like a river flowing. New York, Doubleday, Doran and Co., Inc., 1941. 388 p. [8932

Moore, James. Kilpatrick and our cavalry. New York, International Book Co. [c.1865] 245 p. [8933

Moore, James Hall. Defence of the Mecklenburg Declaration of Independence. Raleigh, Edwards & Broughton Printing Co., 1908. 157 p. [8934

Moore, James Lewis. Cabarrus reborn; a historical sketch of the founding and development of Cannon Mills Company and Kannapolis, by James Lewis Moore and Thomas Herron Wingate. Kannapolis, Kannapolis Publishing Co., Inc., 1940. 102 p. [8935

Moore, John Henry. Noble ancestry and descendants. Wilmington, Linprint Co., 1949. 89 p. [8936

Moore, John Monroe. The long road to Methodist union. New York, Abingdon-Cokesbury Press [1943] 247 p. [8937

——The South to-day. New York, Missionary Education Movement of the United States and Canada, 1916. 251 p. [8938

Moore, John Trotwood. Hearts of hickory; a story of Andrew Jackson and the War of 1812. Nashville, Cokesbury Press, 1926. 454 p. [8939

Moore, John Wheeler. Address delivered at Oakwood Cemetery, May 10th, 1881, by request of the Ladies' Memorial Association of North Carolina. Raleigh, Edwards & Broughton, 1881. 11 p. [8940

——Heirs of St. Kilda. Raleigh, Edwards, Broughton & Co., 1881. 493 p. [8941

——History of North Carolina. Raleigh, Alfred Williams & Co., 1880. 2 v. [8942

Moore, John Wheeler, comp. Roster of North Carolina troops in the war between the states. Raleigh, Ashe & Gatling, 1882. 4 v. [8943

Moore, John Wheeler. School history of North Carolina, from 1584 to 1879. Raleigh, Alfred Williams & Co., 1879. 323 p. [8944

— —School history of North Carolina from 1584 to the present time. 2d ed., rev. & enl. Raleigh, Alfred Williams & Co., 1882 [1881] 359 p. [8945

— ——3d ed., rev. and enl. 1882. 397 p. [8946

— ——4th ed. rev. and enl. 1884. 369 p. [8947

— ——5th ed. 1886. 369 p. [8948

— ——6th ed. rev. and enl. 1886. 369 p. [8949

— ——8th ed. rev. and enl. 1889. 369 p. [8950

— ——14th ed. New York, American Book Co. [c.1882] 369 p. [8951

Moore, Joseph Hampton. Address of J. Hampton Moore, president of the Atlantic Deeper Waterways Association, nineteenth annual convention, Richmond, Va., Sept. 15, 1926. No place, no publisher [1926?] 12 p. [8952

——Address . . . Trenton conference on New Jersey canal project, March 2, 1926. No place, no publisher [1926?] 7 p. [8953

Moore, Lilian. Daniel Boone. New York, Random House [1956] 64 p. [8954

Moore, Louis Toomer. Beautiful Oakdale, 1855-1955. [Wilmington? 1956] 8 p. [8955
——Stories old and new of the Cape Fear region. Wilmington, privately published, 1956. 261 p. [8956

Moore, Lucinda (Sugg) The genealogy of the Macons, Martins, and Crenshaws of North Carolina. No place, no publisher, n.d. 12 p. [8957

[**Moore, Lucinda (Sugg)**] The genealogy of the Sugg and Pender families of Edgecomb County, North Carolina. [Greensboro, Charles G. Harrison, 1928] 11 p. [8958

Moore, Marinda (Branson) The Dixie primer for the little folks. 3d ed. Raleigh, Branson, Farrar & Co., 1863. 32 p. [8959
——The Dixie speller, to follow the First Dixie reader. Raleigh, Branson & Farrar, 1864. 120 p. [8960
——First Dixie reader. Raleigh, Branson, Farrar & Co., 1863. 63 p. [8961
—— ——2d ed. 1864. 62 p. [8962
—— ——3d ed. 1866. 48 p. [8963
——The geographical reader for the Dixie children. Raleigh, Branson and Farrar, 1863. 48 p. [8964
——Primary geography arranged as a reading book for common schools. (2d ed.) Raleigh, Branson & Farrar, 1864. 48 p. Rev. ed. of The geographical reader. [8965

[**Moore, Marinda (Branson)**] comp. Songs of love and liberty, comp. by a North Carolina lady. Raleigh, Branson & Farrar, 1864. 62 p. [8966

Moore, Martin V. The rhyme of the southern rivers. Nashville, Tenn., Publishing House M. E. Church, South [1897] 107 p. [8967

Moore, Matthew Henry. Sketches of the pioneers of Methodism in N. C. and Virginia. Nashville, Southern Methodist Publishing House, 1884. 314 p. [8968

Moore, Maurice. Justice and policy of taxing the American colonies in Great-Britain considered. Wilmington, Printed by Andrew Steuart, 1765. 16 p. [8969

Moore, Walter William. Appreciations and historical addresses. No place, no publisher, n.d. 167 p. [8970
——Exercises in connection with the inauguration of the Rev. Walter W. Moore, . . . as president of Union Theological Seminary, Richmond, Virginia, May 9, 1905. Richmond, Press of L. D. Sullivan & Co., n.d. 50 p. [8971
——The indispensable book. New York, Fleming H. Revell Co. [c.1910] 114 p. [8972
——The life and letters of Walter W. Moore . . . by J. Gray McAllister. Richmond, Va., Union Theological Seminary, 1939. 576 p. [8973
——A real boy scout. Richmond, Presbyterian Committee of Publication, 1920. 53 p. [8974
——The whole man; baccalaureate sermon . . . at the University of North Carolina, Chapel Hill, N. C., May 31st, 1891. Wilmington, Jackson & Bell, 1891. 23 p. [8975

[**Moore, Walter William**] William Hall Kerr. [Baltimore, William J. Dulaney Co., pr., pref. 1895] 32 p. [8976

Moore, Walter William. A year in Europe. Richmond, Va., Presbyterian Committee of Publication, 1904. 366 p. [8977

Moore, William Armistead. Law and order vs. Ku Klux violence; speech . . . delivered in the House of Representatives, Jan. 19, 1870. No place, no publisher, n.d. 8 p. [8978

Moore, William Henry. An historical oration on the life and labors of Rev. Hezekiah Leigh . . . Kinston, N. C., December 8, 1896. [Petersburg, Va., Mitchell Manufacturing Co.] n.d. 15 p. [8979
——Rise and progress of the M. E. Church, South; a centennial address . . . before the Hillsboro District Conference in Chapel Hill, August A. D. 1876. Durham, D. W. Whitaker, pr., 1876. 22 p. [8980
——Virginia Dare: a story of colonial days. [Raleigh] for the Author by Edwards & Broughton, 1904. 67 p. [8981

Moore Co., N. C. Board of Education. Report of the Public Schools of Moore County, 19 - Sanford, 19 - NcU has 1907-1917; 1916/17, with comparative statistics [8982

Moore Co., N. C. Commissioners. Subscription of $50,000 to Chatham Railroad Co. No place, no publisher [1869?] 4 p. [8983

[**Moore's Creek Monumental Association**] Ceremonies at the unveiling of the monu-

ment upon Moore's Creek Battle Ground to the women of the Revolution, August,
1907. No place [1907?] 16 p. [8984

Mooresville, N. C. Board of Trustees of Graded Schools. Mooresville Graded
Schools, 1909/10. [8985

Mooresville, N. C. Chamber of Commerce. Facts about Mooresville, North Carolina. Mooresville [193?] [7] p. [8986
——An invitation to industry from Mooresville. [Mooresville, 1956] [19] p. [8987

Mooresville, N. C. Library. List of books in the Mooresville Free Library . . .
1908. Mooresville, Enterprise Print, 1908. 16 p. [8988

Moravians or United Brethren. A brotherly agreement, adopted by the congrega-
tions at Bethabara, Bethania, Friedland, Friedberg and Hope, in North-Carolina
. . . in . . . 1836. Salem, Printed by Blum & Son, 1837. 8 p. [8989
——Christmas Eve. [Salem, 1856] 4 p. [8990
——Church book of the southern district of the American province of the Moravian
Church, 1898. Salem, Crist & Keehln, pr., n.d. 32 p. [8991
——Circular to the congregation at Salem. [Salem, May, 1871] 2 p. [8992
——Constitution of the United Brethren's home-mission society of N. C. Salem,
Printed by Blum & Son, 1837. 4 p. [8993
——Dank-Psalm zu dem Jubel-Feste und der Einweihung des neuerbauten Kirchen-
Saals der Gemeine in Bethanien am 20sten Merz, 1809. Salisbury, Gedruckt bey
Francis Coupee, n.d. 8 p. [8994

[**Moravians or United Brethren**] Einige Biblische Geschichten Neuen-Testaments
mit kupfern und kurzen evangelischen Liedern für Kinder. Neudietendorf, bei
Heinrich Gottlieb Petsch, 1808. 50 p. [8995

Moravians or United Brethren. Funeral chorals of the Unitas Fratrum or Moravian
Church; [comp. by A. L. Fries] [Winston-Salem, 1905] 23 p. [8996
——Hymn for the festival of the pupils in the Female Academy at Salem, September
24, 1830. Salem, J. C. Blum, pr., 1830. [5] p. [8997
—— ———September 24. Salem, Gazette Office [1841] 5 p. [8998
——Hymns arranged for the communion service of the church of the United Breth-
ren at Salem. Salem, E. A. Vogler, 1867. 35 p. [8999
——Jubel-psalm zum Andenken an den Anfang der ersten Mission der erneuerten
Bruderkirche unter die Heiden, am 21sten August, 1732, Salem, 1832. No place,
no publisher, n.d. 4 p. [9000
——Jubel-psalm zum 4ten May 1830 in Salem in Erinnerung an den 4ten May, 1730,
von Br. Johan B. v. Albertini in Austrag der U.Ae. C. gedichtet. No place, no
publisher, n.d. 6 p. [9001
——Jubelpsalm zum 13ten November, 1841. No place, no publisher, n.d. 4 p. [9002
——Jubelpsalm zum 29sten August, 1841. No place, no publisher, n.d. 4 p. [9003
——Dem Lieben und Würdigen Bruder Friedrich Wilhelm von Marschall, nach zu-
rückgelegten achtzig Lebensjahren und Sechzigjährigen treuem und gesegnetem
Dienst bey der evangelischen Brüderunität am 5ten Februar 1801 von der Gemeine
in Salem. Salisbury, Francis Coupee [1800] 8 p. [9004
——The liturgy and hymns of the American province of the Unitas Fratrum, or, the
Moravian Church. Bethlehem [Pa.] Moravian Publication Office, 1876. 688 p. [9005
——The liturgy and the offices of worship and hymns of the American province of
the Unitas Fratrum. Winston-Salem, Southern Province [c.1908] 479 p. [9006
——Lob-und Dank-psalm zur Jubelfeyer der Gemeine in Salem den 19ten Februar
1816. No place, no publisher, n.d. 5 p. [9007
——Moravian history for Sunday School purposes. [Winston-Salem?] n.d. [6] p. [9008
——The Moravians and their faith. A new and revised edition of Moravian tracts
nos. 1 and 2 combined. Bethlehem, Pa., 1900. (Special Moravian publication
fund committee. Leaflet no. 2) 16 p. [9009
——Ode for September 7th. No place, no publisher, n.d. 4 p. [9010
——Ode for the centenary jubilee of the congregation at Salem, on the 19th and 20th
of February, 1866. Salem, L. V. and E. T. Blum, 1866. 6 p. [9011
——Principles and discipline of the United Brethren's congregation, at Salem, N. C.,
as adopted by the congregation council, May 17th, 1859. Salem, Printed by L. V.
Blum, 1859. 16 p. [9012
——Principles and rules of the Moravian congregation at Salem, N. C., adopted by
congregation council, May 9, 1893. Salem, Crist & Keehln, pr., 1893. 36 p. [9013

——Rules and regulations of the congregation of the United Brethren at Salem, North Carolina. Salem, Printed by Blum & Son, 1850. 16 p. [9014

——Zum Chorfest der grössern Mädchen, 1833. No place, no publisher, n.d. 4 p. [9015

——Zum Chorfest der ledigen Schwestern, 1838, in Salem. [Salem, 1838?] 8 p. [9016

——Zum Grossen Sabbath, den 28ten Merz 1812, in Salem. No place, no publisher, n.d. 4 p. [9017

——Zum 13ten August 1804 in Salem. No place, no publisher, n.d. 4 p. [9018

——Zum 13ten August 1806, in Salem. No place, no publisher, n.d. 4 p. [9019

——Zum 13ten November, 1834, in Salem. No place, no publisher, n.d. 4 p. [9020

——Zur Christnacht, 1798, in Salem. [Salisbury, Francis Coupee? 1798] [4] p. NcU has photostat. [9021

——Zur Christnacht, den 24ten December, 1813, in Salem. No place, no publisher, n.d. 4 p. [9022

——Zur Feier des 13ten August in Salem. No place, no publisher [1849] 4 p. [9023

——Zur funfzigjahrigen Jubelfeier der Einweihung des Kirchensaales in Salem, den 13ten November, 1850. Salem, Gedruckt von Blum und Sohn, 1850. 6 p. [9024

Moravians or United Brethren. Salem Congregation. Charter, rules, and regulations, the Congregation of United Brethren of Salem and its vicinity, Winston-Salem, N. C. Winston-Salem [1931] 28 p. [9025

——Charter, rules, and regulations, "The congregation of United Brethren of Salem and vicinity" as amended and adopted, June 8th, 1909. [Winston-Salem, Union Republican, 1909?] 19 p. [9026

——The rules and regulations of the Salem congregation at Salem, N. C. Adopted by congregation council May 9th, 1893. Winston-Salem, King's Printing House, 1904. 36 p. [9027

——Services memorial of Edmund de Schweinitz, S. T. D. bishop of the Unitas Fratrum. [Salem?] n.d. 10 p. [9028

Mordecai, Alfred. Address. [1880] 16 p. Address at West Point, June 27, 1880. [9029

Mordecai, Ellen (Mordecai) Gleanings from long ago. [Savannah, Braid & Hutton, Inc., c.1933] 125 p. [9030

Mordecai, Samuel Fox. Address at the banquet of the Trinity College Law School alumni, Hotel Malbourne, Nov. 12, 1922. [Durham? 1922] 13 p. [9031

——Domestic relations. Durham, Press of the Seeman Printery, 1908. 39 p. [9032

——The government of North Carolina. New York, Charles Scribner's Sons, 1911. 66 p. [9033

——Law lectures; a treatise, from a North Carolina standpoint, on . . . commentaries of Sir William Blackstone. Raleigh, Edwards & Broughton Printing Co., 1907. 1251 p. [9034

—— ——[2d ed.] Raleigh, Commercial Printing Co., 1916. 2 v. [9035

——Law notes. Durham, 1911-13. 3 v. in 1. Paged continously. [9036

——Bailments and carriers, v. 4. Raleigh, Author, 1920. p. 1383-1481. [9037

[**Mordecai, Samuel Fox**] Legal opinions, 1899-1900, North Carolina Bankers' Association. No place, no publisher [1899] 11 p. [9038

Mordecai, Samuel Fox. Lex scripta; a condensed summary of the most important acts of Parliament . . . treated of in first and second Blackstone, with reference to the statutes of North Carolina covering the same ground. 2d ed. [Durham?] c.1905. 75, 32 p. [9039

——Mechanics' liens in North Carolina. Raleigh, Edwards & Broughton, pr., 1897. 150 p. [9040

——Mordecai's miscellanies. No place, privately printed, n.d. 86 p. [9041

Mordecai, Samuel Fox, ed. Negotiable instruments law in North Carolina. Raleigh, Capital Printing Co., 1899. 95 p. [9042

Mordecai, Samuel Fox. Principal and agent and master and servant; a condensed summary of lectures delivered before the law class of Wake Forest college. Raleigh, Edwards & Broughton, 1900. 42 p. [9043

[**Mordecai, Samuel Fox**] Questions and answers on real property. 2d ed. [Durham, Seeman Printery, 1925] p. 1713-1871 [9044

Mordecai, Samuel Fox, ed. Remedies by selected cases, annotated by Samuel F. Mordecai . . . and Atwell C. McIntosh. Durham [Madison, Wis., State Journal Printing Co.] 1910. 1018 p. [9045

Mordecai, Samuel Fox. Some old friends and new for some young friends and old. Durham, Seeman Printery, 1922. 15 p. [9046

Morehead, John Motley, 1866-1923. [Address, accepting the unanimous call of the Republican convention to the state chairmanship] No place, no publisher, n.d. [4] p. [9047

——Charge originated with eminent Democrats and are not denied, Mr. Morehead fittingly replies to Brook's telegram. [Spray?] 1908. [4] p. [9048

——Morehead's reply to a false and malicious attack. No place, no publisher, n.d. [1] p. [9049

[**Morehead, John Motley**] 1870- The analysis of industrial gases. Chicago, E. H. Sargent & Co. [c.1905] 23 p. [9050

Morehead, John Motley, 1870- Heritage, dreams, and fulfillment of the life and services of Governor John Motley Morehead of North Carolina; an address . . . on the occasion of the dedication of the port terminal at Morehead City, N. C., August 14, 1952. [Chapel Hill, University, 1954] 21 p. Previously pub. under title: North Carolina is on the march. [9051

——The Morehead family of North Carolina and Virginia. New York, privately printed [by the De Vinne Press] 1921. 147 p. [9052

——North Carolina is on the march; an address at Morehead City, N. C., the dedication of the harbors and piers on August 14, 1952. [Chapel Hill, University of North Carolina, 1952] 20 p. [9053

Morehead, Joseph Motley. Address of Joseph M. Morehead, esq., of Guilford, on the life and times of James Hunter, "general" of the Regulators, at Guilford Battle Ground, . . . July 3, 1897. 2d cor. and enl. ed. Greensboro, C. F. Thomas, Printer, 1898. 73 p. [9054

——Address to the battle-ground oak at old Guilford Court-House, Greenesboro, N. C. Greenesboro, J. J. Stone & Co., 1904. [8] p. [9055

——Addresses of Joseph M. Morehead, on the life and times of James Hunter . . . of Professor J. M. Weatherly, on the presentation of David Clark's portrait of John Penn; and of Hon. Charles M. Stedman, on the dedication of the Schenck Museum. Greensboro, Reece & Elam, pr. [1897] 66 p. [9056

——Appeal to the descendants of General Nathanael Greene for his remains, and to Congress for a monument over these, at Guilford Battle Ground, N. C. Greensboro, 1902. 15 p. [9057

[**Morehead, Joseph Motley**] Battle of Guilford Court House, and the preservation of that historic field. [Greensboro, Jos. J. Stone & Co., 1906] [6 p.] [9058

—— ——No publisher [1906] 7 p. [9059

—— ——No publisher [1908] 8 p. [9060

—— ——[Greensboro, The Record Job Office, 1909] [8] p. [9061

[**Morehead Banking Co.**] William Henry Willard, died Sunday, February 6th, 1898. No place, no publisher [1898] [3] p. [9062

Morehead Bluffs, Inc. [Norfolk, Va., Morrie Co.] n.d. 2 p. [9063

Morehead City, N. C. Board of Commissioners. Ordinances of the town of Morehead City, N. C., Jan. 1st, 1923. New Bern, Owen G. Dunn [1923] 38 p. [9064

[**Morehead City, N. C. Junior Chamber of Commerce**] Morehead City, where business and pleasure meet. [Morehead City, 1937?] [16] p. [9065

Morehead City, N. C. Morehead City Hotel Company. President. To the stockholders of the Morehead City Hotel Co. [Durham, 1882] [1] p. [9066

Moreheid, J. N. Lives, adventures, anecdotes, amusements, and domestic habits of the Siamese twins. Raleigh, Printed and published by E. E. Barclay, 1850. 24 p. [9067

[**Morehouse, H. L.**] H. M. Tupper, D. D.; a narrative of twenty-five years' work in the South, 1865-1890. [New York, American Baptist Home Mission Society, pref. 1890] 25 p. [9068

Morehouse, Kathleen (Moore) Rain on the just. New York, Lee Furman, Inc. [c.1936] 319 p. [9069

Morgan, Daniel. Cowpens papers, being correspondence of Gen. Morgan and the prominent actors. Charleston, News and Courier, 1881. 54 p. [9070

Morgan, Dolly Ann. Held by the heights, poems. New York, Exposition Press [1949] 63 p. [9071

——Lines from life in the hills. [High Springs, Fla., Booklover, c.1938] 18 p. [9072

Morgan, Jacob L., ed. History of the Lutheran Church in North Carolina, edited by Jacob L. Morgan [and others] No place, United Evangelical Lutheran Synod of North Carolina, 1953. 407 p. [9073

Morgan, James Morris. Recollections of a Rebel reefer. Boston, Houghton Mifflin Co., 1917. 491 p. [9074

Morgan, Lawrence N. Land tenure in proprietary North Carolina. Chapel Hill, 1912. (James Sprunt historical publications; pub. under the direction of the North Carolina Historical Society. v. 12, no. 1, p. [41]-63) [9075

Morgan, Murray C. Dixie raider, the saga of the C. S. S. Shenandoah. New York, E. P. Dutton, 1948. 336 p. [9076

Morgan, Thomas Alfred. Address to the graduating class of Bowman Gray Medical School of Wake Forest College, September 25, 1944. [New York, Author, 1944?] 15 p. [9077

Morgan, W. Scott. The red light: a story of southern politics and election methods. Moravian Falls, Yellow Jacket Press, 1904. 288 p. [9078

Morgan, William Fred. The life work and travels of William Fred Morgan. [Washington, 1914] 19 p. [9079

Morgan, William Henry. Thinking together about marriage and family . . . [by] William H. Morgan [and] Mildred I. Morgan. New York, Association Press [1955] 178 p. [9080

Morgan's Female Seminary, Salisbury, N. C. The system of education in Professor Morgan's Female Seminary at Salisbury, N. C. Salisbury, Carolina Watchman Office, pr., 1851. 16 p. [9081

Morganton, N. C. Board of Trustees of Graded Schools. Morganton Graded Schools, 190 - Morganton, 190 - NcU has 1905/06, 1906/07 [9082
——Report, 190 - Morganton, 190 - NcU has 1906/07, 1908/09 [9083

Morganton, N. C. First Presbyterian Church. Commemorating the sesqui-centennial of the First Presbyterian Church, Morganton, N. C., October 11-19, 1947. [Morganton? 1947?] 19 p. [9084

Morganton, N. C. Grace Hospital. Report, 19 - Morganton, 19 - NcU has 1918-19 [9085

Morganton, N. C. High School. "The birthright"; a pageant portraying the history of Burke County. Morganton, News-Herald, pr., 1924. [8] p. [9086

Morley, Margaret Warner. The Carolina mountains. Boston, Houghton Mifflin Co., 1913. 397 p. [9087

Morphis, J. M. History of Texas, from its discovery and settlement. New York, United States Publishing Co., 1874. 591 p. [9088

Morrah, Dave. Cinderella Hassenpfeffer, and other tales mein grossfader told. New York, Rinehart & Co., Inc. [1948] 60 p. [9089
——Fraulein Bo-Peepen, and more tales mein grossfader told. New York, Rinehart & Co., Inc. [1953] 79 p. [9090
——Heinrich Schnibble, and even more tales mein grossfader told. New York, Rinehart & Co., Inc. [1955] 111 p. [9091
——Sillynyms. New York, Rinehart & Co. [1956] 93 p. [9092

Morrel, Martha McBride. "Young Hickory," the life and times of President James K. Polk. New York, E. P. Dutton, 1949. 381 p. [9093

Morrill, Madge (Haines) The Wright brothers, first to fly [by] Madge Haines and Leslie Morrill. Nashville, Abingdon Press [1955] 128 p. [9094

Morris, Bettie Watkins. Down home. No place, no publisher, n.d. 4 p. [9095

Morris, Charles. The old South and the new. [Philadelphia? c.1907] 640 p. [9096

Morris, Charles S. Southward via the Piedmont line. Philadelphia, Published for the Piedmont Air-line by Jas. W. Nagle, n.d. 80 p. [9097

Morris, George Blythe. Damphoul thoughts of a small-town doctor. Chicago, 1923. 82 p. [9098

Morris, James A. Woolen and worsted manufacturing in the southern Piedmont. Columbia, University of South Carolina Press, 1952. 197 p. [9099

Morris, Jane Sims (Davison)   Adam Symes and his descendants. Philadelphia, Dorrance and Co. [c.1938]   403 p.   [9100
——The Duke-Symes family. Philadelphia, Dorrance and Co. [c.1940]   264 p. [9101

Morris, John Gottlieb.   The Stork family in the Lutheran Church: or, Biographical sketches of Rev. Charles Augustus Gottlieb Stork, Rev. Theophilus Stork, D. D., and Rev. Charles A. Stork.   Philadelphia, Lutheran Publication Society [c.1886] 263 p.   [9102

Morris, Lloyd R.   Ceiling unlimited, the story of American aviation from Kitty Hawk to supersonics, by Lloyd Morris and Kendall Smith.   New York, Macmillan Co. [1953]   417 p.   [9103

Morris, Percy A.   A field guide to the shells of our Atlantic and Gulf coasts. Rev. and enl. ed.   Boston, Houghton Mifflin, 1951. (The Peterson field guide series [3])   236 p.   [9104

Morris, Whitmore.   A Morris family of Mecklenburg County, North Carolina. [San Antonio? Texas, 1956]   128 p.   [9105

Morrison, Alfred James.   Beginnings of public education in Virginia, 1776-1860. Richmond, Davis Bottom, Supt. of Public Printing, 1917.   195 p.   [9106
——College of Hampden Sidney dictionary of biography, 1776-1825. Hampton Sidney, Va., Hampden Sidney College [1921]   321 p.   [9107
——East by West, essays in transportation. Boston, Four Seas Co., 1920. 177 p. [9108

Morrison, Alfred James, ed.   Six addresses on the state of letters and science in Virginia; delivered chiefly before the Literary and Philosophical Society at Hampden-Sidney College . . . 1824-1835.   Roanoke, Va., Stone Printing and Manufacturing Co., 1917.   55 p.   [9109
——Travels in Virginia in Revolutionary times. [Lynchburg, Va., J. P. Bell Co. Inc., c.1922]   138 p.   [9110

Morrison, Alfred James, tr. and ed.   see **Schöpf, Johann Ludwig von**

Morrison, Cameron.   Cameron Morrison speaks at Chapel Hill, states where he stands. [Charlotte? 1920]   [3] p.   [9111
——Robert Burns; an address delivered before the Caledonian Club of New York, January 25, 1924. No place, no publisher [1924]   7 p.   [9112

Morrison, Fred Wilson.   Equalization of the financial burden of education among counties in North Carolina.   New York, Teachers College, Columbia University, 1925. (Teachers College, Columbia University. Contributions to education, no. 184)   88 p.   [9113

Morrison, J. M.   Aid to loyal North Carolinians.   New York, no publisher, 1861. [1] p.   [9114

Morrison, Joseph L.   The Chapel Hill guide; campus and community. [Chapel Hill, Author, c.1955]   [24] p.   [9115
——Opportunities in business papers.   New York, Vocational Guidance Manuals [1955]   96 p.   [9116

Morrison, Robert Hall, 1798-1889.   Funeral sermon of the Rev. John Robinson, D. D., late pastor of Poplar Tent Church, preached at Poplar Tent, Feb. 22, 1844. Charlotte, Journal, 1844.   15 p.   [9117
——Inaugural address; pronounced at his inauguration as president of Davidson College, N. C., Aug. 2, 1838.   Philadelphia, William S. Martien, 1838.   23 p. [9118

[**Morrison, Robert Hall, 1798-1889**]   Obituary of Major-General Joseph Graham. Raleigh, Edwards and Broughton, n.d.   [1] p.   [9119

Morrison, Robert Hall, 1798-1889.   A report to the Board of Trustees of Davidson College on the importance of the silk culture in the western parts of North & South Carolina.   Charlotte, Charlotte Journal, 1838.   8 p.   [9120

Morrison, Robert Hall, ca.1880-   Biography of Joseph Graham Morrison, captain, Confederate States of America.   No place [1955]   [34] p.   [9121

Morrison, Sarah Parke.   Among ourselves: . . . being·a life story of principally seven generations, especially of the Morris-Trueblood branch. Plainfield, Ind., Publishing Association of Friends, 1901-1904?   3 v.?   [9122

Morriss, Elizabeth (Cleveland)   Adult adventures in reading; practice exercises for adult elementary students. New York, E. P. Dutton & Co., Inc., 1939. 264 p. [9123
—— ——teachers' manual.   31 p.   [9124

——Citizens' reference book; a textbook for adult beginners in community schools. Chapel Hill, University of North Carolina Press, 1927-1928. 2 v. [9125

—— ——1935. 2 v. NcU has v. 2 [9126

Morrow, Decatur Franklin. Then and now; reminiscences and historical romance, 1856-1865. Macon, Ga., Press of the J. W. Burke Co., 1926. 346 p. [9127

Morse, Jedidiah. The American geography. 2d ed. London, Printed for John Stockdale, 1792. 536 p. [9128

——The American universal geography. Boston, I. Thomas and E. T. Andrews, 1793. 2 v. NcU has v. 1. [9129

——Geography made easy: being an abridgment of the American universal geography. 13th edition. Boston, Thomas & Andrews; J. T. Buckingham, printer, 1809. 432 p. [9130

—— ——20th edition. Utica, Published by William Williams, July, 1819. 364 p. [9131

Morton, Oren Frederic. The story of Daniel Boone. Hot Springs, Va., McAllister Publishing Co., 1913. 23 p. [9132

Mortuary. Salisbury, 1872. [1] p. [9133

Mosby, Charles Virgil. Little journeys to the homes of great physicians. William Beaumont—physiologist, Augustus Charles Bernays—surgeon, Williams McKim Marriott—pediatrician. St. Louis, 1937. 66 p. [9134

Mose, pseud. see Bunting, John N.?

Moseley, John Reed. Manifest victory; a quest and a testimony. New York, Harper & Brothers [c.1941] 238 p. [9135

Moses, Edward Pearson. . . . First reader with 4,000 words for spelling by sound. Raleigh, Edwards & Broughton, pr., 1895. 96 p. [9136

——Moses' phonic readers, first- Raleigh, Edwards & Broughton, 1895- v. NcU has v. 1 [9137

——Moses' primer. Richmond, Va., B. F. Johnson Publishing Co. [c.1907] 120 p. [9138

——Moses' readers, number one- Richmond, Va., B. F. Johnson Publishing Co., 1900- v. NcU has no. 1 [9139

Moses, Edward Pearson, joint author, see Noble, Marcus Cicero Stephens

Moss, Paul. The rock was free. Philadelphia, Dorrance & Co. [1945] 174 p. [9140

Moss, William Dygnum. A Christmas message. [Chapel Hill, 1928] 19 p. [9141

[Moss, William Dygnum] The gentle art of living, by Parson Moss. No place, n.d. Various paging. [9142

Moss, William Dygnum. A prayer. [Chapel Hill] n.d. [1] p. [9143

——Sermons and prayers . . . A memorial volume. Chapel Hill, University of North Carolina Press, 1940. 207 p. [9144

——A tragedy of speed; sermon on the wreck of the Titanic, April 21, 1912. Washington, D. C., Washington Heights Presbyterian Church, c.1912. 14 p. [9145

A motor trip veritably to nature's heart in "the Land of the Sky." [Washington, Southern Railway] n.d. 2 p. [9146

Motor transportation of North Carolina, Jan. 1932-March, 1937, v. 1, no. 1-v. 6, no. 3. Charlotte, North Carolina Truck Owners' Association, 1932-1937. NcU has v. 2-6. [9147

Mott, Ed. Black Homer of Jimtown. New York, Grosset & Dunlap, 1900. 286 p. [9148

Mott, Frank Luther. A history of American magazines. Cambridge, Mass., Harvard University Press, 1930-1938. 3 v. [9149

Moulton, C. W. The review of General Sherman's Memoirs examined, chiefly in the light of its own evidence. Cincinnati, R. Clarke & Co., pr., 1875. 87 p. [9150

Moultrie, William. Memoirs of the American Revolution, so far as it related to the states of North and South Carolina, and Georgia. New York, Printed by David Longworth for the Author, 1802. 2 v. [9151

Moultrie, William. Moultrie-Montague Letters, 1781; some related matters. No place, privately printed [1904?] 12 p. [9152

Mount Airy, N. C. Board of Commissioners. The charter of the town of Mount Airy, incorporating the amendments up to and including acts of 1891; together with the ordinances of the town. Winston, Stewarts' Printing Co., 1892. 48 p. [9153

Mount Airy, N. C. Board of School Commissioners. Mount Airy City Public Schools. Mount Airy, 1916. 20 p.   [9154

Mount Allen Junior College. Mt. Olive, N. C. Bulletin, v. 1- 1952/53- Mt. Olive, 1952- NcU has v. [1-4]   [9155

Mount Amoena Seminary, Mount Pleasant, N. C. Catalogue, 18 - Mount Pleasant, 18 - NcU has [1904/05-1918/19]   [9156

Mount Holly, N. C. School Board. Course of study for the Mount Holly Graded School, 1908/09. Mount Holly, 1908. 8 p.   [9157

Mount Mitchell, altitude 6711 feet, top of Eastern America. No place, no publisher, n.d. 16 p.   [9158

[Mount Mitchell Railroad] Top of Eastern America. [Asheville, Inland Press, 1918?] Folder   [9159

Mount Pleasant Collegiate Institute, Mt. Pleasant, N. C. Catalogue, 18 - 18 - NcU has 1858/59, 1859/60, 1861/62, 1867/68-1869/70 [1880/81-1914/15] 1919/20-1926/27, 1929/30, 1930/31   [9160

——Collegiate Institute appeal; a handbook of facts and plans. Salisbury, Collegiate Institute Appeal Headquarters [1924] 19 p.   [9161

——[Commencement and Society programs, 1857-58] NcU has 6 programs   [9162

——Regulations for the discipline and police of cadets. [Mt. Pleasant?] 1927. 22 p.   [9163

—— ——1930. 24 p.   [9164

——Regulations of Mount Pleasant Collegiate Institute. [Mt. Pleasant,?] n.d. 12 p.   [9165

[Mount Zion Baptist Association] A member's manual for the Baptist Church. Raleigh, Edwards, Broughton & Co., pr., 1875. 34 p.   [9166

Mount Zion Baptist Association. Minutes of the session, 1870- 1870- NcU has 1870-1955   [9167

Mountain District Primitive Baptist Association. Minutes, 19 - 19 - NcU has 1955, 1956   [9168

Mountain Park School, Park Mountain, N. C. Catalogue, 19 - Park Mountain, 19 - NcU has 1915/16   [9169

Mountain Sanatarium for Pulmonary Diseases, Asheville, N. C. Report, 18 - Asheville, 18 - NcU has 1877   [9170

Mountain View Institute, Hays, N. C. Catalogue, 191 - Hays, 191 - NcU has 1919/20   [9171

Mountaineer, 19 - Weaverville, Senior Class of Weaver College, 1920- NcU has 1920   [9172

Mowris, James A. A history of the One Hundred and Seventeenth Regiment, New York Volunteers (Fourth Oneida) from the date of its organization, August, 1862, till that of its muster out, June, 1865. Hartford, Conn., Case, Lockwood and Co., pr., 1866. 315 p.   [9173

Moyle, Seth. My friend, O. Henry. New York, H. K. Fly Co., [c.1914] 32 p. [9174

Mozingo, Edgar. Mamma's little rascal, a novel. New York, Exposition Press [1955] 104 p.   [9175

Mülinen, Wolfgang Friedrich von. Christoph von Graffenried, Landgraf von Carolina, Gründer von Neu-Bern. Bern, K. J. Wyss, 1896. 43 p.   [9176

Mull, Larry W. Everybody square dances. [Asheville, Stephens Press, c.1948] [16] p.   [9177

——Scenic Western North Carolina, a vacation guide to the highlands. New York, The William-Frederick Press [c.1946] 45 p.   [9178

Mullen, John M., comp. Facts to know North Carolina. Lincolnton, Mullen Feature Syndicate [c.1937] 124 p.   [9179

—— ——1944. 147 p.   [9180

[Mullen, John M.?] comp. Know your state; do you know these facts about North Carolina? [Charlotte, Mullen Feature Syndicate, c.1933] 15 p.   [9181

Muller, Herbert Joseph. Thomas Wolfe. Norfolk, Conn., New Directions Books [1947] 196 p.   [9182

Mullican, Naamon Spencer. Mullikins and Mullicans of North Carolina. Winston-Salem, The Author [1952?] 218 p. [9183

Mullis, Nellie Hughes. Wings of gold. Dallas, Story Book Press [1956] 48 p. [9184

Mumford, Elizabeth. Whistler's mother; the life of Anna McNeil Whistler. Boston, Little, Brown and Co., 1939. 326 p. [9185

The municipal South, v. 1, no. 1- January, 1954- Charlotte, Clark-Smith Publishing Co., 1954- NcU has v. 1-3 [9186

The municipal year book, 1934- Chicago, International City Managers' Association, 1934- NcU has 1934-1953, 1955 [9187

Murchison, Claudius Temple. King Cotton is sick. Chapel Hill, University of North Carolina Press, 1930. 190 p. [9188

——. . . Resale price maintenance. New York, Columbia University, 1919. (Studies in history, economics and public law, ed. by the Faculty of Political Science of Columbia University. v. LXXXII, no. 2; whole no. 192) 202 p. [9189

Murchison, R. To the voters of the thirteenth congressional district of N. C., comprising Ashe, Iredell, Surry, and Wilkes counties. [Jefferson, no publisher, 1839] 2 p. [9190

Murdoch, Francis J. Duty of the Church with reference to unity among Christians. Wilmington, Wm. L. De Rosset, Jr., n.d. 14 p. [9191

[**Murdoch, Francis J.**] Henry VIII did not found the Church of England. No place, n.d. [4] p. [9192

Murdoch, Francis J. A sermon on the great necessity of confirmation. Greensboro, Pub. at the request of the Vestry of St. Barnabas' Church, 1876. 14 p. [9193

——Sermon on the prohibited degrees. No place, no publisher, n.d. 10 p. [9194

——The substance of a sermon preached in St. Luke's church, Lincolnton, March 5th, 1882 . . . at the ordination of Rev. W. S. Bynum. Greensboro, C. F. Thomas, pr., 1882. 19 p. [9195

Murfree, Mary Noailles see **Craddock, Charles Egbert, pseud.**

Murphey, Archibald DeBow. An oration delivered in Person Hall, Chapel Hill, on the 27th of June, 1827 . . . under the appointment of the Dialectic Society. Raleigh, Printed by J. Gales & Son, 1827. 18 p. [9196

—— ——2d ed. Raleigh, Printed by W. R. Gales, 1843. 23 p. [9197

——To the freeholders of Orange County. [Orange County, June 3, 1814] [2] p. [9198

——To the freeholders of Orange County. No place, The Author [June 27, 1816] 3 p. [9199

[**Murphey, Archibald DeBow**] To the freemen of Orange County. [Raleigh, T. Henderson, pr., Dec. 25, 1813] 8 p. [9200

Murphy, Eliza Wright. Are you building character? [Wilmington, Wilmington Stamp and Printing Co.] n.d. 20 p. [9201

[**Murphy, Eliza Wright**] Dr. George C. Worth, 1867-1936. [Wilmington, First Presbyterian Church, 1937?] 36 p. [9202

Murphy, George H. Children of the candle-light. No place, no publisher, n.d. 42 p. [9203

Murphy, Henry Cruse. The voyage of Verrazzano. New York [Albany, Press of J. Munsell] 1875-[76] 198 p. NcU has copy lacking supplement [1876] [9204

Murphy, Isabel G. The outer banks; photographs, historical sketches, and special events. Kill Devil Hills, Surfside Press [c.1951] [32] p. [9205

Murphy, Joseph Wiggins. Sermon-sketch of the history of St. Matthews Parish, Hillsboro, N. C., delivered by the rector . . . St. Matthews's Day, Sept. 21st, and . . . Oct. 5th, 1890. Washington, no publisher, 1900. 40 p. [9206

Murphy, Maud (King) Edgar Gardner Murphy, from records and memories. New York, Pub. for the Author, 1943. 120 p. [9207

Murphy, Partick Livingston. The care of the insane and the treatment and prognosis of insanity. [Morganton? 1895?] 13 p. [9208

——Colony treatment of the insane and other defectives; read before the meeting of the N. C. Medical Association, June, 1906, Charlotte, N. C. No place, no publisher [1906?] 29 p. [9209

——The treatment and care of the insane in North Carolina: . . . an address delivered before the Agricultural and Mechanical College, Raleigh, N. C., Mar. 16, 1900. No place, no publisher [1900?]   29 p.   [9210

Murphy, Walter.   Memorial address, commemorating the memory of the distinguish-ed members of the Rowan County bar.   [Salisbury, Rowan County Bar Associa-tion, 1938]   37 p.   [9211
——The remarks of Walter Murphy . . . on the occasion of the unveiling of the memorial to the North Carolina Confederate dead, on the field of Gettysburg, July the third, nineteen hundred and twenty-nine.   No place, no publisher, n.d. [3] p.   [9212
——Speech of Hon. Walter Murphy, memorial to the North Carolina Confederate dead on the field of Gettysburg, July the third, nineteen hundred and twenty-nine. No place, no publisher, n.d.   [3] p.   [9213

Murray, Amelia Matilda.   Letters from the United States, Cuba and Canada.   New York, G. P. Putnam, 1856.   410 p.   [9214

Murray, Ephraim C.   History of Alamance Church, 1762-1918.   [Statesville, Brady Printing Co.] n.d.   39 p.   [9215
——Presbyterianism, a historical sketch; a sermon preached at the installation of Rev. Melton Clark as pastor of the First Presbyterian Church, Greensboro, N. C., April 7, 1907.   No place, no publisher, n.d.   14 p.   [9216

Murray, James, 1713-1781.   Letters of James Murray, loyalist; ed. by Nina Moore Tiffany.   Boston, Printed: not pub., 1901.   324 p.   [9217

Murray, James, 1732-1782.   An impartial history of the present war in America. Newcastle upon Tyne, Printed for T. Robson [1782]   2 v.   [9218
——Sermons to asses.   3d ed.   Philadelphia, Re-printed by John Dunlap, 1769. 114 p.   NcU has defective copy, pp. 111-114 wanting.   [9219

Murray, Lindley.   . . . English grammar, adapted to the different classes of learners. Raleigh, Printed by Gales & Seaton, 1811.   296 p.   [9220
—— ——Raleigh, Printed by J. Gales & Son, 1822.   344 p.   [9221
——The English reader: or, Pieces in prose and poetry, selected from the best writers. Newbern, S. Hall, 1805.   306 p.   [9222
——Introduction to the English reader; or, A selection of pieces in prose and poetry; calculated to improve the younger classes of learners in reading.   Raleigh, Printed by J. Gales & Son, 1828.   179 p.   [9223

Murray, Paul.   The Whig Party in Georgia, 1825-1853.   Chapel Hill, Univ. of North Carolina Press, 1948.   (James Sprunt studies in history and political science, v. 29) 219 p.   [9224

Murray, Pauli.   Proud shoes.   New York, Harper [1956]   276 p.   [9225

Murray, Pauli, ed.   States' laws on race and color.   [Cincinnati, Woman's Division of Christian Service, Board of Missions and Church Extension, Methodist Church] 1950 [i.e. 1951]   746 p.   [9226

Murray, Philip Alcemus.   Fishing in the Carolinas.   Chapel Hill, University of North Carolina Press, 1941.   183 p.   [9227

Murray, Raymond Le Roy.   Introduction to nuclear engineering.   New York, Prentice-Hall, 1954.   418 p.   [9228

Murrell, Mrs. Hagar A.   Garnett Training School, Pollocksville, N. C.   No place, n.d.   [2] p.   [9229

Murrett, John C.   . . . Tar heel apostle, Thomas Frederick Price, cofounder of Maryknoll.   New York, Longmans, Green [1944]   260 p.   [9230

Murrill, Hugh A., Jr.   Furniture merchandising and successful salesmanship.   High Point, Southern Furniture Journal [c.1929]   24 v. in 12.   [9231

Muse, Amy.   Beaufort by the sea, history.   Beaufort, Wesleyan Service Guild, Ann Street Methodist Church [1953]   38 p.   [9232

Muse   see Stage coach

Music and dance in the Southeastern States.   New York, Bureau of Musical Re-search [1952]   331 p.   [9233

A musical instructor, containing hints to performers on the piano forte.   Salem, Printed by Blum & Son, 1838.   26 p.   [9234

Musical tempo   see North Carolina Federation of Music Clubs. Bulletin

My name is Durham (Motion picture) Durham, N. C., Community Chest. Made and released by Communication Center, University of North Carolina, 1949. 20 minutes. [9235

My tussle with the devil, and other stories, by O. Henry's ghost. New York, I. M. Y. Co., 1918. 197 p. [9236

Myers, Edward Warren. Form of advertisement, proposal, schedules, contract, bond, and specifications for a system of sanitary sewers at Reidsville, North Carolina. Greensboro, E. W. Myers, [1910] 39 p. [9237

Myers, I. H. Twelve hundred questions and answers on the Bible, by Revs. M. H. and I. H. Myers. 2d ed. Wilmington, no publisher, 1868. 237 p. [9238

[Myrover, James H.] Short history of Cumberland County and the Cape Fear section. [Fayetteville, N. C. Baptist Publishing Co. for the Bank of Fayetteville, 1905] 32 p. [9239

Naglee, Henry Morris. Report of the conduct of the advance of the column for the relief of Little Washington, N. C., April 18th-19th, 1863. Philadelphia, Collins, pr., 1863. 16 p. [9240

Nantahala and Tuckasege Land and Mineral Company. Preliminary report on the lands of the Nantahala & Tuckasege Land and Mineral Association by David Christy. Cincinnati, Wrightson and Co., pr.. 1856. 24 p. NcU has microfilm (negative) from original in U.S. Geological Survey Library, Washington, D.C. [9241
——Second preliminary report of the Nantahala & Tuckasege Land and Mineral Company, for 1858. Cincinnati, Wrightson & Co., pr., 1858. 44 p. [9242

Narrative of facts in the case of Passmore Williamson. Philadelphia, Published by the Pennsylvania Anti-slavery Society, 1855. 24 p. [9243

Narron Central Railroad. Traffic Dept. Local freight tariff on classes and commodities between Narron Central Railroad stations, local freight tariff no. 1. Raleigh, Edwards & Broughton, 1918. 5 p. [9244

Nasby, Petroleum V., pseud. see Locke, David Ross

Nash, Arnold Samuel. [Letter from Arnold and Ethel Nash, Allahabad, India, Nov. 20, 1953] Madras, Ahura Press, 1953. 12 p. [9245

Nash, Arnold Samuel, ed. Protestant thought in the twentieth century. New York, Macmillan Co., 1951. 296 p. [9246

Nash, F. K. Circumcision and baptism, sacraments of the covenant of grace. Fayetteville, Presbyterian Office, 1859. 79 p. [9247

Nash, Francis. Abner Nash; an address . . . delivered at the unveiling of a tablet in New Bern, N. C., June 7th, 1923. 9 p. [9248
——Edmund Strudwick, man and country doctor; an address delivered on . . . the presentation of a portrait of Doctor Strudwick to the State Hospital at Raleigh, Dec. 14, 1926. Raleigh, Edwards & Broughton Co., 1927. 10 p. [9249
——Hillsboro, colonial and revolutionary. Raleigh, Edwards & Broughton, 1903. 100 p. [9250
—— ——Chapel Hill, Orange Printshop, 1953. 96 p. [9251
——Influence of Presbyterianism upon civil liberty; an address delivered at First Presbyterian Church, Raleigh . . . August 6, 1922. [Raleigh? 1922?] 8 p. [9252
——Presentation of portrait of Governor Alexander Martin to the state of North Carolina in the hall of the House of Representatives, at Raleigh, November 16, 1908, by the North Carolina Society of the Sons of the Revolution. [Raleigh? 1909] 19 p. [9253
——The relation of the clerk of the Superior Court to appeals to the Supreme Court. [Raleigh, n.d.] 17 p. [9254
——The special tax bonds of North Carolina and their repudiation. Raleigh, Edwards & Broughton Co., 1926. 8 p. [9255

Nash, Frederick. An address delivered before the members of Eagle Lodge, no. 71, on the anniversary of St. John the evangelist, December 27, 1838. Hillsborough, Dennis Heartt, 1839. 17 p. [9256

Nash, Leonidas Lydwell. Baptism, the nature, mode, and subjects. Greensboro, Christian Advocate, n.d. 16 p. [9257
——Early morning scenes in the Bible. New York, Fleming H. Revell Co. [c.1910] 209 p. [9258

——Recollections and observations during a ministry in the North Carolina Conference, Methodist Episcopal Church, South, of forty-three years. Raleigh Mutual Publishing Co., 1916.   142 p.   [9259
——Regeneration. Fayetteville, Fayetteville Printing and Publishing Co., 1897.
13 p.   [9260
——Spiritual life. Nashville, Methodist Episcopal Church, South, 1898. 203p. [9261

Nash and Kollock School, Hillsboro, N. C. see **Select Boarding and Day School,**
Hillsboro, N. C.   [9262
Nash Co., N. C. Board of County Commissioners. Report on Nash County, North
Carolina, 19 - [Nashville, 19 - NcU has 1920/26   [9263
Nash Co., N. C. Board of Education. Nash county teachers handbook, 1927-1928.
Rocky Mount, Carolina Office Equipment Co. [1927?]   48 p.   [9264
——Report, 19 - [Nashville, 19 - NcU has 1925/26   [9265
Nash Co., N. C. Schools. Fourth and Fifth Grade Teachers. Bulletin of suggestions and information for carrying out a unit of work on pioneer life. No place, no publisher, 1932.   21 p.   [9266
Nash Co., N. C. Schools. Third Grade Teachers. Nature study bulletin. No
place, no publisher, April, 1933.   22 p.   [9267
Nash Co., N. C. Treasurer. Statement for Nash County, 19 - [Nashville, 19 -
NcU has 1920/21   [9268

National Carbon Company, Morganton, N. C. A guide for visitors and defense workers on the National Carbon Company plant. [Asheville, F. E. Vaden, 1942?]
44 p.   [9269

National Child Labor Committee, New York. Child in the cotton mill. New York,
March, 1916.   (Pamphlet no. 260)   10 p.   [9270
——Child welfare in North Carolina. New York City [c.1918]   314 p.   [9271
——North Carolina child labor law. New York [193?]   2 p.   [9272

National Committee for Mental Hygiene. Mental hygiene exhibit and conference to be held in the auditorium, Raleigh, N. C., Nov. 28 to Dec. 3, 1913. Raleigh, Edwards & Broughton [1913?]   7 p.   [9273

National Committee to Observe the 50th Anniversary of Powered Flight. Fifty
years of aviation progress. Wash. [1953]   59 p.   [9174

[National Committee to Observe the 50th Anniversary of Powered Flight] Flight.
[Wash. 1953]   [33] p.   [9275

National Congress of Parents and Teachers. North Carolina. see **North Carolina**
Congress of Parents and Teachers; see also **Names of North Carolina towns, sub-**
head, Parent Teacher Association.

National Council for Protection of Roadside Beauty, New York. The roadsides of North Carolina: a survey. Washington, American Nature Association [1932?]
33 p.   [9276

National Foundation for Infantile Paralysis, Inc., New York. The miracle of Hickory.
New York [1944] (Its Publication no. 53)   [21] p.   [9277

National Industrial Conference Board. The cost of living among wage-earners, Greenville, South Carolina; Pelzer, South Carolina; Charlotte, North Carolina, January and February, 1920. Boston, Mass., c.1920. (Its Special report, no. 8)
25 p.   [9278

National Johnson Club. Document no. 1, National Johnson Club: 1. Address of the National Johnson Club. 2. Testimony of Alexander H. Stephens. No place, no publisher [1866?]   16 p.   [9279
——Document no. 2. Washington, Intelligencer Printing House, 1866. 32 p. [9280

National Man, pseud. see **Rayner, Kenneth**

National Planning Association. Committee of the South. New industry comes to the South; a summary of the report on location of industry. Washington, 1949.
(Its Reports, no. 1)   32 p.   [9281
——Selected studies of Negro employment in the South. Washington [1953- (Its
Reports, no. 6: 1-)   NcU has no. 2   [9282

National Republican Party. North Carolina. Address of the administration convention, held at Raleigh, Dec. 20, 1827: To the freemen of North Carolina. [Raleigh, 1828]   8 p.   [9283

—— ——[With biographical sketch of Wm. Gaston preceding caption title]
8 p.   [9284
—— ——Raleigh, Printed by J. Gales and Son, 1827. 15 p.   [9285

National Republican Party. North Carolina. An address to the freemen of North
Carolina. [Raleigh, Loring, pr., 1836] 12 p.   [9286

[**National Republican Party. North Carolina**] Address to the friends of General
Andrew Jackson in North Carolina. Raleigh, Printed at the Office of the Constitutionalist, October, 1832. 14 p.   [9287

National Republican Party. Virginia. Convention, 1828. Proceedings of the Anti-
Jackson convention. Richmond, Printed by Samuel Shepherd & Co., 1828.
38 p.   [9288
——The Virginia address. [Richmond? 1828] 8 p.   [9289

National Society of the Daughters of the American Revolution see **Daughters of the
American Revolution**

The nation's oldest state university. [Houston, Texas, Star Engraving Co., 1939?]
[7] p.   [9290

Native of Pennsylvania, pseud. see **Williamson, Hugh**

Navy League of the U. S. Eighth annual dinner in honor of the Secretary of the
Navy, Hon. Josephus Daniels, Friday, April eleven, nineteen hundred and thirteen,
The New Willard, Washington. No place, no publisher [1913?] 3 p.   [9291

Nawhunty Baptist Association. Minutes, 18 - [Halifax, Office of the Free Press,
18 - NcU has 1829-1830   [9292

Neale, Mary (Peisley) Some account of the life and religious exercises of Mary
Neale. Dublin, Reprinted, Philadelphia for Joseph Crukshank, 1796. 118 p. [9293

Neathery, John B., joint author, see **Harrell, Eugene G.**

Negro Community League. Purposes and policies. Raleigh, Edwards & Broughton,
1917. 8 p.   [9294

The Negro who can read may vote, the illiterate white man cannot vote. No place,
no publisher [1900?] [1] p.   [9295

Nehemiah, pseud. Strictures on the sentiments of the Kehukee Association. Newbern, Thomas Watson, 1829. 12 p.   [9296

Neilson, Sarah D. 2 decades of progress, 1932-1952. [Columbus, Miss.] Mississippi State College for Women [1952] 31 p.   [9297

[**Nelms, Henning**] . . . The hangman's handyman, by Hake Talbot [pseud.] New
York, Simon and Schuster, 1942. 342 p.   [9298

Nelson, Anson. Memorials of Sarah Childress Polk . . . by Anson and Fanny Nelson.
New York, A. D. F. Randolph & Co. [1892] 284 p.   [9299

Nelson, Thomas. Practical loom fixing. [Charlotte, Ray Printing Co.] 1917.
93 p.   [9300
—— ——[4th ed.] [Charlotte, Charlotte Publishing Co.] 1936. 165 p.   [9301
——Weaving—plain and fancy. Raleigh, For the Author by Edwards & Broughton
Printing Co. [c.1907] 94 p.   [9302

Nesbitt, Lillie B., joint author, see **Wood, Edna Hilliard White**

Neue Nachricht alter und neuer Merckwürdigkeiten, enthaltende ein vertrautes
Gespräch und sichere Briefe von der landschaft Carolina und ubrigen englischen
Pflantz-städten in America. Zürich, 1734. 79 p. NcU has microfilm (negative)
from Library of Congress   [9303

Neuse, 19 - Oriental, Senior Class of Oriental High School, 1923- NcU has
1923   [9304

Neuse-Atlantic Baptist Association. Minutes, 1907- 1907- NcU has [1907-
1929]   [9305

Neuse Baptist Association. Minutes of annual session, 1899- 1899- NcU has
1899-1906, [1915-1928] 1932, 1934-1941   [9306

Neuse River Navigation Co. Annual report, 1852- 1852- NcU has 1853, 1854 [9307

Neuse River Soil Conservation District. Report, 194 - Raleigh, 1949- NcU has
1948   [9308

Nevill, J. Parks. A discourse delivered in the Christian Church, . . . Raleigh . . . in
May, 1859. No place, no publisher, n.d. 16 p.   [9309

——A discourse on the origin and increase of devils on all parts of earth.   Richmond, William H. Clemmitt, pr., 1856.   26 p.   [9310

——Discourse showing that Esau.was the angel that wrestled with Jacob; preached at Wake Bethel, on Sunday, April 11, 1858.   Richmond, Printed for the Author by Wm. H. Clemmitt, 1858.   16 p.   [9311

——A discourse showing that "The earth abideth forever", and that hell and heaven are in this world; delivered in the city of Raleigh, June 14th, 1857.   Richmond, William H. Clemmitt, pr., 1857.   15 p.   [9312

Nevins, Allan.   The American states during and after the Revolution, 1775-1789. New York, Macmillan Co., 1924.   727 p.   [9313

New, Albert.   Four sermons.   Weldon, Weldon Printing Co., 1910.   22 p.   [9314

——Unity and diversity, a sermon preached . . . before the Ven. Archdeacon, the clergy and laity of the Convocation of Raleigh.   [Weldon?] n.d.   [8] p.   [9315

New and complete North Carolina form-book; containing forms of all those legal instruments which the people have occasion to use.   Raleigh, Henry D. Turner, 1858.   344 p.   [9316

—— ——1860.   [9317

—— ——Raleigh, North Carolina Publishing Co., 1867.   [9318

New Bern, N. C.   Board of Aldermen.   Charter of the city of New Bern, North Carolina, also, ordinances of the Board of Aldermen, amended and adopted 1904. Raleigh, Edwards & Broughton, pr., 1903.   120 p.   [9319

New Bern, N. C.   Board of Education.   Report of the Public Schools of the city of New Bern, N. C., 19 - 19 - NcU has 1901/02, 1902/03, 1907/08, 1908/09, 1910/11, 1911/12, 1920/21-1929/1930   [9320

New Bern, N. C.   Centenary Methodist Episcopal Church.   Annual . . . containing messages, reports, directory, assessments, 19 - [New Bern] Owen G. Dunn, 1921- NcU has 1921   [9321

New Bern, N. C.   Centenary Methodist Episcopal Church.   Committee of Ladies. The Elm City cook book.   New Bern, N. S. Richardson and Son, 1896.   72 p. [9322

New Bern, N. C.   Chamber of Commerce.   Craven County, N. C. and New Bern, its capital.   New Bern, Owen G. Dunn, pr. [1913]   19 p.   [9323

——Facts about New Bern . . . and Craven County.   [New Bern, Dunn, 1916?] 6 p.   [9324

——Hunting wild game and fowl near New Bern, North Carolina.   New Bern [1924] Folder.   [9325

New Bern, N. C.   Chamber of Commerce.   New Bern, North Carolina.   [New Bern] [c.1926]   [27] p.   [9326

[New Bern, N. C.   Chamber of Commerce]   New Bern, North Carolina, industrially a modern city with historic traditions.   [New Bern] 1940.   69 p.   [9327

New Bern, N. C.   Chamber of Commerce.   Report, 19 - New Bern, 19 - NcU has 1923, 1926   [9328

New Bern, N. C.   Christ Church.   Juvenile Sewing Society.   Answer to an appeal for benefit of the church, lovingly inscribed to a former pastor, by Esclairmond Claremont.   Newbern, N. S. Richardson, pr., 1871.   27 p.   [9329

New Bern, N. C.   Christ Church.   Sunday School.   Constitution and by-laws . . . established January 16th, 1829.   [Newbern? 1829?]   8 p.   [9330

New Bern, N. C.   Citizens.   [Meeting to make arrangements for paying a suitable tribute of respect to the memory of the Honourable William Gaston] Newbern, 1844.   [1] p.   [9331

New Bern, N. C.   Committee of Inquiry and Correspondence.   The proceedings of the Revolutionary committee of the town of Newbern, North Carolina, 1775. Chicago, Ill., Chicago School of Printing [1938]   4 p.   [9332

New Bern, N. C.   Ladies' Memorial Association.   Confederate memorial addresses, Mon. May 11, 1885, New Bern, N. C.   Richmond, Whittet & Shepperson, 1886. 32 p.   [9333

New Bern, N. C.   Presbyterian Church.   Directory . . . January, 1914.   [New Bern] no publisher, 1914.   23 p.   [9334

New Bern, N. C.   Public School.   175th Anniversary Celebration Committee.   Historical celebration and evening pageant, Thursday, May 4, 1939. [New Bern, 1939] 27 p. [9335

New Bern, N. C. Theater. Dr. Llewellyn Lechmere Wall (of Orange County) will on Wednesday evening, the 16th of May, 1797, administer at the Newbern Theatre, wholesome physic to the mind. No place [1797] [1] p. NcU has photostat (negative) of original in Playbill Collection, Colonial Williamsburg, Inc. [9336

——This evening, Friday, March the 31st, 1797, will be presented, a variety of entertainments. [New Bern, .T Pasteur, pr., 1797] [1] p. NcU has photostat (negative) of original in Playbill Collection, Colonial Williamsburg, Inc. [9337

——To all lovers of wit, satire, character and sentiment. At the Newbern Theatre . . . the 13th of May, 1797. No place [1797] [1] p. NcU has photostat (negative) of original in Playbill Collection, Colonial Williamsburg, Inc. [9338

New Bern, N. C. Water and Sewer Co. Analysis, testimonials, and rates of the Water and Sewer Co. of New Bern. New Bern, N. S. Richardson & Son, pr., 1897. 20 p. [9339

New Bern, cradle of North Carolina. [Raleigh, Edwards and Broughton for] The Garden Club of North Carolina, 1941. Various paging. [9340

[New Bern Historic Celebration and Pageant Committees, 1929] Historic celebration and pageant, June 11th, 1929, New Bern, North Carolina, settled in 1710. [New Bern, 1929] 46 p. [9341

New Bern, N. C., directory, 1904-1905- v. 1- Richmond, Va., Hill Directory Co., 1904- NcU has 1907-08 [9342

The new Cherokee phoenix, v. 1, no. 1- June 30, 1951- Cherokee, 1951- NcU has v. 1, no. 1-10 [9343

New England Educational Commission for Freedmen. Annual report, 186 - Boston, Prentiss & Deland, pr., 1863- NcU has 1863, 1864 [9344

——Extracts from letters of teachers and superintendents of the New England Educational Commission for Freedmen, fourth series, 1864. Boston, David Clapp, pr., 1864. 14 p. [9345

——Extracts from letters of teachers and superintendents of the New-England Freedmen's Aid Society (Educational commission) fifth series, October 15, 1864. Boston, John Wilson and Son, 1864. 20 p. [9346

New Found Baptist Association. Minutes, 19 - 19 - NcU has 1946-1956 [9347

New Garden Meeting of Friends, Guilford Co., N. C. Memoranda of New Garden Meeting of Friends. No place, n.d. 11 p. [9348

——New Garden Monthly Meeting of Friends, organized 1754. No place, 1914. 20 p. [9349

[New Garden Meeting of Friends, Guilford Co., N. C.] The teaching and purpose of Friends. [Guilford College, 1894] 16 p. [9350

New Hampshire. Republican State Convention. Proceedings and address of the New Hampshire Republican State Convention of delegates friendly to the election of Andrew Jackson to the next presidency of the United States, assembled at Concord, June 11 and 12, 1828. Concord, N. H., Patriot Office, 1828. 32 p. [9351

[New Hanover County, N. C. Auditor] . . . Report on examination of books and accounts, 191 - Wilmington, Wilmington Stamp and Printing Co., 1913- NcU has 1913 (containing four years ended Nov. 30, 1912) and 1924/26, 1927/28-1929/30, 1931/32-1946/47 [9352

New Hanover County, N. C. Board of Commissioners. Annual statement, 188 - 188 - NcU has 1886/87, 1889/1890, 1898/99 [9353

[New Hanover Co., N. C. Board of Commissioners] [List of offences tried and disposed of in the Superior and Criminal courts of New Hanover County] [Wilmington, 1888] 7 p. [9354

New Hanover Co., N. C. Board of Education. Report of the Superintendent of Public Instruction, New Hanover County, 19 - Wilmington, 19 - NcU has 1916/17, 1922/23, 1923/24, pts. 1-2, 1924/25, 1925/26 [9355

——Rules and regulations, 1922. No place, no publisher, 1922. 14 p. [9357

New Hanover Co., N. C. Board of health. Our communal health, 19 - [Wilmington] Consolidated Board of Health of Wilmington and New Hanover Co., 19 - NcU has 1935-1939, 1944 [9358

New Hanover Co., N. C. Republican Club. Republican resolutions . . . February 28th, 1909. [Wilmington? 1908] [1] p. [9359

New Hanover Fishing Club. Prize list and annual, 192 - [Wilmington, 192 - NcU has 1927 [9360

New Hope Missionary Baptist Association. Minutes, 18 - 18 - NcU has [1899-1929] [9361

New horizons, v. 1-[2] September, 1945-April, 1949. Chapel Hill, North Carolina League for Crippled Children, 1945-49. NcU has v. 1, September, 1945-February, 1948; (irregular and unnumbered) April, 1948-April, 1949 [9362

New Institute School, Iredell County, N. C. Catalogue, 185 - Salisbury, 185 - NcU has 1854/55 [9363

New Jersey. State Commission for Erection of Monument to Ninth New Jersey Volunteers at New Berne, North Carolina. . . . Report . . . Dedication National Cemetery, New Berne, N. C., May 18, 1905. [Philadelphia] 1905. 112 p. [9364

New liberation see Liberation

New River Baptist Association. Minutes, 18 - 18 - NcU has [1882-1949] [9365

New South (Atlanta) Changing patterns in the new South. [Atlanta, Southern Regional Council, 1955] 116 p. [9366

New South River Baptist Association. Minutes, 192 - 192 - NcU has [1934-1941] [9367

The New Testament Christian, a message from the Eliada Home for Children, v. 1-190 - Asheville, Eliada Home for Children, 190 - NcU has v. [27-37] 38-48 [9368

The new "village smithy", North Carolina version; or, How and where Swipesey's gun was mended. No place, no publisher, n.d. [1] p. [9369

New Wings; an anthology of prose and verse, written . . . by the children of Greensboro Public Schools, Greensboro, North Carolina, v. 1- 1930/31- NcU has v. 1-2 [9370

New World Travel Company. North Carolina teacher's vacation trip. [New York, William Mann Co., pr., 1889] [5] p. [9371

New York (City) Church of the Strangers. Proceedings at the reception of the Rev. Dr. Deems . . . on his return from the East, June 27, 1880. New York, J. J. Little & Co., pr., 1880. 16 p. [9372

New York (City) Citizens. Mass meeting of the citizens of New York, held at the Cooper Institute, Feb. 22d, 1866, to approve the principles announced in the messages of Andrew Johnson. New York, George F. Nesbitt & Co., pr., 1866. 38 p. [9373

New York (City) Common Council. Report of the committee of arrangements . . . upon the funeral ceremonies in commemoration of the death of Gen. Andrew Jackson. New York, 1845. 173 p. [9374

New York (City) Grand Central Art Galleries. Memorial exhibition: paintings, water colors, drawings by Elliott Daingerfield, April 3rd to April 21st, 1934. New York [1934] [15] p. [9375

New York (City) National Park Bank. For sale, $1,142,500 state of North Carolina forty-year four per cent coupon bonds, dated July 1, 1913, payable July 1, 1953. [New York, 1913] [6] p. [9376

New York (City) North Carolina Society see North Carolina Society of New York

New York (City) Public Library. . . . Papers relating to Samuel Cornell, North Carolina Loyalist. New York, 1913. (New York (City) Public library. Bulletin. May, 1913) 44 p. [9377

New York (City) Republican General Committee of Young Men. Address . . . friendly to the election of Gen. Andrew Jackson to the presidency. New York, Alexander Ming, Jr., pr., 1828. 48 p. [9378

New York (City) Southern Society. Year book, 19 - New York, 19 - NcU has 1904/05, 1911/12, 1912/13, 1913/14, 1914/15, 1917/18, 1926-1930 (as one) 1945 [9379

New York (City) Stock Exchange. Committee on Stock List. R. J. Reynolds Tobacco Company. [New York, 1922] [5] p. [9380

New York (State) Republican State Convention. Address. [Albany, N. Y.] Albany Argus Extra [1832?] 24 p. [9381

New York and Southern Railroad and Telegraph Construction Co. Copy of articles of agreement for the purchase of the stock of the state in the Cape Fear and Yadkin Valley Railroad Co. No place, no publisher [1881] 10 p. [9382
——Proposition for the purchase of the stock of the state in the Cape Fear and Yadkin Valley Railroad Co. [1881] 10 p. [9383

Newbern Academy, Newbern, N. C. Laws. Newbern, S. Hall, pr., 1823. 15 p. [9384

Newbold, Nathan Carter, ed. Five North Carolina Negro educators. Chapel Hill, University of North Carolina Press, 1939. 142 p. [9385

Newbury, F. A. Retail catalogue of green-house and border plants for 18 - Magnolia, Rosenvink Gardens, 187 - NcU has Spring and Fall, 1878 [9386

Newell, A. Biography and miscellanies. St. Louis, Nixon-Jones Printing Co., 1894. 248 p. [9387

Newman, Henry Stanley. Memories of Stanley Pumphrey. London, S. W. Partridge & Co. [pref. 1883] 268 p. [9388

Newman, Samuel. Religion and war; an address delivered before the Civitan Club of Greensboro, N. C. [Greensboro] n.d. [4] p. [9389

Newman, William S. The pianist's problems. New York, Harper & Brothers [1950] 134 p. [9390
—— ——rev. and enl. New York, Harper & Brothers [c.1956] 168 p. [9391

Newman, William S., ed. Thirteen keyboard sonatas of the 18th and 19th centuries. Chapel Hill, University of North Carolina Press [c.1947] 175 p. [9392

Newman, William S. Understanding music. New York, Harper & Brothers [1953] 302 p. [9393

Newnan, John, and others. Case of John Newnan and others vs. Wm. Chambers and others. Nashville, Tenn., Printed by E. J. Foster, 1835. 17 p. [9394

Newnan, John. An inaugural dissertation on general dropsy, submitted to the . . . University of Pennsylvania, for the degree of Doctor of Medicine, on the 8th day of May, 1793. Philadelphia, Printed by Parry Hall, 1793. 31 p. [9395

News and Courier, Charleston, S. C. Charleston and Asheville, the City by the Sea to the Land of the Sky. Charleston, 1886. 27 p. [9396

News and observer annual, 188 - Raleigh, News and Observer, 188 - NcU has 1883, 1887 [9397

News and observer classified business and professional directory . . . Raleigh, North Carolina, and vicinity, 1939- [Raleigh, 1939- NcU has 1939 [9398

News Letter see University of North Carolina News Letter

Newsom, Dallas Walton. The history of Duke Memorial Methodist Episcopal Church, South; a paper read . . . at the morning service . . . October 30, 1932. [Durham? 1932?] 32 p. [9399
——Song and dream; poems. Boston, Mass., Stratford Co., 1922. 174 p. [9400

Newsome, Albert Ray. The growth of North Carolina, by Albert Ray Newsome . . . and Hugh Talmage Lefler. Yonkers-on-Hudson, N. Y., World Book Co. [c.1940] 472 p. [9401
——A letter to the Governor; open letter of A. R. Newsome and Hugh T. Lefler to Governor J. M. Broughton. Chapel Hill, 1941. 8 p. [9402
——The presidential election of 1824 in North Carolina. Chapel Hill, University of North Carolina Press, 1939. (James Sprunt studies in history and political science, v. 23, no. 1) 202 p. [9403

Newsome, Albert Ray, ed. Studies in history and political science. Chapel Hill, Univ. of North Carolina Press, 1947. 298 p. [9404

Newsome, Albert Ray, joint author see Lefler, Hugh Talmage

Newton, Harry L. Mr. Seal of North Carolina; a sketch in one scene. Chicago, Dramatic Publishing Co., c.1902. 8 p. [9405

Newton, N. C. Graded School. Graded School bulletin, v. 1- February, 1912- Newton, 1912- NcU has v. [1] [9406

Nichols, George Ward. The story of the great march. New York, Harper & Brothers, 1865. 394 p.   [9407

Nichols, John. Directory of the General Assembly of the state of North Carolina for the session commencing Nov. 19, 1860. No place, John Nichols [1860?] 50 p.   [9408
——For Congress, 4th district, John Nichols, of Wake County; address to the voters of the fourth district. No place [1886?] 8 p.   [9409
——History of Hiram Lodge no. 40, Raleigh, N. C., from 1800 to 1900 inclusive. No place, no publisher, n.d. 56 p.   [9410
——North Carolina; annual address of John Nichols, M. W. Grand Master, December 7th, 1874. Raleigh, Edwards, Broughton & Co., 1875. 13 p.   [9411

Nichols, Spencer Van Bokkelen. The significance of Anthony Trollope. New York, McMurtrie, 1925. 59 p.   [9412

Nicholson, Alfred Osborn Pope. Address delivered before the two literary societies of the University of North-Carolina, June 1, 1853. Raleigh, Printed by W. W. Holden, 1853. 31 p.   [9413

Nicholson, Arnold. Adventures with a prophet. [Philadelphia, Curtis Publishing Co., c.1939] 84 p.   [9414

Nicholson, Meredith. The cavalier of Tennessee. Indianapolis, Bobbs-Merrill Co. [c.1928] 402 p.   [9415
——Little brown jug at Kildare. Indianapolis, Bobbs-Merrill Co. [c.1908] 422 p. [9416
——War of the Carolinas. No place, Thomas Nelson and Sons [pref. 1908] 286 p. Also published under the title The little brown jug at Kildare.   [9417

Nicholson, Roy S. Wesleyan Methodism in the South. Syracuse, N. Y., Wesleyan Methodist Publishing House, 1933. 294 p.   [9418

Nicholson, S. T. Valuable land for sale . . . known as the Fork place. Tarboro, Southerner, 1879. [1] p.   [9419

Nicholson, Thomas. Epistle to Friends in Great Britain; also a testimony concerning Thomas Nicholson of N. C. Carthage, Indiana, Printed by David Marshall, 1888. 8 p.   [9420
——An epistle to Friends in Great Britain, to whom is the salutation of my love. No place, no publisher [1762] 4 p.   [9421

Nicholson, Watson. Anthony Aston, stroller and adventurer; to which is appended Aston's Brief supplement to Colley Cibber's Lives; and A sketch of the life of Anthony Aston, written by himself. South Haven, Mich., Author, 1920. 98 p. [9422

Nicolay, Helen. Andrew Jackson, the fighting president. New York, Century Co. [c.1929] 335 p.   [9423

Niggli, Josephine Morgan. Mexican folk plays. Chapel Hill, University of North Carolina Press [c.1938] 223 p.   [9424
——Mexican village. Chapel Hill, University of North Carolina Press [1945] 491 p.   [9425
——Un pueblo Mexicano. Selecciones from Mexican village. New York, W. W. Norton & Co., Inc. [c.1949] 267 p.   [9426
——Step down, elder brother. New York, Rinehart & Co. [1947] 374 p.   [9427

Niles, John Jacob, comp. . . . Ballads, carols, and tragic legends from the Southern Appalachian mountains. New York, G. Schirmer, Inc. [c.1937] 20 p.   [9428
——Down in yon forest; for four-part chorus of mixed voices *a cappella.* New York, G. Schirmer, Inc. [c.1935-1936] 6 p.   [9429
——. . . More songs of the hill-folk; ten ballads and tragic legends . . . simply arranged with accompaniment for piano. New York, G. Schirmer, Inc. [c.1936] 20 p.   [9430
——Songs of the hill-folk; twelve ballads from Kentucky, Virginia, and North Carolina, collected and simply arranged for the piano. New York, G. Schirmer, Inc. [c.1934] 25 p.   [9431
——Ten Christmas carols from the Southern Appalachian Mountains collected and simply arranged with accompaniment for piano. New York, G. Schirmer, Inc. [c.1935] 22 p.   [9432

Nineteen hundred: Simmons as North Carolina knew him in fusion days. No place, no publisher [1928?] [1] p.   [9433

Nisbet, Alice. Send me an angel. Chapel Hill, University of North Carolina Press [1946] 122 p.   [9434

Nixon, Alfred. Address at the dedication of the Confederate Memorial Hall, Lincolnton, N. C., Aug. 27th, 1908. Lincolnton, News Print for Southern Stars Chapter U. D. C. [1908?] 22 p. [9435

——Address delivered before the Anna Jackson Book Club, in the hall of the Mary Wood School, Lincolnton, N. C., Feb. 22, 1902: Beattie's Ford, a Scotch-Irish settlement on the Catawba. Lincolnton, Journal Printing Co., 1902. 16 p. [9436

——Brief historical sketch of the Hager family of Lincoln County, N. C. No place, no publisher, 1902. 15 p. [9437

——Cross Woodis, character sketch. No place, Journal Print, 1905. 12 p. [9438

——The Finger family of Lincoln County, N. C., with brief sketch of Saint Matthews Church. Lincolnton, Lincoln Journal, 1903. 26 p. [9439

——The Hauss family of Lincoln County, N. C. [Lincolnton] Lincoln Journal, 1905. 10 p. [9440

——History of Daniel's Evangelical Lutheran and Reformed churches, Lincoln Co., N. C. Hickory, A. L. Crouse & Son, pr., 1898. 44 p. [9441

——In memoriam, Ann Elizabeth Henderson. Lincolnton, May 10, 1901. [1] p. [9442

——In memoriam, John Barnett Smith, Nov. 26, 1827-Feb. 2, 1906. Lincolnton, Lincoln Journal, 1906. 12 p. [9443

——In memoriam: Vardry Alexander McBee, 1818-1904. [Lincolnton, 1904] 17 p. [9444

——Major-General Robert F. Hoke. Lincolnton, July 10, 1912. [1] p. [9445

[**Nixon, Alfred**] Quarter-centennial of Rev. R. Z. Johnston's pastorate of Lincolnton Presbyterian Church, Jan. 8, 9, and 10, 1897. Lincolnton, Journal, 1897. 21 p. [9446

Nixon, Alfred. Roster of Confederate soldiers in the war between the states, furnished by Lincoln County, North Carolina, 1861-65. Lincolnton, Journal Print by order of W. J. Hoke Camp, Confederate Veterans, 1905. 64 p. [9447

——Roster of the ex-Confederate soldiers living in Lincoln County, with the address of A. Nixon . . . before the United Daughters of the Confederacy and Confederate veterans . . . Lincolnton, N. C., on Memorial Day . . . May 10th, 1907. Lincolnton, Lincoln County News, 1907. 19 p. [9448

Nixon, Barnaby. Biographical and other extracts from the manuscript writings of Barnaby Nixon. York, Printed and Published by W. Alexander and Son, 1822. 70 p. [9449

——Extracts from the manuscript writings of Barnaby Nixon, deceased. Richmond, J. Warrock, pr., 1814. 54 p. [9450

Nixon, Herman Clarence. . . . Social security for southern farmers. Chapel Hill, University of North Carolina Press, 1936. (Southern policy papers, no. 2) 8 p. [9451

——Southern workers outside the legislative pale. New York City, American Labor Education Service, Inc. in cooperation with the Southern School for Workers, Inc. [1942] 36 p. [9452

Nixon, Joseph Robert. Exercises of Lee and Jackson day, Lincolnton, N. C., Jan. 23, 1915. No place, no publisher [1915?] 15 p. [9453

——The German settlers in Lincoln County and Western North Carolina. Chapel Hill, The University, 1911. (James Sprunt historical publications, v. 11, no. 2) p. [25]-62 [9454

——The Mauney family reunion, Aug. 19th, 1916. No place, Author [1916?] 14 p. [9455

——Unity Presbyterian Church, cradle of state builders. Lincolnton, 1952. [6] p. [9456

Noble, Marcus Cicero Stephens, 1855-1942. A history of the public schools of North Carolina. Chapel Hill, University of North Carolina Press, 1930. 463 p. [9457

——A practical primary arithmetic, by M. C. S. Noble . . . and Mrs. F. L. Stevens. New York, Charles Scribner's Sons, 1911. 177 p. [9458

——The Williams' reader for beginners. To precede the "First reader." By M. C. S. Noble and E. P. Moses. Raleigh, Alfred Williams & Co., 1893. 43 p. [9459

—— ——1895. [9460

Noble, Marcus Cicero Stephens, 1899- Practical measurements for school administrators. Scranton, Pa., International Textbook Co., 1939. 330 p. [9461

——Pupil transportation in the United States. Scranton, Pa., International Textbook Co., 1940. 541 p. [9462

——The socialized motive. Rockville Centre, N. Y., Acorn Publishing Co. [c.1934] 138 p.   [9463

——War-time pupil transportation; the place of highway transportation in American education and its post-war possibilities. Washington, D. C., National Highway Users Conference [1944]   31 p.   [9464

Noblin, Stuart. The Grange in North Carolina, 1929-1954. Greensboro, North Carolina State Grange, 1954.   59 p.   [9465

——Leonidas LaFayette Polk, agrarian crusader. Chapel Hill, University of North Carolina Press, 1949.   325 p.   [9466

Nocalore, being the transactions of the North Carolina Lodge of Research no. 666, A. F. & A. M., v. 1-11, 1931-1941. [Monroe? 1931-1941] NcU has v. 1-11.   [9467

Nola Chucky Primitive Baptist Association. Minutes, 18 - 18 - NcU has 1901   [9468

Nolan, Jeanette (Covert) Andrew Jackson. New York, J. Messner [1949] 178 p. [9469

——O. Henry; the story of William Sydney Porter. New York, J. Messner, Inc. [1943]   263 p.   [9470

——Patriot in the saddle. New York, J. Messner, Inc. [1945]   239 p.   [9471

Nolen, John. Asheville city plan, 1922. Asheville, no publisher, 1922.   48 p. [9472

——New towns for old; achievements in civic improvement in some American small towns. Boston, Marshall Jones Co. [c.1927]   177 p.   [9473

Nolumus, pseud. The Blue Ridge Railroad; a series of articles originally published in the Charleston mercury. No place [Printed by A. E. Miller, 1859]   47 p. [9474

Non Quis, pseud. see Guion, Haywood Williams

Norburn, Charles Arwed. Streamlining our monetary system. Asheville, Stephens Press [1944]   191 p.   [9475

Norburn, Hope (Robertson) Above the brink and other poems. Philadelphia, Dorrance & Co. [1949]   59 p.   [9476

——Lord Lollypop, a timely allegory. New York, Exposition Press [1952] 36 p. [9477

——Melodies for moppets . . . words and illustrations by Hope R. Norburn, music by Hope T. Robertson. [Asheville?] No publisher [c.1948]   [62] p.   [9478

Norcom, James. An inaugural thesis on jaundice . . . submitted to . . . the University of Pennsylvania; on the 6th day of June, 1799, for the degree of Doctor of Medicine. Philadelphia, Printed by James Carey for Mathew Carey [1799?] 49 p.   [9479

Norden, Laura (Howell) Just about music. Wilmington, Printed by Wilmington Print Co., 1948.   171 p.   [9480

——On upward flight. New York, Exposition Press [1951]   47 p.   [9481

Nordhoff, Charles. Cotton states in the spring and summer of 1875. New York, D. Appleton & Co., 1876.   112 p.   [9482

Norfleet Trio, ed. Ten modern trios for violin, cello, and piano. New York, Carl Fischer [c.1928]   3 v.   [9483

Norfolk, Va. Industrial Commission. Agriculture and food production in and around Norfolk, Va., and its tributary territory, Tidewater, Va. and Eastern North Carolina. [Norfolk, Burke and Gregory] 1911.   71 p.   [9484

Norfolk, Va. Select and Common Councils. Committee on Seaboard and Roanoke Railroad. Report on the present condition of the Seaboard & Roanoke Railroad. Norfolk, Printed by T. G. Broughton & Son, 1849.   20 p.   [9485

Norfolk and Southern Railroad Co. Cities of opportunity in the South. [Norfolk? 190?]   39 p.   [9486

——Corn, cotton, and cattle; the Carolina country. [Norfolk, Va., 1915] 44 p. [9487

——Elizabeth City, N. C., hub of the Albemarle region. [Greensboro, J. Stone & Co., 1904?]   46 p.   [9488

——Industrial opportunities in the "territory that has everything", North Carolina and tidewater Virginia. Norfolk [1949]   [32] p.   [9489

——Opportunities for a home in the South on lines of the Norfolk and Southern, the Atlantic and North Carolina, and Raleigh & Pamlico Sound railroads. Norfolk, Va., Land and Industrial Dept., Norfolk & Southern Railroad Co. [1904?] 20 p. [9490

——Present development and future possibilities of Washington, N. C. [Greensboro, J. Stone & Co., 1905?]   52 p.   [9491

——Proposed extension of Norfolk and Southern Railway from Edenton to Mackey's Ferry, N. C.   Raleigh, Edwards & Broughton Printing Co., 1907.   13 p.   [9492
——Report, 1st- 1910/11- [Norfolk, 1911- NcU has 1910/11-1915/16, 1916-1938, 1943-1954   [9493

Norfolk and Western Railway. Industrial and Shippers Guide. Roanoke, Va. 1916. 310 p.   [9494
——Opportunities in Virginia and North Carolina along the Norfolk and Western Railway. Roanoke, Va., n.d.   32 p.   [9495
——Report, 1896/97- 1897- NcU has 1896/97-1954/55   [9496
——[Virginia and North Carolina] Roanoke, Va. [1916?]   13 p.   [9497

Norfolk and Western Railway. Industrial and Agricultural Department. Mineral resources along the line of the Norfolk and Western Railway. Roanoke, Va., 1931. 39 p.   [9498

Norfolk, Wilmington and Charleston Railroad. Norfolk, Wilmington and Charleston Railroad Company. [Philadelphia, 189?]   27 p.   [9499

Norfolk, Wilmington & Charleston Railroad. Engineer. Engineer's report on Norfolk, Wilmington & Charleston Railroad by Major John Runk. [Philadelphia, 1891] 23 p.   [9500

Norlina, N. C. School Board. Norlina Public School, 191 - Norlina, 191 - NcU has 1916/17, 1917/18   [9501

Norment, Mary C. The Lowrie history, as acted in part by Henry Berry Lowrie. Wilmington, Daily Journal Print, 1875.   159 p.   [9503
—— ——Weldon, Harrell's Printing House, 1895.   140 p.   [9504
—— ——Lumberton, Lumbee Publishing Co. [c.1909]   192 p.   [9505

Norris, Ernest Eden. Let's use reason; an address . . . before the North Carolina Press Association, Asheville, North Carolina, September 12, 1946. [Washington? Southern Railway System? 1946] 16 p.   [9506
——"Men working together . . ." an address before the Raleigh Chamber of Commerce, Raleigh, North Carolina, February 18, 1947. [Washington, Southern Railway, 1947] 12 p.   [9507
——Opportunity unlimited; an address . . . before the Winston-Salem Traffic Club . . . January 29, 1946. [Washington, Southern Railway System, 1946] 16 p. [9508

[**Norris, George S.**] Western North Carolina lands. [Baltimore? 1884?] 27 p. [9509

Norris, Hoke. All the kingdoms of earth. New York, Simon and Schuster [1956] 249 p.   [9510

The North-American and the West-Indian gazeteer. 2d ed.   London, Printed for G. Robinson, 1778. [218] p.   [9511

North-American Land Co. Observations on the North-American Land-Company, lately instituted in Philadelphia . . . to which are added, Remarks on American lands in general . . . in two letters from Robert G. Harper. London, C. Barrell and H. Servanté, 1796. 149 p. NcU has microfilm (negative) from original in American Antiquarian Society Library   [9512

[**North-American Land Co.**] Plan for the settlement of 552,500 acres of land in the district of Morgan, county of Wilkes, in the state of North Carolina. [London, 1796?] 3 p. NcU has photostat   [9513
——Plan of association of the North-American Land Company, established, February, 1795. Philadelphia, Printed by R. Aitken and Son, 1795. 25 p. NcU has photograph.   [9514

The North American tourist. New York, A. T. Goodrich [c.1839] 506 p.   [9515

North Carolina, v. 1- April, 1891- Durham, George P. Hart, 1891- NcU has v. [1]   [9516

North Carolina Academy of Science. Constitution; officers, 1902-1929; membership roll, September, 1928. Chapel Hill, University of North Carolina Press, 1928. 32-45 p.   [9517
——Members, as of June 1, 1941. No place, 1941.   14 p.   [9518

North Carolina accountant, v. 1- October, 1940- [Chapel Hill] 1940- Library has v. [1-6]   [9519

North Carolina agricultural almanac, 1868- Raleigh, Levi Branson, [c.1867-1902] NcU has 1869-1873, 1877-1879, 1882-1893, 1895-1899, 1901, 1903   [9520

North Carolina Agricultural Society. Charter and by-laws. [Raleigh? 1922?]
13 p.   [9521
—— ——[Raleigh] Bynum Printing Co. [1925]   14 p.   [9522
——Condensed financial statement, 1917-1919. Raleigh, 1920.   [8] p. [9523
——North Carolina Agricultural Society. No place, n.d.   4 p.   [9524
——Transactions, 1857- Raleigh, 1857- NcU has 1857   [9525
North Carolina Agricultural Society see also **Agricultural Society of North Carolina**
North Carolina almanac and state industrial guide, 1950-51-1954-55. Raleigh,
Almanac Publishing Co., 1950-1954. NcU has 1950-51-1954-55   [9526
North-Carolina almanack, 17 - Newbern, François X. Martin, 17 - NcU has
1797   [9527
North-Carolina almanack, 17 - Newbern, John C. Osborn & Co., 17 - NcU
has 1799   [9528
North-Carolina almanack, 18 - Raleigh, Printed at the Minerva Press by A. Lucas
[18 - NcU has 1815   [9529
North Carolina Anti-Saloon League. Choice temperance recitations and declama-
tions for use in school commencements, contests, Sunday-Schools, etc. [Raleigh,
Edwards and Broughton Co., n.d.]   16 p.   [9530
——Does prohibition prohibit? Does it pay? Look at Kansas. [Raleigh, Ed-
wards and Broughton Co., n.d.]   16 p.   [9531
——Recent utterances on state prohibition. No place, n.d.   15 p.   [9532
North Carolina. Appomattox Commission. Programme at the unveiling of North
Carolina's monument at Appomattox, April 10, 1905. [Raleigh, 1905] [6] p. [9533
North Carolina Association for Childhood Education. Yearbook, 193 - 193 -
NcU has 1939/40-1942/43   [9534
North Carolina Association for the Prevention of Tuberculosis. NCTA news letter,
v. 1- 193 - Raleigh, 193 - NcU has v. [10-17]   [9535
——Transactions, 190 - Raleigh, 190 - NcU has 1910, 1911   [9536
North Carolina Association of Agricultural Fairs. Bulletin, v. 1- 193 - [Greens-
boro? 193 - NcU has v. [17-21]   [9537
North Carolina Association of Certified Public Accountants, Inc. By-laws, as re-
vised June 14, 1952. [Chapel Hill, 1952]   15 p.   [9538
——Constitution and by-laws . . . as revised, 1947. No place, 1947.   15 p. [9539
——Constitution and by-laws, revised October 20-22, 1932. No place, 1932.
21 p.   [9540
——Directory, 19 - 19 - NcU has 1937, 1939, 1945, 1946, 1950, 1951, 1953,
1955   [9541
——Monthly letter, 19 - Chapel Hill, 19 - NcU has 1953-1956   [9542
——The North Carolina Association of Certified Public Accountants presents this
souvenir booklet of the twenty-fifth anniversary celebration and of the fifth annual
symposium on accounting and taxation. Chapel Hill [1944]   [10] p. [9543
——Report, 19 - 19 - NcU has 1954/55   [9544
——Special publication. No place [1948?]   86 p.   [9545
——Symposium papers, the tenth annual symposium on accounting and taxation,
December, 1949. [Raleigh? 1950?]   64 p.   [9546
—— ——November, 1950. Chapel Hill, 1950.   67 p.   [9547
North Carolina Association of City Superintendents. The Connor-Pharr six months
school bill, by Legislative Committee. No place, 1919.   13 p.   [9548
——Proceedings, 19 - Raleigh, 19 - NcU has 1905, 1909, 1910, 1911 [9549
——Report of Course of Study Committee. No place [pref. 1904]   15 p. [9550
North Carolina Association of County Superintendents of Public Instruction. Pro-
ceedings, 188 - 188 - NcU has 1882, 1883   [9551
North Carolina Association of Insurance Agents. Proceedings, 189 - 189 - NcU
has 1926-1930   [9552
North Carolina Association of Jewish Women. Year Book, 192 - 192 - NcU
has 1929/30-1942/43   [9553
North Carolina Association of Life Underwriters. Year book, 19 - 19 - NcU
has 1950/51-1952/53, 1954/55-1955/56   [9554
North Carolina Association of Plumbing and Heating Contractors. Two-day institute. No place [1928]   4 p.   [9555

North Carolina Association of Real Estate Boards. Who's who in the North Carolina General Assembly, Session of 1935. Greensboro [1934] 27 p. [9556

North Carolina Bankers' Association. Proceedings of the . . . annual convention, 1897-1932. Durham, 1897-1932. NcU has 1897-1900, 1905, 1908-1917, 1919, 1921-1922, 1924, 1926-1927, 1929-1932. Continues in Tarheel banker, 1933- [9557
——Program, 1897- 1897- NcU has 1924-1928, 1933-1941, 1950-1952 [9558
——Trends in North Carolina banking, 1927-1937, prepared by the Research Committee. Raleigh, c.1938. 152 p. [9559
——Trends in North Carolina banking, 1938-1950. Raleigh, 1939-1951. NcU has 1938-1950 [9560

North Carolina Baptist almanac, 186 - Raleigh, 186 - NcU has 1865 [9561

North Carolina Baptist almanac, 1882- Raleigh, E. T. Bailey, 1881- NcU has 1882-1897, 1900 [9562

North Carolina Baptist Board of Missions see Baptists. North Carolina. Board of Missions

North Carolina Baptist hand-book, 1912- Raleigh, Mutual Publishing Co., 1911- NcU has 1912 [9563

North Carolina Baptist historical papers, v. 1-3, 1896-1900. Henderson, Baptist Historical Society, 1896-1900. NcU has v. 1-3. Continues as issue of Wake Forest student, v. 1-4, 1905-1908, published in October, 1905, September, 1906, September, 1907, March, 1909 [9564

North Carolina Baptist interpreter, v. 1-2, January, 1833-December, 1834. Edenton, T. Meredith, 1833-34. NcU has v. 1-2. Superseded by Biblical recorder, January, 1835- [9565

North Carolina Baptist Orphanage Association. Tract no. 1- 18 - No place, 18 - NcU has no. 3 which includes First annual report, 1884/85 [9566

North Carolina Baptist Society for Foreign and Domestic Missions, 181 - No place, 181 - NcU has 1821 [9567

North Carolina Baptist State Convention see Baptists. North Carolina. State Convention

North Carolina Bar see North Carolina State Bar

North Carolina Bar Association. Addresses at the unveiling and presentation of the bust of William Gaston, delivered in the hall of the House of Representatives, November 24, 1914. Raleigh, Edwards & Broughton Printing Co., 1915. 49 p. [9568
——Addresses at the unveiling and presentation to the state of the statue of Thomas Ruffin, delivered in the hall of the House of Representatives, 1 February, 1915. Raleigh, Edwards & Broughton Printing Co., 1915. 25 p. [9569
——Centennial celebration of the Supreme Court of North Carolina, 1819-1919, held in the Supreme Court room, Raleigh, January 4, 1919. Raleigh, Mitchell Printing Co., 1919. 85 p. [9570
——Charter, constitution, by-laws, and proceedings of the meeting of organization, February, 1899. Chapel Hill, University Press, 1899. 32 p. [9571
——Constitution and by-laws, together with the proceedings of a convention of the bar of the state, held in Raleigh, the 28th of January, 1885. Raleigh, Edwards and Broughton Printing Co., 1885. 20 p. [9572
——North Carolina Bar Association, special meeting to celebrate the centennial of the Supreme Court of North Carolina. No place, no publisher [1919] [5] p. Program. [9573
——Proceedings of the North Carolina Bar Association at a meeting held in Raleigh, the 14th of October, 1885. Raleigh, Edwards, Broughton & Co., 1886. 14 p. [9574
——Report, 1899- Raleigh, 1899- NcU has 1899-1938 [9575
—— ——Index . . . edited by Dennis A. Dooley. New York, Baker, Voorhis & Co., 1942. 640 p. Includes all state bar association reports as well as N. C. [9576

North Carolina Beekeepers Association. The North Carolina beekeeper, no. 1- 1917- Raleigh, 1917- NcU has no. 1-5 [9577

North Carolina Bible Society. Bible societies in North Carolina. No place, n.d. [1] p. [9578
——Circular. [Raleigh, January, 1814] 2 p. [9579
——Constitution. No place [181?] [1] p. [9580
——Report, 1816- Raleigh, J. Gales, 1816- NcU has 1815, 1817-1820 [9581

North Carolina. Board of Farm Organizations and Agencies. North Carolina accepts the challenge through a united agricultural program. [Raleigh, 1952] 72 p.   [9582

North Carolina booklet, v. 1-23, May 10, 1901-October, 1926. Raleigh, North Carolina Society, Daughters of the Revolution, 1901-1926. NcU has v. 1-23   [9583
——Index to North Carolina articles, by R. D. W. Connor. (North Carolina library bulletin, v. 1, no. 8, p. 91-98)   [9584
——Index to vols. 1-20, compiled by Grace Stovall. (North Carolina College for Women, Greensboro. Extension bulletin, v. 1, no. 5, May, 1923) 27 p.   [9585
——Index to vols. 21-23, compiled by Felix Eugene Snider. Greenville, East Carolina Teachers College Library, 1941. [7] p. Manuscript.   [9586

North Carolina branch of the Buck family. No place, no publisher, n.d. [2] p. [9587

North Carolina Building and Loan League. Proceedings, 1904- 1904- NcU has 1905, 1909, 1912-1927, 1934   [9588

North Carolina. Bulwinkle Campaign Committee. A. L. Bulwinkle for Congress. No place, 1928. [6] p.   [9589

North Carolina calendar, 1934- Raleigh, Bynum Printing Co., 1934- NcU has 1934, 1936, 1938, 1939, 1941, 1942, 1952-1955   [9590

North Carolina calendar and pictorial history, 1954- Raleigh, North Carolina Research Institute [1954- NcU has 1954-1956   [9591

North Carolina cancer news, v. 1- April, 1947- [Mount Airy?] 1947- NcU has v. [1-5]   [9592

North Carolina Carpenter's State Council. Convention, 19 - 19 - NcU has 1925   [9593

North Carolina Catholic, v. 1- October 6, 1946- Nazareth, North Carolina Catholic Laymen's Association, 1946- NcU has v. 1-11   [9594

North Carolina. Central Railroad. North Carolina Central Railroad from Greensboro, N. C., to Cheraw, S. C. [Greensboro, Greensboro Patriot, pr., 1869] 8 p.   [9595

North Carolina. Central Rough and Ready Club. To the people of North Carolina. No place [1848] 8 p.   [9596

North Carolina Choral Association. Annual festival, 18 - Charlotte, 18 - NcU has 1891   [9597

North Carolina Christian, v. 1- February, 1920- Wilson, North Carolina Disciples of Christ, 1920- NcU has v. 1-37   [9598

North Carolina Christian advocate, v. 1- January 4, 1856- Greensboro, North Carolina and Western North Carolina Conferences, Methodist Church, 1856- NcU has v. [1-8, 16-31, 33-34, 37, 51-53, 65-66] 67-101. Numbering of volumes irregular, 1863-1873. Title varies, 1905?-1907?: Raleigh Christian advocate [9599

North Carolina churchman, v. 1- October, 1909- Raleigh, 1909- NcU has v. 1-45   [9600

[**North Carolina. Citizens**] Petition endorsing HCR 64 and SCR 56. [Raleigh? 1950] 3 p.   [9601
——To the members of the Congress of the United States from the state of North Carolina. No place, n.d. [2] p.   [9602

North Carolina. Citizens' Library Movement. Libraries in North Carolina need state aid. [Warrenton? 1936?] 2 p.   [9603
——North Carolina seeks state aid for public libraries. Warrenton [1938] 10 p. [9604

North Carolina civil engineer, v. 1-2, September, 1939-November, 1941. Greensboro, North Carolina Section of the American Society of Civil Engineers, 1939-1941. NcU has v. 1-2   [9605

North Carolina clubwoman, v. 1- 1923- Greensboro, Extension Department of the Woman's College of the University of North Carolina, 1923- NcU has v. 5-32. Title varies, 1923-June, 1934: Bulletin of the North Carolina Federation of Women's Clubs   [9606

North Carolina coastal fishing & vacation guide, v. 1- 1955- Raleigh, Graphic Press, 1955- NcU has 1955, 1956   [9607

North Carolina College, Mount Pleasant, N. C. see Mount Pleasant Collegiate Institute

North Carolina College Conference. Handbook, 1939- [Raleigh, 1939- NcU has 1939 [9608
——Principles for accrediting institutions of higher learning. No place, 1927. 8 p. [9609
—— ——[1936?] 7 p. [9610
——Proceedings of annual meeting, 1929- [Raleigh, 1929- NcU has 1929, 1936-1954 [9611

North Carolina. Commission on Interracial Cooperation. Building goodwill through conference and cooperation. Chapel Hill, 1931. 8 p. [9612
——[Purpose and plan] No place [1938?] 8 p. [9613

North Carolina. Committee for the Study and Writing of a County or Local History. Suggestions for the study and writing of a county or local history. [Chapel Hill] 1953. 9 p. [9614

North Carolina. Committee of One Thousand. A museum and archives center for North Carolina. Raleigh [1950] 17 p. [9615

North Carolina. Committee on Conservation of Cultural Resources. Minutes. Chapel Hill, 1942. 3 p. [9616

North Carolina. Committee to Recommend Legislation for the Better Enforcement of Prohibition Laws. Report [Raleigh? 1951] 7 p. [9617

North Carolina common school journal, v. 1- September, 1856- Greensboro and Raleigh, State Superintendent of Common Schools, 1856- NcU has v. [1] [9618

[North Carolina Conference for Social Service] Ask yourself why? No place [1922?] 8 p. [9619

North Carolina Conference for Social Service. A charter for North Carolina's children. [Raleigh? 1949] [1] p. [9620
——Declaration of principles. No place [1920?] 4 p. [9621
——The North Carolina Conference for Social Service will have its fourteenth annual convention in Greensboro. [Greensboro? 1926] 12 p. [9622
——Program, first- 1913- No place, 1913- NcU has [1-13] 14-32, 41 [9623
——Security and welfare. No place, 1937. 24 p. [9624
——Social service quarterly, v. 1-5, June, 1913-October, 1917. Raleigh, 1913-1917. NcU has v. 1-5. v. 3, no. 4 not issued; v. 5, no. 2-4 as one. [9625
——A statement on taxation to the . . . General Assembly. Raleigh [1933] 7 p. [9626

North Carolina Conference for Social Service. White House Conference Steering Committee. Children, our most valuable resource. Raleigh, 1951. 36 p. [9627

North Carolina Conference of School and Children's Librarians, Chapel Hill, N. C., September 20, 1952. Proceedings. [Raleigh, 1952] 17 p. [9628

North Carolina Conference of the Methodist Church see Methodist Church (United States) North Carolina Conference; also Methodist Episcopal Church, South. North Carolina Conference

North Carolina Conference on Children in a Democracy, Raleigh, February 6, 1941. Proceedings. [1941] 68 p. [9629

North Carolina Conference on Tuberculosis. Program, 192 - No place, 192 - NcU has 1921-1923 [9630

North Carolina Congress of Colored Parents and Teachers. Bulletin, v. 1- 193 - NcU has v. [7-17] [9631
——Handbook. [Raleigh? 1942?] [22] p. [9632

North Carolina Congress of Parents and Teachers. Child labor and education in North Carolina. No place [1926] 4 p. [9633
——Comparative study of child labor standards and the North Carolina law. Raleigh, 1928. [3] p. [9634
——Proceedings, 1936- 1936- NcU has 1938, 1939 [9635

North Carolina Conservation Congress, Raleigh, N. C., November 17-19, 1952. Conservation and development, compiled . . . by C. Sylvester Green. Raleigh, 1952. 2 v. [9636

North Carolina Corporation, Charlotte, N. C. Report of financial condition of Mecklenburg County, N. C. Charlotte, Rush Printing Co., 1931. 15 p. [9637

North Carolina cotton grower see Carolina co-operator

North Carolina Cotton Growers Cooperative Association. The A, B, C's of co-
operative marketing. Raleigh, n.d. 8 p. [9638
——Agreement and contract. Raleigh [1921] 15 p. [9639
——By-laws and articles of incorporation. Raleigh, 1922. 45 p. [9640
——Handbook on cooperative marketing. Raleigh [1923?] 64 p. [9641
——Marketing agreement. Raleigh, 1922. 8 p. [9642
——Rural North Carolina's greatest need. Raleigh, 1933. 63 p. [9643
——Statement, 192 - Raleigh, 192 - NcU has 1923/24 [9644

North Carolina Cotton Manufacturers' Association. Proceedings, 1906- No place,
1906- NcU has 1917-1932 [9645
——Rules for the purchase of cotton, adopted . . . July 1, 1910. No place [1915?]
11 p. [9646

North Carolina Council of Churches. Minutes, 19 - 19 - NcU has 1943,
1944/45 [9647

North Carolina Council on Economic Education. Economic education. Chapel
Hill, 1954. [16] p. [9648

North Carolina. Craig Portrait Committee. Locke Craig, governor of North Carolina, 1913-1917; exercises in connection with the presentation of Governor Craig's
portrait . . . October 16, 1944. [Raleigh?] 1944. 19 p. [9649

North Carolina Dairy Products Association. Bulletin, no. 1- 1944- [Raleigh]
1944- NcU has no. [2-56] [9650

North Carolina dairy report, v. 1- 1950- [Raleigh] 1950- NcU has v. [1-7] [9651

North Carolina Daughters of Temperance. Farmington Union no. 22. Constitution, by-laws, and rules of order. Raleigh, 1852. 29 p. [9652

North Carolina Daughters of the American Revolution see **Daughters of theAmeri-
can Revolution. North Carolina**

North Carolina Daughters of the Confederacy see **United Daughters of the Confederacy. North Carolina**

North Carolina. Democratic-Conservative Party. Central Executive Committee.
Address. No place, n.d. 12 p. [9653
——Address to the people of North Carolina. No place, 1870. [1] p. [9654
—— ———[1874?] 10 p. [9655
——The late radical state convention . . . a brief outline of the Holden-Kirk war.
No place [187?] 7 p. [9656
——Reasons for amending the constitution. [Raleigh, 187?] 8 p. [9657

[North Carolina. Democratic-Conservative Party. Central Executive Committee]
Thoughts for the people, no. 1-7, 1-11, 1868. [Raleigh, 1868] NcU has no. 1-7,
1-11 [9658
——The voice of patriotism and reason. No place [1868] 4 p. [9659
——Waste of the people's money. No place [1870?] 7 p. [9660

North Carolina. Democratic Party. Executive Committee see **North Carolina.
State Democratic Executive Committee**

[North Carolina Dental Society] The history of the North Carolina Dental Society
with biographies of its founders. Raleigh, 1939. 509 p. [9661

North Carolina Dental Society. Journal, 192 - Raleigh, 192 - NcU has v. [5-13]
14-39 Title varies, 19 - : Bulletin [9662
——Proceedings, 18 -1929. 18 -1929. NcU has 1875-1897, 1902-1904, 1914-
1919, 1923-1929. Continues in its Journal, 1930- [9663

North Carolina Dietetic Association. Bulletin, v. 1- April, 1939- Greensboro,
Home Economics Department of Woman's College of the University of North
Carolina, 1939- NcU has v. [1-8] [9664

North Carolina education, v. 1-18, September 15, 1906-June, 1924; [2d. ser.] v. 1-
September, 1934- Durham, 1906-1908; Raleigh, 1909-1924, 1934- NcU has
v. 1-18; 2d. ser., v. 1-22 [9665

North Carolina Education Association. A century of culture, an historical pageant
commemorating the centennial of public education in North Carolina. [Durham,
Seeman Printery, pr., c.1937] 86 p. [9666
——Code of ethics. [Raleigh?] n.d. [3] p. [9667
——News bulletin, v. 1- December, 1947- Raleigh, 1947- NcU has v. 1-9 [9668

——Program, 192 - [Raleigh, 192 - NcU has [1924-1944] [9669

[North Carolina Education Association. Committee on Legislation] Some North Carolinians on equal pay. No place [1918?] 36 p. [9670

North Carolina Education Association. Committee on Public Information. Education in North Carolina, 1900 and now. Raleigh, Bynum Printing Co., 1930. 62 p. [9671

North Carolina Education Association. Committee on Public Relations. The case for the schools. [Raleigh, 1932?] 37 p. [9672

——Public relations handbook. [Raleigh? 1936?] 30 p. [9673

North Carolina Education Association. Department of Classroom Teachers. Directory of the classroom teachers, 19 - Raleigh, 19 - NcU has 1941/42 [9674

——Suggestions for the work of teachers in local units. Chapel Hill, 1942. 19 p. [9675

——To superintendents of schools . . . the Griffin-MacLean school machinery bill. [Raleigh, 1933] 8 p. [9676

North Carolina Education Association. State Planning Committee. Handbook for local units. [Raleigh? 1940] 56 p. [9677

North Carolina Educational Association. Constitution, by-laws and act of incorporation of the State Educational Association of North Carolina. Greensboro, James W. Albright at the World Office, pr., 1862. 8 p. [9678

North Carolina educational journal, v. 1-5, January 15, 1881-December, 1885. Chapel Hill, Trinity College, 1881-1885. NcU has v. 1-5 [9679

North Carolina engineer, v. 1- September, 1944- Raleigh, North Carolina Society of Engineers, 1944- NcU has v. 1-12 [9680

North Carolina English teacher, v. 1- April, 1943- Chapel Hill, North Carolina English Teachers Association, 1943- NcU has v. 1-13 [9681

North Carolina Equal Suffrage League. Proceedings, 1914?- 1914?- NcU has 1915, 1917, 1918 [9682

North Carolina facts, v. 1-4, January, 1953-January, 1956. Raleigh, North Carolina Research Institute, 1953-1956. NcU has v. 1-4 [9683

North Carolina Farm Bureau Federation. Resolutions adopted at 15th annual convention, Asheville, N. C., February 14th, 1951. No place [1951] 21 p. [9684

——What people who know say about Farm Bureau. No place, 1949. [22] p. [9685

North Carolina farmer, v. 1- June, 1845- Raleigh, J. J. Lemay, 1845- NcU has v. [1-5] [9686

North Carolina farmer, v. 1- May 1876- Raleigh, J. H. Enniss, 1876- NcU has v. [1-13] [9687

North Carolina Farmers' and Mechanics' Association. Charter, by-laws, rules of order, list of officers and stockholders. Goldsboro, Messenger and Monitor Power Press Print, 1872. 8 p. [9688

North Carolina Farmers' Cooperative Council see Farmers' Cooperative Council of North Carolina

North Carolina Farmers' Educational and Cooperative Union see Farmers' Educational and Co-operative Union of America. North Carolina

North Carolina Farmers' Mutual Fire Insurance Association. By-laws, rules and regulations, governing membership, property to be insured, losses, etc. Raleigh, n.d. 14 p. [9689

——Circular and by-laws. Greensboro, C. F. Thomas, n.d. 18 p. [9690

North Carolina Farmers' Protective Association. Charter, articles of agreement, and by-laws. Raleigh, Alford, Bynum & Christophers, pr., 1903. 32 p. [9691

North Carolina Farmers' State Alliance. An appeal to the farmers of North Carolina. [Raleigh, 1903] 4 p. [9692

——Constitution. Raleigh, Edwards and Broughton, 1889. 29 p. [9693

—— ——Raleigh, Edwards and Broughton, 1890. 30 p. [9694

—— ——Raleigh, Informer Printing Co., 1892. 42 p. [9695

—— ——Raleigh, Barnes Brothers, 1894. 44 p. [9696

—— ——Raleigh, Capital Printing Co., 1896. 48 p. [9697

—— ——Goldsboro, Nash Brothers, 1907. 31 p. [9698

—— ——[Wilson, Wilson Printing Co., 1912?] 28 p. [9699

——Proceedings, 1887- 1887- NcU has 1890-1892, 1899-1903, 1905-1910, 1912-
1941 [9700
——Ritual. Raleigh, 1907. 31 p. [9701
—— ——Raleigh, 1915. 22 p. [9702
—— ——No place, n.d. 21 p. [9703
North Carolina Federation of Business and Professional Woman's Clubs. Reports,
19 - 19 - NcU has 1943/44-1949/50 [9704
North Carolina Federation of Home Demonstration Clubs. Report, 1953- [Ra-
leigh, 1954- NcU has 1953 [9705
——Year book for Home Demonstration Clubs, 1934/35- [Raleigh? 1934- NcU
has 1934/35, 1936/37, 1938/39, 1940, 1941, 1942/43, 1945-1948, 1950 [9706
North Carolina Federation of Labor see **North Carolina State Federation of Labor**
North Carolina Federation of Music Clubs. Bulletin, v. 1- 1927- [Elon College?
1927- NcU has v. [1-6] Title varies: Musical tempo [9707
——Handbook and constitution and by laws. [Raleigh, 1956] 48 p. [9708
——Program, 192 - 192 - NcU has 1927, 1932, 1933 [9709
North Carolina Federation of Women's Clubs Bulletin see **North Carolina club-
woman**
[**North Carolina Federation of Women's Clubs**] Golden jubilee. [Mt. Gilead,
Montgomery News, pr., 1941?] [46] p. [9710
——North Carolina Federation of Women's Clubs . . . foundation fund, 1929-1941.
[Mt. Gilead, 1941?] 9 p. [9711
——Year book, 1902/03- 1902- NcU has 1902/03-1955/56. Not issued 1904/05 [9712
North Carolina federationist, v. 1- July, 1938- Salisbury, North Carolina State
Federation of Labor, 1938- NcU has v. [1] 2-20 [9713
North Carolina Fire Underwriters Association. Proceedings, 18 - 18 - NcU
has 1898, 1908, 1911 [9714
North Carolina Folk-Lore Society. The Committee on organization urgently re-
quests you to become a charter member. [Durham, 1913] [3] p. [9715
——To the members. Durham, 1914. [2] p. [9716
North Carolina folklore, v. 1- June, 1948- Chapel Hill, 1948- NcU has v. 1-4 [9717
North Carolina Forestry Association. Forest protection or devastation? Chapel
Hill, 1920. 32 p. [9718
——Forestry notes, v. 1- 193 - 193 - NcU has v. [5-7] [9719
——Report of convention, 19 - Chapel Hill, 19 - NcU has 1917, 1952 [9720
——School contests in forestry, prize essay competition. Chapel Hill, 1916. 8 p. [9721
North Carolina. Forestry Council. A long-range forestry program for North Caro-
lina. [Raleigh] 1950. 23 p. [9722
North Carolina form book. Raleigh, Turner and Hughes, 1841. 172 p. [9723
—— ——1844. 190 p. [9724
North Carolina Freemasons see **Freemasons. North Carolina**
North Carolina Funeral Directors and Embalmers Association. Minutes, 18 -
18 - NcU has 1895, 1907, 1908 [9725
North Carolina future farmers, v. 1- Raleigh, North Carolina Association of Future
Farmers of America, 19 - NcU has v. 20-27 [9726
North Carolina Garden Club see **Garden Club of North Carolina**
North Carolina gardener, July, 1936- Raleigh, Asheville, Garden Club of North
Carolina, 1936- NcU has July, 1936-February, 1942 and v. 12-25. Title varies,
July, 1936-February, 1942: North Carolina gardens [9727
[**North Carolina Gettysburg Memorial Commission**] Ceremonies attending the
presentation and unveiling of the North Carolina memorial on the Battlefield of
Gettysburg, Wednesday, July 3d, 1929. [No place, 1929?] 44 p. [9728
North Carolina Gold-Mine Company. North Carolina Gold-Mine Company.
[Washington, 1806] 20 p. [9729
North Carolina Gold-Mining and Bullion Company, New York. The gold fields of
North Carolina. New York [1891] 24 p. [9730
North Carolina Good Health Association, Inc. "No man, woman, or child anywhere
in North Carolina shall lack hospital service or medical care." Greensboro, 1947.
[6] p. [9731

——The North Carolina Good Health Association, Inc. Durham [1947] [11] p. [9732
——To the good health of all North Carolina. Raleigh, 1946. [16] p.   [9733
[North Carolina Good Roads Association] The development of a state policy in
road building in North Carolina. [Chapel Hill, 1920] 133 p.   [9734
North Carolina Good Roads Association. Good roads convention. Greensboro,
1921. [9] p.   [9735
——Legislation that is being considered by the General Assembly of 1913 in regard
to state aid to counties in public road work. [Raleigh, E. M. Uzzell, pr., 1913?]
4 p.   [9736
——North Carolina Good Roads Association. Chapel Hill [1920?] 5 p.   [9737
——North Carolina Good Roads Association, its personnel, history, accomplishments, policies. No place, n.d. 31 p.   [9738
——Road maps and tour book of Western North Carolina. [Chapel Hill] 1916.
159 p.   [9739
——Suggested bill to provide for the construction and maintenance of a state system
of hard surfaced and other dependable highways. [Raleigh, Edwards and Brough-
ton, 1921?] 26 p.   [9740
North Carolina Grange or Patrons of Husbandry. Important information to pro-
ducers and shippers of cotton, Patrons of Husbandry, and all others! Fayette-
ville, November 23, 1874. [1] p.   [9741
North Carolina guardsman, v. 1- 1884- Winston, North Carolina State Guard,
1884- NcU has v. [1-2, 4]   [9742
North Carolina guernsey news, v. 1-4, August, 1929-December, 1932. Salisbury,
T. D. Brown, 1929-1932. NcU has v. 2-4.   [9743
North Carolina. Harvard Club. Harvard Club of North Carolina, 19 - 19 -
NcU has 1939   [9744
North Carolina Health Council. Directory, North Carolina Health Council, North
Carolina health organizations, 1952- [Raleigh, 1952- NcU has 1952   [9745
North Carolina Heart Association. Heart news, v. 1- November, 1950- Chapel
Hill, 1950- NcU has v. [1-7]   [9746
——Report, 195 - Chapel Hill, 195 - NcU has 1952/53   [9747
North Carolina highway and construction journal, v. 1- March, 1941- Raleigh,
1941- NcU has v. [1]   [9748
North Carolina historical and genealogical record, v. 1-2, January, 1932-July, 1933.
Forest City, Clarence Griffin, 1932-1933. NcU has v. 1-2.   [9749
North Carolina historical and genealogical register, v. 1-2, v. 3, no. 1-3, January,
1900-July, 1903. Edenton, J. R. B. Hathaway [1900-1903] NcU has v. 1-3. [9750
North Carolina Historical Association see North Carolina State Literary and His-
torical Association
North Carolina Hospital Association. Transactions, 1919- 1919- NcU has 1919-
1931   [9751
North Carolina Hospital Care Association, Durham. 20 years of service to the
people of North Carolina. Durham, 1953. [16] p.   [9752
North Carolina Hospital Saving Association, Inc. Group health service plans.
Chapel Hill [1946] 7 p.   [9753
——Hospital Saving Association moves to new quarters. [Chapel Hill, 1951]
[12] p.   [9754
——Report of the executive director, 19 - [Chapel Hill, 19 - NcU has 1936,
1937, 1945 (abridged)   [9755
——39 cents per capita. [Chapel Hill, 1945] Folder.   [9756
——Twenty years of service to people. [Chapel Hill, 1956] [12] p.   [9757
North Carolina. Hospital Study Committee. Report, June, 1953. No place, 1953.
34 p.   [9758
North Carolina Hot Mineral Springs, season 1914, Hot Springs, N. C. [Asheville,
Hackney & Moale, 1914?] 18 p.   [9759
[North Carolina. Human Betterment League, Inc.] You wouldn't expect. [Win-
ston-Salem, 1950] [14] p.   [9760
North Carolina Ice Cream Manufacturer's Association. Minutes, 1918- 1918-
NcU has 1921   [9761

North Carolina Infantry.   25th Regiment, Co. I, 1861-65.   Muster roll.   Asheville, Whiteside Printing Co., n.d.   12 p.   [9762

North Carolina Jersey Cattle Club.   The North Carolina jersey book.   No place, 1943.   24 p.   [9763

North Carolina journal of education, v. 1-7, January, 1858-July? 1864.   Greensboro, Times Office, 1858-1864.   NcU has v. 1-5 [6-7]   [9764

North Carolina journal of education, v. 1-3, August, 1897-July, 1900.   Greensboro, 1897-1900.   NcU has v. 1-3.   Continues, v. 4- as Atlantic educational journal. [9765

North Carolina journal of education, v. 1- September, 1874- Raleigh, Enniss-Harris, 1874- NcU has v. 1-2 [3]   [9766

North Carolina journal of law, v. 1-2, January, 1904-December, 1905.   Chapel Hill, University of North Carolina, 1904-05.   NcU has v. 1-2   [9767

North Carolina.   Junior Chamber of Commerce.   Directory, 19 - High Point, 19 - NcU has 1949/50-1952/53   [9768

North Carolina Just Freight Rate Association.   Freight rates in North Carolina. No place [1913?]   16 p.   [9769

——To the shippers, merchants, farmers and all the people of North Carolina.   No place [1913?]   2 p.   [9770

North Carolina Lady, pseud.   see Moore, Marinda (Branson)

North Carolina Landowners Association.   Coastal plain pastures.   Wilmington, n.d. 8 p.   [9771

——The fourteen points.   No place, n.d.   1 p.   [9772

——The league of counties; thirty-two counties united. [Wilmington] n.d. 5 p. [9773

North Carolina law journal, v. 1-2, March 1900-March 1902.   Tarboro, State Bar Association, 1900-1902.   NcU has v. 1-2.   Discontinued following v. 2, no. 11. [9774

North Carolina law review, v. 1- June, 1922- Chapel Hill, University of North Carolina Press, 1923- NcU has v. 1-35   [9775

——Cumulative index digest, v. 1-14, by E. M. Perkins.   Chapel Hill, University of North Carolina Press, 1937.   69 p.   [9776

—— ——v. 1-26, by Kate Wallach.   Chapel Hill, University of North Carolina Press, 1949.   160 p.   [9777

North Carolina League for Nursing news, v. 1- January, 1953- Chapel Hill, 1953-NcU has v. 1-4   [9778

North Carolina League for Progressive Democracy.   Constitution, adopted in Greensboro, August 12, 1939.   [Greensboro?] 1939.   [3] p.   [9779

North Carolina League of Municipalities.   Report, no. 1- April, 1934- Raleigh, 1934- NcU has no. 1, 6-18, 20-33, 35-41, 47-80   [9780

North Carolina League of Women Voters.   The Australian ballot system.   Durham, n.d.   2 p.   [9781

——Goals for working children, 1931.   [Greensboro, 1931]   [6] p.   [9782

——Monthly news, v. 1-10, 1923-32.   Durham, 1923-32.   NcU has v. [1-6] 7-10 Discontinued following v. 10, no. 1   [9783

——Program of the Legislative Council for 1927.   [Durham, n.d.]   2 p.   [9784

——Vote, vote, vote.   No place [1952]   [4] p.   [9785

North Carolina League of Women Voters.   Committee on the Working Child. North Carolina's children.   [Greensboro, 1930]   [3] p.   [9786

North Carolina Legion news, v. 1- September, 1934- Charlotte, 1934- NcU has v. [1, 10-22]   [9787

North Carolina libraries, v. 1- February, 1942- [Durham, Raleigh] 1942- NcU has v. 1-15   [9788

North Carolina Library Association.   [Bill for state aid for public libraries]   Raleigh, 1941.   [6] p.   [9789

——[Calendar of holidays]   Raleigh, 1941.   [3] p.   [9790

North Carolina Library Association]   Manual for the cooperative indexing of certain North Carolina periodicals.   No place, n.d.   6 p.   [9791

North Carolina Library Association.   North Carolina Library Association, 1940-1941: Code for committees.   No place [1940]   [14] p.   [9792

——Plan for library development in North Carolina. [Greensboro?] 1935.   18 p. [9793

——Program, 19 - 19 - NcU has 1908-1910, 1915-1923, 1927, 1931-1955   [9794

——Report of President and other papers, 19 - 19 - NcU has 1951, 1953 [9795

North Carolina Library Association. Committee on Revision of Library Laws. Report. [Durham, 1933] [5] p. [9796

North Carolina Life Assurance, Annuity, and Trust Co. Charter, act of incorporation, ratified August 13, 1868. Raleigh, Nichols & Gorman, pr., 1868. 7 p. [9797

——Charter, by-laws, rules and regulations. Raleigh, Nichols & Gorman, pr., 1868. 30 p. [9798

North Carolina Literary and Historical Association see **North Carolina State Literary and Historical Association**

North Carolina Live Stock, Dairy, and Poultry Associations. Program, 1915- 1915- NcU has 1915, 1916, 1918-1921 [9799

——Report, 1914- 1914- NcU has 1915-1917 [9800

North Carolina Lutheran, v. 1- 192 - Salisbury, United Evangelical Lutheran Synod of North Carolina, 192 - NcU has v. [19] 20-34 [9801

North-Carolina magazine, political, historical, and miscellaneous, v. 1- August, 1813- Salisbury, Coupee and Crider, 1813- NcU has v. 1, no. 1-5. [9802

North Carolina. Manumission Society. An address to the people of North Carolina on the evils of slavery. Greensborough, William Swaim, pr., 1830. 68 p. [9803

——Constitution of the Manumission Society of North Carolina. No place [1824?] 4 p. [9804

——Minutes of the N. C. Manumission Society, 1816-1834, edited by H. M. Wagstaff. Chapel Hill, University of North Carolina Press, 1934. (James Sprunt historical studies, v. 22, no. 1-2) 230 p. [9805

North Carolina March of Dimes Headquarters, Chapel Hill. Here are the facts about infantile paralysis in North Carolina. Chapel Hill [1948] Folder. [9806

North Carolina Masonic Mutual Life Insurance Co. By-laws. Newbern, Commercial Office, 1867. 6 p. [9807

North Carolina Masonic Temple Association. Charter and by-laws. Raleigh, Nichols & Gorman, 1870. 12 p. [9808

North Carolina Master Masons see **Freemasons. North Carolina. Grand Council of Royal and Select Masters**

North Carolina Master Printers' Association. Proceedings of the Printers' Cost Congress, 1911- Greensboro, 1911- NcU has 1911 [9809

——Why a school of printing at North Carolina State College? No place, n.d. 12 p. [9810

North Carolina Medical College, Charlotte. Catalogue, 18 - Charlotte, 18 - NcU has 1907/08-1909/10 [9811

North Carolina medical journal, v. 1-57, January, 1878-March, 1908. Wilmington, Jackson & Bell, 1878. NcU has v. 1-56. v. 51 omitted in numbering. United with Charlotte medical journal following March, 1908, issue. [9812

North Carolina medical journal, v. 1- January, 1940- Winston-Salem, Medical Society of the State of North Carolina, 1940- NcU has v. 1-17 [9813

North Carolina medical journal, 1858-1860, see **Medical journal of North Carolina**

North Carolina Medical Society see **Medical Society of the State of North Carolina**

North Carolina Mental Hygiene Society, Inc. Directory of mental health resources of North Carolina, 1953- Raleigh, 1953- NcU has 1953 [9814

——Mental health week, 1953- Raleigh, 1953- NcU has 1953 [9815

——News letter, v. 1- February, 1950- Raleigh, 1950- NcU has v. [1-7] [9816

North Carolina Merchant's Association. Facts about taxes in North Carolina. Statesville [1927] 8 p. [9817

——Report on legislation of interest, 1953 regular session. Raleigh [1953] 25 p. [9818

North Carolina Methodist handbook, v. 1-4, 1902-1905. Raleigh, Christian Advocate, 1902-1905. NcU has v. 1-4 [9819

North Carolina Military Academy, Red Springs, N. C. Catalogue, 190 - Red Springs, 190 - NcU has 1906/07 [9820

North Carolina Military Institute, Charlotte, N. C. Catalogue, 1859/60- Charlotte, 1860- NcU has 1859/60 [9821

North Carolina Millstone Co., Parkewood, N. C.   Property to be sold at auction, September 22d, 1888, at Parkewood, Moore County, N. C.   No place [1888?] 22 p.   [9822
——Reasons why bonds of the North Carolina Millstone Co. are a good investment. No place, n.d.   [3] p.   [9823
North Carolina Monumental Association.   [Invitation to unveiling of Confederate monument, Raleigh, N. C., May 20, 1895]   [Raleigh] 1895.   1 p.   [9824
North Carolina Motor Carriers Association Bulletin   see Tarheel wheels
North Carolina municipal news   see Southern city
North Carolina municipal review, v. 1, January-April, 1928.   Chapel Hill, North Carolina Municipal Association, 1928.   NcU has v. 1.   [9825
North Carolina music educator, v. 1-   January-February, 1952-   Salisbury, 1952- NcU has v. 1-4 [5]   [9826
North Carolina Music Festival, Raleigh, N. C.   North Carolina Music Festival, 1906-   Raleigh, 1906-   NcU has 1906, 1908, 1909, 1912, 1915.   Called Raleigh Choral Society, 1909.   [9827
North Carolina Mutual Fire Insurance Co.   Charter, by-laws, etc.   Raleigh, Holden and Wilson, pr., 1859.   16 p.   [9828
North Carolina Mutual Home Insurance Co.   Charter and by laws.   Raleigh, Nichols & Gorman, pr., 1869.   10 p.   [9829
North Carolina Mutual Insurance Co.   Charter, instructions to agents, by-laws, rates and conditions of insurance, &c.   Raleigh, Southern Weekly Post,.pr., 1854. 42 p.   [9830
——Circular, by laws, and act of incorporation.   Raleigh, Seaton Gales, 1846. 30 p.   [9831
—— ——Raleigh, Star, 1848.   28 p.   [9832
North Carolina Mutual Life Insurance Co.   Life insurance, its principles, operations and benefits.   Raleigh, Seaton Gales, 1849.   27 p.   [9833
—— ——Raleigh, North Carolina Institution for the Deaf and Dumb, 1849. 34 p.   [9834
——Report, 1849/50-   Raleigh, 1850-   NcU has 1850/51-1852/53, 1854/55-1857/ 58, 1859/60, 1860/61, 1862/63   [9835
North Carolina National Guard Association.   Minutes, 190 -   190 -   NcU has 1908   [9836
North Carolina National Guardsman, v. 1-2, May, 1930-September, 1931.   Raleigh, 1930-1931   NcU has v. 1-2   [9837
North Carolina Negro Teachers Association.   Minutes, 1881-   1881-   NcU has 1885, 1901, 1924-1926   [9838
North Carolina Nurses' Association.   Official proceedings . . . annual convention, 1903?-   1903?-   NcU has 1934-1936, 1938-1946   [9839
——The thirtieth anniversary of the organization of the North Carolina Association of Nurses.   Raleigh, 1932.   [8] p.   [9840
North Carolina parent teacher bulletin, v. 1-   January, 1922-   Greensboro, 1922- NcU has v. 1-33   [9841
North Carolina Peace Congress.   North Carolina Peace Congress.   No place [1908?] 4 p.   [9842
North Carolina.   People's Party State Executive Committee.   Headquarters.   Raleigh, March 24, 1900.   [1] p.   [9843
——Is the Democratic Party honest?   A statement of facts.   No place [1898?] 24 p.   [9844
——Instructions to judges of election and the law.   No place, 1900.   [1] p.   [9845
——To the people of Sampson County indignant.   No place, 1900.   [1] p.   [9846
——People's Party hand-book of facts, 1898-   Raleigh, 1898-   NcU has 1898   [9847
[North Carolina.   People's Party State Executive Committee]   The proposed franchise amendment.   No place [1900?]   75 p.   [9848
North Carolina.   People's Party State Executive Committee.   The proposed suffrage amendment.   No place [1900?]   16 p.   [9849

[North Carolina. People's Party State Executive Committee] Some correspondence between the state chairmen of two political organizations. No place [1900?] 8 p. [9850

North Carolina. People's Party State Executive Committee. To the Populist voters of the eighteenth senatorial district. No place, n.d. [1] p. [9851

[North Carolina. People's Party State Executive Committee?] What may occur on the day of election. No place [1900?] [1] p. [9852

North Carolina Pharmaceutical Association. Proceedings, 1880-1915. No place, 1880-1915. NcU has 1880-1915. Continues, 1916- in Carolina journal of pharmacy. [9853

——Program, 1880- 1880- NcU has 1909-1919 [1921-1940] [9854

——Yearbook, 1946- [Chapel Hill] 1945- NcU has 1946. [9855

North Carolina Pine Association. Bridgeport standard artistic and practical wood finishing products applied on North Carolina pine. Norfolk, Va., 1919. Folder. [9856

——Bulletin, 19 - Norfolk, Va., 19 - NcU has v. [10] [9857

——North Carolina pine, beautiful, substantial, permanent, economical. [Pittsburgh, Albert P. Hill, n.d.] 24 p. [9858

——North Carolina pine, its beauty for panelled walls. Norfolk, Va., n.d. 15 p. [9859

——North Carolina pine, the wood universal. [Pittsburgh, Albert P. Hill Co.] n.d. 15 p. [9860

——Proceedings, 190 - Norfolk, Va., 190 - NcU has 1906 [9861

——Year book, 190 - Norfolk, Va., 190 - NcU has 1921 [9862

A North Carolina Planter [pseud.] A petition and remonstrance to the President and Congress of the United States. No place [1791] [1] p. NcU has photostat (positive) from originial in New York Public Library [9863

North Carolina planter, v. 1-4, January, 1858-May? 1861. Raleigh, A. M. Gorman, 1858-1861. NcU has v. 1-3 [4] [9864

North Carolina poetry review, v. 1-3, July, 1933-June, 1936. Gastonia, North Carolina Poetry Society, 1933-1936. NcU has v. 1-3. [9865

North Carolina poets, 1930- Newport, Ky., International Writers' League, 1930- NcU has 1930. [9866

North Carolina practical spelling book. Raleigh, Alfred Williams & Co., 1892. 172 p. [9867

North Carolina Presbyterian. Circular. [Fayetteville? 1857] 1 p. [9868

——[Letter from Executive Committee of the Stockholders] [Fayetteville, 1858] 1 p. [9869

——Prospectus. [Fayetteville, 1857] 2 p. [9870

North Carolina Presbyterian see also Presbyterian standard

North Carolina press, v. 1- October, 1926- Morganton, North Carolina Press Association, 1926- NcU has v. [1-3] 20-30 [9871

North Carolina Press Association. Directory of North Carolina newspapers. Morganton, 1940. 18 p. [9872

——Historical records, 1873-1887, compiled by J. B. Sherrill. No place, 1930. 107 p. [9873

——North Carolina, the South's no. 1 state, 19 - Morganton, 19 - NcU has 1942, 1947, 1951, 1952, 1954. Title varies, 1942: Sales opportunities [9874

——Proceedings, 1873- 1873- NcU has 1873, 1881-1885, 1887-1888 [1891-1917] 1919-1926 [9875

——Program of exercises for Bill Nye Day in the public schools. [Charlotte, Observer, 1910?] 16 p. [9876

North Carolina press bulletin, v. 1-4, April 1, 1922-1926. Morganton, North Carolina Press Association, 1922-1926. NcU has v. 1, no. 2-v. 4, no. 3. [9877

North Carolina Primary Teachers' Association. Library Committee. Report. E. M. Uzzell and Co., 1915. 36 p. • [9878

North Carolina Primary Teachers' Association. Text Book and Material Committee. Report, 191 - No place, 191 - NcU has 1912-1914 and one issue without date [9879

North Carolina Psychological Association. Bulletin, v. 1- December, 1948- Raleigh, 1948- NcU has v. [1-5] [9880

[North Carolina Railroad Association] A letter to the members of the General Assembly of North Carolina, subject, State taxes on railroads. [Raleigh, 1939] 16 p. [9881

North Carolina real estate and building record, v. 1- December, 1926- Charlotte, 1926- NcU has v. 1-2 [3] [9882

North Carolina recreation review, v. 1- January, 1948- Raleigh, North Carolina Recreation Society, Inc., 1948- NcU has v. 1-9 [9883

North Carolina Recreation Society, Inc. Rules and regulations for conducting state-wide activities. [Raleigh, 1952] Various paging. [9884

[North Carolina. Republican Party] Address of the Republican members of the General Assembly. No place, n.d. 10 p. [9885

North Carolina Republican Party. Randolph County Executive Committee. Notice! A meeting of the citizens of Randolph County will take place at Ashboro. No place, June 1st, 1870. [1] p. [9886

North Carolina. Republican State Executive Committee. Address. No place [1884?] 8 p. [9887

——Address of the Republican Executive Committee of the third congressional district, Wilmington, N. C., June 17, 1872. Wilmington, S. G. Hall, 1872. 13 p. [9888

——Address to the citizens of the 16th Senatorial district. No place, n.d. 4 p. [9889

——Address to the voters of North Carolina. Raleigh, June 16, 1875. 4 p. [9890

[North Carolina. Republican State Executive Committee] Buzzard nest methods. Statesville [1950?] [11] p. [9891

North Carolina. Republican State Executive Committee. Chairman Simmons says the Democrats made no promises on the suffrage question in 1898. No place [1900?] 2 p. [9892

[North Carolina. Republican State Executive Committee] A Democratic bill of indictment. No place [1906?] [3] p. [9893

——Extract from A. E. Holton's speech at Dobson, Oct. 16th, 1920. [Raleigh, 1920] [2] p. [9895

——Facts and figures. No place [1872] 8 p. [9896

——"For the constitution", for Governor, W. W. Holden. No place [1868] [1] p. [9897

——Jeter Conley Pritchard. No place [1920?] [4] p. [9898

——National Republican ticket: For President, Ulysses S. Grant. No place [1868] [1] p. [9899

——No convention! No place [1871] [2] p. [9900

——Old soldiers called "old and childish and afflicted with diseases". No place [1916?] [8] p. [9901

——Plan of organization. No place [1908] 4 p. [9902

——Plan of organization . . . amended and adopted . . . August 28, 1902. No place [1902] [3] p. [9903

——Platform . . . March 19, 1924. [Durham, Seeman Printery, pr., 1924] 8 p. [9904

——The press clipping news. Raleigh [1932?] Folder. [9905

——Read and circulate! No place [1872?] 8 p. [9906

——A report every taxpayer should read. No place [1915?] [16] p. [9907

——Reports every taxpayer should read. No place [1916?] [16] p. [9908

——Republican hand-book, 1906. Greensboro, 1906. 106 p. [9909

——Republican organization of North Carolina, 1939-1940. [Charlotte, 1940] 86 p. [9910

——Republican state platform . . . August 10, 1910. No place [1910] 4 p. [9911

——To the Republicans of the fourth congressional district. No place, n.d. 4 p. [9912

[North Carolina. Republican State Executive Committee?] To the voters of Granville County. No place [1902?] [1] p. [9913

——Vote the Democratic ticket! Thirteen reasons. No place, n.d. [1] p. [9914

——Where the Democratic fire started. No place [1908?] [3] p. [9915

North Carolina. Resource-Use Education Conference. Proceedings, 1948- Raleigh, 1948- NcU has 1949, 1950 [9916

North Carolina review; literary and historical section, the News and observer, October, 1909-April 6, 1913. Raleigh, 1909-1913. NcU has October, 1909-April 6, 1913. Index in issue of January 7, 1912. [9917

North Carolina. **Rural Health Conference.** Proceedings, 1952- Raleigh, Committee on Rural Health of the Medical Society of the State of North Carolina, 1952-NcU has 1952 (fifth) 1953, 1954, 1955. 1st-4th not published.   [9918

North Carolina Sanitary Association. Report of proceedings of the first annual convention, held at Raleigh, February 6th and 7th, 1889. Raleigh, Edwards and Broughton, 1889. 106 p.   [9919

North Carolina School Board Association. School Board Association, organized May, 1937, a brief history. Chapel Hill, 1941. 22 p.   [9920

North Carolina **School Board Conference, Chapel Hill, May 5, 1937.**
North Carolina School Board Conference. [Chapel Hill?] 1937. 7 p.   [9922

North Carolina Sheriffs' Association. Bulletin of news and views from peace officers of North Carolina, July, 1945- Charlotte, 1945- NcU has [July, 1945-August, 1947]   [9923

North Carolina Shipbuilding Co., Wilmington, N. C. Five years of North Carolina shipbuilding. Wilmington, 1946. 48 p.   [9924
——General safety rules, regulations. Wilmington [1944] 30 p.   [9925

North Carolina. **Social Studies Institute, Chapel Hill, June 12-30, 1944.** Report. [Chapel Hill, 1944] 66 p.   [9926

North Carolina Society for Crippled Children. Report, 19 - Chapel Hill, 19 - NcU has 1946, 1950/51-1952/53   [9927

North Carolina Society for the Preservation of Antiquities. Program, 19 - Raleigh, 19 - NcU has [1942-1955]   [9928
——Report, 19 - Raleigh, 19 - NcU has 1942, 1943   [9929

North Carolina Society for the Prevention of Cruelty to Animals. North Carolina Society for the Prevention of Cruelty to Animals, headquarters, Greensboro, N. C. [Greensboro, 1906?] 3 p.   [9930

North Carolina Society of Civil Engineers see **American Society of Civil Engineers. North Carolina Section**

North Carolina Society of County and Local Historians. [Historical tours of North Carolina counties] [1951?- NcU has Bertie, Brunswick, Buncombe, Camden, Chowan, Guilford, Henderson, Lee, Mecklenburg, Montgomery, Moore, Pender, Polk, Raleigh, Sanford area, Rutherford, Stanly   [9931
——[Minutes, 19 - 19 - NcU has 1946, 1952   [9932

North Carolina Society of Engineers. Bulletin, v. 1-4, March, 1941-June, 1944. Raleigh, 1941-1944. NcU has v. 1-2 [3] 4. Continues as North Carolina engineer, v. 1- September, 1944-   [9933
——Code of practice, adopted January, 1928. [Charlotte, 1928] 31 p.   [9934
——Year Book, 19 -1948. Raleigh, 19 -1948. NcU has 1937, 1939, 1941-1948. Continues 1949- in North Carolina engineer, v. 5-   [9935

North Carolina Society of Mayflower Descendants see **Society of Mayflower Descendants**

North Carolina Society of New York. Constitution, by-laws, and list of officers and members, 19 - [New York, 19 - NcU has 1912/13   [9936
——Speeches delivered at the dinner of the North Carolina Society of New York, at the Hotel Astor, December 7, 1908. [New York, 1908] 56 p.   [9937

North Carolina Society of Pennsylvania. North Carolina at Valley Forge. Philadelphia, 1923. 29 p.   [9938
——North Carolina state Sunday at Valley Forge. [Philadelphia, 1926] 7 p. [9939
——Thirteenth annual North Carolina state Sunday at Valley Forge . . . March 22, 1936. [Philadelphia, 1936?] 8 p.   [9940
——Where General Nash of North Carolina is buried. Philadelphia [1923?] Folder.   [9941

North Carolina Society of the Cincinnati see **Society of the Cincinnati. North Carolina**

North Carolina Society of the Colonial Dames of America see **Colonial Dames of America. North Carolina Society**

North Carolina Society of the Daughters of the American Revolution see **Daughters of the American Revolution. North Carolina Society**

North Carolina Society of the Descendants of the Palatines   see **Descendants of the Palatines.   North Carolina Society**

North Carolina Society of the Sons of the Revolution   see **Sons of the Revolution. North Carolina Society**

North Carolina Sons of Temperance.   Chaplain.   No place, n.d.   2 p.   [9942

——Proceedings, 18 - 18 - NcU has 1851, 1860   [9943

——[Ritual]   No place, n.d.   2 p.   [9944

North Carolina Sons of Temperance.   Davie Division no. 18, Davie County.   Constitution and by-laws.   Raleigh, A. M. Gorman, pr., 1851.   17 p.   [9945

North Carolina Sons of Temperance.   High Brighton Division no. 122, Asheville.   Constitution and by-laws.   Asheville, Messenger, 1851.   24 p.   [9946

North Carolina Sons of Temperance.   Independent Division, Fayetteville.   [Charter]   [Raleigh, 1856]   [1] p.   [9947

North Carolina Sons of Temperance.   Lafayette Division no. 2, Fayetteville.   Bye-laws.   [Fayetteville? 1845?]   4 p.   [9948

North Carolina Sons of Temperance.   Washington Division no. 27, Louisburg.   Constitution and by-laws.   Raleigh, A. M. Gorman, pr., 1851.   23 p.   [9949

North Carolina Standard, Raleigh.   Facts for the people!   Record of W. W. Holden.   [Raleigh, n.d.]   [1] p.   [9950

——Holden's record!   Mr. Holden before he was a candidate, and Mr. Holden now.   [Raleigh] Printed at the Office of the State journal [1861?]   [1] p.   [9951

North Carolina State Art Society   see **North Carolina Art Society**

North Carolina State Association for the Blind.   Directory and historical sketch of organized work for the blind in North Carolina.   Raleigh [1947]   10 p.   [9952

North Carolina State Association of County Commissioners.   Proceedings, 190 - 190 - NcU has 1908, 1912, 1931, 1934   [9953

North Carolina State Association of Democratic Clubs.   Call for a convention.   Raleigh, July 17, 1888.   [1] p.   [9954

North Carolina State Bar.   Proceedings, 1934- [Raleigh] 1934- NcU has 1934-1943   [9955

——Index . . . by Dennis A. Dooley.   New York, Baker, Voorhis & Co., Inc., 1942.   640 p.   [9956

North Carolina state concert, Washington, District of Columbia, January 31, 1934.   [Raleigh, Edwards and Broughton] 1934.   [8] p.   [9957

North Carolina State Conference on Employment.   Problems of the Negro, Raleigh, May 6, 1939.   [Papers] [Raleigh? 1939]   Various paging.   [9958

North Carolina State Dairymen's Association.   Annual report, 1st-2d, 1896-1898.   Raleigh, 1896-1898.   NcU has 1896-1898   [9959

North Carolina.   State Democratic Executive Committee.   Address on the objections to an ad valorem system of taxation.   No place [1859?]   32 p.   [9960

——Address to the freemen and voters of North Carolina. [Raleigh, 1840?] 42 p. [9961

[North Carolina.   State Democratic Executive Committee]   After the speaking is over.   No place [1900?]   [1] p.   [9962

——A brazen steal!   Some lessons of the Wake Republican convention.   No place [1900?]   [1] p.   [9963

——"Butler come back".   His former political career, his present domination of the Republican Party in North Carolina [Raleigh? 1910?]   32 p.   [9964

——Can any reasonable man longer doubt?   No place [1898?]   [1] p.   [9965

——Can you vote?   Raleigh [1914]   [3] p.   [9966

——Chapter from Republican National hand-book, 1910 [Raleigh? 1910?]   4 p. [9967

——Comments on the hand book issued by the Peoples Party State Executive Committee.   No place [1898?]   24 p.   [9968

——Cotton mill operatives as affected by the protective tariff.   [Raleigh? 1910?]   4 p.   [9969

——The Cowles force bill.   [Raleigh? 1910?]   4 p.   [9970

——The Crumpacker bill of 1901.   [Raleigh? 1910?]   8 p.   [9971

——A deadly parallel, showing comparative condition of public schools under Fusion and Democratic administration.   [Raleigh? 1910?]   8 p.   [9972

——North Carolina Democratic hand-book, 1882- Raleigh, 1882- NcU has 1882-1888, 1894, 1898-1916, 1922, 1928, 1932, 1936-1950. Biennial. Not issued 1918, 1920 [9973

——Democracy has made good. [Raleigh, 1918] 48 p. [9974

——The Democratic Executive Committee of Caswell County. [Raleigh? 1898] [3] p. [9975

——The Democratic Party and labor. [Raleigh? 1910?] 4 p. [9976

——Democratic Party of North Carolina, plan of organization. [Raleigh, 1929] 20 p. [9977

——Democratic plan of organization. [Raleigh, Edwards and Broughton, pr., 1904?] 8 p. [9978

——Democratic platform, 1920. Raleigh [1920?] 22 p. [9979

——A disgusted Republican. [Raleigh? 1888?] 4 p. [9980

——Dr. Thompson butts his head. [Raleigh? 1898?] [2] p. [9981

——Dr. Thompson says in his Hand Book [Raleigh? 1898?] [2] p. [9982

——Dr. Tyre York's record. No place [1884] [2] p. [9983

——The evidence against Abernathy. [Raleigh, 1918?] 14 p. [9984

——Farm prices not affected by tariff. [Raleigh? 1910?] 2 p. [9985

——Five lessons for North Carolina voters. No place [1898?] [2] p. [9986

——[The great importance of this election compels me . . .] Raleigh, 1876. [1] p. [9987

——Hon. J. Elwood Cox, witness, etc., in freight rate investigation. [Raleigh, 1910?] 8 p. [9989

——How ad valorem will work. No place, Democratic Press, pr., [1859?] 4 p. [9990

——Keynote speech at Democratic State Convention, June 12, 1936, by J. Melville Broughton. [Raleigh] 1936. 18 p. [9991

——Local self-government. [Raleigh? 1910?] 4 p. [9992

——The Negro Smith scores Populist Johnson. [Raleigh, 1900?] [2] p. [9993

——Negro supremacy against white supremacy in North Carolina. [Raleigh? 1898?] [4] p. [9994

——Opinion of about one hundred and seventy-five North Carolina lawyers that the amendment is constitutional. [Raleigh? 1900] [1] p. [9995

——Ought Hon. H. G. Ewart to be confirmed as judge of the United States District Court for the Western District of North Carolina? [Raleigh? n.d.] 7 p. [9996

——Plan of organization. [Raleigh, 1918?] 20 p. [9997

——Plan of organization. [Raleigh, 1937] 19 p. [9998

—— ———[Raleigh, 1946?] 17 p. [9999

——Proceedings of a convention of the friends of the Hon. Stephen A. Douglas, and the Hon. Herschel V. Johnson. Raleigh, 1860. 15 p. [10000

——Prof. Alexander McIver, life-long Republican, approves the amendment. [Raleigh, 1900] [2] p. [10001

——The Republican Party versus a white man's government. [Raleigh? 1928] 4 p. [10002

——Rules governing a senatorial primary to be held November 5, 1912. [Raleigh, 1912] 6 p. [10003

——Should be lynched! Negro candidate for senator from Edgecombe will help lynch any Negro who votes the Democratic ticket. [Raleigh? n.d.] [2] p. [10004

——Speeches of Hon. F. M. Simmons, Hon. John H. Small, Gov. Charles B. Aycock before the Democratic State Convention at Greensboro, N. C. Raleigh, 1904. 32 p. [10004a

——The state campaign. Raleigh, 1882. [2] p. [10005

——Supplement: The North Carolina Democratic handbook, 1922. [Raleigh, 1922?] 7 p. [10006

——Supplement: The state campaign, September 16, 1882. [Raleigh] 1882] [2] p. [10007

——Taft and the Negro. [Raleigh, E. M. Uzzell & Co., pr., 1908] 12 p. [10008

——Tariff-tables. [Raleigh, 1910?] 6 p. [10009

——Ten years' stewardship of the Democratic Party in North Carolina. [Raleigh, 1910?] 4 p. [10010

——The test of prohibition in the South. [Raleigh? 1932] 10 p. [10011

——To the Democratic Party of North Carolina. Raleigh, September, 1880. 4 p. [10012

——To the people of North Carolina. [Raleigh, 1892] 8 p. [10013

——Trial of white women by Negro justices of the peace at Newbern. [Raleigh, 1898] [2] p.   [10014
——Usurpation of the U. S. Marshal. Raleigh, 1876. [1] p.   [10015
——World's leader. Help Wilson win the War. [Raleigh, Edwards and Broughton Co., 1918] 14 p.   [10016
North Carolina State Federation of Labor. Legislative program . . . adopted . . . August 14, 1934. [Raleigh, 1934?] Folder.   [10017
——Proceedings, 19 - 19 - NcU has 1907, 1924, 1926, 1931, 1936, 1937, 1948-1955   [10018
North Carolina State Firemen's Association. Proceedings, 188 - 188 - NcU has 1897-1903, 1910, 1927, 1929-1934, 1936   [10019
[North Carolina State Grange] A directory of the granges of North Carolina, 1877. No place [1877] [10] p.   [10020
North Carolina State Grange. Proceedings, 1874- 1874- NcU has 1875-1878, 1882-1884, 1886-1887   [10021
North Carolina State Horticultural Farm, Southern Pines. Annual report, 1895-Raleigh [1896?- NcU has 1895, 1896   [10022
——The cow pea. Southern Pines, n.d. 63 p.   [10023
——Experiment farming; an account of the experiment farms established at Southern Pines, N. C. Southern Pines, n.d. 25 p.   [10024
——Experiments with fertilizers. Southern Pines, n.d. 36 p.   [10025
——Plant food, its nature, composition, and most profitable use. Southern Pines, n.d. 80 p.   [10026
——Truck farming. Southern Pines, n.d. 78 p.   [10027
North Carolina State Horticultural Society. Report, 1885- Raleigh, 1885- NcU has 1885, 1886, 1893, 1894   [10028
North Carolina State Life Insurance Co. Charter and by-laws. Raleigh, John Nichols & Co., pr., 1875. 16 p.   [10029
——North Carolina State Life Insurance Co., Raleigh, N. C. Raleigh, Edwards & Broughton Co., pr., 1873. 13 p.   [10030
—— ——Raleigh, John Nichols & Co., pr., 1873. 31 p.   [10031
—— ——1873. 30 p.   [10032
—— ——Raleigh, News Publishing Co., 1874. 14 p.   [10033
——Report, 1873/74?- Raleigh, John Nichols & Co., pr., 1874?- NcU has 1875/76, 1876/77, 1878, 1880   [10034
North Carolina. State Literary and Historical Association. Constitution; together with the call, resolutions, and press notices. Raleigh, 1900. 18 p.   [10035
——Five points in the record of North Carolina in the great war of 1861-5. Report of the committee appointed by the North Carolina Literary and Historical Society. Goldsboro, Nash Brothers, pr., 1904. 79 p.   [10036
——Officers, committees, and roll of charter members, 1900-1. Raleigh, Capital Printing Co., 1901. 8 p.   [10037
——Proceedings and addresses of the . . . annual session, 19 - Raleigh, 19 - NcU has 1905-1922   [10038
——Programs of the State Literary and Historical Association and the North Carolina Folk-Lore Society and the North Carolina State Art Society, 190 - Raleigh, 190 - NcU has [1906-1924] 1926-1956   [10039
North Carolina state ports, v. 1- December, 1953- Wilmington, State Ports Authority, 1953- NcU has v. 1 [2]   [10040
North Carolina State Sunday School Association. Minutes, 1882?- 1882?- NcU has 1890-1892   [10041
North Carolina state teachers' directory, 19 - Winston-Salem, Promotion List Co., 19 - NcU has 1904   [10042
North Carolina State Teachers' Educational Association see North Carolina Negro Teachers Association
North Carolina State Veterinary Medical Association. A veterinary history of North Carolina. No place, 1934. 54 p.   [10044
—— ——2d ed. [New Bern, Owen G. Dunn Co.] 1946. 108 p.   [10045
North Carolina Steel and Iron Co. Prospectus. No place [1890?] 30 p. [10046
——Facts. [Greensboro, 1890?] 3 p.   [10047

North Carolina Students for Wallace. Organizing Conference, Chapel Hill, February 28-29, 1948. [Chapel Hill, 1948] [5] p. [10048

North Carolina Sunday School beacon, v. 1- 1900- Raleigh, 1900- NcU has v. [2-7] [10049

North Carolina Symphony Society. Music on the move, 19 - [Chapel Hill] 19 - NcU has 1955, 10th tour [10050

——North Carolina Little Symphony program, 1934- [Chapel Hill, 1934- NcU has [August 23, 1934-1956] [10051

[North Carolina Symphony Society] North Carolina Symphony. [Chapel Hill? 1945] [4] p. [10052

——North Carolina Symphony historical outline. [Chapel Hill, 1952] 5 p. [10053

North Carolina Symphony Society. The North Carolina Symphony Society presents the . . . concert by the North Carolina Symphony Orchestra, first- May 14, 1932-1932- NcU has May 12, 1932-December 18, 1934, first—eighty-third and [1935-1956] [10054

——North Carolina Symphony Society presents the North Carolina Symphony Orchestra, Benjamin Swalin, conductor. [Chapel Hill, 1945] [14] p. [10055

——Program guide, 19 - [Chapel Hill, 19 - NcU has 1950/51 [10056

——Your own North Carolina Symphony, a Tar Heel story of a dream, a reality, and now a plan for tomorrow. [Chapel Hill? 1945] 14 p. [10057

North Carolina Tar Heel farmer, v. 1- 1912?- Goldsboro, Farmers State Alliance, 1912?- NcU has v. [2] [10058

North Carolina teacher, v. 1-13, June, 1883-September, 1895. Raleigh, 1883-1895. NcU has v. 1-13. [10059

North Carolina teacher, v. 1-10, September, 1924-April-May, 1934. Raleigh, North Carolina Education Association, 1924-1934. NcU has v. 1-10. Superseded North Carolina education, 1906-1924, continues as North Carolina education, September, 1934- [10060

North Carolina Teachers' Assembly. Constitution. No place, n.d. [4] p. [10060a

——Constitution and proposed amendments. Raleigh, Mutual Publishing Co., pr., 1912. 14 p. [10061

——Memorial to the General Assembly praying the establishment of a North Carolina normal college . . . with the proposed Act to establish a normal college. [Raleigh, 1886] 8 p. [10062

——The North Carolina Teachers' Assembly. [Raleigh, 1911] [5] p. [10063

——Proceedings and addresses of the 1st-38th, 1884-1921. Raleigh, 1884-1921. NcU has 1884, 1887, 1908-1921. Discontinued, 1922. Proceedings, 1909-1921, published as North Carolina. Department of Public Instruction. Educational bulletin. [10064

——Program, 1884- 1884- NcU has [1885-1896] 1898-1906, 1908-1917, 1919-1922 [10065

[North Carolina Teachers' Assembly. History Committee] Outline of work for the Committee on the history of education in North Carolina. [Wilson? 1909?] [4] p. [10066

North Carolina Teachers' Assembly. Legislative Committee. Report. No place, n.d. [3] p. [10067

——Report. No place [1901] 11 p. [10068

North Carolina Teachers' Association see North Carolina Negro Teachers Association

North Carolina teachers' record, v. 1- January, 1930- Raleigh, North Carolina Negro Teachers' Association, 1930- NcU has v. 1-27 [10069

North Carolina telegraph, v. 1, January 27, 1826-December 29, 1826. Fayetteville [William Hunter for the Editor, Robert H. Morrison] 1826. NcU has v. 1. Following December 29, 1826, united with The Richmond daily visitor. No. 10 omitted in numbering. September 29 not issued. [10070

North Carolina temperance almanac, 18 - Fayetteville, William Whitehead, 18 - NcU has 1834. [10071

North Carolina Tobacco Growers Cooperative Association. Agreement and contract. No place [1920?] 16 p. [10072

North Carolina tourist guide, 1947- Raleigh, The North Carolina Tourist Guide Association, 1947- NcU has 1947-1949 [10073

North Carolina Traffic League, Inc. Data and memoranda for consideration by President Roosevelt in his appointments to membership on the Interstate Commerce Commission. Charlotte, 1933. 3 p. [10074

North Carolina True Reformers. Constitution of subordinate fountains. Oxford, Orphanage Print, 1911. 37 p. [10075

North Carolina view book [Raleigh, Bynum Printing Co., 1943] [64] p. of illus. [10076

North Carolina vocational education, v. 1- April, 1951- Raleigh, North Carolina Vocational Educational Association, 1951- NcU has v. [1-4] [10077

North Carolina Vocational Guidance Association. North Carolina occupations. [Oxford, Oxford Orphanage, pr.] 1938. 80 p. [10078

[North Carolina. Whig Central Committee] Address to the people of North Carolina. No place [1840?] 28 p. [10079

——Report and resolutions unanimously adopted . . . April 4, 1842. [Raleigh, Register, 1842] [1] p. [10080

——To the freemen of North Carolina. No place, n.d. 23 p. [10081

North Carolina white ribbon, v. 1- June, 1896- High Point, Greensboro, Woman's Christian Temperance Union, 1896- NcU has v. [1-11] 12-16 [18] 19-21 [22-26] 27-45 [48] 49-60 [10082

North Carolina. White Supremacy Club. Constitution and by-laws. Raleigh, E. M. Uzzell, pr. [1900?] 8 p. [10083

North Carolina Wild Flower Society. News letter, November, 1954- 1954- NcU has [1954-1956] [10084

North Carolina Women's Clubs see North Carolina Federation of Women's Clubs

North Carolina. Women's Legislative Council see Legislative Council of North Carolina Women

North Carolina writers' news, October, 1956- Chapel Hill, 1956- NcU has October, 1956 [10085

North Carolina year book and business directory, 1901-1937. Raleigh, News and observer, 1901-1937. NcU has 1901-1937. Not issued, 1917-1921 [10086

North Carolina. Young Democratic Clubs. Code of ethics for political campaigns. [Raleigh?] 1951. [1] p. [10087

——Official handbook and directory, 1955- 1955- NcU has 1955 [10088

——Why the Democratic Party? No place, c.1955. 26 p. [10089

North Carolina Young Republican news, v. 1- June, 1953- Charlotte, 1953- NcU has v. 1-2 [3] [10090

North Carolina's future, v. 1- 1947- Raleigh, North Carolina Junior Chamber of Commerce, 1947- NcU has v. [2, 12] [10091

North Carolina's guide to better eating, 195 - [Raleigh, North Carolina Association of Quality Restaurants] 19 - NcU has [1954? 1955?] [10092

North Carolina's war song. No place, no publisher, n.d. [1] p. NcU copy is defective [10093

North Carolinian, pseud. see Hawks, Francis Lister

The North Carolinian, v. 1- 189 - Morganton, North Carolina School for the Deaf, 189 - NcU has v. 31-39, 41-42, 44 [10094

The North Carolinian, v. 1- March, 1955- Raleigh, William Perry Johnson and Russell B. Bidlack, 1955- NcU has v. 1-2 [10095

A North Carolinian Author. Experimental reflections. Nashville, Tenn., Printed and sold by T. G. Bradford, 1817. 147 p. [10096

North Greenville Baptist Association. Minutes, 1888- 1888- NcU has 1888 [10097

The North State artisan, v. 1- October, 1889- Durham, H. E. Seeman, 1889- NcU has v. [1] [10098

North State Improvement Co. Charter and by-laws, and report of the secretary and treasurer. Greensboro, J. S. Hampton & Co., 1885. 43 p. [10099

——Report of the secretary and treasurer, 188 - Greensboro, Thomas, 188 - NcU has 1889 [10100

North State Pottery Co., Sanford, N. C. The North State Pottery, creators of artistic North Carolina pottery. [Southern Pines, Foss and Morris, pr.] n.d. [6] p. [10101

North State School, Asheville, N. C. [Catalogue, 191 - Asheville, 191 - NcU has 1916/17 [10102

North-Western North Carolina Railroad. Amended charter, proceedings of general meeting of stockholders . . . also proceedings of the second annual meeting. Salem, L. V. Blum, pr., 1869. 24 p. [10103

——Charter, proceedings of meetings, by-laws. Salem, L. V. Blum, pr., 1868. 12 p. [10104

North Wilkesboro, N. C. Chamber of Commerce. North Wilkesboro, Wilkes County, North Carolina, town of opportunities. North Wilkesboro [1940?] [30] p. [10105

Northampton Co., N. C. Schools. The spirit and the ladder; an historical pageant of Northampton County . . . presented by schools of the county on the Court House green at Jackson, N. C., April 22, 1921. Jackson, Northampton Printing Co., 1921. [11] p. [10106

Northampton school events, v. 1- 192 - Jackson, Northampton County Schools, 1928- NcU has v. [2-3] [10107

Northcott, H. C. Biography of Rev. Benjamin Northcott. Cincinnati, Western Methodist Book Concern, pr., 1875. 111 p. [10108

Northern colony in the Mid-South. Greensboro, Hardie & Jordan, n.d. 28 p. [10109

Northrop, Henry Davenport. Life and deeds of General Sherman. Philadelphia, Globe Bible Publishing Co. [c.1891] 568 p. [10110

Northup, Herbert. Story of the life of Herbert Northup. No place, no publisher, n.d. 3 p. [10111

Northwest North Carolina Development Association, Inc. Northwest North Carolina industrial location factors. Winston-Salem [1956] unpaged [10112

Norton, Clarence Clifford. The Democratic party in ante-bellum North Carolina, 1835-1861. Chapel Hill, University of North Carolina Press, 1930. (James Sprunt historical studies, v. 21) 276 p. [10113

Norton, Frank Henry. The days of Daniel Boone. New York, American News Co. [c.1883] 406 p. [10114

—— ——New York, New York Publishing Co., 1895. [10115

Norton, John Nicholas. Life of Bishop Ravenscroft. New York, General Protestant Episcopal Sunday School Union, 1858. 152 p. [10116

Norwood, Hayden. The marble man's wife, Thomas Wolfe's mother. New York, Charles Scribner's Sons, 1947. 200 p. [10117

[Norwood, James] To the voters of Orange County. No place [Author?] n.d. 4 p. [10118

Norwood, John Wall, 1802-1885. Address of J. W. Norwood, of Orange, delivered before the State Agricultural Society . . . at the annual fair on the 20th October, 1871. No place, no publisher [1871] 10 p. [10119

[Norwood, John Wall] 1876- Fifty thousand miles with Uncle Sam's army, by Uncle Dudley [pseud.] Waynesville, Enterprise Publishing Co., 1912. 95 p. [10120

Nouvelle relation de la Carolina, par un gentil-homme françois arrivé, depuis deux mois, de ce nouveau pais. A La Haye, Chez Meyndert Uytweff [!] [1686?] 36 p. NcU has photostat (negative) [10121

Nowell, William Cullen. Lectures on the book of Revelation. Raleigh, Edwards & Broughton Printing Co., 1910. 191 p. [10122

Nowitzky, George I. Norfolk; the marine metropolis of Virginia, and the sound and river cities of North Carolina. Norfolk, Va., Author, 1888. 216 p. [10123

Nowitzky's monthly; the Tar-heel magazine and traveller's guide, v. 1- Sept. 1884- Raleigh, George I. Nowitzky, 1884- NcU has v. 1, no. 1-6 [10124

Nuermberger, Ruth Anna (Ketring) The free produce movement; a Quaker protest against slavery. Durham, Duke University Press, 1942. (Historical papers of the Trinity college historical society. Series XXV) 147 p. [10125

Number 2: Oppression of the people. No place, no publisher [187?] 13 p. [10126

Nunn, Romulus Armistead. Memorial address on Hon. Alfred Decatur Ward . . . 13 May, 1940 . . . before the Craven County Bar Association. No place, no publisher [1940] 16 p. [10127

Nye, Edgar Wilson. Baled hay . . . by Bill Nye. Chicago, Morrill, Higgins & Co., 1893. 320 p. [10128

——Bill Nye and Boomerang; or, The tale of a meek-eyed mule. Chicago, Homewood Publishing Co., 1893. 286 p. [10129

——Bill Nye, his own life story, continuity by Frank Wilson Nye. New York, Century Co. [c.1926] 412 p. [10130

——Bill Nye's chestnuts old and new. Chicago, W. B. Conkey [c.1888, 1894] 286 p. [10131

——Bill Nye's comic history of England. Chicago, Thompson & Thomas [c.1896] 195 p. [10132

——Bill Nye's history of the United States. Philadelphia, J. B. Lippincott Co. [1894] 329 p. [10133

——Bill Nye's red book. Chicago, Thompson & Thomas [c.1891] 389 p. [10134

——Bill Nye's remarks. Chicago, Thompson & Thomas, 1900. 504 p. [10135

——Bill Nye's sparks. New York, Hurst & Co., c.1901. 181 p. [10136

——The funny fellow's grab-bag, by Bill Nye and other funny men. New York, J. S. Ogilvie Publishing Co., c.1903. 123 p. [10137

——A guest at the Ludlow. New York, New York Book Co., 1913. 186 p. [10138

——Nye and Riley's wit and humor (poems and yarms) by James Whitcomb Riley & Bill Nye. Chicago, Thompson & Thomas [c.1900] 236 p. [10139

O. Henry, pseud. see **Porter, William Sydney**

The O. Henry calendar, 1917. New York, Doubleday, Page & Co. [1916?] [53] p. [10140

An O. Henry note book. No place, no publisher, n.d. [6] p. [10141

O. Henry papers; containing some sketches of his life together with an alphabetical index to his complete works. New rev. ed. Garden City, N. Y., Doubleday, Page & Co. [192?] 68 p. [10142

[**Oak Grove Monthly Meeting of Friends, Wayne Co., N. C.**] Memorial of Abbie A. Hollowell. Philadelphia, William H. Pile's Sons, 1922. 9 p. [10143

Oak leaves, 190 - Raleigh, Astrotekton and Philaretian Societies of Meredith College, 1904- NcU has 1915-1918 [10144

Oak Ridge Military Institute, Oak Ridge, N. C. Catalogue, 18 - Oak Ridge, 18 - NcU has 1880/81 [1888/89-1935/36] 1937/38-1949/50, 1951/52-1955/ 56 [10145

——Early years of a century of service; centennial commencement, May 25-26, 1952. Oak Ridge, 1952. 24 p. [10146

——Oak Ridge Military Institute . . . founded 1852, a four-year military junior college. [Oak Ridge, 1935?] [9] p. [10147

—— ——[Raleigh, Edwards and Broughton, 1935?] [22] p. [10148

—— ——[1938?] [21] p. [10149

—— ——[1942] [29] p. [10150

Oakland Heights. [St. Louis, Miller & Spalding] n.d. 19 p. [10151

Oakley, Wiley. Roamin' with the roamin' man of the Smoky Mountains. Gatlinburg, Tenn., Mountain Press [c.1940] 64 p. [10152

Oates, John Alexander. The story of Fayetteville and the upper Cape Fear. [Fayetteville? 1950] 868 p. [10153

Oath. No place, no publisher, 1867. [1] p. [10154

Ober, Frederick Albion. Sir Walter Raleigh. New York, Harper & Brothers, 1909. 303 p. [10155

Oberholser, Harry Church. The mammals and summer birds of Western North Carolina. Biltmore, Biltmore Forest School, June, 1905. 7 p. [10156

——Notes on the mammals and summer birds of Western North Carolina. Biltmore, Biltmore Forest School, September, 1905. 24 p. [10157

O'Berry, Annie L., joint author, see **Oettinger, Edna W.**

Obituaries, funeral, and proceedings of the bar, in memory of Wm. H. Battle. Raleigh, Uzzell & Wiley, pr., 1879. 32 p. [10158

Obituaries of George D. Boyd, Eliza C. Boyd, Andrew J. Boyd, Sallie A. Boyd. No place, no publisher, n.d. 20 p. [10159

Obituary [Adolphus L. Erwin] No place, no publisher [1855] [1] p. [10160

Obituary [Mrs. Margaret A. Thompson] Baltimore, J. Murphy and Co., 1881. [1] p.   [10161

Obituary: Old Ball is dead. No place, no publisher, n.d. 8 p.   [10162

[**O'Brien, William F.**] History of the Catholic Church of Durham, North Carolina, 1871-1944. No place, no publisher [194?] 20 p. ,   [10163

Observations on the five candidates for the Commons in E - C - , N. C., 1826. No place, no publisher [1826?] [1] p.   [10164

Observer Printing House, Charlotte, N. C. A story of the "tellers of stories". [Charlotte, Observer] n.d. 16 p.   [10165

Occoneechee Farm, Hillsboro, N. C. Berkshires or Tamworths on every farm; how to get a registered pig by sending us one dollar. Hillsboro [191?] 18 p. [10166

——Catalogue of trottingbred and thoroughbred horses owned at Occoneechee farm. [New York, John Polhemus Printing Co.] 1894. 32 p.   [10167

——If it comes from Occoneechee it's all right. No place, no publisher, n.d. [15] p.   [10168

——Occoneeche poultry farm, Durham, N. C. [Durham, Educator Co., pr.,] n.d. 63 p.   [10169

Ochs, Johann Rudolff. Americanischer Wegweiser, oder Kurtze und eigentliche Beschreibung der englischen Provintzen in Nord America sonderlich aber der Landschafft Carolina. Bern, 1711. 102 p.   [10170

O'Connell, Jeremiah Joseph. Catholicity in the Carolinas and Georgia. New York, D. & J. Sadlier & Co. [1879] 647 p.   [10171

Odd Fellows. North Carolina see **Independent Order of Odd Fellows. North Carolina**

Odeneal, John H. The carrier's address to the patrons and friends of the Raleigh register. [Raleigh?] December 25, 1831. [1] p.   [10172

O'Donnell, Jane (Chesney) Life of the late Gen. F. R. Chesney, by his wife and daughter [Louisa F. Chesney and Jane C. O'Donnell] 2d ed. London, Eden, Remington & Co., 1893. 477 p.   [10173

Odum, Eugene Pleasants. Fundamentals of ecology. Philadelphia, W. B. Saunders Co., 1953. 384 p.   [10174

Odum, Howard Washington. Alabama, past and future [by] Howard W. Odum [and others] Chicago, Textbook Division, Science Research Associates, 1941. 401 p.   [10175

——American democracy anew . . . by Howard W. Odum [and others] New York, H. Holt and Co. [c.1940] 614 p.   [10176

——An American epoch; southern portraiture in the national picture. New York, H. Holt and Co. [c.1930] 379 p.   [10177

Odum, Howard Washington, ed. American masters of social science . . . by Howard W. Odum [and others] New York, H. Holt and Co. [c.1927] 411 p. [10178

Odum, Howard Washington. American regionalism . . . by Howard W. Odum and Harry Estill Moore. New York, H. Holt and Co. [c.1938] 693 p.   [10179

——American social problems. New York, H. Holt and Co. [c.1939] 549 p. [10180

——American sociology; the story of sociology in the United States through 1950. New York, Longmans, Green, 1951. 501 p.   [10181

——An approach to public welfare and social work. Chapel Hill, University of North Carolina Press, 1926. 178 p.   [10182

——A clear vision for North Carolina; an address delivered at the 40th annual meeting of the North Carolina Conference for Social Service, Asheville, May 5, 1953. [Raleigh, 1953?] 6 p.   [10183

——Cold blue moon, Black Ulysses afar off. Indianapolis, Bobbs-Merrill Co. [c.1931] 277 p.   [10184

Odum, Howard Washington, ed. In search of the regional balance of America, edited . . . by Howard W. Odum . . . and Katharine Jocher. Chapel Hill, University of North Carolina Press, 1945. 162 p.   [10185

Odum, Howard Washington. An introduction to social research, by Howard W. Odum . . . and Katharine Jocher. New York, H. Holt and Co. [c.1929] 488 p. [10186

——Man's quest for social guidance. New York, H. Holt and Co. [c.1927] 643 p.   [10187

——The Negro and his songs . . . by Howard W. Odum . . . and Guy B. Johnson. Chapel Hill, University of North Carolina Press, 1925.   306 p.   [10188
——Negro workaday songs, by Howard W. Odum and Guy B. Johnson.   Chapel Hill, University of North Carolina Press, 1926.   278 p.   [10189

Odum, Howard Washington, ed.   Public welfare in the U. S.   Philadelphia, American Academy of Political and Social Science, 1923.   (Annals of the American academy of political and social science, Jan. 1923, v. 105)   282 p.   [10190

Odum, Howard Washington.   Race and rumors of race.   Chapel Hill, University of North Carolina Press [1943]   245 p.   [10191
——Rainbow round my shoulder; the blue trail of Black Ulysses.   Indianapolis, Bobbs-Merrill [c.1928]   323 p.   [10192
——The regional approach to national social planning, with special reference to a more abundant South.   New York, Foreign Policy Association; Chapel Hill, University of North Carolina Press, 1935.   31 p.   [10193
——Social and mental traits of the Negro.   New York, 1910.   303 p.   Thesis (Ph.D.)—Columbia University.   [10194
——. . . Sociology and social problems.   Chicago, American Library Association, 1925.   (Reading with a purpose. [8])   32 p.   [10195

Odum, Howard Washington, ed.   Southern pioneers in social interpretation.   Chapel Hill, University of North Carolina Press, 1925.   221 p.   [10196

Odum, Howard Washington.   Southern regions of the United States.   Chapel Hill, University of North Carolina Press, 1936.   664 p.   [10197
——Symbol and reality of consolidation; acceptance of the fifth annual O. Max Gardner award, anniversary dinner, Woman's College of the University of North Carolina, March 22, 1953.   [Chapel Hill? 1953]   [7] p.   [10198
——Systems of public welfare, by Howard W. Odum and D. W. Willard.   Chapel Hill, University of North Carolina Press, 1925.   302 p.   [10199
——Understanding society; the principles of dynamic sociology.   New York, Macmillan Co., 1947.   749 p.   [10200
——The way of the South; toward the regional balance of America.   New York, Macmillan Co., 1947.   350 p.   [10201
——Wings on my feet; black Ulysses at the wars.   Indianapolis, Bobbs-Merrill Co. [c.1929]   308 p.   [10202

Oertel, Johannes Adam Simon.   Some of the teachings of modern art.   Hartford, Conn., M. H. Mallory and Co., pr., 1873.   15 p.   [10203
——William Cullen Bryant's 'Waiting by the gate' illustrated by J. A. Oertel.   New York, Geo. T. James, 1872.   8 plates.   [10204

Oertel, Mrs. Johannes Adam Simon.   Hand in hand through the happy valley. Brooklyn, Published for the benefit of the Children's Ward, St. John's Hospital, Church Charity Foundation, 1881.   97 p.   [10205

Oertel, John Frederick.   Moonshine.   Macon, Ga., J. W. Burke Co., 1926. 146 p. [10206
——A vision realized, a life story of Rev. J. A. Oertel.   Milwaukee, Young Churchman Co., 1917.   233 p.   [10207

Oettinger, Edna W.   The North Carolina garden year book . . . compiled by Edna W. Oettinger and Annie L. O'Berry, the Garden Club of the Goldsboro Woman's Club.   No place, no publisher, n.d.   51 p.   [10208

Official directory of law enforcement officers in North Carolina, 19   -   [Wilmington? 19   -   NcU has 1933, 1934/35, 1935/36, 1938/39, 1939/40, 1946-1949, 1951-1953, 1955   [10209

The official guide to Cherokee, 19   -   Cherokee, Earle Hitch, 19   -   NcU has 1954   [10210

Official program of the one hundredth anniversary celebration, city of Greensboro, N. C.   [Greensboro, Harrison Press, 1908]   [7] p.   [10211

Ogburn, Dorothy.   Death on the mountain.   Boston, Little, Brown, and Co., 1931. 286 p.   [10212

Ogg, John B.   To the General Assembly of the State of North-Carolina.   Raleigh, 1827.   3 p.   NcU has photostat (negative)   [10213

Ogilby, Edward L.   A clear statement for thinking men; an address delivered in Charlotte, N. C.   No place, no publisher, n.d.   8 p.   [10214

Ogilby, John. America: being the latest, and most accurate description of the New World. London, Printed by the Author, 1671. 674 p. [10215

[Oglesby, Isador Boyd] Are secondary and collegiate schools of business forgetting the little man on the corner? [Durham, Hillside Park High School, 1938] [10] p. [10216

O'Grady, John. Levi Silliman Ives, pioneer leader in Catholic charities. New York, P. J. Kenedy & Sons, 1933. 98 p. [10217

Ohio Jackson Convention, Columbus, Ohio, July 14, 1824. Address to the people of Ohio on the important subject of the next presidency by the committee appointed for that purpose. Cincinnati, Looker and Reynolds [1824] 16 p. [10218

O'Kelly, C. Grant. N. C. C. loyalty (a song) words and music. [Durham? Author, c.1936] [2] p. [10219

[O'Kelly, James] The author's apology for protesting against the Methodist Episcopal government. Hillsborough, Reprinted at the request of the friends of the author, Dennis Heartt, pr., 1829. 120 p. [10220

O'Kelly, James. The divine oracles consulted; or, An appeal to the law and testimony. Hillsborough, D. Heartt, pr., for the Author, 1820. 58 p. [10221

——Essay on Negro-slavery. Philadelphia, Printed by Prichard & Hall, 1789. 48 p. [10222

Old Eastern Baptist Association. Minutes, 1866?- 1866?- NcU has [1895-1929] [10223

Old faith contender and sovereign grace and pilgrim, v. 1- 187 - Elon College, Primitive Baptist Church, 1879- NcU has v. [22] 23-34 [10224

Old Field Teacher, pseud. see Hart, Alban J.

Old Hickory Association. Official souvenir program, 1917-1919, memories 30th Division. [Nashville, Tenn., 1921] 28 p. [10225

Old homes and gardens of North Carolina. Chapel Hill, University of North Carolina Press [c.1939] 34 p. 100 plates. [10226

Old North State almanac, 18 - Brooklyn, N. Y., Lyon Manufacturing Co., 18 - NcU has 1895-1908 [10227

Old North State Medical, Dental and Pharmaceutical Society, Inc. Program, 18 - 18 - NcU has 1937, 1947 [10228

Old-School Abolitionist, pseud. Views of an Old-School Abolitionist on "Impeachment". No place, n.d. [2] p. [10229

Old Shylock, pseud. The North Carolina system of expenditures vs. the constitution. No place [188?] [2] p. [10230

Oldham, Edward A. North Carolina's industrial development, read before the eleventh annual convention of the North Carolina Press Association at Waynesville, July 4th, 1883; 2d ed. Winston, S. C., Western Sentinel Publishing House, 1883. 15 p. [10231

[Oldmixon, John] The British Empire in America, containing the history of the discovery, settlement, progress and state of the British colonies . . . of America. 2d ed., cor. and amended. London, Printed for J. Brotherton, 1741. 2 v. [10232

Olds, Fred A., comp. An abstract of North Carolina wills from about 1760 to about 1800, supplementing Grimes' Abstract of North Carolina wills, 1663 to 1760. Oxford, privately printed by The Orphan's Friend, 1925. 326 p. [10233

—— ——2d ed. Baltimore, Md., Southern Book Co., 1954. 330 p. [10234

Olds, Fred A. Story of the counties of North Carolina. [Oxford, Orphanage Press, 1921] 64 p. [10235

Olds, Helen (Diehl) Peanut butter mascot. New York, Julian Messner, Inc. [1953] 61 p. [10236

Olds, Lewis P. Language as the voice of latitude . . . an address delivered before the Philomathesian and Euzelian societies of Wake Forest College, N. C., June 11th, 1868. 2d ed. New York, 1868. 80 p. [10237

——Philosophy and practice of faith. New York, Carlton & Phillips, 1853. 353 p. [10238

Oldys, William. The life of Sir Walter Ralegh. No place, no publisher, n.d. 696 p. [10239

Olin Mathieson news, v. 1- January, 1955- Pisgah Forest, Ecusta Paper Corporation, 1955- NcU has v. 1-2   [10240

Oliphant, Edward. The history of North America and its United States. 2d ed. Edinburgh, For R. Paul, 1801. 408 p.   [10241

Olive, Johnson. One of the wonders of the age; or, The life and times of Rev. Johnson Olive, Wake Co., N. C. Raleigh, Edwards, Broughton & Co., 1886. 314 p.   [10242

Olive branch see Weekly message

Oliver, David Dickson. The Society for the Propagation of the Gospel in the province of North Carolina. Raleigh, Commercial Printing Co. [for the University of North Carolina] 1910. (James Sprunt historical publications, v. 9, no. 1) p. [5]-23   [10243

Oliver, Frances Motley. Poems. No place, Author, 1942. [23] p.   [10244

Oliver, William B. The covenant of fraternity, a sermon preached before Cross Creek Lodge, no. 4, I. O. O. F. . . . June 15th, 1890. Fayetteville, Fayetteville Printing and Publishing Co., 1890. 14 p.   [10245

Oliver, William H. An address to the National Silver Convention, at Saint Louis. [Newbern?] n.d. [16] p.   [10246

——Blockade-running by the state of North Carolina, 1863-4. Newbern, no publisher [1895] 2 p.   [10247

Oliver, William H., comp. Extracts from the laws from A. D. 1715 to A. D. 1868. [Newbern, 1891] [4] p. (In regard to spelling the name of Newbern)   [10248
——Extracts from the laws from A. D. 1723 in regard to spelling the name of the town or city of Newbern, N. C. [Newbern, 1891] [4] p.   [10249

Oliver, William H. Mr. William H. Oliver's address on the silver question at Newbern, N. C. No place, no publisher, n.d. 4 p.   [10250
——Wheat and flour wanted. [Graham? Author] August 15, 1863. [1] p. [10251
——Write Newbern correctly, that is, in accordance with law. [Newbern, 1891] 4 p.   [10252

Olivia Raney Library, Raleigh, N. C. Exercises at the opening of the Olivia Raney Library . . . January twenty-fourth, 1901. Raleigh, Capital Printing Co., 1901. 31 p.   [10253

[Olmsted, Denison] Outlines of the lectures on chemistry, mineralogy & geology, delivered at the University of North-Carolina; for the use of the students. Raleigh, Printed by J. Gales, 1819. 44 p.   [10254

Olmsted, Frederick Law. The Cotton Kingdom; a traveller's observations on cotton and slavery in the American slave states. New York, Mason Brothers, 1861. 2 v.   [10255
—— ——ed. . . . by Arthur M. Schlesinger. New York, Alfred A. Knopf, 1953. 626 p.   [10256
——A journey in the seaboard slave states. New York, Dix & Edwards, 1856. 723 p.   [10257
—— ——New York, Mason Brothers, 1863.   [10258
—— ——New York, G. P. Putnam's Sons, 1904. 2 v.   [10259
——Journeys and explorations in the cotton kingdom. London, Sampson Low, Son & Co., 1861. 2 v.   [10260

Olmsted, Stanley. At top of Tobin. New York, Dial Press, 1926. 497 p. [10261

Omega Psi Phi Fraternity, Inc. Sixth district. Annual district meeting, 19 - No place, 19 - NcU has 1946   [10262

On Saturday last the Duplin Rifles were re-organized. Kenansville, no publisher, Dec. 23, 1861. [1] p.   [10263

One of the Fools, pseud. see Tourgée, Albion Winegar

O'Neall, John Belton. Address delivered before the Eumenean Society of Davidson College, N. C. . . . Aug. 8, 1850, the annual commencement. Charlotte, Hornets' Nest, 1850. 16 p.   [10264

O'Neill, Jean. Cotton Top. New York, Lothrop, Lee and Shepard [1953] Unpaged.   [10265

Onslow Rod and Gun Club. By-laws, 19 - [Raleigh? 19 - NcU has September 30, 1920, January 10, 1921   [10266

Oogoocoo, 19 - Cullowhee, The Senior Class of Cullowhee Normal and Industrial School, 19 - NcU has 1918 [10267

Oosting, Henry John. The study of plant communities, an introduction to plant ecology. San Francisco, W. H. Freeman, 1948. 389 p. [10268

Operations Thirtieth Division, Old Hickory. No place, no publisher, n.d. 22 p. [10269

[Orange Co., N. C. Board of Education?] The Orange County bond issue concerns you. [Chapel Hill? 1949] [6] p. [10271

[Orange Co., N. C. Board of Education] Orange County schools: bond issue election March 27, 1956. [Hillsboro, 1956] [6] p. [10272

Orange Co., N. C. Board of Education. Orange County teachers' handbook, 1927-28- [Durham, Seeman Printery, 1927- NcU has 1927-28 [10273

——Report of the Public Schools of Orange County, 19 - [Hillsboro, 19 - NcU has 1909/10 [10274

[Orange Co., N. C. Citizens] To the freemen of Orange County. [Orange County, March 18, 1823] 7 p. [10275

Orange Co., N. C. Democratic Executive Committee. Four years of Republican economy in Orange County. No place [1920] [1] p. [10276

——Josiah Turner on independent candidates. [Hillsboro? 1874?] [1] p. [10277

Orange Co., N. C. Republican Executive Committee. An appeal to our neighbors in Orange County, both Democrats and Republicans. No place [1944] [1] p. [10278

[Orange Co., N. C. Tax Assessors] Notice—Tax in kind—Notice—Confederate tax. No place, no publisher [Aug. 11, 1864] [1] p. [10279

Orange County school news, v. 1-3, Dec., 1921-Feb., 1925. Chapel Hill, Orange County Board of Education and Dept. of Rural Education in the University of North Carolina, 1921-1925. NcU has v. 1-3. [10280

Orange County Society for the Promotion of Agriculture, the Mechanic Arts, and Manufactures. County fair, 1854. Hillsborough, D. Heartt & Son, 1854. [1] p. [10281

Orange Grove School, Hillsboro, N. C. Catalogue, 18 - Hillsboro, 18 - NcU has 1907/08, 1908/09 [10282

Orange—Person—Chatham District, N. C. Health Department. Report, 1937-Chapel Hill, 1937- NcU has 1937, 1939, 1943 [10283

Orange Presbyterian, v. 1- October, 1946- Greensboro, Orange Presbytery, 1946-NcU has v. [1-8] [10284

Orange Presbytery see Presbyterian Church in the U. S. Synod of N. C. Orange Presbytery

Orange Printshop, Chapel Hill, N. C. The Orange Printshop guide. [Chapel Hill] n.d. 16 p. [10285

Order of Independent Carpet Baggers of North Carolina. Constitution. No place, n.d. 8 p. NcU has photostat (negative) from original in New York Public Library [10286

Original Bear Creek Primitive Baptist Association. Minutes, 18 - 18 - NcU has [1927-1941] [10287

Original Free Will Baptist Church. North Carolina. Minutes, 1913- 1913- NcU has 1925, 1955 [10288

Original Free Will Baptist Church. North Carolina. Albemarle Conference. Minutes, 1945- 1945- NcU has 1946, 1947, 1949, 1951-1955 [10289

Original Free Will Baptist Church. North Carolina. Cape Fear Conference. Minutes, 1857?- 1857?- NcU has 1951 [10290

Original Free Will Baptist Church. North Carolina. Central Conference, 18 - 18 - NcU has 1879, 1886, [1924-1930] [10291

Original Free Will Baptist Church. North Carolina. Eastern Conference. Minutes, 1896?- 1896?- NcU has [1951-1955] [10292

Original Free Will Baptist Church. North Carolina. Rockfish Conference. Minutes, 1909?- 1909?- NcU has [1947-1955] [10293

Original Free Will Baptist Church. North Carolina. Union Conference. Minutes, 1891?- 1891?- NcU has 1894 [10294

Original Free Will Baptist Church. North Carolina. Western Conference. Minutes, 1887?- 1887?- NcU has 1892 [1933-1955]   [10295

Ormond, Jesse Marvin. By the waters of Bethesda. Nashville, Tenn., Department of Education and Promotion, Board of Missions, Methodist Episcopal Church, South, 1936. 153 p.   [10296

——The country church in North Carolina. Durham, Duke University Press, 1931. 369 p.   [10297

O'Rourke, John T. A report of a study of the dental needs and facilities of North Carolina. No place [1947?] Various paging.   [10298

——Summary of a report on the dental needs and facilities of North Carolina. [Raleigh? 1947?] 22 p.   [10299

Orphans' friend and Masonic journal, v. 1- 187 - Oxford, Oxford Orphanage, 187 - NcU has v. [7-42] 43 [44-47] 48-81   [10300

Osborn, Charles. Journal of that faithful servant of Christ, Charles Osborn. Cincinnati, Printed by Achilles Pugh, 1854. 172 p.   [10301

Osborn, Hartwell. Trials and triumphs; the record of the Fifty-fifth Ohio Volunteer Infantry. Chicago, A. C. McClurg & Co., 1904. 364 p.   [10302

Osborne, Arthur Dimon. The capture of Fort Fisher by Major General Alfred H. Terry . . . read before the New Haven Colony Historical Society, October 23, 1911. New Haven, Tuttle, Morehouse & Taylor Press, 1911. 21 p.   [10303

[Osborne, Mrs. D. C.] Under golden skies. Raleigh, Edwards & Broughton, pr., 1898. 485 p.   [10304

Osborne, Francis I. Presentation of portrait of the Hon. Joseph Harvey Wilson by his son, G. E. Wilson . . . address of Judge Osborne, delivered before the Supreme Court of N. C., April 21st, 1914. Raleigh, Edwards & Broughton Printing Co., 1914. 22 p.   [10305

Osborne Association. Osborne Association survey report on North Carolina prison system. [Raleigh? North Carolina State Highway and Public Works Commission, Prison Department? 1950] Various paging.   [10306

Osbourn, James, comp. North Carolina sonnets; or, A selection of choice hymns for the use of the Old School Baptists. Baltimore, The Compiler, 1844. 406 p. [10307

Osbourn, James. A spiritual poem on animated graves dedicated to the people of Caswell County, North Carolina; to which is added, A poetical address to the female Christians of the same county. Baltimore, Printed by John D. Toy, 1829. 40 p.   [10308

Otey, James Hervey. Trust in God, the foundation of the Christian minister's success; a sermon preached at the consecration of the Right Reverend William Mercer Green . . . Jackson, Miss. . . . Feb. 24th, 1850. New York, Stanford and Swords, 1850. 43 p.   [10309

Otis, James, pseud. see Kaler, James Otis

Otts, John Martin Philip. Unsettled questions. New York, Fleming H. Revell Co. [c.1893] (Davidson College divinity lectures, Otts Foundation. 1st series. 1893) 169 p.   [10310

Ought "Yankee" traitors rule the nation? Being a single fact submitted to the consideration of the loyal men of the North by a North Carolina backwoodsman. New York, W. Henry & Co., 1866. 10 p. NcU has microfilm (negative) from original in Library of Congress   [10311

Our communal health, 191 - Wilmington, Consolidated Boards of Health of Wilmington and New Hanover County, 191 - NcU has [1915-17] 1918-21   [10312

Our fatherless ones, v. 1- 189 - Barium Springs, Presbyterian Orphans' Home, 189 - NcU has v. [10-18]   [10313

Our Lady's orphan boy, v. 1- 190 - Nazareth, Orphan Boys of Catholic Orphanage, 190 - NcU has v. [10-14]   [10314

Our living and our dead, devoted to North Carolina, her past, her present and her future. Official organ N. C. branch, Southern Historical Society, v. 1-3, v. 4, no. 1, September, 1874-March, 1876. Raleigh, S. D. Pool [1874-76] NcU has v. 1-4. Preceded by a weekly newspaper of same title, July 2, 1873-August 5, 1874, v. 1-2. NcU has v. 1-2.   [10315

Our missionary news, v. 1- 192 - Smithfield, Woman's Missionary Union of the
Methodist Episcopal Church, South, 192 - NcU has v. [6-8]   [10316

Our mountain work in Asheville Presbytery, v. 1- 192 - Weaverville, Home
Mission Committee of Asheville Presbytery, 192 - NcU has v. 34-46   [10317

Our neighbors, v. 1- October, 1942- Charlotte, H. L. Reaves, 1942- NcU has
v. 1, no. 1   [10318

Our patriots of America: North Carolina. Winston-Salem, National Patriotic Publishers, c.1944. v. 1   [10319

Our weekly, v. 1- 1872- Charlotte, J. O. H. Nuttall, 1872- NcU has v. [2] [10320

Our young men, v. 1- 1887- Raleigh, Young Men's Christian Associations of
North Carolina, 1887- NcU has v. 2, no. 2   [10321

Out of doors in the Blue Ridge. [Nashville, Tenn., Benson Printing Co.] 1916.
15 p.   [10322

——1917. 13 p.   [10323

——n.d. 16 p.   [10324

——[Nashville, Williams Printing Co., 1920] 15 p.   [10325

Outlaw, Albert Timothy. Grove Presbyterian Church, Kenansville, N. C., bicentennial celebration, Nov. 29, 1936. No place, Author [1936?] [1] p. [10326

——The historical background of Duplin County, North Carolina. [Kenansville,
Author, 1948?] [1] p.   [10327

Outlaw, Albert Timothy, comp. Official directory of Duplin County, North Carolina, 1749-1935. [Kenansville? Author, 1935] 16 p.   [10328

Outlaw, Albert Timothy. Outlaw genealogy, including English records. Wilson,
P. D. Gold Publishing Co., c.1930. 71 p.   [10329

Outlaw, Edward Ralph. Old Nag's Head; personal recollections and some history
of the region. [Elizabeth City? 1952] Unpaged.   [10330

Outrages in North Carolina, no. 1- 1870- No place, no publisher, 1870- NcU
has no. 2-4   [10331

Outreach; organ of the Southern Industrial Institute, v. 1- November, 1911-
Charlotte, The Institute, 1911- NcU has v. 1, no. 1   [10332

Outterson, Leslie A. Unto the hills, a novel. New York, Vantage Press [1950]
216 p.   [10333

Overdyke, William Darrell. The Know-Nothing Party in the South. [Baton
Rouge] Louisiana State University Press [c.1950] 322 p.   [10334

Overman, Lee Slater. Vote for Overman, congressional record of Lee S. Overman,
candidate for United States senator. Washington [1928?] 8 p.   [10335

—— ——Raleigh [1926] 8 p.   [10336

Owen, John. Trial of John Owen, charged with the murder of Patrick Conway . . .
1810. Raleigh, Printed by Thomas Henderson, Jr., 1810. 28 p.   [10337

Owen, Mary Barrow, ed. Old Salem, North Carolina. . . . Sponsored by the Garden
Club of North Carolina. [Winston-Salem, Lithographed by Winston Printing Co.,
c.1941] 173 p.   [10338

Owen, R. Blinn. Hail to our boys in France; a patriotic song by R. Blinn Owen,
words by Aline Hughes. Written in 1918 for the chorus class of St. Mary's School.
No place, no publisher, n.d. 2 p.   [10339

Owen, Richard. Report of a geological examination, made on certain lands and
mines, in the counties of Haywood, Madison, Buncombe, Jackson, and Macon,
N. C., and in Cocke county, Tennessee. Indianapolis, Indianapolis Printing and
Publishing House, 1869. 19 p.   [10340

Owens, Hamilton. Practical problems of making a newspaper; an address delivered
at the Newspaper Institute at Chapel Hill, Jan. 13-15, 1926. No place, no publisher [1926] 7 p.   [10341

Owens, Robert Bruce. Christ church, Rowan County; an historical sketch. [Char-
lotte, Presbyterian Standard, 1921] 20 p.   [10342

—— ——Charlotte [1942] 24 p.   [10343

Ownbey, Richard L. The Christian's religion, its meaning and mission. Nashville,
Tenn., Cokesbury Press [c.1932] 178 p.   [10344

——A Christian and his money. Nashville, Abingdon-Cokesbury Press [1947] 124 p.   [10345

——Evangelism in Christian education. Nashville, Tenn., Abingdon-Cokesbury Press [c.1941]   160 p.   [10346

Owsley, Frank Lawrence.   Plain folk of the Old South.   [Baton Rouge] Louisiana State University Press, 1949.   235 p.   [10347

——State rights in the Confederacy.   Chicago, Ill., University of Chicago Press [c.1925]   289 p.   [10348

Oxford, N. C.   Board of Commissioners.   Charter and ordinances of the town of Oxford . . . ordinances revised and adopted . . . March 1901.   [Oxford? 1901?] 33 p.   [10349

——Charter, ordinances, and franchises of the town of Oxford, North Carolina . . . in effect on and after May 13, 1913.   Oxford, Oxford Orphan Asylum [1913?] 151 p.   [10350

——Contract for system of water works and electric lights in Oxford, N. C.   [Oxford? 1904]   [18] p.   [10351

——Notice . . . Resolution . . . adopted by the Board of Commissioners . . . on the 18th day of January, 1917.   [Oxford, 1917]   [1] p.   [10352

[Oxford, N. C.   Board of Commissioners]   Ordinances of the town of Oxford relating to water closets and dry closets, adopted August 15, 1911.   [Oxford, 1911] [3] p.   [10353

——Sanitary ordinances of the town of Oxford, N. C.   [Oxford, Oxford Orphan Asylum] n.d.   16 p.   [10354

Oxford, N. C.   Chamber of Commerce.   "All about" Oxford, Granville County, N. C.   [Lynchburg, Va., J. P. Bell Co., pr.] n.d.   [8] p.   [10355

Oxford, N. C.   Granville County Court House Centennial Committee.   1840-1940 . . . souvenir program, Oxford . . . June 30, 1940.   [Oxford? 1940]   23 p.   [10356

Oxford, N. C.   Junior Chamber of Commerce.   Oxford, North Carolina, live wire town with progress on its mind.   [Oxford] 1953.   [27] p.   [10357

Oxford, N. C.   Library.   Catalogue of books in the Oxford Library.   [Oxford?] 1911.   [9] p.   [10358

Oxford, N. C.   Villeford Club.   The Villeford Club, by-laws and house rules, incorporated March 9, 1905.   Oxford, Public Ledger, pr., 1905.   [10] p.   [10359

Oxford, N. C.   Woman's Club.   The Woman's Club, 190 -   Oxford, 190 -   NcU has 1907/08, 1912/13, 1916/17 [1927/28-1940/41]   [10360

Oxford, N. C.   Woman's Club.   Literature and Library Extension Department. Two hundred tested recipes.   [Oxford? 1920.   91 p.   [10361

Oxford College, Oxford, N. C.   Catalogue, 185 -   Oxford, 185 -   NcU has 1860/61, [1903/04-1923/24]   [10362

Oxford, county seat of Granville County, North Carolina.   [Oxford? 1913?] [3] p.   [10363

Oxford Land, Improvement, and Manufacturing Company, Oxford, N. C.   Prospectus.   Raleigh, E. M. Uzzell, pr. [1890]   6 p.   [10364

Oxford literary and educational monthly, v. 1-   August, 1881-   Oxford, J. C. Horner and J. H. Mills, 1881-   NcU has v. [1]   [10365

Oxford Orphanage, Oxford, N. C.   Annual report to the Grand Lodge of North Carolina, A. F. & A. M., 18   -   18   -   NcU has 1914-1945   Called Oxford Orphan Asylum, 18   -   1922   [10366

——Orphan Asylum, Oxford, N. C.   [Oxford?] n.d.   4 p.   [10367

——Pictorial history.   [Oxford, 1922]   unpaged   [10368

The P & N and D & S magazine; a monthly magazine . . . of the employees of the Piedmont & Northern Railway and the Durham & Southern Railway, v. 1-   1945- Charlotte, 1945-   NcU has v. 1-12.   Title varies: Semaphore   [10369

Pace, E. M.   Leaf tobacco; how to grow it, and . . . make it pay.   Raleigh, Raleigh Tobacco Association, 1902.   19 p.   [10370

——. . . Tobacco, how to grow it, and . . . make it pay.   New Bern, New Bern Tobacco Warehouse Co., n.d.   19 p.   [10371

——Wilson has advantages over all competitors for high prices in selling tobacco and country produce.   Raleigh, Edwards & Broughton, pr., 1906.   15 p.   [10372

Padgett, Dora A., comp.   The Howard family of Ocracoke Island, N. C.   Washington, Compiler [1955?]   41 p.   [10373
Page, Abraham, pseud.   see Holt, John Saunders
Page, Dorothy Myra.   Gathering storm; a story of the black belt.   New York, International Publishers, 1932.   374 p.   [10374
——Southern cotton mills and labor.   New York, Workers Library Publishers [c.1929]   96 p.   [10375
Page, Frank.   Profits earned by the highways of North Carolina . . . address at the annual meeting, Vermont State Chamber of Commerce, Rutland, Vermont, June 8, 1928.   [Chicago, Portland Cement Assn., 1928]   [5] p.   [10376
Page G. G.   Battle of Kings Mountain, fought Oct. 7, 1780.   Kings Mountain, Herald Publishing House, 1926.   32 p.   [10377
—— ——3d ed., rev. and enl.   1929.   [28] p.   [10378
——Battle of Moore's Creek Bridge.   Kings Mountain, Herald Publishing House, n.d.   9 p.   [10379
——Page's perfect spelling tablet.   Maxton, Author, n.d.   Unpaged.   [10380
——A patriotic address to the Shelby Kiwanis Club at Cleveland Springs Hotel, Oct. 7, 1926 . . . the 146th anniversary of the Battle of Kings Mountain.   No place, no publisher [1926]   7 p.   [10381
Page, Gertrude Cook.   Illusion, and other poems.   Richmond, Va., Dietz Press, 1940.   85 p.   [10382
Page, Harlan.   Motives to early piety.   [Raleigh, General Tract Agency, June, 1861]   (Selected for the soldiers.   No. 322)   4 p.   [10383
Page, Henry Allison.   Some campaign letters.   No place, no publisher [1902] 84 p.   [10384
Page, Hubbard Fulton.   Lyrics and legends of the Cape Fear country.   [Durham, Christian Printing Co.] 1932.   163 p.   [10385
Page, Myra   see Page, Dorothy Myra
Page, Ralph Walter.   Philadelphia's first surplus; address before the Democratic women's luncheon club, the Republican women's luncheon club and the Economy league of Pennsylvania.   [Philadelphia, no publisher] 1941.   9 p.   [10386
Page, Robert Newton.   Demonstration vs. theory; why spend . . . on experiment when public terminals . . . at South Atlantic and Gulf ports have no effect on railroad freight rates?   [Raleigh, Mitchell Printing Co., 1924]   14 p.   [10387
Page, Walter Hines.   A publisher's confession.   New ed.   Garden City, N. Y., Doubleday, Page & Co., 1923.   245 p.   [10388
—— ——1924.   [10389
——The rebuilding of old commonwealths.   New York, Doubleday, Page & Co., 1902.   153 p.   [10390
—— ——1905.   [10391
—— ——1926.   [10392
——The school that built a town.   New York, Harper & Brothers [1952]   109 p. Originally published under the title, The rebuilding of old commonwealths. [10393
[Page, Walter Hines]   The southerner, a novel; being the autobiography of Nicholas Worth [pseud.]   New York, Doubleday, Page & Co., 1909.   424 p.   [10394
Page, Walter Hines.   Union of two great peoples; a speech delivered at Plymouth, Aug. 4th, 1917.   London, Hodder and Stoughton, 1917.   15 p.   [10395
——Walter H. Page's Christmas letter to his grandson.   Garden City, N. Y., Doubleday, Page & Co., 1924.   9 p.   [10396
A pageant of the lower Cape Fear, written in collaboration by citizens of Wilmington in North Carolina, with the supervision of Frederick Henry Koch.   Wilmington, Wilmington Printing Co. [1921]   130 p.   [10397
Pahlow, Gertrude.   Cabin in the pines.   Philadelphia, Penn Publishing Co. [c.1935] 316 p.   [10398
Paine, Dorothy C.   A maid of the mountains.   Philadelphia, G. W. Jacobs & Co. [1906]   348 p.   [10399
Paine, Gregory Lansing, ed.   Southern prose writers; representative selections. New York, American Book Co. [1947]   392 p.   [10400

Paine, Robert. Life and times of William M'Kendree, bishop of the Methodist Episcopal Church. Nashville, Publishing House of the Methodist Episcopal Church, South, 1869-1870. 2 v. [10401

Painter, Charles Cornelius Coffin. The Eastern Cherokees. Philadelphia, Indian Rights Association [1888] 16 p. [10402

Paisley, John Walter. The voice of Mizraim [poems] New York, Neale Publishing Co., 1907. 122 p. [10403

Palairet, Jean. Description abrégée des possessions angloises et françoises du continent septentrional de l'Amérique. Londres, J. Nourse, 1755. 62 p. [10404

Palmer, Abraham John. The history of the Forty-eighth Regiment New York State Volunteers, in the war for the union. Brooklyn, Pub. by the Veteran Association of the Regiment, 1885. 314 p. [10405

Palmer, B. W., comp. Land titles of the Swan Island Club, Inc. No place, privately printed by Geo. H. Ellis Co., 1929. 36 p. [10406

Palmer, Benjamin Morgan. Baconism and the Bible; an address delivered before the Eumenean and Philanthropic societies of Davidson College, N. C., Aug. 11, 1852. Columbia, S. C., Printed by A. S. Johnston, 1852. 31 p. [10407

——Christianity, the only religion for man; a discourse delivered before the graduating class of the University of N. C., June 4, 1855. Raleigh, Carolina Cultivator, 1855. 41 p. [10408

Palmer, Jude. Homestead. North Montpelier, Vt., Driftwind Press, 1942. 44 p. [10409

——Oroondale, verses reminiscent of an old homestead, by Sabra Palmer. Hutchings, Martin Chesley, Jude Palmer. North Montpelier, Vt., Driftwind Press, 1943. 78 p. [10410

[Palmer, Jude] Stray blooms that fall into a wreath. [Montpelier, Vt.] Driftwind Press, 1945. 64 p. [10411

Palmer, Katherine Stedman. The fat frog of Pau. New York, Neale Publishing Co., 1919. 26 p. [10412

Palmer, Theodore Sherman. Some possibilities of game protection in North Carolina ... History of game protection in North Carolina, by Judge Francis D. Winston; addresses delivered at the annual meeting of the Audubon Society of N. C. ... Greensboro, N. C., March 12, 1904. Greensboro, J. M. Reece & Co., pr. [1904] 19 p. [10413

Palmer Memorial Institute, Sedalia, N. C. Catalogue, 19 - Sedalia, 19 - NcU has 1919/20, 1930/31, 1937/38, 1940/41 [10414

Pamlico Baptist Association. Minutes, 1932- 1932- NcU has 1932-1936 [10415

Pamlico, Oriental and Western Railroad Co. First mortgage five per cent thirty years gold bonds, $550,000 to Knickerbocker Trust Company of New York City, trustee, dated July 1, 1903. No place, 1903. 30 p. [10416

Pape, Charles O. Chapel Hill quick step. Baltimore, George Willig, c.1866. 5 p. [10417

"Paramount issues"; Democrats invent a new one every four years to save the endangered republic—Parallel of 1864 and 1890. [St. Paul] no publisher [1900] 4 p. [10418

Parapsychology bulletin, no. 1- March, 1946- Durham, Duke University, 1946- NcU has no. 1-40 [10419

Paris, John. A sermon preached before Brig. Gen. Hoke's brigade, at Kinston, N. C., on the 28th of February, 1864, by ... chaplain Fifty-fourth Regiment, N. C. Troops, upon the death of twenty-two men ... executed ... for the crime of desertion. Greensborough, A. W. Ingold & Co., 1864. 15 p. [10420

Parish news letter, v. 1- Sept. 12, 1953- Salisbury, St. Luke's Episcopal Church, 1953- NcU has v. 1-2 [10421

Park, Herbert W. Physical education. Greensboro, Public Schools, 1923. 3 v. in 1. [10422

Park, James. History of the First Presbyterian Church in Knoxville, Tenn.; a discourse before the congregation ... July 2, 1876. Knoxville, Ramage & Co., pr., 1876. 29 p. [10423

Park, Roy H., comp. Going forward together; the story of the cotton association and the FCX. [Raleigh] North Carolina Cotton Growers Cooperative Association [1939?] 16 p. [10424

Park to park annual see Eastern national park to park guide

Parker, Alton Brooks. Address before the State Bar Association of North Carolina at Hendersonville, Thursday, July 11th, 1907. No place [1907?] 35 p. [10425

[**Parker, Annie (Moore)**] Just a kind memento, by Grandma, Dec. 25, 1910. Raleigh, Commercial Printing Co., 1910. 210 p. [10426

Parker, Coralie. History of taxation in North Carolina during the colonial period, 1663-1776. New York, Columbia University Press, 1928. 178 p. [10426a

Parker, Donald Dean. Local history; how to gather it, write it, and publish it. Rev. and ed. by Bertha E. Josephson. No place, no publisher [1944] 186 p. [10427

Parker, Haywood. Folklore of the North Carolina mountaineer . . . A paper read before the Pen and Plate Club, Asheville, N. C., 1906. [Asheville, 1906?] 12 p. [10428

——The mission schools of the Missionary District of Asheville . . . A report made to the convention at Morganton, 1908. Asheville, Hackney & Moale Co. [1908?] 11 p. [10429

——Recollections and observations of the Reconstruction era. [Asheville? Author] n.d. 16 p. [10430

Parker, James B. Poetic scene of McKinley, by James B. Parker and Leon Czolgosz. [Charlotte] Observer Printing House, c.1902. 12 p. [10431

Parker, James Peele. Hemlock twigs and balsam sprigs. [Black Mountain] Black Mountain Printery [c.1921] 31 p. [10432

Parker, John Johnston. Address . . . before the Bar Association of the city of Richmond, at Richmond, Virginia, on October 25, 1946. [Richmond, Lawyers Publishing Co., Inc., 1946?] 16 p. [10433

——. . . Democracy in government. Charlottesville, Va., The Michie Co., 1940. 116 p. [10434

——Is the constitution passing? Address before the American Bar Association at Grand Rapids, Michigan, August 30, 1933. No place, no publisher, 1933. 16 p. [10435

[**Parker, John Johnston**] To the members of the General Assembly of North Carolina. [Monroe, Author, 1920] 3 p. [10436

Parker, John William. The pageant of education; in celebration of the hundredth anniversary of the beginning of public education in North Carolina . . . the Hillside Theatre, Western Carolina Teachers College. Cullowhee, Western Carolina Teachers College, 1936. 47 p. [10437

[**Parker, Joseph Roy**] ed. The Ahoskie era of Hertford County. Ahoskie, Parker Brothers, Inc. [c.1939] 751 p. [10438

Parker, Joseph Roy, Jr. Index to Colonial and state political history of Hertford County, N. C., by Judge Benjamin Brodie Winborne, Murfreesboro, N. C., 1906. Windsor, 1956. [28] p. [10439

Parker, Junius. The increasing governmental powers and activities; address . . . at the twenty-third annual session of the North Carolina Bar Association. Charlotte, July 6, 1921. 17 p. [10440

——Memorial address, delivered before the Supreme Court of North Carolina, Raleigh, N. C., December 10, 1935. [New York? Author, 1936?] 12 p. [10441

Parker, Marian. Mountain mating. New York, Pageant Press [1954] 344 p. [10442

Parker, Roscoe Edward, ed. The Middle English stanzaic versions of the life of Saint Anne. London, Pub. for the Early English Text Society by H. Milford, 1928. (Early English text society. Original series, no. 174. 1928 [for 1927]) 139 p. [10443

Parker, T. B. Address to North Carolina Tobacco Growers Association. [Raleigh? 1900?] 3 p. [10444

——Catalogue . . . high-grade buggies, road wagons, surreys, farm wagons, barouches, road carts, phaetons, 1st- 18 - Hillsboro, 18 - NcU has 1898 (25th) [10445

Parker, Thomas Valentine. The Cherokee Indians. New York, The Grafton Press [c.1907] 116 p. [10446

Parker, William Harwar. Recollections of a naval officer, 1841-1865. New York, C. Scribners' [!] Sons, 1883. 372 p. [10447

Parker, Willis A. Our friendly neighbors. [Asheville, Stephens Press, c.1945] [27] p. [10448

Parker, Wixie E., ed. A checklist of scientific periodicals and of selected serials in the libraries of Duke University, North Carolina State College, the University of North Carolina, and the Woman's College of the University of North Carolina. Durham [Duke University Library] 1954. 385 p. [10449

Parker-Hunter Realty Co., Raleigh, N. C. Cameron Park, its purpose, its attainments, and its future outlook, 1910-14. [Raleigh, Edwards & Broughton Printing Co., 1914?] 11 p. [10450

Parkhurst, Varanus P., defendant. Proceedings of a court of inquiry in regard to reports made by Maj. M. J. McCafferty and others, of misconduct at the Battle of Roanoke Island, February 8, 1862, by Capt. V. P. Parkhurst. Fitchburg, Curtis and Bushnell, pr., 1864. 55 p. [10451

Parkins, Almon Ernest. The South, its economic-geographic development. New York, J. Wiley & Sons, Inc., 1938. 528 p. [10452

Parkins, Maurice Frank. City planning in Soviet Russia, with an interpretative bibliography. [Chicago] University of Chicago Press [1953] 257 p. [10453

Parks, George Bruner. . . . Richard Hakluyt and the English voyages. New York, American Geographical Society, 1928. (American Geographical Society. Special publication no. 10) 289 p. [10454

Parr, D. Preston, Jr. . . . A lecture delivered under the auspices of the Thompson Orphanage guild, Tarboro, Dec. 1889. No place, no publisher [1889?] 14 p. [10455

Parris, John A. The Cherokee story. Asheville, Stephens Press, c.1950. 122 p. [10456

——Oconaluftee. Cherokee, Cherokee Historical Association, c.1954. 6 p. [10457

——Roaming the mountains with John Parris. Asheville, Citizen-Times Pub. Co., 1955. 246 p. [10458

——. . . Springboard to Berlin. New York, Thomas Y. Crowell Co., 1943. 401 p. [10459

Parrish, Dillwyn. Hung for a song; a novel of the lives . . . of Major Stede Bonnet and Blackbeard the pirate. New York, Farrar & Rinehart [c.1934] 279 p. [10460

Parrish, John. Remarks on the slavery of the black people, addressed to the citizens of the U. S. Philadelphia, Kimber, Conrad & Co. for the Author, 1806. 66 p. [10461

Parson, Donald. Surely the author. Boston, Mass., J. W. Luce & Co., 1944. 64 p. [10462

Parsons, Brinckerhoff, Hall and Macdonald, Engineers, New York. An engineering and fiscal study of North Carolina's highways. New York, 1954. 123 p. [10463

——Survey and report on the inland ports and waterways of North Carolina. New York, 1954. Various paging. [10464

Parton, James. Life of Andrew Jackson. New York, Mason Brothers, 1860. 3 v. [10465

Paschal, George Washington. History of North Carolina Baptists. Raleigh, General Board, North Carolina Baptist State Convention, 1930-1955. 2 v. [10466

——A history of printing in North Carolina; a detailed account of the pioneer printers, 1749-1800, and of the Edwards & Broughton Company, 1871-1946. Raleigh, Edwards & Broughton Co., 1946. 313 p. [10467

——History of Wake Forest College. Wake Forest, Wake Forest College, 1935-1943. 3 v. [10468

——. . . A study of Quintus of Smyrna. Chicago, 1904. 82 p. Thesis (Ph.D.)—University of Chicago, 1900. [10469

Paschal, Herbert Richard. A history of colonial Bath. Raleigh, Edwards & Broughton Co. [for] The Committee on the Two Hundred and Fiftieth Anniversary, 1955. 69 p. [10470

Paschal, Joel Francis. Mr. Justice Sutherland, a man against the state. Princeton, Princeton University Press, 1951. 267 p. [10471

[**Pascoe, Charles Frederick**] comp. Classified digest of the records of the Society for the Propagation of the Gospel in Foreign Parts, 1701-1892. London, Pub. at the Society's Office, 1893. 980 p. [10472

Pascoe, Charles Frederick.   Two hundred years of the S. P. G.: an historical account of the Society for the Propagation of the Gospel . . . 1701-1900.   London, Pub. at the Society's Office, 1901.   2 v.   [10473

Pasquotank Historical Society, Elizabeth City, N. C.   Yearbook, 1954-1955-   [Elizabeth City, 1955-   NcU has 1954-1955   [10474

Pastoral hints on a few points of order and doctrine for the parishioners of St. John's Church, Rutherfordton, N. C.   No place, no publisher, n.d.   12 p.   [10475

Paterson, James H.   History of the North Carolina head camp, Woodmen of the World, 1909-1935.   [Charlotte? 1936?]   87 p.   [10476

Patrick, Clarence Hodges.   Alcohol, culture, and society.   Durham, Duke University Press, 1952.   (Duke University Press sociological series [no. 8]) 176 p. [10477

Patrick, Rembert Wallace.   Jefferson Davis and his cabinet.   Baton Rouge, Louisiana State University Press, 1944.   401 p.   [10478

Patrick Livingston Murphy, M. D., 1848-1907; presentation of a portrait to the State Library, Raleigh, N. C. and a tablet to the State Hospital, Morganton, N. C.   Raleigh, Edwards & Broughton Co., 1915.   32 p.   [10479

The patriots of the Revolution of '76.   Boston, G. W. Tomlinson, 1864.   20 p. [10480

Patten, Marjorie.   The arts workshop of rural America; a study of the rural arts program of the Agricultural Extension Service.   New York, Columbia University Press, 1937.   202 p.   [10481

Patterson, Lindsay.   North Carolina's contribution to the law; an address before the Law School of the University of Indiana, at Bloomington . . . May 7, 1906. [Charlotte, Observer, 1906]   26 p.   [10482

Patterson, Rebecca.   The riddle of Emily Dickinson.   Boston, Houghton Mifflin, 1951.   434 p.   [10483

Patterson, Robert Leet.   Irrationalism and rationalism in religion.   Durham, Duke University Press, 1954.   155 p.   [10484

——The philosophy of William Ellery Channing.   New York, Bookman Associates [1952]   298 p.   [10485

Patterson, Rufus Lenoir, tr.   A literal translation of Demosthenes On the crown, translated from the Greek, by James Chalmers, . . . revised and corrected from his manuscript, by F. S. Goode and R. L. Patterson, Chapel Hill, N. C.   New York, Printed for the Authors, 1849.   81 p.   [10486

Patterson School, Legerwood, N. C.   Announcement, 19 - 19 - NcU has 1921/ 22, 1931/32   [10487

[Patterson School, Legerwood, N. C.]   The Patterson school, Legerwood, N. C., a southern school that gives poor boys a chance.   [Lenoir, News, 1914?]   16 p. [10488

——Patterson school, Legerwood rural station, Lenoir, North Carolina.   [Lenoir] n.d.   [16] p.   [10489

Patterson school news, v. 1- 191 - Legerwood, 191 - NcU has v. [19-22]   [10489a

Pattillo, Henry.   A geographical catechism, to assist those who have neither maps nor gazetteers.   Halifax, Printed by Abraham Hodge, 1796.   62 p.   [10490

—— ——Chapel Hill, The University Press, 1909.   (University reprints, no. 1) 62 p.   [10491

——The plain planter's family assistant.   Wilmington [Del.] James Adams, pr., 1787.   63 p.   NcU has microfilm (negative)   [10492

——Sermons, &c.   Wilmington [Del.] Printed by James Adams for the Author, 1788. 295 p.   [10493

Patton, Frances (Gray)   The finer things of life.   New York, Dodd, Mead [1951] 248 p.   [10494

——Good morning, Miss Dove.   New York, Dodd, Mead [1954]   218 p.   [10495

—— ——New York, Pocket Books, Inc. [1956]   165 p.   [10496

—— ——London, Victor Gollancz, Ltd., 1956.   217 p.   [10497

——A piece of luck.   New York, Dodd, Mead [1955]   248 p.   [10498

Patton, James.   Biography of James Patton.   [Asheville, c.1850]   34 p.   [10499

——Letter of James Patton . . . to his children.   No place, no publisher, 1930. 38 p.   [10500

Patton, James Welch.   Unionism and reconstruction in Tennessee, 1860-1869. Chapel Hill, University of North Carolina Press, 1934.   267 p   [10501

Patton, James Welch, joint author, see Simkins, Francis Butler

Patton, Robert Logan. Law of Christian giving. Shelby, Cleveland Star, 1898. 18 p. [10502

Patton, Robert Williams. An inspiring record in Negro education; historical summary of the work of the American Church Institute for Negroes . . . February 14, 1940. New York, National Council, Protestant Episcopal Church [1940?] 19 p. [10503

Patton, Sadie (Smathers) Buncombe to Mecklenburg: speculation lands. Forest City, Western North Carolina Historical Association, 1955. 47 p. [10504

——Ghost stories and legends of the mountains. Hendersonville, Blue Ridge Specialty, pr., 1935. 48 p. [10505

——Saint James Episcopal Church, Hendersonville, N. C. . . . 1843-1950. [Hendersonville] Western North Carolina Historical Association [1953?] 34 p. [10506

——A sketch of Flat Rock. Flat Rock, Vagabond School of the Drama, Inc., n.d. [2] p. [10507

——Sketches of Polk County history. [Hendersonville?] 1950. 161 p. [10508

——Smathers from Yadkin Valley to Pigeon River; Smathers and Agner families. Hendersonville, 1954. 56 p. [10509

——The story of Henderson County. Asheville, Miller Printing Co. [1947] 290 p. [10510

Patton, Thomas Walton. European letters to the Asheville Citizen; description of the tour of the North Carolina teachers during the summer of 1889. Asheville, Citizen, 1889. 68 p. [10511

Patty, John C. Life of Lucius Bunyan Compton, the mountain evangelist. Cincinnati, Revivalist Press [c.1914] 307 p. [10512

Pau, Charlotte see Alford, Mrs. Alexander Eccles Bryan

Paul, Hiram Voss. History of the town of Durham, N. C. Raleigh, Edwards, Broughton & Co., 1884. 256 p. [10513

—— ——2d ed. Durham, Author, 1884. 138 p. [10514

Paxton, Thomas. List of roses, grape vines, shrubs, &c. for sale by Thomas Paxton, florist, Chapel Hill, N. C., 18 - No place, 18 - NcU has Fall of 1860 and Spring of 1861 (as one) [10515

Payne, Anne Blackwell. Released; a book of verse. Chapel Hill, University of North Carolina Press, 1930. 63 p. [10516

Payne, Bruce Ryburn. Common words commonly misspelled. Richmond, B. F. Johnson Publishing Co. [c.1910] 121 p. [10517

——Public elementary school curricula. New York [Silver, Burdett and Co.] 1905. 200 p. [10518

Payne, Bruce Ryburn, joint ed. see Mims, Edwin, ed.

Payne, Emma Hawkins. A winter garden of verse. Dallas, Tex., The Kaleidograph Press [1939] 265 p. [10519

Payne, Henry Mace. Report on property of the Black Ankle Mining Corporation lying in Montgomery County, North Carolina. Washington, D. C., January, 1933. 19 p. [10520

——The undeveloped mineral resources of the South. Washington, D. C., American Mining Congress, 1928. 368 p. [10521

Payson, William Farquhar. John Vytal, a tale of the lost colony. New York, Harper & Bros., 1901. 318 p. [10522

Payton, Mildred Bright. Lay o' the land. [Siler City? 1953?] [20] p. [10523

Peabody Conference on Dual Education in the South. Education and racial adjustment. Atlanta, Executive Committee of the Conference [1931] 78 p. [10524

Peabody Education Fund. . . . Proceedings of the Trustees at their . . . meeting, [1st]-60th; [1867]-1914. Cambridge [1869?]-1914. NcU has 1st-21st, 1867-1882; 24th, 1885; 26th-60th, 1887-1914 [10525

Peace, Mary Emma. Darky days in Dixie, colorful sayings of old-time Negroes of the deep South. San Antonio, Tex., The Naylor Co., 1941. 38 p. [10526

Peace, Samuel Thomas. Christmas greetings, 1932- No place, 1932- NcU has 1932-1954 [10527

——Leaves of leisure. Raleigh, Edwards and Broughton, 1931. 47 p. [10528

——"Zeb's black baby", Vance county, North Carolina; a short history. Henderson, 1955. 457 p. [10529

Peace, William. Memorial of William Peace to the legislature of North-Carolina. [Raleigh? 185?] 3 p. [10530

Peace College, Raleigh, N. C. Catalog, 18 - Raleigh, 18 - NcU has [1872/73-1909/10] 1913/14-1950/51, 1952/53-1955/56 [10531
——A pageant of the history of the College, 1872-1947. Raleigh, 1947. [23] p. [10532

Peace College, Raleigh, N. C. Alumnae Association. Constitution and by-laws. Raleigh, 1918. 11 p. [10533

Peace Institute for Young Women; book of views. [Raleigh, Peace Institute, 1927?] [11] p. [10534

Peace institute, Raleigh, North Carolina. [Raleigh, Peace Institute] n.d. Folder [10535

Peach blossom, v. 1- August, 1923- Pinehurst, Peach Blossom Publishing Co., 1923- NcU has v. [1] [10536

[Peacock, Dred] In memoriam, William Henry Branson, born May 23, 1860, died March 24, 1899. [Greensboro, Printed by Joseph J. Stone, pref. 1899] 112 p. [10537

Peake, Elmore Elliott. The Darlingtons. New York, McClure, Phillips & Co., 1900. 416 p. [10538

Pearce, J. J. Pearce cotton; awarded a medal at the last fair of the Cape Fear Agricultural Society. [Hilliardston, Nash Co., 1874] [1] p. [10539

Pearce, J. Winston. I believe. Nashville, Broadman Press [1954] 120 p. [10540

Pearsall, Alfred W. Some pleasant recollections of a winter spent in the sunny South. Huntington, N. Y., Author, c.1925. 58 p. [10541

Pearsall, Clarence Eugene, ed. History and genealogy of the Pearsall family in England and America. [San Francisco, Printed by H. S. Crocker Co., Inc.] 1928. 3 v. [10542

Pearsall, Thomas Jenkins. Speech before State School Board Association, Chapel Hill, North Carolina, November 18th [1955] [Chapel Hill, 1955] 9 p. [10543

Pearse, Arthur Sperry. Animal ecology. 2d ed. New York, McGraw-Hill Book Co., Inc., 1939. 642 p. [10544
——The emigrations of animals from the sea. Dryden, N. Y., Sherwood Press [1950] 210 p. [10545
——Hell's bells. Durham, Seeman Printery, Inc., 1941. 121 p. [10546
—— ——No place, no publisher, n.d. 4 p. Corresponds to chapter 5 of the book of this title. [10547
——The migrations of animals from sea to land. Durham, Duke University Press, 1936. 176 p. [10548

Pearson, Charles Chilton. The readjuster movement in Virginia. New Haven, Yale University Press, 1917. (Yale historical publications. Miscellany, IV) 191 p. [10549

Pearson, Cora Wallace. Bluets and buttercups. No place, no publisher, n.d. 24 p. [10550

Pearson, James Larkin. Autobiographical sketch. No place, no publisher, n.d. 20 p. [10551
——Castle gates (a book of poems) Moravian Falls, Pearson Printing Co., 1908. 108 p. [10552
——Early harvest. Guilford College, Pearson Publishing Co. ,1952. 104 p. [10553
——Early poems. Moravian Falls, Pearson Bros., 1903. 28 p. [10554
——Fifty acres, and other poems. Wilkesboro, Pearson Publishing Co., 1933. 44 p. [10555
—— ——1937. 88 p. [10556
——Pearson's poems. Moravian Falls, Pearson Bros., 1906. 42 p. [10557
——Pearson's poems. Boomer, The Author, 1924. 374 p. [10558
——Pilgrimage to Mount Vernon. Moravian Falls, Pearson Bros., 1905. 31 p. [10559
——Plowed ground, humorous and dialect poems. Guilford College, Pearson Publishing Co., 1949. 96 p. [10560

Pearson, Jesse A. Fellow citizens. No place, no publisher [1816] [1] p. [10561
——Fellow citizens. No place, no publisher [1816] [1] p. [10562

[Pearson, Joseph] Circular. Washington, no publisher, 1815. 16 p. [10563

[Pearson, Richmond] Actual condition and prospects of the North Carolina State Life Insurance Company, discussed by a stockholder. No place, no publisher, n.d. 13 p. [10564

Pearson, Richmond. Buncombe County stock law. No place, no publisher [188?] 15 p. [10565

[Pearson, Richmond] Town against the country; Pearson stands by the country people. No place, no publisher [188?] 2 p. [10566

Pearson, Richmond Mumford. Law lectures. Raleigh, Edwards, Broughton & Co., 1879. 523 p. [10567

——R. M. Pearson's circular. [Salisbury] no publisher [1835] 8 p. [10568

Pearson, Thomas Gilbert. Adventures in bird protection; an autobiography. New York, D. Appleton-Century Co., Inc., 1937. 459 p. [10569

——The bird study book. Garden City, Doubleday, 1917. 258 p. [10570

——International cooperation for bird preservation. [New York, International Committee for Bird Preservation, 1938?] 5 p. [10571

——Notes on wildlife protection in Chile. New York, International Committee for Bird Preservation [1940] [6] p. [10572

——Stories of bird life. Richmond, B. F. Johnson Publishing Co., 1901. 236 p. [10573

——Tales from birdland. Garden City, N. Y., Doubleday, Page & Co., 1920. 237 p. [10574

——Where game laws are needed. New York, International Committee for Bird Preservation, 1938. [8] p. [10575

[Pearson, William Simpson] Memoir of Joseph J. Erwin of Bellevue, Burke county, North Carolina. Statesville, Landmark, 1880. 14 p. [10576

——Monon ou; or, Well-nigh reconstructed; a political novel, by Brinsley Matthews [pseud.] New York, E. J. Hale & Son, 1882. 279 p. [10577

Peattie, Donald Culross. Journey into America. Boston, Houghton Mifflin Co., 1943. 276 p. [10578

——A natural history of Pearson's Falls, and some of its human associations. Tryon, [Garden Club] n.d. 66 p. [10579

Peattie, Elia (Wilkinson) Annie Laurie and Azalea. Chicago, Reilly & Britton Co. [c.1913] 295 p. [10580

——Azalea; the story of a girl in the Blue Ridge Mountains. Chicago, Reilly & Britton Co. [c.1912] [10581

Peattie, Roderick, ed. The Great Smokies and the Blue Ridge. New York, Vanguard Press [1943] 372 p. [10582

Peck, Charles Henry. The Jacksonian epoch. New York, Harper and Brothers, 1899. 472 p. [10583

Peckham, Harry Houston. Fancy's guest, and other verses. [Raleigh? Author?] c.1911. 23 p. [10584

Peco contact, v. 1- September, 1918- Asheville, Piedmont Electric Co., 1918- NcU has v. [1-] [10585

Pee Dee Baptist Association. Minutes, 181 - 181 - NcU has [1848-1888] 1929- 1955 [10586

Peele, Herbert. Mr. Albemarle; some quotations from Herbert Peele's editorials and Peelings; compiled by his wife, Kate. Winston-Salem, Collins Co. [1955] 205 p. [10587

Peele, John R. From North Carolina to southern California without a ticket. [Tarboro?] Edwards & Broughton Printing Co., 1907. 134 p. [10588

Peele, William Joseph. Civil government of North Carolina and the United States. Richmond, B. F. Johnson Publishing Co. [c.1907] 279 p. [10589

——Index to the law of exemptions in North Carolina of homestead and personal property. Raleigh, Alfred Williams & Co., 1892. 107 p. [10590

Peele, William Joseph, comp. Lives of distinguished North Carolinians. Raleigh [North Carolina Publishing Society] 1898. 605 p. [10591

Peele, William Joseph. Pen-picture of Wilson Caldwell, colored, late janitor of the University of N. C. No place, no publisher, n.d. 7 p. [10592

Peeler, John W., comp. A record and history of the Peeler family. Charlotte, Queen City Printing Co., 1935. 248 p. [10593

Peery, Beverley DuBose (Hamer) To make men free; a dramatic episode commemorating the Fayetteville Convention of 1789, by Beverley and William Peery. [Chapel Hill? 1939] 33 p.   [10594
——United we stand; a dramatization of North Carolina's entering the Union, by Beverley and William Peery. [Chapel Hill? 1939] 17 p.   [10595

Peet, Harvey Prindle. Address delivered in Commons Hall, at Raleigh, on the occasion of laying the corner stone of the North Carolina Institution for the Instruction of the Deaf and Dumb, April 14th, 1848. New-York, Egbert, Hovey & King, pr., 1848. 47 p.   [10596

Pegg, Carl Hamilton, ed. American society and the changing world. New York, F. S. Crofts & Co., 1942. 601 p.   [10597

Pegg, Carl Hamilton. Contemporary Europe in world focus. New York, Holt [1956] 692 p.   [10598
——Sentiments républicains dans la presse parisienne lors de la fuite du roi. Paris, Mellottée, n.d. 11 p.   [10599

Pegg, J. P. The holly and the oak, and other poems. [Seaboard, Author, 1948?] 42 p.   [10600

Pegram, Sherley. Sherley; book of poems, choice and rare. Richmond, Va., Hermitage Press, 1911. 191 p.   [10601

Pegram, William Howell. A sketch of Randolph County, N. C., showing its resources and possibilites. Greensboro, Thomas, Reece and Co., 1884. 14 p. [10602

Pegues, Albert Witherspoon. Our Baptist ministers and schools. Springfield, Willey & Co., 1892. 622 p.   [10603

Pell, Edward Leigh. The bright side of humanity; glimpses of life in every land. Richmond, Va., B. F. Johnson Publishing Co. [1900] 602 p.   [10604
——Bringing up John. New York, Fleming H. Revell Co. [c.1920] 192 p. [10605
——Dwight L. Moody. Richmond, Va., B. F. Johnson Publishing Co., 1900. 704 p.   [10606
——Secrets of Sunday-School teaching. New York, Fleming H. Revell Co. [c.1912] 201 p.   [10607
——What did Jesus really teach about war? New York, Fleming H. Revell Co. [c.1917] 180 p.   [10608

Pell, George Pierce. Attachment and garnishment. Raleigh, Edwards & Broughton Printing Co., 1918. (Pell's monographs on the law of North Carolina, no. 2) 108 p.   [10609
——. . . Courts of justices of the peace. Raleigh, Edwards & Broughton Printing Co., 1919. (Pell's monographs on the law of North Carolina, no. 3) p. [107]- 189   [10610
——Mechanics' and materialmen's liens on buildings. Raleigh, Capital Printing Co., 1926. (Pell's monographs on the law of North Carolina, no. 6) p. 306- 329.   [10611
——On the law of deeds. Raleigh, Edwards & Broughton Printing Co., 1918. (Pell's monographs on the law of N. C., no. 1) 67 p.   [10612
——Pell's forms of pleading and practice for North Carolina. Cincinnati, O., W. H. Anderson Co., 1912. 926 p.   [10613

[Pell, William E.] comp. The southern Zion's songster. Raleigh, N. C. Christian Advocate Publishing Co., 1864. 128 p.   [10614

Pelley, William Dudley. The door to revelation; an intimate biography. Asheville, The Foundation Fellowship [c.1936] 312 p.   [10615
——Nations-in-law. Asheville, The Author, 1934. 349 p.   [10616

Pell's notes, v. 1- 19 - Richmond, Va., Robert Harding, 19 - NcU has v.11, no. 4, Nov. 1908   [10617

Pelton, Mabell Shippie Clarke. A Tar-Heel baron. Philadelphia, J. B. Lippincott Co., 1903. 354 p.   [10618

Pemberton, Virginia Carroll. Letters from Italy, Switzerland and Germany. Cincinnati, Press of Jennings and Graham [c.1912] 196 p.   [10619

Pen and ink, v. 1- 1942- Raleigh, The Thistle Press, 1942- NcU has v. 1 [10620

Pen and Plate Club, Asheville, N. C. see Asheville, N. C. Pen and Plate Club

Pendexter, Hugh. Red belts. Garden City, N. Y., Doubleday, Page & Co., 1920. 246 p.   [10621

Pendleton, George Hunt. Oration . . . delivered at Charlotte, N. C. at the celebration of the 109th anniversary of the Mecklenburg Declaration of Independence May 20, 1884. Washington, R. O. Polkinhorn & Son, pr., 1884. 8 p. [10622

Pendleton, Louis Beauregard. Corona of the Nantahalas. New York, Merriam Co. [c.1895] 199 p. [10623

Pendleton, Mrs. V. L. Last words of Confederate heroes. Raleigh, Mutual Publishing Co., 1913. 13 p. [10624

Pendray, Edward. Men, mirrors, and stars. New York, Funk & Wagnalls Co., 1935. 339 p. [10625

Penick, P. T. A memorial of Mrs. Robert Bingham, Bingham School, N. C. [Raleigh, Edwards & Broughton] 1886. 24 p. [10626

Penland School of Handicrafts, Inc., Penland, N. C. Mountain milestones. Penland, 1954. 22 p. [10627

——Session, 19 - Penland, 19 - NcU has [1939-1955] [10628

——Weaver's hornbook, tale of what is weaving where [by] Sally Kesler. [Penland, 1949] [42] p. [10629

Penland School of Handicrafts, Inc., Penland, N. C. see also **Appalachian Mountain Community Centre, Penland, N. C.; Appalachian School, Penland, N. C.**

Penn, Irvine Garland. The Afro-American press and its editors. Springfield, Mass., Willey & Co., 1891. 565 p. [10630

Penn, Jefferson. My black mammy. No place, privately printed [c.1942] 58 p. [10631

The Penn family of Virginia. New York, William M. Clemens, 1915. 12 p. [10632

Pennell, Joseph Stanley. The history of Rome Hanks and kindred matters. New York, C. Scribner's Sons, 1944. 363 p. [10633

Pennington, Edgar Legare. . . . The Church of England and the Reverend Clement Hall in colonial North Carolina. Hartford, Conn., Church Missions Publishing Co., 1937. 51 p. [10634

Pennsylvania. Salisbury Memorial Commission. Pennsylvania at Salisbury, North Carolina; ceremonies at the dedication of the memorial . . . of the soldiers of Pennsylvania who perished in the Confederate prison at Salisbury . . . 1864 and 1865. [Harrisburg, C. E. Aughinbaugh, 1912] 70 p. [10635

Pennsylvania Historical and Museum Commission. Daniel Boone homestead, Exeter Township, Berks county, birthplace of Daniel Boone, November 2, 1734. Harrisburg, 1955. Folder. [10636

Pennsylvania Infantry. 121st Regt., 1862-1865. History of the 121st Regiment Pennsylvania Volunteers. Rev. ed. Philadelphia, Pa., Press of Catholic Standard and Times, 1906. 299 p. [10637

Penry, Alice (Armfield) Home spun gems. Winston-Salem, 1931. 80 p. [10638

——Woven threads. Winston-Salem, Clay Printing Co., 1938. 73 p. [10639

Pentecostal Holiness Church. North Carolina Convocation. Minutes, 1895- 1895- NcU has 1918 [10640

Pentecostal Holiness Church. Western North Carolina Conference. Minutes, 19 - 19 - NcU has 1939 [10641

Pentuff, James R. Christian evolutionists answered, and President W. L. Poteat's utterances reviewed. No place, privately printed [c.1925] 100 p. [10642

The people against the bank. [Raleigh, T. Loring, pr., 1836?] 12 p. [10643

Peoples Advocate, Fayetteville, N. C. Josiah W. Bailey battling for certain great causes. [Raleigh, 1924?] 4 p. [10644

People's Building and Loan Association, Raleigh, N. C. Charter and by-laws, chartered March 2, 1870. Raleigh, Nichols & Gorman, pr., 1870. 16 p. [10645

People's rights bulletin, v. 1-2, January, 1936-March, 1937. Chapel Hill, Southern Committee for People's Rights, 1936-1937. NcU has v. 1-2. [10646

Pepper, George Whitfield. Ireland—Liberty springs from her martyrs' blood; an address . . . delivered at Raleigh, N. C., Dec. 20th, 1867. Boston, Published by Patrick Donahoe, 1868. 32 p. [10647

——The national cause: its sanctity and grandeur; oration delivered at Raleigh . . . July 4th, 1867. Raleigh, Branson, Farrar and Co., 1867. 29 p. [10648

——Personal recollections of Sherman's campaigns, in Georgia and the Carolinas. Zanesville, O., Published by Hugh Dunne, 1866.   522 p.   [10649

Perkins, Edgar L.   Essay on the evils of intemperance and the remedy.   Raleigh, A. M. Gorman, pr., 1850.   26 p.   [10650

Perkins, Edgar L., comp.   Ready wisdom; being a collection of the . . . sayings of wise men in all ages.   Raleigh, Star Office, 1848.   176 p.   [10651

Perkins, Edwin Marvin, comp.   Cumulative index-digest of The North Carolina law review, volumes one to fourteen, 1922-1936.   Chapel Hill, University of North Carolina Press, 1937.   69 p.   [10652

Perkins, Maxwell Evarts.   Editor to author, the letters of Maxwell E. Perkins. New York, Charles Scribner's Sons, 1950.   315 p.   [10653

Perkins, William Robertson.   An address on the Duke Endowment . . . delivered before the Spex Club at Lynchburg, Virginia, October 11, 1929.   Charlotte, Duke Endowment [1929]   63 p.   [10654

Perry, G. W.   A treatise on turpentine farming.   Newbern, Muse & Davies, 1859. 163 p.   [10655

Perry, O. H.   Truth vindicated, with reference to the Book of Job.   Raleigh, Biblical Recorder, 1875.   43 p.   [10658

Perry, Stella George S.   The defenders.   New York, Frederick A. Stokes Co., 1927. 411 p.   [10659

Perry, William H.   The hornet's nest no. 2; or, Intemperance and its cure.   Sparta, Star Publishing Co., 1903.   102 p.   [10660

Person, H. K.   Religious slavery, incompatible with civil freedom; an oration delivered before the Euzelian and Philomathesian societies at Wake Forest Institute, July 4, 1836.   Raleigh, Printed by J. Gales and Son, 1836.   16 p.   [10661

Person, Willie Mangum.   Address . . . on the floor of the Senate of North Carolina in behalf of the Franklin County educational bill, February 15, 1917.   [Raleigh?] 1917.   8 p.   [10662

Personne, pseud.   see **DeFontaine, Felix Gregory**

Peschau, F. W. E.   Souvenir of special services . . . in celebration of ten years as pastor and people, St. Paul's Evangelical Lutheran church, Rev. F. W. E. Peschau, D. D., pastor, February 28th, March 2, 1892.   Wilmington, no publisher [1892] 31 p.   [10663

Peterman, Alexander L.   Elements of civil government; a text-book.   New York, American Book Co. [1891] 240 p. With a supplement for North Carolina. [10664

Petersburg, Va. General Military Hospital for the North Carolina Troops.   The General Military Hospital for the North Carolina Troops in Petersburg, Virginia. Raleigh, Strother & Marcom, pr., 1861.   8 p.   [10665

Petersburg and Greensville and Roanoke Railroad.   Report, 18 - Raleigh, Seaton Gales, 18 - NcU has 1851/52, 1852/54   [10666

Petersburg Railroad.   Annual report to the stockholders, 18 - Petersburg, Ellyson, 18 - NcU has 1847/48, 1859, 1860, 1861, 1865   [10667

——Proceedings of the stockholders, 18 - Petersburg, J. R. Lewellen, pr., 18 - NcU has 1855   [10668

Peterson, Belle.   A beautiful bird without a name.   Louisville [Ky.] Author, 1886. 328 p.   [10669

—— ——Louisville, Courier-Journal Job Printing Co., 1883.   [10670

——One word, and a tear; The wounded dove, the story of Lenore Parolee.   St. Louis, Author, 1875.   248 p.   [10671

——Rose Sherwood.   4th ed.   Louisville, Ky., Courier-Journal for the Author, 1880.   133 p.   [10672

Peterson, Clarence Stewart.   The American pioneer in forty-eight states.   New York, William-Frederick Press, 1945.   190 p.   [10673

——Bibliography of county histories of the 3050 counties in the 48 states . . . Prepared in 1935 (2982 counties) Revised 1944.   Baltimore, Md., c.1944.   49 numb. 1.   [10674

—— ——1955 supplement to bibliography of county histories of the 3111 counties in 1946-47 revised edition.   [Baltimore] c.1955.   11 p.   [10675

——First governors of the forty-eight states.   New York, Hobson Book Press, 1947. 110 p.   [10676

Peterson, Mattie J.   Little Pansy, a novel; and, Miscellaneous poetry by the same author.   Wilmington, Messenger, 1890.   54 p.   [10677

Peterson, Paul Willard.   Natural singing and expressive conducting; with a foreword by Walter Golde.   Winston-Salem, J. F. Blair, 1955.   156 p.   [10678

Petherick, Thomas.   Report of the Silver Hill Mining Co., Davidson County, N. C., with report of Thomas Petherick, mining engineer.   New York, no publisher, 1860.   16 p.   [10679

Petry, Ray C.   Christian eschatology and social thought.   New York, Abingdon Press [c.1956]   415 p.   [10680

Petry, Ray C., ed.   No uncertain sound; sermons that shaped the pulpit tradition. Philadelphia, Westminster Press [1948] 331 p.   [10681

——Preaching in the great tradition.   Philadelphia, Westminster Press [1950] 122 p.   [10682

Pettigrew, Charles.   Last advice of the Reverend Charles Pettigrew to his sons, 1797.   No place, no publisher, n.d.   12 p.   [10683

[Pettigrew, Charles]   A series of letters, in which an attentive perusal of Mr. Edward's candid reasons for renouncing the principles of Antipaedobaptism is seriously recommended.   Edenton, Printed by James Wills, 1807.   89 p.   [10684

[Pettigrew, James Johnston]   Notes on Spain and the Spaniards, in the summer of 1859.   ... by a Carolinian (J. J. P.)   Charleston [S. C.] Presses of Evans & Cogswell, 1861.   430 p.   [10685

Peurifoy, George W.   see Purify, George W.

Peyton, John Lewis.   The American crisis; or, Pages from the note-book of a state agent during the Civil War.   London, Saunders, Otley and Co., 1867.   2 v. in 1.   [10686

Pfeiffer Junior College, Misenheimer, N. C.   A brief history, Pfeiffer Junior College. Misenheimer [1952]   12 p.   [10687

——Bulletin, v. 1- 193 - 193 - NcU has v. [1] [10-24]   Became Pfeiffer College, 195 -   [10688

Pfister, Karin.   Zeit und Wirklichkeit bei Thomas Wolfe.   Heidelberg, Carl Winter, 1954.   (Anglistische Forschungen.   Begründet von Professor Dr. Johannes Hoops. Heft 89)   139 p.   [10689

Pfohl, Bernard J.   The Salem band.   Winston-Salem [Wachovia Historical Society] 1953.   85 p.   [10690

Pfohl, John Kenneth.   The Moravian Church.   [Winston-Salem? Author?] n.d. 8 p.   [10691

——The seeking shepherd ... delivered in the Home Moravian Church, March 21, 1920.   No place, no publisher [1920]   15 p.   [10692

Pfohl, John Kenneth, joint author,   see Fries, Adelaide Lisetta

Pharr, Henry Newton.   Pharrs and Farrs with other descendants from five Scotch-Irish pioneers in America.   New Orleans, The Author, 1955.   604 p.   [10693

Pharr, Walter W.   Funeral sermon on the death of Capt. A. K. Simonton.   Salisbury, J. J. Bruner, pr., 1862.   12 p.   [10694

——Short history of the life, character and death of Capt. John B. Andrews.   No place, no publisher, n.d.   4 p.   [10695

Phelps, Charles.   To the freemen of Wilkes County.   Salisbury, Philo White, July 2, 1825.   [1] p.   [10696

Phi Gamma Delta.   Epsilon, North Carolina University.   100 years of Epsilon of Phi Gamma Delta, 1851-1951 ... March 31, 1951. [Chapel Hill, 1951] [16] p. [10697

[Phifer, Charles Henry]   Genealogy and history of the Phifer family.   [Charlotte, Presbyterian Standard Publishing Co., 1910]   53 p.   [10698

Philadelphia.   College of Physicians.   Report of the autopsy of the Siamese twins, together with other interesting information concerning their life.   Philadelphia, J. B. Lippincott & Co., 1874.   39 p.   [10699

Philadelphia.   Democratic Committee of Correspondence.   Clay and Polk; the difference between them on the tariff question.   Philadelphia, Office of the Pennsylvanian [1844]   8 p.   [10700

Philadelphia and North Carolina Mining and Smelting Company. Report on the gold mines . . . with maps and the act of incorporation. Philadelphia, J. H. Schwacke, 1847. 17 p. NcU has microfilm (negative) from original in Library of Congress   [10701

Philanthropos, pseud. see **Pettigrew, Charles**

Philip, Uncle, pseud. see **Hawks, Francis Lister**

Philips, Frederick. Memorial Day in Edgecombe . . . roster of Edgecombe troops. No place, no publisher, n.d. [2] p.   [10702

Phillips, Agnes Lucas. On things inferior, and other poems. Washingtonville, N. Y., Clough-Bush Press [c.1936] 37 p.   [10703
——One clear call, a novel about nursing. New York, Exposition Press [1955] 120 p.   [10704
——Within these gates; poems. Richmond, Va., Dietz Press, 1938. 52 p. [10705

Phillips, Alexander Lacy. The call of the home land; a study in home missions. [Richmond? Va., c.1906] 173 p.   [10706
——The geography of Palestine. Richmond, Va., Presbyterian Committee of Publication, 1906. 58 p.   [10707
——Historical sketch of the Presbyterian Church of Fayetteville, N. C.; address delivered in the Presbyterian Church of Fayetteville, Feb. 3d, 1889. Fayetteville, J. E. Garrett, pr., 1889. 44 p.   [10708

Phillips, Charles. A manual of plane and spherical trigonometry. Raleigh, Printed by William Cooke, 1857. 200 p.   [10709
——"May, 1775"; article on the alleged Mecklenburg Declaration of Independence. Greensboro, Thomas, Reece & Co., pr., 1887. 30 p.   [10710

[Phillips, Charles] A memoir of the Rev. Elisha Mitchell . . . together with the tributes of respect to his memory. Chapel Hill, J. M. Henderson, 1858. 88 p. [10711

Phillips, Dorothy (Evans) Big-enough boat. Chicago, Follett Pub. Co. [1956] 96 p.   [10712

Phillips, James. Elements of the conic sections, comp. for the use of the students of the University of North Carolina. New York, George Long, 1828. 48 p. [10713

Phillips, John Roberts. The story of my life. No place, no publisher [pref. 1923] 87 p.   [10714

[Phillips, S. K.] From a Presbyterian pastor; an address delivered at the State Baraca-Philathea convention of North Carolina, Charlotte, N. C., April 15, 1913. [Greensboro? North Carolina Baraca-Philathea Associations? 1913?] [10] p. [10715

Phillips, Samuel Field. Address at the installation of the Law School of the Columbian University, in the new lecture hall, Oct. 8, 1884. Washington, The University, 1884. 15 p.   [10716
——Address delivered before the Union and Mountain Springs divisions of the Sons of Temperance at Hillsborough, on the fourth of July, 1850. Hillsborough, The Society, 1850. 31 p.   [10717
——Remarks in the House of Commons of the called session of the legislature, Jan. 1866 . . . upon . . . admitting Negro evidence in courts of justice. Raleigh, no publisher, 1866. 8 p.   [10718
——Some topics in Roman history of special importance to the American scholar; an address before the Eumenean and Philanthropic societies of Davidson College. Fayetteville, Printed by Edward J. Hale & Son, 1854. 29 p.   [10719
——Speech at Concord, Cabarrus County, July 4th, 1870. No place [Standard, 1870?] 10 p.   [10720
——Speech on accepting the nomination for attorney general. No place, no publisher [1870?] Various paging.   [10721

Phillips, Ulrich Bonnell. History of transportation in the eastern cotton belt to 1860. New York Columbia University Press, 1908. 405 p.   [10722
——Life and labor in the old South. Boston, Little, Brown, and Co., 1929. 375 p.   [10723

Phillips, Ulrich Bonnell, ed. Plantation and frontier documents: 1649-1863. Cleveland, O., A. H. Clark Co., 1909. 2 v.   [10724

Phillips, William Battle. Algebra and acid phosphate. Wilmington, DeRosset, Meares & Co., pr., 1885. 6 p.   [10725

——Contributions to scientific and technical publications, 1883-1913. [Austin, Texas, Author, 1913] 19 p. [10726

——North Carolina phosphates; in part a report to the Navassa Guano Co. Wilmington, Mercantile Waterpower Presses, 1883. 19 p. [10727

——Notes on the smelting processes at Freiberg, by Walter H. Brown and W. B. Phillips. Freiberg, Saxony, Gerlach's Printing Office, 1886. 32 p. [10728

Phipsicli, 1913- Elon College, Senior Class of Elon College, 1913- NcU has 1913, 1915 [10729

Phisterer, Frederick. . . . Statistical record of the armies of the United States. New York, C. Scribner's Sons, 1883. (Campaigns of the Civil War. Supplementary vol. [XIII]) 343 p. [10730

Pica, v. 1- 1949?- Columbia, S. C., The Printing Industry of the Carolinas, Inc., 1949?- NcU has v. [5] 6-8 [10731

Picayune, v. 1- September, 1923- Moyock, Currituck County Board of Education, 1923- NcU has v. [1-4] [10732

Pickard, Walter. Burlington dynamite plot. [New York, International Labor Defense, 1935?] 23 p. [10733

Pickens, Andrew Lee. Skyagunsta, the border wizard owl, Major-General Andrew Pickens (1739-1817) Greenville, S. C., Observer Printing Co., c.1934. 161 p. [10734

Pickens, Israel. Circular to the citizens of Burke, Rutherford, Lincoln, Buncombe, and Haywood, N. Carolina. [Washington, Author, 1812] 12 p. [10735

——Israel Pickens address to his constituents. Wash., February 20, 1815. [3] p. [10736

——Israel Pickens' letter to his constituents. [Washington, Author, Aug. 2, 1813] [2] p. [10737

—— ——Wash., April 16, 1814. [3] p. [10738

Pickens, Robert Sylvester. Storm clouds over Asia. New York, Funk & Wagnalls Co., 1934. 251 p. [10739

Pickett, Clarence E. Friends and international affairs; the Ward lecture given at Guilford College on Founders Day, October 22, 1952. Guilford College, 1952. 23 p. [10740

Piedmont Area Industrial Relations Conference, Winston-Salem, N. C., May 23 and 24, 1946. Summation . . . prepared by William B. Barton. [Winston-Salem?] 1946. 5 p. [10741

Piedmont Baptist Association. Minutes, 1894- 1894- NcU has 1896-1899, 1901-1907, 1909-1915, 1931-1936, 1939, 1944-1950 [10742

Piedmont High School, Lawndale, N. C. Catalogue, 189 - [Lawndale, 189 - NcU has 1903/04-1908/09, 1916/17, 1918/19, 1921/22 [10743

Piedmont Railroad. General rules applying to officers and employees. Richmond, Gary's Steam Printing House, 1873. 85 p. [10744

—— ——1875. 32 p. [10745

——[Indenture by and between Piedmont Railroad Company, Southern Railway Company, and Central Trust Company of New York.] [New York, 1894] 7 p. [10746

——[Report of engineer and superintendent of Richmond and Danville Railroad and Piedmont Railroad, North Carolina Division, and Northwestern N. C. Railroads] 18 - [Richmond, 18 - NcU has 1874-75 [10747

Pierce, Charles F. History and camp life of Company C. Fifty-first Regiment, Massachusetts Volunteer Militia, 1862-1863. Worcester, Printed by C. Hamilton, 1886. 130 p. [10748

Pierce, Ovid Williams. The plantation. Garden City, N. Y., Doubleday & Co., Inc., 1953. 217 p. [10749

——La plantation. Roman traduit de l'américain par Hubert Audigier. Paris, Plon [1955] 254 p. [10750

Pierce, Truman Mitchell. White and Negro schools in the South: an analysis of bi-racial education [by] Truman M. Pierce [and others] Englewood Cliffs, N. J., Prentice-Hall, 1955. 338 p. [10751

Pierpont, Francis Harrison. Letter of Governor Pierpont, to His Excellency the President and the honorable Congress of the United States, on the subject of abuse of military power in the command of General Butler in Virginia and North Carolina. Washington, McGill & Witherow, pr., 1864. 60 p. NcU has microfilm (negative) from original in Library of Congress [10752

Pierson, Mary Bynum (Holmes) Graduate work in the South. Chapel Hill, University of North Carolina Press, 1947. 265 p. [10753

Pierson, William Whatley. The administration of minimum standards for the master's degree, William W. Pierson . . . Calvin B. Hoover . . . a paper presented before the conference of deans of southern graduate schools . . . Memphis, Tennessee, October 23-24, 1940. No place, no publisher, 1940. 33 p. [10754

——A course on Latin-American history for women's clubs. [Chapel Hill] University of North Carolina, c.1917. 31 p. [10755

——. . . Hispanic-American history, 1826-1920. [New York, Institute of International Education] 1921. (The Institute of international education. International relations clubs, syllabus no. VII) 36 p. [10756

——Hispanic-American history: a syllabus. Rev. and enl. Chapel Hill, University of N. C. Press, 1926. 169 p. [10757

——Latin America and the peace; address delivered at the closing exercises of the special session for Mexican teachers, winter of 1943. Chapel Hill, 1943. 5 p. [10758

Pierson, William Whatley, ed. Studies in Hispanic-American history. Chapel Hill, University of North Carolina Press, 1927. (James Sprunt historical studies, v. 19, no. 2) 133 p. [10759

Pierson, William Whatley. Syllabus of Hispanic-American history. 3d ed. Chapel Hill, University of North Carolina, 1920. 44 p. [10760

——A syllabus of Latin-American history. 2d edition. [Chapel Hill] University of North Carolina, c.1916-17. 36 p. [10761

Pierson, William Whatley, joint ed. see Godfrey, James Logan, ed.

Pigott, Levi Woodbury. Scenes and incidents in the life of a home missionary; with a biographical sketch of Fenner S. Pigott. Norfolk, Va., no publisher, 1901. 160 p. [10762

Pike, H. L. Address at the celebration of emancipation day, at Raleigh, N. C., Jan. 1870. Raleigh, Standard, 1870. 8 p. [10763

Pilgrim Holiness Church. Southern District Assembly. Proceedings, 1911?- 1911?- NcU has 1926 [10764

The pilot, v. 1- 1913- Greensboro, Pilot Life Insurance Company, 1913- NcU has v. [9-13] and 2nd series [1926-1931] [10765

The pilot, v. 1- 193 - [Leaksville?] Senior Class of Leaksville High School, 1937- NcU has v. 4, 1940 [10766

Pilot Mountain Baptist Association. Minutes, 1886- 1886- NcU has [1891-1906] 1935-1940 [10767

Pinchot, Gifford. Biltmore forest, the property of Mr. George W. Vanderbilt. Chicago [R. R. Donnelley & Sons Co.] 1893. 49 p. [10768

Pinckney, Henry Laurens. "The spirit of the age," an address delivered before the two literary societies of the University of North-Carolina. Raleigh, Printed by J. Gales & Son, 1836. 30 p. [10769

Pine burr, 1912- Buie's Creek, Senior Class of Buie's Creek Academy, 1912- NcU has 1912, 1915, 1916 [10770

Pine burr, 192 - Lincolnton, Lincolnton High School, 1922- NcU has 1922 [10771

Pine knot, 191 - [Wilson] Student Body Publication Committee of Atlantic Christian College, 1912- NcU has 1913 [10772

Pine Level, N. C. Board of Commissioners. Ordinances of the town of Pine Level, N. C. Raleigh, Edwards & Broughton Printing Co. [1907] 16 p. [10773

—— ——No place, no publisher [1919] 14 p. [10774

Pine needles, 1920- Greensboro, North Carolina College for Women, 1920- NcU has 1920-1923, 1926 [10775

Pinebluff, N. C., amid the long leafed pines. No place, no publisher [1903?] 16 p. [10776

Pinehurst, N. C. Mid-pines Country Club. Mid-pines Country Club, North Carolina. No place, no publisher, n.d. 16 p. [10777

Pinehurst; a health resort in North Carolina. [Pinehurst?] n.d. 48 p. [10778

Pinehurst, North Carolina. [Boston, Rand Avery Supply Co. Print, 1930] 31 p. [10779

Pinehurst, North Carolina; a brief description of the leading health and recreation resort of the South. [New York, Presbrey for Leonard Tufts, c.1905] 63 p. [10780

Pinehurst, N. C., founded by James W. Tufts; a brief description of the leading health and recreation resort of the South. [Boston, Smith & Porter, pr.] n.d. 63 p.   [10781
——Boston, Leonard Tufts [1908?]   63 p.   [10782
——[1915?]   [10783
——[191?]   [10784

Pinehurst outlook, v. 1-   1896-   Pinehurst, Outlook Publishing Co., 1896- NcU has v. 34-38   [10785

Pinehurst, the ideal winter home.   No place, no publisher [1900?]   47 p.   [10786

Pinehurst, the premier winter resort of America.   [New York, Frank Presbrey Co.] n.d.   30 p.   [10787
——[1924?]   31 p.   [10788

Pineland College, Salemburg, N. C.   Catalogue, 1912/13- Salemburg, 1913- NcU has 1912/13-1915/16, [1939/40-1953/54]   Called Pineland School for Girls, 1912/ 13-?   [10789

Pingel, Martha Mary.   Catalyst; an interpretation of life.   New York, Exposition Press [1951]   64 p.   [10790

The Pinnacles, v. 1- 1916- Banner Elk, Lees-McRae College, 1916- NcU has v. [11-36, 40]   [10791

Pinnix, Esther Searle.   History of the museum of the Wachovia History Society. [Winston-Salem? 1937?]   7 p.   [10792

Pinnix, Frances Mullen.   The Pinnix definer, in three grades, by F. M. and H. C. Pinnix.   Philadelphia, Press of J. B. Lippincott Co. [1904]   243 p.   [10793

Pinnix, Hannah Courtney (Baxter)   Chaney's stratagem.   Boston, C. M. Clark Publishing Co., 1909.   314 p.   [10794
——A watch-key; a novel by Kerr.   Raleigh, Edwards & Broughton, 1889. 291 p.   [10795

Pioneer, 1924- Kannapolis, Kannapolis High School, 1924- NcU has 1924   [10796

Pioneer, v. 1-v. 2, no. 7, September, 1926-March, 1928.   Statesville, North Carolina Auxiliary of the League of American Pen Women, 1926-28.   NcU has v. 1-v. 2, no. 7   [10797

Pioneer life in the West; comprising the adventures of Boone, Kenton, Brady, Clarke, the Whetzels, and others.   Philadelphia, John E. Potter [c.1858]   332 p.   [10798

Piper, Alexander Abbey.   Peter Piper's poems.   New York, Henry Harrison [c.1944] 96 p.   [10799
——Song of the winds.   [Federalsburg, Md., J. W. Stowell Printing Co., c.1937] 114 p.   [10800

Pipkin, Charles Wooten.   . . . Social legislation in the South.   Chapel Hill, University of North Carolina Press, 1936. (Southern policy papers, no. 3) 42 p. [10801

Pippin, Inc., Zebulon, N. C.   Catalogue, 1930- 1930- NcU has 1930   [10802

Pitkin, Timothy.   A statistical view of the commerce of the United States of America. 2d ed.   New York, Published by James Eastburn, 1817.   445 p.   [10803

Pitt County, N. C.   Board of Education.   Suggestions for teaching beginners to read.   Greenville, 1917.   [4] p.   [10804

Pitt County, N. C.   Court.   Rules of the Court of Pitt County, adopted at the February term, 1859.   No place, no publisher [1859?]   [1] p.   [10805

Pittman, Reden Herbert, ed.   Biographical history of Primitive or Old School Baptist ministers of the U. S.   Anderson, Ind., Herald Publishing Co. [c.1909] 406 p.   [10806

Pittman, Thomas Merritt.   Nathaniel Macon; an address on the occasion of the unveiling of a monument . . . at Guilford Battle Ground, July 4, 1902.   Greensboro, Guilford Battle Ground Co., n.d.   19 p.   [10807
——Preparation for Baptist work in North Carolina.   No place, no publisher, n.d. 11 p.   [10808

Placid, Father see Kleppel, Placid, Father

Plan for the settlement of 552,500 acres of land in the district of Morgan, county of Wilkes, in the state of North Carolina. [London, Barrell and Servanté, 1796] 3 p.   [10809

Plan pour former un etablissement en Caroline. [A La Haye, Meindert Uytwerf, 1686] 15 p. NcU has microfilm (negative) from original in the John Carter Brown Library   [10809a

Plant Food Institute of North Carolina and Virginia, Inc. The Plant Food Institute of North Carolina and Virginia, Incorporated. Raleigh, n.d. [4] p.   [10810

——The story of fertilizers (origin, manufacture, and use) Raleigh, 1940. 61 p.[10810a

A plea for Federal union, North Carolina, 1788; a reprint of two pamphlets, with an introduction by Hugh T. Lefler. Charlottesville, Tracy W. McGregor Library, Univ. of Virginia, 1947 [i.e. 1948] 79 p.   [10811

Pleasant Garden Academy. [Greensboro, Pleasant Garden Academy, 1876?] 4 p.   [10811a

Pleasant Grove Baptist Association. Proceedings, 1866- 1866- NcU has 1867 [10812

Pleasant Hill Baptist Church, Cleveland Co., N. C. The Pleasant Hill Baptist Church constituted February 7, 1851, centennial, historical sketch, 1851-1951. No place, 1951. 30 p.   [10813

Please protect our boys. No place, no publisher, n.d. 1 p.   [10814

Plenn, Doris Troutman. The green song. New York, D. McKay Co. [1954] 126 p.   [10815

Pliny, pseud. Series of political letters addressed to a particular friend. Halifax, Office of the Free Press, 1825. 14 p.   [10816

Plyler, Alva Washington. The iron duke of the Methodist itinerancy; an account of the life and labors of Rev. John Tillett. Nashville, Cokesbury Press, 1925. 216 p.   [10817

Plyler, Marion Timothy. Bethel among the oaks. Nashville, Tenn., Cokesbury Press, 1924. 217 p.   [10818

——Men of the burning heart: Ivey, Dow, Doub. By Marion Timothy Plyler [and] Alva Washington Plyler. [Raleigh, Commercial Printing Co., pref. 1918] 223 p.   [10819

——Thomas Neal Ivey, golden-hearted gentleman. Nashville, Tenn., Cokesbury Press, 1925. 166 p.   [10820

——Through eight decades, as minister, editor, author. Durham, Seeman Printery, Inc., 1951. 138 p.   [10821

Poate, Ernest M. Behind locked doors; a detective story. New York, Chelsea House [c.1923] 320 p.   [10822

——Pledged to the dead. New York, Chelsea House [c.1925] 320 p.   [10823

——Trouble at Pinelands. New York, Chelsea House [c.1922] 316 p.   [10824

Pochmann, Henry August. Bibliography of German culture in America to 1940. Madison, University of Wisconsin Press, 1953. 483 p.   [10825

Pocket directory of the furniture manufacturers of the southern states, 1923- High Point, Furniture Press Co., 1923- NcU has 1923   [10826

Poe, Charles Aycock. Climate of fear; a drama. Raleigh, The Author, c.1954, 1955. 101 p.   [10827

Poe, Clarence Hamilton. Asia's great lesson for the South; a paper read at the fourteenth Conference for Education in the South, Jacksonville, Fla., April 21st, 1911. No place, no publisher [1911?] 16 p.   [10828

——Col. Leonidas Lafayette Polk, his services in starting the N. C. State College of Agriculture and Engineering. No place, no publisher [1926] 14 p.   [10829

——. . . Farm life, problems and opportunities. Chicago, American Library Association, 1931. (Reading with a purpose, no. 62) 36 p.   [10830

——Five hundred dollars more a year for the average southern farmer . . . an address before the Southern Commercial Congress, Washington, D. C., Dec. 8, 1908. No place, no publisher [1908?] 15 p.   [10831

——How farmers co-operate and double profits. New York, Orange Judd Co., 1915. 244 p.   [10832

[Poe, Clarence Hamilton] Mrs. Susan Dismukes Poe, 1846-1911. No place, no publisher, n.d. [7] p.   [10833

Poe, Clarence Hamilton. North Carolina of tomorrow; president's address at sixteenth annual session State Literary and Historical Association, Raleigh, Dec. 7, 1915. [Raleigh, Edwards & Broughton, 1916?] 11 p.   [10834

——Rural problems and the rural community; address delivered at meeting of National Conference of Charities and Corrections, Memphis, Tenn., May 10, 1914. No place, no publisher [1914?]   15 p.   [10835
——A southerner in Europe; being fourteen newspaper letters . . . written with especial reference to southern conditions.   Raleigh, Mutual Publishing Co. [c.1908] 140 p.   [10836
——The stars I have tried to follow.   [Raleigh, Progressive Farmer Co., 1954] 7 p.   [10837
——What Dr. Knapp did for southern farmers; address delivered at the Southern Commercial Congress, Nashville, Tenn., Apr. 17, 1912.   No place, no publisher [1912?]   15 p.   [10838
——What North Carolina farmers expect of the legislature.   No place, no publisher, n.d.   4 p.   [10839
——Where half the world is waking up; the old and the new in Japan, China, the Philippines, and India.   Garden City, N. Y., Doubleday, Page & Co., 1911. 276 p.   [10840
——White farm communities should have right of self-protection.   Raleigh, Progressive Farmer, 1913.   1 p.   [10841
——William B. Poe [1839-1907] an imperfect tribute.   [Raleigh, Author, pref. 1909] [7] p.   [10842

Poe, Clarence Hamilton, joint author,   see Burkett, Charles William; also, Connor, Robert Digges Wimberly

Poetic thrills, the poets folio; a journal of verse, v. 1- Nov.-Jan., 1925-26- Wilmington, George W. Cameron, 1926- NcU has v. 1-v. 7, no. 1   Title varies, 1925-26: Bookmakers folio   [10843

Pogue, Joseph Ezekiel.   America's power resources . . . By Chester G. Gilbert and Joseph E. Pogue.   New York, Century Co., 1921.   326 p.   [10844
——Economics of petroleum. New York, John Wiley & Sons, Inc., 1921. 375 p. [10845
——Oil and the Americas; an address . . . before the Inter-American Institute of the University of North Carolina at Chapel Hill on Thursday, June 22, 1944.   [New York? 1944]   28 p.   [10846
——Oil in Venezuela.   [New York, Chase National Bank, Petroleum Dept., 1949] 49 p.   [10847

Poland, C. Beauregard.   North Carolina's glorious victory, 1898; sketches of able Democratic leaders and statesmen.   [Raleigh, Author, 1898?]   58 p.   [10848
——Twentieth century statesmen, North Carolina's political leaders, 1900-1901. No place, no publisher, n.d.   62 p.   [10849

The political and public character of James K. Polk of Tennessee.   No place, no publisher [1844?]   20 p.   [10850

The political mirror; or, Review of Jacksonism.   New York, Published by J. P. Peaslee, 1835.   316 p.   [10851

Polk, James Knox, pres. U. S.   Address of James K. Polk to the people of Tennessee, April 3, 1839.   Columbia, Tenn., J. H. Thompson, pr., 1839.   28 p.   [10852
——Address to the people of Tennessee.   Nashville, 1841.   40 p.   [10853
——The diary of James K. Polk during his presidency, 1845 to 1849.   Chicago, A. C. McClurg & Co., 1910.   4 v.   [10854
——Polk; the diary of a president, 1845-1849, covering the Mexican War, the acquisition of Oregon, and the conquest of California and the Southwest.   London, Longmans, Green and Co., 1929.   412 p.   [10855
—— ——1952.   [10856

Polk, Leonidas.   Address of the commissioners for raising the endowment of the University of the South.   New Orleans, B. M. Norman, 1859.   16 p.   Leonidas Polk and Stephen Elliott   [10857
——Extracts from the journal of the twenty-third annual convention of the Protestant Episcopal Church, in the Diocese of Louisiana.   New Orleans, Bulletin Book and Job Office, 1861.   24 p.   [10858

Polk, Leonidas Lafayette.   An address by the Hon. L. L. Polk . . . before the interstate Convention of Farmers, held in De Give's Opera House, Atlanta, Ga., August 16, 17, 18, 1887.   Atlanta, Jas. P. Harrison & Co., pr., 1887.   7 p. [10859
——Agricultural depression . . . speech before the senate committee on agriculture and forestry, April 22, 1890. Raleigh, Edwards & Broughton, pr., 1890. 32 p. [10860

——Extract from the Raleigh daily news, June 8th, 1880. [Raleigh, Author, 1880] 2 p. Correspondence relating to his resignation as North Carolina Commissioner of Agriculture. [10861

——The protest of the farmer; address to Citizens Alliance no. 4, of Washington, D. C., at Concordia Hall, April 14, 1891. No place, no publisher [1891?] 24 p. [10862

Polk, Tasker. Address; delivered at an entertainment given by the young ladies of Warrenton, N. C. for the benefit of "The Warren guards". Henderson, Ludington & Aycock, pr. [1887?] 8 p. [10863

[Polk, William Harrison] Polk family and kinsmen. [Louisville, Ky., Bradley, 1912] 742 p. [10864

Polk, William Mecklenburg. Leonidas Polk, bishop and general. New ed. New York, Longmans, Green, and Co., 1915. 2 v. [10865

Polk, William Tannahill. Books and the minds of men. No place, privately printed, 1934. 8 p. [10866

——The fallen angel, and other stories. Chapel Hill, University of North Carolina Press [1956] 180 p. [10867

——North Carolina prophets and the twentieth century. No place, no publisher [1936] 14 p. [10868

——Southern accent: from Uncle Remus to Oak Ridge. New York, William Morrow and Co. [1953] 264 p. [10869

[Polk County Centennial Commission, Inc.] Polk County centennial, May 8-14, 1955; souvenir historical booklet. [Tryon] 1955. 32 p. [10870

[Polk Diphtheria Cure Company, Boston] Diphtheria, its cause and cure. [Boston, Goodwin and Driske, pr., 1884?] 36 p. [10871

Pollard, Edward Alfred. Lee and his lieutenants. New York, E. B. Treat & Co., 1867. 851 p. [10872

[Pollock, John Alfred] The fair lady of Halifax, by Ronleigh de Conval. Raleigh, Edwards & Broughton Printing Co., 1920. 403 p. [10873

Pollock, Thomas Clark, ed. Thomas Wolfe at Washington Square, by Thomas Clark Pollock and Oscar Cargill. New York, New York University Press, 1954. 163 p. [10874

Polsky, Thomas. The cudgel. New York, E. P. Dutton & Co., 1950. 223 p. [10875

Pomona Terra-cotta Co., Pomona, N. C. Farm drain tile; drainage and how to drain. Pomona, n.d. 15 p. [10876

Pool, Bettie Freshwater. America's battle cry and other new war songs set to old familiar tunes. [Elizabeth City, Linotype Printery, 1918] 20 p. [10877

——The Eyrie, and other southern stories. New York, Broadway Publishing Co. [c.1905] 108 p. [10878

——Literature in the Albemarle. Baltimore, Md., Baltimore City Printing and Binding Co. [c.1915] 335 p. [10879

——Under Brazilian skies. Elizabeth City, Geo. P. E. Hart, [c.1908] 59 p. [10880

Pool, John. Address delivered before the two literary societies of the University of North Carolina, June 6th, 1860. Chapel Hill, John B. Neathery, 1860. 15 p. [10881

——Address of the Hon. John Pool to the people of North-Carolina. [Raleigh, Standard Book and Job Office Print, 1867] 14 p. [10882

——Address of John Pool to the people of North Carolina. [Washington, no publisher, 1871] 2 p. [10883

——The Cherry letter, by Ex-Senator Pool . . . the solid South—why solid. Washington, 1880. 8 p. [10884

Pool, Maria Louise. Against human nature, a novel. New York, Harper & Brothers, 1895. 361 p. [10885

——Dally. New York, Harper & Brothers, 1893. 280 p. [10886

——A golden sorrow. Chicago, H. S. Stone & Co., 1898. 441 p. [10887

——In Buncombe county. Chicago, H. S. Stone & Co., 1896. 295 p. [10888

—— ——1898. [10889

—— ——1906. [10890

——In the first person; a novel. New York, Harper & Brothers, 1896. 315 p. [10891

——Mrs. Keats Bradford; a novel. New York, Harper & Brothers, 1892. 309 p. [10892

——The red-bridge neighborhood. New York, Harper & Brothers, 1898. 369 p. [10893

——Roweny in Boston; a novel. New York, Harper & Brothers, 1892. 348 p. [10894

——Sand 'n' bushes. Chicago, H. S. Stone & Co., 1899. 364 p. [10895

——The two Salomes. New York, Harper & Brothers, 1893. 372 p.   [10896

[Pool, Ralph I.] comp. Pool family of Pasquotank, North Carolina. [Norfolk, Va.] n.d. [1] p.   [10897

——White. [Norfolk, Va.] n.d. [1] p.   [10898

[Pool, Solomon] Address. To the alumni and friends of the University of North Carolina. [Chapel Hill, 1871] 8 p.   [10899

Poole, George R. Occurrence of gem corundum in North Carolina. Charlotte, 1956. 4 p.   [10900

Poore, Benjamin Perley. The life and public services of Ambrose E. Burnside. Providence, R. I., J. A. & R. A. Reid, 1882. 448 p.   [10901

Pope, Frederick Russell. Within a Quaker college, and other last poems. [Guilford College] Guilford College, 1940. 87 p.   [10902

Pope, Liston. Millhands & preachers, a study of Gastonia. New Haven, Yale University Press, 1942. (Yale studies in religious education. xv) 369 p.   [10903

Pope, W. C. Leisure moments, a collection of short writings . . . in prose and rhyme. Raleigh, Edwards & Broughton Printing Co., 1919. 102 p.   [10904

Poppenheim, Mary Barnett. The history of the United Daughters of the Confederacy, by Mary B. Poppenheim—Maude Blake Merchant [and others] Richmond, Garrett and Massie, Inc. [c.1938] 226 p.   [10905

Porcher, Francis Peyre. Resources of the southern fields and forests, medical, economical, and agricultural. Charleston, Steam-power Press of Evans & Cogswell, 1863. 601 p.   [10906

—— ——New ed., rev. Charleston, Walker, Evans & Cogswell, pr., 1869. 733 p.   [10907

Porter, David Dixon. The naval history of the Civil War. New York, Sherman Publishing Co., 1886. 843 p.   [10908

Porter, Duval. Wasted talents exemplified by the history of a few obscure persons. Part second, Byrd's survey, or, Sketches of men, places, and things. Leaksville, Darlington and Sons, pr., 1890. CXV p.   [10909

Porter, Leona (Bryson) The family of Weimar Siler, 1755-1831. Franklin, Committee appointed at the 100th Meeting [of the family] 1951. 178 p.   [10910

Porter, Martha Byrd (Spruill) Straight down a crooked lane. Richmond, Va., Dietz Press, Inc., 1945. 234 p.   [10911

—— ——John Marshall Press, 1945. 233 p.   [10912

——Tomorrow is another day, a comedy of manners. New York, Exposition Press [1952] 268 p.   [10913

Porter, Nannie (Francisco) The romantic record of Peter Francisco "a Revolutionary soldier", Nannie Francisco Porter, author, Catherine Fauntleroy Albertson, co-author. Staunton, Va., Printed by the McClure Co., Inc., 1929. 103 p.   [10914

Porter, Samuel Judson. The gospel of beauty. New York, George H. Doran Co. [c.1922] 118 p.   [10915

——The shepherd heart. Philadelphia, American Baptist Publication Society [c.1907] 63 p.   [10916

——Yearning upward. [Fayetteville, Author, 1902] 40 p.   [10917

[Porter, William .Sydney] Best stories of O. Henry [pseud.] Garden City, N. Y., Sun Dial Press, 1945. 338 p.   [10918

—— ——New York, Modern Library [1945]   [10919

——Cabbages and kings, by O. Henry [pseud.] New York, McClure, Phillips & Co., 1904. 344 p. First edition.   [10920

—— ——Garden City, N. Y., Doubleday, Page & Co., 1916. 312 p.   [10921

—— ——1920.   [10922

——The complete works of O. Henry [pseud.] Garden City, N. Y., Doubleday, Page & Co. [c.1911] 1396 p.   [10923

—— ——1931.   [10924

—— ——Kingswood, Surrey, Associated Bookbuyers' Co. [1936]   [10925

—— ——Garden City, Doubleday, Doran, 1936.   [10926

—— ——Manuscript edition. Garden City, N. Y., Doubleday, Page and Co., 1912. 12 v.   [10927

—— ——Foreword by Harry Hansen. Garden City, N. Y., Doubleday & Co., Inc., 1953. 2 v.   [10928

——The four million, by O. Henry [pseud.] Garden City, N. Y., Doubleday, Page & Co., 1914. 261 p. [10929
—— ——1920. [10930
——The gentle grafter, by O. Henry [pseud.] New York, The McClure Co., 1908. 235 p. First edition. [10931
—— ——[Garden City, N. Y.] Doubleday, Page & Co., 1919. 237 p. [10932
—— ——1920. [10933
——The gift of the Magi, a Christmas story by O. Henry [pseud.] Baltimore, Norman T. A. Munder, 1923. 16 p. [10934
—— ——Valley Cottage, N. Y., privately printed, 1925. 15 p. [10935
——Heart of the West, by O. Henry [pseud.] New York, The McClure Co., 1907. 334 p. First edition [10936
—— ——[Garden City, N. Y.] Doubleday, Page & Co., 1920. 313 p. [10937
——. . . Let me feel your pulse, by O. Henry [pseud.] New York, Doubleday, Page & Co., 1910. 38 p. First edition. [10938
——Letters to Lithopolis, from O. Henry [pseud.] to Mabel Wagnalls. Garden City, N. Y., Doubleday, Page & Co., 1922. 59 p. [10939
——More O. Henry, one hundred more of the master stories introduced by James Hilton. London, Hodder & Stoughton [1933] 1128 p. [10940
——O. Henry encore; stories and illustrations by O. Henry [pseud.] usually under the name, The Post man, discovered and edited by Mary Sunlocks Harrell. New York, Doubleday, Doran & Co., Inc., 1939. 247 p. First edition. [10941
——O. Henryana; seven odds and ends, poetry and short stories, by O. Henry [pseud.] Garden City, N. Y., Doubleday, Page & Co., 1920. 89 p. First edition. [10942
——O. Henry's own trial; brief for W. S. Porter in the appeal of his case. [Austin, Texas, Trueman E. O'Quinn, c.1940] 18 p. [10943
——Options, by O. Henry [pseud.] New York, Harper & Brothers, 1909. 323 p. First edition. [10944
—— ——[Garden City, N. Y.] Doubleday, Page & Co., 1920. 257 p. [10945
——The pocket book of O. Henry [pseud.] thirty short stories, ed. and with an introd. by Harry Hansen. N[ew] Y[ork] Pocket Books [1948] 291 p. [10946
——Postscripts, by O. Henry [pseud.] with an introduction by Florence Stratton. New York, Harper & Brothers, 1923. 202 p. First edition. [10947
——The ransom of Red Chief, and other O. Henry stories for boys. Garden City, N. Y., Doubleday, Page & Co., 1918. 329 p. [10948
——Roads of destiny, by O. Henry [pseud.] New York, Doubleday, Page & Co., 1909. 376 p. First edition. [10949
—— ——[Garden City, N. Y.] 1920. 312 p. [10950
——Rolling stones, by O. Henry [pseud.] Garden City, N. Y., Doubleday, Page & Co., 1912. 292 p. First edition. [10951
—— ——1920. [10952
——Selected stories from O. Henry [pseud.] ed. by C. Alphonso Smith. Garden City, N. Y., Doubleday, Page & Co., 1922. 255 p. [10953
—— ——New York, Odyssey Press [1942] [10954
——Sixes and sevens, by O. Henry [pseud.] Garden City, N. Y., Doubleday, Page & Co., 1911. 283 p. First edition. [10955
—— ——1920. [10956
——Strictly business; more stories of the four million, by O. Henry [pseud.] New York, Doubleday, Page & Co., 1910. 310 p. First edition. [10957
—— ——Garden City, N. Y., 1920. [10958
——Ten plays from O. Henry [pseud.]; authorized dramatizations by Addison Geery Smith. New York, S. French, 1934. 159 p. [10959
——The trimmed lamp, and other stories of the four million, by O. Henry [pseud.] New York, McClure, Phillips & Co., 1907. 260 p. First edition. [10960
—— ——[Garden City, N. Y.] Doubleday, Page & Co., 1920. [10961
—— ——1922. [10962
——The voice of the city; further stories of the four million, by O. Henry [pseud.] New York, The McClure Co., 1908. 243 p. First edition. [10963
—— ——[Garden City, N. Y.] Doubleday, Page & Co., 1920. 244 p. [10964
——The voice of the city and other stories by O. Henry [pseud.] A selection, with an introduction, by Clifton Fadiman. New York, The Limited Editions Club, 1935. 220 p. [10965

——Waifs and strays; twelve stories, by O. Henry [pseud.] together with a representative selection of critical and biographical comment. Garden City, N. Y., Doubleday, Page and Co., 1917. 308 p. First edition.   [10966
—— ——1920. 305 p.   [10967
——Whirligigs, by O. Henry [pseud.] New York, Doubleday, Page & Co., 1910. 314 p. First edition.   [10968
—— ——[Garden City, N. Y.] 1920.   [10969

Porterfield, Austin Larimore. Crime, suicide and social well-being in your state and city [by] Austin L. Porterfield and Robert H. Talbert. Fort Worth, 1948. 121 p.   [10970

Porterfield, Bettilu. The pleasure is mine . . . verse. Durham [Seeman Printery, Inc.] 1940. 38 p.   [10971

Portsmouth and Roanoke Railroad. President. Reply to the address of Capt. Francis E. Rives to the public. Norfolk, Va., Broughton, 1844. 23 p.   [10972

Portsmouth and Roanoke Railroad. Stockholders. Report of the committee appointed by the stockholders . . . to negotiate the sale of one half the Weldon Bridge. Portsmouth, John T. Hill, 1840. Film.   [10973

Portsmouth and South Mills Railway. Prospectus relating to the Portsmouth and South Mills Railway. Portsmouth, Va., W. A. Fiske, pr., n.d. 7 p.   [10974

Post graduate medical education in North Carolina, 1929-1939. No place, no publisher [1939?] [12] p.   [10975

Post-Oak circuit, by a member of the Red River conference; edited by Thomas O. Summers. Nashville, Tenn., Southern Methodist Publishing House, 1886. 351 p.   [10976

Poteat, Edwin McNeill, 1861-1937. The scandal of the cross. New York, Harper & Brothers, 1928. 189 p.   [10977
——The withered fig tree; studies in stewardship. Philadelphia, The Judson Press [c.1921] 74 p.   [10978

Poteat, Edwin McNeill, 1892-1955. Centurion, a narrative poem. New York, Harper & Brothers, 1939. 182 p.   [10979
——Coming to terms with the universe. New York, Association Press, 1931. 85 p.   [10980
——Four freedoms and God. New York, Harper & Brothers [1943] 155 p. [10981
——God makes the difference; studies in the faith of nature and the nature of faith. New York, Harper & Brothers [1951] 242 p.   [10982
——Jesus and the liberal mind. Philadelphia, The Judson Press [1934] 237 p. [10983
——Jesus' belief in man. New York, Abingdon Press [1956] 159 p.   [10984
——Last reprieve? New York, Harper & Brothers [1946] 105 p.   [10985
——Mandate to humanity; an inquiry into the history and meaning of the Ten Commandments. Nashville, Abingdon-Cokesbury Press [1953] 238 p.   [10986
——Over the sea, the sky. New York, Harper & Brothers [1945] 70 p.   [10987
——Parables of crisis. New York, Harper & Brothers [1950] 255 p.   [10988
——Reverend John Doe, D. D.; a study of the place of the minister in the modern world. New York, Harper & Brothers, 1935. 127 p.   [10989
——The social manifesto of Jesus. New York, Harper & Brothers, 1937. 255 p. [10990
——These shared His power. [New York] Harper & Brothers [c.1941] 180 p. [10991
——Thunder over Sinai; studies in the moral attitudes of Jesus. New York, Harper & Brothers, 1936. 118 p.   [10992

Poteat, Gordon. A Greatheart of the South, John T. Anderson, medical missionary. New York, George H. Doran Co. [c.1921] 123 p.   [10993

Poteat, Hubert McNeill, tr. Marcus Tullius Cicero: Brutus. On the nature of the Gods. On divination. On duties. Chicago, University of Chicago Press [1950] 660 p.   [10994

Poteat, Hubert McNeill. Practical hymnology. Boston, Richard G. Badger [c.1921] 130 p.   [10995
——Repetition in Latin poetry with special reference to the metrical treatment of repeated words. New York, 1912. 79 p. Thesis (Ph. D.) Columbia University   [10996

Poteat, Hubert McNeill, ed. Selected letters of Cicero. Boston, D. C. Heath & Co. [c.1916] 201 p.   [10997

——Selected epigrams of Martial. New York, Prentice-Hall, Inc., 1931. 261 p. [10998
——Selected letters of Pliny. Boston, D. C. Heath and Co. [c.1937]   216 p.   [10999
Poteat, William Louis. The call to heroism. No place, no publisher, 1935. 16 p. [11000
——Can a man be a Christian to-day?   Chapel Hill, University of North Carolina
Press, 1925.   110 p.   [11001
——Education and depression; address delivered before the Southern Conference on
Education, Chapel Hill, N. C., November 5, 1931.   [Chapel Hill, University of
North Carolina?] 1931.   12 p.   [11002
——Laboratory and pulpit; the relation of biology to the preacher and his message.
Philadelphia, Griffith and Rowland Press, 1901.   103 p.   [11003
——The new peace; lectures on science and religion.   Boston, R. G. Badger [c.1915]
160 p.   [11004
——The place of the orphanage in the Christian program.   Thomasville, Charity
and Children Press, 1914.   12 p.   [11005
——Putting the kingdom first.   Raleigh, Edwards & Broughton Printing Co., 1913.
19 p.   [11006
——Religion in education; address before the Southern Baptist Convention, Bal-
timore, May 14, 1910. Nashville, Baptist Sunday School Board [1910?] 12 p. [11007
——Stop-light.   Nashville, Tenn., Broadman Press [c.1935]   91 p.   [11008
——The way of victory.   Chapel Hill, University of North Carolina Press, 1929.
83 p.   [11009
——Youth and culture. [Wake Forest] Wake Forest College Press, 1938. 150 p. [11010
Pothier, Robert Joseph.   Treatise on obligations, considered in a moral and legal
view; tr. from the French . . . [by F. X. Martin?]   Newbern, Martin and Ogden,
1802.   2 v. in 1.   [11011
Potter, Henry.   The office and duty of a justice of the peace, and a guide to sheriffs,
coroners, clerks, constables, and other civil officers; according to the laws of North
Carolina.   Raleigh: Printed by and for Joseph Gales, 1816.   418 p.   [11012
—— ——2d ed.   Raleigh, J. Gales & Son, 1828.   448 p.   [11013
[**Potter, Robert**]   An account of the attempt made by Jesse A. Bynum . . . to murder
Robert Potter. No place, no publisher [182?]   26 p.   [11014
——Address . . . to the people of Granville County.   [Faustus Castle, no publisher,
1832]   86 p.   [11015
Potter, Robert.   Argument addressed to the Supreme Court of North Carolina, at
June term, 1825, on the constitutionality of the civil jurisdiction conferred . . . on
single justices of the peace. Raleigh, Printed by J. Gales & Son, 1826. 11 p. [11016
[**Potter, Robert**]   Head of Medusa; a mock-heroic poem.   Halifax [Office of the Free
Press] 1827.   86 p.   [11017
Potter, Robert.   A statement of the circumstances connected with the affair between
Jesse A. Bynum and himself. [Halifax, Office of the Free Press, 1825] 26 p. [11018
Potwin, Marjorie Adella.   Cotton mill people of the Piedmont.   New York, Colum-
bia University Press, 1927.   (Studies in history, economics and public law, ed. by
the Faculty of Political Science of Columbia University, no. 291)   166 p.   [11019
Pou, Edward William.   Record of Republican Party and its plea to the South; ex-
tract from speech, June 16, 1910.   No place, no publisher [1910?]   8 p.   [11020
Pou, James Hinton.   No compromise peace; founders' day address, Trinity College,
Trinity Park, Durham, N. C., Oct. 2, 1917.   Raleigh, Edwards & Broughton
Printing Co. [1917?]   9 p.   [11021
[**Pou, James Hinton**]   Protection for soldiers and sailors.   [Raleigh, N. C.   Council
of Defense, ca. 1918]   8 p.   [11022
Pound, Merritt Bloodworth.   Benjamin Hawkins, Indian agent.   Athens, Uni-
versity of Georgia Press [1951]   270 p.   [11023
Powell, Emma H.   New Bern, North Carolina, founded by De Graffenried in 1710.
No place [c.1905]   33 p.   [11024
Powell, Harold.   Deacon beacons, by Harold Powell and Tommy Olive.   Wake
Forest, 1953.   56 p.   [11025
Powell, William Stevens.   Frontiersmen, makers of America.   Charlotte, Charlotte
Zone Buick Dealers, 1951.   10 p.   [11026
——St. Luke's Episcopal Church, 1753-1953.   Salisbury, St. Luke's Episcopal
Church, 1953.   76 p.   [11027

Powers, George W. The story of the Thirty-eighth Regiment of Massachusetts Volunteers. Cambridge, Dakin and Metcalf, 1866. 308 p.   [11028

Powers, Mary Rebecca (Watson) comp. . . . Our clan of Johnsons. Kinston, 1940. 126 p.   [11029

Pownall, Thomas. A topographical description of such parts of North America as are contained in the (annexed) map of the middle British colonies, &c. in North America. London, J. Almon, 1776. 46 p.   [11030

Pranque, pseud. A country dance and its consequences. Tarboro, January 10th, 1879. [1] p.   [11031

Pratt, Fletcher. Preble's boys; Commodore Preble and the birth of American sea power. New York, William Sloane Associates, [1950] 419 p.   [11032

Pratt, Joseph Hyde. Answers to questions that are being asked regarding the bond issue for good roads in Orange County. No place, no publisher [1912] 3 p. [11033

——Recreation. Chapel Hill, 1927. 14 p.   [11034

——Suggestions for organization and work on good roads days, Nov. 5 and 6, 1913. No place, no publisher [1913?] 4 p.   [11035

——Western North Carolina . . . by Joseph Hyde Pratt and Frederic Q. Boyer. [Asheville, Inland Press] 1925. 60 p.   [11036

Preble, George Henry. The chase of the Rebel steamer of war Oreto . . . into the Bay of Mobile. Cambridge, Printed for private circulation, 1862. 60 p.   [11037

Predeek, Albert. A history of libraries in Great Britain and North America, tr. by Lawrence S. Thompson. Chicago, American Library Assn., 1947. 177 p. [11038

Prentiss, George L. Discourse in memory of Thomas Harvey Skinner. New York, Anson D. F. Randolph & Co. [1871?] 145 p.   [11039

Presbrey, Frank Spencer. The empire of the South. [Washington] Southern Railway, 1899. 181 p.   [11040

[**Presbrey, Frank Spencer**] Land of the Sky. No place, Richmond and Danville Railroad, n.d. 14 p.   [11041

——The Land of the Sky. [New York, Frank Presbrey Co. for Southern Railway Co.] n.d. 32 p.   [11042

Presbrey, Frank Spencer. The Land of the Sky and beyond. [New York, 1894] [32] p.   [11043

—— ——[Fleming, Schiller & Carnrick Press, 1896?]   [11044

—— ——Asheville plateau. [Passenger Dept., Southern Railroad] n.d.   [11045

——The Southland. [New York?] The Southern Railway Co., 1898. [183] p. Also issued in 1899 under title: The empire of the South.   [11046

——A souvenir of Asheville and thereabouts. New York, Author, n.d. [43] p. [11047

Presbyter, pseud. see Van Antwerp, David D.

Presbyter of N. C., pseud. Letters on the church. Newbern, N. S. Richardson, pr., 1883. 27 p.   [11048

Presbyterian Church in the U. S. The book of church order . . . as adopted by the General Assembly of 1879. Richmond, Presbyterian Committee of Publication [1883?] 117 p.   [11049

—— ——by the General Assembly of 1869. Richmond, Presbyterian Committee of Publication, 1869. 43 p.   [11050

——Minutes of the General Assembly of the Presbyterian Church in the Confederate States of America. Columbia, Evans & Cogswell, 1864. 342 p.   [11051

Presbyterian Church in the U. S. General Assembly. Memorial volume of the Westminster Assembly. 1647-1897. 2d ed. Richmond, Va., Presbyterian Committee of Publication [1897] 297 p.   [11052

Presbyterian Church in the U. S. Synod of Appalachia. Minutes, 19 - 19 - NcU has 1920-1956   [11053

Presbyterian Church in the U. S. Synod of Appalachia. Holston Presbytery. Minutes, 19 - 19 - NcU has [1921-1947]   [11054

Presbyterian Church in the U. S. Synod of the Carolinas. A pastoral letter by the Associate Presbytery of the Carolinas to the people under their care. Charlotte, Printed by Lemuel Bingham, 1826. 46 p.   [11055

——A pastoral letter from the Synod of the Carolinas, through the medium of their commission to the churches under their care. Salisbury, Printed by Francis Coupee, 1802. 24 p.   [11056

——A pastoral letter, from the Synod of the Carolinas, to the churches under their care. Fayetteville, Printed by Sibley and Howard, 1790. 44 p. Title page and p. 43-44 wanting in NcU copy [11057

——A pastoral letter by the Synod of the Carolinas to the churches under their care. Augusta, Hobby and Bunce, 1810. 46 p. [11058

Presbyterian Church in the U. S. Synod of North Carolina. Centennial addresses . . . delivered at Alamance Church, Greensboro, N. C., Oct. 7, 1913. [Greensboro, Jos. J. Stone & Co., pr., 1913?] 82 p. [11059

——Minutes of the session of the Synod of North Carolina, 1813- 1813- NcU has [1844-1847] 1849-1863, 1866-1873, 1875, 1877-1954 [11060

——A pastoral letter from the Synod of North Carolina to the churches under its care, adopted at Charlotte, 10th Nov., 1845. Fayetteville, Printed by Edward J. Hale, 1846 13 p. [11061

——Roll of churches, elders, and deacons in the Synod of North Carolina, 19 - NcU has 1921 [11062

——Synopsis, memorial of Synod of North Carolina to trustees and faculty of University of North Carolina. No place [1926?] [3] p. [11063

Presbyterian Church in the U. S. Synod of North Carolina. Albemarle Presbytery. Manual, containing its history, roll of ministers, roll of churches, officers, agents, committees, standing rules, together with rules of parliamentary order; adopted . . . 1892. Henderson, D. E. Aycock, 1893. 91 p. [11064

——Minutes, 1889- 1890- NcU has 1889-1895 [1897-1928] 1929-1953. [11066

Presbyterian Church in the U. S. Synod of North Carolina. Albemarle Presbytery. Woman's Missionary Union. Constitution and by-laws. Raleigh, Edwards & Broughton Co., 1910. 4 p. [11067

Presbyterian Church in the U. S. Synod of North Carolina. Asheville Presbytery. Minutes, 18 - 18 - NcU has 1921-1928 [11068

Presbyterian Church in the U. S. Synod of North Carolina. Committee on Educational Institutions. Report on the educational institutions survey. [Raleigh] 1955. 100 p. [11069

Presbyterian Church in the U. S. Synod of North Carolina. Concord Presbytery. Addresses delivered at the sesquicentennial celebration of Concord Presbytery, Bethpage Church, October 16, 1945. Morganton [1945] 15 p. [11070

——Manual . . . rev., April, 1888. Richmond, Va., Whittet & Shepperson, pr., 1888. 59 p. [11071

——Manual . . . rev., 1942. No place, 1942. 51 p. [11072

——Minutes, 18 - 18 - NcU has 1853, 1854, 1873 [1892-1907] 1908-1952, 1955 [11073

Presbyterian Church in the U. S. Synod of N. C. Convention of Elders and Deacons, Greensboro, 1858. Minutes of the convention . . . February 24th and 25th, 1858. Fayetteville, North Carolina Presbyterian Office, 1858. 20 p. [11074

Presbyterian Church in the U. S. Synod of N. C. Convention of Elders and Deacons, Raleigh, 1859. Minutes of the convention . . . February 15th and 16th, 1859. Fayetteville, Printed at the Presbyterian Job Office, 1859. 20 p. [11075

Presbyterian Church in the U. S. Synod of N. C. Convention of Elders and Deacons, Fayetteville, 1861. Minutes of the convention . . . March 6th and 7th, 1861. Fayetteville, The Presbyterian, 1861. 33 p. [11076

Presbyterian Church in the U. S. Synod of N. C. Fayetteville Presbytery. Home missions in Fayetteville Presbytery; study booklet for 1940. No place [1940?] 52 p. [11077

——Minutes, 18 - 18 - NcU has 1844 [1855-1907] 1908-1914, 1921-1941 [11078

——One hundred and twenty-fifth anniversary addresses, Fayetteville Presbytery, delivered at Centre Church, Maxton, N. C., October 11, 1938. No place, no publisher [1938?] 16 p. [11079

Presbyterian Church in the U. S. Synod of North Carolina. King's Mountain Presbytery. Manual . . . adopted at stated meeting, October 29, 1924, rev. 1954. No place [1954] 18 p. [11080

——Minutes, 19 - 19 - NcU has 1917-1920, 1922-1955 [11081

Presbyterian Church in the U. S. Synod of North Carolina. Mecklenburg Presbytery. Minutes, 18 - 18 - NcU has 1926-1948, 1953-1955 [11082

——The semi-centennial of Mecklenburg Presbytery, 1869-1919, held in Steele Creek Church, Mecklenburg County, N. C., Sept. 17th, 1919. No place, no publisher [1919?]   53 p.   [11083

Presbyterian Church in the U. S. Synod of North Carolina. Orange Presbytery. An address from the Presbytery of Orange to the churches under their care on the subject of educating poor and pious youth for the gospel ministry. Raleigh, William Boylan, pr., 1806.   13 p.   [11084

——Manual . . . adopted September, 1872. Raleigh, John Nichols, 1873. 38 p. [11085

—— ——rev. and adopted October, 1882. Salem, L. V. & E. T. Blum, 1883. 42 p.   [11086

—— ——Henderson, D. E. Aycock, pr., 1893.   91 p.   [11087

—— ——rev. 1895. Reidsville, R. I. Mayo, pr., 1895.   126 p.   [11088

—— ——3d revision, 1908. [Richmond, Va.] Whittet & Shepperson, pr., 1908. 80 p.   [11089

—— ——rev. 1953. No place, 1953.   91 p.   [11090

——Minutes, 18 - 18 - NcU has 1829-1837 [1854-1861] 1882-1891 [1892-1896] 1897-1907 [1908-1919] 1922-1954, 1956   [11091

Presbyterian Church in the U. S. Synod of North Carolina. Orange Presbytery. Board of Agency. Address in behalf of an institution for the education of youth . . . proposed . . . near Greensborough in the county of Guilford. Chapel Hill, Isaac C. Patridge, 1833. 10 p.   [11092

Presbyterian Church in the U. S. Synod of North Carolina. Orange Presbytery. Woman's Presbyterial Auxiliary. Constitution and by-laws. No place, n.d. 8 p.   [11093

——Proceedings, 18 - 18 - NcU has 1917   [11094

Presbyterian Church in the U. S. Synod of North Carolina. Wilmington Presbytery. Manual, adopted, November, 1883. Wilmington, Jackson & Bell, pr., 1883. 27 p.   [11095

——Minutes, 18 - 18 - NcU has [1913-1919] 1920-1955   [11096

Presbyterian Church in the U. S. Synod of North Carolina. Winston-Salem Presbytery. Minutes, 1923- 1923- NcU has 1923-1935 [1936-1937] 1938-1956 [11097

Presbyterian Church in the U. S. Synod of North Carolina. Woman's Missionary Union. Minutes, 18 - 18   NcU has 1906, 1907, 1911   [11098

Presbyterian Church in the U. S. Synod of North Carolina. Woman's Synodical Auxiliary. Minutes, 1913- 1913- NcU has 1923-1954   [11099

Presbyterian High School, Mebane, N. C. Catalogue, 1893/94?- 1894?- NcU has 1895/96   [11100

Presbyterian home, v. 1- April, 1953- High Point, Presbyterian Home, Inc., 1953- NcU has v. 1-2   [11101

Presbyterian Junior College for Men, Maxton, N. C. Bulletin, v. 1- 1929- Maxton, 1929- NcU has v. [1-18]   [11102

——Your college? [Maxton] n.d.   9 plates   [11103

Presbyterian Mission School for Colored Boys and Girls, Wake Forest, N. C. Catalogue, 1905/06?- 1906?- NcU has 1906/07   [11104

Presbyterian news, v. 1- September, 1935- Greensboro, Home Mission Committee of the Synod of North Carolina, 1935- NcU has v. 1-21   [11105

Presbyterian Orphans' Home, Barium Springs, N. C. Charter of the regents . . . with additions and amendments . . . August, 1924. Barium Springs [1924?] 8 p.   [11106

——Presbyterian Orphans' Home, Barium Springs, North Carolina [Barium Springs, 1941]   32 p.   [11107

——Report, 19 - Barium Springs, 19 - NcU has 1921-1925, 1926/27-1929/ 30   [11108

The Presbyterian preacher; or, Monthly sermons from American Presbyterian ministers, v. 1- 1829- Fayetteville, Evangelical Printing Office, 1829- NcU has v. 1, no. 2, 4   [11109

Presbyterian standard, v. 1-72, 1858-1931. Charlotte, Presbyterian Standard Publishing Co., 1858-1931. NcU has v. [1-9] and new series v. [1-27] 28 [29, 40-64] 65-66 [67] 68-72, v. 30-39 omitted in numbering. Title varies: North Carolina Presbyterian   [11110

Presbyterian Standard. Circular to the ministers and members of the Presbyterian churches and congregations in N. Carolina. [Fayetteville? 1857] [1] p. [11111
——[Letter from executive committee of the stockholders] [Fayetteville, 1858] [1] p. [11112
——Prospectus. [Fayetteville, 1857] 2 p. [11113

Prescott, Helen Malvina Blount. Genealogical memoir of the Roulhac family in America. Atlanta, Ga., American Publishing & Engraving Co., 1894. 109 p. [11114

The present state of Carolina with advice to the setlers, by R. F. London, Printed by John Bringhurst, 1682. 36 p. NcU has photostat from the original in the Henry E. Huntington Library [11115

[Presentation and unveiling of the statue of Charles Duncan McIver, in Capitol Square, Raleigh, N. C., May 15, 1912, 11 O'clock A.M.] [Raleigh, 1912] [2] p. [11116

Presentation of a flag from the city of Bern, Switzerland, to the city of New Bern, N. C., U. S. A. New Bern, N. S. Richardson, 1896. 12 p. [11117

The presentation of the portrait of the late Benjamin Rice Lacy to the state of North Carolina, held in the House of Representatives . . . November the twelfth, nineteen hundred and twenty-nine, Raleigh, North Carolina. [Raleigh] Friends of the late Benjamin Rice Lacy [1930] 41 p. [11118

The presidential question; addressed to the people of the United States. New York, Sickels, pr., 1828. 16 p. [11119

Preston, Carleton Estey. The high school science teacher and his work. New York, McGraw-Hill Book Co., Inc., 1936. 272 p. [11120

Preston, Edmund Randolph. Lee at Lexington. [Charlotte? Author? pref. 1913] [14] p. [11121
—— ——Charlotte, Charlotte Herald [pref. 1923] 15 p. [11122
—— ——[Ancon, Canal Zone, Author, pref. 1935] 16 p. [11123

Preston, George Riley. Thomas Wolfe, a bibliography. New York, C. S. Boesen, 1943. 127 p. [11124

Preston, John S. Celebration of the Battle of King's Mountain, Oct. 1855, and the address of the Hon. John S. Preston. Yorkville, S. C., Published by Miller & Melton, 1855. 108 p. [11125

Preston, Thomas Wilson. Historical sketches of the Holston valleys. Kingsport, Tenn., Kingsport Press, 1926. 186 p. [11126

Price, Isaiah. History of the Ninety-seventh Regiment, Pennsylvania Volunteer Infantry . . . 1861-65. Philadelphia, Author, 1875. 608 p. [11127

Price, Jonathan. A description of Occacock Inlet. Newbern, François-X. Martin, 1795. 8 p. NcU has photostat (positive) [11128

[Price, Julian] A pattern for southern progress. [Greensboro? Jefferson Standard Life Insurance Co., 1938?] [16] p. [11129

Price, Merle. The heart has its daybreak. Emory University, Ga., Banner Press [1950] 60 p. [11130
——Splendid rumor. Emory University, Ga., Banner Press [1953] 60 p. [11131

Price, Natalie Whitted. Sketches in lyric prose and verse. Chicago, R. F. Seymour [c.1920] 80 p. [11132

Price, Richard Nye. Holston Methodism, v. 1-5. Nashville, Tenn., Publishing House of the M. E. Church, South, 1903-1914. 5 v. [11133

Price, Rolland Ernest. Rutherford County: economic and social. [Durham] K. S. Tanner [1918] 61 p. [11134

Pridgen, Tim. Courage, the story of modern cockfighting. Boston, Little, Brown and Co., 1938. 263 p. [11135
——Tory oath. Garden City, N. Y., Doubleday, Doran and Co., Inc., 1941. 371 p. [11136
——West goes the road. Garden City, N. Y., Doubleday, Doran and Co., Inc., 1954. 226 p. [11137

Primitive Baptist, v. 1- 1835/36- Tarborough, George Howard, 1836- NcU has v. 1-11 [24-26, 35] [11138

The Primitive Baptist year book, 1946- Elon College, Primitive Baptist Publishing House & Library [c.1947- NcU has 1946, 1947 [11139

Primitive Baptists. North Carolina. Confession of faith. Raleigh, Primitive Baptist Office, 1850. Various paging [11140

Primitive Baptists. North Carolina. Associations see Name of the individual association

Primrose, Ella P. A sketch of the school of the Misses Nash and Miss Kollock, Hillsboro, North Carolina. [Raleigh, Mrs. W. S. Primrose, 1926] 13 p. [11141

Prince, Joseph Hardy. An address, delivered at Faneuil Hall, July 4, 1828, at the Jackson celebration in Boston. Boston, True and Greene, pr., 1828. 35 p. [11142

Prince, William Meade. The southern part of heaven. New York, Rinehart & Co., Inc. [1950] 314 p. [11143

Pringle, Patrick. Jolly Roger, the story of the great age of piracy. New York, W. W. Norton and Co., Inc. [1953] 294 p. [11144

Pritchard, Jesse Eli. Asheboro—as I remember it. Radio address, Station WGWR. [Asheboro, n.d.] 4 p. [11145

——A brief history of Giles Chapel Methodist Church. No place, Giles Chapel Methodist Church, 1952. 12 p. [11146

——An historical tour of Randolph County. Asheboro, Radio Station WGWR, 1948. 3 p. [11147

——A history of the Central Methodist Church of Asheboro, North Carolina. [Asheboro] Central Methodist Church, 1951. 25 p. [11148

Pritchard, Jeter Conley. "The brightest day of Republicanism": address delivered before the Republican State Convention at Greensboro, N. C., Aug. 28, 1902. No place, no publisher [1902?] 20 p. [11149

——Memorial address and resolutions adopted by the Asheville Bar . . . August, 1911, in honor of . . . Joseph Shepard Adams. Asheville, Inland Press, 1911. 20 p. [11150

——Judge J. C. Pritchard on prohibition . . . speech at Wilmington . . . March 14, 1908. [Raleigh, Edwards and Broughton Printing Co.] n.d. 16 p. [11151

——The judiciary; address delivered at the annual banquet of the Dialectic and Philanthropic societies of the University of North Carolina, Chapel Hill, May 30, 1908. No place, no publisher, n.d. 21 p. [11152

——The moral and intellectual development of the people of Western North Carolina; an address delivered before the graduating class of the Normal and Collegiate Institute, Asheville, N. C., June, nineteen hundred and seven. No place, no publisher, 1907. 15 p. [11153

——Speech delivered at Greensboro, N. C., June 2, 1900. No place, no publisher [1900?] 15 p. [11154

Pritchard, McKinley. Tribute to Richmond Pearson. No place, no publisher, n.d. 5 p. [11155

Pritchard, Thomas Henderson. Death of Col. Samuel L. Arrington, of Montgomery, Ala. Goldsboro, Mail Job Printing Office, 1880. 8 p. [11156

——The literary attractions of the Bible; an address delivered before the Clio Society of Oxford Female College, May 27, 1857. Richmond, H. K. Ellyson, 1857. 44 p. [11157

——No infant baptism in the Bible. Raleigh, Edwards, Broughton & Co., 1876. 139 p. [11158

——Religious liberty and the Baptists; a Thanksgiving sermon preached in the Raleigh Baptist Church, Nov. 28th, 1872. Raleigh, Edwards & Broughton, pr., 1872. 22 p. [11159

Pritchett, Charles Herman. The Tennessee Valley Authority. Chapel Hill, University of North Carolina Press, 1943. 333 p. [11160

Private devotion. [Raleigh? General Tract Agency?] n.d. (Selected for the soldiers. No. 406) 4 p. [11161

Proceedings of a convention of the presidents, superintendents and other officials of southern railways, for the promotion of immigration to the South . . . Atlanta, Jan. 4th, 1869. Atlanta, Atlanta Intelligencer, 1869. 15 p. [11162

Program of celebration and dedication of the Greene memorial monument at Guilford Court House Battlefield, July 3rd, 1915. No place, no publisher [1915?] 2 p. Tentative program. [11163

Program of the exercises at the unveiling of portrait of Thomas Hall Battle, City Court Room in the Municipal Building, Rocky Mount, N. C., November 5th, 1937. [Rocky Mount, Telegram Presses, 1937] 20 p. [11164

Program of the sixth annual convention of the Lloyd clan unveiling a marker in memory of Thos. F. Lloyd, Carrboro . . . Oct. 22, 1941. No place [1941?] 8 p. [11165

Program: Unveiling of monument to 1. Heroes of King's Mountain that went through Gillespie Gap; 2. Heroes of Etchoe Pass . . . 3. North and South Carolina troops, 30th Division, that broke Hindenburg Line, Gillespie Gap, July 4th, 1927. No place, no publisher [1927?] 14 p. [11166

Programme of celebration and dedication of the Greene memorial monument at Guilford Court House battlefield, July 3rd, 1915. No place, no publisher, 1915. 2 p. [11167

The progressive farmer and southern farm gazette, v. 1- 1886 - Raleigh [Agricultural Publishing Co.] 1886- NcU has v. [1-5, 7, 8, 11-20] 21 [22] 23 [24] 25-32 [33] 34-71 [11168

Progressive Farmer, Raleigh, N. C. More jobs . . . through new rural industries. Raleigh [1947] 16 p. [11169

Prohibition laws do not prohibit? Why? No place, no publisher, n.d. 1 p. [11170

Prohibition or saloons and distilleries—Which? No place, no publisher [1902?] 24 p. [11171

Prominent people of North Carolina; brief biographies. Asheville, Evening News Publishing Co., 1906. 128 p. [11172

Prophetic religion, v. 1- Black Mountain, Fellowship of Southern Churchmen, 193 - NcU has [5-14] [11173

Proposals for establishing a number of farms like those of New England, New York . . . and Delaware, on the south side of the western districts of North Carolina, for the mutual benefit of the settlers, and of the trade of Charleston, Wilmington (N. C.) Fayetteville, Georgetown (S. C.) Augusta, and Savannah, and of the planters on the sea-coast of the two Carolinas. No place, no publisher, 1816. 16 p. [11174

Proposals for issuing a periodical in the city of Raleigh, which will be exclusively devoted to polite literature and science, entitled The emerald. No place, no publisher, n.d. [1] p. [11175

The proposed amendments to the constitution of North Carolina; an address to voters. [Raleigh, Commercial Printing Co.] 1914. 10 p. [11176

Proposed changes in the lien laws of North Carolina. [Charlotte, Queen City Printing Co.] n.d. 7 p. [11177

The proposed franchise amendment; some constitutional discussion with declarations from Vance, Saunders, Ransom, Scales, Fowle, and others. No place, no publisher [1900] 75 p. [11178

Proposed memorial to O. Henry. [Raleigh, Mutual Publishing Co.] n.d. 7 p. [11179

Proposed North Carolina state memorial, commemorative and historical, Raleigh, North Carolina. [Norfolk, Va., Rossel Edward Mitchell and Co.] n.d. 1 p. [11180

Proposition for a convention. No place, no publisher, n.d. [1] p. [11181

Prosody of the Latin language . . . revised and amended for the use of colleges and academies. Raleigh, Star Office by T. Henderson, 1809. 12 p. [11182

Prospectus: Branson magazine of genealogies. [Raleigh, Levi Branson] n.d. 12 p. [11183

Prospectus of a proposed history of Western North Carolina . . . to be pub. under the auspices of Edward Buncombe chapter, D. A. R. No place, n.d. 8 p. [11184

Prospectus of souvenir history of the Wharton Orphanage for the Care of Destitute Children. No place, no publisher, n.d. 24 p. [11185

Protestant Episcopal Church in the Confederate States of America. The catechism of the Protestant Episcopal Church in the Confederate States. Raleigh, Church Intelligencer, 1862. 8 p. [11186

——Catechism to be taught orally to those who cannot read; designed especially for the instruction of the slaves. Raleigh, Church Intelligencer, 1862. 47 p. [11187

——Journal of proceedings of an adjourned convention of bishops, clergymen and laymen . . . held in Christ church, Columbia, S. C., from Oct. 16th to Oct. 24th, inclusive . . . 1861. Montgomery, Advertiser, 1861. 45 p.   [11188
——Journal of the proceedings of the general council . . . held in St. Paul's Church, Augusta, Georgia, from Nov. 12th to Nov. 22d, inclusive . . . 1862. Augusta, Ga., Chronicle and Sentinel, 1863. 215 p.   [11189
——Proceedings of a meeting of bishops, clergymen, and laymen . . . at Montgomery, Ala., July 3rd, 1861. Montgomery, Barrett, Wimbish & Co., 1861. 28 p. [11190
——Proposed constitution and digest of revised canons . . . reported to the adjourned convention of bishops, clergymen and laymen of said church, held in Christ Church, Columbia, S. C. in Oct. 1861. Columbia, R. W. Gibbes, 1861. 61 p.   [11191

Protestant Episcopal Church in the U. S. A. The order of service for the consecration of the Reverend William Jones Gordon, Jr., to be bishop of the Missionary District of Alaska, Church of the Good Shepherd, Raleigh, North Carolina . . . May 18th, 1948. [Raleigh?] 1948. 27 p.   [11192

Protestant Episcopal Church in the U. S. A. Department of Sewanee. Missionary Council. Report of commission on "settlement work and training schools for church workers among the cotton mill operatives of the South"; sixth Missionary Council . . . held at Charlotte, N. C., October 29-31, 1912. No place [1912?] 15 p.   [11193

Protestant Episcopal Church in the U. S. A. Diocese of East Carolina. Constitution and canons together with the rules of order . . . adopted by the Convention of 1886. Wilmington, Wm. L. DeRosset, 1886. 36 p.   [11194
——Journal of the convention, 1883- 1883- NcU has 1883-1955   [11195
——Pilgrimage to old Fort Raleigh, Roanoke Island, North Carolina, Aug. 20, 1587-May 20, 1908. New Bern, Owen G. Dunn, pr. [1908?] 41 p.   [11196

Protestant Episcopal Church in the U. S. A. Diocese of North Carolina. Address to the several dioceses of the Protestant Episcopal Church in the United States, on the subject of the division of dioceses, by a committee appointed by the convention of the Diocese of North Carolina, May, 1868. Wilmington, Wm. H. Bernard's Printing and Publishing House, 1868. 37 p.   [11197

[**Protestant Episcopal Church in the U. S. A. Diocese of North Carolina**] Church work among colored people in the Diocese of North Carolina. [Raleigh, St. Augustine's Printery] n.d. [2] p.   [11198

Protestant Episcopal Church in the U. S. A. Diocese of North Carolina. Circular [Raleigh, 1870] [1] p.   [11199
——Circular. [Edenton? Hodge & Wills? 1793] [1] p. NcU has photostat (negative)   [11200
——Constitution and canons, together with the rules of order. No place, no publisher, n.d. 22 p.   [11201
——Constitution and canons . . . Printed by order of the Convention of 1834. No place, n.d. 8 p.   [11202
——Constitution and canons, together with the rules or order . . . Rev. and adopted May 1866. No place, n.d. 16 p.   [11203
—— ——Wilmington, Wm. H. Bernard's Printing and Publishing House, 1868. 20 p.   [11204
—— ——Raleigh, Edwards & Broughton, pr., 1873. 27 p.   [11205
—— ——Wilmington, Jackson & Bell, pr., 1879. 26 p.   [11206
—— ——No place, 1882. 34 p.   [11207
—— ——Charlotte, Hirst Printing Co., 1888. 35 p.   [11208
—— ——Raleigh, Alford, Bynum & Christophers, pr., 1901. 36 p.   [11209
—— ——Raleigh, Edwards & Broughton Printing Co., 1913. 30 p.   [11210
—— ——[Charlotte, Presbyterian Standard Publishing Co.] 1921. 35 p. [11211
—— ——[Raleigh, Edwards & Broughton Co.] 1926. 37 p.   [11212
—— ——No place, 1935. 35 p.   [11213
——Journal of the convention of the Diocese of North Carolina, 1817- 1817- NcU has 1817-1955   [11214
——Journal of the first and second conventions . . . held in Newbern on the 24th of April, 1817, and in Fayetteville on the 2d of April, 1818. Fayetteville, Printed at the Observer Office, 1821. [Reprinted, 1882] 22 p.   [11215

——Minutes of the proceedings of the clergy and lay delegates of the Protestant Episcopal churches of North-Carolina, convened by appointment, the 24th day of April, 1817, in Christ's Church, in the town of Newbern. Fayetteville, Printed at the Observer Office [1817] 7 p. [11216

——Proceedings of the convention . . . convened at Fayetteville in the state of North Carolina, April 2, 1818. Wilmington, Printed by William Hollinshead for Thomas Loring, 1818. 11 p. [11217

——Report of the committee of the convention of the Diocese of North Carolina on the proposed changes in the Book of Common Prayer, A. D. 1886. Raleigh, Edwards, Broughton & Co., 1886. 11 p. [11218

——Statement of the difficulties between the Diocese of North Carolina and Dr. Ives . . . prepared by a committee appointed by the convention of 1853. Fayetteville, Printed by Edward J. Hale & Son, 1853. 29 p. [11219

Protestant Episcopal Church in the U. S. A. Diocese of North Carolina. Archdeaconry for Work Among Colored People. Minutes, 1901- 1901- NcU has 1905, 1906, 1909-1911, 1913, 1914, 1920, 1927, 1942 [11220

Protestant Episcopal Church in the U. S. A. Diocese of North Carolina. Colored Clergy and Congregations. Convocation, 1901- 1901- NcU has 1903, 1904 [11221

Protestant Episcopal Church in the U. S. A. Diocese of North Carolina. Convocation of Raleigh. Constitution. No place, n.d. 3 p. [11222

Protestant Episcopal Church in the U. S. A. Diocese of North Carolina. Missionary Society. An address of the Missionary Society of the Protestant Episcopal Church in the state of North-Carolina. No place [1817] 6 p. [11223

Protestant Episcopal Church in the U. S. A. Diocese of North Carolina. Social Service Commission. The report . . . to the convention, 1917. No place, no publisher [1917?] [6] p. [11224

Protestant Episcopal Church in the U. S. A. Diocese of North Carolina. Woman's Auxiliary to the Board of Missions. Annual report, 1883- 1883- NcU has [1883-1897] [1904-1911] 1912-1945, 1954-1956 [11225

Protestant Episcopal Church in the U. S. A. Diocese of South Carolina. Song sheet compiled for Young People's Service leagues of the Carolina Diocese. Columbia, S. C., The State Co., 1931. 41 p. [11226

Protestant Episcopal Church in the U. S. A. Diocese of Western North Carolina. Constitution and canons, including certain changes of the constitution proposed at the convention of 1923. No place, Published by order of the Convention, 1923. 36 p. [11227

——Constitution and canons; together with certain canons of the general convention and the rules of order of the Diocese. No place, Published by order of the Convention, 1924. 35 p. [11228

—— ——1929. [11229

——Journal, 1922- 1922- NcU has 1922-1954 [11230

[Protestant Episcopal Church in the U. S. A. Domestic and Foreign Missionary Society] The church's work among the Negroes, the Good Samaritan Hospital, Charlotte, N. C. 2d ed. [New York, Calumet Press, 1902] [4] p. [11231

Protestant Episcopal Church in the U. S. A. Missionary District of Asheville. Constitution and canons, 1904. Boston, Protestant Episcopal Church, General Convention, 1904. 31 p. [11232

—— ——No place, no publisher, 1919. 30 p. [11233

——District of Asheville. Asheville, 1904. [1] p. [11234

—— ——Gastonia, June, 1917. [1] p. [11235

——Journal, 1895-1922. 1895-1922. NcU has 1895-1899, 1901-1906, 1908-1922. Continues as Diocese of Western North Carolina, 1923- [11236

Protestant Episcopal Church in the U. S. A. Missionary District of Asheville. Lay Readers' Association. Constitution. Morganton, T. G. Cobb [1897?] 8 p. [11237

Protestant Episcopal Freedmen's Commission. Occasional paper, Jan. 1866. Boston, Rand and Avery, 1866. 29 p. [11238

Protestant Episcopalian, pseud. see Hawks, Francis Lister

Proudfit, Alexander. Tidings of great joy for all people, a sermon preached before the Washington Bible Society, Granville, January 31, 1816. Salem, Dodd and Stevenson, pr., 1816. 32 p. [11239

Prout, H. H. Gifts in the treasury; a sermon on diocesan missions, preached at the convention in St. Paul's Church, Edenton, N. C., May, 1858. Fayetteville, Printed by Edward J. Hale & Son,.1858. 16 p. [11240

Pruitt, Anne, joint author, see **Wood, Harriette**

Public financing, 192 - Trinity, Bruce Craven, 1924- NcU has February, March, April, 1924 [11241

Public Ledger, Oxford, N. C. The Public Ledger cook book, containing 300 recipes submitted by Oxford and Granville County ladies. Oxford, n.d. 79 p. [11242

Public Library Workshop Committee. Which way tomorrow? Public Library Workshop, Winston-Salem, N. C., April 27-29, 1955. No place [1955] 66 p. [11243

Public meeting and correspondence. No place, no publisher [1876] 8 p. [11244

Public service, v. 1- 1924- Raleigh, North and South Carolina Public Utility Information Bureau, 1924- NcU has v. 1-4 [11245

Public Welfare Institute, Chapel Hill, N. C., July 18-22, 1938. Reports of the Committee on social trends and practices and twelve discussion groups. Chapel Hill, Division of Public Welfare and Social Work, University of North Carolina [1938] 65 p. [11246

Public Welfare Institute, Chapel Hill, N. C., October 24-27, 1939. Reports of the forums and summary by the Committee on social work trends and practices. [Raleigh, State Board of Charities and Public Welfare, 1939?] 22 p. [11247

Publicola, pseud. see **Iredell, James, 1751-1799**

Puckett, Newbell Niles. Folk beliefs of the southern Negro. Chapel Hill, University of North Carolina Press, 1926. 644 p. [11248

Puett, Minnie Stowe. History of Gaston County. Charlotte, Observer Printing House, Inc., 1939. 218 p. [11249

[**Pugh, Jesse Forbes**] Journeys through Camden County. [Camden? Author, 1953?] 19 p. [11250

Pugh, Mabel. Little Carolina blue bonnet. New York, Thomas Y. Crowell Co. [c.1933] 171 p. [11251

Pugh, Whitmell H. An inaugural essay on the supposed powers of nature in the cure of disease; submitted to the . . . University of Pennsylvania, on the sixth day of June, one thousand eight hundred and four, for the degree of Doctor of Medicine. Philadelphia, 1804. 30 p. [11252

Pullen, John T. Prayer and its answer . . . 4th ed. Raleigh, Clarence E. Mitchell, 1936. 151 p. [11253

——What saith the scripture? Raleigh, Edwards & Broughton, pr., 1900. 139 p. [11254

Pullen, William Russell. A check list of legislative journals issued since 1937 by the states of the United States of America. Chicago, American Library Association, 1955. 59 p. [11255

Pullias, Earl Vivon. Variability in results from new-type achievement tests. Durham, Duke University Press, 1937. (Duke university research studies in education [no. 2]) 100 p. [11256

Purcell, J. B. Wilmington in health and disease. Wilmington, Journal, 1867. 51 p. [11257

Purdy, Alexander Converse. An adequate leadership for Friends meetings; the Ward lecture given at Guilford College on Founders Day, November 10, 1950. Guilford College [1950] 22 p. [11258

Purify, George W. Denominational tree, or map, showing at one view the origin, date, descent, and by whom the different Christian denominations were founded. Chapel Hill, Author, c.1876. [1] p. [11259

——A history of the Sandy Creek Baptist Association from its organization in A.D. 1758 to A.D. 1858 . . . being an enlargement of the centenary sermon . . . at Love's Creek Meeting-house, Chatham County, N. C. on the 3d day of October, 1858. New-York, Sheldon & Co., 1859. 329 p. [11260

——Mr. Scoville's review unmasked. Hillsborough, Printed by D. Heartt & Son, 1855. 35 p. [11261

——Pedobaptist immersions. Forestville, Baptist Bible and Publication Society, 1854. 67 p. [11262

——Scriptural history of Judas Iscariot. Hillsborough, Printed by D. Heartt & Son, 1853. 32 p.   [11263

——A sermon. Nashville, Southwestern Publishing House, 1858. 96 p.   [11264

——The tekel of Methodism; history of Episcopal Methodism in which its claims to being a church of Christ are investigated. Chapel Hill, Gazette, 1858. 47 p. [11265

Purry, Jean Pierre. Memorial presented to His Grace, my lord the Duke of Newcastle . . . upon the present condition of Carolina. Augusta, Ga. [Savannah, Ga., J. H. Estill, pr.] 1880. 24 p.   [11266

Purviance, David. The biography of Elder David Purviance with his memoirs. Dayton, O., B. F. & G. W. Ells, 1848. 304 p.   [11267

——————[Reprinted Kimberlin Heights, Tenn., Alva Ross Brown, 1940] 278 p.   [11268

Purviance, Samuel D. To the freemen of Fayetteville district. [Fayetteville, 1800] [1] p. NcU has photostat (negative)   [11269

Pusey, William Allen. The Wilderness road to Kentucky. New York, George H. Doran Co. [c.1921] 131 p.   [11270

Puseyite developments; or, Notices of the New York ecclesiologists, dedicated to their patron, the Rt. Rev. Bishop Ives, of North Carolina, by a layman. New York, Berford & Co., 1850. 20 p.   [11271

Putnam, Albigence Waldo. History of middle Tennessee; or, Life and times of General James Robertson. Nashville, Tenn., Printed for the Author, 1859. 668 p.   [11272

Putnam, Arthur Alwyn. A selection from the addresses, lectures and papers, with a biographic sketch, of Arthur A. Putnam. Cambridge, Riverside Press, 1910. 183 p.   [11273

Putnam, Eben. Lieutenant Joshua Hewes; a New England pioneer, and some of his descendants. [New York] Privately printed [J. F. Tapley Co.] 1913. 656 p. [11274

Putnam, George Rockwell. Lighthouses and lightships of the United States. New and rev. ed. Boston, Houghton Mifflin Co., 1933. 324 p.   [11275

Putnam, Nina (Wilcox) The inner voice. New York, Sheridan House [c.1940] 309 p.   [11276

Putnam, Samuel Henry. The story of Company A, Twenty-fifth Regiment, Mass. Vols. in the war of the rebellion. Worcester, Putnam, Davis and Co., 1886. 324 p.   [11277

Pyle, Howard. Howard Pyle's Book of pirates. New York, Harper & Brothers, 1921. 246 p.   [11278

——The story of Jack Ballister's fortunes. New York, Century Co., 1895. 420 p. [11279

Quail Roost Farm, Rougemont, N. C. Quail Roost Maxim Guernsey sale, 1940- Sparks, Md., Louis M. Merryman and Sons, 1940- NcU has 1947, 8th sale [11280

Quaker, v. 1- 191 - Guilford College, Senior Class of Guilford College, 19 - NcU has 1914, 1916/17, 1918   [11281

Quarles, Benjamin. The Negro in the Civil War. Boston, Little, Brown and Co. [1953] 379 p.   [11282

Quarterly review of higher education among Negroes, v. 1- January, 1933- [Charlotte, Johnson C. Smith University] 1933- NcU has v. 1-23   [11283

Quarterly review of literature, v. 1, Autumn, 1943-Summer, 1944. [Chapel Hill] 1943-44. NcU has v. 1. Moved to New Haven Conn., following v. 1, no. 4. [11284

Quarterman, James. Reply to the speech of the Rev. F. L. Hawks, which he delivered in Philadelphia, October 11th, 1844, before the General Convention of the Protestant Episcopal Church. Flushing, Author, 1844. 24 p.   [11285

Quattlebaum, Paul. The land called Chicora; the Carolinas under Spanish rule, with French intrusions, 1520-1670. Gainesville, University of Florida Press, 1956. 153 p.   [11286

Queen City Printing Co., Charlotte, N. C. New York comes to North Carolina. Charlotte, c.1926. 11 p.   [11287

Queen's College, Charlotte, N. C. Bulletin, 191 - 191 - NcU has [1913-1956] [11288

——Catalogue, 18 - Charlotte, 18 - NcU has 1898/99, 1905/06, 1909/10, 1911/ 12, 1912/13 Continues as its Bulletin, 1913?- Called, -1913: Presbyterian College for Women; 192 - Queen's-Chicora College   [11289

Qui, pseud.   see LaSelle, Evelyn

Quick, William Harvey.   Negro stars in all ages of the world.   Richmond, Va., S. B. Adkins & Co., pr., 1898.   447 p.   [11290

Quincy, G. R.   The Reidsville racket store.   [Reidsville] n.d.   [1] p.   [11291

Quinn, David Beers.   Raleigh and the British Empire.   London, Hodder & Stoughton for the English Universities Press [1947]   284 p.   [11292

Quinn, David Beers, ed.   The Roanoke voyages, 1584-1590; documents to illustrate the English voyages to North America under the patent granted to Walter Raleigh in 1584.   London, Hakluyt Society, 1955.   (Works issued by the Hakluyt Society, 2d ser., no. 104)   2 v.   [11293
——The voyages and colonising enterprises of Sir Humphrey Gilbert.   London, Hakluyt Society, 1940.   (Works issued by the Hakluyt Society, 2d ser., no. 83, 84, 1938-1939)   2 v.   [11294

Quint, Alonzo Hall.   The record of the Second Massachusetts Infantry, 1861-65. Boston, J. P. Walker, 1867.   528 p.   [11295

Quintard, Charles Todd, comp.   The Confederate soldiers' pocket manual of devotions, compiled by Rev. C. T. Quintard, chaplain, 1st Tennessee Regiment. Charleston, S. C., Evans & Cogswell, pr., 1863.   80 p.   Title page wanting in NcU copy   [11296
—— ——96 p.   [11297

Quips and cranks, 1895-   Davidson College, Eumenean and Philanthropic Societies, 1895-   NcU has 1895, 1898, 1901, 1920, 1923, 1926, 1934, 1937, 1938   [11298

Rabb, Susie.   Rail fence reveries.   [Cedar Mountain] 1952.   63 p.   [11299

Raby, Mattie Pearl.   Voice of acceptance.   New York, Vantage Press [c.1953] 42 p.   [11300

The racket, January, 1889-   Gamewell, Eliza Pfeiffer Houck, 1889-   NcU has [1889-1892]   [11301

Radcliffe, Edward J.   The Radcliffes of Carolina; a genealogical record.   No place, no publisher [1936?]   [4] p.   [11302
—— ——[1938?]   [9] p.   [11303

Radical falsehood exposed!   Grant's attorney general exposes the falsehoods of Senator Morton and Spencer's Ku-Klux speeches.   [1870]   8 p.   [11304

Radicue Primitive Baptist Association.   Minutes, 188 - 188 -   NcU has [1910-1931]   [11305

Raeford Institute, Raeford, N. C.   Catalogue, 1895/96?-   1896?-   NcU has 1897/98, 1902/03, 1905/06   [11306

Ragsdale, George Young.   Johnston County: economic and social, by W. M. Sanders, Jr. [and] G. Y. Ragsdale.   [Smithfield, Smithfield Observer] 1922.   82 p. [11307

[Railroad meeting, Chatham County, N. C., Aug. 1, 1828]   [Hillsborough, D. Heartt, pr., 1828]   8 p.   [11308

Raine, James Watt.   The land of saddle-bags; a study of the mountain people of Appalachia.   New York, Pub. jointly by Council of Women for Home Missions and Missionary Education Movement of the United States and Canada [c.1924] 260 p.   [11309

Raleigh, N. C.   Associated Charities.   Annual report, 190 -   Raleigh, 190 -   NcU has 1904/05, 1906/08, 1915-19   [11310
——Constitution and by-laws . . . adopted February 18, 1905.   [Raleigh? 1905?] 8 p.   [11311

Raleigh, N. C.   Atlantic Joint Stock Land Bank.   New issue, $1,500,000.   [Raleigh? 1922?]   3 p.   [11312

[Raleigh, N C.   Aycock Memorial Association]   Presentation and unveiling of memorial tablet, Charles Brantley Aycock, Goldsboro, North Carolina, November 1, 1929.   No place, no publisher, n.d.   25 p.   [11313

Raleigh, N. C.   Board of Aldermen.   Charter and ordinances of the city of Raleigh, revised, codified, and indexed . . . by Armistead Jones and son; adopted July, 1912. Raleigh, E. M. Uzzell & Co., pr., 1912.   348 p.   [11314
——Charter of the city of Raleigh . . . adopted by the Board of Aldermen, May 1st, 1885.   Raleigh, P. W. Wiley & Co., 1885.   153 p.   [11315

——Indebtedness of the city of Raleigh, May 1st, 1875.   Raleigh, Edwards, Broughton and Co., 1875.   38 p.   [11316
——Ordinance regulating horse and cow stables in the city of Raleigh, adopted Oct. 6, 1905.   Raleigh, Edwards & Broughton, pr., 1905.   4 p.   [11317
——Ordinance regulating the sale of milk in the city of Raleigh, adopted Aug. 4, 1905.   Raleigh, Edwards & Broughton, pr., 1905.   6 p.   [11318
——Ordinances of the city of Raleigh, revised, codified and indexed . . . by J. N. Holding, city attorney; adopted September 3, 1897.   Raleigh, E. M. Uzzell, pr., 1897.   186 p.   [11319
—— ——revised, codified and indexed . . . by W. L. Watson; adopted Aug. 3, 1900.   Raleigh, Alford, Bynum & Christophers, pr., 1900.   196 p.   [11320
——Resolutions opposing the bill offered by the good government association of Raleigh.   No place, no publisher [1909]   9 p.   [11321
Raleigh, N. C.   Board of Commissioners.   Charter and ordinances of the city of Raleigh, North Carolina.   Raleigh, Nichols, Gorman & Neathery, pr., 1867. 59 p.   [11322
——Charter of the city of Raleigh, revised and consolidated by the General Assembly . . . at the session of 1856-57.   Raleigh, Holden and Wilson, 1857.   37 p.   [11323
—— ——prefaced by a recapitulation of the various acts, ordinances, and resolutions concerning the city.   Raleigh, Daily News, 1876.   125 p.   [11324
——The code of the city of Raleigh, North Carolina; the charter as amended and the general ordinances . . . effective May 1, 1940.   Charlottesville, Va., The Michie Co., 1940.   401 p.   [11325
——Condensed view of the acts of the General Assembly and ordinances of the Commissioners for the government of the city of Raleigh; as rev. . . . March, 1816. Raleigh, J. Gales, pr., [1816]   19 p.   [11326
——Consolidated ordinances of the city of Raleigh, adopted . . . August, 1929 . . . the city charter.   Raleigh, Capital Printing Co., 1929.   182 p.   [11327
——Laws for the government of the city of Raleigh . . . from the first act of incorporation to 1838; comp. by W. C. G. Carrington.   Raleigh, Raleigh Register, 1838.   59 p.   [11328
—— ——from the first act of incorporation to 1854.   Raleigh, J. Gales, pr., 1854. 85 p.   [11329
——[Ordinance for improvement of sidewalks] [Raleigh, no publisher, 1869] 1 p.   ·   [11330
——Ordinance regulating the operation of motor vehicles in the city of Raleigh, N. C., October 10, 1916.   Raleigh, Edwards and Broughton Printing Co., 1916. 7 p.   [11331
——Ordinances and by-laws of the Board of Commissioners for the government of the city of Raleigh . . . from the year 1803 to 1854.   Raleigh, Seaton Gales, 1854. 85 p.   [11332
——Ordinances of the city of Raleigh, adopted April 8th, 1870.   Raleigh, Wm. A. Smith & Co., 1870.   35 p.   [11333
—— ——adopted Jan. 6th, 1873.   Raleigh, John Nichols & Co., 1873.   48 p. [11334
Raleigh, N. C.   Board of Health.   . . . Contagious and infectious diseases sanitation.   Raleigh, n.d.   15 p.   [11335
——Monthly bulletin, v. 1- 19 - Raleigh, 19 - NcU has v. 4, no. 12, Dec. 1916; v. 7, no. 3, Mar. 1917; v. 7, no. 10-11, Oct.-Nov. 1917   [11336
——The prevention of contagious and infectious diseases, by Thomas M. Jordan. Raleigh [191?]   13 p.   [11337
Raleigh, N. C.   Capital Club.   Charter, constitution and by-laws.   Raleigh, E. M. Uzzell, 1891.   21 p.   [11338
Raleigh, N. C.   Cemetery Association.   Charter and by-laws; chartered Feb. 26, 1869.   Raleigh, Nichols & Gorman, pr., 1870.   38 p.   [11339
—— ——Edwards & Broughton Printing Co., 1917.   37 p.   [11340
——Oakwood Cemetery.   [Raleigh, 1872]   3 p.   [11341
Raleigh, N. C.   Chamber of Commerce.   The case of Raleigh for the University medical school of North Carolina.   [Raleigh] n.d.   [3] p.   [11342
[Raleigh, N. C.   Chamber of Commerce]   Facts and figures about Raleigh in the heart of North Carolina's progress.   [Raleigh, 1925?]   8 p.   [11343

Raleigh, N. C. Chamber of Commerce. Industrial directory of manufacturers, processors, wholesale distributors, contractors, branch offices, consulting engineers, located in Raleigh, North Carolina, Raleigh, 19 - NcU has March 15, 1952 [11344

——Motorist information through Raleigh, North Carolina. Raleigh, n.d. 8 p.

[Raleigh, N. C. Chamber of Commerce] [Program of Raleigh Auditorium dedication week, Oct. 17-20, 1911] No place, no publisher [1911] [15] p. [11345

Raleigh, N. C. Chamber of Commerce. Raleigh . . . an epitome of the city's growth, progress, and industries. [Raleigh, Edwards & Broughton Printing Co.] n.d. 16 p. [11346

—— ——[1906?] 31 p. [11347

——Raleigh, the capital city of North Carolina. Raleigh, Edwards & Broughton Printing Co. [1912?] 16 p. [11348

——Raleigh, North Carolina, the capital of the "good roads state". [Raleigh, Edwards & Broughton Printing Co., 1932?] Folder [11349

——Raleigh, North Carolina, the progressive capital of a progressive state. [Raleigh, 1934] [10] p. [11350

——Raleigh, the historical capital city, its institutions, wealth and resources. [Raleigh, Commercial Printing Co., 1924?] 28 p. [11351

——Report, 19 - 19 - NcU has 1908/09, 1909/10, 1916/17 [11352

[Raleigh, N. C. Chamber of Commerce] Souvenir of dedication, Raleigh Memorial Auditorium, Raleigh, North Carolina. Raleigh [1932] [16] p. [11353

Raleigh, N. C. Chamber of Commerce. The sunny South . . . Raleigh, N. C. will suit you. [Raleigh, Edwards & Broughton Printing Co.] n.d. 16 p. [11354

——Visitors' and newcomers' guide to Raleigh, North Carolina; roster, Raleigh Chamber of Commerce. [Raleigh, 1941?] 35 p. [11355

—— ——[1943?] 41 p. [11356

—— ——[1945] 48 p. [11357

Raleigh, N. C. Chamber of Commerce and Industry. The city of Raleigh, N. C. and vicinity, conditions and resources. [Raleigh, Edwards & Broughton, 1894] 132 p. [11358

——[Raleigh . . . prepared by George Allen] [Raleigh, Edwards & Broughton, 1897?] 20 p. [11359

——Raleigh, commercial, financial, educational. Raleigh, Edwards & Broughton [1910] 55 p. [11360

——Raleigh, N. C., within fifteen hours of New York City. [Raleigh, Edwards & Broughton, 1897?] 20 p. [11361

——Raleigh of today, the capital city of North Carolina. [Raleigh? 1904?] 28 p. [11362

[Raleigh, N. C. Christ Church] [At a special meeting of the Vestry of Christ's Church, Raleigh, held on the 18th day of June, 1840] [Raleigh? 1840?] 8 p. [11363

Raleigh, N. C. Christ Church. Centennial ceremonies held in Christ Church parish, Raleigh, North Carolina, A. D. 1921, including historical addresses. Raleigh, Bynum Printing Co., 1922. 55 p. [11364

——Christ Church, Raleigh, North Carolina, parish directory, 1938. [Raleigh?] 1938. 27 p. [11365

—— ——[Raleigh] 1940. 36 p. [11366

——Christ Church parish, Rev. M. M. Marshall, rector. Raleigh, n.d. 4 p. [11367

[Raleigh, N. C. Christ Church] Notes upon Dr. Freeman's appendix to the documents connected with his resignation as rector of Christ's Church, Raleigh, by one of the vestry. [Raleigh, 1840] 28 p. [11368

Raleigh, N. C. Christ Church. Parish directory, Christ Church, the Rev. Milton A. Barber, rector. [Raleigh?] 1927. [25] p. [11369

——Service commemorating the one hundredth anniversary of the laying of the cornerstone of Christ Church, Raleigh, North Carolina, December twelfth, 1948. [Raleigh, 1948] 27 p. [11370

——[Statement showing facts and figures in regard to the finances of the Church for the past few years] Raleigh, June 1st, 1878. [2] p. [11371

Raleigh, N. C. Church of the Good Shepherd. . . . Translation of the body of the late Rt. Rev. Theodore Benedict Lyman . . . fourth bishop of North Carolina, Ascension Day, May 21, 1914, 5:30 P.M. [Raleigh, 1914] [2] p. [11372

Raleigh, N. C. Clearing House Association. Raleigh, the city at the crossways. Raleigh, Edwards & Broughton Printing Co., 1914. 7 p. [11373

Raleigh, N. C. Committee on Federal Farm Loan Bank. A natural and economic territory for a federal farm loan bank district with Raleigh as the location of the bank. No place [1916] 59 p. [11374

Raleigh, N. C. Convention of the Friends of the Hon. Stephen A. Douglas and the Hon. Hershel V. Johnson. Proceedings; together with the speech of Hon. Stephen A. Douglas. [Raleigh, no publisher, 1860] 15 p. [11375

Raleigh, N. C. Council. City of Raleigh, North Carolina, budget, 19 - Raleigh, 19 - NcU has 1950/51, 1952/53-1955/56 [11376
——Report, 1947/48- Raleigh [1948- NcU has 1947/48 [11377
——Statements of financial condition, 19 - Raleigh, 19 - NcU has June 30, 1953; 1953/54 [11378

Raleigh, N. C. Edenton St. Methodist Episcopal Church, South. Directory . . . 1888. Raleigh, Observer, 1888. 45 p. [11379
——Published as an affectionate tribute by the Edenton St. M. E. Church, South, and the Edenton St. Sunday School of Raleigh, N. C. Raleigh, Mitchell Printing Co. [1927] 79 p. [11380

Raleigh, N. C. Elementary Education Council. Bulletin, v. 1- 192 - Raleigh, 192 - NcU has v. 3, no. 2, January, 1930; v. 3, no. 3, March, 1930 [11381

Raleigh, N. C. First Baptist Church. Directory, Feb. 1904. Raleigh, Edwards & Broughton, pr., 1904. 25 p. [11382
—— ——December, 1916. Raleigh, Mutual Publishing Co., 1916. 45 p. [11383
——Manual and directory . . . Oct. 1, 1900. Raleigh, Alford, Bynum & Christophers, pr., 1900. 40 p. [11384
——Manual of the First Baptist Church . . . April, 1874. Raleigh, John Nichols & Co., 1874. 36 p. [11385

Raleigh, N. C. First Baptist Church. Sunday-School. Annual reports of the officers, 188 - Raleigh, Uzzell and Gatling, 1884- NcU has 1883, 1884 [11386

Raleigh, N. C. First Presbyterian Church. Capital City recipes, by the ladies of the Presbyterian Church of Raleigh, N. C. Raleigh, Capital Printing Co., 1900. 82 p. [11387
——First Presbyterian Church, Raleigh, North Carolina, 1816-1941. [Raleigh, 1941] [15] p. [11388
——Directory and historical sketch, February, 1906, Alfred H. Moment, D. D., pastor. [Raleigh] 1906. 29 p. [11389

Raleigh, N. C. First Presbyterian Church. Sunday School Library. Catalogue of the Sunday School library of the First Presbyterian Church, Raleigh, N. C. [Raleigh] n.d. 27 p. [11390

[Raleigh, N. C. First Presbyterian Church. Vanguard Class] In memoriam. [Raleigh] n.d. [1] p. [11391

Raleigh, N. C. First Presbyterian Church. Woman's Auxiliary. Woman's Auxiliary of the First Presbyterian Church, 19 - Raleigh, 19 - NcU has 1939/40 [11392

Raleigh, N. C. Franklin Debating Society. Constitution, adopted February the 14th, 1832. No place, 1832. [1] p. [11393

Raleigh, N. C. Good Government Association. Act to secure more efficient municipal government. Raleigh, Edwards & Broughton Printing Co., n.d. 16 p. [11394

Raleigh, N. C. Greeters' Club. It's great to live in Raleigh. Raleigh [c.1939] unpaged [11395

Raleigh, N. C. Health and Street Cleaning Department. Annual report, 18 - Raleigh, 18 - NcU has 1904 (sixteenth) [11396
——Department of Board of health and street cleaning; from City ordinances, chapter XXII. Raleigh, Alford, Bynum & Christophers, pr., 1900. 27 p. [11397

Raleigh, N. C. Housing Authority. Raleigh housing, 193 - Raleigh, 193 - NcU has 1939/41, 1944/45 [11398

Raleigh, N. C. League of Women Voters. Raleigh city government; a handbook for citizens. Raleigh, 1952. 65 p. [11399

Raleigh, N. C. Mayor and City Officers. Annual report, 18 - Raleigh, 18 - NcU has 1883-1893, 1896-1906, 1909-1910 [11400

Raleigh, N. C. Mechanics and Investors Union. Articles of association and by-laws. Raleigh, Edwards & Broughton, pr., 1893. 19 p.   [11401

——A building and loan association and depository for monthly savings. No place, no publisher [1895?] 4 p.   [11402

Raleigh, N. C. Mechanics' Building and Loan Association. Charter and by-laws. Raleigh, Nichols & Gorman, 1870. 16 p.   [11403

Raleigh, N. C. Meeting of Warehousemen, Leaf Tobacco Dealers, Manufacturers and Farmers, Feb. 27, 1893. Proceedings. No place, no publisher, n.d. 4 p. [11404

Raleigh, N. C. Merchants' Association. Official program, Raleigh's Mardi Gras, Nov. 8th and 9th, 1922. [Raleigh, Capitol Printing Co., 1922] 16 p.   [11405

Raleigh, N. C. National Bank. Report of the President to the stockholders at their annual meeting, 188 - 188 - NcU has 1891   [11406

Raleigh, N. C. North Side Land Co. Prospectus of the North Side Land Company of Raleigh, N. C. No place, no publisher, n.d. Folder   [11407

Raleigh, N. C. Parker-Hunter Realty Co. Ten years in the history of Raleigh, North Carolina. Raleigh [1910?] 16 p.   [11408

Raleigh, N. C. Peace Society. Report, 1819/20- Raleigh, T. Henderson, pr., 1820- NcU has 1819/20   [11409

Raleigh, N. C. Police Commission. Rules, regulations and instructions for the government of the police force of the city of Raleigh, adopted . . . May, 1882. Raleigh, Edwards, Broughton and Co., 1882. 22 p.   [11410

Raleigh, N. C. Richard B. Harrison Public Library. 20 yrs. Richard B. Harrison Public Library, Raleigh, N. C. [Raleigh, 1955] [16] p.   [11411

Raleigh, N. C. Rotary Club. A history of the Rotary Club of Raleigh, North Carolina, 1914-1955. [Raleigh, 1955] 79 p.   [11412

——Rotary Club of Raleigh, constitution, by-laws and list of members. [Raleigh] 1921. 39 p.   [11413

——Silver jubilee meeting, Rotary Club of Raleigh, 1914-1939, Hotel Sir Walter, Monday, May twenty-second, nineteen thirty-nine. [Raleigh, 1939] 10 p. [11414

Raleigh, N. C. Saint Saviour's Church. Some notes in regard to Saint Saviour's (Church) and the new Edgar Haywood Memorial Parish House at Saint Saviour's in Raleigh, North Carolina. Raleigh, 1941. 19 p.   [11415

Raleigh, N. C. School Committee. Course of study and directions to teachers in the Raleigh Public Schools. Raleigh, Clifton, Scarborough and Co., 1898. 32 p.   [11416

——Curriculum bulletin, no. 1- 192 - Raleigh, 1928- NcU has no. 2-6   [11417

——Raleigh schools; a plain statement. [Raleigh?] n.d. 4 p.   [11418

——Rules and regulations of the Raleigh Township Graded Schools for 1907-1908. Raleigh, E. M. Uzzell & Co., 1907. 20 p.   [11419

——Rules and regulations with the course of study for the Public Schools of Raleigh Township. Raleigh, 1882. 20 p.   [11420

Raleigh, N. C. Tabernacle Baptist Church. Directory, July 1, 1903. No place, no publisher, n.d. 48 p.   [11421

Raleigh, N. C. Watauga Club. Need of an industrial school in North Carolina, together with the estimates of the cost of establishing and maintaining it; a memorial to the General Assembly by the Watauga Club of Raleigh, N. C. Raleigh, Daily Chronicle, 1885. 8 p.   [11422

Raleigh, N. C. Woman's Club. The Woman's Club of Raleigh, N. C. [Raleigh, 1922] 48 p.   [11423

——Yearbook, 19 - Raleigh, 19 - NcU has [1914/15-1932/33]   [11424

Raleigh, North Carolina, a summary of important facts about the city. Richmond, Hill Directory Co., Inc. [1926] 8 p.   [11425

Raleigh, N. C. directory, 1903- Richmond, Va., Hill Directory Co., 1903- NcU has 1903, 1905-06, 1907-08, 1909-10, 1911-12, 1913-14, 1915-16, 1917, 1918-19, 1919-20, 1921-22, 1922-23, 1923-24, 1924, 1925-1930, 1931-33, 1934-1942, 1948 [11426

Raleigh, N. C.; photographs in black. New York, Albertype Co. for George C. Heck and Henry E. Litchford, c.1891. [1] p. 16 plates   [11427

Raleigh Academy, Raleigh, N. C. Laws of the Raleigh Academy with the plan of education annexed, as revised in the year 1811. Raleigh, Printed by Gales & Seaton, 1811. 23 p. [11428

Raleigh and Augusta Air Line Railroad. Proceedings of the stockholders, 18 - Raleigh, 18 - NcU has 1889 [11429

Raleigh and Eastern North Carolina Railroad. Act of incorporation and prospectus. No place, no publisher [1903?] 9 p. [11430
——Proposed Raleigh and Eastern North Carolina Railroad Company from the Capital to Atlantic tide-water. No place, no publisher [1902] 11 p. [11431

Raleigh and Gaston Railroad.[1] Deed of trust to Edmund Randolph Robinson, of New York, William Nevins Whelen, of Philadelphia, and William E. Anderson, of Raleigh, North Carollna, to secure . . . the interest and principal of . . . bonds. No place [1873] 16 p. [11432
——First mortgage eight per cent bonds. [Raleigh, 1874] [2] p. [11433
——Proceedings of the annual meeting of the stockholders, 1835?- 1835?- NcU has 1852-1893 [11434
——Regulations governing employees in the passenger and freight transportation service of the Raleigh and Augusta Airline, Raleigh and Gaston, and Seaboard and Roanoke Railroad Co's, July, 1881. Raleigh, Edwards and Broughton, 1881. 33 p. [11435
——Report, 1836/37-1892/93? 1837?- NcU has 1836/37-1842/43, 1849/50-1851/ 52, 1853/54, 1867/68-1869/70, 1872/73 [11436
——Rules and regulations for the government of the Raleigh & Gaston Railroad Co. . . . to take effect February 1, 1871. Raleigh, Nichols & Gorman, 1871. 37 p. [11437
——Souvenir, presentation ceremonials of a silver service to Dr. W. J. Hawkins, retiring president . . . September 29th, 1875. Raleigh, Printed at the Daily News Book and Job Office, 1875. 8 p. [11438
——Through freight prices from Petersburg to stations on the Raleigh & Gaston Railroad via Gaston, May 1st, 1859. No place, 1859. [1] p. [11439
——To the stockholders. [Raleigh, 1871] 2 p. [11440

Raleigh and Pamlico Sound Railroad. Specifications for construction. No place, no publisher, n.d. 8 p. [11441

Raleigh Baptist Association. Minutes, 18 - Raleigh, 18 - NcU has 1807, 1810, 1836 [1851-1862] 1876-1886 [1900-1908] [1922-1934] 1949-1955 [11442

Raleigh Building and Loan Association, Raleigh, N. C. Charter and by-laws of the Raleigh Building and Loan Association. Charleston, S. C., Walker, Evans & Cogswell Co., 1909. 20 p. [11443
——The Raleigh Building and Loan Association. [Raleigh, Edwards and Broughton Printing Co.] n.d. [13] p. [11444
—— ——Raleigh [1915?] [22] p. [11445

Raleigh Christian Advocate see North Carolina Christian Advocate

Raleigh city directory, 188 - Raleigh, Turner, McLean & Losee Directory Co., 188 - NcU has 1886 [11446

Raleigh city directory, 188 - Raleigh, Edwards and Broughton for James Richards, 188 - NcU has 1883 [11447

Raleigh Club, Raleigh, N. C. Constitution. Raleigh, Edwards & Broughton, pr., 1872. 10 p. [11448

Raleigh Cotton Mills. Annual report made to stockholders, 18 - Raleigh, 18 - NcU has 1891 [11449

Raleigh Country Club, Raleigh, N. C. Constitution and by-laws, 1911. Raleigh, Commercial Printing Co. [1911?] 18 p. [11450
—— ——1914. [Raleigh, 1914] [11451

Raleigh Female Seminary, Raleigh, N. C. Catalogue, 18 - Raleigh, 18 - NcU has 1871/72, 1872/73, 1876/77 [11452

Raleigh Female Tract Society. . . . Report, Raleigh, Printed by J. Gales, 18 - NcU has 1820, fourth annual, containing Constitution and bye-laws. [11453

1. The state disposed of its stock in this railroad in 1866. Publications prior to that date are listed in Thornton, Official Publications of the Colony and State of North Carolina. Chapel Hill, 1954.

Raleigh Garden and Nursery. Descriptive catalogue of fruit and ornamental trees, shrubs, vines, roses. Raleigh, N. C. Institution for the Deaf & Dumb and the Blind, n.d. 71 p. [11454

—— ——32 p. [11455

—— ——16 p. [11456

——Descriptive catalogue of fruit trees, vines and plants cultivated and for sale by S. Otho Wilson. [Raleigh?] 1879. 20 p. [11457

——Illustrated descriptive catalogue of fruit trees, vines &c., specially adapted to the southern states . . . 7th ed. Raleigh, Edwards, Broughton & Co. [1884?] 32 p. [11458

Raleigh High School, Raleigh, N. C. Raleigh High School, 1875/76- Raleigh, 1875- NcU has 1875/76 [11459

Raleigh Male Academy, Raleigh, N. C. Catalogue, 1878/79?- 1879?- NcU has [1880/81-1896/97] [11460

Raleigh Marble Works, Raleigh, N. C. Some testimonials, voluntarily given without solicitation. Raleigh, Edwards and Broughton, n.d. 20 p. [11461

——Some work erected by Raleigh Marble Works, Cooper Brothers, proprietors. [Raleigh, Edwards & Broughton] n.d. 16 p. [11462

Raleigh Military Academy, Raleigh, N. C. Catalogue, 184 - 184 - NcU has 1847/48 [11463

Raleigh National Bank of North Carolina. The Raleigh National Bank of North Carolina, United States depository . . . authorized Sept. 12th, 1865. Raleigh, Biblical Recorder, 1865. 16 p. [11464

Raleigh Savings Bank. Charter and by-laws of the Raleigh Savings Bank, incorporated 1885. Raleigh, E. M. Uzzell, pr., 1887. 11 p. [11465

Raleigh Teachers' Mutual Aid Society, Raleigh, N. C. By-laws of the Raleigh Teachers' Mutual Aid Society, chartered January 9, 1915. Raleigh, Edwards and Broughton, 1915. 7 p. [11466

Raleigh Telephone Co. Raleigh Telephone Company, the home company. Raleigh, Edwards and Broughton, 1902. [15] p. [11467

The Raleigh Times classified business and numerical telephone directory of Raleigh, 192 - Raleigh, 192 - NcU has 1922 [11468

Raleigh Township, Wake Co., N. C. School Committee. Report of the Raleigh Township Graded Schools, 188 - Raleigh, 188 - NcU has 1883/84-1888/89, 1895/96, 1907/08-1917/18 [11469

Raleigh Water Company. Quarterly rates, with rules and regulations. Raleigh, 1897. 15 p. [11470

Ramond, John Stanislaus, comp. Among southern Baptists, v. 1- 1936-37- Shreveport, La., Compiler [1936- NcU has v. 1. [11471

Ramp, A. T., pseud. see Doak, Henry Melvil

Ramsaur, William Hoke. The letters of William Hoke Ramsaur. [Jacksonville, Fla., c.1928] 180 p. [11472

Ramsay, David. Histoire de la Révolution d'Amérique par rapport à la Caroline Méridionale. A Londres, chez Froullé, 1787. 2 v. [11473

——The history of the American Revolution. New ed. London, Printed for John Stockdale, 1793. 2 v. [11474

——The history of South Carolina, from its first settlement in 1670, to the year 1808. Charleston, Published by David Longworth, 1809. 2 v. [11475

——The history of the Revolution of South-Carolina, from a British province to an independent state. Trenton, Printed by Isaac Collins, 1785. 2 v. [11476

——Ramsay's History of South Carolina, from its first settlement in 1670 to the year 1808. Newberry, S. C., Published by W. J. Duffie, 1858. 2v. in 1. [11477

Ramsay, James Graham. An address delivered before Mocksville Lodge No. 134, on Thursday, November 4, 1852, the centennial anniversary of the initiation of George Washington into Masonry. Salisbury, Miller and James, Printers for the Lodge, 1853. 28 p. [11478

——Address delivered before the young ladies of Concord Female College at Statesville, May 29th, 1863. No place, no publisher, n.d. 20 p. [11479

——Circular: To the freemen of the eighth congressional district. No place, Oct. 16th, 1883. [1] p. [11480

——Duty of literary men to their country; an address delivered before the alumni of Davidson College, N. C., Aug. 9th, 1849. Salisbury, Bruner & James, pr., 1849. 16 p. [11481

——Education of the masses of the people; an address delivered at the request of the Athenaean Society before the literary societies of Catawba College, on the 16th day of Nov., 1854. Salisbury, Miller and James, pr., 1854. 28 p. [11482

——Historical sketch of Third Creek Church, in Rowan County, N. C; read at the centennial, May 13th, 1892. Concord, Times Book and Job Presses, 1892. 18 p. [11483

—— ——also, Historical address of Rev. John K. Fleming at the centennial of the building, July 24th, 1935. Statesville, Brady Printing Co., 1937. 67 p. [11484

——Love of country; an address delivered before the Ciceronian and Platonic societies of the United Baptist Institute, Taylorsville, N. C., May 31, 1860. Salisbury, J. J. Bruner, pr., 1860. 16 p. [11485

——Semi-centennial speech at Summerville, Rowan County, N. C., Wednesday, July 4th, 1894. Winston, Republican Steam Print, 1894. 15 p. [11486

——Union or disunion! The great day of our country has come! . . . Speeches of Dr. James G. Ramsay and Thomas N. Crumpler, Esq., in the legislature of North Carolina. Salisbury, Printed at Carolina Watchman Office, February 6, 1861. 16 p. [11487

Ramsay, John A. Public speaking! [Salisbury] Watchman Print, n.d. [1] p. [11488

Ramsay, T. N. Sketches of the great battles in 1861, in the Confederate States of America . . . also, Sketches of Jefferson Davis and A. H. Stephens. Salisbury, J. J. Bruner, 1861. 32 p. [11489

Ramsay, W. B. History of the First Presbyterian Church, Hickory, N. C., 1873-1923. No place, no publisher, n.d. 8 p. [11490

[Ramsey, D. Hiden] The story of Biltmore Forest. [Asheville] privately printed, 1925. [7] p. [11491

Ramsey, James Gattys McGregor. The annals of Tennessee, to the end of the eighteenth century. Charleston, John Russell, 1853. 744 p. [11492

—— ——Philadelphia, Lippincott, Grambo & Co., 1853. 744 p. [11493

—— ——1860. [11494

—— ——[Charleston, John Russell, 1853. Reprinted, Kingsport, Tenn., Kingsport Press for Judge David Campbell Chapter of D. A. R., 1926] 832 p. [11495

Ramsey, Robert W. Milestones backward run; the story of Beta Theta Pi at Davidson, 1858-1940, by Robert W. Ramsey, '40, Albert C. Winn, '42. Davidson, Phi Alpha Chapter of Beta Theta Pi, 1940. 112 p. [11496

Ramsey's Durham directory for the year 189 - Durham, N. A. Ramsey, 189 - NcU has 1892 [11497

Ranck, George Washington . . . Boonesborough, its founding, pioneer struggles, Indian experiences . . . and Revolutionary annals. Louisville, Ky., J. P. Morton & Co., pr., 1901. (Filson Club publications, no. 16) 286 p. [11498

Rand, James Hall. The North Carolina Indians. Chapel Hill, The University, 1913. (James Sprunt historical publications, v. 12, no. 2) 41 p. [11499

Randleman, N. C. Rotary Club. Part 1: The story of Naomi Wise . . . Part 2: Reminiscences of Randolph County, by J. A. Blair. Part 3: History of Randleman, N. C. Randleman, 1944. Various paging. [11500

Randolph, Edgar Eugene. Chemical engineering practice. Norman, Okla., University Litho Publishers [1953] 100 p. [11501

Randolph, Vance. Down in the holler; a gallery of Ozark folk speech [by] Vance Randolph & George P. Wilson. Norman, University of Oklahoma Press [1953] 320 p. [11502

Randolph Baptist Association. Minutes, 19 - 19 - NcU has 1955 [11503

Randolph Co., N. C. Superintendent of Schools. School improvement and local taxation. Asheboro, 1909. 5 p. [11504

Rands, Minnie Frost. The Prince of Peace; a story-drama in ten episodes. Washington, D. C. Privately printed by Mrs. R. D. Rands, 1938. 85 p. [11505

Raney, C. W. "Old Popcastle", its history and mysteries. [Raleigh, Edwards & Broughton Printing Co., 1917] 8 p. [11506

Raney, Richard Beverly. Handbook of orthopaedic surgery, by Alfred Rives Shands, Jr. . . . in collaboration with Richard Beverly Raney. St. Louis, C. V. Mosby Co., 1940. 567 p. [11507

——A primer on the prevention of deformity in childhood, by Richard Beverly Raney. . . . in collaboration with Alfred Rives Shands, Jr. Elyria, O., National Society for Crippled Children, Inc., 1941. 188 p. [11508

Raney, Thomas Hansard. The improved Raney canner . . . sold by T. H. Raney, Chapel Hill, N. C. No place, no publisher, 1916. 15 p. [11509

—— ——[Raleigh, Edwards and Broughton] n.d. 30 p. [11510

——Practical instructions in home and market canning for use with the improved Raney and Rialto canning outfits. [Raleigh, Edwards and Broughton for] Raney Canner Co., Chapel Hill, c.1905. 19 p. [11511

Rankin, Carl Emmett. The University of North Carolina and the problems of the cotton mill employee. [New York, c.1936] 212 p. Thesis (Ph. D.)—Columbia University, 1935. [11512

Rankin, Harriet Sutton, comp. History of First Presbyterian Church, Fayetteville, North Carolina, from old manuscripts and addresses. No place, no publisher, 1928. 160 p. [11513

Rankin, Jesse. Funeral sermon occasioned by the death of Mrs. Amy Webb, delivered on the 24th day of May, 1835, at Ebenezer Church, Granville County, N. C. Richmond, T. W. White, pr., 1835. 12 p. [11514

Rankin, Robert Stanley. The Government and administration of North Carolina. New York, Thomas Y. Crowell Co. [1955] (American commonwealth series, v. 31) 429 p. [11515

——Political science in the South. University, Ala., Bureau of Public Administration, University of Alabama, 1946. (Its Publications, 24) 61 p. [11516

——. . . Readings in American government. New York, D. Appleton-Century Co., Inc. [c.1939] 644 p. [11517

——When civil law fails; martial law and its legal basis in the United States. Durham, Duke University Press, 1939. 224 p. [11518

Rankin, Samuel Meek. History of Buffalo Presbyterian Church and her people, Greensboro, N. C. [Greensboro, Jos. J. Stone & Co., pr., 1934] 230 p. [11519

——The Rankin and Wharton families and their genealogy. [Greensboro, J. J. Stone & Co., pr., 1931] 295 p. [11520

Rankin, Watson Smith. The influence of vital statistics on longevity . . . an address delivered at the sixth annual meeting of the Association of Life Insurance Presidents at New York, December 5, 1912. No place [1912?] 8 p. [11521

——James Buchanan Duke (1856-1925) a great pattern of hard work, wisdom, and benevolence. New York, Newcomen Society in North America, 1952. 24 p. [11522

——Joseph Howell Way; an appreciation by his friend. No place, no publisher [1927?] 18 p. [11523

——Richard Henry Lewis; an appreciation. No place, no publisher, n.d. 13 p. [11524

——The small general hospital; prepared for the Trustees of the Duke Endowment by W. S. Rankin, H. E. Hannaford, and H. P. Van Arsdall. Charlotte, Duke Endowment [1928] (Duke endowment. Bulletin, no. 3) 47 p. [11525

—— ——Rev. 1932. 125 p. [11526

Rankin, William. Sketches of the most important battles of the Revolution, explanatory of The vine of liberty. New York, Printed and Published by Warren C. Butler, 1849. 95 p. [11527

Ransom, Matt Whitaker. Address delivered before the Dialectic and Philanthropic societies of the University of North Carolina, June 4th, 1856. Raleigh, Carolina Cultivator Office, 1856. 23 p. [11528

Ransom then and Ransom now; the first federal interference in North Carolina on the application of Ex-Senator Ransom and the Democratic leaders. No place, no publisher, n.d. [1] p. [11529

Raper, Arthur Franklin. Sharecroppers all [by] Arthur F. Raper and Ira DeA. Reid. Chapel Hill, University of North Carolina Press, 1941. 281 p. [11530

——Tenants of the Almighty. New York, Macmillan Co., 1943. 403 p. [11531

——The tragedy of lynching. Chapel Hill, University of North Carolina Press, 1933. 499 p. [11532

Raper, Charles Lee. The church and private schools of North Carolina; a historical study. Greensboro, J. J. Stone, pr., 1898. 247 p. [11533
——North Carolina, a royal province, 1729-1775; the executive and legislature. Chapel Hill, University Press, 1901. 71 p. Thesis (Ph. D.)—Columbia University. [11534
——North Carolina; a study in English colonial government. New York, Macmillan Co., 1904. 260 p. [11535
——The principles of wealth and welfare; economics for high schools. New York, Macmillan Co., 1906. 336 p. [11536
——Railway transportation; a history of its economics and of its relation to the state. New York, G. P. Putnam's Sons, 1912. 331 p. [11537
Raper, Kenneth Bryan. A manual of the penicillia, by Kenneth B. Raper and Charles Thom. Baltimore, Williams & Wilkins Co., 1949. 875 p. [11538
Ratchford, Benjamin Ulysses. American state debts. Durham, Duke University Press, 1941. 629 p. [11539
——Berlin reparations assignment . . . by B. U. Ratchford and Wm. D. Ross. Chapel Hill, Univ. of North Carolina Press [1947] 259 p. [11540
Ratchford, Benjamin Ulysses, joint author, see Hoover, Calvin B.
The Rattler, 190 - Raleigh, Senior Class of the Raleigh High School, 190 - NcU has 1909, 1917, 1921 [11541
Ravenscroft, John Stark. The correspondence published by Professor Mitchell with Bishop Ravenscroft's answer to his letter of the 12th of February last. Raleigh, J. Gales & Son, 1825. 24 p. [11542
——Correspondence respecting two publications which appeared in the Raleigh Register, in the month of December, 1824, between Bishop Ravenscroft and Professor Mitchell. Raleigh, J. Gales and Son, pr., 1825. 30 p. [11543
——Doctrines of the church vindicated from the misrepresentations of Dr. John Rice. Raleigh, Printed by J. Gales & Son, 1826. 166 p. [11544
——Revelation the foundation of faith; a sermon preached in St. Luke's Church Salisbury, N. C. at the ordination of the Rev. Philip B. Wiley . . . May 24th, 1829. Fayetteville, Printed by Edward J. Hale, 1829. 12 p. [11545
——A sermon delivered on the anniversary of the Female Benevolent Society, Raleigh . . . 25th July, 1824. Raleigh, Printed by J. Gales & Son, 1824. 16 p. [11546
——Sermon on regeneration; preached at St. James Church, Philadelphia, May 30th, 1820. Washington, Printed by Davis and Force, July, 1820. 16 p. [11547
——A sermon on the Christian ministry, delivered in St. Peter's Church, Washington, on . . . April 24th, at the ordination of the Rev. Joseph Pierson as priest, and of the Rev. C. C. Brainerd as deacon. Fayetteville, Printed by Edward J. Hale, 1825. 16 p. [11548
——Sermon on the church; delivered before the annual convention of the Protestant Episcopal Church of N. C. Newbern, Printed by Pasteur and Watson, 1824. 24 p. [11549
—— ——Annapolis, Published by G. Shaw, 1825. 22 p. [11550
——A sermon preached before the Bible Society of N. C. on Sunday, Dec. 12, 1824. Raleigh, Printed by Bell and Lawrence, 1825. 22 p. [11551
——A sermon preached in St. Paul's Church, Alexandria, at the opening of the Virginia Convention, May 11, 1820. Philadelphia, William Fry, pr., 1820. 31 p. [11552
——Sermon, preached on Sunday, Dec. 20, 1829, at the consecration of Christ Church, Raleigh, N. C. New York, N. Y. Protestant Episcopal Press, 1830. 16 p. [11553
——Some of the arguments in favour of Episcopacy, forcibly stated. [Charleston, A. E. Miller, pr.] n.d. 46 p. [11554
——To members of the Protestant Episcopal Church in the parish of St. James's, Mecklenburg County, this discourse is humbly presented as a token of his regard. Richmond, Printed by John Warrock, 1824. 16 p. [11555
[Ravenscroft, John Stark?] A tract, on the subject of, and mode of administering the Christian sacrament of baptism. No place, no publisher, n.d. 38 p. [11556
Ravenscroft, John Stark. Works, to which is prefixed a memoir of his life. New York, Protestant Episcopal Press, 1830. 2 v. [11557
—— ——2d ed. Fayetteville, Printed by Edward J. Hale & Son, 1856. 2 v. [11558

Ravenscroft School, Raleigh, N. C. [Catalogue], 193 - Raleigh, 193 - NcU has 1943/44-1950/51 [11559

Ray, John E. Our danger signal. Asheville, Asheville Printing Co., 1892. 58 p. [11560
——A trip abroad. Raleigh, Edwards, Broughton & Co., 1882. 247 p. [11561

[Ray, Neill W.] Sketch of the Sixth Regiment, N. C. State Troops (Infantry) No place, no publisher, n.d. 44 p. [11562

Ray, Worth Stickley. Colonial Granville County and its people. [Austin, Texas] Author, 1945. p. 193-312. Off-print from his The lost tribes of North Carolina[11563
——The lost tribes of North Carolina. Austin, Texas, Published by the Author, 1947. 714 p. [11564
——The Mecklenburg signers and their neighbors. Austin, Texas, The Author, 1946. p. 315-558. Off-print from his The lost tribes of North Carolina [11565

Ray, Worth Stickley, comp. Ray's Index and digest to Hathaway's North Carolina historical and genealogical register. Austin, Texas, The Compiler, 1945. 192 p. Off-print from his The lost tribes of North Carolina [11566

Ray, Worth Stickley. Tennessee cousins; a history of Tennessee people. Austin, Texas, The Compiler [1950] 811 p. [11567

Raymond, Dora (Neill) Captain Lee Hall of Texas. Norman, University of Oklahoma Press, 1940. 350 p. [11568

Raymond, Ida, pseud., see **Tardy, Mary T.**

Raymond, Zillah, pseud., see **Frayser, Lou H.**

Raynal, Guillaume Thomas Francois. Tableau et révolutions des colonies angloises dans l'Amérique Septentrionale. Amsterdam, Chez la Compagnie des Libraries, 1781. 2 v. [11569

Rayner, Kenneth. Address at the examination of the students of Union Academy, and the inauguration of the new academy buildings at Harrellsville, Hertford County, N. C., August 2, 1854. Murfreesborough, Murfreesborough Gazette, 1854. 19 p. [11570
——Address delivered before the graduating class of the United States Military Academy, West Point, June 17th, 1853. New York, John F. Trow [1853?] 30 p. [11571
——Address, delivered before the N. C. State Agricultural Society, at the second annual fair of the society . . . Oct. 19th, 1854. Raleigh, Southern Weekly Post, 1854. 40 p. [11572

[Rayner, Kenneth] Life and times of Andrew Johnson, seventeenth president of the United States . . . by a national man. New York, D. Appleton and Co., 1866. 363 p. [11573

Rayner, Kenneth. Speech in the convention of 1835. No place, Executive Committee of Wake County Democratic Club, n.d. 11 p. [11574

Read, Jesse, joint author, see **Burkitt, Lemuel**

Read, Opie Percival. The Jucklins. Chicago, Laird & Lee [c.1896] 291 p. [11575
—— ——(Opie Read's select works) [11576

Read the record. No place, no publisher [1912] [4] p. [11577

Reade, Edwin Godwin. Address before the convention of the legal profession of N. C., at Asheville, N. C., July 9th, 1884. Raleigh, Edwards, Broughton & Co., 1884. 16 p. [11578
——Address delivered before the literary societies of Wake Forest College, North Carolina, June 12, 1851. Raleigh, A. M. Gorman, pr., 1851. 16 p. [11579
——Address . . . before the law class of Judge Strong, at Raleigh, May 31st, 1878. No place, no publisher [1878?] [1] p. [11580
——Letter of Hon. Edwin G. Reade . . . to his constituents. Washington, American Organ, pr., 1856. 15 p. [11581
——Oration delivered, Wednesday, Sept. 7, 1881, at the laying of the cornerstone of the new building designed for the male department of the Oxford Orphan Asylum. No place, no publisher, n.d. 4 p. [11582

[Reade, Edwin Godwin] Vindication of the legal profession against the unjust accusations contained in an address delivered by William Hooper at Wake Forest College, in June, 1857, by "An advocate". Raleigh, A. M. Gorman, pr., 1858. 24 p. [11583

Reade, Lila. Peggy of the hills. Timberlake [The Author] 1953. 107 p. [11584

[Reade, Willoughby] Fallen at his post, "God's finger touched him and he slept"; Rev. Elias Dodson, died in Wilmington, N. C., December 13, 1882. [Wilmington? 1882?] [2] p. [11585

Readings from Shakspeare and other poets! . . . Mrs. Heavlin of Granville . . . will read. Raleigh, no publisher, Nov. 20, 1861. [1] p. [11586

Reasons for building the Central Railroad, with the charter. Fayetteville, Edward J. Hale and Son, 1856. 38 p. [11587

Reasons for the creation of Moseley County; to the Honourable General Assembly of N. C. No place, no publisher, n.d. 4 p. [11588

Reaves, William Perry. The conservation of the health, teeth, voice, hearing and sight. [Greensboro, privately printed, c.1912] 35 p. [11589

——Physiology and hygiene of the body and mind. [Greensboro, Author] c.1912. 35 p. [11590

Rebekah State Assembly. Independent Order of Odd Fellows. North Carolina see Independent Order of Odd Fellows. North Carolina. Rebekah State Assembly

Reckitt, William. Some account of the life and gospel labours of William Reckett . . . also, Memoirs of the life, religious experiences, and gospel labours of James Gough. Philadelphia, Printed and sold by Joseph Crukshank, 1783. 184 p. [11591

Reconstructed farmer; a monthly magazine, v. 1- May, 1869- 1869- Tarboro, James R. Thigpen and John S. Dancy, 1869- NcU has v. [1] 2-5 [11592

Record, Wilson. The Negro and the Communist Party. Chapel Hill, University of North Carolina Press [1951] 340 p. [11593

A record of fifty years, 1867-1917. No place, no publisher, n.d. 39 p. [11594

The record of Marion Butler. No place, no publisher [1916] [4] p. [11595

The record; the acceptance of the leadership of Marion Butler by the Republican state convention. [Raleigh, E. M. Uzzell, 1913?] 23 p. [11596

Records and documents pertaining to the title of the Western N. C. Railroad, eastern and western divisions. No place, no publisher, n.d. 256 p. [11597

Recreation review, v. 1- January-February, 1948- Raleigh, North Carolina Recreation Society, Inc., 1948- NcU has v. 1-8 [11598

The red and white, v. 1- 189 - Raleigh, Athletic Association of the State College of Agriculture and Engineering, 1899- NcU has v. [3-6] 7 [8-14, 16-18] [11599

Red Cross see American Red Cross

The red guidon; a souvenir of Fort Bragg and activities of civilian military training camp, Fort Bragg, North Carolina, 192 - Fort Bragg, 192 - NcU has 1929, 1930, 1932 [11600

Red Men. Grand Council of North Carolina. Record of proceedings, 1898- 1899- NcU has 1898-1952. No meeting in 1918. [11601

Red Oak Farm-Life High School, Nash County, N. C. Catalogue, 1915/16- [Rocky Mount] 1916?- NcU has 1915/16-1918/19, 1921/22, 1922/23 [11602

Red Springs Seminary see Flora Macdonald College

[Redcay, Edward Edgeworth] comp. Public secondary schools for Negroes in the Southern States of the United States . . . as of October 1, 1933. [Washington, D. C.] 1935. (Trustees of the John F. Slater fund. Occasional papers, no. 29) 72 p. [11603

Redd, F. Marion. Voice of Charlotte . . . Fourth talk . . . broadcasted over . . . WBT by Charlotte Chamber of Commerce . . . September 10, 1930. Charlotte [1930?] [8] p. [11604

Reddick, De Witt Carter, ed. Church and campus; Presbyterians look to the future from their historic role in Christian higher education [by] J. J. Murray [and others] Richmond, Va., John Knox Press [1956] 178 p. [11605

Redding, Jay Saunders. No day of triumph. New York, Harper & Brothers [1942] 342 p. [11606

——To make a poet black. Chapel Hill, University of North Carolina Press, 1939. 142 p. [11607

Reedy Creek Missionary Baptist Association. Minutes, 19 - 19 - NcU has 1913, 1914 [11608

Redhead, John A. Getting to know God, and other sermons. Nashville, Abingdon Press [c.1954] 126 p. [11609

Redpath, James. The roving editor: or, Talks with slaves in the Southern States. New York, A. B. Burdick, 1859. 349 p. [11610

Redway, Jacques Wardlaw. Natural advanced geography, by Jacques W. Redway and Russell Hinman. New York, American Book Co. [c.1898] 162 p. [11611

Reece, Joseph Isaac. The two interpretations of life—the personal and the Sachlich. Chapel Hill, University of North Carolina, 1910. (Worth prize thesis. 1910) 18 p. [11612

Rees, Edward Jeffries. Christ speaks from Calvary. Nashville, Cokesbury Press [c.1935] 172 p. [11613
——Easter's path to Pentecost. New York, Fleming H. Revell Co. [c.1937] 160 p. [11614
——In remembrance of Me. Nashville, Cokesbury Press [c.1932] 144 p. [11615

Reeves, George M. Thomas Wolfe et l'Europe. Paris, Jouve, Editeur, 1955. Thèse (Doctorat)—Université de Paris. 158 p. [11616

Reformed Church in the U. S. Classis of North Carolina. Historic sketch of the Reformed Church in North Carolina. Philadelphia, Pa., Publication Board of the Reformed Church in the United States [c.1908] 327 p. [11617
——Minutes, 1831?- 1831?- NcU has 1899, 1913 [1926-1938] [11618

Register, Edward Chauncey. Practical fever nursing. Philadelphia, W. B. Saunders Co., 1907. 352 p. [11619

Registered Service International, Greensboro, N. C. America's coastal highway; a motor trail in sound of the surf. Greensboro, n.d. 40 p. [11620

Regulus, pseud. see Husband, Herman

Rehder, Jessie Clifford. East wind's back. Atlanta, Ernest Hartsock [c.1929] 44 p. [11621
——Remembrance way, a novel. New York, Putnam [1956] 255 p. [11622

Reichel, Levin Theodore. A history of Nazareth Hall, from 1755 to 1855: and of the reunions of its former pupils, in 1854 and 1855. Philadelphia, J. B. Lippincott & Co., 1855. 162 p. [11623
——The Moravians in North Carolina. Salem, O. A. Keehln, 1857. 206 p. [11624

Reid, Albert Clayton. Christ and the present crisis. Wake Forest, Wake Forest College Press, 1936. 94 p. [11625
——Christian education; an address delivered to Baptist State Convention of North Carolina, November 12, 1952. [Raleigh, Edwards & Broughton, 1952?] 8 p. [11626
——Elements of psychology. New York, Prentice-Hall, Inc., 1938. 409 p. [11627
——Invitation to worship. New York, Abingdon-Cokesbury Press [1942] 157 p. [11628
——Man and Christ. Durham, Duke University Press, 1954. 90 p. [11629
——100 chapel talks. Nashville, Abingdon Press [c.1955] 304 p. [11630
——Resources for worship. New York, Abingdon-Cokesbury Press [1949] 154 p. [11631

Reid, Christian, pseud. see Tiernan, Frances Christine (Fisher)

Reid, David Settle. Circular to his constituents. No place, no publisher [1845] 8 p. [11632
——Circular of Hon. David S. Reid . . . to his constituents. Washington, Printed at the Congressional Globe Office, 1847. 8 p. [11633
——To the people of North Carolina. Reidsville, June 28th, 1850. [1] p. [11634

Reid, F. L. . . . Lines written after having a hemorrhage from the lungs. No place, no publisher, 1876. [1] p. [11635

Reid, James Wright. Life, sermons, and speeches of Rev. Numa F. Reid . . . by his sons, Jas. W. Reid and Frank L. Reid. New York, E. J. Hale & Son, 1874. 536 p. [11636

Reid, John Calvin. We knew Jesus; a series of Lenten messages. Grand Rapids, W. B. Eerdmans Pub. Co., 1954. 148 p. [11637

Reid, Paul Apperson. Gubernatorial campaigns and administrations of David S. Reid, 1848-1854. Cullowhee, Western Carolina College, 1953. (Western Carolina college. Bulletin, v. 30, no. 3) 119 p. [11638

Reid, Samuel Leslie. The life of Christ. Chapel Hill, University of North Carolina, 1918. (Worth prize thesis. 1918) 31 p. [11639

Reidsville, N. C. Board of Aldermen. Charter and ordinances of the town of Reidsville . . . in force from and after Sept. 1, 1891. Reidsville, 1891. 58 p. [11640

Reidsville, N. C. Board of Commissioners. Rules, rates, and ordinances of Reidsville Waterworks and Electric Light Plant. Reidsville, 1899. 12 p. [11641

Reidsville Seminary, Reidsville, N. C. Catalogue, 190 - 190 - NcU has 1906/07, 1907/08 [11642

Reilly, J. S. Wilmington. Past, present & future. [Wilmington, 1884?] 130 p. [11643

Reincke, Abraham. A register of members of the Moravian Church, and of persons attached to said church in this country and abroad, between 1727 and 1754. Bethlehem, Pa., H. T. Clauder, pr., 1873. 144 p. [11644

The rejected addresses together with the prize address . . . on the opening of the new Park Theatre in the city of New York. New York, Nathaniel Smith, 1821. 182 p. "Address written at Newbern, N. C.", p. 142-144 [11645

Religion and health, the magazine . . . to bridge the gap between religion and medicine, v. 1- February, 1952- Durham, Religion and Health Corporation, 1952- NcU has v. 1-5 [11646

Religious anniversaries held at Fayetteville, N. C., March 17th, 18th, 19th, 20th, and 21st, 1835. Richmond, Printed by J. Macfarlan, 1835. 22 p. [11647

Remarks on Mr. Gaston's address to the freemen of the counties of Wayne, Greene, Lenoir, Jones, Craven and Carteret. [Newbern, Watson & Hall, pr., 1808] 44 p. [11648

Renaissance Meeting in the Southeastern States. Renaissance papers, 1955- 1956- NcU has 1955, 1956 [11649

Rencher, Abraham. Circular address to his constituents. [Washington, no publisher, March 13, 1843] 16 p. [11650

——Circular to his constituents of the tenth congressional district of North Carolina. Washington, 1831. 7 p. [11651

——Circular to the freemen of the tenth Congressional district of North Carolina. March 9, 1839. [Washington? 1839?] 13 p. [11652

——Speech of Hon. Abraham Rencher, of Chatham, delivered in the Democratic State Convention of North Carolina, May 14, 1852. No place, no publisher, 1852. 4 p. [11653

——To the freemen of the tenth congressional district of North Carolina. Washington, no publisher, 1835. 15 p. [11654

——To the people of the tenth congressional district of North Carolina. Washington, no publisher, 1837. 8 p. [11655

The repentance of Judas. [Charlotte, Protestant Episcopal Church Publishing Association] n.d. (No. 4) 8 p. [11656

Repiton, A. Paul. Judgment reversed, being an answer to "Arrest, trial and conviction" sent forth by "James McDaniel" against The companion and review, by Elder A. Paul Repiton. Wilmington, Thomas Loring, 1847. 19 p. [11657

The Republican sentiment of New Hampshire, July 4, 1828, exhibited in her anniversary celebrations. No place, no publisher [1828?] 31 p. [11658

The Republican state convention at Greensboro. No place, no publisher [1908] [7] p. [11659

Republican State Executive Committee. North Carolina see North Carolina. Republican State Executive Committee [11660

Resource-Use education, v. 1- October, 1945- Chapel Hill, 1945- NcU has v. 1-2 [3-5] [11661

Retail Dealers' Protective Union. Reference book of Raleigh, N. C., and vicinity, 188 - No place, 188 - NcU has 1885-1886 [11662

Retailer, v. 1- 192 - Raleigh, North Carolina Merchants Association, 192 - NcU has v. 32-33 [11663

The re-union of non-resident natives of North Carolina at Greensboro, October 12th and 13th, 1903; invitation and information. [Greensboro? 1903?] [11] p. [11664

The reveille, v. 1- 193 - Raleigh, Student Division, Baptist State Convention, 193 - NcU has v. [8-11] [11665

Reveillé to taps, v. 1- 1909?- Asheville, Bingham School, 1909?- NcU has v. 1, no. 2, 1910 [11666

Revier, Vernon, pseud. see Huger, Arthur Deveron

Review of Bishop Ives' reasons for renouncing Protestantism. Baltimore, John D. Toy, pr., 1855. 31 p. [11667

Review of Dr. R. J. Breckinridge's letters on The rights of ruling elders, from the Princeton review, April, 1844. Princeton, N. J., Printed by John T. Robinson, 1844. 32 p. [11668

Review of the "Doctrines of the church vindicated from the misrepresentations of Dr. John Rice and the integrity of revealed religion defended against the 'no comment principle' of promiscuous Bible societies, by the Right Rev'd John S. Ravenscroft. Richmond, Printed at the Franklin Press, 1827. 214 p. [11669

A review of the "Trials of a mind, in its progress to Catholicism," by an ex-clergyman. Philadelphia, Thomas Curtis, 1855. 252 p. [11670

Reviewer, v. 1-5, Feb. 15, 1921-Oct., 1925. Richmond, Va., 1921-23; Chapel Hill, University of North Carolina Press, 1925. NcU has v. 1-5, v. 5 only published in Chapel Hill. Merged in Southwest review, Dallas, Texas, 1936. [11671

Reviews and press notices about James Larkin Pearson. Wilkesboro, Pearson Publishing Co., 1933. 12 p. [11672

——Boomer, James Larkin Pearson, 1934. 32 p. [11673

Reviews and press notices concerning the poetry of James Larkin Pearson. Guilford College, Pearson Publishing Co., 1947. 32 p. [11674

Revill, Janie, comp. A compilation of the original lists of Protestant immigrants to South Carolina, 1763-1773. Columbia, S. C., The State Co., 1939. 163 p. [11675

Rex Hospital, Raleigh, N. C. Alumnae Association. Bulletin: v. I, Alumnae homecoming day, 1894-1938, November 10, 1938, Raleigh, N. C. Raleigh, 1938. 42 p. [11676

Reynolds, Charles Albert. "Justice" calls for the facts; why have the Democratic newspapers . . . become so silent about who furnished the carpet-bag bonds to Cuba? No place, n.d. [4] p. [11677

Reynolds, Henry. "The State of Wilkes". [North Wilkesboro? North Wilkesboro Kiwanis Club? 1930] [8] p. [11678

Reynolds, J. L. The man of letters: an address delivered before the literary societies of Wake Forest College . . . June 14, 1849. Richmond, H. K. Ellyson, pr., 1849. 23 p. [11679

Reynolds, Quentin James. The Wright brothers, pioneers of American aviation. New York, Random House [1950] 183 p. [11680

Reynolds, Richard J. Tobacco Co., Winston-Salem, N. C. Financial statement, 19 - [Winston-Salem] 19 - NcU has 1935-1954 [11681

——R. J. Reynolds tobacco company $60,000,000 3 per cent debentures, due October 1, 1973. Winston-Salem, 1948. 44 p. [11682

Reynolds, Robert Rice. Gypsy trails. Asheville, Advocate Publishing Co. [1923?] 127 p. [11683

——Radio address by Senator Robert R. Reynolds on aliens and the unemployment problem, over . . . National Broadcasting System . . . January 12. No place, n.d. 3 p. [11684

——Wanderlust. New York, Broadway Publishing Co., 1913. 98 p. [11685

Rhine, Joseph Banks. Extra-sensory perception. Boston, Mass., Boston Society for Psychic Research, 1934. 169 p. [11686

——New frontiers of the mind. New York, Farrar & Rinehart, Inc. [c.1937] 275 p. [11687

——New worlds of the mind. New York, William Sloane Associates, Inc., 1953. 339 p. [11688

——The reach of the mind. New York, William Sloane Associates, Inc. [1947] 234 p. [11689

—— ——1948. [11690

Rhoades, Josephine L. The Guilford College history play to commemorate the twenty-seventh anniversary of the rechartering of New Garden Boarding School as Guilford College . . . May 31, 1915. [Guilford College, Printed by Joseph Moore Purdie, 1915?] 55 p. [11691

[Rhoades, Verne] Representative Biltmore forest plantations, visited by the Southern Forestry Congress, Asheville, N. C., July 11-15, 1916. [Asheville?] no publisher, 1916. 9 p. [11692

Rhode Island. New Berne Monument Commission. Report made to the General Assembly at its January session, 1910. Providence, R. I., E. L. Freeman Co., 1910. 54 p. [11693

Rhode Island Artillery. 5th Regt., 1861-1865. History of the Fifth Regiment of Rhode Island Heavy Artillery, during three years and a half of service in North Carolina, January, 1862-June, 1865. Providence, Snow & Farnham, 1892. 382 p. [11694

Rhodes, Raleigh E. Address at Memorial Day exercises, May 30, 1910, Arbor Vitae Cemetery, Madera, California. No place, no publisher, n.d. 13 p. [11695

Rhodes, Thomas Daniel. The crest of the little wolf; a tale of "the young Lovell" and the Wars of the Roses. Cincinnati, Robert Clarke Co., 1904. 181 p. [11696
——Nonsense rhymes, sketches and fragments. [Asheville, Advocate Printing Co.] 1927. 41 p. [11697

Rhodes, William Henry. Caxton's book: a collection of essays, poems, tales and sketches. San Francisco, A. L. Bancroft and Co., 1876. 300 p. [11698
——The Indian Gallows, and other poems. New York, Edward Walker, 1846. 153 p. [11699

Rhodes Military Institute, Kinston, N. C. Catalogue, 1902/03?- Kinston, 1903?- NcU has 1904/05 [11700

Rhyne, Jennings Jefferson. Some southern cotton mill workers, and their villages. Chapel Hill, University of North Carolina Press, 1930. 214 p. [11701

[Riccoboni, Marie Jeanne (de Heurles Laboras de Mézières)] Letters of Adelaide de Sancerre: To Count de Nance. Newbern, 1801. 160 p. Tr. by François-Xavier Martin [11702

Rice, David. Sermon on the present revival of religion in this country. Raleigh, Reprinted by William Boylan for Leonard Prather & William Paisley, 1805. 39 p. [11703

[Rich Square, N. C. Monthly Meeting of Friends] Memorial of Abraham Fisher Philadelphia, Wm. H. Pile's Sons, pr., 1911. 12 p. [11704

Richards, Allan Rene. War labor boards in the field. Chapel Hill, University of North Carolina Press, 1953. (James Sprunt studies in history and political science, v. 35) 281 p. [11705

Richards, Horace Gardiner. Geology of the coastal plain of North Carolina. Philadelphia, American Philosophical Society, 1950. (Transactions of the American Philosophical Society. August, 1950. New Ser., v. 40, part 1) 83 p. [11706

Richards, W. P. To the freemen of Davidson County. Science Grove, no publisher, 1846. [1] p. [11707

Richards, William A. Courses of study in business education. Greensboro, 1941. 60 p. [11708
——[Program of distributive education] [Greensboro, 1940] 21 p. [11709

Richards, Mrs. William A. Sharing family life; homemaking education for seventh grades of the Greensboro city schools. Greensboro, 1940. 37 p. [11710

Richardson, Albert Deane. The secret service, the field , the dungeon, and the escape. Hartford, Conn., American Publishing Co., 1865. 512 p. [11711
—— ——Washington, National Tribune, 1897. [11712

Richardson, Ethel (Park) comp. American mountain songs compiled by Ethel Park Richardson, edited and arranged by Sigmund Spaeth. [New York] Greenberg [c.1927] 120 p. [11713
—— ——[1956, c.1955] [11714

Richardson, Frank. From sunrise to sunset; reminiscences. Bristol, Tenn., King Printing Co., Leroi Press, 1910. 242 p. [11715

Richardson, Frank Howard. A doctor's letters to expectant parents. New York, Children, the parents' magazine and W. W. Norton & Co., Inc. [c.1929] 118 p.[11716
——How to get along with children. Atlanta, Tupper & Love [1954] 172 p. [11717
——The nervous child and his parents. New York, G. P. Putnam's Sons, 1928. 400 p. [11718

——The nursing mother. New York, Prentice-Hall [1953] 204 p.   [11719
——Parenthood and the newer psychology. New York, G. P. Putnam's Sons, 1926.
200 p.   [11720
——The pre-school child and his posture; a program of corrective exercises . . . by
Frank Howard Richardson and Winifred Johnson Hearn. New York, G. P.
Putnam's Sons, 1930. 220 p.   [11721

Richardson, Harry Van Buren. Dark glory, a picture of the church among Negroes
in the rural South. New York, Pub. for Home Missions Council of North America
and Phelps-Stokes Fund by Friendship Press [1947] 209 p.   [11722

[Richardson, Henry Smith] Annals of an American family. [Greensboro, privately
printed, 1953] 292 p.   [11723

Richardson, John Wessley. Strong delusions; "The light turned on". No place,
The Author [c.1913] 293 p.   [11724

Richardson, William H. The government of North Carolina. Lincoln, University
Publishing Co., 1929. 64 p.   [11725

Richardson's Virginia and North Carolina almanack see **The Warrock-Richardson
Maryland, Virginia and North Carolina almanack**

Richings, G. F. Evidences of progress among colored people. 8th ed. Philadelphia, G. S. Ferguson Co., 1902. 575 p.   [11726

Richmond, John McCrory. Chapter Sigma of Chi Psi, 1855-1861, University of
North Carolina. No place, no publisher, n.d. 8 p.   [11727

Richmond and Danville Railroad. Excursion guide to the Virginia springs and
health resorts of Western North Carolina and North Georgia. [New York, Printed
at Leve & Alden's Publication Dept., 1883] 72 p.   [11728
——Proceedings of the annual meeting of stockholders, 1848- Richmond, 1848-
NcU has 1848, 1865-1870 [1872-1890]   [11729
——Summer of 1882 among the health resorts of North-east Georgia, Upper South
Carolina, Western North Carolina, and Virginia. [New York, Aldine Press,
1882?] 44 p.   [11730
——Summer resorts and points of interest of Virginia, Western North Carolina and
North Georgia. New York, C. G. Crawford, pr., 1884. 94 p.   [11731
——Through rates and proportions for through tickets by the great central route
between the North and the South via Richmond, Va. and Greensboro, N. C.
Richmond, Gary & Clemmitt, pr., 1866. 56 p.   [11732
——. . . Time-table. No place, 18 - NcU has no. 14, N. C. Division, 1873; no. 1,
Raleigh division, 1875; no. 39, N. C. Division, 1886.   [11733
——Western North Carolina Railroad scenery, Land of the Sky. No place, n.d.
12 plates.   [11734

[Richmond & Petersburg Railroad] Richmond & Weldon route . . . tariff of rates
for transporting local freights over the Richmond and Weldon route, to take effect
June 25th, 1873. No place [1873] [1] p.   [11735

Richmond Co., N. C. Board of Education. Public Schools of Richmond County.
[Rockingham] 19 - NcU has 1906, announcement; 1907/08, 1908/09, report [11736

[Richmond Co., N. C. Citizens] The new county of Scotland. No place [1899]
8 p.   [11737

Ricks, Peirson. Bye-bye breeches. Philadelphia, Dorrance & Co. [c.1936] 112 p. [11738
——The hunter's horn. New York, C. Scribner's Sons, 1947. 361 p.   [11739

Riddick, Robert A. Musings of a bachelor . . . with introduction and three poems
by Maj. John W. Moore. Raleigh, Christian Advocate, 1899. 116 p.   [11740

[Riddick, Thomas M.] Solid facts for the people. No place, no publisher, 1889.
28 p.   [11741

Riddick, Wallace Carl. Inauguration of Wallace Carl Riddick, president of North
Carolina College of Agriculture and Mechanic Arts, Thurs. Feb. the twenty-
second, 1907. [Raleigh, Edwards & Broughton Printing Co., 1917] 15 p. [11742
——Lectures on building materials and the construction of buildings. Raleigh,
Edwards & Broughton Printing Co., 1908. 73 p.   [11743

Riddick, Wiley Goodman. Thoughts promotive of the higher life. Raleigh, Edwards & Broughton Printing Co., 1910. 279 p.   [11744

Riddle, Carl Brown, ed. College men without money. New York, Thomas Y.
Crowell Co. [1914] 287 p.   [11745

Riddle, Carl Brown. Thirty-six. No place, no publisher [c.1915]   16 p.   [11746
——Trailing the truth. Elon College, Southern Christian Publishing Co., 1914. 88 p.   [11747

Riddle, Ida Golding. Wachovia's Easter. [Winston-Salem, Barber Printery, 1914] 5 p.   [11748

Ridenhour, Charles E. Historical sketch of St. John's Evangelical Lutheran Church, Concord, N. C., delivered at the home coming service, August 29th and 30th, 1925. [Concord? St. John's Evangelical Lutheran Church, 1925?]   8 p.   [11749

Ridgeway Nurseries, Ridgeway, N. C. Descriptive catalogue of southern and acclimated fruit trees, grape vines, strawberries. Ridgeway, 1870. 43 p.   [11750

Ridley, Bromfield Lewis. Battles and sketches of the Army of Tennessee. Mexico, Mo., Missouri Printing & Publishing Co., 1906. 662 p.   [11751

Rienzi, pseud. see **Potter, Robert**

Rights, Douglas Le Tell. The American Indian in North Carolina. Durham, Duke University Press, 1947. 296 p.   [11752
——The beginnings of Bethabara—in Wachovia, the first Moravian settlement in North Carolina. Winston-Salem, Wachovia Historical Society, 1953. 7 p. [11753
——Moravian church history in question and answer. Winston-Salem, Author, 1936. 15 p.   [11754
——Traces of the Indian in Piedmont North Carolina. No place, no publisher [1923?] 7 p.   [11755
——A voyage down the Yadkin-Peedee River. Winston-Salem, no publisher, 1929. 79 p.   [11756

Riley, Benjamin Franklin. A history of the Baptists in the Southern States east of the Mississippi. Philadelphia, American Baptist Publication Society, 1898. 376 p.   [11757

Riley, Leslie Walter. Bibliography of production management literature. Chapel Hill, School of Business Administration Library, University of North Carolina [1955] 51 p.   [11758

Ripley, Katharine (Ball) Sand in my shoes. New York, Brewer, Warren & Putnam, 1931. 332 p.   [11759

Ripley, Lila. Heart songs. Hendersonville, Times Printing House, n.d. 62 p. [11760

Rippy, James Fred. . . . The capitalists and Colombia. New York, Vanguard Press [c.1931] 256 p.   [11761
——Crusaders of the jungle, by J. Fred Rippy and Jean Thomas Nelson. Chapel Hill, University of North Carolina Press [c.1936] 401 p.   [11762
——Historical evolution of Hispanic America. New York, F. S. Crofts & Co., 1933. 580 p.   [11763
——Joel R. Poinsett, versatile American. Durham, Duke University Press, 1935. 257 p.   [11764
——. . . Rivalry of the United States and Great Britain over Latin America (1808-1830) Baltimore, Johns Hopkins Press, 1929. (The Albert Shaw lectures on diplomatic history, 1928) 322 p.   [11765

[Rivenback, Mrs. R. W.] Pauline; or, The girl of Piney Dell, by Mita Leon. Wilmington, S. G. Hall, pr., 1883. 149 p.   [11766

Rivers, Joel. The power and excellence of religion exemplified in the happy conversion and triumphant death of Miss Ruina J. Williams. New York, J. Emory and B. Waugh, n.d. 8 p.   [11767

Rivers, Richard Henderson. The life of Robert Paine, D. D., bishop of the Methodist Episcopal Church, South. Nashville, Tenn., Southern Methodist Publishing House, 1884. 314 p.   [11768

[Rivers, William James] A chapter on the colonial history of the Carolinas. Baltimore, J. Murphy & Co., 1885. 67 p.   [11769
——A sketch of the history of South Carolina to . . . 1719. Charleston, McCarter & Co., 1856. 470 p.   [11770

Rives, John G. Anniversary address delivered before the Edgecomb Medical Society, Tarborough, North Carolina, Nov. 1853. Raleigh, Printed by William W. Holden, 1854. 16 p.   [11771

Rix, Guy Scoby. History and genealogy of the Ricks family of America. Salt Lake City, Skelton Publishing Co., 1908. 184 p.   [11772

Rixey, Randolph Picton. The Rixey genealogy, with references to the Morehead, Hunton, Gibbs, Hall . . . and other allied families. Lynchburg, Va., Printed by J. P. Bell Co., 1933. 427 p.   [11773

Roanoke Baptist Association. Minutes, 1908- 1908- NcU has 1908-1910 [1928-1955]   [11774

Roanoke Baptist review, v. 1-v. 5, no. 6, May, 1951-October, 1955. Greenville, 1951-1955. NcU has v. 1-5   [11775

Roanoke Collegiate Institute, Elizabeth City, N. C. Catalogue, 1896/97?- Elizabeth City, 1897?- NcU has 1914/15, 1916/17   [11776

Roanoke Colony Memorial Association. Articles of incorporation, by-laws, and other matter. No place, no publisher [1894?] 8 p.   [11777
—— ——1899. 7 p.   [11778
——The first English settlements on Roanoke Island, 1584-1587. Manteo [c.1937] 38 p.   [11779
——Raleigh's colony on Roanoke Island, North Carolina, 1584-1590. [Baltimore, no publisher, 1893] 3 p.   [11780
——Virginia Dare Day; annual celebration . . . Old Fort Raleigh, Roanoke Island . . . August 18, 1926. Raleigh, Edwards & Broughton Co., 1926. 16 p. [11781

[Roanoke Colony Memorial Association. President] To the Board of directors and stockholders. [Edenton? 1912] 11 p.   [11782

Roanoke Island Historical Association, Inc. The lost colony, souvenir and program; 1587-1937, 350th anniversary celebration. Manteo, c.1937. 48 p.   [11783
—— ——1938. 52 p.   [11784
—— ——[1939] 64 p.   [11785
—— ——[1940] 68 p.   [11786
—— ——[1941] 64 p.   [11787
—— ——[1946] 56 p.   [11788
——The lost colony year book, 1947- Manteo, 1947- NcU has 1947-1955 [11789
——To make history and tourist wealth for North Carolina. [Elizabeth City] 1934. [10] p.   [11790

[Roanoke Island Historical Association, Inc.] When you come to Dare. [Manteo, 1938] [16] p.   [11791

Roanoke Missionary Baptist Association. Minutes, 1866?- 1866?- NcU has [1871-1925]   [11792

Roanoke Navigation and Water-power Co. Prospectus. Raleigh, Edwards & Broughton, pr., 1892. 19 p.   [11793
——Roanoke Navigation and Water-power Company: Important! Inquire within. [Weldon? 1891] 8 p.   [11794
——The Roanoke Navigation and Water Power Company, situated on the Roanoke River . . . its charter, the charters of the Roanoke Navigation Company. Weldon, Harrell's Book and Job Printing House, 1887. 57 p.   [11795

Roanoke Navigation Co. Important sale! . . . the franchise, rights, and privileges of the Roanoke Navigation Company. Weldon, Harrell, pr., Dec. 1, 1881. [1] p.   [11796
——Report, 182 - 182 - NcU has 1826/27, 1829/30, 1853/54   [11797
——Report of the directors to the stockholders on the subject of locking into the river at Weldon. Halifax, Office of the Free Press, 1824. 14 p.   [11798

Roanoke Navigation Co. Engineer. Roanoke Canal! Engineer's report. [Weldon, Harrell, pr., 1860] 4 p.   [11799

Roanoke Navigation Co. Treasurer. Report to the president and directors, 18 - [Weldon], 18 - NcU has 1836/38   [11800

[Roanoke Rapids, N. C. Lions Club] Semi-centennial celebration, July 2d, 3rd, 4th, 1947, Roanoke Rapids, N. C. [Roanoke Rapids] 1947. 64 p.   [11801

Roanoke Rapids, N. C. Public Schools. Roanoke Rapids school facts. [Roanoke Rapids, Herald Printing Co., 1933] 16 p.   [11802

Roanoke Rapids Herald, Roanoke Rapids, N. C. Roanoke Rapids, a prosperous and progressive industrial city. [Roanoke Rapids, 1940?] [14] p.   [11803

Roanoke River Basin Association. John H. Kerr dam dedication ceremony sponsored by Roanoke River Basin Association . . . October 3, 1952. No place, 1952. [14] p.   [11804

Roaring River Primitive Baptist Association. Minutes, 18 - 18 - NcU has 1873, 1914   [11805

Robbins, D. P. Descriptive sketch of Winston-Salem, its advantages and surroundings. Winston, Sentinel Job Print, 1888. 96 p.   [11806

Robbins, E. C. Wholesale trade-list, hardy and rare broad-leaved evergreens, ornamental trees, shrubs, vines, ferns, and herbaceous plants of the Blue Ridge Mountains, 19   Ashford, 19   NcU has 1923/24, 1924/25, 1924 (Christmas) 1925/26, Fall and Spring, 1926/27, Fall and Spring, 1929 (Autumn)   [11807

Robbins, William McKendree. Speech of Hon. William M. Robbins. No place, no publisher, n.d. 13 p.   [11808

Robbins Mills, Inc. Report, 194   New York, 194   NcU has 1948/49   [11809

Robeson Baptist Association. Minutes, 1883?-   1883?-   NcU has [1886-1906] 1911-1948, 1953   [11810

Robeson County High and Farm Life School, Philadelphus, N. C. Announcement, 1913/14?- 1913?- NcU has 1916/17   [11811

Robersonville, N. C. Peoples Building and Loan Association. Constitution and by-laws. [Raleigh, Edwards & Broughton Printing Co., 1917?] 16 p.   [11812

Robert, Joseph Clarke. The story of tobacco in America. New York, A. A. Knopf, 1949. 296 p.   [11813
——The tobacco kingdom; plantation, market, and factory in Virginia and North Carolina, 1800-1860. Durham, Duke University Press, 1938. 286 p. [11814

Robert, T. A narrative of the life of the Rev. Mr. George Whitefield . . . with the history of his travels. London, J. Bunyan [1780?] 259 p.   [11815

Roberts, A., pseud. see Hobart-Hampden, Augustus Charles

Roberts, Dita. A short historical sketch of Christ Church parish, New Bern, N. C., 1715-1911. [New Bern, Owen G. Dunn, pr.] n.d. 26 p.   [11816

Roberts, Elliott. One river—seven States; TVA relations in the development of the Tennessee River. Knoxville, Bureau of Public Administration, University of Tennessee, 1955. (University of Tennessee record. Extension series, v. 31, no. 1) 100 p.   [11817

Roberts, Mrs. F. C. Historical incidents; what "our women in the war" did and suffered. Beaufort, St. Paul's School Printing Dept., 1909. 14 p. [11818

Roberts, John K. History of Union Presbyterian Church, for the home coming, August 10-11, 1910. Carthage, Kelly Printing Co., n.d. 43 p.   [11819

Roberts, Percy. Sketch of the Hon. Thomas Courtland Manning, LL.D., chief-justice of Louisiana. Philadelphia, Chas. Robson & Co., 1880. 31 p.   [11820

Roberts, Ruth Newman. The heart speaks, poems. New York, Crown Publications [c.1947] 64 p.   [11821

Robertson, Archibald Thomas, 1863-1934. A grammar of the Greek New Testament in the light of historical research. New York, Hodder & Stoughton [c.1914] 1360 p.   [11822
——An introduction to the textual criticism of the New Testament. London, Hodder & Stoughton, Lt. [c.1925] 300 p.   [11823
——Jesus as a soul-winner, and other sermons. New York, Fleming H. Revell Co. [c.1937] 158 p.   [11824
——Life and letters of John Albert Broadus. Philadelphia, American Baptist Publication Society, 1901. 462 p.   [11825
——Luke the historian, in the light of research. New York, C. Scribner's Sons, 1920. 257 p.   [11826
——A short grammar of the Greek New Testament. New York, A. C. Armstrong & Son, 1908. 240 p.   [11827
——Some minor characters in the New Testament. Nashville, Tenn., Sunday School Board of the Southern Baptist Convention, 1928. 182 p.   [11828

Robertson, Archibald Thomas, fl. 1945. Slow train to yesterday, a last glance at the local. Boston, Houghton Mifflin Co., 1945. 189 p.   [11829

Robertson, Ben. Travelers' rest. Clemson, S. C., The Cottonfield Publishers [c.1938] 268 p.   [11830

Robertson, George F. A small boy's recollections of the Civil War. Clover, S. C., The Author, 1932. 116 p.   [11831

Robertson, Judge Buxton. America as a liberator; graduating oration delivered at the University of N. C., Chapel Hill, N. C., 1905. No place, no publisher, n.d. 7 p. [11832

Robertson, Judge Buxton, ed. Gems of truth in stories of life. Burlington [c.1932] 143 p. [11833

Robertson, Judge Buxton. Guide-posts for the school room. [Burlington, Press of Burlington Printing Co., c.1918] 87 p. [11834

——The importance of study by the pupil and some ways to secure it. No place, no publisher, 1921. 8 p. [11835

——Some suggestions for school committeemen of Cabarrus County. No place, no publisher, 1920. 15 p. [11836

Robertson, Stewart. Introduction to modern journalism. New York, Prentice-Hall, Inc., 1930. 339 p. [11837

Robertson, William. The history of America, books IX. and X. containing the history of Virginia to the year 1688; and of New England to the year 1652. Philadelphia, Printed from the London ed. by J. Humphreys, 1799. 196 p. [11838

Robeson, Anne Glenn. Betty and scarlet bunny, a three act fairy play; adapted . . . from "The adventures of Betty and scarlet bunny" by W. A. Lillycrop. Wilmington, W. A. Lillycrop, c.1932. 48 p. [11839

Robeson Baptist Association. Minutes, 188 - 188 - NcU has 1884-1886, 1911-1923, 1925-1945 [11840

[Robeson Co., N. C. High School Teachers Association] A course of study for the high schools of Robeson County. No place [1917] 8 p. [11841

Robins, Sidney Swaim. A criticism of Herbert Spencer's "First principles". Chapel Hill, University of North Carolina, 1904. (Worth prize thesis. 1904) 23 p. [11842

——A letter on Robins family history. Asheboro, Durham Printing Co. [1955] 40 p. [11843

Robinson, Anthony Lewin. William McDougall . . . a bibliography, together with a brief outline of his life. Durham, Duke University Press, 1943. 54 p. [11844

Robinson, Benjamin. Dolores; a tale of dissappointment and distress. New York, E. J. Hale & Sons, 1868. 180 p. [11845

Robinson, Blackwell Pierce. The history of escheats. Chapel Hill, University of North Carolina, 1955. 62 p. [11846

——A history of Moore County, North Carolina, 1747-1847. Southern Pines, Moore County Historical Association, 1956. 270 p. [11847

Robinson, Blackwell Pierce, ed. see Federal Writers Project. North Carolina. The North Carolina guide

Robinson, Charles Mulford. A city plan for Raleigh. Raleigh, The Woman's Club of Raleigh, 1913. 99 p. [11848

Robinson, Conway. An account of discoveries in the West until 1519, and of voyages to and along the Atlantic coast of North America from 1520 to 1573. Richmond, Printed by Shepherd and Colin, 1848. 491 p. [11849

Robinson, Frank Torrey. History of the Fifth Regiment, M. V. M. Boston, W. F. Brown & Co., pr., 1879. 237 p. [11850

Robinson, Melvin. Riddle of the Lost Colony. New Bern, Owen G. Dunn Co. [1946] 64 p. [11851

Robinson, William Morrison. The Confederate privateers. New Haven, Yale University Press, 1928. 372 p. [11852

Robison, Bartram. Den on the several demises of Bartram Robison and others vs. Allen Barefield; case agreed. No place, no publisher [1815?] 24 p. [11853

[Rochefort, Charles de] Recit de l'estat present des celebres colonies de la Virginie, de Marie-Land, de la Caroline, du nouveau Duché d'York, de Penn-Sylvania, & de nouvelle Angleterre. Rotterdam, Chez Reinier Leers, 1681. 43 p. NcU has microfilm (negative) from New York Public Library [11854

Rochelle, James Henry. Life of Rear Admiral John Randolph Tucker. Washington, Neale Publishing Co., 1903. 112 p. [11855

Rockingham, N. C. Board of Commissioners. Town of Rockingham, Richmond County, North Carolina; $40,000.00 of thirty-year straight coupon bonds, interest five per cent, payable semi-annually. Raleigh, Edwards & Broughton Printing Co., 1907. 20 p.   [11856

Rockingham, N. C. Board of School Trustees. Course of study, rules and regulations, Rockingham Public Schools, adopted . . . 1913. Rockingham, The Post [1913?] 20 p.   [11857

Rockingham, N. C. Water Committee. Water rates and plumbing ordinance of the town of Rockingham, adopted June 12, 1908. Raleigh, Edwards & Broughton, 1909. 20 p.   [11858

[**Rockingham Co., N. C. Commissioner (John M. Galloway)**] Rockingham County finances; an appeal for justice. No place [1886?] 4 p.   [11859

Rockingham Co., N. C. Republican Executive Committee. Notice! There will be a convention of the Republican Party of Rockingham County held at Reidsville . . .Aug. 21, 1880. [Reidsville, 1880] [1] p. Signed: C. A. Reynolds, chm'n. [11860

Rockingham Co., N. C. Sheriff (J. S. Johnston) Attention, fellow citizens! [Reidsville?] September 10, 1880. [1] p.   [11861

Rockingham County Library, Reidsville, N. C. Report, 19 - Reidsville, 19 - NcU has 1946/47-1950/51, 1954/55   [11862

Rockwell, Ethel Theodora. Children of old Carolina; an historical pageant of N. C. for children. Chapel Hill, University Extension Division, c.1925. (Its Extension bulletin. April 1, 1925. v. 4, no. 12) 63 p.   [11863

—— ——No place, no publisher, n.d. 3 p. Program.   [11864

Rockwell, James Chester. Chrystella; the echo of a dream. Vineland, Rockwell, Taylor and Co., 1887. 23 p.   [11865

Rockwell, Kiffin Yates. War letters of Kiffin Yates Rockwell, foreign legionnaire and aviator, France, 1914-1916. Garden City, N. Y., Country Life Press, 1925. 202 p.   [11866

Rockwell, Paul Ayres. Three centuries of the Rockwell family in America, 1630-1930. Paris, privately printed, 1930. 83 p.   [11867

[**Rocky Mount, N. C. Board of Aldermen**] Building code of the city of Rocky Mount, July 1, 1941. [Rocky Mount] 1941. 43 p.   [11868

Rocky Mount, N. C. Board of Aldermen. Code of the city of Rocky Mount . . . together with its charter, adopted May 17, 1913. Rocky Mount, Telegram [1913?] 44 p.   [11869

—— ——adopted February 7, 1929. [1929?] 35 p.   [11870

[**Rocky Mount, N. C. Board of Aldermen**] Code of the city of Rocky Mount, revised October 6th, 1938. Rocky Mount, 1938. 38 p.   [11871

[**Rocky Mount, N. C. Board of Aldermen. Finance Committee**] Financial statement, 19 - [Rocky Mount, 19 - NcU has 1912/13, 1914/15, 1942/43, 1944/ 45-1946/47   [11872

Rocky Mount, N. C. Chamber of Commerce. Rocky Mount, North Carolina, fastest growing city in the state. [Rocky Mount] n.d. 8 p.   [11873

[**Rocky Mount, N. C. Chamber of Commerce**] Rocky Mount, North Carolina, where industry and agriculture combine with the finer things of life. [Rocky Mount, 1926?] [24] p.   [11874

Rocky Mount, N. C. Daughtridge Club. For governor of N. C., E. L. Daughtridge. Raleigh, Allied Printing Trades [1916?] 15 p.   [11875

Rocky Mount, N. C. Emergency Housing Committee. Report, 1946- Rocky Mount, 1946- NcU has 1946,   [11876

Rocky Mount, N. C. Missionary Baptist Church. Building Committee. Read carefully, this letter, asking assistance from you! Rocky Mount, 1880. [1] p. [11877

Rocky Mount Mills, Rocky Mount, N. C. Highlights in the progress of cotton spinning. Rocky Mount [1944] 64 p.   [11878

——Playing the game at Rocky Mount Mills. Rocky Mount [1951] 38 p. [11879

—— ——[1953] 35 p.   [11880

——Rocky Mount Mills, a case history of industrial development, 1818-1943. Rocky Mount, c.1943] 50 p.   [11881

Rocky River Baptist Association. Minutes, 1867?- 1867?- NcU has [1871- 1883]   [11882

Rocwel, A. M. A fragment of phrenology . . . together with the character of Mr. Thos. Avent & Master James Avent. Washington, Alfred L. Price, pr., 1842. 24 p. [11883

Rodgers, Andrew Denny. American botany, 1873-1892. Princeton, Princeton University Press, 1914. 340 p. [11884

Rodgers, Eric W. [Development of the Roanoke River basin] Scotland Neck [1947?] 17 p. [11885

Rodgers, James Pinckney. Life of Rev. James Needham, the oldest Methodist preacher. Pilot Mountain, Surry Printing House, 1899. 52 p. [11886

Rodman, William Blount. Address delivered before the two literary societies of Wake Forest College, on the 9th June, 1846, at the solicitation of the Philomathesian Society. Raleigh, W. W. Holden, 1846. 28 p. [11887

Rodman, William Blount. Eulogy on Andrew Jackson; delivered in the Presbyterian Church at Washington, N. C. on the 26th day of June, 1845. Tarboro, Printed by George Howard, Jr., 1845. 8 p. [11888

Roe, Alfred Seelye. The Fifth Regiment Massachusetts Volunteer Infantry in its three tours of duty 1861, 1862-'63, 1864. Boston, Mass., Fifth Regiment Veteran Association, 1911. 510 p. [11889

——The Twenty-fourth Regiment, Massachusetts Volunteers, 1861-1866. Worcester, Mass., Twenty-fourth Veteran Association, 1907. 573 p. [11890

Roe, Edward Payson. Hornet's nest. New York, Dodd, Mead and Co. [c.1892] 193 p. [11891

Rogers, Andrew J., comp. Brief history, formation and growth of the First Baptist Church of Raleigh, N. C. . . . roster of members, 1927. Raleigh, Capital Printing Co., 1927. 16 p. [11892

Rogers, Edward H. Reminiscences of military service in the Forty-third Regiment, Massachusetts Infantry, during the great Civil War, 1862-63. Boston, Franklin Press, 1883. 210 p. [11893

Rogers, Henry Munroe. Memories of ninety years. Boston, Houghton Mifflin Co. 1928. 409 p. [11894

Rogers, James. The executioner, being a true account . . . of what happened to the man, who burnt the Rev. John Rogers. Philadelphia, Published by Wm. Beastall, n.d. 63 p. [11895

Rogers, James A. Columbus County, North Carolina, 1946. Whiteville, The News-Reporter, 1946. 108 p. [11896

Rogers, James R. The Cane Ridge meeting-house . . . to which is appended the Autobiography of B. W. Stone and a Sketch of David Purviance, by William Rogers. 2d ed. Cincinnati, Standard [c.1910] 237 p. [11897

Rogers, James Webb. Madame Surratt, a drama in five acts. Washington, D. C., T. J. Brashears, pr., 1879. New York, Reprinted, W. Abbatt, 1912. (The magazine of history with notes and queries. Extra no. 20) 161 p. [11898

—— ——4th ed. Washington, D. C., Press of Judd & Detweiler, Inc. [c.1926] 135 p. [11899

Rogers, John, ed. Biography of Elder Barton Warren Stone, written by himself, with additions and reflections by Elder John Rogers. Cincinnati, Published for the Author by J. A. & U. P. James, 1847. 404 p. [11900

Rogers, Joseph Morgan. . . . Thomas H. Benton. Philadelphia, G. W. Jacobs & Co. [1905] 361 p. [11901

Rogers, Lettie (Hamlett) Landscape of the heart. New York, Random House [1953] 248 p. [11902

——South of heaven. New York, Random House [1946] 278 p. [11903

——The storm cloud. New York, Random House [1951] 309 p. [11904

Rogers, Lou. Tar heel women. Raleigh, Warren Publishing Co. [1949] 284 p. [11905

Rogers, Robert. A concise account of North America. London, Printed for the Author, and sold by J. Millan, 1765. 264 p. [11906

Rogers, Samuel L. Indictment quashed! No place, no publisher, 1912. [2] p. [11907

Rogers, William White. Individualism. Chapel Hill, University of North Carolina, 1912. (Worth prize thesis. 1912) 12 p. [11908

Rogers' Asheville. Photogravures. New York, The Albertype Co. [1895] 40 plates [11909
—— ——[1896] 12 plates [11910

Rollins, Kathleen. Impassioned foothills. New York, Arcadia House, 1937. 287 p. [11911
——Love's tapestry. New York, Arcadia House [c.1935] 286 p. [11912

Rollins, Thomas Scott. Speech of Chairman Thomas S. Rollins at the Republican state convention. No place, no publisher [1904?] 7 p. [11913

The romance of Edith. No place, no publisher, n.d. 11 p. [11914

Rondthaler, Alice K. The story of Ocracoke. [Ocracoke, Channel Press, 1949] 6 p. [11915

Rondthaler, Edward. The Memorabilia of fifty years, 1877 to 1927. Raleigh, Edwards & Broughton Co., 1928. 520 p. [11916
——Appendix . . . 1928, 1929, 1930. Raleigh, Edwards & Broughton Co., 1931. 58 p. [19116a
——The use of the lot in the Moravian Church; paper read before the Wachovia Historical Society, October 21, 1901. [Winston-Salem? 1901?] 8 p. [11917

Rondthaler, Katharine Boring. "Tell me a story". Bethlehem, Pa., Comenius Press, 1948. [60] p. [11918

Roosevelt, Franklin Delano, pres. U. S. Roosevelt and Daniels, a friendship in politics. Edited . . . by Carroll Kilpatrick. Chapel Hill, University of North Carolina Press [1952] 226 p. [11919

Roosevelt, Theodore, pres. U. S. Thomas H. Benton. Boston, Houghton Mifflin [c.1886-1914] 372 p. [11920
——The winning of the West. New York, G. P. Putnam's Sons, 1889-96. 4 v. [11921
—— ——1894-1910. 4 v. [11922

Root, Albert S. Leading truck crops of the Wilmington section. Wilmington, Carolina Trucking Development Co., n.d. 50 p. [11923

Roper, Moses. A narrative of the adventures and escape of Moses Roper, from American slavery. 3d ed. London, Harvey and Darton, 1839. 193 p. [11924

Rose, Charles Grandison. The development of Hebrew law. Chapel Hill, University Press, 1900. (N. C. University. Philosophy Dept. Worth prize thesis. 1900) 12 p. [11925
——The lawyer, his privileges and responsibilities; address before the North Carolina Bar Association, Chapel Hill, July 23, 1931. Raleigh, Edwards & Broughton Co. [1931] 13 p. [11926

Rose, Duncan. Madeline . . . a love story. Fayetteville, Cape Fear Press [c.1898] 158 p. [11927
——The resources and industries of Cumberland County and Fayetteville, North Carolina. No place, Commissioners of Cumberland County and Mayor and Aldermen of Fayetteville [1897] 42 p. [11928
——The romantic career of a naval officer, Federal and Confederate: Captain Maffitt. [Spray, Author, 1935] 68 p. [11929

Rose, Wickliffe. School funds in ten southern states. [Nashville, Tenn., Foster, Webb & Parker] 1909. 98 p. [11930

Ross, Fred E. Jackson Mahaffey, a novel. Boston, Houghton Mifflin [c.1951] 308 p. [11931

Ross, Ishbel. Through the lich-gate; a biography of the Little Church Around the Corner. New York, W. F. Payson, 1931. 164 p. [11932

Ross, James, fl. 1882. Life and times of Elder Reuben Ross, by his son. Philadelphia, Printed by Grant, Faires & Rodgers [introd. 1882] 426 p. [11933

Ross, James, 1911- . . . They don't dance much. Boston, Houghton Mifflin Co., 1940. 296 p. [11934
—— ——[New York] New American Library [1952] 191 p. Abridged. [11935

Ross, Jane Amelia. The logic of the spiritual process. Chapel Hill, Department of Philosophy, University of North Carolina, 1937. (Studies in philosophy, no. 11) 46 p. [11936

Ross, Laura. The Renaissance; crowned with the Mildred Williams Buchan prize. Chapel Hill, University of North Carolina, 1933. 7 p. [11937

Ross, Michael H.   The third party tradition in North Carolina.   Greensboro, 1947.
29 p.   [11938

Ross, Otho Bescent.   European problems; some new syntheses as stimulated by a
tour May and June, 1948.   [Charlotte, Author, 1948]   19 p.   [11939
——The place of the church in religion.   Chapel Hill, University of North Carolina,
1904.   (Worth prize thesis.   1905)   11 p.   [11940

Ross Williamson, Hugh.   Sir Walter Raleigh.   London, Faber and Faber [1951]
215 p.   [11941

Rotary International.   Fifty-Seventh District.   Conference, 1935, Raleigh, North
Carolina, May 16th and 17th.   [Raleigh] 1935.   27 p.   [11942
——Program and information, annual conference of the fifty-seventh district, Rotary
International, Pinehurst, N. C., May 9th and 10th, 1937.   No place, 1937.
32 p.   [11943

Rotary International.   189th District.   Program and information, annual conference
of the 189th district, Rotary International, Pinehurst, North Carolina, May 7-8,
1944; district governor, Robert W. Madry, host club, Chapel Hill.   No place,
1944.   40 p.   [11944

Rotary International.   278th District.   Minutes, 19 - 19 - NcU has 1950,
1953   [11945

Round Hill School, Union Mills, N. C.   Catalogue, 1899/1900?-   Union Mills, 1900?-
NcU has 1908/09, 1918/19   [11946

Rounds, Glen.   Buffalo harvest.   New York, Holiday House [1952]   141 p. [11947
——Hunted horses.   New York, Holiday House [1951]   154 p.   [11948
——Lone muskrat.   New York, Holiday House [1953]   124 p.   [11949
——Rodeo; bulls, broncs and buckaroos.   [New York] Holiday House [1949]
157 p.   [11950
——Stolen pony.   New York, Holiday House [1948]   154 p.   [11951

Rountree, George.   Argument on behalf of the Cape Fear bar pilots, by George
Rountree and J. O. Carr.   Raleigh, Edwards & Broughton, n.d.   35 p.   [11952
——The Supreme Court of the United States; an address delivered before the Bar
Association of North Carolina . . . 1902. No place, no publisher, n.d. 16 p. [11953

Rountree, George, joint author,   see Carr, James Ozborn

Rountree, Maude McIver, comp.   The Cross of Military Service ("C. M. S.")
History and records of men of lineal Confederate descent who served honorably In
the Army, Navy or Marine Corps of the United States or its allies during the . . .
World War.   Vol. I.   [Jackson, Tenn., Press of McCowat-Mercer Printing Co.]
1927.   311 p.   [11954

Rountree Family Association.   Dedication of the Rountree Church memorial . . .
April 27, 1947.   No place, 1947.   [3] p.   Program.   [11955

Rouse, Alice Riddle (Read)   The Reads and their relatives.   Cincinnati, Johnson &
Hardin Press, 1930.   688 p.   [11956

Rouse, Irving.   An anthropological bibliography of the eastern seaboard, ed. by
Irving Rouse and John M. Goggin.   New Haven, The Federation, 1947 [i.e. 1948]
(Eastern States Archeological Federation. Research publication no. 1) 174 p. [11957

Routh, Martha.   Memoir of the life, travels, and religious experience of Martha
Routh. York, Printed and published by W. Alexander and Son, 1822. 317 p. [11958

Rowan Baptist Association.   Minutes, 1927?- 1927?- NcU has 1945-1955 [11959

Rowan County, N. C.   Auditor.   Rowan County, North Carolina, financial statement, June 30, 1930.   [Salisbury] 1930.   [22] p.   [11960

Rowan Co., N. C.   Board of Superintendents of Common Schools.   Report of the
chairman of the board, 1852/53.   [Salisbury? 1853]   [1] p.   [11961

[Rowan Co., N. C.   Bicentennial Committee]   Rowan County's bicentennial celebration, April 12-18, 1953, featuring the dramatic historical spectacle "Rowan
200".   [Salisbury, 1953]   76 p.   Program.   [11962

Rowan Co., N. C.   Citizens.   To the freemen of the counties of Mecklenburg, Rowan,
and Cabarrus.   No place, no publisher, n.d.   [1] p.   [11963

Rowan Co., N. C.   Clerk of Superior Court.   List of taxable property in the county
of Rowan? North Carolina, anno 1778, transcribed from several lists . . . (also
. . . Tax lists of 1784)   Washington, Annie Walker Burns [1953]   49 p.   [11965

Rowan Co., N. C. Court. Patrol regulations for the county of Rowan; printed by order of the county court . . . 1825. Salisbury, Printed by Philo White, 1825. 7 p. [11966

[Rowan Co., N. C. Democratic Executive Committee] Democratic speaking at Mt. Ulla school house. [Salisbury, 1916?] [1] p. [11967
——Wilson and cotton! [Salisbury? 1916] [1] p. [11968

Rowan Co., N. C. Physicians. Table of fees. Salisbury, 1854. [1] p. [11969

Rowan County Medical Society. Constitution and by-laws of Rowan County Medical Society. [Salisbury?] n.d. 4 p. [11970
——Fee table. [Salisbury?] n.d. [1] p. [11971

Rowe, Claude Watson. How and where lawyers get practice; 780 lawyers' answers to the question. Durham, Judiciary Publishing Co. [1955] 212 p. [11972
——The lawyers' proof of the hereafter. 4th ed. Philadelphia, John C. Winston Co. [1941] 246 p. [11973

Rowe, John. A treatise on the five material points of the Arminian creed. Wilson, Printed at the Office of "Zion's Landmarks", 1870. 32 p. [11974

Rowe, Nellie M. Discovering North Carolina. Chapel Hill, University of North Carolina Press, 1933. 363 p. [11975
——My magic storyland. Chicago, A. Whitman & Co. [c.1929] 125 p. [11976

Rowe, Walter Wheat. History of the Baptists of Greensboro, N. C. with particular reference to . . . the First Baptist Church, 1850-1926. [Greensboro, Printed by Jos. J. Stone and Co.] n.d. 75 p. [11977

Rowell, John Wesley. Brief history of Waxhaw Baptist Church and the family of Godfreys. Matthews, The Author [c.1939] 96 p. [11978

Rowland, Eron Orpha (Moore) Andrew Jackson's campaign against the British. New York, Macmillan Co., 1926. 424 p. [11979

Rowland, Henry Augustus. The elect saved by faith. New-York, D. Fanshaw, pr., 1833. 31 p. [11980
——The real glory of a church; a dedication sermon preached in Fayetteville, North-Carolina, at the opening of the Presbyterian Church . . . re-built and dedicated August 12th, 1832. New-York, J. Leavitt and J. P. Haven, 1832. 34 p. [11981

Rowland, Joseph Medley. Blue Ridge breezes. Richmond, Appeals Press, 1918. 535 p. [11982
——The Hill Billies. Nashville, Tenn., Cokesbury Press, 1924. 298 p. [11983

Rowley, Erastus. Discourse delivered before the Asheville lodge of the order of Free Masons, June 24th, 1848. Asheville, Thos. W. Atkin, pr., 1848. 16 p. [11984

Rowse, Alfred Leslie. Sir Richard Grenville of the Revenge. Boston, Houghton Mifflin Co., 1937. 365 p. [11985

Roxboro, N. C. Board of Trustees of Public Schools. Report, 1902/03?- 1903?-NcU has 1905/06 [11986

Royal Arcanum. North Carolina. Official reports of grand council, officers and Journal of proceedings of the annual session, 18 - Raleigh, Edwards & Brough-ton, 18 - NcU has 1902-1931 [11987

Royal Knights of King David. Lady Knights Department. Constitution and general laws. No place, no publisher, n.d. 32 p. [11988

Royall, William. A treatise on Latin cases and analysis. New York, Sheldon & Co., 1860. 129 p. [11989

Royall, William L. Reply to "A fool's errand, by one of the fools". 2d ed. New York, E. J. Hale & Son, 1881. 95 p. [11990
—— ——3d ed. 160 p. [11991

Royster, Edith. Instructions for primary teachers in Wake County. Raleigh, Edwards & Broughton Co. for Board of Education of Wake County, 1915. 39 p. [11992

Royster, Hubert Ashley. The adventurous life of Edward Warren Bey. [Raleigh? Author? 1937?] 23 p. [11993
——Appendicitis. New York, D. Appleton and Co., 1927. 370 p. [11994
——Edmund Strudwick, surgeon. No place, no publisher, n.d. 7 p. [11995

[Royster, Hubert Ashley] Historical sketch of the University of North Carolina medical department at Raleigh. [Chapel Hill?] The Alumni Association, 1941. 72 p. [11996

Royster, Hubert Ashley.   Medical morals and manners.   Chapel Hill, University of
North Carolina Press, 1937.   333 p.   [11997
——Muscle; a lecture delivered by invitation before the students of Wake Forest
College, March 12, 1896.   No place, no publisher, n.d.   15 p.   [11998
——Types of modern doctors.   No place, no publisher [1906]   16 p.   President's
address, Tri-State Medical Association, February 27-28, 1906.   [11999

Royster, James Finch.   Guide to composition, by James Finch Royster . . . and
Stith Thompson.   Chicago, Scott, Foresman and Co. [c.1919]   204 p.   [12000

Royster, James Finch, ed.   The Tudor Shakespeare: Love's labour's lost.   New
York, Macmillan Co., 1912.   149 p.   [12001

Royster, James Finch.   Practice sheets for English composition, by James Finch
Royster . . . and Stith Thompson.   Chicago, Scott, Foresman and Co. [c.1918]
83 leaves   [12002

Royster, James Finch, joint author,   see Elson, William Harris

Royster, Nat L.   Once to every heart.   New York, Exposition Press [1947] 95 p. [12003

Royster, Wisconsin Iowa.   Edmund Burke Haywood; memorial address read before
the Raleigh Academy of Medicine, April 28, 1894.   Raleigh, Edwards & Broughton, pr., 1895.   21 p.   [12004
—— ——Raleigh, Bynum Printing Co., 1933.   18 p.   [12005

Royster memorial studies, edited by Louis B. Wright [and others]   Chapel Hill,
University of North Carolina Press, 1931.   329 p.   [12006

Ruark, Fletcher.   Poems.   Windsor, Ont., Curtis Co., Ltd. [c.1931]   79 p.   [12007

Ruark, Robert Chester.   Horn of the hunter.   Garden City, N. Y., Doubleday &
Co., Inc., 1953.   315 p.   [12008
——I didn't know it was loaded.   Garden City, N. Y., Doubleday & Co., Inc., 1948.
255 p.   [12009
——One for the road. Garden City, N. Y., Doubleday & Co., Inc., 1949. 253 p. [12010
——Something of value.   Garden City, N. Y., Doubleday and Co., Inc., 1955.
566 p.   [12011

Rubin, Louis Decimus, ed.   Southern renascence: the literature of the modern
South, edited by Louis D. Rubin, Jr. and Robert D. Jacobs.   Baltimore, Johns
Hopkins Press, 1953.   450 p.   [12012

Rubin, Louis Decimus.   Thomas Wolfe; the weather of his youth.   Baton Rouge,
Louisiana State University Press [1955]   183 p.   [12013

Rucker, Elizabeth (Hoyle)   The genealogy of Peiter Heyl and his descendants, 1100-
1936.   Shelby, Z. J. Thompson and others [c.1938]   1539 p.   [12014

Ruddiman, Thomas.   The rudiments of the Latin tongue . . . 25th ed.   Raleigh,
Printed at the Star Office by Thomas Henderson, Jr., 1809.   155 p.   [12015

[Rudy, Abraham?]   Our United States; a national song.   Raleigh, Edwards &
Broughton Printing Co. [c.1913]   [2] p.   [12016

Ruffin, Thomas, 1824-1889.   A card.   Hillsboro, no publisher, July 22, 1874.
[1] p.   [12017

Ruffin, Thomas, 1873-   Address before the N. C. Bar Association at Hendersonville,
N. C. . . . July 12, 1907.   Raleigh, Edwards & Broughton Printing Co., n.d.
13 p.   [12018

Ruffin, N. C. School Committee.   The community of Ruffin.   Ruffin, 1926.
3 p.   [12019

Ruffner, Henry.   Strictures on a book, entitled, "An apology for the book of Psalms.
By Gilbert M'Master."   2d ed.   Charlotte, Printed by Lemuel Bingham, 1825.
64 p.   [12020

Rules of Virginia and North Carolina for cock-fighting.   Richmond, Printed by
James M. Ford, 1860.   12 p.   NcU has photostat (positive)   [12021

Rules to be observed in the trial of horses for speed.   No place, no publisher, n.d.
[1] p.   [12022

Rumley, Robert Parker.   "De dry bones in de valley", a sermon reported by Orville
Knight Smith.   Asheville, Published by A. Y. Pearson [1896]   [20] p.   [12023

Rumple, Jethro.   A history of Rowan County, North Carolina.   Salisbury, J. J.
Bruner, 1881.   508 p.   [12024

—— ——Salisbury, Elizabeth Maxwell Steele Chapter, D.A.R. [1916] 618 p.[12025
—— ——[1929]   428 p.   [12026

Runyan, Morris C.   Eight days with the Confederates and capture of their archives, flags, &c by Company "G" Ninth New Jersey Vol.   Princeton, N. J., Wm. C. C. Zapf, pr., 1896.   44 p.   [12027

Rupp, Israel Daniel.   . . . A collection of thirty thousand names of German, Swiss Dutch, French, Portuguese and other immigrants in Pennsylvania.   Philadelphia, Leary, Stuart Co., 1927.   495 p.   [12028
—— ——Index by M. V. Koger.   [Pennington Gap, Va., M. V. Koger, 1936] 232 p.   [12029

Rural directory and mailing list of Edgecombe County, N. C., 19 - Raleigh, Edwards & Broughton Printing Co., 19 - NcU has 1920   [12030

Rush, Benjamin.   An inquiry into the effects of ardent spirits upon the human body and mind.   6th edition.   Raleigh, Printed by Thomas Henderson, Jr., 1813. 36 p.   [12031

Rush, Christopher.   Short account of the rise and progress of the African M. E. Church in America, written by Christopher Rush . . . with the aid of George Collins.   New York, The Author, 1866.   106 p.   [12032

Russ, John P. H.   To the voters of Wake County.   No place [1862]   [1] p.   [12033

Russell, Daniel Lindsay.   To the voters of the third congressional district of North Carolina.   No place, The Author, n.d.   [1] p.   [12034

Russell, Elbert.   A book of chapel talks.   Nashville, Cokesbury Press [c.1935] 222 p.   [12035
——Elbert Russell, Quaker, an autobiography.   Jackson, Tenn., Friendly Press [c.1956]   376 p.   [12036
——The history of Quakerism.   New York, Macmillan Co., 1942.   586 p.   [12037
——The inner light in the history and present problems of the Society of Friends. [Guilford College] North Carolina Friends Historical Society [1946]   (Its Publication no. 1)   24 p.   [12038
——The message of the Fourth Gospel.   Nashville, Cokesbury Press [c.1932] 200 p.   [12039
——More chapel talks.   Nashville, Cokesbury Press [c.1938]   222 p.   [12040

Russell, Harry Kitsun, ed.   Literature in English; ed. by H. K. Russell, William Wells [and] Donald A. Stauffer.   New York, Henry Holt & Co. [1948] 1174 p. [12041

Russell, Josiah Cox, ed.   The shorter Latin poems of Master Henry of Avranches relating to England [edited by] Josiah Cox Russell . . . and John Paul Heironimus. Cambridge, Mass., Mediaeval Academy of America, 1935.   (Its Studies and documents, no. 1)   162 p.   [12042

Russell, Lindsay.   A Tar Heel goes to town, Detroit, London, New York, 1870-1949. Wilmington, The Author [1948]   15 p.   [12043

Russell, Phillips.   Benjamin Franklin, the first civilized American.   New York, Brentano's, 1926.   323 p.   [12044
——Emerson, the wisest American.   New York, Brentano's, 1929.   320 p.   [12045
——Flowings.   [London, Caledonian Press] n.d.   10 p.   [12046
——Fumbler.   New York, Macaulay Co. [c.1928]   332 p.   [12047
——The glittering century.   New York, C. Scribner's Sons, 1936.   326 p.   [12048
——Harvesters.   New York, Brentano's [c.1932]   302 p.   [12049
——Jefferson, champion of the free mind. New York, Dodd, Mead, 1956. 374 p. [12050
——John Paul Jones: man of action.   New York, Brentano's, 1927.   314 p.   [12051
——Meal and honey.   [London, Westminster Press, 1924]   11 p.   [12052
——Red tiger: adventures in Yucatan and Mexico.   New York, Brentano's, 1929. 335 p.   [12053
——William the Conqueror.   New York, C. Scribner's Sons, 1933.   334 p.   [12054
——The woman who rang the bell; the story of Cornelia Phillips Spencer.   Chapel Hill, University of North Carolina Press [1949]   293 p.   [12055

Russell, Texie Horton Barlowe   see Barlowe, Texie Horton

Russell, Sir William Howard.   My diary North and South.   New York, Harper & Brothers, 1863.   225 p.   [12056

Russell Sage Foundation, New York.   Library.   The southern highlander.   New York [1932]   (Its Bulletin, no. 115.   October, 1932)   4 p.   [12057

Ruth, Thomas L.   My own life as an outcast husband.   [Wilmington] The Author, c.1901.   111 p.   [12058

Rutherford, Mildred Lewis.   The South in history and literature . . . from . . . 1607, to living writers.   [Atlanta, Franklin-Turner, 1907]   866 p.   [12059

Rutherford College, Rutherford College, N. C.   Catalogue, 18   -   Rutherford College, 18   -   NcU has [1900/01-1912/13] 1914/15-1922/23 [1924/25-1928/29]   [12060

Rutherford County club directory, 1923-   1923-   NcU has 1923   [12061

Rutherfurd, John.   The importance of the colonies to Great Britain.   London, Printed for J. Millan, 1761.   46 p.   [12062

Rutland, Robert Allen.   The birth of the Bill of Rights, 1776-1791.   Chapel Hill, Published for the Institute of Early American History and Culture by the University of North Carolina Press [1955]   243 p.   [12063

Ryan, James T.   The port terminal bill; address before the High Point Rotary Club on October 2d, 1924.   [High Point, C. F. Long and others, 1924]   15 p.   [12064

Ryan, Lee Winfree.   French travelers in the Southeastern United States, 1775-1800. Bloomington, Ind., The Principia Press, Inc., 1939.   107 p.   [12065

Ryan, Will Carson, ed.   Secondary education in the South, edited . . . by W. Carson Ryan . . . J. Minor Gwynn . . . [and] Arnold K. King.   Chapel Hill, University of North Carolina Press, 1946.   269 p.   [12066

Ryan, Will Carson.   Studies in early graduate education.   New York, Carnegie Foundation for the Advancement of Teaching, 1939.   (Its Bulletin, no. 30) 167 p.   [12067

Ryder, C. J.   The "poor men of Lyons" in our southern mountains.   [New York, American Missionary Association Bible House, 1905?]   7 p.   [12068

Ryle, John Charles.   A call to prayer.   [Raleigh, General Tract Agency] n.d. 15 p.   [12069

Sabbath School Teacher, pseud.   A collection of Sabbath School hymns . . . for the benefit of the children in the Confederate States.   Raleigh, Raleigh Register Steam-power Press, 1863.   62 p.   [12070

——The Sabbath School wreath.   Raleigh, Raleigh Register, 1863.   94 p.   [12071

—— ——4th ed.   Raleigh, [Raleigh Standard for] Sunday School and Publication Board, 1866.   104 p.   [12072

Sabine, Lorenzo.   American loyalists.   Boston, Charles C. Little and James Brown, 1847.   733 p.   [12073

——Biographical sketches of loyalists of the American Revolution.   Boston, Little, Brown, and Co., 1864.   2 v.   A new and enlarged edition of "The American loyalists."   [12074

Sacred Heart Junior College, Belmont, N. C.   Catalogue, 189   -   Belmont, 189 - NcU has 1905/06, 1940/41, 1952/54, 1955/56   [12075

Saint Augustine's College, Raleigh, N. C.   Catalogue, 186   -   Raleigh, 186   -   NcU has [1882/83-1917/18] 1919/20-1933/34   [12076

——A brief statement of the history and present condition of Saint Augustine's Normal School and Collegiate Institute.   [Raleigh] 1883.   8 p.   [12077

——Saint Augustine's record, v. 1- 189 - Raleigh, 189 - NcU has v. [10-59]   [12078

St. Clair, Kenneth Edson.   The administration of justice in North Carolina during Reconstruction, 1865-1876.   University, Ohio, Ohio State University Press, 1940. (Its Abstracts of doctoral dissertations.   1940, no. 31)   p. 317-324   [12079

St. Cloud, Virgil.   Pioneer blood.   Raleigh, Edwards & Broughton Co., 1948. 312 p.   [12080

Saint Genevieve of the Pines, Asheville, N. C.   Catalogue, 191   -   Asheville, 191 - NcU has 1912/13-1916/17 [1947/48?] 1953/55 (as one)   [12081

Saint John's Episcopal Church, Williamsboro, N. C.   St. John's Episcopal Church. [Henderson, Committee on the Restoration of St. John's Church] n.d.   [4] p. [12082

Saint Leo's Hospital, Greensboro, N. C.   St. Leo's Hospital . . . incorporated 1906. [Greensboro] n.d.   34 p.   [12083

Saint Mary's College, Belmont, N. C.   see Belmont Abbey College, Belmont, N. C.

Saint Mary's Junior College, Raleigh N. C. Book of views. [Raleigh] n.d. 16 p. [12084

—— ——[1917?]   Folder.   [12085

——Bulletin, ser. 1- 1905- Raleigh, 1905- NcU has ser. [1-7, 9, 13-14] 15-23 [24-33] 34-38 [39-45] Called Saint Mary's School; also, Saint Mary's School and Junior College [12086
——Catalogue, 184 - Raleigh, 184 - NcU has [1879/80-1905/06] Continues as its Bulletin, 1905- [12087
——Catalogue of drawings and paintings by the pupils of the Art Department, session, 1882-83, Raleigh, Uzzell & Gatling, pr. [1883?] [8] p. [12088
——Manual of Saint Mary's School. Raleigh, Carolina Cultivator, 1857. 75 p. [12089
——Panoramic view of Saint Mary's School, Raleigh, N. C. Raleigh [1913] 1 plate [12090
——Records about new buildings and endowment. [Raleigh, Edwards & Broughton Printing Co.] n.d. 8 p. [12091
——Saint Mary's. [Raleigh] n.d. [24] p. [12092
——Saint Mary's alumnae song book. Raleigh, 1921. 6 p. [12093
——Saint Mary's and the challenge of our time. [Raleigh, 1952?] 16 p. [12094
——Saint Mary's calendar, 1907. [Raleigh, 1906] [7] p. [12095
——Saint Mary's in the grove. [Raleigh, 1920?] [12] p. [12096
——Saint Mary's School and Junior College. [Raleigh, 1930] [15] p. [12097
—— ——[1944] [24] p. [12098
——Saint Mary's song book. Raleigh, 1915. 24 p. [12099
——Saint Mary's songs, Alumnae luncheon. [Raleigh, 1922] [4] p. [12100

Saint Mary's muse, v. 1- 1878- Raleigh, Saint' Mary School, 1878- NcU has v. [2-4] 5-6 [7] and issues of 1896-1899 not numbered, 9-14, 18-21 [22-26] [12101

Saint Paul's School, Beaufort, N. C. Catalogue, 1899/1900?- Beaufort, 1900?- NcU has 1906/07, 1909/10 [12102

Salem, N. C. Forsyth Immigration Agency. Forsyth County, North Carolina; a description of its resources and a review of its industries. Raleigh, State Chronicle Print, 1884. 31 p. [12103

Salem Baptist Association. Minutes, 18 - 18 - NcU has 1877, 1878 [12104

Salem Boys' School, Salem, N. C. Catalogue, 18 - Salem, 18 - NcU has 1900/01, 1902/03, 1904/05 [12105

Salem College, Winston-Salem, N. C. Alumnae Memorial Hall . . . May 22, 1916 . . . "Romeo and Juliet", Gounod. No place [1916?] 11 p. [12106
——Alumnae record, no. 1-v. 71, 1879?-1949. 1879?-1949. NcU has no. [2-400] 401-426 [427-469] 470-480 [481-485] and v. 51-54, 66-67 [69-71] Title varies, 1879-191 : Academy. Continues as its Bulletin, v. 1- October, 1949- [12107
——Bulletin, v. 1- 1908- Winston-Salem, 1908- NcU has v. [1-3] [12108
——Bulletin [2d ser.] v. 1- October, 1949- Winston-Salem, 1949- NcU has v. [1-6] [12091
——Catalogue, 18 - Winston-Salem, 18 - NcU has [1859/60-1926/27] 1933/34-1950/51. Issued at intervals as its Alumnae record, or, as its Bulletin. Called Salem Academy; also, Salem Academy and College [12110
——A masque of collegiate futurity, Salem, May twenty-ninth, nineteen thirteen. No place [1913?] 18 p. [12111
——175th anniversary, Salem College, 1772, 1947. [Winston-Salem, 1947] 24 p. [12112
——Salem Academy and College. [Winston-Salem] n.d. portfolio of plates [12113
—— ——[1910] portfolio of plates [12114
—— ——n.d. 8 p. [12115
——Salem College and vicinity. [Winston-Salem] n.d. [4] p. [12116
——Salem College, including Academy and preparatory departments. [Winston-Salem] n.d. 8 p. [12117
——Salem tells its story of the education of American girls. [Winston-Salem, 1946?] [10] p. [12118
——The social book, Salem Academy and College. [Winston-Salem, 1912] 21 p. [12119
——Terms and conditions of the boarding school for female education in Salem, N. C. Salem [1870?] [1] p. [12120
——Within these pages we hope to share with you something of the life and spirit of Salem College. [Winston-Salem, 1945] [23] p. [12121

Salem Primitive Baptist Association. Minutes, 1910- 1910- NcU has 1910-1936 [1939-1951] [12122

Salemburg Academy, Salemburg, N. C. Catalogue, 187 - Salemburg, 187 - NcU has 1904/05, 1907/08 [12123

Sales Management, New York. Complete ranking of 233 metropolitan county areas in 13 sales classifications by dollar volume . . . plus complete North Carolina county-city data. Greensboro, Greensboro News and Record, 1955. 100 p. [12124

——Complete ranking of 225 metropolitan county areas in 13 sales classifications by dollar volume. Greensboro, Greensboro News and Record, 1953. 64 p. [12125

Sales-Sayles, Hall Fletcher. The history of the Sale-Sales-Sayles families. [Asheville? 1955] 43 p. [12126

Salisbury, N. C. Board of Aldermen. Code of the city of Salisbury . . . April 28, 1899. Raleigh, Edwards & Broughton, pr., 1899. 136 p. [12127

Salisbury, N. C. Board of Commissioners. The charter, the amendments thereto, and ordinances of the town of Salisbury . . . July, 1865. Salisbury, J. J. Bruner, pr., n.d. 31 p. [12128

Salisbury, N. C. Chamber of Commerce. Chamber of Commerce, Salisbury, North Carolina. [Salisbury, 1902?] 13 p. [12129

——Geographic location, industries, wealth . . . government, Salisbury. Salisbury [194?] [6] p. [12130

——Industrial analysis, Salisbury (Rowan County) North Carolina. [Salisbury] 1956. 17 p. [12131

[**Salisbury, N. C. Chamber of Commerce**] Salisbury, North Carolina. [Salisbury, [195?] [22] p. [12132

——Why you should prosper in Salisbury. [Salisbury, 193?] 20 p. [12133

Salisbury, N. C. Finance Committee. Financial statement of the city of Salisbury, N. C., 19 - 19 - NcU has June 1, 1905-March 1, 1909 [12134

Salisbury, N. C. First Presbyterian Church. Manual . . . April, 1913. Salisbury, Wm. H. Stewart, pr., 1913. 36 p. [12135

[**Salisbury, N. C. Frank B. John School. Sixth Grade**] The making of North Carolina. Salisbury, n.d. 12 p. [12136

Salisbury, N. C. Hospital Committee. An appeal for the sick and wounded soldiers. [Salisbury, 1863] [1] p. [12137

Salisbury, N. C. Industrial Club. Salisbury, North Carolina. [Salisbury, 1913?] 7 p. [12138

Salisbury, N. C. Lutheran Church. A misstatement in the "Episcopal journal" of Bishop Ravenscroft corrected. Salisbury, Printed by Philo White, 1827. 7 p. [12139

Salisbury, N. C. Old Hickory Club. . . . Eighteenth anniversary of the Old Hickory Club of Salisbury, N. C. [Charlotte, Charlotte Observer] 1903. 24 p. [12140

Salisbury, N. C. Saint Luke's Episcopal Church. Parish news letter, v. 1- 1953- NcU has v. [1] 2-5 [12140a

Salisbury, N. C. Schools. Brand preference survey (foods) of 1486 families at Salisbury, North Carolina, 1st- 194 - Salisbury, 194 - NcU has 5th, 1951 [12141

Salisbury, North Carolina, Rowan county. No place, no publisher [190?] 16 p. [12142

Salisbury and Taylorsville Plank Road Co. Charter and by-laws. Salisbury, Printed at the Carolina Watchman Office, 1851. 8 p. [12143

Salisbury Normal and Industrial Institute, Salisbury, N. C. Catalogue, 19 - 19 - NcU has 1919/20 [12144

Salisbury Pink Granite Company. Prospectus of the Salisbury Pink Granite Company. [Kansas City, Mo., 1903?] [10] p. [12145

Salisbury-Spencer North Carolina city directory, 1907- Asheville, Piedmont Directory Co., Inc., c.1907- NcU has 1917, 1922-23, 1926-27 [12146

Salley, Alexander Samuel. . . . The boundary line between North Carolina and South Carolina. Columbia, S. C., Printed for the Commission by the State Co., 1929. (Bulletins of the Historical Commission of South Carolina, no. 10) 38 p. [12147

——The Lords Proprietors of Carolina. [Columbia, S. C.] Joint Committee on Printing, General Assembly of South Carolina, 1944. 16 p. [12148

Salley, Alexander Samuel, ed. . . . Narratives of early Carolina, 1650-1708. New York, C. Scribner's Sons, 1911. 388 p. [12149

Salley, Alexander Samuel. . . . The origin of Carolina. Columbia, S. C. Printed for the Commission by the State Co., 1926. (Bulletins of the Historical Commission of South Carolina, no. 8) 22 p. [12150

——The true Mecklenburg "Declaration of Independence." Columbia, S. C., The Author, 1905. 18 p.   [12151

Salley, Katherine (Batts) ed. Life at Saint Mary's. Chapel Hill, University of North Carolina Press, 1942. 288 p.   [12152

Salls, Helen Harriet. Pensive citadels. Emory University, Ga., Banner Press [c.1931] 41 p.   [12153

——Pine-needles, by Helen Harriet Salls and Grace Jean Salls. [Oxford? Oxford Orphanage Press] 1921. 24 p.   [12154

Saluda magazine of, for, and by Saluda folks and their friends, v. 1-3, April, 1936-July, 1938. Saluda, Excelsior Printers, 1936-1938. NcU has v. 1-3.   [12155

Sampson Co., N. C. Board of Education. Report of the industrial work of the colored schools of Sampson County, 19 - Wilmington, 1913- NcU has 1910/13, called Third annual, including resume of first and second reports.   [12156

——Report of the Public Schools of Sampson County, 19 - [Clinton, 19 - NcU has 1911/13, 1916/17   [12157

[Sampson Co., N. C. Republican Executive Committee?] Honorable record made by the Populist and Republican officials of Sampson County. No place [1906?] 30 p.   [12158

Sampson County school record, v. 1- November, 1914- Clinton, 1914- NcU has v. 1-2   [12159

Sampson County year book, v. 1, no. 1- 1945-46- Clinton, Mrs. Taft Bass [1946-NcU has 1945-46   [12160

Sams, Conway Whittle. The conquest of Virginia, the first attempt. Norfolk, Va., Keyser-Doherty for the Author, 1924. 547 p.   [12161

——The conquest of Virginia: the forest primeval. New York, G. P. Putnam's Sons, 1916. 432 p.   [12162

Samuel A. Ashe for treasurer. No place, no publisher [1908?] 4 p.   [12163

Samuel Fox Mordecai: presentation of a portrait by the alumni of the Duke University School of Law. [Durham, Duke University, 1932?] 57 p.   [12164

Samuels, J. E. Dr. J. P. Barrett, editor of the Herald of gospel liberty, and "The Noachin curse"; an answer. 2d ed. Franklinton, Afro-Christian Publishing Association, n.d. 10 p.   [12165

Sanborn, Ruth Burr. Murder on the Aphrodite. New York, Macmillan Co., 1935. 299 p.   [12166

——. . . These are my people. New York, Thomas Y. Crowell Co., 1941. 306 p. [12167

Sand Hill Board of Trade. The Sand Hill section of North Carolina. Aberdeen, Sand Hill Board of Trade [1915] 63 p.   [12168

Sandburg, Carl. Abraham Lincoln; the prairie years and the war years. New York, Harcourt, Brace [1954] 762 p.   [12169

——Always the young strangers. New York, Harcourt, Brace [1953] 445 p. [12170

Sandburg, Carl, ed. The American songbag. New York, Harcourt [c.1927] 495 p.   [12171

Sandburg, Carl. Complete poems. New York, Harcourt, Brace [1950] 676 p. [12172

Sandburg, Carl, ed. New American songbag. New York, Broadcast Music [1950] 107 p.   [12173

Sandburg, Carl. Remembrance Rock. New York, Harcourt, Brace [1948] 1067 p.   [12174

Sanders, Charles Richard. Coleridge and the Broad church movement. Durham, Duke University Press, 1942. 307 p.   [12175

——The Strachey family, 1588-1932. [Durham] Duke University Press, 1953. 337 p.   [12176

[Sanders, Daniel Clarke] A history of the Indian wars with the first settlers of the United States, to the commencement of the late war. Rochester, N. Y., Printed by Edwin Scranton, 1828. 196 (i.e. 192) p.   [12177

—— ——Reprinted [Rochester, 1893]   [12178

Sanders, George N. Appendix to the Life and times of Duncan K. McRae; with his letter of resignation to Gov. Vance. Raleigh, Standard Print., 1864. 48 p. [12179

Sanders, Wiley Britton. Juvenile courts in North Carolina. Chapel Hill, University of North Carolina Press, 1948. 210 p.   [12180

Sanders, Wiley Britton, ed. Negro child welfare in North Carolina, a Rosenwald study. Chapel Hill, Pub. for the North Carolina State Board of Charities and Public Welfare by the University of North Carolina Press, 1933. 326 p. [12181

Sanders, William Marsh, joint author, see **Ragsdale, George Young**

Sandhill Farm Life School, Vass, N. C. Catalogue, 191 - Vass, 191 - NcU has 1918/19 [12182

Sands, Francis Preston Blair. The last of the blockade and the fall of Fort Fisher. [Washington, 1902] (Military Order of the Loyal Legion of the United States. Commandery of the District of Columbia. War papers, 40) 30 p. [12183
——A volunteer's reminiscences of life in the North Atlantic Blockading Squadron, 1862-'5. [Washington, 1894] (Military Order of the Loyal Legion of the United States. Commandery of the District of Columbia. War papers, 18 [i.e. 20]) 27 p. [12184

Sandy Creek Baptist Association. Minutes, 18 - 18 - NcU has [1849-1869] 1876-1886 [1895-1955] [12185

Sandy Run Baptist Association. Minutes, 189 - 189 - NcU has [1902-1925] 1944-1955 [12186

Sanford, Edward T. Blount College and the University of Tennessee. [Knoxville, Tenn.] University of Tennessee [1894?] 119 p. [12187

[**Sanford, N. C. Board of Aldermen**] Ordinances and charter, town of Sanford, North Carolina. [Sanford] 1916. 43 p. [12188

Sanford, N. C. First Presbyterian Church. The First Presbyterian Church, Sanford, North Carolina, golden jubilee. [Sanford, 1944] 25 p. [12189

Sargent, Daniel. All the day long. James Anthony Walsh, cofounder of Maryknoll. New York, Longmans, Green & Co. [c.1941] 259 p. [12190

Sartorio, Enrico. A brief history of the Waldensians. No place, no publisher, 1921. 15 p. [12191

Sass, Herbert Ravenel. Hear me, my chiefs! New York, W. Morrow & Co., 1940. 256 p. [12192

Satchwell, S. S. Address on immigration delivered before the North Carolina Immigration Association at a meeting held at Goldsboro, N. C., on the second of April, 1869. Weldon, Roanoke News' Book and Job Print [1869] 22 p. [12193
——An address on the welfare of the medical profession delivered before the State Medical Society, at Warrenton, N. C. on the 20th May, 1868. Wilmington, Engelhard & Price, 1868. 23 p. [12194
——Annual address before the Alumni Association of the University of the City of New York, Medical Department, March 4th, 1873. [New York? 1873?] 25 p.[12195
——The influence of material agents in developing man, an address delivered before the literary societies of Wake Forest College . . . June, 1858. Wilmington, C. E. & R. Burr, pr., 1858. 31 p. [12196
——Memoir of Dr. W. H. McKee . . . delivered at Wilson, N. C., May 19, 1875, by S. S. Satchwell . . . and at Raleigh, N. C., June 2d, 1875, by William G. Hill. Raleigh, Edwards, Broughton & Co., pr., 1875. 16 p. [12197
——Memorial of Otis Frederick Manson. No place, no publisher [1888?] 8 p. [12198
——Obstacles to medical progress, annual address delivered before the Medical Society of the State of North Carolina, at Edenton, N. C., April, 1857. Wilmington, Fulton & Price, 1857. 26 p. [12199
——Treatment of fever and inflammation, an essay on the topography and prevailing diseases of New Hanover County, N. C., read before the annual meeting of the North Carolina Medical Society, held at Wilmington, N. C., May 25, 1870. Wilmington, Engelhard & Price, 1870. 69 p. [12200

Satterfield, Frances Gibson. Charles Duncan McIver, 1860-1906. [Atlanta, Ruralist Press, Inc., 1942] 66 p. [12201

Saunders, James, 1765-? A genealogical table for the use of Joseph H. Saunders, written by his father, James Saunders, town of Edenton, North Carolina, A. D. 1824. Wilmington, Engelhard & Price, 1866. 20 p. [12202

Saunders, James, fl. 1846. A brief history of the imprisonment of James Saunders, of North Carolina, son of the Hon. R. M. Saunders, our minister to Spain, at the New Hampshire Insane Asylum. Boston, D. H. Ela & Co., pr., 1846. 11 p. [12203

Saunders, James Edmonds. Early settlers of Alabama . . . with notes and genealogies by his granddaughter, Elizabeth Saunders Blair Stubbs. New Orleans, L.
Graham & Son, Ltd., pr., 1899. 530 p.   [12204

Saunders, Jason Lewis. Justus Lipsius; the philosophy of Renaissance stoicism.
New York, Liberal Arts Press, 1955. 228 p.   [12205

Saunders, Richard R., comp. Open doors and closed windows of the First Baptist
Church of Reidsville, North Carolina. Reidsville, 1948. 308 p.   [12206

Saunders, Romulus Mitchell. Address delivered before the two literary societies of
Wake Forest College, June 9, 1852. Raleigh, W. W. Holden, pr., 1852. 43 p. [12207

——Address to the people of North Carolina. [Washington, The Author, 1843]
8 p.   [12208

——To the freemen of Stokes, Guilford, Rockingham, and Caswell. [Caswell County,
The Author, June 7, 1824] [3] p.   [12209

Saunders, William Laurence. History of the great seal of the state of North Carolina. Raleigh, 1893. 11 p.   [12210

——Lessons from our North Carolina records, an address read before the faculty and
students of Trinity College, November 27, 1888. [Durham] Trinity College, 1889.
(Its Publications, no. 1) 26 p.   [12211

—— ——[Durham? 1888] 27 p. Proof sheets with notes of the author in manuscript.   [12212

Saunders, William Oscar. The book of Ham. Elizabeth City, The Independent
[c.1924] 24 p.   [12213

——A concept of life and other Saunders editorials. Elizabeth City, The Independent, 1921. 68 p.   [12214

——A concept of life and other editorial cocktails. A rev. and enl. ed. [Elizabeth
City, The Independent, c.1932] 72 p.   [12215

——Heard on Main Street: the book of the bank clerk and the soda jerker. Elizabeth City, The Independent, 1927. 63 p.   [12216

—— ——[Elizabeth City, Swan Publishing Co., c.1934] 77 p.   [12217

——The newer Testament, being a modern attempt to bring down to date all that is
actually known about creation, God, the devil, and a future life. Elizabeth City,
The Author, 1908. [1] p. The page is blank.   [12218

Saunders, William Oscar, ed. A souvenir handbook of the Wright Memorial.
Elizabeth City, The Independent [c.1935] 29 p.   [12219

——Two historic shrines, the Wright Memorial and Fort Raleigh on Roanoke Island.
Elizabeth City, The Editor [c.1937] 30 p.   [12220

Savage, Henry. River of the Carolinas: the Santee. New York, Rinehart [1956]
435 p.   [12221

Savage, James W. The loyal element of North Carolina during the war; a paper read
before the Nebraska Commandery of the Loyal Legion of the United States, May 5,
1886. Omaha, Neb. [Omaha Republican Print] 1886. 8 p.   [12222

Savage, John. The life and public services of Andrew Johnson . . . including his
state papers, speeches and addresses. New York, Derby & Miller, 1866. 408,
130, 19 p.   [12223

Saville, Thorndike. The cause and correction of red water troubles. [Chapel Hill?
The Author?] n.d. 35 p.   [12224

——The relation of flood control to drainage; address before tenth annual drainage
convention held at Washington, N. C., March 31 and April 1, 1920. Raleigh, Edwards & Broughton Printing Co., 1920. 7 p.   [12225

Sawyer, Elmer Warren. Insurance as interstate commerce. New York, McGraw-
Hill Book Co., Inc., 1945. 169 p.   [12226

Sawyer, Harriet Adams. Souvenir of Asheville, or the sky-land. St. Louis, Nixon-
Jones Printing Co., 1892. 104 p.   [12227

Sawyer, Lemuel. Auto-biography of Lemuel Sawyer, formerly member of Congress
from North Carolina. New York, The Author, 1844. 48 p.   [12228

——A biography of John Randolph, of Roanoke, with a selection from his speeches.
New York, W. Robinson, 1844. 132 p.   [12229

——Blackbeard, a comedy, in four acts, founded on fact. Washington, Davis and
Force (Franklin's Head) pr., 1824. 66 p.   [12230

[Sawyer, Lemuel] The wreck of honor; or, Adventures in Paris, &c. A tragedy in five acts, translated from the French by John Dunlap, Esq. York, T. Scott, 1828. 87 p. [12231

Sawyer, Matthias Enoch. A treatise on primitive or secondary disguised or misplaced fever, as a single disease. New York, Peabody & Co., 1831. 307 p. [12232

Sawyer, Samuel T. An address to the freemen of the town of Edenton, declining a poll. Edenton, Miscellany Office, 1833. 7 p. [12233

Saxe-Weimer-Eisenach, Bernhard, Duke of. Reize naar en door Noord-Amerika, 1825-1826. Te Dordrecht, Bij, Blusse en van Braam, 1829. 2 v. [12234

Saxton, Eugene Francis. The O. Henry index, containing some little pictures of O. Henry together with an alphabetical guide to his complete works. Garden City, N. Y., Doubleday, Page & Co. [1917?] 48 p. [12235

Sayakini, 19 - Salisbury, Catawba College, 19 - NcU has 1955 [12236

Scaife, Hazel Lewis. History and condition of the Catawba Indians of South Carolina. Philadelphia, Office of the Indian Rights Association, 1896. 24 p. [12237

Scales, Alfred Moore. The Battle of Fredericksburg; an address before the Association of the Virginia Division of the Army of Northern Virginia at Richmond, Va., on Thursday evening, November 1, 1883. Washington, R. O. Polkinhorn & Son, pr., 1884. 23 p. [12238

Scales, Junius Irving. Mr. Scales' platform; the newspapers of the state with great unanimity loud in its praise. No place, no publisher, n.d. 5 p. [12239

[Scanlon, David Howard] Genealogy of the O'Scanlon family. [Durham, Author, 1938] 23 p. [12240

Scanlon, David Howard. An historical sketch of Shenandoah Normal College, Virginia, 1883-1896, founded by George Washington Hoenshel. No place, no publisher, 1941. 24 p. [12241

Scarborough, Dorothy. A song catcher in southern mountains; American folk songs of British ancestry. New York, Columbia University Press, 1937. 476 p. [12242

Scenic Chapel Hill, North Carolina. [Chapel Hill? 1924] 16 p. [12243

Schaare, C. Richard. The life of Daniel Boone in picture and story. New York, Cupples & Leon Co. [c.1934] 56 p. [12244

[Schafer Brothers, New York] Petition addressed to the General Assembly of North Carolina by certain holders of North Carolina bonds issued in aid of the Western North Carolina Rail Road. [Raleigh, Edwards & Broughton, pr.] 1901. 26 p.[12245

Schaffle, Evalyn. Verses. New York, H. Harrison [c.1938] 63 p. [12246

Scharf, John Thomas. History of the Confederate States Navy from its organization to the surrender of its last vessel. New York, Rogers & Sherwood, 1887. 824 p. [12247

—— ——2d ed. Albany, N. Y., Joseph McDonough, 1894. [12248

Schauinger, Joseph Herman. William Gaston, Carolinian. Milwaukee, Bruce Publishing Co. [1949] 242 p. [12249

[Schaw, Janet] Journal of a lady of quality; being the narrative of a journey from Scotland to the West Indies, North Carolina, and Portugal, in the years 1774 to 1776, ed. by Evangeline Walker Andrews, in collaboration with Charles McLean Andrews. New Haven, Yale University Press, 1921. 341 p. [12250

—— ——London, Oxford University Press, 1934. 349 p. [12251

—— ——New Haven, Yale University Press, 1939. 351 p. [12252

[Schenck, Carl Alwin] ed. The Biltmore immortals, biographies of 50 American boys graduating from the Biltmore Forest School which was the first school of American forestry on American soil. [Darmstadt, Germany, L. C. Wittich, pr., 1953] 342 p. [12253

Schenck, Carl Alwin. Biltmore lectures on sylviculture. Albany, N. Y., Brandow Printing Co., 1907. 184 p. [12254

——The Biltmore story . . . ed. by Ovid Butler. St. Paul, American Forest History Foundation, Minnesota Historical Society, 1955. 224 p. [12255

——Lectures on forest policy: Second part, Forestry conditions in the United States. [Biltmore, The Author? 1904] 108 p. [12256

——Our yellow poplar. [Biltmore? The Author?] n.d. 34 p. [12257

——Report on Highland Forest. [Biltmore, 1907] 30 p. [12258

Schenck, David. A historical address, delivered, Saturday, May 5th, 1888, at the Guilford Battle Ground. Subject: The Battle of Guilford Court House, fought Thursday, March 15, 1781. Greensboro, Thomas Brothers, pr., 1888. 74 p. [12259

——Historical sketch of the Schenck and Bevens families, with an appendix. Greensboro, Thomas, Reece & Co., pr., 1884. 45 p. [12260

——North Carolina, 1780-'81, being a history of the invasion of the Carolinas by the British army under Lord Cornwallis in 1780-'81, with the particular design of showing the part borne by North Carolina in that struggle for liberty and independence, and to correct some of the errors of history in regard to that state and its people. Raleigh, Edwards & Broughton, pr., 1889. 498 p. [12261

——Personal sketches of distinguished delegates of the state convention, 1861-2, North Carolina. Greensboro, Thomas, Reece & Co., pr., 1885. 23 p. [12262

——A short sketch of the life of Eli W. Caruthers, D. D. Greensboro, Reece & Elam, pr., 1901. 4 p. [12263

[Schenck, David] comp. Sketches of Maj.-Gen. Stephen Dodson Ramseur. [Greensboro? 1892?] Various paging. A collection of various publications reissued with a special title page and preface. [12264

Schenck, John Franklin. Child labor legislation. No place, no publisher, 1913. 20 p. [12265

——Uncle Sam's petted and spoiled children have been scratching "Papa" in the face, and what else could "Papa" expect? [Lawndale, Author, 1943] [3] p. [12266

Schenck, Lewis Bevens. The Presbyterian doctrine of children in the covenant. New Haven, Yale University Press, 1940. 188 p. [12267

Schenkkan, Robert Frederic, ed. Fourteen plays for the church [ed. by] Robert Schenkkan and Kai Jurgensen. New Brunswick, Rutgers University Press, 1948. 268 p. [12268

Scherer, James Augustin Brown. Cotton as a world power; a study in the economic interpretation of history. New York, Frederick A. Stokes Co. [c.1916] 452 p. [12269

——The Holy Grail; six kindred addresses and essays. Philadelphia, J. B. Lippincott Co., 1905. 210 p. [12270

——Japan defies the world. Indianapolis, Bobbs-Merrill Co. [c.1938] 311 p. [12271

——The Japanese crisis. New York, Frederick A. Stokes Co. [c.1916] 148 p. [12272

——The nation at war. New York, George H. Doran Co. [c.1918] 285 p. [12273

——The romance of Japan through the ages. New York, George H. Doran Co. c.1926] 326 p. [12274

——The tree of light. New York, Thomas Y. Crowell Co. [c.1921] 125 p. [12275

——Young Japan; the story of the Japanese people, and especially of their educational development. Philadelphia, J. B. Lippincott Co., 1905. 328 p. [12276

Schieffelin, Samuel Bradhurst. The President and Congress; a hint to the South, a warning to the North. New York, Gray and Green, 1867. 16 p. [12277

Schlözer, August Ludwig, von. Neue Erdbeschreibung von Amerika. Bern, Walthard, 1777. 4 v. [12278

Schöpf, Johann David. Travels in the Confederation, 1783-1784, from the German of Johann David Schoepf, tr. and ed. by Alfred J. Morrison. Philadelphia, W. J. Campbell, 1911. 2 v. [12279

[Schofel, Johann W. A.] Hirum Harum; ein Satirisch-Komischer, original-Roman. Salem in Nordkarolina, bei H. Bagge, 1789. 276 p. The North Carolina imprint is a false one the book having been printed in Nurnberg by Schneider and Weigel. [12280

Schonwald, James T. The child; a treatise on the diagnosis and treatment of the diseases of children, according to the simple laws of nature, without medicaments. Philadelphia, L. A. Wollenweber, pr., 1851. 250 p. [12281

School bond catechism; some questions as to Raleigh's future. [Raleigh, Capital Printing Co., 1922] 13 p. [12282

School bulletin v. 1- February, 1915- Greenville, Pitt County Schools, 1915- NcU has v. [1-2] [12283

School supplement, v. 1- , 1897- Raleigh, Superintendent and teachers of the Raleigh Public Schools, 1897- NcU has v. 1 [12284

Schoolteacher, v. 1- January, 1887- Winston, J. L. Tomlinson and W. A. Blair, 1887- NcU has v. 1-2 [12285

Schuchert, Charles. Stratigraphy of the eastern and central United States. New York, J. Wiley & Sons, Inc. [1943] (His Historical geology of North America, v. II) 1013 p.   [12286

Schumacher, Francis Xavier. Sampling methods in forestry and range management, by F. X. Schumacher . . . and R. A. Chapman. Durham [Seeman Printery] 1942. (Duke University. School of Forestry. Bulletin, 7) 213 p.   [12287

Schuyler, Hamilton. A fisher of men: Churchill Satterlee, priest and missionary. New York, E. S. Gorham, 1905. 202 p.   [12288

Schwarze, Edmund. History of the Moravian missions among the southern Indian tribes of the United States. Bethlehem, Pa., Times, 1923. (Moravian Historical Society. Transactions, Special series, v. 1) 331 p.   [12289

Schweinitz, Emil Alexander de. Ueber Octylderivate des Thiophens und Benzols. Göttingen, E. A. Huth, 1886. Inaugural-Dissertation (Ph. D.) Georg-Augusts-Universität zu Göttingen. 37 p.   [12290

Schweinitz, Lewis David von. Specimen florae Americae Septentrionalis crypto-gamicae, sistens, muscos hepaticos huc usque in Am. Sept. observatos. Raleigh, J. Gales, pr., 1821. 27 p.   [12291

——Synopsis fungorum Carolinae superioris secundum observationes Ludovici Davidis de Scweinitz [!] ed. à D. F. Schwaegrichen. No place, no publisher [1822] 105 p.   [12292

Schwenning, Gustav Theodor, ed. Management problems, with special reference to the textile industry. Chapel Hill, University of North Carolina Press, 1930. 266 p.   [12293

Schwenning, Gustav Theodor, joint author, see Anderson, Edward Hutchings

Scimitar and song, v. 1- July, 1938- Jonesboro, Lura Thomas McNair, 1938-NcU has v. 1-19   [12294

Scotland County, N. C. Board of Education. Report, 19 - [Laurinburg?] 19 -NcU has 1914/15   [12295

Scotland Neck, N. C. Board of Trustees of the Graded School. Scotland Neck Graded School, 191 - 191 - NcU has 1910/11   [12296

Scott, Eugene Crampton, comp. Ministerial directory of the Presbyterian Church, U. S., 1861-1941. Austin, Tex., Von Boeckmann-Jones Co., 1942. 826 p. [12297

Scott, George G. Budgetary system of accounting adopted by Buncombe County. [Charlotte, Presbyterian Standard Publishing Co., 1925?] 24 p.   [12298

——State budget system and budgetary accounting. [Charlotte, Observer Printing Co. 1924] 23 p.   [12299

Scott, Job. Journal of the life, travels and gospel labors of that faithful servant and minister of Christ, Job Scott. New York, Isaac Collins, 1797. 360 p.   [12300

Scott, Joseph. A geographical dictionary of the United States of North America, containing a general description of each state. Philadelphia, Printed by Archibald Bartram for Thomas Armstrong, 1805. [584] p.   [12301

——The United States gazetteer, containing an authentic description of the several states. Philadelphia, Printed by F. and R. Bailey, 1795. [292] p.   [12302

Scott, Nancy N., ed. A memoir of Hugh Lawson White, judge of the Supreme Court of Tennessee, member of the Senate of the United States, etc., etc., with selections from his speeches and correspondence. Philadelphia, J. B. Lippincott & Co., 1856. 455 p.   [12303

Scott, W. H. The history of the Rogers case from July 22 to September 4, with the speech of Rev. W. H. Scott before the Governor of Massachusetts and the Attorney-General and Rev. W. H. Scott's address to the President of the United States on February 26, 1902. No place, The Author? [1902?] 16 p.   [12304

Scott, William Amasa. The repudiation of state debts; a study in the financial history of Mississippi, Florida, Alabama, North Carolina, South Carolina, Georgia, Louisiana, Arkansas, Tennessee, Minnesota, Michigan, and Virginia. New York, T. Y. Crowell & Co. [1893] (Library of economics and politics, R. T. Ely, ed., no. 2) 325 p.   [12305

Scott, William L., tr. A literal version of Demosthenes' Select orations, translated from the Greek, by William L. Scott, of Guilford. Raleigh, Weekly Post, pr., 1852. 51 p.   [12306

Scott, William W.   Annals of Caldwell County.   Lenoir, News-Topic Print [1930?]
162 p.   [12307
——"Gentleman" John Perkins.   Lenoir, Lenoir News-Topic, n.d.   84 p.   [12308
Scott, Winfield.   Infantry tactics; or, Rules of the exercise and manoeuvres of in-
fantry . . . Evaluations of the line.   Raleigh, State Journal, 1862.   66 p.   [12309
Scottish rite bulletin, v. 1- 191 - Wilmington, Scottish Rite Freemasons in the
Valley of Wilmington, 191 - NcU has v. [4-16; new series, v. 1, no. 2-37]   [12310
Scottish Society of America.   Charter and by-laws, together with the annual address
delivered by Rev. A. H. McArn, at a meeting of the Society at Red Springs, N. C.,
May, 1910.   Raleigh, Edwards & Broughton, pr., 1911.   27 p.   [12311
——Fifth annual session . . . Fayetteville, North Carolina, May, 1914.   Fayette-
ville, Judge Printing Co., 1914.   32 p.   [12312
Scoville, O.   Review of a pamphlet published by Rev. George W. Purify, in which
the doctrines of Calvinistic election and reprobation, and the impossibility of falling
from grace are affirmed.   Raleigh, William C. Doub, 1854.   125 p.   [12313
The scriptural doctrine of water baptism; with an appendix.   Hillsborough, Dennis
Heartt, 1824.   22 p.   [12314
Scripture illustrations of the all-sufficiency of Christ.   [Raleigh, Strother and
Marcom, n.d.]   (Selected for the soldiers, no. 421)   4 p.   [12315
Scruggs, Lawson Andrew.   Women of distinction, remarkable in works and invin-
cible in character.   Raleigh, L. A. Scruggs, 1893.   382 p.   [12316
Seaboard Air Line Railway.   Carolina fruit hills.   [Richmond, Va., Byrd Press,
1920?]   40 p.   [12317
——The corporate history of the Seaboard Air Line Railway Company.   Norfolk,
Va., Burke & Gregory, Inc., 1922.   137 p.   [12318
——Dedication of the new Hamlet yard, Hamlet, North Carolina, January 31, 1955.
No place [1955]   [11] p.   [12319
——Education in the South; schools, colleges and universities along the Seaboard Air
Line.   Portsmouth, Va., n.d.   96 p.   [12320
——North Carolina and Virginia; Seaboard Air Line handbook.   Park Place, N. Y.,
C. G. Crawford, pr. [1883?]   54 p.   [12321
——Reply to the order of the Honorable Board of Railroad Commissioners of the
state of North Carolina to show cause why passenger rates on its lines within that
state should not be reduced, January 27th, 1898.   No place [1898]   8 p.   [12322
——Report, 1900/01- [Norfolk, Va.] 1901- NcU has 1900/01-1903/04, 1905/06-
1915/16, 1916-1954   [12323
——Sand hill area of the Carolinas.   Norfolk, Va., n.d.   16 p.   [12324
——Seaboard Air Line Railway shippers guide.   New York, Wynkoop Hallenbeck
Crawford Co., c.1914)   560 p.   [12325
——Seaboard Air Line winter resorts.   [Chicago, Poole Brothers, 1915]   46 p. [12326
——Seaboard game trails.   [St. Augustine, Fla., Record Co.] n.d.   16 p.   [12327
——Sketches of the South.   Portsmouth, Va. [c.1905]   48 p.   [12328
——The South, your textile opportunity.   [Savannah, Ga., M. S. & D. A. Byck Co.,
1924]   38 p.   [12329
[Seaboard Air Line Railway]   The Southern Pines, Moore County, N. C.   No place,
n.d.   4 p.   [12330
Seaboard Air Line Railway.   Southern Pines, North Carolina, the highest point in
the long leaf pine region and the healthiest place in America.   [New York, C. G.
Crawford's Print, 1886?]   24 p.   [12331
——Winter resorts located on and reached via the Seaboard Air Line.   Portsmouth,
Va., 1897-98   207 p.   [12332
——Wintering in the South.   Chicago, Poole Brothers, n.d.   70 p.   [12333
Searight, Frank Thompson, ed.   American press humorists' book.   "Bill" Nye
monument edition.   Los Angeles, no publisher, 1907.   Unpaged.   [12334
Sears, Barnas.   Address on the objects and advantages of normal schools.   Durham,
W. T. Blackwell & Co., pr., 1878.   12 p.   [12335
Seashore Hotel, Wrightsville Beach, N. C.   Seashore Hotel, Wrightsville Beach,
No. Carolina.   [Wrightsville Beach] n.d.   14 p.   [12336
[Seaton, Josephine]   William Winston Seaton of the "National intelligencer", a
biographical sketch.   Boston, J. R. Osgood and Co., 1871.   385 p.   [12337

Seawell, Benjamin Lee. The genealogy, with historical and personal comments, of the known descendants of Col. Benjamin Seawell, Sr., and Lucy Hicks. South Pasadena, Calif. [L. C. Mock, pr.] 1935. 139 p.   [12338

Seawell, Herbert Floyd. An address, the country lawyer, delivered at the twenty-first annual session of the North Carolina State Bar Association at Greensboro, August 6th, 1919. No place, no publisher [1919?] 22 p.   [12339

Seawell, Joseph Lacy. A horse, a preacher, and a humming bird. No place, no publisher, n.d. 13 p.   [12340

——Law tales for laymen. Raleigh, Alfred Williams & Co., 1925. 314 p.   [12341

——The trial of Jesus. [Raleigh, 1923] 31 p.   [12342

Seawell, Meade. Songs from the sandhills. Baltimore, Md., Saulsbury Publishing Co. [c.1919] 72 p.   [12343

Seaworthy, Gregory, pseud. see **Throop, George Higby**

The secret given away. No place, no publisher [1900?] 2 p.   [12344

[**Security Life and Annuity Company, Greensboro, N. C.**] North Carolina, Guilford County, Greensboro. [Greensboro, Jos. J. Stone, pr., 1903?] [8] p.   [12345

See here! A federal Whig trap. No place, no publisher [1840?] [1] p.   [12346

Seebohm, Benjamin, ed. Memoirs of William Forster. London, Alfred W. Bennett, 1865. 2 v.   [12347

Seeing the Smokies, the Great Smoky Mountains National Park. [Asheville, Stephens Press, c.1946] [15] p.   [12348

Seeman, Ernest. The hand of education in the South, a program of broad objectives proposed for the orientation of education in the Southern States along lines compatible with geographic need and the ideals of a planned society. No place [1933?] 37 p.   [12349

——Square pegs; some thoughts on the prevention and salvage of vocational misfits, addressed to young people, parents, employers, and the misfit. [Durham, 1929?] [16] p.   [12350

——The tobacco-waterpower monopoly and the public schools. [Chicago? Author? 1940?] (Occasional political papers by Ernest Seeman) [2] p.   [12351

Seeman, William. Down Goose Creek; being a ten-year-old boy's own account of a journey by stream and swamp from Carolina foothills to the sea. New York, Fleming H. Revell Co. [c.1931] 200 p.   [12352

Seeman Printery, Inc., Durham, N. C. Fifty years, the Seeman Printery, Inc., established 1885, Durham, N. C. [Durham, 1935] [25] p.   [12353

Seeman's magazine, v. 1-2, January, 1930-November, 1931. Durham, Seeman Printery, Inc., 1930-1931. NcU has v. 1-2. Discontinued following November, 1931.   [12354

Seitz, Don Carlos. Braxton Bragg, general of the Confederacy. Columbia, S. C., State Co., 1924. 544 p.   [12355

——Famous American duels, with some account of the causes that led up to them and the men engaged. New York, Thomas Y. Crowell Co. [c.1929] 345 p.   [12356

——Uncommon Americans, pencil portraits of men and women who have broken the rules. Indianapolis, Bobbs-Merrill Co. [c.1925] 328 p.   [12357

Selden, Samuel. First steps in acting. New York, F. S. Crofts & Co., Inc., 1947. 344 p.   [12358

——Frederick Henry Koch, pioneer playmaker; a brief biography, by Samuel Selden and Mary Tom Sphangos. Chapel Hill, University of North Carolina Library, 1954. (Its Library Extension publication, v. 19, no. 4) 92 p.   [12359

Selden, Samuel, ed. International folk plays. Chapel Hill, University of North Carolina Press [1949] 285 p.   [12360

Selden, Samuel. An introduction to playwriting. New York, F. S. Crofts & Co., Inc., 1946. 120 p.   [12361

Selden, Samuel, ed. Organizing a community theatre. Cleveland, O., National Theatre Conference, 1945. 127 p.   [12362

Selden, Samuel. A player's handbook; the theory and practice of acting. New York, F. S. Crofts & Co., 1934. 252 p.   [12363

——Producing America's outdoor dramas, by Samuel Selden, with Paul Green. Chapel Hill, University of North Carolina Press, 1954. (University of North Carolina extension bulletin, v. 33, no. 4)   44 p.   [12364
——The stage in action.   New York, F. S. Crofts & Co., 1941.   324 p.   [12365
——Stage scenery and lighting; a handbook for non-professionals, by Samuel Selden . . . and Hunton D. Sellman.   New York, F. S. Crofts & Co., 1930.   398 p. [12366
—— ——Revised ed.   1940.   435 p.   [12367
——A syllabus of dramatic practice, prepared for the courses in acting, rehearsal and performance, and play direction (English 61, 62, and 63) at the University of North Carolina . . . Part I. Acting.   [Chapel Hill] The Author, c.1933.   77 p.   [12368
Selders, Adelbert.   The collegiate tenderfoot who made good.   [Albemarle] Selders Weekly, c.1923.   [108] p.   [12369
——The mountain queen.   [Albemarle] Stanly Republican, c.1924.   127 p.   [12370
——The native son who loses his identity.   [Albemarle] Stanly Republican and Selders' Weekly, 1924.   128 p.   [12371
Select Boarding and Day School, Hillsboro, N. C.   Soiree musicale, 18 - Hillsboro, 18   -   NcU has June 25, 1868, June 21, 1877, June 10, 1891   [12372
Select Boarding and Day School, Hillsborough, N. C.   Hillsboro, 1864.   [1] p. [12373
Selective service organization for the state of North Carolina.   No place, no publisher [1918?]   35 p.   [12374
Self dedication to God.   [Raleigh, Strother and Marcom] n.d.   (Selected for the soldiers, no. 407)   4 p.   [12375
Sellers, Hazel.   Faith of our fathers; a book of sketches of old North Carolina churches.   No place, The Author, 1940.   [51] p.   [12376
Sellers, James Benson.   The prohibition movement in Alabama, 1702 to 1943. Chapel Hill, University of North Carolina Press, 1943.   (James Sprunt studies in history and political science, v. 26, no. 1)   325 p.   [12377
Semaphore   see The P & N and D & S magazine
Semple, Ellen Churchill.   American history and its geographic conditions.   Boston, Houghton, Mifflin and Co., 1903.   466 p.   [12378
Semple, Robert Baylor.   A history of the rise and progress of the Baptists in Virginia. Richmond, John O'Lynch, pr., 1810.   446 p.   [12379
——   ——Rev. and extended by G. W. Beale.   Richmond, Va., Pitt and Dickinson, 1894.   536 p.   [12380
Senour, Fauntleroy.   Major General William T. Sherman, and his campaigns.   Chicago, H. M. Sherwood, 1865.   477 p.   [12381
Senter Primitive Baptist Association.   Minutes, 18 - 18 - NcU has 1900 [1921-1955]   [12382
Separk, Joseph Henry.   Gastonia and Gaston County, North Carolina.   [Kingsport, Tenn., Kingsport Press, Inc., 1936]   169 p.   [12383
——   ——1846-1949.   Gastonia [1950?]   237 p.   [12384
Sergeant Manufacturing Company, Greensboro, N. C.   List no 13, North Carolina Foundry, Machine and Agricultural Works.   Greensboro, Thomas, Reece & Co., pr., 1884.   52 p.   [12385
Settle, Thomas.   Southern politics.   No place, no publisher, n.d.   27 p.   [12386
Setzer, Pearl.   The building of Catawba; a historical pageant.   No place, no publisher [1925]   50 p.   [12387
Seven Mile Primitive Baptist Association.   Minutes of the annual session, 1881?-1881?-   NcU has [1911-1926] 1929-1945, 1955   [12388
Seventh commandment.   No place, no publisher, n.d.   11 p.   [12389
Seward, William Henry.   Exposé de la situation politique et militaire aux États-Unis . . . Protestation des habitants de la Caroline du Nord contre la continuation de la guerre.   Paris, E. Dentu, 1863.   32 p.   [12390
Seybert, Adam.   Statistical annals.   Philadelphia, Thomas Dobson & Son, 1818. 803 p.   [12391
Seymour, Flora Warren (Smith)   Daniel Boone, pioneer.   New York, Century Co. [c.1931]   206 p.   [12392
Seymour, William.   Journal of the southern expedition.   Wilmington, Del., Historical Society of Delaware, 1896.   42 p.   [12393

[Shackelford, E. A. B.] Virginia Dare; a romance of the sixteenth century. New York, T. Whittaker, 1892. 207 p. [12394

Shackford, James Atkins. David Crockett, the man and the legend. Chapel Hill, University of North Carolina Press [1956] 338 p. [12395

Shaffer, A. Webster. Hon. Geo. F. Hoar, chairman, Senate Committee on Elections, &c., Sir. Raleigh, July 8th, 1890. [3] p. [12396

——In the matter of the official irregularities and malpractice in the fourth collection district of N. C. Raleigh, no publisher, 1879. 82 p. [12397

Shaffer, Edward Terry Hendrie. Carolina gardens. New York, Huntington Press, 1937. 289 p. [12398

—— ——Chapel Hill, University of North Carolina Press, 1939. 326 p. [12399

Shaffner, John Francis. Diary of Dr. J. F. Shaffner, Sr., commencing September 13, 1863, ending February 5, 1865. [Winston-Salem?] Privately printed, n.d. 67 p. [12400

Shaftesbury, Anthony Ashley Cooper, 1st earl of, 1621-1683. The Shaftesbury papers and other records relating to Carolina, and the first settlement of Ashley River prior to the year 1676, prepared for publication by Langdon Cheves. Charleston, South Carolina Historical Society, 1897. (Its Collections, v. 5) 523 p. [12401

Shanks, Henry Thomas. The secession movement in Virginia, 1847-1861. Richmond, Va., Garrett and Massie [c.1934] 296 p. [12402

Shannonhouse, Royal Graham, ed. St. Bartholomew's Parish, Pittsboro, N. C., 1833-1933. No place, no publisher, 1933. 54 p. [12403

Shapiro, Albert Abraham. A beginner's Spanish grammar. Chapel Hill, University Press [c.1924] 263 p. [12404

Sharp, Cecil James. American-English folk-songs from the Southern Appalachian Mountains. New York, G. Schirmer, Inc. [c.1918] (Schirmer's American folk-song series, set 21) 27 p. [12405

——American-English folk-ballads from the Southern Appalachian Mountains. [c.1918] (Schirmer's American folk-song series, set 22) 31 p. [12406

——English folk songs from the Southern Appalachians . . . ed. by Maud Karpeles. London, Oxford University Press, H. Milford, 1932. 2 v. [12407

Sharp, Susie Marshall. Plain talk "about the recurring incidents which get the courts and the press into each other's hair"; an address before the members of the Eastern North Carolina Press Association in convention at Fayetteville, November 6, 1954. Ahoskie, [1954] 15 p. [12408

Sharp Institute, Intelligence, N. C. [Catalogue, 1900/01?- 1901?- NcU has 1904/05-1906/07 [12409

Sharpe, Bill see Sharpe, William P.

Sharpe, Robert Boies. The real war of the theaters. Boston, D. C. Heath and Co., 1935. (The Modern Language Association of America. Monograph series, 5) 260 p. [12410

Sharpe, Stella Gentry. Tobe. Chapel Hill, University of North Carolina Press, 1939. 121 p. [12411

Sharpe, William P. Fishing Carolina's coast; a guide. Wilmington, Marina Publishing House, Inc., c.1949. 66 p. [12412

——A new geography of North Carolina. Raleigh, Sharpe Publishing Co. [c.1954] v. 1 [12413

——Tar on my heels; a press agent's note book. Winston-Salem, The Tar Heels, 1946. 229 p. [12414

Shaw, Cornelia Rebekah. Davidson College. New York, Fleming H. Revell Co. [c.1923] 307 p. [12415

——War record, Davidson College, 1917-1918. Charlotte, Presbyterian Standard, 1923. 133 p. [12416

Shaw, Easdale. The history of the North Carolina branch of the International Order of the King's Daughters and Sons. Raleigh, Capital Printing Co., 1929. 30 p. [12417

Shaw, George Clayton. John Chavis, 1763-1838, a remarkable Negro who conducted a school in North Carolina for white boys and girls. [Binghamton, N. Y., Vail-Ballou Press, Inc., c.1931] 60 p. [12418

Shaw, Helen Louise. British administration of the southern Indians, 1756-1783. [Lancaster, Pa., Lancaster Press, Inc.] 1931. 205 p. [12419

Shaw, Henry Wheeler see **Billings, Josh, pseud.**

Shaw, Jessie Owen. The Johnsons and their kin of Randolph. Washington, 1955. 214 p. [12420

Shaw, William A. Benediction of infants and baptism of believers. New-York, Lewis Colby for the Author, 1848. 56 p. [12421
——Lectures on the utility of temperance societies. Washington, N. C., 1832. 65 p. [12422

Shaw University, Raleigh, N. C. Bulletin, v. 1- 1920- Raleigh, 1920- NcU has first series v. [1-5] second series v. [1-25] discontinued following May, 1924. Resumed publication 1931. [12423
——Catalogue, 18 - Raleigh, 18 - NcU has 1876/77, 1878/79 [1891/92-1918/19] 1924/25-1930/31 Issued as its Bulletin, 1919/20-1923/24, 1931- [12424
——General catalogue of the officers and students of Shaw University, 1875-1882. Raleigh, Edwards, Broughton & Co., 1882. 32 p. [12425
——Shaw University, Raleigh, North Carolina. [Boston, Frank Wood, 1902] 18 p. [12426
——That they may better serve. Raleigh, 1945. 24 p. [12427

Shaw University, Raleigh, N. C. Medical Department. Catalogue, 18 - Raleigh, 18 - NcU has 1894/95, 1895/96, 1898/99, 1907/08, 1908/09, 1911/12 [12428

Shaw University, Raleigh, N. C. President. Report to the Trustees, and to the Secretary of the American Baptist Home Mission Society, 18 - [Raleigh, 18 - NcU has 1897/98 [12429

Shearer, Elizabeth (Gessner) Prayer meeting papers. Richmond, Va., Presbyterian Committee of Publication, 1914. 142 p. [12430

Shearer, Ernest Charles. Robert Potter, remarkable North Carolinian and Texan. [Houston, Tex.] University of Houston Press, 1951. 133 p. [12431

Shearer, James William. The Shearer-Akers family, combined with "The Bryan line" through the seventh generation. [Somerville, N. J., Somerset Messenger] 1915. 171 p. [12432

Shearer, John Bunyan. Bible course syllabus. Richmond, Va., B. F. Johnson Publishing Co., 1895-1896. 3 v. [12433
——Hebrew institutions, social and civil. Richmond, Va., Presbyterian Committee of Publication [c.1910] 170 p. [12434
——Modern mysticism; or, The covenants of the spirit, their scope and limitations. Richmond, Va., Presbyterian Committee of Publication [c.1905] 116 p. [12435
——One hundred brief Bible studies. Richmond, Va., Presbyterian Committee of Publication, 1912. 229 p. [12436
——The Scriptures, fundamental facts and features. Richmond, Va., Presbyterian Committee of Publication [c.1908] 166 p. [12437
——Selected Old Testament studies. Richmond, Va., Presbyterian Committee of Publication [c.1909] 223 p. [12438
——The sermon on the mount: a study. Richmond, Va., Presbyterian Committee of Publication [c.1906] 146 p. [12439
——Studies in the life of Christ. Richmond, Va., Presbyterian Committee of Publication, 1907. 172 p. [12440

Sheets, Henry. History of the Liberty Baptist Association. Raleigh, Edwards & Broughton Co., 1907. 255 p. [12441
——Who are Primitive Baptists? Raleigh, Edwards & Broughton Co. [1908?] 96 p. [12442

[**Sheffield, John Baker Holroyd**] Observations on the commerce of the American states; with an appendix. Dublin, P. Bryne, 1784. 10, 7, 287 p. [12443

Sheffield, Joseph E. To the public. Newbern, October 13, 1814. [1] p. [12444

[**Shelby, Isaac**] Battle of King's Mountain. To the public. No place, no publisher [1823] 24 p. [12445

[**Shelby, N. C. Chamber of Commerce**] Shelby, North Carolina, for pleasant living. [Shelby, 1947?] [16] p. [12446

Shelton Tobacco Curing Co., Asheville, N. C. The planter's guide for cultivating and curing tobacco. Boston, Getchell Brothers [1875] 27 p. [12447

Shepard, Charles. To the freemen of the fourth congressional district of North Carolina. [Washington, Joseph Etter, pr., 1838] 8 p. [12448

Shepard, Charles Upham. Description of gold and copper mines at Gold Hill, Rowan County, N. C. No place, no publisher [1853] 18 p. [12449

Shepard, George Edward. Interscholastic athletics [by] George E. Shepard [and] Richard E. Jamerson. New York, McGraw-Hill, 1953. 276 p. [12450

Shepard, James Biddle. An address delivered before the citizens, mechanics, and guards of the city of Raleigh, July 4, 1839. Raleigh, T. Loring, 1839. 25 p. [12451

——An address delivered before the two literary societies of Wake Forest College, June 17, 1841. Raleigh, North Carolina Standard, 1841. 26 p. [12452

——An address delivered before the two literary societies of the University of North Carolina, in Gerard Hall, June 5, 1844. Raleigh, T. Loring, pr., 1844. 18 p. [12453

——Introductory lecture, read before the Raleigh Mechanics Association, at the opening of their course, July 12, 1841. Raleigh, North Carolina Standard, 1841. 31 p. [12454

——Speech delivered at the great Republican meeting, in the county of Granville, in the presidential canvass of 1840. Raleigh, North Carolina Standard, 1840. 37 p. [12455

Shepard, James Edward. Our mutual tasks . . . broadcast over state-wide radio system, February 16, 1946. [Durham, 1946] [6] p. [12456

——Radio address: Racial relationships in North Carolina. [Durham] n.d. 7 p. [12457

Shepard, Odell. Holdfast Gaines, by Odell Shepard and Willard Shepard. New York, Macmillan Co., 1946. 647 p. [13458

Shepard, William Biddle. An address delivered before the two literary societies of the University of North-Carolina, June 27, 1838. Raleigh, Raleigh Register, 1838. 29 p. [12459

Shepherd, Grant. The silver magnet, fifty years in a Mexican silver mine. New York, E. P. Dutton & Co., [c.1938] 302 p. [12460

Shepherd, Henry Elliott. A commentary upon Tennyson's In memoriam. New York, Neale Publishing Co., 1908. 135 p. [12461

——An elementary grammar of the English language. Baltimore, J. B. Piet, 1881. 128 p. [12462

——An historical reader for the use of classes in academies, high schools, and grammar schools. New York, D. Appleton and Co., 1882. 345 p. [12463

——Historical readings for the use of teachers' reading circles. New York, American Book Co. [c.1893] 424 p. [12464

——History of the English language from the Teutonic invasion of Britain to the close of the Georgian era. New York, E. J. Hale & Son, 1874. 227 p. [12465

——Life of Robert Edward Lee. New York, Neale Publishing Co., 1906. 280 p. [12466

——Narrative of prison life at Baltimore and Johnson's Island, Ohio. Baltimore, Commercial Printing and Stationery Co., 1917. 22 p. [12467

Shepherd, James Edward. An address on the life and character of Judge David Schenck, delivered at Guilford Battle Ground, on the occasion of the unveiling of a monument to his memory, July 4, 1904. Greensboro, Guilford Battle Ground Co., n.d. 20 p. [12468

——A statement by Judge Shepherd. No place, no publisher [1888?] 18 p. [12469

——Supplement: To the public. No place, no publisher [1888?] [2] p. [12470

Sheppard, Muriel (Earley) Cabins in the laurel . . . with illustrations by Bayard Wootten. Chapel Hill, University of North Carolina Press [c.1935] 313 p. [12471

Sheppe, Edwin S. Suggestions to teachers, word studies. Richmond, Va., B. F. Johnson Publishing Co. [c.1908] 20 p. [12472

——Word studies; advanced book. Richmond, Va., B. F. Johnson Publishing Co., [c.1905] 126 p. [12473

——Word studies; primary book. Richmond, Va., B. F. Johnson Publishing Co. [c.1905] 96, 10 p. [12474

Shepperd, Augustine H. To the freemen of the fourth congressional district of North Carolina. [Washington] J. & G. S. Gideon, pr. [1849] 4 p. [12475

Sheps, Cecil George. Needed research in health and medical care; a bio-social approach, by Cecil G. Sheps and Eugene E. Taylor. Chapel Hill, University of North Carolina Press [1954] 216 p. [12476

Sherman, Frederic Fairchild. Landscape and figure painters of America. New York, privately printed, 1917. 71 p. [12477

Sherman, George R. Assault on Fort Gilmer and reminiscences of prison life. Providence, R. I., Rhode Island Soldiers and Sailors Historical Society, 1897. (Its Personal narratives of events in the war of the rebellion, 5th ser., no. 7) 79 p. [12478

Sherman, Philemon Tecumseh. General Sherman in the last year of the Civil War. [New York, Robert Crier Cooke] 1908. 21 p. [12479

Sherman, William Tecumseh. General and field orders, campaign of the armies of the Tennessee, Ohio, and Cumberland, Maj. Gen. W. T. Sherman, commanding, 1864-5. St. Louis, R. P. Studley and Co., 1865. 250 p. [12480

——General Sherman's official account of his great march through Georgia and the Carolinas. New York, Bunce & Huntington, 1865. 214 p. [12481

——Major-General Sherman's reports . . . Official copy, complete. New York, Beadle and Co. [1865?] (Beales's dime series) 84 p. [12482

——Memoirs of Gen. W. T. Sherman, written by himself, with an appendix, bringing his life down to its closing scenes, also a personal tribute and critique of the memoirs, by Hon. James G. Blaine . . . 4th ed., rev., cor., and complete. New York, C. I. Webster & Co., 1891. 2 v. in 1. [12483

Sherrill, Clarence Osborne. Military map reading. [Leavenworth, Kan., Ketcheson Printing Co., 1909] 46 p. [12484

——Military topography for the mobile forces, including map reading, surveying and sketching . . . 2d ed. [Menasha, Wis., George Banta Publishing Co., c.1912] 353 p. [12485

——A simple method of collection of sales taxes that is fair to the consumer, the retailer, and the state. [Cincinnati, O.? The Author] c.1935. 14 p. [12486

Sherrill, George Raymond. Criminal procedure in North Carolina as shown by criminal appeals since 1890. Chapel Hill, University of North Carolina Press, 1930. 173 p. [12487

[**Sherrill, John B.**] Forty years on the same newspaper at Concord, North Carolina. No place, no publisher [1925] 16 p. [12488

Sherrill, Martin V. The mode of Christian baptism. 2d ed. Monroe, Enquirer Steam Power Presses, 1879. 52 p. [12489

Sherrill, Miles Osborne. A soldier's story; prison life and other incidents in the war of 1861-5. Raleigh, Edwards & Broughton Co., n.d. 23 p. [12490

Sherrill, William Lander. Annals of Lincoln County, North Carolina. Charlotte, [Observer Printing House, Inc.] 1937. 536 p. [12491

——Brief history of Rev. Samuel Lander, Senior, and his wife, Eliza Ann (Miller) Lander . . . their two sons, William Lander and Samuel, and their grandson, Samuel A. Weber. [Greensboro, Advocate Press] 1918. 63 p. [12492

Sherwood, George Frederick Tudor, comp. American colonists in English records . . . a guide to direct references in authentic records, passenger lists not in "Hotten". London G. Sherwood, 1932-1933. 2 v. [12493

Sherwood, Henry Noble. Makers of the new world. Indianapolis, Bobbs-Merrill Co. [c.1936] 301 p. [12494

Shewmake, Edwin F. Working with words, form A. New York, Harper and Brothers [c.1951] 122 p. [12495

Shields, James M. Just plain larnin'. New York, Coward-McCann, Inc., 1934. 344 p. [12496

Shillitoe, Thomas. An address to Friends in Great Britain and Ireland. Elizabeth City, Society of Friends, 1822. 24 p. [12497

Shiloh Missionary Baptist Association. Minutes, 19 - 19 - NcU has [1911-1922] [12498

Shine, Hill, ed. Booker memorial studies; eight essays on Victorian literature in memory of John Manning Booker, 1881-1948. Chapel Hill, University of North Carolina Press [1950] 183 p. [12499

Shine, Hill. Carlyle's fusion of poetry, history, and religion by 1834. Chapel Hill, University of North Carolina Press, 1938. 85 p. [12500

——The Quarterly review under Gifford; identification of contributors, 1809-1824, by Hill Shine and Helen Chadwick Shine.   Chapel Hill, University of North Carolina Press, 1949.   108 p.   [12501

Ship canal to unite the waters of Albemarle, Currituck, and Pamlico sounds with Chesapeake Bay.   Raleigh, Holden and Wilson, pr., 1854.   29 p.   [12502

Shipley, Hester E.   see Williams, Sarah Stone

Shipley, Maynard.   The war on modern science; a short history of the fundamentalist attacks on evolution and modernism. New York, A. A. Knopf, 1927. 415 p. [12503

Shipman, Dessie, comp.   A book of poems and hymns. [Gastonia, Gaston Times Printery, 1890?]   23 p.   [12504

Shipman, Mitchell L.   North Carolina, land of opportunity and achievement; address . . . before the North Carolina Society of Pennsylvania, Philadelphia, March 24, 1924. [Raleigh, 1924]   5 p.   [12505

Shipp, Albert Micajah.   The history of Methodism in South Carolina. Nashville, Tenn., Southern Methodist Publishing House, 1883.   648 p.   [12506

Shober, Francis Edwin.   Dear Sir: Having announced myself as a candidate for clerk of the next House of Representatives . . . Salisbury, November 4th, 1875. [1] p.   [12507

[Shober, Gottlieb]   A comprehensive account of the rise and progress of the blessed reformation of the Christian Church, by Doctor Martin Luther . . . and how the church, established by him, arrived and progressed in North America; as also, The constitution and rules of that church in North Carolina and adjoining states, as existing in October, 1817. Baltimore, Schaeffer & Maund, pr., 1818. 213 p. [12508

——Review of a pamphlet, issued from the press of the Western Carolinian in Salisbury, N. C., written by David Henkel. Salisbury, Bingham and White, pr., 1821. 64 p.   [12509

Shoemaker, Don C.   Middle East journey. [Asheville, Asheville Citizen-Times Co., 1952]   54 p.   [12510

——Remarks . . . before the University of Michigan School of Journalism, November 12, 1956. [Ann Arbor? 1956]   19 p.   [12511

[Shoemaker, Don C.] comp.   Toward United Nations; a memorial to Franklin Delano Roosevelt, brief excerpts from addresses and public papers, 1933-1945. [Asheville, Stephens Press, 1945]   [9] p.   [12512

A short account of the happy death of Mrs. Frances Lambeth. Greensborough, William Swaim, pr., 1830.   8 p.   [12513

A short sketch of Belmont Abbey, the canonical erection of the Abbatia Nullius, and the silver abbatial jubilee of Right Reverend Leo Haid. Belmont, Belmont Abbey Press, 1910.   51 p.   [12514

A short sketch of the life of Major E. J. Hale, issued by the Fayetteville Committee, October 1, 1910. [Fayetteville?] n.d.   8 p.   [12515

[A short sketch of the progress of the congregation of the First Baptist Church of New Bern, N. C.]   15 p.   Title page wanting in NcU copy.   [12516

Shotwell, Randolph Abbott, comp.   New Bern mercantile and manufacturers' business directory and N. C. farmers' reference book. New Bern, W. I. Vestal, 1866. 56 p.   [12517

Shryock, Richard Harrison.   The development of modern medicine; an interpretation of the social and scientific factors involved. Philadelphia, University of Pennsylvania Press, 1936.   442 p.   [12518

——   ——New York, A. A. Knopf, 1947.   457 p.   [12519

——Georgia and the Union in 1850. Philadelphia, 1926.   406 p. Thesis (Ph. D.) University of Pennsylvania.   [12520

[Shuck, Lewis Hall]   Joan of Arc, the maid of Orleans; a poem delivered at Wake Forest College, North Carolina, June 12, 1856. Richmond, Va., J. W. Randolph, 1856.   21 p.   [12521

Shuford, Augusta.   Colonial North Carolina. Cincinnati, Elbert & Richardson Co., 1927.   33 p.   [12522

Shuford, George A., joint author   see Conway, C. B.

Shuford, Julius H.   A historical sketch of the Shuford family. Hickory, A. L. Crouse & Son, pr., 1902.   156 p.   [12523

Shuford, Mary Frances. Midge. New York, D. Appleton & Co., 1929. 245 p. [12524
Shull, Lena Mearle. Dark salt. Dexter, Mo., Candor Press, 1954. 32 p. [12525
——Night is always kind. Dallas, Kaleidograph Press [1948] 69 p. [12526
Shurter, Edwin Du Bois, ed. Oratory of the South, from the Civil War to the present time. New York, Neale Publishing Co., 1908. 336 p. [12527
Shute, John Raymond. The chapel of the seer. Monroe, Nocalore Press, 1950. 63 p. [12528
——The golden dawn. Monroe, Nocalore Press, 1950. 78 p. [12529
——The happy mayor. Monroe, Nocalore Press, 1951. 79 p. [12530
——His Honor, the heretic. Monroe, Nocalore Press, 1950. 76 p. [12531
——Nocalore initials for use in Masonic publications. Monroe, n.d. [1] p. [12532
——Prose poems and other trivia. Monroe, Nocalore Press, 1954. 71 p. [12533
——The quest. Monroe, Nocalore Press, 1951. 78 p. [12534
——Quintology. Monroe, Nocalore Press [1954] 77 p. [12535
——Roanoke Council no. 1, Royal and Select Masters. Monroe, North Carolina Lodge of Research, no. 666, A. F. & A. M., 1932. 164 p. [12536
—— ——2d ed. [12537
——The Seer, his parables and tales. Monroe, Nocalore Press, 1950. 94 p. [12538
——Soft tolls the bell. Monroe, Nocalore Press [1953] 64 p. [12539
——A song in the night. Monroe, Nocalore Press, 1952. 64 p. [12540
——Tales of yore retold. Monroe, Nocalore Press, 1938. 57 p. [12541
——Twilight in the temple. Monroe, Nocalore Press, 1950. 72 p. [12542
——Voice of the vault. Monroe, North Carolina Lodge of Research, no. 666, A. F. & A. M., 1933. 97 p. [12543
Sieber, Herman Alexander. In this the Marian year. Chapel Hill, Old Well Publishers [1955] 27 p. [12544
——Something the West will remember; a poem. Chapel Hill, Old Well Publishers, 1956. 18 p. [12545
Siewers, Charles Nathaniel. Forsyth County, economic and social. [Chapel Hill, Department of Rural Social Economics, University of North Carolina] 1924. 110 p. [12546
Sights and insights, 190 - Winston-Salem, Senior Class of Salem College, 190 - NcU has 1910, 1937 [12547
Sigma Alpha Epsilon. North Carolina XI. Chapter letter, 19 - [Chapel Hill, 190 - NcU has 1900/01 [12548
Sigma Alpha Epsilon. Pennsylvania Sigma Phi. History and catalogue of the Sigma Alpha Epsilon Fraternity. Harrisburg, Pa., Meyers Printing House, 1893. 599 p. [12549
Sigma Chi. North Carolina Alpha Tau. The Tar Heel Sig, Alpha Tau of Sigma Chi, University of North Carolina. [Chapel Hill, 1918] 8 p. [12550
Sigmund, Jay G. The saints get together; a play in one act, by Jay G. Sigmund and Betty Smith. Chicago, T. S. Denison Co. [c.1937] 21 p. [12551
——The silvered rope, a Biblical drama in one act, by Jay G. Sigmund and Betty Smith. Chicago, T. S. Denison & Co. [1938] 17 p. [12552
——They released Barabbas; a one-act play for Easter and other occasions, by Jay G. Sigmund and Betty Smith. Franklin, O., Eldredge Entertainment House, Inc., c.1939. 18 p. [12553
The signal, v. 1, July 1, 1852-March, 1853. Washington, G. S. Gideon, 1852-53. NcU has v. 1. Discontinued following March, 1853. No numbers issued Nov. 1852-Feb. 1853. [12554
Sikes, Earl Ray. State and federal corrupt-practices legislation. Durham, Duke University Press, 1928. 321 p. [12555
Sikes, Enoch Walter. Confederate States Congress. Raleigh, Edwards & Broughton Co., 1903. 29 p. [12556
——The growth of the nation, 1837 to 1860, from the beginning of Van Buren's administration to the close of that of Buchanan, by Enoch Walter Sikes and William Morse Keener. Philadelphia, G. Barrie & Sons [1905] 489 p. [12557
——The transition of North Carolina from colony to commonwealth. Baltimore, Johns Hopkins Press, 1898. (Its Studies in historical and political science, ser. XVI, nos. 10, 11) 84 p. [12558

Sikes, J. R. The Biblical reason why prohibition is wrong. Loudonville, O., P. H. Stauffer, 1886. 110 p.   [12559
——Pen pictures of prohibition and prohibitionists. Loudonville, O., P. H. Stauffer, 1887. 57 p.   [12560

[Sikes, Thomas Eugene] McArthur family record. Columbus, Ga., Gilbert Printing Co., 1911. 95 p.   [12561

Siler, Frank. Memorial address delivered at the funeral of Jackson Johnston, April 12, 1902. [Franklin? 1902?] 8 p.   [12562

Siler, Margaret R. Cherokee Indian lore and Smoky Mountains stories. Bryson City, Bryson City Times, 1938. 111 p.   [12563

The Siler family. Franklin, Franklin Press, 1906. 39 p.   [12564

Sill, James B. Historical sketches of churches in the Diocese of Western North Carolina Episcopal Church. Asheville, Church of the Redeemer, 1955. 207 p. [12565

Simkins, Francis Butler. A history of the South [2d ed., rev., enl.] New York, A. A. Knopf, 1953. 655 p.   [12566
——The South, old and new; a history, 1820-1947. New York, A. A. Knopf, 1947. 527 p.   [12568
——The women of the Confederacy, by Francis Butler Simkins and James Welch Patton. Richmond, Va., Garrett and Massie, Inc. [c.1936] 306 p.   [12569

Simmons, Enoch Spencer. A solution of the race problem in the South, an essay. Raleigh, Edwards & Broughton Presses, 1898. 150 p.   [12570

Simmons, Furnifold McLendell. Address before Democratic state convention, at Greensboro, N. C., July 16, 1902; Address of Hon. A. M. Scales. Raleigh, E. M. Uzzell, pr., 1902. 16 p.   [12571
——Exposure and denunciation of the Tammany-Smith-Raskob-DuPont coalition for the destruction of prohibition, restricted immigration, and Jeffersonian Democratic principles; speech . . . delivered at New Bern, N. C., Friday, October 12, 1928. Charlotte, News Printing House, 1928. 8 p.   [12572
——F. M. Simmons, statesman of the new South, memoirs and addresses, compiled and edited by J. Fred Rippy. Durham, Duke University Press, 1936. 535 p. [12573
——Senator Simmons' record and his reply to Governor Kitchin's attack. No place, no publisher [1912?] 7 p.   [12574
——Speech delivered at Charlotte, N. C., Oct. 17th, 1904, discussing national and state issues in the campaign of 1904. Raleigh, Edwards & Broughton Co., 1904. 16 p.   [12575
——Speech to the National Democratic Club of New York on Jefferson Day, April 13th, 1908, in response to the toast "The White House and the Democracy". No place, no publisher [1908?] 8 p.   [12576

Simmons, James Frederick. Rural lyrics, elegies, and other short poems. Philadelphia, J. B. Lippincott & Co., 1885. 228 p.   [12577
——The welded link and other poems. Philadelphia, J. B. Lippincott & Co., 1881. 264 p.   [12578

Simmons, Virginia Lee. Whitecaps. [Yellow Springs, O., The Antioch Press, 1942] 79 p.   [12579

Simms, William Gilmore. The history of South Carolina. Charleston, S. Babcock & Co., 1840. 355 p.   [12580

[Simms, William Gilmore] Life in America; or, The wigwam and the cabin. Aberdeen, G. Clark and Son, 1848. 311 p.   [12581

Simms, William Gilmore. The life of Francis Marion. 8th ed. New York, G. F. Cooledge & Brother [1846?] 347 p.   [12582

Simms, William Gilmore, ed. The life of Nathanael Greene, major-general in the army of the Revolution. New York, Derby & Jackson, 1856. 393 p.   [12583

Simms, William Gilmore. Southward ho! A spell of sunshine. New York, A. C. Armstrong & Co., 1882. 472 p.   [12584
——Views and reviews in American literature, history, and fiction. New York, Wiley and Putnam, 1845. 238 p.   [12585

Simms, William Gilmore, ed. War poetry of the South. New York, Richardson & Co., 1866. 482 p.   [12586
——The wigwam and the cabin. New and rev. ed. New York, A. C. Armstrong & Son, 1882. 472 p.   [12587

[Simms, William Gilmore] The Yemassee; a romance of Carolina. New York, Harper & Brothers, 1835. 2 v. [12588
—— ——1844. 2 v. in 1. [12589
Simms, William Gilmore. The Yemassee, edited for the use of schools with introduction and notes. New York, University Publishing Co. [c.1898] 191 p. [12590
—— ——edited with introduction and notes by M. Lyle Spencer. Atlanta, B. F. Johnson [c.1911] 441 p. [12591
Simon, Charlie May (Hogue) Younger brother, a Cherokee Indian tale. New York, E. P. Dutton and Co., Inc., 1942. 182 p. [12592
Simonton Female College, Statesville, N. C. Catalogue, 18 - 18 - NcU has 1876/77 [12593
Simpson, Ann K. The trial of Mrs. Ann K. Simpson. Fayetteville, E. J. Hale & Son, 1851. 200 p. [12594
Simpson, Carrie Lewis. Picture poems. New York, Vantage Press [1956] 59 p. [12595
Simpson, Frances (Best) A beautiful woman on a southern plantation. Boston, Meader Publishing Co. [1946] 136 p. [12596
Simpson, George Lee. The Cokers of Carolina; a social biography of a family. Chapel Hill, University of North Carolina Press [1956] 327 p. [12597
[Simpson, John Wells] History of the First Presbyterian Church of Greensboro, North Carolina, 1824-1945. [Greensboro, Piedmont Press, 1947] 369 p. [12598
Simpson, William Hays. Life in mill communities. Clinton, S. C., P. C. Press [1943] 105 p. [12599
——The small loan problem of the Carolinas; with a commentary on regulation in Virginia. [Clinton, S. C., Presbyterian College Press, c.1941] 154 p. [12600
——Southern textile communities. [Durham? 1948] 139 p. [12601
——Workmen's compensation in South Carolina. [Durham? 1949] 156 p. [12602
Sims, Henry Upson. The genealogy of the Sims family of Virginia, the Carolinas, and the Gulf states. Kansas City, Mo., E. L. Mendenhall, Inc., pr. [1940?] 238 p. [12604
Sims, Marian (McCamy) Beyond surrender, a novel. Philadelphia, J. B. Lippincott Co. [1942] 492 p. [12605
——Call it freedom. Philadelphia, J. B. Lippincott Co. [c.1937] 319 p. [12606
——The city on the hill, a novel. Philadelphia, J. B. Lippincott Co. [c.1940] 356 p. [12607
——Memo. to Timothy Sheldon. Philadelphia, J. B. Lippincott Co. [c.1938] 252 p. [12608
——Morning star. Philadelphia, J. B. Lippincott Co. [c.1934] 320 p. [12609
——Storm before daybreak. Philadelphia, J. B. Lippincott Co. [1946] 295 p.[12610
Sinclair, Upton Beall. Bill Porter, a drama of O. Henry in prison. Pasadena, Calif., The Author [c.1925] 58 p. [12611
Sink, Margaret Jewell. Davidson County, economic and social. [Chapel Hill, Department of Rural Social Economics, University of North Carolina, 1925] 86 p. [12612
Sink, Margaret Jewell, joint author, see Matthews, Mary Green
Sir Walter Raleigh Memorial Association. North Carolina, Sir Walter Raleigh. [Raleigh? 1921?] 7 p. [12613
Sitterson, Joseph Carlyle. The secession movement in North Carolina. Chapel Hill, University of North Carolina Press, 1939. (The James Sprunt studies in history and political science, v. 23, no. 2) 285 p. [12614
——Sugar country; the cane sugar industry in the South, 1753-1950. [Lexington] University of Kentucky Press [1953] 414 p. [12615
Skaggs, Alma (Stone) ed. Serials currently received in southern libraries, a union list. Chapel Hill, University of North Carolina Library, 1936. 194 p. [12616
Skaggs, Marvin Lucian. North Carolina boundary disputes involving her southern line. Chapel Hill, University of North Carolina Press, 1941. (James Sprunt studies in history and political science, v. 25, no. 1) 250 p. [12617
Skeeter, 19 - New Bern, Stonewall High School, 19 - NcU has 1924 [12618
Sketch of the Duplin Rifles. No place, no publisher [1895?] 12 p. [12619

Sketch of the Forty-third Regiment, North Carolina troops. [Raleigh? 1895?] 26 p.   [12620

A sketch of the life and service of General William Ruffin Cox, including the address of Hon. Frank S. Spruill at the presentation of portrait . . . to the state of North Carolina. Richmond, Va., Whittet and Shepperson, 1921. 41 p.   [12621

Sketch of the life of Gen. Andrew Jackson, late president of the United States, interspersed with numerous personal anecdotes. Worcester, Mass., H. J. Howland, pr., 1845. 16 p.   [12622

Sketches of the county of Rockingham, N. C. Leaksville, Gazette Job Print, 1884. 31 p.   [12623

Sketches of the graduating class of Davidson College, North Carolina, 1872-1876. [Davidson? 1916?] 41 p.   [12624

Skidmore, Hubert. Hill doctor. New York, Doubleday, Doran & Co., Inc., 1940. 307 p.   [12625

Skillman, Lula Hunter, ed. Davis: History of the descendants of Peter Davis, 1752-1952. 2d ed. [Gainesville, Fla., The Editor] 1953. 52 p.   [12626

Skinner, Constance Lindsay. Pioneers of the old Southwest; a chronicle of the dark and bloody ground. New Haven, Yale University Press, 1919. 304 p.   [12627

Skinner, Joseph Blount. Letter on the subject of the Albemarle fisheries. No place, no publisher [1846] 8 p.   [12628

Skinner, Milton Philo. A guide to the winter birds of the North Carolina sandhills. Albany, N. Y., 1928. 301 p.   [12629

Skinner, Thomas Edward. Sermons, addresses and reminiscences, to which is appended briefs, sketches, and skeletons of sermons. Raleigh, Edwards, Broughton & Co., 1894. 437 p.   [12630

——A discourse delivered, June 10, 1827, in the Fifth Presbyterian Church of Philadelphia, commemorative of its dedication. Philadelphia, I. Ashmead, 1827. 28 p.   [12631

Skitt, pseud. see Taliaferro, Harden E.

Sky-land; stories of picturesque North Carolina, v. 1-2, June, 1913-September, 1915. Charlotte, 1913-1915. NcU has v. 1-2. Discontinued following v. 2, no. 5, September, 1915.   [12632

Slappey, Mary McGowan. Firelosophy and inspiration; narrative, poetry, drama. Boston, Christopher Publishing House [c.1936] 151 p.   [12633

Slaughter, Frank Gill. Air surgeon. Garden City, N. Y., Doubleday, Doran and Co., Inc., 1943. 306 p.   [12635

——Apalachee gold: the fabulous adventures of Cabeza de Vaca. Garden City, N. Y., Doubleday and Co., 1954. 254 p.   [12636

—— ——New York, A. A. Wyn, Inc. [c.1954] 256 p.   [12637

——Divine mistress. Garden City, N. Y., Doubleday and Co., 1949. 340 p. [12638

——East side General. Garden City, N. Y., Doubleday and Co., 1952. 311 p. [12639

—— ——Garden City, N. Y., Permabooks [1953] 347 p.   [12640

——Flight from Natchez. Garden City, N. Y., Doubleday and Co., 1955. 284 p. [12641

——Fort Everglades. Garden City, N. Y., Doubleday and Co., 1951. 340 p. [12642

——The Galileans, a novel of Mary Magdalene. Garden City, N. Y., Doubleday and Co., 1953. 307 p.   [12643

——The golden isle. Garden City, N. Y., Doubleday and Co., 1947. 373 p. [12644

——The healer. Garden City, N. Y., Doubleday and Co., 1955. 316 p.   [12645

——Immortal Magyar: Semmelweis, conqueror of childbed fever. New York, Henry Schuman [1950] 211 p.   [12646

——In a dark garden. Garden City, N. Y., Doubleday & Co., Inc. 1946. 435 p. [12647

——The road to Bithynia, a novel of Luke, the beloved physician. Garden City, N. Y., Doubleday and Co., 1951. 330 p.   [12648

——Sangaree. Garden City, N. Y., Doubleday and Co., 1948. 306 p.   [12649

——The scarlet cord; a novel of the woman of Jericho. Garden City, N. Y., Doubleday, 1956. 352 p.   [12650

——The song of Ruth; a love story from the Old Testament. Garden City, N. Y., Doubleday and Doran, 1954. 317 p.   [12651

—— ——New York, Premabooks [1955] 288 p.   [12652

——Spencer Brade, M. D. Garden City, N. Y., Doubleday, Doran and Co., 1942. 375 p. [12653
——Storm Haven. Garden City, N. Y., Doubleday and Co., 1953. 282 p. [12654
——The stubborn heart. Garden City, N. Y., Doubleday and Co., 1950. 307 p. [12655
—— ——[New York] New American Library [1952] (Signet book) 336 p. [12656
——That none should die. New York, Doubleday, Doran and Co., 1941. 423 p. [12657
——A touch of glory. Garden City, N. Y., Doubleday, Doran and Co., 1945. 329 p. [12658
——The warrior. Garden City, N. Y., Doubleday, 1956. 255 p. [12659

Sledd, Benjamin. At Lexington, a memorial poem. [Raleigh, Mutual Publishing Co., 1913] 12 p. [12660
——From cliff and scaur, a collection of verse. New York, G. P. Putnam's Sons, 1897. 100 p. [12661
——Watchers of the hearth. Boston, Gorham Press, 1902. 84 p. [12662

Sloan, John Alexander. North Carolina in the war between the states. Washington, Rufus H. Darby, 1883. 170 p. Appendix: Roster of North Carolina officers. [12663
——Reminiscences of the Guilford Grays, Co. B., 27th N. C. Regiment. Washington, R. O. Polkinhorn, pr., 1883. 129 p. [12664

Sloan, Samuel. Specifications of the workmanship and materials to be used in the erection and construction of the Western State Asylum for the Insane, at Morganton, Burke County, N. C. Philadelphia, McLaughlin Brothers, pr., 1875. 36 p. [12665

Sloo, James R., comp. John Herring of New Hanover County, N. C., and some of his descendants, 1705-1941, compiled by James R. Sloo and Pauline Herring Sloo. Raleigh, The Compilers [1941] 81 p. [12666

Sloop, Mary T. (Martin) Miracle in the hills, by Mary T. Martin Sloop, with LeGette Blythe. New York, McGraw-Hill [1953] 232 p. [12667

Small, John Humphrey. Bridges over navigable waters; address . . . at the convention of the Atlantic Deeper Waterways Association, Richmond, Virginia, September 17th, 1926. [Philadelphia, Atlantic Deeper Waterways Association, 1926] [4] p. [12668
——Free zones for American ports; address before the Georgia Press Association . . . ebruary 16, 1924. [Savannah, 1924] [6] p. [12669

Small, John Kunkel. Ferns of the Southeastern States. Lancaster, Pa. [Science Press Printing Co.] 1938. 517 p. [12670
——Flora of the Southeastern United States. 2d ed. New York, The Author, 1913. 1394 p. [12671
——Manual of the southeastern flora. New York, The Author, 1933. 1554 p. [12672

Small, Victor Robert. I knew 3000 lunatics. New York, Farrar & Rinehart, Inc., [c.1935] 273 p. [12673

Smathers, Frank. The last pioneer of Western North Carolina. Coral Gables, Fla., Glade House, 1956. 42 p. [12674

Smathers, George Henry. The history of land titles in Western North Carolina. Asheville, Miller Printing Co., 1938. 148 p. [12675

[Smedes, Aldert] Hints on the rite of confirmation addressed to the pupils of St. Mary's School. Raleigh, 1857. 28 p. [12676
—— ——Charlotte, Protestant Episcopal Publishing Association [1864?] (No. 9) 16 p. [12677
——"She hath done what she could"; or, The duty and responsibility of woman, a sermon preached in the chapel of St. Mary's School, by the rector. Raleigh, Seaton Gales, pr., 1851. 16 p. [12678

Smedes, Henrietta Rhea. Agricultural graphics, North Carolina and the United States, 1866-1922. Chapel Hill, University of North Carolina Press [1923] (Its University Extension Division. Bulletin [v. 2, no. 13]) 51 p. [12679
——In many moods, verses by Henrietta R. Smedes and John Esten Cooke Smedes. New York, Exposition Press [1951] 96 p. [12680

Smiley, John S. History of Tennessee River Baptist Association, from the year 1830 to the year 1892. Bryson City, Times Print, 1893. 166 p. [12681

Smith, Abbot Emerson. Colonists in bondage; white servitude and convict labor in America, 1607-1776. Chapel Hill, Institute of Early American History and Culture at Williamsburg, Va., by the University of North Carolina Press, 1947. 435 p. [12682

Smith, Alexander B. The mode and subjects of baptism. Charleston, S. C., Southern Christian Advocate Office, 1844. 112 p. [12683

Smith, Aristides S. The early British church in no way indebted to the Church of Rome for its establishment. No place, no publisher [1891] 21 p. [12684

[**Smith, Aristides S.**] Holy baptism; a conversation. Tarboro, S. Mary's Guild, Calvary Church, n.d. 19 p. [12685

Smith, Arthur Charlton. The soul of man is man entirely. Fayetteville, The Author, n.d. 144 p. [12686

Smith, Ashbel. The cholera spasmodica, as observed in Paris in 1832, comprising its symptoms, pathology, and treatment, illustrated by cases. New York, Peter Hill, sold also by J. Gales and Son, Raleigh, and at the Office of the Western Carolinian, Salisbury, 1832. 80 p. [12687

Smith, Austin Wheeler. The Dickson-McEwen and allied families genealogy. Cookeville, Tenn., Author, 1945. 512 p. [12688

Smith, Betty. Un albero cresce a Brooklyn. [Verona] Arnoldo Mondadori, 1953. 483 p. [12689

——The boy, Abe, a one act play. Boston, Baker's Plays [c.1944] 15 p. [12690

——The copper bracelet, by Betty Smith and Robert Finch. Syracuse, N. Y., Willis N. Bugbee Co., c.1938. 12 p. [12691

——His last skirmish, a play in one act, by Betty Smith and Robert Finch. New York, S. French, c.1937. 29 p. [12692

——Le lys de Brooklyn, traduit par Maurice Beerblock. [Paris] Hachette [1948] 431 p. [12693

——Mannequin's maid, a play in one act. Chicago, T. S. Denison & Co. [1939] 24 p. [12694

——Murder in the snow, a one-act drama of the West, by Betty Smith and Robert Finch. New York, S. French, c.1938. 29 p. [12695

——Naked angel, a comedy in one act, by Betty Smith and Robert Finch. New York, S. French, c.1937. 26 p. [12696

——Near closing time, a comedy-drama in one act, by Betty Smith and Robert Finch. Chicago, T. S. Denison & Co. [c.1939] 16 p. [12697

——A night in the country, a comedy in one act, by Betty Smith and Robert Finch. Evanston, Ill., Row, Peterson & Co. [c.1930] 36 p. [12698

——Popcastle Inn, a comedy-drama in one act, by Betty Smith and Robert Finch. New York, S. French [1937] 31 p. [12699

——The professor roars. Chicago, Dramatic Publishing Co. [c.1938] 28 p. [12700

——Tomorrow will be better, a novel. New York, Harper & Brothers [1948] 274 p. [12701

——A tree grows in Brooklyn, a novel. New York, Harper & Brothers [1943] 443 p. [12702

—— ——Philadelphia, Blakiston Co. [c.1943] 376 p. [12703

—— ——New York, Harper & Brothers [1943] [1947] 420 p. [12704

——A tree grows in Brooklyn, a musical play by Betty Smith and George Abbott, based on Betty Smith's novel. Lyrics by Dorothy Fields. New York, Harper & Brothers [1951] 179 p. [12705

Smith, Betty, comp. 25 non-royalty one-act plays for all-girl casts. New York, Greenberg [1942] 359 p. [12706

Smith, Betty. Western ghost town, a play in one act by Betty Smith and Robert Finch. Chicago, T. S. Denison & Co. [c.1939] 24 p. [12707

——Youth takes over; or, When a man's sixteen, a comedy of high school days in three acts, by Betty Smith and Robert Finch. New York, S. French, c.1939. 101 p. [12708

Smith, Betty, joint author, see Sigmund, Jay G.

Smith, Blanche (Lucas) comp. North Carolina's Confederate monuments and memorials. [Raleigh] North Carolina Division, United Daughters of the Confederacy, 1941. 131 p. [12709

Smith, Bryant. The present status of international arbitration. Mohonk Lake, N. Y., Lake Mohonk Conference on International Arbitration, 1913. 14 p. [12710

Smith, Buckingham. Inquiry into the authenticity of documents concerning a discovery in North America claimed to have been made by Verrazzano; read before the New York Historical Society, Tuesday, October 4th, 1864. New York, John F. Trow, pr., 1864. 31 p. [12711

Smith, C. D. A brief history of Macon County, North Carolina. Franklin, Franklin Press, 1891. 15 p. [12712

——A brief history of Macon County, North Carolina, by Dr. C. D. Smith and The topography of Macon County, by W. A. Curtis. Franklin, Franklin Press, 1905. 24 p. [12713

[**Smith, C. D.**] Magnetic iron ore found on the Western North Carolina Railroad near Asheville, N. C.; analysis made by A. R. Ledoux & Company, New York. [Asheville, D. S. Watson] n.d. 1 p. [12714

Smith, C. D. Semi-centennial sermon delivered before the Holston Conference, Methodist Episcopal Church, South, at its session in Asheville, N. C., October, 1888. Asheville, Randolph and Kerr, 1888. 16 p. [12715

Smith, Charles Alphonso. The American short story. Boston, Ginn and Company, 1912. 50 p. [12716

—— ——Berlin [August Scherl] 1910. 36 p. [12717

——Americanism. [Easton, Md., Easton Publishing Co. 1917?] 6 p. [12718

——Die amerikanische Literatur. Berlin, Weidmann, 1912. 388 p. [12719

——Common errors in English. [Annapolis, Md., U. S. Naval Academy, 1922] 4 p. [12720

——The crisis. Raleigh, Mitchell Printing Co., 1922. 7 p. [12721

——Edgar Allan Poe; how to know him. Indianapolis, Bobbs-Merrill Co. [c.1921] 350 p. [12722

Smith, Charles Alphonso, ed. Essays on current themes, selected and edited. Boston, Ginn and Co. [c.1923] 467 p. [12723

Smith, Charles Alphonso. The freshman mind. [Boston, Ginn and Co.] n.d. Folder. [12724

——Interpretative syntax. Baltimore, Modern Language Association of America, 1900. 19 p. [12725

——Keynote studies in keynote books of the Bible. New York, Fleming H. Revell Co. [c.1919] (James Sprunt lectures delivered at the Union Theological Seminary in Virginia [1917]) 202 p. [12726

Smith, Charles Alphonso, ed. Literary contrasts, selected and edited. Boston, Ginn and Co. [c.1925] 432 p. [12727

Smith, Charles Alphonso. New words self-defined. Garden City, N. Y., Doubleday, Page & Co., 1919. 215 p. [12728

—— ——1920. [12729

——New York Southern Society; an address on "Literature in the South" delivered before the Society on April 10th, 1908. [New York] New York Southern Society, 1908. 19 p. [12730

——The novel in America. [Washington] Teachers' Annuity and Aid Association of the District of Columbia [1903?] (Teachers' institute course, 1902, 1903) 11 p. [12731

——O. Henry biography. New York, Doubleday, Page & Co., 1916. 258 p. [12732

—— ——1918. [12733

—— ——1921. [12734

—— ——London, Hodder and Stoughton, 1916. 258 p. [12735

——An Old English grammar and exercise book, with inflections, syntax, selections for reading, and glossary. New ed., rev. Boston, Allyn & Bacon [c.1896] 193 p. [12736

—— ——[c.1903] 193 p. [12737

——An open letter. [Chapel Hill, The Author, February 2, 1909] [1] p. [12738

——Order of words in Anglo-Saxon prose. Baltimore, Modern Language Association of America, 1893. 39 p. Thesis (Ph. D.) Johns Hopkins University. [12739

——Our language. Richmond, Va., B. F. Johnson Publishing Co., [c.190?] 3? v. NcU has v. 2, 3 [12740

——Our language, Smith and McMurray; grammar. Richmond, Va., B. F. Johnson Publishing Co., 1903. 263 p. [12741

——The publication department of the southern Presbyterian Church; an address delivered in connection with the dedication of the new Presbyterian publishing house, Richmond, Va., March 27, 1904. Richmond, Va., Presbyterian Committee of Publication [1904?] 28 p.   [12742

——Repetition and parallelism in English verse; a study in the technique of poetry. New York, University Publishing Co., 1894. 76 p.   [12743

Smith, Charles Alphonso, ed. Short stories, old and new. Boston, Ginn and Co. [c.1916] 292 p.   [12744

Smith, Charles Alphonso. The significance of history in a democracy. [Greens-boro, Guilford Battle Ground Co., 1909] 10 p. Cover title: Clio.   [12745

——The Smith-McMurray language series, Book one-three? by C. Alphonso Smith and Lida B. McMurry. Richmond, Va., B. F. Johnson Publishing Co. [c.1919] 3? v.   [12746

——Southern literary studies, a collection of literary, biographical, and other sketches; with a biographical study by F. Stringfellow Barr. Chapel Hill, University of North Carolina Press, 1927. 192 p.   [12747

——The student body of the University of Virginia. [Charlottesville?] n.d. 8 p.[12748

——Studies in English syntax. Boston, Ginn & Co. [c.1906] 92 p.   [12749

——What can literature do for me? Garden City, N. Y., Doubleday, Page & Co., 1913. 228 p.   [12750

——Why young men should study Shakespeare. New York, University Society [c.1902] 8 p.   [12751

Smith, Charles Lee. [Inauguration as president of Mercer University, November 24, 1905] Macon, Ga., Mercer University, 1905. (Its Quarterly bulletin, Ser. 1, no. 2) 62 p.   [12752

——The money question. St. Louis, Mo., Shirley Press, 1894. 32 p.   [12753

Smith, Charles Page. James Wilson, founding father, 1742-1798. Chapel Hill, University of North Carolina Press [c.1956] 426 p.   [12754

Smith, Claiborne, joint author, see Smith, Stuart Hall

[Smith, Daniel] A short description of the state of Tennessee, lately called the Territory of the United States, south of the River Ohio; to accompany and explain a map of that country. Philadelphia, Printed for Mathew Carey by Land and Ustick, March 9, 1796. 36 p.   [12755

Smith, Edith Hutchins. Drought, and other North Carolina yarns. Winston-Salem, J. F. Blair, 1955. 153 p.   [12756

——El tigre! Mexican short stories. Winston-Salem, John F. Blair, 1956. 178 p. [12757

Smith, Edwin W. Aggrey of Africa, a study in black and white. New York, Doubleday and Co., Inc., 1929. 292 p.   [12758

Smith, Egbert Watson. The creed of Presbyterians. New York, Baker and Taylor Co. [1901] 223 p.   [12759

——The creed of Presbyterians. Rev. ed. Richmond, Va., John Knox Press [c.1941] 214 p.   [12760

——The desire of all nations. Garden City, N. Y., Doubleday, Doran & Co., Inc., 1928. 193 p.   [12761

——From one generation to another. Richmond, Va., Executive Committee of Foreign Missions, Educational Department, Presbyterian Church, by John Knox Press [c.1945] 136 p.   [12762

——A protest against prejudice. [Tuscaloosa, Ala., Presbyterian General Assembly's Committee on Colored Evangelization, 1909] 15 p.   [12763

——The temperance question; a sermon preached in the First Presbyterian Church of Greensboro, N. C. [Greensboro?] n.d. 8 p.   [12764

Smith, Frances Patterson. Song and shadow. No place, privately printed [1953?] 29 p.   [12765

Smith, Franklin L. Oration in commemoration of the Mecklenburg Declaration of Independence, delivered at Charlotte, on 20th May, 1835. Charlotte, Holton, 1835. 14 p.   [12766

Smith, Grover Cleveland. T. S. Eliot's poetry and plays; a study in sources and meaning. [Chicago] University of Chicago Press [1956] 338 p.   [12767

Smith, Gustavus Woodson. Confederate war papers: Fairfax Court House, New Orleans, Seven Pines, Richmond and North Carolina. New York, Atlantic Publishing and Engraving Co., 1884. 381 p.   [12768

Smith, Hay Watson. Evolution and Presbyterianism. Little Rock, Allsopp and Chapple, 1923. 115 p. [12769

Smith, Henry Louis. Memorial address: Life and character of John J. Fray, A. M., first president, North Carolina Teachers' Assembly. Raleigh, A. Williams & Co., 1886. 10 p. [12770

——This troubled century, selected addresses. Chapel Hill, University of North Carolina Press, 1947. 203 p. [12771

——Your biggest job, school or business; some words of counsel for red-blooded young Americans who are getting tired of school. New York, D. Appleton & Co., 1920. 79 p. [12772

Smith, Hildreth Hosea. The Robertsonian system of teaching French, with rules of pronunciation and a full vocabulary. Chapel Hill, James M. Henderson, 1858. 110 p. [12773

Smith, Hilrie Shelton. Changing conceptions of original sin; a study in American theology since 1750. New York, Charles Scribner's Sons, 1955. 242 p. [12774
——Faith and nurture. New York, C. Scribner's Sons, 1941. 208 p. [12775

Smith, Isaac H. How long shall the present state of affairs exist? New Bern [Author] 1899. [1] p. [12776

Smith, Ivory Harvey, ed. Life lines, a collection of inspiring poetry and prose, by Ivory Harvey Smith and Isabelle Tolbert Smith. [Charlotte, Observer Printing House for the Editors, c.1952] 144 p. [12777

[Smith, James] Civil practice in the court of pleas and quarter sessions of North Carolina in ordinary cases. Raleigh, no publisher, 1846. 458 p. [12778

Smith, James Strudwick. To the electors of Orange County. Hillsborough, The Author, July 1st, 1829. [1] p. [12779

——To the voters of Wake, Person, and Orange. Hillsborough, The Author, March 29, 1844. [1] p. [12780

Smith, John. The generall historie of Virginia, New-England, and the Summer Isles. London, Printed by J. D. and J. H. for Michael Sparkes, 1624. 96, 105-248 p. NcU has microfilm. [12781

——Travels and works of Captain John Smith . . . edited by Edward Arber . . . Edinburgh, J. Grant, 1910. 2 v. [12781a

——Works, 1608-1631 . . . edited by Edward Arber. Birmingham, England [The Editor] 1884. (The English scholar's library, no. 16) 984 p. [12782

Smith, John Eliphalet. A laboratory guide for beginners in geology. Chapel Hill [Lancaster, Pa., Press of the New Era Printing Co.] 1917. 91 p. [12783

Smith, John William. Building a railroad (1832-1952) The Seaboard Air Line, its beginnings and its contributions. New York, Newcomen Society in North America, 1952. 32 p. [12784

Smith, Leonidas L. Masonic address delivered at the laying of the cornerstone of St. John's College at Oxford, North Carolina . . . 1855. Raleigh, Register Office, pr., 1855. 16 p. [12785

Smith, Lloyd M., joint author, see Johnson, Leonard E.

Smith, Mary Kelly (Watson) Some meagre recollections of Mammy, by Mrs. J. Henry Smith. [Greensboro, 1914] [15] p. [12786

Smith, Mary Loomis. John Charles McNeill. Raleigh, Meredith College, 1926. (Its Bulletin, ser. 19, no. 2) 39 p. [12787

Smith, Mary Shannon. Union sentiment in North Carolina during the Civil War. [Raleigh, Meredith College, 1915] (Its Bulletin, ser. 9, no. 1) 21 p. [12788

Smith, Michael. To sermon, preached in Christ-Church, in Newbern, in North-Carolina, December the 27th, 1755. Newbern, James Davis, 1756. 19 p. NcU has photograph [12789

Smith, Millie. The history of the Carolina twins, told in their own peculiar way by one of them. Buffalo, Buffalo Courier Printing House, n.d. 22 p. [12790

Smith, Moody B. Address delivered before the two literary societies of Davidson College, N. C., July 15th, 1857. Wilmington, Fulton and Price, 1857. 30 p. [12791

Smith, Orren Randolph. The stars and bars; speech by Major Orren Randolph Smith; Report of "Stars and Bars" Committee. No place, no publisher, n.d. 13 p.   [12792

Smith, R. P. Some results of mission work in the mountains of North Carolina. [Asheville, no publisher, 1905] 20 p.   [12793

Smith, Mrs. Ravenel see **Pelton, Mabell Shippie Clark**

Smith, Reed, ed. American anthology of old world ballads . . . settings by Hilton Rufty. New York, J. Fischer & Bro. [c.1937] 70 p.   [12794

Smith, Richard H. Organization of the Protestant Episcopal Church of the Confederate States, A. D. 1861, and its reunion with the Protestant Episcopal Church in the U. S., A. D. 1865. Weldon, Harrell's Cheap Book and Job Printing House, 1882. 11 p.   [12795

Smith, Robert Sidney. The Spanish guild merchant; a history of the consulado, 1250-1700. Durham, Duke University Press, 1940. 167 p.   [12796

Smith, Samuel Denny. The Negro in Congress, 1870-1901. Chapel Hill, University of North Carolina Press, 1940. 160 p.   [12797

Smith, Stuart Hall. The history of Trinity Parish, Scotland Neck, Edgecomb Parish, Halifax County [by] Stuart Hall Smith [and] Claiborne T. Smith, Jr Scotland Neck [Christian Printing Co., Durham] 1955. 115 p.   [12798

[Smith, Susan McGee (Heck)] The love that never failed. [Charlottesville, Va., Michie Co., pr., 1928] 110 p.   [12799

Smith, Thomas Marshall. Legends of the war of independence, and of the earlier settlements in the West. Louisville, Ky., J. F. Brennan, 1855. 397 p.   [12800

Smith, William. A true and faithful narrative of the proceedings of the House of Burgesses of North-Carolina, met in assembly for the said Province at Newbern, February 5th, 1739. [Boston? 1740?] 52 p. NcU has photograph   [12801

Smith, William Alexander. The Anson Guards, Company C, Fourteenth Regiment, North Carolina Volunteers, 1861-1865. Charlotte, Stone Publishing Co., 1914. 368 p.   [12802

——Family tree book, genealogical and biographical, listing the relatives of General William Alexander and of W. Thomas Smith. Los Angeles, William Thomas Smith, 1922. 304 p.   [12803

Smith, William B. The mysteries of Freemasonry. Raleigh, Wm. B. Smith & Co., 1866. 41 p.   [12804

——The North Carolina gold circular. Raleigh, Wm. B. Smith & Co., 1866. 31 p.   [12805

Smith, William Cunningham. Bible study: 1. Why study the Bible. 2. The Bible teacher. 3. Some fundamentals in Bible teaching. Greensboro, Sunday School Association [1915] 37 p.   [12806

——Charles Duncan McIver. [Greensboro, J. J. Stone, pr., 1907] 30 p.   [12807

——Jonah; a lecture delivered before the Men's Bible Class of the First Presbyterian Church, Greensboro, N. C. Greensboro, J. J. Stone, pr., n.d. 7 p.   [12808

——Studies in American authors. Greensboro, North Carolina State Normal & Industrial College, 1913. (Its Bulletin, v. 3, no. 2) 171 p.   [12809

[Smith, William H.] Circular to the friends of the University in regard to specimens of natural history. Raleigh, News, 1876. 15 p.   [12810

Smith, William Henry, 1833-1896. A political history of slavery. New York, G. P. Putnam's Sons, 1903. 2 v.   [12811

Smith, William Henry, 1839-1935. Speakers of the House of Representatives of the United States, with personal sketches of the several speakers, with portraits. Baltimore, Md., S. J. Gaeng, 1928. 261 p.   [12812

Smith, William Hugh. Radical falsehood exposed; U. S. troops sent to North Carolina to conquer a radical victory at the elections. Washington, 1870. 4 p.   [12813

Smith, William Loughton. A comparative view of the constitutions of the several states with each other, and with that of the United States. Philadelphia, J. Thompson, 1796. 34 p.   [12814

Smith, William Robert Lee. A great trio, Fuller, Jeter, Yates; three lectures delivered on the Gay Foundation before the Southern Baptist Theological Seminary,

Louisville, Ky., March, 1896. Nashville, Tenn., Sunday School Board, Southern Baptist Convention [1896] 115 p. [12815

Smith, William Robert Lee. The story of the Cherokees. Cleveland, Tenn., The Church of God Publishing House, 1928. 229 p. [12816

Smith, Willis. Citizenship and the bill of rights in war time; annual address . . . North Carolina Bar Association at Pinehurst, North Carolina, May 16, 1942. [Raleigh? 1942] 15 p. [12817

Smithfield, N. C. Board of Education. Report of Superintendent of Public Schools, 19 - 19 - NcU has 1917/18 [12818

Smith's River Association. Minutes, 18 - 18 - NcU has 1868 [12819

Smithson, William T., ed. Methodist pulpit, South. 2d ed. Washington, Henry Polkinhorn, pr., 1859. 426 p. [12820

—— ——3d ed. Washington, W. T. Smithson, 1859. 456 p. [12821

Smithwick, Noah. The evolution of a state; or, Recollections of old Texas days, by Noah Smithwick . . . compiled by his daughter, Nanna Smithwick Donaldson. Austin, Tex., Gammel Book Co. [c.1900] 354 p. [12822

Smoot, James Edward, comp. Marshal Ney before and after execution. Charlotte, Queen City Printing Co., 1929. 460 p. [12823

Smyth, J. Jones. An address delivered before the Philanthropic and Eumenean societies of Davidson College, North Carolina . . . on Wednesday, August 8, 1855. Raleigh, Office of the Carolina Cultivator, pr., 1855. 32 p. [12824

Smyth, John Ferdinand Dalziel. A tour in the United States of America. Dublin, Price, Moncrieffe, 1784. 2 v. [12825

Smyth, Thomas. The voice of God in calamity; or, Reflections on the loss of the steam-boat Home, October 9, 1837; a sermon delivered in the Second Presbyterian Church, Charleston, on Sabbath morning, October 22, 1837. 2d ed. Charleston, Jenkins & Hussey, 1837. 32 p. [12826

Smythe, Charles W. Our own elementary grammar, intermediate between the primary and high school grammars, and especially adapted to the wants of the common schools. Greensboro, Sterling, Campbell & Albright, 1863. 148 p.[12827

——Our own primary grammar for the use of beginners. Greensborough, Sterling and Campbell, 1861. 72 p. [12828

—— ——2d ed. Greensboro, Sterling, Campbell and Albright, 1862. [12829

—— ——3d ed. 1863. [12830

——Our own school grammar, designed for our schools and academies, as a sequel to the Primary grammar. Greensborough, Sterling, Campbell & Albright, 1862. 208 p. [12831

Snell, George Dixon. The shapers of American fiction, 1798-1947. New York, E. P. Dutton & Co., Inc., 1947. 316 p. [12832

Snell, John Leslie, Jr., ed. The meaning of Yalta; Big Three diplomacy and the new balance of power. Baton Rouge, Louisiana State University Press [1956] 239 p. [12833

[Snelling, William Joseph] A brief and impartial history of the life and actions of Andrew Jackson . . . by a free man. Boston, Stimpson and Clapp, 1831. 216 p.[12834

Snips and cuts, 1910- Charlotte, Students of Alexander Graham High School, 1910- NcU has 1920, 1922 [12835

Snow, Edward Rowe. Famous lighthouses of America. New York, Dodd, Mead and Co., 1955. 314 p. [12837

——Mysteries and adventures along the Atlantic coast. New York, Dodd, Mead and Co., 1948. 352 p. [12836

——Pirates and buccaneers of the Atlantic coast. Boston, Yankee Publishing Co. [1944] 350 p. [12838

——Secrets of the North Atlantic islands. New York, Dodd, Mead and Co., 1950. 339 p. [12839

——Strange tales from Nova Scotia to Cape Hatteras. New York, Dodd, Mead, and Co. [1949] 322 p. [12840

Snow, W. H. Snow's modern barn system of raising and curing tobacco. 3d ed. Baltimore, Friedenwald Co., 1895. 31 p. [12841

Snow, William Parker. Southern generals, their lives and campaigns New York, Charles B. Richardson, 1866. 500 p. [12842

Snowden, James Ross. Extract from the Report on the mint at Charlotte, N. C., and upon the gold mines of that region to the Director of the U. S. Mint, May 22d, 1877. Philadelphia, F. G. Odenheimer & Co., pr. [1877] 4 p.   [12843

Snyder, William A. An historical sketch of St. Paul's Evangelical Lutheran congregation, Wilmington, N. C. [Wilmington, The Fiftieth Anniversary Committee, 1908?] 49 p.   [12844

Sober second thought, extra for the presidential campaign of 1844. New York, Daniel E. Sickles, 1844. [2] p.   [12845

Social forces, v. 1- November, 1922- Chapel Hill, University of North Carolina Press, 1922- NcU has v. 1-34   [12846

The social register of North Carolina, edited by Mary F. Henderson. No place, 1936. 94 p.   [12847

The social register, Richmond, North Carolina, Charleston, Savannah, Augusta, 188 - Atlanta, 188 - NcU has 1908   [12848

Society of American Foresters, Washington. A survey of state forestry administration in North Carolina, under the direction of a joint committee of the Society of American Foresters and the Charles Lathrop Pack Forestry Foundation. [Washington?] Society of American Foresters [1946] 38 p.   [12849

Society of Colonial Wars. Annual register of officers and members, constitution of the General Society. New-York [DeVinne Press] 1894. 215 p.   [12850

—— ——New York [J. Pott & Co., pr.] 1895. 301 p.   [12851

—— ——1898. 586 p.   [12852

——Second supplement to the General register . . . 1911. New York [D. Taylor & Co., pr.] 1911. 415 p.   [12853

Society of Mayflower Descendants. North Carolina. Society of Mayflower Descendants in the state of North Carolina. Asheville [1924] 24 p.   [12854

—— ——[1926] 14 p.   [12855

—— ——[1928?] 33 p.   [12856

—— ——[1931?] 37 p.   [12857

Society of the Burnside Expedition and of the Ninth Army Corps, organized February 8th, 1869. No place, n.d. [2] p.   [12858

Society of the Cincinnati. Roster, 18 - [Washington] 18 - NcU has 1920, 1938, 1941, 1944, 1953, 1956. Includes a section for North Carolina members.[12859

Society of the Cincinnati. North Carolina. By laws, adopted, July 4th, 1896. No place [1896?] 3 p.   [12860

——Dinner given to the General Society by the North Carolina Society . . . Asheville, May 10th, 1917. [Asheville? 1917?] [11] p.   [12861

——Minutes, 189 - 189 - NcU has [1903-1923]   [12862

——North Carolina Society of the Cincinnati. No place [1903] [6] p.   [12863

—— ——[1904] [8] p.   [12864

—— ——1906. 11 p.   [12865

—— ——[1907] [10] p.   [12866

—— ——[1912] 12 p.   [12867

—— ——[1913] 12 p.   [12868

—— ——[1915] 11 p.   [12869

—— ——[1918] 12 p.   [12870

—— ——[1921] 12 p.   [12871

—— ——[1922] 12 p.   [12872

—— ——1931. 14 p.   [12872a

——North Carolina Society of the Cincinnati . . . past and present members, compiled by John Collins Daves, 22 April 1922. No place [1922] 23 p.   [12873

——The Society of the Cincinnati. No place, n.d. [9] p.   [12874

Society of the Descendants of the Palatines. North Carolina. Register. [New Bern] 1945. [14] p.   [12875

Soldier list. [Greensboro? 1919?] [4] p. A roster of soldiers from Greensboro serving in World War I.   [12876

The soldier's hymn-book for camp worship. No place, Soldiers' Tract Association, M. E. Church, South, 1863. 63 p.   [12877

Soldiers of the great war . . . compiled by W. M. Haulsee, G. F. Howe [and] A. C. Doyle. Washington, Soldiers Record Publishing Association [c.1920] 3 v. [12878

Soley, James Russell. Admiral Porter. New York, D. Appleton and Co., 1903. 499 p. [12879

——The blockade and the cruisers. New York, C. Scribner's Sons, 1883. 257 p. [12880

—— ——London, Sampson Low, Marston & Co., 1898. 257 p. [12881

Solicitor see **Wachovia**

Solomon, J. B. The old paths and the good way, a sermon preached on the occasion of the dedication of the Sharon Baptist Meeting House, Warren County, N. C., September 20th, 1857. Richmond, Va., H. K. Ellyson, 1857. 26 p. [12882

Some account of General Jackson, drawn up from the Hon. Mr. Eaton's very circumstantial narrative, and other well-established information respecting him, by a gentleman of the Baltimore bar. Baltimore, H. Vicary, Matchell, pr., 1828. 272 p. [12883

Some queer Americans and other stories. New York, Akron, O., Werner Co. 1899. [72] p. [12884

Some Tennessee heroes of the Revolution, compiled from pension statements. Chattanooga, Tenn., Lookout Publishing Co. [1934?] [36] p. [12885

——Pamphlet no. II. [1935?] [39] p. [12886

——Pamphlet III. [1937?] [33] p. [12887

——Pamphlet no. IV. [1939?] [31] p. [12888

——Pamphlet no. V. [1944?] [34] p. [12889

——Pamphlet no. VI. n.d. [33] p. [12890

Some unsolicited comment on Mr. Hammer's brief on Jackson. No place, no publisher, n.d. 4 p. [12891

Somers, Nathan. Proposals for clearing land in Carolina, Pensilvania, East Jersy, West-Jersy, or any other parts of America. London, John Pringhurst, 1682. [1] p. NcU has photostat [12892

Somers, Robert. The Southern States since the war, 1870-1. London & New York, Macmillan and Co., 1871. 286 p. [12893

Somerset Sesquicentennial Association, Somerset, Pa. Sketches of Somerset. Somerset, Pa. [1954] 96 p. [12894

Somerville, Edith Anna Oenone. The states through Irish eyes. Boston, Houghton Mifflin Co. [c.1930] 199 p. [12895

Somerville Female Institute, Leasburg, N. C. Catalogue, 18 - Leasburg, 18 - NcU has 1854/55, 1859/60 [12896

Something of a partial review of Greensboro's public school facilities and a few facts and figures showing the absolute, immediate need for a central high school building, April, 1904. Greensboro, J. M. Reece & Co., 1904. 36 p. [12897

Sommerville, Charles William. The history of Hopewell Presbyterian Church for 175 years from the assigned date of its organization, 1762, prepared for publication by Jane D. Carson . . . [and] Betty Guy Sommerville. [Charlotte, Observer Printing House, 1939] 323 p. [12898

Sondley, Foster Alexander. An address of welcome to the National Association of State Libraries at its session held at Asheville, North Carolina, May, 1907. Asheville, 1907. 12 p. [12899

——Alexander-Davidson reunion, Swannanoa, N. C., August 26, 1911; addresses by F. A. Sondley . . . and Theo. F. Davidson. [Asheville? 1911?] 53 p. [12900

——Asheville and Buncombe County, by F. A. Sondley; Genesis of Buncombe County, by T. F. Davidson. Asheville, Citizen, 1922. 200 p. [12901

——Descent of the Scottish Alexanders, a genealogical sketch, with discussions of some historic matters. [Asheville, Hackney and Moale Co., c.1912] 73 p. [12902

——The Hickory-Nut Gorge. No place, no publisher, n.d. 62 p. [12903

——A history of Buncombe County, North Carolina. Asheville, Advocate Printing Co., 1930. 2 v. [12904

——The Indian's curse; a legend of the Cherokees. [Asheville? The Author] n.d. 16 p. [12905

——My ancestry. Asheville, privately printed, 1930. 289 p. [12906

——The origin of the Catawba grape and other sketches. Asheville, privately printed, 1918. 47 p. [12907

——Samuel Davidson . . . an address delivered at the commemorative exercises when the monument was unveiled, September 25th, 1913. [Asheville? 1913] 22 p. [12908

Sons of Confederate Veterans. North Carolina Division. Harry Burgwyn Camp no. 166, Raleigh. By-laws. Raleigh, Alford, Bynum & Christophers, 1900. 13 p.[12909
——Charter members, including records of ancestors. Raleigh, Alford, Bynum & Christophers, 1900. 13 p.   [12910
Sons of the American Revolution. North Carolina Society. Lineage book of past and present members of the North Carolina Society of Sons of the American Revolution. [Raleigh] 1951. 322 p.   [12911
——North Carolina Society, Sons of the American Revolution, organized February 22, 1911. No place [1911?]   19 p.   [12912
—— ——No place [1944?]   15 p.   [12913
Sons of the American Revolution. North Carolina Society. Mecklenburg Chapter, Charlotte. Mecklenburg in the Revolution, 1740-1783. [Charlotte, 1931] 114 p.   [12914
Sons of the Revolution. North Carolina Society. By-laws, and charter . . . to which is prefixed the constitution of the General Society. Raleigh, Edwards & Broughton, pr., 1894.   27 p.   [12915
—— ——Raleigh, Commercial Printing Co., 1909.   27 p.   [12916
——Membership and ancestral register, by-laws and charter, including the constitution of the General Society. Raleigh, 1898.   57 p.   [12917
——North Carolina Society of the Sons of the Revolution. Raleigh, 1894. [3] p. [12918
——The North Carolina Society of the Sons of the Revolution and its past patriotic activities. [Raleigh, 1926?]   [3] p.   [12919
——North Carolina Society of the Sons of the Revolution; objects of the Society and qualifications for membership therein. [Raleigh] n.d.   4 p.   [12920
——Presentation of portrait of Governor William Richardson Davie to the state of North Carolina, in the Senate chamber at Raleigh, November 15, 1910. [Raleigh, 1910?]   19 p.   [12921
——Prospectus. Raleigh, 1894.   10 p.   [12922
South and world affairs, February? 1938- Chapel Hill, Southern Council on International Relations, 1938-   NcU has v. [1] 2-10   [12923
The South-Atlantic, v. 1- November, 1877- Wilmington, 1877- NcU has v. 1, 2 [3] 4, 5, 6 [7]   [12924
South Atlantic and North Western Railroad. Prospectus. No place, Samuel Hall [1887]   18 p.   [12925
South Atlantic bulletin, v. 1- May, 1935- [Chapel Hill] South Atlantic Modern Language Association] 1935- NcU has v. 1-10 [11] 12-21   [12926
South Atlantic Modern Language Association. South Atlantic studies for Sturgis E. Leavitt, edited by Thomas B. Stroup and Sterling A. Stoudemire. Washington, Scarecrow Press, 1953.   215 p.   [12927
The South Atlantic quarterly, v. 1- January, 1902- Durham, Duke University, 1902- NcU has v. 1-55   [12928
The South Atlantic quarterly. Fifty years of the South Atlantic quarterly [by] William Baskerville Hamilton. Durham, Duke University Press, 1952. 397 p.[12929
South Carolina (Colony) The colonial records of South Carolina . . . ed. by J. H. Easterby. Columbia, Historical Commission of South Carolina, 1951- NcU has v. 1-4   [12930
South Carolina. Commission on Railroad Between Charleston and Cincinnati. Report. Columbia, S. C., Telescope Office, 1836.   34 p.   [12931
——Report on the subject of the proposed railroad from Charleston to Cincinnati and Louisville. Knoxville, Tenn., Ramsey and Craighead, 1836.   15 p.   [12932
South Carolina. Laws, Statutes, etc. Charter of the Charlotte and South Carolina Railroad Company, as granted by the legislature of South Carolina, December 18, 1846. No place, n.d.   22 p.   [12933
——Joint acts. No place, n.d.   14 p.   Relating to Wilmington and Manchester Railroad.   [12934
South Fork Baptist Association. Minutes, 1879?- 1879?- NcU has [1882-1955] [12935
The South in the building of the nation. Richmond, Va., Southern Historical Publication Society [c.1909-13]   13 v.   [12936
South River Baptist Association. Minutes, 18 - 18 - NcU has 1877, 1879-1886 1897, 1906   [12937

South Roanoke Baptist review, v. 1- November, 1955- Greenville, South Roanoke Baptist Association, 1955- NcU has v. 1 [12938

South Sandy Creek Baptist Association. Minutes, 1950- 1950- NcU has 1950-1955 [12939

South Yadkin Baptist Association. Minutes, 1874?- 1874?- NcU has 1876-1886 [1891-1955] [12940

Southard, Lawrence Gedding. Andrew Johnson, the constitutionalist address delivered before the Schubert Club, Jonesboro, Tennessee, March 4, 1931. No place, no pubisher [1931?] 22 p. [12941

Southeastern Baptist Theological Seminary. Bulletin, v. 1- July, 1951- Wake Forest, 1951- NcU has v. [1-6] [12942

Southeastern Library Association. Papers and proceedings of biennial conference, 19 - 19 - NcU has 1926-1938, 1946, 1948, 1956. No meetings in 1942, 1944 [12943
——Program, 1920- 1920- NcU has 1924, 1926, 1929, 1934, 1936, 1946. [12944

Southeastern road builder, v. 1- 1951- Raleigh, Southeastern Publishing Corporation, 1951- NcU has v. [1] [12945

Southeastern States Cooperative Library Survey. Libraries of the Southeast . . . ed. by Louis R. Wilson and Marion A. Milczewski. Chapel Hill, Southeastern Library Association, 1949. 301 p. ` [12946

[Southeastern Tariff Association] [North Carolina, mercantile risks, revised schedules] No place [1908] 79 p. [12947

Southeastern Tariff Association. Tariff of minimum rates. Atlanta, 1882. 14 p.[12948
——Tariff of minimum rates . . . amended and re-adopted . . . July 3, 1884. Revised and re-adopted, December 1, 1887. No place, 1887. 107 p. [12949

Southern advertising and publishing, v. 1- November, 1925- Greensboro, 1925- NcU has v. 1-6. Published in Atlanta, July, 1928- [12950

Southern Appalachian Water Power Conference. Proceedings, 1st- 1922- Knoxville, Tenn. [1922- NcU has 1922, 1923, 1927 [12951

Southern architect, v. 1- May, 1954- Charlotte, North Carolina Chapter of American Institute of Architects, 1954- NcU has v. 1-3 [12952

Southern Assembly, Lake Junaluska, N. C. Southern Assembly . . . for conference, training, rest, inspiration, recreation. [Waynesville, 1913?] 32 p. [12953

The Southern Association quarterly, v. 1-12, February, 1937-February, 1948. [Durham, Duke University Press, 1937-1948. NcU has v. 1-12 [12954

Southern Baptist Assembly, Ridgecrest, N. C. The Ridgecrest story. Nashville, Tenn., Broadman Press [c.1955] 64 p. [12955
——The Southern Baptist Assembly. Raleigh, Mutual Publishing Co., 1915. 12 p. [12956

Southern Baptist Convention. North Carolina Baptists and southern Baptists working together. [Nashville? Tenn. 1929?] 71 p. [12957

Southern Baptist Convention. Educational Commission. Schools in the Baptist system in North Carolina, 1917. No place, n.d. 38 p. [12958

Southern Biblical Assembly, Asheville, N. C., 1925. Manual. No place, American Society of Religious Education [1895?] 20 p. [12959

Southern Book Exchange, Raleigh, N. C. Rare and valuable North Carolina books for sale. Raleigh, n.d. [2] p. [12961

Southern business guide, 1879-80- New York, United States Central Publishing Co., 1879?- NcU has 1879-80, 1885-86 [12962

Southern city, v. 1- August, 1937- [Raleigh, Southern Municipal News Publishing Co.] 1937- NcU has v. 1-12, 2d ser. v. 1-8. Title varies, August, 1937-May, 1939: North Carolina municipal news; June, 1939-June, 1940: Southern municipal news [12963

Southern Committee for People's Rights, Chapel Hill, N. C. The Southern Committee for People's Rights. [Chapel Hill, 1936] [2] p. [12964

Southern Conference. Constitution and by-laws, 1934, adopted at Charlottesville, Virginia, February 24, 1934. No place [1934?] [15] p. [12965

——Winter sports roster and press data, 19 - [Durham? 19 - NcU has 1952/53, v. 3 [12966

Southern Conference for Education and Industry. March of thought and achievement in the South, 1898-1915. [Washington, National Capitol Press] 1916. 22 p. [12967

——The Southern Conference for Education and Industry. [Chattanooga? 1915] 20 p. [12968

Southern Conference for Human Welfare. For your children too. [Nashville, Tenn., 1945] [30] p. [12969

Southern Conference on Race Relations, Durham, N. C., October 20, 1942. A basis for inter-racial cooperation and development in the South; a statement by southern Negroes. [Norfolk, Va., Journal and Guide, 1942] 8 p. [12970

——Statement of purpose . . . A list of those that attended the Conference. No place [1942?] 16 p. [12971

Southern Conference-Seminar on Teaching and Research in Rural Sociology, Blue Ridge, N. C. Proceedings . . . August 26-30, 1940. [Charlottesville, Va., 1940] 196 p. [12972

Southern Conservatory of Music, Durham, N. C. [Catalogue, 18 - Durham. 18 - NcU has 1903/04, 1928/29 [12973

Southern economic journal, v. 1- October, 1933- Athens, Ga., Chapel Hill, N. C., Southern Economic Association [1933- NcU has v. 1-23. Published at Chapel Hill, January, 1936- v. 3- [12974

Southern educator, v. 1- 1890- Durham, The Educator Co., 1890- NcU has v. [1-3] . [12975

Southern Fertilizing Co., Richmond, Va. Reports of tobacco growers in Virginia and North Carolina on the action of the tobacco fertilizers prepared by the Southern Fertilizing Co. Richmond, Va., 1874. 47 p. [12976

——Tobacco in Virginia and North Carolina. Richmond, Va., Clemmitt and Jones [1877] 31 p. [12977

Southern field and fireside, new ser. v. 1- 1863?- Raleigh, W. B. Smith, 1863?- NcU has v. [1-2] [12978

Southern Forestry Congress. Proceedings, 1st- 1916- Chapel Hill, 1916- NcU has 1916, 1920, 1st-2d [12979

——Words of wisdom heard at the Southern Forestry Congress, Asheville, North Carolina, July, 1916. Chapel Hill, North Carolina Forestry Association, 1917. 6 p. [12980

Southern fur animal and poultry digest see **American fur** animal and poultry digest

Southern furniture journal, v. 1-63, 1901-June, 1932. High Point, 1901-1932. NcU has v. [17] 18-21, 33-34, 43-63. Discontinued following June, 1932. Title varies, 1931-32: Furniture merchandising [12981

[**Southern Furniture Market Association**] Furniture center of the South, Southern Furniture Exposition Building, High Point, North Carolina. High Point, 1944. [6] p. [12982

Southern Furniture Market Association. What's new at the southern market. [Charlotte, Queen City Printing Co., 1928?] 16 p. [12983

Southern furniture market news see **Furniture South**

Southern furniture record see **Furniture South**

Southern garden see **Southern life,** home and garden magazine

Southern garment manufacturer, v. 1- August, 1941- Charlotte, Textile Cutters Publishing Co., 1941- NcU has v. 1. Published in Atlanta, v. 1, no. 9-¦ [12984

Southern good roads, v. 1- January, 1910- Lexington, Southern Good Roads Publishing Co., 1910- NcU has v. 1-17 [18] 19-21 [22] [12985

Southern historical monthly, v. 1, no. 1-2, January-February, 1876. Raleigh, S. D. Pool, 1876. Superseded Our living and our dead. Discontinued following v. 1, no. 2, February, 1876. [12986

Southern Historical Society. Southern Historical Society papers, v. 1-38, 1878-1910, new ser., no. 1- 1914- Richmond, Va. [1876]- NcU has v. 1-50 [12987

—— ——An author and subject index to the Southern Historical Society papers, v. 1-38, comp. by Mrs. Kate Pleasants Minor. Richmond, D. Bottom, 1913. (Virginia State Library, Richmond. Bulletin, v. 6, no. 3-4) p. [47]-139 [12988

Southern History Association. Constitution, officers, list of members, September, 1904. Washington, 1904. 13 p. [12989

——Publications, v. 1-11, January, 1897-November, 1907. Washington, 1897-1907. NcU has v. 1-11. [12990

Southern home and garden see **Southern life,** home and garden magazine

Southern home journal, v. 1- 1904?- Winston-Salem, Southern Publishing Co., 1904?- NcU has v. [2] [12991

Southern homeseeker and investor's guide, v. 1-10, January, 1909-June, 1918. Roanoke, Va., Norfolk and Western Railroad, 1909-1918. NcU has v. [1-3] 4-9 [10] Discontinued following v. 10, no. 3 [12992

Southern Humanities Conference. The industrial South challenges the humanities; papers presented at the ninth annual meeting of the Southern Humanities Conference, by Morris B. Abram and others. Chapel Hill, Orange Printshop, 1956. (Southern Humanities Conference. Bulletin, no. 6) 28 p. [12993

Southern illustrated age, v. 1- August 14, 1875- Raleigh, R. T. Fulghum, 1875- NcU has v. [1] [12994

Southern index, v. 1- March, 1850- Ashborough, B. Craven, 1850- NcU has v. [1] [12995

Southern Indian studies, v. 1- April, 1949- Chapel Hill, Archeological Society of North Carolina and Research Laboratories of Anthropology of the University, 1949- NcU has v. 1-6 [12996

Southern Industrial Institute, Charlotte, N. C. Catalog, 19 - Charlotte, 19 - NcU has 1922/23 [12997

Southern Interstate Immigration Convention, Asheville, N. C. Proceedings . . . December 17, 18, 19, 1890, and of the Southern Interstate Immigration Executive Committee, convened in Asheville, N. C., December 18 and 19, 1890. [Asheville?] n.d. 56 p. [12998

Southern jeweler, v. 1- 1926- Greensboro, 1926- NcU has v. [1] [12999

Southern journal of health, v. 1- March, 1885- Asheville, H. P. Gatchell, 1885- NcU has v. [1] [13000

Southern Land and Development Company, Charlotte, N. C. Creighton Heights. [Charlotte, Observer, 1911] [20] p. [13001

[**Southern Land Company, New York?**] The North Carolina Hyde Park settlement. [New York, 1870?] 32 p. [13002

Southern life, v. 1-3, April, 1938-1941? Raleigh, J. B. Warren, 1938-1941? NcU has v. [1] Title varies: Southern home and garden [13003

Southern Life and Trust Company, Greensboro, N. C. Statement, 1903?- Greensboro, 1903?- NcU has 1921 [13004

Southern life, home and garden magazine, v. 1-3?, April, 1938-1941? Raleigh, Southern Home and Garden Publishing Co., 1938-1941? NcU has v. [1-3] [13004a

Southern medical journal, v. 1- January, 1899- LaGrange, Southern Medical Publishing Co., 1899- NcU has v. [1, 7] [13005

Southern medicine and surgery, v. 1-104, 1892-1953. Charlotte, Charlotte Medical Journal Co., 1892-1953. NcU has v. 1-7 [8-32] 58 [59-80] 84-115. Absorbed Carolina medical journal, 1908, and continued its numbering, v. 58- Title varies, 1892-January, 1921: Charlotte medical journal; February-December, 1953: Southern general practitioner of medicine and surgery. Consolidated with American journal of clinical medicine to continue as Clinical medicine, following December, 1953, published at Wilmette, Illinois. [13006

Southern Methodist handbook, 1906- Raleigh, Commercial Printing Co., 1906- NcU has 1906-1912, 1914, 1918 [13007

The Southern Methodist pulpit, v. 1- January, 1848- Greensborough, Swaim & Sherwood, 1848- NcU has v. [1-3] 4 [5] [13008

Southern municipal news see **Southern city**

Southern National Highway Association. Constitution approved by convention of Southern and Western States, held at Asheville, North Carolina, February 12, 1913. [Asheville? 1913] 15 p. [13009

Southern Normal, Lexington, N. C. Catalogue, 1884/85- Lexington, 1885- NcU has 1884/85, 1885/86 [13010

The southern packet; a monthly miscellany of southern books and ideas, v. 1-5, June, 1945-December, 1949. Asheville [Stephens Press] 1945-1949. NcU has v. 1-5 [13011

The southern packet, Asheville, N. C. The Southern packet booklist; a reprint of 215 titles reviewed or listed from June, 1945, through December, 1946. Asheville [1947] 11 p. [13012

The southern philosopher, v. 1- January, 1952- Chapel Hill, L. O. Katsoff, 1952- NcU has v. 1-2 [3, 5] [13013

Southern Pines, N. C. Chamber of Commerce. An invitation to the Air Force Academy to establish in Moore County, North Carolina. [Southern Pines, 1950] [10] p. [13014

Southern Pines, N. C. Piney Woods Inn. Piney Woods messenger, Southern Pines, N. C. Southern Pines, n.d. 8 p. [13015

Southern Pines, North Carolina, "capitol of sunshine land". No place [Seaboard Air Line Railway] n.d. 16 p. [13016

Southern Pines, North Carolina, superb climate, fine hotels, fine golf courses. [Southern Pines, 1916] 32 p. [13017

Southern Pines, North Carolina, "the land of sunshine". No place, no publisher [1922?] 24 p. [13018

Southern Pines Sanitorium, Southern Pines, N. C. Southern Pines Sanitorium . . . a private institution for the treatment of tuberculosis. [Charlotte, Queen City Printing Co., 1913?] 12 p. [13019

Southern Pines, the nation's winter home and playground. [Charlotte, Queen City Printing Co.] n.d. [13] p. [13020

Southern Policy Conference. 1st, Atlanta, 1935. Southern policy. [New Orleans, 1935] 27 p. [13021

Southern Policy Conference, 2d, Chattanooga, 1936. Second Southern Policy Conference report. Chapel Hill, University of North Carolina Press, 1936. (Southern policy papers, no. 8) 23 p. [13022

Southern policy papers, no. 1- 1936- Chapel Hill, University of North Carolina Press, 1936- NcU has no. 1-10 [13023

[Southern Power Company, Charlotte, N. C.] Power and the new South. [Charlotte, Queen City Printing Co.] n.d. [16] p. [13024

Southern Presbyterian College, Charlotte, N. C., see Queen's College, Charlotte, N. C.

Southern Presbyterian College and Conservatory of Music, Red Springs, N. C., see Flora Macdonald College, Red Springs, N. C.

Southern Presbyterian journal, v. 1- May, 1942- Weaverville, Southern Presbyterian Journal Co., 1942- NcU has v. 1-15 [13025

Southern public utilities magazine see **Duke power** magazine

Southern pulpit, v. 1- March, 1840- Fayetteville, 1840- NcU has v. [1] [13026

Southern Railway. Andrews Fountain, Round Knob, N. C. [Washington, 1912] 3 p. [13027

——Asheville—its wonderful tourist hotels and golf courses. [Washington] n.d. 24 p. [13028

——[Asheville, the ideal autumn and winter resort city] [Washington] n.d. 16 p.[13029

——Autumn and winter in the Land of the Sky. [Washington] n.d. 16 p. [13030

——Boys' camps and girls' camps in the mountains. [Washington] n.d. 13 p.[13031

——Camping on Mount Mitchell. [New York, Redfield-Kendrick-Odell Co.] for Southern Railway, 1916. 32 p. [13032

——Carolina special through the "Land of the Sky". [New York, Redfield-Kendrick-Odell Co., pr.] n.d. Folder. [13033

——Community life in Western North Carolina, the Land of the Sky. [Milwaukee, Wright and Joys, pr., for Southern Railway, 1914?] 40 p. [13034

——Community life in Western North Carolina. [Washington, c.1913] 39 p.[13035
——The country of the Southeast. [Baltimore, Summers, pr., for the Southern Railway] n.d. 32 p. [13036
——Famous winter resort points. [Washington, 1914?] 14 p. [13037
——First consolidated mortgage deed, Southern Railway Company to Central Trust Company of New York, trustee, dated October 2d, 1894. New York, C. G. Burgoyne [1894?] 97 p. [13038
——The floods of July, 1916; how the Southern Railway organization met an emergency. [Washington] 1917. 131 p. [13039
——Fruit growing in the South. [Washington] n.d. 16 p. [13040
——Gold fields along the Southern Railway. Washington, 1897. 30 p. [13041
——Golf in wonderland, Asheville—Biltmore Forest, Western North Carolina. [Washington] n.d. 13 p. [13042
——"I will lift up my eyes to the mountains, from whence cometh my strength." [Chicago, Poole Brothers for Southern Railway, 1898] 34 p. [13043
——Industrial and shippers' directory of the Southern Railway. Washington, 1914. 479 p. [13044
——Iron, coal, gold, marble, clay, bauxite, corundum, and other deposits. Washington, 1899. 27 p. [13045
——Lake Lure and how to get there. [Washington] n.d. 1 p. [13046
——Land of the Sky. [Washington, 1917] Folder. [13047
——The Land of the Sky; a picturesque country on the Southern Railway. [New York, Frank Presbrey Co.] 1905. [32] p. [13048
—— ——1907. [13049
——Land of the Sky, Asheville, Hendersonville, Waynesville, North Carolina. [Washington] n.d. [28] p. [13050
——Land of the Sky, glorious mountains of Western North Carolina. [Washington, 1914] 30 p. [13051
——The Land of the Sky in the mountains of Western North Carolina. Washington [1921] 2 p. [13052
——The Land of the Sky is a beautiful country. [Washington] 1918. 34 p. [13053
——The Land of the Sky, picturesque country, Southern Railway. [Washington] 1911. 26 p. [13054
——Land of the Sky, Southern Appalachian Mountains, in story and picture. [Washington, 1926] [46] p. [13055
——[Land of the Sky, Southern Railway] [Washington, 1912] 10 p. [13056
——Land of the Sky, Southern Railway, premier carrier of the South. [Washington, c.1913] 11 p. [13057
——Land of the Sky, Western North Carolina. [Washington] n.d. 12 p. [13058
——The Land of the Sky, Western North Carolina. [New York, American Bank Note Co., for Southern Railway c.1914] [36] p. [13059
——The Land of the Sky, Western North Carolina mountains. [Washington, 1922] 39 p. [13060
[Southern Railway] No "bad faith" say railroad presidents; history of negotiations with legislative commission. [Washington?] 1913. 16 p. [13061
Southern Railway [North Carolina] [Washington, 1911?] 35 p. [13062
——Opportunities along the Southern Railway. [Washington, 1899] [16] p. [13063
——Report, 1st- 1894/95- Washington, 1895- NcU has 1894/95-1916/17, 1917-1954 [13064
——Rich country of the South. [Washington] n.d. 32 p. [13065
——[Rules to govern the railroads operated by the Southern Railway Company] [Washington, 1899] 202 p. [13066
——"Samaritan of the South" is the Southern Railway. [Washington, 1898] 38 p. [13067
——Shooting and fishing in the South. New York, Frank Presbrey Co., c.1897] 63 p. [13068
——The southern field, v. 1- 1895?- Washington, 1895?- NcU has v. [2, 3, 6, 12-22] [13069
——Southern Railway Company: Index to existing contracts in volumes I-X, compiled by George R. Anderson. Washington, 1915. 118 p. [13070
——Southern Railway system, 1911-1920, a record of growth. [Washington, 1922] 13 p. [13071
——The Southern serves and sells the South. [Washington, 1945] [48] p. [13072

——Station directory no. 18 - [Washington?] 18 - NcU has February 15, 1899, no. 4 and supplement; July 1, 1912, no. 5   [13073

——Summer homes and resorts. Chicago, Poole Brothers, pr., 1896. 29 p. [13074

—— ———[1899] 38 p.   [13075

——Summer in the Land of the Sky. [Chicago, Poole Brothers, pr., 1912] 31 p.[13076

—— ———1913.   [13077

—— ———[1914] 35 p.   [13078

——Summer resorts, hotels and boarding houses . . . golf clubs, boys' camps and girls' camps in the mountains. [Washington] 1922. Folder.   [13079

——Summer service to Asheville. [Washington] n.d. 3 p.   [13080

——Summer vacations, Southern Appalachian Mountains, Land of the Sky. [New York, Redfield-Kendrick-Odell Co., Inc., pr., 1925] 30 p.   [13081

—— ———[1926?] 34 p.   [13082

——The sunny South . . . Some interesting drawings by E. H. Suydam. Washington, 1924. Unpaged. Four drawings of Asheville and vicinity.   [13083

——Textile directory, January, 1927, Southern Railway system. [Washington, 1927] 20 p.   [13084

——Tryon, North Carolina, in the famous "thermal belt" of the Western North Carolina mountains. [Washington, 1927] 3 p.   [13085

——Virginia, North Carolina, South Carolina, Georgia, Alabama, Mississippi, East Tennessee, Kentucky. Washington [1897?] 13 p.   [13086

——Western North Carolina section at a glance. Washington c.1913. 64 p. [13087

——Where to go this winter. [Washington, 1916] 68 p.   [13088

——Winter homes in the South, 1911-12. Washington [1911] 56 p.   [13089

—— ———1912-13. [1912] 56 p.   [13090

—— ———1913-14. [1913] 62 p.   [13091

—— ———1914-15. [1914] 19 p.   [13092

Southern Regional Education Board. The South's regional education program, a progress report. [Atlanta, 1951] 15 p.   [13093

The Southern review, v. 1, January-October, 1920. [Asheville, Southern Review Publishing Co., 1920] NcU has v. 1. Not issued February, 1920   [13094

A Southern sampler; an anthology of prose and poetry by writers of the South [1st-New York, Harbinger House] c.1941- NcU has 1st-2d ser.   [13095

Southern sanitarium, v. 1- 1896- Raleigh, L. A. Scruggs, 1896- NcU has v. [1, 3, 4]   [13096

Southern slavery considered on general principles; or, A grapple with abstractionists, by a North Carolinian. New York, D. Murphy's Son, pr., 1861. 24 p.   [13097

Southern social register, 1st- 1950/51- [Williamsburg, Va., Southern Social Register Foundation] 19 - NcU has 1952/53 (2d)   [13098

Southern Summer School for Women Workers in Industry, Little Switzerland, N. C. The 1935 scrap book. Little Switzerland, 1935. 45, 5 p.   [13099

——Report of the director, 19 - 19 - NcU has 1937 (11th)   [13100

Southern Synod standard, v. 1- 18 - Salisbury, Southern Synod, Evangelical and Reformed Church, 18 - NcU has v. [47-62]   [13101

Southern textile bulletin see Textile bulletin

Southern tobacco journal, v. 1- 1887- Winston-Salem, 1887- NcU has v. [17] [26] 44-71 (v. 44, 46-50 repeated in numbering)   [13102

Southern tourist and diversion, v. 1- December, 1921- Asheville, Grady Hunt, 1921- NcU has v. 1-2 [3-10, 13]   [13103

Southern Vineyard Company, Philadelphia, Pa. Eastern North Carolina, the land of opportunity, the home of the scuppernong grape. Philadelphia [1906?] 30 p.   [13104

Southern watchman, v. 1- August, 1873- Ringwood, Moore Brothers, 1873- NcU has v. [1]   [13105

Southern wings, v. 1- April, 1947- High Point, Atlantic Publications, 1947- NcU has v. [1]   [13106

Southland, v. 1-2, October, 1897-August, 1898. Greenville, Henry T. King, 1897-1898. NcU has v. 1, no. 1-3, v. 2, no. 1-8, 10   [13107

Southland, v. 1- December, 1898- Asheville, A. H. McQuilkin, 1898- NcU has v. [1-2] and 2d ser. v. [1] Title varies, 1898-1900: Southern pictures and pencillings [13108

Southport, N. C. Board of Aldermen. Ordinances of the city of Southport, North Carolina. [Raleigh, Edwards & Broughton Co.] 1916. 23 p. [13109

Southport, N. C. Chamber of Commerce. Before the State Ship and Water Transportation Commission: Brief on behalf of a state owned and operated port terminal at the mouth of the Cape Fear River, or Southport. Raleigh, Commercial Printing Co. [1923] 98 p. [13110

——Compulsory pilotage; resolutions and papers . . . showing why the present laws should not be changed. No place, no publisher, n.d. 5 p. [13111

Southport-Chicago syndicate. No place, no publisher [1895?] Various paging. [13112

Southwick, Albert Plympton. Bijou: the foundling of Nag's Head. New York, American News Co., 1889. 186 p. [13113

Souvenir calendar, New Berne, N. C. No place [J. L. Hill Printing Co.] 1903. 18 plates [13114

Souvenir calendar, ye old Bath Town, 1705-1905. No place, L. T. Rodman, c.1904. [19] p. [13115

Souvenir of Asheville, N. C. Asheville, J. N. Morgan and Co., n.d. 10 plates [13116

Souvenir of Asheville, N. C., and North Carolina "in the Land of the Sky". Asheville, Brown Book Co., n.d. 22 plates [13117

——Asheville, Southern Post Card Co., n.d. 16 plates [13118

Souvenir of Durham, North Carolina. [Durham, Seeman Printery, 1902?] 4 p. [13119

Souvenir of Greensboro, N. C., photogravures. Brooklyn, Albertype Co., c.1910. 12 plates [13120

A souvenir of Prof. J. R. Blake and his friends, compiled by one of them. No place, no publisher, n.d. 166 p. [13121

Spalding, Arthur Whitefield. The hills o' Ca'liny. Takoma Park, Washington, D. C., Review and Herald Publishing Association [c.1921] 192 p. [13122

——Men of the mountains. Nashville, Tenn., Southern Publishing Association [c.1915] 320 p. [13123

Spanish explorers in the southern United States, 1528-1543: The narrative of Alvar Nuñez Cabeça deVaca, ed. by Frederick W. Hodge . . . The narrative of the expedition of Hernando de Soto by the gentleman of Elvas, ed. by Theodore H. Lewis. New York, C. Scribner's Sons, 1907. (Original narratives of early American history) 411 p. [13124

Spann, Meno. First interlinear German reader. Chapel Hill, University of North Carolina Press, 1937. 75 p. [13125

——Second interlinear German reader. Chapel Hill, University of North Carolina Press, 1938. 120 p. [13126

Sparks, Elizabeth Hedgecock. North Carolina and Old Salem cookery. Kernersville, 1955. 226 p. [13127

Sparrow, Mrs. L. W. A history of Mt. Carmel Church, RFD no. 3, Chapel Hill, North Carolina, sesquicentennial year, 1803-1953. [Chapel Hill, 1953] 24 p. [13128

Sparrow, Patrick Jones. The duty of the educated young men of this country, an address delivered before the Eumenean and Philanthropic societies of Davidson College, N. C., July 31st, 1839. Raleigh, Turner & Hughes, 1839. 32 p. [13129

——The inaugural address, pronounced at his inauguration as Professor of Languages in Davidson College, N. C., August 2, 1838. Philadelphia, William S. Martien, 1838. 24 p. [13130

Spartanburg and Asheville Railroad. The charters of the S. & A. R. R. and G. & F. B. R. R. companies, together with the articles of consolidation of the two companies. Spartanburg, S. C., Model Job and Book Printing Office, 1876. 31 p. [13131

——Engineer's report of the survey and location of the Spartanburg and Asheville Railroad, 1875. Hendersonville, Advertiser, pr., [1875?] 7 p. [13132

Spearman, Walter. Dead man's bluff, a three-act play by Walter Spearman and Joe Abrams. Charlotte, Herald Press, Inc., 1937. 48 p. [13133

——Death of the swan, a romantic tragedy. Charlotte, Herald Press, Inc., c.1937. 16 p. [13134

——Transient.   Charlotte, Herald Press, Inc., c.1937.   20 p.   [13135

Spears, John Wesley.   The origin of law (crowned with the Mildred Williams Buchan prize)   Chapel Hill, University of North Carolina, 1928.   (University of North Carolina.   Department of Philosophy)   11 p.   [13136

Spears, Marshall Turner.   The meaning of law.   Chapel Hill, University of North Carolina, Philosophy Department, 1914.   (Worth prize thesis, 1914)   12 p. [13137

Speas, Jan Cox.   Bride of the MacHugh, a novel.   Indianapolis, Bobbs-Merrill Co. [1954]   315 p.   [13138

——My Lord Monleigh.   Indianapolis, Bobbs-Merrill Co. [1956]   309 p.   [13139

Speas, Mamie L.   A trilogy of war poems.   Raleigh [1947?]   [6] p.   [13140

Speck, Frank Gouldsmith.   Cherokee dance and drama, by Frank G. Speck and Leonard Broom in collaboration with Will West Long.   Berkeley, University of California Press, 1951.   106 p.   [13141

[**Speculation Land Co.**]   For sale: the quantity of 389,565 acres of farm lands.   No place [1800?]   [1] p.   NcU has photostat (negative)   [13142

——North Carolina.   The following minutes concerning the state of North-Carolina will tend to shew the situation and prospects of that state.   No place [1800?] [1] p.   NcU has photostat (negative)   [13143

Speed, John.   An epitome of Mr. John Speed's Theatre of the empire of Great Britain and of his Prospect of the most famous parts of the world.   In this new edition are added the Description of . . . New England, New York, Carolina, Florida, Virginia, Maryland.   London, Thomas Basset, 1676.   276 p.   [13144

Speed, John Gilmer.   Gilmers in America, with a genealogical record compiled by Louisa H. A. Minor.   New York, privately printed, 1897.   200 p.   [13145

Speed, Thomas.   The Wilderness road, a description of the routes of travel by which the pioneers and early settlers first came to Kentucky.   Louisville, Ky., J. P. Morton & Co., 1886.   (Filson Club publications, no. 2)   75 p.   [13146

Spellman, Cecil Lloyd.   Rough steps on my stairway; the life history of a Negro educator.   New York, Exposition Press [1953]   273 p.   [13147

Spence, Hersey Everett.   A guide to the study of the English Bible.   Durham, Trinity College Press, 1922.   177 p.   [13148

——Holidays and holy days, plays, pageants and programs for many occasions.   Greensboro, Piedmont Press, 1946.   203 p.   [13149

——"I remember"; recollections and reminiscences of Alma Mater.   Durham, Seeman Printery, 1954.   278 p.   [13150

——Old Testament dramas.   Durham, Duke University Press, 1936.   142 p. [13151

——Reveries in rhyme.   Durham, Durham Book and Stationery Co., 1913. 120 p.   [13152

——Ruth; a dramatization of Biblical history.   Nashville, Tenn., Cokesbury Press [c.1924]   67 p.   [13153

Spence, Thomas Hugh.   Catalogues of Presbyterian and Reformed institutions: I. As historical sources.   II. In the Historical Foundation.   Montreat, Historical Foundation, 1952.   39 p.   [13154

——North State refrain.   Montreat, 1941.   23 p.   [13154a

——The Presbyterian congregation on Rocky River.   Concord, Rocky River Presbyterian Church, 1954.   238 p.   [13155

Spencer, Cornelia (Phillips)   Circular respectfully addressed to the ladies of North Carolina.   [Chapel Hill? 1876?]   2 p.   [13156

——First steps in North Carolina history.   Rev· ed.   New York, American Book Company [c.1888]   272 p.   [13157

—— ——Raleigh, A. Williams & Co., 1889.   (Alfred Williams & Co.'s North Carolina historical series, no. 1)   272 p.   [13158

—— ——1890.   [13159

—— ——1892.   [13160

——The last ninety days of the war in North Carolina.   New York, Watchman Publishing Co., 1866.   287 p.   [13161

[**Spencer, Cornelia (Phillips)**]   Memorial sketch of Mrs. Richard H. Lewis.   [Chapel Hill?] Privately printed [1886?]   37 p.   [13162

——Obituary.   Chapel Hill, privately printed [1874?]   [2] p.   The subject is Lucy M. Battle.   [13163

Spencer, Cornelia (Phillips)   Selected papers; edited with an introduction by Louis R. Wilson.   Chapel Hill, University of North Carolina Press [1953]   753 p. [13164
——The song of the old alumnus, U. N. C.   [Burlington? James Lee Love? 1946] [2] p.   [13165
——University centennial song.   [Chapel Hill? 1895?]   [1] p.   [13166
[Spencer, Cornelia (Phillips)]   The University of N. C. [by] C. P. S.   (Air "God save the Queen)   [Chapel Hill?] n.d.   [1] p.   [13167
——University of North Carolina, Thursday, June 6th, 1867: Hymn.   [Chapel Hill? 1867]   [1] p.   [13168
Spencer, J. E.   Tales told in the hills.   [Rockingham? The Author?] 1939.   40 p. [13169
Spencer, Mary Kerr.   Dreams at twilight.   No place, no publisher, n.d.   8 p. [13170
Spencer, Samuel R.   Booker T. Washington and the Negro's place in American life.   Boston, Little, Brown [1955]   212 p.   [13171
Spencer, William Oliver.   A plea for prompt and thorough action in gunshot and other wounds of the abdomen, with reports of cases; address delivered before the the Medical Society of North Carolina, May 23-25, 1905.   Raleigh, Edwards & Broughton Co., 1905.   11 p.   [13172
Spencer, N. C.   Board of School Trustees.   Spencer Public City School, 19 - Spencer, 19 -   NcU has 1917/18   [13173
Spengler, Joseph John.   France faces depopulation.   Durham, Duke University Press, 1938.   313 p.   [13174
——French predecessors of Malthus; a study in eighteenth-century wage and population theory.   Durham, Duke University Press, 1942.   398 p.   [13175
Sphangos, Mary Tom, joint author,   see Selden, Samuel
Spilman, Bernard Washington.   Baptists in Sunday School history.   Nashville, Tenn., Sunday School Board of the Southern Baptist Convention, c.1907.   21 p.   [13176
——John Alexander Oates; a personal tribute.   No place, no publisher [1936?] 17 p.   [13177
——The Mills Home; a history of the Baptist Orphanage movement in North Carolina.   Thomasville, Mills Home [1932]   238 p.   [13178
——The new convention normal manual for Sunday School workers by B. W. Spilman, L. P. Leavell, P. E. Burroughs, Sunday School Board, Southern Baptist Convention, Nashville, Tenn.; translated and adapted by Pinston Hsu.   Canton, China, China Baptist Publication Society, 1923.   [128] p.   In Chinese with Chinese and English titles.   [13179
——Normal studies for Sunday School workers: 1. The Sunday School.   Nashville, Tenn., Baptist Sunday School Board, 1902.   89 p.   [13180
——One hundred years of Baptist Sunday School work in North Carolina, 1830-1930.   No place, no publisher [1930]   13 p.   [13181
——Ridgecrest, past, present, future, with foreword by C. Sylvester Green.   Ridgecrest, Southern Baptist Assembly, 1928.   22 p.   [13182
——Sixty years old today, January 22, 1931.   No place, The Author [1931] [13] p.   [13183
——A study in religious pedagogy based on Our Lord's interview with the woman of Samaria.   New York, Fleming H. Revell Co. [c.1920]   88 p.   [13184
Spinner, the annual of the Gastonia High School, 19 -   Gastonia, 19 -   NcU has 1922   [13185
The spirit of the Great Smokies; a pageant commemorating the one-hundredth anniversary of the great removal, 1835-1935, October 2d and 3d, 1935, Cherokee Indian Reservation.   Cherokee, 1935.   16 p.   [13186
Spirit of the press in regard to Judge Graham's candidacy for western membership of Corporation Commission.   No place, no publisher, n.d.   [2] p.   [13187
The spirit of the Roanoke; a pageant of Halifax County history, designed and written in collaboration by Halifax County teachers under the direction of A. E. Akers . . . and Annie M. Cherry.   Roanoke Rapids, Herald Publishing Co., 1921.   78 p. [13188
Spirittine Chemical Co., Wilmington, N. C.   Spirittine Chemical Company, established 1878, incorporated 1900, oldest operating pine wood distillers in United States.   Wilmington, National Press, pr. [1924?]   [12] p.   [13189
Spivey, A. D.   Historical sketch, Ellerbe, N. C., town, schools, springs.   [Rockingham, Post-Dispatch, 1936]   [10] p.   [13190

Spot-Light, 19 - [Barium Springs, High School of Presbyterian Orphan Home, 19 - NcU has 1924-1927, 1938, 1942, 1944, 1949   [13191

Sprague, Frederick H. Sixth congressional district: Fellow citizens. Salisbury, July 23, 1870. [1] p.   [13192

Spraker, Ella Hazel (Atterbury) The Boone family; a genealogical history of the descendants of George and Mary Boone who came to America in 1717; containing many unpublished bits of early Kentucky history, also a biographical sketch of Daniel Boone, the pioneer, by one of his descendants. Rutland, Vt., Tuttle Co., 1922. 691 p.   [13193

Spratt, James B. A song and a hope for every one. Charlotte [Pound & Moore Co.] 1937. 83 numb. leaves.   [13194

Springfield Memorial Association. Annual meeting, 19 - [High Point? 19 - NcU has 1942   [13195

Sprinkle, Rebecca K. A house for Leander. New York, Abingdon-Cokesbury Press [1953] 47 p.   [13196

——Parakeet Peter. Chicago, Rand McNally Co., c.1954. unpaged.   [13197

Spruce Pine, N. C. Chamber of Commerce. Spruce Pine, the trading center of a steadily growing vacation, farming, and industrial section in the mountains of North Carolina. Spruce Pine [1947?] [6] p.   [13198

Spruill, Corydon Perry. Graduate credit for workshop courses. [New Orleans, Tulane University, 1941?] 14 p.   [13199

Spruill, Frank Shepherd. Presentation of portrait of Honorable Asa Biggs to United States District Court; address by F. S. Spruill . . . acceptance by Judge H. G. Connor, at Raleigh, N. C., January 18, 1915. Raleigh, E. M. Uzzell & Co., pr., 1915. 24 p.   [13200

Spruill, Julia (Cherry) Women's life and work in the southern colonies. Chapel Hill, University of North Carolina Press, 1938. 426 p.   [13201

Sprunt, James. Chronicles of the Cape Fear River; being some account of historic events on the Cape Fear River. Raleigh, Edwards & Broughton Printing Co., 1914. 594 p.   [13202

——Chronicles of the Cape Fear River, 1660-1916. 2d ed. Raleigh, Edwards & Broughton Printing Co., 1916. 732 p.   [13203

——A colonial apparition, a story of the Cape Fear. Wilmington, Le Gwin Brothers, 1898. 28 p.   [13204

—— ——Wilmington, Harper's Steamboat Line, 1909. 16 p.   [13205

——Derelicts; an account of ships lost at sea in general commercial traffic and a brief history of blockade runners stranded along the North Carolina coast, 1861-1865. Wilmington, 1920. 304 p.   [13206

[**Sprunt, James**] Information and statistics respecting Wilmington, North Carolina, being a report of the President of the Produce Exchange. Wilmington, Jackson & Bell, pr., 1883. 252 p.   [13207

——Tales and traditions of the lower Cape Fear, 1661-1896. Wilmington, LeGwin Brothers, 1896. 215 p.   [13208

Spurgeon, Charles Haddon. Twenty-three sermons, selected from two thousand and sixty-one published discourses, by A. G. and J. M. McManaway. Richmond, Va., Everett Waddey, 1890. 396 p.   [13209

Squibb, Robert. Gardener's calendar for North-Carolina, South-Carolina, and Georgia, with amendments and additions. Charleston, S. C., Printed and sold by W. P. Young, 1813. 162 p.   [13210

——The gardener's calendar for the states of North-Carolina, South-Carolina, and Georgia, with appendix, containing a variety of particular and general information on husbandry and horticulture. Charleston, S. C., P. Hoff, 1827. 176 p. [13211

Staab, Hermann Henry, comp. Contemporary French readings in commerce, economics, history, and sociology, with the editorial assistance of Hugo Giduz. Chapel Hill, University of North Carolina, 1938. 84 p.   [13212

——Cours de français commercial par H. H. Staab. Chapel Hill, University of North Carolina, 1940. 65 p.   [13213

——French commercial correspondence, by H. H. Staab and Hugo Giduz. Ann Arbor, Mich., Edwards Brothers, Inc., 1935. 162 p.   [13214

Stack, Amos Morehead. Sketches of Monroe and Union County . . . by Stack & Beasley. Charlotte, News and Times, pr., 1902. 115 p. [13215

Stacy, Laura E. Home folks. Morganton, Savage Print Shop, 1952. 83 p. [13216

Stacy, Walter Parker. Memorial address delivered before the North Carolina Bar Association, Wrightsville Beach, N. C., July 1, 1926. Raleigh, Bynum Printing Co. [1926] 11 p. [13217

Stafford, William Gaston. Poems. Raleigh, Edwards, Broughton & Co., 1873. 98 p. [13218

Stage coach, 1900?- Raleigh, Students of Saint Mary's Junior College, 1900?- NcU has [1900-1942] 1955. Title varies, 1900?-1924: Muse [13219

Stagg, John W. The race problem in the South; an address delivered before the Unity Club of New Bedford, Mass., April 27, 1900. Charlotte, Presbyterian Publishing Co., 1900. [34] p. [13220

——A sermon preached in the Second Presbyterian Church, Charlotte, N. C., December 30, 1900. Charlotte, Presbyterian Publishing Co., 1901. 19 p. [13221

Stamey, Enoch Lafayette. The corridor of life, and other poems. Nashville, Tenn., Methodist Publishing House [c.1933] 126 p. [13222

——Family history of Enoch Lafayette Stamey. No place, no publisher, 1923. 8 p. [13223

——Re-echoes of faith. Nashville, Tenn., Publishing House, Methodist Episcopal Church, South, 1936. 128 p. [13224

Stanbury, Walter Albert. Preventing the next war; peace-makers in a war-making world; a sermon delivered in Central Methodist Church, Asheville, North Carolina, February 27, 1938. No place, no publisher [1938]? 20 p. [13225

——Victories of the cross. Nashville, Tenn., Cokesbury Press [c.1955] 192 p. [13226

Stancil, James C. Statement of fact, fourth congressional district, North Carolina, Delegates James C. Stancil and Willis G. Briggs to the National Republican Convention, Chicago, Ill., June 16, 1908. No place, no publisher [1908] 10 p. [13227

Standard Oil Company of New Jersey. Esso fishing and hunting guide to North Carolina. [Charlotte, c.1946] [34] p. [13228

——Know your own state: North Carolina. No place [c.1925] 44 p. [13229

Stanfield, S. A. Address delivered before the Adelphian Society of the Caldwell Institute, February 6th, 1850, on occasion of their fourteenth anniversary. Hillsborough, Dennis Heartt, pr., 1850. 16 p. [13230

[Stanford, Richard] [Circular to his constituents] March 2, 1813. Washington, 1813. [3] p. [13231

——[Letter to his constituents, June 24, 1808] Orange County, 1808. [1] p. [13232

Stanley McCormick School, Burnsville, N. C. Announcement, 19 - Burnsville, 19 - NcU has 1915/16. Continues as its Bulletin, 1923?- [13233

——Bulletin, v. 1- 1923?- Burnsville, 1923?- NcU has v. [1-2] [13234

Stanly, Edward. Letter from Hon. Edward Stanly, military governor of North Carolina, to Col. Henry A. Gilliam, refuting certain charges and insinuations made by Hon. George E. Badger, in behalf of the southern Confederacy. [New Bern? 1862] 10 p. [13235

——Letter from Mr. Stanly, of N. C., to Mr. Botts, of Virginia. Washington City, Sept. 23d, 1840. 7 p. [13236

——A military governor among abolitionists; a letter from Edward Stanly to Charles Sumner. New York, 1865. 48 p. [13237

Stanly, John, joint author, see Bryan, John Heritage

Stanly Baptist Association. Minutes, 1885?- 1885?- NcU has 1897 [1907-1924, 1950-1955] [13238

Stanly Co., N. C. Board of Education. Report of the public schools, 19 - [Albemarle?] 19 - NcU has 1914/15 [13239

Stanly Co., N. C. Health Department. Report, 193 - [Albemarle?] 193 - NcU has 1938/39 [13240

Stansbury, Charles Frederick. The Lake of the Great Dismal; with a preface by Don Marquis. New York, Albert & Charles Boni, 1925. 238 p. [13241

Stanton, Daniel. A journal of the life, travels, and gospel labours of a faithful minister of Jesus Christ, Daniel Stanton. Philadelphia, Printed and sold by Joseph Crukshank, 1772. 184 p. [13242

Stanton, Samuel Ward. Steam navigation on the Carolina sounds and the Chesapeake in 1892. Salem, Mass., Steamship Historical Society of America, 1947. (Its Reprint series, no. 4) 31 p. [13243

Starbuck, Victor Stanley. Come, let us adore Him . . . a play of the nativity. Chicago, Dramatic Publishing Co. [1932] 54 p. [13244

——Saul, king of Israel. Chapel Hill, University of North Carolina Press, 1938. 290 p. [13245

——Wind in the pines. New Haven, Yale University Press, 1923. 82 p. [13246

Starkey, Marion Lena. The Cherokee nation. New York, A. A. Knopf, 1946. 355 p. [13247

Starr, Emmet. History of the Cherokee Indians and their legends and folk lore. Oklahoma City, Okla., Warden Co., 1921. 680 p. [13248

The Stars and stripes in rebeldom; a series of papers written by federal prisoners (privates) in Richmond, Tuscaloosa, New Orleans, and Salisbury, N. C. Boston, T. O. H. P. Burnham, 1862. 137 p. [13249

The State, a weekly survey of North Carolina, v. 1- June 3, 1933- Raleigh, The Sharpe Publishing Co., 1933- NcU has v. 1-23. Title varies: The State, down home in North Carolina [13250

——State subject index, 1933 through 1952, compiled by the Staff of the Rowan Public Library, Salisbury, N. C. [Salisbury] n.d. 166 p. [13251

State agricultural journal, v. 1- July, 1875- Raleigh, State Grange, 1875- NcU has v. [1] [13252

State Company, Columbia, S. C. A bar of song and its author. Columbia, S. C. The State Co. [1914?] 8 p. [13253

State employees' news, v. 1- 1955- Raleigh, North Carolina State Employees' Association, 1955- NcU has v. [1-2] [13254

State Guard: turn on the lights, the testimony of two old soldiers who wore the gray when there was some danger in doing so, and who recognize the right of the state to prescribe any color and style of dress for her regular soldiery. Wilmington, Jackson & Bell, 1891. 14 p. [13255

Statesville, N. C. Board of Aldermen. Charters, laws, ordinances, and rules of the city of Statesville. Statesville, The Landmark, 1885. 80 p. [13256

——The code of the city of Statesville, North Carolina, 1947. Charlottesville, Michie City Publications Co., 1947. 349 p. [13257

Statesville, N. C. Board of Commissioners. Ordinances of the town of Statesville, adopted, March, 1879. Statesville, Statesville American, pr., 1879. 15 p. [13258

Statesville, N. C. Board of Education. Statesville Public Schools. [Statesville, 1904] 24 p. [13259

[Statesville, N. C. Chamber of Commerce] Agricultural and industrial survey; Iredell County . . . Alexander County . . . June 24, 1942. [Statesville] 1942. [21] p. [13260

Statesville, N. C. Chamber of Commerce. Facts and figures of Statesville, N. C., and Iredell County. [Statesville, 1928] 28 p. [13261

Statesville, N. C. Citizens. Memorial to the General Assembly of North Carolina, session 1852. [Raleigh? 1852?] 8 p. [13262

Statesville, N. C. First Presbyterian Church. History, year book and directory. Statesville, 1933. Unpaged. [13263

——Manual . . . November, 1927. [Statesville] 1927. 45 p. [13264

——175th anniversary . . . a brief history of the church. [Statesville, 1939] [16] p. [13265

Statesville Air Line Railway. Charters, financial, engineering and traffic reports, covering 62 miles of proposed railroad from Statesville, North Carolina, to Mt. Airy, North Carolina. Statesville, Brady, pr. [1912?] 30 p. [13266

Statesville Christian advocate, v. 1- 1886?- Statesville, James Wilson, 1886?- NcU has v. [1, 5] [13267

Statesville Female College, Statesville, N. C. Catalogue, 18 - Statesville, 18 - NcU has 1905/06, 1906/07, [1912/13-1915/16]   [13268

Statesville, the best town in North Carolina. [Statesville? 1926] 24 p.   [13269

Staton, Kate Elony (Baker) comp. Old southern songs of the period of the Confederacy, the Dixie trophy collection. New York, S. French, c.1926. 146 p. [13270

Stearns, Walter M. Haywood Hall. [Raleigh] Wake County Committee of the North Carolina Society of the Colonial Dames of America, c.1948. 12 p.   [13271

Stebbing, William. Sir Walter Ralegh, a biography. Oxford, Clarendon Press, 1891. 413 p.   [13272

Stedman, Andrew. Murder and mystery, history of the life and death of John W. Stephens, state senator of North Carolina, from Caswell County. [Greensboro, Printed at the Patriot Office, 1870] 40 p.   [13273

Stedman, Charles. The history of the origin, progress, and termination of the American war. London, Printed for the Author, and sold by J. Murray, 1794. 2 v.   [13274
—— ——Dublin, P. Wogan [etc.] 1794. 2 v.   [13275

Stedman, Charles Manly. Memorial address, delivered May 10th, 1890, at Wilmington, N. C.; A sketch of the life and character of General William MacRae, with an account of the Battle of Ream's Station. Wilmington, Wm. L. DeRosset, Jr., pr. [1890?] 27 p.   [13276

Stedman's Salem magazine, v. 1- January, 1858- Salem, Andrew J. Stedman, 1858- NcU has v. 1, no. 1 and 2d series v. 1, no. 1, published at Raleigh, May, 1858.   [13277

Steel, Samuel Augustus. The folded banner. No place, no publisher, n.d. 5 p. [13278

Steele, Christie, pseud. Where the world kneels, a novel. Culler, W. C. Phillips, pr., 1893. 118 p.   [13279

Steele, Max. Debby. New York, Harper & Bros. [1950] 304 p.   [13280
——Nichts gegen Debby! Roman. Hamburg, Marion von Schröder [c.1950] 326 p.   [13281

Steele, William O. The golden root. New York, Aladdin Books, 1951. 76 p. [13282
——John Sevier, pioneer boy. Indianapolis, Bobbs-Merrill Co. [1953] 192 p. [13283
——The story of Daniel Boone. New York, Grosset & Dunlap [1953] 175 p. [13284
——Wilderness journey. New York, Harcourt, Brace and Co. [1953] 209 p. [13285

Steffey, Sidney D. A brief history of St. John's Evangelical Lutheran Church of Cabarrus County, N. C. Concord, Times Steam Book and Job Presses, 1899. 69 p.   [13286

Stein, Harry B. Legacy; essays. New York, Exposition Press [1954] 64 p. [13287

Steger, Harry Peyton. O. Henry, who he is and how he works. [New York, Doubleday, Page & Co.] n.d. [6] p.   [13288

Stein, Sanford Ivan. One more Spring. [Chapel Hill, 1940] 87 p.   [13289

Steiner, Jesse Frederick. Community organization, a study of its theory and current practice. New York, Century Co., 1925. 395 p.   [13290
——Education for social work. Chicago, University of Chicago Press [1921] 99 p.   [13291
——The North Carolina chain gang; a study of county convict road work, by Jesse F. Steiner . . . and Roy M. Brown. Chapel Hill, University of North Carolina Press, 1927. 194 p.   [13292

[Stellings, E. G. and Co.] The city of Wilmington, North Carolina. [Wilmington, Wilmington Stamp and Printing Co.] n.d. 24 p.   [13293

Stem, Thad, Jr. The jackknife horse, poems. Raleigh, Wolf's Head Press, 1954. 59 p.   [13294

Stenhouse, James Alan. Exploring old Mecklenburg. [Charlotte, 1952] 50 p. [13295
——Journeys into history; to record the historical places in Mecklenburg and the lands which were once a part thereof. No place, 1951. 11, 10 p.   [13296

[Stephens, George Myers] Mountain Dance & Folk Festival. [Asheville, Asheville Chamber of Commerce, c.1945] [11] p.   [13297
—— ——[c.1955] [14] p.   [13298

Stephens, George Myers. The Smokies guide. Asheville, Stephens Press [c.1941] [64] p.   [13299

Stephens, George Myers, joint author, see Lunsford, Bascom Lamar

Stephenson, Gilbert Thomas. The business relation between God and man, a trusteeship. [Nashville, Tenn., Sunday School Board of the Southern Baptist Convention] 1921. 112 p. [13300

——English executor and trustee business through the eyes of an American trust man. New York, Harper & Brothers, 1930. 262 p. [13301

——Estates and trusts. New York, Appleton-Century-Crofts, Inc. [1949] 450 p. [13302

—— ——Rev. ed. New York, Appleton-Century Crofts, Inc. [1955] 450 p. [13303

——Guide-posts in preparing wills, by G. T. Stephenson and A. H. Eller. Winston-Salem, Barber Printing Co., 1919. 79 p. [13304

——The life story of a trust man; being that of Francis Henry Fries, president of the Wachovia Bank and Trust Company, Winston-Salem, North Carolina, since February 16, 1893. New York, F. S. Crofts & Co., 1930. 267 p. [13305

——Living trusts, including life insurance trusts. New York, F. S. Crofts & Co., 1926. 431 p. [13306

——The pastor beloved; an appreciation of Dr. Henry Alfred Brown, pastor of the First Baptist Church of Winston-Salem, N. C. Nashville, Tenn., Sunday School Board of the Southern Baptist Convention [c.1925] 126 p. [13307

——Trust business in common law countries. New York, Research Council, American Bankers Association [c.1940] 911 p. [13308

——What a life insurance man should know about trust business. New York, F. S. Crofts & Co., 1932. 199 p. [13309

——Wills. New York, F. S. Crofts & Co., 1928. 327 p. [13310

——Your family and your estate. [New York, Prentice-Hall, Inc., 1951] 64 p. [13311

Stephenson, Wendell Holmes. The political career of General James H. Lane. Topeka, Kansas State Printing Plant, 1930. (Publications of the Kansas State Historical Society, v. 3) 196 p. Thesis (Ph. D.) University of Michigan, 1928. [13312

——The South lives in history; southern historians and their legacy. Baton Rouge, Louisiana State University Press [1955] 163 p. [13313

Sterling, Richard. Our own first reader; for the use of schools and families, by Richard Sterling . . . and J. D. Campbell. Greensboro, Sterling, Campbell and Albright [1864] 96 p. [13314

——Our own fourth reader; for the use of schools and families. Greensboro, Sterling & Albright [c.1865] 319 p. [13315

——Our own primer; for the children [by Richard Sterling and J. D. Campbell] 3d ed. Greensboro, Sterling, Campbell & Albright, 1863. 32 p. [13316

——Our own second reader; for the use of schools and families, by R. Sterling . . . and J. D. Campbell. Greensboro, Sterling, Campbell and Albright [1862] 168 p. [13317

——Our own spelling book; for the use of schools and families, by Richard Sterling . . . and J. D. Campbell. Greensboro, Sterling, Campbell & Albright [c.1862] 128 p. [13318

—— ——2d ed. 1863. 112 p. [13319

—— ——3d ed. [c.1862] 112 p. [13320

——Our own third reader; for the use of schools and families, by Richard Sterling and J. D. Campbell. Greensboro, Sterling, Campbell & Albright, 1862. 208 p. [13321

—— ——[1862] 224 p. [13322

Sterling, Richard, comp. Sterling's southern orator, containing standard lectures in prose and poetry and recitation in schools and colleges. New-York, Owens and Agar, 1867. 544 p. [13323

Sterling, Richard. Sterling's southern [first?]-fifth reader; for the use of schools and families. New York, Owens and Agar, 1866-68. 5 v. NcU has 2d-5th. [13324

—— ——Macon, J. W. Burke & Co., 186?- NcU has 4th-5th [13325

Stern, William. Allgemeine Psychologie auf personalistischer Grundlage. Haag, M. Nijhoff, 1935- NcU has v. 1 [13326

——General psychology from the personalistic standpoint . . . translated by Howard Davis Spoerl. New York, Macmillan Co., 1938. 589 p. [13327

Sterne, Emma (Gelders) How Rabbit stole fire; a Cherokee legend, by Emily Broun [pseud.] New York, Aladdin Books [1954] unpaged. [13328

Sterner, Richard Mauritz Edvard. The Negro's share; a study of income, consumption, housing and public assistance. New York, Harper & Brothers [1943] 433 p. [13329

Stevens, Adeline T. (Chapman) joint author, see Noble, Marcus Cicero Stephens

Stevens, Benjamin Franklin, comp. and ed. The campaign in Virginia, 1781; an exact reprint of six rare pamphlets on the Clinton-Cornwallis controversy, with very numerous important unpublished manuscript notes, by Sir Henry Clinton. London, 1888. 2 v. [13330

Stevens, Frank Lincoln. Diseases of economic plants, by F. L. Stevens . . . and J. G. Hall. New York, Macmillan Co., 1910. 513 p. [13331
——A practical advanced arithmetic, by F. L. Stevens, Tait Butler, Mrs. F. L. Stevens. New York, Charles Scribner's Sons, 1911. 386 p. [13332
——A practical arithmetic, by F. L. Stevens . . . Tait Butler . . . Mrs. F. L. Stevens. New York, C. Scribner's Sons, 1909. 386 p. [13333

Stevens, Henry. Thomas Hariot, the mathematician, the philosopher and the scholar. London, privately printed, 1900. 213 p. [13334

[Stevens, John] ed. A new collection of voyages and travels . . . For the month of December, 1708. To be continu'd monthly. London, J. Knapton, 1708-[10] NcU has December, 1708, May, 1709, January, 1710 (defective) [13335
——A new collection of voyages and travels. London, Printed for J. Knapton, 1711. 2 v. NcU has v. 1 [13336

Stevens, Ross Oliver. Talk about wildlife, for hunters, fishermen and nature lovers. Raleigh, Bynum Printing Co. [1944] 229 p. [13337

Stevens, Thomas Wood. Official programme: The pageant of Charlotte and old Mecklenburg, Charlotte, N. C., May 18-22, 1925. [Charlotte, Queen City Printing Co. for the Charlotte Pageant Association, 1925] 14 p. [13338
——The pageant of Charlotte and old Mecklenburg, written for the sesquicentennial of the Mecklenburg Declaration of Independence, May 20, 1775. Charlotte, Charlotte Pageant Association [c.1925] 121 p. [13339

Stevenson, Augusta. Andy Jackson, boy soldier. Indianapolis, Bobbs-Merrill Co. [1942] 196 p. [13340
——Daniel Boone, boy hunter. Indianapolis, Bobbs-Merrill Co. [1943] 194 p. [13341
——Wilbur and Orville Wright, boys with wings. Indianapolis, Bobbs-Merrill Co. [1951] 192 p. [13342

Stevenson, George S. The educated farmer; an oration before the Euzelian and Philomathesian societies of Wake Forest College, North Carolina, delivered June 13, 1855. Raleigh, A. M. Gorman, pr., 1855. 16 p. [13343

Stevenson, Samuel Harris. History and genealogical record of the Stevenson family from 1748 to 1926, by Rev. S. H. Stevenson, Rev. J. A. Harris, and Hon. W. F. Stevenson. No place, no publisher, n.d. 238 p. [13344

Steward, Davenport. Sail the dark tide. Atlanta, Tupper & Love [1954] 310 p. [13345

Stewart, Alexander. The validity of infant baptism. Newbern, Printed by James Davis, 1758. 40 p. NcU has photograph of original in Harvard University Library. [13346

Stewart, Donald H. The ministry of understanding. [Chapel Hill? Privately printed] n.d. 16 p. [13347

Stewart, George W. The Babylonish garment; or, Innovation opposed and exposed, being an answer to Elder W. A. Chastain's book and Monitor article on the subject of humanly protracted meetings. [Raleigh, Edwards & Broughton Co., 1915] 70 p. [13348

Stewart, George W., comp. The Primitive pathway, its mileposts and sign-boards; or, Many historic truths and facts concerning the doctrine and order of the Church of God, as understood and contended for by the Primitive or Old School Baptists. No place, no publisher, n.d. 108 p. [13349

Stewart, George W. The two witnesses; or, The way of salvation as taught in the scriptures. Raleigh, Printed for the Author by Edwards & Broughton, 1905. 407 p. [13350
——Warning against evolution; reply to a leading lawyer and statesman of Alabama. Raleigh, Edwards & Broughton Printing Co., 1923. 32 p. [13351

Stewart, Henry. Macon County, North Carolina. Highlands, Blue Ridge Association Press, 1902. [30] p.   [13352

Stewart, Matilda H., comp. Markers placed by the North Carolina Daughters of the American Revolution, 1900-1940. [Raleigh, Edwards & Broughton, pr., 1940?] 73 p.   [13353

Stewart, Pamela Helen Hansford (Johnson) see Johnson, Pamela Hansford

Stick, David. Fabulous Dare; the story of Dare County, past and present. Kitty Hawk, Dare Press [1949] 71 p.   [13354

——Graveyard of the Atlantic; shipwrecks of the North Carolina coast. Chapel Hill, University of North Carolina Press [1952] 276 p.   [13355

——List of vessels probably lost on the North Carolina coast. Kill Devil Hills, The Author, 1952. 4 p. Supplement to his Graveyard of the Atlantic.   [13356

[Stickney, F. S.] comp. Biographic sketches of Fenner Bryan Satterthwaite; together with the obituary proceedings of the Washington bar, etc. Norfolk, Va., Virginian Steam Print, 1887. 85 p.   [13357

Stikeleather, Laura A. E. Verses. [Asheville? Privately printed] n.d. 12 p. [13358

Stillman, Albert Leeds. Drums beat in old Carolina. Chicago, John C. Winston Co. [c.1939] 244 p.   [13359

Stillwell, E. H. Notes on the history of Western North Carolina: Part 1. A handbook and syllabus with assignments and questions for class use. Cullowhee, Cullowhee State Normal School, 1927. 144 p.   [13360

Stinceon Institute and Commercial School, Orrum, N. C. Catalogue, 190 - Orrum, 190 - NcU has 1906/07   [13361

[Stinson, Daniel Green] The Gaston family. No place, no publisher, n.d. 12 p. [13362

Stith, William. The history of the first discovery and settlement of Virginia. Virginia, Printed: London, Reprinted for S. Birt, 1753. viii, 331 (i.e. 341) v, 34 p. 295-304 repeated.   [13363

Stockard, Henry Jerome. Fugitive lines. New York, G. P. Putnam's Sons, 1897. 93 p.   [13364

——On Hatteras bar. Raleigh, Art Publishing Co., n.d. [1] p.   [13365

——Poems; decorations by Mabel Pugh. Raleigh, Bynum Printing Co. [c.1939] 94 p.   [13366

——A study in southern poetry, for use in schools, colleges, and the library. New York, Neale Publishing Co., 1911. 346 p.   [13367

Stockard, Sallie Walker. The history of Alamance. Raleigh, Capital Printing Co., 1900. 166 p.   [13368

——The history of Guilford County, North Carolina. Knoxville, Tenn., Gaut-Ogden Co., pr., 1902. 197 p.   [13369

——Lily of the valleys. No place, no publisher [1901] 84 p.   [13370

Stockton, Frank Richard. Buccaneers and pirates of our coasts. New York, Macmillan Co., 1898. 325 p.   [13371

—— ——1924.   [13372

—— ——1954.   [13373

——Kate Bonnet; the romance of a pirate's daughter. New York, D. Appleton and Co., 1902. 420 p.   [13374

Stockwell, Roy, comp. John Graves (1703-1804) and his descendants. Kansas City, 1954. 246 p.   [13375

Stokes, J. Ernest. The relation of the general practitioner to gynecology; paper read before the State Medical Society at its fifty-fifth annual meeting, 1908. No place, no publisher [1908?] 12 p.   [13376

Stokes, Montfort. To the freemen of the counties of Rowan, Randolph and Cabarrus in the state of North Carolina. Salisbury, September 6, 1804. [1] p.   [13377

Stokes Co., N. C. Citizens. To the people of Stokes County. Stokes County, October 5, 1846. [1] p.   [13378

Stone, Charles Haywood. The Stones of Surry. Charlotte, Observer Printing House [1951] 272 p.   [13379

Stone, David Williamson. "An honest tale speeds best, being plainly told". [Raleigh, The Author, November 17, 1823] 3 p.   [13380

Stone, Harold Alfred. City manager government in Charlotte (North Carolina) by Harold A. Stone, Don K. Price [and] Kathryn H. Stone, for the Committee on Public Administration of the Social Science Research Council. Chicago, Public Administration Service, 1939. ([Public Administration Service, Chicago] Publication no. sp. 9) 53 p. [13381

Stone, Irving. The President's lady; a novel about Rachel and Andrew Jackson. Garden City, N. Y., Doubleday, 1951. 338 p. [13382

Stone, Walton Edgar. Walton Stone, a Bunyan, Boone, Crockett, a Robinson Crusoe. [New York, J. J. Little & Co., pr.] 1931. 345 p. [13383

Stone Mountain Baptist Association. Minutes, 1897?- 1897?- NcU has 1906, 1946-1955 [13384

Stoney, William Shannon. Historical sketch of Grace Church, Morganton, North Carolina. No place, no publisher, 1935. 50 p. [13385

Stoney Creek Presbyterian Church, Alamance County, N. C. Church year book, history and directory of Stoney Creek (1776) Shiloh (1913) Burlington Second (1913) Presbyterian churches, May 7, 1933. Burlington, 1933. [38] p. [13386

Stony Fork Baptist Association. Minutes, 18 - 18 - NcU has 1897, 1904 [13387

Storm, W. W. Wilmington—where the Cape Fear rolls to the sea. Wilmington [Wilmington Stamp and Printing Co. for the Author, 1933] 128 p. [13388

Story, Thomas. The life of Thomas Story, carefully abridged, in which the principal occurences and the most interesting remarks and observations are retained, [edited] by John Kendall. London, Printed and sold by James Phillips, 1786. 383 p. [13389

[**Stott, Juanita**] The wedding of Miss Senior Class and Mr. Life of Service; a class night play. Raleigh, The Author [c.1939] 16 p. [13390

Stoudemire, Sterling Aubrey. Cuentos de España y de América. Boston, for Reynal & Hitchcock by Houghton Mifflin Co. [1942] 237 p. [13391

Stoudemire, Sterling Aubrey, joint ed. see **Adams, Nicholson Barney, ed.**

Stoudemire, Sterling Aubrey, joint author, see **Leavitt, Sturgis Elleno**

Stout, Charles D., comp. Some old poems. Asheboro, The Author, 1895. 64 p. [13392

Stout, Herald Franklin. The Staudt-Stoudt-Stout family of Ohio and their ancestors at home and abroad. No place, no publisher [1934] 276, 79 p. [13393

Stout, L. H. Reminiscences of General Braxton Bragg. Hattiesburg, Miss., The Book Farm, 1942. (Heartman's historical series, no. 63) 23 p. [13394

Stout, Wilbur White. A Carolina folk-play: In Dixon's kitchen, a comedy of a country courtship, by Wilbur Stout, written in collaboration with Ellen B. Lay. [Atlanta, Ga., Ruralist Press, 1925?] 6 p. [13395

——The logic of language growth; a prize thesis in competition for the Mildred Williams Buchan prize in philosophy. [Chapel Hill] Department of Philosophy, University of North Carolina, 1922. 9 p. [13396

Stovall, Eugenia (Orchard) A son of Carolina. New York, Neale Publishing Co., 1909. 369 p. [13397

Stovall, Floyd. American idealism. Norman, University of Oklahoma Press, 1943. 235 p. [13398

Stovall, Floyd, ed. The development of American literary criticism, by Harry H. Clark [and others] Chapel Hill, University of North Carolina Press, 1955. 262 p. [13399

Stover, John F. The railroads of the South, 1865-1900; a study in finance and control. Chapel Hill, University of North Carolina Press [1955] 310 p. [13400

Stowe, Harriet Elizabeth (Beecher) Dred; a tale of the great Dismal Swamp, together with Anti-slavery tales and papers, and Life in Florida after the war. Boston, Houghton, Mifflin and Co., 1896. (Riverside edition. The writings of Harriet Beecher Stowe, v. 3-4) 2 v. [13401

——Dred; a tale of the great Dismal Swamp. Boston, Phillips, Sampson and Co., 1856. 2 v. [13402

——A key to Uncle Tom's cabin; presenting the original facts and documents upon which the story is founded, together with corroborative statements verifying the truth of the work. London, T. Bosworth, 1853. 511 p. [13403

Stowe, Robert Lee. Early history of Belmont and Gaston County, North Carolina, with preface. [Belmont, The Author] 1951. 61 p. [13404

Stowell, Jay Samuel. Methodist adventures in Negro education. New York, Methodist Book Concern [c.1922]   190 p.   [13405

Strachey, William. The historie of travaile into Virginia Britannia . . . edited from the original manuscript . . . by R. H. Major. London, Hakluyt Society, 1849. (Works issued by the Hakluyt Society [No. VI])   203 p.   [13406
——The historie of travell into Virginia Britania (1612) edited by Louis B. Wright and Virginia Freund. London, Hakluyt Society, 1953. (Works issued by the Hakluyt Society, 2d ser., no. 103)   221 p.   [13407

Strange, Robert, 1796-1854. An address delivered before the Peithessophian and Philoclean societies of Rutgers College. New-Brunswick, John Terhune's Press, 1840.   36 p.   [13408
——An address delivered before the two literary societies of the University of North Carolina, June, 1837. Raleigh, J. Gales and Son, pr., 1837.   46 p.   [13409
——Address delivered before the Fayetteville Independent Light Infantry Company, December 4, 1850. To which is appended a history of the company contained in an address delivered before the corps on the semi-centennial anniversary (August 23d, 1843) by Edward Lee Winslow. Fayetteville, Edward J. Hale & Son, 1850. 48 p.   [13410

[Strange, Robert] 1796-1854. Eoneguski; or, The Cherokee chief, a tale of past wars, by an American. Washington, Franck Taylor, 1839.   2 v.   [13411

Strange, Robert, 1796-1854. Eulogy on the life and character of William Rufus King, delivered in Clinton, on the 1st day of June, 1853. Raleigh, William W. Holden, Standard Office, pr., 1853.   14 p.   [13412
——Life and character of Hon. Wm. Gaston; a eulogy, delivered by appointment of the officers and members of the Fayetteville bar, on Monday, November 11, 1844. Fayetteville, E. J. Hale, pr., 1844.   29 p.   [13413
——The pursuits of life; an address, delivered at the request of the Philanthropic Society before the literary societies of Davidson College, on the 8th day of August, 1849. Fayetteville, E. J. Hale, pr., 1849.   28 p.   [13414

Strange, Robert, 1857-1914. Church work among the Negroes in the South . . . preached on the evening of the fifth Sunday in Lent at Grace Episcopal Church. Chicago, Western Theological Seminary, 1907. (The Hale memorial sermon, no. 2)   30 p.   [13415
——A memorial sermon on Dr. Armand J. DeRosset, preached in St. James' Church, December 12th, 1897. [Wilmington] Vestry of St. James' Church [1897] 14 p. [13416

Stranger's hand-book of Henderson County and Hendersonville, N. C. Hendersonville, J. D. Davis, pr. [1885?]   32 p.   [13417

Strassburger, Ralph Beaver. Pennsylvania German pioneers; a publication of the original lists of arrivals in the port of Philadelphia from 1727 to 1808, by Ralph Beaver Strassburger . . . ed. by William John Hinke. Norristown, Penn., Pennsylvania German Society, 1934. (Pennsylvania German Society. Proceedings, v. 42-44)   3 v. Many of these immigrants finally settled in Piedmont North Carolina.   [13418

Stratton, Daniel. Sermon on the religious instruction of children. Newbern, Newbernian, 1850.   23 p.   [13419

Stratton, Eleanor. Course of study in English, Asheville High School, Asheville, North Carolina, adopted June, 1919. [Asheville? 1919?]   16 p.   [13420

Stratton, Florence. The white plume; or, O. Henry's own short story, by Florence Stratton and Vincent Burke. Beaumont, Tex., E. Szafir & Son Co. [1931] 30 p.   [13421

Strayer, George Drayton. Centralizing tendencies in the administration of public education; a study of legislation for schools in North Carolina, Maryland, and New York since 1900. New York, Teachers College, Columbia University, 1934. (Teachers College, Columbia University. Contributions to education, no. 618) 123 p.   [13422

Street, James Howell. The biscuit eater. New York, Dial Press, 1941.   88 p. [13423
——Captain Little Ax. Philadelphia, Lippincott [1956]   377 p.   [13424
——The Civil War; an unvarnished account of the late but still lively hostilities. New York, Dial Press [1953]   144 p.   [13425
——Drengen og Lady. [Copenhagen] Thorkild Becks Forlag [1955]   219 p. [13426
——Good-bye, my Lady. Philadelphia, Lippincott [1954]   222 p.   [13427

——The high calling. Garden City, N. Y., Doubleday, 1951. 308 p.   [13428
——James Street's South; edited by James Street, Jr. Garden City, N. Y., Doubleday, 1955. 282 p.   [13429
——Mingo Dabney. New York, Dial Press, 1950. 383 p.   [13430
——The Revolutionary War; being a de-mythed account of how the thirteen colonies turned a world upside down, New York, Dial Press, 1954. 180 p.   [13431
——Tap roots. New York, Dial Press, 1946. 593 p.   [13432
——Tomorrow we reap, by James Street & James Childers. New York, Dial Press, 1949. 384 p.   [13433
——The velvet doublet. Garden City, N. Y., Doubleday, 1953. 351 p.   [13434
Street, Julia Montgomery. Fiddler's fancy. Chicago, Follett [1955] 157 p. [13435
——Street lights. [Winston-Salem, Cynthia Hensel, 1949] [15] p.   [13436
Strickland, Crump J. Electricity and Christianity. Charlotte, Elizabeth Publishing Co. [c.1938] 96 p.   [13437
——The storage battery. Charlotte, The Author, c.1927. 104 p.   [13438
Stringfield, Lamar. Cripple Creek; from the southern mountains. New York, Carl Fischer [c.1928] 20 p.   [13439
——Georgia buck. Charlotte, Brodt Music Co., c.1950. (Brodt band series, no. 1) 9 p. 37 single sheets.   [13440
——The legend of John Henry; a symphonic ballad for full orchestra. New York, J. Fischer and Brother [c.1936] 2 v.   [13441
——Mountain song; from the southern mountains. New York, Carl Fischer [c.1930] 7 p.   [13442
——The mountain song (Opera in one act, based on the life and traditions of the famous Anderson Clan in Western North Carolina) [Chapel Hill, 1931] 40 p. Libretto only.   [13443
——Peace; a sacred cantata for mixed voices. [Charlotte, Brodt Music Company, c.1949] 36 p.   [13444
——Shout freedom! Charlotte, The Author, c.1948. [1] p.   [13445
Stringfield, Lamar, joint author, see Lunsford, Bascom Lamar

[Stringfield, Margaret] The Cherokee in romance, tragedy, and song in the Great Smokies. [Waynesville, The Author, c.1946] 40 p.   [13446
Stringfield, Margaret. "Occoneechee" fair maid of the forest; a Cherokee operetta in three acts. Waynesville, Margaret Stringfield [1950?] 60 p.   [13447
Strong, Charles Miller. History of Mecklenburg County medicine. [Charlotte, News Printing House, 1929] 143 p.   [13448
Strong, George Vaughan. Francis Herbert, a romance of the Revolution, and other poems. New York, Leavitt, Trow and Co., 1847. 100 p.   [13449
Strong, Hugh. The grave of genius, a poem. Greensboro, Sterling and Albright, pr., 1866. 31 p.   [13450
Strong, Ludlow Potter, comp. List of direct descendants of the de Rosset family. [New York? Compiler? 1948?] 48 p.   [13451
Strong, Paschal Neilson. Behind the Great Smokies. Boston, Little, Brown and Co., 1932. 246 p.   [13452
——West Point wins. Boston, Little, Brown and Co., 1930. 267 p.   [13453
Strong, Robert Cown. Every-day law; or, The law of usual contracts, by Robert C. Strong, assisted by Claude B. Denson. Raleigh, Edwards & Broughton Printing Co. [c.1907] 355 p.   [13454
[Strong, Titus] Candid examination of the Episcopal Church in two letters to a friend. Salisbury, Philo White, pr., 1824. 24 p.   [13455
Stroup, Thomas Bradley, comp. Humanistic scholarship in the South; a survey of work in progress, comp. by Thomas B. Stroup with the assistance of Rembert W. Patrick [and others] [Chapel Hill] University of North Carolina Press, 1948. (Southern Humanities Conference. Bulletin, no. 1) 165 p.   [13456
Stroupe, Henry Smith. The religious press in the South Atlantic States, 1802-1865; an annotated bibliography with historical introduction and notes. Durham, Duke University Press, 1956. (Historical papers of the Trinity College Historical Society, ser. 32) 172 p.   [13457
Strout, E. A., Company. North Wilkesboro, Wilkes County, N. C. Boston [1928?] Folder.   [13458

Strudwick, Edmund. An address before the Medical Society of the State of North Carolina, at its first annual communication, in Raleigh, April, 1850. Raleigh, William W. Holden, pr., 1850. 14 p.   [13459

Strudwick, Frederick Nash. Opinions as expressed by Hon. Fred Strudwick and Hon. John W. Graham. No place, no publisher [1900?] 1 p.   [13460

Stryker, Lloyd Paul. Andrew Johnson; a study in courage. New York, Macmillan Co., 1929. 881 p.   [13461

Stuart, James. Three years in North America. Edinburgh, Printed for R. Cadell, 1833. 2 v.   [13462

[Stubbs, Harry W.] Memorial of James Edwin Moore. No place, no publisher, n.d. 11 p.   [13463

Studebaker, Robert B. History of Eagle Lodge, Ancient, Free and Accepted Masons, Hillsboro, N. C., 1791-1937. [Chapel Hill, Orange Printshop] n.d. 104 p. [13464

Student journal, v. 1- January, 1933- Chapel Hill, North Carolina Federation of Students, 1933- NcU has v. 1, no. 1; 2, no. 1   [13465

Studies in philology, v. 1- 1906- Chapel Hill, Philological Club of the University of North Carolina, University Press, 1906- NcU has v. 1-53   [13466

Stuhlman, Otto. An introduction to biophysics. New York, J. Wiley & Sons [1943] 375 p.   [13467

——Physics laboratory experiments. Ann Arbor, Edwards Brothers, 1924. 70 p.   [13468

Sturges, Wesley Alba. Cases and materials on the law of administration of debtors' estates. St. Paul, West Publishing Co., 1933. 1141 p.   [13469

Stutts, G. D., comp. Picked up here and there. No place, no publisher [1900] 42 p.   [13470

—— ——3d ed. Raleigh, Edwards & Broughton, pr., 1907. 39 p.   [13471

Styron, Arthur Herman. The cast-iron man; John C. Calhoun and American democracy. New York, Longmans, Green and Co., 1935. 426 p.   [13472

——The last of the cocked hats; James Monroe & the Virginia dynasty. Norman, University of Oklahoma Press, 1945. 480 p.   [13473

——The three pelicans; Archbishop Cranmer and the Tudor juggernaut. New York, H. Smith & R. Hass [c.1932] 414 p.   [13474

Sugden, Herbert Wilfred. The grammar of Spenser's Faerie queene. Philadelphia, Linguistic Society of America, University of Pennsylvania, 1936. (Language dissertations, no. 22) 228 p.   [13475

Suggestions for the establishment of a polytechnic school in North Carolina. Fayetteville, E. J. Hale, 1856. 15 p.   [13476

Suggestions to Baptist Christians. Hendersonville, J. J. Davis, 1887. 22 p. [13477

Sullivan, Willard P., comp. The history of the 105th regiment of engineers, divisional engineers of the "Old Hickory" (30th) Division, compiled by Willard P. Sullivan . . . Harry Tucker . . . associate. New York, George H. Doran Co. [c.1919] 466 p.   [13478

Summerbell, N. A history of the Christian Church from A. M. 4004 to A. D. 1852. Raleigh, Christian Sun Office, J. W. Chadwick, pr., 1852. 334 p.   [13479

Summey, George. Modern punctuation, its utilities and conventions. New York, Oxford University Press, American Branch, 1919. 265 p.   [13480

Sumner, Charles. The one man power vs. Congress; address at the Music Hall, Boston, October 2, 1866. Boston, Wright and Potter, 1866. 24 p.   [13481

Sumner, F. W. The true or inner significance of life. Boston, Christopher Publishing House [1951] 149 p.   [13482

Sumner, William Graham. Andrew Jackson as a public man; what he was, what chances he had and what he did with them. Boston, Houghton, Mifflin and Co., 1892. 402 p.   [13483

——Andrew Jackson. Boston, Houghton, Mifflin and Co., 1899. 503 p.   [13484

Sunnyside Press, Monroe, N. C. The Sunnyside sampler; a specimen book of types and ornaments. Monroe, The Sunnyside Press, 1933. [47] p.   [13485

Surry Baptist Association. Minutes, 1903- 1903- NcU has 1905, 1910, 1955[13486

Suskin, Albert, joint author, see **Kelling, Lucile**

Sutherland, Stella Helen. Population distribution in colonial America. New York, Columbia University Press, 1936. 353 p. [13487

Sutton, Cantey (Venable) ed. History of art in Mississippi. Gulfport, Miss., Dixie Press, 1929. 177 p. [13488

Sutton, Edward H. Three times in jail. Baltimore [1887?] 12 p. [13489

Sutton, Felix. Daniel Boone. New York, Grosset & Dunlap [1956] 69 p. [13490

Sutton, Louis Valvelle. Saving topsoil and preventing floods; an address before the North Carolina Chapter of the Soil Conservation Society of America, North Carolina State College, October 20, 1951. [Raleigh, 1951] 11 p. [13491

Sutton, Margaret. Jemima, daughter of Daniel Boone. New York, C. Scribner's Sons, 1942. 251 p. [13492

Sutton, W. J. An open letter to Hon. W. R. Allen and others. No place, no publisher [1898] 2 p. [13493

Swaim, Mary L. The Greensboro press, read before the Guilford Literary and Historical Association, April 4, 1907. [Greensboro? 1907?] [1] p. [13494

Swain, David Lowry. British invasion of North Carolina in 1776; a lecture delivered before the Historical Society of the University of North Carolina, Friday, April 1st, 1853. No place, no publisher, n.d. 24 p. [13495

——Catalogue of the Swain Collection of Autograph Letters. Raleigh, E. M. Uzzell, pr., 1885. 8 p. [13496

——Early times in Raleigh; addresses . . . at the dedication of Tucker Hall, and on the occasion of the completion of the monument to Jacob Johnson. Raleigh, Walters, Hughes & Co., 1867. 41, 21 p. [13497

Swalin, Benjamin Franklin. The violin concerto; a study in German romanticism. Chapel Hill, University of North Carolina Press, 1941. 172 p. [13498

The swamp outlaws of North Carolina. Philadelphia, Old Franklin Publishing House, c.1872. 62 p. [13499

The swamp outlaws; or, The North Carolina bandits, being a complete history of the modern Rob Roys and Robin Hoods. New York, R. M. DeWitt [1872] 84 p. [13500

Swan, Herbert S. The Durham plan. [Durham? 1927?] 88 p. [13501

The swan, 19 - Hobucken, Hobucken High School, 19 - NcU has 1928 [13502

Swank, Harold Allen. The glory of a nation. Greensboro, H. A. Swank Co., c.1921. 125 p. [13503

Swanson, Ernst Werner, ed. Public education in the South today and tomorrow, a statistical survey, edited by Ernst W. Swanson and John A. Griffin. Chapel Hill, University of North Carolina Press [1955] 137 p. [13504

Sweet, William Warren, ed. The Methodists, a collection of source materials. Chicago, University of Chicago Press [1946] 800 p. [13505

Swepson, George W., defendant. State vs. Geo. W. Swepson. [Graham? 1876] [1] p. [13506

Swift, Bulus B. Legislative goals for North Carolina children, 1931. [Raleigh, Legislative Council of North Carolina Women] 1931. [6] p. [13507

Swift, Joseph Gardner. The memoirs of Gen. Joseph Gardner Swift. [Worcester, Mass., F. S. Blanchard & Co.] 1890. 292, 58 p. [13508

Swift, Wiley Hampton. Henry Horace Williams, teacher. [Greensboro, 1909] 8 p. [13509

Swink, David Maxwell. The state idea, its development. Chapel Hill, University Press, 1901. (University of North Carolina, Philosophy Department. Worth prize thesis, 1901) 16 p. [13510

Swink, Louis Melancthon. An examination into the origin and rise of civil law. Chapel Hill, University Press, 1894. (University of North Carolina, Philosophy Department. Worth Prize thesis, 1894) 24 p. [13511

Swint, Henry Lee. The northern teacher in the South, 1862-1870. Nashville, Tenn., Vanderbilt University Press, 1941. 221 p. [13512

Swope, Rodney R. The struggle for a diocese; being an account of the struggle to secure the erection of the Missionary District of Asheville, North Carolina, into a diocese. [Asheville? Protestant Episcopal Diocese of Western North Carolina? 1919?] 15 p. [13513

Sydnor, Charles Sackett. The development of Southern sectionalism, 1819-1848. [Baton Rouge] Louisiana State University Press, 1948. (A History of the South, v. 5)   400 p.   [13514

——A gentleman of the old Natchez region, Benjamin L. C. Wailes.   Durham, Duke University Press, 1938.   337 p.   [13515

——Gentlemen freeholders; political practices in Washington's Virginia.   Chapel Hill, University of North Carolina Press for the Institute of Early American History and Culture at Williamsburg, Va. [1952]   180 p.   [13516

Synod of North Carolina see **Presbyterian Church in the U. S. Synod of North Carolina**

Syrett, Harold Coffin.   Andrew Jackson; his contribution to the American tradition. Indianapolis, Bobbs-Merrill [1953]   298 p.   [13517

Syrian-American Association of North Carolina.   Grand mahrajan, Lebanon Syrian-American Association, Raleigh, North Carolina, June 20-21, 1937.   [Raleigh? 1937?]   20 p.   [13518

Taft, William Howard.   The South and the national government; an address delivered at the dinner of the North Carolina Society of New York, at the Hotel Astor, December 7, 1908.   [New York? 1908?]   16 p.   [13519

Take time to be a good citizen.   No place, no publisher, 1949.   4 p.   [13520

Talbert, Ernest William.   Classical myth and legend in Renaissance dictionaries . . . by DeWitt T. Starnes and Ernest William Talbert.   Chapel Hill, University of North Carolina Press [c.1955]   517 p.   [13521

Talbot, Hoke, pseud. see **Nelms, Henning**

Talbot, Mary Elizabeth.   Rurality; original desultory tales.   Providence, R. I., Marshall and Hammond, pr., 1830.   196 p.   [13522

Tales of female heroism.   London, James Burns, 1846.   210 p.   [13523

Taliaferro, Carol D.   Memorial address, delivered before the Supreme Court of North Carolina, Raleigh N. C., November 10, 1942.   [Raleigh, 1942]   14 p. [13524

Taliaferro, Harden E.   Carolina humor.   Richmond, Va., Dietz Press, 1938. 87 p.   [13525

[**Taliaferro, Harden E.**]   Fisher's River (North Carolina) scenes and characters, by "Skitt" [pseud.] "who was raised thar".   New York, Harper & Brothers, 1859. 269 p.   [13526

—— ——2d ed.   Eona, Va., Excelsior Printing Co., n.d.   155 p.   [13527

Talton, John Thomas.   Illustrated handbook of Clayton, North Carolina, and vicinity.   2d ed.   [Clayton?] Author, 1936.   73 p.   [13528

—— ——Raleigh, Edwards & Broughton Printing Co., 1909.   50, 10 p.   [13529

Tannehill, Ivan Ray.   The hurricane hunters.   New York, Dodd, Mead, 1955. 271 p.   [13530

——Hurricanes, their nature and history, particularly those of the West Indies and the southern coasts of the United States.   Princeton, Princeton University Press, 1942.   265 p.   [13531

Tanner, Henry Schenck.   The American traveller; or, Guide through the United States.   4th ed.   Philadelphia, The Author, 1839.   144 p.   [13532

——Memoir on the recent surveys, observations, and internal improvements in the United States.   2d ed.   Philadelphia, The Author, 1830.   108 p.   [13533

Tapp, Sidney Calhoun.   The glory of North Carolina.   [San Antonio, Tex., The Author, 1929]   [3] p.   [13534

——The story of Anglo-Saxon institutions.   New York, G. P. Putnam's Sons, 1904. 245 p.   [13535

——The struggle.   New York, A. Wessels Co., 1906.   324 p.   [13536

Tappan, George L.   Andrew Johnson-not guilty.   New York, Comet Press Books [1954]   139 p.   [13537

Tar-Bo-Rah, 19 - [Tarboro, Senior Class of Tarboro High School] 19 - NcU has 1916   [13538

Tar Heel barrister, v. 1- November, 1952-   Chapel Hill, Law School Association, University of North Carolina, 1952- NcU has v. 1-4   [13539

The Tar Heel churchman, no. 1- 1949?-   Chapel Hill, Student Vestry of the Chapel of the Cross, 1949?- NcU has no. 2-7, one unnumbered issue and v. [4]   [13540

Tar Heel nurse, v. 1- 1939?- Raleigh, North Carolina Nurses' Association, 1939?-
NcU has v. [4-16] [13541

Tar Heel underwriter see **Dixie underwriter**

Tar Heel Universalist, v. 1- 1932- Mt. Olive, Universalist Convention of North
Carolina, 1932- NcU has v. [1, 9-25] [13542

Tar Heel woman, v. 1- August? 1930- Hickory, North Carolina Federation of
Business and Professional Women's Clubs, 1930- NcU has v. [2-7] 8-15 [16-19]
20-26 [27] [13543

Tar Heels united, v. 1- April, 1946- Charlotte, National Conference of Christians
and Jews, N. C. Area, 1946- NcU has v. [1-4] [13544

Tar River Baptist Association. Minutes, 1831?- 1831?- NcU has [1846-1867]
1878-1886 [1903-1919] 1922-1955 [13545

Tar River Primitive Baptist Association. Minutes, 1897?- 1897?- NcU has [1917-
1929] [13546

Tarboro, N. C. Calvary Episcopal Church. Year book and directory, 19 - Tarboro, 19 - NcU has 1926 [13547

[Tarboro, N. C. Chamber of Commerce] Tarboro means business! [Tarboro,
1948?] [32] p. [13548

Tarboro, N. C. Commissioners. Patrol regulations for the town of Tarborough.
[Tarboro] n.d. [1] p. [13549
——Town ordinances. [Tarboro, 1850?] [1] p. [13550

Tarboro, N. C. Jockey Club. Rules and regulations over the Tarboro course.
Tarboro, Tarboro Press, n.d. [1] p. [13551

Tarboro, N. C. School Board. Report of the Public Schools, 1911/12- Tarboro,
1913- NcU has 1911/12 [13552

Tarboro and Edgecombe County. [Charlotte, J. A. Lorente] 1913. 48 p. [13553

Tarboro Male Academy, Tarboro, N. C. Catalogue, 18 - Tarboro, 18 - NcU
has 1896/97 [13554

Tarbox, Increase Niles. Sir Walter Ralegh and his colony in America. Boston,
Prince Society, 1884. 329 p. [13555

Tarbox, Lela Prescott. Poems and illustrations with a prose supplement. New
Bern, Owen G. Dunn Co., 1954. 63 p. [13556

[Tardy, Mary T.] The living female writers of the South. Philadelphia, Claxton,
Remsen & Haffelfinger, 1872. 568 p. [13557
——Southland writers. Philadelphia, Claxton, Remsen & Haffelfinger, 1870. 2 v.
NcU has extract of section dealing with North Carolina, v. 2, pp. 827-858 [13558

Tarheel banker, v. 1- July, 1922- Raleigh, North Carolina Bankers' Association,
1922- NcU has v. 1-35 [13559

Tarheel social studies bulletin, v. 1- October, 1953- Durham, North Carolina
Council for the Social Studies, 1953- NcU has v. 1-4 [13560

Tarheel wheels, v. 1- 1944?- Raleigh, North Carolina Motor Carriers Association,
1944?- NcU has v. 11-13 [13561

Tarleton, Sir Banastre, bart. A history of the campaigns of 1780 and 1781, in the
southern provinces of North America. London, Printed for T. Cadell, 1787,
518 p. [13562
—— ——Dublin, Printed for Coles, etc., 1787. 533 p. [13563

Tartan, Beth see **Sparks, Elizabeth Hedgecock**

[Tate, Mabel] comp. Women and the war in North Carolina. [Greensboro, Department of History, State Normal and Industrial College, 1918] [10] p. [13564

Tate, Robert. Rev. Robert Tate's history of Black River Chapel. Wilmington,
National Press, Inc., 1925. (Publications of the Scottish Institute of America.
Bulletin, no. 1) [7] p. [13565

[Tate, William J.] Brochure of the twenty-fifth anniversary celebration of the first
successful airplane flight, 1903-1928, Kitty Hawk, N. C., December 17, 1928. No
place, The Author, 1928. 12 p. [13566

Tatsch, Jacob Hugo. Freemasonry in the thirteen colonies. New York, Macoy
Publishing and Masonic Supply Co., 1929. 245 p. [13567

The Tattler, 19 - Greensboro, Student Body of Greensboro Female College, 19 - NcU has 1903 [13568

Tatum, Georgia Lee. Disloyalty in the Confederacy. Chapel Hill, University of North Carolina Press, 1934. 176 p. [13569

Tatum, Howell. Major Howell Tatum's journal while acting topographical engineer (1814) to General Jackson, ed. by John Spencer Bassett. Northampton, Mass., Smith College, Department of History, 1921-1922. (Its Studies in history, v. 7, no. 1-3) 138 p. [13570

Tau, 19 - Greenville, Greenville High School, 19 - NcU has 1918, 1921 [13571

Tauber, Maurice Falcolm. Louis R. Wilson: a biographical sketch. Chapel Hill, Friends of the Library, 1956. 18 p. [13572

[Tax Payer] Opposition-ad valorem; what it is and how it would work. No place, [Democratic Press Print, n.d.] 13 p. [13573

Taxes! Taxes! Taxes! No place, P. F. White, sh'ff., June 22, 1859. [1] p. [13574

Tayleure, Clifton W. Horseshoe Robinson; or, The Battle of King's Mountain, a legendary patriotic drama in three acts. New York, Samuel French, c.1858. (French's Standard drama, no. 213) 40 p. [13575

Tayloe, David Thomas. Address of Dr. D. T. Tayloe (of Washington, N. C.) president of the Medical Society of the State of N. C. . . . 1905. Raleigh, Edwards & Broughton, 1905. 12 p. [13576

Taylor, Carter. The Reidsville survey. No place, no publisher, 1930. 50 p. [13577

Taylor, Charles Elisha. Gilbert Stone, the millionaire. Wake Forest, privately printed, 1891. 15 p. [13578

——How far should a state undertake to educate; or, A plea for the voluntary system in the higher education. Raleigh, Edwards & Broughton, 1894. 48 p. [13578a

Taylor, Charles Elisha, joint author, see **Yates, Matthew Tyson**

Taylor, Eva Germaine Rimington. Late Tudor and early Stuart geography, 1583-1650. London, Methuen & Co. [1934] 322 p. [13578b

Taylor, George Aiken. A sober faith; religion and Alcoholics Anonymous. New York, Macmillan Co., 1953. 108 p. [13578c

Taylor, George Coffin. Essays of Shakespeare; an arrangement by George Coffin Taylor. New York, G. P. Putnam's Sons [1947] 144 p. [13578d

——Milton's use of Du Bartas. Cambridge, Mass., Harvard University Press, 1934. 129 p. [13579

——Shakespeare's debt to Montaigne. Cambridge, Harvard University Press, 1925. 66 p. [13579a

Taylor, George Coffin, ed. Shakespeare's Hamlet. Interlinear edition prepared by George Coffin Taylor . . . and Reed Smith. Boston, Ginn and Co. [c.1936] 206 p. [13579b

——Shakespeare's Julius Caesar. Interlinear edition prepared by George Coffin Taylor . . . and Reed Smith. Boston, Ginn and Co. [c.1936] 155 p. [13579c

——Shakespeare's Macbeth. Interlinear edition prepared by George Coffin Taylor . . . and Reed Smith. Boston, Ginn and Co. [c.1936] 144 p. [13579d

——Shakespeare's Merchant of Venice. Interlinear edition prepared by George Coffin Taylor . . . and Reed Smith. Boston, Ginn and Co. [c.1936] 164 p. [13580

Taylor, Hannis. Due process of law and the equal protection of the laws. Chicago, Callaghan and Co., 1917. 988 p. [13580a

——The freedom of the press. Washington, Judd & Detweiler, pr. [1892?] 54 p. [13580b

——The origin and growth of the American Constitution. Boston, Houghton Mifflin Co., 1911. 676 p. [13580c

—— ——1889. 2 v. [13580d

——Science of jurisprudence. New York, Macmillan Co., 1908. 676 p. [13581

——A treatise on international public law. Chicago, Callaghan & Co., 1901. 912 p. [13581a

Taylor, Harden Franklin. Survey of marine fisheries of North Carolina, by Harden F. Taylor and a staff of associates. Chapel Hill, University of North Carolina Press, 1951. 555 p. [13581b

Taylor, J. M. Memorial of J. M. Taylor to the General Assembly. Raleigh, Star, 1852. 8 p. [13581c

Taylor, Job. Brief Masonic educational course for four meetings. [Oxford] Orphanage Press [1921] 14 p.   [13582

Taylor John. Some account of the discovery of gold in the United States of America, of the progress of mining there, and of the formation and future prospects of the North Carolina Gold Mining Company. No place, no publisher, n.d. 8 p. [13583

Taylor, John Louis. An address delivered to the Grand Lodge of North-Carolina at their annual communication at Raleigh, in 5804. Raleigh, Wm. Boylan, 1804. 14 p.   [13584
——A charge delivered to the Grand Jury of Edgecombe Superior Court, at the Spring term of 1817, exhibiting a view of the criminal law of North Carolina. Raleigh, J. Gales, 1817. 47 p.   [13585

Taylor, Peter Hillsman. A long Fourth, and other stories. New York, Harcourt, Brace and Co. [1948] 166 p.   [13586
——A woman of means. New York, Harcourt, Brace and Co. [1950] 160 p. [13587

Taylor, Richard C. Reports on the Washington Silver Mine in Davidson County, N. C. Philadelphia, E. G. Dorsey, pr., 1845. 40 p.   [13588

Taylor, Rosser Howard. Ante-bellum South Carolina; a social and cultural history. Chapel Hill, University of North Carolina Press, 1942. (James Sprunt studies in history and political science, v. 25, no. 2) 201 p.   [13589
——The free Negro in North Carolina. Chapel Hill, University Press, 1920. (James Sprunt historical publications, v. 17, no. 1) p. [3]-26   [13590
——Slaveholding in North Carolina, an economic view. Chapel Hill, University of North Carolina Press, 1926. (James Sprunt historical publications, v. 18, no. 1-2) 103 p.   [13591

Taylor, Thomas E. Running the blockade; a personal narrative of adventures, risks, and escapes during the American Civil War. London, John Murray, 1896. 180 p.   [13592
——   ——3d ed. 1897.   [13593

Taylor, Thomas J. History of the Tar River Association. No place, Tar River Association [1924?] 334 p.   [13594

Taylor, Tyre Crumpler. The logic of law; a prize thesis in competition for the Graham Kenan fellowship. [Chapel Hill] Department of Philosophy, University of North Carolina, 1922. 16 p.   [13595

Taylor, Vincent Frank. David Crockett, the bravest of them all, who died in the Alamo. San Antonio, Naylor Co. [1955] 79 p.   [13596

Taylor, Walter P. Land wildlife resources of the South. Richmond, Va., Dietz Press, Inc. for the Southern Association of Science and Industry, 1949. 97 p. [13597

Taylorsville Baptist Association. Minutes, 1852?- 1852?- NcU has 1858, 1859 [13598

Taylorsville Collegiate Institute, Taylorsville, N. C. Catalogue, 18 - 18 - NcU has 1898/99, 1908/09 (called Prospectus)   [13599

Tazewell, Littleton Waller. A review of the proclamation of President Jackson, of the 10th of December, 1832. Norfolk, Va., J. D. Ghiselin, 1888. 112 p. [13600

Teale, Edwin Way. North with the Spring. New York, Dodd, Mead and Co. [1951] 366 p.   [13601

Tecoan, 1923- Greenville, Students of East Carolina College, 1923- NcU has 1924-1927, 1931, 1933, 1945   [13602

Tedder, Daniel Allen. Pike and minnow and other poems. Shelby, The Author, n.d. 16 p.   [13603
——Snake tales. Shelby, The Author, n.d. 12 p.   [13604

[Temple, Oliver Perry] John Sevier, citizen, soldier, legislator, governor, statesman, 1744-1815. Knoxville, Tenn., Zi-Po Press, 1910. 24 p.   [13605

Tenella, pseud. see Clarke, Mary Bayard (Devereux)

Tennent, Gaillard S. The Indian path in Buncombe County. [Asheville, Stephens Press, 1950] [5] p.   [13606

Tennessean, pseud. see Haywood, John

[Tennessee. Andrew Jackson Statue Commission] Program of exercises attending the unveiling of the statue of General Andrew Jackson . . . in Statuary Hall of the national Capitol. [Nashville? 1928] [4] p.   [13607

Tennessee. State Democratic Central Committee. Vindication of the Revolutionary character and services of the late Col. Ezekiel Polk, of Mecklenburg, N. C. [Nashville, John P. Heiss, 1844?] 16 p. [13608

Tennessee River Baptist Association. Minutes, 1862?- 1862?- NcU has 1880, 1882, 1889, 1896 [13609

Tennessee Valley Authority. Recreational development of the southern highlands region. [Knoxville, 1938] 61 numb. leaves [13610

——Here are children; a report on conservation contests conducted in several counties of North Carolina and Tennessee during the school term of 1940-41. [Knoxville?] 1941. 44 p. [13611

Tennessee Valley Authority. Library. A bibliography of the Tennessee Valley Authority, prepared by Harry C. Bauer, technical librarian [Knoxville? 1935] 25 numb. leaves. [13612

—— ——Supplement, January/June, 1935- [Knoxville? 1935- NcU has January-June, 1935, 1936, 1939-40, 1941, 1941-42, 1943, 1943-44, 1945-46, 1947-48, 1955 [13613

——Tennessee Valley resources; their development and use. Knoxville, 1947. 2,145 p. [13614

Tenney, Mary (McWhorter) Communion tokens, their origin, history, and use, with a treatise on the relation of the sacrament to the vitality and revivals of the church. Grand Rapids, Mich., Zondervan Publishing House [c.1936] 195 p. [13615

Terrell, Pinkney Lawson. Una Grames, a southern girl in war times. Statesville, Bunyan, pr., 1902. 48 p. [13616

Territory of the United States, South of the River Ohio. Governor, 1790-1796 (Blount) The Blount journal, 1790-1796. [Nashville, Tenn., Benson Printing Co., 1955] 157 p. [13617

Terry, C. E., comp. Health survey of Raleigh. Raleigh, Edwards and Broughton Co., 1918. 29 p. [13618

Textile bulletin, v. 1- March 2, 1911- Charlotte, Clark Publishing Co., 1911- NcU has v. [1] 15, 21, 22-23 [24-25] 25-28 [29] 30-74, 76-81 [13619

Textile Workers Union of America. TWUA sings. No place [1945] 14 p. [13620

Textiles review, v. 1- January, 1946- Gastonia, Textiles, Inc., 1946- NcU has v. [1] 4-11 [13621

The textorian, v. 1- 1928?- Greensboro, Cone Mills Corporation, 1928?- NcU has v. 29 [30] [13622

Thatch, Edward see **Teach, Edward**

Thayer, John. An account of the conversion of the Reverend Mr. John Thayer. 6th ed. Wilmington, Bowen and Howard, 1789. 42 p. NcU has photograph from original in Sondley Library, Asheville. [13623

They are against the free schools; the facts about the great amount of illiteracy in North Carolina. No place [1900?] 4 p. [13624

They refuse to show the books; taxpayers denied information . . . Bailey resigns in disgust. [Raleigh, Edwards and Broughton Co., 1898] 10 p. [13625

This week in the Land of the Sky, v. 1- Asheville, Miller Publishing Co., 18 - NcU has v. 98-101 [13626

Thomas, C. O. H. An address, "The necessity of ministerial unity", delivered at Bull-Head, N. C., October 10, 1906, Tarboro District Conference, African Methodist Episcopal Zion Church . . . also his Fraternal message. Raleigh, Edwards and Broughton Co., 1906. 20 p. [13627

Thomas, Charles A. G. Sunday afternoons with a congregation of children. [Raleigh, Capital Printing Co.] 1901. 97 p. [13628

Thomas, Charles R., joint author see **Winslow, D. H.**

Thomas, Cyrus. The Cherokees in pre-Columbian times. New York, N. D. C. Hodges, 1890. (Fact and theory papers, no. 4) 97 p. [13629

Thomas, Ethel. The better way; a story founded on facts, showing the happy results of co-operation between labor and capital, and the reward of faithful and loyal service of mill operatives. Charlotte, Mill News Printing Co., 1918. 225 p. [13630

Thomas, Florence. Course of study in home economics for the Public Schools of Charlotte, grades seventh, eighth and ninth. [Charlotte, 1926?] 80 p. [13631

Thomas, George Finger. Spirit and its freedom. Chapel Hill, University of North Carolina Press, 1939. 149 p. [13632

Thomas, James Augustus. A pioneer tobacco merchant in the Orient. Durham, Duke University Press, 1928. 339 p. [13633
——Trailing trade a million miles. Durham, Duke University Press, 1931. 314 p. [13634

Thomas, Jeannette (Bell) Blue Ridge country. New York, Duell, Sloan & Pearce [1942] 338 p. [13635

Thomas, Joseph. Discourse, dedicated to the world, on the benevolent institutions of Sunday Schools, delivered in Kernstown, October 18th, 1818. Winchester, Va., J. Foster, 1818. 31 p. [13636
——The life of the pilgrim Joseph Thomas, containing an accurate account of his trials, travels and gospel labours up to the present date. Winchester, Va., J. Foster, 1817. 372 p. [13637
——The life, travels, and gospel labors of Eld. Joseph Thomas, more widely known as the "White Pilgrim" to which are added his poems. New York, M. Cummings, 1861. 266 p. [13638
——Poems, religious, moral and satirical, by Joseph Thomas, the pilgrim; to which is prefixed a compend of the life, travels and gospel labours of the author. Lebanon, O., Printed at the office of the Western Star, 1829. 264 p. [13639
——A poetical descant on the primeval and present state of mankind; or, The pilgrim's muse. Winchester, Va., J. Foster, pr., 1816. 219 p. [13640
——The travels and gospel labors of Joseph Thomas, minister of the gospel and elder in the Christian Church. Winchester, Va., J. Foster, pr., n.d. 107 p. [13641

Thomas, Joseph Miller. Differential Systems. New York, American Mathematical Society, 1937. (American Mathematical Society. Colloquium publications, v. 21) 118 p. [13642
——Elementary mathematics in artillery fire. New York, McGraw-Hill Book Co., Inc., 1942. 256 p. [13643

Thomas, Leonard R. The story of Fort Fisher. [Ocean City, N. J., The Author? 1915?] 16 p. [13644

Thomas, Theresa. Tall grey gates. New York, D. Ryerson, Inc. [c.1942] 245 p. [13645

Thomas, Wendell Marshall. On the resolution of science and faith. New York, Inland Press [1947] 300 p. [13646
——Toward a more democratic social order. New York, Exposition Press [1956] 64 p. [13647

Thomas, William H. Glimpses of West Africa; with an introduction by Rev. A. A. Graham. Raleigh, Capital Printing Co., 1921. 116 p. [13648

[**Thomas Crawford,** his ancestors and descendants] No place, no publisher [1949?] 116 p. [13649

Thomas Hume Cup Committee. Report to contributors, Thomas Hume cup, offered to the high schools of North Carolina for excellence in journalism by former students of Thomas Hume. [Chapel Hill? 1928] 3 p. [13650
——Thomas Hume . . . Professor of English Literature in the University of North Carolina, 1885-1908. [Chapel Hill, n.d.] [3] p. [13651

Thomas Walton Patton, born May 8th, 1841, died November 6th, 1907; a biographical sketch. No place, no publisher, 1907. 55 p. [13652

[**Thomasville, N. C. Chamber of Commerce**] In the heart of the Piedmont section, Thomasville, N. C. [Thomasville, 1939] [10] p. [13653

Thomasville, North Carolina, city directory, 19 - Asheville, Carolina Directory Co., 19 - NcU has 1933, 1943-44, 1947-48 [13654

Thomes, William Henry. Running the blockade; or, U. S. secret service adventures. Boston, Lee and Shepard, 1876. 474 p. [13655

Thompson, Adele Eugenia. Polly of the pines; a patriot girl of the Carolinas. Boston, Lothrop, Lee & Shepard Co. [1906] 313 p. [13656

Thompson, C. C. The Christ; an illustrated poem covering the following phases of the life of Christ: The nativity, His reception, the temptation, His works, His passion, His burial and resurrection, and the ascension. New York, Broadway Publishing Co., 1903. 55 p.   [13657

Thompson, Cyrus. The art of living; the President's address delivered before the Medical Society of the State of North Carolina, April 15, 1919. No place [1919?] 15 p.   [13658
—— ——[Raleigh, 1919] 14 p.   [13659
——Dr. Thompson's great speech. No place, no publisher [1898?] 23 p.   [13660
——An old remedy; an address delivered at the close of Warrenton High School, Warrenton, N. C., on May 26, 1914. Charlotte, Observer [1914?] 18 p.   [13661
——Public sentiment in the state and in the individual; the annual oration delivered before the Medical Society of the State of North Carolina, Wrightsville Beach, June 22, 1910. Raleigh, Mutual Printing Co., 1910. 33 p.   [13662

Thompson, Edgar Tristram. Agricultural Mecklenburg and industrial Charlotte, social and economic. Charlotte, Charlotte Chamber of Commerce [1926?] 317 p.   [13663
——Race and region, a descriptive bibliography compiled with special reference to the relations between whites and Negroes in the United States, by Edgar T. Thompson and Alma Macy Thompson. Chapel Hill, University of North Carolina Press, 1949. 194 p.   [13664

Thompson, Edgar Tristram, ed. Race relations and the race problem, a definition and an analysis. Durham, Duke University Press, 1939. 338 p.   [13665

Thompson, Edward John. Sir Walter Ralegh, last of the Elizabethans. New Haven, Yale University Press, 1936. 416 p.   [13666

Thompson, Elizabeth Hardy, ed. A. L. A. glossary of library terms, with a selection of terms in related fields, prepared under the direction of the Committee on Library Terminology of the American Library Association by Elizabeth H. Thompson. Chicago, American Library Association, 1943. 159 p.   [13667

Thompson, G. M., joint author, see **Bennett, Mark**

Thompson, Henry Paget. Into all lands; the history of the Society for the Propagation of the Gospel in Foreign Parts, 1701-1950. London, S. P. C. K., 1951. 760 p.   [13668

Thompson, Holland. The age of invention; a chronicle of mechanical conquest. New Haven, Yale University Press, 1921. (The chronicles of America series, v. 37) 267 p.   [13669

Thompson, Holland, ed. The book of knowledge; the children's encyclopedia; editors-in-chief, Holland Thompson . . . Arthur Mee. New York, Grolier Society [c.1926] 20 v. Other editions were published in 1928, 1929, 1930, 1933, 1934, 1935, 1937, 1938, 1940, 1941.   [13670

Thompson, Holland. From the cotton field to the cotton mill; a study of the industrial transition in North Carolina. New York, Macmillan Co., 1906. 284 p.   [13671
——The new South; a chronicle of social and industrial evolution. New Haven, Yale University Press, 1919. (The chronicles of America series, v. 42) 250 p. [13672
—— ——·1921.   [13673

Thompson, Lawrence Sidney. Arthur Schopenhauer; in informal talk to students. Lexington, Ky., University of Kentucky Libraries, 1950. 6 p.   [13674
——Faust; a bicentennial review. Louisville, Ky., University of Kentucky Library [1951?] 10 p.   [13675
——The Kentucky novel, by Lawrence S. Thompson and Algernon D. Thompson. [Lexington] University of Kentucky Press [1953] 172 p.   [13676
——The mysticism of Rainer Maria Wilke: from Las Stunden-Buch to the Duinese elegies. [Lexington, Ky., The Author, 1949] 6 p.   [13677
——Students' guide to the use of the Western Michigan College Library. Rev. ed. Kalamazoo, Western Michigan College Library, 1948. 14 p.   [13678
——Wilhelm Waiblinger in Italy. Chapel Hill, University of North Carolina Press [1953] (University of North Carolina studies in the Germanic languages and literatures, no. 9) 105 p.   [13679

Thompson, Lawrence Sidney, tr. see **Predeek, Albert**

Thompson, Roy. Around Europe in 80 feedboxes! Winston-Salem, Flagler Publishing Co. [c.1956] 184 p.   [13680

Thompson, Samuel Hunter. The Highlanders of the South. New York, Eaton & Mains [c.1910] 86 p.   [13681

[**Thompson, William Tappan**] Wilmington Theatre . . . Mr. George Bailey being home on a visit from Lee's army in Virginia will appear in his celebrated character of "Major Jones" in the comedy of Major Jones' courtship. [Wilmington?] February 7th, 1865. [1] p.   [13682

Thompson Orphanage and Training Institution, Charlotte, N. C. The building for small children. [Charlotte, 1922] [4] p.   [13683
——Report, 1st- 1887/88- Charlotte, 1888- NcU has 1887/88-1890/91   [13684

Thompson School, Siler City, N. C. Catalogue, 1880/81?- Siler City, 1881?- NcU has 1886/87, 1889/90   [13685

Thompson's Bromine-Arsenic Springs Company, Ashe Co., N. C. Thompson's Bromine-Arsenic Springs Company, Ashe Co., N. C. Richmond, Va., Andrews, Baptist and Clemmett, 1887. 24 p.   [13686
——A medicinal beverage. [Saltville, Va.] n.d. 24 p.   [13687

Thomson, Katherine Byerly. Memoirs of the life of Sir Walter Raleigh. Philadelphia, Gihon & Smith, 1816. 287 p.   [13688

Thomson, Roy Bertrand. An examination of basic principles of comparative forest valuation. Durham [Seeman Printery] 1942. (Duke University. School of Forestry. Bulletin, 6) 99 p.   [13689

Thoreau, Henry David. Sir Walter Raleigh. Boston, Bibliophile Society, 1905. 106 p.   [13690

Thoreau news letter, 1936?- Chapel Hill, Raymond Adams, 1936?- NcU has [1936-1944]   [13691

Thornburgh, Laura. The Great Smoky Mountains. New York, Thomas Y. Crowell Co., [c.1937] 147 p.   [13692

[**Thornburgh, Laura**] The Great Smoky Mountains. Rev. and enl. ed. New York, Thomas Y. Crowell Co. [1942] 177 p.   [13693

Thorndike, Edward Lee. 144 smaller cities. New York, Harcourt, Brace and Co. [c.1940] 135 p.   [13694

Thorne, J. Williams. North Carolina in the 19th century. The great ecclesiastical trial of J. Williams Thorne, representative from Warren County, who was expelled for opinion [!] sake, by the House of Representatives of North Carolina, on February 24th, 1875. [Raleigh? 1875?] 68 p.   [13695

Thorne, Jack, pseud. see Fulton, David Bryant

Thorne, John Julius. Humble hours of solitude. Wilson, P. D. Gold Publishing Co., 1904. 198 p.   [13696

Thorne, Samuel. The journal of a boy's trip on horseback. New York, privately printed, 1936. 47 p.   [13697

Thornton, Marcellus Eugene. The lady of New Orleans; a novel of the present. London, Abbey Press [c.1901] 330 p.   [13698
——My "budie" and I. London, F. Tennyson Neely [c.1899] 273 p.   [13699

Thornton, Mary Lindsay. Official publications of the colony and state of North Carolina, 1749-1939; a bibliography. Chapel Hill, University of North Carolina Press, 1954. 347 p.   [13700

Thornwell, James Henley. Our danger and our duty. Raleigh, Raleigh Register Steam Press, 1863. (Evangelical Tract Society, Petersburg, Va., no. 215) 16 p.   [13701

Thorpe, John Houston, comp. Roster of Nash County Confederate soldiers, and copy of Edgecombe County roster. Raleigh, Edwards & Broughton, 1925. 135 p.   [13702

Thorpe, Sheldon B. The history of the Fifteenth Connecticut Volunteers in the war for the defense of the Union, 1861-1865. New Haven, Price, Lee & Adkins Co., 1983. 362 p.   [13703

Those excessive fees. No place, no publisher [1908] Various paging.   [13704

Thoughts for the people, no. 1- Raleigh, Sentinel, 186 - NcU has no. 4, 8, 9, 10, 11   [13705

Thrall, William Flint. A handbook to literature, with an outline of literary history, English and American, by William Flint Thrall . . . and Addison Hibbard. Garden City, N. Y., Doubleday, Doran & Co., Inc. [c.1936]   579 p.   [13706

Three Forks Baptist Association. Minutes, 1841?- 1841?- NcU has 1882-1885, 1895, 1904 [1928-1956]   [13707

Thrift, Charles Tinsley. Are Methodists willing to face the facts? No place, no publisher, n.d.   [12] p.   [13708
——The model church. [Farmville, N. C., The Author] c.1923.   [14] p.   [13709
——A modern scholar, modern scholarship and the form baptism, Methodism and the perilous times, some remarkable Baptist utterances. [Greensboro, Methodist Board of Publication] c.1922.   38 p.   [13710
——The possibility of falling from grace, versus once in grace, always in grace, and why Methodist preachers move so much. [Moyock, The Author] c.1925. [40] p.   [13711
——The romance of the gospel . . . Introduction by Rev. Marion T. Plyler. Greensboro, Piedmont Press, 1934-   NcU has v. 1   [13712
——A short collection of poems and hymns . . . and a poem by Ruth Nell Thrift. [Durham, The Author] c.1949.   [17] p.   [13713
——Why John the Baptist sprinkled the multitudes at the River Jordan. [Greensboro, North Carolina Christian Advocate] c.1921.   24 p.   [13714

Thrift, v. 1- May, 1902- Durham, Thrift Publishing Co., 1902- NcU has v. [1-4] [13715

[Throop, George Higby] Bertie; or, Life in the old field, a humorous novel, by Capt. Gregory Seaworthy [pseud.] with a letter to the author from Washington Irving. Philadelphia, A. Hart, 1851.   242 p.   [13716
——Nag's Head; or, Two months among "The Bankers". A story of sea-shore life manners, by Gregory Seaworthy [pseud.] Philadelphia, A. Hart, 1850. 180, 12 p.   [13717
NcU has defective copy completed by photographic reproduction.   [13718

Thruston, Gates Phillips. The antiquities of Tennessee and the adjacent states and the state of aboriginal society in the scale of civilization represented by them. Cincinnati, R. Clarke & Co., 1890.   369 p.   [13719

Thruston, Lucy (Meacham) Jenifer. Boston, Little, Brown, and Co., 1907. 298 p.   [13720

Thwaites, Reuben Gold. Daniel Boone. New York, D. Appleton & Co., 1913. 257 p.   [13721
—— ——1935.   [13722

Tiemann, Bernard J. Our North Carolina. New York, The Author, n.d. 2 p. [13723
—— ——[c.1905] [1] p.   [13724

[Tiernan, Frances Christine (Fisher)] After many days, a novel, by Christian Reid [pseud.] New York, D. Appleton and Co., 1877.   212 p.   [13725
—— ——1890.   [13726
——Armine. New York, Christian Press Association Publishing Co. [c.1884] 359 p.   [13727
—— ——Baltimore, McCauley & Kilner [c.1884]   [13728
——Bonny Kate. New York, D. Appleton and Co., 1891.   222 p.   [13729
——Carmela. Philadelphia, H. L. Kilner & Co. [c.1891]   371 p.   [13730
——Carmen's inheritance. Philadelphia, To-day Printing and Publishing Co., 1873.   89 p.   [13731
——The chase of an heiress. New York, G. P. Putnam's Sons [c.1898] 261 p. [13732
——A child of Mary. 2d ed. Notre Dame, Ind., Joseph A. Lyons, 1887. 352 p. [13733
——A comedy of elopement. New York, D. Appleton and Co., 1893.   261 p. [13734
——The daughter of a star. New York, Devin-Adair [c.1913]   349 p.   [13735
——A daughter of Bohemia. New York, D. Appleton and Co., 1874.   222 p. [13736
——A daughter of the Sierra. St. Louis, B. Herder, 1903.   367 p.   [13737
——Ebb-tide, and other stories. New York, D. Appleton & Co., 1872. 166 p. [13738
——Fairy gold. Notre Dame, Ind., Ave Maria Press [c.1897]   357 p.   [13739
——A far-away princess. New York, Devin-Adair [c.1914]   406 p.   [13740
——A gentle belle. New York, D. Appleton and Co., 1879.   142 p.   [13741
—— ——1891.   142 p.   [13742
——Heart of steel. New York, D. Appleton and Co., 1883.   543 p.   [13743
——Hearts and hands. New York, D. Appleton and Co., 1889.   99 p.   [13744

——His victory. Notre Dame, Ind., Ave Maria Press, 1887. (Ave Maria series, no. 8) 82 p.   [13745
——The Land of the Sky; or, Adventures in mountain by-ways. New York, D. Appleton and Co., 1876. 130 p.   [13746
—— ——1883.   [13747
—— ——1888.   [13748
—— ——1889.   [13749
—— ——1892.   [13750
—— ——1907.   [13751
——The land of the sun; visitas Mexicanas. New York, D. Appleton and Co., 1894. 355 p.   [13752
——The light of the vision. Notre Dame, Ind., Ave-Maria Press [c.1911] 362 p. [13753
——A little maid of Arcady. Philadelphia, H. L. Kilner & Co., [c.1893] 284 p. [13754
——The lost lode, and Stella's discipline. Philadelphia, H. L. Kilner [c.1882] 278 p.   [13755
——Mabel Lee. New York, D. Appleton and Co., 1872. 162 p.   [13756
—— ——1892.   [13757
——The man of the family. New York, G. P. Putnam's Sons, 1897. 336 p. [13758
——Miss Churchill, a study. New York, D. Appleton and Co., 1889. 294 p. [13759
——Morton House. New York, D. Appleton and Co., 1872. 266 p.   [13761
—— ——1889.   [13760
——Nina's atonement, and other stories. New York, D. Appleton and Co., 1873. 154 p.   [13762
——The picture of Las Cruces; a romance of Mexico. New York, D. Appleton and Co., 1896. 275 p.   [13763
——Princess Nadine. New York, G. P. Putnam's Sons, 1908. 340 p.   [13764
——A question of honor. New York, D. Appleton and Co., 1876. 501 p. [13765
—— ——1878.   [13766
——Roslyn's fortune. New York, D. Appleton and Co., 1885. 288 p.   [13767
——A summer idyl. New York, D. Appleton and Co., 1878. 211 p.   [13768
—— ——1879.   [13769
——Under the southern cross; a war drama in four acts. Raleigh, Capital Printing Co., 1900. 106 p.   [13770
——Under the southern cross; a drama of the war of secession, by Christian Reid [pseud.] presented by the Salisbury Dramatic Club under auspices of the Daughters of the Confederacy for benefit of the Davis monument, Meroney's Opera House, June 8th and 9th, 1900. Salisbury, Salisbury Daily Sun Print, [1900] 2 p. Program.   [13771
——Valerie Aylmer. New York, D. Appleton and Co., 1871. 221 p.   [13772
——1891.   [13773
——The Wargrave trust. New York, Benziger Brothers, 1912. 384 p.   [13774
——Weighed in the balance. Boston, Malier, Callanan & Co., 1900. 500 p. [13775
——A woman of fortune. New York, Benziger Brothers [1896] 285 p.   [13776
Tiffany, Francis. Life of Dorothea Lynde Dix. Boston, Houghton, Mifflin and Co., 1890. 392 p.   [13777
[Tilden, Mrs. Charles W. F.] Two Christmases of long ago, by A. Fitch La Mar [pseud.] Greensboro, no publisher, 1901. 26 p.   [13778
Tillery, Annie V. Dream verses. [Rocky Mount, Transcript Press, 1913] 52 p. [13779
Tillett, Charles Walter, 1857-1936. Al Smith and fair play. [Charlotte, The Author, 1928] [13] p.   [13780
——De senectute, a birthday gift, an offering of the heart. [Charlotte, Southern Printing Co.] 1932. [3] p.   [13781
——Ginger and pepper; evolution and reminiscences. [Charlotte, The Author] 1926. 19 p.   [13782
——"Inasmuch . . . " a Christmas allegory. [Charlotte, The Author, 1932] [3] p.[13783
——A letter of explanation. [Charlotte, 1932] 12 p.   [13784
——"Lindy". [Charlotte, Observer Printing House, 1927] [2] p.   [13785
——To each and every of my friends unto whom these presents shall come—Greeting. Charlotte, The Author, 1926. 96 p.   [13786
Tillett, Charles Walter, 1888-1952. An alumnus reports a sightseeing trip through the University. Chapel Hill, General Alumni Association [1939] 10 p.   [13787
Tillett, Nettie Sue., ed. How writers write; essays by contemporary authors. New York, Thomas Y. Crowell Co. [c.1937] 222 p.   [13788

——Image and incident, specimens of description and narration, selected by Nettie S. Tillett . . . and Minnie Clare Yarborough. New York, F. S. Crofts and Co., 1933. 308 p. [13789

Tillett, Wilbur Fisk. The doctrines and polity of the Methodist Episcopal Church, South. Part first, by Rev. Wilbur F. Tillett . . . Part second, by Rev. James Atkins. Nashville, Tenn., Publishing House of the M. E. Church, South, 1905. 172 p. [13790

——The paths that lead to God; a new survey of the grounds of theistic and Christian belief. New York, George H. Doran Co. [c.1924] 581 p. [13791

——Providence, prayer and power. Nashville, Tenn., Cokesbury Press, 1926. 338 p. [13792

Tilley, Ethel. Book of the ages; a course for junior high groups in the vacation church school. Teachers book. Nashville, For Cooperative Publication Association by Abingdon Press [1956] 144 p. [13793

Tilley, Nannie May. The bright-tobacco industry, 1860-1929. Chapel Hill, University of North Carolina Press [1948] 754 p. [13794

——The Trinity College Historical Society, 1892-1941. Durham, Duke University Press, 1941. 133 p. [13795

Timberlake, Edward Walter, Jr. Questions on the law of real property. No place, no publisher, n.d. 50 p. [13796

Timberlake, Henry. Lieut. Henry Timberlake's Memoirs, 1756-1765; with annotation, introduction and index by Samuel Cole Williams. Johnson City, Tenn., Watauga Press, 1927. 197 p. [13797

——The memoirs of Lieut. Henry Timberlake. London, Printed for the Author, 1765. 160 p. [13798

——Memoirs, 1756-1765, with annotation, introduction and index by Samuel Cole Williams. Marietta, Ga., Continental Book Co., 1948. 197 p. [13799

Tinker, Edward. Trial of Edward Tinker, mariner, for the wilful murder of a youth called Edward, at Carteret Superior Court, September term, 1811. Newbern, Printed and sold by Hall & Bryan and T. Watson, 1811. 95 p. [13800

Tinsley Military Institute, Winston-Salem, N. C. Catalogue, 1909/10- Winston-Salem, 1910- NcU has 1909/10, 1910/11 [13801

Tippett, James Sterling. Abraham Lincoln, humble and great. Chicago, Beckley-Cardy [1951] 154 p. [13802

——Henry and his friends. Yonkers-on-Hudson, N. Y., World Book Co. [c.1939] 187 p. [13803

——Henry and the garden. Yonkers-on-Hudson, N. Y., World Book Co. [c.1936] 46 p. [13804

——Here and there with Henry. Yonkers-on-Hudson, N. Y., World Book Co. [1943] 250 p. [13805

——I know some little animals. New York, Harper & Brothers [c.1941] 40 p. [13806

——Jesus lights the Sabbath lamp. Nashville, Abingdon-Cokesbury Press, c.1953. [23] p. [13807

——Teacher's manual for Henry and the garden, Stories about Henry, Henry and his friends. Yonkers-on-Hudson, N. Y., World Book Co. [c.1939] 74 p. [13808

——Tools for Andy. New York, Abingdon-Cokesbury Press [1951] 47 p. [13809

Tippett, Thomas. When southern labor stirs. New York, J. Cape & H. Smith [1931] 348 p. [13810

Tisdale, James W. A southerner's reflections about the 1954 U. S. Supreme Court decision concerning racial segregation in public schools. [Asheville, Jarrett's Press, Inc., c.1956] 28 p. [13811

The Tither, v. 1-4, June, 1918-August, 1921. Burlington, C. B. Biddle, 1918-1921. NcU has v. [1-4] [13812

To arms! Those who would be free themselves must strike the blow! Now is the time to volunteer! [Raleigh] Raleigh Register, pr. [1861?] [1] p. [13813

To Julia. No place, no publisher, n.d. 8 p. [13814

To the citizens of the United States and particularly to the citizens of New-York, New-Jersey, Delaware and Pennsylvania, Maryland and North-Carolina, on the propriety of choosing Republican members to their state legislatures. [New York? 1800] 6 p. Signed: A Republican farmer. NcU has microfilm. [13815

To the Democrats of Beaufort County. No place, no publisher [1920] [1] p. [13816

To the General Assembly of North Carolina. No place, Independent Oil Companies, n.d. 3 p. [13817

To the people, Democrats and Whigs! No place, no publisher, n.d. [1] p. [13818

To the people of North-Carolina. [Raleigh, North-Carolina Standard, 1856] 16 p. [13819

To the voters of North Carolina; facts, figures, and arguments against the so-called prohibition bill. No place, no publisher [1881?] [2] p. [13820

Tobacco almanac, 18 - Wilson, Watson's Warehouse, 18 - NcU has 1897 [13821

Tobacco Growers' Cooperative Association of Virginia, North Carolina, and South Carolina. Tobacco Growers Cooperative Association agreement and contract. [Raleigh, 1921] 15 p. [13822

Todd, Charles Cecil. Kissing and conspiring, containing some telephone history of interest to the people of Eastern North Carolina. [New Bern, O. G. Dunn] c.1928. 59 p. [13823

——The new directory for the directors of Carolina Telephone & Telegraph Company. [Tarboro, The Author, 1929] [11] p. [13824

——Unimpeachable. [Tarboro, 1929] 22 p. [13825

Todd, Richard Cecil. Confederate finance. Athens, University of Georgia Press [1954] 258 p. [13826

Todd, Vincent Hollis. Baron Christoph von Graffenried's New Bern adventures. No place [1913?] 124 p. Thesis (Ph. D.)—University of Illinois. [13827

Toisnot Baptist Association. Minutes, 18 - 18 - NcU has 1830 [13828

Tolar, William J., defendant. Proceedings in the case of the United States against Duncan G. McRae, William J. Tolar, David Watkins, Samuel Phillips and Thomas Powers, for the murder of Archibald Beebee at Fayetteville, North Carolina, on the 11th day of February, 1867, together with the argument of Ed. Graham Haywood, special judge advocate . . . Reported by Chas. Flowers and Chas. P. Young. Raleigh, Published for R. Avery, 1867. 398 p. [13829

——Trial of the murderers of Archibald Beebee: Argument of Ed. Graham Haywood. Raleigh, Published for R. Avery, 1867. 94 p. [13830

Tomlinson, Ambrose Jessup. Diary of A. J. Tomlinson; editorial notes by his son, Homer A. Tomlinson. New York, Church of God, World Headquarters [1949- NcU has v. 1 [13831

Tomlinson, Everett Titsworth. The mysterious rifleman; a story of the American Revolution. New York, D. Appleton and Co., 1921. 244 p. [13832

——Scouting with Daniel Boone. New York, D. Appleton & Co., 1931. 303 p. [13833

Tomlinson, Homer Aubrey. Mountain of the Lord's house [Queens Village, N. Y., Churches of God of Greater New York, c.1941] 41 p. [13834

——There shall be wings . . . Part one of seven. Queens Village, N. Y., Churches of God of Greater New York, c.1941. 21 p. [13835

Tomlinson, John S. Assembly sketch book, North Carolina. Raleigh, Edwards, Broughton & Co., 1879-1893. NcU has 1879, 1883, 1885, 1887, 1889, 1893. 1879 was printed by News Steam Book and Job Office with title: Tar Heel sketch-book. [13836

Tomorrow, v. 1- 1943- Lexington, Allied Church League, 1943- NcU has v. 1-3 [4-5] [13837

Tompkins, Daniel Augustus. Address at Lenoir, N. C., September 18, 1902, at a public meeting held to celebrate the change of the C. and N. W. Railway from narrow to broad gauge. Charlotte, Observer, 1902. 12 p. [13838

——An address made before the Cotton Manufacturers Association of South Carolina at its annual meeting held in Charleston, South Carolina, January 9, 1909. Charlotte, Observer Printing House, c.1909. 11 p. [13839

——American commerce, its expansion; a collection of addresses and pamphlets relating to the extension of foreign markets for American manufactures. Charlotte, The Author, 1900. 154 p. [13840

——A builder of the new South; being the story of the life work of Daniel Augustus Tompkins, by George Tayloe Winston. Garden City, N. Y., Doubleday, Page & Co., 1920. 403 p. [13841

——Building and loan associations, the means for co-operative savings by southern working people. [Charlotte] Observer Co., 1910. 52 p.   [13842

[Tompkins, Daniel Augustus] Company K, Fourteenth South Carolina Volunteers. Charlotte, Observer Co., 1897. 36 p.   [13843

Tompkins, Daniel Augustus, ed. Condition of hospitals. [Charlotte, Author? 1906?] 12 p.   [13844

Tompkins, Daniel Augustus. Cotton and cotton oil. Charlotte, The Author, 1901. 2 v.   [13845

——The cotton gin; the history of its invention. Charlotte, The Author, 1901. 62 p.   [13846

——Cotton, its marketing and equalizing, supply, demand and price. [Charlotte, Observer Printing House, 1905] 5 p.   [13847

——Cotton mill, commercial features; a text-book for the use of textile schools and investors. Charlotte, The Author, 1899. 240 p.   [13848

——Cotton mill processes and calculations; an elementary text book for the use of textile schools and for home study. Charlotte, The Author, 1899. 312 p. [13849

——Cotton mills; an address delivered at Winnsboro, S. C. [Charlotte, Observer Print] n.d. 14 p.   [13850

——Cotton seed oil, history and commercial features. Charlotte [Observer Printing House] 1902. 71 p.   [13851

——Cotton; the mill man's point of view. [Charlotte, Observer Printing House] 1904. 11 p.   [13852

——Cotton, to equalize supply and demand. [Charlotte? The Author, c.1905] [2] p.   [13853

——Cotton values in textile fabrics; a collection of cloth samples, arranged to show the value of cotton when converted into various kinds of cloth. Charlotte, The Author, 1900. 18 numbered leaves.   [13854

——Cultivation, picking, baling and manufacturing of cotton from a southern standpoint; a paper read at the meeting of the New England Cotton Manufac- turer's Association, at Atlanta, Ga., October 25, 1895. No place, no publisher [1895?] 19 p.   [13855

——The currency. [Charlotte, The Author?] 1909. 7 p.   [13856

——Currency reform, needs of the South. Charlotte, Observer Printing House, 1897. 8 p.   [13857

——Fourth of July address at Gastonia, 1902. [Charlotte, Observer Printing House] n.d. 15 p.   [13858

——History of Mecklenburg County and the city of Charlotte, from 1740 to 1903. Charlotte, Observer Printing House, 1903. 2 v.   [13859

——Home acquiring and industrial insurance; how these may be correlated for the benefit of the family of working people; an address made before the National Civic Federation, November, 1909, in New York. [Charlotte, Observer Co., 1909?] 18 p.   [13860

——Manufactures; an address at the first annual dinner of the Progressive Associa- tion of Edgecombe County, Hotel Farrar, Tarboro, N. C., December 28, 1899. Charlotte, Observer Printing House, 1900. 22 p.   [13861

——Markets for American goods; an address before the New England Cotton Manu- facturers' Association at their Washington meeting, October 16, 1900. No place, no publisher, n.d. 31 p.   [13862

——The money value of education and training. [Charlotte? The Author?] n.d. [2] p.   [13863

——National expansion, traditional policy of the United States. Charlotte, Ob- server Printing House, 1899. 14 p.   [13864

——New books. Charlotte, The Author, c.1905. 31 p.   [13865

——Nursing and nurses, a monograph; being a historical resume of the profession; an address before the graduating nurses of the Charlotte Sanatorium, 1909. Char- lotte, Observer Printing House, 1909. 12 p.   [13866

——A plan to raise capital for manufacturing. New York, Clark & Zugalia, 1894. 11 p.   [13867

——A plan to raise capital for manufacturing with appendix on technical education. 5th ed. Charlotte, The Author, 1900. 62 p.   [13868

——Road building and broad tires; a brief history of Mecklenburg's good roads to- gether with some arguments in favor of broad tires for all vehicles. 4th ed. Char- lotte, Observer Printing House, 1901. 22 p.   [13869

——Road building and repairs. Charlotte, Observer Printing House, 1909. 26 p. [13870

——Road-building in a southern state. [Charlotte? Observer Printing House? 1894?] 12 p. [13871

—— ——2d ed. Charlotte, Observer Printing House, 1897. 17 p. [13872

——The tariff. [Charlotte, Observer Co., 1909?] 14 p. [13873

——The tariff and reciprocity; an address delivered before the Georgia Industrial Association, Atlanta, Georgia, May 15, 1905. [Charlotte, Observer Co., 1905] 22 p. [13874

——Unification and enlargement of American interests; address delivered at the Southern Cotton Spinners Association, Charlotte, N. C., May 11, 1900. [Charlotte? The Author? 1900?] 11 p. [13875

Tompkins, Dorothy Louise (Campbell) Culver. State government and administration; a bibliography. [Berkeley] Bureau of Public Administration, University of California [1955, c.1954] 269 p. [13876

Tompkins, John R. Family notes; being recollections and data gathered by John R. Tompkins of Mobile, Alabama. [Mobile? The Author?] n.d. 30 p. [13877

Toole, Henry Irwin. Substance of a speech delivered at the Court House in Washington, Beaufort County, on the 5th of March, 1845. No place, no publisher, n.d. [1] p. [13878

——To the voters of Edgecombe, Halifax, Nash, Franklin, Warren, Wake and Johnston counties. No place, 1847. [1] p. [13879

Torrey, Bradford. A world of green hills; observations of nature and human nature in the Blue Ridge. Boston, Houghton, Mifflin and Co., c.1898. 285 p. [13880

Totten, Henry Roland. Laboratory guide in pharmaceutical botany and pharmacognosy. 3d ed. [Chapel Hill] Book Exchange, University of North Carolina, 1937. 47 p. [13881

Totten, Henry Roland, joint author, see **Coker, William Chambers**

Tourgée, Albion Winegar. An appeal to Caesar. New York, Fords, Howard & Hulbert, 1884. 422 p. [13882

——Bricks without straw; a novel. New York, Fords, Howard & Hulbert [c.1880] 521 p. [13883

[**Tourgée, Albion Winegar**] The "C" letters, as published in The North State. Greensboro, The North State, 1878. 54 p. [13884

Tourgée, Albion Winegar. Figs and thistles; a western story. New York, Fords, Howard & Hulbert [c.1879] 538 p. [13885

[**Tourgée, Albion Winegar**] A fool's errand, by one of the fools. New York, Fords, Howard & Hulbert, 1879. 361 p. [13886

—— ——[c.1879] [13887

—— ——1880. [13888

Tourgée, Albion Winegar. A fool's errand, by one of the fools. The famous romance of American history. New, enlarged and illustrated edition to which is added by the same author: Part 2. The invisible empire, a concise review of the epoch on which the tale is based. New York, Fords, Howard & Hulbert, c.1880. 521 p. [13889

——Hot plowshares, a novel. New York, Fords, Howard and Hulbert [1883] 610 p. [13890

——The invisible empire: Part 1. A new, illustrated, and enlarged edition of A fool's errand, by one of the fools. Part 2. A concise review of recent events showing the elements on which the tale is based. New York, Fords, Howard & Hulbert [c.1879, 1880] 521 p. [13891

——John Eax and Mamelon; or, The South without the shadow. New York, Fords, Howard & Hulbert [c.1882] 300 p. [13892

——A royal gentleman, and 'Zouri's Christmas. New York, Fords, Howard & Hulbert [c.1881] 529 p. [13893

—— ——1884. [13894

——The story of a thousand; being a history of the service of the 105th Ohio Volunteer Infantry, in the war for the Union from August 21, 1862 to June 6, 1865. Buffalo, S. McGerald & Son, 1896. 409 p. [13895

——Toinette, a tale of the South. New York, Fords, Howard & Hulbert, [c.1874] 529 p. Published in 1881 under title: A royal gentleman. [13896

Touring; the travel directors reference book, "the Land of the Sky" and the Great Smoky Mountains National Park, 1933-1941. Asheville, Southland Tourist Publishing Co., 1933-1941. NcU has v. [2] 4-7 [13897

Tousey, Sanford. Daniel Boone. New York, Rand McNally & Co., c.1939. [36] p. [13898

——Airplane Andy. Garden City, N. Y., Doubleday, Doran & Co., Inc., 1942. 43 p. [13899

Towle, George Makepeace. Ralegh; his exploits and voyages. Boston, Lee and Shepard [1902] 273 p. [13900

Townsend, Mabel Anges. A history of Iona Presbyterian Church. No place, no publisher [1940?] 50 p. [13901

Townsend, Meta (Folger) In the Nantahalas. Nashville, Tenn., Publishing House, M. E. Church, South [c.1910] 186 p. [13902

——On golden hinges. New York, Broadway Publishing Co. [1917 320 p. [13903

——Songs in the night. Lenoir, privately printed, 1952. 53 p. [13904

Townsend, Richard Walter. The passing of the Confederate. New York, Neale Publishing Co., 1911. 20 p. [13905

Toy, Jane Bingham. Agatha, a play. [Chapel Hill?] n.d. 8 p. [13906

Toy, Walter Dallam, ed. Die Journalisten; Lustspiel in vier Akten, von Gustav Freytag. Boston, D. C. Heath & Co., 1889. 160 p. [13907

—— ——New ed. [c.1916] 202 p. [13908

——Molière's Les précieuses ridicules. Boston, D. C. Heath and Co. [c.1899] 62 p. [13909

Tracy, Don. Carolina corsair. New York, Dial Press, 1955. 375 p. [13910

——Roanoke renegade. New York, Dial Press, 1954. 367 p. [13911

—— ——New York, Pocket Books, Inc. [1955] 346 p. [13912

——Second try. Philadelphia, Westminster Press [1954] 189 p. [13913

Tracy, J. Perkins. The blockade runner. New York, Street & Street [c.1896] 267 p. [13914

Traill, Henry Duff. Shaftesbury (the first Earl). New York, D. Appleton and Co., 1886. 218 p. [13915

Transylvania Baptist Association. Minutes, 1882?- 1882?- NcU has 1950-1955 [13916

Transylvania Co., N. C. Board of Education. Report of the Public Schools, 19 - Brevard, 19 - NcU has 1905/11. [13917

Travelers' Protective Association of America. North Carolina Division. Commercial history of the state of North Carolina. Charlotte, Ray Printing Co., 1908. 137 p. [13918

Traver, Lorenzo. Burnside expedition in North Carolina. Battles of Roanoke Island and Elizabeth City. Providence, R. I., N. B. Williams & Co., 1880. (Personal narratives of events in the war of the rebellion, being papers read before the Rhode Island Soldiers and Sailors Historical Society, 2d ser., no. 5) 31 p. [13919

Travis, Joseph. Autobiography . . . with short memoirs of several local preachers and an address to his friends; edited by T. O. Summers. Nashville, Tenn., Methodist Episcopal Church, South, 1855. 238 p. [13920

—— ——1856. [13921

Trease, Geoffrey. Sir Walter Raleigh, captain & adventurer. New York, Vanguard Press [1950] 248 p. [13922

Trelsoe, Sereca, pseud. see Henry, Beulah Louise

Trenholme, Louise (Irby) The ratification of the federal constitution in North Carolina. New York, Columbia University Press, 1932. (Columbia University Studies in history, economics and public law, no. 363) 282 p. [13923

Trent, William Johnson. Development of Negro life insurance enterprises. Philadelphia, 1932. 62 numbered leaves. Thesis (M. B. A.)—University of Pennsylvania. [13924

Trent River Oakey Grove Missionary Baptist Association. Minutes, 1873?- 1873?- NcU has 1902, 1903 [13925

Trenton High School, Trenton, N. C. Catalogue, 1890/91?- 1891?- NcU has 1896/98 [13926

Trescot, William Henry. Memorial of the life of J. Johnston Pettigrew, Brig. Gen. of the Confederate States Army. Charleston, John Russell, 1870. 65 p. [13927

A tribute . . . Major Seaton Gales. No place, no publisher [1878] 22 p. [13928

A tribute to the memory of the Rev. Francis L. Hawks. New York, Bible House, 1867. 71 p. [13929

A tribute . . . Weston R. Gales. No place, no publisher [1848] 28 p. [13930

Trigg, Harold L. A philosophy of race relations. Raleigh, North Carolina Commission on Interracial Cooperation [1938] 15 p. [13931

Trinity alumni register, v. 1-10, April, 1915-December, 1924. Durham, Trinity College, 1915-1924. NcU has v. 1-10. Superseded, January, 1925, by Alumni register of Duke University [13932

Trinity archive, v. 1-37, 188 - Durham, Students of Trinity College, 188 - 1925. NcU has v. [1, 7-37] Superseded, v. 38- by Archive, Students of Duke University [13933

Trinity College, Durham, N. C. Catalogue, 1850/51-1923/24. Trinity and Durham, 1851-1924. NcU has [1850/51-1859/60] 1867/68-1892/93, 1894/95-1923/24. Continues as Duke University, Durham, N. C. Catalogue, 1924/25- [13934

——Constitution and by-laws, together with general enactments of the Trustees. Durham, 1903. 12 p. [13935

——Exercises at the unveiling of the Washington Duke memorial statue, and biographical sketch, Trinity Park, Durham, N. C., June 10, 1908. [Durham? 1908] 30 p. [13936

——Trinity College, Durham, N. C. [Durham] 1907. 15 plates [13937

—— ——1912. 40 p. [13938

—— ——Durham, Greater Trinity Club, 1919. 24 p. [13939

Trinity College, Durham, N. C. Columbian Literary Society. Catalogue of the books of Columbian Literary Society. Greensboro, Patriot Job Office, n.d. 46 p. [13940

Trinity College, Durham, N. C. Hesperian Literary Society. Constitution and by-laws. [Durham, Seeman Printery] 1919. 22 p. [13941

Trinity College, Durham, N. C. Law Department. Prospectus. [Durham? 1904] 6 p. [13942

Trinity College, Durham, N. C. Library. Estimate of . . . books for Trinity College Library, Durham, N. C. [Durham 190?] 47 p. [13943

——Formal opening. Durham, 1903. 26 p. [13944

Trinity College, Durham, N. C. President. Report, 18 - [Durham, 18 - NcU has [1900/01-1907/08] 1910/11-1923/24 [13945

Trinity College, Durham, N. C. Trinity College Historical Society. Historical papers, series 1-14, 1897-1922. Durham, 1897-1922. NcU has ser. 1-14. Continues as Duke University, Durham, N. C. Trinity College Historical Society Historical papers, ser. 15- 1925- [13946

Trinity High School, Trinity, N. C. Announcement, 1891/92- Trinity, 1891- NcU has [1891/92-1909/10] [13947

——Catalogue, 1891/92?- Trinity, 1892?- NcU has [1897/98-1911/12] [13948

Trinity Park High School, Durham, N. C. Catalogue, 1898/99?- Durham, 1899?- NcU has [1900/01-1914/15] [13949

Trinity School, Chocowinity, N. C. Catalogue, 1876/77?- Chocowinity, 1877?- NcU has [1900/01-1906/07] [13950

Tri-State Medical Association. Transactions, 1899-1921. 1899-1921. NcU has 1905-1921. Continues in Southern medicine and surgery, 1922- [13951

Tri-State tobacco grower, v. 1-6, 1922-1926. Raleigh, Tobacco Growers Cooperative Association of Virginia, North Carolina, and South Carolina, 1922-1926. NcU has v. 3-5 [6] Discontinued following v. 6, no. 2, August, 1926 [13952

Trogdon, W. T. Special notice to the voters of Asheboro Township. [Asheboro, 1869] [1] p. [13953

Trogdon, William Franklin. Trogdon family history. No place, The Author, c.1926. 117 p. [13954

Tross, Joseph Samuel Nathaniel. This thing called religion. Charlotte, 1934. 132 p. [13955

Trott, Nicholas. The laws of the British plantations in America, relating to the church and the clergy, religion and learning. London, Printed for B. Cowse, 1721. 435 p. NcU has extract with separate title page: The laws of the province of North Carolina . . . p. 83-104. [13956

Trowbridge, John Townsend. The drummer boy; a story of Burnside's expedition. Boston, J. E. Tilton, 1863. 334 p. [13957

——A picture of the desolated states; and the work of the restoration, 1865-1868. Hartford, Conn., L. Stebbins, 1868. 690, 46 p. [13958

——The South; a tour of its battlefields and ruined cities. Hartford, Conn., L. Stebbins, 1867. 590 p. [13959

Troy, John C. Scriptural comments, with a brief personal sketch of the Author. Charlotte, Observer, 1897. 61 p. [13960

——Scriptural comments, volume II, with supplement. Charlotte, Observer, 1898. 161 p. [13961

True, John Preston. On guard! Against Tory and Tarleton; containing adventures of Stuart Schuyler, major of cavalry during the Revolution. Boston, Little, Brown and Co., 1909. 302 p. [13962

Truett, George Washington. Christmas messages. Chicago [Moody Press, 1945] 79 p. [13963

——"Follow thou Me." New York, R. Long & R. R. Smith, Inc., 1932. 241 p. [13964

——A quest for souls, comprising all the sermons preached and prayers offered in a series of gospel meetings held in Fort Worth, Texas, June 11-24, 1917 . . . compiled and edited by J. B. Cranfill. Dallas, Tex., Texas Baptist Book House [c.1917] 379 p. [13965

——Some vital questions . . . edited by Powhatan W. James. Grand Rapids, Mich., Wm. B. Eerdmans Publishing Co., 1946. (Truett memorial series, v. 1) 192 p. [13966

——These gracious years. New York, Richard R. Smith, Inc., 1929. 82 p. [13967

——We would see Jesus, and other sermons . . . compiled and edited by J. B. Cranfill. New York, Fleming H. Revell Co. [c.1915] 224 p. [13968

Truett, Randle Bond. Trade and travel around the southern Appalachians before 1830. Chapel Hill, University of North Carolina Press, 1935. 192 p. [13969

Truitt, John Galloway. Across the years; a collection of poems. Richmond, Va., Central Publishing Co., c.1949] 159 p. [13970

Truman, Harry S. pres. U. S. [Letter greeting the people of Goldsboro, North Carolina, on the occasion of that city's one hundredth anniversary] Washington, September 22, 1947. Printer's type mounted on wood block. [13971

Trumbo, Dalton. The remarkable Andrew, being the chronicle of a literal man. Philadelphia, J. B. Lippincott Co. [c.1941] 350 p. [13972

Trumbull, Henry Clay. The knightly soldier; a biography of Major Henry Ward Camp. New and rev. ed. Philadelphia, J. D. Wattles, 1892. 323 p. [13973

Trumper, Virginia M., joint author, see **Lyle, Guy Redvers**

The trumpet, v. 1-3, March 26, 1886-November 14, 1888. Lincolnton, L. B. and T. C. Wetmore, 1886-1888. NcU has v. [1-3] [13974

Truslow, Alice. A new Carolina folk-play: Pensioner, a play of present day social conditions. [Chapel Hill, Carolina Playmakers? 1935] 32 p. [13975

Truth, pseud. To Hamilton C. Jones, editor of the "Carolina watchman". No place, no publisher, n.d. 1 p. [13976

Truth, a Catholic magazine, v. 1- April, 1897- Raleigh, 1897- NcU has v. [1] 2-4 [5-9] [13977

Truth about Western North Carolina. [Charlotte, Jeff Palmer, 1926] [23] p. [13978

The truth concerning Pitt County finances. No place [1896?] [1] p. [13979

Truth's advocate and monthly anti-Jackson expositor, by an association of individuals, January-October, 1828. Cincinnati, Lodge, L'Hommedieu, and Hammond, 1828. 400 p. [13980

Tryals for high-treason and other crimes, with proceedings on bills of attainder, and impeachments for three hundred years past. London, Printed for D. Browne, 1720. NcU has Part III: Proceedings upon the bill of indictment of high treason prefer'd against Anthony Cooper [1st] Earl of Shaftesbury. p. 797-824. [13981

Tryon, North Carolina. Spartanburg, S. C., Band and White, n.d. 11 p. [13982

Tryon, N. C., "Switzerland of America". No place, E. E. Missildine, n.d. Folder. [13983

Tryon Palace Commission. Tryon Palace, New Bern, first permanent capital of North Carolina. [New Bern, 1956] Folder. [13984

[Tryon Toy-Makers & Wood Carvers, Tryon, N. C.] Delightful Tryon toys. [Biltmore, Gollifox Press] n.d. [11] p. [13985

Tuckasiege Baptist Association. Minutes, 1830?- 1830?- NcU has 1876, 1877, 1879, 1880, 1889, 1953, 1955 [13986

Tucker, George. The life of Thomas Jefferson. Philadelphia, Carey, Lea & Blanchard, 1837. 2 v. NcU has v. 2 with material on the Mecklenburg Declaration of Independence. [13987

Tucker, Glenn. Poltroons and patriots; a popular account of the War of 1812. Indianapolis, Bobbs-Merrill [1954] 2 v. [13988

——Tecumseh, vision of glory. Indianapolis, Bobbs-Merrill [1956] 399 p. [13989

Tucker, Harry, joint compiler, see Sullivan, Willard P., comp.

Tucker, Helen. Remembrance. Boston, B. Humphries [c.1951] 48 p. [13990

Tucker, Joel W. God sovereign and man free; a discourse. Fayetteville, Presbyterian Office, 1862. 22 p. [13991

——God's providence in war; a sermon delivered to his congregation, in Fayetteville, on Friday, May 16th, 1862. Fayetteville, Presbyterian Office, 1862. 12 p. [13992

——The guilt and punishment of extortion; a sermon preached before his congregation in Fayetteville, on Sunday, the 7th of September, 1862. Fayetteville, Presbyterian Office, 1862. 16 p. [13993

Tucker, John Randolph. The Bible or atheism. [Raleigh? General Tract Agency?] n.d. 31 p. [13994

Tucker, Mae S. Textiles, a bibliography of the materials in the Textile Collection at the Public Library of Charlotte and Mecklenburg County. Charlotte, Public Library, 1952. 49 p. [13995

Tucker, S. E. Hello folks! Letters of a Mediterranean cruise. No place, no publisher [1934?] 64 p. [13996

Tunis, John Roberts. Highpockets. New York, W. Morrow, 1948. 189 p. [13997

——Son of the valley. New York, W. Morrow, 1949. 192 p. [13998

Tupper, Martin Farquhar. Raleigh, his life and his death; a historical play in five acts. London, John Mitchell, 1866. 81 p. [13999

Turlington, Edgar Willis. Mexico and her foreign creditors. New York, Columbia University Press, 1930. (Columbia University. Council for Research in the Social Sciences. Mexico in international finance and diplomacy, v. 1) 449 p. [14000

Turlington Institute, Smithfield, N. C. Catalogue, 1886/87?- Smithfield, 1887?- NcU has 1896/97. Called Smithfield Collegiate Institute, 1886-1891 [14001

Turnbull, Robert James. Bibliography of South Carolina, 1563-1950. Charlottesville, University of Virginia Press [1956] 5 v. [14002

Turner, Alice Lucile. A study of the content of the Sewanee review, with historical introduction. Nashville, Tenn., George Peabody College for Teachers, 1931. (Contributions to education, George Peabody College for Teachers, no. 80) 291 p. Thesis (Ph. D.)—George Peabody College for Teachers, 1930. [14003

Turner, Arlin. George W. Cable, a biography. Durham, Duke University Press, 1956. 391 p. [14004

Turner, Audrey. Betty Starling, private secretary. New York, Lantern Press [1955] 223 p. [14005

Turner, George Edgar. Victory rode the rails; the strategic place of the railroads in the Civil War. Indianapolis, Bobbs-Merrill [1953] 419 p. [14006

Turner, John Clyde. The gospel of the grace of God. Nashville, Tenn., Broadman Press [1943] 165 p. [14007

——Our Baptist heritage. Nashville, Tenn., Sunday School Board of the Southern Baptist Convention [1945] 133 p. [14008

——Soul-winning doctrines. Nashville, Tenn., Sunday School Board of the Southern Baptist Convention [1943] 133 p. [14009

——A truth in a smile.   Nashville, Tenn., Broadman Press [c.1941]   101 p.   [14010

Turner, Joseph Kelly.   History of Edgecombe County, North Carolina, by J. Kelly Turner and Jno. L. Bridgers, Jr.   Raleigh, Edwards & Broughton Printing Co., 1920.   486 p.   [14011

[**Turner, Josiah**]   Mr. Albert Holmes.   [Hillsborough, 1897]   4 p.   [14012

Turner, Josiah.   Speech, delivered in the Court House at Raleigh, N. C., Friday night, October 13th, 1865.   [Raleigh, 1865]   2 p.   [14013

——State vs. Josiah Turner, indictment for libel; evidence of George W. Swepson, Raleigh, N. C., 1876.   [Raleigh? 1876?]   90 p.   [14014

[**Turner, Josiah**]   To the honorable members of the House of Representatives now in session.   [Raleigh?] n.d.   [1] p.   [14015

——To the voters of the Senatorial district, composed of the counties of Orange, Person, and Caswell.   [Hillsboro? 1876]   12 p.   [14016

——Turner to his constituents.   No place, n.d.   8 p.   [14017

Turner, Orren Jack.   Lightly lies the earth, a novel.   New York, Vantage Press [1955]   304 p.   [14018

Turner, Robert Harry.   The tobacco auction murders.   New York, Ace Books [1954]   131 p.   [14019

Turner & Co.'s Durham directory . . . to which is added a business directory, and an appendix of useful information, also a farmers list, 1889-90-   Danville, Va., E. F. Turner & Co., 1889-   NcU has 1889-90   [14020

Turner's North Carolina almanac, 1838-   Raleigh, Turner and Hughes, [1837- Merged with Blum's almanac, 19   - and identical with it with the exception of the cover.   NcU has 1838-1946   [14021

Turpin, James A.   The serpent slips into a modern Eden; or, Nancy Kerlee and her crime.   Raleigh, Edwards & Broughton Printing Co., 1923.   80 p.   [14022

Turrentine, George Ruford.   The Turrentine family.   [Russellville, Ark.]   The Author, 1954.   128 p.   [14023

Turrentine, Samuel Bryant.   A romance of education; a narrative including recollections and other facts connected with Greensboro College.   Greensboro, Piedmont Press [1946]   314 p.   [14024

Tuttle, Benson Hill.   Spring in Verdun.   San Antonio, Southern Literary Institute, 1936.   [30] p.   [14025

Tuttle, Louise (Jennings) Acres of beauty. New York, Fortuny's [c.1936] 188 p.[14026

Tuttle, Romulus Morrison.   Tuttle's poems.   Dallas, Tex., W. M. Warlick, 1905. 444 p.   [14027

Tuttle, Worth   see **Hedden, Worth Tuttle**

Tuttle Advertising Agency, Greensboro, N. C.   North Carolina "the garden spot of the world".   Greensboro [1923?]   4 p.   [14028

Tyler, John Edward.   "Bertie at Gettysburg" and other poems.   No place, no publisher, n.d.   69 p.   [14029

Tyng, Stephen H.   Memoir of the Reverend Gregory T. Bedell.   2d ed.   Philadelphia, Henry Perkins, 1836.   402 p.   [14030

Tyson, Bryan   [Circular reviewing his pamphlet A ray of light]   Brown's Mills, The Author, 1862.   [1] p.   [14031

——The institution of slavery in the Southern States, religiously and morally considered in connection with our sectional troubles.   Washington, H. Polkinhorn, pr., 1863.   60 p.   [14032

——Object of the administration in prosecuting the war.   Washington, McGill & Witherow, pr , 1869.   16 p.   First published in 1864.   [14033

——A ray of light; or, A treatise on the sectional troubles, religiously and morally considered.   Brower's Mill, The Author, 1862.   171 p.   [14034

——To the hon. . . . member of the Senate in Congress assembled.   No place, no publisher [1863?]   [1] p.   [14035

[**Tyson, Bryan**]   To the honorable the members of the Senate and House of Representatives in Congress assembled.   [Washington, The Author? 1869] 10 p. [14036

Tyson and Jones Buggy Company, Carthage, N. C.   Tyson and Jones Buggy Co., Carthage, North Carolina, established, 1859, incorporated, 1889.   Cincinnati, Cohen & Co., n.d.   40 p.   [14037

Ucker, Clement S. Forestry, its place in the economic life of the South; two addresses made at the eighth annual meeting of the North Carolina Forestry Association . . . by C. S. Ucker . . . and . . . by J. A. Mitchell. Chapel Hill, North Carolina Forestry Association, 1918. 24 p.   [14038

Ufford, Frances Ellingwood. Among deserving girls in the South; a glimpse of thirty-five years work. No place, no publisher [c.1915] 30 p.   [14039

Ullman, Berthold Louis, ed. De laboribus Herculis. Turici, In aedibus Thesauri mundi [1951] 2 v.   [14040

Ullman, Berthold Louis. Mens sana. Fiftieth annual Phi Beta Kappa address, Alpha Chapter of North Carolina. [Chapel Hill, 1954] 18 p.   [14041

——Studies in the Italian Renaissance. Roma, Edizioni di Storia e Letteratura, 1955. (Storia e letteratura, 51) 393 p.   [14042

Ulmer, Mary, ed. To make my bread, preparing Cherokee foods, edited by Mary Ulmer and Samuel E. Beck. Cherokee, Museum of the Cherokee Indian [c.1951] 71 p.   [14043

Umsted, Lillie (Devereux) see Blake, Lillie (Devereux)

Uncle Dudley, pseud. see Norwood, John Wall

Uncle Philip, pseud. see Hawks, Francis Lister

Understanding the big corporations, by the editors of Fortune. New York, R. M. McBride & Co. [c.1934] 292 p.   [14044

Underwood, Adin Ballou. The three years' service of the Thirty-Third Mass. Infantry Regiment, 1862-1865 . . . the march to the sea and through the Carolinas. Boston, A. Williams & Co., 1881. 299 p.   [14045

Underwood, Raye Miller. The complete book of dried arrangements. New York, M. Barrows [1952] 193 p.   [14046

Underwood, Samuel Alexander. Backing up to heaven. Albemarle, The Author, c.1937. 24 p.   [14047

Underwood, Thomas Bryan. Legends of the ancient Cherokee. Asheville, Stephens Press [c.1956] 32 p.   [14048

Union Baptist Association. Minutes, 1844- 1844- NcU has [1844-1854, 1893-1955]   [14049

Union Baptist Association (Negro) Minutes, 19 - 19 - NcU has 1908, 1915   [14050

Union Co., N. C. Board of Education. Report of the Public Schools, 19 - Monroe, 19 - NcU has 1911/13, 1914/15, 1915/17   [14051

Union Home School, Moore Co., N. C. Address to the public and stockholders. No place [1893?] 3 p.   [14052

——Charter, ratified, March 6th, 1893. Sanford, Cole's Printing House [1893?] 3 p.   [14053

——Circular letter, re-opening of the Union Home School, on Monday, August 14th, 1893. No place [1893?] [1] p.   [14054

——Notice: Some of the superior advantages offered. No place [1894?] [1] p.   [14055

——Programme of the closing exercises, 189 - 189 - NcU has 1895   [14056

——Report of directors to the stockholders. No place [1894] [1] p.   [14057

Union Institute, Unionville, N. C. Catalogue, 1886/87?- 1887?- NcU has 1891/92, 1908/09   [14058

Union labor record, v. 1- 190?- Wilmington, 190?- NcU has v. [35-41]   [14059

Union Link Mutual Indemnity Association of North Carolina. Constitution and by-laws. Raleigh, Edwards & Broughton Co., 1906. 6 p.   [14060

Union Primitive Baptist Association. Minutes, 1874?- 1874?- NcU has [1915-1931]   [14061

United American Free Will Baptist Church. North Carolina. Minutes, 18 - 18 - NcU has 1845, 1857   [14062

United American Free Will Baptist Church. North Carolina. North East Conference. Minutes, 19 - 19 - NcU has 1922, 1927   [14063

United American Free Will Baptist Church. North Carolina. North West Conference. Minutes, 19 - 19 - NcU has 1925   [14064

United American Free Will Baptist Church. North Carolina. Sunday School Convention. Constitution as revised by special committees on revision who met at Ayden, N. C., December 1-2, 1921. No place, n.d.   20 p.   [14065

United Baptist Association. Minutes, 1860?- 1860?- NcU has 1862, 1866, 1868, 1869   [14066

United Brotherhood of Carpenters and Joiners of America. North Carolina State Council. North Carolina carpenters' state convention year book, 19   - 19   - NcU has 1920   [14067

United Commercial Travellers. Grand Council of the Carolinas. Session, 1907?- 1907?- NcU has 1911, 1920   [14068

United Confederate Veterans. Official program, 39th annual reunion, Charlotte, N. C. . . . June 4, 5, 6, 7, 1929. [Charlotte, Washburn Printing Co.] 1929. Unpaged   [14069

United Confederate Veterans. History Committee. Report, by Judge George L. Christian. No place, no publisher, n.d.   16 p.   [14070

United Confederate Veterans. Stars and Bars Committee. Report . . . Richmond reunion, June 1 to 3, 1915. No place [1915?]   16 p.   [14071

United Confederate Veterans. North Carolina Division. Brochure, 1861-65. No place [1905?]   57 p.   [14072

——Confederate songs. Durham, Seeman Printery, n.d.   16 p.   [14073

——Organization (as existing October 23, 1899) headquarters, brigades, camps. No place, [1899?]   12 p.   [14074

[United Confederate Veterans. North Carolina Division] Reunion at Greensboro, N. C., August 20, 1902. [Greensboro? 1902]   [3] p.   [14075

United Confederate Veterans. North Carolina Division. Mecklenburg Camp no. 382. To increase the pensions of Confederate veterans. [Charlotte? 1906] [1] p.   [14076

United Confederate Veterans. North Carolina Division. New Hanover County Camp. In memoriam: Wilmington's tribute of respect of Ex-President Jefferson Davis. Wilmington, Messenger, pr., 1890.   36 p.   [14077

United Confederate Veterans. North Carolina Division. Zebulon Vance Camp, Asheville. Confederate veterans' benefit to create a burial fund for their indigent comrades, Grand Opera House, Thursday, April 1st, 1897. [Asheville, 1897] [7] p.   [14078

United Daughters of the Confederacy. Ritual, prepared by Mrs. J. D. Beale, Montgomery, Alabama. No place [1943?]   [1] p.   [14079

United Daughters of the Confederacy. Jefferson Davis National Highway Committee. Jefferson Davis National Highway. Louisville, Ky. [1930]   44 p. [14080

United Daughters of the Confederacy. North Carolina Division. Constitution and by-laws, as revised October, 1929. No place, n.d.   23 p.   [14081

——The dedication and unveiling of the memorial to Orren Randolph Smith, 1827- 1913, who in February of 1861 designed the Stars and Bars, the first official flag of the Confederacy. [Fletcher? 1930]   [4] p.   [14082

——Minutes of the annual meeting, 1897- 1897- NcU has 1897-1905, 1907-1911, 1914-1955. Not issued in 1918.   1897 and 1898 published as one.   [14083

——Prize essays . . . Mrs. J. W. Parker, historian, 1935-36. [Raleigh, Edwards and Broughton Co., 1936]   178 p.   [14084

——Prize essays . . . Mrs. J. J. Andoe, historian, 1940-41. [Raleigh, Edwards and Broughton Co., 1941]   147 p.   [14085

——Prize essays, 1941-42 . . . Mrs. W. L. Johnson, historian. [Raleigh, Edwards and Broughton Co.] n.d.   143 p.   [14086

——Prize essays . . . Mrs. Eugene Thomas Robeson, historian, 1944-45. [Raleigh, Edwards and Broughton Co., 1946?]   118 p.   [14087

——Prize essays . . . Mrs. A. T. St. Amand, historian [1943, 1946, 1947] [Wilmington, Wilmington Printing Co.] 1947.   129 p.   [14088

——Program, the unveiling and the dedication of the Robert E. Lee marker on the Dixie Highway at old historic Calvary Episcopal Church, Fletcher, North Carolina. No place, 1926.   [4] p.   [14089

United Daughters of the Confederacy. North Carolina Division. Asheville Chapter. Souvenir of the general convention . . . held November 16-22, 1930, at the George Vanderbilt Hotel, Asheville, N. C. [Asheville, 1930] 47 p.   [14090

United Daughters of the Confederacy. North Carolina Division. Cape Fear Chapter, Wilmington. Constitution. Wilmington, Review Job Print, 1895. 8 p.   [14091

——Constitution and by-laws . . . as revised, December, 1902. Wilmington, Wm. L. DeRosset, Jr., pr., 1903. 8 p.   [14092

[United Daughters of the Confederacy. North Carolina Division. Granville Grays Chapter, Oxford] [Cornerstone of Confederate monument laid Monday, May 10th, 1909, with impressive ceremony] [Oxford, Orphanage Press, 1909?] 28 p. [14093

United Daughters of the Confederacy. North Carolina Division. J. E. B. Stuart Chapter, Fayetteville. [Invitation to unveiling of a marker on the site of the Confederate Arsenal at Fayetteville, N. C.] [Fayetteville, 1928] [1] p.   [14094

——War days in Fayetteville, North Carolina; reminiscences of 1861 to 1865. [Fayetteville, Judge Printing Co., 1910] 60 p.   [14095

United Daughters of the Confederacy. North Carolina Division. Pamlico Chapter, no. 43, Washington. The Confederate reveille, memorial edition. Raleigh, Edwards & Broughton, pr., 1898. 162 p.   [14096

United Daughters of the Confederacy. North Carolina. Robert F. Hoke Chapter, Salisbury. Festa al fresco . . . July 6th, to 11th inclusive, 1903, Salisbury, N. C. Salisbury, Royall-Barber, pr. [1903?] 27 p.   [14097

——In Mrs. Tiernan's garden, Friday, June 8, 1906, Laila, an operetta, by Mrs. G. W. Stratton, for the benefit of the monument fund. [Salisbury, 1906] 3 p. [14098

——Programme, unveiling Confederate Monument, May 10, 1909. Salisbury, 1909. [6] p.   [14099

United Evangelical Lutheran Synod of North Carolina. Constitution. Wilmington, Lutheran Publication Co., pr., 1888. 35 p.   [14100

——Constitution. Newberry, S. C., Aull & Houseal, 1890. 45 p.   [14101

——Kurzer Bericht von den Conferenzen . . . Jahr 1803-Jahr 1810. New Market, A. Henkel, 1811. 34 p.   [14102

——Minutes of the annual convention, 18 - 18 - NcU has 1803-1817 (German ed.) 1811-1812, 1819 (German ed.) 1821, 1825 (German ed.) 1826-1827 [1841-1881] 1883-1893 [1895-1898] 1901-1915, 1917, 1919-1921, 1923-1955. Not published in 1926   [14103

——Minutes of the Evangelical Lutheran Synod of North Carolina from 1803-1826, twenty-three conventions, translated from the German protocol by Rev. F. W. E. Peschau. Newberry, S. C., Aull & Houseal, pr., 1894. 67 p.   [14104

United Evangelical Lutheran Synod of North Carolina. Luther League. Minutes, 1920- 1920- NcU has 1920-1927, 1929-1938, 1940   [14105

United Fruit Growers of Western North Carolina, Inc. By-laws. North Wilkesboro, Hustler Publishing Co. [1912?] 26 p.   [14106

United Sons of Confederate Veterans. North Carolina Division. Harry Burgwyn Camp No. 166, Raleigh. By-laws. Raleigh, Alford, Bynum & Christophers, pr., 1900. 13 p.   [14107

——Charter members, including records of ancestors through whom they derive eligibility. Raleigh, Alford, Bynum & Christophers, pr., 1900. 13 p.   [14108

Universalist Church in the U. S. Women's National Missionary Association. North Carolina under the Women's National Missionary Association. No place [1915] [12] p.   [14109

University Commission on Southern Race Questions. Four open letters to the college men of the South. No place [1919] 8 p.   [14110

——Five letters. No place, Trustees of the John F. Slater Fund, 1927 (Occasional papers, no. 24) 22 p.   [14111

——Minutes [1st-8th meetings, 1912-1917] [Lexington, Va.] n.d. 75 p.   [14112

University Methodist church bulletin, 1925- Chapel Hill, Joint Commission of the North Carolina and Western North Carolina Conferences, 1925- NcU has April, 1925   [14113

The University of North Carolina magazine, 1844-1947/48. Chapel Hill, 1844-1948. Publication suspended 1845-51, 1862-77, 1879-81, June, 1895-Nov. 1897. Ceased publication following May, 1948 issue. Volumes are numbered in five series. Title varies. NcU has 1844-1947/48.   [14114

The University of North Carolina news letter, v. 1- November, 1914- Chapel Hill, 1914- NcU has v. 1-42   [14115

University Publishing Company, New York. North Carolina official introduction of school books. Raleigh, July 21, 1879. [1] p.   [14116

Unveiling of monument erected in Capitol Square, Raleigh, to Charles Brantley Aycock, born November 1, 1859, governor of North Carolina, 1901-5, died April 12, 1912. [Raleigh] 1924. 3 p.   [14117

Upchurch, J. Sherwood. I did not come from him, neither did you. Raleigh, Mitchell, pr. [1926] [1] p.   [14118

Upchurch, John Jordan. The life, labors and travels of Father J. J. Upchurch, founder of the Ancient Order of United Workmen . . . Rev. and ed. by Sam. Booth. San Francisco, Calif., A. T. Dewey, 1887. 264 p.   [14119

Upchurch, Mollie Johnson. Three score years and ten. [Oxford, Oxford Orphanage, pr., 1937] 107 p.   [14120

Upchurch, Thomas Benton. The story of my life. Oxford, Oxford Orphanage Press, n.d. 70 p.   [14121

Upchurch, William Merriman. Durham County: economic and social [by] W. M. Upchurch and M. B. Fowler. [Chapel Hill] Department of Rural Economics and Sociology, University of North Carolina [1918] 62 p.   [14122

Uplift, v. 1- June, 1909- Concord, Stonewall Jackson Manual Training and Industrial School, 1909- NcU has v. [1-12] 13-44   [14123

Upper Country Line Primitive Baptist Association. Minutes, 1907?- 1907?- NcU has [1911-1955]   [14124

Upson, Theodore Frelinghuysen. With Sherman to the sea; the Civil War letters, diaries & reminiscences of Theodore F. Upson, edited with an introduction by Oscar Osburn Winther. University Station, Baton Rouge, La., Louisiana State University Press, 1943. 181 p.   [14125

Utilization of seaweeds from the South Atlantic and Gulf coasts for agar and its decomposition by bacteria. Durham, Duke University Press, 1946. (Duke University. Marine Station. Bulletin, no. 3) 80 p.   [14126

Utley, Mrs. E. F. see Carter, Eva M.

Vacationing in North Carolina; 1930 all year resorts. [Greensboro] Carolina Motor Club, 1930. 32 p.   [14127

The vaccine inquirer; or, Miscellaneous collections relative to vaccination, by a society of physicians, nos. [1-5]]Baltimore? Vaccine Institution? 1824?] 234 p.   [14128

Vail, Nicholas. The advantages of the Chicago & South-Atlantic Railroad, as set forth in the report of Major Nicholas J. Vail, January 1, 1874. Chicago, Chas. Francis, pr., for the Board of Directors, 1874. 44 p.   [14129

Vail, Ruth (Newbold) River acres. Dallas, Tex., The Kaleidograph Press [c.1936] 103 p.   [14130

——The year's at the Spring. Emory University, Ga., Banner Press [c.1954] 78 p.   [14131

Valdese Manufacturing Company, Valdese, N. C. Valdese, North Carolina, incorporated in 1920. [Valdese?] 1920. 12 p.   [14132

Valentine, Herbert Eugene. Story of Co. F, 23d Massachusetts Volunteers, in the war for the Union, 1861-1865. Boston, W. B. Clarke & Co., 1896. 166 p. [14133

Valle Crucis School, Valle Crucis, N. C. Announcement, 189 - Valle Crucis 189 - NcU has 1934/35, 1941/42   [14134

——Valle Crucis Mission School, located in the Appalachian Mountains. Valle Crucis, 1923. 4 p.   [14135

Valle Crucis Summer School for Religious Education. Valle Crucis Summer School for Religious Education, July 5th-17th. Valle Crucis, [1926] Folder.   [14136

Valley River Baptist Association. Minutes, 18 - 18 - NcU has 1879   [14137

[Van Antwerp, David D.] The principles of church history adapted to the young, by a presbyter of the Diocese of North Carolina. New York, H. B. Durand, 1863. 284 p.   [14138

—— ——2d ed. [c.1869]   [14139

Van Buren, Caroline. Five little Martins and the Martin house. Boston, Marshall Jones Co. [c.1930] 286 p.   [14140

Van Doren, John. Big money in little sums; a study of small contributions in political party fund-raising prepared for the Louis H. Harris Memorial Fund. Chapel Hill, Institute for Research in Social Science, University of North Carolina, 1956. 82 p.   [14141

Van Eeden-Colony in N. Carolina, U. S. A.; information for settlers, with a letter by Dr. Frederik Van Eeden. Amsterdam, W. Versluys, 1912. 83 p. Dutch and English on alternate pages.   [14142

Van Hook, Robert. To the citizens of Person County. Raleigh, 1822. [1] p. [14143
—— ——1823. [1] p.   [14144

Van Landingham, Mary Oates (Spratt) Glowing embers. [Charlotte, Observer Printing House, c.1921] 307 p.   [14145

Van Lindley Nursery Company, Pomona, N. C. Descriptive catalogue of fruit trees, vines, &c. 185 - Greensboro, 185 - NcU has 1853-56, 1868-69, 1870-72, 1899, 1902? 1912?, 1917, 1918, 1920, 1926, 1927   [14146
——The how and the why of happy home grounds. Pomona, n.d. [3] p.   [14147
——How to plant and cultivate an orchard. [Greensboro, C. F. Thomas, pr., 1901?] 41 p.   [14148
—— ——[1902?] 39 p.   [14149
—— ——[1904?] 39 p.   [14150
—— ——[1908?] 30 p.   [14151
——Plantings for southern homes. [Greensboro?] n.d. 16 p.   [14152
——What, where, and how to plant. [Greensboro, Joseph J. Stone, pr.] n.d. 40 p.   [14153

[Van Noppen, Addie (Donnell)] The battle field of Guilford Court House. [Greensboro, Guilford Battle Chapter of the Daughters of the American Revolution, 1915] [16] p.   [14154

[Van Noppen, Charles Leonard] Are the people being enslaved by the banks? [Greensboro, The Author, 1930] 12 p.   [14155

Van Noppen, Charles Leonard. Charles L. Van Noppen, Greensboro, N. C., candidate for Congress from the sixth district. [Greensboro, The Author, 1931] Folder.   [14156

Van Noppen, Charles Leonard. Death in cellophane. Greensboro, The Author [c.1937] 104 p.   [14157
——Impeachments, and What is the matter with Durham? [Greensboro, The Author, 1932] Folder.   [14158

[Van Noppen, Charles Leonard] The industrial banks must be destroyed. [Greensboro, The Author, 1930] 8 p.   [14159

Van Noppen, Charles Leonard. Killing the goose, then what? Greensboro, The Author, c.1936. 86 p.   [14160
——Mecklenburg Declaration of Independence written in 1800. Lynchburg, Va., Brown-Morrison Co., n.d. 3 p.   [14161

[Van Noppen, Charles Leonard] North Carolina selling indulgences. [Greensboro, The Author, 1930] 8 p.   [14162

Van Noppen, Charles Leonard. Open letters; organized graft. [Greensboro, The Author, 1931] Folder.   [14163
——Paid to steal and The story of the ox and of the ass. [Greensboro, The Author, 1932] Folder.   [14164

[Van Noppen, Charles Leonard] The people be damned; the shame of Greensboro. [Greensboro, The Author, 1930] 8 p.   [14165

Van Noppen, Charles Leonard. A polemic and an appeal to the North Carolina legislature. [Greensboro, The Author, 1935] [4] p.   [14166
——Stolen—$750,000. [Greensboro, 1931?] [1] p.   [14167
——The story of an eccentric solo player, Charles L. Van Noppen, Democratic candidate for Congress from the sixth district. [Greensboro, The Author, 1931] Folder.   [14168

[Van Noppen, Charles Leonard]   The supineness of the North Carolina Historical Association and the ignorance of the North Carolina Society of Colonial Dames. [Greensboro, 1912]   [3] p.   [14169

Van Noppen, Charles Leonard.   Thirty pieces of silver.   [Greensboro, The Author, 1932]   Folder.   [14170

Van Noppen, Leonard Charles.   The challenge; war chants of the allies, wise and otherwise.   London, Elkin Mathews, 1919.   112 p.   [14172

Van Noppen, Leonard Charles, comp.   In memoriam, George Washington Watts, born August 18, 1851, died March 7, 1921.   [Greensboro?] Privately printed, 1922. 157 p.   [14173

[Van Noppen, Leonard Charles]   Who is Bashti Beki.   [Lynchburg, Va., Brown-Morrison Co., c.1912]   32 p.   [14174

—— ——36 p.   Advance sheets of his Armageddon.   [14175

Van Orden, William H.   General William T. Sherman.   New York, Street & Smith [c.1895]   201 p.   [14176

Van Tyne, Claude Halstead.   The loyalists in the American Revolution.   New York, P. Smith, 1929.   360 p.   [14177

Van Wyck, Augustus.   Address before the literary societies of University of North Carolina.   Raleigh, Edwards, Broughton & Co., 1886.   20 p.   [14178

Vance, David.   Literary advancement; seven thousand dollars may be gained for the small sum of four in the Newton Academy lottery.   Columbia, S. C., D. and J. J. Faust, January 25, 1810.   [1] p.   [14179

Vance, David, joint author,   see Henry, Robert

Vance, James J.   The philosophy of emphasis; one of a course of lectures delivered at University of North Carolina, 1881.   Baltimore, J. B. Piet [c.1881]   54 p. [14180

Vance, Marguerite.   The Jacksons of Tennessee.   New York, E. P. Dutton & Co., Inc., 1953.   181 p.   [14181

Vance, Robert Brank.   Heart-throbs from the mountains.   Nashville, Southern Methodist Publishing House, 1887.   149 p.   [14182

Vance, Rupert Bayless.   All these people; the nation's human resources in the South in collaboration with Nadia Danilevsky.   Chapel Hill, University of North Carolina Press, 1945.   503 p.   [14183

——Exploring the South, by Rupert B. Vance, John E. Ivey, Jr. and Marjorie N. Bond; aids to learning by Mary Sue Beam Fonville.   Chapel Hill, University of North Carolina Press [1949]   404 p.   [14184

——Farmers without land [New York, Public Affairs Committee] 1937.   (Public affairs pamphlets, no. 12)   31 p.   [14185

——How the other half is housed; a pictorial record of sub-minimum farm housing in the South.   Chapel Hill, University of North Carolina Press, 1936.   (Southern policy papers, no. 4)   [16] p.   [14186

——Human factors in cotton culture; a study in the social geography of the American South.   Chapel Hill, University of North Carolina Press, 1929.   346 p.   [14187

——Human geography of the South; a study in regional resources and human adequacy.   Chapel Hill, University of North Carolina Press, 1932.   596 p.   [14188

—— ——2d ed.   1935.   [14189

——New farm homes for old; a study of rural public housing in the South by Rupert B. Vance . . . Gordon W. Blackwell . . . with the collaboration of Howard G. McClain.   University, University of Alabama Press, 1946.   245 p.   [14190

——Regional planning and social trends in the South. [Chapel Hill] 1934. 18 p. [14191

——Regional reconstruction; a way out for the South.   New York, Foreign Policy Association, 1935.   31 p.   [14192

——Research memorandum on population redistribution within the United States. New York, Social Science Research Council [1938]   (Social Science Research Council.   Bulletin, 42)   134 p.   [14193

——The South's place in the nation.   [Washington, Public Affairs Committee] 1936. (Public Affairs pamphlet, no. 6)   32 p.   [14194

—— ——1941.   (Public Affairs pamphlet, no. 6, rev.)   31 p.   [14195

Vance, Rupert Bayless, ed.   The urban South [by] Rupert B. Vance and Nicholas J. Demerath, editors, with the assistance of Sara Smith and Elizabeth M. Fink. Chapel Hill, University of North Carolina Press, 1954.   307 p.   [14196

Vance, William Reynolds. Address before the North Carolina Bar Association, at Asheville, N. C., 1915. Wilmington, Wilmington Stamp & Printing Co. [1915?] 22 p. [14197

Vance, Zebulon Baird. Address at the Guilford Battle Ground, May 4, 1889. [Greensboro] Reece & Elam, pr. [1889] 15 p. [14198

——Address delivered before the graduating class and literary societies of Wake Forest College, June 26th 1872. [Wake Forest] Philomathesian Society, 1872. 22 p. [14199

——Addresses of Hon. Z. B. Vance of North Carolina and Hon. D. W. Voorhees of Indiana at the opening of the International Cotton Exposition at Atlanta, Georgia, October 5, 1881. Washington, R. O. Polkinhorn, pr., 1881. 24 p. [14200

——The duties of defeat; an address delivered before the two literary societies of the University of North Carolina, June 7th, 1866. Raleigh, William B. Smith & Co., 1866. 25 p. [14201

——Life and character of Hon. David L. Swain, late president of the University of North Carolina; a memorial oration delivered in Gerard Hall, on commencement day, June 7, 1877. Durham, W. T. Blackwell & Co.'s Steam Presses, 1878. 20 p. [14202

——The political and social South during the war; a lecture delivered before John A. Andrew Post, no. 15, G. A. R., in Boston, Massachusetts, Dec. 8, 1866. Washington, R. O. Polkinhorn, pr., 1886. 20 p. [14203

——Reduction of war taxes! Revenue reform! The great speech delivered in the Senate of the United States, February 14, 1883; facts for the people. No place [Virginia Democratic Executive Committee? 1884?] [2] p. [14204

——The scattered nation; with an introductory sketch of the author, by Willis Bruce Dowd. New York, J. J. Little & Co. [1904] 41 p. [14205

—— ——New York, Rational Publishing Co. [c.1904] 42 p. [14206

——The scattered nation. New York, Marcus Schnitzer, 1916. 60 p. [14207

—— ——Raleigh, Alfred Williams & Co., 1928. 59 p. [14208

——Sketches of North Carolina by ex-Governor Vance, together with an elegiac ode and other poems, by James Barron Hope. Norfolk, Va., Norfolk Landmark, 1875. 175 p. [14209

[Vance, Zebulon Baird] To the citizens of the eighth congressional district of North Carolina. [Washington, H. Polkinhorn, pr., 1861] 7 p. [14210

Vance, Zebulon Baird. Vance's speech at Jonesboro. No place, no publisher, n.d. [2] p. [14211

Vance and Settle, their record as public men. [Raleigh, Sentinel Print, 1876?] 4 p. [14212

Vance Co., N. C. Board of Education. Bulletin for county commencement of Vance County, April, 1915, prepared by Lillian V. Gilbert, rural supervisor. Henderson [1915?] 16 p. [14213

—— ——April, 1916. [1916?] 67 p. [14214

——Hand book for school committeemen, Vance County, 1913-1914. [Henderson? 1913?] 8 p. [14215

——Report of the Public Schools of Vance County, 19 - Henderson, 19 - NcU has 1912/14, 1914/15, 1915/16, 1917/19, 1920/21 [14216

Vance Memorial Association of North Carolina. Report of condition of the Association, July 1st, 1902. [Charlotte, 1902?] 9 p. [14217

Van der Linden, Frank. Dark horse. San Antonio, Tex., Naylor Co., 1944. 114 p. [14218

Vanderlip, Frank Arthur. An address delivered at a banquet tendered by the Chamber of Commerce of Wilmington, N. C. to Frank A. Vanderlip, vice-president of the National City Bank of New York. [Wilmington?] n.d. 16 p. [14219

Vanhoy, J. W. Information concerning the Stonewall Jackson Training School. [Concord, Uplift Press] n.d. 19 p. [14220

Vann, Richard Tillman. The things not seen. Nashville, Sunday School Board of the Southern Baptist Convention [c.1931] 183 p. [14221

——What have Baptist colleges to do with fundamentalism and modernism? No place, no publisher [1925?] 19 p. [14222

Vardell, Charles Gildersleeve. Organs in the wilderness. [Winston-Salem, Salem Academy and College, 1944] 15 p. [14223

Vartanian, Parounak Hatch. The law of automobiles in North Carolina. Charlottesville, Va., Michie Co., 1928. 524 p.   [14224
—— ——Charlottesville, Michie Co., 1938. 728 p.   [14225
—— ——3d ed. 1947. 3 v. (1688 p.)   [14226
——The law of corporations in North Carolina (a handbook) Charlottesville, Va., Michie Co., 1929. 719 p.   [14227
——The law of wills in North Carolina. Charlottesville, Va., Michie Co., 1929. 1929. 492 p.   [14228

Vass, Lachlan Cumming. History of the Presbyterian Church in New Bern, N. C., with a resumé of early ecclesiastical affairs in eastern North Carolina, and a sketch of the early days of New Bern, N. C. Richmond, Va., Whittet & Shepperson, pr., 1886. 196 p.   [14229

Vass, S. N. The divine message of the hour. Raleigh, Edwards and Broughton Co. [1908] 41 p.   [14230

Vaughan, Benjamin Grieg. Cheer up, one hundred humorous stories. 2d ed. Asheville, Hackney & Moale Co., n.d. 47 p.   [14231
—— ——rewritten. Asheville, Inland Press, 1918. 93 p.   [14232

Vaughan, Frank. Kate Weathers; or, Scattered by the tempest, a novel. Philadelphia, J. B. Lippincott & Co., 1878. 437 p.   [14233

Vaughan, Frank E. The Albemarle district of North Carolina. Elizabeth City, 1895. 32 p.   [14234

[Vaughan, Frank E.] comp. The Albemarle section of North Carolina traversed by the Norfolk Southern Railroad and its connecting steamboat lines. New York, J. C. Rankin, Jr., pr., 1884. 80 p.   [14235

Venable, Abraham Watkins. Address delivered before the American Whig and Cliosophic societies of the College of New Jersey, June 24th, 1851. Princeton, N. J., J. T. Robinson, pr., 1851. 47 p.   [14236
——Address delivered before the Union Agricultural Society of Virginia and North Carolina, October 25, 1854. Petersburg, Va., Southern Farmer, 1854. 37 p. [14237
——Speech before the two societies at Wake Forest College, delivered Wednesday, June 8th, 1853. Raleigh, A. M. Gorman, pr., 1853. 30 p.   [14238

Venable, Francis Preston. A brief account of radio-activity. Boston, D. C. Heath & Co. [c.1917] 54 p.   [14239
——A course in qualitative chemical analysis. Raleigh, Alfred Williams & Co., 1883. 51 p.   [14240
—— ——[2d ed.] New York, University Publishing Co., 1892. 53 p.   [14241
—— ——1897.   [14242
——Development of periodic law. Easton, Chemical Publishing Co., 1896. 321 p.   [14243
——The duty owed by the educated man to his country; an address delivered before the Alumni Association of Lafayette College, Easton, Pa. Easton, The Association, 1904. [11] p.   [14244
——History of chemistry. Boston, D. C. Heath & Co. [c.1922] 168 p.   [14245
——Inorganic chemistry according to the periodic law, by F. P. Venable . . . and Jas. Lewis Howe. Easton, Pa., Chemical Publishing Co., 1898. 266 p.   [14246
—— ——2d ed. 1907. 422 p.   [14247
——A short history of chemistry. Boston, D. C. Heath & Co., 1894. 163 p. [14248
—— ——3d ed. 1903.   [14249
——Some thoughts on democracy. [Chapel Hill? The Author?] n.d. 10 p.   [14250
——The study of the atom; or, The foundation of chemistry. Easton, Pa., Chemical Publishing Co., 1904. 290 p.   [14251

Veritas, pseud. The Kehukee Association; a series of letters addressed to Mr. C. B. Hassell. Raleigh, Recorder Office, pr., 1845. 35 p.   [14252

Vermiculite and bentonite of Tennessee Valley region. Knoxville, Tenn., Tennessee Valley Authority, 1936. (Its Division of Geology. Bulletin, 5) 51 numb. leaves.   [14253

[Vermont, Adolph] Aux États-Unis; a French reader for beginners, by Aldophe de Monvert [pseud.] Boston, Allyn and Bacon [c.1919] 265, 70 p.   [14254

Vermont, Adolph. Esther Wake; or, The spirit of the Regulators, a play in four acts. Raleigh, Edwards & Broughton Co., 1913. 74 p.   [14255

Verne, Jules. Facing the flag. New York, F. T. Neely [1897] (Neely's library of choice literature, no. 61) 217 p. [14256

——Maitre du monde. Paris, Collection Hetzel, n.d. (Les voyages extraordinaires) 215 p. [14257

Vernon, Charles [pseud.] see **Craven, Braxton**

Verrazzano, Giovanni da. Verrazzano's voyage along the Atlantic coast of North America, 1524. Albany, University of the State of New York, 1916. 16 p. [14258

——Verrɛ zzano's voyage, 1524. Boston, Old South Meeting House, n.d. (Old South leaflets, no. 17) 16 p. [14259

Vestal, Blum H. From the saloon to the pulpit; or, The life of Blum H. Vestal, by himself. Greensboro, The Author [1913] 55 p. [14260

Vester, Kelly G. Food service, a master plan. New York, Pageant Press [1953] 152 p. [14261

Vickers, Thurman G. Pictures of the battlefront of the 324th Infantry, Meuse-Argonne, November 9-11, 1918, photographed by Chaplain T. G. Vickers, April 28-May 2, 1919. [Raleigh?] n.d. [4] p. 100 plates. [14262

Victor Silas Bryant, 1867-1920. [Durham? 1920?] 26 p. [14263

Viehman, Theodore. The centennial pageant and masque of Davidson College, presented by the students and friends of Davidson College on Richardson Field . . . Monday, June 7, 1937, as a feature of the centennial celebration and commencement. [Davidson, 1937] 16 p. [14264

Views in and about Hendersonville. [Hendersonville?] n.d. 19 plates [14265

Views of Montreat, N. C. Brooklyn, N. Y., Albertype Co. for Alice Margaret Dickinson, c.1908. (Rhododendron series, no. 1) 8 plates. [14266

A vindication of the character of the Rever'd David Henkel, residing in Lincoln County, N. C., by the elders, &c. of his several congregations. No place [1820] 12 p. [14267

Vine Hill Academy, Scotland Neck, N. C. [Announcement] 18 - Scotland Neck, 18 - NcU has 1896/97 [14268

——Catalogue, 189 - Scotland Neck, 189 - NcU has 1894/95 [14269

Vining, Elizabeth Janet (Gray) see **Gray, Elizabeth Janet**

The Virginia and North Carolina almanac see **The Warrock**-Richardson Maryland, Virginia, and North Carolina almanack

The Virginia & North-Carolina almanack for the year of our Lord, 18 - Petersburg, Somervill & Conrad, 18 - NcU has 1810, 1813 [14270

Virginia and North Carolina Presbyterian preacher, v. 1- January, 1828- Fayetteville, Colin McIver, 1828- NcU has v. [1] [14271

Virginia-Carolina peanut news, v. 1- April, 1955- Ahoskie, North Carolina Peanut Growers Association, 1955- NcU has v. [1-2] [14272

[Virginia Midland Railway] Summer resorts and points of interest of Virginia, Western North Carolina, and North Georgia. New York, C. G. Crawford, pr., 1884. 95 p. [14273

Virginia Trust Company, Richmond. Heritage of a half century, 1892-1942. Richmond [Whittet & Shepperson, pr.] 1942. 47 p. [14274

Visitor's guide to Asheville, N. C., including hotels, boarding homes, schools, and general information. [Asheville, Asheville Printing Co.] n.d. 66 p. [14275

Vogtle, Alvin Ward. Freight rates and the South; statements by Alvin W. Vogtle and Henry B. Kline. Nashville, Tenn., Vanderbilt University Press, 1943. 52 p. [14276

A voice from heaven. [Raleigh, General Tract Agency, June, 1861] (Selected for the soldiers, no. 243) 4 p. [14277

Voices of Peace, v. 1- December, 1889- Raleigh, Peace Institute, 1889- NcU has v. [1-2] and 2d series, v. [1-4] Discontinued 1895-1919, 1931- [14278

Vollmer, Lula. The hill between; a folk play in three acts. New York, Longmans, Green and Co. [1939] 110 p. [14279

——Moonshine and honeysuckle; a play in three acts. New York, S. French, Inc., c.1934. 99 p. [14280

——Sun-up; a play in three acts. New York, Brentano's [c.1924] 79 p. [14281

Von Glahn, Henry. Brief and argument: Henry von Glahn vs. Zebulon Latimer, ex. of Henry Savage. [Wilmington?] n.d. 14 p.   [14282

Von Ruck, Karl. The management of pulmonary phthisis. Asheville, Citizen Publishing Co., 1889. 44 p.   [14283

Von Ruck Memorial Sanatorium, Asheville, N. C. see Asheville, N. C. Von Ruck Memorial Sanatorium

Vorse, Mary Marvin (Heaton) Strike! New York, H. Liveright [c.1930] 376 p.[14284

Voters of North Carolina, read the whole record. No place, no publisher [1912] 16 p.   [14285

Vox populi, pseud. Appeal to the people of North Carolina. [Raleigh, no publisher, 1869] 12 p.   [14286

Voyages en Virginie et en Floride. Paris, Dvchartre et Van Bvggenhovdt, 1927. 311 p.   [14287

W. T. Lee for corporation commissioner. No place, no publisher, n.d. [14] p. [14288

Waccamaw Baptist Association. Minutes, 18 - 18 - NcU has 1877, 1881-1883   [14288a

Wachovia, v. 1- 190 - Winston-Salem, Wachovia Bank and Trust Co., 190 - Title varies, 190 - December, 1921: Solicitor. NcU has v. [9-13] 14-49 [14289

Wachovia Bank and Trust Company, Winston-Salem. 75 years of progress with the Southeast, 1879-1954. Winston-Salem, 1954. [31] p.   [14290

——Suggested forms of wills and trust agreements for the exclusive use of attorneys at law. Asheville [c.1929] 37 p.   [14291

——The Wachovia and its work. Winston-Salem, n.d. 30 p.   [14292

——What is the answer to today's estate problem? [Winston-Salem, 1929] 20 p.   [14293

Wachovia Historical Society, Winston-Salem. Wachovia Historical Society, Winston-Salem, North Carolina, 19 - [Winston-Salem] 19 - NcU has 1933/34-1955/56   [14294

Wachovia Moravian, v. 1- March, 1893- Winston-Salem, Moravians or United Brethren, 1893- NcU has v. 3-8 [9-10] 11-13, 19-21 [22-25] 26-30 [30-33] 34-35 [36-39] 40-64, 55-60, v. 14-18 omitted in numbering; v. 30 repeated in numbering twice; v. 41-50 omitted in numbering; v. 55-60 repeated in numbering   [14295

Waddel, John Newton. Memorials of academic life: being an historical sketch of the Waddel family. Richmond, Va., Presbyterian Committee of Publication, 1891. 583 p.   [14296

Waddell, Alfred Moore. Address at the unveiling of the Confederate monument, at Raleigh, N. C., May 20th, 1895. Wilmington, LeGwin Brothers, pr., 1895. 21 p.   [14297

——Address before the Philanthropic and Dialectic societies of the University of North Carolina, June, 1876. No place, no publisher, n.d. 23 p.   [14298

——Address to the graduating class of the Medical College of Virginia, at Richmond, Va., March 31st, 1887. Wilmington, S. G. Hall, pr., 1887. 23 p.   [14299

——The ante-bellum university; oration delivered at the centennial celebration of the opening of the University of North Carolina, June 5th, 1895. Wilmington, Jackson & Bell, 1895. 17 p.   [14300

——A colonial officer and his times, 1754-1773; a biographical sketch of Gen. Hugh Waddell, of North Carolina. Raleigh, Edwards & Broughton, 1890. 242 p.[14301

——The Confederate soldier; an address delivered at the written request of 5,000 ex-Union soldiers, at Steinway Hall, New York City, Friday evening, May 3d, 1878, for the benefit of the 47th N. Y. Veteran Volunteers (Miles O'Reilly's regiment) Washington, Joseph L. Pearson, pr., 1878. 23 p.   [14302

——General Francis Nash; an address delivered at the unveiling of a monument to General Nash, voted by Congress, at the Guilford Battle Ground, July 4th, 1906. Greensboro, Guilford Battle Ground Co., 1906. 19 p.   [14303

——A history of New Hanover County and the lower Cape Fear region, 1723-1800. [Wilmington? 1909] 232 p. Called v. 1. No more published.   [14304

——The last year of the war in North Carolina, including Plymouth, Fort Fisher and Bentonsville; an address before the Association Army Northern Virginia, delivered in the hall of the House of Delegates, Richmond, Va., October 28, 1887. Richmond, W. E. Jones, pr., 1888. 31 p.   [14305

——The life and character of William L. Saunders; an oration delivered before the Alumni Association of the University of North Carolina, Tuesday, May 31st, 1892. Wilmington, Jackson & Bell, 1892. 15 p.   [14306

——Our foreign commerce and American shipping; an address delivered by request of the Chamber of Commerce . . . and other bodies of the city of Wilmington, N. C., on Thursday, September 19th, 1878. 20 p.   [14307

——Robert Emmet; an address delivered before the Irish-American societies of Washington, D. C., at Ford's Opera House, March 4th, 1878 (the centennial anniversary of Emmet's birth) Washington, Joseph L. Pearson, pr., 1878. 16 p. [14308

——Socialism in the United States; an address delivered before the literary societies of Trinity College, N. C., June 7th, 1893. [Durham? Trinity College? 1893?] 15 p.   [14309

——Some memories of my life. Raleigh, Edwards & Broughton Printing Co., 1908. 249 p.   [14310

——Some public dangers; an address delivered at Enfield, N. C., Tuesday, June 26, 1894. No place, no publisher [1894?] 15 p.   [14311

Waddell, Charles Edward and Company, Asheville. Twenty-five years of engineering in Western North Carolina, being a record of the works of Charles E. Waddell & Company, 1902 to 1927. [Asheville, Advocate Printing Co., 1928?] [23] p. [14312

Waddell, Gabrielle de Rosset. Digest of prefaces of the Colonial records of North Carolina, volumes 1-X [Raleigh] National Society of the Colonial Dames of America in the State of North Carolina, 1935. 42 p.   [14313

Waddell, Hugh. To the freemen of Orange County. Orange County, November 1, 1835. [1] p.   [14314

Waddell, Maude. Bookgreen ballads and low country lyrics. [Wendell, Gold Leaf Press, 1940?] 16 p.   [14315

——Carolina coast; songs of the southern sea. [Wendell, Gold Leaf Press, pr., 1938?] 25 p.   [14316

——Charleston chimes. [Wendell, Gold Leaf Press, pr., 1939?] 17 p.   [14317

——Melodies of the marshes. [Charleston, S. C.? The Author, 1941] 15 p. [14318

——Ocean echoes. [Charleston, S. C.? The Author, 1941] 16 p.   [14319

——Places. [Charleston, S. C.? The Author, 1945?] [7] p.   [14320

——River reveries. [Charleston, S. C. The Author, 1945] 9 p.   [14321

——Saint Peters-By-The-Sea. [Wendell, Gold Leaf Press, pr., 1940] 19 p. [14322

——Songs of the sea. [Charleston? The Author, 1942?] 17 p.   [14323

——Songs of the South. No place, no publisher [1940?] 16 p.   [14324

——Songs of the South; life work of Maude Waddell. Charleston, S. C., Southern Printing & Publishing Co., 1942. 205 p.   [14325

——Southern poems. No place, no publisher, n.d. 14 p.   [14326

Waddill, Ed. M. The song of the Soldiers' Home, Raleigh, N. C. Raleigh, Edwards & Broughton, 1895. 13 p.   [14327

Waddill, J. M. Circular: To the citizens of Rockingham. Huntsville Township, n.d. [1] p.   [14328

Wade, Julius Jennings. Sports parade; selected columns. [Kannapolis, Williams Printing Co. for James L. Moore and T. H. Wingate, c.1941] 32 p.   [14329

[Wadesboro, N. C. Board of Education] Wadesboro City Schools. [Wadesboro, 1908] 10 p.   [14330

Wadesboro, N. C. Chamber of Commerce. North Carolina, the most talked of state in the South. Wadesboro, Wadesboro Chamber of Commerce [1928?] Folder.   [14331

——A 3-minute story, Wadesboro, N. C., worth several hours of careful study. [Wadesboro, 1928] 3 p.   [14332

——Wadesboro's door of opportunity is open. [Wadesboro, 1928] Folder. [14333

Wadesboro, N. C. Merchants Association. Dear historians. Wadesboro, 1948. [5] p.   [14334

Wager, Paul Woodford, ed. County government across the nation. Chapel Hill, University of North Carolina Press [1950] 817 p.   [14335

Wager, Paul Woodford. County government and administration in North Carolina. Chapel Hill, University of North Carolina Press, 1928. 447 p.   [14336

——North Carolina, the state and its government. New York, Oxford Book Co., 1947. 124 p.   [14337

——One foot on the soil, a study of subsistence homesteads in Alabama. University, Ala., Bureau of Public Administration, University of Alabama, 1945. (Its Publications, no. 19)   230 p.   [14338

Wager, Paul Woodford, joint ed. see Lefler, Hugh Talmage, ed.

Wagstaff, Henry McGilbert. The Concord community; a retrospect. [Roxboro? The Roxboro Courier?] 1941.   12 p.   [14339
——Federalism in North Carolina. Chapel Hill, The University, 1910. (James Sprunt historical publications, v. 9, no. 2)   p. [3]-44   [14340
——Impressions of men and movements at the University of North Carolina, edited with a prefatory note, by Louis R. Wilson. Chapel Hill, University of North Carolina Press [1950]   110 p.   [14341
——State rights and political parties in North Carolina—1776-1861. Baltimore, Johns Hopkins Press, 1906. (Johns Hopkins University. Studies in historical and political science, series xxiv, no. 7-8)   155 p.   [14342
——Wiley Buck and other stories of the Concord community. Chapel Hill, University of North Carolina Press [1953]   118 p.   [14343

Wahiscoan, 19 - [Washington? N. C.] Senior Class of the Washington, N. C., High School, 19 - NcU has 1917   [14344

Waite, Minnie May (Curtis) Verses. [Angwin, Calif., Angwin Bindery, 1942] 104 p.   [14345

Wake Co., N. C. Board of Alcoholic Control. Report, 1937/38- Raleigh, 1938- NcU has 1937/38-1944/45, 1946/47-1949/50   [14346

Wake Co., N. C. Board of Commissioners. Wake County finances, 1867/68- 1871/72. [Raleigh, 1868-1872]   5 broadsides.   [14347

[Wake Co., N. C. Board of Education] Directions to teachers of Public Schools for Negroes, 1915-16. Raleigh [1915?]   16 p.   [14348
——Directions to Wake County teachers. Raleigh, 1911. [6] p.   [14349
——An examination for teachers of Wake County Public Schools. [Raleigh, 1902] [3] p.   [14350

Wake Co., N. C. Board of Education. Handbook for Wake County teachers, 1913- 14. Raleigh [1913?]   28 p.   [14351
—— ——1915-16. [1915?]   28 p.   [14352
—— ——1917-18. [1917?]   23 p.   [14353
—— ——1927-28. Raleigh, 1927.   23 p.   [14354

[Wake Co., N. C. Board of Education] Language and arithmetic for primary teachers in Wake County, 1917. Raleigh, 1917.   68 p.   [14355

Wake Co., N. C. Board of Education. Report of the Wake County Public Schools, 189 - Raleigh, 189 - NcU has 1899/1900, 1900/01, 1904/05, 1905/07, 1907/ 09   [14356

[Wake Co., N. C. Citizens] Constitutional Union resolutions and ticket for Wake County. [Raleigh? 1861?]   [1] p.   [14357

Wake Co., N. C. Cattle Club. Constitution and by-laws. No place, no publisher, n.d. 1 p.   [14358

[Wake Co., N. C. Committee for Smith?] Leroy Jones, Kinston, N. C.; Frank Graham appointed him to West Point as an alternate. [Raleigh? 1950] [1] p. [14359
——The Negro press makes a final appeal. Raleigh, 1950. [1] p.   [14360

Wake Co., N. C. Exposition Committee. Wake County, North Carolina; its resources, its products, and its people. Raleigh, Edwards, Broughton & Co., pr., 1884. 16 p.   [14361

Wake Co., N. C. Treasurer. Annual statement, 18 - Raleigh, 18 - NcU has 1878/79, 1881/82, 1882/83   [14362

Wake County Association for the Betterment of Public Schools. Wake County Association for the Betterment of Public Schools. Raleigh, 1911. 30 p.   [14363
—— ——Raleigh, 1916. 31 p.   [14364

Wake County Bar Association. Brief in support of a bill to be entitled An act to prohibit the unauthorized practice of law in North Carolina. [Raleigh? 1931?] 11 p.   [14365
——Constitution, by-laws, canons of ethics, officers, committees, membership, etc. Raleigh, January, 1930. 34 p.   [14366

——A statute providing for a uniform system for the election and compensation of justices of the peace in North Carolina. [Raleigh? 1934?] 41 p. [14367

Wake County Builders' Exchange. By-laws; organized Dec. 27, 1916. Raleigh, Edwards and Broughton, pr., n.d. 7 p. [14368

Wake County Medical Society. Medical fee bill. [Raleigh] Star Office, n.d. [1] p. [14369

Wake County school news, v. 1- January, 1918- Raleigh, Wake County Board of Education, 1918- NcU has v. [1] and 2d series v. [1] November, 1929- [14370

Wake County Teachers Association. Joint township meeting of the teachers of Wake County, 1906- Raleigh, 1906- NcU has 1906, 1907 [14371

Wake County Working-Men's Association. Resolutions and address. [Raleigh?] 1859. 6 p. [14372

Wake Forest alumni news see Wake Forest magazine

Wake Forest College, Wake Forest, and Winston-Salem, N. C. Bulletin, v. 1- 1899- Wake Forest, 1899- NcU has v. [2, 3] new series, v. 1-3 [4] 5 [7-9] 10-12 [13-17] 18-22 [23-50] [14373

——Catalogue of Wake Forest College, 18 - 1904/05- Wake Forest, 18 - 1905. NcU has [1835/36-1896/97] Continues as its Bulletin, 1898/99-1904/05 new series, v. 1- 1906- [14374

——The charter and laws of the Wake Forest College . . . December, 1838. Raleigh, The Recorder Office, pr., 1839. 15 p. [14375

——Commencement exercises at Wake Forest College, North Carolina, June 7, 1854. Philadelphia, C. Sherman, 1854. 103 p. [14376

——General catalogue of Wake Forest College, 1834/35-1891/92, prepared by C. E. Taylor. Raleigh, Edwards & Broughton, pr., 1892. 199 p. [14377

——Wake Forest College circular of information; history. Raleigh, Edwards & Broughton, pr. [1906?] 20 p. [14378

——Wake Forest College, Wake Forest, N. C. Brooklyn, N. Y., Albertype Co., n.d. [2] p. 15 plates [14379

Wake Forest College, Wake Forest, and Winston-Salem, N. C. Alumni Association. The Wake Forest Alumni Association. Raleigh, Edwards, Broughton & Co., pr., 1886. 16 p. [14380

Wake Forest College, Wake Forest, and Winston-Salem, N. C. Bowman Gray School of Medicine. Journal, v. 1- January, 1944- Winston-Salem, 1944- NcU has v. 1-14 [14381

Wake Forest College, Wake Forest, and Winston-Salem N. C. Library. A catalogue of the library of Charles Lee Smith, edited by Edgar Estes Folk. Wake Forest, Wake Forest College Press, 1950. 654 p. [14382

——Through thirty-one years; report of Mrs. Ethel Taylor Crittenden as librarian . . . 1915-1946. Wake Forest, 1947. (Its Bulletin, new series, v. 42, no. 3) 32 p. [14383

Wake Forest College, Wake Forest, and Winston-Salem, N. C. President. Report, 18 - Wake Forest, 18 - NcU has 1906/07, 1907/08, 1909/10, 1914/15, 1917/18 [14384

Wake Forest College, Wake Forest, and Winston-Salem, N. C. Treasurer. Report, 18 - Wake Forest, 18 - NcU has [1899/1900-1904/05] [14385

Wake Forest Historical Society papers. Raleigh, Edwards & Broughton, Pr., 1899. 58 p. [14386

Wake Forest student, v. 1- 1882?- Wake Forest, Students of Wake Forest College, 1882?- NcU has v. [1-2] 3 [4-7] 8 [9-10] 11 [12] 13 [14] 15-17 [18-21] 22 [23-25] 26-37 [38] 39-47 [48-58] 70-72 [14387

Wakefield, Lawrence. Beating a retreat on the eve of victory. No place, Author [1912] 4 p. [14388

Wakefield, Priscilla (Bell) Excursions in North America. 2d ed. London, Darton, Harvey and Darton, 1810. 420 p. [14389

Wakefield Classical and Mathematical School, Wakefield, N. C. Catalogue, 1882/ 83?- Wakefield, 1883?- NcU has [1898/99-1906/07] [14390

Wakelon High School and Farm Life School, Wakefield, N. C. Catalogue, 1908/09- Wakefield, 1909- NcU has 1908/09, 1911/12-1914/15, 1916/17, 1918/19 [14391

Walcot, James. The new Pilgrim's progress; or, The pious Indian convert, containing a faithful account of Hattain Gelashmin, a heathen, who was baptis'd into the Christian faith by the name of George James.   London, M. Cooper, 1748. 316 p.   [14392

Walcott, Charles Folsom. History of the Twenty-first Regiment, Massachusetts Volunteers, in the war for the preservation of the Union, 1861-1865.   Boston, Houghton, Mifflin and Co., 1882.   502 p.   [14393

Waldman, Milton. Sir Walter Raleigh.   New York, Harper & Brothers, 1928. 255 p.   [14394

Waldo, Samuel Putnam. Memoirs of Andrew Jackson. 3d ed. Hartford, S. Andrus, 1819.   312 p.   [14395

[**Waldo, Samuel Putnam**] Memoirs of the illustrious citizen and patriot, Andrew Jackson . . . By a citizen of Hagers-town, Md.   Chambersburg, Printed for subscribers, 1828.   306 p.   [14396

Waldron, Holman D. With pen and camera thro' the "Land of the sky", Western North Carolina and the Asheville plateau.   Portland, Me., Chisholm Bros., c.1900. [48] p.   [14397

Walker, Alexander. Jackson and New Orleans. New York, J. C. Derby, 1856. 411 p.   [14398

——The life of Andrew Jackson, to which is added an authentic narrative of the memorable achievements of the American army at New Orleans, in the winter of 1814, '15.   Philadelphia, G. G. Evans, 1860.   414 p.   [14399

—— ——Philadelphia, John E. Potter & Co., 1867.   414 p.   [14400

Walker, Alice Evan. What is education? Chapel Hill, 1933. ([North Carolina University] Studies in philosophy, no. 6)   11 p.   [14401

——What is an individual? Chapel Hill, University of North Carolina, Department of Philosophy, 1932.   8 p.   [14402

Walker, David. [Walker's appeal in four articles] . . . written in Boston . . . Sept. 28, 1829.   2d ed. with corrections, &c.   Boston, D. Walker, 1830.   80 p.   NcU has microfilm from defective copy in the Library of Congress with title page mutilated.   [14403

Walker, Felix Hampton. Memoirs of the late the Hon. Felix Walker, of North Carolina . . . ed. by Sam'l R. Walker.   New Orleans, A. Taylor, pr., 1877. 19 p.   [14404

Walker, Harriette Hammer. Busy North Carolina women.   Asheboro [The Author] 1931.   156 p.   [14405

Walker, James Alves. Life of Col. John (Jack) Walker. [Wilmington, The Author, 1902] [9] p.   [14406

Walker, James Garfield. Presbyterianism and the Negro. [Greensboro?] n.d. 92 p.   [14407

Walker, James Robert. Be firm my hope.   New York, Comet Press Books [1955] 114 p.   [14408

——Poetical diets. No place, no publisher [c.1923] 146 p.   [14409

Walker, John M. North Carolina, Dec. 17, 1816; a report on education.   No place, no publisher [1816?]   8 p.   [14410

[**Walker, L. A.?**] The surrender at Greensboro. No place, no publisher, n.d. 7 p.   [14411

Walker, Margaret. For my people . . . with a foreword by Stephen Vincent Benét. New Haven, Yale University Press, 1942.   58 p.   [14412

Walker, Nathan Wilson. The preparation and the selection of teachers for high school and college; presidential address before the Association of Colleges and Secondary Schools of the Southern States, Jackson, Mississippi, December 2, 1926. [Chapel Hill? 1926?]   13 p.   [14413

Walker, Nathan Wilson, joint author, see McBain, Howard Lee

Walker, Nona. Kappy Oliver. New York, Holt [1956] 256 p.   [14414

Walker, S. G. The household catechism on the Decalogue, for proper religious worship, moral and civil culture of children and youth.   Burlington, The Author, 1909.   124 p.   [14415

——Thomas memorials; comprising the biography, death, funeral service, burial rite and reminiscences of Rev. Spencer Thomas and sketches of his churches. Burlington [Southern Christian Publishing Co.] n.d. 74 p. [14416

[Walker, W. R.] Those clerical errors. [Raleigh, Edwards & Broughton, pr., 1895] 4 p. [14417

Wall, Henry Clay. Historical sketch of the Pee Dee Guards (Co. D., 23d N. C. Regiment) from 1861 to 1865. Raleigh, Edwards, Broughton and Co., 1876. 100 p. [14418

Wall, Mary Moore. Lines by a little lady 99 years old. [Oakland, Calif., T. M. Price] 1954. [22] p. [14419

Wall, Mary Virginia. The daughter of Virginia Dare. New York, Neale Publishing Co., 1908. 194 p. [14420

Wallace, J. A. Diligence and perseverance; a sermon delivered in the chapel of Davidson College, October 26th, 1845. Salisbury, The Watchman, n.d. 20 p.[14421

Wallace, John. Carpet bag rule in Florida. Jacksonville, Fla., Da Costa Printing and Publishing House, 1888. 444 p. [14422

Wallace, Lillian Parker. The papacy and European diplomacy, 1869-1878. Chapel Hill, University of North Carolina Press [1948] 349 p. [14423
——A syllabus for the history of civilization, by Lillian Parker Wallace and Alice Barnwell Keith. Raleigh, Technical Press, 1943. 2 v. [14424

Wallace Brothers, Statesville, N. C. Descriptive list of roots, herbs, barks, seeds, flowers, mosses, etc. [Statesville, W. P. Drake, 1884] 47 p. [14425
——The Wallace Brothers Company, collectors of roots, herbs, barks, etc. [Statesville] n.d. [2] p. [14426

Waller, John A. For the Senate! Whither are we drifting? To all good Populists and true reformers of Granville and Person counties. No place [1894?] [1] p. [14427

Wallin, Clarence Monroe. Gena of the Appalachians. New York, Cochrane Publishing Co., 1910. 109 p. [14428

Wallis, James. The Bible defended; being an investigation of the misrepresentations and falsehoods of Thomas Paine's Age of reason, part the second. Halifax, Abraham Hodge, 1797. 115 p. [14429
——An oration on the death of General George Washington, late president of the United States, delivered in Charlotte, February 22, 1800, to the citizens of Mecklenburgh County, and published at the request of the militia officers of said county. Raleigh, Printed by Joseph Gales, 1800. 16 p. [14430

Walls, William Jacob. Joseph Charles Price, educator and race leader. Boston, Christopher Publishing House [1943] 568 p. [14431

Walser, Richard Gaither. Bernice Kelly Harris; storyteller of eastern Carolina. Chapel Hill, University of North Carolina Library, 1955. 52 p. [14432
——Correspondence courses, North Carolina literature, English Ex-374. Raleigh, Division of College Extension, North Carolina State College of Agriculture and Engineering [1953?] 28 p. [14433

Walser, Richard Gaither, ed. The enigma of Thomas Wolfe; biographical and critical selections. Cambridge, Harvard University Press, 1953. 313 p. [14434

Walser, Richard Gaither. Inglis Fletcher of Bandon Plantation. Chapel Hill, University of North Carolina Library, 1952. 79 p. [14435

Walser, Richard Gaither, ed. North Carolina drama. Richmond, Va., Garrett and Massie, 1956. 229 p. [14436
——North Carolina in the short story. Chapel Hill, University of North Carolina Press, 1948. 309 p. [14437

Walser, Richard Gaither, comp. One hundred outstanding books about North Carolina, compiled by Richard Walser and Hugh T. Lefler. [Chapel Hill, University of North Carolina Press, 1956] 15 p. [14438

Walser, Richard Gaither, ed. North Carolina poetry. Richmond, Garrett and Massie, Inc. [c.1941] 196 p. [14439
—— ——Rev. ed. 1951. 200 p. [14440
——A selected bibliography: abstracts of titles from N. C. authors, a selective handbook. [Raleigh, The Editor, 1954] 8 p. [14441

Walser, Zebulon Vance. Flashes of wit and humor of the North Carolina bench and bar; an address at the annual meeting of the North Carolina Bar Association, at Morehead City, July 2d, 1908. No place, no publisher, n.d.   23 p.   [14442

Walsh, John Tomline. The life and times of John Tomline Walsh; with biographical and historical sketches and reflections on contemporary men and things, edited by a member of his family.   Cincinnati, Standard Publishing Co., 1885.   171 p. [14443
——The nature and duration of future punishment.   Richmond, Va., Wm. H. Clemmitt, 1857.   124 p.   [14444
——A review of Free Masonry.   Rev. ed.   New-Berne, Job Office of N. S. Richardson, 1871.   32 p.   [14445

Walter, Thomas. Flora Caroliniana.   London, J. Fraser, 1788.   263 p.   [14446
—— ——Cambridge, Mass., Arnold Arboretum, 1946.   Facsimile ed.   [14447

Walter Hines Page. [New York, Walter Hines Page School of International Relations, 1924?]   19 p.   [14448

Walter Kempner Foundation, Inc., Durham, N. C. The Walter Kempner Foundation, Inc.   Durham, 1950.   [18] p.   [14449

Walton, Loring Baker. Anatole France and the Greek world.   Durham, Duke University Press, 1950.   334 p.   [14450

Walton, Mary Ethel. Words have breath, poems.   Philadelphia, Dorrance & Co. [1951]   (Contemporary poets of Dorrance, 419)   127 p.   [14451

[**Walz, Audrey**]   Dead reckoning [by] Francis Bonnamy, pseud.   New York, Duel, Sloan and Pearce [1943]   248 p.   [14452

Ward, Dallas T. The last flag of truce.   Franklinton [c.1915]   16 p.   [14453

Ward, E. L. C. Address delivered at the tenth annual session of the North Carolina Press Association in Elizabeth City, North Carolina, April 27th, 1882.   No place, no publisher, n.d.   8 p.   [14454

Ward, John William. Andrew Jackson, symbol for an age.   New York, Oxford University Press, 1955.   274 p.   [14455

Ward, Mary Elizabeth (Jones) "Beer by Christmas" and Bertrand Russell drives backward now.   Robersonville, The Author [1932]   [6] p.   [14456

Ward, Millard. Brute.   New York, D. Appleton-Century Co., 1935.   248 p. [14457

Ward, Vernon Albert, Jr. Credo politico.   [Robersonville? 1939]   11 p.   [14458
——International poems.   Robersonville, The Author, 1943.   26 p.   [14459
——One world for humanity.   [Robersonville? The Author 1942]   [4] p.   [14460

Ward Gold-Mine Company. Prospectus of the Ward Gold-Mine Company.   New York, R. C. Root & Anthony [1854?]   15 p.   [14461

Warden, David Baillie. A statistical, political, and historical account of the United States of North America; from the period of their first colonization to the present day.   Edinburgh, A. Constable and Co., 1819.   3 v.   North Carolina, v. 2, p. 364-394.   [14462

Warden, William. Letters written on board His Majesty's ship the Northumberland, and 'at Saint Helena.   Newbern, Published by W. Ivey & J. Scott, 1817. 142 p.   [14463

Wardlaw, Jack. Top secrets of successful selling: thought plus action.   New York, W. Funk [1952]   241 p.   [14464

Ware, Charles Crossfield. Barton Warren Stone, pathfinder of Christian union; a a story of his life and times.   St. Louis, Mo., Bethany Press [c.1932]   357 p. [14465
——Centennial play: Christians' reveille, a drama of the beginnings of North Carolina Disciples of Christ.   Wilson, North Carolina Christian Missionary Convention [1944]   30 p.   [14466
——A history of Atlantic Christian College.   Wilson, Atlantic Christian College [c.1956]   248 p.   [14467
——North Carolina Disciples of Christ; a history of their rise and progress, and of their contribution to their general brotherhood.   St. Louis, Mo., Christian Board of Publication, 1927.   372 p.   [14468
——Onslow's oldest church.   Wilson, Carolina Discipliana Library, 1956. 12 p. [14469
——Rountree chronicles, 1827-1840, documentary primer of a Tar Heel faith. Wilson, North Carolina Christian Missionary Convention, 1947.   64 p.   [14470

Ware, Thomas. Sketches of the life and travels of Rev. Thomas Ware, who has been an itinerant Methodist preacher for more than fifty years. New York, T. Mason and G. Lane, 1839. 264 p. [14471

Ware, William R. Historical sketch and directory of the Central Methodist Episcopal Church, South, Monroe, N. C., 1907. Raleigh, Edwards & Broughton Co., n.d. 40 p. [14472

Warm Springs, Madison County, Western North Carolina. Warm Springs, 1877. 15 p. [14473

——Raleigh, W. H. Ferrell, pr. [1880?] 16 p. [14474

——New York, J. H. Warner [1882] 20 p. [14475

Warne, Joseph A. The duty of supporting the Christian ministry stated and enforced; a circular written for the Neuse Baptist Association and presented at their session, October 14th, 1825. Newbern, Printed by Pasteur & Watson, 1826. 14 p. [14476

Warner, Charles Dudley. On horseback; a tour in Virginia, North Carolina and Tennessee, with notes of travel in Mexico and California. New York, Houghton, Mifflin and Co., 1889. 331 p. [14477

—— ——1888. [14478

Warner, Harold Phillips. First authentic V-mail portrait of World War II, and several short stories. Raleigh, 1948. 84 p. [14479

Warren, Andrew Jackson. Some modern health care problems; an address delivered at the 160th annual commencement of the University of North Carolina at Chapel Hill, N. C., June 7, 1954. [Chapel Hill, 1954] 11 p. [14480

Warren, E. J. Mr. Warren's speech, upon resolution concerning the recent action of the Governor, the Chief Justice, and certain other justices of the Supreme Court, in the Senate of N. C., March 22d, 1871. No place, no publisher [1871?] 13 p.[14481

Warren, Edward. A doctor's experiences in three continents; in a series of letters addressed to John Norris, M. D., of Baltimore, Md. Baltimore, Md., Cushings & Bailey, 1885. 613 p. [14482

——An epitome of practical surgery for field and hospital. Richmond, Va., West & Johnson, 1863. 401 p. [14483

——An introductory lecture delivered before the faculty and class of the Medical Department of Washington University, October 1, 1867. Baltimore, The Sun, pr., 1867. 31 p. [14484

——The rule of life; an address delivered before the two literary societies of Wake Forest College, June 8, 1859. Fayetteville, Edward J. Hale and Son, 1859. 24 p. [14485

Warren, Julius Benjamin. Interpreting the public's schools. Raleigh, Bynum Printing Co., 1929. 48 p. [14486

——North Carolina atlas and outline maps, by Jule B. Warren and L. Polk Denmark. Raleigh, Warren Publishing Co., c.1947. 40 p. [14487

—— ——c.1952. 48 p. [14488

——North Carolina yesterday and today. Raleigh [Edwards & Broughton Co., c.1941] 328 p. [14489

——The people govern North Carolina. Raleigh, Warren Publishing Co., 1946. 219 p. [14490

Warren, Mary Alethea. Historic buildings of Edenton, North Carolina. No place, no publisher [1927?] [20] p. [14491

Warren Co., N. C. Auditor. Report, 19 - 19 - NcU has 1926/27 [14492

Warren Co., N. C. Board of Education. Report, 19 - Warrenton, 19 - NcU has 1912/13 [14493

Warren Wilson Vocational Junior College, Swannanoa, N. C. Catalogue, 1942/43?- Swannanoa, 1943?- NcU has 1955/56 [14494

Warrenton Female Seminary, Warrenton, N. C. Catalogue, 18 - Warrenton, 18 - NcU has 1841/42, 1849/50 [14495

Warrenton High School, Warrenton, N. C. Catalogue, 1896/97?- Warrenton, 1897?- NcU has 1901/02?, 1903/04?, 1904/05-1908/09, 1910/11, 1912/13-1915/16 [14496

The Warrock-Richardson Maryland, Virginia, and North Carolina almanack for the year, 1816- Richmond, Va., Clyde W. Saunders, 1816- NcU has [1820-1853]

1854-1859 (Cottom's edition) 1860-1865 (Wynne's edition) 1868-1898, 1900-1920, 1922-1931, 1933-1935   [14497

Warsaw, N. C.   Board of Trustees of Graded School.   Catalogue, 19   -   Warsaw, 19   -   NcU has 1912/13   [14498

Washburn, Benjamin Earle.   A country doctor in the South Mountains.   Asheville, Stephens Press [1955]   94 p.   [14499

——The health game.   London, J. & A. Churchill, 1930.   202 p.   [14500

——The hookworm campaign in Alamance County, North Carolina.   Raleigh, E. M. Uzzell, 1914.   38 p.   [14501

Washburn, Jim.   Jim, the boy; autobiographical sketches of the author's first 18 years.   Lake Lure, 1952.   115 p.   [14502

Washington, George, pres. U. S.   The diaries of George Washington, 1748-1799, ed. by J. C. Fitzpatrick.   Boston, Houghton, Mifflin and Co., 1925.   4 v.   [14503

——The diary of George Washington from 1789 to 1791, embracing the opening of the first Congress, and his tours through New England, Long Island, and the Southern States.   Richmond, Va., Press of the Historical Society, 1861.   248 p.   [14504

——President Washington's diaries, 1791 to 1799, transcribed and compiled by Joseph A. Hoskins.   Summerfield, The Compiler, 1921.   100 p.   [14505

——Washington's farewell address to the people of the United States, September, 1796.   Raleigh, Star Office by Thomas Henderson, Jr., 1809.   28 p.   [14506

Washington, Lawrence Daniel.   Confessions of a schoolmaster.   San Antonio, Naylor Co., 1939.   354 p.   [14507

Washington, William H.   An address delivered before Manteo Lodge, no. 8, of the I. O. O. F. on its third anniversary, January 13, 1849.   Raleigh, William W. Holden, 1849.   12 p.   [14508

Washington, N. C.   Board of School Trustees.   Report, 1897/98-   Washington, 1898-   NcU has [1898/99-1921/22]   [14509

[Washington, N. C.   Bug House Laboratory]   Bug House Laboratory, sponsors of Washington Field Museum, largest and oldest amateur museum in America. [Washington, 1932?]   19 p.   [14510

Washington, N. C.   Chamber of Commerce.   A survey of Washington, North Carolina, for industrial development.   Washington [1951]   11, 4 p.   [14511

——Washington, Beaufort County, North Carolina, describing its advantages and presenting your opportunities.   [Lynchburg, Va., J. P. Ball Co.] n.d.   38 p. [14512

Washington, N. C.   Grimes Real Estate Company.   Coastal plain region of North Carolina, agricultural, trucking, and fruit lands.   Washington [1899?] 24 p. [14513

Washington, N. C.   St. Peter's Church.   Year book, 19   -   Washington, 19   -   NcU has 1918   [14514

Washington, N. C.   Washington Building and Loan Association.   Constitution and by-laws, and act of incorporation thereof, organized June 15th, 1871.   Baltimore, John Murphy & Co., pr., 1872.   19 p.   [14515

Washington Collegiate Institute, Washington, N. C.   Announcement, 1913/14- Washington, 1913-   NcU has 1913/14   [14516

Washington School, Raleigh, N. C.   Catalogue, 1865/66?-   Raleigh, 1866-   NcU has 1875/76   [14517

Watauga Co., N. C.   Board of Education.   Report of the Public Schools, 19   - [Boone, 19   -   NcU has 1911/12   [14518

The watch-tower: a monthly magazine conducted under the authority of the annual convention of the Disciples of Christ, N. Carolina, 187   -   Newbern, Jno. Tomline Walsh, 187   -   NcU has February, 1874, v. 2, no. 5.   [14519

[Waters, D. P.]   Resources and progress of Wilkes County, North Carolina.   North Wilkesboro, D. J. Carter, 1914.   43 p.   [14520

Waters, Mary Louise.   A short historical sketch, New Bern, N. C.   New Bern, Craven County Committee of Colonial Dames of America [1924]   19 p.   [14521

Waters, N. McGee.   A Christmas meditation.   No place, no publisher, n.d. 16 p.   [14522

Waters Normal Institute, Winton, N. C.   Catalogue, 19   -   Winton, 19   -   NcU has 1905/06, 1914/15, 1915/16   [14523

Wathen, Richard.   Cliffs of fall.   New Orleans, Publications Press, c.1953. 304 p.   [14524

Watkins, Basil M.   A challenge to North Carolina Baptists; an address to the North Carolina Baptist State Convention, July 30, 1946. Greensboro [1946?] 16 p. [14525

Watkins, D. Hatcher, publisher.   The hundred and thirty-first anniversary of the Mecklenburg Declaration of Independence; souvenir program. Charlotte, Ray Printing Co. [1906] 26 p.   [14526

Watkins, Francis N.   Catalogue of the descendants of Thomas Watkins of Chicka-homony, Va. Henderson, Atlas Printing Co., 1899. 50 p.   [14527

Watkins, John Bullock, Jr.   Historic Vance County and "happy, healthy, hustling Henderson". Henderson, Henderson Daily Dispatch Co., 1941. 48 p.   [14528

Watkins, N. J., ed.   The pine and the palm greeting; or, The trip of the northern editors to the South in 1871. Baltimore, J. D. Ehlers & Co's Engraving and Printing House, 1873. 144 p.   [14529

Watkins, Shirley.   Georgina finds herself. New York, Goldsmith Publishing Co. [c.1922] 294 p.   [14530
——Jane lends a hand.   New York, Goldsmith Publishing Co. [c.1923] 300 p.[14531
——Nancy of Paradise cottage.   New York, Goldsmith Publishing Co. [c.1921] 307 p.   [14532
——This poor player.   Philadelphia, Macrae-Smith Co. [c.1929] 454 p.   [14533

Watson, Alfred Augustin.   Divine worship; a sermon preached in St. James Church, Wilmington, N. C., the second Sunday after Trinity, June 9th, 1872. Wilmington, J. A. Engelhard, 1872. 24 p.   [14534

[**Watson, Alfred Augustin**]   Pastoral letter of the Bishop of East Carolina to the clergy and laity of his diocese, read before the council at Fayetteville, N. C., May 25, 1888. No place, no publisher, 1888. 8 p.   [14535

Watson, Alfred Augustin.   Sermon delivered before the annual council of the Diocese of North Carolina, upon the festival of the Ascension, May 14, 1863. Raleigh, Progress Print, 1863. 24 p.   [14536

Watson, Annah Walker (Robinson)   On the field of honor. Detroit, Mich., Sprague Publishing Co. [c.1902] 226 p.   [14537

Watson, C. H., ed.   Colored Charlotte. Charlotte, A. M. E. Zion Job Print [1915] 13 p.   [14538

Watson, Cyrus Barksdale.   Appeal for Democratic unity. No place [1908] [4] p.   [14539

[**Watson, Cyrus Barksdale**]   To the voters of North Carolina. No place, no pub-lisher, n.d. [3] p.   [14540

Watson, Elkanah.   History of the rise, progress, and existing state of the Berkshire Agricultural Society in Massachusetts, with practical directions for societies form-ing in North-Carolina on the Berkshire model. Albany, E. & E. Hosford, 1819. 80 p.   [14541
——Men and times of the Revolution; or, Memoirs of Elkanah Watson, including journals of travels in Europe and America, from 1777 to 1842, with his correspond-ence with public men and reminiscences and incidents of the Revolution, ed. by his son, Winslow C. Watson. New-York, Dana and Co., 1856. 460 p.   [14542
—— ——2d ed.   1857. 557 p.   [14543

Watson, Richard.   An apology for the Bible, in a series of letters addressed to Thomas Paine, author of a book entitled The age of reason. Newbern, Printed by François-X. Martin for Joseph Shute and Durant Hatch, 1797. 77 p.   [14544

Watson, Thomas Edward.   The life and times of Andrew Jackson. Thomson, Ga., Jeffersonian Publishing Co., 1917. 440 p.   [14545

Watson, Thomas Lowe.   The poet of man, a senior speech in the University of North Carolina, to be delivered on Friday, April 29th, 1859. Chapel Hill, James M. Henderson, 1859. 4 p.   [14546

Watson and Hall's North-Carolina almanac, 18 - Newbern, Printed by Watson and Hall, 18 - NcU has 1809   [14547

Watters, Fanny C.   Plantation memories of the Cape Fear River country. [Ashe-ville, Stephens Press, 1944] 45 p.   [14548

Watts, A. L.   Sermon on the final perseverance of the saints, preached in the Presbyterian churches of Lincolnton and Long Creek. Greensboro, The Patriot, 1840. 29 p.   [14549

Watts, George Byron.   The Waldenses in the new world. Durham, Duke University Press, 1941. 309 p.   [14550

[Watts Hospital, Durham, N. C.]   Forty years of service to the sick. [Durham, 1936] 22 p.   [14551

Watts Hospital, Durham, N. C.   Report, 1895- Durham, 1896- NcU has 1895, 1920/21-1927. Not published 1926.   [14552

——The Watts Hospital training course in dietetics. Rev. November, 1945. Durham, 1945. 23 p.   [14553

[Watts Hospital, Durham, N. C.]   Welcome to Watts Hospital. [Durham, 1955?] 32 p.   [14554

Watts Hospital, Durham, N. C.   Board of Lady Visitors. Popular cook book. Durham, Seeman Printery, 1899. 122 p.   [14555

Watts law repudiated by Democrats; Pitt County Democrats opposed to class legislation. No place, no publisher [1904?] [1] p.   [14556

Waxhaw Institute, Waxhaw, N. C.   Catalogue, 1897/98?- Waxhaw, 1898?- NcU has 1901/02   [14557

Way, William, 1876-   History of the New England Society of Charleston, South Carolina, for one hundred years, 1819-1919. Charleston, The Society, 1920. 307 p.   [14558

Way, William, Jr.   The Clinchfield Railroad; the story of a trade route across the Blue Ridge Mountains. Chapel Hill, University of North Carolina Press, 1931. 297 p.   [14559

Wayne Co., N. C.   Board of Education. Wayne County teachers' handbook, 1924-25. [Goldsboro? 1924] 28 p.   [14560

[Waynesville, N. C.   Board of Education] Regulations and course of study adopted by the Board of Trustees, Waynesville Graded Schools, 1906. Oxford, Oxford Orphan Asylum, pr. [1906?] 44 p.   [14561

Waynesville, N. C.   Board of Education. Report of the public schools of Waynesville, 19 - Waynesville, 19 - NcU has 1914/15   [14562

[Waynesville, N. C.   Board of Trade] Waynesville, the favorite resort, North Carolina. [Asheville, Inland Press] n.d. 15 p.   [14563

Waynesville, N. C.   Methodist Episcopal Church, South. Handbook. [Waynesville] 1911. 16 p.   [14564

The Waynesville Inn, Waynesville, N. C., in the "Land of the Sky". [Asheville, French Broad Press, 1900] [8] p.   [14565

Waynesville, the beautiful, Waynesville, N. C. No place, no publisher, n.d. [20] p.   [14566

Waynick, Capus.   North Carolina roads and their builders. Raleigh, Superior Stone Company, 1952. 308 p.   [14567

WBT.   Colossus of the Carolinas, the story of a hobby that became an industry. [Charlotte, 1952?] [23] p.   [14568

——Power for the people. [Charlotte, 1954?] [22] p.   [14569

WBTips, v. 1- 1947?- Charlotte, 1947?- NcU has v. 7 [8]   [14570

WDNC news, a guide to greater radio enjoyment, no. 1-12, v. 2-3, October, 1945-June, 1948. Durham, Radio Station WDNC, 1945-1948. NcU has no. 1-12, v. 2-3. Discontinued following June, 1948, issue.   [14571

We the people of North Carolina, v. 1- May, 1943- Raleigh, North Carolina Citizens Association, 1943- NcU has v. 1-14   [14572

Weatherly, H. T.   A funeral sermon on the death of Mrs. Amy Webb, a member of the Methodist E. P. Church, delivered at Ebenezer Church, Granville County, N. C., May 24, 1835. Richmond, T. W. White, 1835. 11 p.   [14573

Weathers, Ida B.   Rhyme and verse, written by Mrs. Jo H. Weathers (Miss Ida) 1937. Raleigh, John T. Pullen Tract Society [1937?] 37 p.   [14574

Weathers, Lee Beam.   The living past of Cleveland County, a history. [Shelby, Star Publishing Co., 1956] 269 p.   [14575

——Thomas Dixon, North Carolina's most colorful character of his generation, lawyer, minister, author, orator, playwright, actor. [Shelby? 1949?] 15 p. [14576

Weaver, Anderson. A lesson book for Bible study; a four-years course for schools and colleges. Hickory, Clay Printing Co., 1909. 265 p. [14577

[**Weaver, Burnley**] Guide for tourists and visitors in Asheville, No. Carolina, with some hints on seemly behavior whilst in our midst. Biltmore, Gollifox Press, 1933. 21 p. [14578

Weaver, Burnley. The Smokies coloring book. Asheville, Stephens Press [c.1943] 12 plates. [14579

Weaver, Charles Clinton. Internal improvements in North Carolina previous to 1860. Baltimore, John Hopkins Press, 1903. (Johns Hopkins University, Studies in historical and political science, ser. XXI, no. 3-4) 94 p. [14580

Weaver, Charles Preston. The hermit in English literature from the beginnings to 1660. Nashville, George Peabody College for Teachers, 1924. (Its Contributions to education, no. 11) 141 p. [14581

Weaver, Frederick Henry. A report to the Carnegie Corporation of New York on travel performed under a grant for young administrators, February 10-May 17, 1952. Chapel Hill [1952] 80 p. [14582

[**Weaver, Frederick Henry**] Tradition in Chapel Hill, 1793, 1953. [Chapel Hill, Office of the Dean of Students, University of North Carolina, 1953] 16 p. [14583

Weaver, Guy. Rime thoughts and jingle smiles. [Asheville, Biltmore Press, c.1955] 70 p. [14584

Weaver, Richard M. Ideas have consequences. [Chicago] University of Chicago Press [1948] 189 p. [14585

Weaver, Rufus Washington. The spiritual apostolate; a brief treatise upon the problems of personal work. No place, no publisher, 1902. 56 p. [14586

Weaver College, Weaverville, N. C. Bulletin, v. 1- 192?- Weaverville, 192?- NcU has v. [4-10] College closed in 1934. [14587

——Catalogue, 1872/73?- Weaverville, 1873?- NcU has 1889/90, 1906/07, 1909/ 10, 1916/17, 1921/22, 1922/23. Called Weaverville College -190? Continues as its Bulletin, 192?- [14588

Weaver School, Lenoir, N. C. Announcement, 190 - Lenoir, 190 - NcU has 1905/06 [14589

Webb, Charles Aurelius. Asheville, North Carolina, forty-six years in Asheville, 1889-1935, reminiscences and observations. Asheville [The Author] 1935. 28 p. [14590

——Fifty-eight years in Asheville. [Asheville, Citizen-Times Co., 1948] 17 p. [14591

——Mount Mitchell and Dr. Elisha Mitchell. Asheville, Citizen-Times Co., 1946. 24 p. [14592

——North Carolina's amazing progress. No place, no publisher [1923?] 8 p. [14593

Webb, Garland E. Winston-Salem, North Carolina . . . compiled and written by Col. G. Webb and L. E. Norryce. [Roanoke, Va., Stone Printing and Manufacturing Co.] n.d. 26 p. [14594

Webb, John. The Webb and allied families. Louisville, Ky., J. Adger Stewart [1930] 50 p. [14595

[**Webb, John Frederick**] City administrative units. [Oxford? The Author?] n.d. [4] p. [14596

——Local taxation for schools. [Oxford, The Author, 1935?] [3] p. [14597

Webb, John Frederick. The public schools and the constitution. [Oxford, Oxford Orphanage Press, 1942] 7 p. [14598

——To the members of the General Assembly of North Carolina. [Oxford, 1944?] [1] p. [14599

Webb, Lucie Thomas. Grading simplified; a teacher's aid in making out reports and averaging grades. Asheville, Hackney & Moale Co. [c.1908] 21 p. [14600

Webb, Richard. Sidney Lanier, poet and prosodist [by] Richard Webb and Edwin R. Coulson. Athens, University of Georgia Press, 1941. 108 p. [14601

Webb, Sarah (Gorham) The Gorhams of North Carolina. Boston [Wright & Potter Printing Co.] 1928. 18 p. [14602

Webb, William James. Historical sketch of Geneva Presbyterian Church, Granville County, North Carolina, 1833-1933. No place, no publisher, n.d. 15 p. [14603
——Our Webb kin of Dixie. Oxford, W. J. Webb, 1940. 176 p. [14604

Weber, Margaret Isabella (Walker) Planting the cross at Sewanee and other poems. Nashville, Tenn., The Author, 1904. 40 p. [14605

Webster, John R. To the voters of the fifth congressional district. [Reidsville? Webster's Weekly? 1890] [1] p. [14606

Webster, Noah. The elementary spelling-book, revised from Webster and adapted to southern schools by the publisher. Raleigh, Branson, Farrar & Co., n.d. 152 p. [14607

Weed, Katherine Kirtley. Studies of British newspapers and periodicals from their beginning to 1800; a bibliography by Katherine Kirtley Weed and Richmond Pugh Bond. Chapel Hill, University of North Carolina Press, 1946 [i.e. 1947] (Studies in philology, extra series, Dec. 1946, no. 2) 233 p. [14608

Weekes, Refine. The advantages and disadvantages of the marriage state, as entered into with religious or irreligious persons. James Town, J. Stanton, pr., 1836. 39 p. [14609

Weekly message, October 30, 1851-1872. Greensborough, Sidney D. Bumpass, Mrs. Frances M. Bumpass, 1851-1872. NcU has [October 30, 1851-September 28, 1871] [14610

Weeks, Alfred Leonard Edward. Autobiography of Alfred Leonard Edward Weeks and Annie Elizabeth Cooke Weeks, principal and wife of the New Bern Collegiate Industrial Institute, New Bern, N. C. No place, no publisher, n.d. 27 p. [14611
——Victims of circumstances and heroes of the truth. No place, no publisher, n.d. 84 p. [14612

Weeks, Lena (Pittman) God-given messages. Raleigh, Edwards & Broughton Co., 1930. 232 p. [14613
——"In the beginning". [Raleigh, Edwards and Broughton Co.] 1947. 57 p. [14614

Weeks, Neville B. Adoption for school-age children in institutions. New York, Child Welfare League of America, Inc. [1953] (Mary E. Boretz award, 1953) 10 p. [14615

Weeks, Stephen Beauregard. A bibliography of the historical literature of North Carolina. Cambridge, Library of Harvard University, 1895. (Its Bibliographical contributions, no. 48) 79 p. [14616
——Books, magazines, and pamphlets on North Carolina history wanted by Stephen B. Weeks, San Carlos, Arizona. [San Carlos, Arizona, The Author] n.d. [4] p. [14617
——Church and state in North Carolina. Baltimore, Johns Hopkins Press, 1893. (Johns Hopkins University, Studies in historical and political science, ser. XI, 5-6) 65 p. [14618
——A history of the Young Men's Christian Association movement in North Carolina, 1857-1888. Raleigh, Observer Printing Co., 1888. 20 p. [14619
——The press of North Carolina in the eighteenth century; with biographical sketches of printers, an account of the manufacture of paper, and a bibliography of the issues. Brooklyn, Historical Printing Club, 1891. 80 p. [14620
——The religious development in the province of North Carolina. Baltimore, Johns Hopkins Press, 1892. (Johns Hopkins University Studies in historical and political science, ser X, 5-6) 68 p. [14621
——The renaissance: a plea for the Trinity College Library. [Trinity College, Trinity College] n.d. 4 p. [14622
——Southern Quakers and slavery: a study in institutional history. Baltimore, Johns Hopkins Press, 1896. (Johns Hopkins University. Studies in historical and political science, extra vol. XV) 400 p. [14623

[Weeks, Stephen Beauregard] Truth and justice for the history of North Carolina; the Mecklenburg resolves of May 31, 1775 vs. the "Mecklenburg Declaration of May 20, 1775". Greensboro, C. L. Van Noppen [1908?] 16 p. [14624

Weeks, Stephen Beauregard. The Weeks Collection of Caroliniana. Raleigh, E. M. Uzzell, 1907. 31 p. [14624a

Weems, Mason Locke. God's revenge against adultery, awfully exemplified in the following cases of American crim. con.: I. The accomplished Dr. Theodore Wilson (Delaware) who for seducing Mrs. Nancy Wiley had his brains blown out by her

husband. II. The elegant James O'Neale, esq. (North Carolina) who for seducing the beautiful Miss Matilda L'Estrange was killed by her brother. 3d ed. Philadelphia, The Author, 1818. 48 p. [14625
—— ——Philadelphia, Joseph Allen, 1828. 71 p. [14626

Wehman, Henry J., publisher. Wehman's book on the adventures of Daniel Boone. New York, Henry J. Wehman, n.d. 48 p. [14627

Weil, Lionel. A device for safely transplanting long leaf pines and other evergreens. [Raleigh, Commercial Printing Co.] n.d. 15 p. [14628
——Goldsboro and its government from the beginning to the present time. [Raleigh, Mitchell Printing Co., 1923] 34 p. [14629
——Our native trees. [Raleigh, Mitchell Printing Co., 1924] 16 p. [14630

Weill, Kurt. The vocal score of Johnny Johnson; play by Paul Green, music by Kurt Weill. New York, S. French, Inc., c.1940. 94 p. [14631

Weis, Frederick Lewis. The colonial churches and the colonial clergy of the middle and southern colonies, 1607-1776. Lancaster, Mass., Society of the Descendants of the Colonial Clergy, 1938. 140 p. [14632
——The colonial clergy of Virginia, North Carolina, and South Carolina. Boston, 1955. (Publications of the Society of the Descendants of the Colonial Clergy, 7) 100 p. [14633

Welch, Edward Ruskin. A Palestine pilgrimage. Asheville, Asheville Advocate [1922?] 205 p. [14634

Welch, William Lewis. The Burnside expedition and the engagement at Roanoke Island. Providence, The Society, 1890. (Personal narratives of events in the war of the rebellion, being papers read before the Rhode Island Soldiers and Sailors Historical Society, ser. IV, 9) 48 p. [14635

Welfling, Weldon. Savings banking in New York state, a study of changes in savings bank practice and policy occasioned by important economic changes. Durham, Duke University Press, 1939. 205 p. [14636

Welling, James Clarke. Addresses, lectures, and other papers. Cambridge [Mass.] Privately printed, the Riverside Press, 1903. 389 p. [14637

Wellman, Manly Wade. Dead and gone; classic crimes of North Carolina. Chapel Hill, University of North Carolina Press [c.1954] 190 p. [14638
——Flag on the levee. New York, I. Washburn [1955] 209 p. [14639
——Fort Sun Dance. [New York, Dell Publishing Co., 1955] 222 p. [14640
——Giant in gray; a biography of Wade Hampton of South Carolina. New York, C. Scribner's Sons, 1949. 387 p. [14641
——Gray riders: Jeb Stuart and his men. New York, Aladdin Books, 1954. 192 p. [14642
——The haunts of Drowning Creek. [New York] Holiday House [1951] 205 p. [14643
——The last mammoth. New York, Holiday House [1953] 222 p. [14644
——The mystery of Lost Valley. New York, T. Nelson [1948] 176 p. [14645
——The raiders of Beaver Lake. New York, T. Nelson [1950] 160 p. [14646
——Rebel boast: first at Bethel—last at Appomattox. New York, Henry Holt [1956] 317 p. [14647
——Rebel mail runner. New York, Holiday House [1954] 221 p. [14648
——The sleuth patrol. New York, T. Nelson [1947] 192 p. [14649
——To unknown lands. New York, Holiday House [1956] 202 p. [14650
——Wild dogs of Drowning Creek. New York, Holiday House [1952] 221 p. [14651
——Young Squire Morgan. New York, I. Washburn [1956] 172 p. [14652

Wellons, James Willis, comp. Family prayers for morning and evening service. Beltimore, Sherwood & Co., 1874. 227 p. [14653
—— ——3d ed. Raleigh, Edwards & Broughton, 1892. 227 p. [14654

Wellons, William Brock. The Christians, South, not Unitarians in sentiment; a reply to Rev. John Paris' book, entitled, Unitarianism exposed, as it exists in the Christian Church. Suffolk, Va., Christian Sun, 1860. 91 p. [14655
——Life and labors of Rev. William Brock Wellons . . . compiled and edited by his brother, Rev. J. W. Wellons and Rev. R. H. Holland. Raleigh, Edwards, Broughton & Co., 1881. 448 p. [14656

Wells, Bertram Whittier. The natural gardens of North Carolina, with keys and descriptions of the herbaceous wild flowers found therein. Chapel Hill, University of North Carolina Press, 1932. 458 p. [14657

——The remarkable flora of the Great Smoky Mountains. Asheville, North Carolina National Park Commission, n.d. [13] p.   [14658

Wells, Edgar Franklin. The logical development of the concept of value. Chapel Hill, Department of Philosophy, University of North Carolina, 1937. (Buchan prize thesis)   32 p.   [14659

Wells, John Miller. Southern Presbyterian worthies. Richmond, Va., Presbyterian Committee of Publication [c.1936]   240 p.   [14660

Wells, Mary E. Student's own history work book, seventh grade. Smithfield, Wells & Medlin, c. 1929.   40 p.   [14661

Wells, Warner, tr. and ed. Hiroshima diary; the journal of a Japanese physician, August 6-September 30, 1945. Chapel Hill, University of North Carolina Press [1955]   238 p.   [14662

Welt, Louis Gordon. The contribution of the student to education; an address delivered at the opening convocation of the School of Medicine, University of North Carolina at Chapel Hill, September 15, 1954.   Chapel Hill, Medical Foundation of North Carolina, 1954.   13 p.   [14663

Wentworth, Harold. American dialect dictionary. New York, Thomas Y. Crowell Co., 1944.   747 p.   [14664

Wesleyan Methodist Connection (or Church) of America. North Carolina. Minutes, 18 - Syracuse, N. Y., Wesleyan Methodist Publishing Association, 18 - NcU has 1931-1941   [14665

West, John Foster. Up ego! New York, Payton, Paul Publishing Co. [1951] 26 p.   [14666

West W. The North Carolina rose, Dulcimer's song; from Mrs. Stowe's tale of Dred. London, T. E. Purday, n.d.   5 p.   [14667

West Buncombe Baptist Association. Minutes, 1909?- 1909?- NcU has 1914 [14668

West Chowan Baptist Association. Minutes, 1883- 1883- NcU has 1883-1886 [1891-1919] 1921-1945 [1946-1955]   [14669

West-Green Nurseries and Gardens, Guilford County, N. C. Descriptive catalogue of southern and acclimated fruit trees, grape vines, small fruits &c., cultivated and for sale . . . by S. W. Westbrook and C. P. Mendenhall.   High Point, J. H. Moore, 1860.   45 p.   [14670

—— ——Greensboro, Times, pr., 1856.   34 p.   [14671

——Ornamental catalogue of the West-Green Nurseries, Autumn, 1860-Spring, 1861. High Point, J. H. Moore, 1860.   22 p.   [14672

West Roanoke Baptist Association. Minutes, 18 - 18 - NcU has 1925, 1929   [14673

Westbrook Nurseries, Greensboro, N. C. Catalogue of southern and acclimated fruit trees, grape vines, small fruits, and hardy evergreens and shrubbery. Greensboro, Westbrook & Co. [1867?]   32 p.   [14674

Western, pseud. Biography of Joseph Lane. Washington, Congressional Globe Office, 1852.   40 p.   [14675

Western Baptist Convention of North Carolina. Minutes, 18 - 18 - NcU has 1877   [14676

Western Carolina answers the last Sunday's Raleigh News and Observer's attack on the South Atlantic Trans-Continental Railroad bill. [Raleigh? 1907]   24 p. [14677

Western Carolina Male Academy, Mount Pleasant, N. C. see **Mount Pleasant Collegiate Institute**

Western Carolina Teachers College, Cullowhee, N. C. Facts and legends of the Cullowhee region. Cullowhee, 1938. (Its Bulletin, v. 15, no. 4)   21 p.   [14678

——Fiftieth anniversary celebration. Cullowhee, 1939. (Its Bulletin, v. 15, no. 4-5) 48 p.   [14679

——Regional sketches of Western North Carolina. Cullowhee, 1937. (Its Bulletin, v. 14, no. 6)   40 p.   [14680

Western North Carolina Associated Communities. Inventory of assets of Transylvania County.   No place [1948?]   27 p.   [14681

Western North Carolina Baptist Association. Minutes, 18 - 18 - NcU has [1909-1955]   [14682

Western North Carolina Baptist Convention. Minutes, 185 - 185 - NcU has 1861, 1863, 1867, 1886, 1888, 1890, 1891, 1895 [14683

Western North Carolina Historical Association. History bulletin, v. 1- January, 1955- 1955- NcU has v. 1-2 [14684

Western North Carolina Land Company, Charlotte, N. C. Western North Carolina Land Company . . . chartered by the legislature of North Carolina, February 21st, 1874. Norristown, Pa., Daily Herald Steam Printing House, 1877. 20 p. [14685

Western North Carolina, Land of the Sky. Raleigh, Edwards and Broughton Co. [1905?] 15 p. [14686

Western Union Missionary Baptist Association. Minutes, 1906?- 1906?- NcU has 1920 [14687

Westminister School, Rutherfordton, N. C. Catalogue, 190 - Wildmere and Rutherfordton, 190 - NcU has [1905/06-1918/19] [14688
——Points for patrons. Rutherfordton, n.d. [11] p. [14689

Weston, James Augustus. Historic doubts as to the execution of Marshal Ney. New York, T. Whittaker, 1895. 310 p. [14690
—— ——Philadelphia, J. B. Lippincott and Co., 1890. Prospectus. 25 p. [14691
——Services held in the Chapel of Rest, Yadkin Valley, N. C., at the burial of the late Gen. Collett Leventhorpe, with the sermon and a sketch of the life of the deceased. No place, no publisher [1889?] 15 p. [14692

Westray, Samuel Elward. Will, list of heirs, and decree of sale of lands, Thomas H. Battle, executor, Rocky Mount, N. C. [Rocky Mount? 1894] 29 p. [14693

Wetmore, Susannah. Mountain songs of North Carolina collected by Susannah Wetmore and Marshall Bartholomew. New York, G. Schirmer, n.d. 43 p. [14694

Wettach, Robert Hasley, ed. A century of legal education. Chapel Hill, University of North Carolina Press, 1947. (North Carolina. University. Sesquicentennial publications) 146 p. [14695

Wettach, Robert Hasley. Restrictions on a free press; an address delivered at the Newspaper Institute at Chapel Hill, January 13-15, 1926. [Chapel Hill? 1926] 11 p. [14696
——A survey of the powers and duties of the Board of Trustees of the University of North Carolina and of the Executive Committee of the Board of Trustees. [Chapel Hill, University of North Carolina, 1941] 36 p. [14697

Wey, Frederick W. Historical sketches of the missions in charge of the Rev. Fred'k W. Wey, in the missionary jurisdiction of Asheville, N. C. Murphy, Alfred Morgan, pr., 1897. 17 p. [14698

Wharton, Don, ed. The Roosevelt omnibus. New York, A. A. Knopf, 1934. [38] 174 [60] p. [14699

What is conversion. No place, Republished by the T. A. F. in N. C., n.d. 2 p. [14700

What others say, Globe Academy. Globe, Globe Academy, 1887. 12 p. [14701

What people say about St. Augustine's, Raleigh, N. C. [Raleigh, 1917?] Folder. [14702

Wheat, John Thomas. The character and example of St. John the Evangelist; a sermon preached before Columbus Lodge, no. 102, December 27th, 1850, in St. Bartholomew's Church, Pittsboro'. Raleigh, Seaton Gales, pr., 1851. 15 p. [14703
——The communion of saints; a sermon in memory of four beloved children, gone, as we believe, to Paradise. [Greensboro?] New North State Job Print, 1875. 12 p. [14704
——Epithalamium to my dear wife on the sixtieth anniversary of our wedding day, tenth of March, 1885. No place [1885] 12 p. [14705
——The first and most important thing in religion, a sermon. Winchester, Va., Times Office, 1880. 12 p. [14706
——A preparation for the Holy Communion. New York, General Protestant Episcopal Sunday School Union, 1866. 136 p. [14707
——Reminiscences of my pre-nuptial life in homely rhymes for my dear wife on our golden wedding day. Greensboro, New North State Job Print, 1875. 47 p. [14708
——Sermon on the Trinity. No place, no publisher, n.d. 4 p. [14709
——To my dear wife on the sixty-first anniversary of our wedding-day, tenth of March A. D. 1886. No place [1886] 7 p. [14710
——Tributary verses to my dear wife on the eighty-first anniversary of her birthday, twelfth of September, 1886. No place, 1886. 15 p. [14711

Wheatley, Phillis. Memoir and poems of Phillis Wheatley, a native African and a slave; also, Poems by a slave. 3d ed. Boston, I. Knapp, 1838. 155 p. "Poems by a slave" by George Moses Horton.   [14712

Whedbee, Charles. Major William Henry Bagley, clerk of the Supreme Court of North Carolina, 1868-1886; address upon presentation of his portrait . . . acceptance of portrait by Chief Justice Stacy. No place, no publisher [1929?] 15 p. [14713

[**Wheeler, A. O.**] Eye-witness; or, Life scenes in the Old North State, depicting the trials and sufferings of the unionists during the rebellion. By A. O. W. Boston, B. B. Russell and Co., 1865. 276 p.   [14714
———— ————1866.   [14715

Wheeler, Jacob D. A practical treatise on the law of slavery; being a compilation of all the decisions made on that subject in the several courts of the United States, and state courts. New York, A. Pollock, Jr., 1837. 476 p.   [14716

Wheeler, John Hill. An address on the appropriate pursuits of American youth, delivered at Wake Forest College, June 15, 1843, under the appointment of the Euzelian Society. Raleigh, Biblical Recorder Office [1843] 23 p.   [14717
————Catalogue of the library of John H. Wheeler, the historian of North Carolina . . . to be sold at auction, Monday afternoon, April 24, 1882 . . . by Bangs and Co. No place, n.d. 81 p.   [14718
————The early times and men of Albemarle; an oration delivered at Elizabeth City, N. C., on 7th of August, 1877, at request of the Albemarle Historical Society. [Elizabeth City? 1877] [17] p.   [14719
————Historical sketches of North Carolina, from 1584 to 1851. Philadelphia, Lippincott, Grambo and Co., 1851. 2 v. in 1.   [14720
———— ————A reprint of the original edition . . . with a foreword by Magnolia McKay Shuford. New York, F. H. Hitchcock, 1925. 2 v. in 1.   [14721
————North Carolina: her past, present and future; an address delivered before the faculty and students of the University of North Carolina, at the commencement, June 8th, 1870. Raleigh, Standard Print, 1870. 32 p.   [14722
————The lives and characters of the signers of the Mecklenburg Declaration of Independence, of the 20th of May, 1775; delivered at Charlotte, N. C., on the 24th of May, 1875, at the request of the Mecklenburg Historical Society. Charlotte, Observer Book and Job Power Press Print, 1875. 16 p.   [14723
————Reminiscences and memoirs of North Carolina and eminent North Carolinians. Washington, Joseph Shillington, Columbus, O., 1883-1884. First issued as 4 sections, parts 1-2, published in Washington, parts 3-4, in Columbus. NcU has Parts 1-2, 4   [14724
———— ————Columbus, O., Columbus Printing Works, 1884. 478 p.   [14725
————Sketch of the life of Richard Dobbs Spaight of North Carolina. Baltimore, W. K. Boyle, pr., 1880. 29 p.   [14726

[**Wheeler, Samuel J.**] History of the Baptist Church worshipping at Parker's Meeting House, called Meherrin, by the clerk. Raleigh, Recorder Office, pr., 1847. 60 p.   [14727

Where half of our state taxes go. No place, no publisher [1879?] [1] p.   [14728

Where we live, v. 1- January, 1945- Raleigh, United War Fund of North Carolina, 1945- NcU has v. 1-v. 2, no. 1   [14729

The whetstone, v. 1- February, 1924- Durham, North Carolina Mutual Life Insurance Co., 1924- NcU has v. 25-33   [14730

Which will you have for president, Jackson or the Bank? To the democracy of New Haven County. No place, no publisher, n.d. 11 p.   [14731

Whig clarion, Raleigh, N. C. Address of the carrier of the Whig clarion. [Raleigh] December 25, 1843. [1] p.   [14732

Whig Party. North Carolina. Letters of James W. Osborne, Esq., Hon. D. M. Barringer, and A. C. Williamson . . . also, An extract from the letter of Hon. Charles J. Jenkins of Georgia. Charlotte, Western Democrat Office, 1856. 8 p.   [14733

Whipple, Joshuaway, pseud. see Easley, Philip Samuel

Whitaker, Bessie Lewis. The provincial council and committees of safety in North Carolina. Chapel Hill, University Press, 1908. (James Sprunt historical monograph, no. 8) 49 p.   [14734

Whitaker, Fanny de Berniere (Hooper) Spier Whitaker, 1798-1869; a sketch of his life and an account of his family. [Raleigh?] n.d. 32 p. [14735

[Whitaker, Joel] The antrum of Highmore, its diseases and their treatment. [Raleigh, Edwards and Broughton Co., 1907] 9 p. [14736

Whitaker, L. F. The old Carolina state. Boston, Oliver Ditson [c.1860] 5 p.[14737

Whitaker, Richard Harper. Whitaker's reminiscences, incidents and anecdotes. Raleigh, Edwards and Broughton Co., 1905. 488 p. [14738

Whitaker, Walter. Centennial history of Alamance County, 1849-1949 [by] Walter Whitaker in collaboration with Staley A. Cook and A. Howard White. Burlington, Burlington Chamber of Commerce [1949] 270 p. [14739

White, Benjamin T. Three cheers for the happy land. No place, no publisher, n.d. [1] p. [14740

White, Edwin Elverton. Highland heritage; the southern mountains and the nation. New York, Friendship Press [c.1937] 197 p. [14741

White, Ernestine (Dew) Genealogy of some of the descendants of Thomas Dew. Greenville, S. C., 1937. 349 p. [14742

White, Gilbert C. Final report on the establishment of water works, Durham, N. C., November, 1917. [Durham, Seeman Printery, 1917] 19 p. [14743

——Valuation of the plant of the Durham Water Company, Durham, North Carolina. [Durham? 1916?] 74 p. [14744

White, Henry Alexander. Southern Presbyterian leaders. New York, Neale Publishing Co., 1911. 476 p. [14745

White, Howard. The Battle of Alamance, May 16, 1771. Burlington, Chamber of Commerce [1956] 22 p. [14746

White, J. L. A sermon. No place, no publisher [1888] 14 p. [14747

[White, John] The pictures of sondry things collected and counterfeited to the truth in the voyage made by Sr Walter Raleigh, knight, for the discovery of La Virginea. London, British Museum, 1936, 3 p., 2 plates. Prospectus of a facsimile edition. [14749

White, John Ellington. My old Confederate; address delivered before Atlanta Camp, U. C. V., and the Atlanta Chapter, United Daughters of the Confederacy, October 21st, 1906. [Atlanta, Foote and Davies, pr.] 1908. 15 p. [14750

——Our southern mountain region and southern Baptists. Atlanta, Ga., Southern Baptist Convention, n.d. 24 p. [14751

——A solution of the mountain problem. Atlanta, Home Mission Board, Southern Baptist Convention, n.d. 16 p. [14752

——White echoes, by Annie Dove Denmark . . . a volume of echoes from sermons preached by John Ellington White during his pastorate of the First Baptist Church, Anderson, S. C. Nashville, Tenn., Sunday School Board of the Southern Baptist Convention, 1932. 214 p. [14753

[White, Joseph M.?] The presidency. No place, no publisher [1831?] 45 p.[14754

White, Kathrine Keogh. The King's Mountain men; the story of the battle, with sketches of the American soldiers who took part. Dayton, Va., J. K. Ruebush, 1924. 271 p. [14755

White, Leonard Dupee. The Jacksonians; a study in administrative history, 1929-1861. New York, Macmillan Co., 1954. 593 p. [14756

White, M. L. History of the life of Amos Owens, the noted blockader of Cherry Mountain, N. C. Shelby, Cleveland Star [1901?] 55 p. [14757

White, N. D. Torch-lights and stepping-stones from slavery to self-government. [Goldsboro, The Author, c.1920] 204 p. [14758

White, Newman Ivey. American Negro folk-songs. Cambridge, Harvard University Press, 1928. 501 p. [14759

White, Newman Ivey, ed. An anthology of verse by American Negroes, edited with a critical introduction, biographical sketches of the authors, and bibliographical notes by Newman Ivey White . . . and Walter Clinton Jackson. Durham, Trinity College Press, 1924. 250 p. [14760

——The best of Shelley. New York, T. Nelson and Sons, 1932. 531 p. [14761

White, Newman Ivey. Portrait of Shelley. New York, A. A. Knopf, 1945. 482 p. [14762

——Shelley. New York, A. A. Knopf, 1940. 2 v.   [14763

——The unextinguished hearth; Shelley and his contemporary critics. Durham, Duke University Press, 1938. 397 p.   [14764

White, Philip S. Claims of the order, a temperance essay; with a biographical sketch of his life, character, &c, by James W. Edney. Asheville, Messenger Office, 1851. 16 p.   [14765

White, Robert Shaw. History and genealogy of interest to the descendants of Thomas and Sallie Johnson White, late of Petersburg, Va. Raleigh, no publisher, 1910. 16 p.   [14766

White, Samuel C. Original statements of White and Cross. [Raleigh, 1887?] 16 p.   [14767

White, Stephen Van Culen. Address upon the race question in the South, delivered at Salisbury, N. C., before the literary societies of Livingstone College, May 27th, 1890. No place, no publisher, n.d. 16 p.   [14768

——[Selections from the portfolio of S. V. White] [New York, The Author's Daughter, 1893?] [26] p.   [14769

White, Stewart Edward. Daniel Boone, wilderness scout. Garden City, N. Y., Doubleday, Page & Co., 1922. 308 p.   [14770

—— ——edited by Helen E. Hawkins. Boston, Allyn and Bacon [c.1926] 320 p.   [14771

—— ——illustrated by James Daugherty. Garden City, N. Y., Garden City Publishing Co., Inc. [1933] 274 p.   [14772

—— ——Garden City, N. Y., Doubleday & Co., Inc., 1947. 308 p.   [14773

White, Warren T. Industrial development in the Carolinas. Baltimore, Manufacturers Record, 1943. 14 p.   [14774

White, William Allen, ed. Defense for America; the views of Quincy Wright, Charles Seymour, Barry Bingham [and others, including Frank Porter Graham] New York, Macmillan Co., 1940. 205 p.   [14775

The white cane, v. 1- February, 1936- [Raleigh] North Carolina State Association for the Blind, 1936- NcU has v. [1, 5-7] 11-20   [14776

The white man, 1900- Raleigh, White Man Publishing Co., 1900- NcU has June, 1900, July 19, 1900   [14777

White man, read! No place, no publisher, 1898. [2] p.   [14778

White Oak Academy, White Oak, N. C. Catalogue, 1882/83?- White Oak, 1883?- NcU has [1902/03-1907/08]   [14779

White-Oak Baptist Primitive Association. Minutes, 18 - 18 - NcU has 1839, 1870, 1873, [1911-1955]   [14780

Whitfield, Charles Randolph D. Brief history of the Negro Disciples of Christ in Eastern North Carolina. No place, Whitfield Printery, n.d. [19] p.   [14781

Whitehead, Daisy Crump. From me to you. [New York, Alexander Walsh, c.1940] 64 p.   [14782

——Heart lines. [Raleigh, Pittman Printing Co., c.1937] 56 p.   [14783

Whitehead, Paul. Recreations of a presiding elder. Nashville, Southern Methodist Publishing House, 1885. 222 p.   [14784

Whitehead, Richard Henry. The anatomy of the brain; a text-book for medical students. Philadelphia, F. A. Davis Co., 1901. 96 p.   [14785

Whitehead, Russell F., ed. The white pine series of architectural monographs, v. 1- 19 - New York, Russell F. Whitehead, 19 - NcU has v. 13, no. 1-2, v. 15, no. 2.   [14786

Whitehill, Arthur Murray. Food industries in Virginia. Charlottesville, Bureau of Population and Economic Research, University of Virginia, 1950. 23 p.   [14787

——Personnel relations: the human aspects of administration. New York, McGraw-Hill, 1955. 526 p.   [14788

Whiteley, Charles Douglas. Reaching upward; or, Man's age-long search for truth. Grand Rapids, Mich., Zondervan Publishing House [c.1937] 182 p.   [14789

Whitener, Daniel Jay. History of Watauga County, North Carolina, and History of Appalachian State Teachers College, 1899-1949] 112 p.   [14790

——Local history: how to find and write it. Asheville, Western North Carolina Historical Association, 1955. 17 p.   [14791

——Prohibition in North Carolina, 1715-1945. Chapel Hill, University of North Carolina Press, 1945 [i.e. 1946] (James Sprunt studies in history and political science, v. 27) 268 p. [14792

Whitfield, Emma Morehead. Whitfield, Bryan, Smith, and related families. [Westminster, Md., Theodore M. Whitfield, 1948-1950] 2 v. [14793

Whitfield, Theodore. Small duties, a sermon. No place, no publisher, n.d. 20 p. [14794

Whitford, John D. Letter to the editor of the Beaufort Journal, respecting the construction of the Atlantic and North Carolina Railroad, December 26, 1857. Kinston, American Advocate Office, 1858. 16 p. [14795

Whiting, Roberta Harriss. Rose petals. New York, Broadway Publishing Co. [c.1914] 51 p. [14796

Whitley, Edythe Johns (Rucker) Cantrell—Potter—Magness; ancestry of Alvin Edward Potter, Sr. Nashville, Tenn., The Author, 1938. 86 [27] p. [14797

——Hale family. Nashville, Tenn., The Author, 1934. 37 [7] p. [14798

——Notes from deeds in Nash County, North Carolina. Nashville, Tenn., The Author, 1938. 9 p. [14799

——Tennessee genealogical records. Nashville, Tenn., The Author, 1931-1935. 10 v. [14800

Whitlock, Paul Cameron. 75 years ago in Charlotte; address delivered at the annual meeting of the Charlotte Chamber of Commerce. Charlotte, Chamber of Commerce, 1947. Folder. [14801

Whitman, Willson. God's valley; people and power along the Tennessee River. New York, Viking Press, 1939. 320 p. [14802

Whitney, J. H. E. The Hawkins Zouaves (Ninth N. Y. V.) their battles and marches. New York, The Author, 1866. 216 p. [14803

Whitney, Janet. John Woolman, American Quaker. Boston, Little, Brown and Co., 1942. 490 p. [14804

Whitsett, William Thornton. A brief history of Alamance County, North Carolina, with sketches of the Whitesell family and the Huffman family. Burlington, A. D. Pate and Co., pr. [c.1926] (Whitsett historical monographs, no. 4) 32 p. [14805

——Founders of church and state. Whitsett, The Author [c.1926] (Whitsett historical monographs, no. 3) 14 p. [14806

——History of Brick Church and the Clapp family. Greensboro, Harrison Printing Co. [c.1925] (Whitsett historical monographs, no. 2) 28 p. [14807

——Landmarks and pioneers; an address. Whitsett, The Author [c.1925] (Whitsett historical monographs, no. 1) 4 p. [14808

——Saber and song, a book of poems. Whitsett, Whitsett Institute, 1917. 156 p. [14809

Whitsett Institute, Whitsett, N. C. Register, announcement, 1883/84?- Whitsett, 1884?- NcU has 1898/99, 1899/1900, 1900/01-1916/17 [14810

Whitted, J. A. Biographical sketch of the life and work of the late Rev. Augustus Shepard, D. D., Durham, North Carolina. Raleigh, Edwards and Broughton Co., 1912. 69 p. [14811

——A history of the Negro Baptists of North Carolina. Raleigh, Edwards & Broughton Printing Co., 1908. 212 p. [14812

Whitter, Henry. Familiar folk songs as sung by Henry Whitter; songs composed by Henry Whitter. [Crumpler, The Author, 1934?] [26] p. [14813

Whittlesey, Sarah Johnson Cogswell. Bertha the beauty; a story of the southern revolution. Philadelphia, Claxton, Remsen & Haffelfinger, 1872. 382 p. [14814

——Heart-drops from memory's urn. New York, A. S. Barnes & Co., 1852. 342 p. [14815

——The stranger's stratagem; or, The double deceit, and other stories. New York, M. W. Dodd, 1859. 405 p. [14816

Whitworth, Henry P., ed. Carolina architecture and allied arts; a pictorial review of Carolina's representative architecture. Miami, Fla., Carolina Architecture and Allied Arts, 1939. 60, 32 p. [14817

Who endorsed the Helper book! Who were the inciters to bloodshed? No place, no publisher, n.d. [1] p. [14818

The "whole" record sustains Kitchin; Mr. J. W. Bailey denies what is not charged and artfully dodges what is charged. No place, no publisher [1912] 2 p. [14819

Who's who in Durham, North Carolina, being a business directory and list of members of the Durham Chamber of Commerce, 19 - [Durham, 19 - NcU has 1924 [14820

Who's who in the South and Southwest, a biographical dictionary of leading men and women of the Southern and Southwestern States. v. 1. Chicago, Larkin, Roosevelt & Larkin, 1947. 1084 p. [14821

Who's who in the South; a business, professional and social record . . . 1927- Washington, Mayflower Publishing Co., Inc. [c.1927- NcU has 1927 [14822

Why Not Academy and Business Institute, Why Not, N. C. Announcement, 1893/94?- 1894?- NcU has 1903/04, 1904/05 [14823

Why the citizens of Jackson County should have the right to vote upon the question of removing the county seat and public buildings from the town of Webster to the town of Sylva. No place, no publisher, n.d. [2] p. [14824

Wick, James L. How not to run for President, a handbook for Republicans. New York, Vantage Press [1952] 101 p. [14825

[Wicker, Tom] Get out of town [by] Paul Connolly. New York, Fawcett Publications, Inc. [c.1951] (Gold medal books) 164 p. [14826

Wicker, Tom. The kingpin. New York, Sloane, 1953. 343 p. [14827

[Wicker, Tom] So fair, so evil; a Gold medal original by Paul Connelly [pseud.] New York, Fawcett Publications [c.1955] 159 p. [14828

Widgery, Alban Gregory. Christian ethics in history and modern life. New York, Round Table Press, Inc., 1940. 318 p. [14829

——What is religion? New York, Harper and Brothers [1953] 330 p. [14830

Widgery, Claude Brooke. Beginnings; essays, stories, poems. [Durham] printed for private circulation, 1934. 76 p. [14831

The wife who always helped and never hindered; a memorial of Mary Faison Dixon, wife of Amzi Clarence Dixon, who entered the glory from Kuling, China, August 6, 1922. Baltimore, University Baptist Church [1922?] 61 p. [14832

Wiggins, Archibald Lee Manning. The Horace Williams Society presents an informal talk on Horace Williams, philosopher, as I knew him; delivered at its meeting, June, 1952, Chapel Hill, N. C. [Chapel Hill, 1952] [10] p. [14833

Wiggins, Lee Manning. Reason, will, and responsibility. Chapel Hill, Department of Philosophy, University of North Carolina, 1941. (Buchan prize thesis) 41 p. [14834

Wiggins, Ronald Luther. Industrial survey of Raleigh, North Carolina. Raleigh, North Carolina State College, 1948. (Its Dept. of Engineering Research. Bulletin, no. 38) 22 p. [14835

Wiggs, Lewis D. Thirty-nine years with the great I am. [Chapel Hill?] 1952. 154 p. [14836

[Wilburn, Hiram Coleman] Junaluska, the man, the name, the places. [Waynesville, The Author, c.1951] 18 p. [14837

Wilburn, Hiram Coleman. Welborn—Wilburn, history, genealogy; the families in Virginia, North Carolina, and South Carolina. Waynesville, The Author, c.1953. 104 p. [14838

Wilcox, James, defendant. State vs. James Wilcox; from Pasquotank . . . Superior Court, March term, 1902. [Elizabeth City, E. F. Snakenburg, pr., 1902] 169 p. [14839

Wilcox, Mary Emily Donelson. Christmas under three flags; being memories of holiday festivities in the White House with "Old Hickory", in the palace of H. R. H. Prince of Prussia, afterwards Emperor William I, and at the Alamo where the Alcade's daughter. Washington, Neale Co., 1900. 95 p. [14840

Wilde, Irene. Fire against the sky. New York, Liveright Publishing Corporation [c.1938] 144 p. [14841

Wilder, Robert. Mr. G. strings along. New York, G. P. Putnam's Sons [1944] 217 p. [14842

——Written on the wind, a novel. New York, G.P. Putnam's Sons [1946] 338 p.[14843

—— ——New York, Bantam Books [1956] 309 p. [14844

Wile, William C. The ideal place for those suffering from pulmonary troubles. Danbury, Conn., Danbury Medical Printing Co., 1891. 28 p. [14845

Wiley, Bell Irvin. The life of Johnny Reb, the common soldier of the Confederacy. Indianapolis, Bobbs-Merrill Co. [1943]   444 p.   [14846
——Southern Negroes, 1861-1865. New Haven, Yale University Press, 1938. 366 p.   [14847

Wiley, Calvin Henderson. An address delivered before the two literary societies of Wake Forest College on the 12th of June, 1845, at the solicitation of the Euselian Society. Raleigh, North Carolina Standard, 1845. 27 p.   [14848
——Adventures of old Dan Tucker, and his son Walter; a tale of North Carolina. London, Willoughby & Co. [1851] 222 p. American imprint called Roanoke. [14849
——Alamance Church; a historical address delivered at the dedication of its fourth house of worship, on October 18th, 1879. Raleigh, Edwards, Broughton & Co., 1880. 46 p.   [14850

[**Wiley, Calvin Henderson**] Alamance; or, The great and final experiment. New York, Harper & Brothers, 1847. 151 p.   [14851
—— ——New York, Harper & Brothers, 1870. (Library of select novels, no. 104) 151 p.   [14852
——Constitution of North Carolina, with a historical account of its origin and changes . . . by a member of the last legislature. Raleigh, North Carolina Institution for the Deaf and Dumb and the Blind, 1851. 150 p.   [14853

Wiley, Calvin Henderson. Life in the South; a companion to Uncle Tom's cabin. Philadelphia, T. B. Peterson [1852]   144 p. English imprint called Utopia [14854

Wiley, Calvin Henderson, comp. A new and practical form book, containing forms of all those legal instruments important to be known by the people of North Carolina. Raleigh, Weekly Post, 1852. 199 p.   [14855

Wiley, Calvin Henderson. The North-Carolina reader; containing a history and description of North-Carolina, selections in prose and verse, many of them by eminent citizens of the state, historical and chronological tables, and a variety of miscellaneous information and statistics. Philadelphia, Lippincott, Grambo & Co. [1851]   354 p.   [14856
——The North Carolina reader number III. New York, A. S. Barnes & Co., Raleigh, W. L. Pomeroy, 1859. 351 p.   [14857
—— ——1860.   [14858
—— ——1866.   [14859
—— ——1868.   [14860
—— ——1874.   [14861
——Roanoke; or, Where is Utopia? Philadelphia, T. B. Peterson & Brothers [c.1866] 156 p. English imprint called Adventures of old Dan Tucker.   [14862
——Scriptural views of national trials; or, The true road to the independence and peace of the Confederate States of America. Greensboro, Sterling, Campbell & Albright, 1863. 213 p.   [14863

[**Wiley, Calvin Henderson**] A sober view of the slavery question, by a citizen of the South. No place, no publisher [1849?] 8 p.   [14864

Wiley, Calvin Henderson. This week goes to press The North Carolina reader. [Greensboro? The Author, 1851] [1] p.   [14865
——Utopia; an early picture of life at the South. London, Henry Lea, n.d. 222 p. NcU has defective copy, pp. 1-2 wanting. American imprint has title Life in the South.   [14866

Wiley, Philip W. Thoughts in verse; Luther's finding of the Word; Is life worth living, and other verses. No place, privately printed by the Author, 1927. 110 p. [14867

Wiley, William Leon, ed. André Maurois, Climats; abridged and edited with introduction, notes and vocabulary by W. L. Wiley and R. W. Linker. New York, Henry Holt and Co. [c.1936] 225 p.   [14868

Wiley, William Leon. The gentleman of Renaissance France. Cambridge, Harvard University Press, 1954. 303 p.   [14869

Wiley, William Leon, ed. Pierre Le Loyer's version of the Ars amatoria. Chapel Hill, 1941. (University of North Carolina. Studies in the Romance languages and literature, no. 3) 74 p.   [14870

[**Wilkes, Jane Renwick**] History of St. Peter's Hospital, Charlotte, N. C., for thirty years, from January, 1876 to December, 1905. Charlotte, Elam & Dooley, pr., 1906. 28 p.   [14871

Wilkes Co., N. C. Board of Education. Report of the Public Schools of Wilkes County, 19 - North Wilkesboro, 19 - NcU has 1903/04-1920/21 [14872

Wilkes County school news, v. 1- 1922- Hunting Creek, Wilkes County Board of Education, 1922- NcU has v. [2, 5, 6] [14873

Wilkesboro, N. C. Andrew Jackson Committee. An address reported by the Committee appointed at Wilkesboro', 5th February, 1828, to the people composing the counties of Surry, Ashe, Wilkes, and Iredell. Salisbury, Philo White, pr., 1828. 16 p. [14874

Wilkinson, Henry. The information of Capt. Hen. Wilkinson, of what hath passed betwixt him and some other persons, who have attempted to prevail with him to swear high treason against the Earl of Shaftsbury. London, Henry Wilkinson, 1681. 11 p. [14875

Wilkinson, S. The voyages and adventures of Edward Teach, commonly called Black Beard, the notorious pirate. Boston, Book Printing-Office, 1808. 35 p. NcU has microfilm (negative) from original in Library of Congress. [14876

Will, Allen Sinclair. Life of Cardinal Gibbons, archbishop of Baltimore. New York, E. P. Dutton and Co. [c.1922] 2 v. North Carolina mission labors, v. 1, pp. 92-115 [14877

——Life of James, cardinal Gibbons. Baltimore, John Murphy Co. [c.1911] 414 p. [14878

[**Willard, Martin Stevenson**] Letters from a Tar Heel traveler in Mediterranean countries. Oxford, Oxford Orphan Asylum, 1907. 122 p. [14879

Willett, Edward. True blue; or, The writing in cipher. A tale of the Old North State. Glasgow, Cameron and Ferguson, n.d. 41 p. [14880

William Alexander Hoke. [Raleigh] n.d. 6 p. [14881

William Henry Ragsdale, 1855-1914. No place, no publisher, n.d. 40 p. [14882

William Jackson Hicks . . . Julia Louise Hicks. [Greensboro, Joseph J. Stone and Co., pr.] n.d. [14883

Williams, Arnold, ed. A tribute to George Coffin Taylor; studies and essays, chiefly Elizabethan, by his students and friends. [Chapel Hill] University of North Carolina Press [1952] 213 p. [14884

Williams, B. Brown. Mental alchemy; a treatise on the mind, nervous system, psychology, magnetism, mesmerism, and diseases. New York, Fowler and Wells, 1853. 180 p. [14885

Williams, Ben Ames. House divided. Boston, Houghton Mifflin Co., 1947. 1514 p. [14886

Williams, C. W. Chairman Williams answers Chairman Folger and the Democratic press. [Mt. Park? 1932] [4] p. [14887

Williams, Charles Bray. The evolution of New Testament Christology. Boston, Richard C. Badger [c.1928] 215 p. [14888

——A history of the Baptists in North Carolina. Raleigh, Edwards & Broughton, 1901. 214 p. [14889

Williams, Charles Burgess. Corn book for young folk, by Charles Burgess Williams and Daniel Harvey Hill. Boston, Ginn and Co. [c.1920] 250 p. [14890

[**Williams, Charlotte Bryan (Grimes)**] History of the Wake County Ladies Memorial Association, Confederate memorials in Capitol Square, Memorial Pavilion, the House of Memory, and the Confederate Cemetery. Raleigh, [James Johnston Pettigrew Chapter, U. D. C.] 1938. 54 p. [14891

Williams, Edgar D. Practical meteorology, from a sailor's log. Wilmington, The Author, n.d. [1] p. [14892

Williams, Edith Webb. Research in southern regional development. Richmond, Va., Dietz Press, 1948. (Southern Association of Science and Industry. Monograph no. 3) 145 p. [14893

Williams, Edward. Virginia: more especially the south part thereof, richly and truly valued: viz. The fertile Carolina, and no lesse excellent isle of Roanoak, of latitude from 31. to 37. degr . . . 2d ed. London, Printed by T. H. for J. Stephenson, 1650. (Reprint. Force, Peter. Tracts. Washington, 1836-46. v. 3 (1844) no. 11) 62 p. Reprint of the first part of the second edition of this work. [14894

—— ——2d ed. London, Printed by T. H. for J. Stephenson, 1650. 2 pt. in
1 v. NcU has microcard   [14895
Williams, Edward Locke. Christianity, the highest development of religious evolution. Chapel Hill, The University, 1911. (University of North Carolina. Department of Philosophy [Worth prize]) 19 p.   [14896
Williams, Edwin, comp. The addresses and messages of the Presidents of the United
States, inaugural, annual, and special, from 1789 to 1846; with a memoir of each of
the presidents, and a history of their administrations. New York, Edward Walker,
1847. 2 v. v. 2 includes Andrew Jackson and James K. Polk.   [14897
Williams, George Walton. Sketches of travel in the Old and New World. Charles-
ton, S. C., Walker, Evans & Cogswell, pr., 1871. 469 p.   [14898
Williams, Henry G. Address delivered at the examination of the students of Bel-
ford Male Academy, of Franklin County, N. C., June 12, 1857. Raleigh, Holden &
Wilson, pr., 1857. 15 p.   [14899
——To the voters of Nash County. Raleigh, The Author, February 25, 1861.
[1] p.   [14900
Williams, Henry Horace. An address . . . The spirit of truth; basis of remarks sub-
mitted to senior class at their last meeting . . . June 14, 1920. [Chapel Hill]
Horace Williams Philosophical Society, 1949. [3] p.   [14901
——The education of Horace Williams. Chapel Hill, The Author, 1936. 200 p. [14902
——The evolution of logic. Chapel Hill, The Author [c.1925] 181 p. [14903
——The Horace Williams Philosophical Society presents the first lecture of philo-
sophical lectures of 1922-23. [Chapel Hill, Horace Williams Philosophical Society,
1947. [6] p.   [14904
——Logic for living, lectures of 1921-22, edited by Jane Ross Hammer. New York,
Philosophical Library [1951] 281 p.   [14905
——Modern logic. Chapel Hill, The Author [c.1927] 347 p.   [14906
Williams, James, comp. Yadkin County (North Carolina) record book, vol. 1,
1939. Yadkinville, James Williams Printing Co., 1939. 97 p.   [14907
Williams, Joseph A., comp. Selections for devotional exercises. Boone [The Author,
1927] 224 p.   [14908
Williams, Lester Alonzo. Essentials in spelling for high schools [by] L. A. Williams
. . . I. C. Griffin . . . H. W. Chase. Raleigh, Alfred Williams & Co., 1916.
76 p.   [14909
——A study of the Winston-Salem schools [by] L. A. Williams, J. H. Johnston.
[Winston-Salem] High School Press, 1918. 93 p.   [14910
Williams, Lewis. To the citizens of the thirteenth congressional district of North
Carolina. [Washington, February 20, 1819] 3 p.   [14911
—— ——[1821] 3 p.   [14912
—— ——[1824] 3 p.   [14913
—— ——[1825] 3 p.   [14914
—— ——[1826] 3 p.   [14915
—— ——[1827] 3 p.   [14916
—— ——[1828] 3 p.   [14917
—— ——[1829] 3 p.   [14918
—— ——[1830] 3 p.   [14919
—— ——[1831] 3 p.   [14920
—— ——[1832] 4 p.   [14921
—— ——[1833] 12 p.   [14922
—— ——[1834] 24 p.   [14923
—— ——[1835] 15 p.   [14924
—— ——[1836] 16 p.   [14925
—— ——[1837] 23 p.   [14926
—— ——[1838] 16 p.   [14927
—— ——[1840?] p. 23-wanting in NcU copy   [14928
——To the freeman of the counties of Wilkes, Surry, Iredell and Ashe. [Washing-
ton? 1813?] 3 p.   [14929
Williams, Lloyd Haynes. Pirates of colonial Virginia. Richmond, Va., Dietz Press,
1937. 139 p.   [14930
Williams, Patrick Henry. Bonus, ships, terminals, and freight rates. No place, no
publisher [1924] 31 p.   [14931

Williams, Reese F. The star and door of hope; evidence of the divinity of Christ. New York, William-Frederick Press, 1952. 91 p.   [14932

Williams, Robert, d. 1790. Clear views in 1782, concerning the effects of slavery, expressed by Robert Williams, of Carteret County, North Carolina. Cincinnati, Wrightson & Co., pr., 1867. 7 p. NcU has photostat (negative) from original in Columbia University Library.   [14933

Williams, Robert, 1773-1836. [Letter to his constituents] Washington, February 26, 1801. [1] p.   [14934

Williams, Robert Murphy. The Bible and real estate, made at Real Estate Board Meeting in Greensboro, N. C., October, 1943. [Greensboro?] Real Estate Board [1943?] Folder.   [14935

——A birthday message with its traditions and its challenge. [Greensboro] June, 1944. 16 p.   [14936

——God and the passing years, sermon preached . . . Presbyterian Church, the Covenant, June 13, 1943, Greensboro, N. C. [Greensboro? 1943] Folder. [14937

——Presbyterian Home for the Aged, sponsored by the Synod of N. C.; As we therefore have opportunity. [Greensboro, 1948] 7 p.   [14938

——Williams and Murphy records and related families. Raleigh, Edwards and Broughton Co., 1949. 369 p.   [14939

Williams, Robin Murphy, ed. Schools in transition; community experiences in desegregation, edited by Robin M. Williams, Jr., and Margaret W. Ryan. Chapel Hill, University of North Carolina Press [1954] 272 p.   [14940

Williams, Ruth Smith. Abstracts of the wills of Edgecombe County, North Carolina, 1733-1856, by Ruth Smith Williams and Margarette Glenn Griffin. Rocky Mount, Dixie Letter Service, 1956. 392 p.   [14941

Williams, S. Stacker. Historical sketch of Cryptic Masonry in North Carolina, 1822-1883. No place [1883?] 8 p.   [14942

——Historical sketch no. 2 of Cryptic Masonry in North Carolina, 1883-1895. No place [1895?] 11 p.   [14943

Williams, Samuel Clay. Address before the American Arbitration Association, the Chamber of Commerce of the State of New York, and the Merchants Association of New York . . . December 13, 1934. [Washington?] 1934. 8 p.   [14944

——An analysis and discussion of certain features of the proposed amendments to the Agricultural Adjustment Act, H. R. 8492. [Winston-Salem, The Author, 1935] 38 p.   [14945

——Remarks . . . for delivery over the Raleigh, N. C. radio station . . . August 8, 1931 . . . The tobacco industry in North Carolina. No place, no publisher [1931?] 16 p.   [14946

——Remarks before the Rotary Club of Greenville, N. C., Monday night, November 30, 1931. No place, no publisher [1931?] 24 p.   [14947

Williams, Samuel Cole. Beginnings of West Tennessee, in the land of the Chickasaws, 1541-1841. Johnson City, Tenn., Watauga Press, 1930. 331 p.   [14948

——Dawn of Tennessee Valley and Tennessee history. Johnson City, Tenn., Watauga Press, 1937. 495 p.   [14949

Williams, Samuel Cole, ed. Early travels in the Tennessee country, 1540-1800. Johnson City, Tenn., Watauga Press, 1928. 540 p.   [14950

Williams, Samuel Cole. History of the lost state of Franklin. Johnson City, Tenn., Watauga Press, 1924. 371 p.   [14951

—— ——Rev. ed. New York, Press of the Pioneers, 1933. 378 p.   [14952

——Phases of Southwest Territory history (a contribution to the celebration of the sesqui-centennial of the Territory, October 13, 1940) Johnson City, Tenn., Watauga Press, 1940. 26 p.   [14953

——Tennessee during the Revolutionary war. Nashville, Tenn., Tennessee Historical Commission, 1944. 294 p.   [14954

——William Tatham, Wataugan. 2d. rev. and limited ed. Johnson City, Tenn., Watauga Press, 1947. 109 p.   [14955

Williams, Sarah Stone. The man from London town. New York, Neale Publishing Co., 1906. 288 p.   [14956

Williams, Sidney S. From Spottsylvania to Wilmington, N. C., by way of Andersonville and Florence. Providence, Society, 1899. (Personal narratives of events in the war of the rebellion, being papers read before the Rhode Island Soldiers and Sailors Historical Society, ser. V, no. 10)   47 p.   [14957

Williams, William. Journal of the life, travels, and gospel labours of William Williams, dec., a minister of the Society of Friends, late of White-Water, Indiana. Cincinnati, Lodge, L'Hommedieu, and Hammond, pr., 1828.   272 p.   [14958

—— ——Cincinnati, printed; Dublin, Reprinted by Webb and Chapman for William Robinson, 1839.   195 p.   [14959

Williams, William Wash. The quiet lodger of Irving Place.   New York, E. P. Dutton & Co., Inc., 1936.   251 p.   [14960

Williamson, B. P. Sale at auction of trotting bred Hambletonian and Morgan stallions, brood mares, colts and fillies, 18   -   Raleigh, Edwards and Broughton, pr., 18   -   NcU has November 20, 1890, November 11, 1891, November 9, 1894, February 14, 1895   [14961

Williamson, Hugh. The history of North Carolina.   Philadelphia, Thomas Dobson, 1812.   2 v.   [14962

——Observations on the climate in different parts of America, compared with the climate in corresponding parts of the other continent; To which are added, remarks on the different complexions of the human race; with some account of the aborigines of America; being an introductory discourse to the History of North-Carolina. New-York, Printed and sold by T. & J. Swords, 1811.   199 p.   [14963

[**Williamson, Hugh**] The plain dealer; or, Remarks on Quaker politicks in Pennsylvania. Numb. III.   To be continued, by W. D., author of No. I.   Philadelphia, 1764.   24 p.   [14964

——The plea of the colonies, on the charges brought against by Lord M——d, and others,in a letter to His Lordship. London, Printed for J. Almon, 1775. 47 p.[14965

——The plea of the colonies on the charges brought against them by Lord Mansfield, and others, in a letter to His Lordship, by a native of Pennsylvania.   London, 1776.   Philadelphia, Reprinted and sold by Robert Bell, 1777.   38 p.   [14966

Williamson, John Gustavus Adolphus. Caracas diary, 1835-1840; the journal of John G. A. Williamson, first diplomatic representative of the United States to Venezuela; edited by Jane Lucas de Grummond.   Baton Rouge, La., Camellia Publishing Co. [1954]   444 p.   [14967

Williamson, Passmore. Case of Passmore Williamson; report of the proceedings on the writ of habeas corpus issued by the Hon. John K. Kane, judge of the District Court of the United States for the Eastern District of Pennsylvania in the case of the United States of America ex rel. John H. Wheeler vs. Passmore Williamson including the several opinions delivered, and the arguments of counsel, reported by Arthur Cannon.   Philadelphia, Uriah Hunt & Son, 1856.   191 p.   [14968

Williamson, Wilbur Munro. The history of Company L, 120th Infantry.   Lumberton, Freeman Printing Co., 1938.   104 p.   [14969

Willison, John. The mother's catechism, designed as a help to the more easy understanding of the Westminster Assembly's shorter catechism.   New ed., enl. and improved.   Fayetteville, E. J. Hale, pr., 1838.   39 p.   [14970

——The young communicant's catechism, by the Rev. John Willison; with questions and counsel for young converts, by the Rev. Ashbel Green.   Hillsborough, Dennis Heartt, pr., 1821.   72 p.   [14971

Wills, George Stockton. Questions on Longfellow's Hiawatha.   No place, no publisher [1894?]   11 p.   [14972

Willson, H. Bowlby. North Carolina, its debt and financial resources, 1st September 1869.   New York, John Medole, pr., 1869.   32 p.   [14973

Wilmeth, James Lillard, comp. Wilmot—Wilmoth—Wilmeth.   [Charlotte, Washburn Printing Co. for] The Author, Philadelphia, Pa., 1940.   374 p.   [14974

Wilmington, N. C. Brief by the city of Wilmington and the Wilmington Chamber of Commerce in respect to the installation of Navy Surplus Drydock at Maritime Commission Reserve Fleet site at Wilmington, North Carolina, for the preservation of the bottoms of vessels.   Wilmington [1949]   9 p.   [14975

Wilmington, N. C. Bible Society. Constitution of the Bible Society of Wilmington, North Carolina [Wilmington? 1819?]   [3] p.   [14976

Wilmington, N. C. Bicentennial Celebration Commission. Souvenir program, A tale of two centuries, presented by Wilmington Bicentennial Commission, Inc., June 21, 22, 23, 1939. [Wilmington] 1939. [24] p. [14977
——Two centuries of the Wilmington scene, June 18-28, 1939, Federal Art Center, sponsored by Wilmington Museum of Art. Wilmington, 1939. [8] p. [14978

Wilmington, N. C. Board of Aldermen. General tax ordinance for the city of Wilmington, N. C., for the year 1901. Wilmington, S. G. Hall, pr., 1901. 14 p. [14979

[**Wilmington, N. C. Board of Education**] Report, 188 - Wilmington, 188 - NcU has 1885/86 [14980

Wilmington, N. C. Cape Fear Club. Constitution of the Cape Fear Club of Wilmington, N. C. Wilmington, Dispatch Book and Job Printing Establishment, 1866. 10 p. [14981

Wilmington, N. C. Carolina Rice Mills. How to cook Carolina rice. Wilmington [1883?] 6 p. [14982

[**Wilmington, N. C. Chamber of Commerce**] Building code, Wilmington, N. C. [Wilmington? Building Code Publishing Co., c.1925] [48] p. [14983

Wilmington, N. C. Chamber of Commerce. City of Wilmington, the metropolis and port of North Carolina, its advantages and interests; also, A series of sketches of representative business houses, by I. J. Isaacs. Wilmington, Wilmington Stamp, 1912. 111 p. [14984
——City of Wilmington, North Carolina, New Hanover County: Facts about Wilmington as an ideal location for a new industrial plant. [Wilmington, 1946?] 15 p. [14985
——Facts about Wilmington. Wilmington, Wilmington Printing Co. [1923?] Folder. [14986
——An hour's automobile itinerary around the city of Wilmington, North Carolina. Wilmington, n.d. [3] p. [14987
——New Hanover County, sub-tropical region of North Carolina. [Wilmington, 1897] 42 p. [14988
——The port of Wilmington, N. C., marine gateway of the Old North State; a digest of port facilities. Wilmington, Service Printing Co. [1923?] Folder. [14989
——Souvenir of Wilmington, N. C. Brooklyn, N. Y., Albertype Company for the Wilmington Chamber of Commerce [1902?] 20 plates. [14990
——Supplemental brief . . . filed with the State Ship and Water Transportation Commission. Wilmington, Wilmington Printing Co. [1923?] 36 p. [14991
——The tariff on lumber; resolutions adopted by the Wilmington Chamber of Commerce. [Wilmington, 1909] 3 p. [14992
——Where, when, how, why, what in wartime Wilmington, North Carolina. [Wilmington, 1943?] [13] p. [14993
——Wilmington, North Carolina, facts and figures. [Wilmington? 1943?] 15 p. [14994
——Wilmington, North Carolina, past, present and future; history of its harbor, with detailed reports of the work for improving and restoring the same, now being conducted by the U. S. government. Wilmington, J. A. Engelhard, pr., 1872. 84 p. [14995
——Wilmington, North Carolina, South Atlantic port city. [Wilmington, Wilmington Printing Co., 1918?] [15] p. [14996
——Wilmington, North Carolina's only deep water port . . . a digest of port facilities. Wilmington [1930] Folder. [14997
——Wilmington, the leading port city of North Carolina. [Wilmington, 1946?] [9] p. [14998
—— ——1948-49. [Wilmington, 1948?] 12 p. [14999
——Wilmington up-to-date, the metropolis of North Carolina. Wilmington, W. L. de Rosset, 1902. 115 p. [15000

[**Wilmington, N. C. Chamber of Commerce**] The wonderful story of Wilmington, North Carolina, playground of the South [Wilmington, 1929] [20] p. [15001

Wilmington, N. C. Citizens. Counter-memorial of citizens of Wilmington, opposed to taxation for railroad purposes. [Wilmington? 1846] [1] p. [15002

[**Wilmington, N. C. Citizens**] Reasons why the government ought to erect a public building in Wilmington, N. C. [Wilmington?] n.d. [2] p. [15003

Wilmington, N. C. Council. The code of the city of Wilmington, North Carolina, 1946. Charlottesville, Va., Michie City Publications Co., 1946. 238 p. [15004

——Report of operations of the city of Wilmington, North Carolina, 1942/43- [Wilmington, 1943- NcU has 1942/43-1946/47 [15005

——Report on audit of books and accounts, 19 - Wilmington, 19 - NcU has 1925/26-1929/30, 1942/43, 1946/47-1950/51 [15006

Wilmington, N. C. First Presbyterian Church [The dedication of the James Sprunt memorial organ, November 25, 1928] [Wilmington, 1928] 4 p. [15007

——Hand book of the First Presbyterian Church, Wilmington, N. C., 1892-1913, being a continuation of the memorial volumes of 1892. [Wilmington? 1913?] 72 p. [15008

——Program of exercises, centennial anniversary . . . Sunday, April 1st, to Sunday, April 8th, 1917. [Wilmington? 1917?] [6] p. [15009

——Record and manual of the First Presbyterian Church, Wilmington, N. C., 1895-96. [Wilmington, Jackson & Bell, pr., 1896] 37 p. [15010

Wilmington, N. C. Housing Authority. Report, 193 - Wilmington, 193 - NcU has 1948 (with a summary of 1938-1948) 1949, 1950 [15011

Wilmington, N. C. L'Arioso German Club. Constitution and by-laws, officers, patronesses, members; also, Club history as disclosed from old newspaper files and other records, with introduction by Boyden Sparkes. [Wilmington] 1941. [28] p. [15012

Wilmington, N. C. Masonic Temple Corporation. Reports of the president and treasurer, 19 - Wilmington, 19 - NcU has 1903/04, 1906/07 [15013

Wilmington, N. C. Mayor. Report, 18 - Wilmington, 18 - NcU has 1870/71, 1900 (with statistics 1894-1900) [15014

Wilmington, N. C. Ministering Circle. Favorite recipes of the lower Cape Fear. Wilmington [c.1955] 184 p. [15015

Wilmington, N. C. New Hanover Fishing Club. Prize list and annual, 194 - Wilmington, 194 - NcU has 1947 [15016

[Wilmington, N. C. New Hanover High School] New Hanover High School handbook, Wilmington, N. C., January, 1925. Wilmington, 1925. 41 p. [15017

Wilmington, N. C. New Hanover High School. English Department. Student themes, selected from regular classroom work, 1944/45- Wilmington, 1945- NcU has 1945/46, 1948/49 [15018

Wilmington, N. C. New Hanover High School. Faculty. Course of study, New Hanover High School, Wilmington, North Carolina. [Wilmington, 1925?] 74 p. [15019

[Wilmington, N. C. Oakdale Cemetery Co.] Historical sketch of the Oakdale Cemetery Company, with the charter, by-lays [!] and rules governing the grounds generally. Wilmington, Review Job Office, pr. [1911?] 20 p. [15020

Wilmington, N. C. Port-Traffic Association. The Port of Wilmington, North Carolina. Wilmington, 1932. 14 p. [15021

Wilmington, N. C. Real Estate Investment Company. A prospectus of 600,000 acres of North Carolina land offered for sale. Wilmington, State, pr., n.d. 11 p. [15022

——The Real Estate Investment Company of Wilmington, North Carolina, a description of its property; reports of Professor J. A. Holmes and of General W. G. Lewis. Wilmington, Morning Star, 1891. 20 p. [15023

Wilmington, N. C. Safety Committee. Proceedings of the Safety Committee for the town of Wilmington, N. C., from 1774 to 1776. Raleigh, T. Loring, 1844. 76 p. [15024

Wilmington, N. C. St. James Church. 1839-1939: One hundredth anniversary commemorating the building of St. James Church, Wilmington, North Carolina, April 30th and May 1st, 1939, the two hundred and tenth year of the parish; historical notices by Rev. Robert Brent Drane. [Wilmington, William Lord de Rosset, c.1939] [29] p. [15025

—— ——[Wilmington, 1939] [4] p. Program. [15026

——Souvenir bulletin of the opening of the new parish house . . . March 4th, 1924. [Wilmington] 1924. 8 p. [15027

Wilmington, N. C. St. John's Church. Year book, May, 1910. Wilmington, Review Job Office, pr. [1910?] 31 p. [15028

Wilmington, N. C. Social Service League. Wilmington, North Carolina, a guide to points of interest. Wilmington, 1949. 38 p.   [15029

——— ———1950. 50 p.   [15030

Wilmington, N. C. Taft Day Celebration. Publicity Committee. Complimentary smoker in honor of the Tar Heel press. Wilmington, 1909. [32] p.   [15031

Wilmington, N. C. Temple of Israel. 1876, seventy-fifth anniversary, Temple of Israel, Wilmington, North Carolina, May 12, 1951. [Wilmington] 1951. 16 p. [15032

Wilmington, N. C. Tide Water Power Company. Wrightsville Beach. Wilmington [1923?] Folder.   [15033

———Wrightsville Beach . . . season 1930. [Wilmington] 1930. Folder.   [15034

Wilmington, N. C. Winter Park Memorial Presbyterian Church. Dedication, Sunday, March 5th, 1916, 4:15 P.M. [Wilmington? 1916]   3 p.   [15035

Wilmington Baptist Association. Minutes, 1901- 1901- NcU has 1903, 1906, 1926, 1934   [15036

Wilmington College, Wilmington, N. C. Bulletin, no. 1- 194 - Wilmington, 194 - NcU has no. 3-8   [15037

Wilmington directory including a general and city business directory for 1865-66. Wilmington, P. Heinsberger, 1865. 136 p.   [15038

Wilmington Institute, Wilmington, N. C. Announcement, 1850/51?- Wilmington, 1850?- NcU has 1858/59   [15039

Wilmington Light Infantry [Circular to the volunteer military companies throughout the state] Wilmington, April 23, 1860. [1] p.   [15040

———Constitution and by-laws, adopted May 14, 1894. Wilmington, R. P. McClammy, pr., 1894. 20 p.   [15041

——— ———adopted August 19th, 1886. Wilmington, Wm. L. de Rosset, Jr., pr., 1886. 24 p.   [15042

——— ———as revised January, 1877. Wilmington, Mercantile Printing Co., 1877. 23 p.   [15043

——— ———as revised January, 1883, with amendments adopted April, 1884. 20 p.   [15044

Wilmington, North Carolina, and vicinity. [Wilmington, Wm. L. de Rosset, Jr.] n.d. [6] p. 16 plates.   [15045

Wilmington, North Carolina, South Atlantic port city. [Wilmington, Wilmington Printing Co., 1919?] 14 p.   [15046

Wilson, Albert R. The importance of disinfecting the bowel discharges in typhoid fever; read at the Salisbury Health Conference, September 13, 1894. Winston, M. I. & J. C. Stewart, pr., 1895. 8 p.   [15047

Wilson, Alexander. A sermon, preached at Smyrna, Granville County, N. C., August 23rd, 1835, and occasioned by the death of Col. Maurice Smith, ruling elder of the Presbyterian Church at Spring Grove. Milton, Spectator Office, 1835. 9 p.   [15048

Wilson, Alpheus Waters. Missions of the Methodist Episcopal Church, South. Nashville, Tenn., Southern Methodist Publishing House, 1882. 144 p.   [15049

Wilson, Carrie B. History of the North Carolina State Division of the American Association of University Women, 1927-1947. Greensboro, Riser Printing Co., c.1948. 77 p.   [15050

Wilson, Eddie Watts, comp. The gourd: a bibliography. Los Angeles, 1954. 13 p.   [15051

Wilson, Eddie Watts. The gourd in folk literature. [Boston, Gourd Society of America, Inc., 1947] 120 p.   [15052

Wilson, Eddie Watts, joint author, see **Camp, Cordelia**

Wilson, Edwin Mood. The congressional career of Nathaniel Macon . . . followed by letters of Mr. Macon and Willie P. Mangum, with notes by Kemp P. Battle. Chapel Hill [University Press] 1900. (James Sprunt historical monographs, no. 2) 115 p.   [15053

[**Wilson, Ellen Hale**] comp. In memoriam, Mrs. James Sprunt. [Wilmington, privately printed for James Sprunt, c.1916] 121 p.   [15054

Wilson, Frank I. Address delivered before the Wake County Workingmen's Association in the Court House at Raleigh, February 6, 1860. Raleigh, Standard Office, pr., 1860. 22 p. [15055

——Battle of Great Bethel (fought June 10, 1861). Raleigh, Standard Office, pr., 1864. 28 p. [15056

——Sketches of Nassau; to which is added, The devil's ball-alley, an Indian tradition. Raleigh, Standard Office, 1864. 76 p. [15057

——The superiority of the present age; an address delivered before the Franklin Literary Society of Mr. Horner's School, Oxford, N. C., May 27, 1859. Raleigh, Holden and Wilson, 1859. 20 p. [15058

Wilson, George Pickett. A guide to better English. New York, F. S. Crofts & Co., 1946. 527 p. [15059

——Informal oral composition. Boston, Palmer Co. [c.1922] 188 p. [15060

Wilson, George Pickett, joint author, see Randolph, Vance

Wilson, Henry B. The power to heal; a handbook for the practice of healing according to the methods of Jesus. Asheville, Nazarene Press, c.1923. 92 p. [15061

Wilson, J. D. An address delivered at the commencement at Floral College, June, 1853. Fayetteville, E. J. Hale & Son, pr., 1853. 15 p. [15062

Wilson, James W. To the Democrats of North Carolina. No place, no publisher [1902?] 8 p. [15063

Wilson, Joseph Ruggles. Beneficiary ministerial education; the substance of a report adopted by the General Assembly of the Presbyterian Church in the Confederate States of America, at its sessions in Charlotte, N. C., in May, 1864. Richmond, Va., Presbyterian Committee of Publication, 1864. 12 p. [15064

Wilson, Lollie (Cave) Hard to forget; the young O. Henry. Los Angeles, Lymanhouse, 1939. 235 p. [15065

Wilson, Louis Round. Addresses by Vice-President R. Wendell Harrison and Dean Emeritus Louis Round Wilson on the occasion of the 25th anniversary of the establishment of the Graduate Library School, University of Chicago, July 12, 1951. [Chicago, University of Chicago, 1951] 12 p. [15066

——Chaucer's relative constructions. Chapel Hill, University Press, 1906. (Studies in philology, v. 1) 60 p. [15067

Wilson, Louis Round, ed. The chronicles of the Sesquicentennial. Chapel Hill, University of North Carolina Press, 1947. 349 p. [15068

Wilson, Louis Round. County library service in the South; a study of the Rosenwald county library demonstration, by Louis R. Wilson and Edward A. Wight. Chicago, University of Chicago Press [1935] 259 p. [15069

[**Wilson, Louis Round]** ed. Edward Kidder Graham, 1876-1918. Raleigh, Edwards and Broughton Co., 1919. (University of North Carolina record, no. 162, supplement) 38 p. [15070

Wilson, Louis Round. The geography of reading; a study of the distribution and status of libraries in the United States. Chicago, American Library Association and University of Chicago Press [1938] 481 p. [15071

——The high school library, by Louis R. Wilson and others. Chapel Hill, University of North Carolina Press, 1923. (University of North Carolina extension bulletin [vol. II, no. 14]) 48 p. [15072

——Library extension service. Chapel Hill, University of North Carolina [1920] (University of North Carolina extension leaflet, vol. IV, no. 4) 16 p. [15073

——The library in college instruction, a syllabus on the improvement of college instruction through library use, by Louis Round Wilson, Mildred Hawksworth Lowell [and] Sarah Rebecca Reed. New York, H. W. Wilson Co., 1951. 347 p.[15074

——Library planning; a working memorandum prepared for the American Library Association. Chicago, American Library Association, 1944. 93 p. [15075

Wilson, Louis Round, ed. Library trends; papers presented before the Library Institute at the University of Chicago, August 3-15, 1936. Chicago, University of Chicago Press [1937] 388 p. [15076

[**Wilson, Louis Round]** ed. Marvin Hendrix Stacy, 1877-1919. Raleigh, Edwards and Broughton Co., 1919. (University of North Carolina record, no. 163) 22 p [15077

Wilson, Louis Round. Memorandum concerning the background of consolidation. [Chapel Hill, The Author, 1956] 3 p.   [15078

[**Wilson, Louis Round**] ed. Public discussion and debate. Chapel Hill, University of North Carolina [1914] (University of North Carolina record, no. 115) 54 p. [15079

——Report of a survey of the libraries of Cornell University for the Library Board of Cornell University, October, 1847-February, 1948 [by] Louis R. Wilson, Robert B. Downs [and] Maurice F. Tauber. Ithaca, N. Y., Cornell University, 1948. 202 p.   [15080

——Report of a survey of the libraries of the Alabama Polytechnic Institute, November, 1948-March, 1949, by Louis R. Wilson and Robert W. Orr. Auburn, Alabama Polytechnic Institute, 1949. 215 p.   [15081

——Report of a survey of the Library of the University of Notre Dame for the University of Notre Dame, November, 1950-March, 1952 [by] Louis R. Wilson and Frank A. Lundy on behalf of the American Library Association. Chicago, American Library Association, 1952. 195 p.   [15082

——Report of a survey of the Library of Stanford University for Stanford University, November, 1946-March, 1947 [by] Louis R. Wilson and Raynard C. Swank on behalf of the American Library Association. Chicago, 1947. 222 p.   [15083

——Report of a survey of the University of Florida Library for the University of Florida, February-May, 1940, [by] Louis R. Wilson, chairman, . . . A. F. Kuhlman . . . Guy R. Lyle. Chicago, American Library Association, 1940. 120 p.   [15084

——Report of a survey of the University of Georgia Library for the University of Georgia, September-December, 1938, by Louis R. Wilson . . . Ralph M. Dunbar . . . [and] Guy R. Lyle on behalf of the American Library Association. Chicago, American Library Association, 1939. 74 numb. leaves.   [15085

——Report of a survey of the University of South Carolina Library for the University of South Carolina, February-May, 1946, by Louis R. Wilson . . . and Maurice F. Tauber. Columbia, S. C., University of South Carolina, 1946. 134 leaves. [15086

——A report on the Mary Reed Library. [Denver] University of Denver, 1947. 18 p.   [15087

——The role of the library in adult education; papers presented before the Library Institute at the University of Chicago, August 2-13, 1937. Chicago, University of Chicago Press [1937] 321 p.   [15088

Wilson, Louis Round. The university library; its organization, administration and functions, by Louis Round Wilson and Maurice F. Tauber. Chicago, University of Chicago Press [1945] 570 p.   [15089

—— ——2d ed. New York, Columbia University Press, 1956. 641 p. [15090

——Why consolidation should be continued. [Chapel Hill, The Author, 1956] 3 p.   [15091

Wilson, Mary Badger. Canon Brett. New York, Greystone Press [1942] 342 p.[15092

——From nine to five. Philadelphia, Penn Publishing Co. [c.1933] 303 p. [15093

——New dreams for old. New York, A. L. Burt Co., c.1931] 284 p.   [15094

——The painted city; dry-points of Washington life. New York, Frederick A. Stokes Co., 1927. 247 p.   [15095

——Separate star. Philadelphia, Penn Publishing Co. [c.1932] 299 p.   [15096

——Yesterday's promise. Philadelphia, Penn Publishing Co. [c.1934] 306 p. [15097

Wilson, Nathan Hunt Daniel, 1822-1888. An address delivered before the two literary societies of New Institute, Iredell Co., N. C., June 6th, 1855. Salisbury, Office of the Carolina Watchman, 1855. 15 p.   [15098

Wilson, Nathan Hunt Daniel, 1866-1940. Honorable union or a separate existence of peace. Washington, N. C., 1921. 23 p.   [15099

[**Wilson, Nathan Hunt Daniel**] **1866-1940.** Roderick Belton John. No place, no publisher [1931] [4] p.   [15100

Wilson, Peter Mitchel. Southern exposure. Chapel Hill, University of North Carolina Press, 1927. 197 p.   [15101

[**Wilson, Samuel**] An account of the province of Carolina in America; together with an abstract of the patent, and several other necessary and useful particulars, to such as have thoughts of transporting themselves thither. London, Printed by G. Larkin for F. Smith, 1682. 27 p.   [15102

Wilson, Samuel Mackay. Andrew Jackson; an address . . . at the centennial celebration of the Battle of New Orleans. [Louisville, Ky., Westerfield-Bonte Press] 1915. 43 p. [15103

Wilson, Samuel Tyndale. The southern mountaineers. New York, Literature Department, Presbyterian Home Missions, 1906. 164 p. [15104

Wilson, T. B. Family record of Thomas de Fereby and Joseph Wilson of England, continuing through the American line to the year 1915. Fairmont, Wilson Printing Co., n.d. 24 p. [15105

Wilson, Thomas W. To the freemen of the county of Wilkes. No place, no publisher [June 12, 1825] 2 p. [15106

Wilson, Upton Gwynn. My 33 years of life in bed. [Durham] privately printed by Author's family, 1946. 213 p. [15107

Wilson, W. M. [Boot and shoe shop] No place, no publisher, January, 1869. [1] p. Title mutilated in NcU copy [15108

Wilson, William J. Wilson's progressive speller, containing upwards of twelve thousand words, with reading and dictation exercises annexed to each lesson. Baltimore, John Murphy & Co., 1870. 190 p. [15109

Wilson, William Jesse, comp. The Eureka songster; being a small collection of choice songs for family and school use. San Saba, Texas, San Saba Star Print [1912] 22 p. [15110

—— ——Improved 5th ed. 1917. 56 p. [15111

——A few patriotic songs taken from The Eureka songster . . . Special edition for North Carolina. Austin, Texas, Von Boekmann-Jones Co., n.d. 8 p. [15112

Wilson, William Thomas. For the love of Lady Margaret; a romance of the Lost Colony. Charlotte, Stone & Barringer Co., 1908. 305 p. [15113

Wilson, N. C. Chamber of Commerce. Facts about Wilson, North Carolina. Wilson, 1934. 83 p. [15114

[Wilson, N. C. Chamber of Commerce] Come to Wilson, North Carolina on U. S. route 301, the city of beautiful trees. [Wilson, 1940?] Folder. [15115

Wilson, N. C. First Methodist Episcopal Church, South. Directory of membership. [Wilson?] 1919. 32 p. [15116

Wilson, N. C. Kiwanis Club. Kiwanis business directory and souvenir program, Follies of 1921. Wilson Theatre, Wednesday and Thursday, July 6th and 7th, 1921. [Wilson? 1921?] 20 p. [15117

Wilson, N. C. Superintendent of Schools. Wilson City Public Schools, general information for teachers . . . compiled by Charles L. Coon. [Wilson] 1914. 38 p. [15118

Wilson, N. C. directory, v. 1-1908-09- Wilson, and Richmond, Va., Hill Directory Co., c.1908- NcU has 1930, 1941, 1947-48, 1951-52 [15119

Wilson College, Wilson, N. C. Catalogue, 1872- Wilson, 1872- NcU has 1872, 1875/76 [15120

Wilson Collegiate Seminary for Young Ladies, Wilson, N. C. Catalogue, 186 - Wilson, 186 - NcU has 1870/71, 1877/78 [15121

Wilson County, N. C. Board of Education. Directions for Wilson County teachers, 1913-14 . . . [by] Charles L. Coon. Wilson [1913] 11 p. [15122

——Plan of classification of Wilson County public school teachers. Wilson, 1914. 10 p. [15123

Winborne, Benjamin Brodie. The colonial and state political history of Hertford County, N. C. [Murfreesboro?] Printed for the Author by Edwards & Broughton, 1906. 348 p. [15124

——An historical brief of political economy. Raleigh, Edwards & Broughton, pr., n.d. 20 p. [15125

——The Perry family of Hertford County, North Carolina. [Raleigh, Edwards-Broughton Printing Co., 1909] 64 p. [15126

——Speech, delivered at the convention of peanut growers of Virginia, North Carolina, and Tennessee at the Jamestown Exposition, Friday, September 27, 1907. Raleigh, Edwards & Broughton Printing Co., n.d. 15 p. [15127

——The Vaughan family of Hertford County, N. C. [Raleigh, Edwards & Broughton Printing Co.] 1909. 104 p. [15128

——The Winborne family. Raleigh, Edwards & Broughton, pr. [1905] 141 p. [15129

——The Winbornes of old. No place, no publisher, 1911. 38 p. [15130

Winchester, George T. A story of Union County and the History of Pleasant Grove Camp Ground. Mineral Springs, Author [1937] 103 p. [15131

[Windsor, Anne] Humanity and the church by the road. No place, no publisher, n.d. [4] p. [15132

Windsor, Anne, ed. Laughter and heart cries, 1938. Carthage, Moore County News Press, pr., 1938. 35 p. [15133

[Windsor, N. C. Citizens] A souvenir of Windsor, North Carolina. [Asheville, Inland Press] 1913. 32 p. [15134

[Winecoff, J. Eugene L.] The Winecoff family. [Florence, S. C., 1933] 32 p. [15135

Winecoff, Thomas Edward. The one catholic and apostolic church. [Chapel Hill] University of North Carolina Press for the Author, 1898. 37 p. [15136

Winfield, Robert, pseud. see Glascock, Harold

Wingate, Thomas Herron, joint author, see Moore, James Lewis

Wingate, Washington Manly. I have brought my little brother back. [Raleigh, Board of Missions of the North Carolina Baptist State Convention] n.d. (No. 11) 8 p. [15137

——Self-culture; an address delivered before the Oxford Female School, May 27, 1858. Raleigh, Holden and Wilson, pr., 1858. 22 p. [15138

Wingate Junior College, Wingate, N. C. Catalogue, 1896/97?- Wingate, 1897?- Called Wingate School for Boys and Girls. NcU has 1900/02 [1912/13-1955/ 56] [15139

Wingert, Grace (Harper) Our kinsmen, a record of the ancestry and descendants of Griffith Thomas, a pioneer resident of Orange County, North Carolina. [Springfield, O., 1938] 135 p. [15140

Winkler, Angelina Virginia (Walton) Souvenir of the twin cities of North Carolina, Winston-Salem, Forsyth County. Salem, Blums' Steam Power Press Print, 1890. 92 p. [15141

Winkler, John Kennedy. Tobacco tycoon, the story of James Buchanan Duke. New York, Random House [1942] 337 p. [15142

Winslow, D. H. Brains and eggs. [Raleigh, The Author] n.d. 20 p. [15143

——Highway maintenance in North Carolina by D. H. Winslow and Charles R. Thomas. Raleigh, North Carolina State College of Agriculture and Engineering, 1918. (Its State College record, v. 17, no. 2) 18 p. [15144

Winslow, Edward Lee. Oration, delivered before the Fayetteville Independent Light Infantry Company, on the semi-anniversary of the corps, August 23d, 1843. Fayetteville, E. J. Hale, pr., 1843. 29 p. [15145

Winslow, Edward Lee, joint author, see Strange, Robert, 1796-1854

Winslow, Ellen Goode (Rawlings) History of Perquimans County as compiled from records found there and elsewhere. Raleigh, Edwards & Broughton Co., 1931. 488 p. [15146

Winslow, Francis Edward. The Horace Williams Society presents an informal talk on "The free mind in action" delivered at its meeting, June, 1953, Chapel Hill, N. C. [Chapel Hill, 1954] [14] p. [15147

Winslow, Hubbard. Eulogy on the late Prof. E. A. Andrews delivered at New Britain, Conn., May 19, 1858. Boston, Crocker and Brewster, 1858. 50 p. [15148

Winslow, John Cooper. Eta prime of Kappa Sigma, an historical sketch, 1873-1908, being a short narrative of Kappa Sigma's career at old Trinity, with an account of the fraternity at new Trinity to the present time. Durham, Seeman Printery, 1908. 66 p. [15149

Winstanley, pseud. see Coleman, Thaddeus Charles

[Winston, Ellen Engelmann (Black)] History of the State Legislative Council, 1920-1955. Raleigh [1955] 8 p. [15150

Winston, Ellen Engelmann (Black) joint author, see Woofter, Thomas Jackson

Winston, Francis Donnell. Masonry. [Raleigh] Grand Lodge of North Carolina, 1911. 11 p. [15151

Winston, Francis Donnell, joint author, see Palmer, Theodore Sherman

Winston, George Tayloe. Child labor in North Carolina. New York, National Child Labor Committee, 1916. (Its Pamphlet no. 262) 4 p.   [15152
——The Greek, the Roman, and the Teuton; an address delivered before several classical schools of the state. Greensboro, Thomas, Reece & Co., 1884. 20 p. [15153
——Industrial education and the use of machinery essential to the development of North Carolina; an address delivered before the convention of the North Carolina Bankers' Association, at Greensboro, N. C., June 15th, 1900. Charlotte, Merchants and Farmers Bank [1900?] 11 p.   [15154
——Mephistopheles and Iago; lecture delivered March 30, 1887, before the Shakespere Club of the University of North Carolina. No place, no publisher, n.d. 32 p.   [15155
——Oration at Guilford Battle Ground, July 4th, 1895. Subject: The life and times of Major Joseph Winston; to this are added other speeches delivered on this occasion. Greensboro, Guilford Battle Ground Co. [1895?] 46 p.   [15156
Winston, James Horner. Judah P. Benjamin, distinguished at the bars of two nations; an address delivered before the Law Club of Chicago on March 22, 1929. Chicago, privately printed, 1930. 47 p.   [15157
Winston, Joseph. Circular; Joseph Winston to his constituents & fellow citizens. [Washington, February 26, 1807] [3] p.   [15158
——To the citizens of Wilkes County. [Washington, March 20, 1804] [3] p. [15159
[Winston, Laura Annie] ed. In fond and loving memory of Lonnie Hinton Winston. No place, privately printed [1890?] 68 p.   [15160
Winston, Patrick Henry. An address on the subject of convention delivered . . . at Tucker Hall, Wednesday evening, Dec. 2d, 1874. Raleigh, Daily News Print, 1874. 15 p.   [15161
Winston, Robert Watson. Andrew Johnson, the modern Prometheus, an address. No place, no publisher [1931] 13 p.   [15162
——Andrew Johnson, plebian and patriot. New York, H. Holt and Co. [c.1928] 549 p.   [15163
——Aycock, his people's genius; founders' day address, October 12, 1933, University of North Carolina. Chapel Hill, The Alumni Review, 1933. (Supplement, v. 22, no. 2) 24 p.   [15164
——A garland for ashes, an aspiration for the South; address before North Carolina Bar Association, June 28, 1934. [Chapel Hill, The Author] 1934. 12 p.   [15165
——High stakes and hair trigger; the life of Jefferson Davis. New York, H. Holt and Co. [c.1930] 306 p.   [15166
——Horace Williams, gadfly of Chapel Hill. Chapel Hill, University of North Carolina Press, 1942. 309 p.   [15167
——It's a far cry. New York, H. Holt and Co. [c.1937] 381 p.   [15168
——Judge Henry Groves Connor; memorial address before the North Carolina Bar Association, Asheville, N. C., July 2, 1925. No place, no publisher, n.d. 7 p. [15169
——Leonard Henderson; address presenting the portrait of Chief Justice Henderson to the Supreme Court of North Carolina; address of acceptance by Chief Justice Walter Clark. No place, no publisher, n.d. 24 p.   [15170
——Memorial address delivered before the Supreme Court of North Carolina, Raleigh, North Carolina, March 29, 1938. No place, no publisher [1938?] 17 p. [15171
——Memorial Hall, its tablets and memories; acceptance of tablets memorializing Col. Robert Bingham and Senator Matt W. Ransom, University Day, October 12, 1939, University of North Carolina [Chapel Hill] 1939. [3] p.   [15172
——Popular discontent with judicial procedure, its causes considered and some remedies suggested; address before the North Carolina Bar Association at Asheville, July 4, 1913. Raleigh, Mutual Publishing Co., 1913. 23 p.   [15173
——Red Cross and the war; Judge Robert W. Winston at St. Mary's School, Raleigh, North Carolina, May 19, 1918. [Raleigh?] n.d. 5 p.   [15174
——Robert E. Lee, a biography. New York, W. Morrow & Co., 1934. 428 p. [15175
——Talks about law. Raleigh, Edwards & Broughton, 1894. 192 p.   [15176
——Vance and Aycock; acceptance of a joint tablet memorializing Zebulon B. Vance and Charles B. Aycock . . . University Day, October 12, 1941, University of North Carolina. [Chapel Hill, 1941] 8 p.   [15177
——Victor Silas Bryant, truest friend and noblest foe . . . address presenting portrait to Durham bar. [Durham? 1942] 18 p.   [15178
Winston, Sanford. Culture and human behavior. New York, Ronald Press Co. [c.1933] 249 p.   [15179

——Housing of a rural low income group in North Carolina by Sanford Winston and Ethel A. Giles. [Raleigh] North Carolina Conference for Social Service, Housing Committee, 1953. 14 p. [15180

——Illiteracy in the United States. Chapel Hill, University of North Carolina Press, 1930. 168 p. .. [15181

——Leadership in war and peace. Raleigh, North Carolina State College of Agriculture and Engineering, Agricultural Experiment Station, 1946. (Its Special publication, no. 1) 141 p. [15182

——Social aspects of public housing; an evaluation of North Carolina experience. [Raleigh, North Carolina Council of Housing Authorities] 1947. 44 p. [15183

Winston, N. C. Board of School Commissioners. Report of the Public Schools, 1884/85?- Winston, 1885?- NcU has 1887/88, 1910/11, 1912/13. Continues 1913/14- as Winston-Salem, N. C. Board of School Commissioners. Report [15184

Winston, N. C. First Presbyterian Church [Circular] Winston, November, 1860. [1] p. [15185

Winston-Salem, N. C. Anti-Tuberculosis Committee of One Hundred. Tuberculosis and its prevention. Winston-Salem, 1910. 34 p. [15186

Winston-Salem, N. C. Board of Aldermen. Chapters 7, 8, and 9 of the City ordinances pertaining to street traffic, vehicles for hire, motor vehicles. [Winston-Salem?] n.d. 29 p. [15187

——Chapters 10 and 11 of the City ordinances pertaining to water, sewerage and plumbing. [Winston-Salem?] n.d. 29 p. [15188

——City of Winston-Salem, North Carolina, budget, 19 - Winston-Salem, 19 - NcU has 1948/49, 1949/50, 1952/53, 1953/54 summary, 1955/56 summary [15189

——The code of the city of Winston-Salem, North Carolina, 1953; the charter, related laws and general ordinances of the city, enacted as a whole, February 5, 1954. Charlottesville, Va., Michie City Publications Co., 1954. 824 p. [15190

——The general ordinances and the charter of the city of Winston-Salem, North Carolina, adopted, July 21, 1916, compiled by Philip Williams. Winston-Salem, Barber Printing and Stationery Co., 1916. 240, 61 p. [15191

——The general ordinances, and the charter, amendments to the charter of the city of Winston-Salem, North Carolina, adopted, January 22, 1926, compiled by Parrish and Deal, city attorneys. Winston-Salem, Barber Printing Co., 1926. 249, 116 p. [15192

——Ordinances . . . January 29, 1926- [Winston-Salem, 1926- NcU has January 29, 1926-January 3, 1953. Issued serially as loose leaves following authorization [15193

——An ordinance providing revenue and privilege taxes for the city of Winston-Salem for the Year 1927-28 and the following years, adopted May 27, 1927. [Winston-Salem, 1927] 15 p. [15194

——An ordinance regulating storage of gasoline or other volatile inflammable liquids in quantities greater than one gallon in the city of Winston-Salem, N. C., adopted October 12, 1928. [Winston-Salem, 1928?] [4] p. [15195

——Ordinances pertaining to public health. [Winston-Salem] n.d. 59 p. [15196

——Statement of financial information, city of Winston-Salem, North Carolina, 19 - [Winston-Salem, 19 - NcU has 1932-1950, 1952, 1954 [15197

Winston-Salem, N. C. Board of School Commissioners. Course of study for grade schools. Winston-Salem, 1920. 86 p. [15198

——Educational bulletin series, 192 - [Winston-Salem, 192 - NcU has [1929/30-1931/32] [15199

——Report of the Public Schools of the city of Winston-Salem, North Carolina, 1913/14- Winston-Salem, 1914- NcU has 1913/14-1922/23 [15200

——Winston-Salem city Public Schools, a brief statement of their organization and activities, 1927/1928. [Winston-Salem, Richard J. Reynolds High School, pr., 1928] 11 p. [15201

——Winston-Salem city Public Schools, directory of school officials and school buildings, 1927/28. [Winston-Salem, Richard J. Reynolds High School, pr., 1928] 11 p. [15202

——Winston-Salem city Public Schools, 191 - [Winston-Salem, 191 - NcU has 1919/20, 1923/24 [15203

Winston-Salem, N. C. Board of Trade. Souvenir of Winston-Salem, N. C. Brooklyn, N. Y., Albertype Co., n.d. [2] p. 15 plates. [15204

——Winston-Salem, North Carolina, city of diversified industry. Winston-Salem, April, 1916. Folder. [15205

Winston-Salem, N. C. Chamber of Commerce. Directory of manufacturers, Winston-Salem and Forsyth County, North Carolina, 19 - Winston-Salem, 19 - NcU has 1953 [15206

——Historical Winston-Salem. [Winston-Salem] n.d. 16 p. [15207

——Industrial survey, Winston-Salem and Forsyth County, North Carolina. Winston-Salem [1956] 26 p. [15208

——Presenting a three-volume work on Winston-Salem. Condensed ed. [Winston-Salem, 1947] [15] p. [15209

[**Winston-Salem, N. C. Chamber of Commerce**] [Report, 19 - Winston-Salem, 19 - NcU has 1941/42, 1945/46, 1946/47, 1949/50-1955/56 [15210

Winston-Salem, N. C. Chamber of Commerce. A unit on city government with emphasis on the Winston-Salem city government and the city of Winston-Salem, prepared for the teachers of civics in the Winston-Salem Public Schools. Winston-Salem, 1947. 40 p. [15211

——Winston-Salem goes to church. Winston-Salem, 1954. 3, 3 p. [15212

[**Winston-Salem, N. C. Chamber of Commerce**] Winston-Salem, half century of progress. [Winston-Salem, Winston Printing Co., 1935] 48 p. [15213

Winston-Salem N. C. Chamber of Commerce. Winston-Salem, North Carolina, the world's tobacco metropolis. Winston-Salem [1937] Folder. [15214

[**Winston-Salem, N. C. Chamber of Commerce. Bi-centennial Committee**] Souvenir programme, bi-centennial celebration of visit of President George Washington to Salem, 1791, Winston-Salem, May 28, 1932. [Winston-Salem, 1932] [11] p. [15215

Winston-Salem, N. C. Federal Home Loan Bank. Report, 1933?- 1933?- NcU has 1936-1948 [15216

Winston-Salem, N. C. First Baptist Church (Negro) First Baptist Church, Winston-Salem, N. C., 1879-1945, sixty-sixth anniversary. Winston-Salem [c.1945] 44 p. [15217

Winston-Salem, N. C. First Presbyterian Church. Directory, May 1, 1912. [Winston-Salem?] 1912. 29 p. [15218

——Fundamentals; what every young person should know about the scriptures, salvation, the church. [Winston-Salem] 1915. 11 p. [15219

——Golden anniversary, 1862-1912. [Winston-Salem] 1912. 15 p. [15220

[**Winston-Salem, N. C. Home Moravian Church**] Portrait of the Right Reverend J. Kenneth Pfohl, D. D., painted and presented by Otto John Hershel. [Winston-Salem, 1946] [3] p. [15221

Winston-Salem, N. C. Home Moravian Church. 1771-1921: Special services commemorating the 150th anniversary of the organization of the Salem congregation of the Moravian Church . . . 1921. [Winston-Salem] 1921. [14] p. [15222

Winston-Salem, N. C. Industrial Commission. Booklet, no. 1-4, 1931. Winston-Salem, Industrial Commission of Winston-Salem, Inc., 1931. NcU has no. 1-4[15223

Winston-Salem, N. C. Inter-faith Round Table. Fair play; hand book of the Inter-faith Round Table, 1935. Winston-Salem [1935?] [12] p. [15224

Winston-Salem, N. C. Music Festival. Program, 19 - [Winston-Salem, 19 - NcU has 1908 [15225

Winston-Salem, N. C. Old Salem Restoration Committee. Their faith, our heritage. [Winston-Salem, 1952?] [12] p. [15226

Winston-Salem, N. C. Police Department. Auxiliary police manual. Winston-Salem, 1942. 62 p. [15227

Winston-Salem, N. C. Richard J. Reynolds High School. The Richard J. Reynolds High School. Winston-Salem, 1923. 68 p. [15228

—— ——1925. 59 p. [15229

Winston-Salem, N. C. Salem Home. Dorcas Co-Workers. Pages from old Salem cook books. Winston-Salem, 1931. 96 p. [15230

Winston-Salem, N. C. Third Ward Civic League. Constitution, adopted November 21, 1921. [Winston-Salem?] 1921. 6 p. [15231

Winston-Salem, N. C. Twin-City Club. Directory. [Winston-Salem?] 1926. 4 p. [15232

Winston-Salem, N. C. Y. W. C. A. Report, 1908/09- Winston-Salem, 1909-NcU has 1908/09 [15233

Winston-Salem, North Carolina. [Winston-Salem?] No publisher, n.d. 15 p. [15234

The Winston-Salem, N. C. city directory, 19 - Asheville, Piedmont Directory Co., 19 - NcU has 1910, 1918, 1921, 1924 [15235

Winston-Salem's new school program; gifts to public education. [Winston-Salem, City Public Schools Print Shop, 1919] [6] p. [15236

Winston Tobacco Fair, Winston, N. C., November 2, 1898, and facts about Winston-Salem. [Winston-Salem, 1898] 30 p. [15237

[**Winter, Alpheus**] Tryon, Polk County, N. C., a health resort. Hendersonville, N. C., C. M. Kenyon, pr., 1894. 6 p. [15238

Winter, F. Report on the High Shoals property In Gaston County, North Carolina. No place, no publisher [1873] 15 p. [15239

Winterville High School, Winterville, N. C. Catalogue, 1900/01?- Winterville, 1901?- NcU has 1903/04-1906/07, 1908/09 [15240

Winton, George Beverly, ed. The Junaluska conference, a report of the second general missionary conference of the Methodist Episcopal Church, South, held at Lake Junaluska, N. C., June 25-29, 1913. Nashville, Tenn., Board of Missions of the Methodist Episcopal Church, South, 1913. 327 p. [15241

Wisconsin. State Historical Society. Calendar of the Tennessee and King's Mountain papers of the Draper collection of manuscripts. Madison, The Society, 1929. (Wisconsin historical publications, Calendar series, v. 3) 699 p. [15242

Wise, W. Harvey. A bibliography of Andrew Jackson and Martin Van Buren, compiled by W. Harvey Wise, Jr., and John W. Cronin. Washington, Riverford Publishing Co., 1935. (Presidential bibliographical series, no. 5) 72 p. [55243

Wise and timely resolutions . . . adopted by the Duplin County Republican Convention. No place, no publisher [1908?] [7] p. [15244

Witherspoon, John. A review of the sermon preached before the Bible Society of N. Carolina, on Sunday, December 12, 1824, by the Right Reverend John S. Ravenscroft, bishop of the Diocese of North Carolina. Hillsborough, Printed and published by D. Heartt, 1825. 28 p. [15245

Witherspoon, T. D. Materialism in its relations to modern civilization; an address before the Eumenean and Philanthropic societies of Davidson College, North Carolina, delivered in the public hall of the college on Wednesday, June 26, 1877. Raleigh, News, 1877. 27 p. [15246

Withy, George. An affectionate farewell address to Friends in North America. Hillsborough, Printed by Dennis Heartt, 1824. 12 p. [15247

[**Wittemann, Adolph**] Asheville, N. C. [New York, Adolph Wittemann, c.1887] (Adolph Wittemann's souvenir albums) Folder with plates [15248

Wofford, Azile. Know the South; books with southern background for high schools. New York, H. W. Wilson Co., 1943. (Reading for background, no. 15) 94 p. [15249

Wolf, Frederick Adolph. Fungi of the Duke forest and their relation to forest pathology. Durham, Duke University, School of Forestry, 1938. (Its Bulletin, 2) 122 p. [15250

——Tobacco diseases & decays. Durham, Duke University Press, 1935. 454 p. [15251

Wolf, Simon. The American Jew as patriot, soldier and citizen, by Simon Wolf; ed. by Louis Edward Levy. Philadelphia, Levytype Co., 1895. 576 p. [15252

Wolfe, John Harold. Jeffersonian democracy in South Carolina. Chapel Hill, University of North Carolina Press, 1940. (James Sprunt studies in history and political science, v. 24, no. 1) 308 p. [15253

Wolfe, Samuel M. Helper's Impending crisis dissected. Philadelphia, J. T. Lloyd, 1860. 223 p. [15254

Wolfe, Thomas. Angelo, guarda il passato, traduzione di Jole Jannelli Pintor. [Torino] Einaudi [1949] 670 p. First Italian edition of Look homeward, angel. [15255

——Au fils du temps (Of time and the river) roman, traduction R. N. Raimbault, Manoël Faucher et Charles P. Vorce. Paris, Librarie Stock, Delamain et Boutelleau, 1951. 602 p. [15256

——Aux sources du fleuve; roman traduit de l'americain par Pierre Singer. Paris, Stock, 1956. 542 p. French edition of Look homeward, Angel. [15257

——The correspondence of Thomas Wolfe and Homer Andrew Watt; edited by Oscar Cargill and Thomas Clark Pollock. New York, New York University Press, 1954. 53 p. [15258

——The crisis in industry (Crowned with the Worth prize). Chapel Hill, Published by the University, 1919. (University of North Carolina, Department of Philosophy) 14 p. [15259

——De la mort au matin, traduit de l'Americain par R. N. Raimbault et Ch. P. Vorce; préface d'André Bay. Paris, Editions Stock, Delamain et Boutelleau, 1948. 293 p. First French edition. [15260

——Del tiempo y del río; una leyenda de la ansiedad del hombre en su juventud. Buenos Aires, Emecé [1948] 2 v. [15261

——Englen paa torvet. Copenhagen, Arnold Busck, 1941. 2 v. First Danish edition. [15262

——Es führt kein Weg zurück, roman. Hamburg, Rowohlt [1950] 622 p. [15263

——The face of a nation; poetical passages from the writings of Thomas Wolfe. New York, C. Scribner's Sons, 1939. 321 p. [15264

——De fjerne bjerge. Copenhagen, Arnold Busck, 1949. 240 p. [12265

——From death to morning. New York, C. Scribner's Sons, 1935. 304 p. [15266

—— ——New York, Grosset & Dunlap [c.1935] 304 p. [15267

—— ——London, William Heinemann, Ltd. [1936] 280 p. First English edition. [15268

——Gentlemen of the press, a play. Chicago, Ill., W. Targ, Black Archer Press [1942] 27 p. First edition. [15269

——Geweb und Fels, roman. Hamburg, Rowohlt [1953] 690 p. [15270

——Herrenhaus; Schauspiel in drei Akten und einem Vorspiel. Hamburg, Rowohlt [1953] 83 p. [15271

——The hills beyond, with a note on Thomas Wolfe by Edward C. Aswell. New York, Harper & Brothers [c.1941] 386 p. First edition. [15272

—— ——Garden City, N. Y., Sun Dial Press [1943] [15273

—— ——New York, Avon Book Co. [c.1944] 227 p. [15274

—— ——New York, Lion Books, Inc. [1955] 288 p. [15275

——Hinter jenen Bergen. [Hamburg] Rowohlt [1956] 279 p. [15276

——Historien om en roman. Copenhagen, Arnold Busck, 1948. 89 p. [15277

——Huset i den gamla stilen; oversättning av Börje Lindell; radioversion av Henrik Dyfverman. [Stockholm, Alb. Bonniers boktryckeri, 1949] 79 p. [15278

——Letters, collected and edited, with an introduction and explanatory text, by Elizabeth Nowell. New York, Charles Scribner's Sons [1956] 797 p. [15279

——Die leute von Alt-Catawba; erzählungen. Stuttgart, Reclam-Verlag, 1954. 85 p. [15280

——Look homeward, angel, a story of the buried life. New York, C. Scribner's Sons, 1929. 626 p. First edition. [15281

—— ——New York, Grosset and Dunlap [c.1929] 626 p. [15282

—— ——New York, Editions for the Armed Services, Inc., c.1929. 511 p. [15283

—— ——London, William Heinemann, Ltd. [1930] 613 p. [15284

—— ——New York, Bennett A. Cerf, Donald S. Klopfer [c.1934] (The modern library) 626 p. [15285

—— ——illustrated by Douglas W. Gorsline. New York, C. Scribner's Sons, 1947. 662 p. [15286

—— ——[1947, 1952] 662 p. [15287

——Look homeward, angel: II. The adventures of young Gant, with an introduction by Edward C. Aswell. [New York] New American Library [1948] (N. A. L. Signet books, 697) 192 p. [15288

—— ——[1949] 192 p. [15289

——Look homeward, angel; screenplay by Arthur Ripley, first draft. Hollywood, Nero Films, Inc., 1947. 226 p. [15290

——Mannerhouse, a play in a prologue and three acts. New York, Harper and Brothers, 1948. 183 p. First edition. [15291

—— ——London, William Heinemann, Ltd. [1950] 86 p. [15292

—— ——Copenhagen, Steen Hasselbalchs Forlag, 1952. 65 p. [15293

——Marblehead Playhouse, Inc. presents the program of the week: Kay Francis in The web and the rock, August 21-26, 1950. Marblehead, Mass., 1950. [12] p. Program. [15294

——Maxwell E. Perkins, Seattle, Wash., August 13, 1938. No place, no publisher, n.d. [1] p. Print of Wolfe's last letter to Perkins. [15295

——A note on experts: Dexter Vespasian Joyner. New York, House of Books, Ltd., 1939. (The crown octavos, no. 5) [28] p. First edition. [15296

——Of time and the river; a legend of man's hunger in this youth. New York, C. Scribner's Sons, 1935. 912 p. First edition. [15297

—— ——London, William Heinemann, Ltd., 1935. [15298

—— ——New York, Grosset and Dunlap [c.1935] [15299

—— ——New York, C. Scribner's Sons, 1944. [15300

—— ——New York, Sun Dial Press [1944] [15301

——The portable Thomas Wolfe, edited by Maxwell Geismar. New York, Viking Press, 1946. 712 p. [15302

——La ragnatela e la roccia; con un'introduczione di J. B. Priestley e quindici illustrazioni di Angela Motti. [Verona] Mondadori [1955] 702 p. [15303

——Schau heimwärts, Engel! Eine Geschichte vom begrabnen Leben. Berlin, Rowohlt Verlag, 1932. 556 p. [15304

—— ——Hamburg, Rowohlt Verlag [1951] 556 p. [15305

—— ——[1954] 446 p. [15306

—— ——Berlin, Deutsche Buch-Gemainschaft, n.d. 582 p. [15307

——Selections from the works of Thomas Wolfe, edited by Maxwell Geismar. London, William Heinemann, Ltd. [1952] 712 p. [15308

——Short stories. New York, Penguin Books, Inc. [c.1947] 150 p. [15309

—— ——[New York] New American Library [1949] (Signet books) 150 p. [15310

——Spindelvaev og klippe, roman. Copenhagen, Arnold Busck, 1940. 2v. First Danish edition. [15311

——A stone, a leaf, a door; poems, selected and arranged in verse by John S. Barnes, with a foreword by Louis Untermeyer. New York, C. Scribner's Sons, 1945. 166 p. [15312

——Stories. New York, Avon Book Co. [1944] 135 p. [15313

——The story of a novel. New York, C. Scribner's Sons, 1936. 93 p. [15314

—— ——London, William Heinemann, Ltd., 1936. [15315

——Thomas Wolfe short stories: Only the dead know Brooklyn, selections from From death to morning, plus The story of a novel. New York, New American Library [1952] 150 p. [15316

——Thomas Wolfe's letters to his mother, Julia Elizabeth Wolfe, edited with an introduction by John Skally Terry. New York, C. Scribner's Sons, 1943. 368 p. [15317

——To Rupert Brooke. [Paris, privately printed by Lecram Press for Richard Jean Picard] 1948. [3] p. [15318

——Tod der stolze Bruder. München, R. Piper & Coverlag [1953] 61 p. [15319

——La toile et le roc; traduit de l'anglais par José Ravita. [Lausanne] Marguerat [1946] 590 p. [15320

——Uns Bleibt die Erde; die Geschichte eines Romans mit Breifen und 4 Abbildungen. [München, Die Arche, c.1951] 160 p. [15321

——Von Tod zum Morgen; Erzählungen. Hamburg, Rowohlt Verlag [1952] 353 p. [15322

——Von Zeit un Strom, eine Legende vom Hunger des Menschen in der Jugend, Roman. Hamburg, Rowohlt Verlag [1952] 976 p. [15323

——The web and the rock. New York and London, Harper & Brothers, 1939. 695 p. First edition. [15324

—— ——New York, Sun Dial Press [1940] [15325

—— ——London, William Heinemann, Ltd. [1947] 642 p. [15326

——A western journal; a daily log of the great parks trip, June 20-July 2, 1938. [Pittsburgh] University of Pittsburgh Press, 1951. 72 p. [15327

——What is man? [Chicago, privately printed by R. Hunter Middleton, 1942] [8] p. [15328

——the years of wandering in many lands and cities. New York, C. S. Boesen [1949] [10] p. 6 mounted facsims. [15329

——You can't go home again. New York and London, Harper & Brothers [c.1940] 743 p. First edition. [15330

—— ——New York, Grosset & Dunlap [c.1940] 743 p. [15331

—— ——New York, Sun Dial Press [1942] [15332

—— ——London, William Heinemann, Ltd. [1947] 600 p. [15333

Wolfinger, Abraham D. Inauguration as president of Catawba College, Newton, N. C., Wednesday, May 8th, 1918. No place, no publisher, n.d. 8 p. [15334

Woltz, Albert Edgar. North Carolina's new school law; a summary and interpretation of the Hancock act passed by the 1929 session of the North Carolina General Assembly. Raleigh, 1929. 12 p. [15335

Womack, Thomas Brown. Speech, contrasting Democratic and Republican financial administration of state government . . . Extracts from speech of Hon. R. W. Winston . . . Extracts from speech of Hon. John S. Henderson. Raleigh, E. M. Uzzell, pr., 1902. 19 p. [15336

The Woman golfer, v. 1- July, 1946- Greensboro, Woman's Professional Golf Association, Inc., 1946- NcU has v. 1-v. 2, no. 3. [15337

Woman's Christian Temperance Union. North Carolina. Report of the annual session, 1883- 1883- NcU has 1883-1933, 1935-1955 [15338

Woman's Synodical Auxiliary of the Synod of North Carolina see **Presbyterian Church in the U. S. Synod of North Carolina. Woman's Synodical Auxiliary**

Womble, Edgar. Rhyme and reason; word pictures of prominent senators and house leaders, session 1919. Raleigh, Commercial Printing Co., 1919. 134 p. [15339

Womble, Walter L. Love in the mists. Raleigh, Edwards & Broughton Co., 1892. 141 p. [15340

Wonderful spring performing miraculous cures, Thompson's bromine arsenic water . . . springs in Ashe County, N. C. No place, no publisher, n.d. 24 p. [15341

The Wonderful story of High Point. [Danville, Va., Boatwright Press for the manufacturers of High Point, 1906?] [29] p. [15342

Wood, Charles Barnette. First, the fields. Chapel Hill, University of North Carolina Press [c.1941] 308 p. [15343

Wood, Edna Hilliard White. The Herndon-Hunt and allied families by Edna H. W. Wood and Lillie B. Nesbitt. Raleigh, Bynum Printing Co., 1930. 110 p. [15344

Wood, Edward. To the President of the State Agricultural Society of North Carolina. Edenton, 1871. [1] p. [15345

Wood, Edward Jenner. A treatise on pellagra, for the general practitioner. New York, D. Appleton and Co., 1912. 377 p. [15346

Wood, Grahame. Speech delivered at the eightieth session of the Grand Chapter of the Fraternity of Delta Psi, December 29, 1926, on the occasion of the celebration of the refounding of the XI Chapter at the University of North Carolina. No place, no publisher [1926?] 11 p. [15347

Wood, Harriette. Guidance at work in the schools of Craven County, N. C., by Harriette Wood and Anne Pruitt. Richmond, Va., Southern Woman's Educational Alliance, 1930. 99, 9 p. [15348

Wood, Jane Dalziel. Lucy Adelaide Chadbourn, born July 9th, 1876, died May 10th, 1910. [Raleigh, Edwards & Broughton Co., 1910?] 45 p. [15349

——A history of the North Carolina Society of the Colonial Dames of America from March, 1894 to March, 1935. [Wilmington, North Carolina Society of the Colonial Dames of America, 1935] 52 p. [15350

[Wood, Mrs. L. C.] The Haydock's testimony. Philadelphia, Christian Arbitration and Peace Society, 1890. 276 p. [15351

Wood, Martha Mann. Home-made poetry. Winston-Salem [Margaret Van Hoy Wood] 1937. [22] p. [15352

Wood, Otto. Life history of Otto Wood, inmate State Prison, 1926. Raleigh, Commercial Printing Co., 1926. 27 p. [15353

——Wadesboro, Pee Dee Publishing Co., 1931. 67 p. [15354

Wood, Thomas Fanning. James Fergus McRee, M. D. (a biographical sketch with portrait). Wilmington, Jackson & Bell, 1891. 11 p. [15355

——Wilmington flora; a list of plants growing about Wilmington, North Carolina, with date of flowering . . . by Thomas F. Wood and Gerald McCarthy. Raleigh, Edwards, Broughton & Co., pr., 1886. 69 p. [15356

Woodard, Clement Manly. A word-list from Virginia and North Carolina. Greensboro, American Dialect Society, 1946. (Its Publication, no. 6) 46 p. [15357

Woodbury, Augustus. Ambrose Everett Burnside. Providence, R. I., N. Bangs Williams Co., 1882. (Rhode Island Soldiers and Sailors Historical Society. Personal narratives, 2d ser., no. 17) 97 p. [15358

——Major General Ambrose E. Burnside and the Ninth Army Corps. Providence, R. I., S. S. Rider & Brother, 1867. 554 p. [15359

Woodbury, Joye Freeman. Petal dust from my garden. Nashville, Tenn., Broadman Press [c.1941] 142 p. [15360

Woodcock, John Henry. More light, a treatise on tuberculosis written especially for the Negro race. [Asheville, Advocate Publishing Co., c.1924] 192 p. [15361

Woodell, B. H., comp. Digest and hand-book of law and forms. Raleigh, Capital Printing Co., 1899. 139 p. [15362

——A manual of law and forms, with sketch, statistical tables, forms, and parliamentary points for Odd Fellows in North Carolina. Greensboro, C. F. Thomas, pr., 1894. 122 p. [15363

Woodhouse, Edward James. The government of Charlotte. No place, no publisher [1926] 52 p. [15364

Woodhull, Maxwell Van Zandt. A glimpse of Sherman fifty years ago. [Washington, 1914] (Military Order of the Loyal Legion of the United States. Commandery of the District of Columbia. War paper, no. 97) 18 p. [15365

Woodland-Olney High School. Bulletin, June, 1924. New Bern, Owen G. Dunn, pr., 1924. 24 p. [15366

Woodley, Winifred, pseud. see **Hedden, Worth Tuttle**

Woodmason, Charles. The Carolina backcountry on the eve of the Revolution; the Journal and other writings of Charles Woodmason, Anglican itinerant, edited with an introduction by Richard J. Hooker. Chapel Hill, Institute of Early American History and Culture at Williamsburg, Va., by the University of North Carolina Press, 1953. 305 p. [15367

Woodmen of the World. North Carolina Jurisdiction. Minutes, 1909?- 1909?- NcU has 1909 [1921-1949] [15368

Woodrow, James. Albemarle yesterday and today, by James Woodrow and Archie Friend Hassell. New Bern, Owen G. Dunn, pr., 1954. [55] p. [15369

Woods, John Henry Leak. Poems. Durham, Mutual Printery, 1907. 38 p. [15370

Woods, William Sledge, ed. A critical edition of Ciperis de Vignevaux, with introduction, notes, and glossary. Chapel Hill, 1949. (North Carolina. University. Studies in the Romance languages and literatures, no. 9) 229 p. [15371

Woodside, Moya. Sterilization in North Carolina; a sociological and psychological study. Chapel Hill, University of North Carolina Press, 1950. 219 p. [15372

Woodward, L. G. An address delivered before the students and citizens at Richland Academy, Richlands, N. C., July 14th, 1859. Newbern, Daily Progress Print, 1859. 22 p. [15373

Woodward, W. J. Report to Railroad Freight Committee of the Produce Exchange of Wilmington, January, 1887. Raleigh, Edwards, Broughton & Co., 1887. 31 p. [15374

Woody, John W. American history by the topical method, a hand-book. Greensboro, Thomas Brothers, 1892. 91 p. [15375

——The elements of pedagogics. Greensboro, Thomas Brothers, 1891. 152 p. [15376

——History by the topical method, a hand-book. Greensboro, Thomas Brothers, 1889. 120 p. [15377

Woody, Robert Hilliard. South Carolina during Reconstruction, by Francis Butler Simkins [and] Robert Hilliard Woody. Chapel Hill, University of North Carolina Press, 1932. 610 p. [15377a

Woofter, Thomas Jackson. Black yeomanry; life on St. Helena Island. New York, H. Holt and Co. [c.1930] 291 p. [15378

——The plight of cigarette tobacco. Chapel Hill, University of North Carolina Press, 1931. 99 p. [15379

——Seven lean years, by T. J. Woofter, Jr., and Ellen Winston. Chapel Hill, University of North Carolina Press, 1939. 187 p. [15380

——Southern population and social planning. Chapel Hill, University of North Carolina Press, 1936. (Southern policy papers, no. 1) 10 p. [15381

Woolard, Beulah Bailey. Giants of fortune, a play especially adapted for senior class day exercises. New York, S. French, c.1929. 38 p.   [15382
——The graduate's seven guides, a play especially adapted for senior class day exercises. Charlotte, Queen City Printing Co., 1934. 29 p.   [15383
——The knight triumphant, a play especially adapted for senior class day exercises. Charlotte, Queen City Printing Co., 1934. 28 p.   [15384
——The open road, a play especially adapted for senior class day exercises. Charlotte, Herald Press, Inc., 1937. 26 p.   [15385
——Out of the past, a play especially adapted for senior class day exercises. Raleigh, Edwards and Broughton Co., 1933. 24 p.   [15386
——The parting of the braves, a play especially adapted for senior class day exercises. Charlotte, Queen City Printing Co., 1935. 28 p.   [15387
——Pirates' gold, a play especially adapted for senior class day exercises. Raleigh, Edwards and Broughton Co., 1933. 24 p.   [15388
——Renovating Miss Emma, a three-act play. Charlotte, Herald Press, Inc., 1937. 44 p.   [15389
——The senior follies, a play especially adapted for senior class day exercises. Charlotte, Queen City Printing Co., 1936. 32 p.   [15390
——Seniors at the bar, a burlesque class trial especially adapted for senior class day exercises. Charlotte, Queen City Printing Co., 1934. 30 p.   [15391
——The set of the sail, a play expecially adapted for senior class day exercises. New York, S. French, c.1929. 30 p.   [15392
——The world outside, a play especially adapted for senior class day exercises. New York, S. French, c.1929. 30 p.   [15393
——Youth marches on, by Beulah Bailey Woolard and Ann Pitts Hicks, a stirring class day play in three parts. Raleigh, Edwards and Broughton Co., 1937. 28 p.   [15394

Woollen, Betsy Roberts. How does your cotton grow? An educational story for children. Clinton, S. C., Jacobs Press, 1942. 59 p.   [15395

Woolman, John. Journal; edited and with an introduction by Thomas S. Kepler. Cleveland, O., World Publishing Co. [1954] 235 p.   [15396
——A journal of the life, gospel labors, and Christian experiences of that faithful minister of Jesus Christ, John Woolman. London, William Phillips, 1824. 416 p.   [15397
—— ——New York, Collins, Brother & Co., 1845. 309 p.   [15398
——The works of John Woolman. Philadelphia, Joseph Crukshank, pr., 1774. 436 p.   [15399

Woolson, Constance Fenimore. For the Major, a novelette. New York, Harper & Brothers [c.1883] 208 p.   [15400
——Horace Chase, a novel. New York, Harper & Brothers, 1894. 419 p. [15401
——Rodman the keeper; southern sketches. New York, Harper & Brothers, 1886. 339 p.   [15402

Woosley, John Brooks. State taxation of banks. Chapel Hill, University of North Carolina Press, 1935. 133 p.   [15403

[Wooten, Inez] Durham City Schools song book. Durham, Seeman Printery [1910] 47 p.   [15404

Wootten, Bayard (Morgan) Charleston; azaleas and old bricks; photographs by Bayard Wootten, text by Samuel Gaillard Stoney. Boston, Houghton, Mifflin Co., 1937. 24 p. 61 plates.   [15405

Worcester, Joseph Emerson. A gazetteer of the United States, abstracted from The universal gazetteer of the author; with enlargement of the principal articles. Andover, Mass., Printed for the Author by Flagg and Gould, 1818. [360] p. [15406

The worker's voice, v. 1- August, 1944- Winston-Salem, United Tobacco Workers Local 22, 1944- NcU has v. 1 [2, 3]   [15407

[Workman, John Hiliary Andrew] Narrative history of Company K, 324th Infantry, 81st (Stonewall) Division, September 2, 1917 to June 23, 1919. No place, The Author [1919?] 48 p.   [15408

Workshop for College and University Librarians, University of North Carolina, 1948. Report, edited by Agatha Boyd Adams. Chapel Hill, University of North Carolina, School of Library Science, 1948. 46 p.   [15409

World law report, v. 1- 1953- Chapel Hill, Chapel Hill Chapter, United World Federalists, 1953- NcU has v. [2-3]   [15410

Wormley, Ray T.   The party boss; a brief outline of American political history from 1789-1952. Atlanta, 1952. 155 p.   [15411

Worship. No place, n.d.   (T. A. F. in North Carolina) 2 p.   [15412

[Worth, Jonathan] To my constituents of the counties of Randolph and Alamance. [Raleigh, 1861] [1] p.   [15413

Worth, Jonathan. To the people of N. Carolina. Raleigh, October 17, 1865. [1] p.   [15414

Worth, Kathryn. The middle button. New York, Doubleday, Doran & Co., Inc., 1941. 274 p.   [15415
——Sea change. Garden City, N. Y., Doubleday, 1948. 240 p.   [15416
——Sign of Capricornus. New York, A. A. Knopf, 1937. 65 p.   [15417
——They loved to laugh. Garden City, Doubleday, Doran and Co., Inc., 1942. 269 p.   [15418

Worth, Nicholas, pseud. see Page, Walter Hines

Worthington, Dennis. The broken sword; or, A pictorial page in Reconstruction. Wilson, P. D. Gold & Sons, 1901. 326 p.   [15419

Worthington, Samuel Wheeler. Ancient and rare North Caroliniana; a brief resume of some of the early and rare publications on North Carolina from 1524 to 1929. Wilmington, Wilmington Stamp & Printing Co. [c.1939] [10] p.   [15420

Wray, Esther. Old-time recipes, Nu-Wray Inn, established 1850. 3d ed., revised by Rush T. Wray. [Burnsville, 1950?] 23 p.   [15421

Wright, E. A. Education; an address delivered by E. A. Wright, Superintendent of Public Instruction of Wayne County, N. C., before the schools visited during the years 1885-86. Goldsboro, Messenger, 1886. 22 p.   [15422

Wright, James Thomas Carr. The function of mathematics in a state educational program. Nashville, Tenn., George Peabody College for Teachers, 1938. (Its Abstract of Contribution to education, no. 212) 12 p.   [15423

Wright, John. The American negotiator; or, The various currencies of the British colonies in America. London, Printed for the Proprietor, 1765. 326 p.   [15424

Wright, Joshua Granger. Address delivered at the celebration of the Battle of Moore's Creek Bridge, February 27th, 1857. Wilmington, Fulton & Price, pr., 1857. 24 p.   [15425
——An oration delivered 4th July A. D. 1832, at the Presbyterian Church in Wilmington, N. C. Wilmington, Published by the Committee, 1832. 12 p. [15426
——An oration delivered in the Methodist Epsicopal Church, Wilmington, N. C., on the fourth of July A. D. 1851. Wilmington, Herald Book and Job Office, 1851. 22 p.   [15427

Wright, Marcus Joseph. General officers of the Confederate army, officers of the executive departments of the Confederate States, members of the Confederate Congress by states. New York, Neale Publishing Co., 1911. 188 p.   [15428
——Some account of the life and services of William Blount . . . together with a full account of his impeachment and trial in Congress, and his expulsion from the U. S. Senate. Washington, E. J. Gray [c.1884] 142 p.   [15429

Wright, Mary Emily. The missionary work of the Southern Baptist Convention; with introduction by Lansing Burrows. Philadelphia, American Baptist Publication Society [1902] 412 p.   [15430

Wright, Orville. How we invented the airplane; edited and with commentary by Fred C. Kelly. New York, David McKay Co. [1953] 78 p.   [15431

[Wright, Orville] Twenty-five years ago. [Washington, 1928] 23 p.   [15432

Wright, Pattie Julia. Some early verses and compositions, written in her schooldays. [Durham, Seeman Printery for R. H. Wright, 1912] 45 p.   [15433

Wright, Wilbur. Miracle at Kitty Hawk; the letters of Wilbur and Orville Wright, edited by Fred C. Kelly. New York, Farrar, Straus and Young [1951] 482 p. [15434
——The papers of Wilbur and Orville Wright, including the Canute-Wright letters and other papers of Octave Chanute, Marvin W. McFarland, editor. New York, McGraw-Hill [1953] 2 v. (1278 p.)   [15435

Writers' Program. North Carolina. American recreation series. Northport, L. I., Bacon & Wierck, Inc., [c.1941] 32 p. [15436

Writers' Program. North Carolina. Bundle of troubles and other Tarheel tales by workers of the Writers' Program of the Work Projects Administration in the state of North Carolina, edited by W. C. Hendricks. Durham, Duke University Press, 1943. 206 p. [15437

——Charlotte, a guide to the Queen City of North Carolina . . . sponsored by Hornet's Nest Post, no. 9, American Legion. [Charlotte] News Printing House, 1939. (American guide series) 74 p. [15438

——How North Carolina grew . . . sponsored by the North Carolina Historical Commission. Raleigh, The News and Observer, 1941. 98 p. [15439

——How they began—the story of North Carolina county, town, and other place names . . . sponsored by North Carolina Department of Conservation and Development. Raleigh, New York City Harlan Publications, 1941. 73 p. [15440

——Raleigh, capital of North Carolina . . . sponsored by the Raleigh Sesquicentennial Commission. [New Bern, Owen G. Dunn Co., pr., 1942] (American guide series) 170 p. [15441

Writers' Program. Tennessee. God bless the devil! Liars bench tales [by] James R. Aswell [and others] Chapel Hill, University of North Carolina Press, 1940. 254 p. [15442

Wunsch, William Robert, ed. Thicker than water; stories of family life, ed. by W. Robert Wunsch and Edna Albers for the Commission on Human Relations. New York, D. Appleton-Century Co., Inc. [c.1939] 359 p. [15443

Wyatt, Lillian (Reeves) The Reeves, Mercer, Newkirk families; a compilation. [Jacksonville? Fla., 1956] 374 p. [15444

Wyatt, Wilbur Carl. Families of Joseph and Isaac Wyatt, brothers, who were sons of Zachariah ("Sacker") and Elizabeth (Ripley) Wyatt, of Durant's Neck, Perquimans County, North Carolina. Washington, c.1950. 206 p. [15445

Wyche, Ethel Cheshire (Deaver) comp. History of twenty-five years of the Daughters of the American Colonists in North Carolina, 1927-1952. No place, n.d. 36 p. [15446

Wyche, Mary Lewis. The history of nursing in North Carolina, by Mary Lewis Wyche; edited by Edna L. Heinzerling. Chapel Hill, University of North Carolina Press, 1938. 151 p. [15447

Wyeth, John Jasper] Leaves from a diary written while serving in Co. E, 44 Mass., Dep't of No. Carolina, from September, 1862, to June, 1863. Boston, F. L. Lawrence & Co., 1878. 76 p. [15448

Wylde, Marjorie. Upon this rock, by Marjorie Wylde and William Waddell. [Chapel Hill] 1954. 28 p. [15449

Wynn, Moses Warren. This is Dr. Moses Warren Wynn's tract of the Holy Bible. No place, no publisher [1924] 14 p. [15450

Wynne, John Peter. Philosophies of education from the standpoint of the philosophy of experimentalism. New York, 1947. 427 p. [15451

X-Ray, 1907- Oxford, Students of Oxford College, 1907- NcU has 1913 [15452

Yadkin Baptist Association. Minutes, 18 - 18 - NcU has 1876, 1879-1886, 1913 [15453

Yadkin College, Yadkin College, N. C. Welcome! Alumni and friends! The double marker unveiling program of historic Yadkin College, 1856-1924. [High Point? 1941] [7] p. [15454

Yadkin Collegiate Institute, Yadkin College, N. C. Catalogue, 18 - Yadkin College, 18 - NcU has 1902/03 [15455

Yadkin Valley Institute, Boonville, N. C. Catalogue, 1894/95- Boonville, 1895- NcU has 1894/95-1899/1900, 1901/02-1904/05 [1906/07-1916/17] [15456

Yadkinville, N. C. Baptist Church. Dedication service, Sunday, March 20, 1955. [Yadkinville, 1955] [6] p. [15457

Yancey, Henry A. A capital improvement program for the city of Durham, North Carolina. [Durham] 1943. 44 p. [15458

Yancey Collegiate Institute, Burnsville, N. C. Catalog, 1901/02?- Burnsville, 1902?- NcU has 1920/21 [15459

Yancey Co., N. C.   Board of Education.   Teacher Training Department. History and geography of Yancey County. [Burnsville] 1930. 59 p.   [15460

Yancey Co., N. C.   Chamber of Commerce. A word about Yancey. Burnsville, 1926. Folder.   [15461

Yancey County Baptist Association. Minutes, 1888?- 1888?- NcU has [1892-1906]   [15462

Yates, Elizabeth. Brave interval. New York, Coward-McCann [1952] 246 p. [15463

Yates, Matthew Tyson. The story of Yates the missionary, as told in his letters and reminiscences, prepared by Charles E. Taylor. Nashville, Tenn., Sunday School Board, Southern Baptist Convention, 1898. 304 p.   [15464

Yates, Richard Edwin. Zebulon B. Vance as war governor of North Carolina, 1862-1865. Nashville, 1937. 33 p.   [15465

Yates Baptist Association. Minutes, 1949- 1949- NcU has 1949-1953   [15466

[Yerger, George S.] A letter on the doctrine of the church in regard to auricular confession and private absolution, being a review of the positions of the Bishop of North Carolina on these subjects, by a layman of Mississippi. Jackson, Thomas Palmer, pr., 1850. 26 p.   [15467

Yoder, Robert Anderson. The situation in North Carolina. Newton, Enterprise Job Office, 1894. 48 p.   [15468

York, Brantley. An analytical, illustrative and constructive grammar of the English language. 3d ed. Raleigh, W. L. Pomeroy, 1862. 219 p.   [15469

——An analytical, synthetical, and illustrated grammar of the English language [4th ed.] Raleigh, L. Branson, 1879. 295 p.   [15470

——The autobiography of Brantley York. Durham, Seeman Printery, 1910. (The John Lawson monographs of the Trinity College Historical Society, v. 1) 139 p.   [15471

——An illustrative and constructive grammar of the English language. Salisbury, Carolina Watchman, 1854. 112 p.   [15472

—— ——Raleigh, Warren L. Pomeroy, 1860. 231 p.   [15473

——Introduction to the analytical, synthetical, and illustrated grammar; or, A grammar for common schools and beginners. Raleigh, L. Branson, 1880. 126 p.   [15474

——Introduction to the illustrative and constructive grammar; or, A grammar for beginners. Raleigh, W. L. Pomeroy, 1860. 120 p.   [15475

——The man of business and railroad calculator, containing such parts of arithmetic as have a special application in business transactions . . . to which are appended a few of the plainer forms necessary in ordinary business. Raleigh, John Nichols & Co., 1873. 147 p.   [15476

——York's English grammar, revised and adapted to southern schools. 3d ed. Raleigh, Branson, Farrar & Co., 1864. 120 p.   [15477

—— ——3d ed. Raleigh, Branson & Farrar, 1865.   [15478

You are cordially invited to be present at a centennial reception and ball complimentary to Miss Winnie Davis, 1789-1889, November 20th, '89, Fayetteville, N. C. [Fayetteville, Garrett, 1889?] 2 p.   [15479

You should drink more water, and Vade Mecum water is the best, Vade Mecum Spring . . . Stokes County, N. C. Erie, Pa., Erie Lithographing and Printing Co. [1901?] 33 p.   [15480

Young, Charlotte. The heart has reasons. Emory University, Ga., Banner Press [1953] 60 p.   [15481

Young, Edward Hudson. Our Young family in America. Durham, 1947. 315 p.   [15482

Young, Elizabeth Barber. A study of the curricula of seven selected women's colleges of the southern states. New York, Teachers College, Columbia University [c.1932] 220 p.   [15483

Young, Isaac J. Speech delivered at Louisburg, N. C. on the 12th day of March, 1872. No place, no publisher, n.d. 31 p.   [15484

Young, John A. A short dissertation on sheep husbandry in the South, submitted in the form of a report to the Agricultural Society of Mecklenburg County, N. C., at its meeting in April, A. D. 1854. Charlotte, North-Carolina Whig Office, 1854. 14 p.   [15485

Young, Louis G. The Battle of Gettysburg, an address; a just tribute to the part played in the great drama of war by the North Carolina troops. No place, no publisher [1900?] 8 p. [15486

Young, Richard K. The pastor's hospital ministry. Nashville, Broadman Press [1954] 139 p. [15487

Young, Stanley. Young Hickory, a story of the frontier boyhood and youth of Andrew Jackson. New York, Farrar & Rinehart, Inc. [c.1940] 271 p. [15488

Young Men's Christian Associations. Industrial Department. Human relations in industry, annual industrial conference, Blue Ridge, N. C., 191 - No place, no NcU has 1930 (11th) 1931, 1933-1937. [15489

Young Men's Christian Associations. North and South Carolina. Handbook for Carolina pioneers. [Durham, Seeman Printery, 1926?] 27 p. [15490

Young Men's Christian Associations. North and South Carolina. Interstate Committee. Report, 18 - 18 - NcU has 1935/36-1939/40, 1948/49-1951/52 [15491

Young Men's Christian Associations. North Carolina. Minutes of the annual convention, 1877- 1877- NcU has 1882, 1883, 1886-1892 [15492
——Program, 1877- 1877- NcU has 1878, 1893 [15493
——Program of service for the men and boys of North Carolina. Charlotte [Observer Printing House, 1919?] 9 p. [15494
——Report, 18 - 18 - NcU has 1922, 1923, 1925 [15495

Young Men's Christian Associations. North Carolina. Charlotte. A quarter century's work in behalf of young men [Charlotte, Observer] 1899. 40 p. [15496

Young Men's Christian Associations. North Carolina. Durham. Constitution and by-laws, adopted February 7th, 1888. Durham, H. E. Seeman, pr., 1888. 15 p. [15497
——Durham's character factory. [Durham, Seeman Printery, 1919?] 4 p. [15498

Young Men's Christian Associations. North Carolina. Greensboro. The Biblical Room, Cone Memorial, Y. M. C. A., White Oak Branch. [Greensboro? 1937?] [7] p. [15499
——For man efficiency, a Greensboro enterprise for Greensboro's good. [Greensboro? 1910?] 4 p. [15500
——Greensboro's new building for the Y. M. C. A. [Greensboro, Joseph J. Stone, 1911] 5 p. [15501
——Hoops of steel, a book of friendship. [Greensboro?] n.d. 31 p. [15502

Young Men's Christian Associations. North Carolina. Raleigh. Citizens' dinner conference in the interest of a Young Men's Christian Association for Raleigh, Metropolitan Hall, March twenty-third, nineteen eleven. [Raleigh, Edwards & Broughton Co.] 1911. 10 p. [15503
——A civic movement to meet a civic need. [Raleigh, Edwards & Broughton Co., 1911] [16] p. [15504

Young Men's Christian Associations Graduate School, Blue Ridge, N. C. Bulletin, v. 1-1931?- Nashville, Tenn., and Blue Ridge, N. C., 1931?- NcU has v. [4-5] [15505
——Catalog, 191 - Nashville, Tenn. and Blue Ridge, N. C., 191 - NcU has 1919/ 20, 1928/29 [15506

Young Women's Christian Associations. North Carolina. Asheville. Young Women's Christian Association House, the Henrietta. Asheville [1906?] 13 p. [15507

Young Women's Christian Associations. North Carolina. Charlotte. The Constitution and by-laws. [Charlotte, Queen City Printing Co., 1902] 16 p. [15508

Young Women's Christian Associations. North Carolina. Greensboro. The Young Women's Christian Association Home, Greensboro, N. C. [Greensboro? 1908?] 3 p. [15509

Young Women's Christian Associations. Virginia, North Carolina, and South Carolina. Territorial Committee. Report, 1907/09- Charlotte, 1909- NcU has 1907/09, 1910/11 [15510

Your soul—Is it safe? A question for every one. [Raleigh, General Tract Agency] n.d. (For the soldier, no. 16) 16 p. [15511

Zabriskie, George. The mind's geography. New York, A. A. Knopf, 1941. 106 p. [15512

Zeigler, Wilbur Gleason. The heart of the Alleghanies; or, Western North Carolina . . . by Wilbur G. Ziegler and Ben S. Grosscup. Raleigh, A. Williams & Co. [1883] 386 p. [15513

Zimmermann, Erich Walter. World resources and industries; a functional appraisal of the availability of agricultural and industrial resources. New York, Harper & Brothers, 1933. 842 p. [15514

—— ——Rev. ed. [1951] 832 p. [15515

Zion Missionary Baptist Association. Minutes, 1873?- 1873?- NcU has 1888 [15516

Zion Primitive Baptist Association. Minutes, 1902?- 1902?- NcU has 1925, 1928, 1936 [15517

Zion's landmark, v. 1- 1867?- Wilson, 1867?- NcU has v. [2, 3, 8-11, 13-20] 21-22 [23] 24-29 [30] 31-34 [35-36] 37-39 [40-54] 55-70 [71] 72-89 [15518

Zook, George Frederick. Report on a survey of the North Carolina State College of Agriculture and Engineering . . . 1923. Raleigh, Bynum Printing Co., 1923. 22 p. [15519

INDEX

46, 8246, 10505, 11500, 12800, 13204-05, 13208, 14048, 15057, 15437, 15442; *see also* Folklore
Legislative journals, Checklist, 11255
Legislature *see* General Assembly
Leigh, Hezekiah Gilbert (1795-1853) 8979
Lemmond family, 7655
Lenoir, Bessie (1869-1877) 7922
Lenoir, Louisa Avery (1866-1877) 7922
Lenoir, Description, 7662, 7671, 10207; Directory, 8756; First Presbyterian Church, 7665; History, 12307; *see also* Caldwell County
Lenoir County, Finance, 7669; History, 7015; Schools, 7670
Lenoir family, 6077
L'Estrange, Matilda (fl.1800) 14625-26
Letchmore, Anthony (d.1801?)
Leventhorpe, Collett (1815-1889) 14692
Lewis, Cornelia Viola (Battle) (1857-1886) 13162
Lewis, Nell (Battle) (1893?-1956) 8587
Lewis, Richard Henry (1850-1926) 11524
Lewis family, 233, 3589, 7722, 7728
Lewis Mine, Union County, 7419
Lexington, Code, 7732; Directories, 584, 8757
Libel, 5890
Liberalism, 3801, 8587
Liberty Baptist Association, History, 12441
Liberty loan, 4174
Libraries, 621, 747, 3547, 3549, 4716, 4886, 6158, 9603-04, 9616, 9791-96, 10866, 12943, 12946, 15069-73, 15409; Buildings, 2708; Catalogues, 8806, 10449, 13700, 14382, 14718; High school, 4811; Periodicals, 7740-41, 9788; Public, 11243; Special, 8094
Liens (Law) 8503, 9040, 10611, 11177
Lighthouses and lightships, 11275, 12836
Lillington, John Alexander (1725-1786) 796
Lincoln, Abraham (1809-1865) Family, 146, 1939-40, 2470-72
Lincoln County, History, 8111, 9436, 9441-42, 9447-48, 9453-54, 12491; Marriage records, 1572
Lincolnton, High School, 10772; History, 9435; Presbyterian Church, 9446
Lindsay family, 7792
Linville, Eseeola Inn, 4038
Liquor law, 14792
Liquor traffic, 991, 7022, 11560, 14757
Literature, Bibliography, 1725, 3297, 4813-14, 7570-71, 10038; Collections, 968, 1410, 1810, 4856, 5678, 6501-07, 6828, 7575, 8788, 12936, 13095, 14856-61; History and criticism, 4686, 5637, 6986, 7570-71, 8142, 8341, 9917, 10038, 10879, 12012, 12059, 12924, 12926, 12928, 12936, 13556-57, 14145; Outlines, syllabi, 14433; Periodicals, 191, 421, 962, 2901, 4007 4065-66, 7467, 7834-35, 8581, 10797, 11284, 11671, 12924, 12926, 12928 13094;

see also Fiction; Humor; Juvenile literature; Poetry
Little Brittain Presbyterian Church, Rutherford County, 7038
Little Switzerland, 7846-47; Church of the Resurrection, 2353, 2355
Live stock, 1789, 8551, 9799-9800, 10166-69, 10565
Livingstone College, Salisbury, 4374, 12758, 14431
Lloyd family, 11165
Loans, 12600
Lobbying, 5567
Local government, 804, 1279, 5416, 9953, 12963, 14335-36; *see also* Names of counties and towns
Locke, John (1632-1704) 7432, 7600
London, Henry Armand (1846-1918) 6035
London, Isaac Spencer (1926-1947) 7882
London family, 7882
Looms, 6765
Lord's acre plan, 4113
Lords Proprietors, 12148
"Lost Colony" *see* Roanoke Island Colonies
Louisburg College, Louisburg, 7924-30
Louisville, Cincinnati and Charleston Railroad, 999, 2044, 3296, 5834, 12931-32
Love, Thomas (1766-1844) 7946
Lowe, Thomas G. (1815-1869) 7298
Lowrie family, 9503-05, 13499-13500
Loyalists, 2203-05, 3276, 4093-95, 12073-74, 13495, 14177; *see also* Revolution
Lucas, John R. (fl.1823) 13380
Lumber Bridge Independent Company, 14969
Lumberton, Description, 7960-63; Directory, 576; *see also* Robeson County
Lutheran Church, 838-39, 2788, 3341, 4046-51, 5917, 6013-18, 8701, 9073, 9102, 9801, 12508-09, 14100-05, 14806, 14808, 15468
Lyman, Theodore Benedict (1815-1893) 1741, 4209, 11372
Lynch law, 1956, 7524, 11532

M

McAllister family, 114, 8011
McArthur family, 12561
McBee, Vardry Alexander (1818-1904) 9444
McCall family, 8024
McCallum family, 4124
McClamroch family, 8033a
McClure, Alexander Doak (1850-1920) 6652
McCorkle, Samuel Eusebius (1746-1811) 6603
McDaniel, James (fl.1847) 11657
Macdonald, Flora (1720-1790) 594, 1563, 3853, 7047, 7070, 8095-96, 8135, 8208-09, 13523; *see also* Scotch
McDonald, Ralph Waldo (b.1903) 8099
McDougall, William (1871-1938) Bibliography, 11844
McDowell family, 8113
McDuffie, David Gee (1821-1891) 5449